Europe
Europa

Country	Code	Currency	Emergency (100 51 € / 2)	SOS ☎	🛣 Motorway	🚗 (towing)	Country road	🏘 Urban	Toll (MAUT/TOLL)	‰
Österreich / Austria	A	1 Euro (EUR) = 100 Cent	133 / 144	130	100	100	50	▣ ▣	0,5 ‰
Shqipëria / Albania	AL	1 Lek (ALL) = 100 Quindarka	129 /126	120	100	80	40		0,0 ‰
België/Belgique / Belgium	B	1 Euro (EUR) = 100 Cent	101 / 100	120	120	90	50		0,5 ‰
Bălgarija / Bulgaria	BG	1 Lew (BGN) = 100 Stótinki	166 / 150	130	90	90	50	▣ ▣	0,5 ‰
Bosna i Hercegovina / Bosnia and Herzegovina	BIH	Konvert. Marka (BAM) = 100 Fening	92 / 94	120	100	80	60		0,3 ‰
Schweiz/Suisse/Svizzera / Switzerland	CH	1 Franken (CHF) = 100 Rappen	117 / 144	120	100	80	50	▣	0,5 ‰
Kypros/Kibris / Cyprus	CY	1 Euro (EUR) = 100 Cent	199	100	80	80	50		0,5 ‰
Česká republika / Czech Republic	CZ	1 Koruna (CZK) = 100 Haliru	112 / 155	130	130	90	50	▣ ▣	0,0 ‰
Deutschland / Germany	D	1 Euro (EUR) = 100 Cent	110 / 112	(no limit)	(no limit)	100	50		0,5 ‰
Danmark / Denmark	DK	1 Krone (DKK) = 100 Øre	112	130	80	80	50		0,5 ‰
España / Spain	E	1 Euro (EUR) = 100 Cent	112	110	100	90	50	▣	0,5 ‰
Eesti / Estonia	EST	1 Euro (EUR) = 100 Cent	110 / 112	110	110	90	50		0,0 ‰
France / France	F	1 Euro (EUR) = 100 Cent	112	130	110	90	50	▣	0,5 ‰
Suomi/Finland / Finland	FIN	1 Euro (EUR) = 100 Cent	112	120	100	100	50		0,5 ‰
United Kingdom / United Kingdom	GB	1 Pound Sterling (GBP) = 100 Pence	999 / 112	70 mph (112)	70 mph (112)	60 mph (96)	30 mph (48)		0,8 ‰
Ellás (Hellás) / Greece	GR	1 Euro (EUR) = 100 Cent	100 / 166	120	110	90	50	▣ ▣	0,5 ‰
Magyarország / Hungary	H	1 Forint (HUF) = 100 Filler	112	130	110	90	50	▣	0,0 ‰
Hrvatska / Croatia	HR	1 Kuna (HRK) = 100 Lipa	112 / 94	130	110	90	50	▣	0,5 ‰
Italia / Italy	I	1 Euro (EUR) = 100 Cent	112 / 118	130	110	90	50	▣	0,5 ‰
Éire/Ireland / Ireland	IRL	1 Euro (EUR) = 100 Cent	999 / 112	120	100	60/100	50		0,5 ‰
Ísland / Iceland	IS	1 Krona (ISK) = 100 Aurar	112			80/90	50		0,0 ‰
Kosovo / Kosovo	RKS	1 Euro (EUR) = 100 Cent	112 / 92	130	110	80	50		0,5 ‰
Luxembourg / Luxembourg	L	1 Euro (EUR) = 100 Cent	113 / 112	130	90	90	50		0,5 ‰
Lietuva / Lithuania	LT	1 Litas (LTL) = 100 Centas	02 / 03 / 112	110	90	90	50		0,4 ‰
Latvija / Latvia	LV	1 Euro (EUR) = 100 Cent	02 / 03 / 112	110	90	90	50		0,5 ‰
Makedonija / Macedonia	MK	1 Denar (MKD) = 100 Deni	192 / 194	120	100	80	40/60	▣ ▣	0,5 ‰
Norge / Norway	N	1 Krone (NOK) = 100 Øre	112 / 113	90	90	80	50	▣ ▣ ▣	0,1 ‰
Nederland / Netherlands	NL	1 Euro (EUR) = 100 Cent	112	120	100	80	50		0,5 ‰
Portugal / Portugal	P	1 Euro (EUR) = 100 Cent	112	120	100	90	50	▣	0,5 ‰
Polska / Poland	PL	1 Zloty (PLN) = 100 Groszy	112 / 999	130/140	100/120	90/100	50	▣	0,2 ‰
România / Romania	RO	1 Leu (RON) = 100 Bani	112	130	100	90	50	▣ ▣ ▣	0,0 ‰
Rossija / Russia	RUS	1 Rubel (RUB) = 100 Kopeek	02 / 03	110	90	90	60		0,0 ‰
Sverige / Sweden	S	1 Krona (SEK) = 100 Öre	112	110	110/90	70/90	50		0,2 ‰
Srbija / Crna Gora / Serbia / Montenegro	SRB MNE	1 Dinar (CSM) = 100 Para ; Euro	92 / 94	120	100	80	60	▣ ▣	0,3 ‰
Slovenská republika / Slovakia	SK	1 Euro (EUR) = 100 Cent	112 / 155	130	90	90	60	▣ ▣	0,0 ‰
Slovenija / Slovenia	SLO	1 Euro (EUR) = 100 Cent	113 / 112	130	100	90	50	▣	0,5 ‰
Türkiye / Turkey	TR	1 Lira (TRY) = 100 Kurus	155 / 112	120	90	90	50	▣	0,5 ‰
Ukrajina / Ukraine	UA	1 Griwna (UAH) = 100 Kopijken	02 / 03	130	110	90	60		0,0 ‰

© Kunth Verlag GmbH & Co. KG 2014
Königinstraße 11, D-80539 München,
phone +49-89-458020-0, fax +49-89-458020-21
e-mail: info@kunth-verlag.de
www.kunth-verlag.de

Printed in Slovakia

© AA Media Limited 2014
Fanum House, Basing View,
Basingstoke, Hampshire RG21 4EA, UK
ISBN: 978-0-7495-7669-1
       987-0-7495-7670-7
A05233

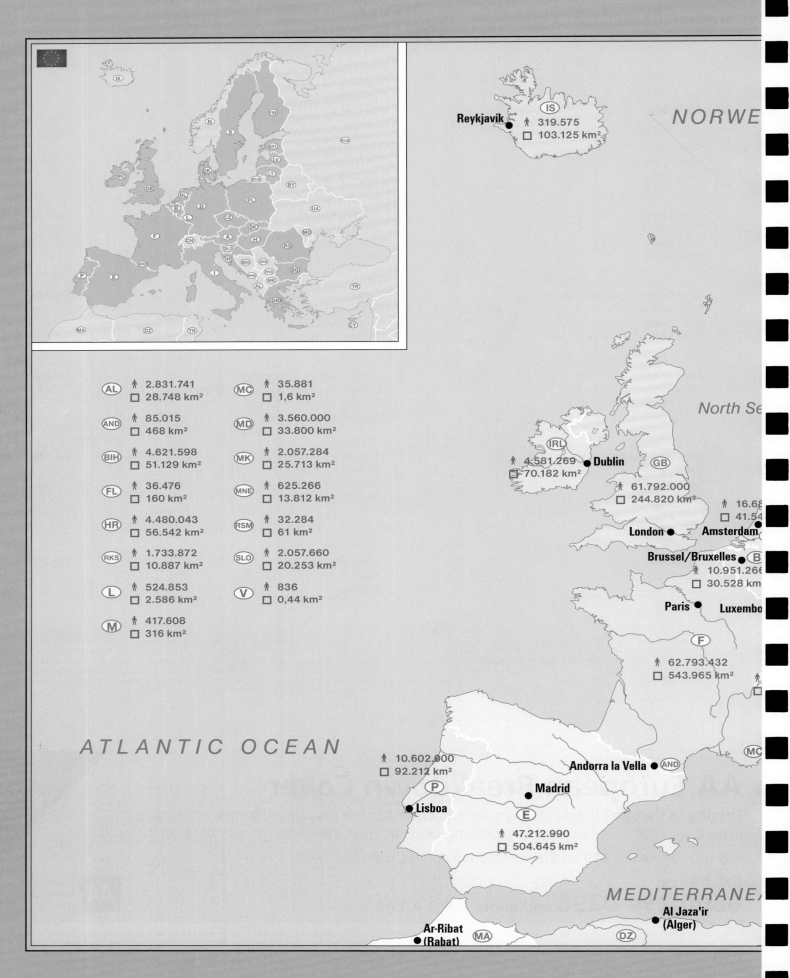

Reykjavík ⊙   🚶 319.575
       ⬜ 103.125 km²

(IS)

NORWE

AL   🚶 2.831.741   MC   🚶 35.881
     ⬜ 28.748 km²   ⬜ 1,6 km²

AND   🚶 85.015   MD   🚶 3.560.000
      ⬜ 468 km²   ⬜ 33.800 km²

BIH   🚶 4.621.598   MK   🚶 2.057.284
      ⬜ 51.129 km²   ⬜ 25.713 km²

FL   🚶 36.476   MNE   🚶 625.266
     ⬜ 160 km²   ⬜ 13.812 km²

HR   🚶 4.480.043   RSM   🚶 32.284
      ⬜ 56.542 km²   ⬜ 61 km²

RKS   🚶 1.733.872   SLO   🚶 2.057.660
      ⬜ 10.887 km²   ⬜ 20.253 km²

L   🚶 524.853   V   🚶 836
    ⬜ 2.586 km²   ⬜ 0,44 km²

M   🚶 417.608
    ⬜ 316 km²

(IRL)
🚶 4.581.269   ● **Dublin**   (GB)
⬜ 70.182 km²
                🚶 61.792.000
                ⬜ 244.820 km²

North Se

🚶 16.68
⬜ 41.54

London ●   **Amsterdam** ●

Brussel/Bruxelles ●   (B)
         🚶 10.951.266
         ⬜ 30.528 km

Paris ●   **Luxembo**

(F)

🚶 62.793.432
⬜ 543.965 km²

(MC)

ATLANTIC OCEAN

🚶 10.602.000   **Andorra la Vella** ●   (AND)
⬜ 92.212 km²

(P)   **Madrid** ●

● **Lisboa**   (E)

         🚶 47.212.990
         ⬜ 504.645 km²

MEDITERRANE

Al Jaza'ir
(Alger) ●

Ar-Ribat
(Rabat) ●   (MA)   (DZ)

GIAN SEA

⊛ 5.404.956
☐ 338.432 km²

Helsinki

⊛ 9.514.406
☐ 450.295 km²

⊛ 4.985.900
☐ 385.199 km²

Oslo

Stockholm

Tallinn (EST)
⊛ 1.340.021
☐ 45.227 km²

⊛ 143.200.000
☐ 17.075.400 km²

Moskva

(S)

(N)

(FIN)

⊛ 2.074.605
☐ 64.589 km²

Riga (LV)

(RUS)

⊛ 5.475.791
☐ 43.094 km²

København

Baltic Sea

⊛ 2.988.381
☐ 65.301 km²

(LT)

(RUS)

Vilnius

(BY)

Minsk

⊛ 9.457.000
☐ 207.595 km²

(DK)

Berlin

(PL)

Warszawa

⊛ 38.501.000
☐ 312.685 km²

Kyjiv

0.000
8 km²

(NL)

⊛ 81.903.000
☐ 357.121 km²

(L)

(D)

(CZ) Praha
⊛ 10.526.685
☐ 78.866 km²

⊛ 5.404.322
☐ 49.034 km²

(SK)

(UA)

⊛ 45.665.281
☐ 603.700 km²

burg

(A) Wien

Bratislava

(H) Budapest

(MD)

Chișinău

(RO)

CH) Bern (FL)

⊛ 8.460.390
☐ 83.878 km²

⊛ 10.005.000
☐ 93.036 km²

7.952.600
41.285 km²

Vaduz

Ljubljana (SLO)

Zagreb

Beograd

⊛ 19.042.936
☐ 238.391 km²

București

Black Sea

⊛ 7.120.666
☐ 77.474 km²

(HR)

(RSM)

Monaco

San Marino

(BIH)

Sarajevo

(SRB)

Priština

⊛ 7.364.570
☐ 110.994 km²

(I)

(MNE)

(RKS)

Sofija (BG)

Roma

(V)

Podgorica

Skopje

Ankara

⊛ 60.626.442
☐ 301.338 km²

(MK)

Tiranë

(AL)

(GR)

(TR)

⊛ 74.724.269
☐ 814.578 km²

AN SEA

⊛ 9.903.268
☐ 131.957 km²

Athína

Tunis

⊛ 1.193.976
☐ 9.251 km²

(CY)

(TN)

	(A)	Österreich
	(AL)	Shqipëria
	(AND)	Andorra
	(B)	België/Belgique
	(BG)	Bâlgarija
	(BIH)	Bosna i Hercegovina
	(BY)	Belarus'
	(MNE)	Crna Gora
	(CH)	Schweiz/Suisse/Svizzera
	(CY)	Kýpros
	(CZ)	Česká Republika
	(D)	Deutschland
	(DK)	Danmark
	(E)	España
	(EST)	Eesti
	(F)	France
	(FIN)	Finland
	(FL)	Liechtenstein
	(GB)	United Kingdom
	(GR)	Elláda
	(H)	Magyarország
	(HR)	Hrvatska
	(I)	Italia
	(IRL)	Éire/Ireland
	(IS)	Ísland
	(RKS)	Kosovo
	(L)	Luxembourg
	(LT)	Lietuva
	(LV)	Latvija
	(M)	Malta
	(MC)	Monaco
	(MD)	Moldova
	(MK)	Makedonija
	(N)	Norge
	(NL)	Nederland
	(P)	Portugal
	(PL)	Polska
	(RO)	România
	(RSM)	San Marino
	(RUS)	Rossija
	(S)	Sverige
	(SK)	Slovenská Republika
	(SLO)	Slovenija
	(SRB)	Srbija
	(TR)	Türkiye
	(UA)	Ukrajina
	(V)	Città del Vaticano

Legend	Zeichenerklärung	1:900 000	Légende	Legenda
Motorway (under construction)	Autobahn (im Bau)		Autoroute (en construction)	Autosnelweg (in aanleg)
Toll motorway	Gebührenpflichtige Autobahn		Autoroute à péage	Tolautosnelweg
Dual carriageway (under construction)	4-oder mehrspurige Autobahn (im Bau)		Double chaussée (en construction)	Hoofdroute, tweebaans (in aanleg)
Primary route (under construction)	Fernstraße (im Bau)		Route principale (en construction)	Hoofdroute (in aanleg)
Main road (under construction)	Wichtige Hauptstraße (im Bau)		Route principale importante (en construction)	Belangrijke verbindingsweg (in aanleg)
Main road	Hauptstraße		Route départementale	Regionale verbindingsweg
Secondary road	Nebenstraße		Route secondaire	Overige wegen
Railway	Eisenbahn		Chemin de fer	Spoorweg
Restricted area	Sperrgebiet		Zone interdite	Verboden gebied
National or nature park	National- und Naturpark		Parc national, parc naturel	Nationaal park, natuurpark
Motorway number	Autobahnnummer	4 2 A22	Numéro autoroute	Nummering Autosnelwegen
Number of main European road	Europastraßennummer	E54	Numéro des routes européennes	Nummering Europaroutes
Other road numbers	Andere Straßennummern	34 28 N22 322	Autre numéro de routes	Wegnummers
Motorway junction number	Autobahnanschlussnummer	22	Numéros d'échangeurs	Afrit met nummer
Motorway junction	Anschlussstelle		Échangeur	Aansluiting
Not suitable / closed for caravans	Für Wohnwagen nicht geeignet / gesperrt		Non recommandé aux caravans - interdite	Voor caravans niet aanbevelen - verboden
Filling station	Autobahntankstelle		Station-service	Tankstation
Restaurant	Autobahnrasthaus		Restaurant	Restaurant
Restaurant with motel	Autobahnrasthaus mit Motel		Hôtel	Restaurant met motel
Major airport	Wichtiger Flughafen		Aéroport important	Belangrijke luchthaven
Airport	Flughafen		Aéroport	Luchthaven
Airfield	Flugplatz		Aérodrome	Vliegveld
Ferry	Autofähre		Ferry	Veerdienst
Border crossing	Grenzübergang		Passage frontalier - douane	Grensovergang
Windmill	Windmühle		Moulin	Windmolen
Lighthouse	Leuchtturm		Phare	Vuurtoren
Place of interest	Sehenswerter Ort	COLMAR	Curiosités	Bezienswaardig

Significant points of interest · Herausragende Sehenswürdigkeiten · Curiosités remarquables · Opvallende bezienswaardigheden

GB	D	F	NL
Major tourist route	Autoroute	Autoroute	Autoroute
Major tourist railway	Bahnstrecke	Ligne ferroviaire	Spoorwegtraject
Highspeed train	Hochgeschwindigkeitszug	Train à Grande Vitesse	Hogesnelheidstrein
Shipping route	Schiffsroute	Itinéraire en bateau	Scheepsroute
UNESCO World Natural Heritage	UNESCO-Weltnaturerbe	Patrimoine naturel de l'humanité de l'UNESCO	UNESCO-wereldnatuurerfgoed
Mountain landscape	Gebirgslandschaft	Paysage de montagne	Berglandschap
Rock landscape	Felslandschaft	Paysage rocheux	Rotslandschap
Ravine/canyon	Schlucht/Canyon	Gorge/canyon	Kloof/canyon
Glacier	Gletscher	Glacier	Gletsjer
Active volcano	Vulkan, aktiv	Volcan actif	Actieve vulkaan
Extinct volcano	Vulkan, erloschen	Volcan éteint	Dode vulkaan
Geyser	Geysir	Geyser	Geiser
Cave	Höhle	Grotte	Grotten
River landscape	Flusslandschaft	Paysage fluvial	Rivierlandschap
Waterfall/rapids	Wasserfall/Stromschnelle	Chute d'eau/rapide	Waterval/stroomversnelling
Lake country	Seenlandschaft	Paysage de lacs	Merenlandschap
Desert	Wüstenlandschaft	Désert	Woestijnlandschap
Oasis	Oase	Oasis	Oase
Depression	Depression	Bassin	Depressie
Fossil site	Fossilienfundstätte	Site fossile	Fossielenplaats
Nature park	Naturpark	Parc naturel	Natuurpark
National park (landscape)	Nationalpark (Landschaft)	Parc national (paysage)	Nationaal park (landschap)
National park (flora)	Nationalpark (Flora)	Parc national (flore)	Nationaal park (flora)
National park (fauna)	Nationalpark (Fauna)	Parc national (faune)	Nationaal park (fauna)
National park (culture)	Nationalpark (Kultur)	Parc national (site culturel)	Nationaal park (cultuur)
Botanic gardens	Botanischer Garten	Jardin botanique	Botanische tuin
Biosphere reserve	Biosphärenreservat	Réserve de biosphère	Biosfeerreservaat
Wildlife reserve	Wildreservat	Réserve animale	Wildreservaat
Zoo/safari park	Zoo/Safaripark	Zoo/parc de safari	Dierentuin/safaripark
Coastal landscape	Küstenlandschaft	Paysage côtier	Kustlandschap
Beach	Strand	Plage	Strand
Island	Insel	Île	Eiland
Underwater reserve	Unterwasserreservat	Réserve sous-marine	Onderwaterreservaat
Spring	Quelle	Source	Bron
UNESCO World Cultural Heritage	UNESCO-Weltkulturerbe	Patrimoine culturel de l'humanité de l'UNESCO	UNESCO-wereldcultuurerfgoed
Remarkable city	Außergewöhnliche Metropole	Métropole d'exception	Buitengewone metropolen
Pre-and early history	Vor- und Frühgeschichte	Préhistoire et protohistoire	Prehistorie en vroegste geschiedenis
Prehistoric rockscape	Prähistorische Felsbilder/Naturvölker	Peintures rupestres préhistoriques	Prehistorische rotstekeningen
The Ancient Orient	Alter Orient	Ancien Orient	Oud-Oriënt
Minoan site	Minoische Kultur	Civilisation minoenne	Minoïsche cultuur
Phoenecian site	Phönikische Kultur	Civilisation phénicienne	Fenicische cultuur
Etruscan site	Etruskische Kultur	Civilisation étrusque	Etruskische cultuur
Greek antiquity	Griechische Antike	Antiquité grecque	Griekse oudheden
Roman antiquity	Römische Antike	Antiquité romaine	Romeinse oudheden
Vikings	Wikinger	Vikings	Vikingen
Places of Jewish cultural interest	Jüdische Kulturstätte	Site juif	Joodse cultuurhist. plaatsen
Places of Islamic cultural interest	Islamische Kulturstätte	Site islamique	Islamitische cultuurhist. plaatsen
Places of Christian cultural interest	Christliche Kulturstätte	Site chrétien	Christelijke cultuurhist. plaatsen
Roman church	Romanische Kirche	Église romane	Romaanse kerk
Gothic church	Gotische Kirche	Église gothique	Gotische kerk
Renaissance church	Renaissance-Kirche	Église renaissance	Renaissance kerk
Baroque church	Barock-Kirche	Église baroque	Barok kerk

GB	D	F	NL
Christian monastery	Christliches Kloster	Monastère chrétien	Christelijk klooster
Cultural landscape	Kulturlandschaft	Paysage culturel	Cultuurlandschap
Historical city scape	Historisches Stadtbild	Cité historique	Historisch stadsgezicht
Impressive skyline	Imposante Skyline	Gratte-ciel	Imposante skyline
Castle/fortress/fort	Burg/Festung/Wehranlage	Château/forteresse/remparts	Burcht/vesting/verdedigingswerk
Castle ruin	Burgruine	Château ruine	Burcht ruine
Tower of interest	Sehenswerter Turm	Tour intéressante	Bezienswaardige toren
Windmill	Windmühle	Moulin	Windmolen
Palace	Palast/Schloss	Palais	Paleis
Technical/industrial monument	Techn./industrielles Monument	Monument technique/industriel	Technisch/industrieel monument
Working mine	Bergwerk in Betrieb	Mine en activité	Mijn in bedrijf
Disused mine	Bergwerk geschlossen	Mine fermée	Mijn buiten bedrijf
Dam	Staumauer	Barrage	Stuwdam
Impressive lighthouse	Sehenswerter Leuchtturm	Très beau phare	Bezienswaardige vuurtoren
Notable bridge	Herausragende Brücke	Pont remarquable	Opvallende brug
Remarkable building	Herausragendes Gebäude	Bâtiment remarquable	Bijzonder gebouw
Tomb/grave	Grabmal	Tombeau	Grafmonument
Monument	Denkmal	Monument	Monument
Memorial	Mahnmal	Mémorial	Gedenkteken
Theater of war/battlefield	Kriegsschauplatz/Schlachtfeld	Champs de bataille	Strijdtoneel/slagvelden
Space mission launch site	Weltraumbahnhof	Base spatiale	Ruimtestation
Space telescope	Weltraumteleskop	Télescope astronomique	Ruimtetelescoop
Market	Markt	Marché	Markt
Festivals	Feste und Festivals	Fêtes et festivals	Feesten en festivals
Museum	Museum	Musée	Museum
State Historical Park	Freilichtmuseum	Musée de plein air	Openluchtmuseum
Theatre	Theater	Théâtre	Theater
World exhibition/World Fair	Weltausstellung	Exposition universelle	Wereldtentoonstelling
Arena/stadium	Arena/Stdion	Arène/stade	Arena/stadion
Race track	Rennstrecke	Circuit automobile	Circuit
Golf	Golf	Golf	Golf
Horse racing	Pferdesport	Équitation	Paardensport
Skiing	Skigebiet	Station de ski	Skigebied
Sailing	Segeln	Voile	Zeilen
Wind surfing	Windsurfen	Planche à voile	Surfen
Surfing	Wellenreiten	Surf	Surfriding
Diving	Tauchen	Plongée	Duiken
Canoeing/rafting	Kanu/Rafting	Canoë/rafting	Kanoën/rafting
Seaport	Seehafen	Port	Zeehaven
Deep-sea fishing	Hochseeangeln	Pêche en mer	Zeevissen
Waterskiing	Wasserski	Ski nautique	Waterskiën
Beach resort	Badeort	Station balnéaire	Badplaats
Leisure bath	Freizeitbad	Piscine découverte	Recreatiebad
Mineral/thermal spa	Mineralbad/Therme	Station hydrothermale	Mineraalbad/thermen
Leisure park	Freizeitpark	Parc de loisirs	Recreatiepark
Casino	Spielcasino	Casino	Casino
Hill resort	Hill Resort	Station de montagne	Hill resort
Mountain refuge/alpine pasture	Berghütte/Alm	Refuge/pâturages	Berghut/alpenweide
Rambling/rambling area	Wandern/Wandergebiet	Randonnées/zone de randonnées	Wandelen/wandelgebied
Viewpoint	Aussichtspunkt	Point de vue	Uitzichtpunt
Mountain railway	Bergbahn	Chemin de fer de montagne	Kabelbaan
Shipwreck	Schiffswrack	Épave de navire	Scheepswrak

Road Distances

	Amsterdam	Athína	Barcelona	Belfast	Beograd	Berlin	Bern	Birmingham	Bordeaux	Bratislava	Bruxelles/Brussel	București	Budapest	Calais	Dublin	Edinburgh	Frankfurt a.M.	Genova	Hamburg	Helsinki	Istanbul	København	Köln	Kyjiv	Le Havre	Lisboa	Ljubljana	London	Luxembourg	Lyon	Madrid	Málaga	Marseille	Milano	Minsk	Moskva	München	Oslo	Paris	Praha	Riga	Roma	Rotterdam	Sankt-Peterburg	Sarajevo	Skopje	Sofija	Stockholm	Strasbourg	Tallinn	Tiranë	Vilnius	Warszawa	Wien	Zagreb
Amsterdam		2827	1566	1286	1720	656	833	734	1082	1211	210	2267	1398	363	1125	1196	443	1216	466	1953	2693	788	263	1943	598	2241	1234	532	360	923	1770	2321	1235	1076	1768	2469	826	1268	502	883	1873	1662	76	2424	1743	2155	2113	1435	602	2183	2217	1665	1209	1148	1330
Athína	2827		2612	3758	1106	2338	2010	3206	2682	1662	2598	1168	1466	2844	3598	3668	2386	1780	2627	3227	1094	2767	2568	2307	2744	3768	1633	2952	2414	2115	3215	3619	2156	1691	2583	3283	2039	3440	2554	1991	2830	1267	2834	3381	1175	701	798	3415	2170	3140	713	2622	2343	1705	1493
Barcelona	1566	2612		2280	1988	1877	915	1728	637	1894	1376	2574	1926	1365	2120	2190	1336	857	1776	3263	2961	2099	1383	3048	1251	1259	1462	1526	1180	639	627	1031	508	978	2989	3690	1343	2578	1071	1715	3093	1366	1525	3645	2014	2422	2380	2746	1130	3450	2360	2886	2430	1829	1597
Belfast	1286	3758	2280		2800	1850	1745	594	1784	2349	1119	3415	2545	925	166	319	1521	2119	1676	3161	3773	1999	1331	3244	1191	2941	2316	776	1347	1672	2474	3009	1983	2057	2957	3660	1856	2478	1206	2025	3062	2651	1226	3601	2864	3241	3193	2647	1540	3373	3296	2864	2401	2227	2405
Beograd	1720	1106	1988	2800		1236	1334	2248	2031	560	1680	592	363	1877	2639	2709	1287	1159	1525	2125	979	1665	1469	1472	1971	3147	534	2046	1500	1464	2594	2998	1535	1036	1480	2181	940	2338	1771	889	1728	1296	1735	2279	305	439	398	2312	1314	2038	748	1520	1051	603	395
Berlin	656	2338	1877	1850	1236		956	1298	1632	683	774	1751	881	927	1689	1760	549	1177	289	1649	2320	434	576	1325	1148	2791	997	1096	743	1238	2320	2879	1549	1038	1150	1850	588	1031	1053	355	991	1518	693	1711	1418	1687	1714	1082	753	1486	1967	1026	590	686	1053
Bern	833	2010	915	1745	1334	956		1167	889	950	637	1920	1136	796	1564	1629	429	450	910	2397	2307	1232	583	2205	752	2044	809	965	453	305	1543	1947	573	318	1992	2693	433	1723	561	806	2183	903	802	2648	1271	1767	1726	1879	238	2320	1706	1943	1448	867	943
Birmingham	734	3206	1728	594	2248	1298	1167		1232	1797	566	2794	1924	373	385	472	968	1567	1124	2609	3221	1447	779	2582	432	2233	1764	191	795	1120	1768	2302	1431	1498	2405	3108	1317	1926	654	1460	2608	2099	674	2913	2278	2682	2641	2095	988	2615	2730	2312	1849	1675	1853
Bordeaux	1082	2682	637	1784	2031	1632	889	1232		1936	891	2616	1967	869	1470	1540	1167	997	1483	2970	3003	1806	1065	2998	686	1162	1503	1030	995	588	691	1242	648	1014	2744	3445	1276	2285	586	1549	2829	1506	1039	3249	2059	2463	2422	2453	964	2944	2389	2641	2185	1870	1639
Bratislava	1211	1662	1894	2349	560	683	950	1797	1936		1203	1071	201	1388	2151	2221	799	1063	968	1751	1640	1109	987	1256	1521	3052	447	1557	1031	1368	2498	2902	1439	940	1201	1902	490	1705	1350	333	1353	1200	1237	1904	723	1007	1034	1756	893	1664	1316	1146	684	65	442
Bruxelles/Brussel	210	2598	1376	1119	1680	774	637	566	891	1203		2227	1357	195	958	1028	402	1023	601	2088	2653	923	212	2163	406	2049	1156	364	230	732	1578	2129	1044	884	1884	2585	737	1403	311	902	1775	1469	151	2389	1702	2113	2072	1570	434	2094	2177	1781	1325	1107	1289
București	2267	1168	2574	3415	592	1751	1920	2794	2616	1071	2227		874	2426	3196	3256	1833	1746	2035	2183	625	2175	2015	947	2585	3735	1122	2592	2077	2052	3182	3586	2122	1624	1357	1790	1525	2713	2356	1399	1786	1884	2286	2366	915	690	383	2764	1906	2096	923	1756	1338	1113	982
Budapest	1398	1466	1926	2545	363	881	1136	1924	1967	201	1357	874		1577	2315	2386	963	1094	1165	1776	1350	1305	1152	1123	1685	3083	460	1722	1195	1399	2529	2933	1470	971	1132	1832	655	1901	1491	529	1356	1231	1411	1907	545	810	769	1952	1067	1666	1119	1148	687	273	344
Calais	363	2844	1365	925	1877	927	796	373	869	1388	195	2426	1577		764	777	600	1189	754	2241	2851	1077	410	2213	273	2025	1382	171	414	759	1554	2105	1070	1023	2038	2738	935	1556	288	1100	1929	1608	304	2543	1905	2311	2270	1724	617	2237	2332	1934	1478	1305	1487
Dublin	1125	3598	2120	166	2639	1689	1564	385	1470	2151	958	3196	2315	764		450	1326	1926	1480	2979	3578	1803	1136	2939	789	2616	2106	546	1145	1479	2146	2717	1792	1751	2770	3470	1677	2288	1019	1826	2874	2342	1030	3272	2618	3040	3033	2450	1343	2969	3101	2672	2204	2031	2213
Edinburgh	1196	3668	2190	319	2709	1760	1629	472	1540	2221	1028	3256	2386	777	450		1430	2021	1586	3071	3683	1909	1241	3043	894	2697	2183	650	1256	1582	2230	2764	1893	1959	2866	3569	1765	2387	1116	1922	2971	2553	893	3375	2682	3143	3102	2556	1450	3070	3206	2773	2310	2137	2315
Frankfurt a.M.	443	2386	1336	1521	1287	549	429	968	1167	799	402	1833	963	600	1326	1430		808	496	1968	2261	818	189	1841	772	2306	801	766	231	700	1835	2341	1012	668	1663	2364	393	1308	573	510	1768	1254	456	2319	1299	1721	1680	1465	223	1882	1785	1560	1104	715	897
Genova	1216	1780	857	2119	1159	1177	450	1567	997	1063	1023	1746	1094	1189	1926	2021	808		1244	2746	2123	1566	971	2210	1104	2013	623	1364	828	475	1459	1863	400	140	2196	2897	628	2057	914	1081	2348	522	1177	2899	1068	1583	1542	2213	613	2674	1482	2141	1679	991	759
Hamburg	466	2627	1776	1676	1525	289	910	1124	1483	968	601	2035	1165	754	1480	1586	496	1244		1502	2646	338	425	1603	997	2639	1184	922	623	1140	2169	2720	1452	1109	1428	2128	776	814	892	646	1280	1669	501	1893	1684	2104	2063	985	703	1588	2170	1324	868	976	1280
Helsinki	1953	3227	3263	3161	2125	1649	2397	2609	2970	1751	2088	2183	1776	2241	2979	3071	1968	2746	1502		3081	1173	1910	1546	2482	4125	2126	2407	2106	2625	3654	4205	2937	2424	882	1107	1974	1019	2387	1641	396	2879	1986	389	2334	2570	2476	517	2189	88	2879	689	1062	1754	2121
Istanbul	2693	1094	2961	3773	979	2320	2307	3221	3003	1640	2653	625	1350	2851	3578	3683	2261	2123	2646	3081		2642	2442	1475	2944	4121	1508	3019	2449	2438	3567	3971	2508	2009	2006	2524	1914	3314	2745	1866	2569	1743	2708	2948	1168	787	580	3289	2287	2879	1015	2361	1943	1580	1368
København	788	2767	2099	1999	1665	434	1232	1447	1806	1109	923	2175	1305	1077	1803	1909	818	1566	338	1173	2642		748	1744	1320	2962	1390	1245	944	1463	2492	3043	1775	1432	1104	1786	981	607	1215	785	912	1911	824	1473	1832	2117	2144	658	1026	1139	2360	919	1009	1116	1472
Köln	263	2568	1383	1331	1469	576	583	779	1065	987	212	2015	1152	410	1136	1241	189	971	425	1910	2442	748		1947	580	2223	984	575	207	746	1752	2303	1058	826	1683	2384	575	1224	485	692	1575	1411	257	2138	1493	1910	1862	1392	354	1883	1967	1580	1124	897	1079
Kyjiv	1943	2307	3048	3244	1472	1325	2205	2582	2998	1256	2163	947	1123	2213	2939	3043	1841	2210	1603	1546	1475	1744	1947		2532	4183	1560	2379	2048	2480	3629	4033	2570	2071	560	852	1749	2343	2336	1405	1045	2331	1977	1378	1652	1645	1320	1591	2003	1461	1859	751	767	1343	1444
Le Havre	598	2744	1251	1191	1971	1148	752	432	686	1521	406	2585	1685	273	789	894	772	1104	997	2482	2944	1320	580	2532		1845	1437	298	531	658	1374	1925	970	1044	2261	2962	1022	1802	197	1230	2153	1638	540	2715	2006	2404	2363	1970	688	2461	2432	2158	1702	1436	1580
Lisboa	2241	3768	1259	2941	3147	2791	2044	2233	1162	3052	2049	3735	3083	2025	2616	2697	2306	2013	2639	4125	4121	2962	2223	4183	1845		2616	2187	2128	1742	626	683	1662	2132	3901	4602	2430	3442	1743	2702	3793	2520	2196	4347	3175	3576	3535	3610	2118	4101	3474	3798	3342	2983	2751
Ljubljana	1234	1633	1462	2316	534	997	809	1764	1503	447	1156	1122	460	1382	2106	2183	801	623	1184	2126	1508	1390	984	1560	1437	2616		1538	942	939	2068	2472	1009	510	1588	2289	409	1999	1240	708	1741	770	1251	2245	554	965	924	2038	782	2051	949	1533	1072	383	140
London	532	2952	1526	776	2046	1096	965	191	1030	1557	364	2592	1722	171	546	650	766	1364	922	2407	3019	1245	575	2379	298	2187	1538		587	918	1720	2254	1229	1260	2202	2905	1120	1724	452	1270	2098	1897	472	2661	2067	2479	2438	1892	786	2098	2542	2109	1646	1473	1651
Luxembourg	360	2414	1180	1347	1500	743	453	795	995	1031	230	2077	1195	414	1145	1256	231	828	623	2106	2449	944	207	2048	531	2128	942	587		517	1634	2158	829	669	1878	2579	523	1427	372	732	1788	1254	355	2352	1494	1906	1864	1595	219	2096	1969	1774	1319	938	1081
Lyon	923	2115	639	1672	1464	1238	305	1120	588	1368	732	2052	1399	759	1479	1582	700	475	1140	2625	2438	1463	746	2480	658	1742	939	918	517		1242	1646	317	448	2354	3044	733	1943	468	1080	2265	983	849	2958	1473	1897	1856	2111	495	2573	1823	2251	1795	1304	1072
Madrid	1770	3215	627	2474	2594	2320	1543	1768	691	2498	1578	3182	2529	1554	2146	2230	1835	1459	2169	3654	3567	2492	1752	3629	1374	626	2068	1720	1634	1242		545	1105	1576	3434	4135	1941	2975	1275	2312	3538	1964	1728	3887	2605	3028	2987	3140	1733	3630	2923	3334	2871	2433	2200
Málaga	2321	3619	1031	3009	2998	2879	1947	2302	1242	2902	2129	3586	2933	2105	2717	2764	2341	1863	2720	4205	3971	3043	2303	4033	1925	683	2472	2254	2158	1646	545		1506	1977	3988	4689	2342	3577	1810	2713	4092	2365	2263	4596	2979	3420	3379	3677	2129	4206	3319	3884	3428	2828	2596
Marseille	1235	2156	508	1983	1535	1549	573	1431	648	1439	1044	2122	1470	1070	1792	1893	1012	400	1452	2937	2508	1775	1058	2570	970	1662	1009	1229	829	317	1105	1506		521	2577	3278	1010	2255	779	1382	2729	909	1160	3234	1544	1965	1924	2422	806	2884	1863	2522	2060	1372	1140
Milano	1076	1691	978	2057	1036	1038	318	1498	1014	940	884	1624	971	1023	1751	1959	668	140	1109	2424	2009	1432	826	2071	1044	2132	510	1260	669	448	1576	1977	521		2077	2778	493	1921	853	865	2229	584	1041	2732	1045	1465	1423	2078	477	2365	1400	2022	1512	872	540
Minsk	1768	2583	2989	2957	1480	1150	1992	2405	2744	1201	1884	1357	1132	2038	2770	2866	1663	2196	1428	882	2006	1104	1683	560	2261	3901	1588	2202	1878	2354	3434	3988	2577	2077		720	1627	1516	2159	1281	484	2338	1800	783	2447	1926	1744	1030	1791	794	2235	191	550	1213	1473
Moskva	2469	3283	3690	3660	2181	1850	2693	3108	3445	1902	2585	1790	1832	2738	3470	3569	2364	2897	2128	1107	2524	1786	2384	852	2962	4602	2289	2905	2579	3044	4135	4689	3278	2778	720		2362	1997	2863	1873	917	3041	2503	697	2382	2496	2265	1464	2570	1014	2938	908	1253	1916	2176
München	826	2039	1343	1856	940	588	433	1317	1276	490	737	1525	655	935	1677	1765	393	628	776	1974	1914	981	575	1749	1022	2430	409	1120	523	733	1941	2342	1010	493	1627	2362		1588	822	381	1608	928	824	2166	962	1374	1332	1627	364	1916	1435	1594	992	406	549
Oslo	1268	3440	2578	2478	2338	1031	1723	1926	2285	1705	1403	2713	1901	1556	2288	2387	1308	2057	814	1019	3314	607	1224	2343	1802	3442	1999	1724	1427	1943	2975	3577	2255	1921	1516	1997	1588		1703	1382	1069	2507	1302	1341	2430	2713	2741	523	1516	986	2956	1331	1605	1712	2068
Paris	502	2554	1071	1206	1771	1053	561	654	586	1350	311	2356	1491	288	1019	1116	573	914	892	2387	2745	1215	485	2336	197	1743	1240	452	372	468	1275	1810	779	853	2159	2863	822	1703		1030	2055	1445	458	2619	1805	2204	2163	1873	488	2363	2262	2061	1605	1237	1377
Praha	883	1991	1715	2025	889	355	806	1460	1549	333	902	1399	529	1100	1826	1922	510	1081	646	1641	1866	785	692	1405	1230	2702	708	1270	732	1080	2312	2713	1382	865	1281	1873	381	1382	1030		1282	1296	909	1777	1044	1334	1362	1427	606	1593	1542	1075	613	333	654
Riga	1873	2830	3093	3062	1728	991	2183	2608	2829	1353	1775	1786	1356	1929	2874	2971	1768	2348	1280	396	2569	912	1575	1045	2153	3793	1741	2098	1788	2265	3538	4092	2729	2229	484	917	1608	1069	2055	1282		2482	1905	561	1916	2173	2078	547	1752	310	2482	291	664	1356	1723
Roma	1662	1267	1366	2651	1296	1518	903	2099	1506	1200	1469	1884	1231	1608	2342	2553	1254	522	1669	2879	1743	1911	1411	2331	1638	2520	770	1897	1254	983	1964	2365	909	584	2338	3041	928	2507	1445	1296	2482		1626	2993	892	1190	1686	2556	1062	2803	975	2284	1823	1135	903
Rotterdam	76	2834	1525	1226	1735	693	802	674	1039	1237	151	2286	1411	304	1030	893	456	1177	501	1986	2708	824	257	1977	540	2196	1251	472	355	849	1728	2263	1160	1041	1800	2503	824	1302	458	909	1905	1626		2260	1757	2167	2126	1469	566	2002	2231	1699	1243	1161	1343
Sankt-Peterburg	2424	3381	3645	3601	2279	1711	2648	2913	3249	1904	2389	2366	1907	2543	3272	3375	2319	2899	1893	389	2948	1473	2138	1378	2715	4347	2245	2661	2352	2958	3887	4596	3234	2732	783	697	2166	1341	2619	1777	561	2993	2260		2447	2665	2571	899	2317	361	2975	714	1157	1849	2216
Sarajevo	1743	1175	2014	2864	305	1418	1271	2278	2059	723	1702	915	545	1905	2618	2682	1299	1068	1684	2334	1168	1832	1493	1652	2006	3175	554	2067	1494	1473	2605	2979	1544	1045	2447	2382	962	2430	1805	1044	1916	892	1757	2447		459	586	2482	1340	2249	498	1691	1250	759	414
Skopje	2155	701	2422	3241	439	1687	1767	2682	2463	1007	2113	690	810	2311	3040	3143	1721	1583	2104	2570	787	2117	1910	1645	2404	3576	965	2479	1906	1897	3028	3420	1965	1465	1926	2496	1374	2713	2204	1334	2173	1190	2167	2665	459		229	2750	1747	2475	311	1957	1488	1040	828
Sofija	2113	798	2380	3193	398	1714	1726	2641	2422	1034	2072	383	769	2270	3033	3102	1680	1542	2063	2476	580	2144	1862	1320	2363	3535	924	2438	1864	1856	2987	3379	1924	1423	1744	2265	1332	2741	2163	1362	2078	1686	2126	2571	586	229		2709	1706	2389	540	1916	1447	999	787
Stockholm	1435	3415	2746	2647	2312	1082	1879	2095	2453	1756	1570	2764	1952	1724	2450	2556	1465	2213	985	517	3289	658	1392	1591	1970	3610	2038	1892	1595	2111	3140	3677	2422	2078	1030	1464	1627	523	1873	1427	547	2556	1469	899	2482	2750	2709		1674	482	3008	838	1198	1764	2120
Strasbourg	602	2170	1130	1540	1314	753	238	988	964	893	434	1906	1067	617	1343	1450	223	613	703	2189	2287	1026	354	2003	688	2118	782	786	219	495	1733	2129	806	477	1791	2570	364	1516	488	606	1752	1062	566	2317	1340	1747	1706	1674		2090	1815	1767	1311	769	927
Tallinn	2183	3140	3450	3373	2038	1486	2320	2615	2944	1664	2094	2096	1666	2237	2969	3070	1882	2674	1588	88	2879	1139	1883	1461	2461	4101	2051	2098	2096	2573	3630	4206	2884	2365	794	1014	1916	986	2363	1593	310	2803	2002	361	2249	2475	2389	482	2090		2793	602	975	1667	2034
Tiranë	2217	713	2360	3296	748	1967	1706	2730	2389	1316	2177	923	1119	2332	3101	3206	1785	1482	2170	2879	1015	2360	1967	1859	2432	3474	949	2542	1969	1823	2923	3319	1863	1400	2235	2938	1435	2956	2262	1542	2482	975	2231	2975	498	311	540	3008	1815	2793		2268	1799	1264	910
Vilnius	1665	2622	2886	2864	1520	1026	1943	2312	2641	1146	1781	1756	1148	1934	2672	2773	1560	2141	1324	689	2361	919	1580	751	2158	3798	1533	2109	1774	2251	3334	3884	2522	2022	191	908	1594	1331	2061	1075	291	2284	1699	714	1691	1957	1916	838	1767	602	2268		466	1158	1525
Warszawa	1209	2343	2430	2401	1051	590	1448	1849	2185	684	1325	1338	687	1478	2204	2310	1104	1679	868	1062	1943	1009	1124	767	1702	3342	1072	1646	1319	1795	2871	3428	2060	1512	550	1253	992	1605	1605	613	664	1823	1243	1157	1250	1488	1447	1198	1311	975	1799	466		689	1056
Wien	1148	1705	1829	2227	603	686	867	1675	1870	65	1107	1113	243	1305	2031	2137	715	991	976	1754	1580	1116	897	1343	1436	2983	383	1473	938	1304	2433	2828	1372	872	1213	1916	406	1712	1237	333	1356	1135	1161	1849	759	1040	999	1764	769	1667	1264	1158	689		376
Zagreb	1330	1493	1597	2405	395	1053	943	1853	1639	442	1289	982	344	1487	2213	2315	897	759	1280	2121	1368	1472	1079	1444	1580	2751	140	1651	1081	1072	2200	2596	1140	640	1473	2176	549	2068	1377	654	1723	903	1343	2216	414	828	787	2120	927	2034	910	1525	1056	376	

All distances in this chart are in kilometres and include any part of the route taken by ferry.

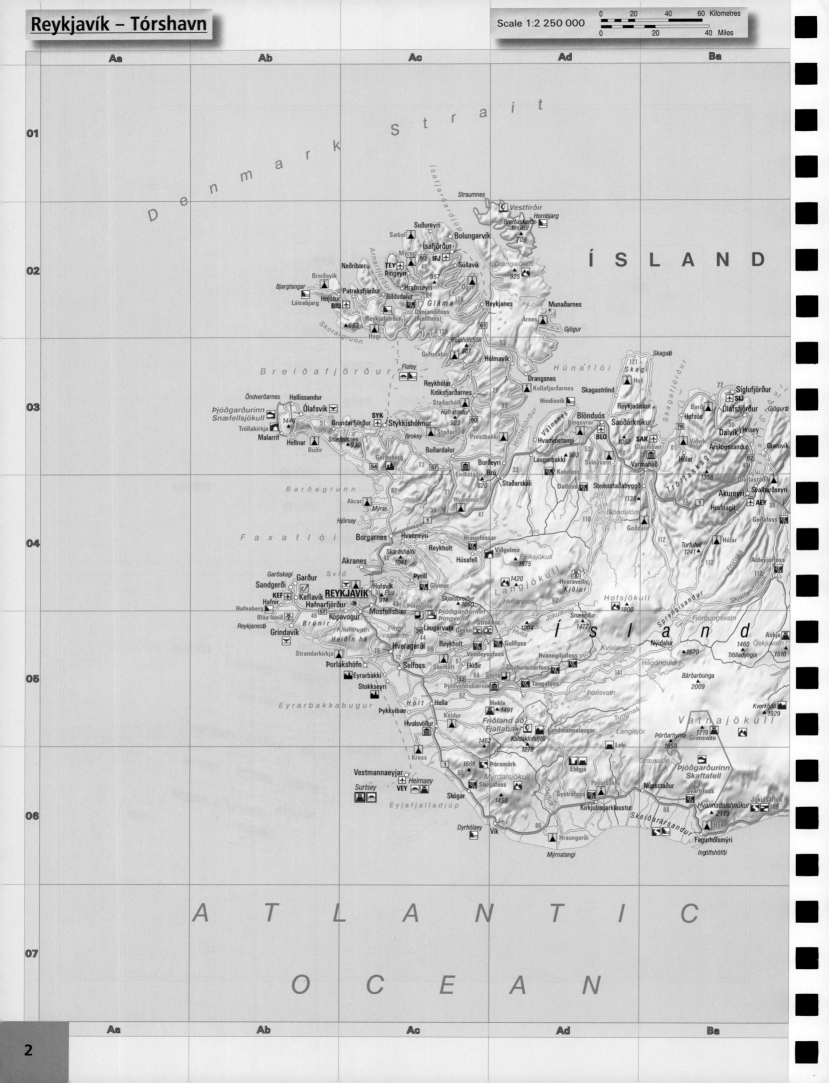

Scale 1:2 250 000

0   20   40   60 Kilometres
0   20   40 Miles

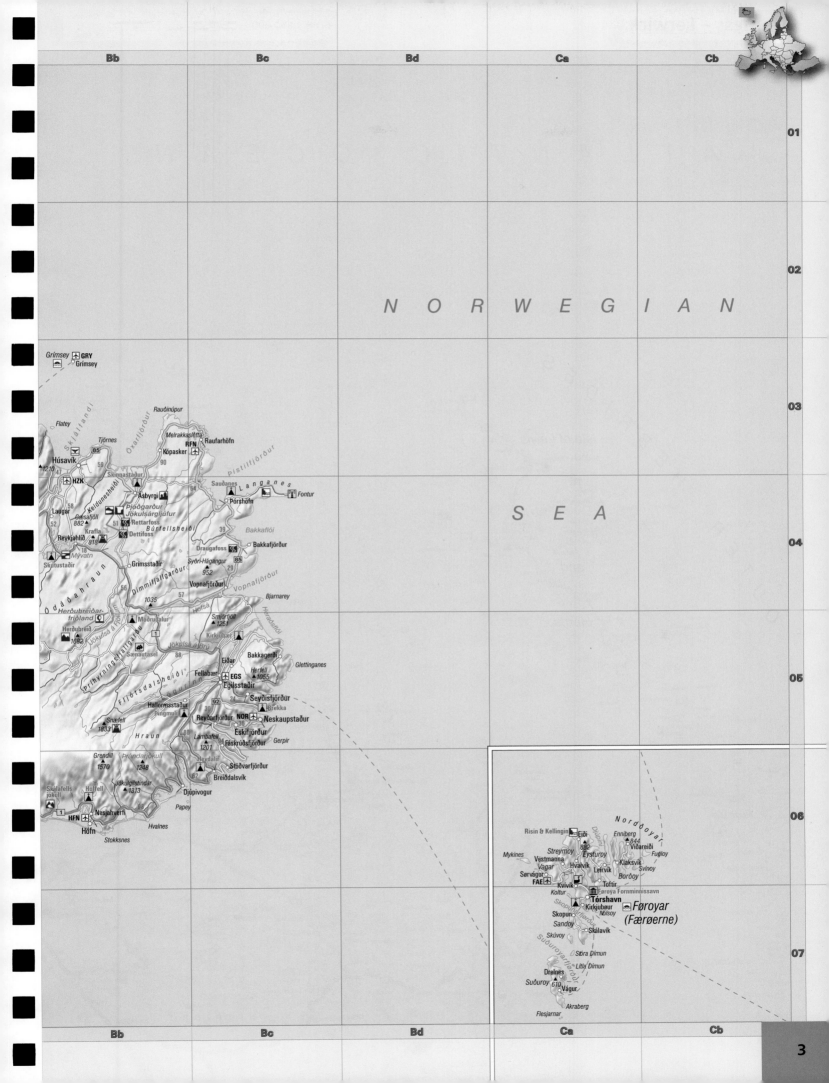

N O R W E G I A N

Grímsey GRY
Grímsey

03

S E A

Flatey
Tjörnes
85
Húsavík
1210 47   59
HZK   Skinnastaðir
58   Ásbyrgi
Laugar   Gæsafjöll   Þjóðgarður
52   882   Jökulsárgljúfur
Krafla   51   Rettarfoss
Reykjahlíð   818   Búrfellsheiði
Dettifoss
Mývatn
Skútustaðir
Grímsstaðir

Rauðinúpur
Melrakkaslétta
Raufarhöfn
RFN
Kópasker
90

Saudanes   L a n g a n e s
Þórshöfn   Fontur
64

Pistilfjörður

Draugafoss
Bakkafjörður
Syðri-Hágangur   85
952   29
Vopnafjörður
1035   57
Bjarnarey
Smjörfjöll
1251
Kirkjubær
Bakkagerði
Eiðar   Herfell
Fellabær   1055
EGS
Egilsstaðir
Hallormsstaður   92
Þingmúli   24
Seyðisfjörður
30   Brekka
Reyðarfjörður   NOR
36   Neskaupstaður
Eskifjörður
Lambafell   Fáskrúðsfjörður
1201   Gerpir

Bakkaflói

04

Vopnafjörður

Herðubreiðar-
friðland
Herðubreið
1682
Sænautasel   88
Þríhyrningsfjallgarður
Snæfell
1833   H r a u n

05

Glettinganes

Herðubreiðarlindir
Ódáðahraun
Dimmifjallgarður
Jökulsá á Fjöllum

Grendill
1570   Þrándarjökull
1248
Heydalir
62   Stöðvarfjörður
Breiðdalsvík
Jökulgilstindar
1313
Djúpivogur
Papey

Skálafells-
jökull
Hoffell
1
HFN
Höfn
Stokksnes

Nesjahverfi
Hvalnes

06

Norðoyar

Risin & Kellingin   Eiði
882   Enniberg
Mykines   Streymoy   844   Viðareiði
Vestmanna   Eysturoy   Fugloy
Vagar   Hvalvík   Klaksvík
Sørvágur   Leirvík   Svínoy
FAE   Kvívík   Borðoy
Koltur   Tóttir
Føroya Fornminnissavn
Tórshavn
Kirkjubøur
Skopun   Nólsoy
Sandoy
Skúvoy   Skálavík

Føroyar
(Færøerne)

Skopunarfjørður

07

Suðuroyarfjørður
Stóra Dímun
Litla Dímun
Drelnes
Suðuroy   610
Vágur
Akraberg
Flesjarnar

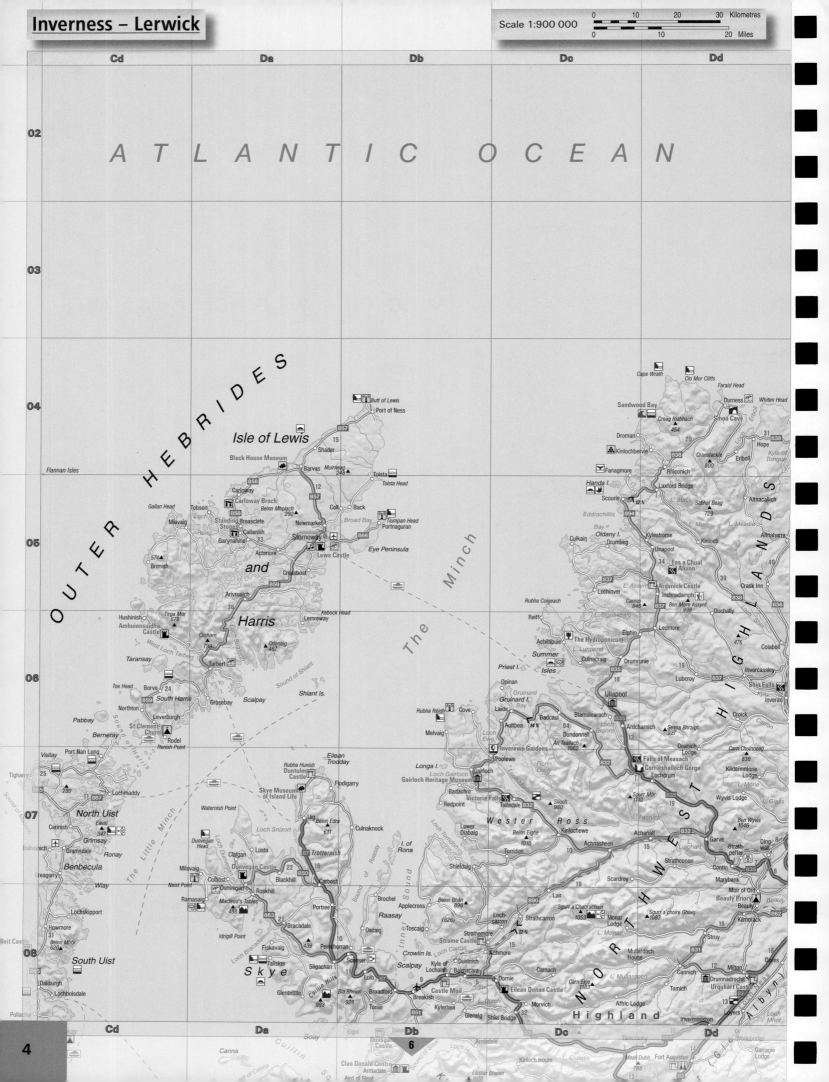

Scale 1:900 000

0 10 20 30 Kilometres
0   10   20 Miles

Cd   Da   Db   Dc   Dd

02

A T L A N T I C   O C E A N

03

04

OUTER HEBRIDES

Flannan Isles

Isle of Lewis

Black House Museum

Butt of Lewis
Port of Ness

857
Shader
15
Barvas
Muirneag
248
Tolsta
Tolsta Head

858
Carloway
857
12
Carloway Broch
Beinn Mholach
292
Coll
Back
Broad Bay
Newmarket
Tiumpan Head
Portnaguran
Stornoway
866
Eye Peninsula
Lews Castle

Gallan Head
Tobson
Miavaig
Loch Roag
Standing Breasclete
Stones
Garynahine
Callanish
33
Achmore
574
Brenish
Crossbost
859
and
Arivruaich
36
Kebock Head
Harris
Lemreway

Hushinish
Amhuinnsuidhe
Castle
Tirga Mór
679
Clisham
799
Crionaig
467

Taransay
Tarbert
West Loch Tarbert
Sound of Shiant

Toe Head
Borve
24
South Harris
859
Grosebay
Scalpay
Shiant Is.

Pabbay
Northton
Leverburgh
St Clement's
Church
Rodel
Renish Point

Berneray

Vallay
Port Nan Long
Tighary
25
230
11
867
Lochmaddy

North Uist
Eaval
347
Carinish
Grimsay
Balivanich
Gramsdale
Ronay

Benbecula
Wiay
Creagorry

Howmore
31
Beinn Mhor
620
Daliburgh
South Uist
Lochboisdale
Pollachar

The Minch

The Little Minch

Cape Wrath
Clo Mor Cliffs
Faraid Head

Sandwood Bay
Durness
Whiten Head
Creag Riabhach
454
Smoo Cave
Droman
Hope
31
838
Kinlochbervie
20
Cranstackie
800
Eriboll
Kyle of Tongue
Fanagmore
Rhiconich
838
Handa I.
Laxford Bridge
Scourie
12%
894
Altnacallich
Eddrachillis
Bay
L. Stack
Sabhal Beag
729
L. More
L. Meadie
Culkein
Oldany I.
Drumbeg
Kylestrome
Kinloch
40
Unapool
34
Eas a Chual
Aluinn
39
Lochinver
837
Ardvreck Castle
Inchnadamph
Crask Inn
838
836
Rubha Coigeach
Canisp
846
Ben More Assynt
998
Duchally
Reiff
Achiltibuie
The Hydroponicum
Elphin
476
Ledmore
Colaboll
Summer
Isles
L. Lurgainn
Drumrunie
19
Invercassley
Priest I.
835
18
Lubcroy
837
Shin Falls
Culnacraig
Opinan
Ullapool
Inveran
Gruinard
Bay
Gruinard I.
835
Croick
Rubha Réidh
Cove
Laide
Badcaul
Blarnalearoch
Ardcharnich
Seana Bhraigh
927
Carn Chuinneag
838
Aultbea
14%
Dundonnell
64
L. Broom
12
Deanich
Lodge
Melvaig
An Teallach
1062
832
Kildermorrie
Lodge
Inverewe Gardens
Falls of Measach
Corrieshalloch Gorge
Lochdrum
L. Morie
Poolewe
Florin
Loch
Longa I.
Gairloch
Sgurr Mór
1110
835
19
Wyvis Lodge
Loch Gairloch
Gairloch Heritage Museum
832
L. Glass
Badachro
Victoria Falls
Ben Wyvis
1046
Redpoint
Talladale
832
Slioch
980
Garve
Strath-
peffer
8
Wester
Ross
Kinlochewe
Achanalt
Ding-
wall
Lower
Diabaig
Beinn Eighe
1010
10
Achnasheen
15
832
L. Luichart
Torridon
Strathconon
835
Scardroy
Marybank
Shieldaig
Lair
890
Lubh
19
Muir of Ord
Beauly Priory
Beauly
Brochel
Applecross
Beinn Bhán
896
Sgurr a'Chaorachain
1053
Loch-
carron
Monar
Lodge
862
(626)
Strathcarron
Sgurr a'ghoire Ghlais
1083
Kilmorack
Oscaig
Toscaig
Stromemore
12%
L. Monar
16
Raasay
Strome Castle
890
Carn Eige
1183
831
Beinn Bhán
439
Crowlin Is.
Achmore
15
Carnach
Mullardoch
House
12
Milton
Kyle of
Lochalsh
Duirinish
Dornie
Affric Lodge
Tomich
Drumnadrochit
Castle Moil
Balmacara
Eilean Donan Castle
Urquhart Castle
Breakish
Morvich
Affric Lodge
Lovers
Kylerhea
Glenelg
Shiel Bridge
32
Highland
Invermoriston

Rubha Hunish
Duntulm
Castle
Eilean
Trodday
Flodigarry
Skye Museum
of Island Life
Uig
87
Trotternish
Beinn Edra
611
Culnaknock
I. of
Rona
Waternish Point
Loch Snizort
Waternish Point
Dunvegan
Head
Claigan
Lusta
16
Milovaig
Dunvegan Castle
22
850
Blackhill
Neist Point
Colbost
Dunvegan
Roskhill
Carbost
Ramasaig
Macleod's Tables
488
Portree
Bracadale
863
21
10
Idrigill Point
Fiskavaig
439
Peinchorran
Sound of Raasay
Oscaig
Inner Sound
Applecross
Loch Torridon

Skye
Talisker
Sligachan
11
Scalpay
Glenbrittle
Cuillin Hills
Bla Bheinn
928
87
Luib
Broadford
Torrin
851

993
Soay
Elgol
Canna
Cuillin
Loch Brittle

Dunsgaith
Castle
6
Arnisdale
Loch Hourn
Kinloch Hourn
Clan Donald Centre
Armadale
Aird of Sleat
Ladhar Bheinn
Meall Dubh
768
Fort Augustus
Garragie
Lodge

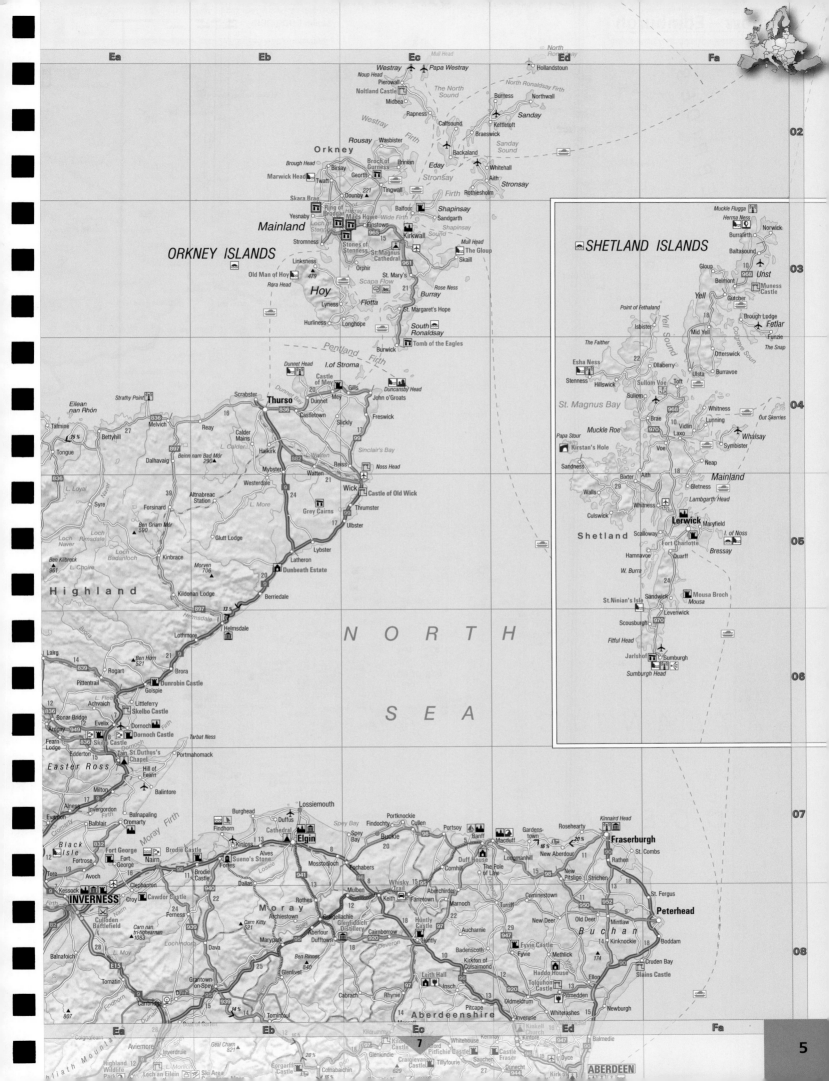

ORKNEY ISLANDS

Westray
Noup Head
Pierowall
Noltland Castle
Midbea
Rapness
Calfsound
Rousay   Wasbister
Orkney
Brough Head   Birsay
Marwick Head   Twatt
Skara Brae
Yesnaby
Ring of Brodgar
Mainland
Maes Howe
Stromness
Stones of Stenness
Linksness
Old Man of Hoy
Røra Head
Hoy
Lyness   Flotta
Hurliness   Longhope
Burwick

Papa Westray
Hollandstoun
North Ronaldsay
Burness   Northwall
Westray Firth   Sanday
Kettletoft
Braeswick
Sanday Sound
Backaland
Eday   Whitehall
Stronsay   Aith   Stronsay
Firth   Rothiesholm
Brinnian
Broch of Gurness   Georth
Dounby   221
Tingwall
Balfour   Shapinsay   Sandgarth
Wide Firth   Shapinsay
Kirkwall   Sound
965   15
St. Magnus Cathedral   961
Orphir
St. Mary's
Scapa Flow   21
Rose Ness
Burray
St. Margaret's Hope
South Ronaldsay
Tomb of the Eagles

Mull Head
The North Sound
North Ronaldsay Firth
Eday
Stronsay
Mull Head
The Gloup
Skaill

SHETLAND ISLANDS

Muckle Flugga
Herma Ness
Burrafirth   Norwick
Baltasound
Gloup   Unst
Belmont   968
Yell   Muness Castle
Gutcher
Point of Fethaland
Mid Yell   Brough Lodge   Fetlar
Isbister   Otterswick   Funzie
The Faither   The Snap
Esha Ness   22
Stenness   Ollaberry   Burravoe
Hillswick   Sullom Voe
St. Magnus Bay   Sullom   Toft
Brae   Whitness
Muckle Roe   968   Lunning   Out Skerries
Papa Stour   Vidlin
Kirstan's Hole   970   Laxo   Whalsay
Sandness   Voe   Symbister
Walls   Neap
Bixter   Aith   18   Mainland
Gletness
Whitness   Lambgarth Head
Culswick   Lerwick   I. of Noss
Shetland   Scalloway   Maryfield
Fort Charlotte
Hamnavoe   Quarff   Bressay
W. Burra   24
Sandwick   Mousa Broch
St.Ninian's Isle   Mousa
Levenwick
Scousburgh   970
Fitful Head
Jarlshof   Sumburgh
Sumburgh Head

NORTH SEA

Eilean nan Rhón
Strathy Point
Talmine   15 %
Tongue   Bettyhill
Melvich
Reay
Scrabster
Thurso   836
Dunnet Bay   Dunnet
Castletown
Calder Mains
Halkirk
Westerdale
Watten   Wick   Castle of Old Wick
Reiss   Noss Head
Mybster   Watten   21
9   24
Thrumster
Grey Cairns   99
17   Ulbster
Lybster
Latheron
Dunbeath Estate
Berriedale
Kildonan Lodge
13 %
Helmsdale
Lothmore
Brora
Dunrobin Castle
Golspie
Littleferry   Skelbo Castle

Dunnet Head
Castle of Mey
Mey   Gills   Duncansby Head
John o'Groats
Slickly   Freswick
Sinclair's Bay
99

Beinn nam Bad Mór 290
L. Calder
882
Altnabreac Station
L. More
Glutt Lodge
Ben Griam Mór 590
Morven 706
Kinbrace
20
Kildonan Lodge
Helmsdale
897
Ben Horn 521
Rogart
Brora
Pittentrail
L. Fleet
Achvaich

Highland
L. Loyal
836
L. Naver
Syre
Forsinard
Loch Naver
Ben Klibreck 961
L. Choire
Loch Rimsdale
Loch Badanloch

Lairg
14
839
Bonar Bridge
Ardgay   949   Evelix   Dornoch
Fearn Lodge   836   Skibo Castle   Dornoch Castle
Edderton   Tain St.Duthus's Chapel
Portmahomack
Tarbat Ness
Hill of Fearn
Balintore

Easter Ross
Milton
Alness
Evanton   Invergordon
Balblair   Balnapaling
Cromarty
Black Isle   832
Fortrose
Tore
Avoch   Fort George   Fort George
Kessock
INVERNESS
Culloden Battlefield
Cawdor Castle
Croy   Nairn
Carn nan tri-tighearnan 1083
Ferness
Balnafoich
L. Moy
Tomatin
807
E15
Carrbridge
Duthil
14 %
Aviemore
Inverdruie
Highland Wildlife Park
Loch an Eilein
Ski Area
Sgoran Mountain
Geal Charn 821

Burghead   Lossiemouth
Duffus   Spey Bay
Findhorn   Cathedral   **Elgin**
Kinloss   Sueno's Stone
Brodie Castle   Alves
Forres   Lossie
Nairn   Mosstodloch   Fochabers
Clephanton   941
Brodie Castle   Dallas
940   Rothes
Moray   Aberlour
Dufftown
Marypark   Glenfiddich Distillery
Carn Kitty 521   Cairnborrow
939   Achiestown   Glenlivet
Ben Rinnes 840
Dava
25
Grantown-on-Spey
939   14 %   Tomintoul
Cabrach
Rhynie
Kildrummy
Aberdeenshire

Spey Bay   Portknockie   Cullen
Findochty   Portsoy
Buckie   Banff   Macduff
Whisky Trail   Duff House
Keith   Aberchirder   Cornhill
Farmtown   The Pole of Law
Mulben   Marnoch   Longmanhill
Huntly Castle   Turriff
Cairnborrow   Huntly   Aucharnie
Badensoch   New Deer
Kirkton of Cushnie   Old Deer
Leith Hall   Insch   Mintlaw
Kinknockie   Boddam
Methlick   174   Cruden Bay
Fyvie Castle   Ellon   Slains Castle
Haddo House
Tolquhon Castle   Pitmedden
Oldmeldrum   Newburgh
Pitcape   Inverurie   Whiterashes

Kinnaird Head
Rosehearty   **Fraserburgh**
20 %   St. Combs
New Aberdour   Rathen
New Pitsligo   Strichen
St. Fergus
Peterhead
950   952
Buchan
Cruden Bay
Slains Castle

Kinkell Church   Whitehouse   Kemnay   Balmedie
Kildrummy Castle   Castle Fraser
Corgarff Castle   Colpy   Craigievar Castle   Tillyfourie   Dunecht   Dyce
Glenkindie   Kirk   **ABERDEEN**

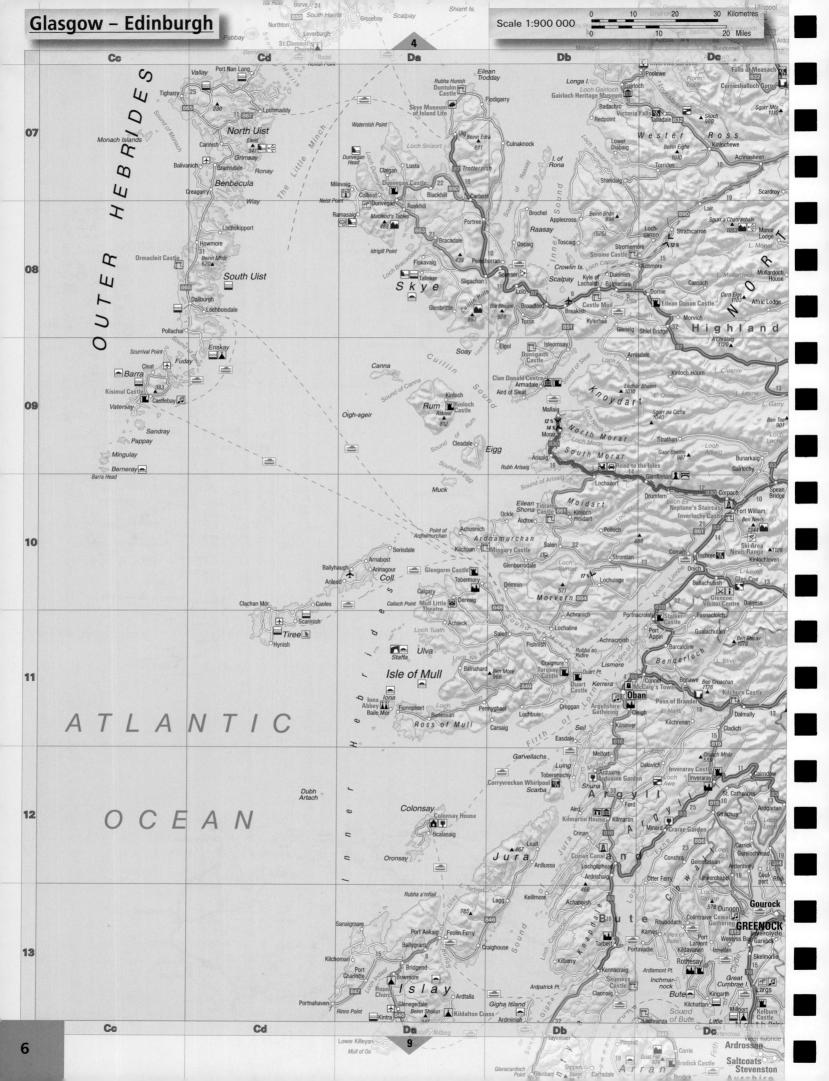

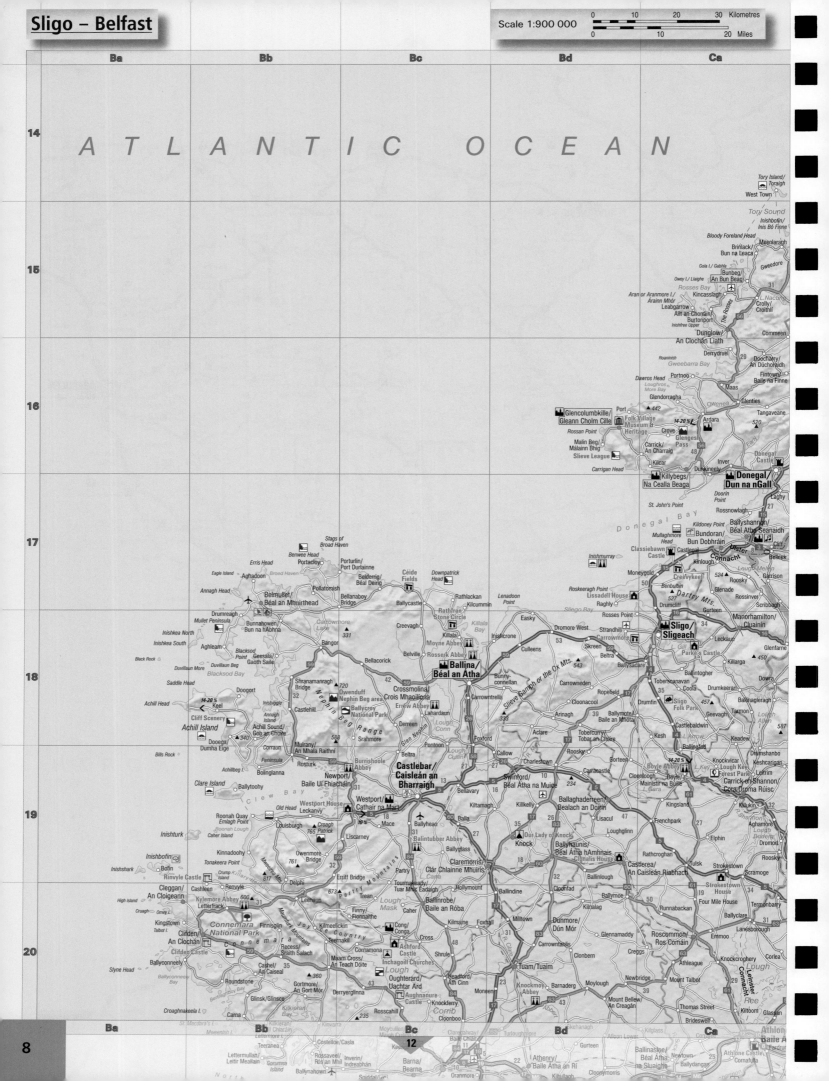

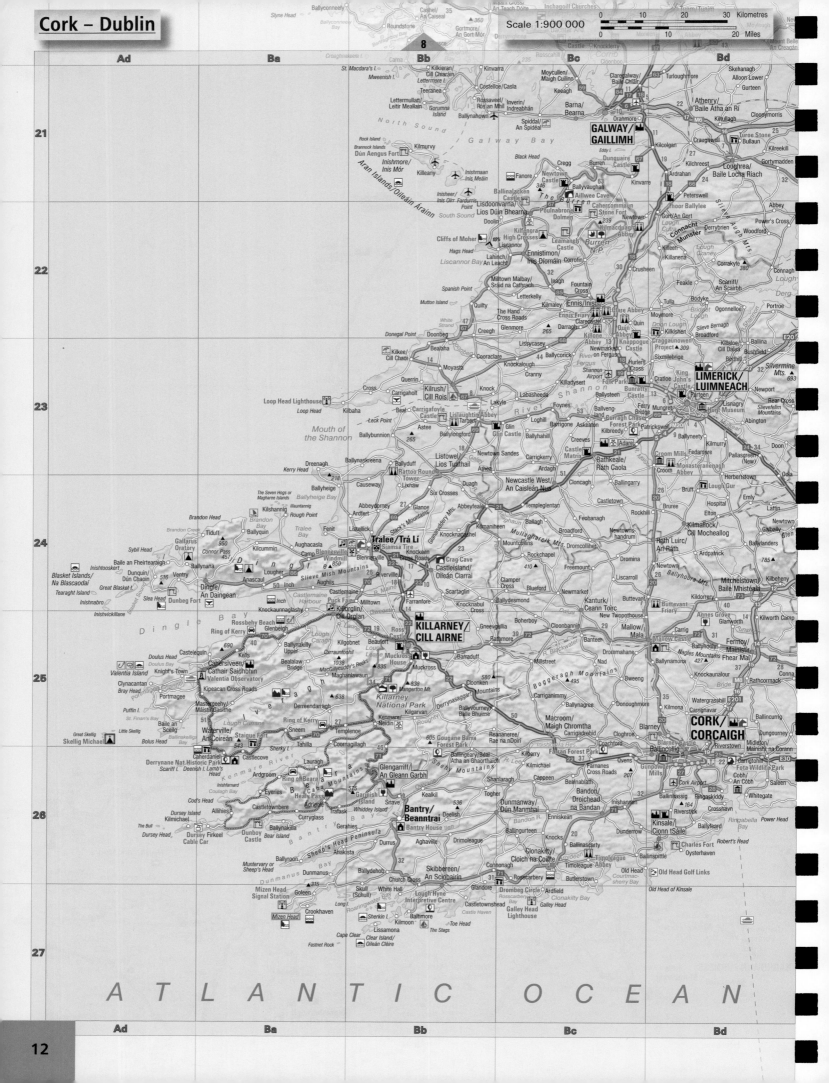

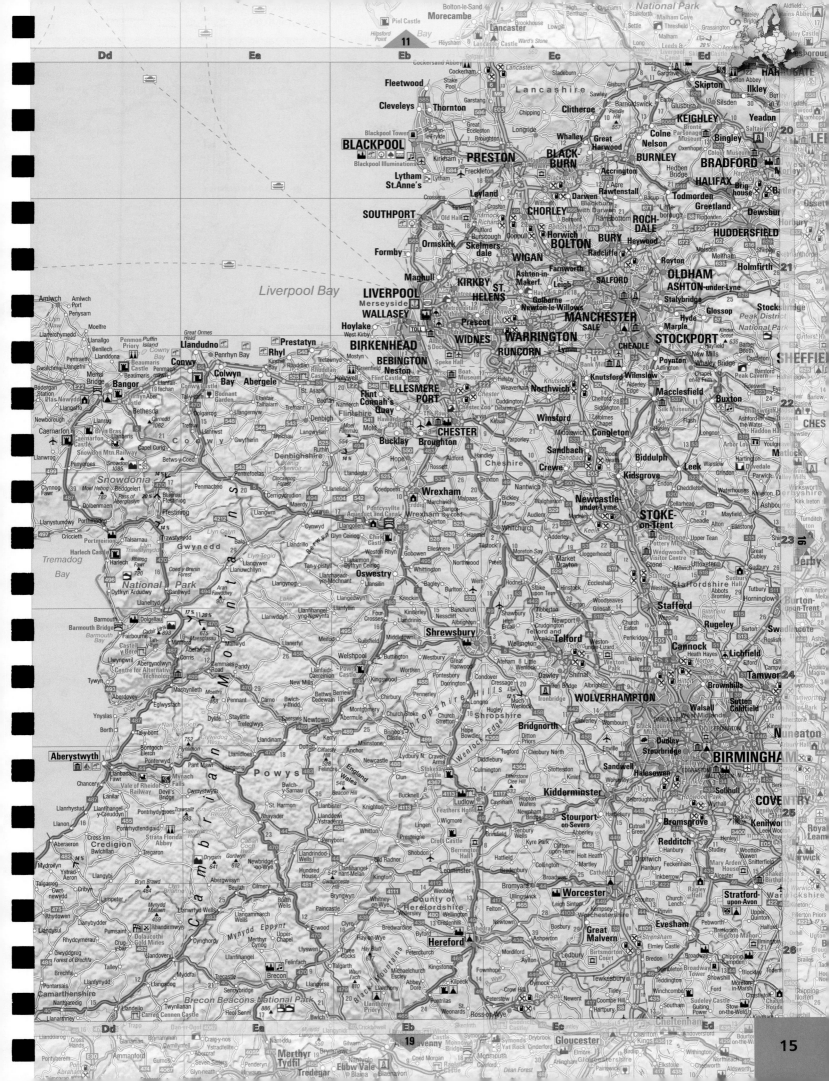

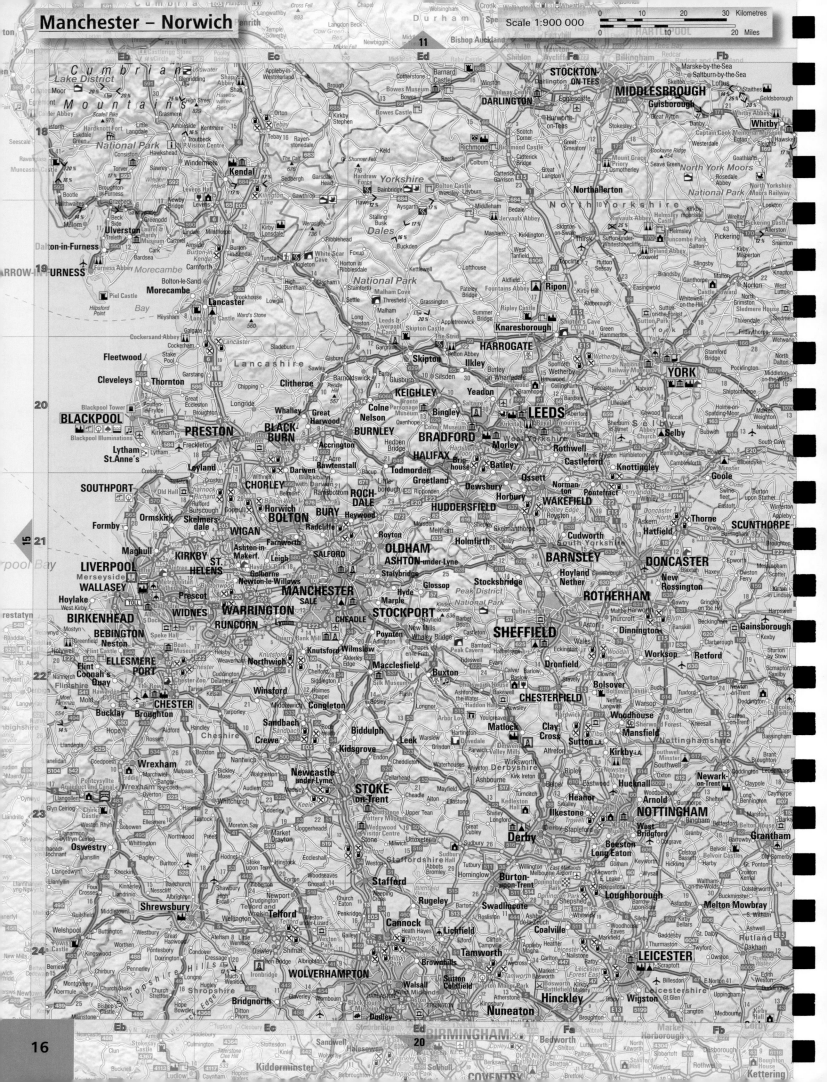

Scale 1:900 000

18

19

N O R T H

20

S E A

21

22

23

24

Robin
Hood's Bay
Ravenscar
Cloughton
17 %
Scarborough Castle
Scarborough
Ayton
Seamer
Brompton
Filey
17 %   Saxton
Humanby
Reighton
Filey Bay
Flamborough
Langtoft   Boynton
Burton Agnes Hall   Flamborough Head
Kilham   Bridlington
Burton   Bridlington
Agnes   Bay
Driffield
Lissett
Bainton   Skipsea
Bedford   Skipsea Castle

East Riding
of Yorkshire
Leven   Hornsea
Sligglesthorne
Minster   South
Beverley   Skirlaugh
Aldbrough
KINGSTON   Burton
UPON HULL   Constable
Skidby   Sproatley   Tunstall
The Deep   Hedon
North   Holy Trinity Church   Withernsea
Ferriby
TOLL   Humber Bridge
outh   New Holland
Ferriby   Barton-upon-Humber
Thornton   Patrington
Curtis   Thornton Abbey   Easington
Immingham   Kilnsea
North Lincolnshire   Spurn
M180   180   Head
Keelby
Brigg   Barnetby   GREAT
le Wold   GRIMSBY
Cleethorpes
Redbourne   North East   Humberston
Caistor   Lincolnshire
Nettleton   Waltham
Moortown   East
Ravendale   North Thoresby
Binbrook   North
Market   Somercotes
Middle   Rasen   Saltfleet
Rasen   Ludborough
Spridlington   Ludford
Dunholme   Hainton   Louth
Fulnetby   Mablethorpe
Wragby   Withern   Sutton on Sea
Scamblesby
Burwell
Baumber   Maltby
le Marsh   Mumby
Alford
LINCOLN   Tetford   Ulceby
High Bridge   Horncastle   Willoughby   Chapel
Bracebridge Heath   St. Leonards
Waddington   Bardney   Partney   Ingoldmells
Lincolnshire   Candlesby
Metheringham   Spilsby   Skegness
Woodhall Spa   Burgh
Navenby   Keal   le Marsh
Scopwick   Coningsby
Billinghay   Stickney
Ruskington   Tattershall   Eastville
Tattershall Castle   Wainfleet All Saints
Cranwell   S. Kyme   Wrangle   Friskney
Kirkby-   Langrick
la-Thorpe   Old Lake
Sleaford   St. Botolph's   Benington
Heckington   Church   Freiston
Wilsford   Boston
Scredington   The Wash
Ropsley   Bicker
Folkingham   Kirton End
Billingborough   Hunstanton   Brancaster   Blakeney
Dowsby   Holbeach   Thornham   Bay   Holkham   Point
Ingoldsby   Gosberton   St. Matthew   Heacham   Burnham   Bay   W.Runton   Cromer
Kirby   Market   N. Creake   Holkham Hall   Blakeney   Kelling   Overstrand
Corby Glen   Underwood   Gedney   Docking   Wells-   Holt   Felbrigg Hall   Thorpe
Pinchbeck   Dove End   next-the-Sea   Market   Mundesley
Saracen's   Lit. Walsingham   Briston
Spalding   Head   Sandringham   Great   Barney   Corpusty   North
Bourne   Whaplode   Long   House   Snoring   Fakenham   Blicking   Walsham
Deeping   Sutton   Sutton   Great Bircham   Barmingham   Hall   Honing
Castle   St. Nicholas   St. James   N. Wootton   East Rudham   Wood Dalling   Aylsham
Bytham   Holbeach   Castle   Brisley   Cawston   Scottow   Hickling
Market   King's Lynn   Rising   Hillington   Weasenham   Reepham   Honing   Green
Deeping   Houghton   St. Peter   Bawdeswell   Coltishall   Winterton-
Stamford   Cowbit   Hall   Guist   Norfolk   on-Sea
Burghley   Walpole   W. Winch   Litcham   Elsing   Hevingham   Broads
House   St. Andrew   Grimston   Hainford   Horning   Ormesby
Wisbech   St. Mary Magdalen   Castle Acre   East   Wroxham   St. Margaret
Marholm   Crowland   W. Winch   Swaffham   Dereham   St. Helen   Bastwick
Peterborough   Sutton   E. Winch   Norfolk   Caister-on-Sea
Nene Valley   St. Edmund   Marham   Yaxham   Costessey   Acle   Great Yarmouth
Railway   Thorney   Wending   NORWICH
King's Cliffe   Eye   Downham   Swaffham   Cranworth   Norwich   Freethorpe
PETERBOROUGH   Whittlesey   Market   Barford   Easton   Castle   Burgh Castle   Hopton
Fotheringhay   Guyhirn   Goodestone   Ashill   Easton   Mulbarton   Loddon   Seething
Bedford   Nordelph   Oxburgh   Watton   Great
Levels   March   Stoke Ferry   Hall   Ellingham   Saxlingham
Welney   Southery   Thompson   Nethergate

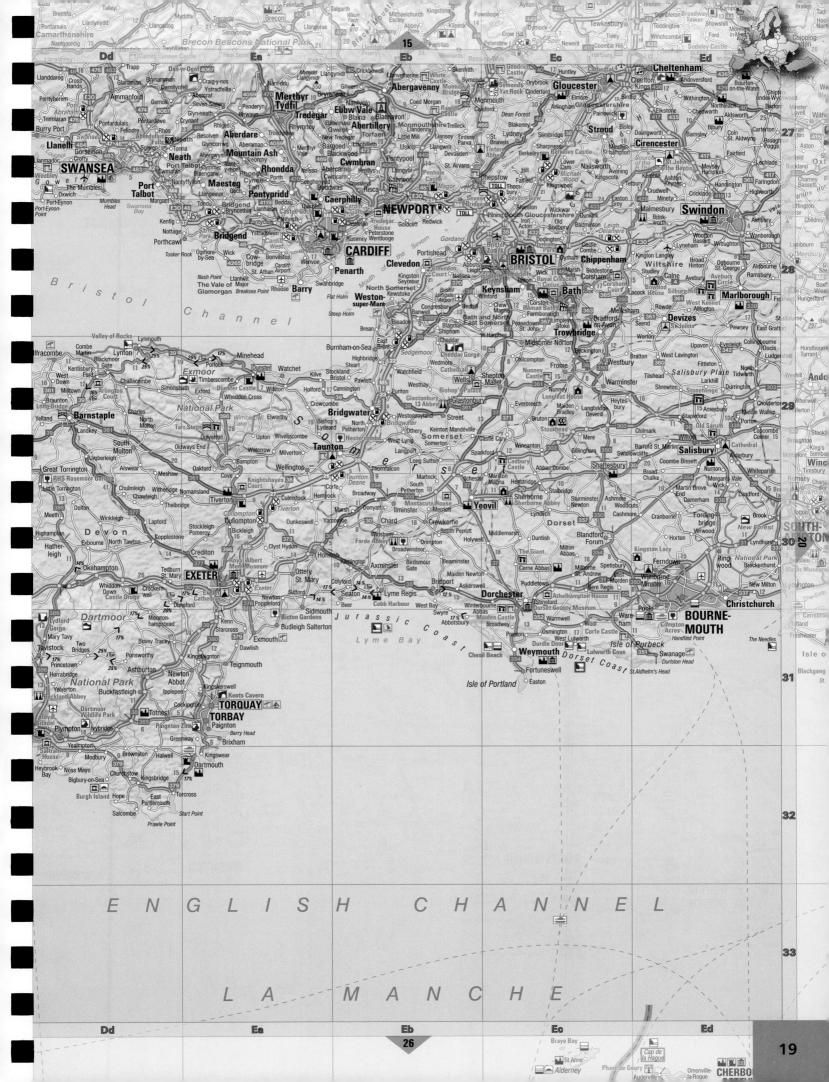

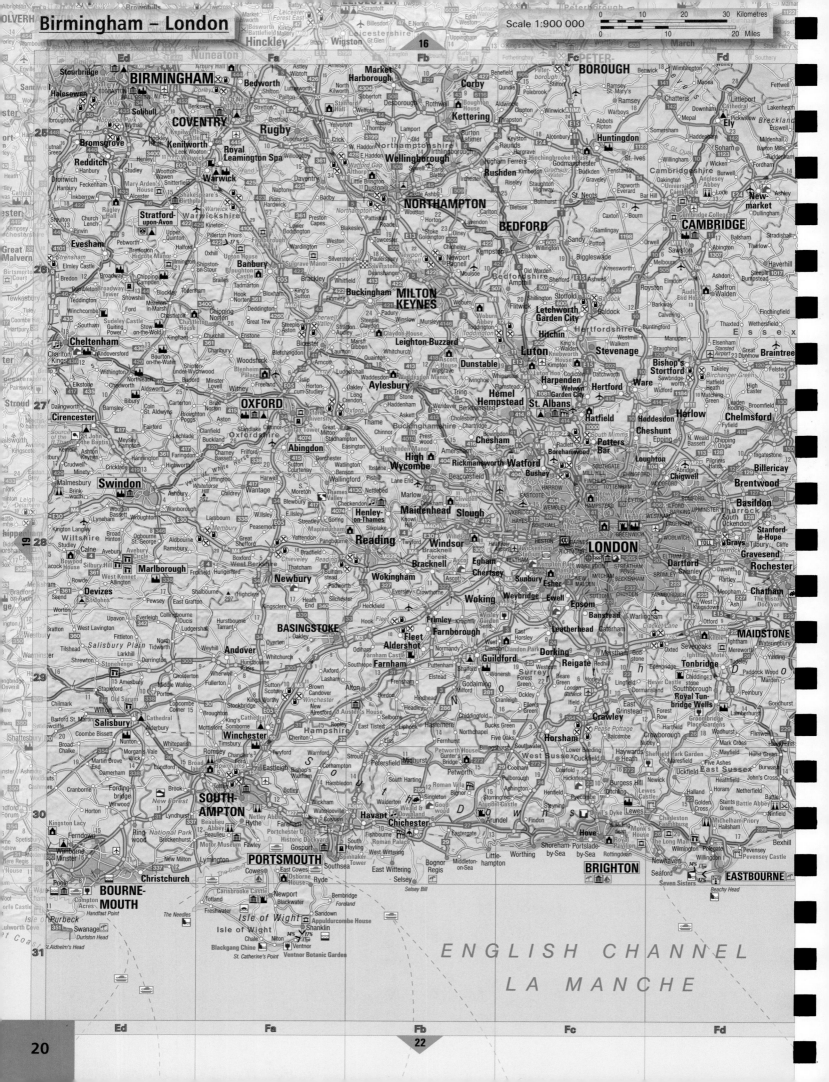

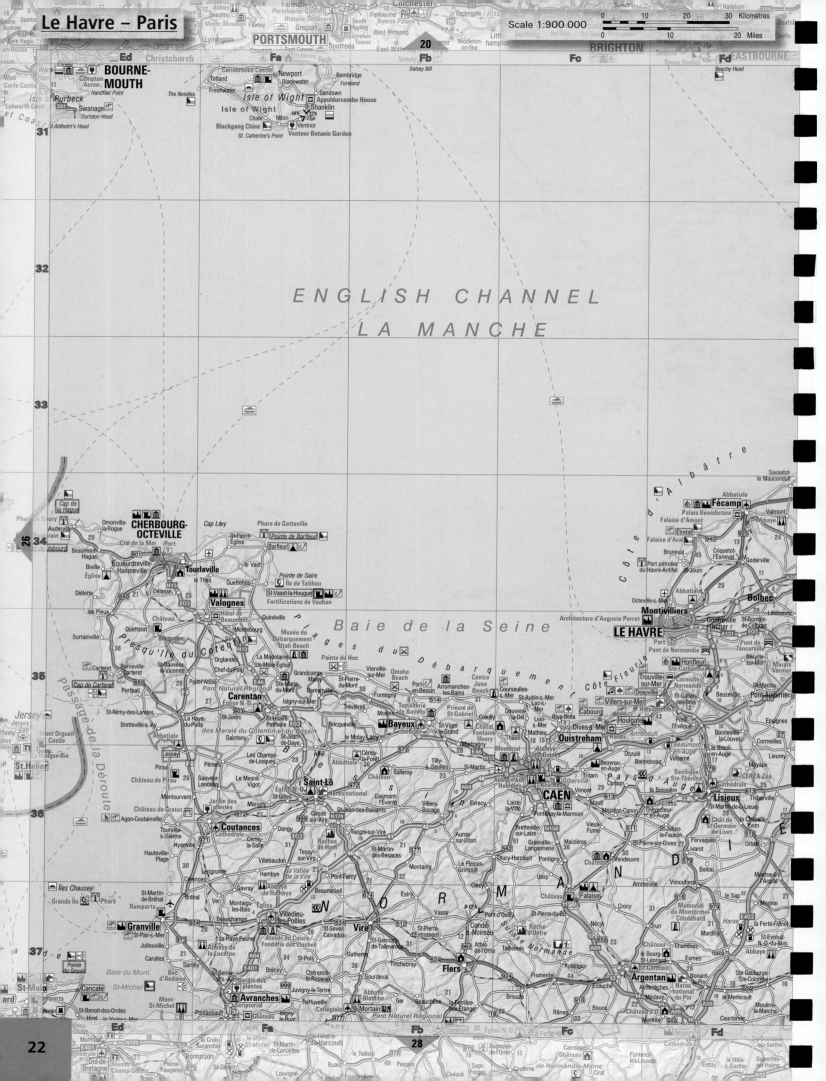

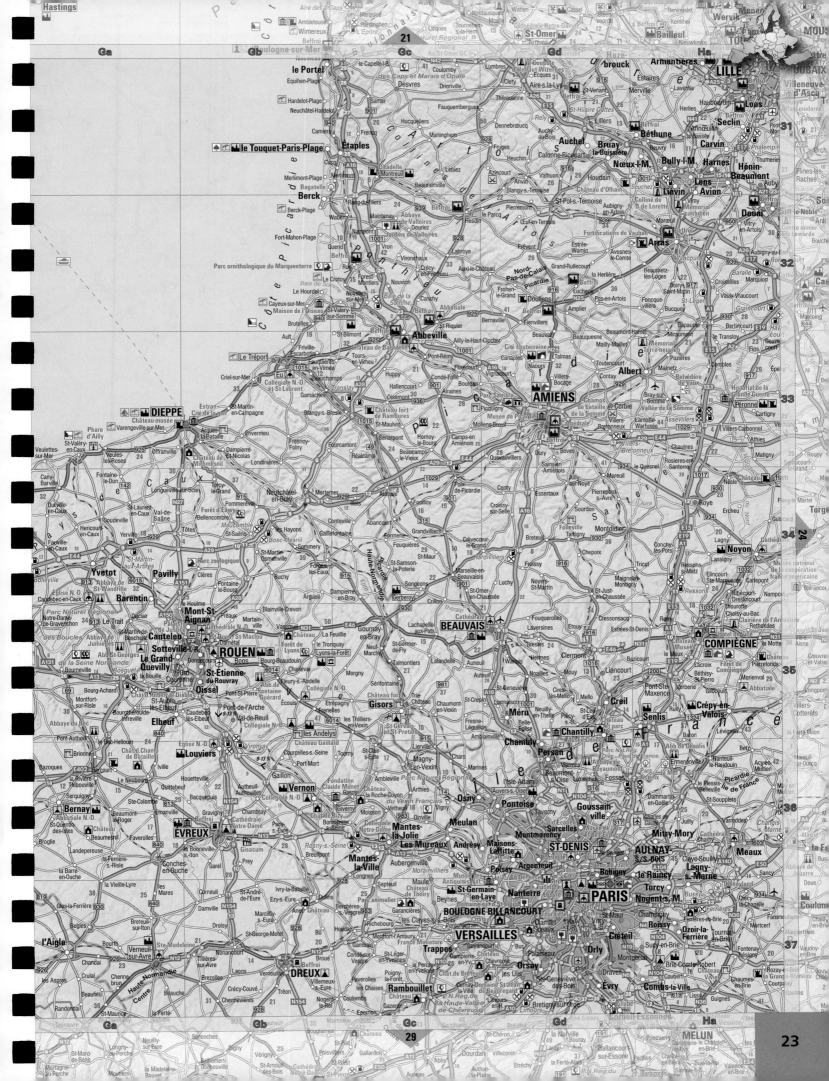

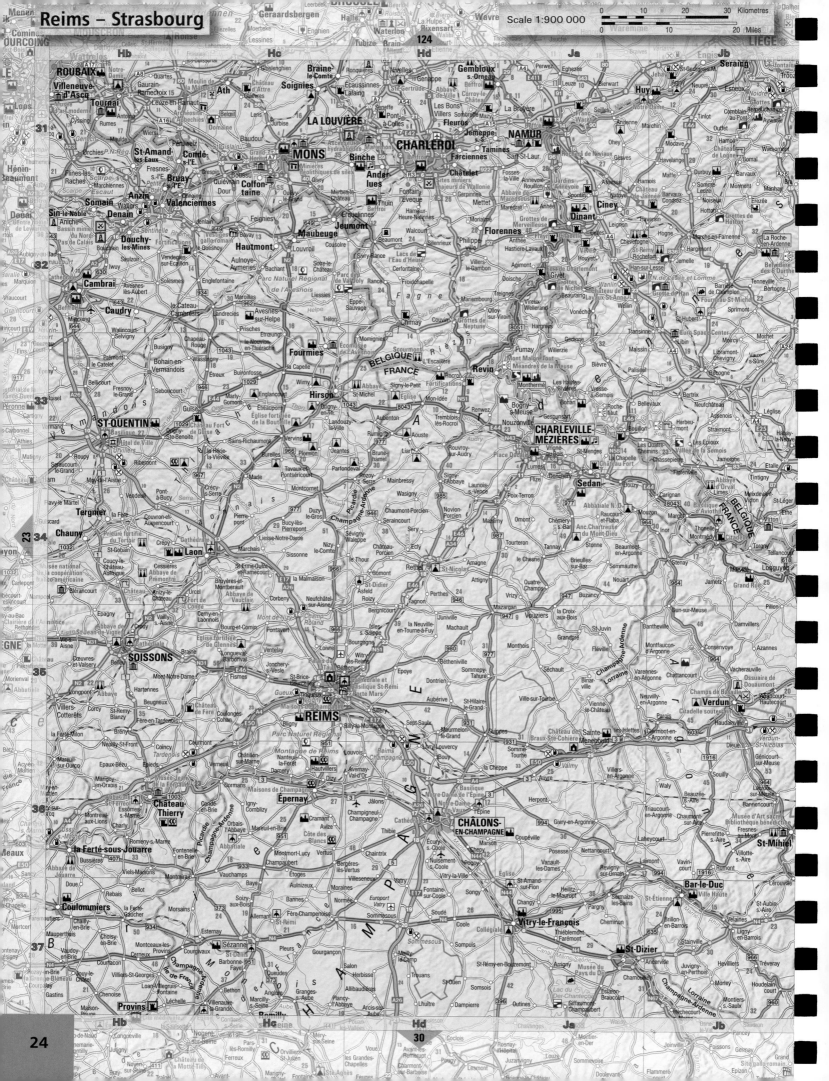

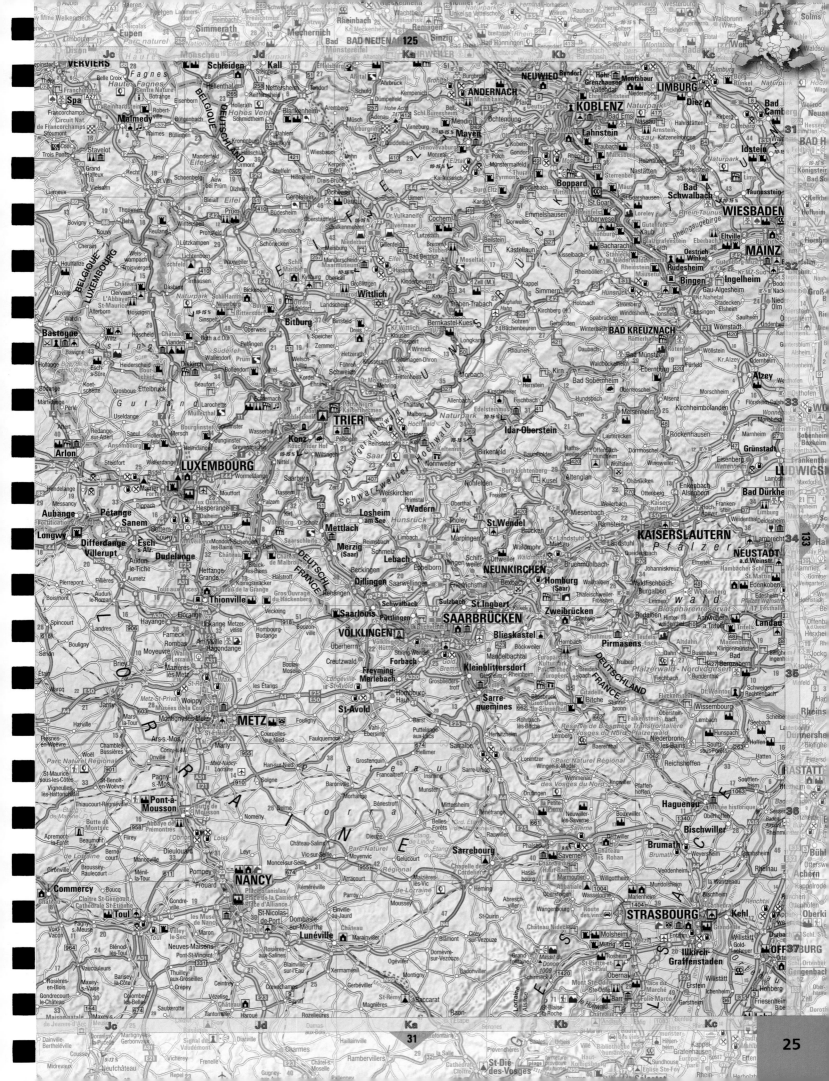

Scale 1:900 000

0   10   20   30 Kilometres
0   10   20 Miles

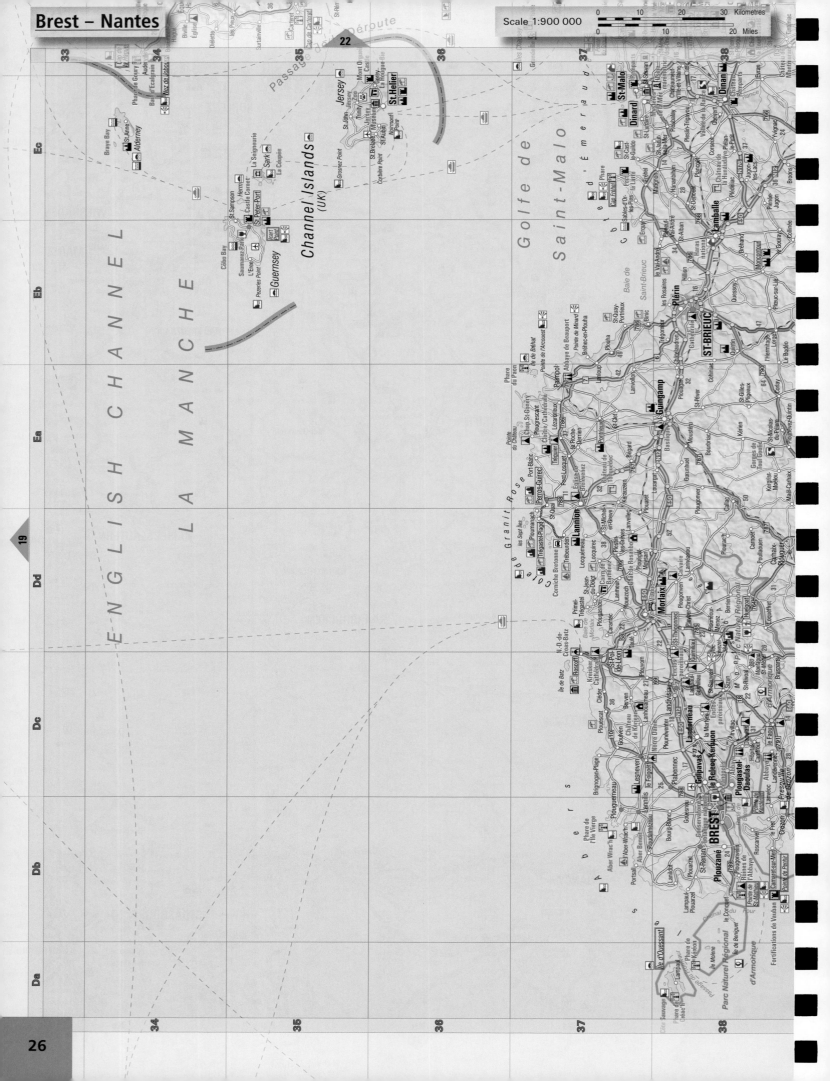

ENGLISH CHANNEL

LA MANCHE

Channel Islands (UK)

Jersey
St.Helier

Guernsey

Golfe de
Saint-Malo

St-Malo
Dinard
Dinan
Lamballe

ST-BRIEUC
Plérin

Guingamp

Lannion

Morlaix

Landerneau
Landivisiau

Roscoff

BREST
Plouzané

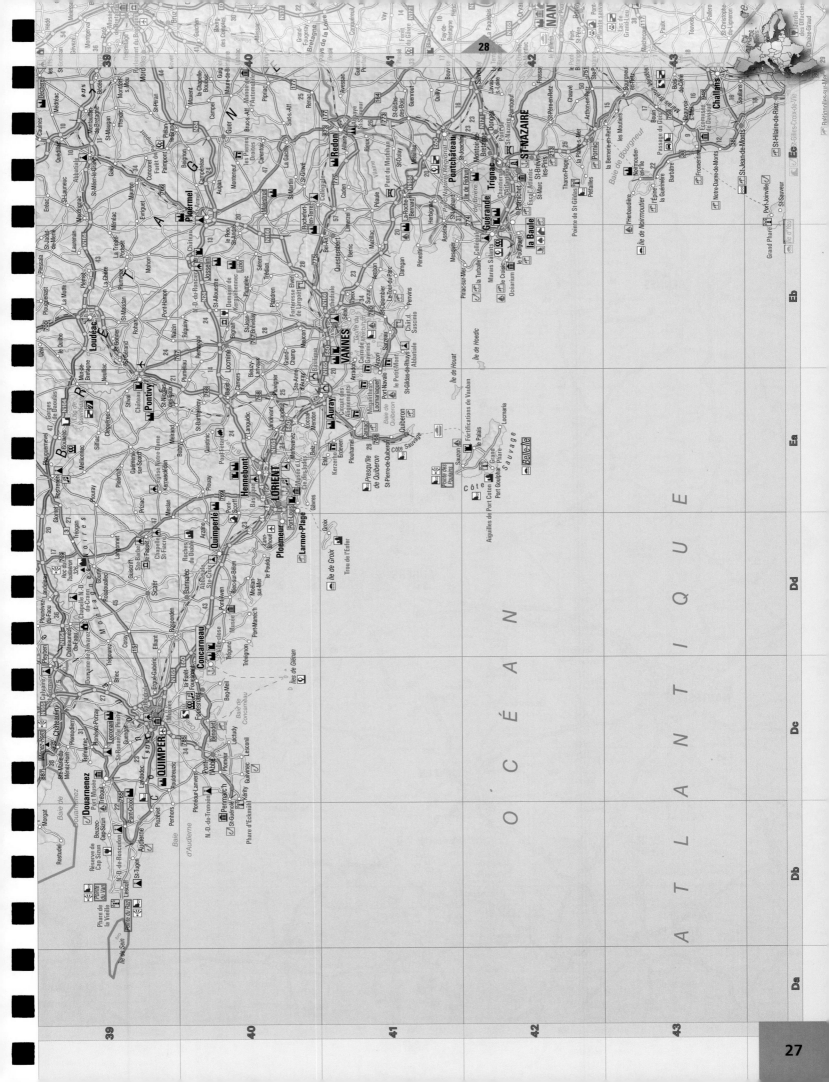

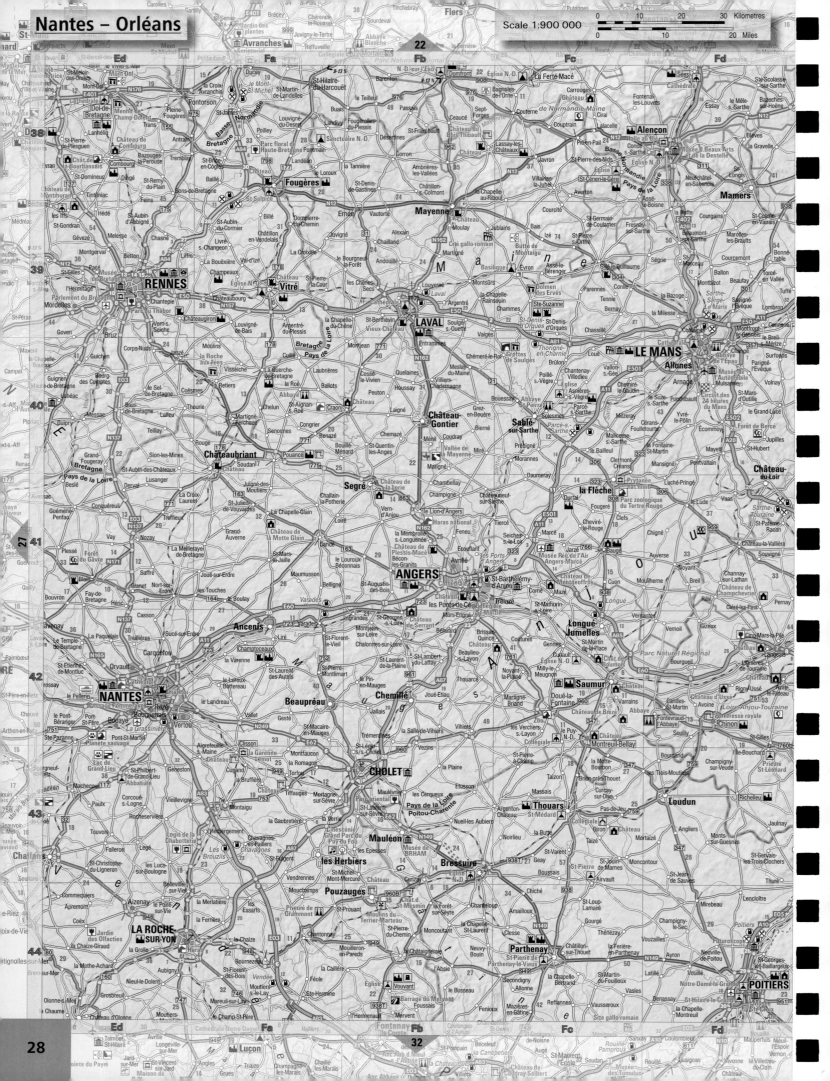

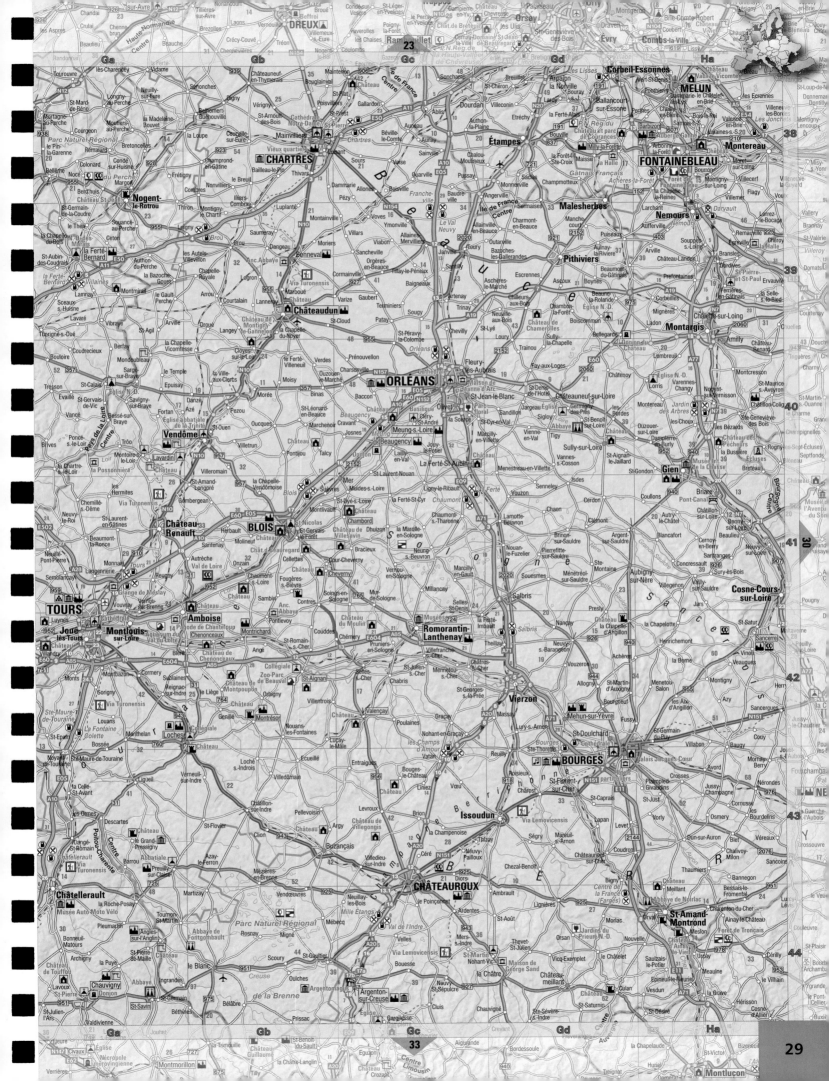

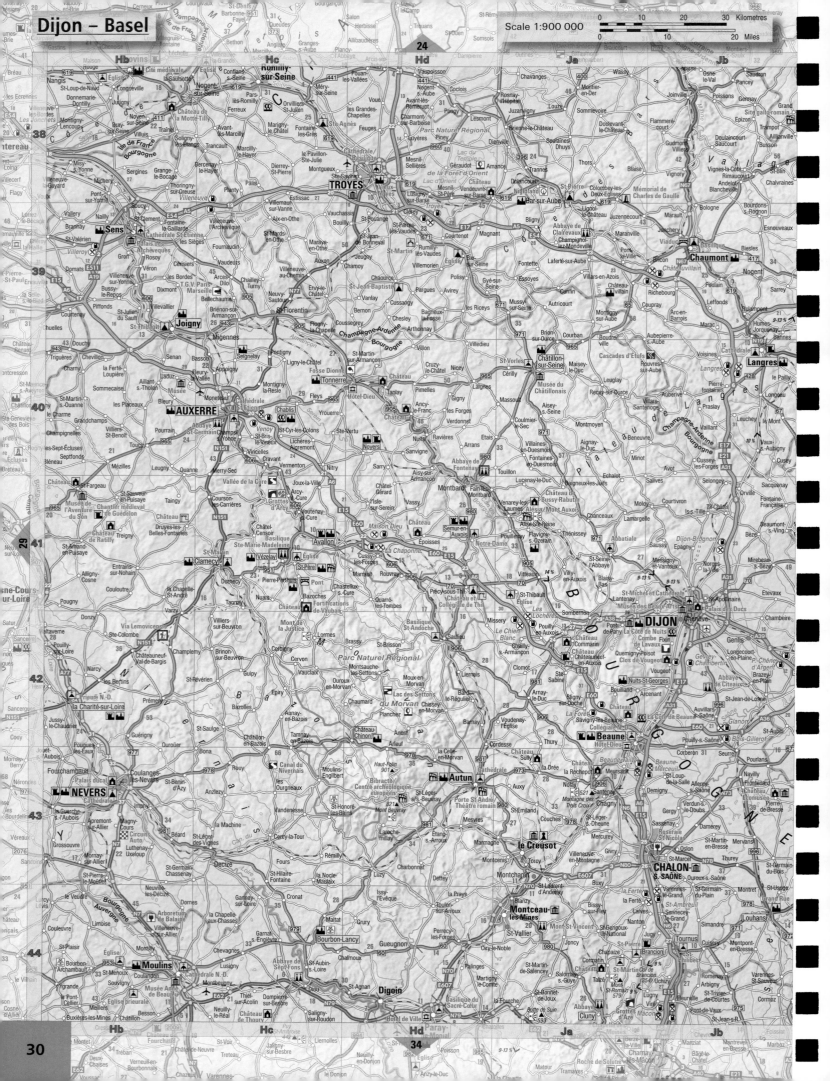

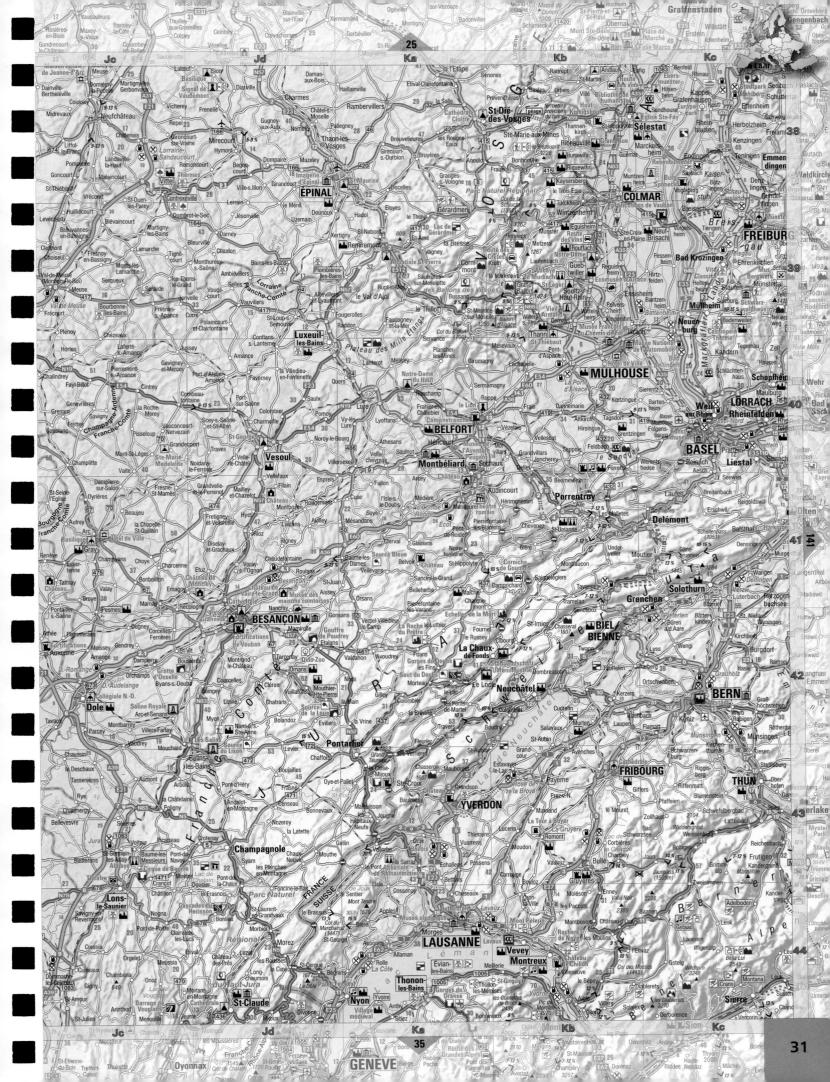

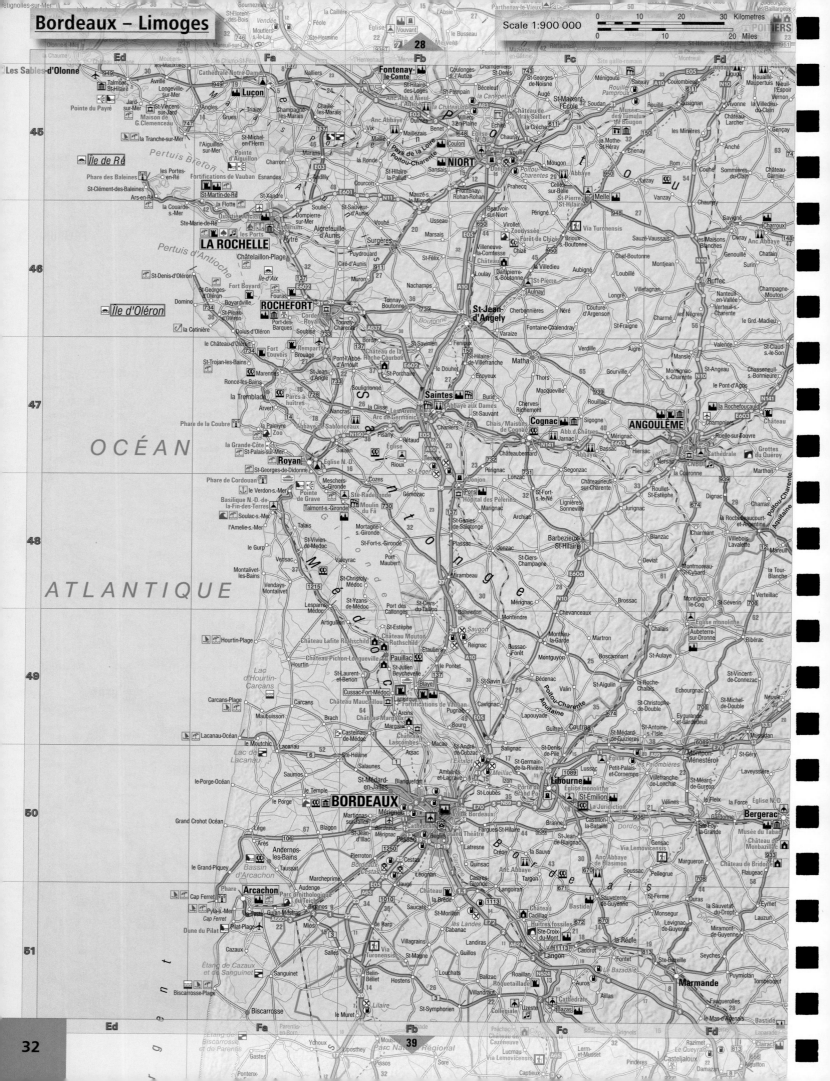

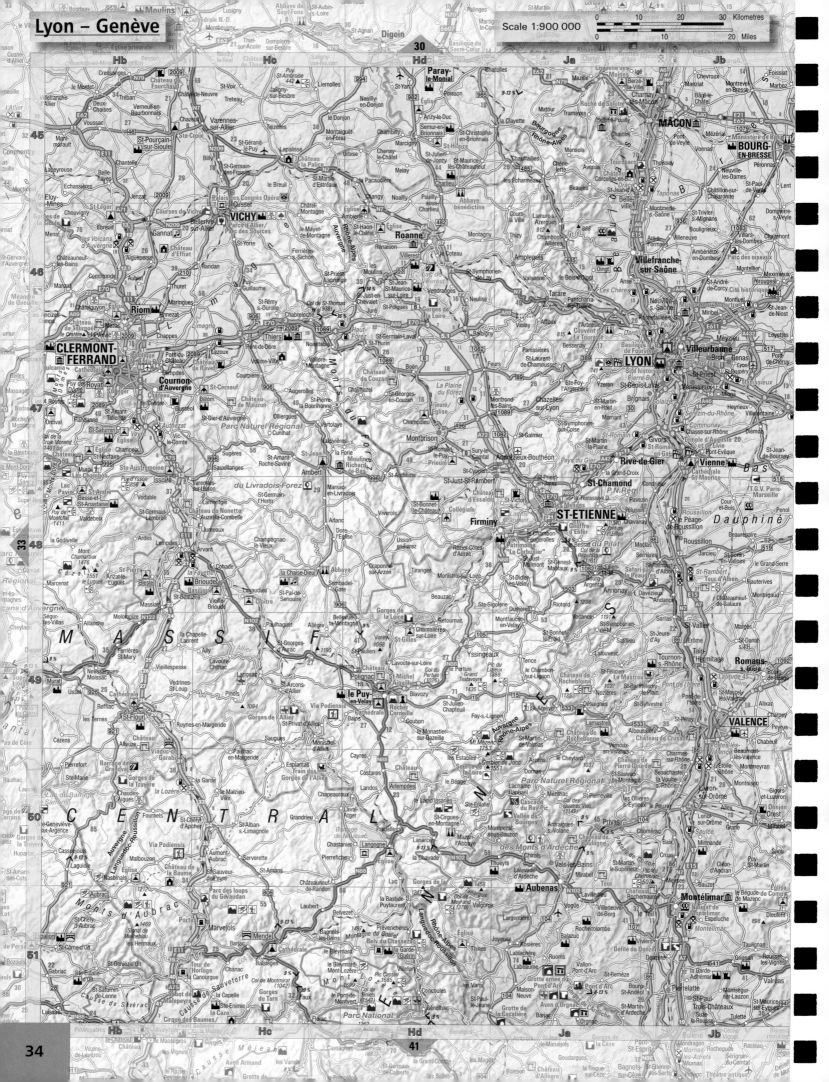

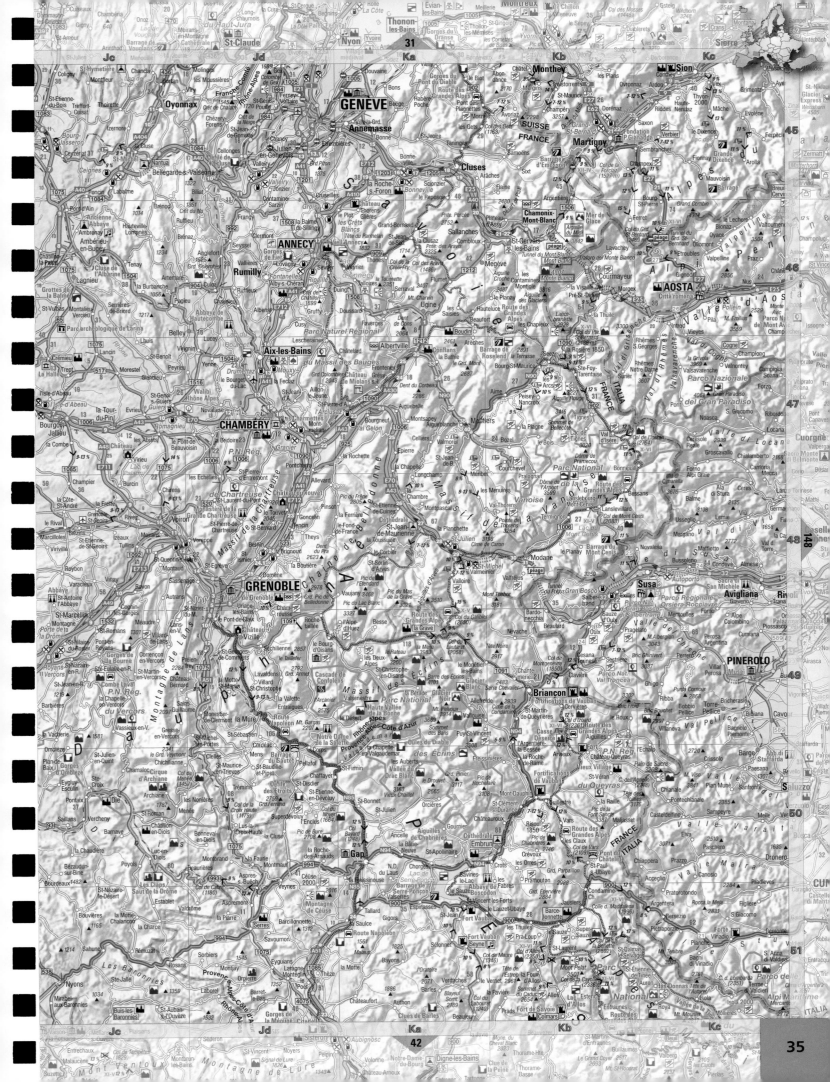

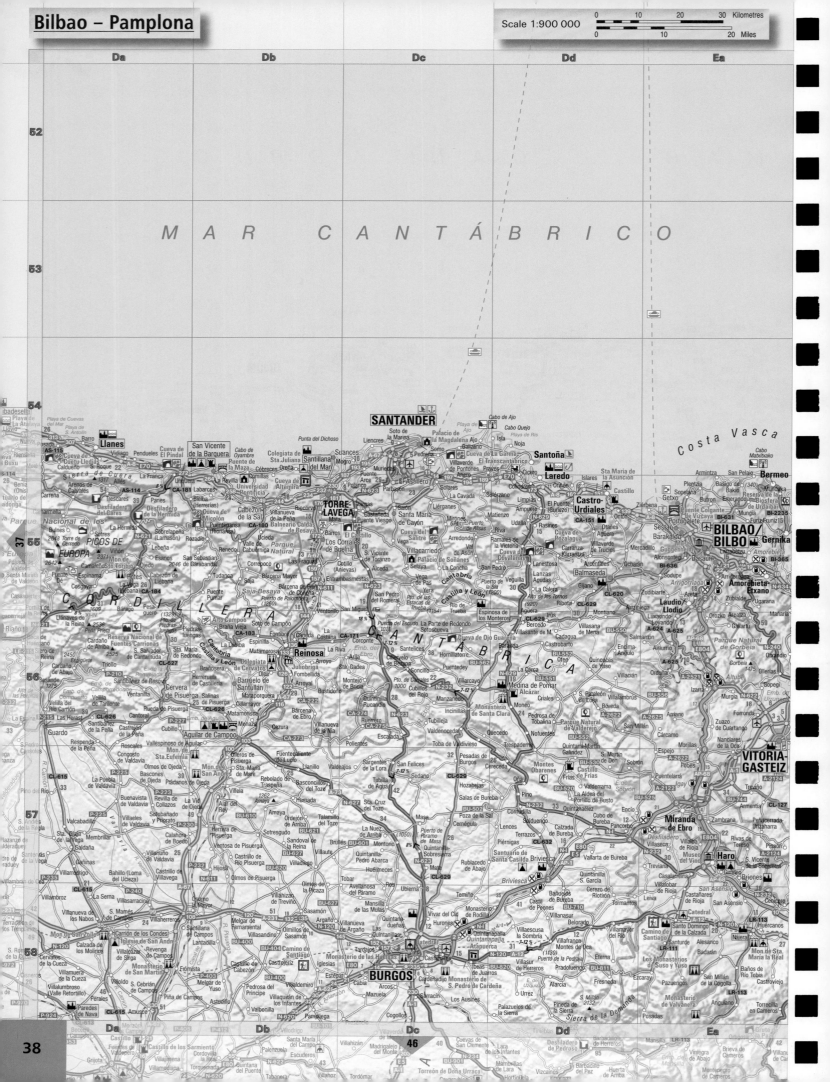

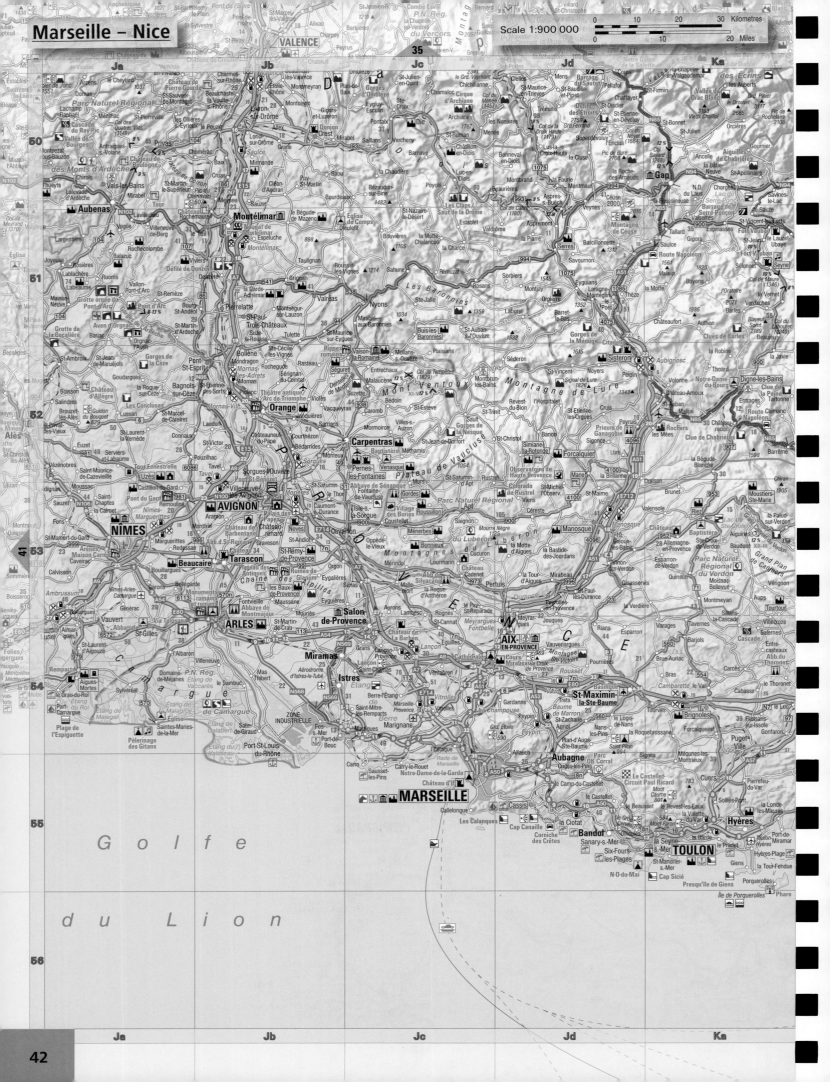

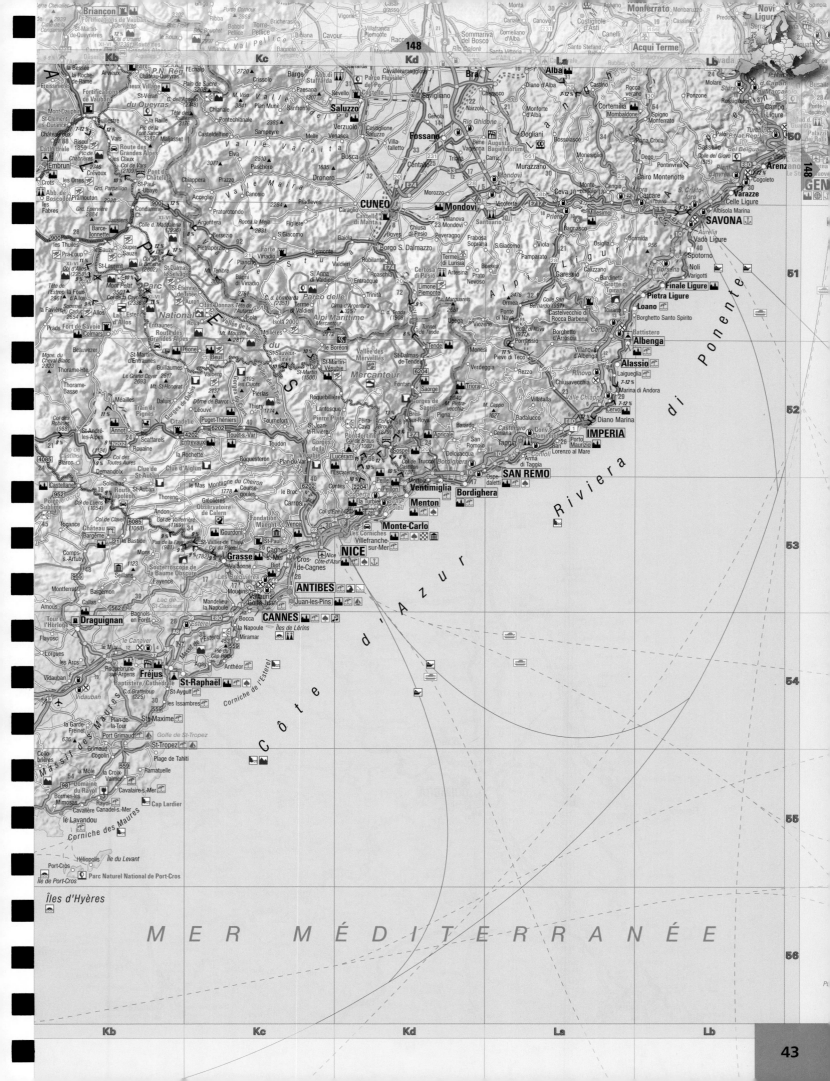

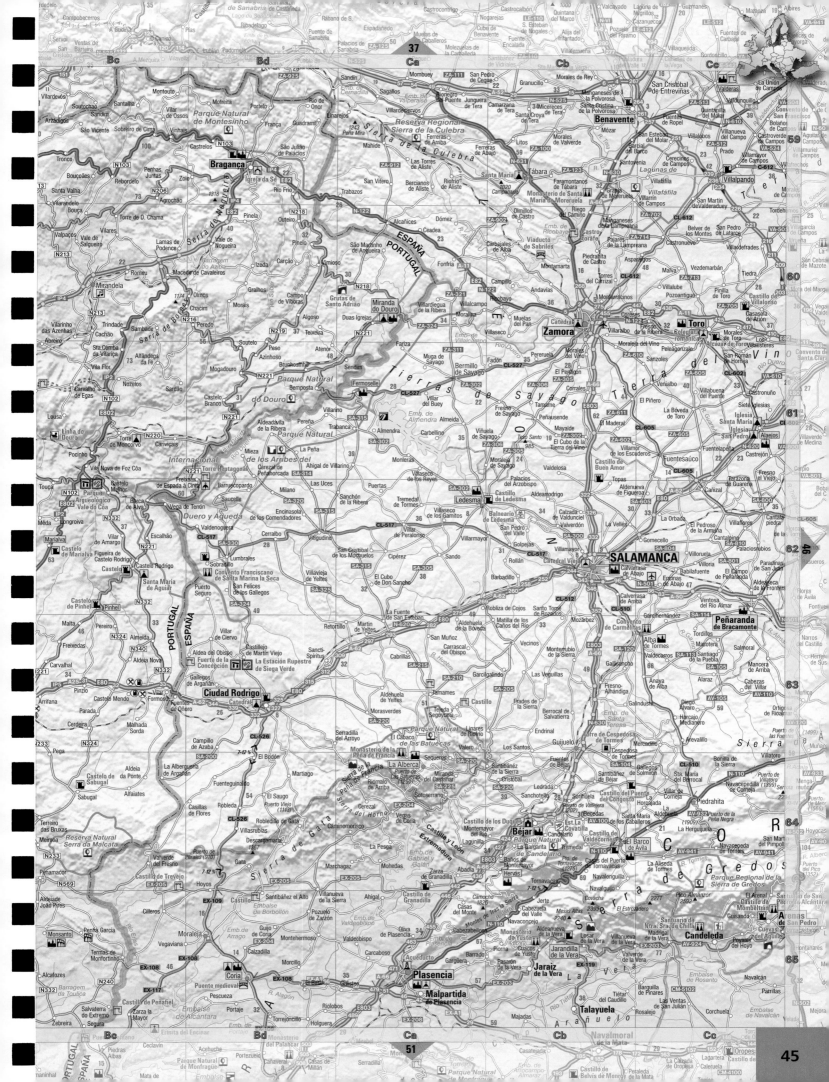

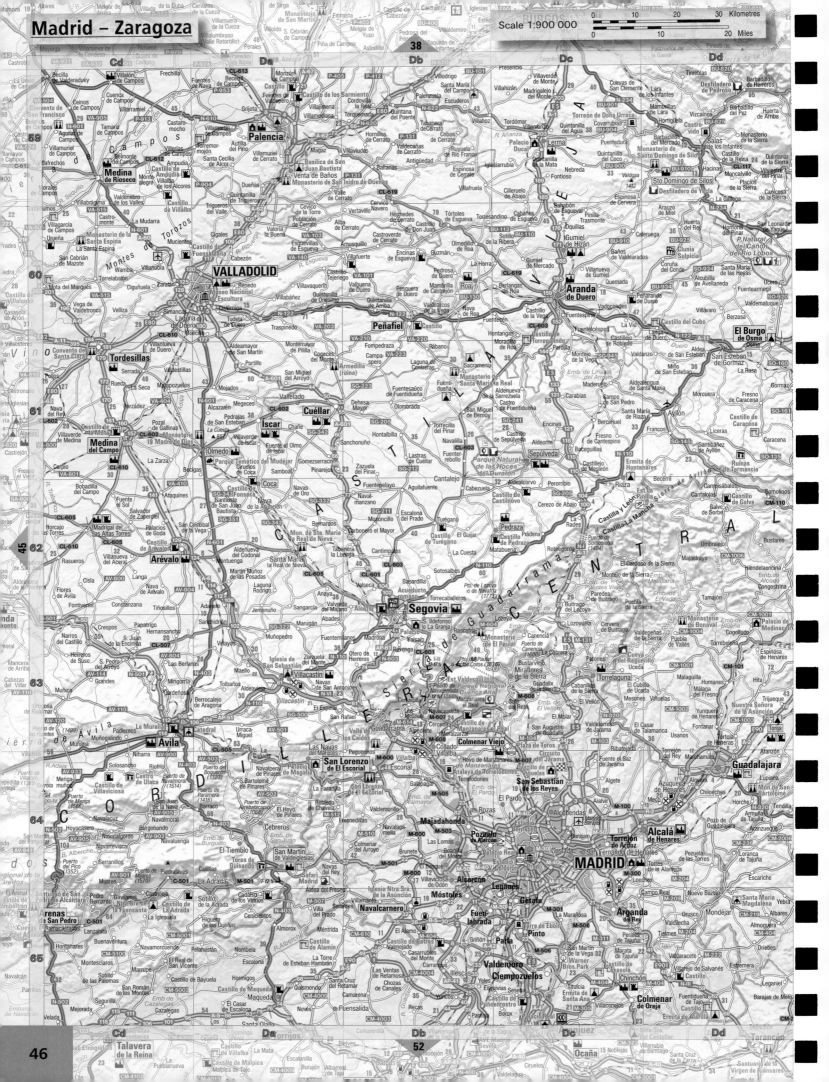

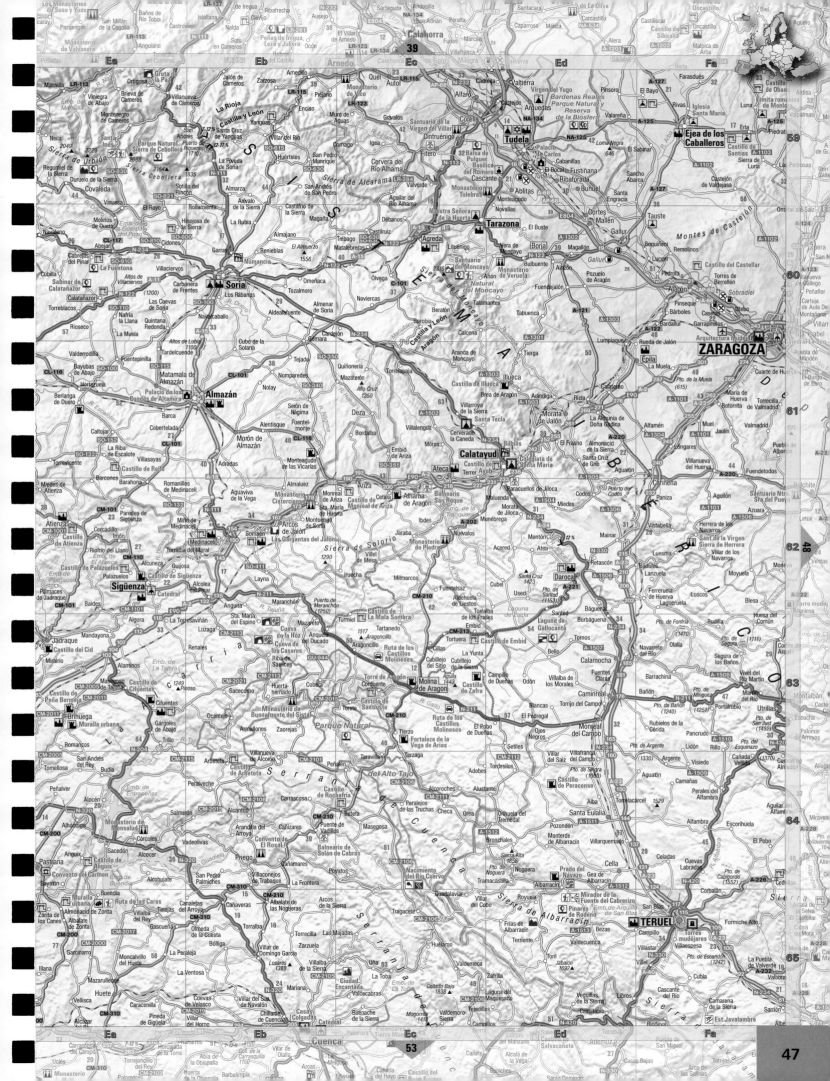

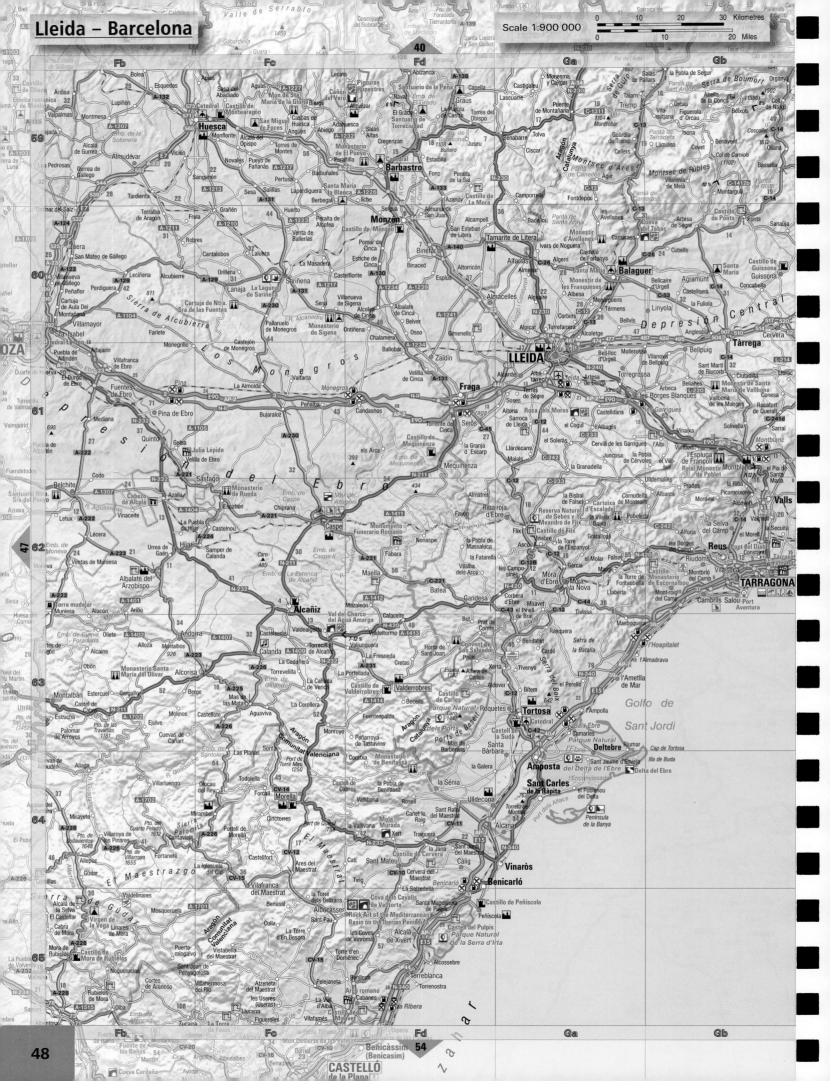

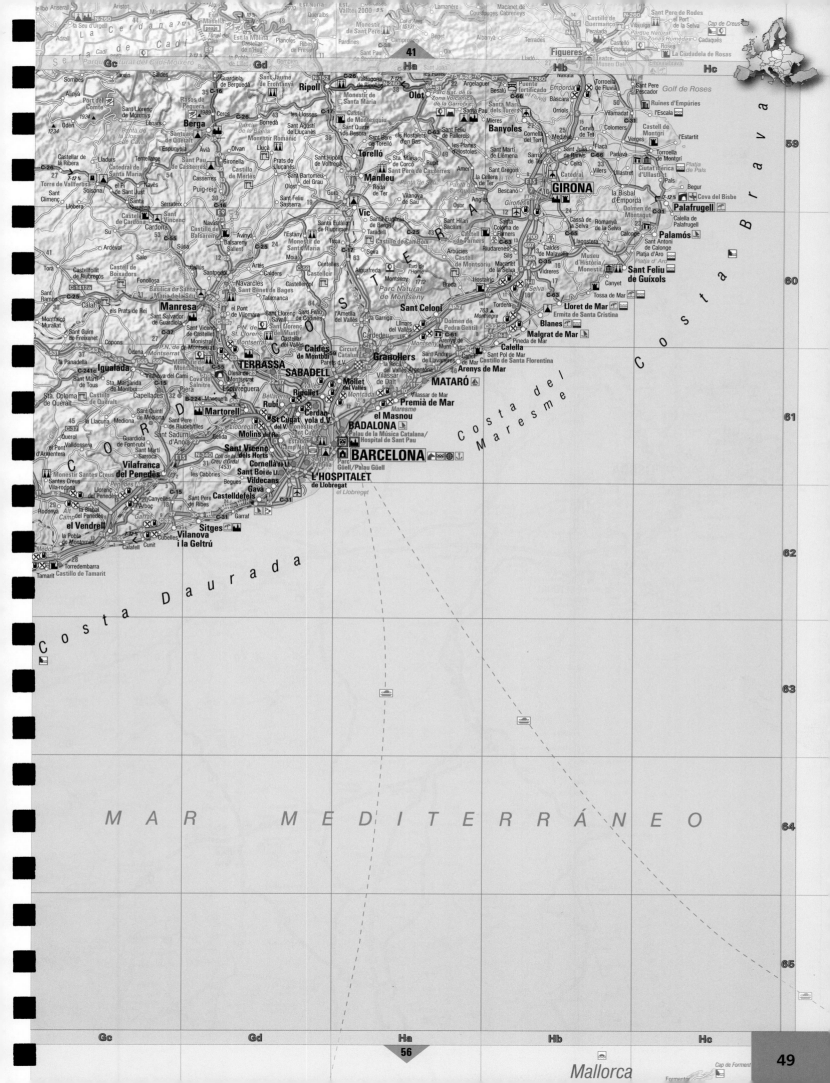

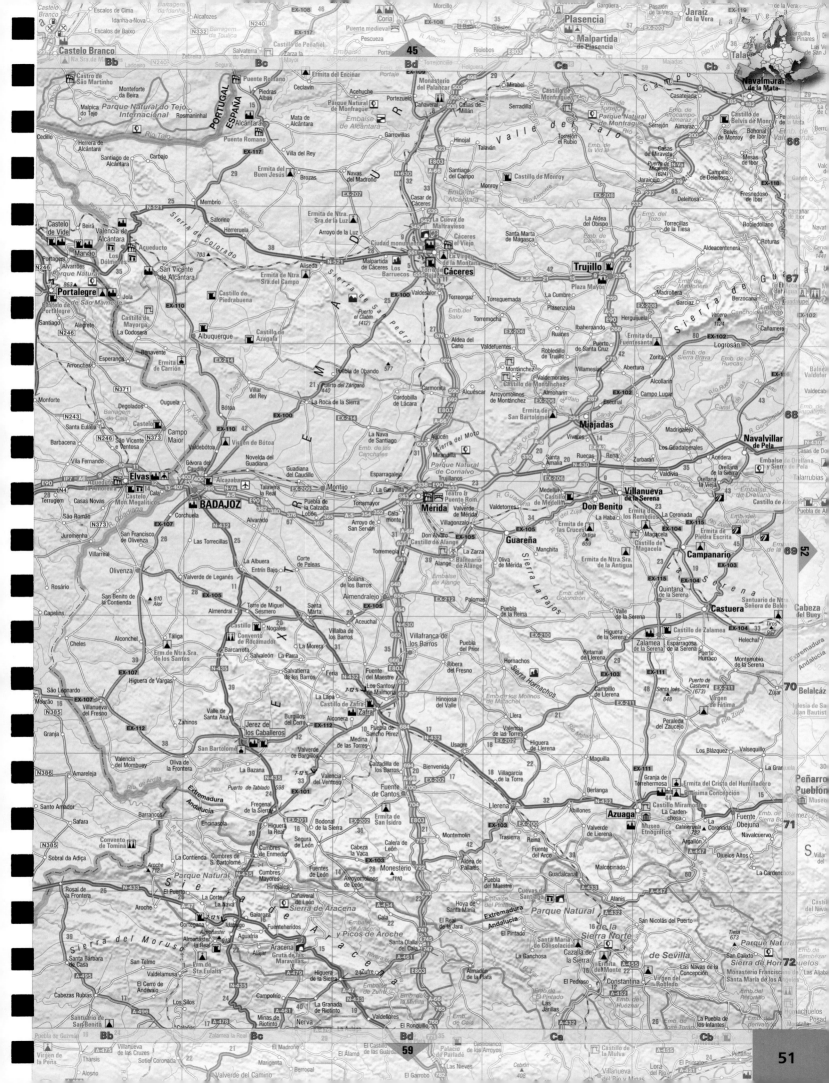

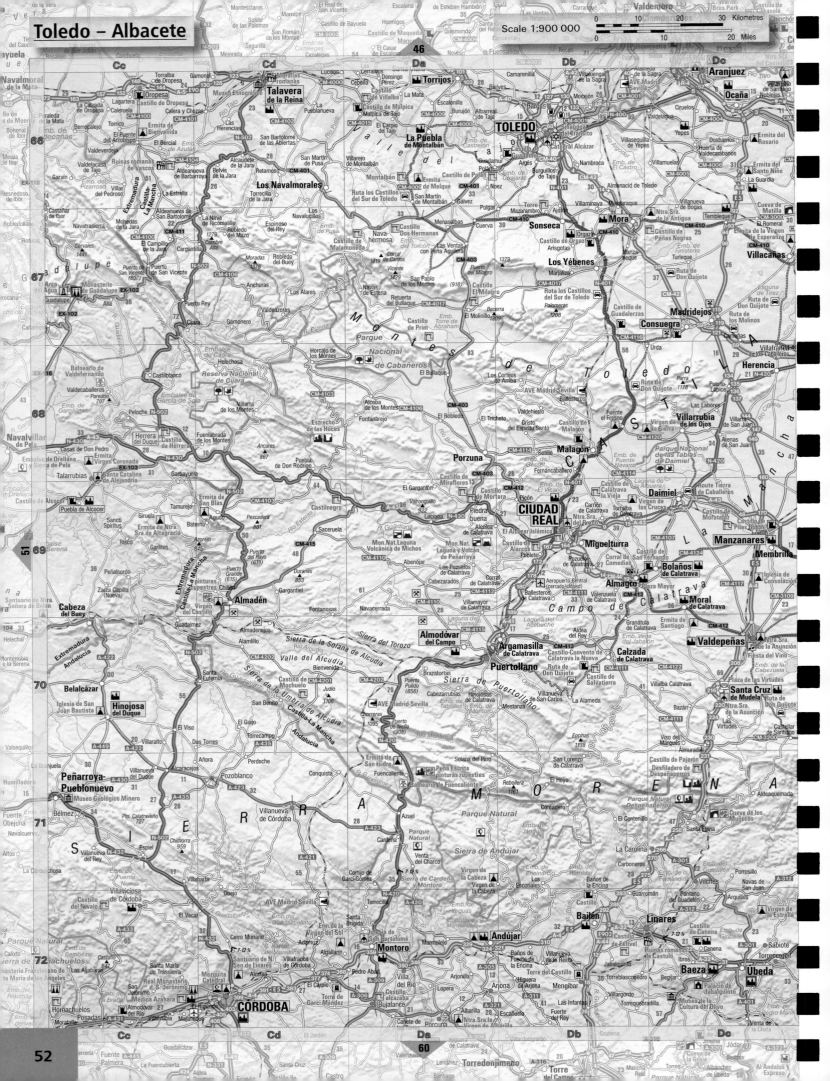

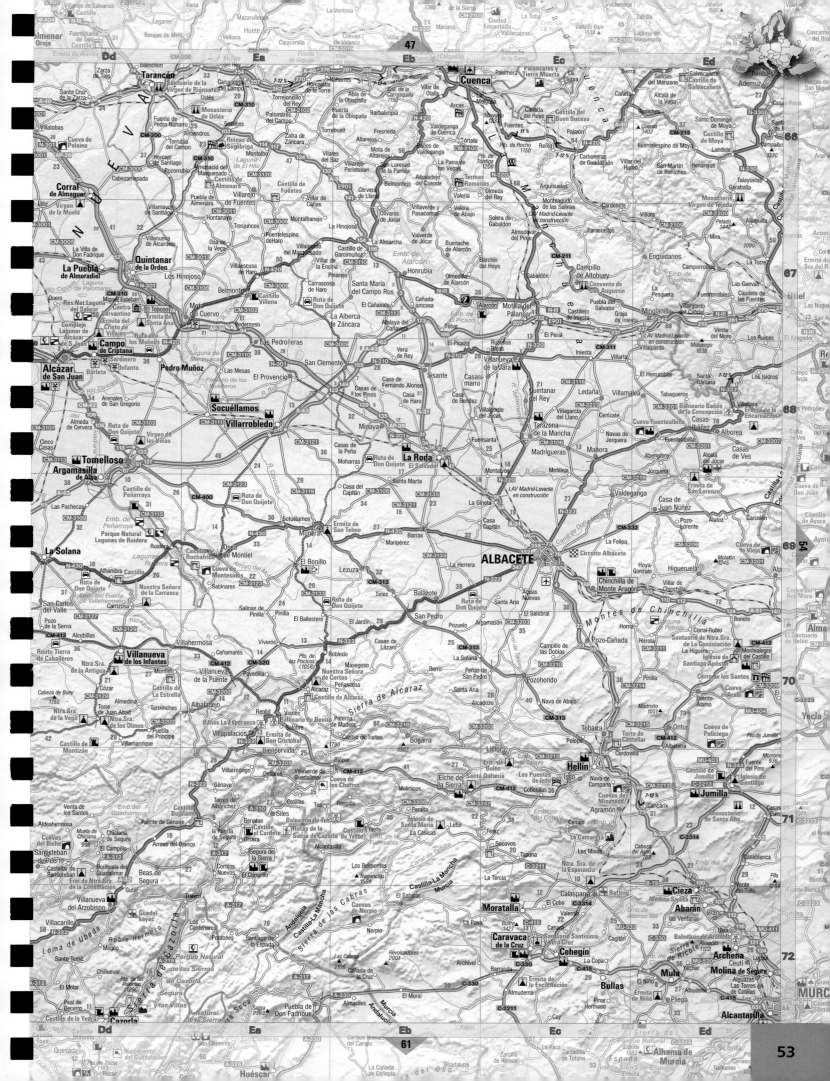

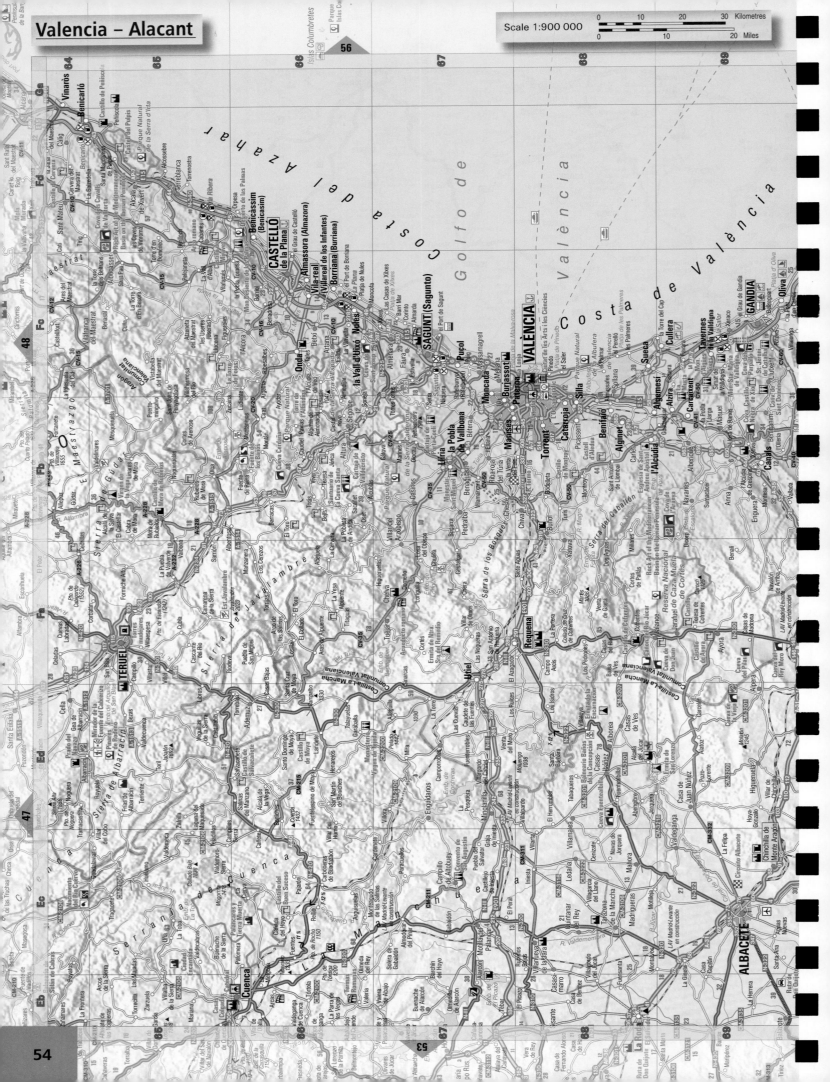

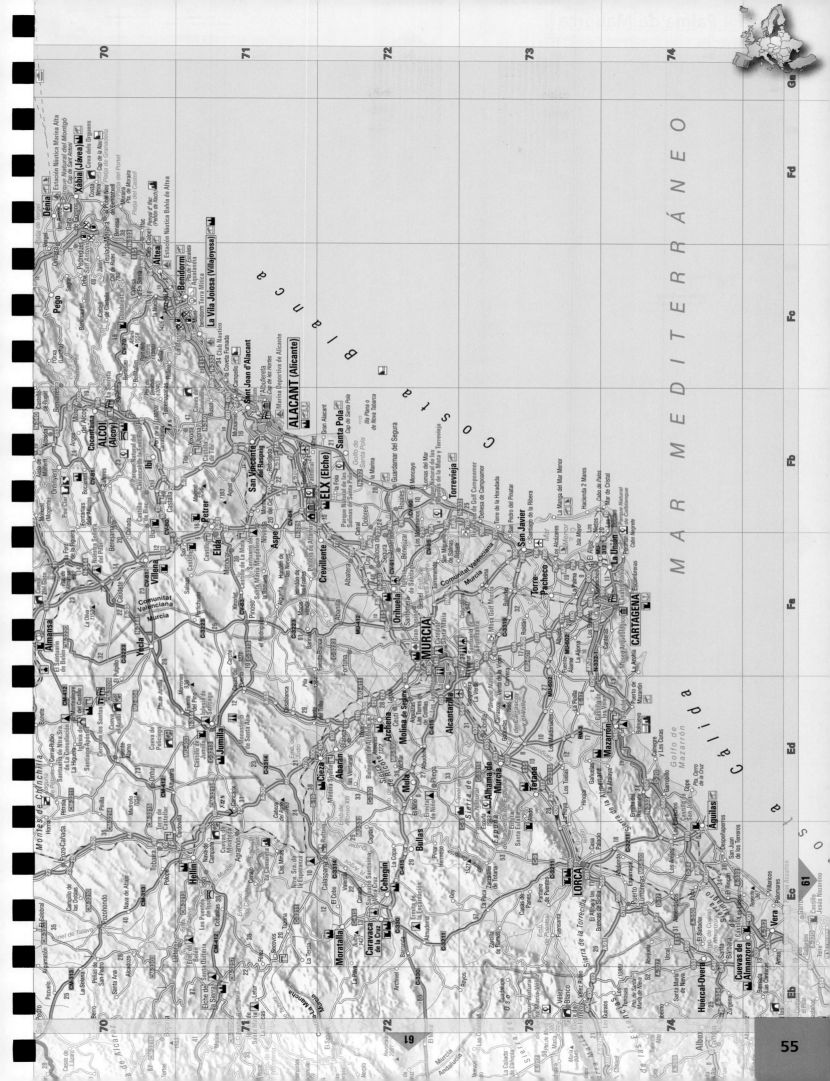

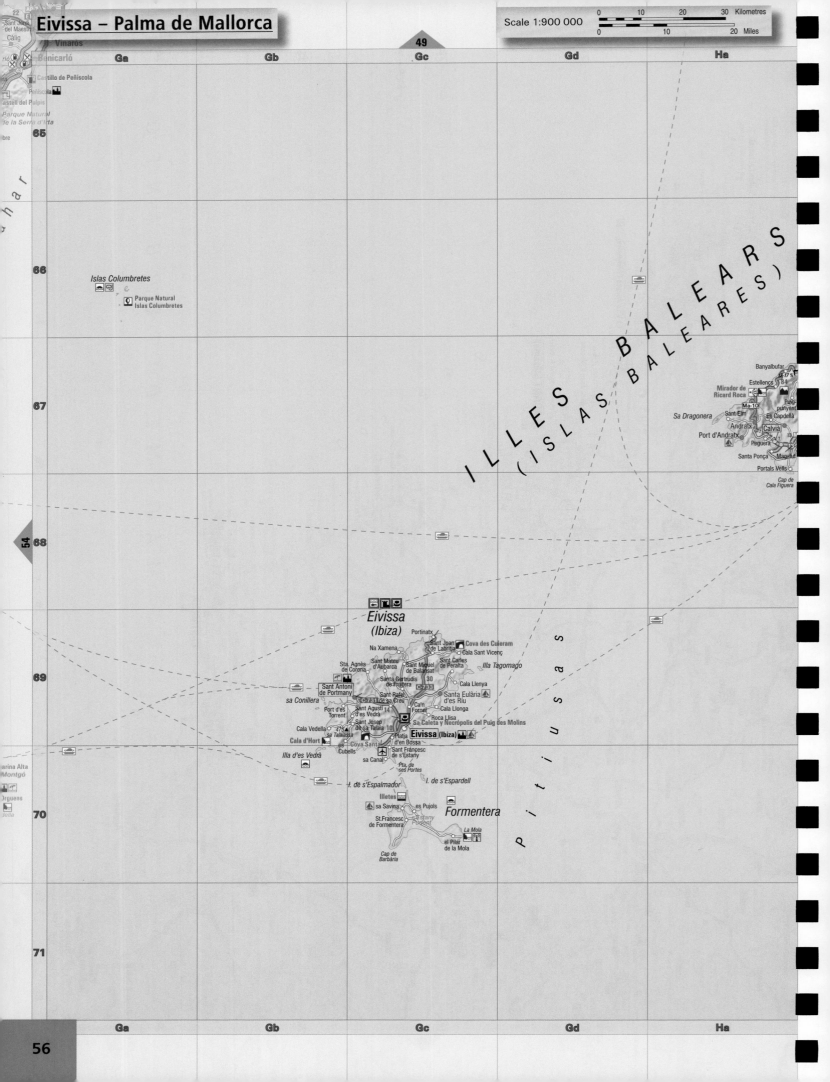

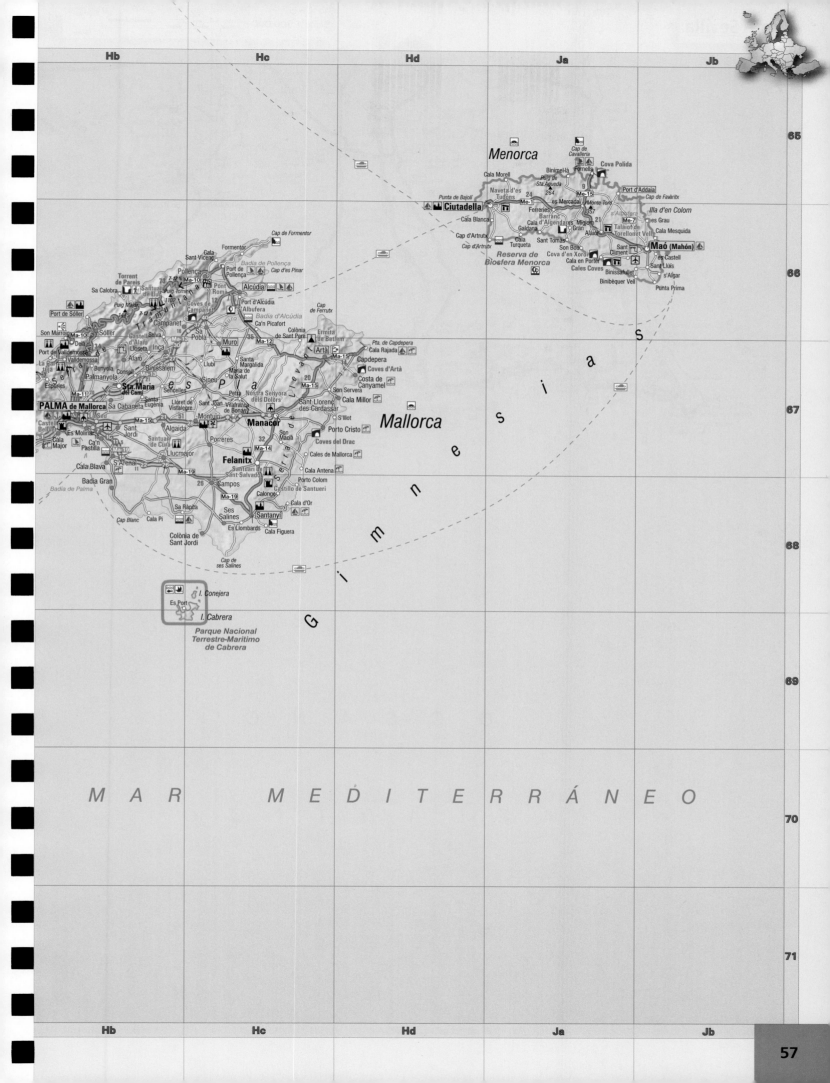

Menorca

Cap de
Cavalleria

Cova Polida

Cala Morell

Binimel·là
Puig de
Sta. Águeda
264
Fornells

Port d'Addaia

Punta de Bajoll
Naveta d'es
Tudons
24
9
Me-15
Cap de Favàritx

Ciutadella
es Mercadal
Monte Toro
357
Me-1
Illa d'en Colom

Cala Blanca
Ferreries
Barranc
Cala d'Algendares
Galdana
Migjorn
Gran
21
Alaior
Talaiot de
Torellonet Vell
Me-7
s'Albufera
es Grau

Cap d'Artrutx
Cala
Turqueta
Sant Tomàs
Son Bou
Cala Mesquida

Cap d'Artrutx
Reserva de
Biosfera Menorca
Cova d'en Xoroi
Cales Coves
Sant
Climent
Cala en Porter
Maó (Mahón)

es Castell
Sant Lluís
s'Algar

Binissafullet
Binibèquer Vell
Punta Prima

Cap de Formentor

Formentor
Cala
Sant Vicenç
Badia de Pollença
Cap d'es Pinar

Torrent
de Pareis
73
7-12
Ma-10
Pollença
Port de
Pollença

Sa Calobra
Santuari
de Lluc
Puig Tomir
Pont
Romà
Alcúdia

Puig Major
12
Coves de
Campanet
Port d'Alcúdia
d'Albufera
Cap de
Ferrutx

Port de Sóller
7-12
Sa
Pobla
Ca'n Picafort
Colònia
de Sant Pere
Ermita
de Betlem

Son Marroig
Ma-10
Sóller
Castell Selva
d'Alaró
16
Muro
Ma-12
Artà
Pta. de Capdepera

Deià
Lloseta
Inca
50
35
Ma-15
Cala Rajada

Port de Valldemossa
Valldemossa
Alaró
Llubí
Santa
Margalida
Capdepera
Coves d'Artà

La Trapa
Bunyola
Palmanyola
Consell
Binissalem
Ma-13
Maria de
la Salut
Petra
Nostra Senyora
dels Dolors
20
Costa de
Canyamel

Espelles
Ma-11
Sta. Maria
del Camí
Santa
Eugènia
Sineu
Sant Joan
Vilafranca
de Bonany
Ma-15
Son Servera
Sant Llorenç
des Cardassar
Cala Millor

PALMA de Mallorca
Sa Cabaneta
Lloret de
Vistalegre
Montuïri
51
S'Illot

Castell
Bellver
Ma-15
21
Sant
Jordi
Algaida
Santuari
de Cura
32
Manacor
Son
Macià
Porto Cristo
Coves del Drac

Cala
Major
Ca'n
Pastilla
Es Molinar
Porreres
Ma-14
Cales de Mallorca

S'Arenal
22
Llucmajor
Felanitx
Santuari de
Sant Salvador
Cala Antena

Cala Blava
26
Campos
Castillo de Santueri
Pòrto Colom

Badia Gran
26
Ma-19
Calonge
Cala d'Or

Badia de Palma
Ses
Salines
Ma-19
Sa Ràpita
Cala Pi
Santanyí
Cala Figuera

Cap Blanc
Es Llombards

Colònia de
Sant Jordi

Cap de
ses Salines

Mallorca

Gimnesias

I. Conejera
Es Port
I. Cabrera

Parque Nacional
Terrestre-Marítimo
de Cabrera

65
66
67
68
69
70
71

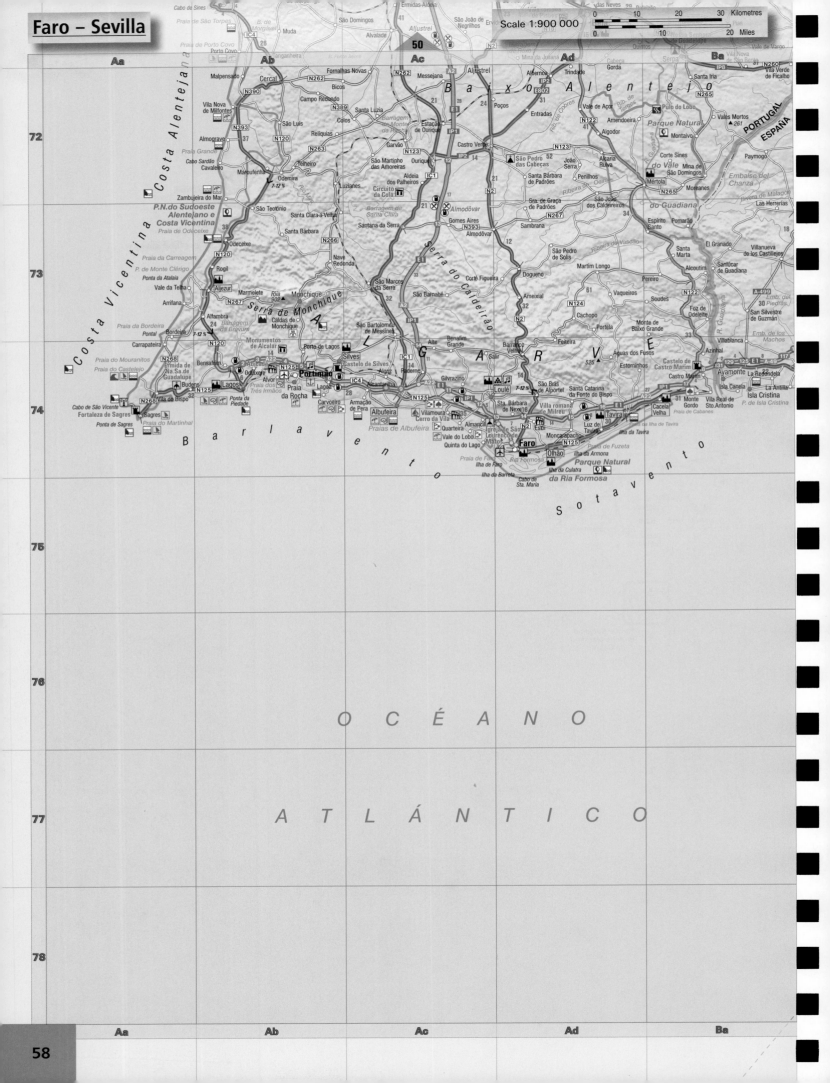

Scale 1:900 000

| 0 | 10 | 20 | 30 Kilometres |
| 0 | | 10 | 20 Miles |

Ga   Gb   Gc   Gd   Ha

04

05

NORWEGIAN SEA

06

07

Lopphavet

Fugløykalven fyr
Fugløya
Grimsholman
Næringen   Fugløykallen
Nordkvaløy   753   Klubben
Torsvåg fyr   Nakkeslett   Burøya   833
Store   Vannareid   Store   Árviksand
Store Måsvær   Burøysund   Skorøya   Nymo
Grøtøy   Laukvik   Helgøy   Sengskroken kpl.   Spenna   Fugløysund   Høgtind   Arnøy
Store Hattøy   731   Bekkestrand   924
Andammen   Hersøya   Helgøy   Vanna   Vannavalen   Lauksund-skardet
Sør-Fugløya   654   Bromnes   (Vannøya)   Amøyhamn
Rebbenesøy   Mikkelvik   Dåfjorda   Vannvåg   Akkarvik
Rebbenesbotn   Steinnes   Skåningbukt   Haugnes
Mjølvik   Árnes   Grunnfjord   Karlsøy   Vorterøyskagen
Sandøya   Engvik   Dafjord   Karlsøy   Nordklubben   Vorterøya
Sør-Grunnfjord   Russel-   Russelvfjellet
Risøy   Skarstjord   Elvebakken   Hansnes   Stakkvik   816   Teigen
Komagvik   Hessfjord   Klokkarvollen
Skars-   Skogsfjord-   Uløya
Ytre   fjorden   vatnet   Gamnes   Uløybukt
Gåsvær   Kårvik   Ringvassøy   Solhzidon   Reinøy   Søreidet   Storvoll   Berglund   1142
Musvær   863   1051   884   Grøtnesdalen   Tverrbakk-   Havnes
Kiberg   Tverrbakktind   tind   Hamnes
Vengsøy   Laukvik   Finnkroken   1320   Styrmannste   Sør-Lenangen   Rotsund
Naustbukt   Nordhella   Latter-   Djupvik
Ullstind   vik   Store   Nordmannvik
Skulsfjord   Skulgam   1094   Lenangstind   1236
Bellvika   Skittenelv   Skotsætet   1596   Oldredalen
Store   863   Botn   Jægelr
Hersøya   Tromvik   Blåmainen   Futrikelv   Oldervik   1398   vatnet   Nordmannvik
Håja   Sessøya   1044   Tønsnes   Jægervatn   Iddonjargqa
Rekvik   Kvaløysletta   Nonstind   Breivikeidet   Svensby   Koppangen   Nokrdmannviktind
843   862   1111   Hov   1236
Tussøya   Ersfjordbotn   Kroken   1441   1489   Oldedalen
Bu   Eidkjosen   Håkøy   Polaria   20   Kjosen   Kvitberg
Vasstrand   Ishavskatedralen   Bensnes   Kåfjord
Sommarøy   Kvaløy   862   Håkøybotn   Tromsdalen   Stortno   91   Skarmunken   91   Odden
TROMSØ   Forneset   Lyngseidet   Løkvoll
Hekkingen fyr   Fjellheisen   858   Fagernes   Bjørnskar-   Skjelnes   Rypedafe   Fossheim
Kjølva   Hillesøy   Vollen   Larsnes   tinden   Ullsfjord   vatnet   Jorbbavarre
414   Sjøtun   Skavberg   1359   Pollen   Reydal
Laukvik   hellerisfninger   Andersdal   1567   Jiekkevarre   Furuflaten   Sandvika
Husøy   Bakkejord   Vikran   Ramfjordnes   Kobbevåg   1833   Abmelaseter
Greipstad   Ansnes   1769   1293   Skognes   Hundberg   Skibotn
Mefjordvær   Jakobnjargga   Stortind   Stordalselv   Lakselv-   42   Falsnes
Senjahopen   Vangshamn   Tennskjer   1323   E8   bukt   1565   Nordlysobservatoriet
Bøvær   Fjordgård   862   Spildra   Slettind   Malangen Krokelv   E6   Brennfjell   39
Bergsøyan   858   Lia   Sommarfjellet   E8
Skaland   Stønnesbotn   Rødbergshamn   1119   Kantornes   1491   39
864   Bukkemoen   Malangseidet   Skrean   Slettmo   E6
Hamn   86   Istindan   Lenvik   Rossfjord   Elvevollen   Aglet
Bygde-   Flatvoll   Mestervik   Heimdal   1514
Gryllefjord   Sætra   919   Nymoen   museum   Straumen   Balsfjord
785 Spøkkel   Gibostad   Tarnev   859
Torsken   fossen   Senja   Skognes   Bjørelvnes   Eidet   Hamn-   859
Andenes fyr   Torsken-   Svartnet/Estvatnet   vågnes   Nordnordfjordbotn
fjorden

Holmenvær   Gunnarnes   560   Fjordfjordeidet   Lunne-   Aursfjord-   Ytre   Bergneset   Nordkjosbotn   18   Cæcca   Riepp
Kaldfarnes   851   879   Tverrelv   856   borg   botn   Iskluusvatn   Myrhaug   Störsteinnes   jawe   Laukvoll
Ørja   Medby   Svanelvmo   86   Karlstad   860   Myrhaug   Markus-   Gouddajavre   141
Finnsnes   855   Rossvoll   Enenfjord-   Segel-vatn   fjellet   Signaldalen
Flakkstadvåg   Vågan   Hemmingsjord   Blåtind   1543
Anderdalen   Kampevoll   nark   Blåhammar
nasjonal-
park

B A R E N T S   S E A

04

Hurtigruten

Skarveneset
Tanahorn
266
Berlevåg
Havnemuseum
Raggonjargga
Kjølnes fyr
Nålneset
Kongsøy-
fjorden
Kongsøya
Veines
Kongsfjord
Rubbedalshøgda
Seiboneset
Makkaur fyr
Korsneset
Syltefjordklubben
Hurtigruten

Raggočærro
467
Læsi
Båtsfjord
427
Syltefjord-
fjellet
402
Harbaken
Blodskytodden
Rein-
øya
Vardø
fyr
Vardøhus festning
Vardø

05

Gulgofjorden
Buefjell
473
Davgge
Oarddovarre
504
Båtsfjordfjellet
481
445
Vesterelva
Sommersete
Syltevikmyra
Syltevikmyra
Perstjorden
Vadsøya
Vardøya

Kongsfjordfjellet
526
Hangalačærro
618
890
891
Gædnja-
javrre
Varangerhalvøya
Skipskjølen
Langryggen
Holmfjellet
239
Kiberg
Indre
Kramvik

Leirpolls-
kogen
Basávže
Jakobselvvidda
Kjøltindan
Komagelva
Kibergneset

Hanadal
Nerasvarre
446
Guovddaoaivve
501
Øvre Hintela
Urfjellet
460
Falkefjellet
545
Bidelva
Skallelv
Komagvær
E75
78
Komagnes

Hana
Varanger
samiske museum
Varangerbotn
17
Nyborg
Dotkomyrene
Nesseby
Biggánjarg
Bunes
Abelsborg
Klubbvik
Mortensnes
Klubben
Vestre
Jakobselv
Paddeby
Graksesteinen
Andersby
E75
49
Vadsøya
Vadsø
Kiby
Saltjern
Vadsøya kulturpark
Gjelhaugan
Frakendalen
Storelva
Vasavatnet
Storskog
Krampenes
Ekkerøy
Søines
Lille Ekkerøy
Store Ekkerøy
Skallneset
Skallelv

06

Vajdaguba
Skorbojevski
243
Guba Bol. Bolokovaja
Ozerki
Poluostrov Rybačij

Vesterelv
Sivertbukt
Grasbakken
Hustufter
E6
81
Byluft
Varangerfjorden

Tšaraoaivi
345
Gæčoaivve
412
Dirge-
javrre
Gallok-
javrre
Korgåsen
419
Skarvfjell
355
Kjerringfjell
416
Garsjøen
Gandvik
Ramtinden
468
Bugøynesfjellet
497
Bugøya
Bugøynes
Endeneset
Valen
Brasfjellet
416
Skogerøyfjellet
445
Skogerøya
Bøkfjord fyr
Trifansneset
Pasvik-
neset
Kjermsøya
Holmengråfjellet
408
Ørentoppen
465
Kong Oscar II's Kapel
Grense
Jakobselv
Guba Mal. Bolokovaja
g.Ejna
299
334
Poluostrov
Srednij
Motovskij zali
07

Villavaara
Ullovarri
344
Bugøyfjord
Norskbukta
Nord-Leirvåg
Jerestad-
vatnet
Steinkjernes
Reinøya
Reinøysund
Lanabukt
Lanabukt
Valatnet
886
Bjørnstad
Eggemoen
504
Liinahamari
Nasynkys
Trifona
Porovara
Novaya Titovka
477
Motovskij zali

Norge
Suomi/Finland
219
Bjørneset
Svanefjellet
Mikkelsnes
Brannfjellet
222
Valbukta
E6
Buholmen
Hesseng
Andersgrotta
Kirkenes
Jakobsnes
Midtgård
Eidet
Elvenes
Tårnet
Karpbukt
Urfjellet
336
Viksjøfjell
391
Korpfjellet
327
Elvenheim
Pečenga
Star Titovka
302
Baraki

Nättämö
Neiden
Skoltefossen
Skolteplassen
St.Georgs
kapell
Lillebekken
Stabbursfjellet
297
Langfjordbotn
Bjørnevatn
885
Fisk-
vatn
Bjørnevatn
Hammerfjella
Væccer
Straumsnes
Norge
Rossija
Vuatser-
javri
A138
31
Myasyukka
23
Zaozersk

971
Kirakkajärvi
Kirehasjärvi
Sevettijärvi
Tševetjärvi
Vainosjärvi
Vainkässimjavri
Store
Samett
Lille
Samett
Brattli
E105
Virtaat
Langli
Strand
Nordvik
Furuhy
Ahmalahti
Kuvernerinkoski
Svanhovd miljøsenter
Svanvik
Utnes
Salmijärvi
21
Suonde
Kuhtajarvi
Vilgiskoddeoaiv
517
Star Titovka
E105
Luostari
Zapoljarnyj
Kolttakylä
65
E105
Ura
08

Tsaraoaivi
Kolmmesjavri
Lávdnjekoahtevarri
233
Ukonselka
Rajapää
331
Utsiktstårn
Svanvatne
Nyheim
Kaulatunturi
Nikel'
g.Kuorpukas
650
Lugitjokk
Porovara
Vidja
09

Rovaselkä
Roavvetšielgi
249
Aarneniemi
Aarninjarga
Suolisjärvi
Tšuolisjärvi
Rautaperä
Sumujärvi
Sumujärvi
Triangelen
Fossheim
Langvatn
Vanhakylä
Petsamontunturit
g.Maaret
528
oz.Urdozero
Kilp

Pekkala
Nitsijärvi
Niiddšijavri
Supru
Suojanperä
Kivisel�
Juovvatšielgi
Kynnejärvi
Koonjalijavri
Kobbfoss
Skogjon
885
Hauge
Kalkupää
357
P10
Pitkäjärvi
g.Suort
495
g.Valestšielj
350
g.Stuorratšielj
419
oz.Terskei-
jaur
oz.Kvodsenaure
g.Kučintundra
578
oz.Kaskeljavre
Jurkino

Partakko
Páártih
Rajavaara
Räijivoadas
252
Skogly
Vaggetem
Nesheim
Rusk-
vatn
Stabburfjellet
214
Nytud
oz.Piedsjaur
oz.Seigijärvi
oz.Vuell-
Akkajävri
Prirečnyj
oz.Kiestjaur
oz.Vuell
Akkajävri
g.Stuorratšielj
g.Tsuossah
342
g.Viijmvid
451
302
Pouloos
10

Inarijärvi
Anarjävri
Øvre Pasvik
nasjonalpark
Onomusvaara
Onomušváári
237
Rajakoski
Nautsi
g.Raunvaar
202
Keinojärvi
Leppävaara
231
Pápjávri
142
g.Keltovaara
283
Virtaniemi
Nellim?
Njelim
g.Neaskimjau
Tshuudhjauratshielj
314
P11
oz.Sovnajavre
Vosmu

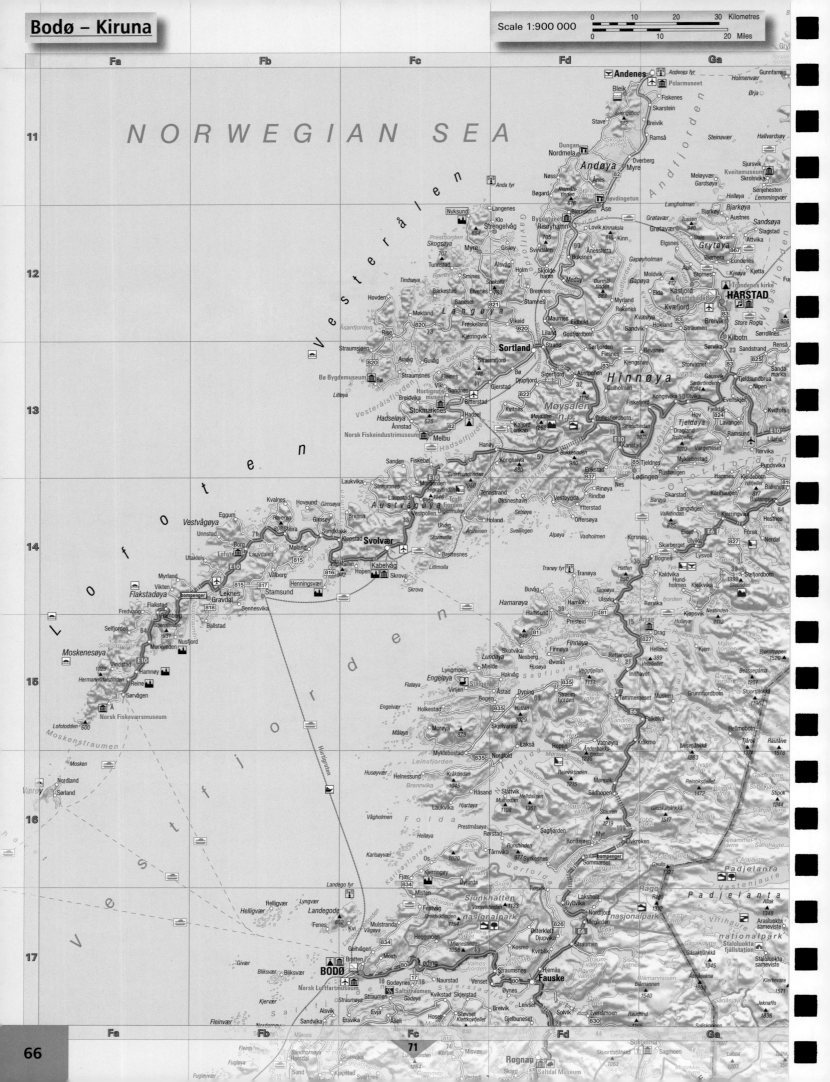

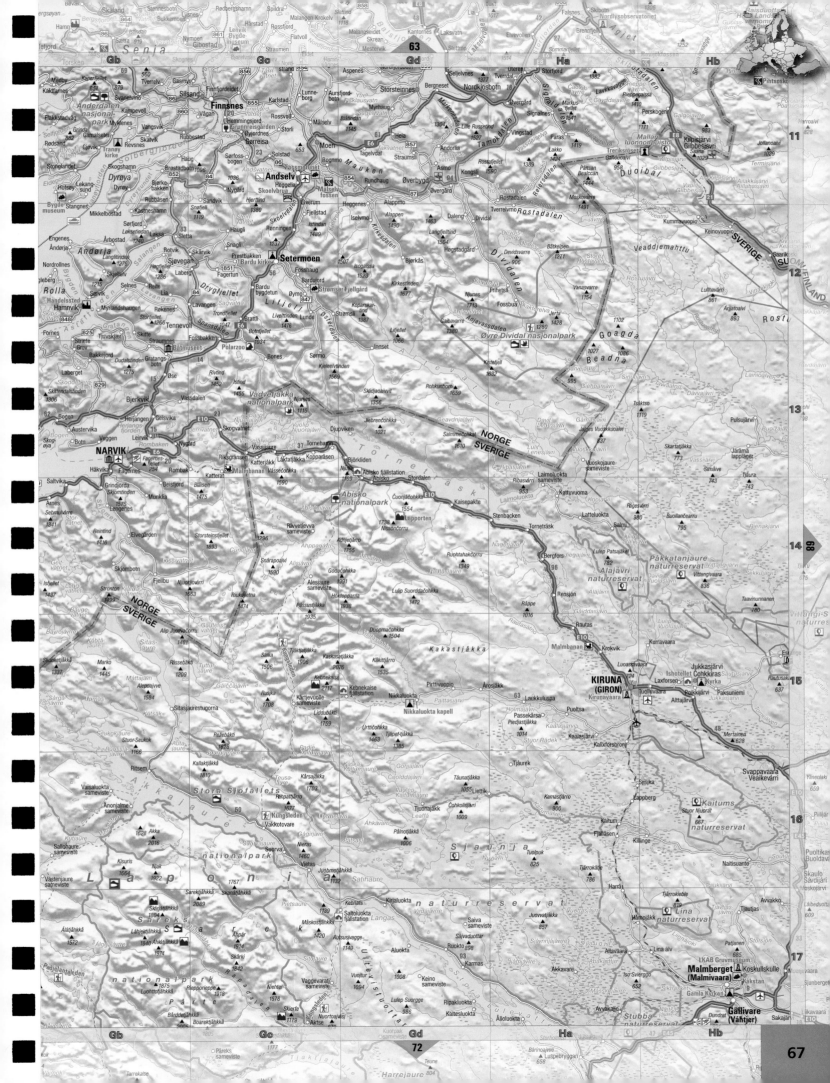

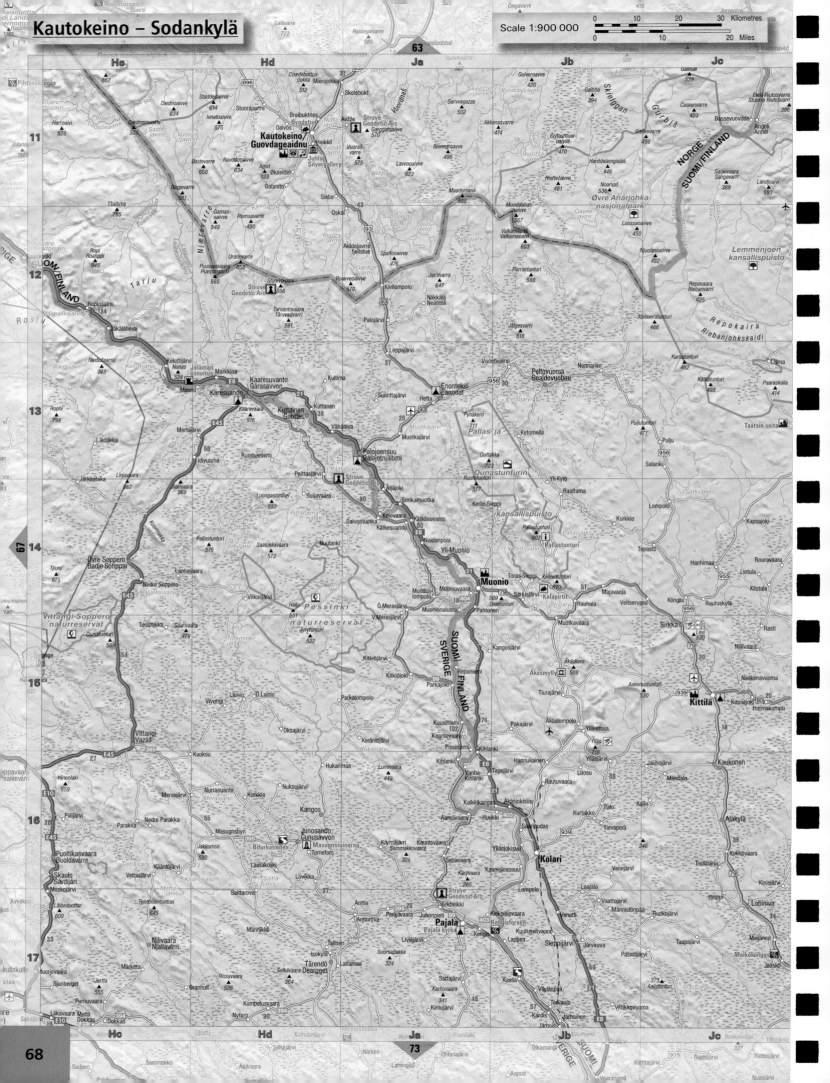

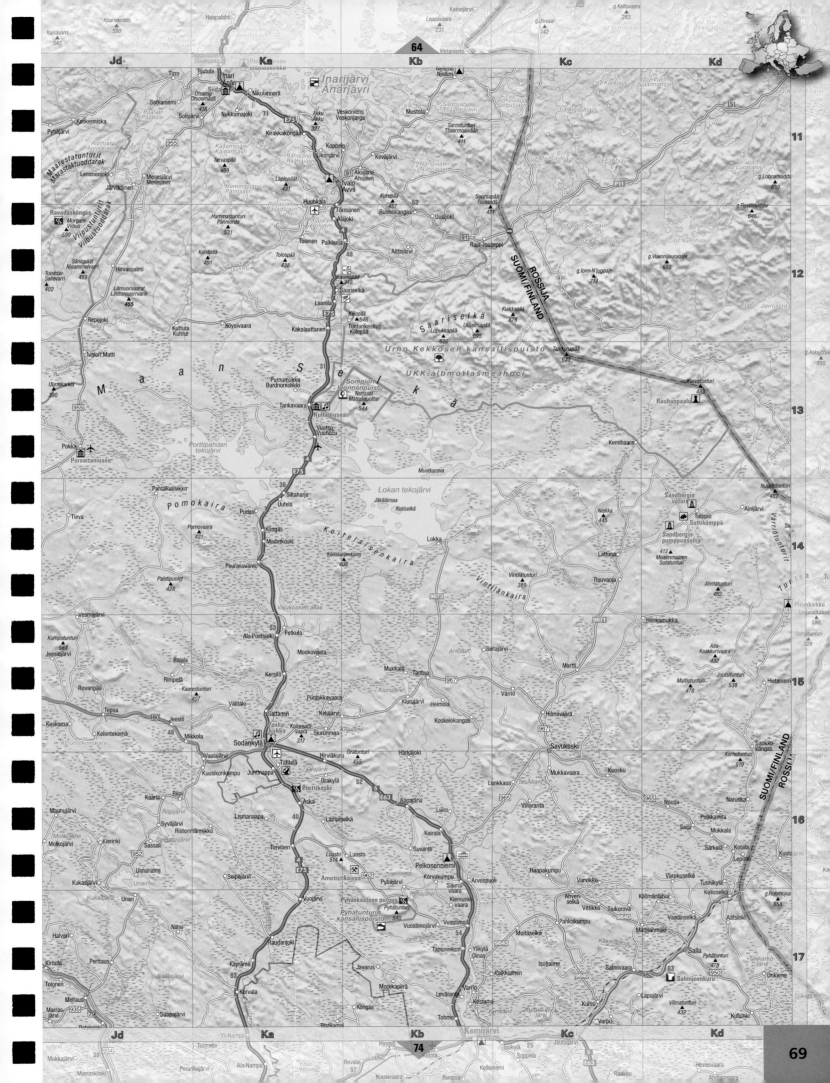

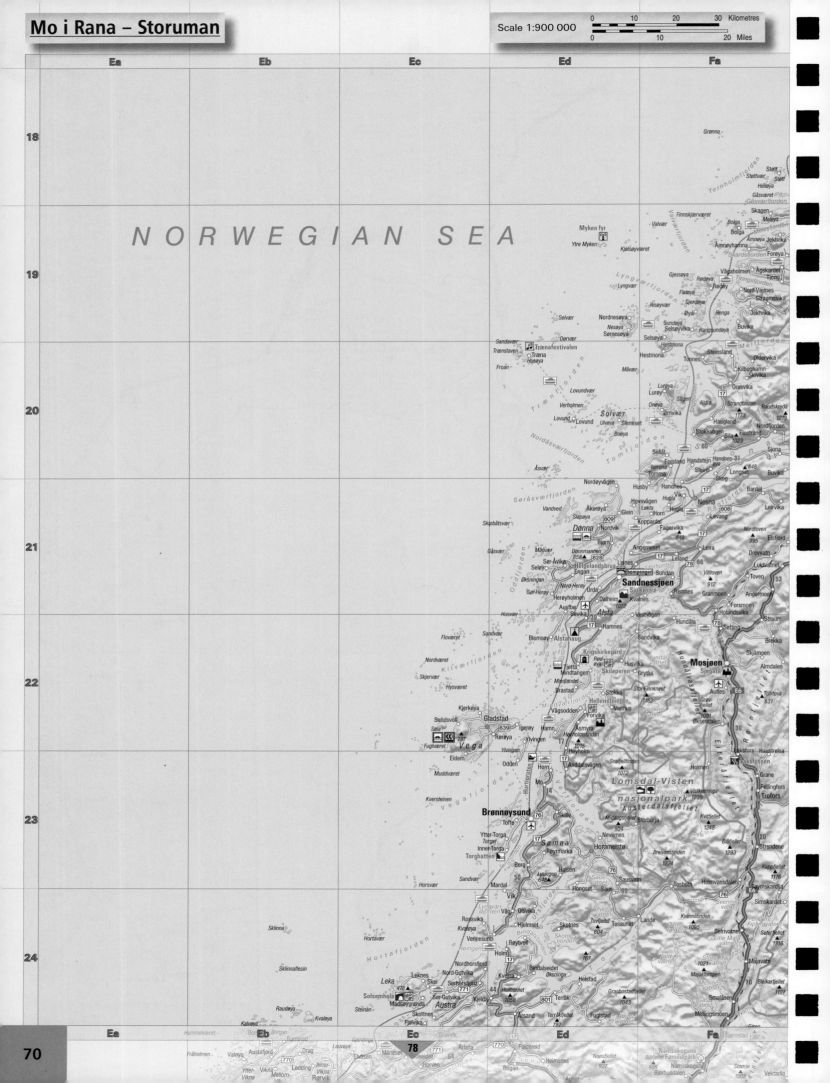

NORWEGIAN SEA

Ea Eb Ec Ed Fa

18

19

20

21

22

23

24

Grønna

Støtt
Støttvær
Helløya
Gåsværøya
Gåsværfjorden
Skagen
Meløya
Bolga
Bolga
Amnøya
Jektvika
Åmøyhamna

Myken fyr
Ytre Myken
Kjølsøyværet
Valvær
Valværfjorden
Finnskjærværet
Vågaholmen
Skardsfjorden
Forøy
Gjessøya
Lyngvær
Lyngværfjorden
Rødøya
Tjongsfjorden
Røgøy
Nord-Væmes
Flatøya
Risvær
Gjerdøya
Øya
Renga
Jektvika
Straumsvika

Selvær
Nordnesøya
Nesøya
Sørnesøya
Selsøyvika
Rangsundøya
Buvika

Dørvær
Træna
Husøya
Hestmona
Tonnes
Steinsland
Oldervika
Skivika

Sandvær
Trænafestivalen
Trænstaven
Froan
Måvær
Hestmona

Lovundvær
Verholmen
Lurøy
Onøya
Stigen
Aldra
Strandtindan
1173
Raudskreda
1215
Nordfjorden

Lovund
Lovund
Ulvøya
Sleneset
Buøya
Sølvær
Ørnvika
Stokkvågen
Sila
Flostrand
1023
Sjona

Åsvær
Sellåt
Forsland
Handstein
Tomma
Handnes
Sjona
848
Steiro
Longset
Buvika

Nordøyvågen
Husby
Handnes
Vik
Skog
Bardal

Seråsværfjorden
Åkerøya
Hovsvågen
Hugla
Nesna
Leirvika

Vandved
Slapøya
Glein
Lokta
Horn
Hugla
Løvang
Levang

Skipbåtsvær
809
Koppardal
808
Fagervika
Nordtoven
995
Elsfjord

Gåsvær
Dønna
Nordvik
848
Drevvatn

Måsvær
Dønnmannen
858
Bjørn
Angerneset
Leira
66
Luktvatnet

Sør-Åvika
828
Lønes
Leland
78
Villtoven
912
Toven
53

Oddfjorden
Seløy
Engan
Helgelandsbrua
bompengen
Sundan

Øksningan
Nord-Herøy
Urda
Sandnessjøen
Remnes
Granmoen
Angermoen

Sør-Herøy
Herøyholmen
Sjusestre
1072
Kvalnes
Forsmoen
Holandsvika

Austbø
Dalheim
Alsta
Vestvågan
Straum

Husvær
Sevika
Hamnes
Hundåla
Softing
78
Brekka

Floværet
Sandvær
Blomsøy
Alstahaug
Sandvika
Skjemoen

Nordværet
Krigskirkegard
Rødøya
Husvika
Hundal vatnet
Mosjøen
Almdalen

Kliværfjorden
Tjøtta
Mindtangen
Skiløperen
Grytåa
Sjøgata
E6

Skjervær
Midlandet
Brastad
Stokka
Stor-Finnknet
1162
Aufles
Grav fjellet
1001
Tolvtuva
831

Hysværet
Hellristninger
Vågsodden
Vistnus
Øksendalen
39

Kjerkøya
Midtværfjorden
Forvika
Ranken vatnet
Laksfors
Haustreisa

Sundsvoll
Gladstad
Igerøy
Hamn
Åsmyra
Hagholmstindan
Holmen
Grane

Søla
839
Rørøya
Ylvingen
1015
Høyholm
Fellingfors
Trofors

Fuglværet
Vega
737
Ylvingen
Anddalsvågen
Snøfjelltinden
1072

Eidem
Odden
Horn
Mo
Lomsdal-Visten
Vistvatnet
Vistkjørringa
1239
Lille Majavatnet
1316

Muddværet
Storvistjorden
nasjonalpark
Austerdalsfjellet

Kversteinen
Brønnøysund
76
Skille
Middagsfjellet
804
Storbørja
Kvitfjellet
1248
20
Strandene

Vegafjorden
Tofte
Ytter-Torga
Torget
Inner-Torga
Torghatten
77
Sømna
Nevernes
Breivasstinden
1224
1293
Blåfjellet
Kappfjellet
1176

Horsvær
Sandvær
Berg
Lysingen
648
Halsen
Røyrmarka
Hommelstø
76
Sausvatn
Saus
Saurstrøm
Tosbotn
Holmvassdalen
Trymskardla

Sklinna
Mardal
Vik
50
Høngset
76
Simskardet

Rossvika
Olsvika
Vennesund
Skotnes
Turvfjellet
804
Tosaunet
Lande
Øyre Vøgen
Kvannlinden
1095
Litle Majavatnet

Hjelmset
Bindalseidet
Terråk
Granbostadfjellet
1043
Store Maja vatnet
1021
Majavatn

Hortavær
Røyngen
Holm
Nordhorsfjord
Nord-Gutvika
Kvelna
Øksninga
Helstad
Majaklumpen

Sklinnaflesin
Leknes
Leka
Skei
Sørborsfjord
Heilhornet
1058
801
Terråk
Fuglstad
767
70
Bleikarfjellet
1121

Raudøya
Kvaløya
Solsemhola
Madseygrenda
Austra
Kjelda
Arsand
Terråkfjellet
782
Mellingsmoen
Smålåsen
Gas Smala vatnet

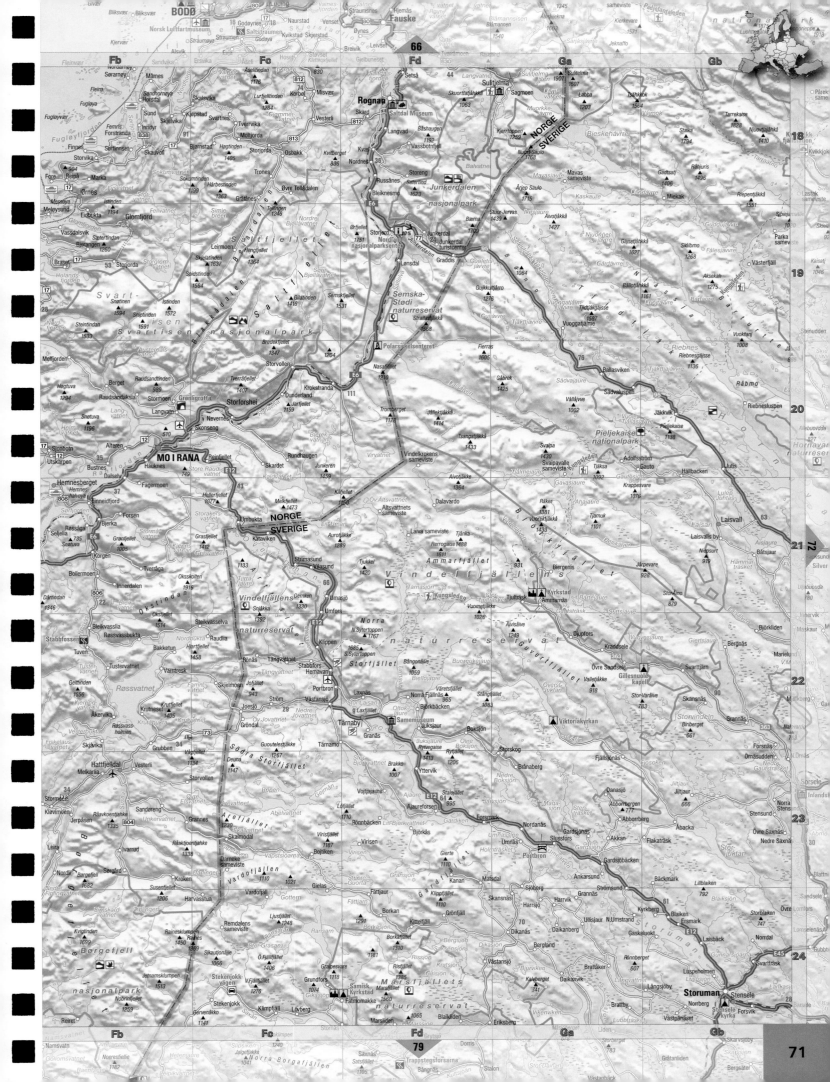

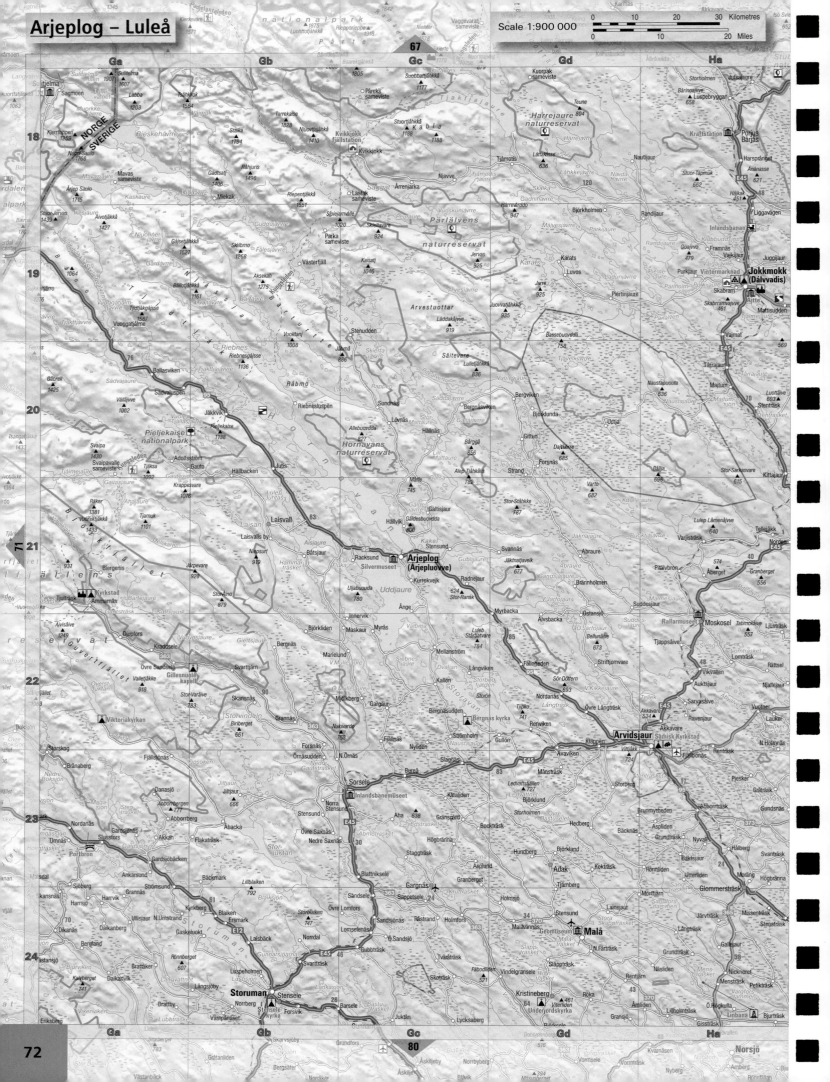

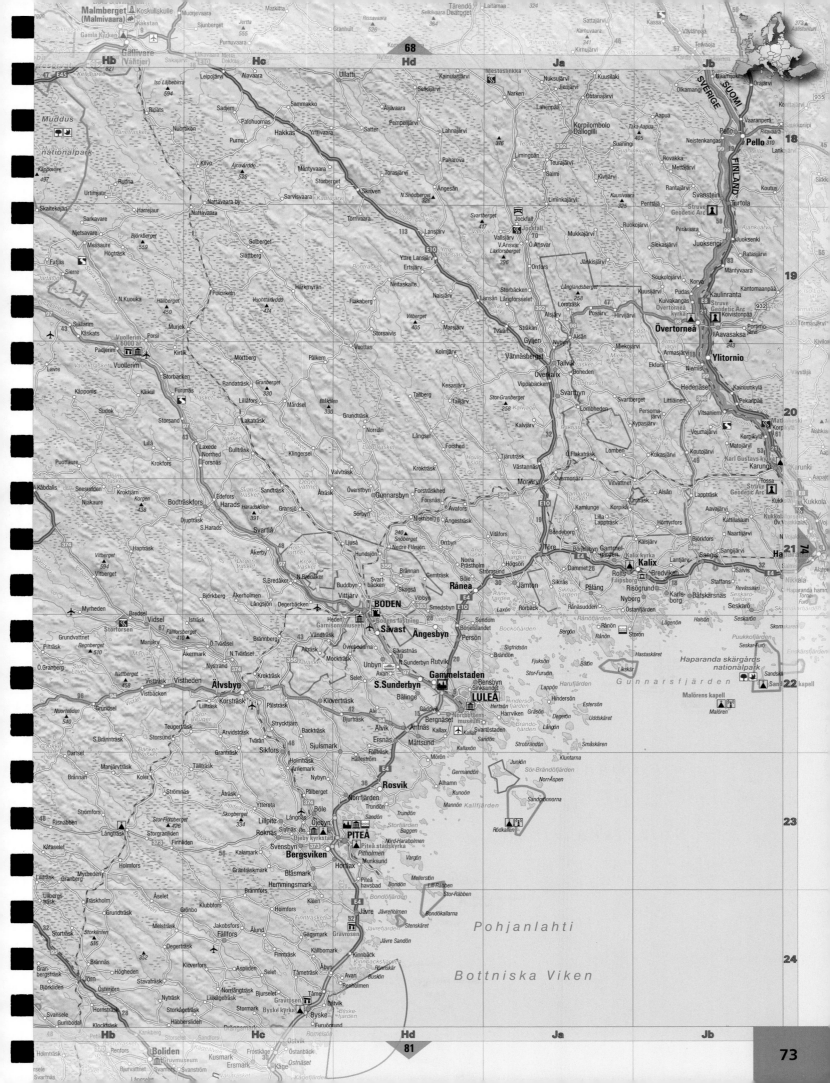

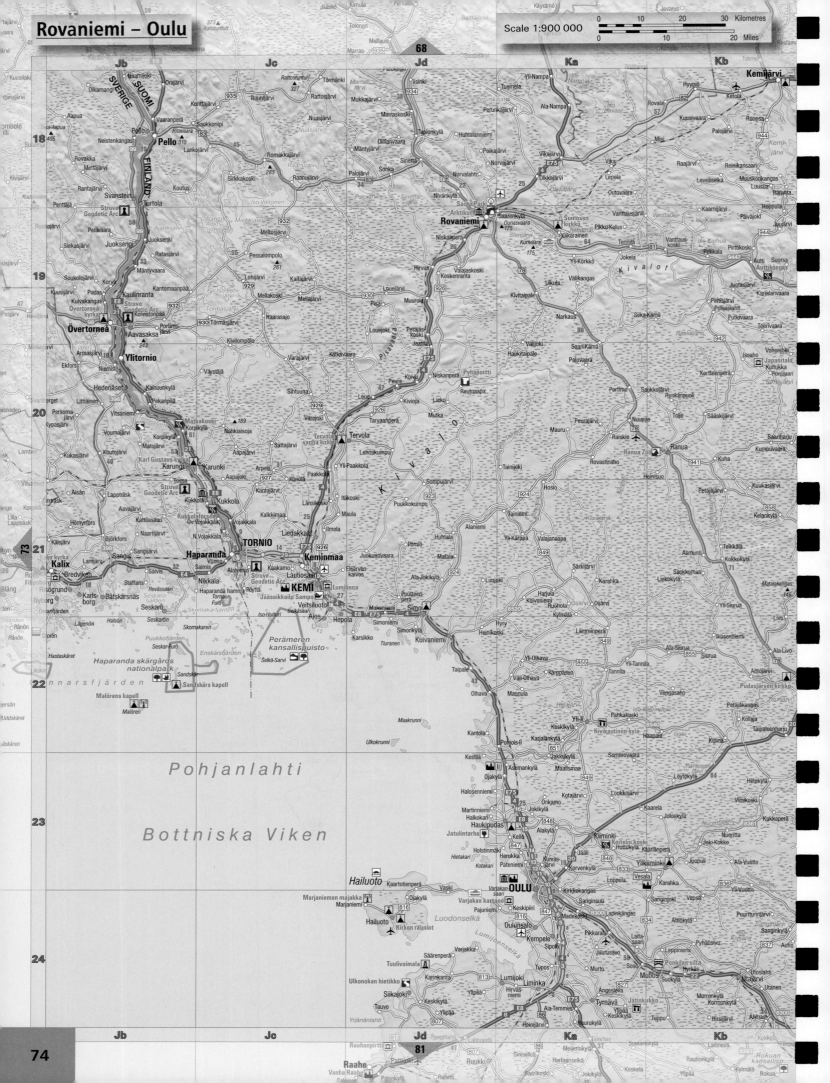

Scale 1:900 000

0 10 20 30 Kilometres
0 10 20 Miles

68

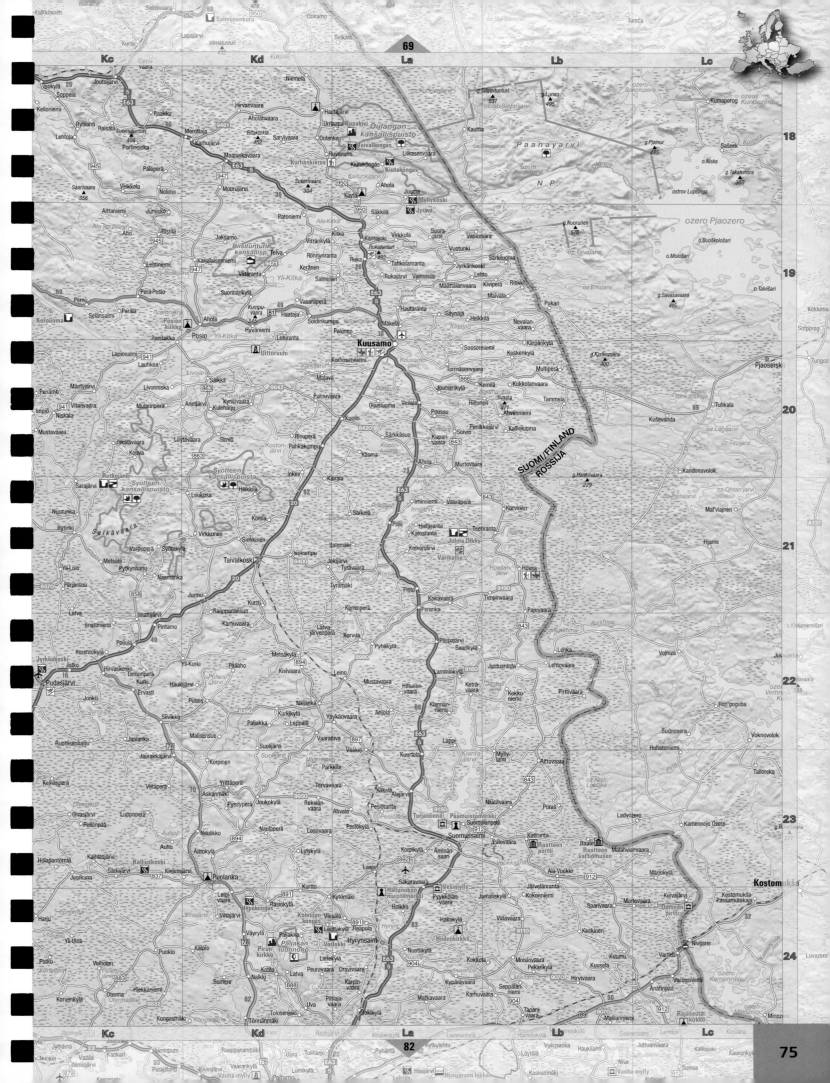

	Bd	Ca	Cb	Cc	Cd

27

28

NORWEGIAN SEA

29

30

31

Hustad

Vikan
Skarset

Bud

664

Husøy
Ona
Bjørnsund

Gossen
Elnesvågen

Steinshamn
Sandøy
Tornes

Myfjorden
Orten
Vågøy

Ulla fyr
Fjørtoft
Tangen
Aukra
Hollingsholm

Nordøyane
Haramsøya
Grunne-
fjorden
Otrøy
662
MOLDE

Storholmen fyr
Flemsøya
Mildøy
668
Sundsbø
Romsdals-
museet

Lepsøya
Midsund
729

Austnes
Tautra
Møldefjorden

Vigrafjorden
Hildre
Ørnes
Fiksdal
Vestnes

Roald
Skjelten
Brattvåg
Skaeringen
Vik

Erkna fyr
Vigra
659
Søvik
661
Vatne
1062
661
Tomrefjord

32
Nordstrand
Hamsund
Stette
Skodje
Sørpvstind
1194
Daugstad

Alnes
Godøy
bompenger
Hoff
Gryttefjorden
Alvik 13
E39
35
Tresfjord
Ospetind
1228

Sørøyane
Graseyane fyr
Brei-
sundet
ÅLESUND
11
Ellingsøy
Aalfjorden
Sjøholt
Vaksvik
Øvstedal

Holme-
fjorden
Runde
Atlanterhavsparken
Spjelkavik
Valla
60
Magerholm
Klokk
Dyrkorn
Overøye

Nerlandsøy
Kvalsvik
Runde
Remøy
Fla
Brandal
Langevåg
Sula
Filsnes
61
Ikornnes
Sykkylven
Brune
Velle 48
650
Stordal
Mo

Skorpa
Kvalsund
Leine
Leinøy
Ulsteinvik
Hareid
Sulesund
Festøy
E39
Arsnes
Tollkyrkja
1478
Drottninghaug
Jølgrøhørnet
1263

Svinøy fyr
Fosnavåg
Tørvik
61
Romdals-
horn
1480
Strandal
Trandal
Stranda
Liabygda

Herøyfjorden
Dimnøy
104
Haddal
Vartdalsfjorden
Vartdal
54
Kvien
Velle
Opshaugvik
Skrenakkhorn
1519
Eidsdal

Sandsøy
Moltustranda
654
653
Bjånes
S u n n m ø r e
Skarasalen
1632
Nordda
60
Flosteinnipa
1514

33
Årvik
Kvamsøy
Sande
Gurskøy
Gursken
652
Røve
Åsen
Ørsta
Kolås
Sæbø
Leknes
Skarasalen
1542
Herdal
655
63
Indreeide

Ervik
Eltvik
Vanylvs-
gapet
Åram
Larsnes
Årvik
61
Jøsok
Berknes
Syvdsnes
Lauvstad
Volda
Vatne
651
Viddal
655
XI-IV

Stadlandet
Sandvik
Koparnes
Børøvatnet
61
Dalsfjord
Folkestad
39
Ørnes-
vinnen

Hoddevika
Leikanger
Hundsnes
Eidså
Fiskå
Vik
Viddal

Sildegapet
620
Syvde

Kråkenes fyr
Skongenes fyr
Sanktan
Sunniva
Selje
61B
Syvde
Iverberg
Dale
Austefjord

Raudeberg
Barmen
Bjørka
Ørnes-
vinnen

Kvalheimsvika
617
Ameltoft
Botnane
Matreska
1332
Tryggestad
Heliesylt
Sørsæter-
fossen

Måløy
Flatraket
61
Almklov
Kalvatn
62
Geirangerfjorden
Geiranger
Norsk
Fjordsenter

Husevågøy
Deknepollen
20
Brygga
Haugsvarden
Bjørkedal
Geiranger

Maurstad
Kinnlsdal
1070 Smørda
39
Holmbuvatn
Lyngvoll
Bjørdal

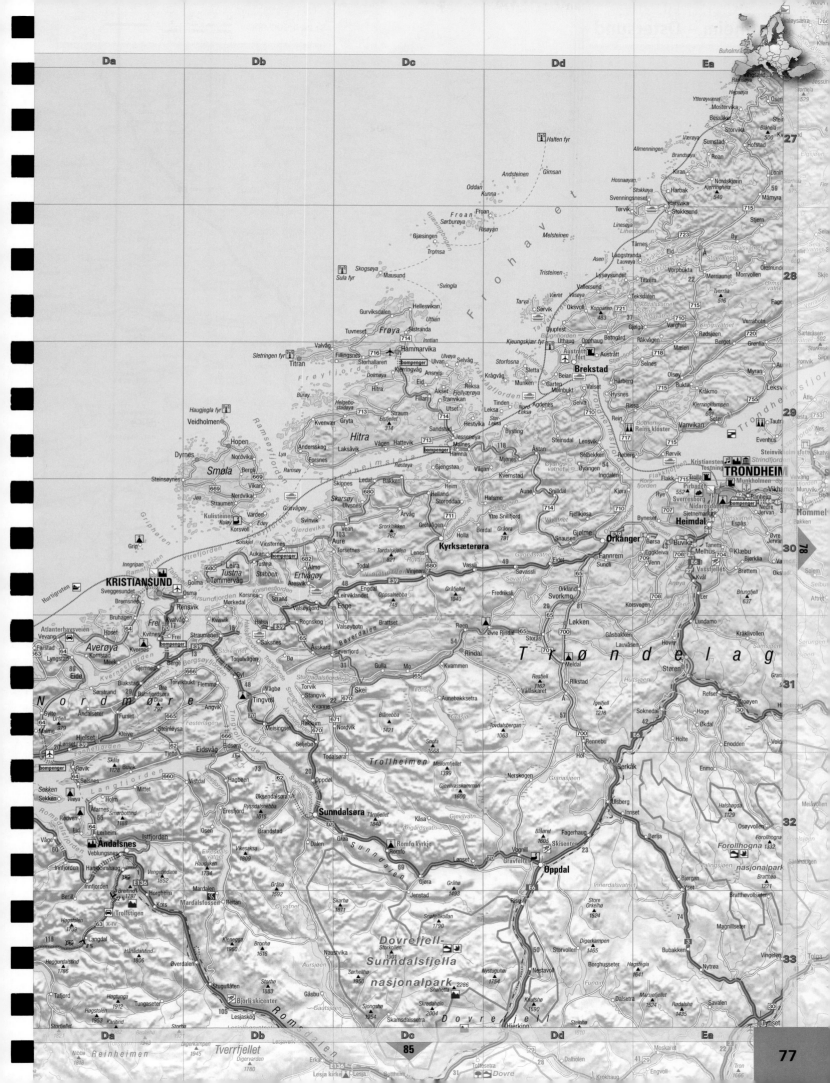

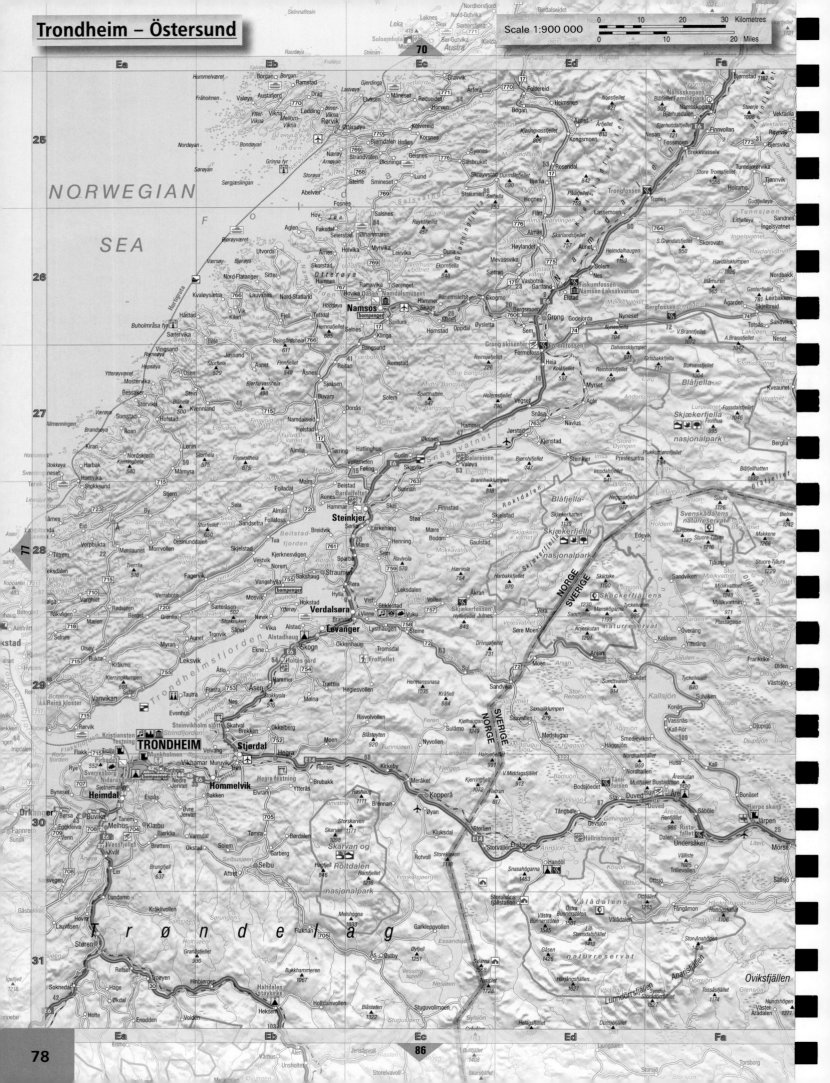

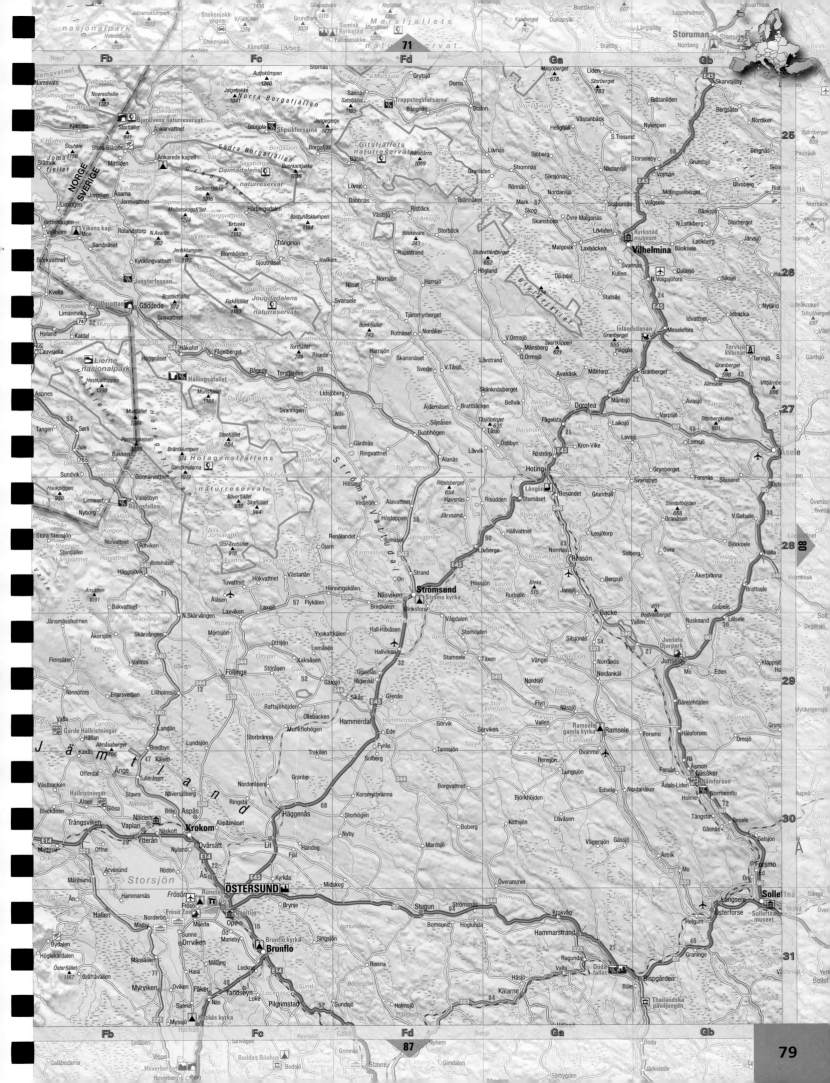

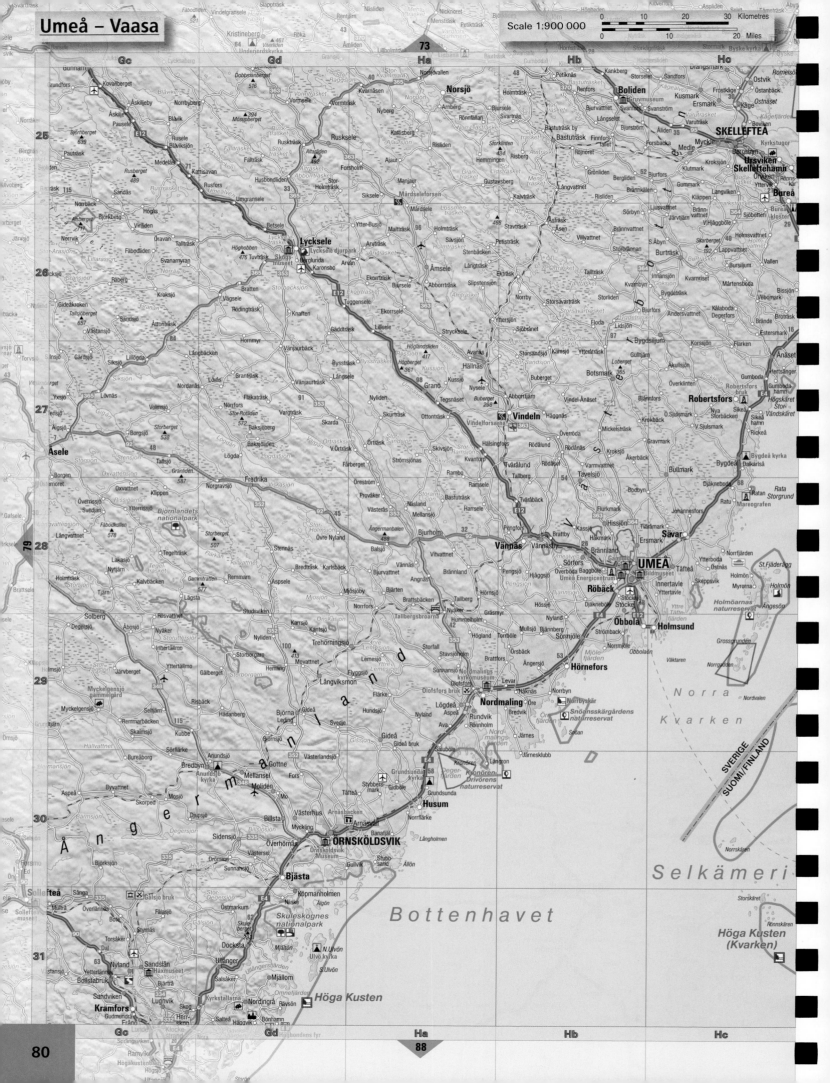

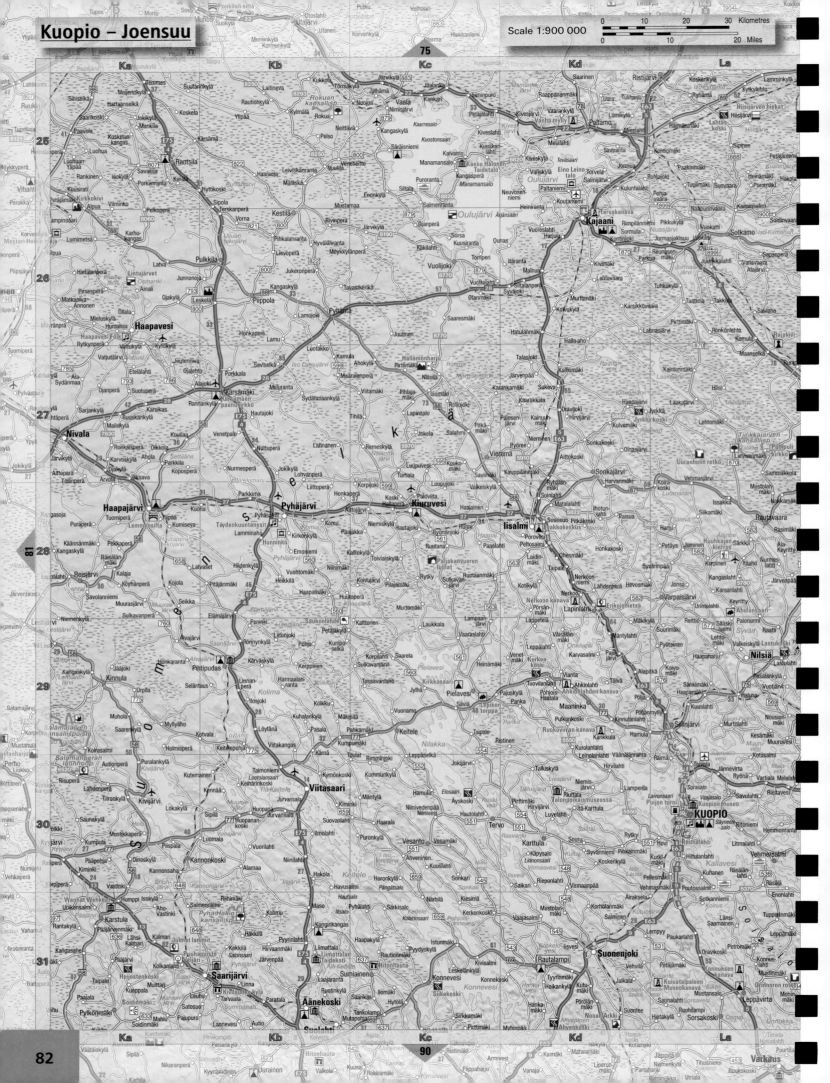

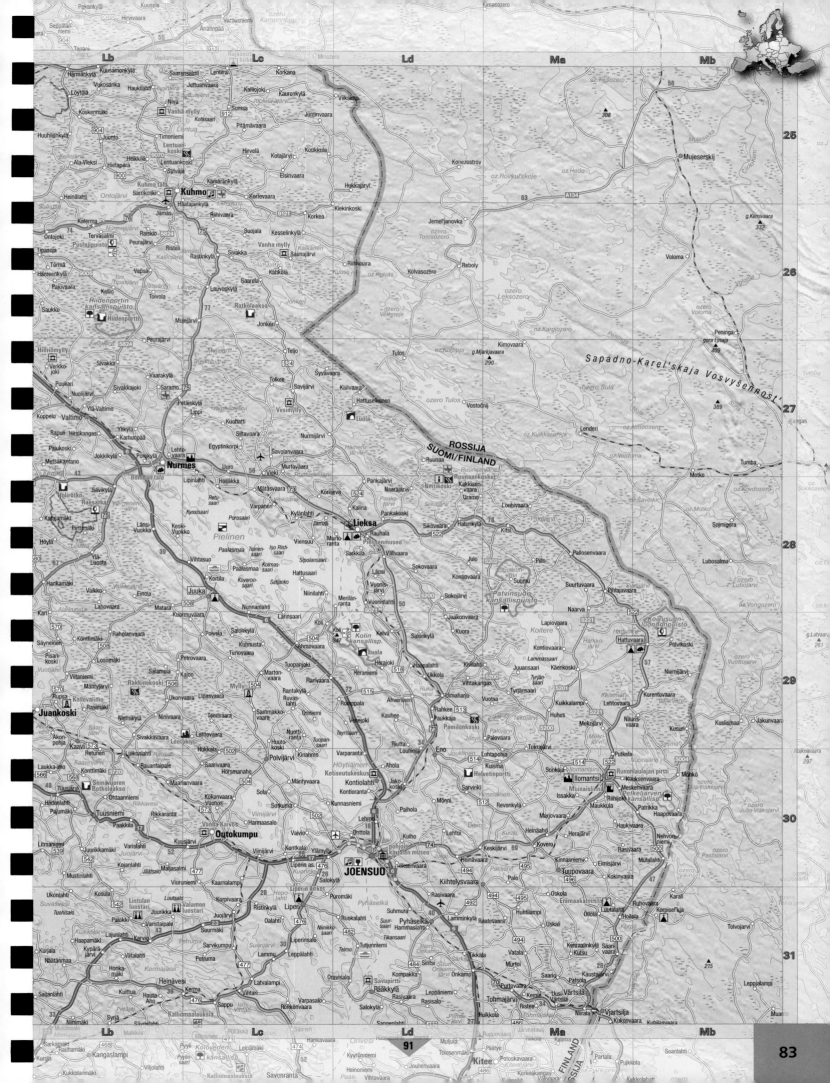

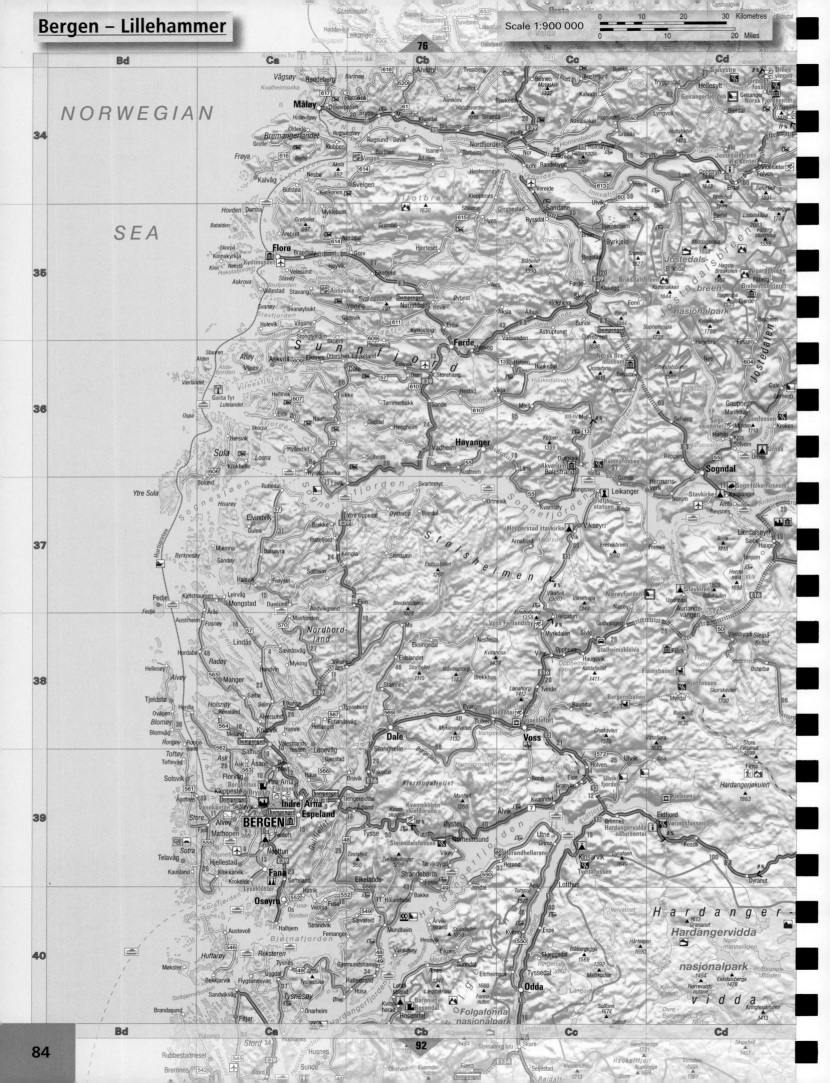

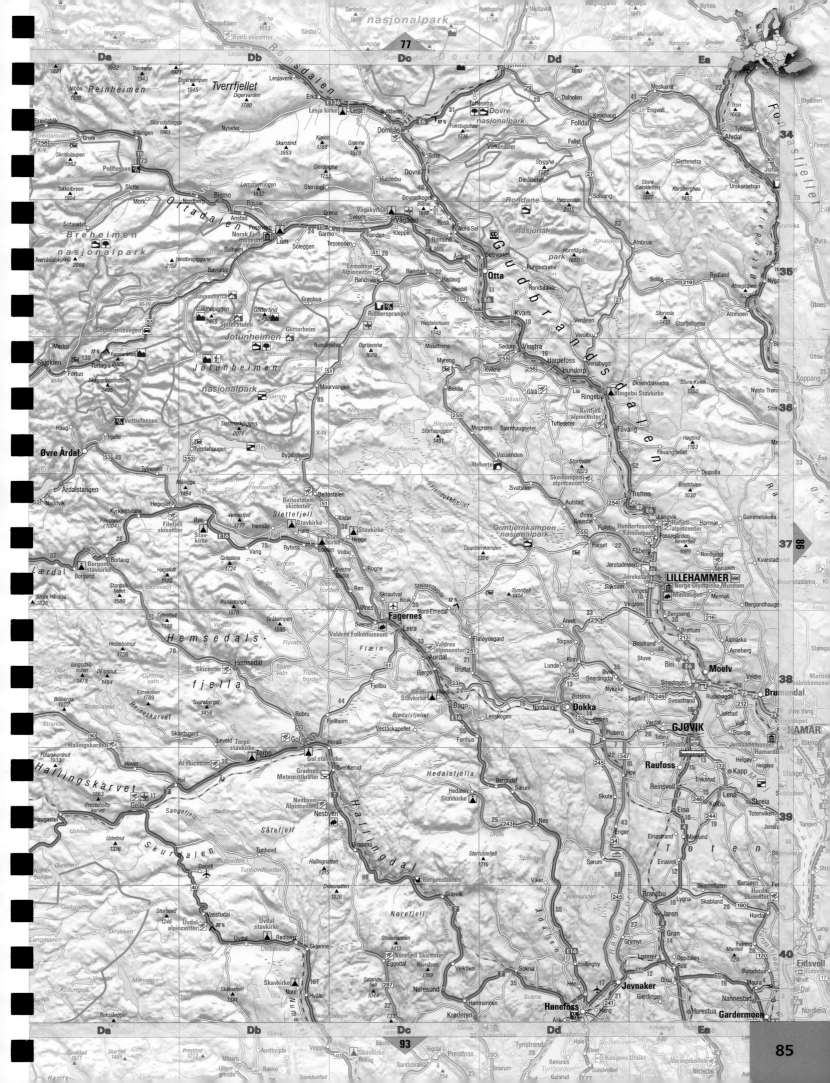

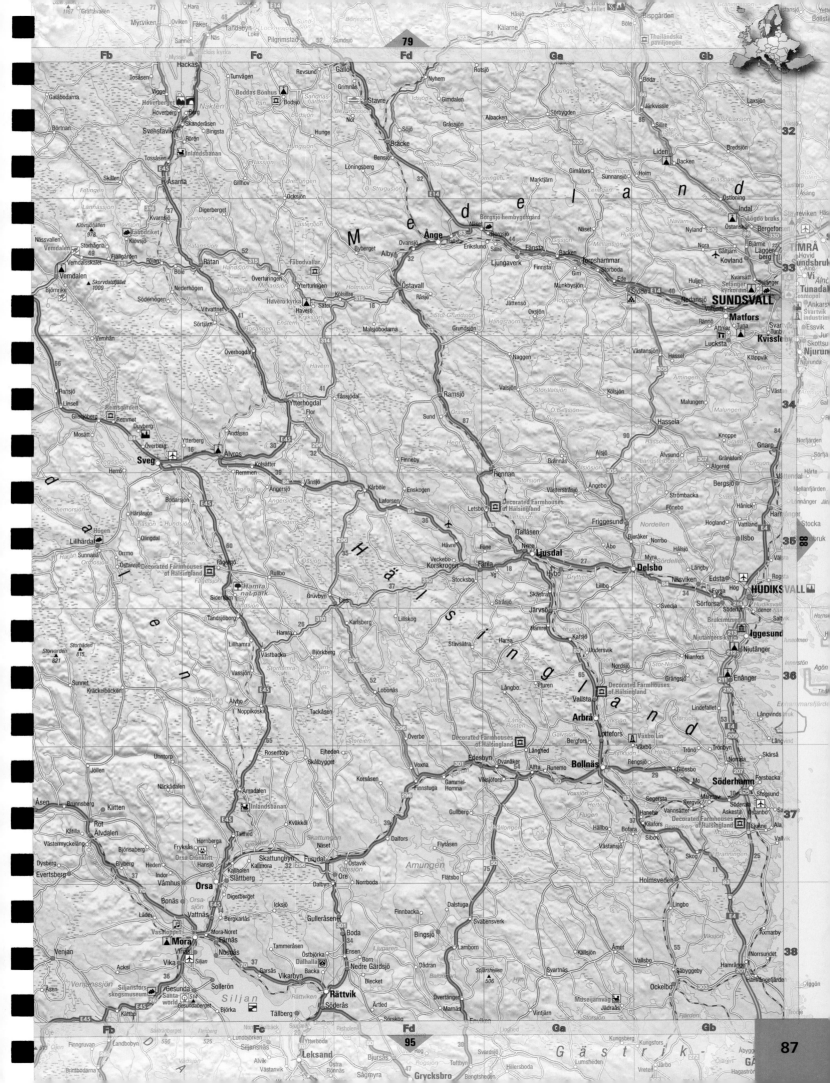

Krämfors
Lunde
Klockestrand
Sprängsviken
Ramvik
Högakustenbron
Högsjö
Utansjö
Viksjö
Aspnäs
Storön
Hemsö
Ålandsbro
Ulvvik
Hemsön
Lungön
Stigsjö
Säbrå
Vågnön
Ljustorp
Åsäng
HÄRNÖSAND
Gånsvik
Antjärn
Murberget
Härnön
Stavreviken
Hässjö
Öje
Bye
Berneforsen
Häggdånger
Söråker
Barsviken
TIMRÅ
Hovid
Sundsbruk
Tynderö
Åvikebukten
Vi
Alnö
Åkerö
Tunadal
Åstön
Cosmopol
Rödön
Åstholmsudde
Ankarsvik
Svartvik
industriminnen
Sundsvallsbukten
Essvik
Juniskär
Skottsund
Njurundabommen
Njurunda
Brämön
Galtströms bruk
Galtström
Ragvaldsnäs
Norrfjärden
Sörfjärden
Hårte
Vitörarna
Mellanfjärden
Lönnånger
Jättholmarna
Harmånger
Stocka
Strömsbruk
Bästdal
Västa
Rogsta
HUDIKSVALL
Bålsön
Kuggörarna
Hornslandet
Klappstenfält
Hölick
Tunaolmen
Iggesund
Njutånger
Innerstön
Agön
Tihällan
Enhammarsfjärden
Långvinds bruk
Långvind
Skärså
Forsbacka
Stugsund
Östanbo
Ljusne
Ala
Vallvik
Axmarby
Norrsun
Iggön
Trödje

Höga Kusten

Selkämeri

Bottenhavet

Bottenhavet

Gävlebukten

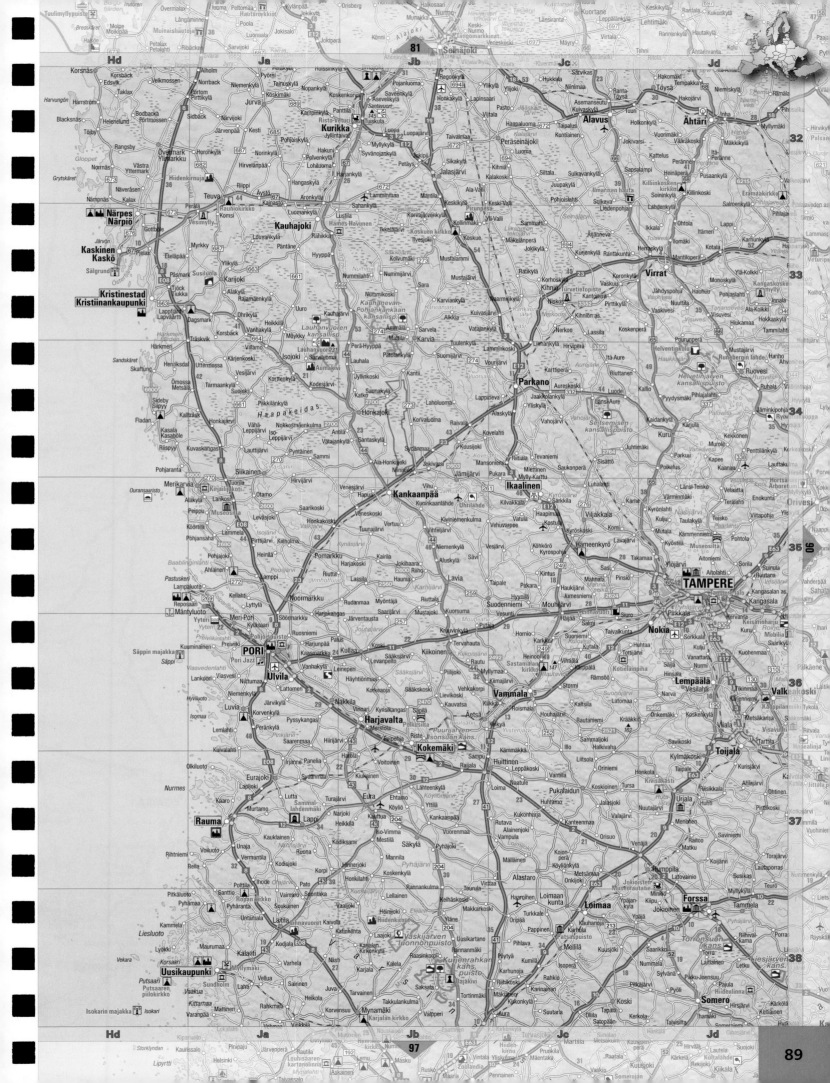

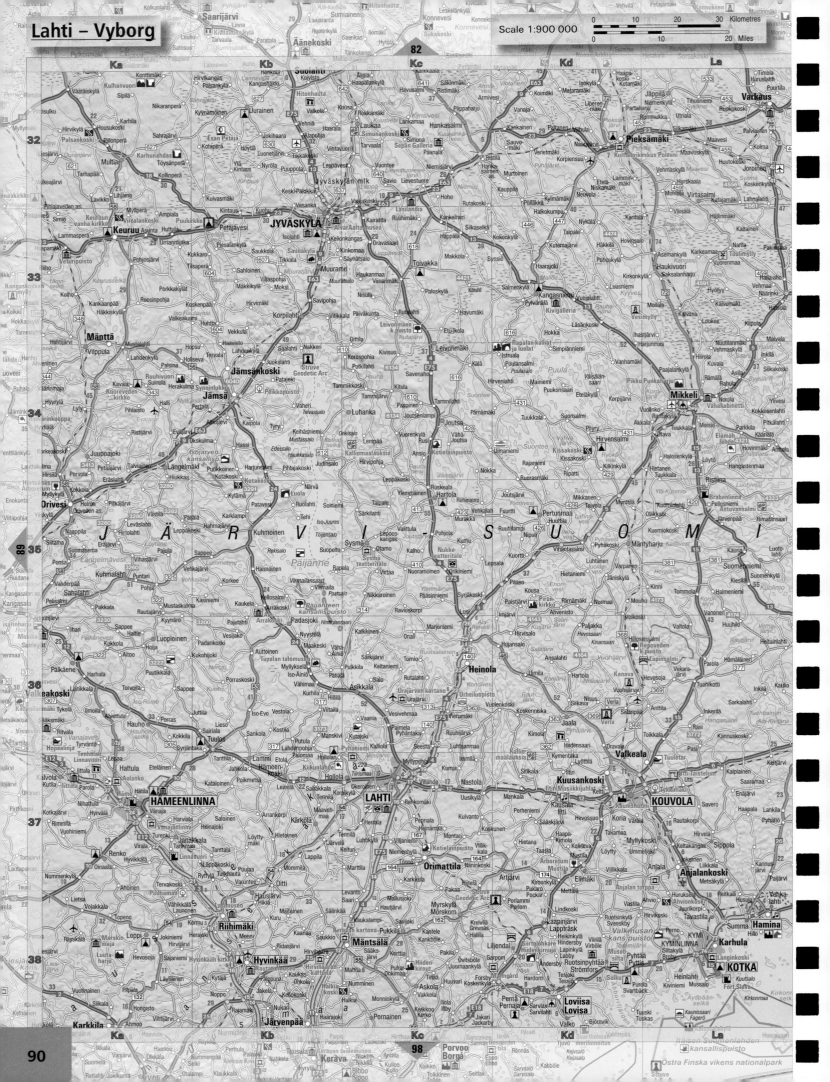

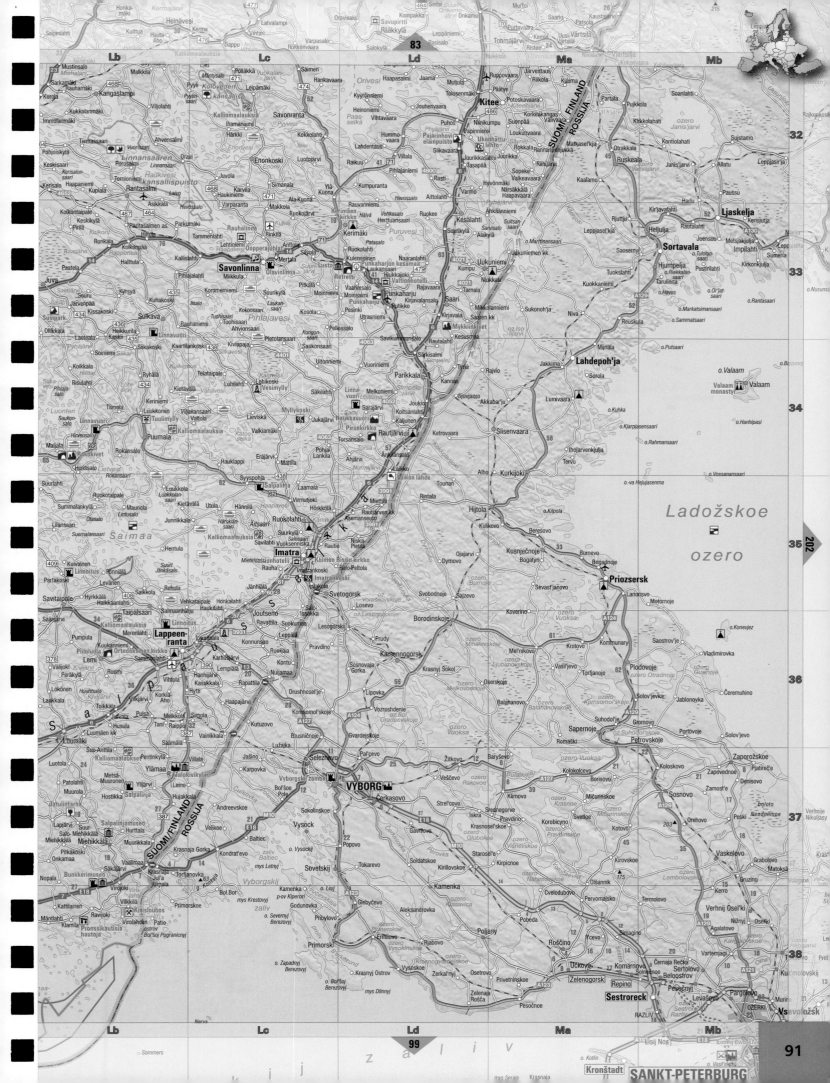

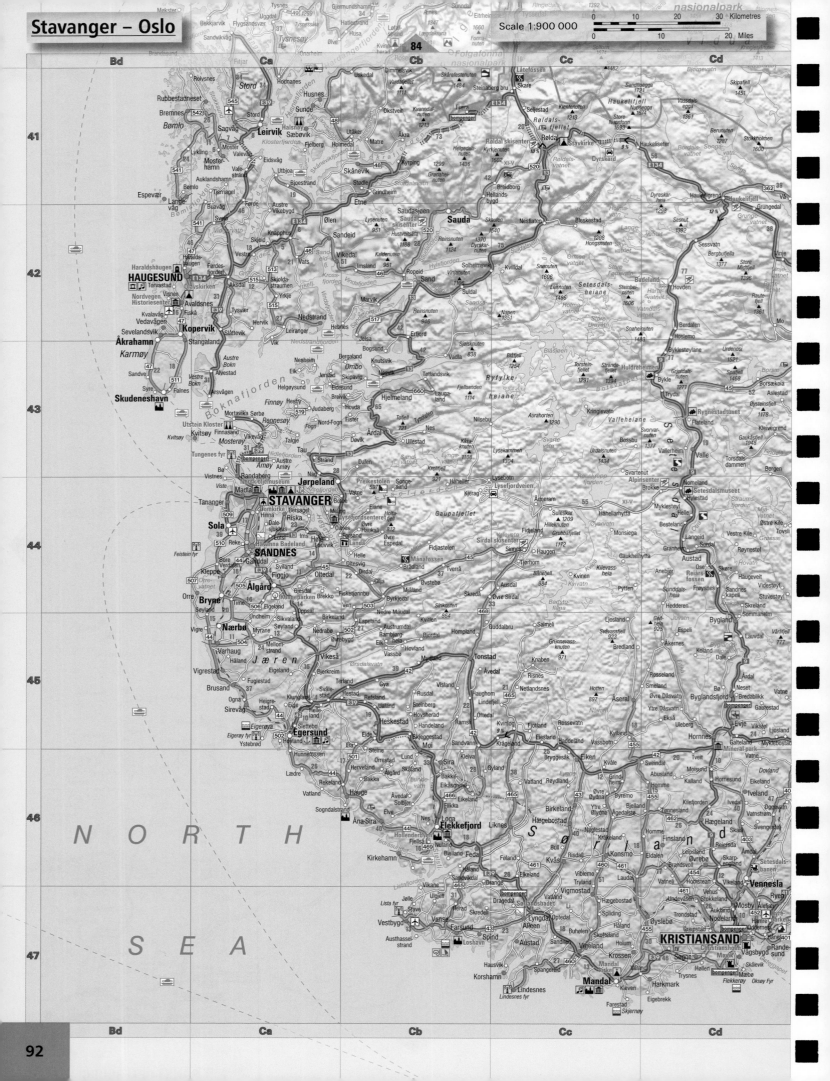

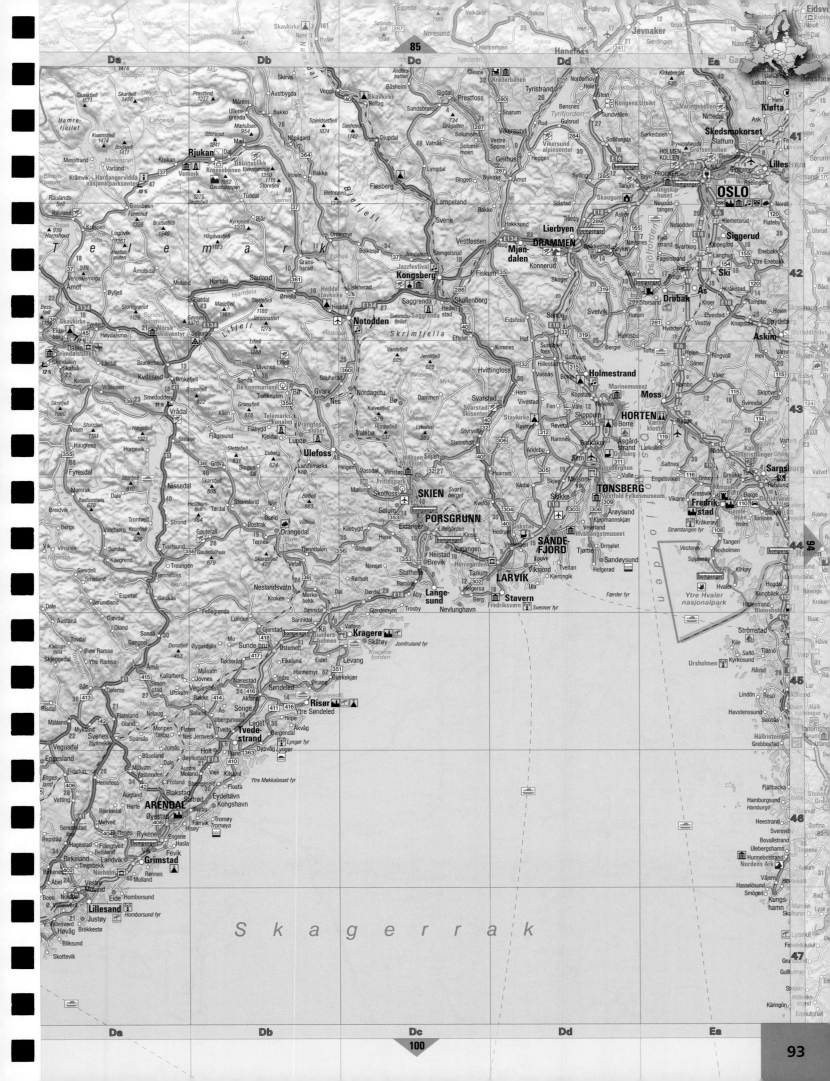

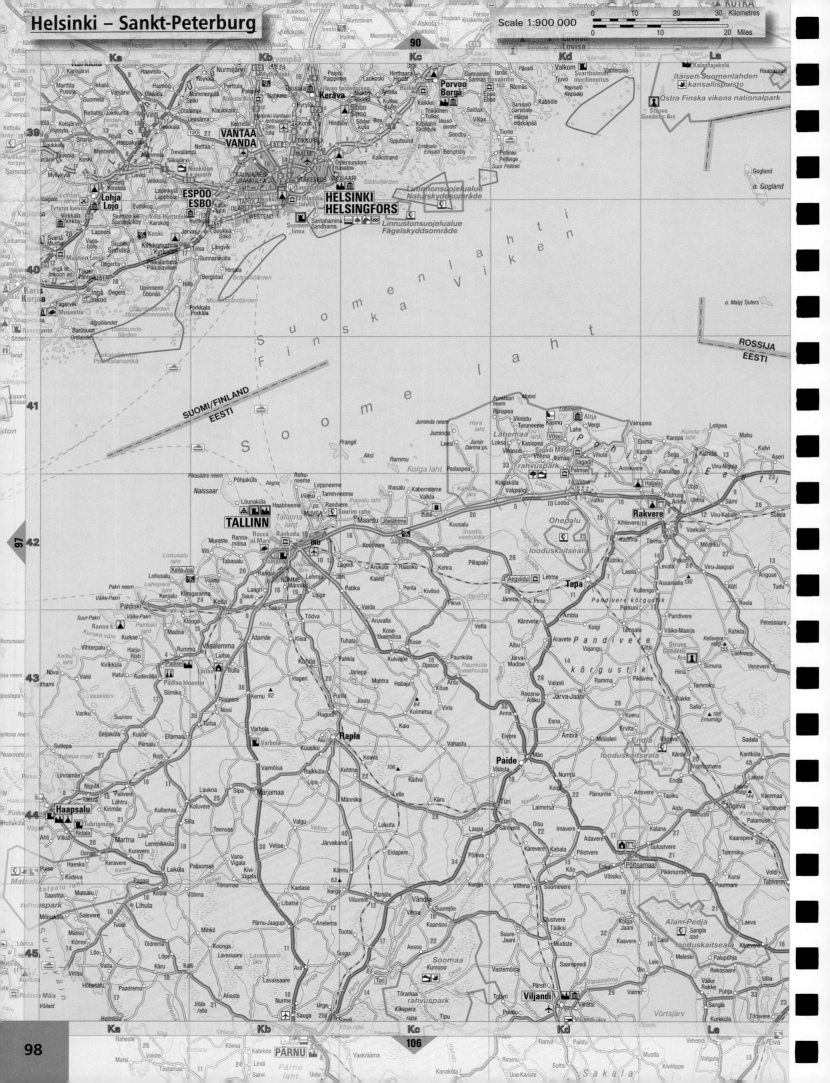

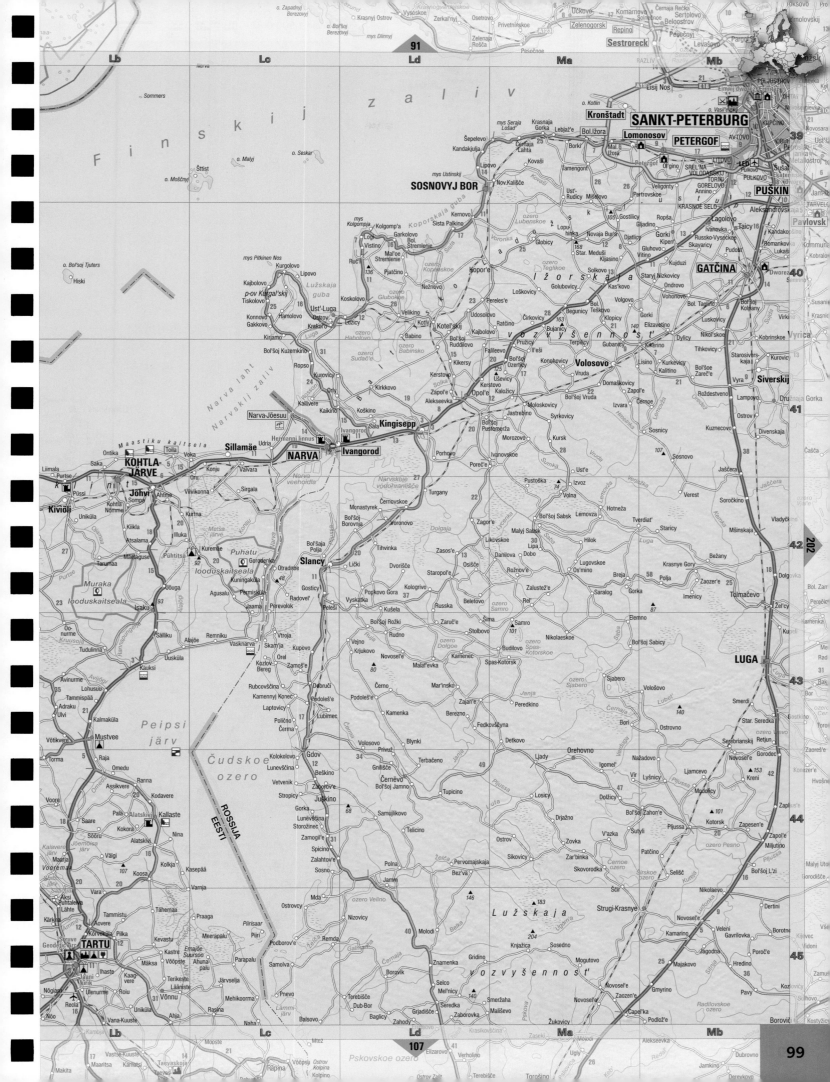

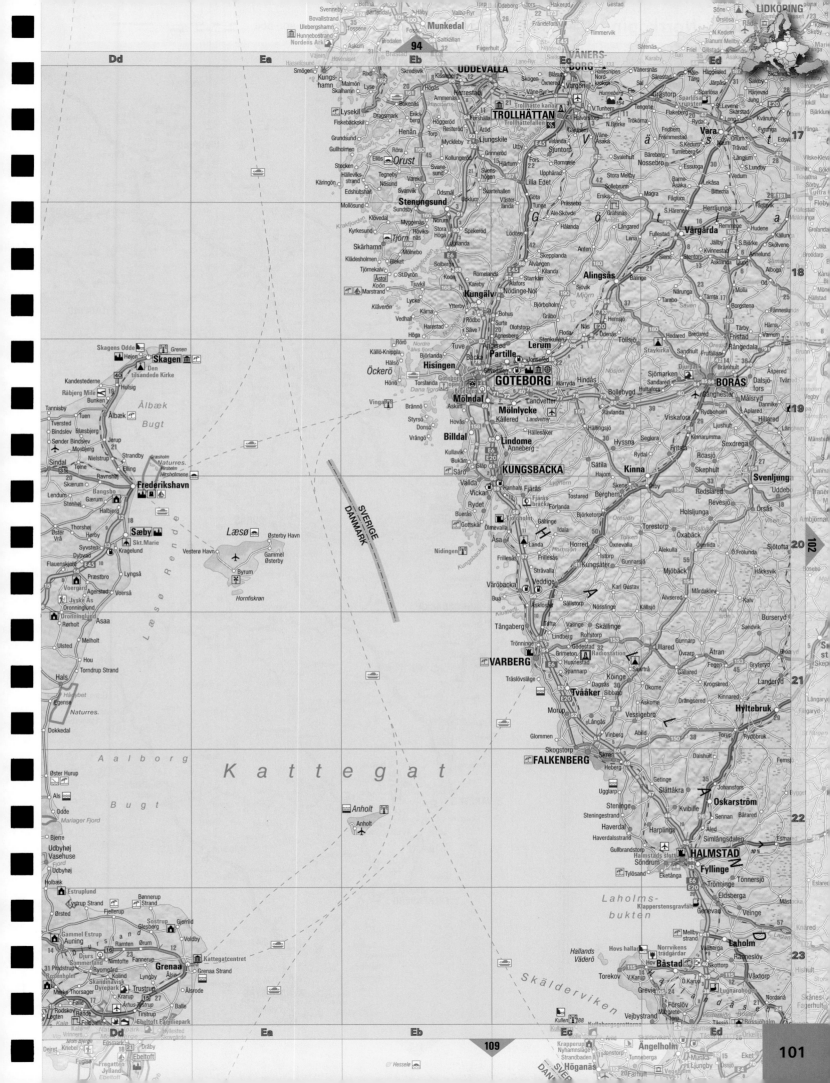

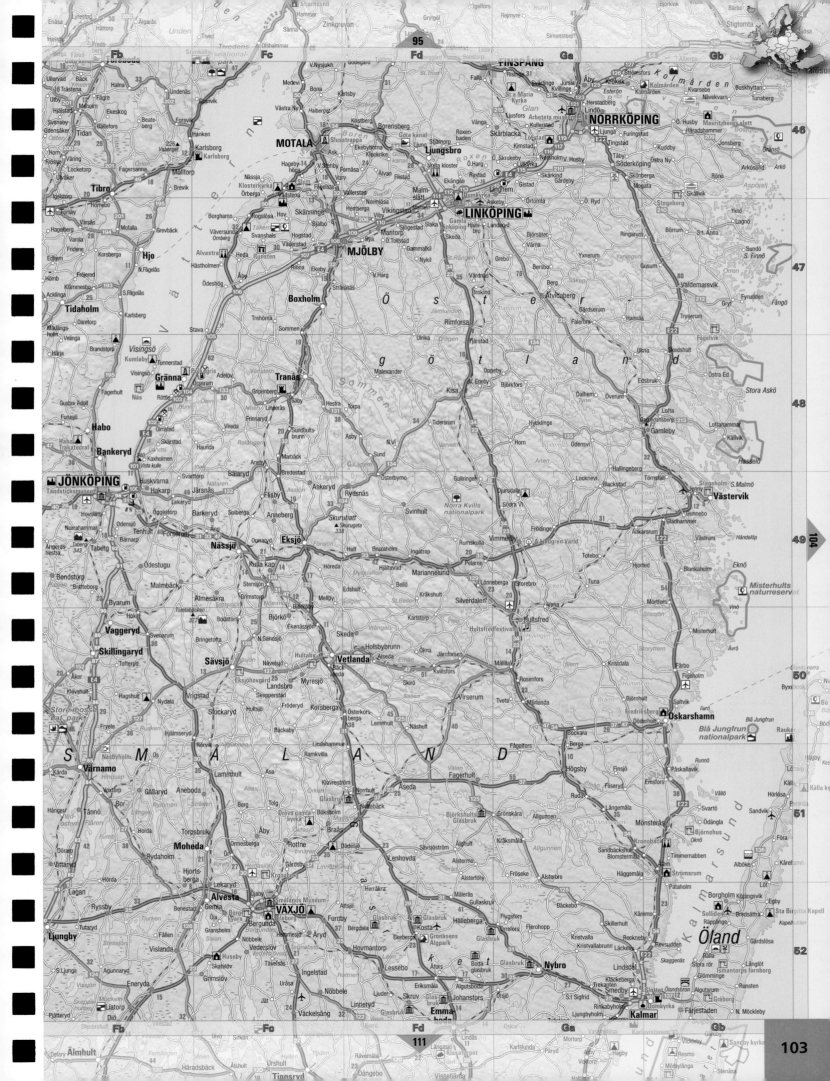

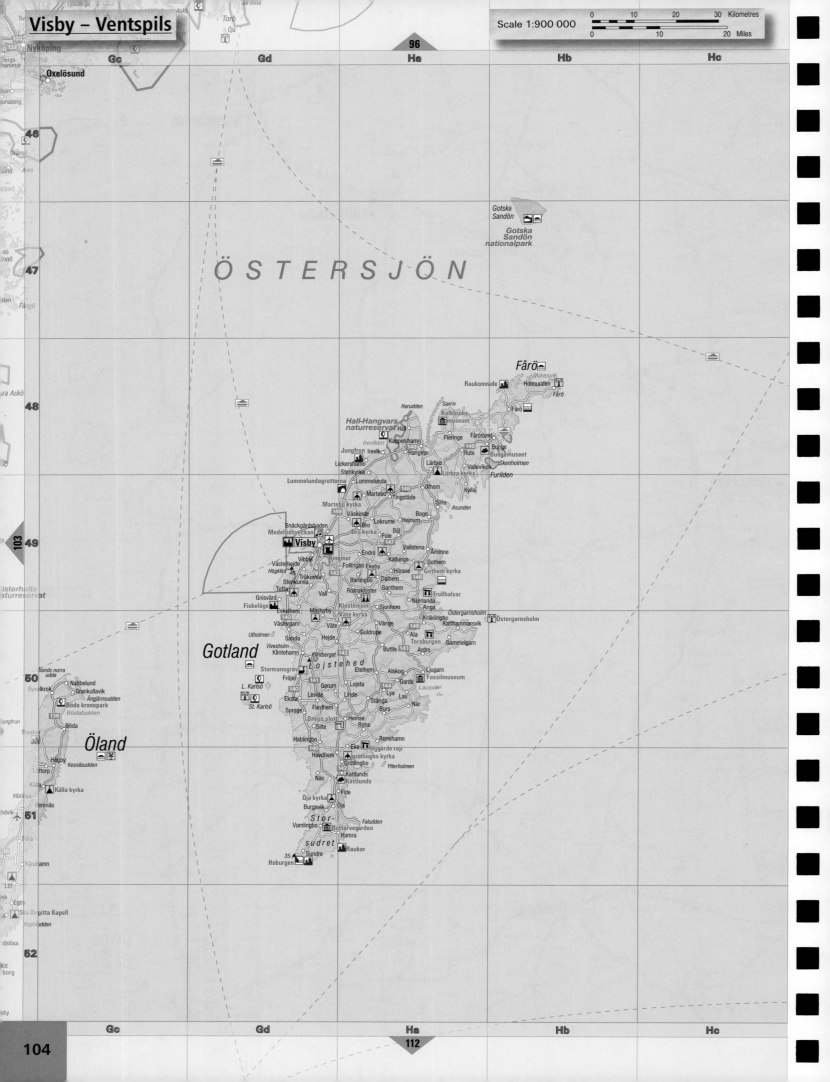

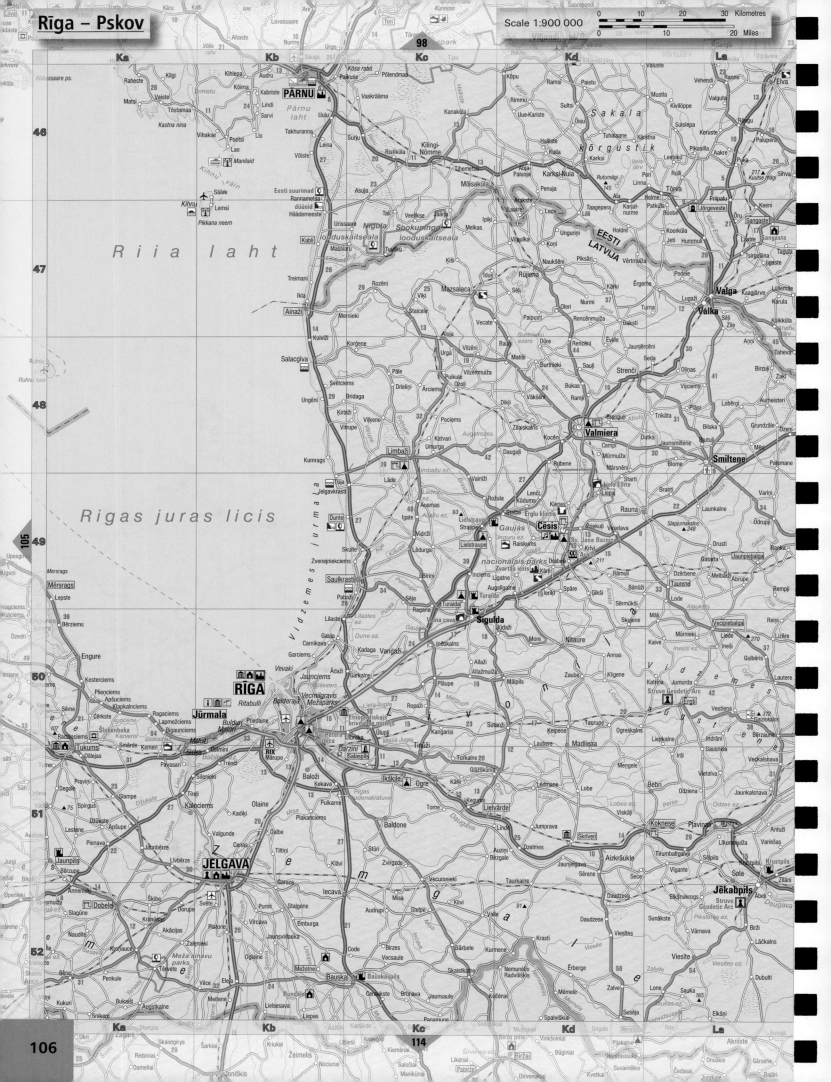

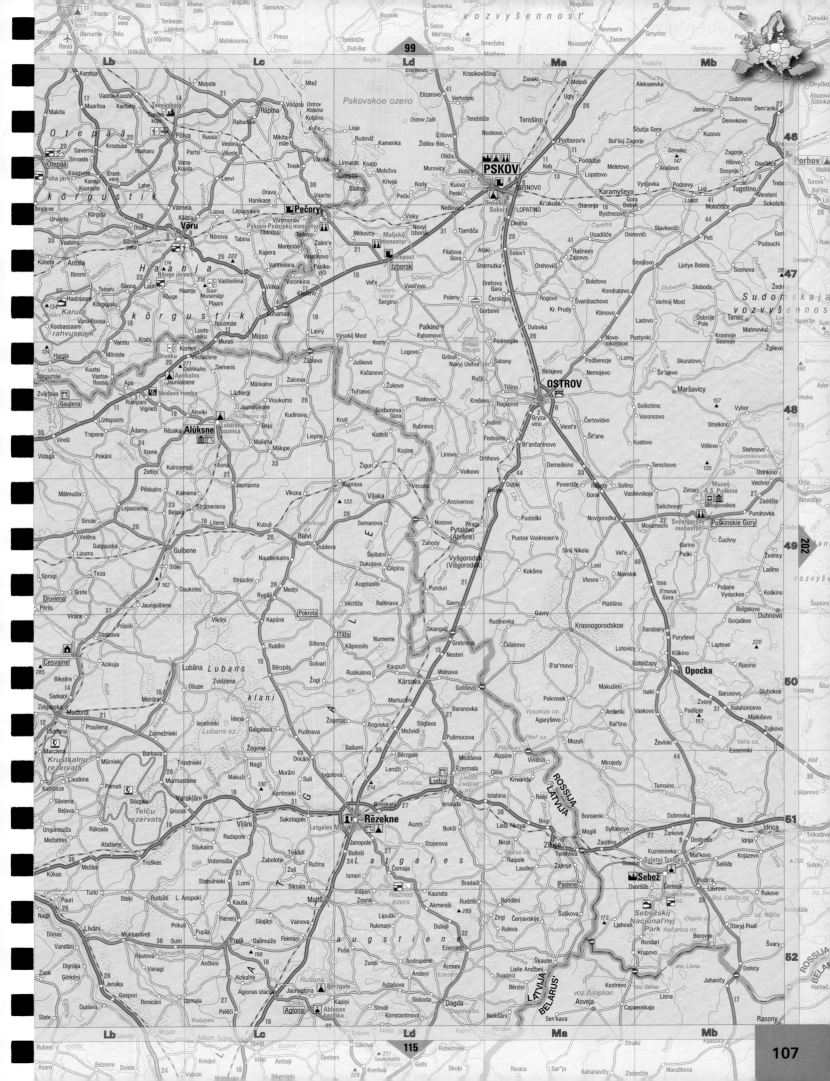

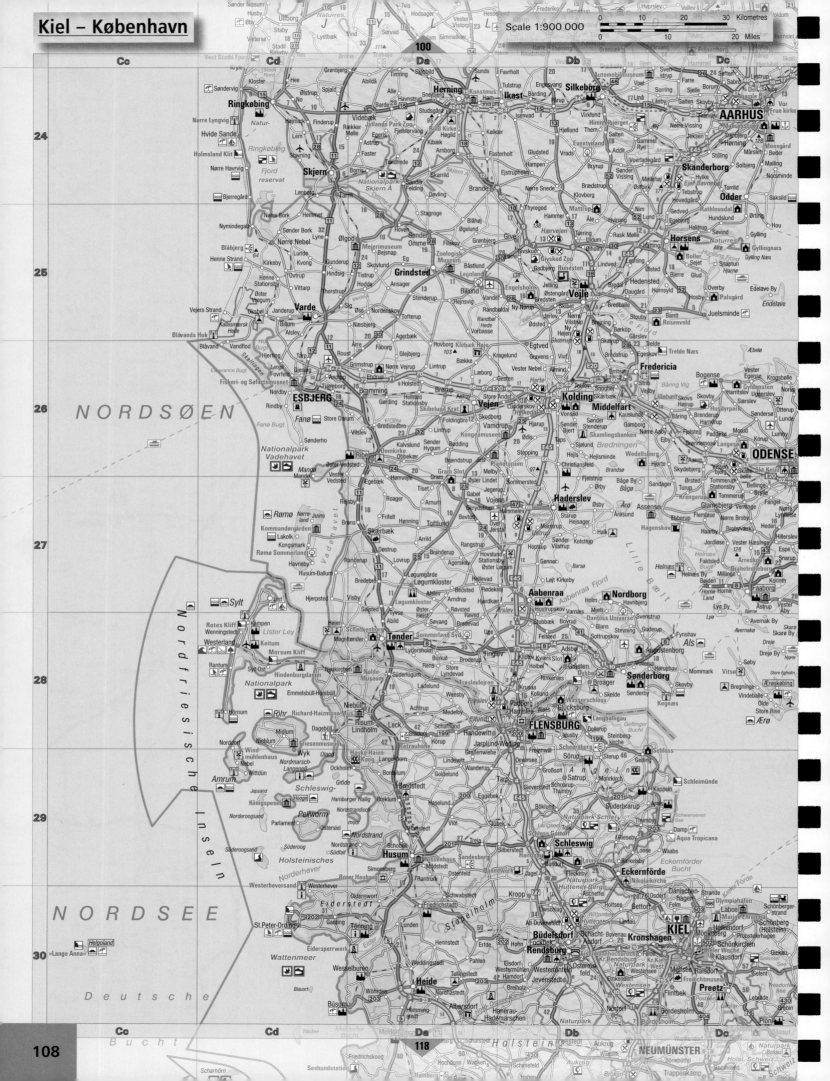

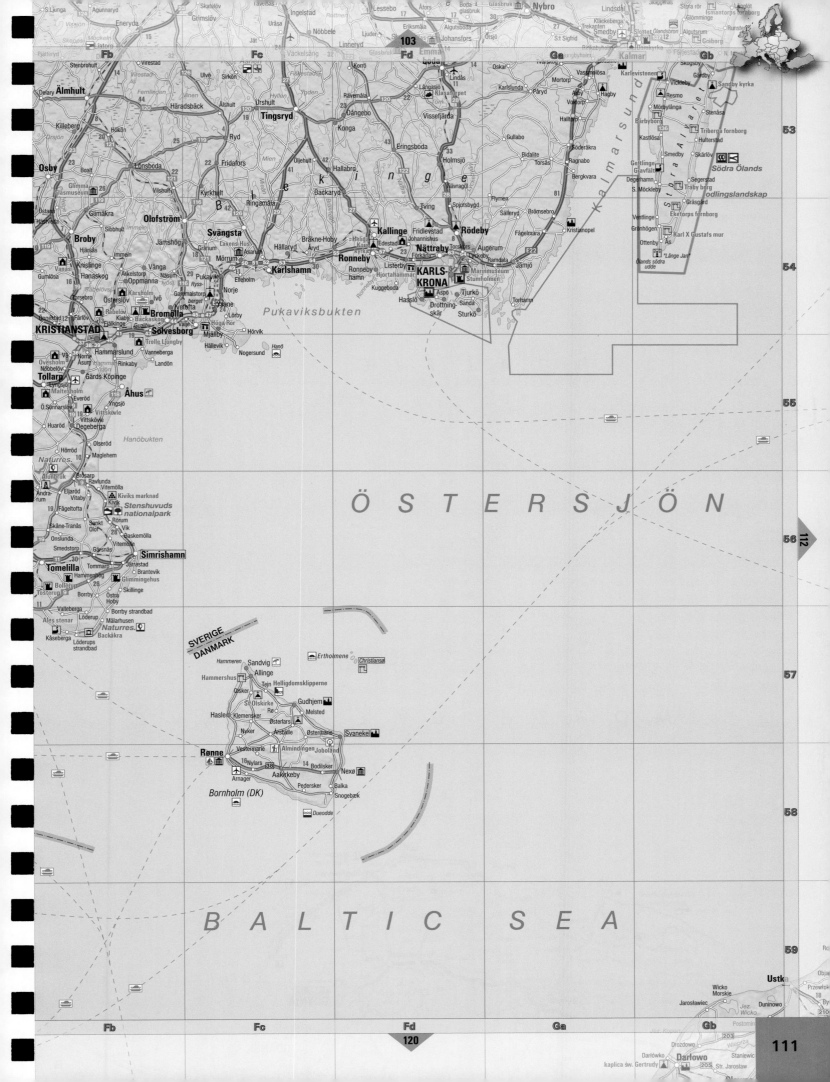

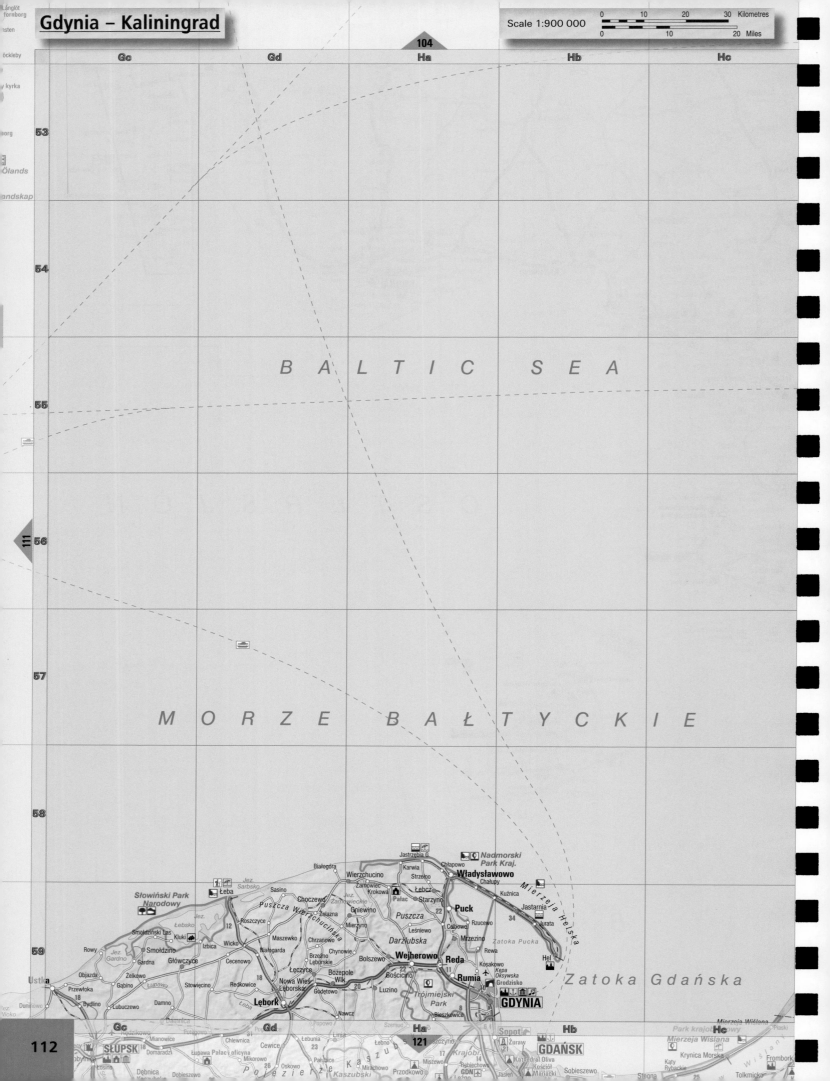

Scale 1:900 000

0   10   20   30   Kilometres

0   10   20   Miles

104

Gc   Gd   Ha   Hb   Hc

53

Länglöt
fornborg

kyrka

Ölands

andskap

54

55

111   56

57

BALTIC SEA

MORZE BAŁTYCKIE

58

59

Jastrzębia G.

Nadmorski
Park Kraj.

Chłapowo

Białogóra   Wierzchucino

Karwia   Strzelno

Władysławowo

Chałupy

Jez.
Sarbsko   Łeba

Sasino   Krokowa   Łebcz   Kuźnica

Słowiński Park
Narodowy

Choczewo   Żarnowiec   Pałac   Starzyno

Jez.
Żarnowieckie   Gniewino

Jastarnia

Jurata

Puszcza Wierzchucińska   Żelazno   Puck

Łebsko   Jez.

Roszczyce   Mierzyno

Puszcza

Rzucewo   34

Kluki   Izbica   Maszewko   Chrzanowo   Leśniewo   Celbowo

Smołdziński Las

12

Wicko   Białogarda   Chynowie   Darzlubska   Mrzezino

Rowy   Jez.
Gardno   Smołdzino   Gardna   Główczyce   Brzeźno
Lęborskie   Bolszewo   Wejherowo   Reda   Rewa

Zatoka Pucka

Hel

Mierzeja Helska

Ustka   Objazda   Cecenowo   Łęczyce   Bożepole Wlk   Gościcino   Rumia   Kosakowo
Oksywska
Kępa

Przewłoka   Żelkowo   Stowięcino   Nowa Wieś
Lęborska   Godętowo   Luzino

18   Gabino   Łupawa   Ręgowice   20

Bydlino   Lubuczewo   Damno   Łeba   Lębork   Nawcz

Duninowo

Vicko

Zatoka Gdańska

Trójmiejski
Park

8   GDYNIA

Bieszkowice

Damnica   Popowo

Mierzeja Wiślana
Park krajobrazowy

Gc   Gd   Ha   Hb   Hc

Rudzikowo   Chlewnica   Łebno   Sopot   Żuraw
Mianowice   Cewice   Linia   23   **121**

SŁUPSK   18   Łupawa Pałac oficyna   Miszewo   Krajobr.   GDAŃSK
Domaradz   Mikorowo   Oskowo   Przodkowo   GDN   Katedral Oliva   Krynica Morska

Łosino   Dębnica   Dobieszewo   Pałubice   Kaszub.   Jasień   Kościół   Mariacki   Sobieszewo   Stegna   25   Tolkmicko

Pojezierze Kaszubskie   Fromb

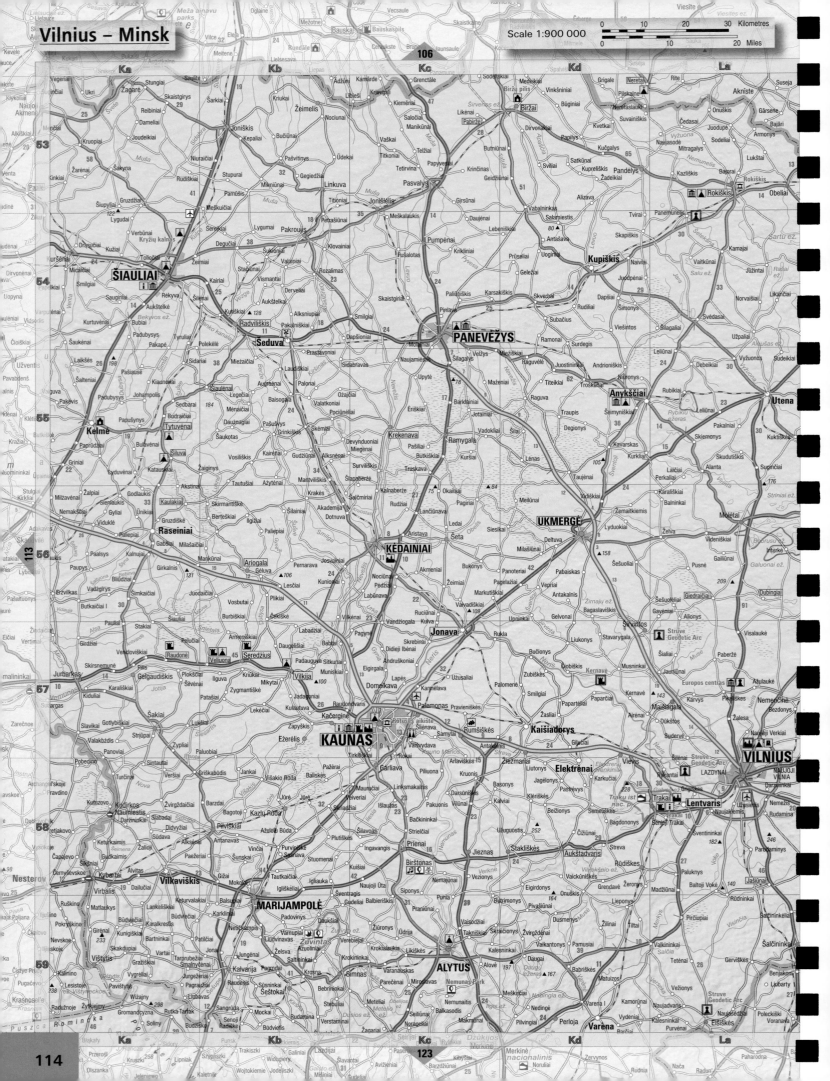

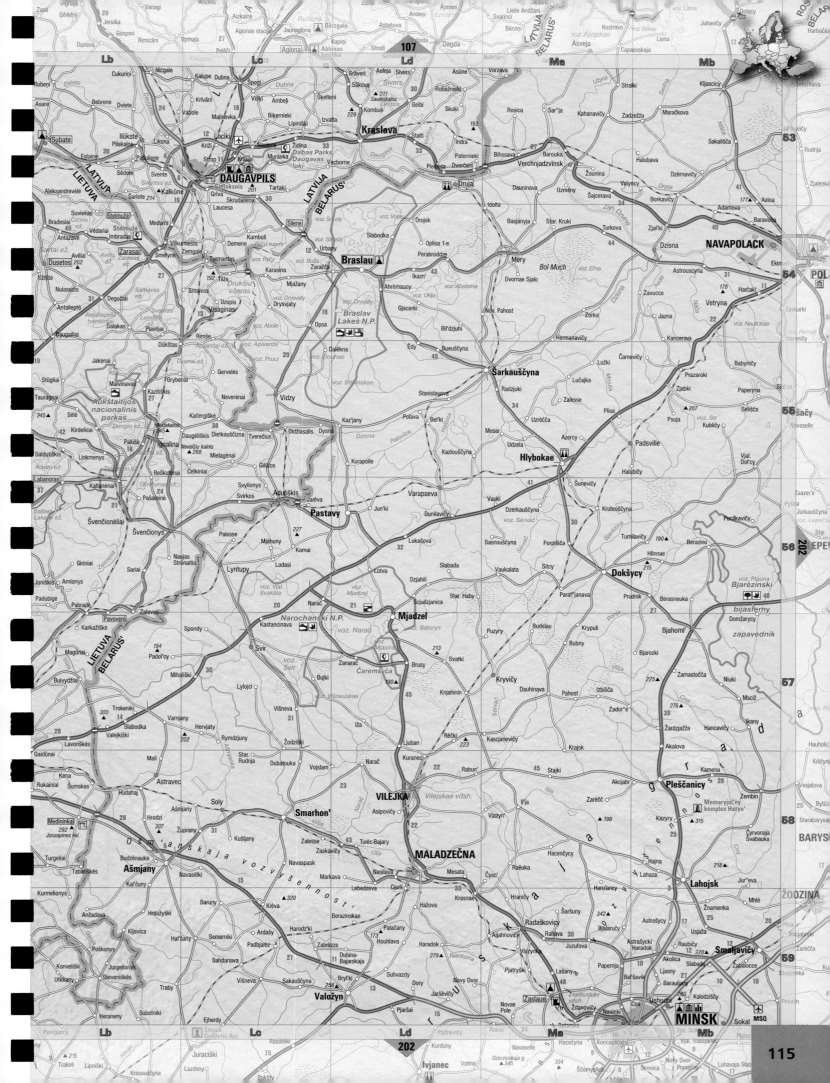

Scale 1:900 000

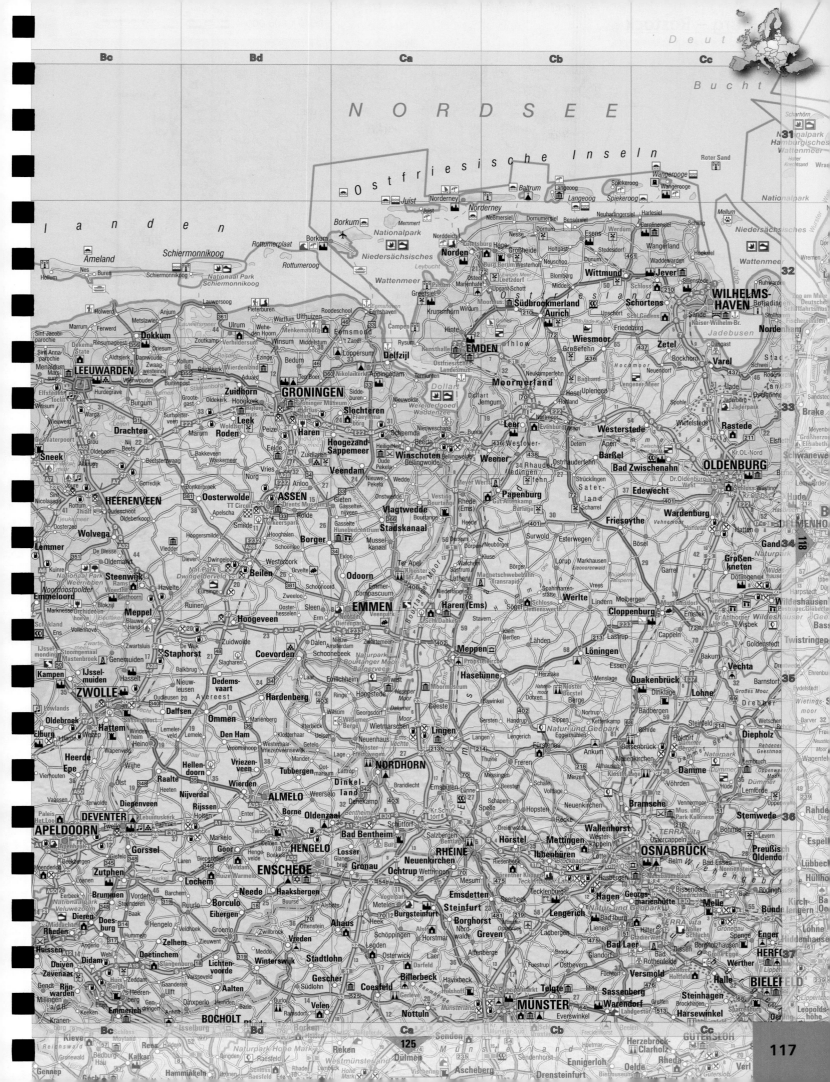

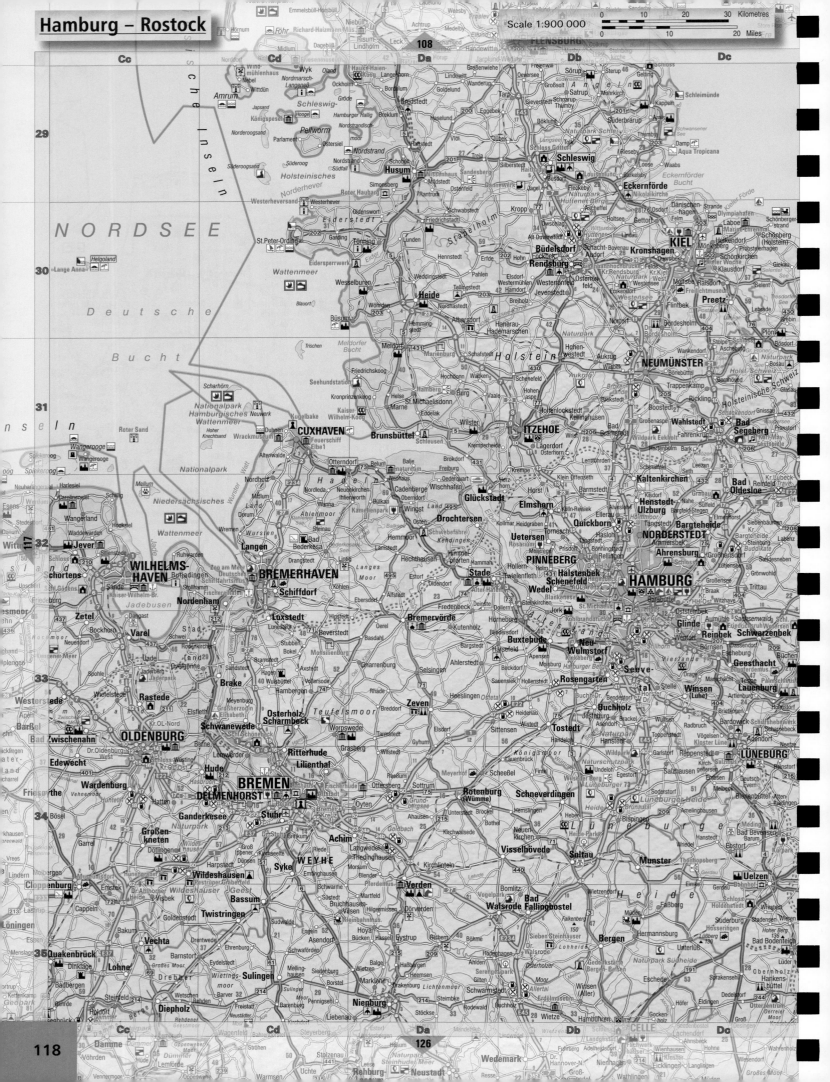

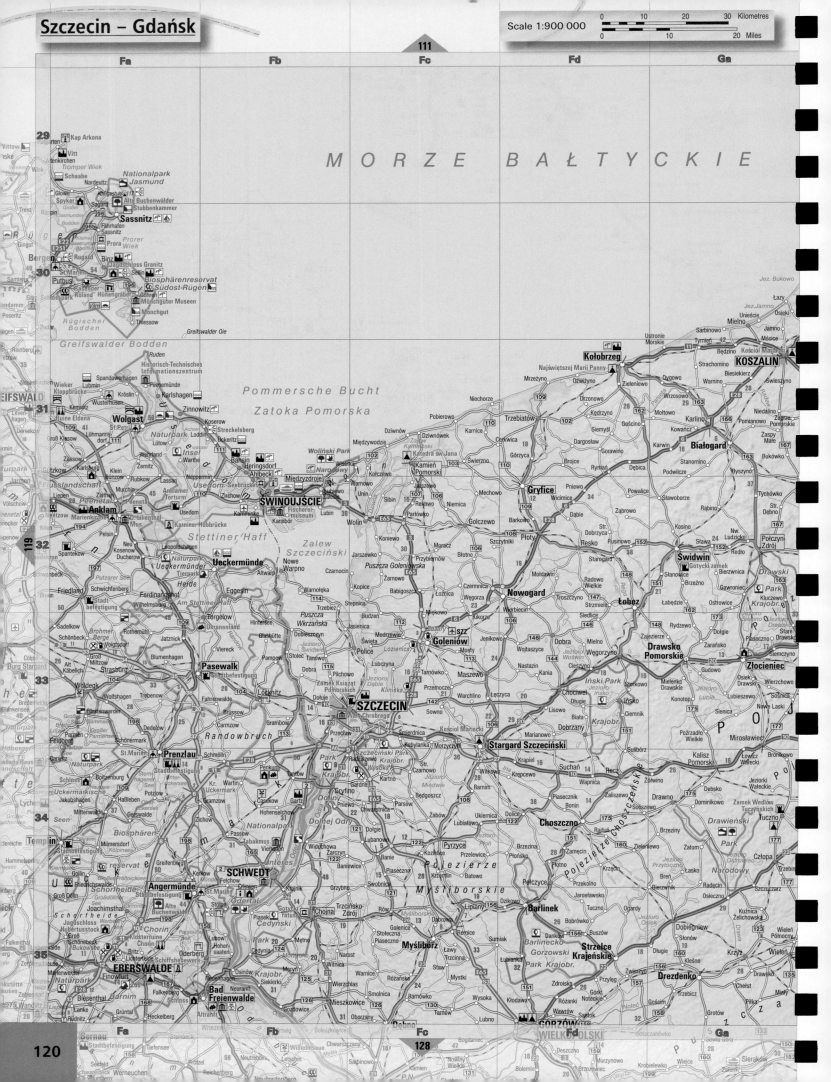

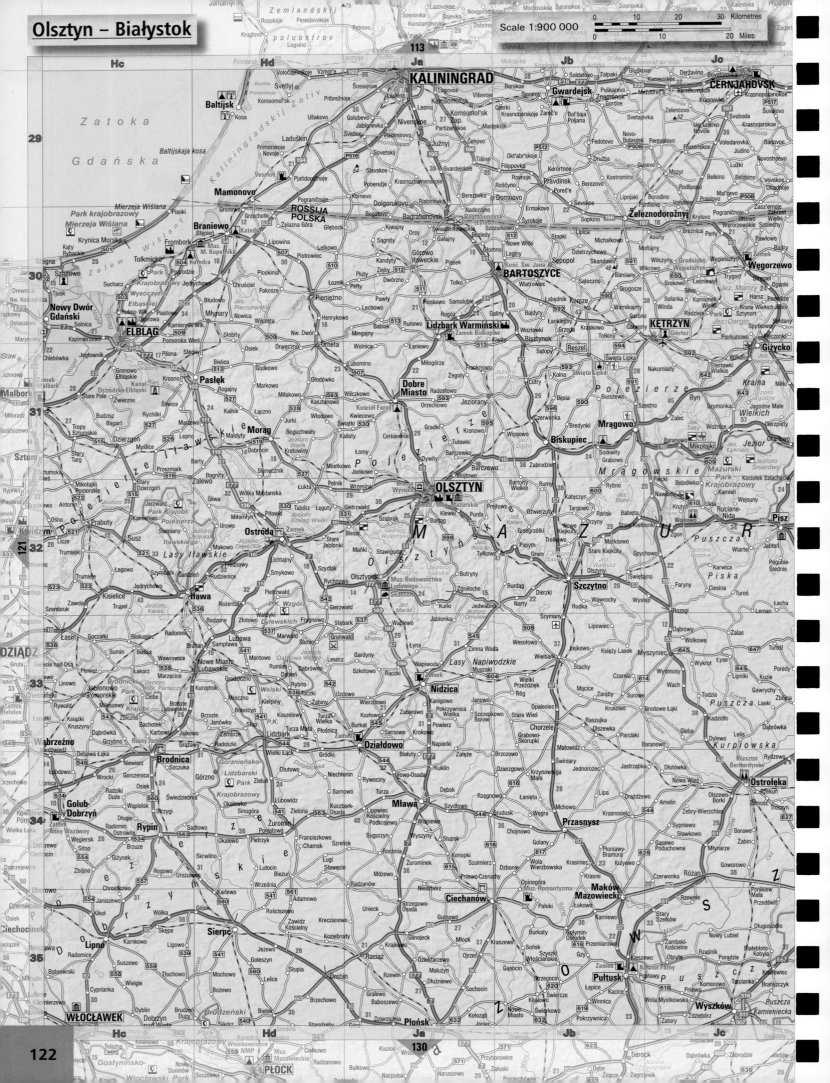

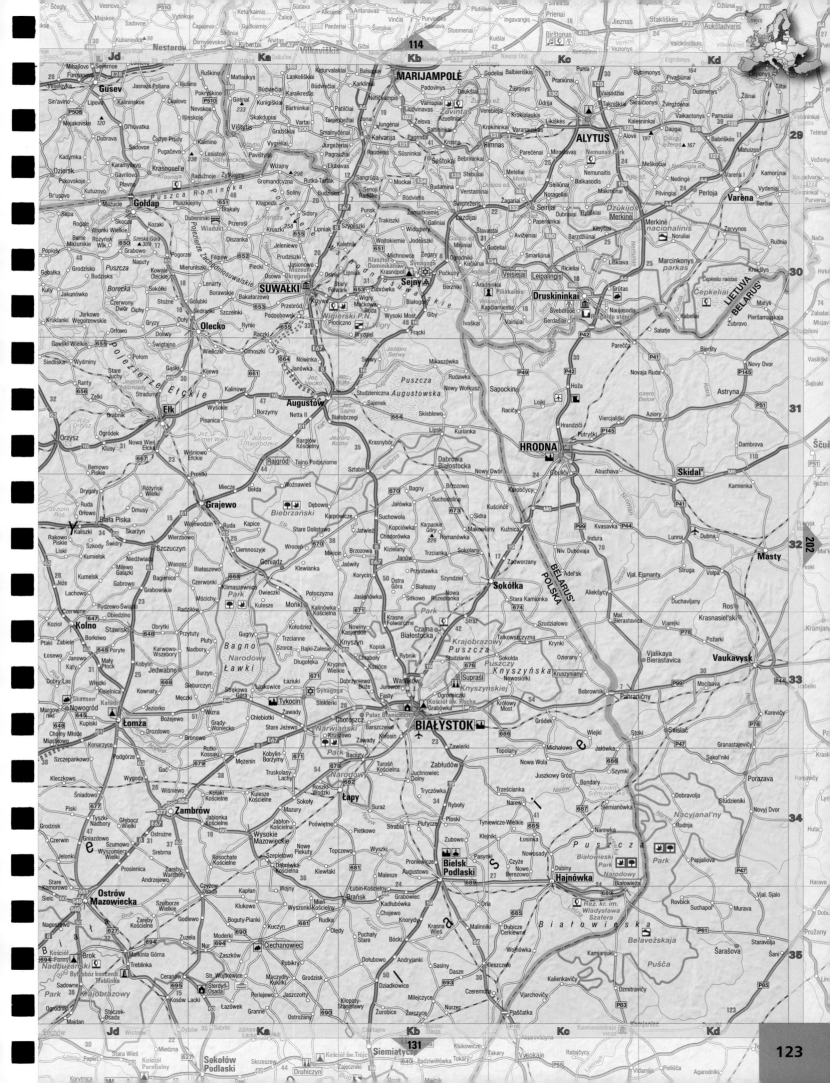

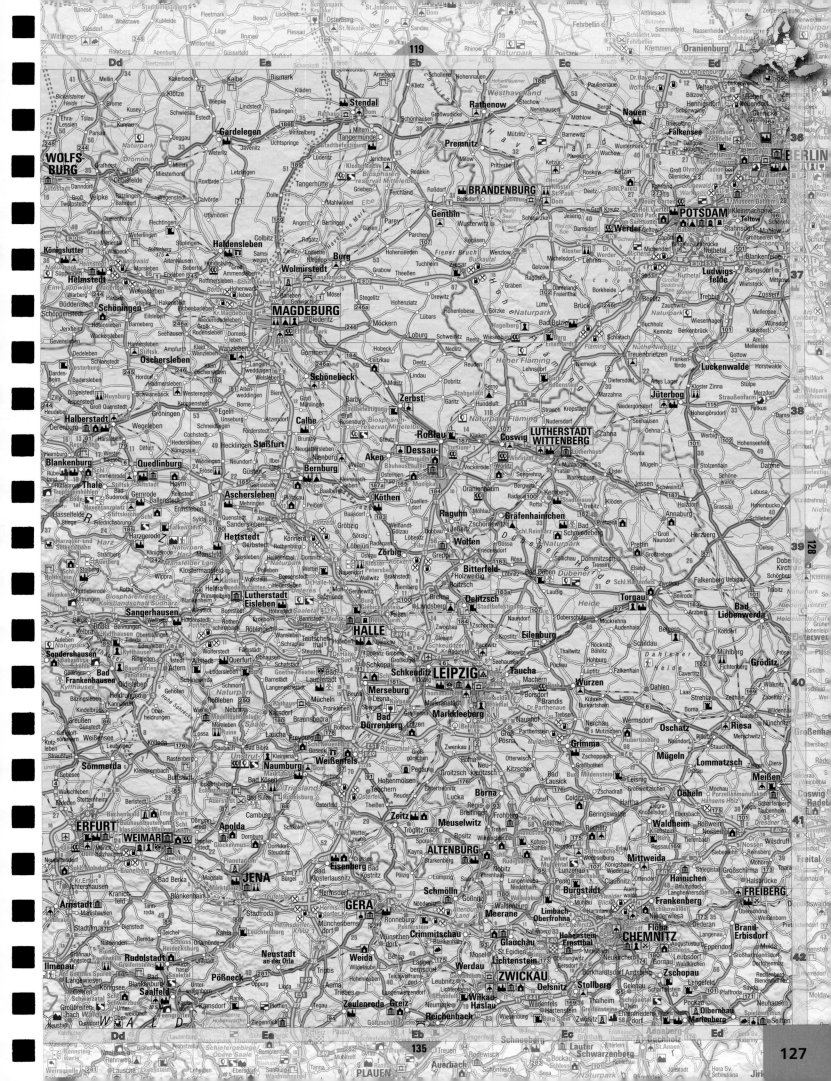

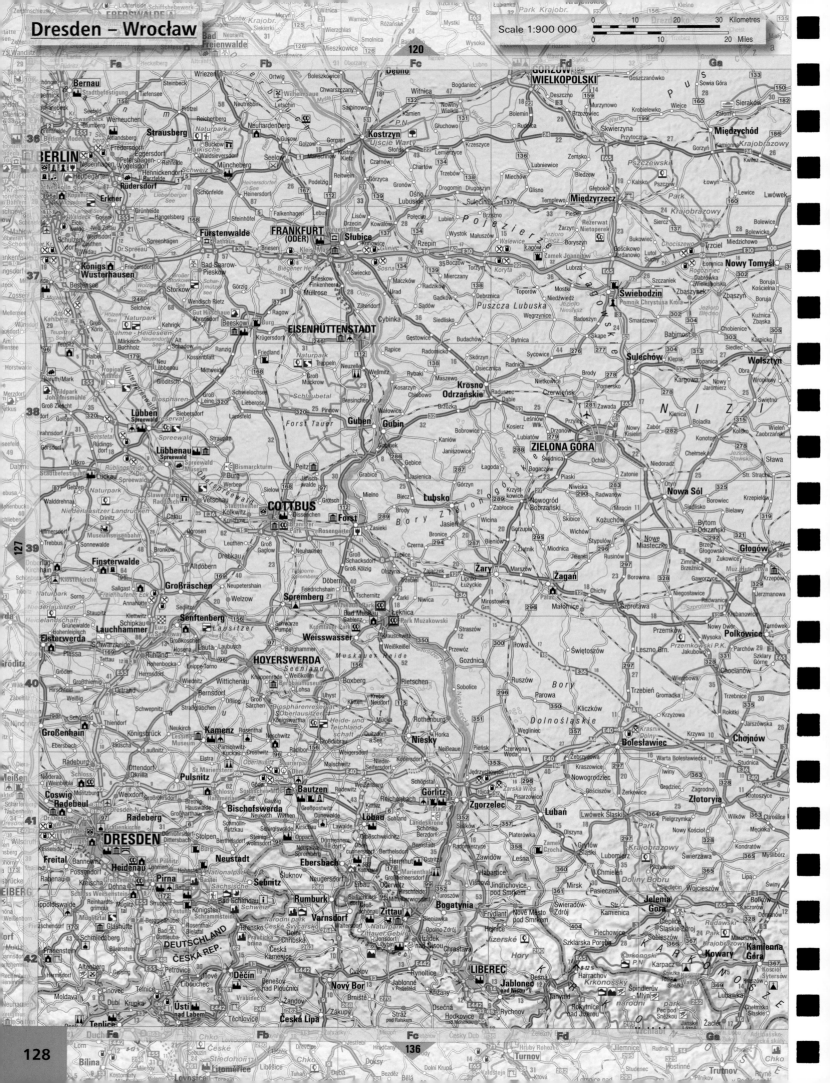

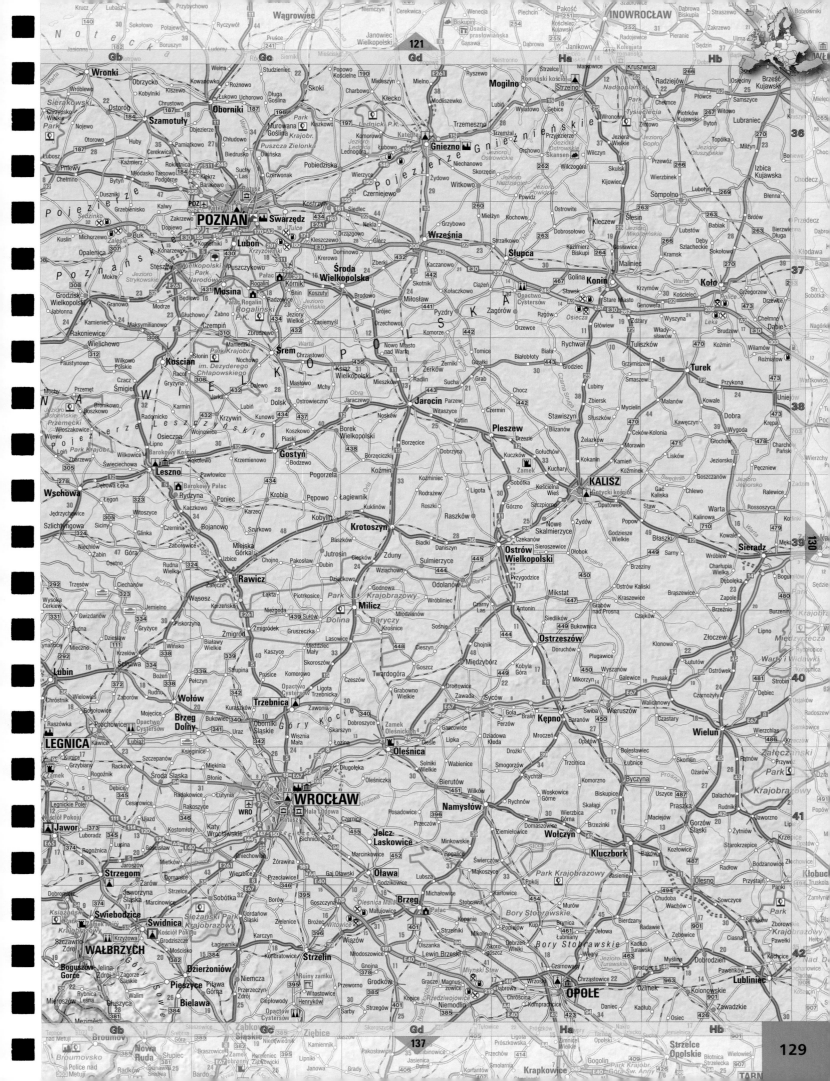

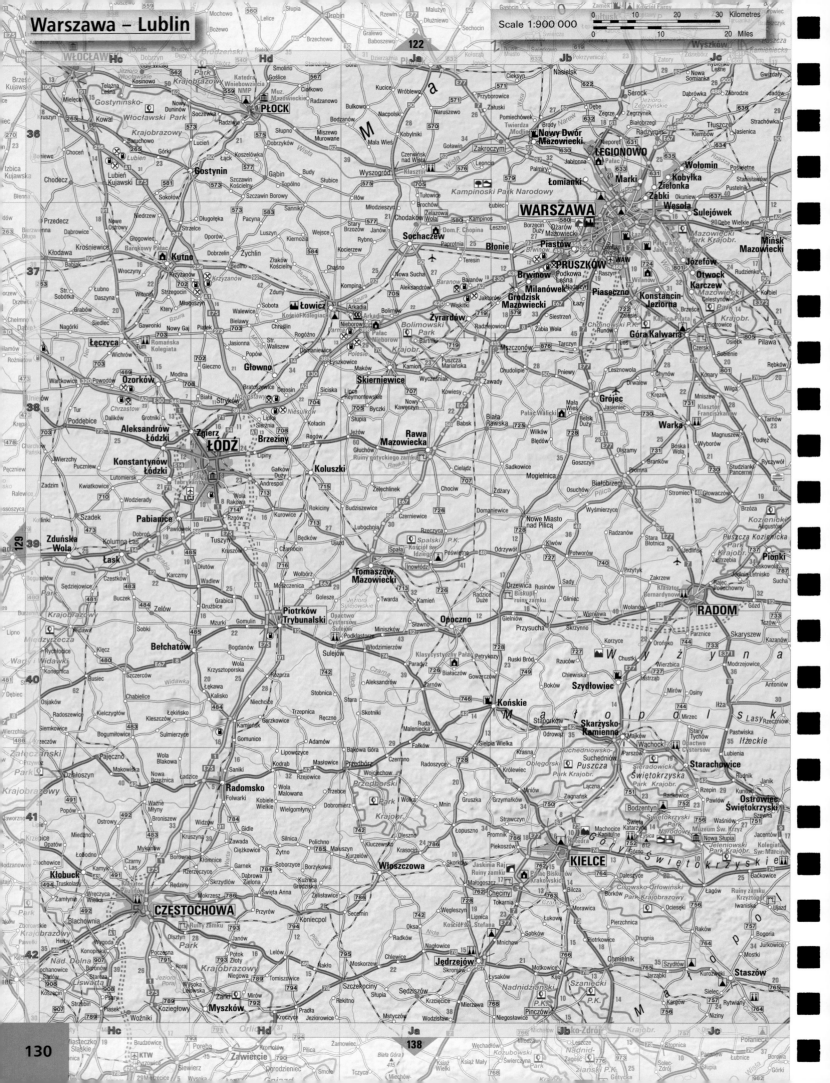

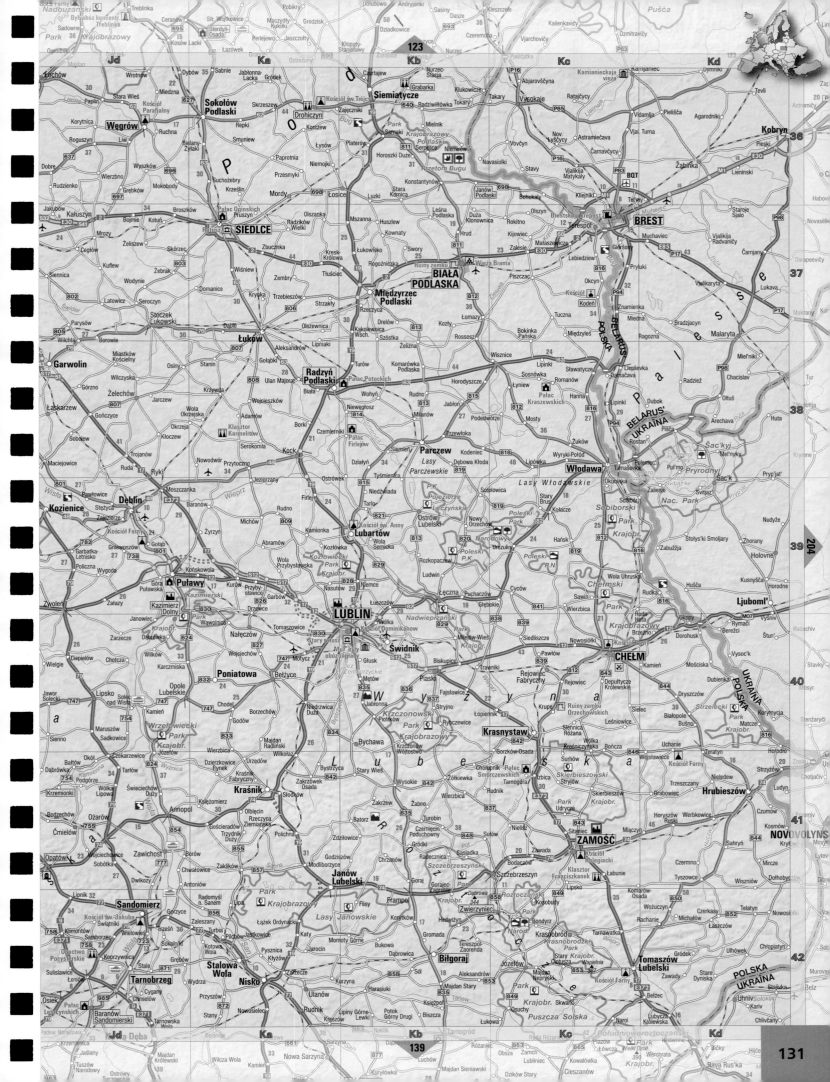

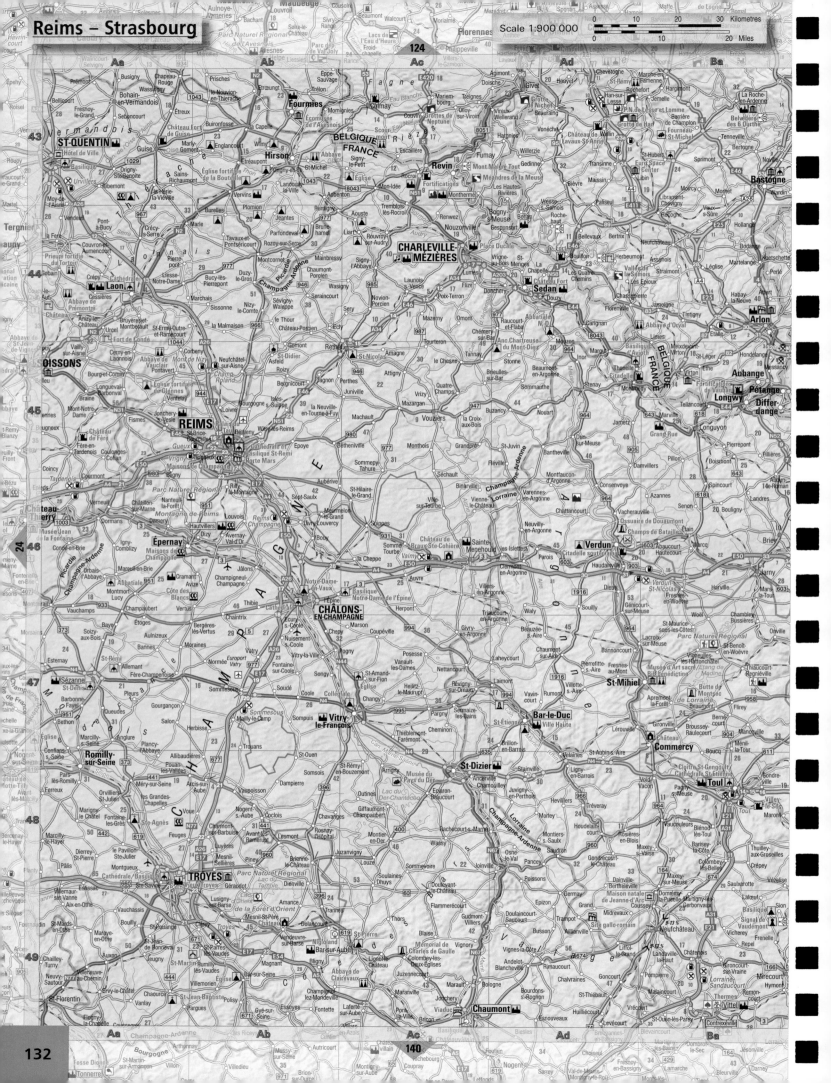

Scale 1:900 000

0 10 20 30 Kilometres
0   10   20 Miles

Aa   Ab   Ac   Ad   Ba

ST-QUENTIN
Hirson
BELGIQUE
FRANCE
Revin
Fourmies
Chimay
Givet
Bastogne
Laon
CHARLEVILLE-MÉZIÈRES
Sedan
Arlon
SOISSONS
Aubange
Longwy
Pétange
Differdange
REIMS
Rethel
Verdun
Épernay
CHÂLONS-EN-CHAMPAGNE
St-Mihiel
Sézanne
Bar-le-Duc
Commercy
Vitry-le-François
Romilly-sur-Seine
St-Dizier
Toul
TROYES
Chaumont
Neufchâteau
Vittel

Aa   Ab   Ac   Ad   Ba

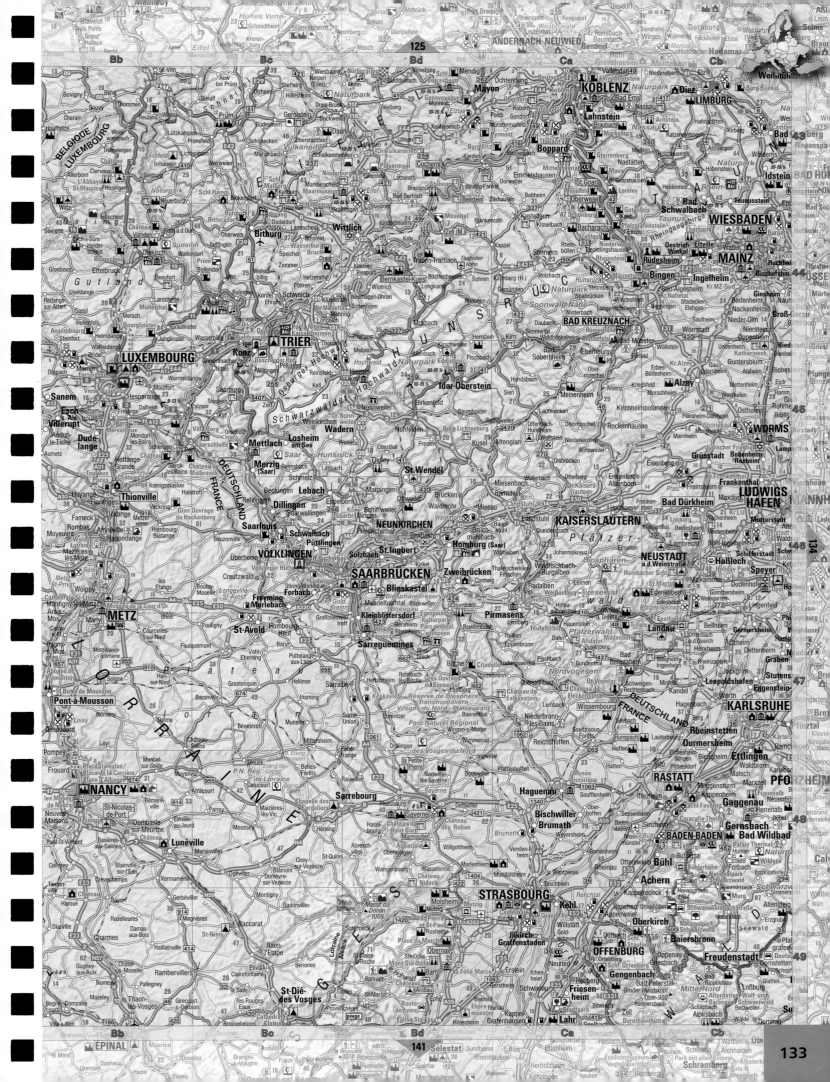

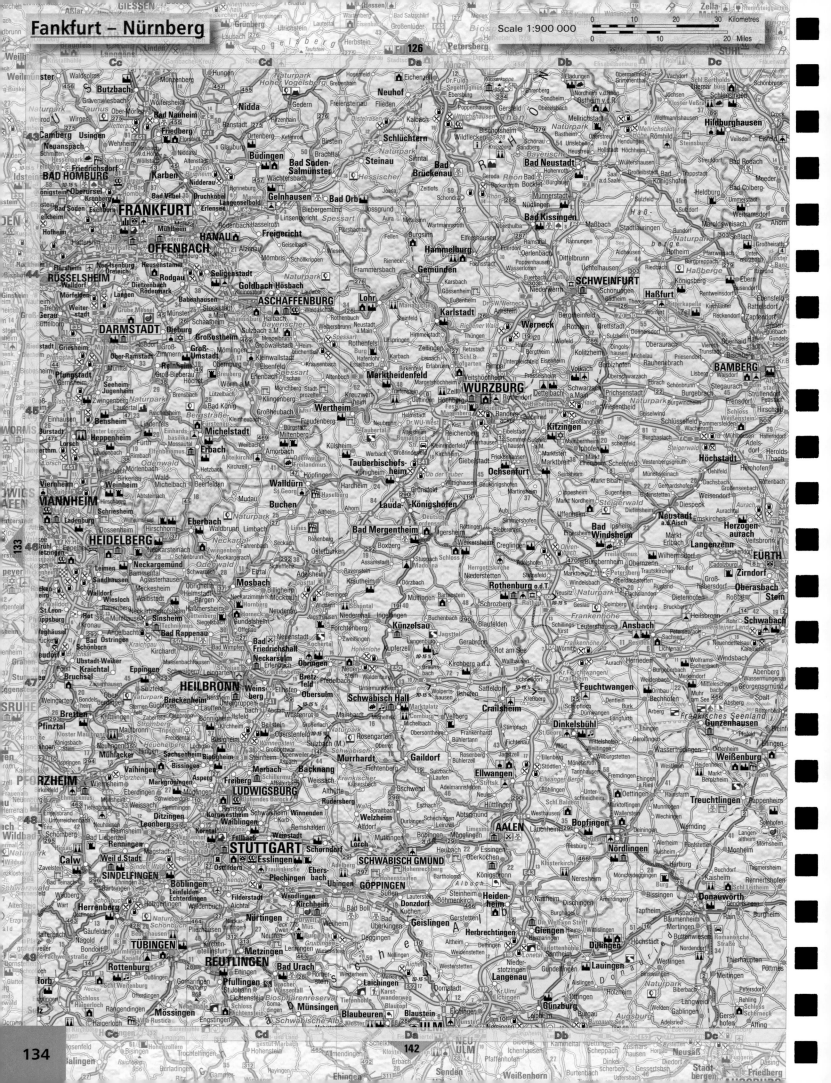

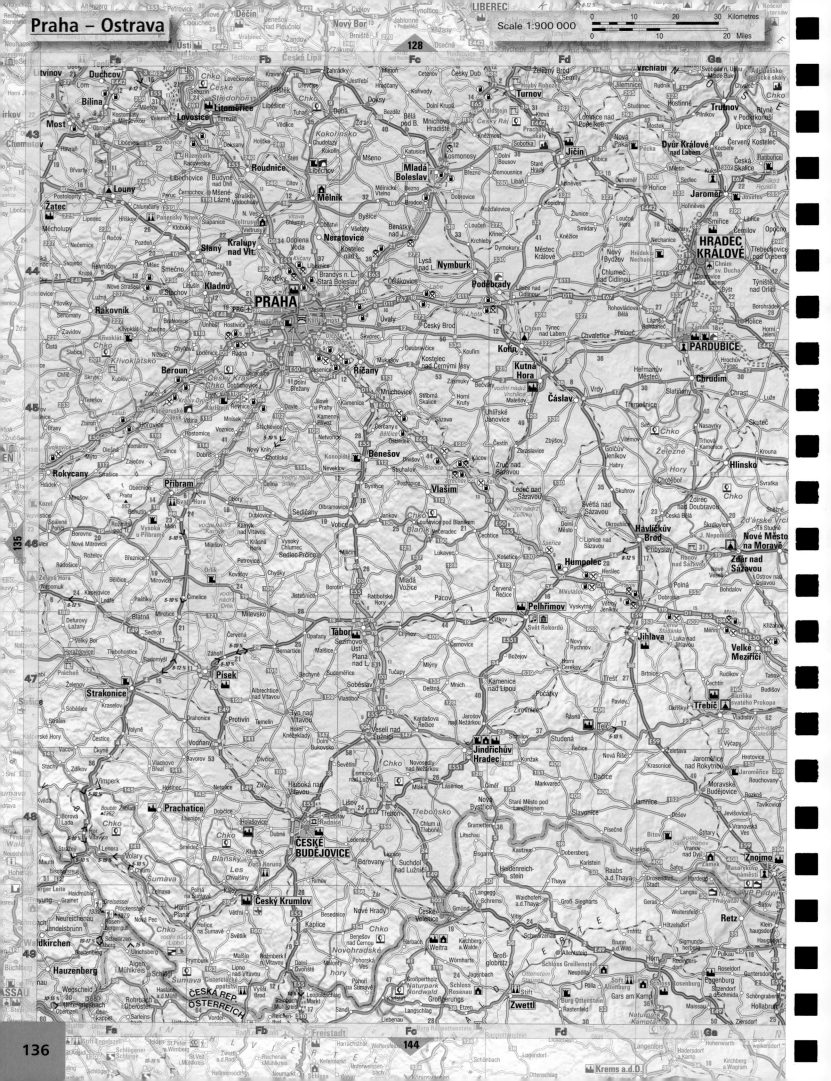

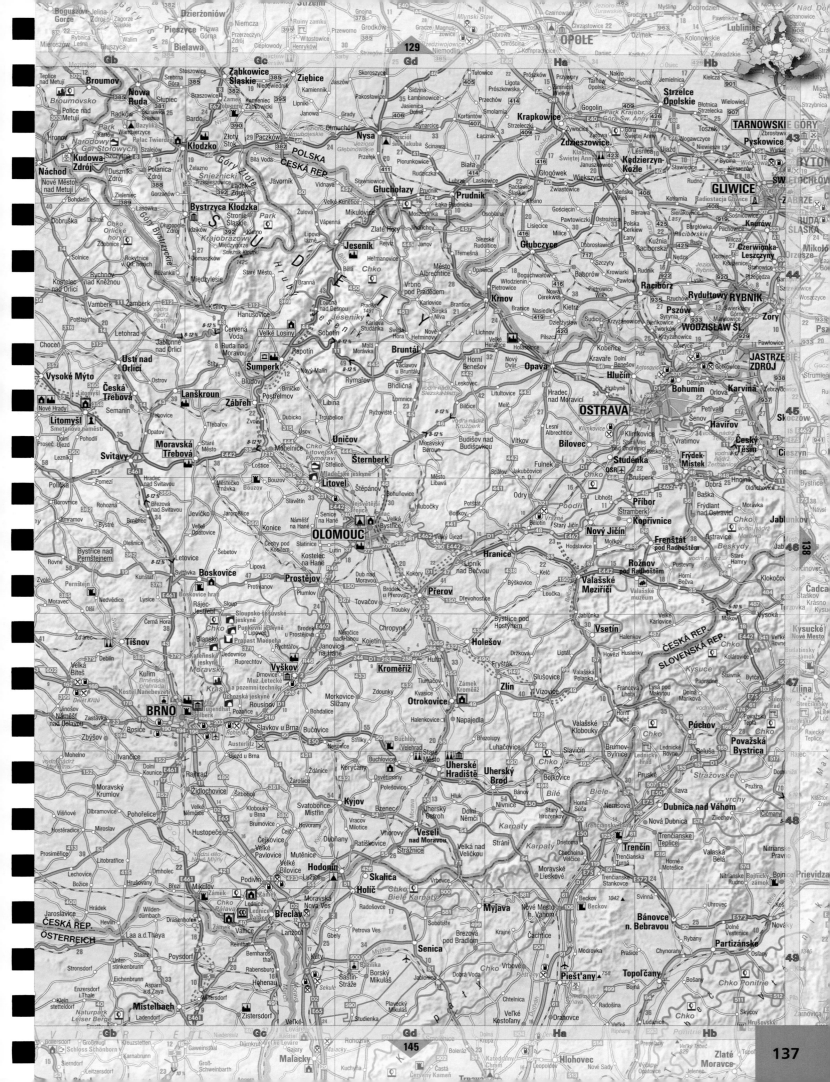

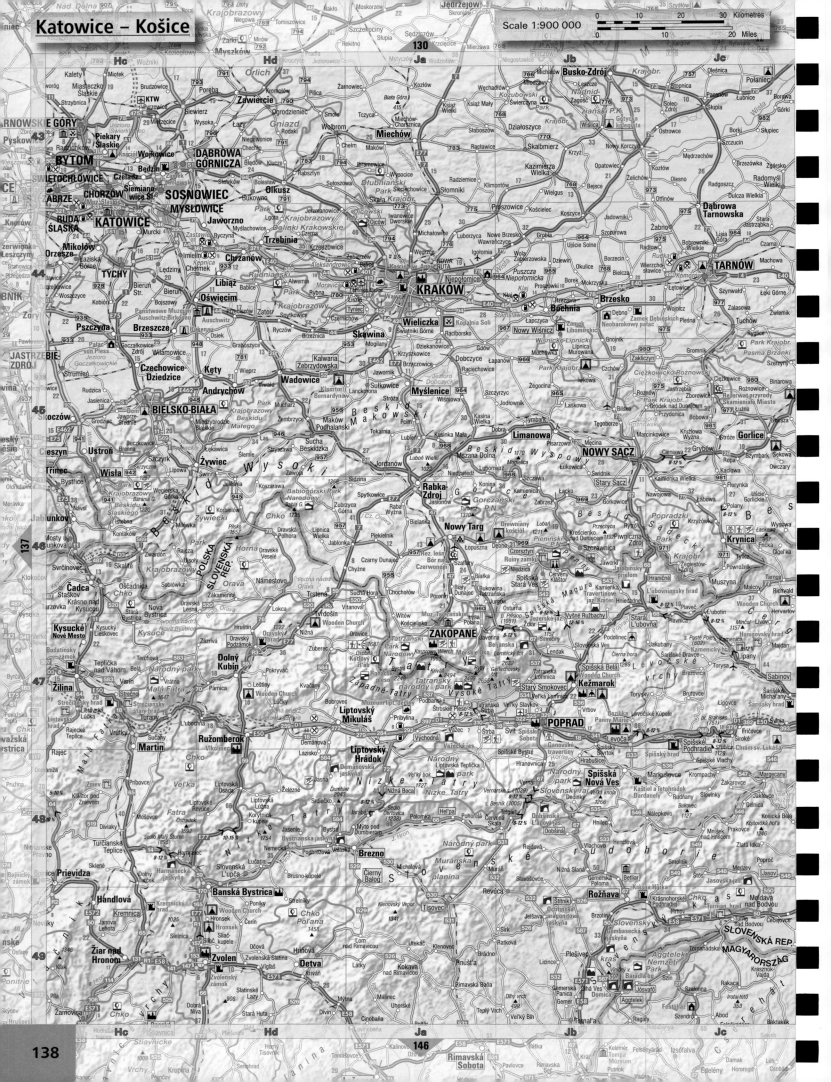

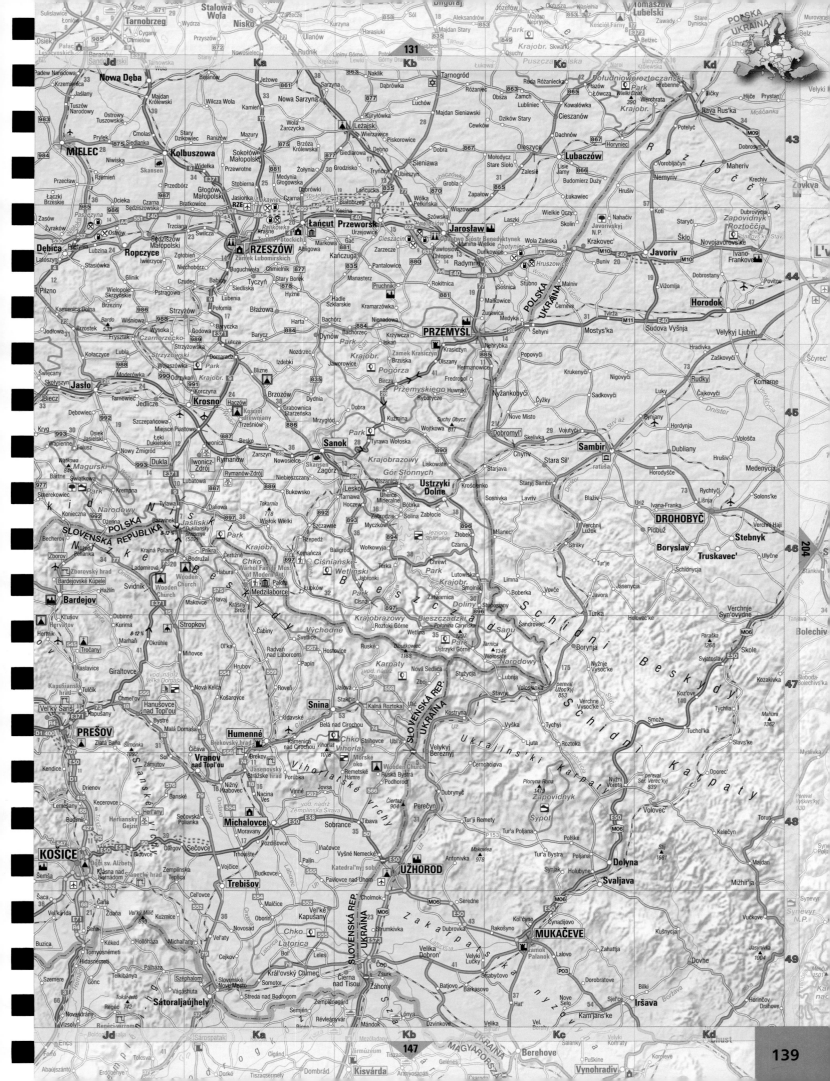

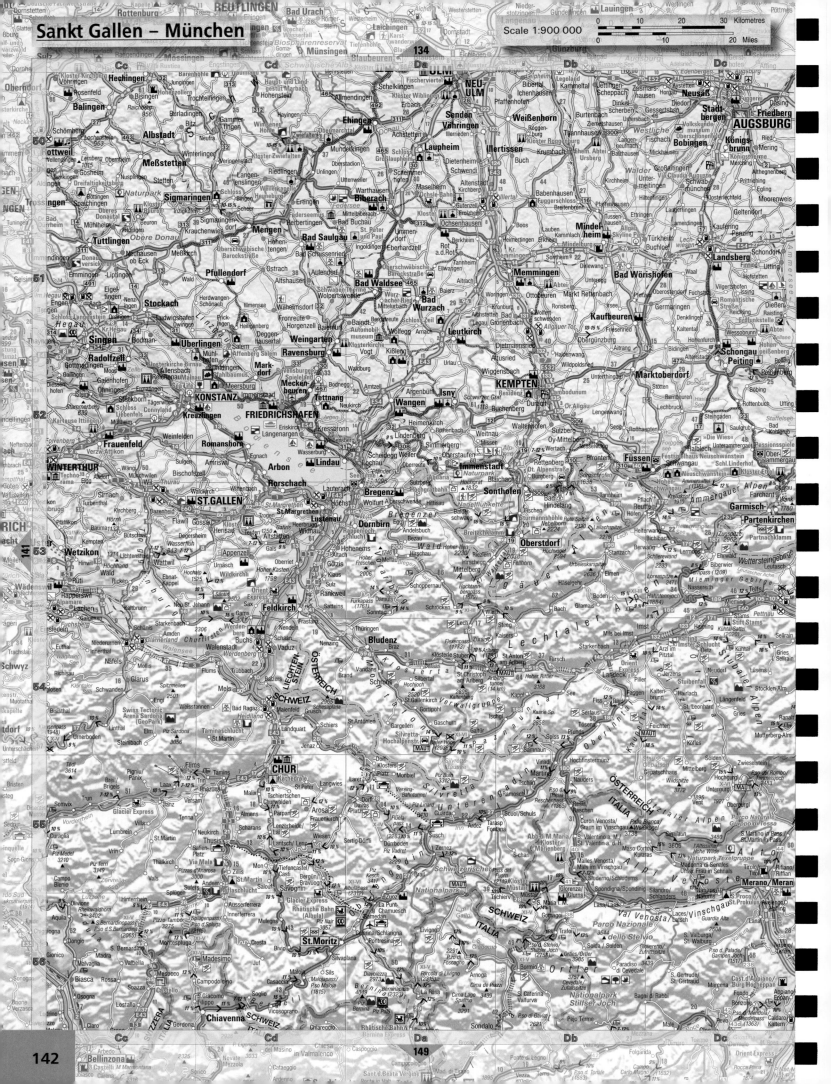

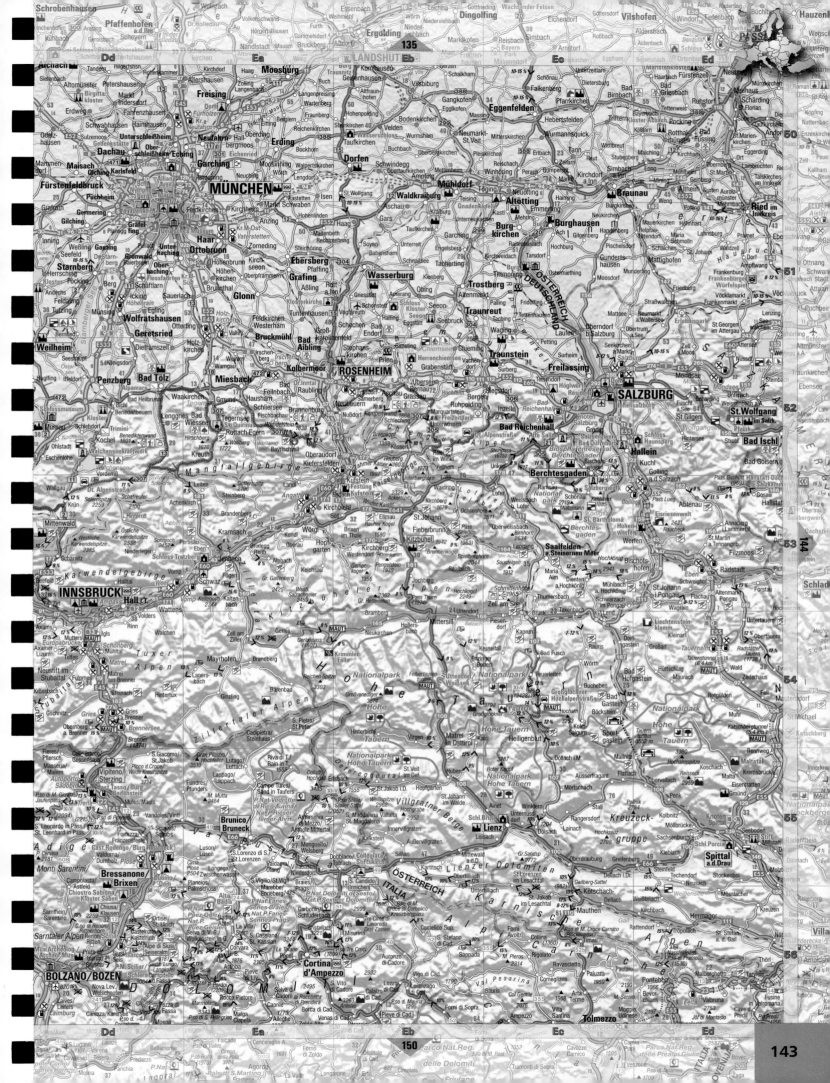

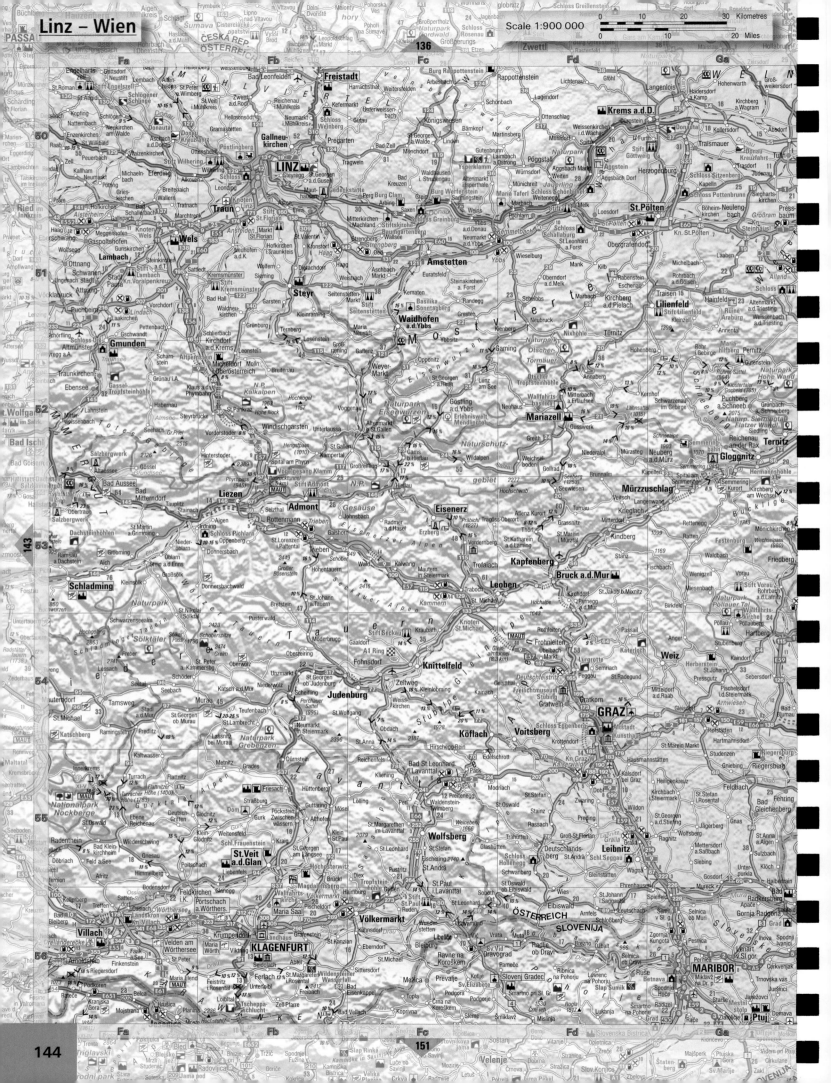

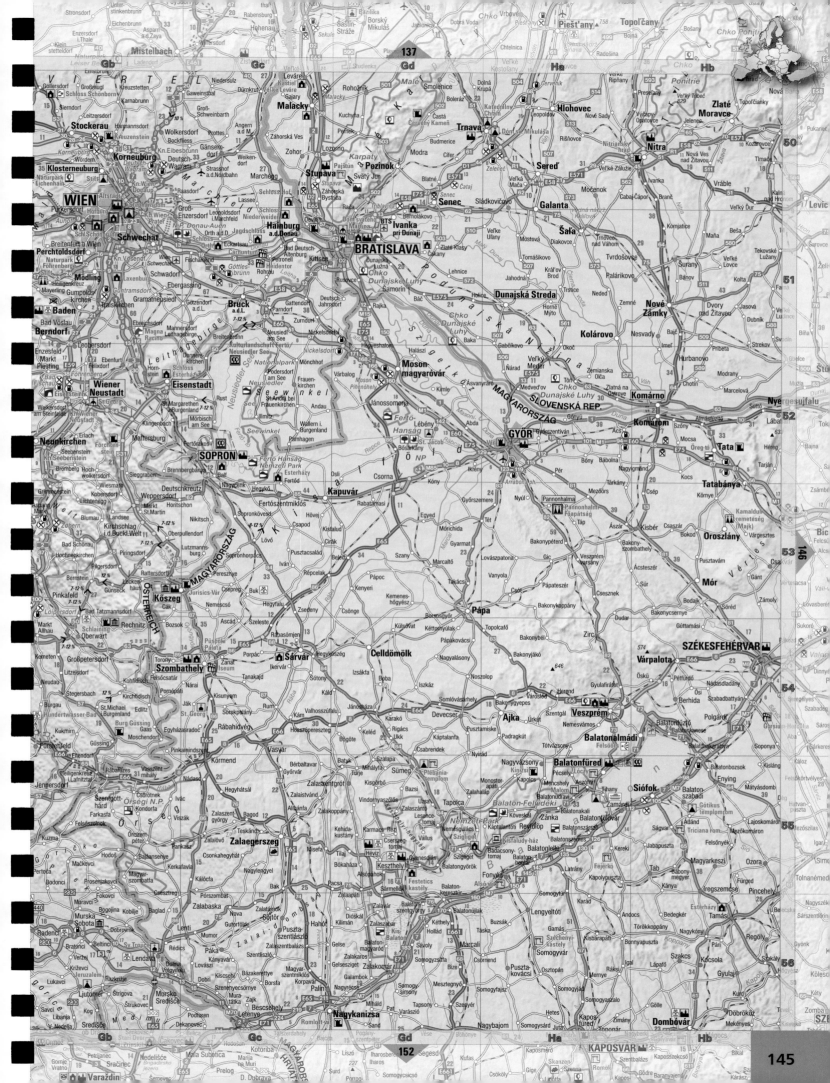

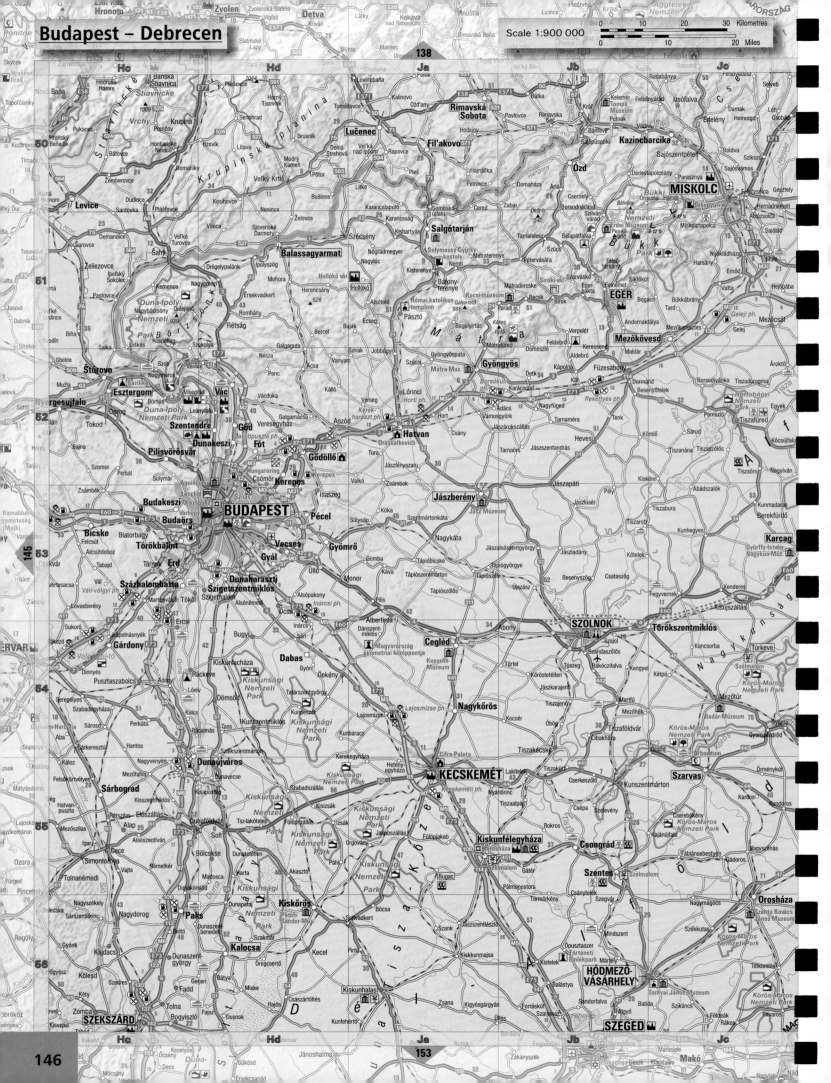

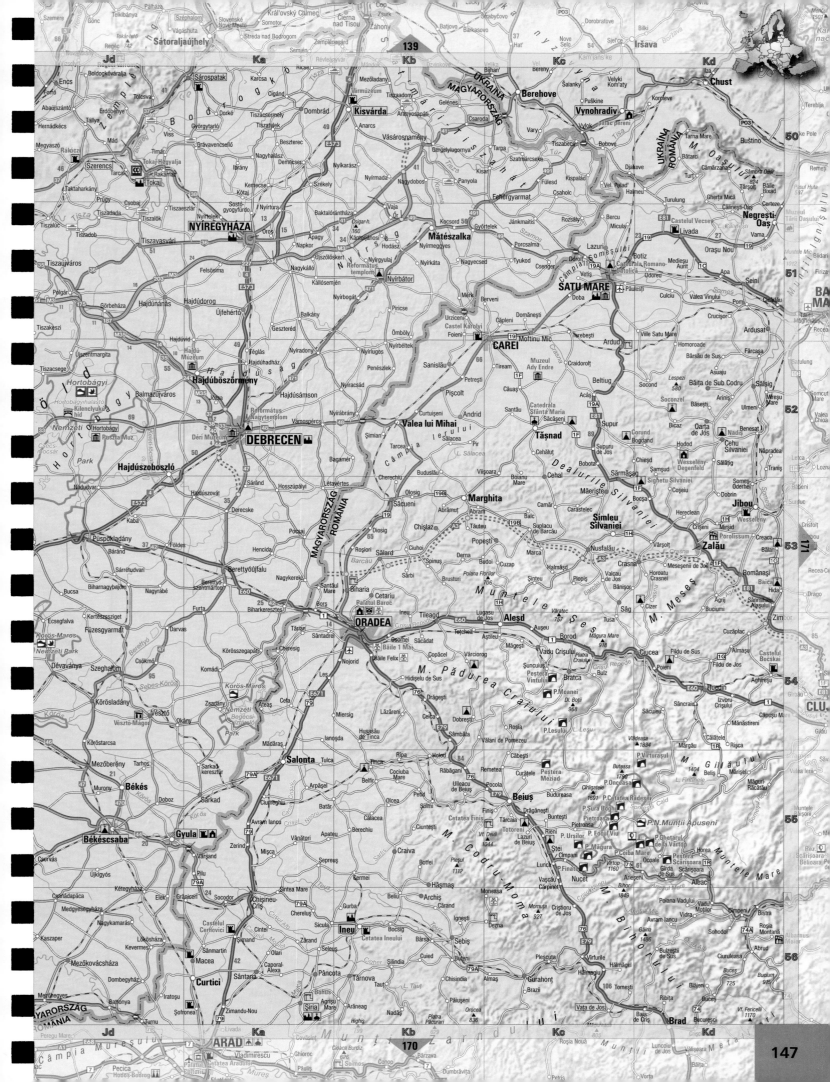

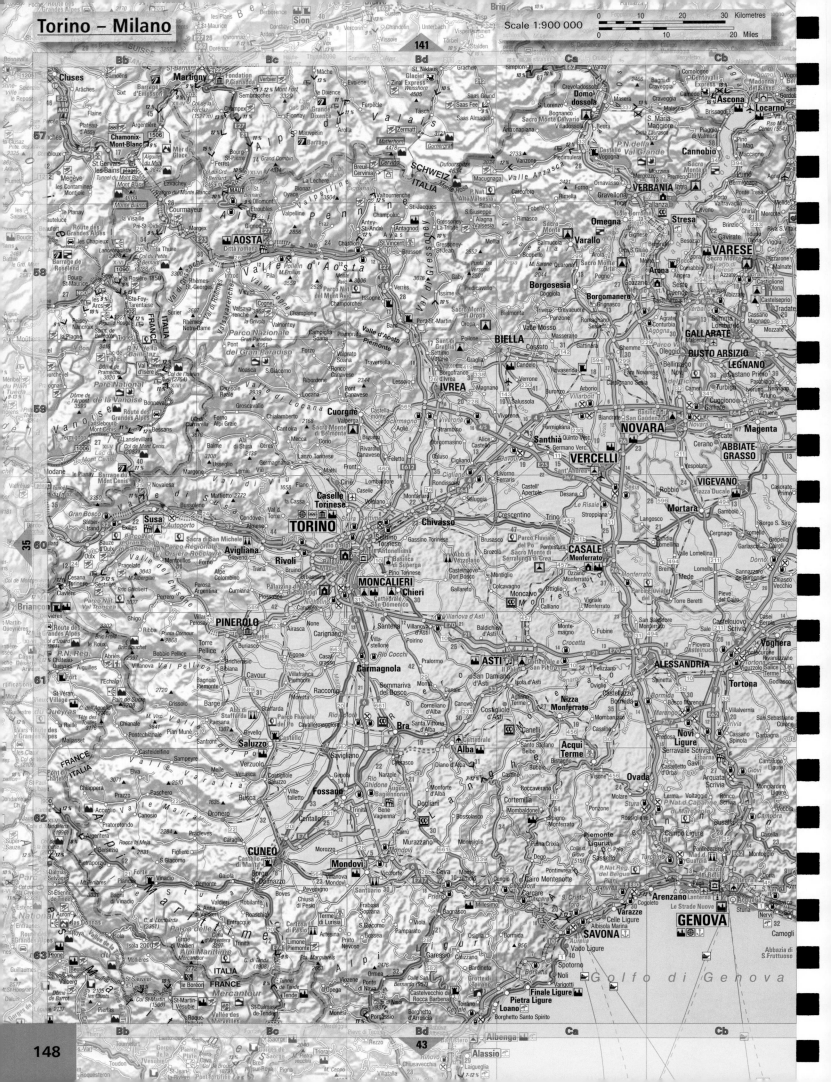

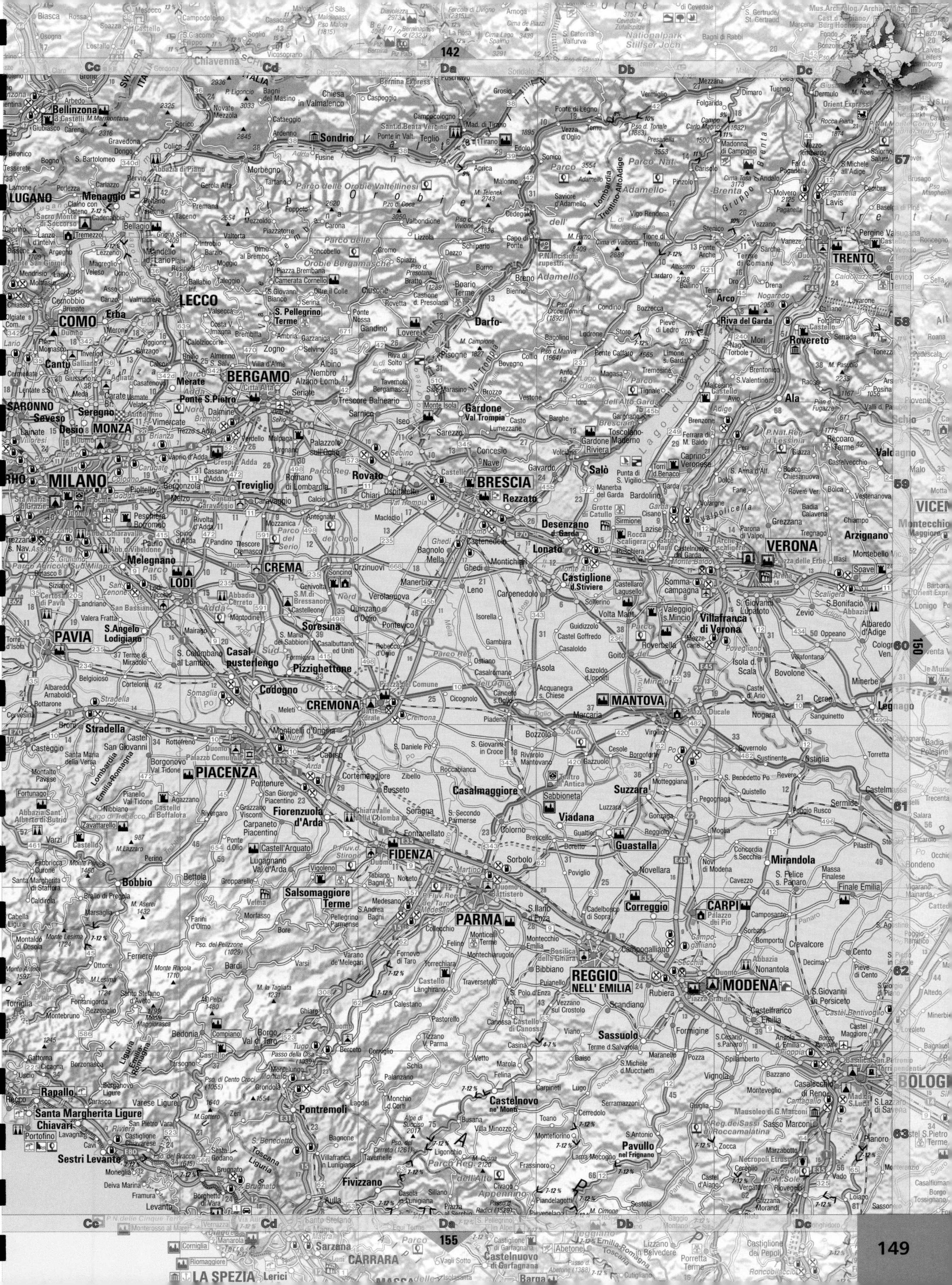

LUGANO
Bellinzona
Giubiasco
Menaggio
Bellagio
COMO
Erba
Cantù
SARONNO
Seveso
Seregno
Desio
MONZA
RHO
MILANO
LECCO
BERGAMO
Ponte S. Pietro
Treviglio
Melegnano
CREMA
LODI
PAVIA
Casalpusterlengo
Pizzighettone
Codogno
CREMONA
Stradella
PIACENZA
Fiorenzuola d'Arda
Salsomaggiore Terme
Bobbio
FIDENZA
PARMA
Collecchio
REGGIO NELL'EMILIA
Sassuolo
MODENA
CORREGGIO
CARPI
Guastalla
Viadana
Casalmaggiore
Suzzara
MANTOVA
Legnago
VERONA
Villafranca di Verona
Valeggio s. Mincio
Desenzano
Lonato
Castiglione d. Stiviere
BRESCIA
Rezzato
Salò
Riva del Garda
Rovereto
Ala
Arco
TRENTO
SONDRIO
Tirano
Chiavari
Rapallo
Santa Margherita Ligure
Portofino
Sestri Levante
Pontremoli
Fivizzano
Sarzana
CARRARA
LA SPEZIA
BOLOGNA

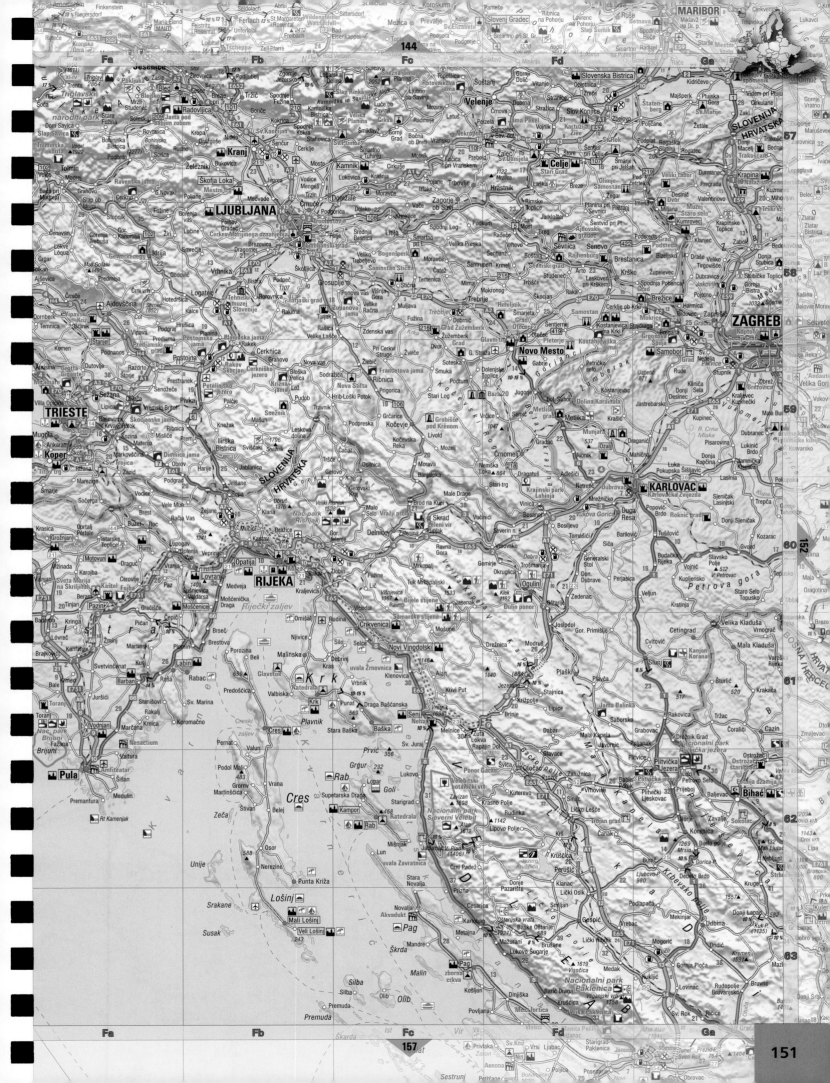

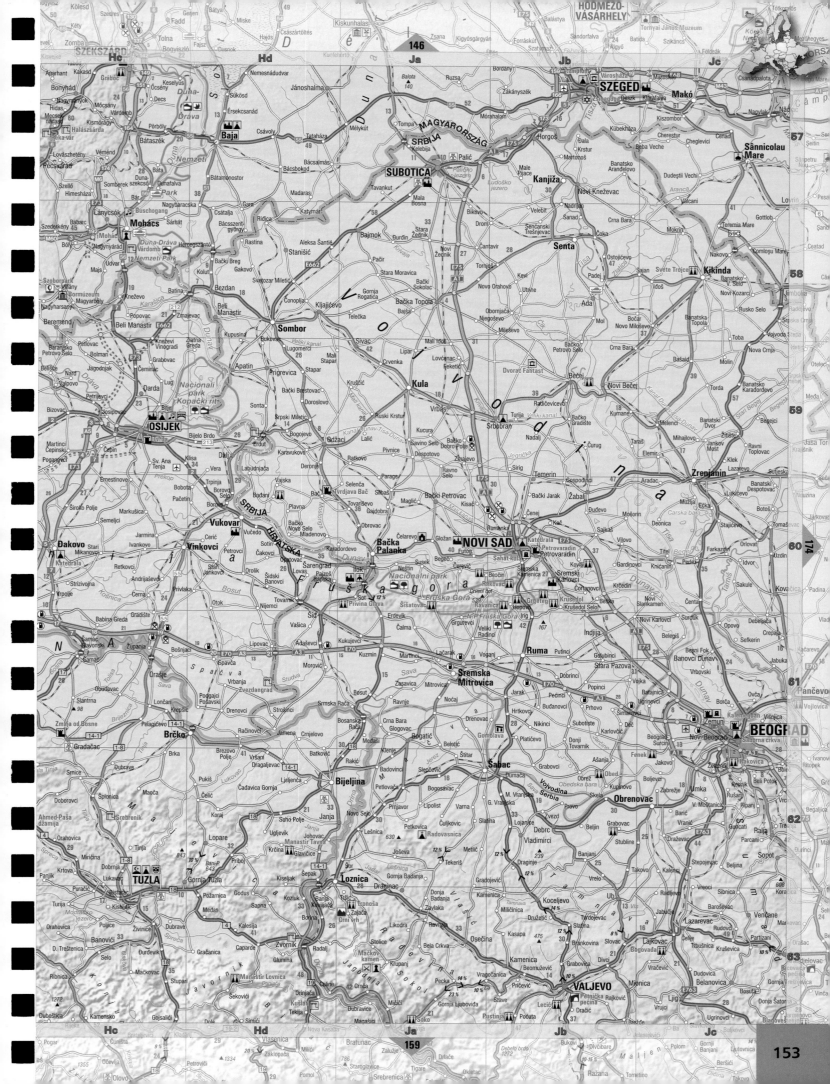

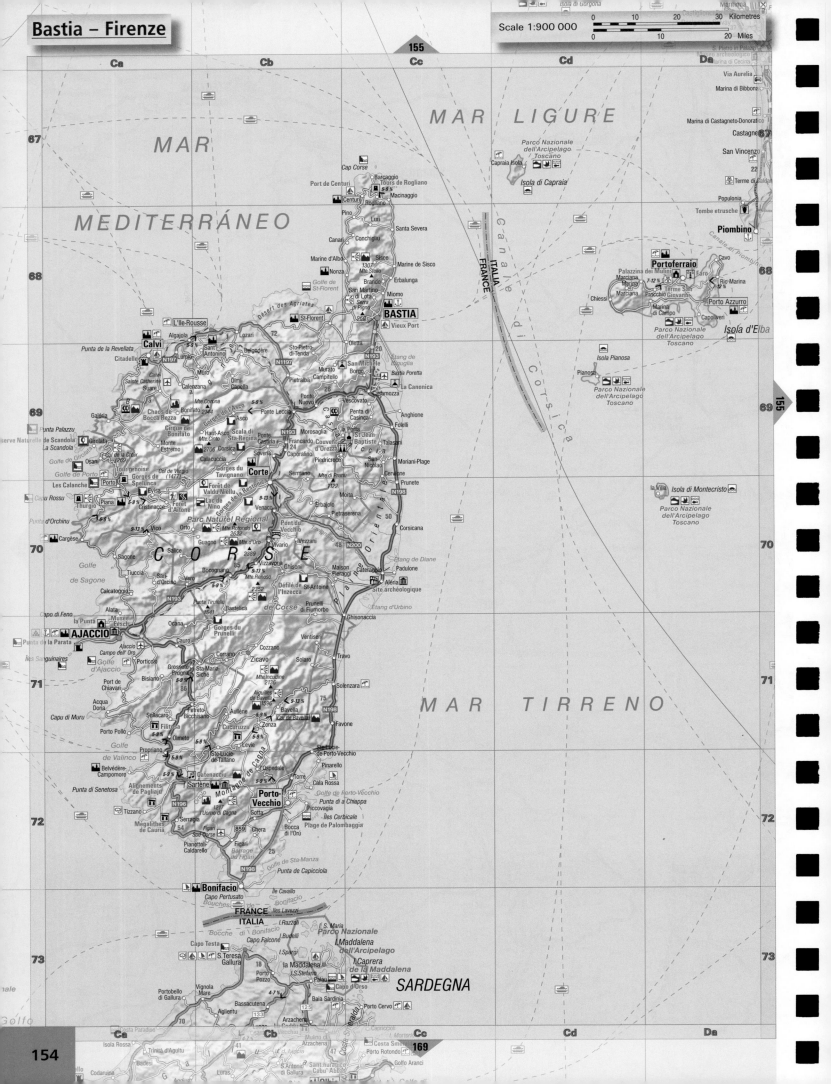

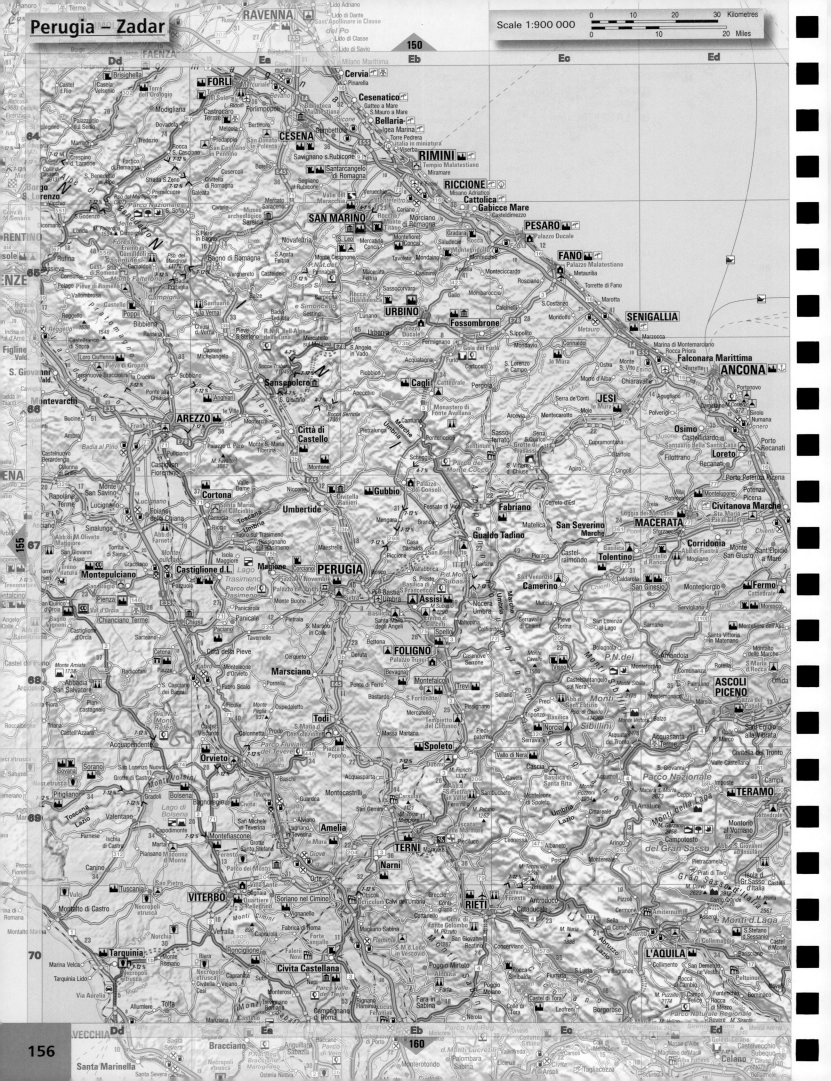

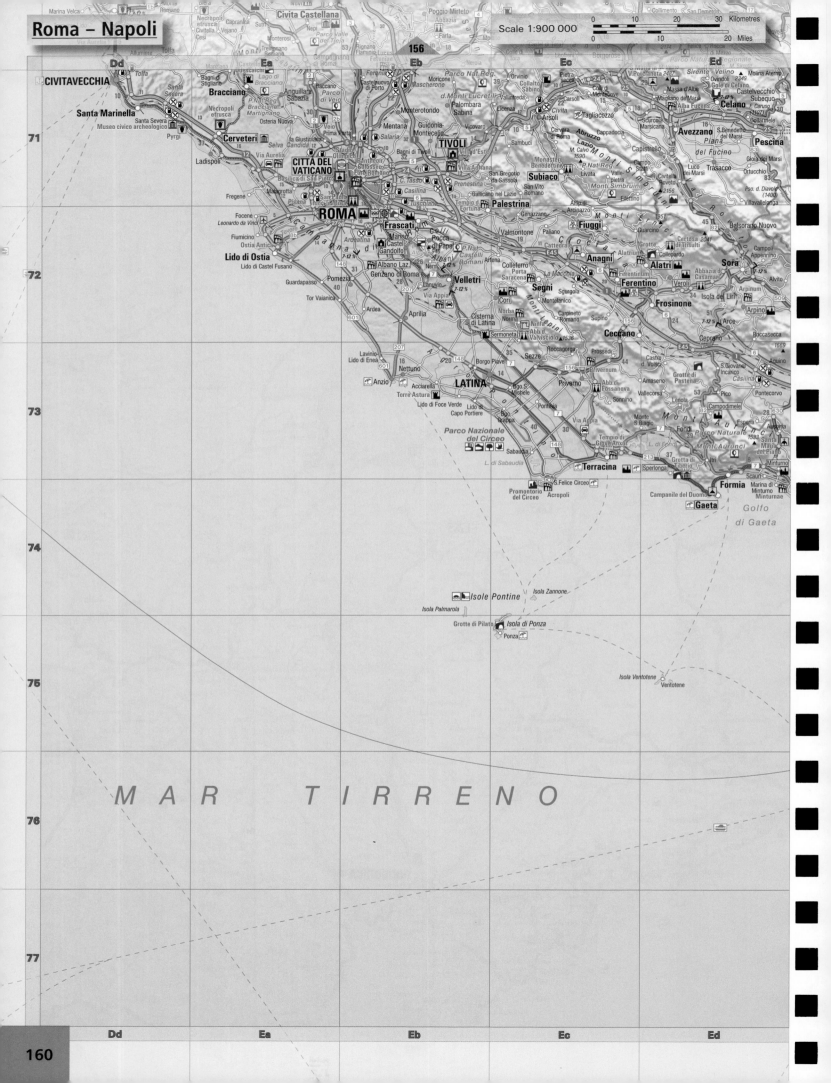

Scale 1:900 000

0   10   20   30 Kilometres
0   10   20 Miles

Gb   Gc   Gd   Ha   Hb

71

Peschici
40 Marinum
Vico del Gargano
Torre di Porticello
Castello **Vieste**
Lido di Portonuovo
Foresta Umbra
Testa del Gargano
M. Sacro
Monte Sant'Angelo 872
Pugnochiuso
Baia d.Zagare
72 Santuario di San Michele
Mattinata

MANFREDONIA
Lido di Siponto
Santa Maria di Siponto
Golfo di Manfredonia
Leonardo Siponto

M A R

Lido di Rivoli
Zapponeta
25
19 73 Margherita di Savoia
Trinitapoli
Mass. Anzani

A D R I A T I C O

BARLETTA
Santo Sepolcro
Colosso
S.Ferdinando di Puglia
Trani Cattedrale
Canne
Canne d. Batt.
Bisceglie
MOLFETTA
Giovinazzo
Canosa di Puglia
Dolmen di Bisceglie
Dolmen di Chianca
S.Spirito
ANDRIA
Palese
Corato
Ruvo di Puglia
Terlizzi
Sovereto
BARI Cattedrale di San Sabino/
Basilica di San Nicola
161 74 Castel del Monte
Bitonto
Palo d.Colle
Modugno
S.Giorgio
Minervino Murge
Mariotto
Torre a Mare
Cattedrale
Grumo Appula
Bitetto
S.Felice
il Balsignano
Capurso
Mola di Bari
Montemilone
Parco Nazionale
680
dell'Alta Murgia
Quasano
Sannicandro di Bari
Adelfia
Noicattaro
Cozze
Rutigliano
Casamassima
S.Benedetto
Polignano a Mare
Spinazzola
Pulo
l'uomo di Altamura
Acquaviva delle Fonti
Conversano
Monopoli
Palazzo S.Gervasio
Cattedrale
Cassano d. Murge
Le Fonti
Turi
Castello
Castellana Grotte
Banzi
Altamura
Sammichele di Bari
Grotte di Castellana
Lamandia
Gnathia/Egnazia
Genzano di Lucania
Casal Sabini
Grotta di Putignano
Savelletri
Acerenza
Monte Sannace
Putignano
Selva di Fasano
Torre Canne
75 **Gravina in Puglia**
Gioia del Colle
Noci
Monticelli
Marina di Ostuni
Pietragalla
Irsina
Santeramo in Colle
Alberobello
Fasano
Forenza
Oppido Lucano
Trulli
Locorotondo
Montalbano
Santa Sabina
Cancellara
Mass. Cangiulli
S.Basilio
Cisternino
Lido Specchiolla
Vaglio Basilicata
Mass. Montanaro
Ostuni
Carovigno
Punta Penne
Tolve
S.Chirico Nuovo
Mass. di Matera
Via Appia
S.Martino
Crispta di S.Biagio
BRINDISI
845
Matera
Mottola
Martina Franca
S.Vito d.Normanni
1078
Chiese rupestri
Palagianello
Massafra
Ceglie Messapica
Crispta di S. Giovanni
Tricarico
Grottole
Laterza
Castellaneta
Crispiano
Villa Castelli
Civita
Parco delle Chiese rupestri del Materano
Ginosa
Palagiano
Monte-mesola
S.Michele Salentino
Albano di Lucania
Castello del Malconsiglio
Mesagne
Grottaglie
Oria
Latiano
Miglionico
Montescaglioso
Perrone
Francavilla Fontana
S.Pietro Vernotico
P.Nat.Gallipoli Cognato
Salandra
Abb.d.S.Michele Arcangelo
Chiatona
Lido Azzurro
Torre Santa Susanna
Cellino S.Marco
Pietrapertosa
Pomarico
Tavoliere di Lecce
Castelmezzano
S.Giorgio Jonico
Necropoli e Mura Messapiche
San Donaci
76 Piccole Dolomiti Lucane
S.Mauro Forte
Castellaneta Marina
Mus.Arch.Naz.
S.Marzano
Erchie
Squinzano
Laurenzana
Ferrandina
Riva dei Tessali
Carosino
Campi Salentina
Stigliano
Marina di Ginosa
TARANTO
Fragagnano
S.Pancrazio Salentino
Corleto Perticara
Gorgoglione
Cirigliano
Bernalda
Talsano
Pulsano
Sava
Guagnano
Guardia Perticara
Craco
Tempio Tavole Palatine
Manduria
Aliano
Metapontum
Lizzano
Avetrana
Salice Salentino
Monte-murro
Missanello
Montalbano Jonico
Lido di Metaponto
Saturo
Torricella
Veglie
Parco Nazionale Val d'Agri Lagonegrese
Tinchi
Marina di Pulsano
Leverano
Pisticci
Maruggio
Librari
Campomarino
Specchiarica
77 Spinoso
S.Arcangelo
S.Maria d'Anglona
Tursi
Siris Heraklea
Torre Lapillo
Porto Cesareo
M. Sirino 2005
Chiaromonte
Valsinni
Scanzano Jonico
Nardò
Fardella
Nova Siri
Policoro
Episcopia
S.Giorgio Lucano
Lido di Policoro
Latronico
Roccanova
Castronuovo di S.Andrea
Rocca imperiale
Marina di Nova Siri
Riserva Naturale Marina Porto Cesareo
Santa Caterina
Senise
Colobraro
Canna
Santa Maria al Bagno
Noepoli
Francavilla sul Sinni
Oriolo
Montegiordano Marina
Città vecchia
Castelluccio Inferiore
S.Severino
S.Costantino
Gallipoli

Golfo di Taranto

Parco Nazionale Basilicata Calabria
Terranova di Pollino
Amendolara
Alessandria del Carretto
Capo Spulico
Rotonda
Albidona
Marina di Amendolara

Golfo di Taranto

Santa Maria al Bagno
Neviano
Maglie
Santa Marina
Capo d'Otranto
Città vecchia
Parabita
Collepasso
Nociglia
Muro Leccese
Poggiardo
Grotta dei Cervi
163 Gallipoli
Chiesa di Casaranello
Casarano
Supersano
Diso
Santa Cesarea Terme
Ruffano
Montesano Salentino
Castro Marina
Grotta Romanelli/ Grotta Zinzulusa

Gd | Ha | Hb | Hc | Hd

Taviano
Giuggianello
Tricase
173
Racale
Alliste
Specchia
Tricase Porto
Ugento
Presicce
Messano
Marina Serra
Marina di Novaglie
Ausentum
Salve
Gagliano del Capo
Torre San Giovanni
Patù
Marini
Torre Vado
Marina di Leuca
Capo S.Maria di Leuca

78

Capo Trionto
Mirto
27
Staz.d.Mandatoriccio-Campana
Cariati
P. Fiume Nicà
Mandatoriccio
Terravecchia
Campana
Crucoli
P. Alice
Santuario di Apollo Aleo
Umbriatico
Cirò
Cirò Marina
Savelli
Melissa
Torre Melissa
Verzino
Petelia
Strongoli
Marina di Strongoli
Cerenzia
Rocca di Neto
Fasana
Caccuri
Cotronei
Santa Severina
Gabella Grande
Castello
CROTONE
Petilia Policastro
S.Mauro Marchesato
Mus.Arch.Naz.
Tempio di Hera Lacinia
Mesoraca
Cutro
Capo Colonna
Sersale
Salica
S. Anna
Cropani
Isola di Capo Rizzuto
Steccato
Fortezza aragonese
Cropani Marina
Botricello
Capo Rizzuto
le Castella
Area Marina Protetta Capo Rizzuto
Capo Rizzuto

79

80

81

M A R   I O N I O

Golfo di

Squillace

82

83

M A R

M E D I T E R R A N E O

84

Gd | Ha | Hb | Hc | Hd

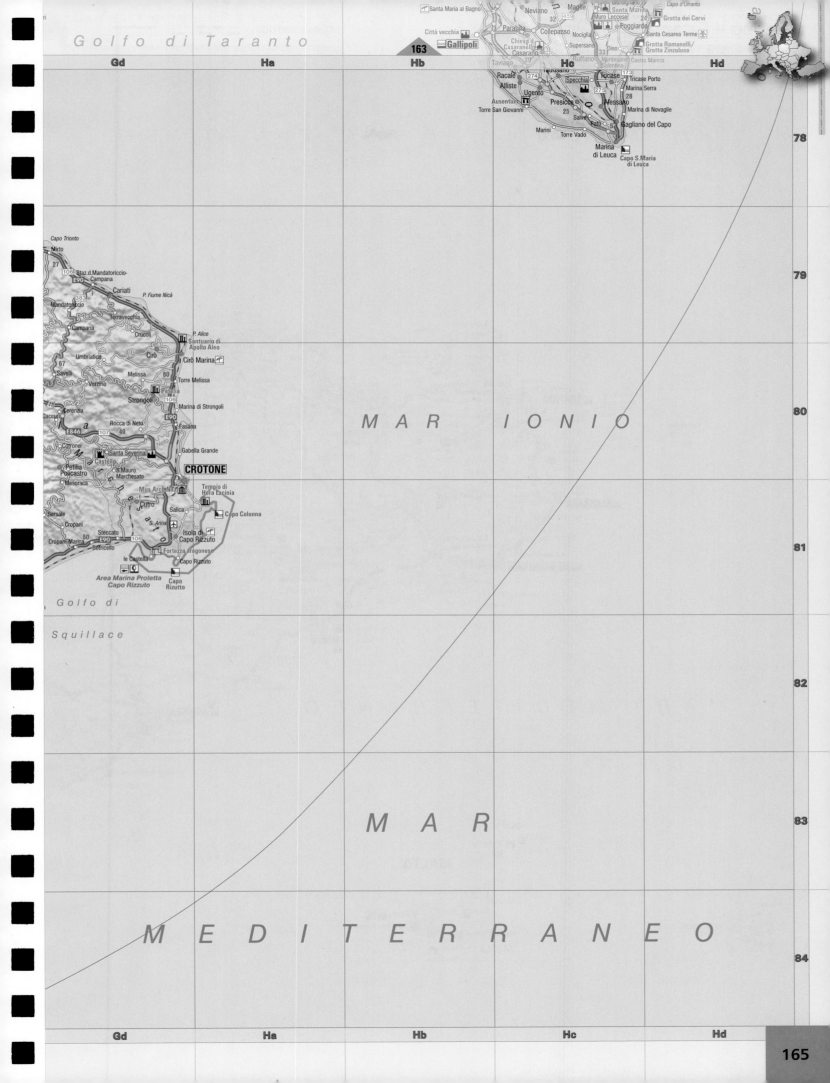

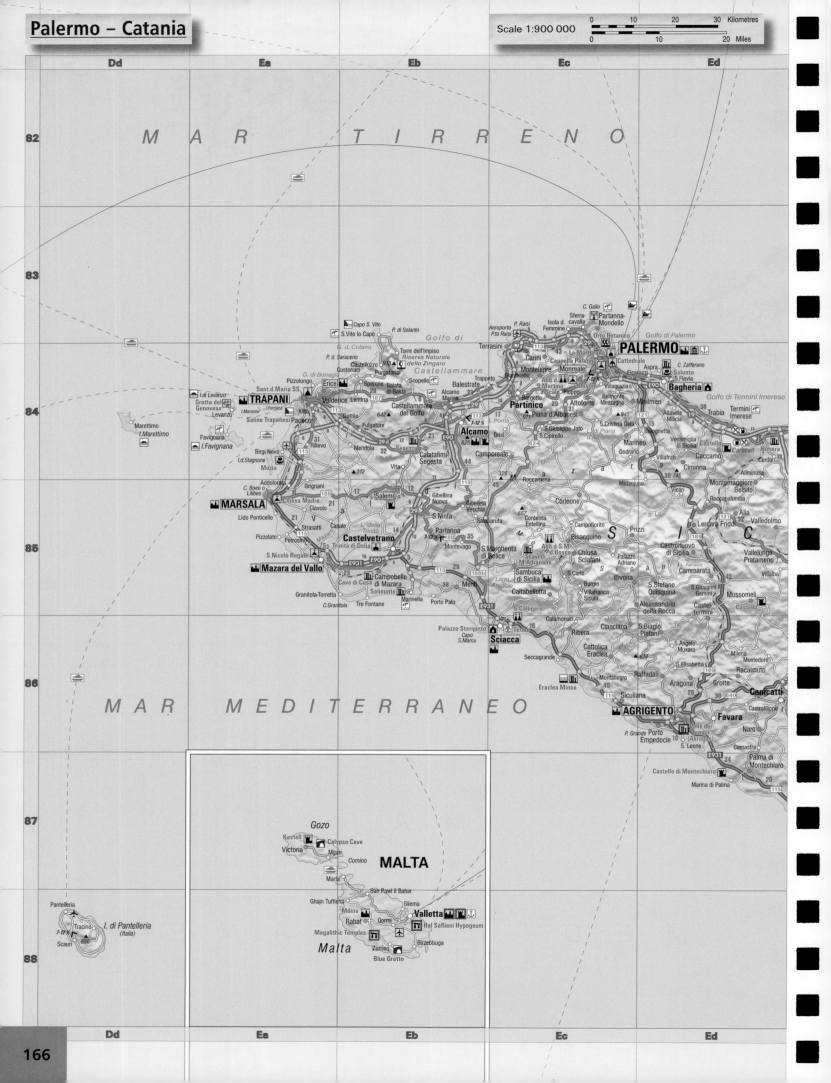

Scale 1:900 000

| 0 | 10 | 20 | 30 | Kilometres |
| 0 | | 10 | | 20 Miles |

M A R   T I R R E N O

Golfo di Palermo

Capo S. Vito
S.Vito lo Capo
G. d. Cofano
P. d. Saraceno
Pizzolungo
Sant.d.Maria SS.
Erice
TRAPANI
I.di Levanzo
Grotta del
Genovese
Levanzo
I.Marettimo
Marettimo
Favignana
I.Favignana
I.Marettimo

P. di Solanto
Torre dell'Impiso
Riserva Naturale
dello Zingaro
Castelluzzo   913
Custonaci
Purgatorio
Sperone   Balata
Scopello   di Baida
Valderice   Lentina
Xitta   Dattilo
Saline Trapanesi
Pacero
Rilievo
Birgi Novo
I.d.Stagnone
Mozia
C. Boeo o
Lilibeo
Addolorata
Grignani
MARSALA
Lido Ponticello
Strasatti
Pizzolato   Casale
Petrosino
S.Nicolò Regale
Mazara del Vallo
Cave di Cusa
Granitola-Torretta
C.Granitola
Tre Fontane

Golfo di
Castellammare
Castellammare
del Golfo
Alcamo
Marine
Fulgatore   642
Mendola
Guddia   Segesta
I. Rubini
Vita   312
Calatafimi
Segesta
Salemi
Gibellina
Nuova
Gibellina
Vecchia
S.Ninfa
L. della
Trinità   Partanna
Ss. Trinità di Delia   7-12%
Castelvetrano   Montevago
Campobello
di Mazara
Selinunte
Marinella
Porto Palo

Aeroporto
P.ta Raisi   P. Raisi
Isola d.
Femmine
Sferra-
cavallo
C. Gallo
Partanna-
Mondello
Orto Botanico
Carini   Cinisi   La Martorana
Montelepre   Cappella Palatina
PALERMO
Cattedrale
Monreale
S. Martino   Duomo
Borgetto   Pioppo   Villagrazia s
Giardinello   Altofonte
Trappeto   Mezzagno
Balestrate   Partinico   Misilmeri
Alcamo   825   Grisi   Piana d.Albanesi
971   S. Giuseppe Jato   S.Cristina Gela
L.Poma   S.Cipirello   d. Piana
Camporeale   624
Roccamena   326
Mezzojuso
Contessa
Entellina   Corleone
557
Campofiorito
Salaparuta   Bisacquino
S. Margherita
di Belice   Chiusa
Scavi di   Sclafina
M.Adranone   Palazzo
Sambuca   Adriano
di Sicilia   S. Carlo
Burgio   Bivona
Menfi   Villafranca
Lago   Sicula
Arancio   Caltabellotta
S.Calogero   Calamonaci
Ribera
Palazzo Steripinto   Cattolica
Capo   Terme   Eraclea
S.Marco   Montallegro
Sciacca   Eraclea Minoa
Seccagrande   Siculiana
AGRIGENTO
P. Grande   Porto
Empedocle   Valle dei
Templi
(Akragas)
S. Leone

Aspra
Ficarazzi
Solunto
S.Flavia
C. Zafferano
Bagheria
Golfo di Termini Imerese
Belmonte   Termini
Ventimiglia   Imerese
di Sicilia   Castello
Marineo   Caccamo   Caracoli
Godrano   Villafrati   Himera
Vicari   Ciminna   Cerda
Alliminusa
Montemaggiore
Belsito
Roccapalumba
Alia
Valledolmo
Lercara Friddi
Prizzi   Castronuovo
di Sicilia   Vallelunga
Pratameno
S.Stefano   Cammarata
Quisquina   S.Giovanni
Gemini   Villalba
Aleassandria   Mussomeli
della Rocca   Castel-
Castel-   termini
termini   Castello
Cianciana
S.Biagio   Milena
Platani   Montedoro
S.Angelo   Racalmuto
Muxaro   189
Raffadali   Aragona   Grotte   **Canicatti**
40   Castelfilippo
Favara   Naro
Castello di Montechiaro
Camastra
Palma di
Montechiaro
Marina di Palma

M A R   M E D I T E R R A N E O

Gozo
Kastell
Victoria   Calypso Cave
Mgarr
Comino
MALTA
Marfa
Ghajn Tuffieha   San Pawl il Bahar
Mdina   Sliema
Rabat   **Valletta**
Megalithic Temples   Qormi   Hal Saflieni Hypogeum
Zurrieq   Birzebbuga
Blue Grotto
Malta

Pantelleria
Tracino   836
Scauri
I. di Pantelleria
(Italia)

Golfo

VIBO

Isole Eolie o Lipari

I. Stromboli
Stromboli 924
San Vincenzo
Ginostra

Marina di Zambrone
Tropea
Torre Ruffa
Capo Vaticano
Joppolo
Nicotera

82

I. Basiluzzo
I. Lisca Bianca
S. Pietro
I. Panarea

Golfo di
Gioia

S. Ferdinando
Eranova
Marina di Gioia Tauro
Gioia Tauro

I. Filicudi
Malfa
S. Marina Salina
I. Salina
Rinella
P. Grottazza
Acquacalda
P. Castagna

Filicudi Porto
C. Graziano
Pecorini

I. Alicudi
Alicudi Porto

Pianoconte
Canneto
I. Lipari
Lipari
Mus.Arch.Eoliano
P. Ctapazza
Vulcano Porto
I. Vulcano
Vulcano Piano
P. Bandiera

Palmi
Museo Etnografico
Bagnara Calabra

83

Capo di Milazzo
Golfo di Milazzo
Milazzo
Tono

C. Rasocolmo
Sparta
Castanea d'Furie
Mortelle
P. del Faro
Faro
Torre

111

Scilla

Capo d'Orlando
C. Calavà
Gioiosa Marea
Brolo
Golfo di Patti
Barcellona
Pozzo di Gotto
Olivarella S.Giorgio
Villafranca Tirrena
Spadafora

Divieto
Paradiso
Villa S. Giovanni
Galati Marina

MESSINA
REGGIO DI CALABRIA

164

Cefalù
Duomo
Castello
C. Plaia
Capo Raisigerbi
S. Stefano d.Camastra
Fiumara d'Arte
Marina di Caronia
Patti
S. Angelo di Brolo
Tindari
Naso
Falcone
Castroreale
Terme
Mazzarra S.Andrea
Castroreale

Sinopoli
Roghudi

84

Parco dei Nebrodi
Castel di Tusa
Tusa
Halaesa
Reitano
Mistretta
Rocca di Capri Leone
Sant'Agata di Militello
Acquedolci
Caronia
Capizzi
S. Fratello
Longi
Tortorici
Floresta
Randazzo
Montalbano Elicona
S.Piero Patti
Raccuia
Ucria
S. Filippo d.Fragala
Mon.d. S.Filippo

Bronte
Parco dell'Etna
Monte Etna (Mongibello) 3323
Rif Sapienza

85

ILIA
Petralia Sottana
Petralia Soprana
Gangi
Geraci Siculo
Colle del Contrasto
Nicosia
Cattedrale
Sperlinga
Cesarò
Troina
Cerami
Agira
Gagliano Castelferrato
Regalbuto

Adrano
Biancavilla
S. Maria di Licodia
Città antica
Belpasso
Nicolosi
Paternò
Misterbianco

Acireale
Aci Trezza
Faraglioni dei Ciclopi
Aci Castello

86

Caltanissetta
Enna
Calascibetta
Leonforte
Assoro
Villarosa
Valguarnera Caropepe
Raddusa
Castel di Iudica
Gerbini

CATANIA
Gelso Bianco
Lido di Plaia
Fontanarossa

Golfo
di Catania

Piazza Armerina
Villa Romana del Casale
Aidone
Morgantina
Barrafranca
Pietraperzia
Mazzarino
Ramacca
Palagonia
Scordia
Lentini
Carlentini
Agnone

Augusta
Megara Hyblaea
Golfo di Augusta

87

Riesi
Butera
Caltagirone
Grammichele
Mineo
Francofonte
Pedagaggi
Sortino
Melilli
Priolo Gargallo
Penisola Magnisi

GELA
Museo Archeologico
Licodia Eubea
Vizzini
Buccheri
Ferla
Cassaro
Necropoli di Pantalica
Solarino
Floridia

SIRACUSA
Teatro Greco/Siracusa antica
Ortigia

Licata
Museo Archeologico

Golfo di Gela

88

Vittoria
Comiso
RAGUSA
Modica
Scicli
Chiaramonte Gulfi
Monterosso Almo
Palazzolo Acreide
Akrai
Canicattini Bagni
Rosolini
Ispica

NOTO
Avola
Lido di Noto
Eloro

Scoglitti
Camarina
S. Croce Camerina
Marina di Ragusa
Donnalucata
Sampieri
Marina di Modica
Pozzallo
Ispica
Riserva Naturale Oasi faunistica di Vendicari
Marzamemi
Pachino
Capo Passero
Portopalo di C.Passero

Golfo di Noto

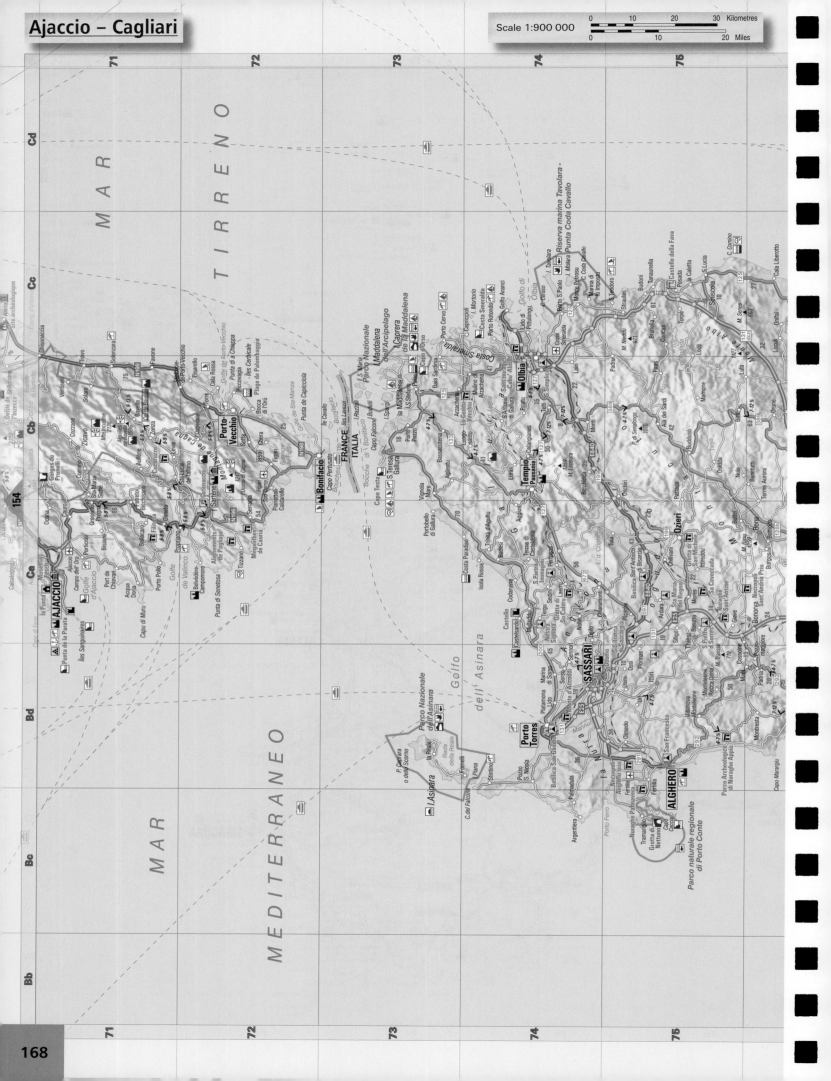

Scale 1:900 000

| | 0 | 10 | 20 | 30 | Kilometres |
| | 0 | | 10 | | 20 | Miles |

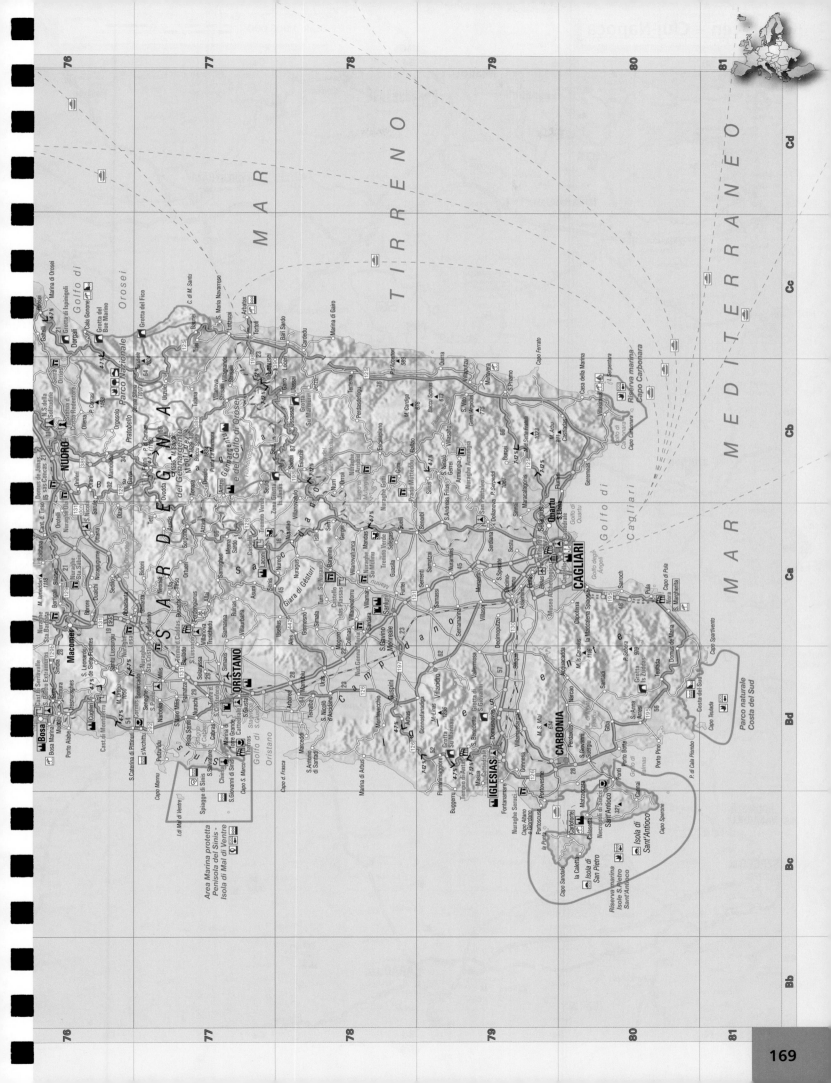

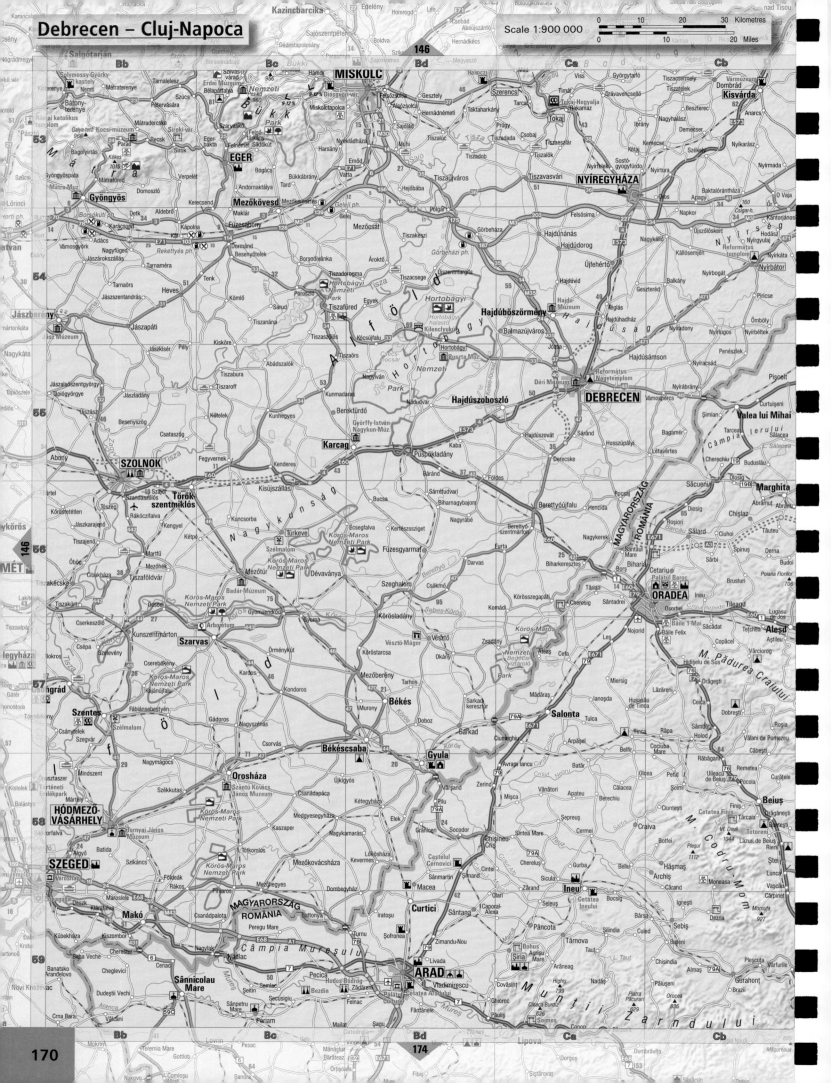

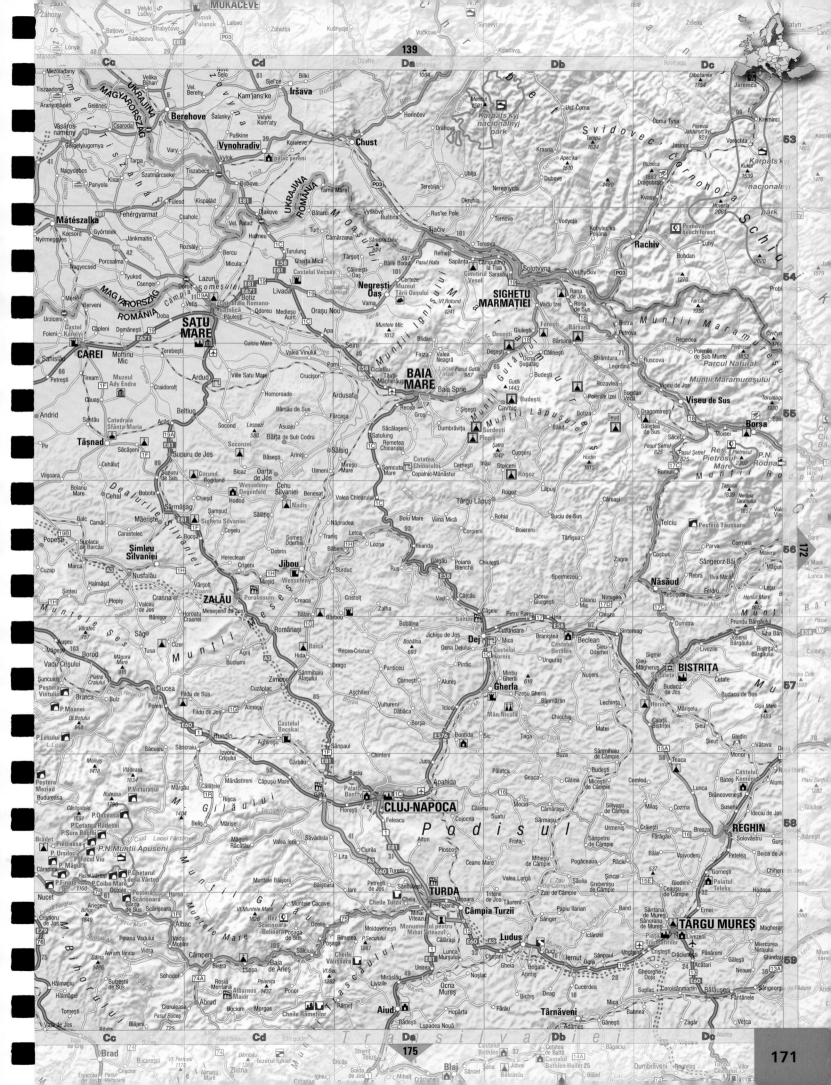

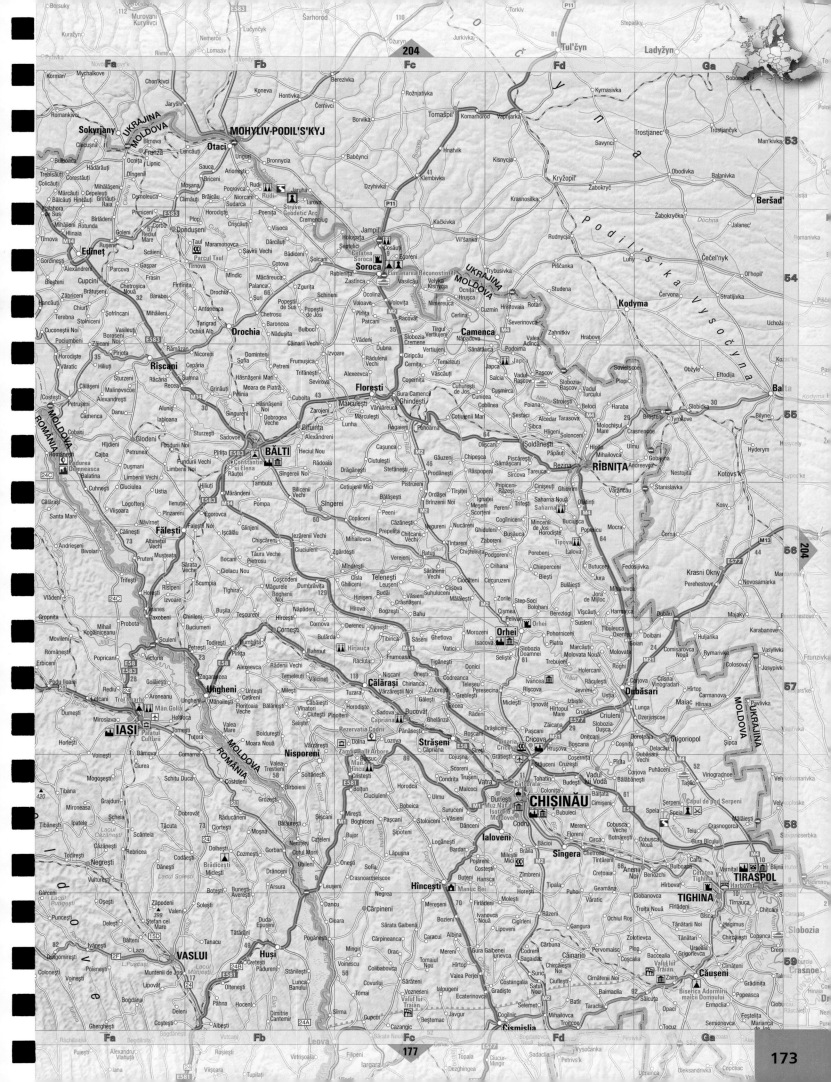

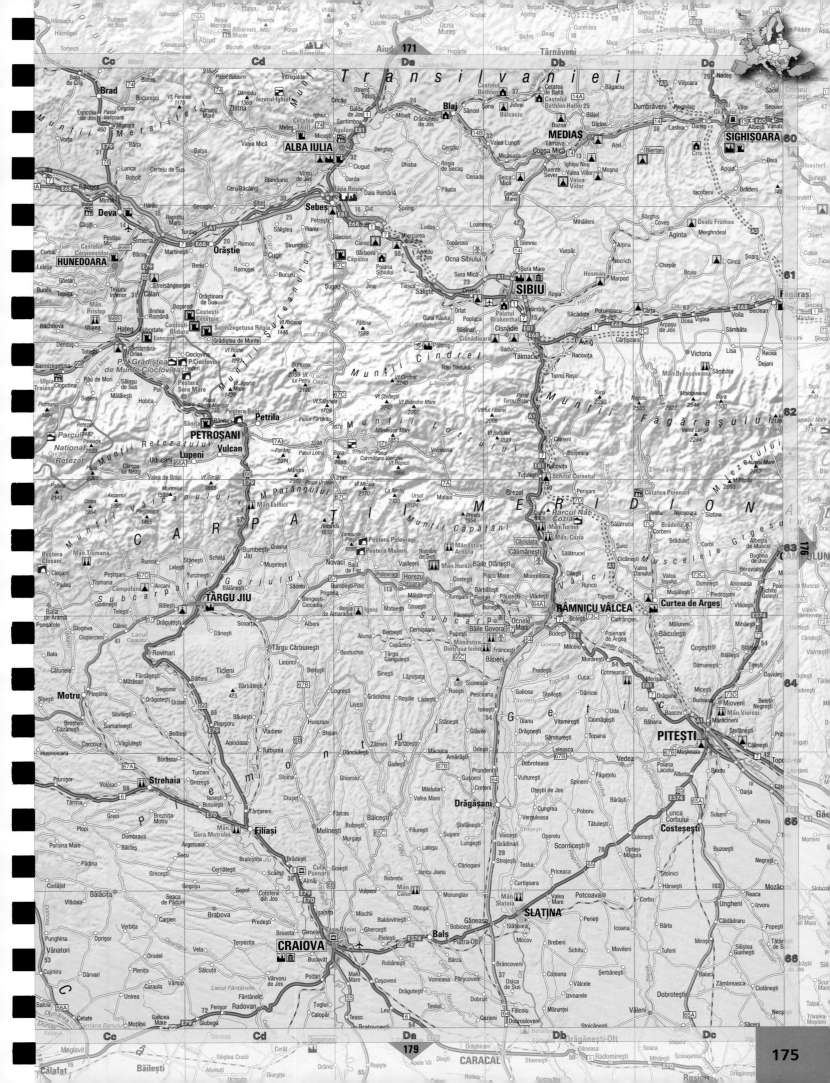

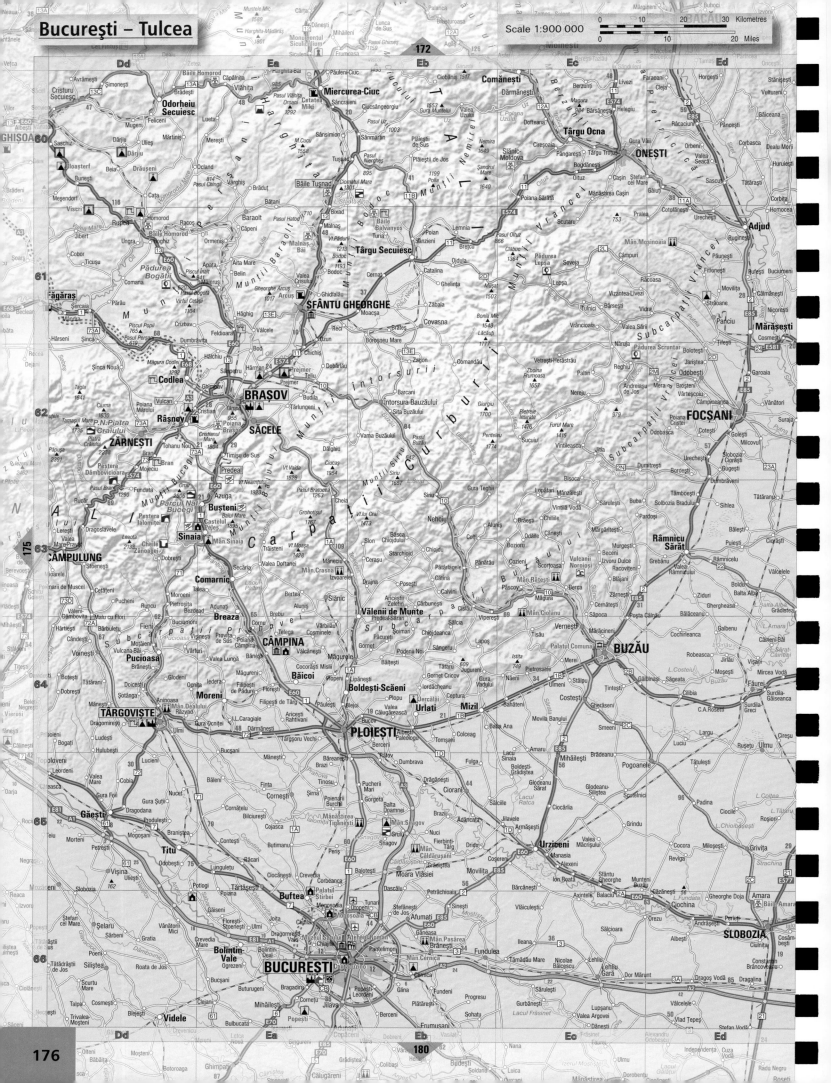

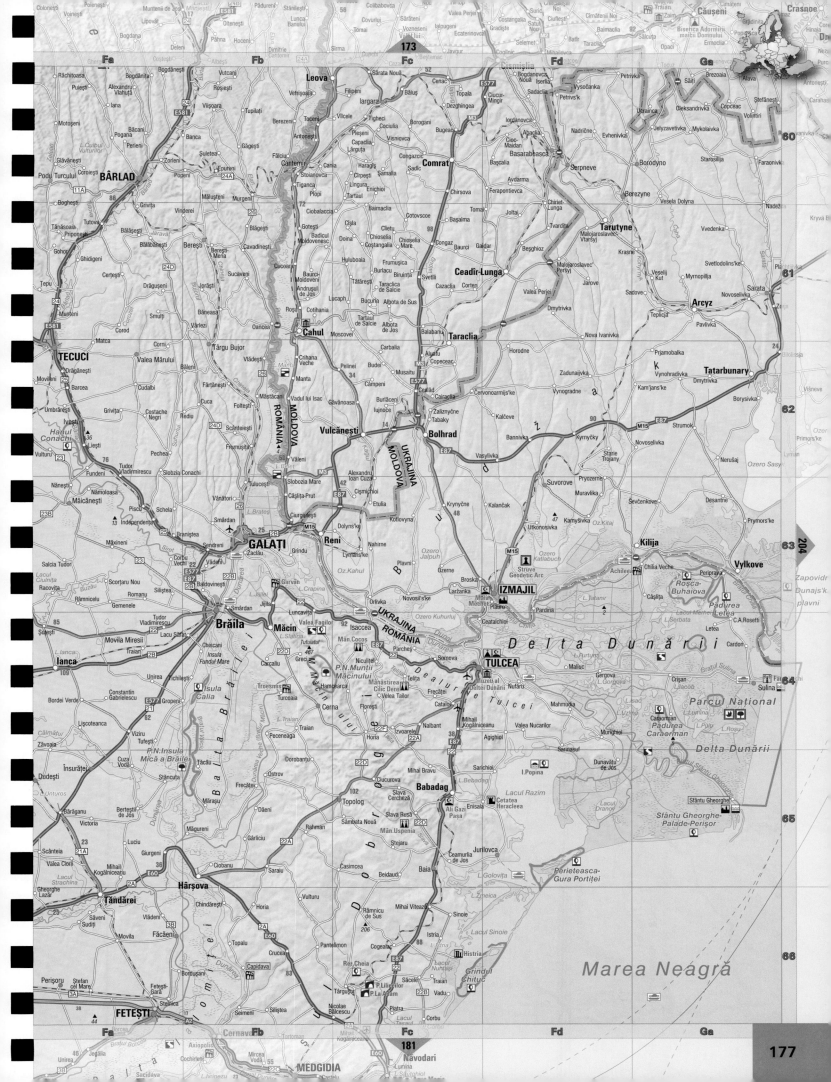

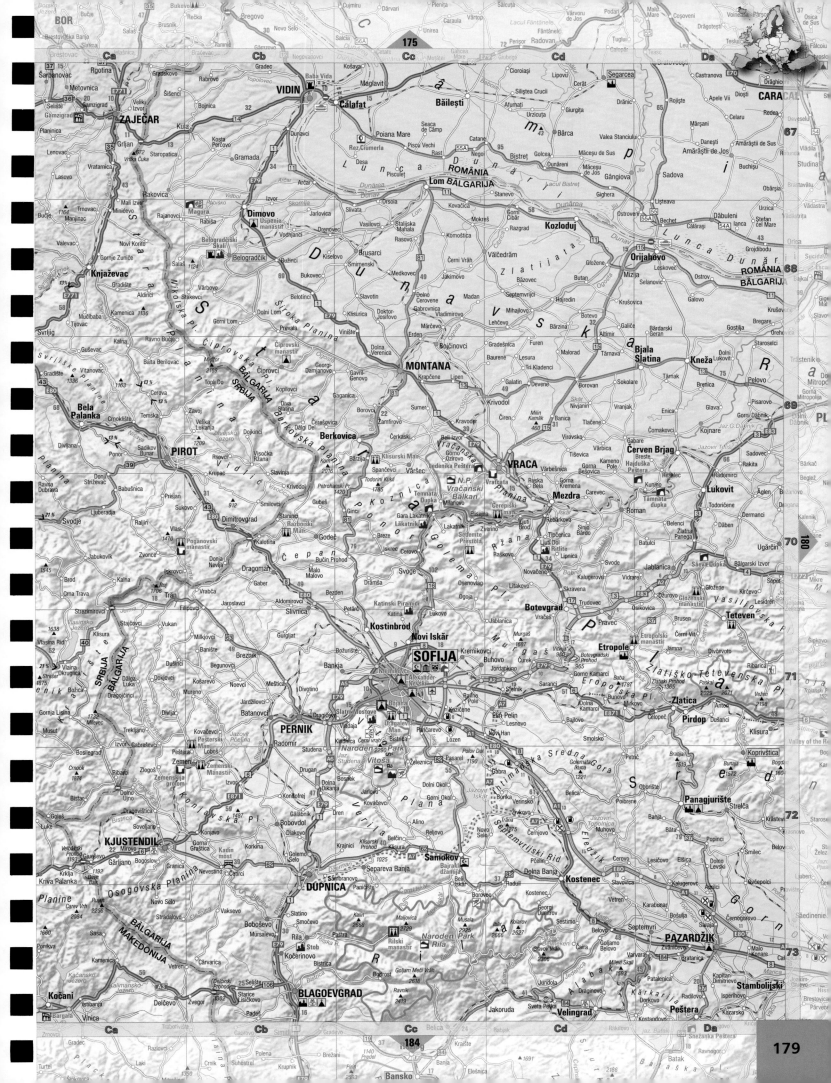

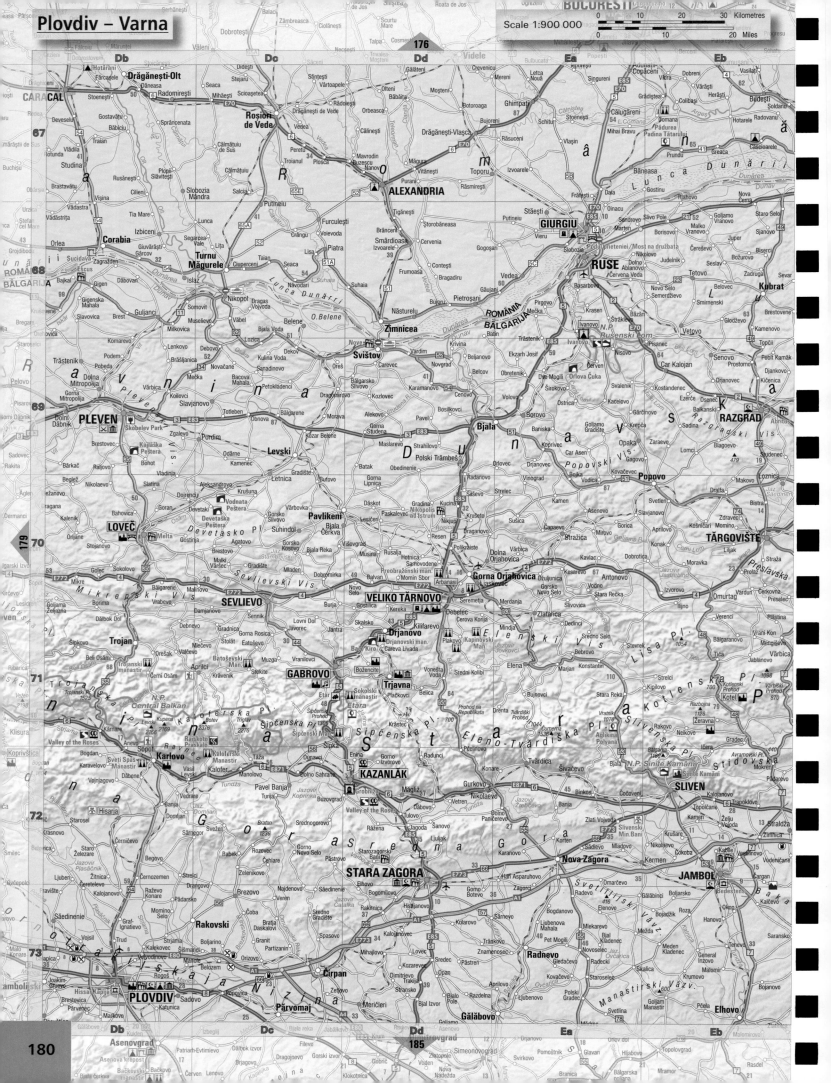

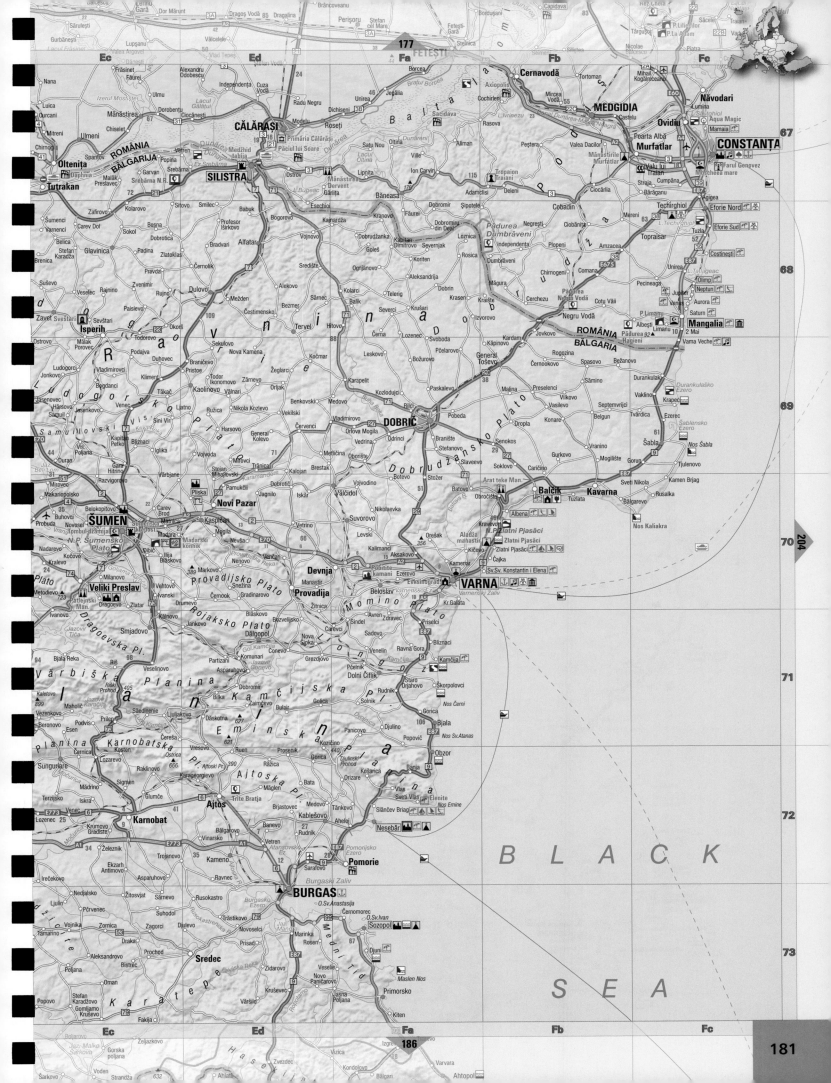

Scale 1:900 000

| 0 | 10 | 20 | 30 Kilometres |
| 0 | 10 | 20 Miles |

74

75

163
77

76

78

79

80

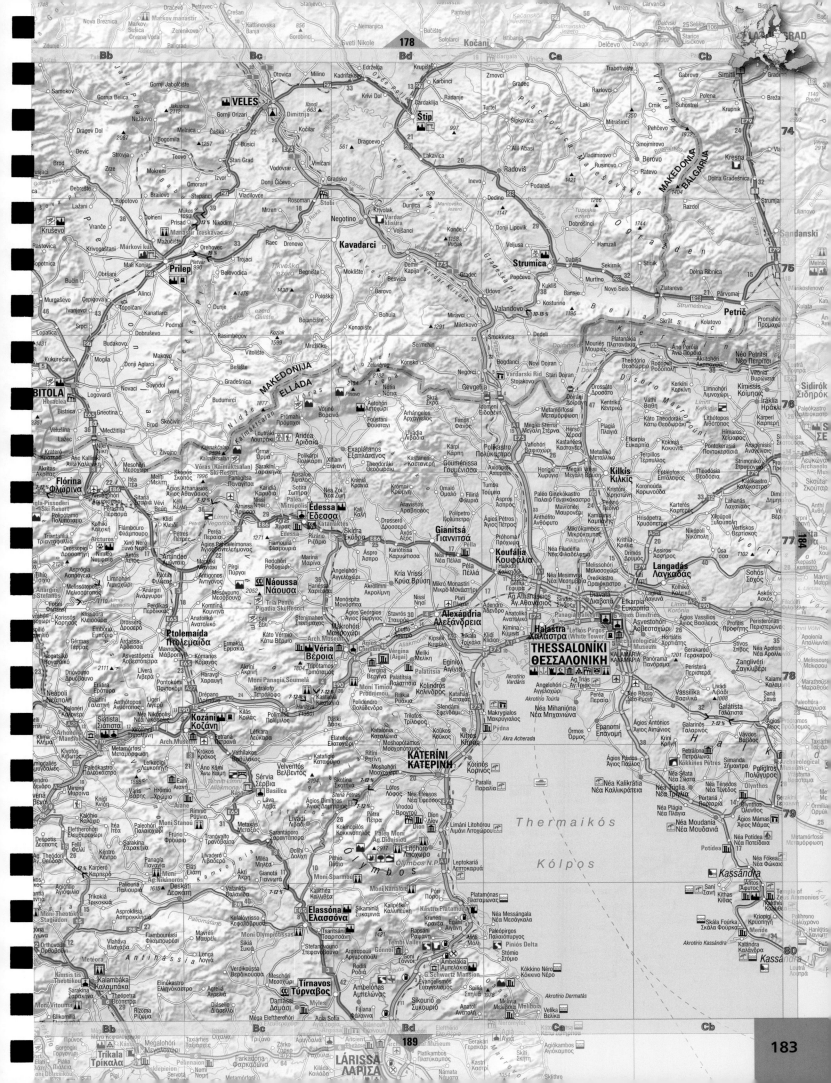

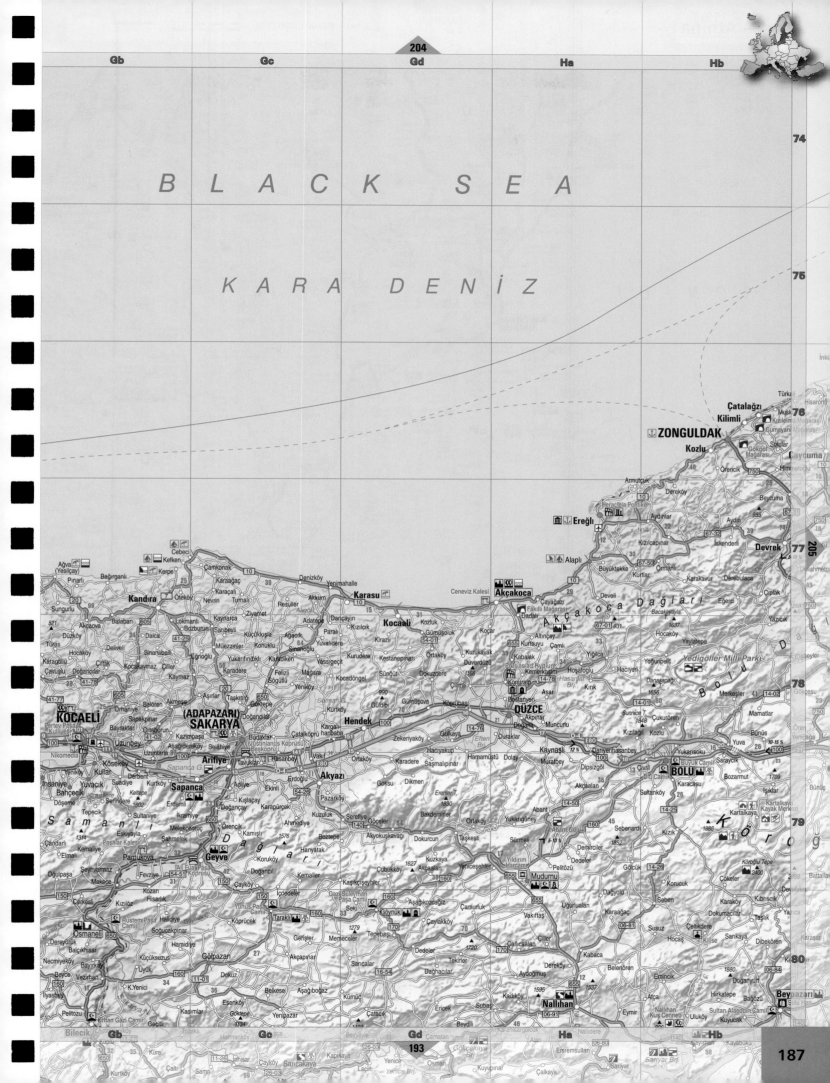

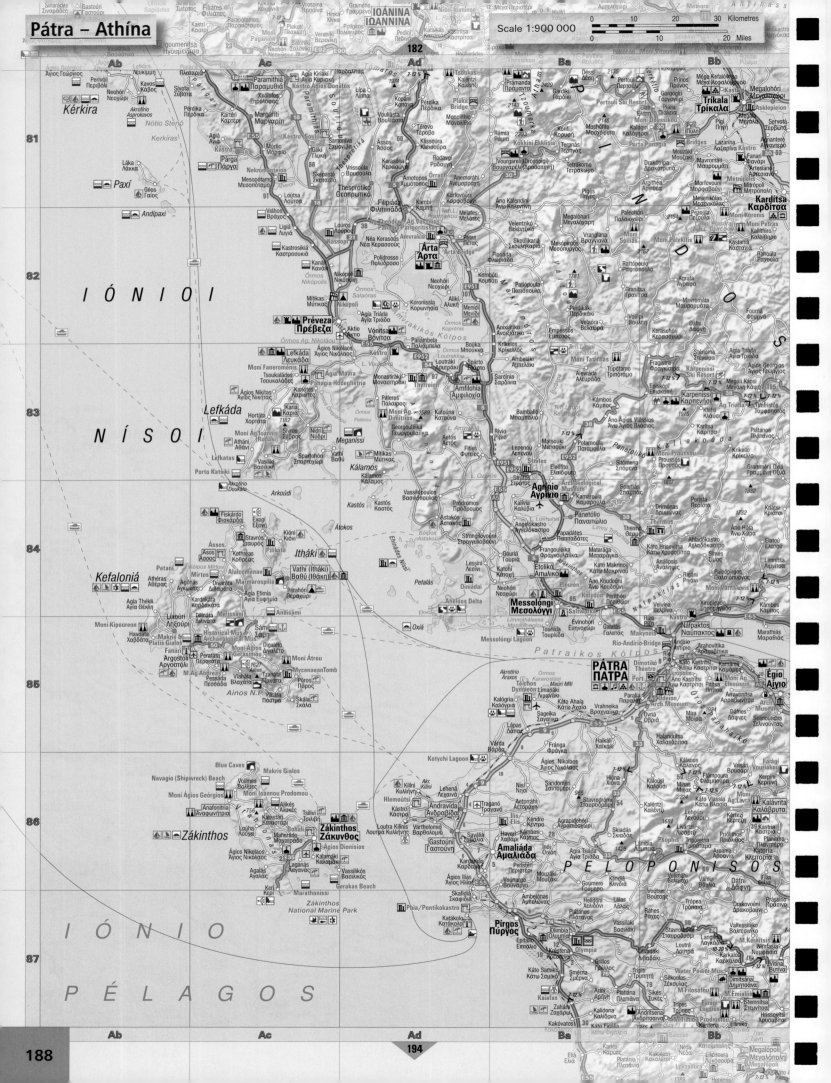

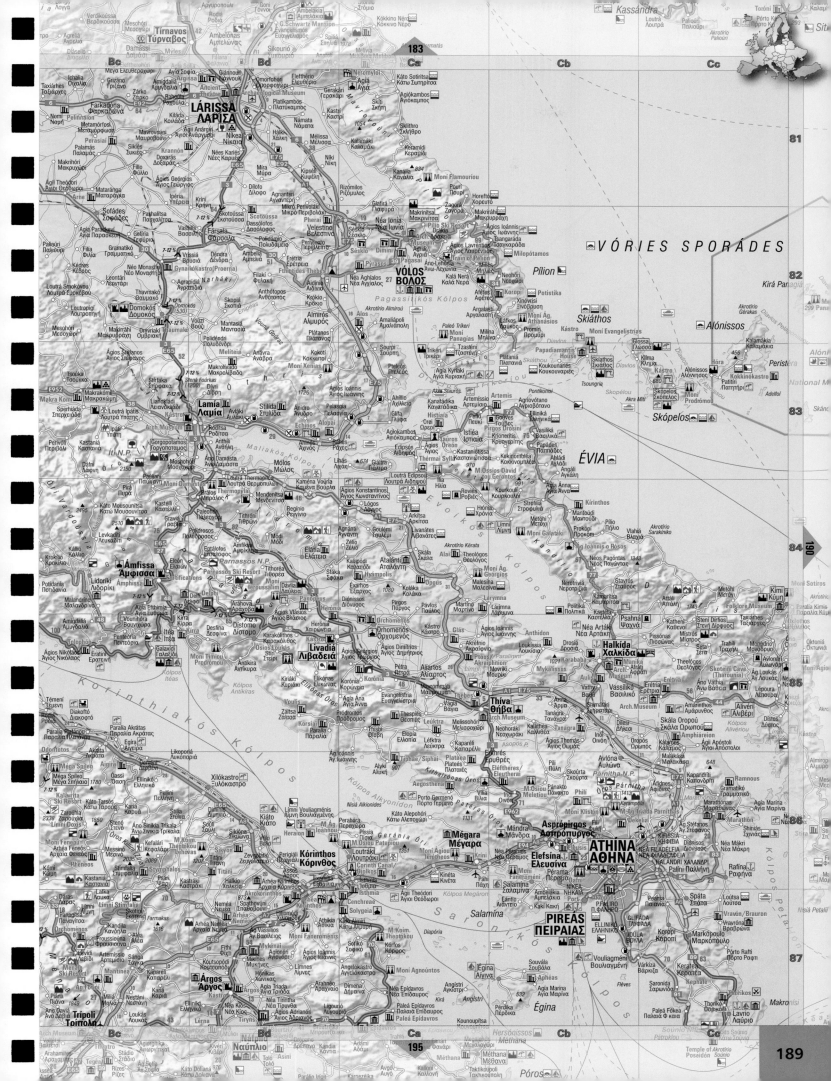

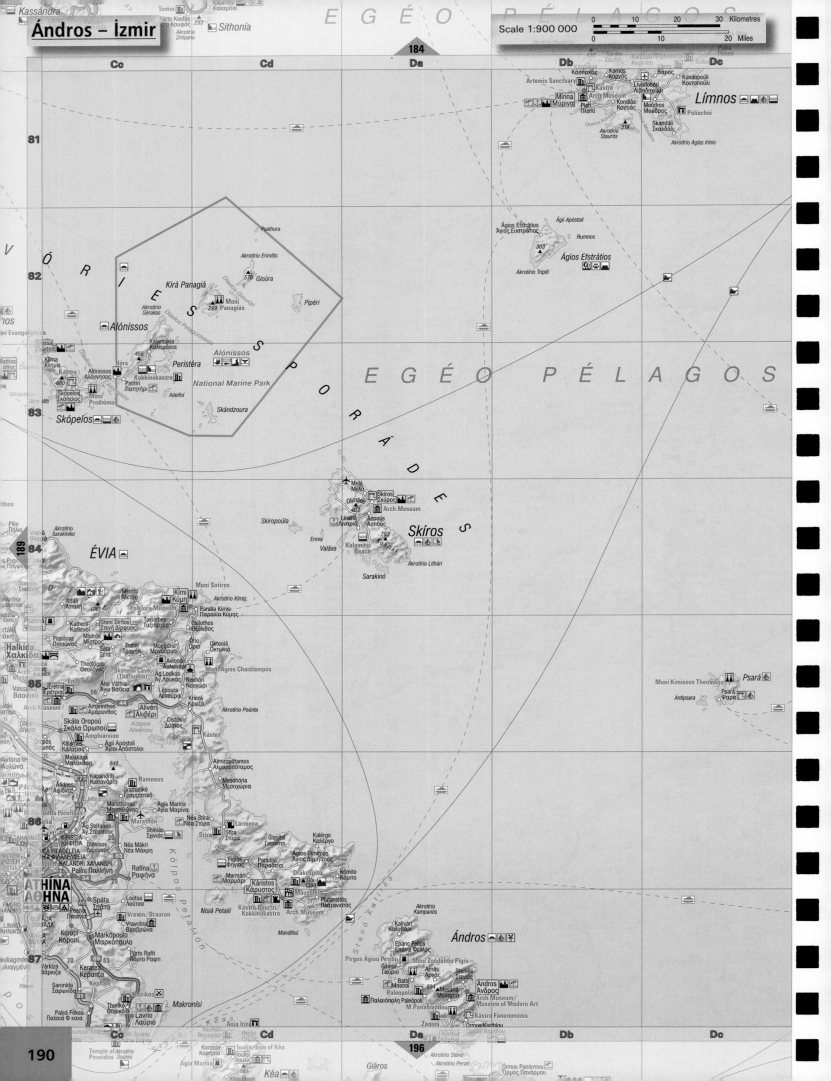

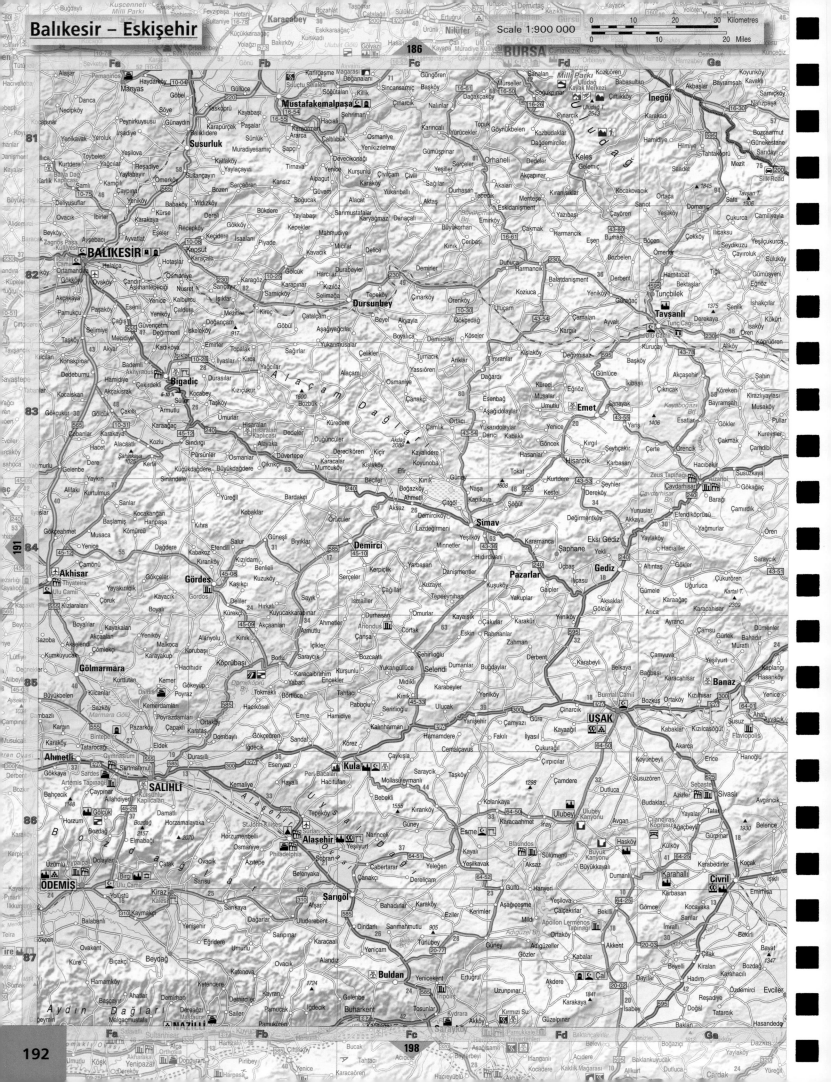

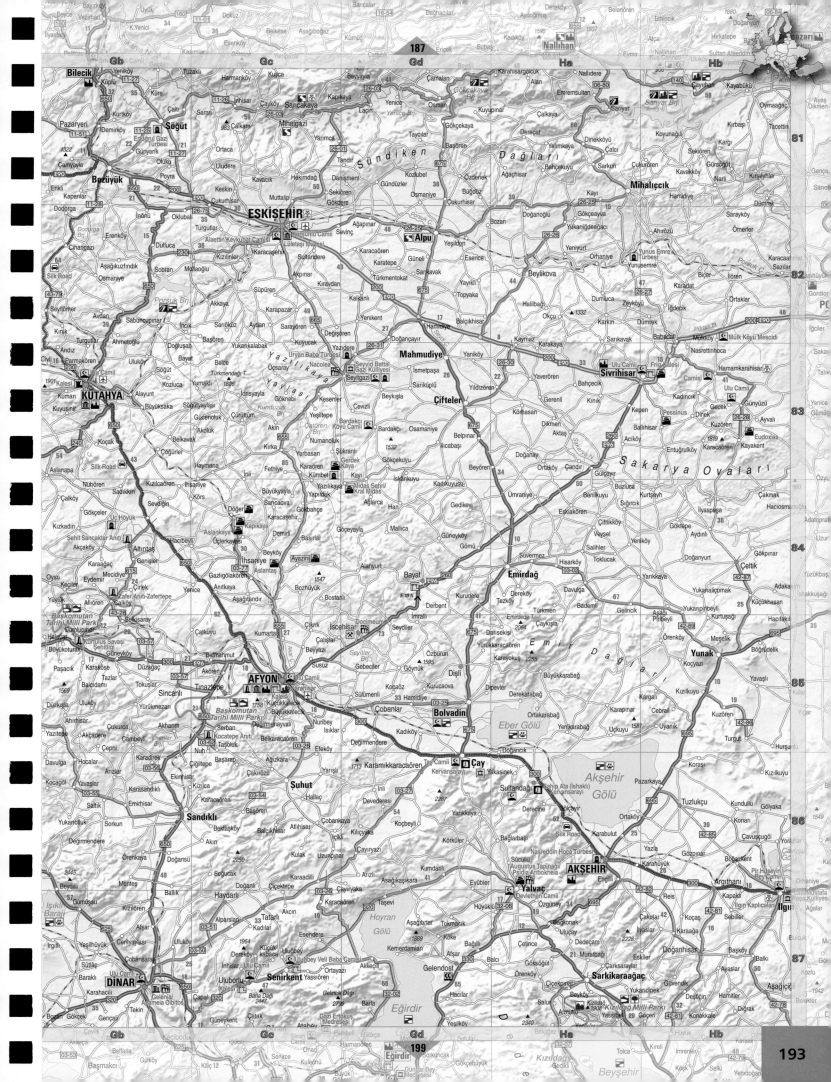

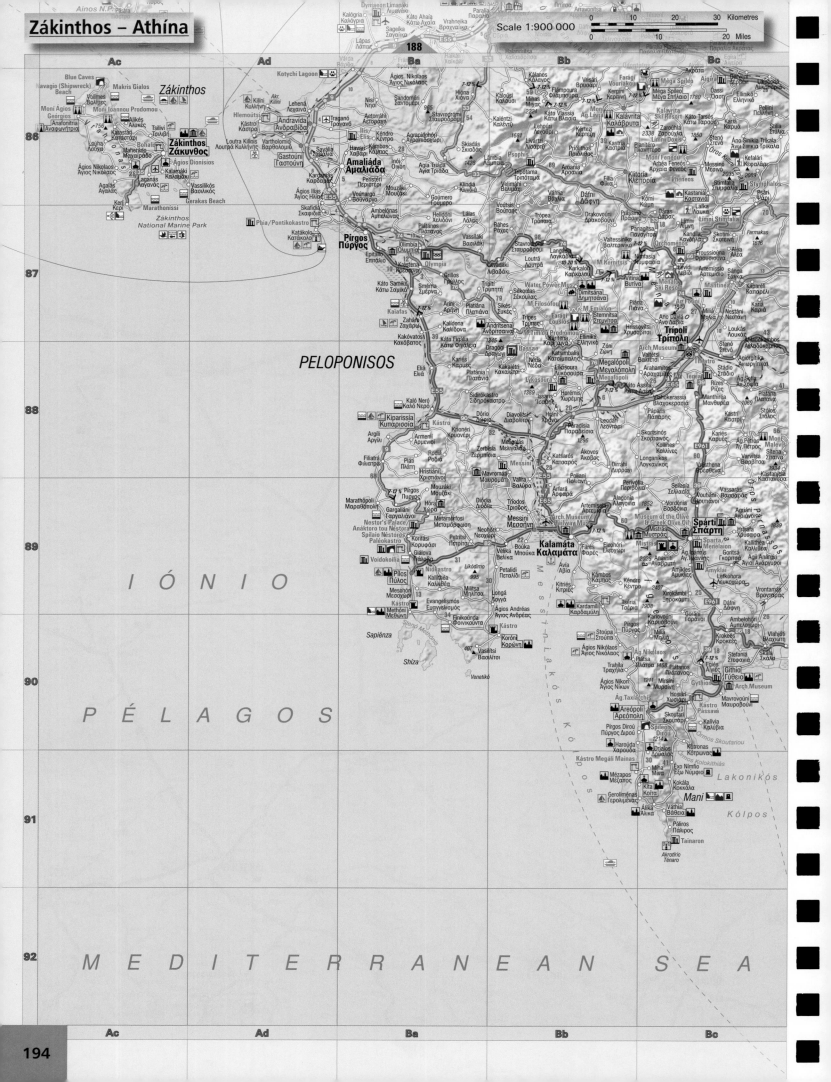

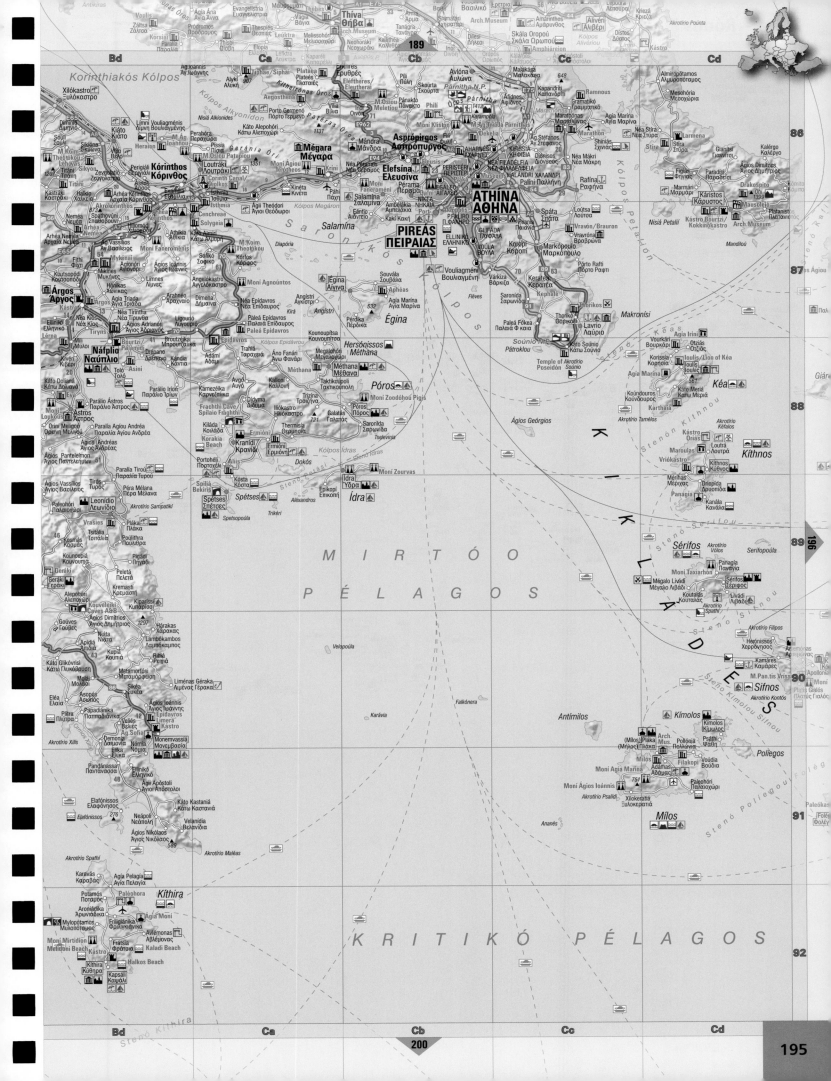

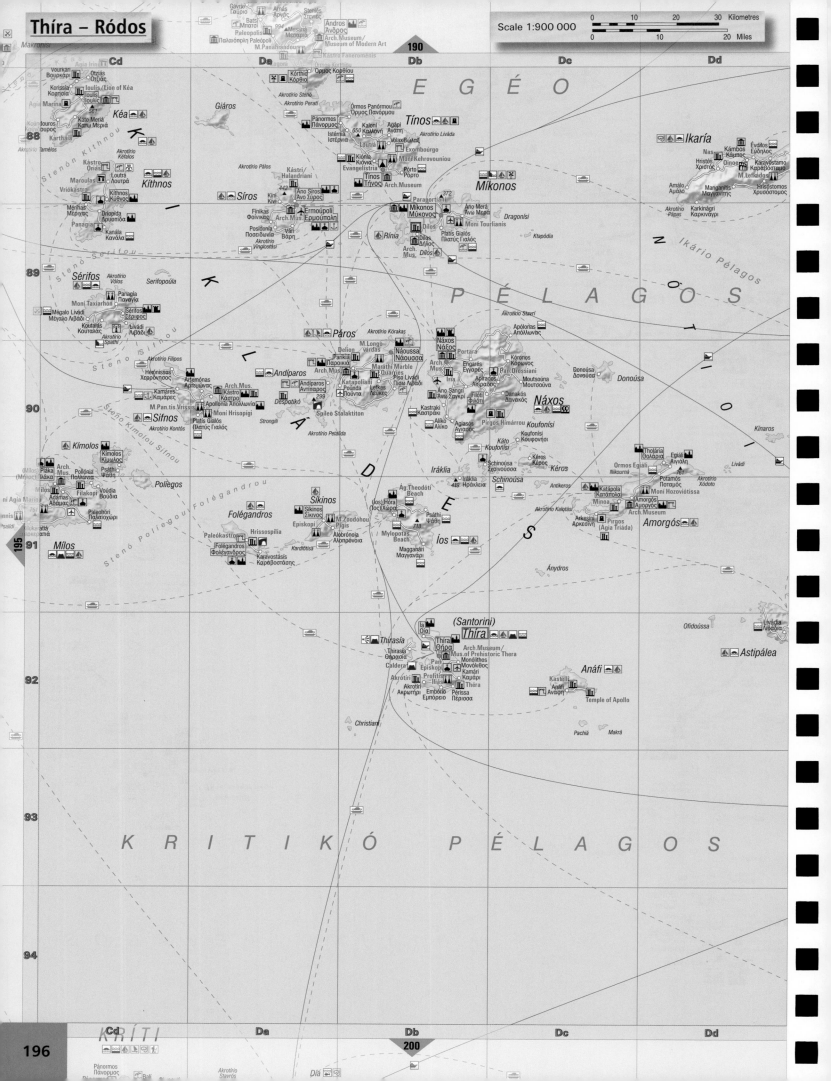

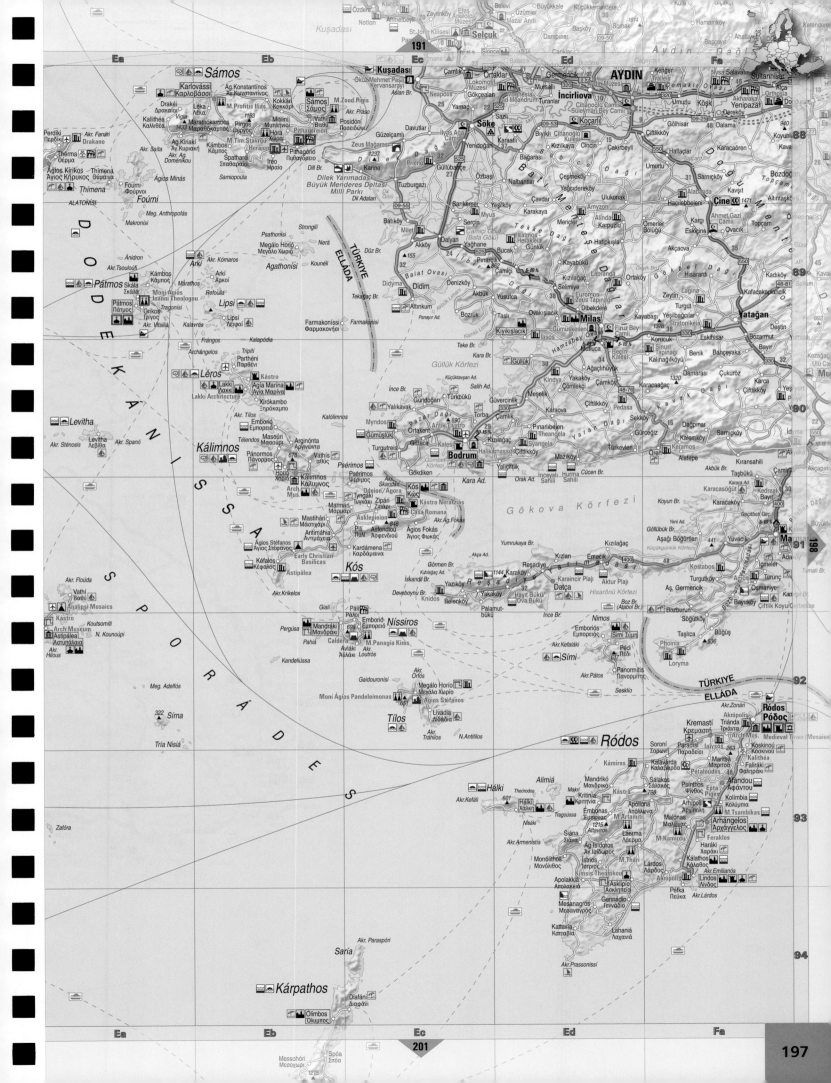

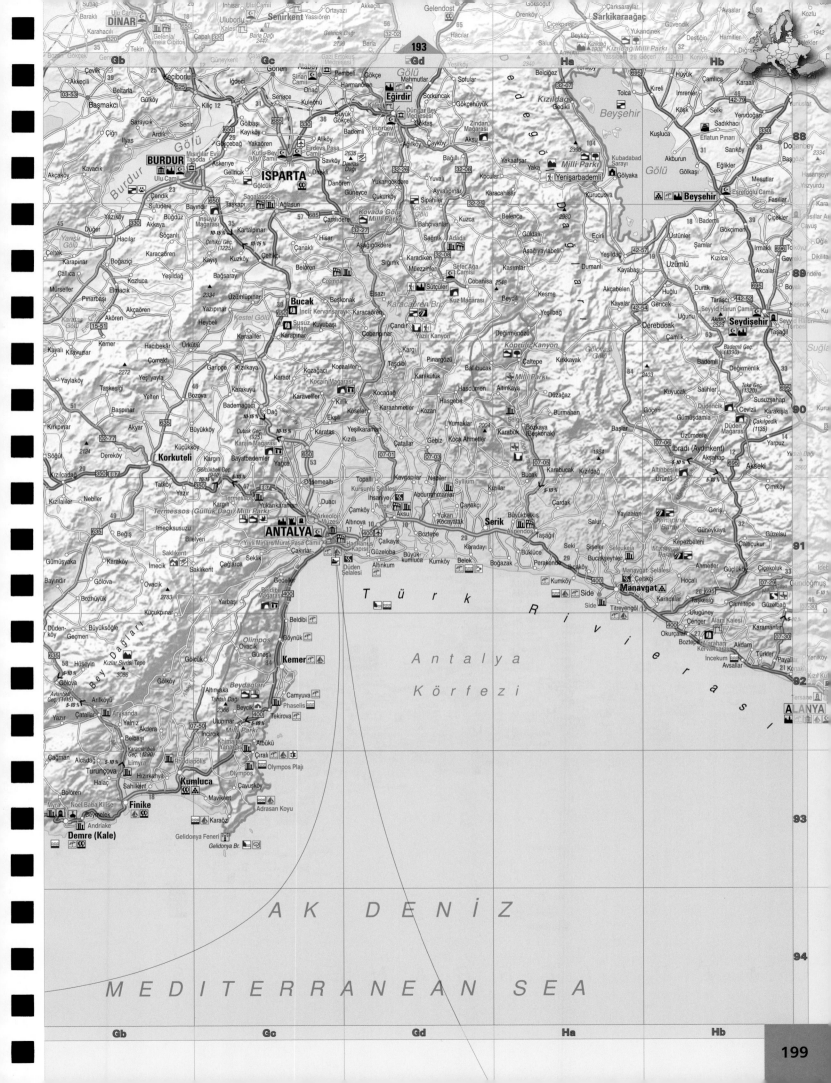

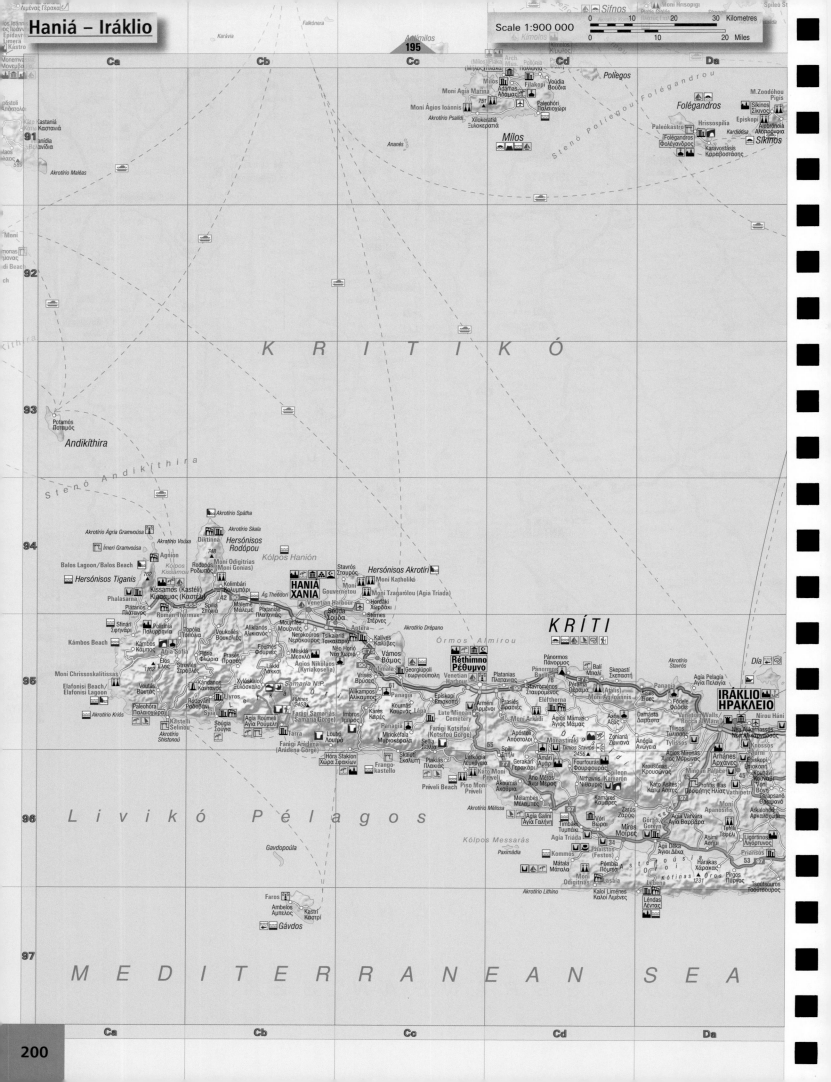

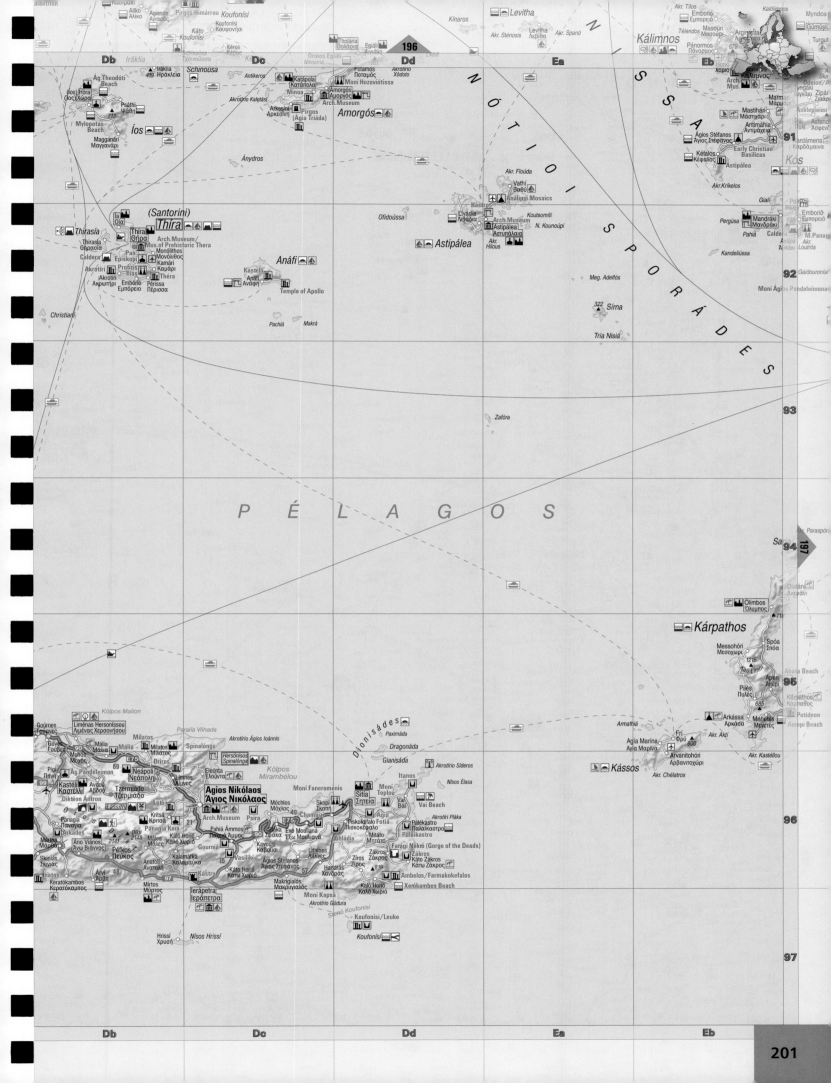

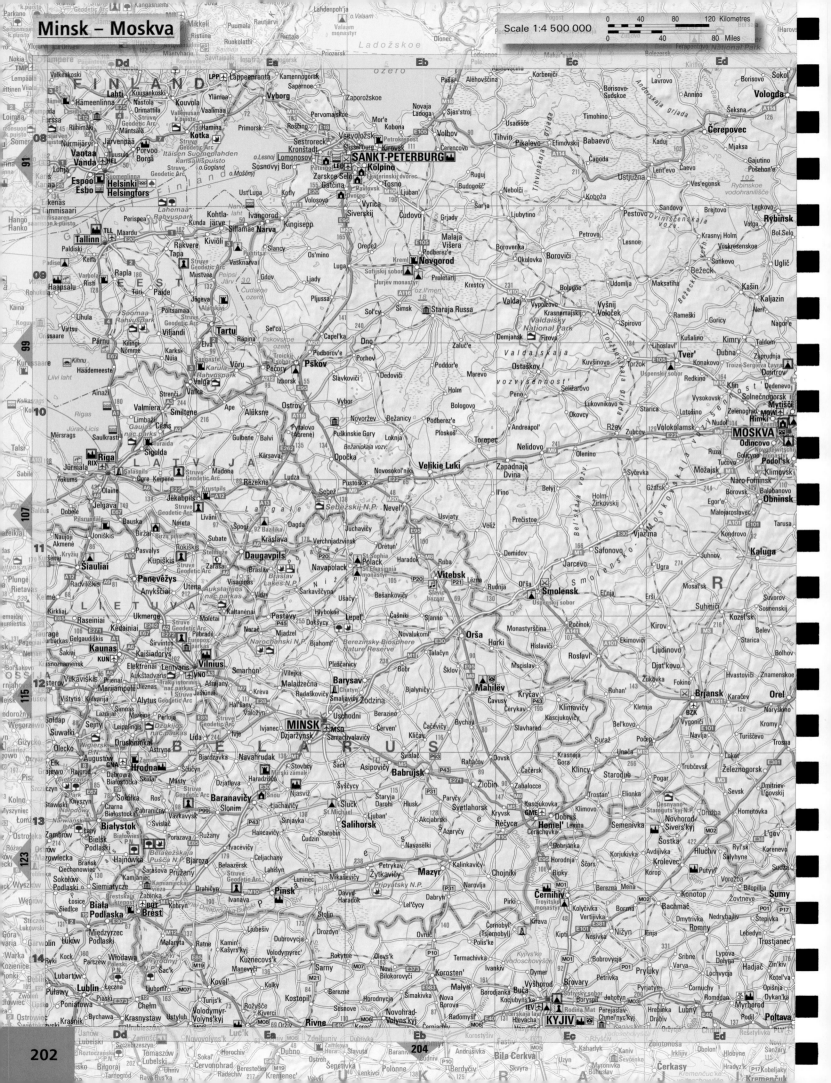

Scale 1:4 500 000

0   40   80   120 Kilometres
0   40   80 Miles

204

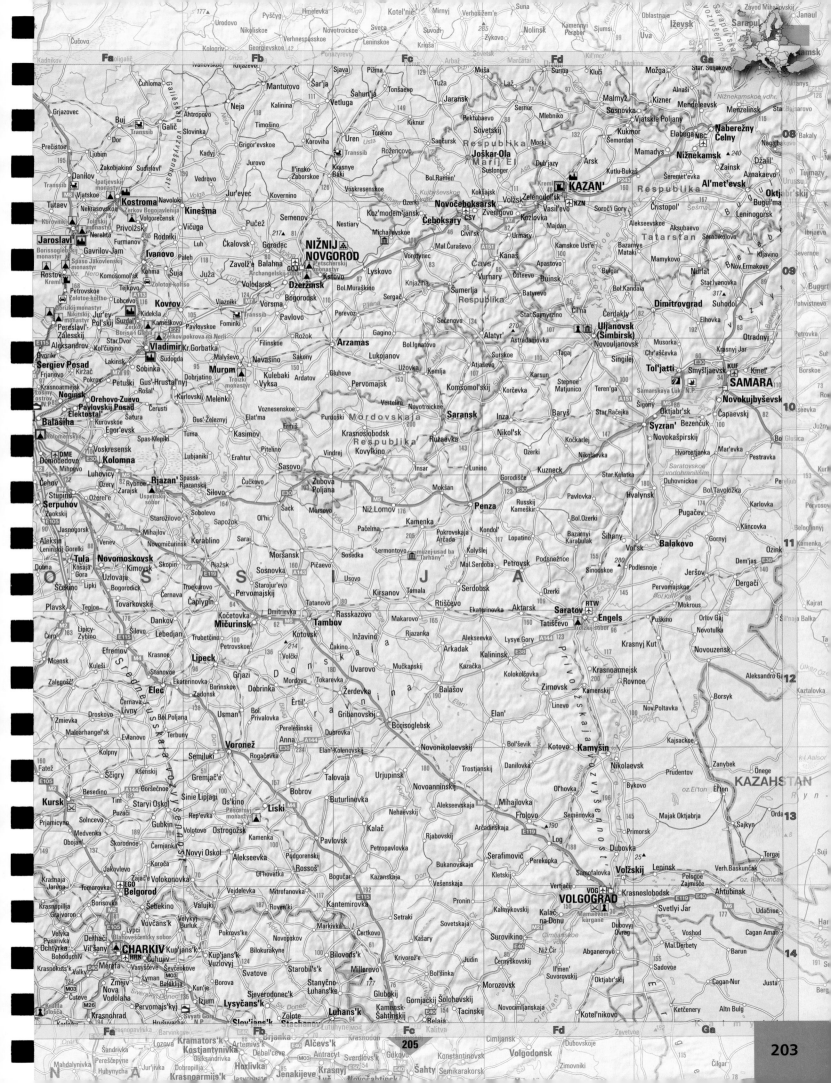

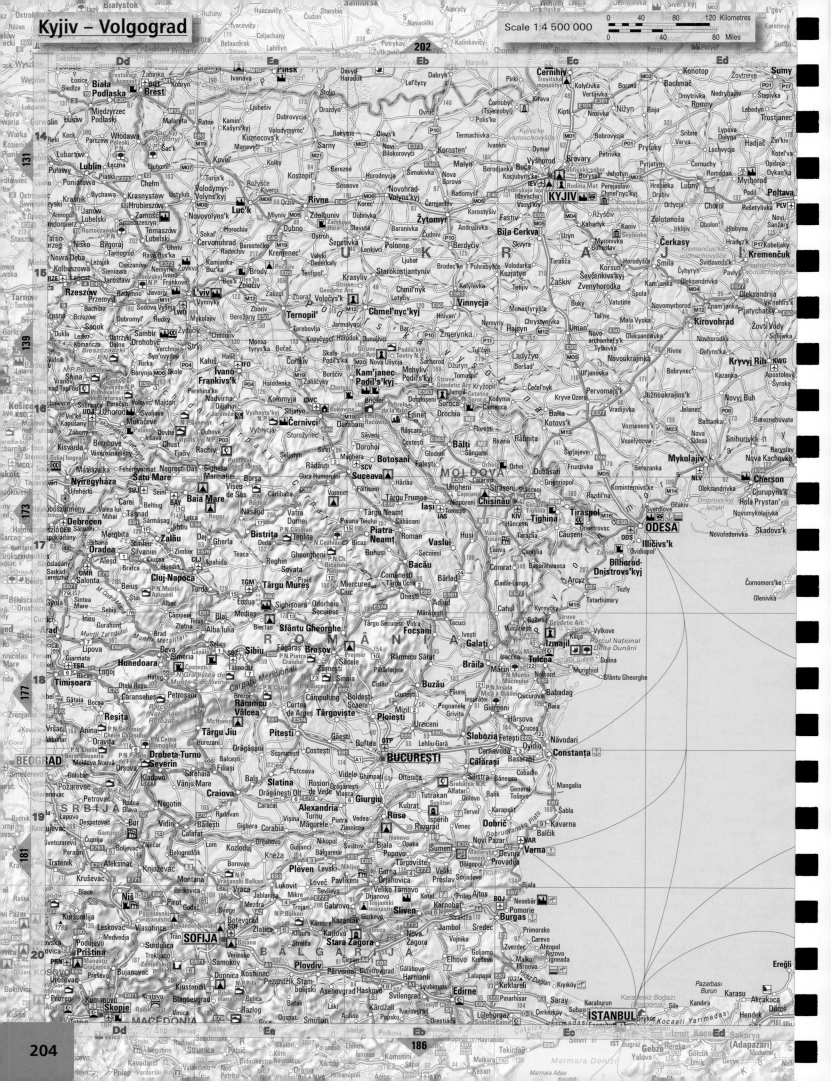

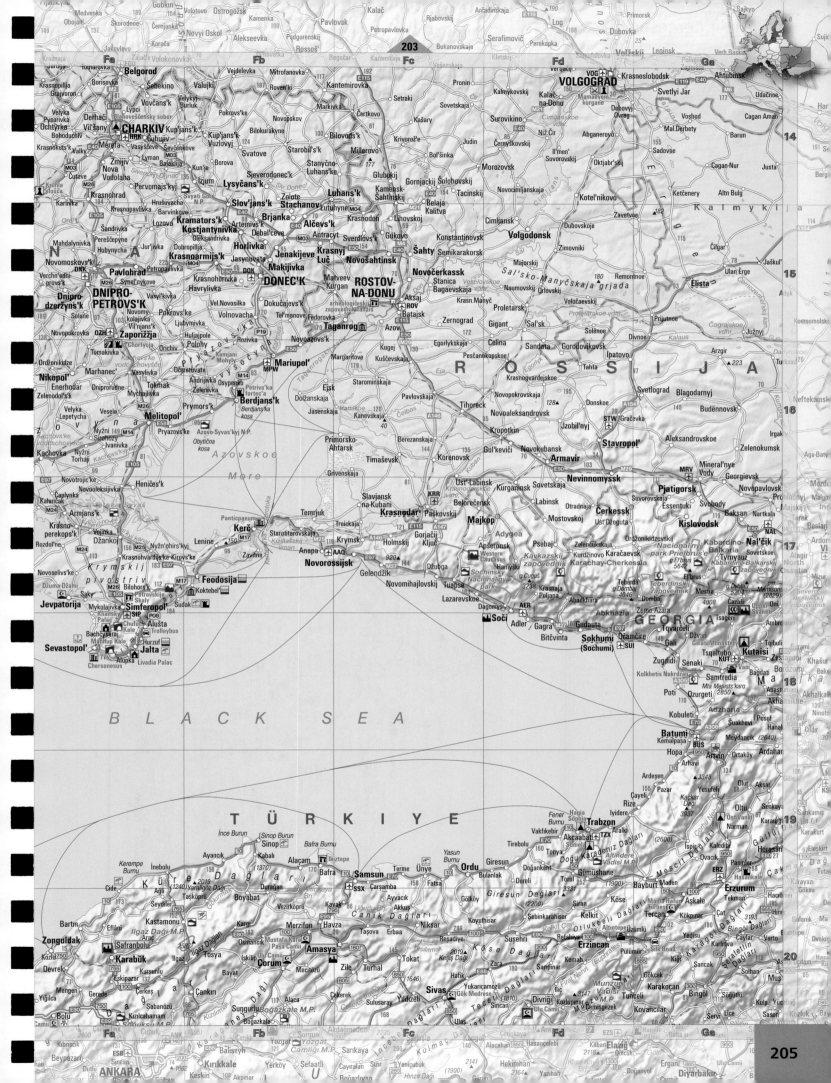

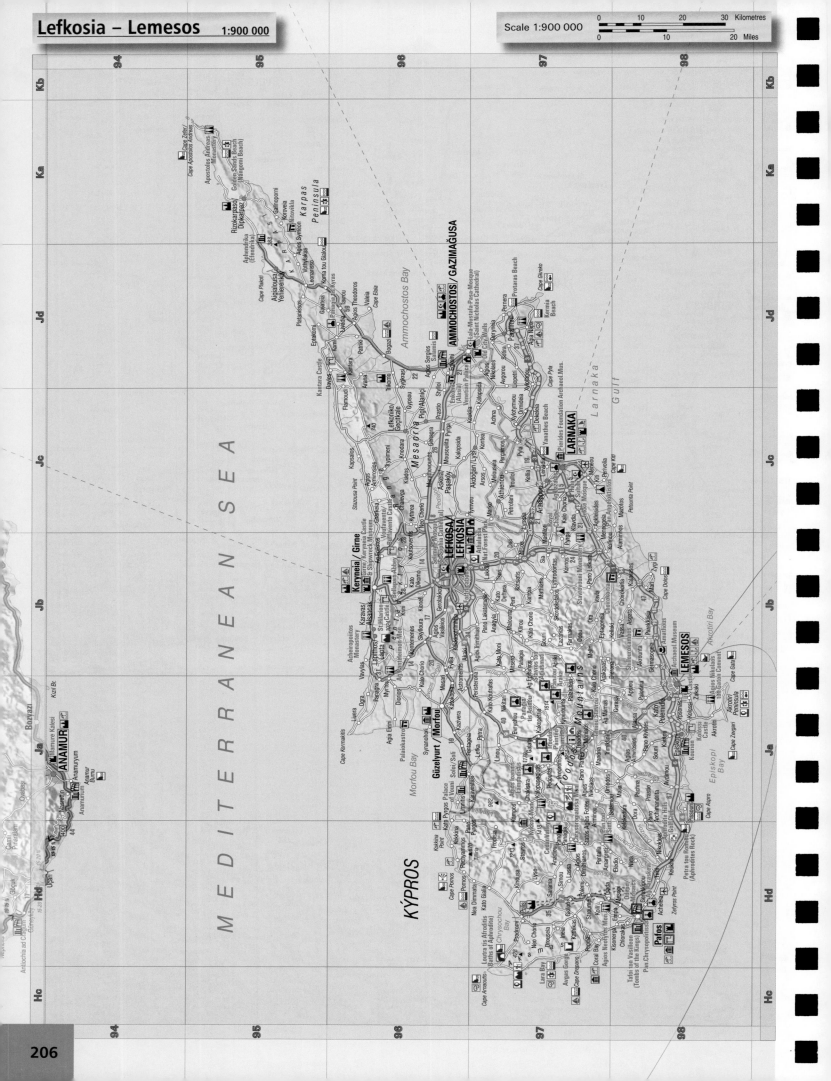

Scale 1:900 000

0 10 20 30 Kilometres
0 10 20 Miles

2. Mai RO 181 Fc68
23. August RO 181 Fc68

A

Å N 66 Fa15
Å N 77 Dd31
Å N 78 Ea28
Aabenraa DK 108 Db27
Aabybro DK 100 Dc20
Aach D 142 Cc51
Aachen D 125 Bb41
Aadorf CH 142 Cc52
Aakirkeby DK 111 Fc58
Aakre EST 106 La46
Aalborg DK 100 Dc21
Aalburg NL 124 Ba37
Aalen D 134 Db48
Aalestrup DK 100 Db22
Aalsmeer NL 116 Ba36
Aalst B 124 Ac40
Aalten NL 125 Bd37
Äänekoski FIN 82 Kb31
Aapajärvi FIN 69 Kb16
Aapajärvi FIN 74 Jc20
Aapajoki FIN 74 Jc20
Aapua S 74 Jb18
Aarau CH 141 Ca53
Aarberg CH 141 Bc54
Aarburg CH 141 Ca53
Aardenburg NL 124 Ab38
Aareavaara S 68 Ja16
Aarhus DK 108 Dc24
Aarneniemi FIN 65 Kb09
Aarninjarga FIN 65 Kb09
Aars DK 100 Db22
Aarschot B 124 Ad40
Aarup DK 108 Dc26
Aaşağınova TR 185 Ec80
Ääsmäe EST 98 Kb43
Aatsinki FIN 69 Kd17
Aavajärvi S 73 Jb21
Aavasaksa FIN 73 Jb19
Åbacka S 72 Gb23
Abaclia MD 177 Fd60
Abad E 36 Bb53
Abades E 46 Da63
Abadía E 45 Ca64
Abadín E 36 Bc54
Abádszalók H 146 Jc53
A Baiuca E 36 Ad54
Abalar TR 185 Eb76
Abaliget H 152 Hb57
A Baña E 36 Ad55
Abancourt F 23 Gc34
Abanilla E 55 Fa72
Abano Terme I 150 Dd60
Abant TR 187 Ha79
Abarán E 55 Ed72
Abárzuza E 39 Ec57
Abaucourt-Hautecourt F 24 Jb35
Abaújszántó H 147 Jd50
Abaurrea Alta E 39 Fa56
Abaurrea Baja E 39 Fa56
Abbadia San Salvatore I 156 Dd68
Abbasanta I 169 Ca76
Abbas Combe GB 19 Ec29
Abbekås S 110 Fa57
Abberley GB 15 Ec25
Abbeville F 23 Gc33
Abbey IRL 12 Bd22
Abbey Dore GB 15 Eb26
Abbeydorney IRL 12 Bb24
Abbeyfeale IRL 12 Bb24
Abbeyleix IRL 13 Cb22
Abbiategrasso I 148 Cb59
Abborrberg S 71 Ga23
Abborrberget S 95 Gb43
Abborrtjärn S 80 Hb27
Abborrträsk S 72 Ha23
Abborrträsk S 80 Ha26
Abbots Bromley GB 16 Ed23
Abbotsbury GB 19 Eb31
Abbots Leigh GB 19 Eb28
Abbots Ripton GB 20 Fc25
Abbytown GB 11 Eb17
Abda H 145 Gd52
Abdürrahim TR 185 Ea78
Abdurrahmanlar TR 199 Gd91
Abejar E 47 Ea60
Abejuela E 54 Fa66
Abejuela E 61 Ec74
Åbel N 93 Da46
Abela P 50 Ab71
Ābeļi LV 106 La52
Abellá E 36 Ba55
Abella de la Conca E 48 Gb59
Abelsborg N 65 Kb06
Abelvær N 78 Eb25
Abenberg D 134 Dc47
Abengibre E 54 Ed68
Abenójar E 52 Da69
Abensberg D 135 Ea48
Aber GB 15 Dd22
Aberaeron GB 15 Dd25
Aberaman GB 19 Ea27
Aberangell GB 15 Ea24
Abercarn GB 19 Eb27
Aberchirder GB 7 Ec08
Abercraf GB 19 Ea27
Aberdare GB 19 Ea27
Aberdaron GB 14 Dc23
Aberdeen GB 7 Ed09
Aberdovey GB 15 Dd24
Abereiddy GB 14 Db26
Aberfeldy GB 7 Ea11
Aberford GB 16 Fa20
Aberfoyle GB 7 Dd12
Abergavenny GB 19 Eb27
Abergele GB 15 Ea22
Åberget S 72 Ha21
Abergwesyn GB 15 Ea25
Abergwynfi GB 19 Ea27
Abergynolwyn GB 15 Dd24
Aberlady GB 11 Ec13
Aberlour GB 7 Eb08
Abermule GB 15 Eb24
Abernyte GB 7 Eb11
Aberporth GB 14 Dc25
Abersoch GB 14 Dc23
Abertamy CZ 135 Ec43
Abertillery GB 19 Eb27
Abertura E 51 Ca68
Aberystwyth GB 15 Dd25
Abetone I 155 Db64
Abganerovo RUS 203 Fd14
Abia de la Obispalía E 53 Eb66
Abiego E 48 Fc59
Abild DK 108 Da28
Abild S 102 Ed51
Abildå DK 108 Da24
Abingdon GB 20 Fa27
Abington GB 10 Ea14
Abington GB 20 Fd26
Abington IRL 12 Bd23
Abisko S 67 Gd14
Abizanda E 48 Fd59
Abja-Paluoja EST 106 Kd46
Abla E 61 Dd75
Ablanica BG 184 Cd75
Ablis F 29 Gc38
Ablitas E 47 Ed59
Abmelaseter N 62 Ha10
Åbo FIN 97 Jb39
Åbo S 78 Ed29
Åbo S 87 Ga35
Abod H 138 Jc49
Abondance F 35 Kb45
Abony H 146 Jb54
Aborim P 44 Ad59
Åbosjö S 80 Gc29
Aboyne GB 7 Ec09
Abram RO 171 Cc56
Abramów PL 131 Ka39
Abrămuț RO 170 Cb56
Abrantes P 50 Ad66
Abraure S 72 Gd21
Abreiro P 45 Bc60
Abrene RUS 107 Ld49
Abrene = Pytalovo RUS 202 Ea10
Abreschviller F 25 Kb37
Abridge GB 20 Fd27
Abriès F 36 Kb49
Abrud RO 171 Cd59
Abruka EST 105 Jc47
Abrupe LV 106 La49
Absberg D 134 Dc47
Absdorf A 144 Ga50
Abstatt D 134 Cd47
Abtei A 144 Fb56
Abtei I 143 Ea56
Abtenau A 143 Ed53
Abtsgmünd D 134 Da48
Abtsteinach D 134 Cc46
Abula EST 105 Jc46
Abusland N 92 Cd46
Åby N 93 Dc44
Åby S 103 Ga46
Åby S 103 Fc47
Åby S 103 Fc51
Åbyen DK 100 Dc19
Åbyggeby S 95 Gb39
Åbyn S 73 Hc24
Åbyskov DK 109 Dd27
Åbytorp S 95 Fc44
A Cañiza E 36 Ba57
Acâş RO 171 Cc55
Acătari RO 171 Dc59
Acate I 167 Fb87
Accadia I 161 Fd74
Acceglio I 148 Bb62
Accettura I 162 Gb76
Acciarella I 160 Eb73
Acciaroli I 161 Fc77
Accrington GB 15 Ec20
Accumoli I 156 Ec69
Acebuche E 59 Bc75
Acedera E 51 Cb68
Acedo E 39 Eb57
Acehuche E 51 Bd66
Acered E 47 Ed62
Acerenza I 162 Gb75
Acerno I 161 Fc75
Acerra I 161 Fb74
Aceuchal E 51 Bd70
Ach A 143 Ec51
Achahoish GB 6 Db13
Achanalt GB 4 Dd07
Achel B 124 Ba39
Acheleia CY 206 Hd98
Achenkirch A 143 Ea53
Achères F 29 Ha42
Achern D 133 Ca48
Achill Sound IRL 8 Bb18
Achiltibuie GB 4 Dc06
Achim D 118 Cd34
Achleck GB 6 Da11
Achmore GB 4 Da05
Achmore GB 4 Db08
Achna CY 206 Jc97
Achnacroish GB 6 Db11
Achnasheen GB 4 Dc07
Achosnich GB 6 Da10
Achranich GB 6 Db11
Achslach D 135 Ec48
Achstetten D 142 Da50
Achvaich GB 5 Ea06
Aci Castello I 167 Fd86
Aci Catena I 167 Fd85
Acıdere TR 198 Fc88
Acıdere TR 198 Fd88
Acıköy TR 193 Ha83
Acıpayam TR 198 Fd89
Acireale I 167 Fd85
Aci Trezza I 167 Fd85
Aciveiro E 36 Ba56
Acklinga S 102 Fa47
Acksi S 87 Fb38
Aclare IRL 8 Bd18
Acle GB 17 Gb24
A Coruña E 36 Ba54
Acquacadda I 169 Bd80
Acquacalda I 167 Fc82
Acqua Doria F 154 Ca71
Acquaformosa I 164 Gb78
Acquafredda I 161 Ga77
Acqualagna I 156 Eb66
Acquanegra sul Chiese I 149 Db60
Acquapendente I 156 Dd68
Acquaro I 164 Gb82
Acquasanta Terme I 156 Ed68
Acquasparta I 156 Eb69
Acquaviva delle Fonti I 162 Gd75
Acquaviva Picena I 157 Fa68
Acquedolci I 167 Fb84
Acqui Terme I 148 Ca62
Acri I 164 Gc79
Ács H 145 Ha52
Acsa H 146 Hd52
Ácsteszér H 145 Hb53
Acton GB 20 Fc28
Acy-en-Multien F 23 Ha36
Ada SRB 153 Jb58
Adács H 146 Ja52
Adahuesca E 48 Fc59
Adak S 72 Gd23
Adakasım TR 193 Hb84
Adakavas LT 113 Jd56
Adaköy TR 197 Fa91
Ådalsbruk N 86 Eb38
Ådals-Liden S 79 Gb30
Adámas GR 195 Cd91
Adamclisi RO 181 Fb67
Adámi GR 195 Ca88
Adamów PL 130 Hd40
Adamów PL 131 Ka38
Adamowo PL 122 Hd35
Ādams LV 107 Lb48
Adamsfjord N 64 Jd06
Adămuş RO 175 Db60
Adamuz E 60 Cd72
Adâncata RO 172 Ec55
Adâncata RO 176 Eb65
Ádánd H 145 Hb55
Adanero E 46 Da62
Adapazarı = Sakarya TR 187 Gc78
Adare IRL 12 Bc23
Adaševci SRB 153 Hd61
Adatepe TR 187 Gc78
Adatepe TR 191 Eb82
Adaúfe P 44 Ad59
Adavere EST 98 Kd44
Ādaži LV 106 Kb50
Ādaži LV 106 Kc50
Adderley GB 15 Ec23
Addit DK 108 Db24
Addolorata I 166 Ea85
Adelán E 36 Bc53
Adelboden CH 141 Bd55
Adelebsen D 126 Da39
Adelfia I 162 Gd74
Adelheidsdorf D 126 Db36
Adelmannsfelden D 134 Da48
Adelöv S 103 Fc48
Adelschlag D 135 Dd48
Adelsdorf D 134 Dc45
Adelsheim D 134 Cd46
Adelshofen D 134 Db46
Adelsö S 96 Gc43
Adelsried D 134 Dc49
Ademuz E 54 Ed66
Adenau D 125 Bd42
Adenbüttel D 126 Dc36
Adendorf D 118 Dc33
Adendro GR 183 Ca77
Adenstedt D 126 Db38
Adıgüzeller TR 192 Fd87
Adil TR 191 Ed84
Adinkerke B 21 Gd29
Adjud RO 176 Ed61
Ådland N 84 Cb39
Adlešiči SLO 151 Fd60
Adlington GB 16 Ed22
Adliswil CH 141 Cb53
Adliye TR 186 Fd80
Adliye TR 187 Gc79
Adlkofen D 135 Eb49
Admont A 144 Fb53
Ådneram N 92 Cc44
Adobes E 47 Ed64
Adolfsberg S 95 Fd44
Adolfsström S 71 Ga20
Adony H 146 Hc54
Adorf D 126 Cd40
Adorf D 135 Eb43
Adra E 61 Dd76
Adradas E 47 Eb61
Adraku EST 99 Lb43
Adrall E 40 Gc58
Adrano I 167 Fc85
Adria I 150 Ea61
Adriani GR 184 Da76
Adriers F 33 Ga45
Adrigole IRL 12 Ba26
Adsbøl DK 108 Db28
Aduard NL 117 Bd33
Adunaţi RO 176 Ea63
Adunaţii-Copăceni RO 180 Ea67
Adutiškis LT 115 Lc56
Adzes LV 105 Jb51
Ādžūni LT 114 Kb53
Aegviidu EST 98 Kd42
Ænes N 84 Cb40
A Ermida E 36 Ba56
Ærøskøbing DK 108 Dc28
Aerzen D 126 Da37
Aesch CH 141 Bd52
Aesoo EST 98 Kc45
A Estrada E 36 Ad56
Aetohóri GR 183 Bd76
Aetomilitsa GR 182 Ad78
Aetópetra GR 182 Ac80
Aetorráhi GR 188 Ba86
Aetós GR 183 Bb77
Aetós GR 188 Ad83
Äetsä FIN 89 Jb36
Afándou GR 197 Fa93
Åfarnes N 77 Da32
Afétes GR 189 Ca82
Affalterbach D 134 Cd48
Affing D 134 Dc49
Affoltern CH 141 Cb53
Affoux F 34 Ja46
Affric Lodge GB 6 Dc08
Afídnes GR 189 Cc86
Afionas GR 182 Aa79
Áfitos GR 183 Cb80
Aflenz Kurort A 144 Fd53
A Fonsagrada E 37 Bd55
Åfors S 103 Fd52
A Forxa E 36 Bb58
A Forxa (Punxín) E 36 Ba57
Afragola I 161 Fb75
Afráti GR 189 Cb85
Africo Nuovo I 164 Gb84
Afritz A 144 Fa55
Afşar TR 192 Fb87
Afşar TR 193 Gb87
Afşar TR 193 Gd87
Aftret N 78 Eb30
Afumaţi RO 176 Eb66
Afumaţi RO 179 Cd67
Afyon TR 193 Gc85
Aga N 84 Cc40
Ağaçbeyli TR 192 Ga86
Ağaçhisar TR 193 Ha81
Ağacık TR 187 Gc78
Ağaçlı TR 186 Fc77
Ağaçlıhüyük TR 197 Ed90
Ağaköy TR 185 Ec80
Agalás GR 188 Ac86
Agápi GR 196 Db88
Agapia RO 172 Eb57
Ağapınar TR 193 Gd82
Ågarden N 78 Fa26
Agaryševo RUS 107 Ma50
Agâş RO 172 Eb59
Agatovo BG 180 Dc70
Agay F 43 Kc54
Agazzano I 149 Cc61
Agde F 41 Hc55
Ågedalstø N 92 Cc46
Agen F 40 Ga52
Åger E 48 Ga59
Agerbæk DK 108 Da25
Agerskov DK 108 Da27
Agersø DK 109 Ea27
Agersted DK 101 Dd20
Agger DK 100 Cd21
Aggersund DK 100 Db21
Aggius I 168 Ca74
Aggsbach Dorf A 144 Fd50
Aggsbach Markt A 144 Fd50
Aggtelek H 138 Jb49
Aghadoon IRL 8 Bb17
Aghagallon GB 9 Da17
Aghamore IRL 8 Ca19
Aghavannagh IRL 13 Cd23
Aghaville IRL 12 Bb26
Aghireşu RO 171 Cd57
Aghleam IRL 8 Bb18
Agiá GR 188 Ac81
Agiá GR 189 Ca81
Agía Ána GR 189 Ca85
Agía Ánna GR 189 Cb84
Agía Efimía GR 188 Ac84
Agía Efthimía GR 189 Bc84
Agía Eirini CY 206 Ja96
Agía Galíni GR 200 Cd96
Agía Kiriakí GR 188 Ac81
Agía Kyriaki GR 189 Ca83
Agía Marína GR 189 Cc86
Agía Marína GR 195 Cb87
Agía Marína GR 197 Eb90
Agía Marína GR 201 Eb95
Agía Napa CY 206 Jd97
Agía Paraskeví GR 182 Ad79
Agía Paraskeví GR 189 Bc82
Agía Paraskeví GR 191 Ea83
Agía Pelagía GR 195 Bd91
Agía Pelagía GR 200 Da95
Agía Roúmeli GR 200 Cb95
Agíasma GR 184 Dc77
Agiásmata GR 191 Dd85
Agía Sofía GR 189 Bd81
Agía Sofía GR 194 Bc88
Agiasós GR 196 Db90
Agiássos GR 191 Ea83
Agía Thékli GR 188 Ab84
Agía Triáda GR 188 Ad82
Agía Triáda GR 188 Ba86
Agía Triáda GR 188 Bb83
Agía Triada GR 195 Bd87
Agía Triás GR 183 Ca78
Agía Varvára GR 200 Da96
Agigea RO 181 Fc67
Agighiol RO 177 Fd64
Ágii Anárgiri GR 189 Bd81
Ágii Anárgiri GR 194 Bc89
Ágii Apóstoli GR 189 Cc85
Ágii Apóstoli GR 195 Bd91
Ágii Déka GR 200 Da96
Ágii Theódori GR 189 Bc81
Ágii Theódori GR 189 Ca86
Ağılköy TR 199 Gd88
Agimont B 132 Ad43
Aginta RO 175 Dc61
Agiófillo GR 183 Bb79
Ágio Gála GR 191 Dd85
Ágioi Pántes GR 182 Ac80
Agioi Trimithias CY 206 Jb97
Agiókambos GR 189 Ca81
Agiókambos GR 189 Ca83
Agionas stacija LV 107 Lc52
Agionóri GR 195 Bd87
Ágio Pnévma GR 184 Cc76
Agiorgítika GR 194 Bc88
Ágios GR 189 Ca83
Ágios Adrianós GR 195 Bd87
Ágios Ahílios GR 182 Ba77
Agios Amvrosios CY 206 Ja98
Agios Amvrosios CY 206 Jc96
Ágios Andréas GR 194 Bb89
Ágios Andréas GR 195 Bd88
Ágios Antónios GR 183 Cb78
Ágios Athanásios GR 183 Bc77
Ágios Athanássios GR 183 Ca77
AgiosDimitrianos CY 206 Hd97
Ágios Dimítrios GR 183 Bd79
Ágios Dimítrios GR 189 Ca85
Ágios Dimítrios GR 190 Cd86
Ágios Dimítrios GR 195 Bd90
Ágios Efstrátios GR 190 Db82
Agios Epifanios CY 206 Jb97
Agios Epiktitos CY 206 Jb96
Ágios Fokás GR 197 Ec91
Ágios Geórgios GR 182 Ab80
Ágios Geórgios GR 183 Bd78
Ágios Geórgios GR 188 Bb83
Ágios Geórgios GR 189 Ca85
Ágios Germanós GR 182 Ba76
Ágios Harálambos GR 184 Dc78
Ágios Ilías GR 188 Ad86
Ágios Ioánnis GR 189 Bd83
Ágios Ioánnis GR 189 Ca82
Ágios Ioánnis GR 189 Ca83
Ágios Ioánnis GR 189 Ca85
Ágios Ioánnis GR 189 Ca85
Ágios Ioánnis GR 194 Bc89
Ágios Ioánnis GR 195 Bd87
Ágios Ioánnis GR 195 Bd90
Ágios Isídoros GR 197 Ed93
Ágios Kiriakí GR 197 Ea88
Ágios Kírikos GR 197 Ea88
Ágios Konstantínos GR 189 Bd84
Ágios Konstantínos GR 197 Eb88
Ágios Lavréntios GR 189 Ca82
Ágios Loukás GR 189 Cc85
Agios Mamas CY 206 Ja97
Ágios Mámas GR 183 Cb79
Ágios Mámas GR 200 Cd95
Ágios Mathéos GR 182 Ab80
Ágios Míronas GR 200 Da96
Ágios Nikitas GR 188 Ac83
Agios Nikolaos CY 206 Ja97
AgiosNikolaos CY 206 Jd97
Ágios Nikólaos GR 184 Cc79
Ágios Nikolaos GR 188 Ac86
Ágios Nikólaos GR 188 Ad83
Ágios Nikólaos GR 188 Ba86
Ágios Nikólaos GR 189 Bc85
Ágios Nikólaos GR 194 Bb90
Ágios Nikólaos GR 195 Bd91
Ágios Nikólaos GR 201 Dc96
Ágios Níkon GR 194 Bb90
Ágios Pandeleímonas GR 183 Bc77
Ágios Panteleímon GR 195 Bd88
Ágios Pávlos GR 183 Cb79
Ágios Pétros GR 183 Ca77
Ágios Pétros GR 194 Bc88
Ágios Pródromos GR 183 Cb78
Agios Sergios CY 206 Jd96
Ágios Stéfanos GR 189 Bc83
Ágios Stéfanos GR 189 Cc86
Ágios Stéfanos GR 197 Eb91
Ágios Stéfanos GR 201 Dc96
Agios Symeon CY 206 Jd95
Agios Theodoros CY 206 Jd96
Ágios Thomás GR 189 Cb85
Agios Vasileios CY 206 Jb96
Ágios Vassílios GR 183 Cb78
Ágios Vassílios GR 195 Bd87
Ágios Vassílios GR 195 Bd89
Ágios Vlásios GR 189 Bd84
Agira I 167 Fb85
Agivey GB 9 Cd15
Ağızkara TR 193 Gc86
Agkleisides CY 206 Jc97
Ağla TR 198 Fc90
Ağlarca TR 193 Gd84
Ağlaşan TR 186 Fd80
Aglasterhausen D 134 Cc46
Ağlasun TR 199 Gc89
Agle N 78 Ed27
Aglen BG 179 Da70
Aglen N 78 Eb26
Ağli TR 205 Fa20
Agliano Terme I 148 Ca61
Agliè I 148 Bd59
Aglientu I 168 Cb73
Aglona LV 107 Lc52
Agna I 150 Ea61
Agnano Terme I 161 Fa75
Agnanterí GR 189 Bd81
Agnanteró GR 188 Bb81
Agnánti GR 189 Cb84
Agnantiá GR 183 Bb80
Agnesberg S 102 Ec48
Agno CH 148 Cb57
Agnone I 161 Fb72
Agnone Bagni I 167 Fd86
Agoitz E 39 Ed57
Agónas GR 188 Ac84
Agon-Coutainville F 22 Ed36
Agordo I 150 Ea57
Agost E 55 Fb71
Ågotnes N 84 Bd39
Ágra GR 191 Dd83
Agrafa GR 188 Bb82
Agramón E 53 Ec71
Agramunt E 48 Gb60
A Graña E 36 Ba57
Agrapidiá GR 189 Bc82
Agrapidohóri GR 188 Ba86
Ágras GR 183 Bc77
Agrate Conturbia I 148 Cb58
Ágreda E 47 Ec60
Agreliá GR 183 Bc80
Agriá GR 189 Ca82
Agriani GR 184 Cd76
Agriáni GR 194 Bc89
Agrigent = Agrigento (Sizilien) I 166 Ed86
Agrigento I 166 Ed86
Agrij RO 171 Cd57
Agriliá Kiatígou GR 191 Eb84
Agrínio GR 188 Ba84
Agriovótano GR 189 Cb83
Agrişu Mare RO 170 Ca59
Agrochão P 45 Bc59
Agropoli I 161 Fc76
Ågskardet N 70 Fa19
Ag. Theódori GR 183 Bb79
Aguadulce E 60 Cc74
Aguadulce E 61 Ea76
Aguafría E 59 Bc72
Agualada E 36 Ad54
Agua Longa P 44 Ad60
A Guarda E 36 Ac58
Aguarón E 47 Ed61
Aguas E 48 Fc59
Aguasantas E 36 Ad57
Águas de Moura P 50 Ab69
Águas dos Fusos P 58 Ad74
Águas Frias P 44 Bb59
Aguas Nuevas E 53 Ec69
Aguatón E 47 Fa64
Aguaviva E 48 Fc63
Aguaviva de la Vega E 47 Eb62
A Gudiña E 36 Bc58
Agudo E 52 Cd69
Águeda P 44 Ad63
Agüera E 38 Dd55
Agüera E 38 Dd56
Agüerina E 37 Ca55
Agüero E 39 Fb58
Aguessac F 41 Hb52
Agugliano I 156 Ed66
Aguiar P 50 Ad70
Aguiar da Beira P 44 Bb62
Aguiar de Sousa P 44 Ad61
Aguilafuente E 46 Db62
Aguilar de Campoo E 38 Db56
Aguilar de Campos E 46 Cd59
Aguilar de Codés E 39 Eb57
Aguilar de la Frontera E 60 Cd74
Aguilar del Alfambra E 48 Fb64
Aguilar del Río Alhama E 47 Ec59
Águilas E 61 Ec74
Aguilón E 47 Fa62
Aguiño E 36 Ac56
Agunnaryd S 103 Fb52
Agusalu EST 99 Lc42
Agustín E 36 Bc55
Ağva TR 187 Gb77
Aha S 72 Gc23
Ahakista IRL 12 Ba26
Aham D 135 Eb49
Aharávi GR 182 Ab79
Aharnés GR 189 Cb86
Ahaste EST 98 Kb45
Ahat TR 192 Ga85
Ahatlar TR 192 Fa87
Ahatlı TR 198 Ga92
Ahaus D 125 Ca37
Ahausen D 118 Da34
Åheim N 84 Cb34
Aheloj BG 181 Fa72
Ahievren TR 185 Ec78
Ahigal E 45 Ca65
Ahigal de Villarino E 45 Ca61
Ahillio GR 189 Ca83
Ahillones E 51 Ca71
Ahimehmet TR 186 Fa76
Ahinós GR 184 Cc77
Ahinós GR 189 Bd83
Ahırhisar TR 193 Gb85
Ahırözü TR 193 Hb82
Ahja EST 99 Lb45
Ahjärvi FIN 91 Ld34
Ahjola FIN 75 La22
Ähkäänniemi FIN 91 Ld33
Ahkiolahti FIN 82 Kd29
Ahládi GR 189 Cb83
Ahladiá GR 184 Cd75
Ahladohóri GR 184 Cc76
Ahladókambos GR 194 Bc88
Ahladókastro GR 188 Bb84
Ahlainen FIN 89 Ja35
Ahlajärvi FIN 89 Jd37
Ahlatlı TR 185 Ed74
Ahlbeck D 120 Fb32
Ahlden D 118 Da35
Ahlen D 125 Cb38
Ahlerstedt D 118 Da33
Ahli EST 98 Ka44
Ahmas FIN 74 Kb24
Ahmediye TR 187 Gc79
Ahmetbey TR 185 Ed76
Ahmetbey TR 186 Fc80
Ahmetbeyler TR 191 Ec83
Ahmetbeyli TR 191 Ec87
Ahmetçe TR 185 Ed75
Ahmetçe TR 191 Ea82
Ahmet Gazi Camii (Eskiçine) TR 197 Fa89
Ahmetler TR 185 Ed74
Ahmetler TR 191 Ea82
Ahmetler TR 192 Fc85
Ahmetler TR 199 Hb91
Ahmetli TR 191 Ec87
Ahmetli TR 192 Fa86
Ahmetli TR 192 Fc84
Ahmetoğlu TR 193 Gb82
Ahmoo FIN 90 Ka38
Ahmovaara FIN 83 Lc29
Ahnatal D 126 Da40
Ahnsbeck D 126 Dc36
Aho FIN 75 Kc19
Ahoghill GB 9 Cd16
Ahoinen FIN 90 Ka37
Ahokylä FIN 82 Kc27
Ahola FIN 74 La18
Ahola FIN 75 Kd19
Ahola FIN 75 La20
Ahola FIN 81 Jc30
Ahola FIN 82 Ka27
Ahola FIN 83 Ld30
Aholanvaara FIN 74 Kd18
Aholfing D 135 Eb48
Aholming D 135 Ec49
Ahonkylä FIN 81 Jb31
Ahonperä FIN 81 Jd26
Ahorn D 134 Db46
Ahorn D 134 Dc44
Aho-Vastinki FIN 82 Ka31
Ahrbergen D 133 Cb43
Ahrbrück D 125 Bd42
Ahrensbök D 119 Dd31
Ahrensburg D 118 Dc32
Ahrensdorf D 128 Fb37
Ahrensfelde-Blumberg D 128 Fa36
Ahrenshagen D 119 Ec30
Ahrenshoop D 119 Ec30
Ahrweiler, Bad Neuenahr- D 125 Bd42
Ähtäri FIN 89 Jd32
Ähtärinranta FIN 81 Jd31
Ähtävä FIN 81 Jb29
Ahtiala FIN 97 Jd39
Ahtme EST 99 Lb42
Ahtopol BG 186 Fa74
Ahtropovo RUS 203 Fb08
Ahtubinsk RUS 203 Ga14
Ahujärvi FIN 69 Kb11
Ahun F 33 Gd46
Ahunapalu EST 99 Lc45
Åhus S 111 Fb55
Ahvela FIN 75 La23
Ahveninen FIN 82 Kc30
Ahveninen FIN 83 Ld29
Ahveninen FIN 90 Ka34
Ahvenisto FIN 90 Kd35
Ahvenniemi FIN 75 Lb20
Ahvensaari FIN 97 Ja40
Ahvensalmi FIN 91 Lb32
Ahvenselkä FIN 69 Kc17
Ahvio FIN 90 La38
Ahvionsaari FIN 91 Lc33
Aia E 39 Ec55
Aia E 39 Ec56
Aialvir E 46 Dc64
Aibaladejo del Cuende E 53 Eb66
Aibar E 39 Ed57
Aich A 144 Fa53
Aicha D 135 Ed49
Aichach D 135 Dd49
Aichhalden D 141 Cb50
Aichstetten D 142 Da51
Aichtal D 134 Cd49
Aiddejavrre fjellstue N 68 Ja12
Aidenbach D 135 Ed49
Aidhausen D 134 Db44
Aidínio GR 189 Bd82
Aidone I 167 Fb86
Aidonohóri GR 184 Cc77
Aidu EST 98 La44
Aiello Calabro I 164 Gb80
Aielo de Malferit E 55 Fb70
Aigen A 144 Fb53
Aigen im Mühlkreis A 136 Fa49
Aigialousa CY 206 Jd95
Aigle CH 141 Bb56
Aiglsbach D 135 Ea49
Aignan F 40 Fd54
Aignay-le-Duc F 30 Ja40
Aigre F 32 Fc47
Aigrefeuille-d'Aunis F 32 Fa46
Aigrefeuille-sur-Maine F 28 Fa43
Aiguafreda E 49 Ha60
Aiguebelle F 35 Ka47
Aigueblanche F 35 Ka47
Aiguefonde F 41 Ha54
Aigueperse F 34 Hb46
Aigues-Mortes F 42 Ja54
Aigues-Vives F 41 Hb55
Aiguilles F 35 Kb49
Aiguillon F 40 Fd52
Aiguines F 42 Ka53
Aigurande F 33 Gc45
Äijäjoki FIN 68 Ja14
Äijälä FIN 90 Kc32
Aijala FIN 97 Jd40
Äijänneva FIN 89 Jc33
Äijävaara S 73 Hd18
Ailefroide F 35 Ka49
Aillant-sur-Tholon F 30 Hb40
Aillas F 32 Fc51
Aillevillers-et-Lyaumont F 31 Jd39
Aillianville F 31 Jc38
Aillon-le-Jeune F 35 Jd47
Ailly-le-Haut-Clocher F 23 Gc33
Ailly-sur-Noye F 23 Gd34
Ailt an Chorráin IRL 8 Ca15
Aimargues F 42 Ja54
Aime F 35 Kb47
Ainali FIN 81 Jc27
Ainali FIN 82 Ka26
Ainay-le-Château F 29 Ha44
Ainaži LV 106 Kb47
Ainet A 143 Ec55
Ainhoa F 39 Ed55
Ainijärvi FIN 69 Kd14
Ainring D 143 Ec52
Ainsa E 40 Fd58
Ainzón E 47 Ed60
Airaines F 23 Gc33
Airaksela FIN 82 Kd31
Airasca I 148 Bc61
Aird GB 6 Db12
Aird Mhór IRL 13 Ca26

Aird of Sleat – Almaceda

Aird of Sleat GB 6 Db09
Airdrie GB 10 Ea13
Airel F 22 Fa36
Airénai LT 114 Kd57
Aire-sur-l'Adour F 40 Fc54
Aire-sur-la-Lys F 23 Gd31
Airisto FIN 97 Jb40
Airola I 161 Fb74
Airolo CH 141 Cb56
Airvault F 28 Fc43
Aisa E 39 Fb57
Aisey-sur-Seine F 30 Ja40
Aislingen D 134 Db49
Aissey F 31 Jd41
Aisy-sur-Armançon F 30 Hd40
Aita Mare RO 176 Ea61
Aiterhofen D 135 Ec48
Aith GB 5 Ec02
Aith GB 5 Fa04
Aitolahti FIN 89 Jd35
Aiton RO 171 Da58
Aitona E 48 Ga61
Aitoniemi FIN 89 Jd35
Aitoo FIN 90 Ka36
Aitrach D 142 Da51
Aitrang D 142 Db52
Aittaniemi FIN 75 Kc19
Aittijoki FIN 64 Jc08
Aittojärvi FIN 74 Kb22
Aittojärvi FIN 82 Kc28
Aittokoski FIN 82 Kd27
Aittokylä FIN 75 Kd23
Aittolahti FIN 91 Ld32
Aittoperä FIN 82 Ka27
Aittovaara FIN 75 Lb23
Aiud RO 171 Da59
Äivo FIN 81 Jb28
Aix-en-Othe F 30 Hc39
Aix-en-Provence F 42 Jc54
Aixe-sur-Vienne F 33 Gb47
Aix-les-Bains F 35 Jd47
Aizdzire LV 105 Jd51
Aizenay F 28 Ed44
Aizkalne LV 107 Lc52
Aizkraukle LV 106 Kd51
Aizkuja LV 107 Lb50
Aizpūre LV 107 Ma51
Aizpute LV 105 Jb52
Aizviki LV 113 Jb53
Ajaccio F 154 Ca71
Ajain F 33 Gd45
Ajaur S 80 Ha25
Ajaureforsen S 71 Fd23
Ajdovščina SLO 151 Fa58
Ajka H 145 Ha54
Ajo E 38 Dc54
Ajofrín E 52 Db66
Ajos FIN 74 Jc21
Ajševica SLO 151 Fa58
Ajtos BG 181 Ed72
Akācijas LV 106 Ka52
Akácliget H 152 Ha58
Akademija LV 114 Kb56
Akaki CY 206 Jb97
Akalan TR 192 Fd81
Akalan TR 198 Fd89
Akarca TR 192 Ga86
Åkarp S 110 Ed56
Äkäsjokisuu FIN 68 Jb16
Äkäslompolo FIN 68 Jb15
Akasztó H 146 Hd55
Akbaş TR 191 Ed82
Akbaş TR 198 Fd88
Akbaşlar TR 192 Ga81
Akbük TR 197 Ec89
Akburun TR 199 Hb88
Akçaabat TR 205 Fd19
Akçaalan TR 187 Gd79
Akçaalan TR 187 Ha79
Akçaalan TR 192 Fa85
Akçaanlan TR 192 Fb85
Akçabelen TR 199 Ha89
Akçadere TR 193 Gb85
Akçakavak TR 198 Fb91
Akçakaya TR 192 Fa82
Akçakese TR 186 Ga77
Akçakısrak TR 192 Fa83
Akçaköy TR 193 Gb84
Akçaköy TR 198 Ga88
Akçakoyun TR 191 Ec81
Akcalar TR 199 Hb89
Akçaören TR 199 Gb89
Akçaova TR 187 Gb78
Akçaova TR 197 Fa89
Akçapınar TR 187 Gc80
Akçapınar TR 191 Ea81
Akçapınar TR 192 Fd81
Akçapınar TR 198 Fb90
Akçaşehir TR 192 Ga83
Akçat TR 186 Ga79
Akçay TR 191 Eb82
Akçay TR 198 Ga92
Akcın TR 193 Gc87
Akcjabrski BY 202 Eb13
Akçokoca TR 187 Ha77
Akdam TR 199 Hb92
Akdera TR 199 Gb92
Akdere TR 192 Fd87
Akdoğan = Lysi CY 206 Jc97
Aken D 127 Eb38
Aken = Aachen D 125 Bb41
Åker S 95 Gb44
Åker S 103 Fb50
Åkerbäck S 80 Hb27
Åkerbränna S 79 Gb28
Åkerby S 73 Hc21
Åkerby S 96 Gc41
Åkerholmen S 73 Hc21
Åkermark S 73 Hc22
Åkernes N 92 Cd45
Åkerö S 88 Gc33
Åkerøya N 70 Ed21
Åkersberga S 96 Gd43
Åkersjön S 79 Fb29
Akersloot NL 116 Ba35
Åkers styckebruk S 95 Gb44
Åkervika N 71 Fb22
Akhan TR 198 Fd88
Akharım TR 193 Gb85
Akhisar TR 192 Fa84
Akin TR 193 Gc83
Akın TR 193 Gc86
Akkala FIN 90 La34
Akkan S 71 Ga23
Akkaor TR 198 Fd92
Akkarfjord N 63 Hd06
Akkarfjord N 63 Hd05
Akkarvik N 62 Ha08
Akkavare S 67 Ha17
Akkavare S 72 Ha22
Akkaya TR 192 Fd84
Akkaya TR 193 Gc82
Akkaya TR 198 Fb89
Akkaya TR 198 Fd91
Akkaya TR 199 Gb89
Akkeçili TR 193 Gd87
Akkeçili TR 199 Gb88
Akkent TR 192 Fd87
Akköy TR 191 Ea81
Akköy TR 192 Fd87
Akköy TR 197 Ec89
Akkrum NL 117 Bc33
Akkum TR 187 Gc77
Akkuş TR 205 Fc20
Akland N 93 Db45
Aklar TR 198 Fd92
Akmeņdziras LV 105 Jb49
Akmenė LT 113 Jd53
Akmeniai LT 114 Kc56
Akmeniši LV 107 Ld52
Akmeņe TR 187 Gb78
Akniste LV 114 La53
Akoluk TR 193 Gc83
Akonpohja FIN 83 Lb29
Akören TR 185 Ed75
Akören TR 186 Fb77
Akören TR 193 Gc85
Akören TR 199 Gb89
Akoúmia GR 200 Cd96
Ákovos GR 194 Bb88
Akpınar TR 186 Fc77
Akpınar TR 187 Ha78
Akpınar TR 191 Eb81
Akpınar TR 193 Gc82
Akpınar TR 198 Fd90
Åkra N 92 Bd43
Åkra N 92 Cb41
Åkrahamn N 92 Bd42
Akran N 78 Ec28
Akranes IS 2 Ac04
Akráta GR 189 Bc85
Akréfnio GR 189 Ca85
Åkrestrømmen N 86 Eb35
Akri GR 183 Bc79
Akriní GR 183 Bc78
Akrítas GR 183 Bb77
Akritohóri GR 183 Cb76
Akrogiáli GR 184 Cc77
Akrolímni GR 183 Bd77
Akropótamos GR 184 Cd77
Akrotiri CY 206 Ja98
Akrotíri GR 196 Db92
Akrounta CY 206 Jb98
Akşahap TR 199 Hb90
Aksaj RUS 205 Fc15
Aksakal TR 186 Fa80
Aksaklar TR 192 Fd84
Aksakovo BG 181 Fa70
Akşar TR 198 Fd90
Akşar TR 205 Ga19
Aksaz TR 185 Ec79
Aksaz TR 192 Fc84
Aksaz TR 192 Fd86
Aksdal N 92 Ca42
Akşehir TR 193 Ha86
Akseki TR 198 Fb88
Akseki TR 199 Hb90
Akselendi TR 192 Fa85
Akset N 77 Dc29
Äksi EST 99 Lb45
Aksicim TR 186 Fa76
Aksla N 84 Cc35
Akstinai LT 114 Ka56
Aksu TR 186 Fd80
Aksu TR 193 Ha85
Aksu TR 193 Hc18
Aksu TR 199 Gd88
Aksu TR 199 Gd91
Aksubaevo RUS 203 Ga09
Aktarsk RUS 203 Fd12
Aktaş TR 192 Fc81
Aktaş TR 193 Ha83
Aktio GR 188 Ad82
Aktse S 67 Gc17
Akujärvi FIN 69 Kb11
Åkullsjön S 80 Hc27
Akureyri IS 2 Ba04
Åkvåg N 93 Db45
Akyaka TR 198 Fb90
Akyar TR 192 Fa82
Akyar TR 199 Gb90
Akyayla TR 192 Fc82
Akyazı TR 187 Gc79
Akyazı TR 198 Fd93
Akyer TR 198 Fb89
Akyokuşkavağı TR 187 Gd79
Ål N 85 Db39
Ala EST 106 Kd46
Ala I 149 Dc58
Ala S 87 Gb37
Ala S 104 Ha50
Aláattin TR 198 Fd89
Alabey TR 185 Ec78
Alaca TR 205 Fb20
Alacaatlı TR 192 Fa83
Alacaklar TR 191 Ec83
Alaçam TR 192 Fc83
Alaçam TR 205 Fb19
Alacant E 55 Fb71
Alacaoğlu TR 185 Ed76
Alacat TR 192 Fc81
Alaçati TR 191 Ea86
Alacón E 48 Fb62
Alà dei Sardi I 168 Cb75
Ala di Stura I 148 Bc59
Alaejos E 45 Cc61
Alafors S 102 Ec48
Alagna Valsesia I 148 Bd58
Alagoa P 50 Ba67
Alagón E 47 Fa60
Alagonia GR 194 Bb89
Alahärmä FIN 81 Jb30
Ala-Honkajoki FIN 89 Jb34
Alainenjoki FIN 89 Jc37
Alaior E 57 Ja66
Alájar E 59 Bc72
Alajärvi FIN 75 La23
Alajärvi FIN 81 Jc30
Alajärvi FIN 82 La26
Alajõe EST 99 Lb43
Alajoki FIN 69 Ka12
Alajoki FIN 82 Ka27
Ala-Jokikylä FIN 74 Jd21
Alakylä FIN 82 La28
Ala-Keyritty FIN 82 La28
Ala-Kolkki FIN 89 Jd33
Ala-Kuona FIN 91 Lc32
Alakylä FIN 68 Jc16
Alakylä FIN 74 Ka23
Alakylä FIN 81 Jd28
Alakylä FIN 81 Jb31
Alakylä FIN 89 Ja35
Alakylä FIN 89 Ja33
Alakylä FIN 91 Ld33
Ala-Livo FIN 74 Kb22
Alamaa FIN 82 Kb30
Alameda E 60 Cd74
Alameda de la Sagra E 52 Db66
Alamedilla E 60 Dc74
Alaminnos CY 206 Jc98
Alaminos E 47 Ea63
Alamillo E 52 Cd70
Alan HR 151 Fc61
Alan TR 193 Ha81
Ala-Nampa FIN 74 Ka18
Alanäs S 79 Fd27
Alancık TR 191 Ed81
Åland S 96 Gc42
Alandız TR 192 Fb87
Alandroal P 50 Ba69
Ålandsbro S 88 Gc32
Alange E 51 Bd69
Alaniçi = Pigi CY 206 Jc96
Alaniemi FIN 74 Jd21
Alanis E 59 Ca72
Alanta LT 114 La55
Alanyolu TR 192 Fb85
Alanyurt TR 193 Gd84
Alap H 146 Hc55
Alapää FIN 81 Jd27
Alapitkä FIN 82 Kd29
Alaplı TR 187 Ha77
Alapohja FIN 90 Kb32
Ala-Postojoki FIN 69 Ka15
Alappmo N 67 Gd11
Alaraz E 45 Cc63
Alarcia E 38 Dd58
Alarcón E 53 Eb67
Alar del Rey E 38 Db57
Alaró E 57 Hb67
Alarup AL 182 Ad76
Alaşar TR 192 Fa81
Alaşehir TR 192 Fb86
Ålåsen S 79 Fc28
Ala-Siurua FIN 74 Kb22
Alaskylä FIN 89 Jc34
Alassa CY 206 Ja98
Alassio I 43 La52
Alastaro FIN 89 Jc37
Ala-Sydänmaa FIN 82 Ka27
Alata F 154 Ca70
Ala-Temmes FIN 74 Ka24
Alatepe TR 197 Fa90
Alatornio FIN 74 Jc21
Alatoz E 54 Ed69
Alatri I 160 Ed72
Alatskivi EST 99 Lb44
Alatyr' RUS 203 Fd09
Alava MD 177 Ga60
Alavaara S 73 Hc18
Ala-Valli FIN 89 Jb32
Alavattnet S 79 Fd28
Alaveteli FIN 81 Jc28
Ala-Vieksi FIN 83 Lb25
Alavieska FIN 81 Jd26
Ala-Viirre FIN 81 Jc27
Ala-Vuokki FIN 75 Lb23
Ala-Vuotto FIN 74 Kb23
Alavus FIN 89 Jc32
Alayaka TR 192 Fb83
Alaylı TR 186 Ga80
Alayunt TR 193 Gb83
Alba E 36 Bb54
Alba E 47 Ed64
Alba I 148 Bd61
Alba RO 172 Ec54
Alba Adriatica I 157 Fa68
Albac RO 171 Cc59
Albacete E 53 Ec69
Albacken S 87 Ga32
Alba de Cerrato E 46 Da60
Alba de Tormes E 45 Cc63
Albæk DK 101 Dd19
Albaida E 55 Fb70
Albaina E 38 Ea57
Alba Iulia RO 175 Da60
Albaladejo E 53 Ea70
Albalate de Cinca E 48 Fd60
Albalate del Arzobispo E 48 Fb62
Albalate de las Nogueras E 47 Eb65
Albalate de Zorita E 47 Ea65
Alban F 41 Ha53
Albánchez E 61 Eb75
Albánchez de Úbeda E 60 Dc73
Albaneto I 156 Ec69
Albano di Lucania I 162 Gb76
Albano Laziale I 160 Eb72
Albanyà E 41 Hb58
Albarca E 48 Gb62
Albaredo Arnaboldi I 149 Cc60
Albaredo d'Adige I 149 Dc60
Albarellos E 36 Ba56
Albares E 46 Dd65
Albarracín E 47 Ed64
Albarreal de Tajo E 52 Da66
Albas F 33 Gb51
Albatana E 55 Ed70
Albatàrrec E 48 Ga61
Albatera E 55 Fa72
Albbruck D 141 Ca52
Albelda de Iregua E 39 Eb58
Albena BG 181 Fb70
Albendín E 60 Da73
Albenga I 43 La52
Albeni RO 175 Cd64
Albeniz E 39 Eb56
Albens F 35 Jd46
Albentosa E 54 Fb66
Albercastle GB 14 Db26
Alberese I 155 Dc69
Ålberga S 95 Ga44
Ålberga S 95 Gb45
Albergaria-a-Nova P 44 Ad62
Albergaria-a-Velha P 44 Ad62
Alberguería E 36 Bb58
Alberique E 54 Fb69
Alberite E 39 Eb58
Albernoa P 58 Ad72
Alberobello I 162 Ha75
Alberona I 161 Fd73
Alberoni I 150 Eb60
Albersdorf D 118 Da30
Albert F 23 Ha33
Albertirsa H 146 Ja53
Albertville F 35 Ka47
Albesa E 48 Ga60
Albeşti RO 172 Ed55
Albeşti RO 173 Fb59
Albeşti RO 175 Dc60
Albeşti RO 176 Ed66
Albeşti RO 181 Fc68
Albeştii de Muscel RO 175 Dc63
Albeşti Paleologu RO 176 Eb64
Albi F 41 Gd53
Albias F 40 Gc52
Albidona I 164 Gc78
Albigowa PL 139 Ka44
Albina MD 173 Fc59
Albineţul Vechi MD 173 Fa56
Albinia I 155 Dc69
Albino I 149 Cd58
Albires E 37 Cc58
Albisola Marina I 148 Ca63
Albizzate I 148 Cb58
Alblasserdam NL 124 Ad37
Albocàsser E 54 Fd65
Alboga S 102 Ed48
Alböke S 103 Gb51
Alboloduy E 61 Ea75
Albolote E 60 Db75
Albondón E 60 Dc76
Alborea E 54 Ed68
Albota RO 175 Dc65
Albota de Jos MD 177 Fc61
Albota de Sus MD 177 Fc61
Alboussière F 34 Jb49
Albox E 61 Eb74
Albrechtice nad Vltavou CZ 136 Fb47
Albrighton GB 15 Eb24
Albrighton GB 15 Ec24
Albstadt D 142 Cc50
Albu EST 98 Kd43
Albudeite E 55 Ed72
Albufeira P 58 Ac74
Albujón E 55 Fa73
Albuñol E 60 Dc76
Albuñuelas E 60 Db76
Albuquerque E 51 Bc67
Alby S 87 Fd33
Alby-sur-Chéran F 35 Jd46
Alcácer do Sal P 50 Ac70
Alcáçovas P 50 Ad70
Alcadağ TR 199 Gb93
Alcadozo E 53 Ec70
Alcafozes P 45 Bc65
Alcaine E 48 Fb63
Alcalá de Gurrea E 48 Fb59
Alcalá de Henares E 46 Dd64
Alcalá de la Selva E 54 Fb65
Alcalá de la Vega E 54 Ed66
Alcalá del Júcar E 54 Ed68
Alcalá del Opispo E 48 Fc59
Alcalá de los Gazules E 59 Ca77
Alcalá del Río E 59 Ca73
Alcalá del Valle E 60 Cc75
Alcalà de Xivert E 54 Fd65
Alcalá la Real E 60 Db74
Alcamo I 166 Eb84
Alcamo Marina I 166 Eb84
Alcampell E 48 Fd60
Alcanadre E 39 Ec58
Alcanar E 48 Ga64
Alcanede P 50 Ab66
Alcanena P 50 Ac66
Alcañices E 45 Ca60
Alcañiz E 48 Fc62
Alcántara E 51 Bc66
Alcantarilha P 58 Ac74
Alcantarilla E 53 Ea71
Alcantarilla E 55 Ed72
Alcantud E 47 Eb64
Alcaracejos E 52 Cc71
Alcaraz E 53 Ea70
Alcaria P 44 Bb64
Alcaria Rulva P 58 Ad72
Alcarràs E 48 Ga61
Alcaucín E 60 Da76
Alcaudete E 60 Da73
Alcaudete de la Jara E 52 Cd66
Alcázar del Rey E 47 Ea65
Alcázar de San Juan E 53 Dd68
Alcazarén E 46 Da61
Alceda E 38 Dc55
Alcedar MD 173 Fd55
Alcester GB 20 Ed25
Alčevs'k UA 205 Fb15
Alcı TR 198 Fd90
Alcıtepe TR 185 Ea80
Alcobaça P 50 Ab66
Alcoba de los Montes E 52 Da68
Alcobendas E 46 Dc64
Alcocer E 47 Ea64
Alcochete P 50 Ab68
Alcoentre P 50 Ab67
Alcohujate E 47 Ea64
Alcoi E 55 Fb70
Alcolea E 60 Cd72
Alcolea E 61 Dd75
Alcolea de Calatrava E 52 Da69
Alcolea de Cinca E 48 Fd60
Alcolea del Pinar E 47 Eb62
Alcolea del Río E 59 Ca73
Alcoletge E 48 Ga60
Alcollarín E 51 Cb68
Alconbury GB 20 Fc25
Alconchel E 51 Bb70
Alconera E 51 Bd70
Alcóntar E 61 Ea74
Alcorcón E 46 Db64
Alcorisa E 48 Fc63
Alcoroches E 47 Ec64
Alcossebre E 54 Fd65
Alcoutim P 58 Ba73
Alcover E 48 Gb62
Alcoy E 55 Fb70
Alcsútdoboz H 146 Hc53
Alcubierre E 48 Fb60
Alcubilla de Avellaneda E 46 Dd60
Alcubillas E 53 Dd70
Alcublas E 54 Fb66
Alcúdia E 57 Hc66
Alcudia de Gaudix E 61 Dd75
Alcuéscar E 51 Bd68
Alcuneza E 47 Ea62
Aldborough GB 11 Fa19
Aldbourne GB 20 Ed28
Aldbrough GB 17 Fc20
Aldeacentenera E 51 Cb67
Aldeadávila de la Ribera E 45 Bd61
Aldea del Cano E 51 Bd67
Aldea del Fresno E 46 Db64
Aldea del Obispo E 45 Bd63
Aldea del Rey E 52 Db70
Aldea de Pallarés E 51 Bd71
Aldea de San Esteban E 46 Dd61
Aldeahermosa E 53 Dd71
Aldealafuente E 47 Eb60
Aldealcorvo E 46 Dc62
Aldealengua de Santa Maria E 46 Dc61
Aldeamayor de San Martín E 46 Da61
Aldeanueva de Barbarroya E 52 Cc66
Aldeanueva de la Vera E 45 Cb65
Aldeanueva de San Bartolomé E 52 Cc67
Aldeaquemada E 52 Dc71
Aldea Quintana E 60 Cc73
Aldearrodrigo E 45 Cb62
Aldeaseca de la Frontera E 45 Cc62
Aldeavieja E 46 Da63
Aldebrő H 146 Jb52
Aldeburgh GB 21 Gb26
Aldehuela de la Bóveda E 45 Ca63
Aldehuela de Liestos E 47 Ec62
Aldehuela de Yeltes E 45 Ca63
Aldeia da Mata P 50 Ba67
Aldeia da Ponte P 45 Bc64
Aldeia da Serra P 50 Ba69
Aldeia de João Pires P 45 Bc65
Aldeia dos Palheiros P 58 Ac72
Aldeia Gavinha P 50 Ab67
Aldeia Velha P 50 Ad68
Aldenhoven D 125 Bc41
Aldenueva de Figueroa E 45 Cc62
Aldenueva de la Serrezuela E 46 Dc61
Aldenueva del Codonal E 46 Da62
Aldeonte E 46 Dc61
Alderbury GB 20 Ed29
Aldernäset S 79 Fd27
Aldersbach D 135 Ed49
Aldershot GB 20 Fb29
Aldfield GB 11 Fa19
Aldford GB 15 Eb22
Aldinci MK 178 Bb73
Aldinci SRB 179 Ca68
Aldingen D 142 Cc50
Aldomirovci BG 179 Cb70
Aldover E 48 Ga63
Aldsworth GB 20 Ed27
Aldtsjerk NL 117 Bc33
Aldwincle GB 20 Fc25
Ale S 73 Hd22
Aléa GR 194 Bc87
Åleby S 94 Fa41
Åled S 102 Ed52
Aledo E 55 Ed73
Ålefjær N 92 Cd47
Alegrete P 51 Bb67
Alëhovščina RUS 202 Eb08
Alekovo BG 180 Dd69
Alekovo BG 181 Ed68
Aleksandrevėlė LT 115 Lb53
Aleksandrija BG 181 Fa68
Aleksandrija LT 113 Jb53
Aleksandro Gaj RUS 203 Ga12
Aleksandrov RUS 203 Fa10
Aleksandrovac SRB 178 Bb68
Aleksandrovo BG 180 Dc70
Aleksandrovo BG 181 Ec73
Aleksandrovskaja RUS 99 Mb40
Aleksandrovskoe RUS 205 Ga16
Aleksandrów PL 130 Ja37
Aleksandrów PL 130 Ja40
Aleksandrów PL 131 Ka38
Aleksandrów PL 131 Kb42
Aleksandrów Kujawski PL 121 Hb35
Aleksandrów Łódzki PL 130 Hc38
Aleksa Šantić SRB 153 Hd58
Alekseevka RUS 99 Ld41
Alekseevka RUS 107 Mb46
Alekseevka RUS 203 Fb13
Alekseevka RUS 203 Fc12
Alekseevskaja RUS 203 Fc13
Alekseevskoe RUS 203 Ga09
Aleksin RUS 202 Ed11
Aleksinac SRB 178 Bd68
Aleksinac Bujmir SRB 178 Bd68
Älekulla S 102 Ed50
Ålem S 103 Gb51
Ålen N 86 Eb32
Alençon F 28 Fd38
Alenica SRB 159 Jc64
Alenquer P 50 Ab68
Alentisque E 47 Eb61
Alepohóri GR 195 Bd89
Alepoú GR 182 Ab80
Alera E 39 Ed58
Alerheim D 134 Dd48
Aléria F 154 Cc70
Alès F 41 Hd52
Ales I 169 Ca78
Alesanco E 38 Ea58
Aleşd RO 170 Cb57
Alesjaure sameviste S 67 Gc14
Ale-Skövde S 102 Ec48
Alessandria I 148 Cb61
Alessandria del Carretto I 164 Gc78
Alessandria della Rocca I 166 Ec85
Alessano I 165 Hc78
Ålesund N 76 Cc32
Alet-les-Bains F 41 Gd56
Alevráda GR 188 Ba83
Alexain F 28 Fb39
Alexándreni MD 173 Fa54
Alexándreni MD 173 Fb55
Alexandreşti MD 173 Fa55
Alexándria GR 183 Bd78
Alexandria RO 180 Dd67
Alexandroúpoli GR 185 Dd78
Alexandru Ioan Cuza MD 177 Fc63
Alexandru I.Cuza RO 172 Ed57
Alexandru Odobescu RO 181 Ed67
Alexandru Vlahuţă RO 177 Fa60
Alexeevca MD 173 Fb57
Alexeevca MD 173 Fc55
Alexeni RO 176 Ec65
Alfacar E 60 Dc75
Alfajarín E 48 Fb61
Alfambra E 47 Fa64
Alfambra P 58 Ab73
Alfamén E 47 Fa61
Alfândega da Fé P 45 Bc61
Alfano I 161 Fd77
Alfara de Carles E 48 Fd63
Alfarela de Jales P 44 Bb60
Alfarelos P 44 Ac64
Alfarim P 50 Aa69
Alfarnate E 60 Da75
Alfaro E 47 Ec59
Alfarràs E 48 Ga60
Alfatar BG 181 Ed68
Alfaz del Pi E 55 Fc70
Alfdorf D 134 Da48
Alfedena I 161 Fa72
Alfeld D 126 Db38
Alfeld D 135 Ea46
Alfhausen D 117 Cb36
Alfonsine I 150 Ea63
Alford GB 7 Ec09
Alford GB 17 Fd22
Alforja E 48 Gb62
Ålfoten N 84 Cb34
Alfreton GB 16 Fa23
Alfstedt D 118 Da32
Alfta S 87 Ga37
Älga S 94 Ec42
Algaida E 57 Hb67
Algajola F 154 Ca68
Algallarín E 60 Cd72
Algamitas E 60 Cc75
Älganå S 94 Ec44
Algar E 59 Ca76
Älgarås S 95 Fb45
Älgård N 92 Ca44
Älgård N 92 Cb46
Algarinejo E 60 Da74
Algarrobo E 60 Da76
Algatocin E 59 Cb76
Algeciras E 59 Cb78
Algemesí E 54 Fb68
Älgered S 87 Gb34
Algermissen D 126 Db37
Algerri E 48 Ga60
Algestrup DK 109 Eb27
Algete E 46 Dc64
Alghero I 168 Bd75
Älghult S 103 Fd51
Algimia de Almonacid E 54 Fb66
Alginet E 54 Fb68
Algodonales E 59 Cb75
Algodor P 58 Ad72
Algora E 47 Ea63
Algoso P 45 Bd60
Algoz P 58 Ac74
Älgsjö S 80 Gc27
Alguaire E 48 Ga60
Alguazas E 55 Ed72
Algueña E 55 Fa71
Algutsboda S 103 Fd52
Algutsrum S 103 Gb52
Algyő H 146 Jb56
Alhabia E 61 Ea75
Alhadas P 44 Ac64
Alhama de Almería E 61 Ea76
Alhama de Aragón E 47 Ec62
Alhama de Granada E 60 Da75
Alhama de Murcia E 55 Ed73
Alhambra E 53 Dd69
Alhamn S 73 Hd23
Alharilla E 52 Da72
Alhatlı TR 191 Ed83
Alhaurín de la Torre E 60 Cd76
Alhaurín el Grande E 60 Cd76
Alhojärvi FIN 90 Kb34
Alholm FIN 89 Ja32
Alhóndiga E 47 Ea64
Ålhus N 84 Cc35
Ali I 167 Fd84
Alia I 166 Ed85
Alía E 52 Cc67
Aliaga E 48 Fb64
Aliağa TR 191 Eb85
Aliaguilla E 54 Ed67
Aliano I 162 Gb77
Aliártos GR 189 Ca85
Alibánfa H 145 Gc55
Alibey TR 191 Eb83
Alibeyli TR 191 Ed85
Aliç TR 185 Eb77
Alicante E 55 Fb71
Alice Castello I 148 Bd59
Aliçlıkuyu TR 198 Fd91
Alicudi Porto I 167 Fb82
Alicún de Ortega E 61 Dd73
Alidemirci TR 191 Ed82
Åliden S 80 Hc25
Alifakı TR 192 Fa84
Alife I 161 Fb73
Alija del Infantado E 37 Cb58
Alijó P 44 Bb61
Álika GR 194 Bc91
Alikampos GR 200 Cc95
Alikés GR 188 Ac86
Aliki GR 184 Db78
Aliki GR 188 Ad82
Alikianós GR 200 Cb95
Aliko GR 196 Db90
Aliköy TR 192 Ga83
Aliköy TR 199 Gc88
Alikurt TR 198 Fd88
Alikylä FIN 81 Jc28
Alil Abasi MK 183 Ca74
Aliman RO 181 Fa67
Alimena I 167 Fa85
Aliminusa I 166 Ed84
Alınca TR 198 Fd92
Alinci MK 183 Bb75
Alingsås S 102 Ec48
Alino BG 179 Cc72
Alins E 40 Gb58
Alinyà E 49 Gc59
Alionys LT 114 La56
Aliseda E 51 Bc67
Alise-Sainte-Reine F 30 Ja41
Alistráti GR 184 Cd77
Ali Terme I 167 Fd84
Alivéri GR 189 Cc85
Alixan F 34 Jb49
Alizava LT 114 Kd53
Aljaraque E 59 Bb74
Aljezur P 58 Ab73
Aljinovići SRB 159 Jb66
Aljucén E 51 Bd68
Aljustrel P 50 Ac71
Alken B 124 Ba40
Alkiškiai LT 113 Jd53
Alkkia FIN 89 Jb33
Alkmaar NL 116 Ba34
Alkoven A 144 Fa50
Alkpınar TR 186 Fa76
Alksėnai LT 114 Ka58
Alksnėnai LT 113 Jc54
Alksnėnai LV 114 Kb55
Alksniupiai LT 114 Kb54
Alkhdiyen TR 192 Fa86
Allai I 169 Ca77
Allaines-Mervilliers F 29 Gc39
Allainville-en-Beauce F 29 Gd39
Allaire F 27 Ec41
Allaman CH 140 Ba55
Allanche F 34 Hb49
Allariz E 36 Bb58
Allasac F 33 Gc49
Allauch F 42 Jd55
Allavaara S 67 Ha17
Allažmuiža LV 106 Kc50
Alle CH 141 Bc52
Alle DK 108 Da24
Alleen N 92 Cc47
Alleghe I 143 Ea56
Alleknjarg N 64 Ka07
Allemagne-en-Provence F 42 Ka53
Allemant F 24 Hc37
Allen IRL 13 Cc21
Allenbach D 133 Bd45
Allendale Town GB 11 Ed16
Allendorf D 126 Cd42
Allendorf, Bad Sooden- D 126 Db40
Allenheads GB 11 Ed17
Allensbach D 142 Cc52
Allensteig A 136 Fd49
Allenstein = Olsztyn PL 122 Ja32
Allepuz E 48 Fb64
Allerborn L 133 Bb43
Allerey-sur-Saône F 30 Jb43
Allersberg D 135 Dd47
Allershausen D 143 Ea50
Allerslev DK 109 Eb28
Allerston GB 16 Fb19
Allerum S 110 Ec54
Allés E 38 Da55
Alleuze F 34 Hb49
Allevard F 35 Jd48
Allex F 34 Jb50
Allgunnen S 103 Ga51
Allhallows GB 21 Ga28
Allibaudières F 24 Hd37
Alligny-Cosne F 30 Hb41
Allihies IRL 12 Ba26
Allinge DK 111 Fc57
Allington GB 20 Ed28
Allıören TR 193 Gb84
Alliste I 165 Hc78
Allistragh GB 9 Cd18
Allmendingen D 142 Da50
Allo E 39 Ec57
Alloa GB 7 Ea12
Allogny F 29 Gd42
Ålloluokta S 67 Ha17
Allonby GB 11 Eb17
Allones F 28 Fd40
Allones F 29 Gc38
Allonne F 28 Fc44
Allons F 40 Fc52
Alloon Lower IRL 12 Bd21
Allos F 43 Kb51
Alloue F 33 Ga46
Alloza E 48 Fb63
Allstedt D 127 Ea40
Allumiere I 156 Dd70
Ally F 33 Gd49
Ally F 34 Hc49
Almaça P 44 Ad64
Almaceda P 44 Ba65

Almacelles - Ansnes

Almacelles E 48 Fd60
Almaciles E 61 Eb72
Almada P 50 Aa69
Almadén E 52 Cd69
Almadén de la Plata E 59 Bd72
Almadenejos E 52 Cd70
Almagro E 52 Db69
Almăj RO 175 Cd65
Almajano E 47 Eb60
Almaluez E 47 Eb62
Almancil P 58 Ac74
Almansa E 55 Fa70
Almanza E 37 Cd57
Almaraz E 51 Cb66
Almarda E 54 Fc67
Almargen E 60 Cc75
Almarza E 47 Eb59
Almås N 78 Ed26
Almaş RO 170 Cb59
Almásfüzitő H 145 Hb52
Almassora E 54 Fc66
Almaşu RO 171 Cd57
Almaşu Mare RO 175 Cd60
Almatret E 48 Fd62
Almazán E 47 Eb61
Almazora E 54 Fc66
Almberget S 94 Fa39
Almby S 95 Fd44
Almdalen N 70 Fa22
Alme D 126 Cc39
Almeda de Cervera E 53 Dd68
Almedijar E 54 Fb66
Almedina E 53 Dd70
Almedinilla E 60 Da74
Almeida E 45 Ca61
Almeida P 45 Bc63
Almeirim P 50 Ac67
Almelo NL 117 Bd36
Almenar E 48 Ga60
Almenara E 54 Fc67
Almenar de Soria E 47 Eb60
Almendar TR 186 Fd77
Almendra E 45 Ca61
Almendral E 51 Bc69
Almendralejo E 51 Bd69
Almendricos E 61 Ec74
Almendros E 53 Ea66
Almenêches F 22 Fd37
Almenno San Salvatore I 149 Cd58
Almens CH 142 Cd55
Almensilla E 59 Bd74
Almere NL 116 Ba35
Almere-Buiten NL 116 Ba35
Almere-Haven NL 116 Ba36
Almería E 61 Ea76
Almerimar E 61 Dd76
Almesåkra S 103 Fc49
Almese I 148 Bc60
Al'met'evsk RUS 203 Ga08
Älmhult S 111 Fb53
Almidar E 61 Dd74
Almind DK 108 Db26
Almiropótamos GR 190 Cd86
Almirós GR 189 Bd82
Almklov N 84 Cb34
Almlia N 78 Eb27
Almlia N 78 Eb28
Ålmo N 77 Db30
Almodôvar P 58 Ac73
Almodóvar del Campo E 52 Da70
Almodóvar del Pinar E 53 Ec67
Almodóvar del Río E 60 Cc72
Almogia E 60 Cd76
Almograve P 58 Ab72
Almoguera E 46 Dd65
Almoharín E 51 Ca68
Almonacid de la Sierra E 47 Ed61
Almonacid del Marquesado E 53 Ea66
Almonacid de Toledo E 52 Db66
Almonacid de Zorita E 47 Ea65
Almonáster la Real E 59 Bc72
Almonte E 59 Bc74
Almoradí E 55 Fb72
Almoraima E 59 Cb77
Almorox E 46 Da65
Almoster P 44 Ac65
Almourol P 50 Ac66
Almsele S 79 Gb27
Älmsta S 96 Ha41
Almstedt D 126 Db37
Almudaina E 55 Fc70
Almudema E 61 Ec72
Almudévar E 48 Fb59
Almuñécar E 60 Db76
Almunge S 96 Gd42
Almunia de San Juan E 48 Fd60
Almuradiel E 52 Dc70
Almussafes E 54 Fb68
Alna N 93 Ea41
Alnaši RUS 203 Ga08
Alnes N 76 Cc32
Alness GB 5 Ea07
Alnö S 88 Gc33
Alnwick GB 11 Fa15
Alobrónoia GR 196 Da91
Alocén E 47 Ea64
Aloja LV 106 Kc47
Alomartes E 60 Db74
Alónissos GR 189 Cc83
Alonsontegí E 38 Ea55
Álora E 60 Cd76
Alosno E 59 Bb73
Alovė LT 114 Kc59
Alovera E 46 Dd64
Alozaina E 60 Cc76
Alp E 41 Gd58
Alpagut TR 192 Fb81
Alpalhão P 50 Ba67
Alparslan TR 193 Gc87
Alpbach A 143 Ea53
Alpe Colombino I 148 Bc60
Alpe di Siusi I 143 Dd56
Alpedrete E 46 Db63
Alpedrinha P 44 Bb65
Alpen D 125 Bc38
Alpera E 54 Ed69
Alphen NL 124 Ad38
Alphen aan de Rijn NL 116 Ad36
Alpheton GB 21 Ga26
Alpiarça P 50 Ac67
Alpicat E 48 Ga60
Alpirsbach D 133 Cb49
Alpnach Dorf CH 141 Ca54
Alpu TR 193 Gd82
Alpua FIN 82 Ka25
Alpuente E 54 Fa66
Alpullu TR 185 Ec76
Alqueva P 50 Ba71
Alquézar E 48 Fd59
Als DK 101 Dd22
Alsån S 73 Ja19
Alsån S 73 Jb21
Alsancak = Karavas CY 206 Jb96
Alsasua E 39 Ec56
Alsdorf D 125 Bc41
Alseda S 103 Fd50
Alsėdžiai LT 113 Jc54
Alsen S 79 Fb30
Alsenz D 133 Ca45
Alsfeld D 126 Cd42
Ålsgårde DK 109 Ec24
Alsheim D 133 Cb45
Ålshult S 111 Fc53
Alsike S 96 Gc42
Alsjärv S 73 Ja19
Alsjö S 87 Ga34
Alskog S 104 Ha50
Alsleben D 127 Ea39
Alslev DK 108 Cd25
Alslev DK 108 Da27
Ålsø DK 101 Dd23
Alsónémedi H 146 Hd53
Alsópáhok H 145 Gd55
Alsópakony H 146 Hd53
Alsószentiván H 146 Hc55
Alsótold H 146 Ja51
Alsózsolca H 146 Jc51
Alsrode DK 101 Dd23
Alstad N 78 Eb29
Alstadt S 110 Ed56
Alstätte D 125 Bd37
Alster S 94 Fa43
Alsterbro S 103 Ga51
Alsterfors S 103 Fd51
Alstermo S 103 Fd51
Alston GB 11 Ec17
Alstrup DK 109 Dd25
Alsunga LV 105 Jb51
Ålsvåg N 66 Fd12
Alsvik N 66 Fb17
Alsviķi LV 107 Lc48
Alswear GB 19 Dd29
Alta N 63 Hd08
Älta S 96 Gd44
Altach A 142 Cd53
Altamura I 162 Gc75
Altarejos E 53 Eb66
Altaussee A 144 Fa52
Altavilla Irpina I 161 Fc74
Altavilla Milicia I 166 Ed84
Altavilla Silentina I 161 Fd76
Altbüron CH 141 Ca53
Altdöbern D 128 Fb39
Altdorf CH 141 Cb54
Altdorf D 135 Dd46
Altdorf D 135 Eb49
Alt Duvenstedt D 118 Db30
Alte P 58 Ac74
Altea E 55 Fc70
Altedo I 150 Dd62
Alteglofsheim D 135 Eb48
Alteidet N 63 Hc08
Altena D 125 Cb40
Altenahr D 125 Bd42
Altenbeken D 126 Cd38
Altenberg D 128 Fa42
Altenberge D 125 Ca37
Altenbuch D 134 Cd45
Altenburg D 127 Eb41
Altendorf D 135 Dd45
Altendorf D 135 Eb46
Altenfelden A 144 Fa50
Altenglan D 133 Ca45
Altenhausen D 127 Dd37
Altenhof D 119 Ec33
Altenkirchen (Rügen) D 119 Ed29
Altenkirchen (Westerwald) D 125 Ca42
Altenkrempe D 119 Dd31
Altenkunstadt D 135 Dd44
Altenmarkt bei Sankt Gallen A 144 Fc52
Altenmarkt D 143 Eb51
Altenmarkt an der Triesting A 144 Ga51
Altenmarkt im Isperthale A 144 Fc50
Altenmarkt im Pongau A 143 Ed53
Altenmedingen D 118 Dc34
Altenstadt D 134 Cd43
Altenstadt D 135 Eb45
Altenstadt D 142 Da50
Altenstadt D 142 Dc52
Altensteig D 133 Cb49
Altenthann D 135 Eb48
Altentreptow D 119 Ed32
Altenwalde D 118 Cd31
Altenweddingen D 127 Ea38
Alter do Chão P 50 Ba67
Alteren N 71 Fb20
Altertheim D 134 Da45
Altes Lager D 127 Ed38
Altfraunhofen D 143 Eb50
Altfriesack D 119 Ec35
Althegnenberg D 142 Dc50
Altheim A 143 Ed50
Altheim D 134 Cd46
Altheim D 134 Da49
Althofen A 144 Fb55
Althorne GB 21 Ga27
Althütte D 134 Da48
Altimir BG 179 Cd69
Alţina RO 175 Db61
Altınçay TR 187 Ha78
Altınkaya TR 199 Ha90
Altınkum TR 197 Ec89
Altınkum TR 199 Gd91
Altınova TR 186 Ga79
Altınova TR 191 Eb83
Altınova TR 199 Gd91
Altıntaş TR 185 Eb77
Altıntaş TR 192 Ga84
Altıntaş TR 193 Gb84
Altıntaşköyü TR 198 Fb88
Altınyaka TR 199 Gc92
Altınyayla TR 198 Ga91
Altipiani di Arcinazzo I 160 Ec72
Alt Käbelich D 120 Fa33
Altkalen D 119 Ec32
Altkirch F 31 Kb40
Altlandsberg D 128 Fa36
Altmannstein D 135 Ea48
Altmünster A 144 Fa52
Altnabreac Station GB 5 Eb05
Altnacallich GB 4 Dd05
Altnaharra GB 4 Dd05
Altnamackan GB 9 Cd18
Altn Bulg RUS 203 Ga14
Altnes N 63 Hd07
Altobordo E 61 Ec74
Alto da Serra P 50 Ab67
Alto de la Madera E 37 Cc54
Altofonte I 166 Ec84
Altomonte I 164 Gb79
Altomünster D 143 Dd50
Alton GB 16 Ed23
Alton GB 20 Fb29
Altopascio I 155 Db65
Altorricón E 48 Fd60
Altötting D 143 Ec50
Alträsk S 73 Hc22
Altrip D 134 Cc46
Alt Ruppin D 119 Ec35
Altsasu E 39 Ec56
Alt Schadow D 128 Fa38
Alt Schönau D 119 Ec33
Altshausen D 142 Cd51
Altstätten CH 142 Cd53
Altsvattnets sameviste S 71 Fd21
Alttajärvi S 67 Hb15
Alttojärvi FIN 69 Kb12
Altuna S 95 Gb42
Altura E 54 Fb66
Altusried D 142 Db52
Altwarp D 120 Fb32
Alu EST 98 Kb43
Aluatu MD 177 Fc62
Alūksne LV 107 Lc48
Ålum DK 100 Dc23
Ålund S 73 Hc24
Alunda S 96 Gd41
Aluniş MD 173 Fa55
Aluniş RO 171 Da57
Aluniş RO 171 Dc58
Aluniş RO 176 Ea63
Aluniş RO 176 Eb63
Alunu RO 175 Da64
Aluokta S 67 Gd17
Alupka UA 205 Fa18
Aluskylä FIN 89 Jb35
Alušta UA 205 Fa18
Alustante E 47 Ed64
Alvaiázere P 44 Ad65
Alvajärvi FIN 82 Ka29
Alvalade P 50 Ac71
Älvan S 103 Fd46
Älvängen S 102 Ec48
Alvarado E 51 Bc69
Alvarenga P 44 Ad61
Alvares P 44 Ad65
Álvaro P 44 Ba65
Alvarrões P 51 Bb67
Alvdal N 85 Ea34
Älvdalen S 87 Fb37
Alvegal P 50 Ad66
Alverca do Ribatejo P 50 Ab68
Alversund N 84 Ca38
Alves GB 5 Eb07
Alveslohe D 118 Db32
Alvesta S 103 Fc52
Alvestad N 92 Ca43
Alveston GB 19 Ec28
Alvettula FIN 90 Ka36
Älvho S 87 Fc36
Alviano I 156 Ea69
Alvignac F 33 Gc50
Alvik N 76 Cc32
Ålvik N 84 Cc39
Alvik S 73 Hd22
Alvik S 95 Fc39
Alvitas LT 114 Ka58
Alvito I 160 Ed72
Alvito P 50 Ad70
Älvkarleby S 96 Gc39
Älvkarleö S 96 Gc39
Alvor P 58 Ab74
Alvorge P 44 Ac65
Alvøy N 84 Ca39
Älvros S 87 Fc34
Älvsbacka S 93 Fd41
Älvsbacka S 94 Fa42
Älvsbyn S 73 Hc22
Älvsered S 102 Ed50
Älvsund S 87 Gb34
Alwernia PL 138 Hd44
Alwinton GB 11 Ed15
Alyki GR 189 Ca86
Alyth GB 7 Eb11
Alytus LT 114 Kc59
Alzano Lombardo I 149 Cd58
Alzenau D 134 Cd44
Alzey D 133 Cb45
Alzira E 54 Fb69
Alzola E 39 Eb55
Alzon F 41 Hc53
Amadora P 50 Aa68
Amagne F 24 Hd34
Amailloux F 28 Fc44
Åmål S 94 Ed44
Amalfi I 161 Fb76
Amaliáda GR 188 Ba86
Amaliápoli GR 189 Ca82
Amálo GR 196 Dd88
Amance F 30 Ja38
Amance F 31 Jd40
A Manchica E 36 Ba57
Amandola I 156 Ed68
Amange F 31 Jc42
Amantea I 164 Gb80
Amara RO 176 Ed66
Amarante P 44 Ba61
Amárantos GR 182 Ad78
Amărăşti RO 175 Da65
Amărăştii de Jos RO 179 Da67
Amărăştii de Sus RO 179 Da67
Amareleja P 51 Bb71
Amares P 44 Ad59
Amargreti CY 206 Hd98
Amári GR 200 Cd96
Amárinthos GR 189 Cc85
Amaru RO 176 Ec64
Amaseno I 160 Ec73
Amasya TR 205 Fc20
Amatrice I 156 Ec69
Amay B 124 Ba41
Amaya E 38 Db57
Ambarès et-Lagrave F 32 Fb50
Ambarkaya TR 198 Fd91
Ambas E 37 Cc54
Ambazac F 33 Gb46
Ambeláki GR 188 Ba83
Ambelákia GR 183 Bc80
Ambelákia GR 195 Cb87
Ambeļi LV 115 Lc53
Ambelía GR 182 Ad80
Ambeliá GR 189 Bd82
Ambelohóri GR 182 Ba80
Ambelohóri GR 194 Bc90
Ambelónas GR 182 Ac80
Ambelónas GR 183 Bd80
Ambelónas GR 194 Ba87
Ambelos GR 200 Cb97
Amberg D 135 Ea46
Ambérieu-en-Bugey F 35 Jc46
Ambérieux-en-Dombes F 34 Jb46
Ambert F 34 Hc47
Ambialet F 41 Ha53
Ambierle F 34 Hd46
Ambiévillers F 31 Jd39
Ambjörby S 94 Fa40
Ambjörnarp S 102 Fa50
Ambla EST 98 Kd43
Amblainville F 23 Gd35
Amble GB 11 Fa15
Ambleside GB 11 Eb18
Ambleteuse F 21 Gb30
Ambleville F 23 Gc36
Amboise F 29 Gb42
Ambon F 27 Eb41
Ämbra EST 98 Kd43
Ambra I 156 Dd66
Ambrault F 29 Gd44
Ambria I 149 Cd58
Ambrières-les-Vallées F 28 Fb38
Ambronay F 35 Jc46
Åmdal N 92 Cd46
Amden CH 142 Cc54
Ameixial P 58 Ad73
Amel B 125 Bb42
Amele LV 105 Jc49
Åmelfot N 84 Cb34
Amelia I 156 Ea69
Amélie-les-Bains-Palalda F 41 Ha58
Amelin PL 122 Jc34
Amelinghausen D 118 Dc34
Amelunxen D 126 Da38
Amendoeira P 58 Ad72
Amendolara I 164 Gc78
Amer E 49 Ha59
Amerang D 143 Eb51
A Merca E 36 Ba58
Amerongen NL 125 Bb37
Amersfoort NL 116 Bb36
Amersham GB 20 Fb27
Amesbury GB 20 Ed29
Amezketa E 39 Ec56
A Mezquita E 36 Bc58
Amfiklia GR 189 Bd84
Amfilohía GR 188 Ad83
Amfípolis GR 184 Cd77
Ámfissa GR 189 Bc84
Amieira P 50 Ba70
Amiens F 23 Gd33
Amieva E 37 Cd55
Amigdaliá GR 189 Bc81
Amigdaliá GR 189 Bc85
Amigdaliés GR 182 Ba79
Amíkles GR 194 Bc89
Amillano E 39 Ec57
Amilly F 29 Ha40
Amindeo GR 183 Bb77
Åminne FIN 81 Hd31
Åminne S 104 Ha49
Amla N 84 Cd37
Åmli N 93 Da45
Amliden S 72 Ha24
Amlwch GB 15 Dd21
Amlwch Port GB 15 Dd21
Ämmälä FIN 89 Jb33
Ammanford GB 19 Dd27
Ämmänsaari FIN 75 La23
Ammarnäs S 71 Ga21
Åmmeberg S 95 Fc45
Ammenäs S 102 Eb47
Ammern D 126 Dc40
Ammersbek D 118 Dc32
Ammerthal D 135 Ea46
Ammerzoden NL 124 Ba37
Ammeville F 22 Fd36
Ammochostos CY 206 Jd96
Amnehärad S 95 Fb45
Amnéville F 25 Jd35
Åmnøyhamna N 70 Fa19
Amoliani GR 184 Cd79
Amöneburg D 126 Cd41
Amorbach D 134 Cd45
Amorebieta E 38 Ea55
Amorgós GR 196 Dc91
Amóri GR 185 Eb76
Amorosa P 44 Ac59
Amorosi I 161 Fb74
Åmot N 85 Dd38
Åmot N 86 Eb37
Åmot N 93 Dd41
Åmot N 93 Da42
Åmot S 87 Ga38
Amot S 94 Ed42
Amotfors S 94 Ec42
Amotopos GR 188 Ad81
Åmotsdal N 93 Da42
Amou F 39 Fb54
Amous F 43 Kb53
Ampfing D 143 Eb50
Ampflwang A 143 Ed51
Ampfurth D 127 Dd38
Ampiala FIN 90 Ka33
Amplepuis F 34 Ja46
Amplier F 23 Gd32
Ampola FIN 97 Jc40
Amposta E 48 Ga64
Ampthill GB 20 Fc26
Ampudia E 46 Cd59
Ampuero E 38 Dd55
Amriswil CH 142 Cd52
Amroth GB 18 Dc27
Åmsele S 80 Ha26
Amsteg CH 141 Cb55
Amstelveen NL 116 Ba35
Amsterdam NL 116 Ba35
Amstetten A 144 Fc51
Amtoft DK 100 Da21
Amtsberg D 127 Ec42
Amtzell D 142 Da52
Amulree GB 7 Ea11
Amurrio E 38 Ea56
Amusco E 38 Da58
Amusquillo E 46 Db60
Amvrossía GR 184 Dc77
Amzacea RO 181 Fb68
Ån S 79 Fb31
Anacapri I 161 Fa76
Anadiou CY 206 Hd97
Anadolufeneri TR 186 Fd77
Anáfi GR 196 Dc92
Anafonitria GR 188 Ac86
Anagénisis GR 183 Cb76
Anagni I 160 Ec72
Anagyia CY 206 Jb97
Análipsis GR 188 Bb84
Anapa RUS 205 Fb17
Ânâr FIN 69 Ka11
Anarcs H 147 Kb50
Anárgiri GR 183 Bb77
Anascaul IRL 12 Ba24
Anäset S 80 Hc27
Åna-Sira N 92 Cb46
Änätinpää FIN 75 Lc24
Anatolí GR 183 Bd80
Anatolí GR 201 Db96
Anatolikó GR 183 Bc78
Anatolikó GR 183 Ca78
Anavainen FIN 97 Ja39
Anávatos GR 191 Dd86
Anávra GR 189 Bd83
Anavrití GR 194 Bc89
Anaya E 46 Da62
Anaya de Alba E 45 Cc63
An Bun Beag IRL 8 Ca15
Ançã P 44 Ac64
An Cabhán IRL 9 Cb19
An Caiseal IRL 8 Bb20
An Caisleán Nua IRL 12 Bc24
An Caisleán Riabhach IRL 8 Bd19
Ance LV 105 Jc49
Ancelle F 35 Ka50
Ancenis F 28 Fa42
Ančenki RUS 107 Ma50
Ancerville F 24 Ja37
An Charraig IRL 8 Ca16
An Chathair IRL 13 Ca24
Anché F 32 Fd45
Anchor GB 15 Eb25
Anchuras E 52 Cd67
Ancín E 39 Eb57
Ancíverovo RUS 107 Ld49
Ančkini LV 107 Lc52
An Clochán IRL 8 Bb20
An Clochán IRL 9 Cb16
An Clochán Liath IRL 8 Ca15
An Cloigeann IRL 8 Ba20
An Cóbh IRL 12 Bd26
An Coireán IRL 12 Ba25
Ancona I 156 Ed66
An Creagán IRL 8 Bd20
Ancroft GB 11 Ed14
Ancy-le-Franc F 30 Hd40
An Daingean IRL 12 Ba24
Andalo I 149 Dc57
Åndalseter N 77 Da31
Åndalsnes N 77 Da32
Andance F 34 Jb48
Andåsen S 87 Fc34
Andau A 145 Gc52
Andavías E 45 Cb60
Anddalsvågen N 70 Ed23
Andebu N 93 Dd43
Andechs D 143 Dd51
Andeer CH 142 Cd55
Andelfingen CH 141 Cb52
Andelot-Blancheville F 30 Jb38
Andelot-en-Montagne F 31 Jd43
Andelsbuch A 142 Da53
Andelst NL 125 Bb37
Andenäs S 94 Fa40
Andenes N 66 Ga11
Andeņi LV 107 Ld52
Andenne B 124 Ad42
Andermatt CH 141 Cb55
Andernach D 125 Ca42
Andernos-les-Bains F 32 Fa50
Andersby FIN 90 Kd38
Andersby N 65 Kc06
Anderslöv S 110 Ed56
Andersskog N 77 Db29
Anderstorp S 102 Fa50
Andersvattnet S 80 Hc26
Andijk NL 116 Bb34
Andilly F 32 Fa45
Andíparos GR 196 Da90
Andirio GR 188 Bb85
Andız TR 193 Gb83
Andlau F 25 Kb37
Andoain E 39 Ec55
Andocs H 145 Ha56
Andoins F 40 Fc55
Andon F 43 Kb53
Andorf A 143 Ed50
Åndørja N 67 Gb12
Andorlia N 67 Gd11
Andornaktálya H 146 Jb51
Andorra E 48 Fb63
Andorra la Vella AND 40 Gc58
Andosilla E 39 Ec58
Andouillé F 28 Fb39
Andover GB 20 Fa29
Andoversford GB 20 Ed27
Andrarum S 111 Fb56
Andrăşeşti RO 176 Ed66
Andratx E 56 Ha67
Andravída GR 188 Ad86
Andreapol' RUS 202 Ec10
Andreas GB 10 Dd18
Andreevca MD 173 Ga55
Andreiaşu de Jos RO 176 Ec62
Andrespol PL 130 Hd39
Andrest F 40 Fd55
Andrésy F 23 Gd36
Andretta I 161 Fd75
Andrézieux-Bouthéon F 34 Ja47
Andria I 162 Gb74
Andrid RO 171 Cc55
Andrieşeni RO 173 Fa56
Andrijaševci HR 153 Hc60
Andrijevica MNE 159 Jb68
Andrijivka UA 205 Fb16
Andrioniškis LT 114 Kc55
Andrítsena GR 194 Bb87
An Droichead Nua IRL 13 Cc22
Ándros GR 190 Da87
Andrup DK 108 Cd26
Andrupene LV 107 Ld52
Andruśivka UA 204 Eb15
Andruškoniai LT 114 Kc57
Andruşul de Jos MD 177 Fb61
Andrychów PL 138 Hd45
Andryjanki PL 123 Kb35
Andrzejewo PL 123 Jd34
Andselv N 67 Gc11
Andsnes N 63 Hb07
An Dúchoraidh IRL 8 Ca16
Andújar E 52 Da72
Anduze F 41 Hd52
Andvikgrend N 84 Ca37
Anebakelv N 63 Hb09
Anebjør N 92 Cd44
Aneboda S 103 Fc51
Aneby S 103 Fc48
Anelema EST 98 Kb45
Anemoráhi GR 188 Ad81
Anenii Noi MD 173 Ga58
Anero E 38 Dc55
Ånes N 66 Fd11
Ånessletta N 66 Fd12
Anet F 23 Gb37
Anetjärvi FIN 75 Kd20
Anevo BG 180 Db72
Anfo I 149 Db58
Ång S 103 Fc49
Anga S 104 Ha49
Angáli GR 189 Cb83
Angarn S 96 Gd43
Angé F 29 Gb42
Ånge S 72 Gc21
Ånge S 79 Fb30
Ånge S 87 Fd33
Ängebäck S 94 Ec43
Ängebo S 87 Ga35
Angelbachtal D 134 Cc47
Angelburg D 126 Cc41
Ängelholm S 110 Ed54
Angeli FIN 68 Jc11
Angelniemi FIN 97 Jc40
Angelohóri GR 183 Bd77
Angelohóri GR 183 Ca78
Angelókastro GR 188 Ba84
Angelókastro GR 195 Ca87
Ängelsberg S 95 Ga41
Angelstad S 102 Fa52
Anger A 144 Ga54
Angera I 148 Cb58
Angerdshestra S 103 Fb49
Angered S 102 Ec49
Angerlo NL 125 Bc37
Angermoen N 70 Fa21
Angermünde D 120 Fa35
Angern D 127 Ea37
Angern an der March A 145 Gc50
Angerneset N 70 Ed21
Angers F 28 Fb41
Ångersjö S 80 Hb29
Ångersjö S 87 Fc35
Angerville F 29 Gd38
Ångesån S 73 Hd18
Angesbyn S 73 Hd22
Ängesleva FIN 74 Ka24
Angesträsk S 73 Hd21
Anghiari I 156 Ea66
Anghione F 154 Cc69
Angista GR 184 Cd77
Angístri GR 195 Ca87
Angistro GR 184 Cc75
Angla EST 97 Jc45
Anglards-de-Salers F 33 Ha49
Angle GB 18 Db27
An Gleann Garbh IRL 12 Bb26
Anglefort F 35 Jd46
Angles F 32 Fa45
Anglès F 41 Ha54
Anglès E 49 Ha59
Anglesola E 48 Gb60
Angles-sur-l'Anglin F 29 Ga44
Anglet F 39 Ed54
Angliers F 28 Fd43
Anglure F 24 Hc37
Angnäs S 80 Ha28
Angoncillo E 39 Eb58
An Gort IRL 12 Bd22
An Gort Mór IRL 8 Bb20
Angoulême F 32 Fd47
Angri I 161 Fb75
Ängskär S 96 Gd40
Ängsö S 95 Gb43
Angstedt, Gräfinau- D 127 Dd42
Ångsvik S 96 Ha43
Angüés E 48 Fc59
Anguiano E 38 Ea58
Anguillara Sabazia I 160 Ea71
Anguillara Veneta I 150 Ea61
Anguita E 47 Eb62
Anguix E 47 Ea64
Anguse EST 98 La42
Angvik N 77 Db31
Anhée B 124 Ad42
Anholt D 125 Bc37
Anholt DK 101 Eb22
Aniane F 41 Hc54
Aniche F 24 Hb32
Ánidro GR 189 Bd83
Aniés E 39 Fb58
Ånimskog S 94 Ec45
Anina RO 174 Ca63
Aninoasa RO 175 Cd64
Aninoasa RO 175 Dc63
Aninoasa RO 176 Dd64
Aniñón E 47 Ed61
Anitkaya TR 193 Gc84
Anixiátiko GR 188 Ba82
Anizy-le-Château F 24 Hb34
Anjala FIN 90 La37
Anjalankoski FIN 90 La37
Anjan S 78 Ed29
Anjum NL 117 Bc32
Ankaran SLO 151 Fa59
Ankarsrum S 103 Ga49
Ankarsund S 71 Ga23
Ankarsvik S 88 Gc33
Ankarvattnet S 79 Fb25
Änkilänsalo FIN 91 Ld34
Anklam D 120 Fa32
Ankum D 117 Cb35
An Leacht IRL 12 Bc22
An Longfort IRL 9 Cb20
Anloo NL 117 Bd34
An Mhala Raithní IRL 8 Bb19
An Móta IRL 13 Cb21
An Muileann gCearr IRL 9 Cb20
Anna E 54 Fb69
Anna EST 98 Kd43
Anna LV 107 Lc48
Anna RUS 203 Fb12
Annaberg A 144 Fd52
Annaberg-Buchholz D 135 Ed43
Annaberg im Lammertal A 143 Ed53
Annaburg D 127 Ed39
Annacloy GB 9 Da18
Annahütte D 128 Fa39
Annalong GB 9 Da19
Annan GB 11 Eb16
Anna Paulowna NL 116 Ba34
An Nás IRL 13 Cc22
Annas LV 106 Kd50
Annayalla IRL 9 Cd18
Anneberg S 102 Ec49
Anneberg S 103 Fc49
Annecy F 35 Jd46
Annel FIN 68 Jc11
Annelund S 102 Ed48
Annemasse F 35 Ka45
Annenieki LV 106 Ka52
Annental A 144 Ga51
Annerstad S 102 Fa52
Annestown IRL 13 Cb25
Annevoie-Rouillon B 124 Ad42
Annfield Plain GB 11 Ed17
Aņņi LV 106 La48
Annikvere EST 98 Kd41
Annino RUS 99 Mb39
Annino RUS 202 Ed08
Annonay F 34 Ja48
Annonen FIN 82 Ka26
Annopol PL 131 Jd41
Annot F 43 Kb52
Annstad N 66 Fc13
Annweiler amTrifels D 133 Ca47
Áno Ágios Vlássios GR 188 Ba83
Áno Damásta GR 189 Bd83
Áno Daviá GR 194 Bc87
Áno Drossiní GR 185 Dd77
Annœullin F 23 Ha31
Áno Fanári GR 195 Ca88
Anógia GR 200 Da95
Áno Hóra GR 188 Bb84
Áno Kalendíni GR 188 Ba82
Áno Kalliníki GR 183 Bb76
Áno Kariófito GR 184 Db76
Áno Kastrítsi GR 188 Bb85
Áno Kómi GR 183 Bc79
Áno Korakiána GR 182 Ab80
Áno Koudoúni GR 188 Ba84
Áno-Lehónia GR 189 Ca82
Áno Mathráki GR 182 Aa79
Áno Merá GR 196 Db89
Áno Méros GR 200 Cd96
Añón E 47 Ec60
Ånonjalme sameviste S 67 Gb16
Áno Poróia GR 183 Cb76
Añora E 52 Cc71
Áno Sangri GR 196 Db90
Áno Sinikia Trikala GR 189 Bc86
Áno Síros GR 196 Da88
Anost F 30 Hd42
Anould F 31 Ka38
Áno Váthia GR 189 Cc85
Áno Viános GR 201 Db96
Áno Vrondoú GR 184 Cc76
Anoye F 40 Fc55
Anquela del Ducado E 47 Eb63
An Ráth IRL 12 Bd24
Anröchte D 126 Cc39
An Ros IRL 13 Da21
Ans DK 100 Db23
Ansac-sur-Viènne F 33 Ga46
Ansager DK 108 Da25
Ansalahti FIN 90 Kd36
Ansbach D 134 Dc47
An Scairbh IRL 12 Bb22
An Sciobairín IRL 12 Bb26
Anse F 34 Ja46
An Seanchaisleán IRL 9 Cc20
Ansedonia I 155 Dc69
Anselküla EST 105 Jc47
Anserall E 40 Gc58
Ansião P 44 Ac65
Ansignan F 41 Ha57
Ansio FIN 90 Kc34
Ansku FIN 97 Jd40
Ansnes N 62 Gc10
Ansnes N 77 Dc29

Ansó – Åsenhöga

Ansó E 39 Fb57
An Spidéal IRL 12 Bc21
Anspoki, L. LV 107 Lc52
Anstad N 85 Db35
Anstruther GB 7 Ec12
Antagnod I 148 Bd58
Antakalnis LT 114 Kc57
Antakalnis LT 114 Kd56
Antalieptė LT 115 Lb54
Antalya TR 199 Gc91
Antanavas LV 114 Kb58
An tAonach IRL 13 Ca22
Antas E 61 Ec75
Antas P 44 Bb62
Antašava LT 114 Kd54
Antas de Ulla E 36 Bb56
Antazavė LT 115 Lb54
An Teach Dóite IRL 8 Bb20
An Teampall Mór IRL 13 Ca23
Antegluonis LT 113 Jd56
Antegnate I 149 Cd59
Antemil (Cerceda) E 36 Ba54
Anten S 102 Ec48
Antequera E 60 Cd75
Anterselva di Mezzo I 143 Ea55
Antey-Saint-André I 148 Bd58
Anthée B 124 Ad42
Anthéor F 43 Kc54
Anthí GR 184 Cc77
Anthili GR 189 Bd83
Anthófito GR 183 Ca77
Antholz Mittertal I 143 Ea55
Anthorn GB 11 Eb16
Anthótopos GR 183 Bb78
Anthótopos GR 189 Bd82
Anthy F 31 Ka44
Antibes F 43 Kc53
Antignano I 155 Da66
Antigonos GR 183 Bc77
Antigüedad E 46 Db59
Antikira GR 189 Bd85
Antilä FIN 89 Jb34
Antillo I 167 Fd84
Antimáhia GR 197 Eb91
An tinbhear Mór IRL 13 Cd23
Antinrova S 68 Ja17
Ántissa GR 191 Dd83
Antjärn S 88 Gc32
Antnäs S 73 Hd22
Anton BG 179 Da71
Antonești MD 177 Fb60
Antoneuca MD 173 Fb54
Antonimina I 164 Gb83
Antonin PL 122 Hc32
Antonin PL 129 Ha39
Antoniów PL 130 Jc40
Antoniów PL 131 Jd41
Antonovo BG 180 Ea70
Antonsthal D 135 Ec43
Antracyt UA 205 Fb15
Antraigues-sur-Volane F 34 Ja50
Antrain F 28 Ed38
Antrim GB 9 Da17
Antrodoco I 156 Ec70
Antronapiana I 148 Ca57
Antskog FIN 97 Jd40
Antsla EST 107 Lb47
Anttila FIN 90 La36
Anttila FIN 98 Kc39
Anttis S 68 Ja17
Anttola FIN 90 La34
Anttola FIN 91 Lc33
An Tulach IRL 13 Cc23
Antuži LV 106 La51
Antwerpen B 124 Ac39
An Uaimh IRL 9 Cd20
Anundsjö S 80 Gd30
Anversa di Abruzzi I 161 Fa71
Anvin F 23 Gd31
Anxeriz E 36 Ad54
Anykščiai LT 114 Kd55
Anzat-le-Luguet F 34 Hb48
Anzi I 161 Ga76
Anzin F 24 Hb32
Anzing D 143 Ea51
Anzio I 160 Eb73
Anzlezy F 30 Hc43
Anzola dell'Emilia I 149 Dc62
Anzur E 60 Cd74
Anzy-le-Duc F 34 Hd45
Aoiz E 39 Ed57
Aosta I 148 Bc58
Aouste F 24 Hd33
Aovere EST 99 Lb45
Apa H 146 Hc54
Apa RO 171 Cd54
Apače SLO 144 Ga56
Apagy H 147 Ka51
Apahida RO 171 Da58
Aparhant H 153 Hc57
Apastovo RUS 203 Fd09
Apața RO 176 Ea61
Apateu RO 170 Ca58
Apatin SRB 153 Hd59
Apatovac HR 152 Gc57
Ape LV 107 Lb48
Apecchio I 156 Eb66
Apeldoorn NL 117 Bc36
Apelern D 126 Da37
Apele Vii RO 179 Da67
Apelscha NL 117 Bd34
Apen D 117 Cb33
Apenburg D 119 Dd35
Apensen D 118 Db33
Apéri GR 201 Eb95
A Peroxa E 36 Bb57
Apice I 161 Fc74
Apidiá GR 195 Bd90
Apiés E 48 Fc59
Apírados GR 196 Dc90
Apiro I 156 Ec66
Aplared S 102 Ed49
Apliki CY 206 Jb97
A Pobra de Caramiñal E 36 Ac56
Apolakkiá GR 197 Ed93
Apold RO 175 Dc60
Apolda D 127 Ea41
Apoldu de Jos RO 175 Da61
Apóllona GR 197 Fa93
Apollonia GR 196 Da90
Apólonas GR 196 Dc89
Apolonía GR 184 Cc78
Apóstoli GR 200 Cd95
Apostolove UA 204 Ed16
Appel D 118 Db33
Äppelbo S 95 Fb40
Appeltern NL 125 Bb37
Appenweier D 133 Ca49
Appenzell CH 142 Cd53
Appiano I 142 Dc56
Appingedam NL 117 Ca33
Appleby GB 16 Fb21
Appleby-in-Westmorland GB 11 Ec18
Appleby Magna GB 16 Fa24
Applecross GB 4 Db08
Appledore GB 21 Ga29
Apples CH 140 Ba55
Appletreewick GB 11 Ed19
Äpplö FIN 97 Ja40
Appoigny F 30 Hc40
Apremont F 28 Ed44
Apremont-la-Forêt F 25 Jc36
Apremont-sur-Allier F 30 Hb43
Aprica I 149 Da57
Apricale I 43 Kd52
Apricena I 161 Fd72
Aprigliano I 164 Gc80
Aprīķi LV 105 Jb51
Aprilci BG 179 Da73
Aprilci BG 180 Dc71
Aprilia I 160 Eb72
Aprilovo BG 180 Ea73
Aprilovo BG 180 Eb70
Ápsalos GR 183 Bc77
Apsella I 156 Eb65
Apšeronsk RUS 205 Fc17
Apsiou CY 206 Ja98
Apšuciems LV 106 Ka50
Apšupe LV 106 Ka51
Apt F 42 Jc53
Aquila CH 142 Cc56
Aquileia I 150 Ed59
Aquilonia I 161 Fd74
Aquino I 160 Ed73
Arabaalan TR 185 Ed80
Arabacıbozköy TR 191 Ed84
Arabba I 143 Ea56
Araç TR 205 Fa20
Aracena E 59 Bc72
Arâches F 35 Ka45
Aračinovo MK 178 Bc73
Arad RO 170 Bd59
Aradac SRB 153 Jc60
Aradeo I 163 Hc77
Aradippou CY 206 Jc97
Aradninkai LV 123 Kb30
Araglin IRL 13 Ca25
Aragnouet F 40 Fd57
Aragona I 166 Ed86
Aragoncillo E 47 Ec63
Aragüés del Puerto E 39 Fb57
Arahamítes GR 194 Bc88
Arahnéo GR 195 Bd87
Aráhova GR 189 Bd84
Arahovítika GR 188 Bb85
Arakapas CY 206 Jb97
Arakste LV 106 Kd47
Araklı TR 205 Fd19
Aralla E 37 Cb56
Åram N 76 Cb33
A Ramallosa E 36 Ac58
Aramits F 39 Fb56
Aramon F 42 Jb53
Arana CY 206 Jd96
Aranaz E 39 Ec56
Aranda de Duero E 46 Dc60
Aranda de Moncayo E 47 Ec61
Arándiga E 47 Ed61
Arandilla del Arroyo E 47 Eb64
Arăneag RO 170 Ca59
Aranga E 36 Bb54
Aranjuez E 52 Dc66
Arantzazu E 39 Eb56
Aranyosapáti H 147 Kb50
Aranzueque E 46 Dd64
Araovacık TR 191 Ed81
Ararca TR 192 Fb81
Årås N 84 Ca37
Aras de Alpuente E 54 Fa66
Araševo RUS 107 Mb46
Arasi I 164 Ga84
Arasluokta sameviste S 66 Ga17
Aratores E 39 Fb57
Áratos GR 185 Dd77
Arauzo de Miel E 46 Dd60
Aravete EST 98 Kd43
Aravissós GR 183 Bd77
Arazede P 44 Ac64
Arbanasi BG 180 Dd70
Arbas F 40 Gb56
Arbás E 37 Cc56
Arbatax I 169 Cc77
Arbeca E 48 Gb61
Arbedo CH 149 Cc57
Arberg D 134 Dc47
Arbesbach A 144 Fc50
Arbeteta E 47 Eb64
Arbigny F 30 Jb44
Arbing A 144 Fc51
Arbinovo MK 182 Ba75
Arbirlot GB 7 Ec11
Arboga S 95 Ga43
Arbois F 31 Jc43
Arbon CH 142 Cd52
Arbonne-la-Forêt F 29 Ha38
Arbore RO 172 Eb55
Arborea I 169 Bd78
Arborio I 148 Ca59
Årbostad N 67 Gb12
Årbotten S 94 Ed42
Arbrå S 87 Ga36
Arbroath GB 7 Ec11
Arbúcies E 49 Ha60
Arbuniel E 60 Dc73
Arbus I 169 Bd78
Arby S 111 Ga53
Arc F 31 Jc41
Arca P 44 Ad63
Arcachon F 32 Fa51
Arčadinskaja RUS 203 Fd13
Arcallana E 37 Ca54
Arcani RO 175 Cc63
Arčar BG 179 Cb67
Arcas E 53 Eb66
Arce I 160 Ed72
Arcen NL 125 Bc39
Arcenant F 30 Ja42
Arc-en-Barrois F 30 Jb39
Arcens F 34 Ja50
Arcentales E 38 Dd55
Arces-Dilo F 30 Hc39
Arc-et-Senans F 31 Jc42
Arcevia I 156 Ec66
Arcey F 31 Ka40
Archangel'skoje RUS 113 Jd58
Archena E 55 Ed72
Archiac F 32 Fc48
Archiane F 35 Jc50
Archidona E 60 Cd75
Archiestown GB 7 Eb08
Archigny F 29 Ga44
Archiș RO 170 Cb58
Archivel E 61 Eb72
Arcidosso I 156 Dd68
Ārciems LV 106 Kc48
Arcille I 155 Dd68
Arcins F 32 Fb49
Arcis-sur-Aube F 30 Hd38
Arco I 149 Dc58
Arco de Baúlhe P 44 Ba60
Arco de las Salinas E 54 Fa66
Arcos E 36 Bb56
Arcos E 38 Dc58
Arcos de Jalón E 47 Eb62
Arcos de la Frontera E 59 Ca76
Arcos de la Sierra E 47 Eb65
Arcos de Valdevez P 44 Ad59
Arcy-sur-Cure F 30 Hc41
Arcyz UA 204 Ec17
Arda BG 184 Db75
Ardagh IRL 12 Bc23
Ardahan TR 205 Ga18
Årdal N 92 Cb43
Årdal N 92 Cd45
Årdala S 95 Gb45
Ardales E 60 Cc76
Årdalstangen N 85 Da37
Ardan IRL 13 Cb21
Ardanairy IRL 13 Cd23
Ardara I 168 Ca75
Ardara IRL 8 Ca16
Árdassa GR 183 Bb78
Ardatov RUS 203 Fb10
Ardbeg GB 9 Da14
Ardcharnich GB 4 Dc06
Ardea I 160 Eb72
Ardee IRL 9 Cd19
Ardeluța RO 172 Eb59
Arden DK 100 Dc22
Ardenno I 149 Cd57
Ardentes F 29 Gc44
Ardentinny GB 6 Dc12
Ardenza I 155 Da66
Ardeoani RO 172 Ec59
Ardes F 34 Hb48
Ardeșen TR 205 Ga19
Ardèvol E 49 Gc60
Ardez CH 142 Da55
Ardfert IRL 12 Bb24
Ardfinnan IRL 13 Ca24
Ardgartan GB 6 Dc12
Ardgay GB 5 Ea06
Ardglass GB 10 Db18
Ardgroom IRL 12 Ba26
Ardılı TR 199 Gb88
Ardino BG 184 Dc75
Ardisa E 48 Fb59
Ardkeen GB 10 Db18
Ardleigh GB 21 Ga26
Ardlussa GB 6 Db12
Ardminish GB 6 Db13
Ardmore IRL 13 Ca26
Ardon CH 141 Bc56
Ardón E 37 Cc57
Ardore Marina I 164 Gb83
Ardpatrick IRL 12 Bd24
Ardrahan IRL 12 Bd21
Ardre S 104 Ha50
Ardres F 21 Gc30
Ardrishaig GB 6 Db12
Ardrossan GB 10 Dc14
Ardshankill GB 9 Cb17
Ardstraw GB 9 Cc16
Ardtalla GB 6 Da13
Ardtoe GB 6 Db10
Ardu EST 98 Kc43
Arduaine GB 6 Db12
Ardud RO 171 Cd55
Ardusat RO 171 Da55
Ardwell GB 10 Dc17
Åre S 78 Fa30
Areatza E 38 Ea56
Årebrot N 84 Ca35
Arèches F 35 Ka47
Arefu RO 175 Dc63
Aremark N 94 Eb44
Aremberg D 125 Bd42
Arenales de San Gregorio E 53 Dd68
Arenas E 60 Da76
Arenas de Cabrales E 38 Da55
Arenas del Rey E 60 Db75
Arenas de San Juan E 52 Dc68
Arenas de San Pedro E 45 Cc65
Arendal N 93 Da46
Arendonk B 124 Ba39
Arendsee D 119 Ea35
Arengosse F 39 Fb53
Arenshausen D 126 Db40
Arentsminde DK 100 Dc21
Arenys de Mar E 49 Ha61
Arenys de Munt E 49 Ha60
Arenzano I 148 Cb63
Areópoli GR 194 Bc90
Ares E 36 Ba54
Arès F 32 Fa50
Ares del Maestrat E 48 Fc64
Aresing D 135 Dd49
Årestrup DK 100 Dc22
Aresvik N 77 Db30
Areta E 38 Ea55
Aréthoussa GR 184 Cc77
Arette F 39 Fb56
Arevalillo E 45 Cc63
Arévalo E 46 Cd62
Arévalo de la Sierra E 47 Eb59
Arez P 50 Ba66
Arezzo I 156 Dd66
Arfará GR 194 Bb89
Argalasti GR 189 Cb82
Argallón E 51 Cb71
Argamasilla de Alba E 53 Dd69
Argamasilla de Calatrava E 52 Db70
Argamasón E 53 Ec70
Arganda E 46 Dc65
Arganil P 44 Ad64
Argaño E 38 Dc58
Argegno I 149 Cc58
Argein F 40 Gb56
Argelaguer E 49 Ha59
Argelès-Gazost F 40 Fc56
Argelès-Plage F 41 Hb57
Argelès-sur-Mer F 41 Hb57
Argelita E 54 Fc66
Argemil P 44 Bb60
Argenbühl D 142 Da52
Argenta I 150 Dd62
Argentan F 22 Fc37
Argentat F 33 Gd49
Argente E 47 Fa64
Argentera I 148 Bb62
Argenteuil F 23 Gd36
Argentiera I 168 Bc74
Argentière F 35 Kb45
Argentona E 49 Ha61
Argenton-Château F 28 Fc43
Argenton-sur-Creuse F 29 Gc44
Argentré F 28 Fb39
Argentré-du-Plessis F 28 Fa39
Argent-sur-Sauldre F 29 Gd41
Arges E 55 Fb70
Argés E 52 Db66
Argetoaia RO 175 Cd65
Argíli GR 194 Ba88
Arginónta GR 197 Eb90
Argirádes GR 182 Ab80
Argiropoúli GR 183 Bd80
Argıthanı TR 193 Hb86
Argithéa GR 188 Bb81
Árgos GR 195 Bd87
Árgos Orestikó GR 182 Ba78
Argostóli GR 188 Ac85
Argovë AL 182 Ac78
Arguedas E 47 Ed59
Argueil F 23 Gb34
Argüero E 37 Cc54
Arguisuelas E 53 Ec66
Argy F 29 Gb43
Arhánes GR 200 Da96
Arhángelos GR 183 Bd76
Arhángelos GR 197 Fa93
Arhavi TR 205 Ga19
Arhéa Feneós GR 189 Bc86
Arhéa Kórinthos GR 195 Bd87
Arhéa Neméa GR 195 Bd87
Arhípoli GR 197 Fa93
Ariano Irpino I 161 Fd74
Ariano nel Polesine I 150 Ea61
Arıca TR 192 Ga84
Ariceștii Zeletin RO 176 Eb63
Ariceşti Rahtivani RO 176 Ea64
Aridéa GR 183 Bc76
Arielli I 157 Fb70
Arienzo I 161 Fb74
Arieșeni RO 171 Cc59
Arifiye TR 187 Gc79
Arifköyü TR 199 Gb92
Arija E 38 Dc56
Arıklar TR 192 Fc83
Arıklı TR 191 Eb82
Arild S 110 Ec54
Arileod GB 6 Da10
Arileod GB 9 Da14
Arilje SRB 178 Ad67
Arinagh IRL 8 Bd18
Arinagour GB 9 Da14
Aringo I 156 Ec69
Aríni GR 194 Ba87
Ariniș RO 171 Cd55
Ariño E 48 Fb62
Arinsal AND 40 Gc57
Arinsal AND 40 Gc57
Arinthod F 31 Jc44
Ariogala LV 114 Kb56
Arionești MD 173 Fb53
Arisaig GB 6 Db09
Ariscal E 59 Bd74
Arisgotas E 52 Db67
Aristava LT 114 Kc56
Aristot E 40 Gc58
Arisvere EST 98 Kd44
Arísvi GR 185 Dd77
Aritzo I 169 Cb77
Arive E 39 Fa56
Arivruaich GB 4 Da05
Ariza E 47 Ec61
Arızlar TR 193 Gb86
Arızlı TR 193 Gd86
Årjäng S 94 Ec43
Arjeplog S 72 Gc21
Årjepluovve S 72 Gc21
Arjona E 52 Da72
Arjonilla E 52 Da72
Arjuzanx F 39 Fb53
Arkadak RUS 203 Fc12
Arkadia PL 130 Ja37
Arkalohóri GR 200 Da96
Arkássa GR 201 Eb95
Arkelstorp S 111 Fb54
Arkesíni GR 196 Dc91
Arkhyttan S 95 Ga40
Arki GR 197 Eb89
Arkitsa GR 189 Ca84
Arklow IRL 13 Cd23
Arkna EST 98 La42
Arkösund S 103 Gb46
Ärla S 95 Gb44
Arlanc F 34 Hc48
Arlaviškės LT 114 Kc57
Arlempdes F 34 Hd50
Arles F 42 Jb54
Arles-sur-Tech F 41 Ha58
Arleuf F 30 Hd42
Arlingham GB 19 Ec27
Arló H 146 Jb50
Arlon B 132 Ba44
Arlöv S 110 Ed56
Arlucea E 39 Eb57
Arluno I 148 Cb59
Árma GR 189 Cb85
Armação de Pera P 58 Ac74
Armadale GB 6 Db09
Arma di Taggia I 43 La52
Armağan TR 185 Ed75
Armagh GB 9 Cd18
Armallones E 47 Eb63
Armamar P 44 Bb61
Ārmani LV 107 Ld52
Armășești RO 176 Ec65
Armasjärvi S 73 Jb20
Armata GR 182 Ad79
Armavir RUS 205 Fd16
Armellada E 37 Cb57
Armen AL 182 Ab77
Arméni GR 200 Cc95
Armenií GR 194 Ba88
Armeniș RO 174 Cb63
Armeniškiai LV 114 Kb57
Armenohóri GR 183 Bb77
Armenteira E 36 Ad56
Armentia E 38 Ea57
Armentières F 23 Ha31
Armilla E 60 Db75
Arminou CY 206 Ja97
Armintza E 38 Ea54
Armivesi FIN 90 Kd32
Armjans'k UA 205 Fa17
Armo I 164 Ga84
Armólia GR 191 Db86
Armonys LT 114 La53
Armoy GB 9 Da15
Armuña de Tajuña E 46 Dd64
Armungia I 169 Cb79
Armutçuk TR 187 Ha77
Armutçuk TR 191 Ec82
Armutlu TR 185 Ed80
Armutlu TR 186 Fc79
Armutlu TR 191 Ed86
Armutlu TR 192 Fa83
Armutlu TR 192 Fb85
Armutlu TR 193 Ha87
Armutlu TR 198 Ga92
Arnabost GB 6 Da10
Arnabost GB 9 Da14
Arnaccio I 155 Da65
Arnach D 142 Da51
Arnac-Pompadour F 33 Gb48
Arnac-sur-Dourdou F 41 Hb54
Arnafjord N 84 Cc37
Arnage F 28 Fd40
Arnager DK 111 Fc58
Arnás GR 190 Da87
Ärnäs S 86 Fa38
Arnäsvall S 80 Ha30
Arnavutköy TR 186 Fc77
Arnavutköy TR 186 Fc79
Arnay-le-Duc F 30 Ja42
Arnberg S 80 Ha25
Arnborg DK 108 Da24
Arnbruck D 135 Ec47
Arncott GB 20 Fa27
Arndrup DK 108 Da27
Arnéa GR 184 Cc78
Arneberg N 86 Ea38
Arneburg D 127 Eb36
Arnedillo E 47 Eb59
Arnedo E 47 Ec59
Arnemark S 73 Hc23
Arnemuiden NL 124 Ab38
Årnes N 62 Gd08
Arnes N 67 Gb14
Årnes N 78 Eb26
Årnes N 94 Eb41
Arnesby GB 16 Fa24
Arnfels A 144 Fd56
Arnhem NL 125 Bb37
Arnionys LT 115 Lb56
Arnis D 108 Dc29
Arnisdale GB 6 Db09
Árnissa GR 183 Bc77
Arnö S 95 Gb45
Arnö S 96 Gc43
Arnoga I 142 Da56
Arnold GB 16 Fa23
Arnoldstein A 144 Fa56
Arnøyhamn N 62 Ha08
Arnprior GB 7 Dd12
Arnsberg D 125 Cb39
Arnschwang D 135 Ec47
Arnsdorf D 128 Fb41
Arnside GB 11 Eb19
Arnstadt D 127 Dd42
Arnstein D 134 Db44
Arnstorf D 135 Ec49
Arnum DK 108 Da27
Aroanía GR 188 Bb86
Aroche E 59 Bb72
Aröd S 102 Eb47
Ároktő H 146 Jc52
Arola FIN 64 Ka07
Arola I 148 Ca58
Arolla CH 148 Bc57
Arona I 148 Cb58
Aroneanu RO 173 Fa57
Aroniádika GR 195 Bd92
Aronkylä FIN 89 Ja32
Åros N 93 Dd42
Arosa CH 142 Cd55
Arosa P 44 Ba60
Árosjåkk S 67 Gd15
Årøsund DK 108 Db27
Arouca P 44 Ad62
Arousa E 36 Ac56
Årøysund N 93 Dd44
Arpacık TR 198 Fd91
Arpajon la Norville F 29 Gd38
Arpășel RO 170 Ca57
Arpașu de Jos RO 175 Dc61
Arpela FIN 74 Jc20
Arpino I 160 Ed72
Arquà Petrarca I 150 Dd60
Arquata del Tronto I 156 Ec68
Arquata Scrivia I 148 Cb62
Arques F 21 Gd30
Arques-la-Bataille F 23 Gb33
Arquillos E 52 Dc72
Arrabal (Oia) E 36 Ac58
Arrach D 135 Ec47
Arracourt F 25 Ka37
Arradon F 27 Eb41
Arraiolos P 50 Ad69
Arrakoski FIN 90 Kb35
Arrankorpi FIN 90 Kb37
Arrans F 30 Hd40
Arras AL 178 Ad73
Arras F 23 Ha32
Arrasate Mondragon E 39 Eb56
Arraute-Charritte F 39 Fa55
Arravonítsa GR 188 Bb85
Arre DK 108 Da26
Arreau F 40 Fd56
Arredondo E 38 Dc55
Årrenjarka S 72 Gc18
Arrens F 40 Fc56
Arreza e Madhe AL 182 Ac77
Arrianá GR 185 Dd77
Arriano E 38 Ea56
Arriate E 60 Cc76
Arrie S 110 Ed56
Arrien F 40 Fc55
Arrifana P 44 Ad64
Arrifana P 45 Bc63
Arrifana P 58 Aa73
Arrigny F 24 Ja37
Arrigorriaga E 38 Ea55
Arrild DK 108 Da27
Arríondas (Parres) E 37 Cd54
Arro E 40 Fd58
Arroiabe E 39 Eb56
Arrojo E 37 Cb55
Arromanches-les-Bains F 22 Fb35
Arronches P 51 Bb68
Arróniz E 39 Ec57
Arrou F 29 Gb39
Arrovo del Ojanco E 53 Dd71
Arroyal E 38 Db56
Arroyo E 38 Db56
Arroyo de la Luz E 51 Bd67
Arroyo de la Plata E 59 Bd73
Arroyo de San Serván E 51 Bd69
Arroyomolinos de León E 51 Bd71
Arroyomolinos de Montánchez E 51 Ca68
Arruazu E 39 Ec56
Arryheernabin IRL 9 Cb15
Ars E 40 Gc58
Arsac F 32 Fb50
Årsand N 70 Ed24
Årsballe DK 111 Fc57
Arsbeck D 125 Bc40
Ars-en-Ré F 32 Ed45
Arsgue F 39 Fb54
Arsiè I 150 Dd58
Arsiero I 150 Dd58
Arsk RUS 203 Fd08
Árskógssandur IS 2 Ba03
Årslev DK 109 Dd27
Årsnes N 76 Cc33
Arsoli I 160 Ec71
Arsos CY 206 Jc97
Ars-sur-Formans F 34 Jb46
Ars-sur-Moselle F 25 Jc35
Årsta havsbad S 96 Gd44
Årsunda S 95 Gb39
Arsura RO 173 Fb58
Arsvågen N 92 Ca43
Árta GR 188 Ad82
Artà E 57 Hc67
Artajona E 39 Ec57
Artana E 54 Fc66
Arta Terme I 143 Ec56
Artazu E 39 Ec57
Artegna I 150 Ec57
Artemare F 35 Jc46
Ärtemark S 94 Ec44
Artemíssia GR 194 Bb89
Artemíssio GR 189 Ca83
Artemíssio GR 194 Bc87
Artemivs'k UA 205 Fb15
Artemónas GR 196 Da90
Artemovka RUS 113 Jc57
Arten I 150 Ea58
Artena I 160 Ec72
Artenay F 29 Gc39
Artern D 127 Dd40
Artés E 49 Gd60
Artesa de Lleida E 48 Ga61
Artesa de Segre E 48 Gb60
Artesianó GR 188 Bb81
Artesina I 148 Bb63
Arth CH 141 Cb54
Arthez-de-Béarn F 39 Fb55
Arthies F 23 Gc36
Arthon-en-Retz F 27 Ec42
Arthonnay F 30 Hd39
Arthurstown IRL 13 Cc25
Artieda E 39 Ed57
Arties E 40 Ga57
Artiguelouve F 39 Fb55
Artiguillon F 32 Fb49
Artix F 39 Fb55
Artjärvi FIN 90 Kd37
Ärtled S 87 Fd38
Artlenburg D 118 Dc33
Arto SLO 151 Fd58
Artozqui E 39 Ed56
Ärtrik S 79 Gb30
Artvin TR 205 Ga19
Artziniega E 38 Dd56
A Rúa E 36 Bc57
Arudy F 39 Fb56
Aruküla EST 98 Kc42
Arum NL 116 Bb33
Arundel GB 20 Fb30
Aruvalla EST 98 Kc43
Årvåg N 77 Dc30
Arvagh IRL 9 Cb19
Arvån S 80 Ha26
Arvanitohóri GR 201 Eb96
Arvant F 34 Hc48
Arvert F 32 Fa47
Arvesund S 79 Fb30
Árvi GR 201 Db96
Arvidsjaur S 72 Ha22
Arvidsträsk S 73 Hc22
Arvieux F 35 Kb50
Arvik N 76 Ca33
Årvik N 76 Ca33
Arvika S 94 Ed42
Årviksand N 62 Ha08
Årvikstrand N 84 Cb40
Arville F 29 Ga39
Arville F 29 Ha39
Arvola FIN 82 Ka27
Arvospouli FIN 69 Kb16
Arvträsk S 80 Ha26
Åryd S 103 Fc52
Åryd S 111 Fc54
Arzachena I 168 Cb73
Arzacq-Arraziguet F 39 Fb54
Arzádigos E 45 Bc59
Arzamas RUS 203 Fc10
Arzano F 27 Dd40
Arzberg D 127 Ed39
Arzberg D 135 Eb44
Arzgir RUS 205 Ga16
Arzignano I 149 Dc59
Arzl im Pitztal A 142 Dc54
Arzon F 27 Eb41
Arzúa E 36 Ba55
Arzulu TR 185 Ed77
As B 125 Bb40
Aš CZ 135 Eb44
Ås N 78 Ec31
Ås N 93 Ea42
Ås N 93 Db45
Ås S 79 Fc30
Ås S 111 Gb54
Åsa S 102 Ec50
Åsa S 103 Fc51
Asaa DK 101 Dd21
Aşağıboğaz TR 187 Gc80
Aşağı Böğürtlen TR 197 Fa91
Aşağıçeşme TR 192 Fd87
Aşağıçiğil TR 193 Hb87
Aşağı Çobanisa TR 191 Ed85
Aşağıdereköy TR 187 Gc78
Aşağıdolaylar TR 192 Fc83
Aşağı Germencik TR 197 Fa91
Aşağıgökdere TR 199 Gd89
Aşağıgünlüce TR 198 Fc90
Aşağıgürlek TR 198 Fc91
Aşağıkaraçay TR 198 Fd88
Aşağıkaşıkara TR 193 Gd86
Aşağıkozcağız TR 187 Gd80
Aşağıkuzfındık TR 193 Gb82
Aşağıokçular TR 185 Ea80
Aşağı Piribeyli TR 193 Hb84
Aşağısamlı TR 198 Fc88
Aşağısevindikli TR 185 Ed77
Aşağıtandır TR 193 Gc84
Aşağıtırtar TR 193 Gd87
Aşağıyağcılar TR 192 Fc82
Aşağıyaylabeli TR 199 Ha89
Asak N 94 Eb44
Asamati MK 182 Ba76
Åsane N 84 Ca39
Åsäng S 88 Gc32
Asanja SRB 153 Jb62
Asar TR 187 Ha78
Asare LV 115 Lb53
Åsaren N 85 Dc35
Åsarna S 79 Fb25
Åsarna S 87 Fb32
Åsarp S 102 Fa48
Asarum S 111 Fc54
Asasp-Arros F 39 Fb56
Asău RO 172 Ec59
Asbach D 125 Ca42
Asbach-Bäumenheim D 134 Dc49
Åsbro S 95 Fc45
Asby S 103 Fd48
Ásbyrgi IS 3 Bb04
Ascád H 145 Gc54
Ascain F 39 Ed55
Ascea I 161 Fd77
Ascha D 135 Ec48
Aschach an der Donau A 144 Fa50
Aschaffenburg D 134 Cd44
Aschau D 143 Eb51
Aschau D 143 Eb53
Aschbach-Markt A 144 Fc51
Ascheberg D 118 Dc31
Ascheberg D 125 Cb38
Ascheffel D 118 Db30
Aschères-le-Marché F 29 Gd39
Aschersleben D 127 Ea39
Așchileu RO 171 Da57
Asciano I 156 Dd67
Asco F 154 Cb69
Ascó E 48 Ga62
Ascoli Piceno I 156 Ed68
Ascoli Satriano I 161 Ga74
Ascona CH 148 Cb57
Ascot GB 20 Fb28
Ascoux F 29 Gd39
Åse N 66 Fd12
A Seara E 36 Ba57
Åsebyn S 94 Ec43
Åseda S 103 Fd51
Åsele S 79 Gb27
Åseli S 73 Hb24
Åseli N 66 Fc17
Asemankylä FIN 74 Ka23
Asemankylä FIN 90 La33
Asemanseutu FIN 81 Jb31
Asemanseutu FIN 89 Jc32
Åsen N 76 Cc33
Åsen N 78 Eb29
Åsen S 80 Hb26
Åsen S 87 Fb38
Åsen S 87 Fb37
Asendorf D 118 Cd35
Asendorf D 118 Db33
Åsenhöga S 102 Fa50

Asenovgrad – Bad Bertrich

Asenovgrad BG 184 Db74
Asenovo BG 180 Ea70
Åsensbruk S 94 Ec45
Åseral N 92 Cc45
Aseri EST 98 La41
Åserud N 94 Eb42
Asevelikylä FIN 89 Jb32
Asfáka GR 182 Ad80
Asfeld F 24 Hd34
Asfendioú GR 197 Ec91
Asferg DK 100 Dc22
Asfordby GB 16 Fb24
Åsgårdstrand N 93 Dd43
Asgata CY 206 Jb98
Ash GB 20 Fd28
Åshagen S 94 Ed41
Åshammar S 95 Gb39
Ashbourne GB 16 Ed23
Ashbourne IRL 13 Cd21
Ashburton GB 19 Dd31
Ashbury GB 20 Ed28
Ashby-de-la-Zouch GB 16 Fa24
Ashdon GB 20 Fd26
Ashford GB 21 Ga29
Ashford IRL 13 Cd22
Ashford-in-the-Water GB 16 Ed22
Ashill GB 17 Ga24
Ashington GB 11 Fa16
Ashington GB 20 Fc30
Ashkirk GB 11 Ec14
Ashley GB 20 Fd26
Ashmore GB 19 Ec30
Ashperton GB 15 Ec26
Ashton-in-Makerfield GB 15 Ec21
Ashton Keynes GB 20 Ed27
Ashton-under-Lyne GB 16 Ed21
Ashwater GB 18 Dc30
Ashwell GB 16 Fb24
Ashwell GB 20 Fc26
Ashwellthorpe GB 17 Gb24
Asiago I 150 Dd58
Asikkala FIN 90 Kc36
Asikkala FIN 91 Lb32
Asila FIN 90 La34
Asími GR 200 Da96
Asipovičy BY 202 Eb13
Aşırlar TR 187 Gc78
Ask N 84 Ca39
Ask N 85 Dd40
Ask N 93 Ea41
Ask S 103 Fc46
Ask S 110 Ed55
Aska FIN 69 Ka16
Askainen FIN 97 Ja39
Aşkale TR 205 Ga20
Askanmäki FIN 75 Kd23
Askeaton IRL 12 Bc23
Askeby S 103 Ga47
Askeia CY 206 Jc96
Asker N 93 Dd42
Askerıye TR 199 Gc88
Askern GB 16 Fa21
Askeröd S 110 Fa55
Askersby S 95 Fd44
Askersund S 95 Fc45
Askerswell GB 19 Eb30
Askeryd S 103 Fc49
Askesta S 87 Gb37
Askett GB 20 Fb27
Åskilje S 80 Gc25
Åskiljeby S 80 Gc25
Askim N 93 Ea42
Askim S 102 Eb49
Asklanda S 102 Ed48
Asklipío GR 197 Ed93
Åskloster S 102 Ec50
Askø By DK 109 Ea28
Askola FIN 90 Kc38
Askome S 102 Ec51
Asköping S 95 Ga44
Askós GR 183 Cb77
Askov DK 108 Da26
Askum S 102 Eb46
Askvoll N 84 Ca36
As Lamas E 36 Bb58
Aslanapa TR 193 Gb83
Aslanlar TR 191 Ec87
Aslestad N 92 Cd43
Aslıhantepeciği TR 192 Fa82
Åsljunga S 110 Fa54
Asma E 36 Bb56
Asmalı TR 186 Fa79
Asmali TR 198 Fd90
Åsmansbo S 95 Fd40
Åsmarka N 86 Ea38
Asmíni GR 189 Ca83
Ašmjany BY 202 Ea12
Asmo N 67 Gd11
Åsmon S 79 Gb30
Asmundtorp S 110 Ed55
Asmunti FIN 74 Kb21
Åsmyra N 70 Ed22
Asnæs DK 109 Ea25
Åsnes N 78 Eb27
Åsnes Finnskog N 94 Ec39
As Neves E 36 Ad58
Asnières-sur-Vègre F 28 Fc40
As Nogais E 36 Bc56
Asola I 149 Da60
Asolo I 150 Ea58
Asopós GR 195 Bd90
Asos GR 188 Ac84
Asp DK 100 Da23
Aspach D 134 Cd48
Aspai E 36 Bb55
Aspang Markt A 145 Gb53
Aspariegos E 45 Cc60
Asparn an der Zaya A 137 Gb49
Asparuhovo BG 181 Ec72
Asparuhovo BG 181 Ed71
Aspås S 79 Fc30
Aspåsnäset S 79 Fc30
Aspatria GB 11 Eb17
Aspberget S 86 Ec38
Aspe E 55 Fb71
Aspeå S 80 Ha29
Aspeå S 80 Gc30
Aspeboda S 95 Fd39
Aspenes N 62 Gd10
Aspenstedt D 127 Dd38
Äspered S 102 Ed49
Asperen NL 124 Ba37
Asperg D 134 Cd48
Asperöd S 110 Fa56
Aspet F 40 Ga56
Aspliden S 72 Ha23
Aspliden S 73 Hc24
Asplund S 72 Gc23
Aspnäs S 88 Gc32
Aspnes N 79 Fb27
Aspö S 95 Gb43
Aspö S 111 Fd54
As Pontes de García Rodríguez E 36 Bb54
Aspoús GR 190 Da84
Aspra I 166 Ed84
Aspremont F 42 Jd51
Aspres-sur-Buëch F 35 Jd50
Áspro GR 183 Bd77
Asprógia GR 183 Bb77
Asproklisiá GR 183 Bb80
Asprópirgos GR 189 Cb86
Áspros GR 183 Ca77
Asproválta GR 184 Cc78
Aspsele S 80 Gd28
Assamalla EST 98 La42
Assamstadt D 134 Da46
Assat F 40 Fc55
Assé-le-Bérenger F 28 Fc39
Assé-le-Boisne F 28 Fc38
Assemini I 169 Ca79
Assen NL 117 Bd34
Assenois B 132 Ba44
Assens DK 100 Dc22
Assens DK 108 Dc27
Assentoft DK 100 Dc23
Assérac F 27 Ec41
Asserbo DK 109 Eb24
Assergi I 156 Ed70
Assesse B 124 Ad42
Assier F 33 Gd51
Assikvere EST 99 Lb44
Ássiros GR 183 Cb77
Assisi I 156 Eb67
Åsskard N 77 Db31
Aßlar D 126 Cc42
Aßling D 143 Ea51
Asso I 149 Cc59
Asson F 40 Fc56
Assoro I 167 Fb85
Ássos GR 188 Ad81
Ássos GR 189 Bd86
Åsta N 86 Eb37
Åstad N 66 Fd15
Astaffort F 40 Ga53
Astakós GR 188 Ad84
Åstan N 77 Dd29
Astašova LV 107 Ld52
Aste EST 105 Jc46
Åsteby S 94 Ed40
Astee IRL 12 Bb23
Asten A 144 Fb51
Asten NL 125 Bb39
Astfeld I 143 Dd56
Asti I 148 Ca61
Aştileu RO 170 Cb57
Astipálea GR 197 Ea92
Åstol S 102 Eb48
Aston GB 16 Fa22
Aston GB 20 Fa27
Astorga E 37 Cb57
Åstorp S 110 Ed54
Astradamovka RUS 203 Fd10
Astráin E 39 Ec57
Åsträsk S 80 Hb26
Astromeritis CY 206 Ja96
Ástros GR 195 Bd88
Astrup DK 100 Dc19
Astrup DK 100 Dc22
Astrup DK 108 Da24
Åstrup DK 108 Dc27
Astruptunet N 84 Cc35
Astryna BY 202 Dd13
Astudillo E 38 Db58
Asuaju RO 171 Cd55
Asuja EST 106 Kc46
Asūne LV 107 Ld52
Asuni I 169 Ca77
Asunta FIN 90 Ka33
Asuny PL 122 Jc30
Ásványráró H 145 Gd52
Asvestohóri GR 183 Cb78
Asvestópetra GR 183 Bb78
Ászár H 145 Ha53
Aszód H 146 Hd52
Aszófő H 145 Ha55
Atabey TR 186 Fd78
Atabey TR 199 Gc88
Atajate E 59 Cb76
Ataki RUS 107 Ma47
Atalánti GR 189 Ca84
Atalaya del Cañavate E 53 Eb67
Atanzón E 46 Dd64
Ataquines E 46 Cd62
Atarte E 60 Db75
Atašiene LV 107 Lb51
Atbükü TR 199 Gc92
Atça TR 187 Hb80
Atça TR 197 Fa88
Atea E 47 Ed62
Ateaş RO 170 Ca57
Ateca E 47 Ec61
Ateham GB 15 Ec24
Aţel RO 175 Db60
Ateleta I 161 Fa71
Atella I 161 Ga75
Atena Lucana I 161 Ga76
Atessa I 161 Fb71
Atháni GR 188 Ac83
Athboy IRL 9 Cc20
Áth Cinn IRL 8 Bc20
Athea IRL 12 Bb23
Athée F 31 Jc42
Athenry IRL 12 Bd21
Athéras GR 188 Ab84
Atherstone GB 16 Fa24
Athesans F 31 Ka40
Athienou CY 206 Jc97
Athies F 23 Ha33
Athíkia GR 195 Bd87
Athína GR 189 Cb86
Athis-de-l'Orne F 22 Fb37
Athleague IRL 8 Ca20
Athlone IRL 13 Ca21
Athy IRL 13 Cc22
Atid RO 172 Dd59
Atienza E 47 Ea62
Atina I 161 Fa72
Aţintiş RO 171 Db59
Atios E 36 Ba53
Atjaševo RUS 203 Fc10
Atla EST 105 Jb46
Atlanterra E 59 Ca78
Atlıhisar TR 193 Gc86
Åtlo N 78 Eb29
Atnbrua N 85 Ea35
Atnmoen N 85 Ea35
Ätran S 102 Ed51
Atrani I 161 Fb75
Åträsk S 73 Hc23
Åträsk S 73 Hc21
Atri I 157 Fa69
Atripalda I 161 Fc75
Atsalama EST 99 Lb42
Attáli GR 189 Cc84
Attendorn D 125 Cb40
Attenkirchen D 135 Ea49
Attersee A 143 Ed52
Attert B 132 Ba44
Attigny F 24 Hd34
Attimis I 150 Ed57
Attiökylä FIN 74 Kb24
Attleborough GB 21 Ga25
Attlebridge GB 17 Gb24
Attmar S 87 Gb33
Attnang-Puchheim A 144 Fa51
Åttonträsk S 80 Gc26
Attrup DK 100 Db21
Attsjö S 103 Fc52
Attu FIN 97 Jb40
Attvika N 66 Ga12
Åtvidaberg S 103 Ga47
Atzara I 169 Ca77
Atzendorf D 127 Ea38
Atzeneta del Maestrat E 54 Fc65
Au D 135 Ea49
Aub D 134 Db46
Aubagne F 42 Jd55
Aubange B 132 Ba45
Aubazine F 33 Gc49
Aubel B 125 Bb41
Aubenas F 34 Ja50
Aubenton F 24 Hd33
Aubepierre-sur-Aube F 30 Jb39
Aubergenville F 23 Gc36
Aubérive F 24 Hd35
Auberive F 30 Jb40
Aubeterre-sur-Dronne F 32 Fd49
Aubiat F 34 Hb46
Aubiet F 40 Ga54
Aubigné F 32 Fc46
Aubigny F 28 Ed44
Aubigny-au-Bac F 24 Hb32
Aubigny-en-Artois F 23 Gd32
Aubigny-sur-Nère F 29 Gd41
Aubin F 33 Gd51
Aubonne CH 140 Ba55
Aubrac F 34 Hb51
Aubusson F 33 Gd46
Auby F 23 Ha31
Auce LV 105 Jd52
Auch F 40 Ga54
Aucharnie GB 7 Ec08
Auchavan GB 7 Eb10
Auchel F 23 Gd31
Auchencairn GB 10 Ea17
Auchenmaig GB 10 Dc16
Auchentiber GB 10 Dd14
Auchronie GB 7 Ec10
Auchterarder GB 7 Ea12
Auchtermuchty GB 7 Eb12
Auchy-au-Bois F 23 Gd31
Aucun F 40 Fc56
Audenge F 32 Fa51
Audenhain D 127 Ec40
Auderville F 22 Ed34
Audevälja EST 98 Ka43
Audierne F 27 Db39
Audincourt F 31 Ka41
Audla EST 105 Jd46
Audlem GB 15 Ec23
Audru EST 106 Kb46
Audruicq F 21 Gc30
Audrupi LV 106 Kc52
Audun-le-Roman F 25 Jc34
Audun-le-Tiche F 25 Jc34
Aue D 135 Ec43
Auer I 150 Dd57
Auerbach D 135 Ea45
Auerbach D 135 Eb43
Auerbach D 135 Ed49
Auerswalde D 127 Ec42
Auetal D 126 Da37
Aufferville F 29 Ha39
Aufhausen D 135 Eb48
Aufles N 70 Fa22
Aufseß D 135 Dd45
Augan F 27 Ec40
Augé F 32 Fc45
Augerolles F 34 Hc47
Augerum S 111 Fd54
Aughacasla IRL 12 Ba24
Augher GB 9 Cc17
Aughils IRL 12 Ba24
Aughnacloy GB 9 Cc18
Aughrim IRL 13 Ca21
Aughrim IRL 13 Cd23
Augland N 93 Da46
Augmėnai LV 114 Kb55
Augsburg D 142 Dc50
Augsligatne LV 106 Kd49
Augstasils LV 107 Ld49
Augstkalne LV 106 Ka52
Augusta I 167 Fd87
Augustdorf D 126 Cd38
Auguste LV 113 Jc53
Augustenborg DK 108 Db28
Augustów PL 123 Ka31
Augustów PL 130 Jc39
Augustowo PL 123 Kb34
Augustusburg D 127 Ed42
Auho FIN 75 Kc23
Auiņi LV 105 Jc52
Aukan N 77 Db30
Aukland N 92 Cd47
Auklandshamn N 92 Ca41
Aukra N 76 Cd31
Aukrug D 118 Db31
Aukštadvaris LT 114 Kd58
Aukštelkai LT 114 Kb54
Aukštelkė LT 114 Ka54
Auktsjaur S 72 Ha22
Auleben D 127 Dd40
Auleja LV 107 Ld52
Aulendorf D 142 Cd51
Aulesti E 39 Eb55
Auletta I 161 Fd76
Aulla I 149 Cd63
Aullène F 154 Cb71
Aulnay F 32 Fc46
Aulnay-la-Riviere F 29 Gd39
Aulnay-sous-Bois F 23 Gd36
Aulnizeux F 24 Hc37
Aulnoye-Aymeries F 24 Hc32
Aulstad N 85 Dd37
Ault F 23 Gb33
Aultbea GB 4 Dc06
Aulum DK 100 Da23
Aulus-les-Bains F 40 Gb57
Auma D 127 Ea42
Aumale F 23 Gc34
Aumeisteri LV 106 La48
Aumetz F 25 Jc34
Aumont F 31 Jc43
Aumont-Aubrac F 34 Hc50
Aumühle D 118 Dc33
Aun N 66 Ga12
Aunay F 29 Gc38
Aunay-en-Bazois F 30 Hc42
Aunay-sur-Odon F 22 Fb36
Aune N 77 Dd30
Auneau F 29 Gc38
Aunebakksetra N 77 Dc31
Aunet N 78 Ed25
Aunet N 78 Ed26
Aunet N 78 Eb27
Aunet N 78 Ea29
Auneuil F 23 Gc35
Auning DK 101 Dd23
Aunslev DK 109 Dd27
Aups F 42 Ka53
Aura D 134 Da44
Aura FIN 89 Jc38
Aurach D 134 Db47
Aurachtal D 134 Dc46
Auray F 27 Ea41
Aurdal N 85 Dc38
Aure N 77 Db30
Aureskoski FIN 89 Jc34
Aurice F 39 Fb53
Aurich D 117 Cb32
Aurignac F 40 Ga55
Aurillac F 33 Ha50
Auriol F 42 Jd54
Aurisina I 151 Fa59
Auritz E 39 Ed56
Aurlandsvangen N 84 Cd38
Aurolzmünster A 143 Ed50
Auron F 43 Kc51
Aurons F 42 Jc53
Auronzo di Cadore I 143 Eb56
Aurora RO 181 Fc68
Auros F 32 Fc51
Aursfjordbotn N 67 Gc11
Aursmoen N 94 Eb41
Ausa Corno I 150 Ed59
Ausås S 110 Ed54
Auschwitz = Oświęcim PL 138 Hd44
Ausdal N 92 Cc44
Ausejo E 39 Eb58
Auşeu RO 171 Cc57
Auskarnes N 64 Ka05
Ausonia I 160 Ed73
Ausserferrera CH 142 Cd56
Ausserfragant A 143 Ec55
Außervillgraten A 143 Eb55
Aussonne F 40 Gb54
Austad N 92 Cd44
Austad N 92 Cc47
Austafjord N 78 Eb25
Austanå N 93 Da45
Austbø N 70 Ed21
Austbygda N 93 Db41
Austefjord N 84 Cc34
Austervika N 67 Gb13
Austevoll N 84 Ca40
Austhasselstrand N 92 Cb47
Austis I 169 Ca77
Austmarka N 94 Ec41
Austnes N 66 Ga12
Austnes N 76 Cc32
Austpollen N 66 Fd13
Austrått N 77 Dd29
Austre Amøy N 92 Ca43
Austreim N 84 Cb36
Austre Moland N 93 Db46
Austre Vikebygd N 92 Ca42
Austrheim N 84 Ca38
Austrumdal N 92 Cb45
Auterive F 40 Gc55
Auteuil F 23 Gd35
Autheuil-Authouillet F 23 Gb36
Authon F 42 Ka51
Authon-du-Perche F 29 Ga39
Authon-la-Plaine F 29 Gc38
Autilla del Pino E 46 Da59
Autio FIN 74 Kb24
Autio FIN 81 Jd31
Autio FIN 82 Kb31
Autionperä FIN 82 Ka30
Autol E 47 Ec59
Autrans F 35 Jc48
Autrèche F 29 Gb41
Autrey F 31 Jc41
Autricourt F 30 Ja39
Autry-le-Châtel F 29 Ha41
Autti FIN 74 Kb19
Auttoinen FIN 90 Kb36
Autun F 30 Hd43
Auvåg N 66 Fc13
Auverse F 28 Fd41
Auvers-sur-Oise F 23 Gd36
Auvillar F 40 Ga53
Auvillars-sur-Saône F 30 Jb42
Auvre F 24 Ja36
Auw bei Prüm D 133 Bc43
Auxerre F 30 Hc40
Auxi-le-Château F 23 Gd32
Auxon F 30 Hc39
Auxonne F 31 Jc42
Auxy F 30 Ja43
Auzances F 33 Ha46
Auzat-la-Combelle F 34 Hc48
Auziņas LV 106 Ka51
Auziņi LV 106 Kd51
Auziņi LV 107 Ld51
Åva FIN 97 Hd39
Ava S 80 Ha29
Avafors S 73 Hd21
Availles-Limouzine F 33 Ga46
Avaldsnes N 92 Bd42
Avallon F 30 Hc41
Avan S 73 Hd22
Avan S 73 Hd24
Avanäs S 80 Ha27
Avant-lès-Marcilly F 30 Hc38
Avant-lès-Remerupt F 30 Hd38
Ávas GR 185 Dd77
Avasjö S 79 Gb27
Avaträsk S 79 Ga27
Avaviken S 72 Gd22
Avcılar TR 186 Fa75
Avcılar TR 191 Eb82
Avcıoğlu TR 198 Fd91
Avdan TR 186 Ga80
Avdan TR 191 Ed83
Avdan TR 193 Gb82
Avdan TR 198 Fc89
Avdarma MD 177 Fd60
Avdebo DK 109 Eb25
Avdijivka UA 202 Ed13
Avdimou CY 206 Ja98
Ávdira GR 184 Db77
Avdoú GR 201 Db96
Avebury GB 20 Ed28
Åvedal N 92 Cb45
Åvedal N 92 Cb46
A Veiga E 36 Bc58
Aveiras de Cima P 50 Ab67
Aveiro P 44 Ac62
Avelengo I 142 Dc56
Avella I 161 Fb74
Avellanosa del Páramo E 38 Dc58
Avellino I 161 Fc75
Avenas F 34 Ja45
Avenches CH 141 Bc54
Avening GB 19 Ec27
Åvensor FIN 97 Ja40
Avereest NL 117 Bd35
Avernak By DK 108 Dc28
Avernay-Val-d'Or F 24 Hd36
A Ver-o-Mar P 44 Ac60
Aversa I 161 Fa74
Averton F 28 Fc38
Aves P 44 Ad60
Avesnes-le-Comte F 23 Gd32
Avesnes-lès-Aubert F 24 Hb32
Avesnes-sur-Helpe F 24 Hc32
Avessac F 27 Ec41
Avesta S 95 Ga41
Avetrana I 162 Hb76
Avezzano I 160 Ed71
Avgan TR 192 Fd86
Avgancık TR 192 Ga86
Avgerinós GR 182 Ba78
Avgó GR 195 Ca88
Avgorou CY 206 Jd97
Avía GR 194 Bb89
Avià E 49 Gd59
Aviano I 150 Eb58
Aviemore GB 7 Ea09
Avigliana I 148 Bc60
Avigliano I 161 Ga75
Avignon F 42 Jb53
Avignonet-Lauragais F 40 Gc55
Ávila E 46 Cd63
Avilés E 37 Cb54
Aviliai LT 115 Lb54
Avilley F 31 Jd41
Avinurme EST 99 Lb43
Avinyó E 49 Gd60
Avio I 149 Dc58
Avion F 23 Ha31
Avión E 36 Ba57
Avirey F 30 Hd39
Avis P 50 Ad68
Åvist FIN 81 Jb29
Avize F 24 Hc36
Avižieniai LT 123 Kc30
Avláki GR 189 Bd83
Avláki GR 197 Ec92
Avlémonas GR 195 Bd92
Avlíótes GR 182 Aa79
Avlóna GR 189 Cb86
Avlonári GR 189 Cc85
Avô P 44 Ba64
Avoca IRL 13 Cd23
Avoch GB 5 Ea07
Avoine F 28 Fd42
Avola I 167 Fd88
Avord F 29 Ha43
Avoriaz F 35 Kb45
Avot F 30 Jb40
Avoudrey F 31 Ka42
Avrămeni RO 172 Ed54
Avrămeşti RO 176 Dd60
Avram Iancu RO 170 Ca58
Avram Iancu RO 171 Cc59
Avranches F 22 Fa37
Avren BG 185 Dd76
Avren BG 181 Fa71
Avrig RO 175 Db61
Avrillé F 28 Fb41
Avrillé F 32 Ed45
Avsallar TR 199 Hb92
Avtovac BIH 159 Hc67
Avtovo RUS 99 Mb39
Avvakajjo S 67 Ha17
Avvakko S 67 Hb17
Avvil FIN 69 Ka11
Avžže N 68 Ja11
Axalp CH 141 Ca55
Axamer Lizum A 143 Dd54
Axams A 143 Dd54
Axat F 41 Gd57
Axberg S 95 Fd43
Axel NL 124 Ab39
Axente Sever RO 175 Db60
Axford GB 20 Fa29
Axintele RO 176 Ec66
Axioúpoli GR 183 Ca76
Ax-les-Thermes F 41 Gd57
Axmarby S 87 Gb38
Axminster GB 19 Eb30
Axós GR 183 Bd77
Axós GR 200 Cd95
Axstedt D 118 Cd33
Axvall S 102 Fa47
Ayamonte E 58 Ba74
Ayancık TR 205 Fb19
Ayas I 148 Bd58
Ayaslar TR 193 Hb87
Ayaz E 36 Bb56
Ayazini TR 193 Gc84
Ayazkent TR 191 Ec83
Aydan TR 193 Gc82
Aydin TR 187 Hb77
Aydin TR 197 Ed88
Aydıncık TR 185 Dd80
Aydınkent = İbradı TR 199 Hb90
Aydınlar TR 186 Fb76
Aydınlar TR 187 Hb77
Aydınlar TR 191 Ed84
Aydınlı TR 186 Fd78
Aydınlı TR 193 Hb84
Aydoğdu TR 186 Ga80
Aydoğmuş TR 187 Ha80
Aydoğmus TR 198 Fd89
Ayen F 33 Gb49
Ayer CH 141 Bd56
Ayerbe E 39 Fb58
Ayguesvives F 40 Gc55
Aylesbury GB 20 Fb27
Aylesham GB 21 Gb29
Ayllón E 46 Dd61
Aylsham GB 17 Gb24
Aylton GB 15 Ec26
Aynac F 33 Gc50
Ayódar E 54 Fc66
Ayora E 54 Fa69
Ayr GB 10 Dd14
Ayrancı TR 192 Ga85
Ayron F 28 Fd44
Ayşebacı TR 192 Fa82
Aysgarth GB 11 Ed19
Äyskoski FIN 82 Kc30
Aystetten D 142 Dc50
Äystö FIN 89 Ja32
Ayton GB 11 Ed13
Ayton GB 17 Fc19
Aytré F 32 Fa46
Ayvacık TR 191 Ea82
Ayvacık TR 191 Ec85
Ayvacık TR 191 Ed85
Ayvacık TR 192 Ga85
Ayvacık TR 205 Fc20
Ayvalı TR 192 Fd82
Ayvalı TR 193 Hb83
Ayvalık TR 191 Eb83
Ayvalıpınar TR 199 Gd88
Ayvanpazarı TR 186 Ga79
Ayvatlar TR 191 Ec83
Ayvatlat TR 192 Fa82
Aywaille B 124 Ba42
Azaila E 48 Fb62
Azambuja P 50 Ab68
Azanja SRB 174 Bb65
Azannes F 24 Jb35
Azanúy E 48 Fd59
Azaruja P 50 Ba69
Azaryčy BY 202 Eb13
Azatlı TR 185 Eb76
Azay-le-Ferron F 29 Gb43
Azay-le-Rideau F 28 Fd42
Azé F 29 Gb40
Azeitada P 50 Ac67
Azincourt F 23 Gd31
Azinhal P 58 Ba74
Azinheira dos Barros P 50 Ac71
Azinhoso P 45 Bd61
Azıtepe TR 192 Fb86
Aziziye BG 185 Ed74
Azizler TR 192 Ga86
Azkoitia E 39 Eb55
Aznakaevo RUS 203 Ga08
Aznalcázar E 59 Bd74
Aznalcóllar E 59 Bd73
Azoia P 44 Ab65
Azov RUS 205 Fc15
Azpeitia E 39 Eb55
Azuaga E 51 Cb71
Azuara E 47 Fa62
Azuel E 52 Da71
Azuga RO 176 Ea63
Ažulaukė LT 114 La57
Ažuolu Būda LV 114 Kb58
Azuoliniai LV 114 Kb59
Azuqueca de Henares E 46 Dd64
Azur F 39 Fa53
Azurara P 44 Ac60
Azy F 29 Ha42
Ažytėnai LV 114 Kb55
Azzano Decimo I 150 Eb58
Azzate I 148 Cb58

B

Ba SRB 159 Jc64
Baak NL 125 Bc37
Baal D 125 Bc40
Baalberge D 127 Ea39
Baamonde E 36 Bb54
Baar CH 141 Cb53
Baarland NL 124 Ab38
Baarle-Nassau B 124 Ad38
Baarlo NL 125 Bc39
Baarn NL 116 Bb36
Baasdorf D 127 Eb39
Baba Ana RO 176 Eb64
Babadag RO 177 Fc65
Babadağ TR 198 Fc88
Babadat TR 193 Hb82
Babadere TR 191 Eb82
Babaeski TR 185 Ec76
Babaevo RUS 202 Ec08
Băbăiţa RO 180 Dd67
Babakale TR 191 Ea82
Babaköy TR 192 Fa81
Băbana RO 175 Dc64
Babarc H 153 Hc58
Babasultan TR 192 Fd81
Babek BG 180 Dc72
Babenhausen D 134 Cd44
Babenhausen D 142 Db50
Băbeni RO 171 Da56
Băbeni RO 175 Db64
Babensham D 143 Eb51
Babiak PL 122 Ja30
Babiak PL 129 Hb37
Babiak PL 130 Hc37
Babica PL 139 Ka44
Babice PL 138 Hd44
Babići BIH 158 Gd64
Băbiciu RO 180 Db67
Babięta PL 122 Jb32
Babigoszcz PL 120 Fc32
Babilafuente E 45 Cc62
Babimost PL 128 Ga37
Babina Greda HR 153 Hc61
Babin Most KSV 178 Bb70
Babino RUS 99 Ld40
Babino Polje HR 158 Ha69
Babin Potok HR 151 Fd62
Babjak BG 184 Cd74
Babljak MNE 159 Ja68
Babócsa H 152 Gd58
Bábolna H 145 Ha52
Bábonymegyer H 145 Hb55
Baborów PL 137 Ha44
Baboszewo PL 122 Ja35
Babriškės LT 114 Kd59
Babrujsk BY 202 Eb13
Babrungas LT 113 Jc54
Babsk PL 130 Ja38
Babtai LV 114 Kb57
Babuk BG 181 Ed68
Babušnica SRB 179 Ca70
Bač SRB 153 Hd60
Băcani RO 177 Fa60
Bača pri Modreju SLO 151 Fa57
Bacares E 61 Ea75
Bacău RO 172 Ed59
Bačavani BIH 152 Gc61
Baccano I 160 Ea71
Baccarat F 25 Ka37
Baccealia MD 173 Ga59
Baccon F 29 Gc40
Baceno I 141 Ca56
Băceşti RO 172 Ed58
Bach A 142 Db53
Bach D 135 Eb48
Bach F 40 Gc52
Bachant F 24 Hc32
Bacharach D 133 Ca44
Bachčysaraj UA 205 Fa18
Bachmač UA 202 Ed14
Bachórz PL 139 Ka44
Bachórzec PL 139 Kb44
Bachotek PL 122 Hc33
Băcia RO 175 Cc61
Bačina SRB 178 Bc67
Băcioi MD 173 Fd58
Baciu RO 171 Da58
Baciuty PL 123 Kb34
Back GB 4 Db05
Bäck S 103 Fb46
Backa S 87 Fc38
Backa S 96 Ha41
Backa S 102 Eb49
Backaby S 103 Fc50
Backaland GB 5 Ec02
Bačka Palanka SRB 153 Ja60
Backaryd S 111 Fd53
Bačka Topola SRB 153 Ja58
Backberg S 95 Gb39
Backbodarna S 95 Fc40
Backby FIN 81 Jb28
Backe S 79 Ga28
Bäcke S 94 Ec45
Backebo S 103 Ga52
Bäckefors S 94 Ec45
Backen S 87 Gb32
Backen S 87 Gb33
Backgränd FIN 97 Jd40
Bački Breg SRB 153 Hd58
Bački Brestovac SRB 153 Hd59
Bački Jarak SRB 153 Jb60
Bačkininkai LT 114 Kc58
Bački Petrovac SRB 153 Ja60
Bački Sokolac SRB 153 Ja58
Bäckmark S 72 Gb23
Backnang D 134 Cd48
Bäcknäs S 72 Gd23
Bačko Dobro Polje SRB 153 Ja59
Bačko Gradište SRB 153 Jb59
Bačko Novo Selo SRB 153 Hd60
Bačko Petrovo Selo SRB 153 Jb59
Bačkovo BG 184 Db74
Bäckseda S 103 Fc50
Backträsk S 73 Hc22
Băcleş RO 175 Cc65
Bacoli I 161 Fa75
Bacor Olivar E 61 Dd74
Bacova Mahala BG 180 Dc69
Bacqueplus F 23 Gb36
Bácsalmás H 153 Hd57
Bácsbokod H 153 Hd57
Bácsszentgyörgy H 153 Hd58
Bacton GB 21 Ga25
Bacup GB 16 Ed20
Bad Abbach D 135 Ea48
Badachro GB 4 Db07
Badacsonytomaj H 145 Ha55
Bad Aibling D 143 Ea52
Badajoz E 51 Bc69
Badalona E 49 Ha61
Badalucco I 43 La52
Badarán E 38 Ea58
Bad Arolsen D 126 Cd40
Bad Aussee A 144 Fa53
Bad Bederkesa D 118 Cd32
Bad Bentheim D 117 Ca36
Badbergen D 117 Cc35
Bad Bergzabern D 133 Ca47
Bad Berka D 127 Dd41
Bad Berleburg D 126 Cc40
Bad Berneck im Fichtelgebirge D 135 Ea44
Bad Bertrich D 133 Bd43

Bad Bevensen – Balsthal

Bad Bevensen D 118 Dc34
Bad Bibra D 127 Ea40
Bad Birnbach D 143 Ec50
Bad Blankenburg D 127 Dd42
Bad Bleiberg A 144 Fa56
Bad Blumau A 144 Ga54
Bad Bocklet D 134 Db43
Bad Bodenteich D 118 Dc35
Bad Boll D 134 Da49
Bad Brambach D 135 Eb44
Bad Bramstedt D 118 Db31
Bad Breisig D 125 Ca42
Bad Brückenau D 134 Da43
Bad Buchau D 142 Cd51
Badby GB 20 Fa25
Bad Camberg D 133 Cb43
Badcaul GB 4 Dc06
Bad Colberg-Heldburg D 134 Dc43
Badderen N 63 Hc08
Bad Deutsch-Altenburg A 145 Gc51
Bad Doberan D 119 Eb31
Bad Driburg D 126 Cd38
Bad Düben D 127 Ec39
Bad Dürkheim D 133 Cb46
Bad Dürrenberg D 127 Eb40
Bad Dürrheim D 141 Cb51
Badeborn D 127 Dd38
Bądecz PL 121 Gc34
Bad Eilsen D 126 Cd37
Badellou E 48 Ga60
Bad Elster D 135 Eb44
Badelunda S 95 Gb42
Bademağacı TR 199 Gc90
Bademler TR 191 Eb86
Bademli TR 185 Dd80
Bademli TR 191 Eb84
Bademli TR 191 Eb86
Bademli TR 192 Fa83
Bademli TR 193 Ha84
Bademli TR 198 Ga89
Bademli TR 199 Gd88
Bademli TR 199 Hb89
Bademli TR 199 Hb90
Bad Ems D 133 Ca43
Baden A 145 Gb51
Baden CH 141 Cb52
Baden-Baden D 133 Cb48
Bad Endbach D 126 Cc41
Badendiek D 119 Eb32
Bad Endorf D 143 Eb51
Badenhausen D 126 Db38
Badenscoth GB 7 Ec08
Badenweiler D 141 Bd51
Baderna HR 151 Fa61
Badersleben D 127 Dd38
Badesi I 168 Ca74
Bad Essen D 117 Cc36
Bad Feilnbach D 143 Ea52
Bad Frankenhausen D 127 Dd40
Bad Freienwalde D 120 Fb35
Bad Friedrichshall D 134 Cd47
Bad Fusch A 143 Ec54
Bad Füssing D 143 Ed50
Bad Gandersheim D 126 Db38
Bad Gastein A 143 Ec54
Bad Gleichenberg A 144 Ga55
Bad Gögging D 135 Ea48
Bad Goisern A 143 Ed52
Bad Gottleuba-Berggießhübel D 128 Fa42
Bad Griesbach D 143 Ed50
Bad Grund D 126 Db38
Bad Hall A 144 Fb51
Bad Harzburg D 126 Dc38
Bad Heilbrunn D 143 Dd52
Bad Herrenalb D 133 Cb48
Bad Hersfeld D 126 Da41
Bad Hindelang D 142 Db53
Bad Hofgastein A 143 Ec54
Bad Homburg D 134 Cc43
Bad Honnef D 125 Bd42
Bad Hönningen D 125 Ca42
Badia I 143 Ea56
Badia Calavena I 149 Dc59
Badia Gran E 57 Hb68
Badia Polesine I 150 Dd61
Badia Pratagia I 156 Dd65
Badia Tedalda I 156 Ea65
Bad Iburg D 125 Cb37
Bădiceni MD 173 Fb54
Badicul Moldovenesc MD 177 Fb61
Badingen D 127 Ea36
Badirga TR 186 Fc80
Bad Ischl A 143 Ed52
Badje-Sohppar S 68 Hc14
Bad Karlshafen D 126 Da39
Bad Kemmeriboden CH 141 Ca54
Bądki PL 121 Hb32
Bad Kissingen D 134 Db44
Bad Kleinen D 119 Ea32
Bad Kleinkirchheim A 144 Fa55
Bad Klosterlausnitz D 127 Ea41
Bad Kohlgrub D 142 Dc52
Bad König D 134 Cd45
Bad Königshofen D 134 Dc43
Bad Kösen D 127 Ea41
Bad Köstritz D 127 Eb41
Bądkowo PL 121 Hb35
Bad Kreuzen A 144 Fc50
Bad Kreuznach D 133 Ca44
Bad Krozingen D 141 Bd51
Bad Laasphe D 126 Cc41
Bad Laer D 126 Cc37
Bad Langensalza D 126 Dc41
Bad Lauchstädt D 127 Ea40
Bad Lausick D 127 Ec41
Bad Lauterberg D 126 Dc39
Bad Leonfelden A 144 Fb50
Bad Liebenstein D 126 Db42
Bad Liebenwerda D 127 Ed40
Bad Liebenzell D 134 Cc48
Bad Lippspringe D 126 Cd38
Badljevina HR 152 Gd59
Bad Lobenstein D 135 Ea43
Bad Marienberg D 125 Cb42
Bad Meinberg, Horn- D 126 Cd38
Bad Mergentheim D 134 Da46
Badminton GB 19 Ec28
Bad Mitterndorf A 144 Fa53
Bad Münder D 126 Da37
Bad Münster-Ebernburg D 133 Ca45
Bad Münstereifel D 125 Bd42
Bad Muskau D 128 Fc39
Bad Nauheim D 134 Cc43
Bad Neuenahr-Ahrweiler D 125 Bd42
Bad Neustadt D 134 Db43
Bad Oeynhausen D 126 Cd37
Badolato I 164 Gc82
Badolato Marina I 164 Gc82
Badolatosa E 60 Cd74
Bad Oldesloe D 118 Dc32
Badonviller F 25 Ka37
Bad Orb D 134 Cd43
Badovinci SRB 153 Ja62
Bad Peterstal-Griesbach D 133 Cb49
Bad Pyrmont D 126 Da38
Bad Radkersburg A 144 Ga56
Bad Ragaz CH 142 Cd54
Bad Rappenau D 134 Cd47
Bad Reichenhall D 143 Ec52
Bad Rippoldsau-Schapbach D 133 Cb49
Bad Rodach D 134 Dc43
Bad Rothenfelde D 126 Cc37
Bad Saarow-Pieskow D 128 Fb37
Bad Sachsa D 126 Dc39
Bad Säckingen D 141 Ca52
Bad Salzdetfurth D 126 Db37
Bad Salzschlirf D 126 Da42
Bad Salzschlirf D 126 Da42
Bad Salzuflen D 126 Cd37
Bad Salzungen D 126 Db42
Bad Sankt Leonhard im Lavanttal A 144 Fc55
Bad Sassendorf D 126 Cc39
Bad Saulgau D 142 Cd51
Bad Schallerbach A 144 Fa50
Bad Schandau D 128 Fb42
Bad Schmiedeberg D 127 Ec39
Bad Schönau A 145 Gb53
Bad Schönborn D 134 Cc47
Bad Schussenried D 142 Cd51
Bad Schwalbach D 133 Cb43
Bad Schwartau D 119 Dd31
Bad Schwarzsee CH 141 Bc55
Bad Segeberg D 118 Dc31
Bad Sobernheim D 133 Ca45
Bad Soden D 134 Cc44
Bad Soden-Salmünster D 134 Cd43
Bad Sooden-Allendorf D 126 Db40
Bad Staffelstein D 135 Dd44
Bad Steben D 135 Ea43
Bad Suderode D 127 Dd39
Bad Sulza D 127 Ea41
Bad Sülze D 119 Ec31
Bad Tatzmannsdorf A 145 Gb54
Bad Teinach-Zavelstein D 134 Cc48
Bad Tennstedt D 126 Dc41
Bad Tölz D 143 Dd52
Bad Überkingen D 134 Da49
Badules E 47 Ed62
Bad Urach D 134 Cd49
Bad Vellach A 144 Fb56
Bad Vilbel D 134 Cc43
Bad Vöslau A 145 Gb51
Bad Waldsee D 142 Da51
Bad Wiessee D 143 Ea52
Bad Wildbad D 133 Cb48
Bad Wildungen D 126 Cd40
Bad Wilsnack D 119 Eb35
Bad Wimpfen D 134 Cd47
Bad Windsheim D 134 Db46
Bad Wörishofen D 142 Db51
Bad Wurzach D 142 Da51
Bad Zell A 144 Fc50
Bad Zwesten D 126 Cd41
Bad Zwischenahn D 118 Cc33
Baek D 119 Eb34
Bække DK 108 Da26
Bækmarksbro DK 100 Cd23
Bælum DK 100 Dc22
Baena E 60 Da73
Baerenthal F 25 Kb35
Baesweiler D 125 Bc41
Baeza E 52 Dc72
Bafra TR 205 Fb19
Bagà E 41 Gd58
Băgaciu RO 175 Db60
Bagaladi I 164 Ga84
Bagamér H 147 Kb52
Bağarası TR 197 Ed88
Bagart PL 122 Hc31
Bagaslaviškis LT 114 Kd56
Bağbaşı TR 192 Ga85
Bagdononys LT 114 Kd58
Bågede S 79 Fc27
Bâgé-le-Châtel F 34 Jb45
Bagenalstown IRL 13 Cc23
Bagenkop DK 109 Dd29
Bages F 41 Hb57
Baggböle S 80 Hb28
Baggbrod S 95 Fd42
Baggetorp S 95 Ga45
Bagheria I 166 Ed84
Bagienice PL 123 Jd32
Bağıllı TR 193 Gd87
Bağıllı TR 199 Gd88
Bağırganlı TR 187 Gb77
Bağkonak TR 193 Ha87
Baglad H 145 Gb56
Bağlarbaşı TR 193 Ha86
Bagley GB 15 Eb23
Bağlıağaç TR 198 Fd92
Baglicy RUS 99 Ld45
Bagn N 85 Dc38
Bagnac-sur-Célé F 33 Gd51
Bagnaia I 156 Ea70
Bagnara Calabra I 164 Ga83
Bagnarola I 150 Dd62
Bagnasco I 148 Bd63
Bagnères-de-Bigorre F 40 Fd56
Bagnères-de-Luchon F 40 Ga57
Bagneux-la-Fosse F 30 Hd39
Bagni Contursi I 161 Fd75
Bagni del Masino I 149 Cc57
Bagni di Craveggia I 148 Cb57
Bagni di Lucca I 155 Db64
Bagni di Mondragone I 161 Fa74
Bagni di Petriolo I 155 Dc67
Bagni di Rabbi I 142 Dc56
Bagni di Stigliano I 160 Ea71
Bagni di Tivoli I 160 Eb71
Bagni di Vinadio I 148 Bb63
Bagni San Cataldo I 161 Ga75
Bagnity PL 122 Hd31
Bagno I 161 Ga72
Bagno di Romagna I 156 Ea65
Bagnoles-de-l'Orne F 28 Fc38
Bagnoli di Sopra I 150 Ea60
Bagnoli Irpino I 161 Fc75
Bagnolo Mella I 149 Da59
Bagnolo Piemonte I 148 Bc61
Bagnols F 33 Ha48
Bagnols-en Forêt F 43 Kb54
Bagnols-les-Bains F 34 Hc51
Bagnols-sur-Cèze F 42 Jb52
Bagnone I 149 Cd63
Bagnoregio I 156 Ea69
Bagny PL 123 Kb32
Bågø By DK 108 Db27
Bagod H 145 Gc55
Bagojë AL 182 Ab75
Bagolino I 149 Db58
Bagolyirtás H 146 Ja51
Bagotoji LV 114 Kb58
Bağözü TR 187 Hb80
Bagrationovsk RUS 122 Ja30
Bagrdan SRB 174 Bc66
Bağsaray TR 199 Gc89
Báguena E 47 Ed62
Bagüés E 39 Fa58
Bağyurdu TR 191 Ed86
Bahabón de Esgueval E 46 Dc60
Bahadınlı TR 191 Ec82
Bahadır TR 192 Ga85
Bahadırlar TR 192 Fc87
Baharlar TR 191 Eb82
Bahçeağıl TR 186 Fa76
Bahçecik TR 187 Gb79
Bahçecik TR 192 Fa86
Bahçecik TR 193 Ha83
Bahçedere TR 191 Eb82
Bahçedere TR 191 Ec84
Bahçeköy TR 185 Eb78
Bahçeköy TR 186 Fa76
Bahçekuyu TR 193 Ha81
Bahçeli TR 191 Ea82
Bahçeyaka TR 197 Fa90
Bahçıvanlar TR 199 Gd89
Bahillo (Loma del Ucieza) E 38 Da57
Bahmut MD 173 Fb57
Bahna RO 172 Ec58
Bahnea RO 171 Dc59
Bahovica BG 180 Db70
Bahrdorf D 127 Dd36
Bahrenborstel D 126 Cd36
Bahrendorf D 127 Ea38
Bahşayış TR 186 Fc77
Bahu MD 173 Fc56
Baia I 161 Fa75
Baia RO 172 Eb56
Baia RO 177 Fc65
Baia de Aramă RO 175 Cc63
Baia de Criș RO 175 Cc60
Baia de Fier RO 175 Da63
Baia delle Zagare I 162 Gb72
Baia Domizia I 161 Fa74
Baia Mare RO 171 Da55
Baiano I 161 Fb74
Baiardo I 43 Kd52
Baia Sardinia I 168 Cb73
Baia Sprie RO 171 Da55
Băicoi RO 176 Ea64
Băiculești RO 175 Dc64
Baides E 47 Ea62
Baienfurt D 142 Cd51
Baierbrunn D 143 Dd51
Baiersbronn D 133 Cb49
Baiersdorf D 135 Dd46
Baierz D 142 Da51
Baigneaux F 29 Gc39
Baigneux-les-Juifs F 30 Ja41
Baile an Fheirtearaigh IRL 12 Ad24
Baile an Mhóta IRL 8 Bd18
Baile an Róba IRL 8 Bc20
Baile an Sceilg IRL 12 Ad25
Baile Átha IRL 13 Cc22
Baile Átha an Rí IRL 12 Bd21
Baile Átha Cliath IRL 13 Cd21
Baile Átha Fhirdhia IRL 9 Cd19
Baile Átha Luain IRL 13 Ca21
Baile Átha Troim IRL 9 Cc20
Băile Bixad RO 171 Da54
Băile Borșa RO 171 Dc55
Baile Brigín IRL 9 Cd20
Baile Chláir IRL 12 Bc21
Băile Felix RO 170 Cb57
Băile Govora RO 175 Db64
Băile Herculane RO 174 Cb64
Baile Locha Riach IRL 12 Bd21
Baile Mhic Andáin IRL 13 Cb24
Baile Mhistéala IRL 12 Bd24
Baile Mór GB 6 Da11
Bailén E 52 Db72
Baile na Finne IRL 8 Ca16
Baile na Lorgan IRL 9 Cd19
Băile Olănești RO 175 Db63
Băilești RO 179 Cc67
Băile Tușnad RO 176 Ea60
Baile Ui Fhiacháin IRL 8 Bc19
Baile Ui Mhatháin IRL 9 Cb20
Baillieborough IRL 9 Cc19
Baillé F 28 Fa38
Bailleau-le-Pin F 29 Gb38
Bailleul F 21 Ha30
Bailo E 39 Fb58
Bailyhaugh GB 6 Da10
Bailyhaugh GB 9 Da14
Baimaclia MD 173 Fd59
Baimaclia MD 177 Fc61
Baiñas E 36 Ac55
Bainbridge GB 11 Ed18
Bain-de-Bretagne F 28 Ed40
Baindt D 142 Da51
Bains F 34 Hd49
Bains-les-Bains F 31 Jd39
Bainton GB 17 Fc20
Baio E 36 Ac54
Baiona E 36 Ac58
Bairro P 50 Ac66
Bais F 28 Fc39
Baiso I 149 Db63
Băișoara RO 171 Cd58
Baisogala LV 114 Kb55
Băița RO 175 Cc60
Băița de Sub Codru RO 171 Cd55
Băiuș MD 177 Fc60
Băiuț RO 171 Db55
Baix F 34 Jb50
Baja H 153 Hd57
Bajáansenye H 145 Gb55
Baja de Arieș RO 171 Cd59
Bajāri LV 114 La53
Bajč SK 145 Hb51
Bajcsa H 152 Gc57
Bajdyty PL 122 Jb30
Bajevka RUS 113 Ja58
Bajgora KSV 178 Bb70
Bajina Bašta SRB 159 Ja64
Bajkal BG 180 Db68
Bajki-Zalesie PL 123 Ka33
Bajlovce MK 178 Bd72
Bajlovo BG 179 Cd71
Bajmok SRB 153 Ja58
Bajna H 146 Hc52
Bajorai LT 114 La53
Bajovo Polje MNE 159 Hd67
Bajram Curr AL 159 Jc69
Bajša SRB 153 Ja58
Bak H 145 Gc55
Baka SK 145 Gd51
Bakacak TR 185 Ec80
Bakałarzewo PL 123 Ka30
Bakar HR 151 Fb60
Bakdemirler TR 187 Gd79
Bakel NL 125 Bb38
Bakewell GB 16 Ed22
Bakır TR 191 Ed84
Bakırköy TR 186 Fb80
Bakka N 92 Cb46
Bakka N 93 Db41
Bakkafjörður IS 3 Bc04
Bakkagerði IS 3 Bc05
Bakke N 84 Cb40
Bakke N 92 Cb46
Bakke N 93 Dd42
Bakke N 93 Db45
Bakkeby N 63 Hb09
Bakkejord N 62 Gc10
Bakkejord N 67 Gb13
Bakken N 77 Dc29
Bakken N 78 Eb30
Bakken N 79 Fb27
Bakketun N 71 Fb22
Bakkeveen NL 117 Bd33
Bakko N 93 Db41
Baklalı TR 186 Fc77
Baklan TR 192 Ga87
Baklançakırlar TR 198 Fd88
Baklankuyucak TR 198 Ga88
Baklia N 85 Dc36
Bakonybél H 145 Ha54
Bakonycsernye H 145 Hb53
Bakonygyepes H 145 Ha54
Bakonyjákó H 145 Ha54
Bakonykoppány H 145 Ha53
Bakonypéterd H 145 Ha53
Bakonyszombathely H 145 Ha53
Bąków PL 129 Hb41
Bąkowa Góra PL 130 Ja41
Baksan RUS 205 Ga17
Baksjöberg S 80 Gd27
Baksjöliden S 80 Gd27
Baktakék H 146 Jc50
Baktalórántháza H 147 Kb51
Baktsjaur S 72 Ha23
Bakum D 117 Cc35
Bakvattnet S 79 Fb28
Bäl S 104 Ha49
Bala GB 15 Ea23
Bala RO 171 Dc58
Bala RO 175 Cc64
Balaban TR 186 Fa75
Balaban TR 186 Fc77
Balaban TR 187 Gb78
Balabancık TR 185 Eb77
Balabancık TR 185 Ec78
Bălăbănești MD 173 Fd58
Bălăbănești RO 177 Fa61
Balabanlı TR 185 Ed77
Balabanlı TR 191 Ea82
Balabanlı TR 192 Fa87
Balabanovo RUS 202 Ed11
Balabanu MD 177 Fc61
Bălăceanu RO 176 Ed63
Balaci RO 175 Dd66
Bălăcița RO 175 Cc66
Balaciu RO 176 Ec66
Balaguer E 48 Ga60
Balahna RUS 203 Fb09
Balahoncevo RUS 107 Mb50
Balaklija UA 203 Fa14
Balakovo RUS 203 Ga11
Bălan RO 171 Cd56
Bălan RO 172 Ea59
Balanegra E 61 Dd76
Bălănești MD 173 Fb57
Bălănești RO 175 Cd63
Balaruc-les-Bains F 41 Hd54
Bälaryd S 103 Fc49
Bălășești MD 173 Fc56
Bălășești RO 177 Fa61
Balašiha RUS 203 Fa10
Balasinești MD 172 Ed54
Balašov RUS 203 Fc12
Balassagyarmat H 146 Hd51
Balástya H 146 Jb56
Balata di Baida I 166 Eb84
Balata di Modica I 167 Fc87
Balatcık TR 191 Ed87
Balatdanişment TR 192 Fd82
Bălați RO 172 Ed57
Balatina MD 173 Fa55
Balatonakali H 145 Ha55
Balatonakarattya H 145 Hb54
Balatonalmádi H 145 Hb54
Balatonboglár H 145 Ha55
Balatonbozsok H 145 Hb55
Balatonföldvár H 145 Ha55
Balatonfüred H 145 Ha55
Balatonfűzfő H 145 Hb54
Balatongyörök H 145 Gd55
Balatonkenese H 145 Hb54
Balatonkeresztúr H 145 Gd56
Balatonlelle H 145 Ha55
Balatonmagyaród H 145 Gd56
Balatonszabadi H 145 Hb55
Balatonszárszó H 145 Ha55
Balatonszemes H 145 Ha55
Balatonszentgyörgy H 145 Gd56
Balatonudvari H 145 Ha55
Balatonújlak H 145 Gd56
Bălăurești MD 173 Fb58
Bălăușeri RO 171 Dc59
Balazote E 53 Eb69
Balazuc F 34 Ja51
Balbeggie GB 7 Eb11
Balbieriškis LT 114 Kc59
Balbigny F 34 Hd46
Balbiši LV 107 Ld51
Balblair GB 5 Ea07
Balboa E 37 Bd56
Balbriggan IRL 9 Cd20
Balc RO 171 Cc56
Bâlca RO 172 Eb54
Balcani RO 172 Ec59
Bălcăuți MD 173 Fa53
Bălcăuți RO 172 Eb55
Bălcești RO 175 Da65
Balcı TR 191 Ed81
Balcı TR 193 Gd87
Balcıdamı TR 193 Gb85
Balčik BG 181 Fb70
Balçık TR 186 Ga78
Balçıkhisar TR 187 Gb80
Balçıkhisar TR 193 Gc86
Balçıkhisar TR 193 Gd82
Balcılar TR 185 Eb80
Balcılar TR 191 Ed86
Balcombe GB 20 Fc29
Balderschwang D 142 Da53
Baldichieri d'Asti I 148 Bd61
Baldock GB 20 Fc26
Baldone LV 106 Kc51
Baldos P 44 Bb62
Baldovinești RO 175 Da66
Baldovinești RO 177 Fb63
Bale HR 151 Fa61
Baleix F 40 Fc55
Baleizão P 50 Ad71
Balen B 124 Ba39
Băleni RO 176 Ea65
Băleni RO 177 Fb62
Balenos LT 113 Jd53
Balerma E 61 Dd76
Balești RO 175 Cc63
Balești RO 176 Ed63
Balestrand N 84 Cc36
Balestrate I 166 Eb84
Balf H 145 Gc52
Balfour GB 5 Ec03
Balfron GB 7 Dd12
Balgale LV 105 Jd50
Bălgaranovo BG 180 Eb71
Bălgarene BG 180 Db70
Bălgarene BG 180 Dc69
Bălgarevo BG 181 Fb70
Bălgari BG 186 Fa74
Bălgarin BG 185 Ea74
Bălgarovo BG 181 Ed72
Bălgarska poljana BG 185 Ea74
Bălgarski Izvor BG 179 Da70
Bălgarsko Slivovo BG 180 Dd69
Balge D 118 Da35
Bälgviken S 95 Gb44
Bali GR 200 Cd95
Balice PL 138 Ja44
Baligród PL 139 Kb46
Balik BG 181 Fa68
Balıkesir TR 192 Fa82
Balıklı TR 185 Ed79
Balıklıçeşme TR 185 Ec80
Balıklıdere TR 192 Fb81
Balıklıova TR 191 Ea86
Bălilești RO 175 Dc64
Balinderry IRL 13 Ca22
Bälinge S 73 Hd22
Bälinge S 96 Gc41
Bälinge S 96 Gc45
Bälinge S 102 Ec48
Bälinge S 110 Fa54
Balingen D 142 Cc50
Balingsta S 96 Gc42
Balinț RO 174 Ca60
Balintore GB 5 Ea07
Baliskės LV 114 Kb58
Balivanich GB 5 Cd07
Balizac F 32 Fb51
Balje D 118 Da31
Baljevac BIH 151 Ga62
Baljevac SRB 178 Ba68
Balk NL 116 Bb34
Balka DK 111 Fd58
Balkanski BG 180 Eb69
Balkány H 147 Ka51
Balkasodis LT 114 Kc59
Balkbrug NL 117 Bd35
Balkı TR 193 Hb87
Balkıca TR 198 Fd89
Balla IRL 8 Bc19
Ballaban AL 182 Ac77
Ballabio Inferiore I 149 Cd58
Ballachullish GB 6 Dc10
Ballagh IRL 12 Bc24
Ballaghaderreen IRL 8 Bd19
Ballancourt-sur-Essone F 29 Gd38
Ballangen N 66 Ga14
Ballantrae GB 10 Dc16
Ballao I 169 Cb78
Ballasalla GB 10 Dc19
Ballasviken S 71 Ga20
Ballater GB 7 Ec09
Balle DK 101 Dd23
Baile Bhuirne IRL 12 Bb25
Ballefors S 103 Fb46
Ballen DK 109 Dd25
Ballenstedt D 127 Dd39
Balleroy F 22 Fb36
Ballerup DK 109 Ec25
Ballesteros E 52 Db68
Ballesteros de Calatrava E 52 Db69
Ballı TR 185 Ec78
Ballıbucak TR 199 Gd90
Ballıca TR 186 Ga78
Ballickmoyler IRL 13 Cc23
Ballıhisar TR 193 Hb83
Ballık TR 193 Gb86
Ballık TR 198 Fd91
Ballina IRL 8 Bc18
Ballina IRL 12 Bd23
Ballinafad IRL 8 Ca19
Ballinagleragh IRL 8 Ca18
Ballinakill IRL 13 Cb23
Ballinalee IRL 9 Cb20
Ballinamore IRL 9 Cb19
Ballinascarty IRL 12 Bc26
Ballinasloe IRL 13 Ca21
Ballinclea IRL 13 Cd22
Ballincollig IRL 12 Bd26
Ballincurrig IRL 12 Bd25
Ballindine IRL 8 Bd20
Balling DK 100 Da22
Ballingarry IRL 12 Bc24
Ballingarry IRL 13 Ca22
Ballingarry IRL 13 Cb23
Ballingeary IRL 12 Bb26
Ballingslöv S 110 Fa54
Ballingurteen IRL 12 Bc26
Ballinhassig IRL 12 Bd26
Ballinlough IRL 8 Bd19
Ballino I 149 Db58
Ballinrobe IRL 8 Bc20
Ballinspittle IRL 12 Bc26
Ballintogher IRL 8 Ca18
Ballinunty IRL 13 Ca23
Ballinure IRL 13 Ca24
Ballıpınar TR 186 Fa79
Ballivor IRL 9 Cc20
Ballobar E 48 Fd61
Balloch GB 10 Dd13
Balloch GB 10 Dd15
Ballon F 28 Fd39
Ballon IRL 13 Cc23
Balloo Cross Roads GB 10 Db18
Ballota E 37 Ca54
Ballots F 28 Fa40
Ballsh AL 182 Ab77
Ballsnes N 66 Ga14
Ballstad N 66 Fb15
Ballvengland IRL 12 Bc23
Ballybay IRL 9 Cc18
Ballybofey IRL 9 Cb16
Ballyboghill IRL 13 Cd21
Ballybogy GB 9 Cd15
Ballybrittas IRL 13 Cc22
Ballybunnion IRL 12 Bb23
Ballycanew IRL 13 Cd24
Ballycastle GB 9 Da15
Ballycastle IRL 8 Bc17
Ballyclare GB 9 Da17
Ballyclare IRL 8 Ca20
Ballycolla IRL 13 Cb22
Ballyconneely IRL 8 Ba20
Ballyconnell IRL 9 Cb18
Ballycorick IRL 12 Bc23
Ballycotton IRL 13 Ca26
Ballydangan IRL 13 Ca21
Ballydehob IRL 12 Bb26
Ballydesmond IRL 12 Bb24
Ballyduff IRL 12 Bb23
Ballyduff IRL 13 Ca25
Ballyfad IRL 13 Cd23
Ballyfeard IRL 12 Bd26
Ballyferriter IRL 12 Ad24
Ballygalley GB 9 Da16
Ballygarrett IRL 13 Cd24
Ballygawley GB 9 Cc17
Ballyglass IRL 8 Bc19
Ballygowan GB 9 Da17
Ballygrant GB 6 Da13
Ballyhahill IRL 12 Bc23
Ballyhalbert GB 10 Db17
Ballyhaunis IRL 8 Bd19
Ballyhean IRL 8 Bc19
Ballyheerin IRL 9 Cb15
Ballyheige IRL 12 Ba24
Ballyhillin IRL 9 Cc14
Ballyhooly IRL 12 Bd25
Ballyhornan GB 10 Db18
Ballyjamesduff IRL 9 Cc19
Ballykeel GB 9 Da18
Ballylanders IRL 12 Bd24
Ballylongford IRL 12 Bb23
Ballylooby IRL 13 Ca24
Ballylynan IRL 13 Cc22
Ballymacarbry IRL 13 Ca25
Ballymack IRL 13 Cb24
Ballymacoda IRL 13 Ca26
Ballymacrevan GB 9 Da17
Ballymahon IRL 9 Cb20
Ballymena GB 9 Da16
Ballymoe IRL 8 Bd20
Ballymoney GB 9 Cc16
Ballymoney GB 9 Cd15
Ballymore IRL 9 Cb20
Ballymore Eustace IRL 13 Cd22
Ballymote IRL 8 Bd18
Ballymurphy IRL 13 Cc24
Ballynabola IRL 13 Cc24
Ballynacarrigy IRL 9 Cb20
Ballynacourty IRL 13 Ca25
Ballynagore IRL 13 Cb21
Ballynagree IRL 12 Bc25
Ballynahinch GB 9 Da18
Ballynahown IRL 12 Bb21
Ballynahown IRL 13 Ca21
Ballynakilla IRL 12 Ba26
Ballynakilly Upper IRL 12 Ba25
Ballynamona IRL 12 Bd25
Ballynamult IRL 13 Ca25
Ballynana IRL 12 Ad24
Ballynaskreena IRL 12 Bb23
Ballyneety IRL 12 Bd23
Ballynure GB 9 Da16
Ballypatrick IRL 13 Cb24
Ballyporeen IRL 13 Ca24
Ballyquin IRL 12 Ba24
Ballyragget IRL 13 Cb23
Ballyroebuck IRL 13 Cd23
Ballyroon IRL 12 Ba26
Ballysadare IRL 8 Ca18
Ballyshannon IRL 8 Ca17
Ballyshannon IRL 13 Cc22
Ballysteen IRL 12 Bc23
Ballytoohy IRL 8 Bb19
Ballyvaughan IRL 12 Bc21
Ballyvourney IRL 12 Bb25
Ballyvoy GB 9 Da15
Ballywater GB 10 Db17
Ballywilliam IRL 13 Cc24
Balmacara GB 4 Da05
Balmahmut TR 193 Gc85
Balmaseda E 38 Dd55
Balmazújváros H 147 Jd52
Balme I 148 Bc59
Balmedie GB 7 Ed09
Balmerino GB 7 Eb11
Balminnoch GB 10 Dc16
Balmonte E 37 Bd54
Balmuccia I 148 Ca58
Balnafoich GB 7 Ea08
Balnahard GB 6 Da11
Balnapaling GB 5 Ea07
Balneario de Panticosa E 40 Fc57
Balninkai LT 114 La56
Baloira E 36 Ad56
Bálojotnjálbmi FIN 68 Ja13
Balören TR 187 Gb78
Balotești RO 176 Eb65
Baloži LV 106 Kb51
Balquhidder GB 7 Dd11
Balrath IRL 9 Cd20
Balș RO 175 Da66
Balsa P 44 Bb60
Balșa RO 175 Cd60
Balsa de Ves E 54 Fa68
Balsareny E 49 Gd60
Balsfjord N 62 Gd10
Balsham GB 20 Fd26
Balsicas E 55 Fa73
Balsièges F 34 Hc51
Balsjö S 80 Ha28
Balsorano Nuovo I 160 Ed72
Balsovo RUS 99 Lc45
Bålsta S 96 Gc43
Balsthal CH 141 Bd53

Balsupiai – Bebertal

Balsupiai LV 114 Kb59
Balta UA 204 Ec16
Balta Albă RO 176 Ed63
Balta Berilovac SRB 179 Ca69
Balta Doamnei RO 176 Eb65
Baltanás E 46 Db59
Baltar E 36 Bb58
Baltasound GB 5 Fa03
Bălţata MD 173 Fd58
Băltăteşti RO 172 Ec57
Balta Verde RO 174 Cb66
Bălteni RO 173 Fa59
Bălteni RO 175 Cd64
Bălţeşti RO 176 Eb64
Bălti MD 173 Fb55
Baltijsk RUS 113 Hd59
Baltimore IRL 12 Bb27
Baltinava LV 107 Ld49
Baltinglass IRL 13 Cc22
Bal'tino RUS 107 Ma50
Baltoji Vokė LT 114 La58
Bałtów PL 131 Jd41
Baltrušaičiai LT 113 Jd57
Balugães P 44 Ad59
Băluseni RO 172 Ed55
Balvan BG 180 Dd70
Balve D 125 Cb39
Balvi LV 107 Lc49
Balya TR 191 Ed82
Balze I 156 Ea65
Balzers FL 142 Cd54
Balzo I 156 Ed68
Bambalió GR 188 Ba83
Bamberg D 134 Dc45
Bamble N 93 Dc44
Bamburgh GB 11 Fa14
Bamford GB 16 Ed22
Bammental D 134 Cc46
Bampton GB 19 Ea29
Banafjäl S 80 Ha30
Banagher IRL 13 Ca21
Banarlı TR 185 Ed77
Banatska Dubica SRB 174 Bb62
Banatska Palanka SRB 174 Bc64
Banatska Topola SRB 153 Jc58
Banatska Topola SRB 174 Bb60
Banatski Despotovac SRB 174 Bb62
Banatski Dvor SRB 153 Jc59
Banatski Karlovac SRB 174 Bc63
Banatsko Aranđelovo SRB 170 Bb59
Banatsko Karađorđevo SRB 153 Jc59
Banatsko Novo Selo SRB 174 Bb63
Banatsko Veliko Selo SRB 174 Bb60
Banaz TR 192 Ga85
Banbridge GB 9 Da18
Banbury GB 20 Fa26
Banca RO 177 Fb60
Band RO 171 Db59
Bande E 36 Ba58
Bandeira E 36 Ba56
Bandenitz D 119 Ea33
Bandholm DK 109 Ea28
Bandirma TR 186 Fa80
Bando I 150 Ea62
Bandol F 42 Jd55
Bandon IRL 12 Bc26
Băneasa RO 177 Fb61
Băneasa RO 180 Ea67
Băneasa RO 181 Fa67
Bañeres E 55 Fb70
Bånes N 63 Hc08
Băneşti RO 176 Ea64
Banevo BG 181 Ed72
Banff GB 5 Ec07
Bångnäs S 79 Fd25
Bangor GB 10 Db17
Bangor GB 15 Dd22
Bangor IRL 8 Bb18
Bangor-is-y-coed GB 15 Eb23
Bangsund N 78 Ec26
Bangueses E 36 Ba58
Banica BG 179 Cd69
Banie PL 120 Fc34
Banie Mazurskie PL 123 Jd30
Baniewice PL 120 Fc34
Baniska BG 180 Ea69
Bănişor RO 171 Cc57
Banište BG 179 Cb71
Băniţa RO 175 Cd62
Banja BG 184 Cc74
Banja BG 179 Da72
Banja BG 180 Db72
Banja BG 180 Ea72
Banja BG 181 Fa72
Banja BIH 159 Ja65
Banja SRB 159 Ja66
Banja e Kukës AL 182 Ad79
Banja Koviljača SRB 153 Hd63
Banjaloka SLO 151 Fc60
Banja Luka BIH 152 Gd62
Banjani SRB 153 Jb62
Banja Vrućica BIH 152 Hb62
Banje KSV 178 Ba69
Banjica KSV 178 Ad70
Banjica SRB 159 Jc68
Banjište MK 182 Ad74
Banjska KSV 178 Ba69
Bankekind S 103 Ga47
Bankeryd S 103 Fb48
Bankja BG 179 Cc71
Banloc RO 174 Bc62
Bannalec F 27 Dd40
Bännbäck S 95 Gb41
Bannegon F 29 Ha43
Bannes F 24 Hc37
Bannes F 30 Jb39
Bannewitz D 128 Fa41
Bannockburn GB 7 Ea12
Bannoncourt F 24 Jb36
Bannow IRL 13 Cc25
Banon F 42 Jd52
Bañón E 47 Fa63
Banos de Alicún de las Torres E 61 Dd74
Baños de Benasque E 40 Ga57
Baños de Fuente de la Encina E 52 Db72
Baños de la Encina E 52 Db71
Baños de Molgas E 36 Bb58
Baños de Montemayor E 45 Cb64
Baños de Río Tobia E 38 Ea58
Baños de Valdearados E 46 Dc60
Baños de Valdeganga E 53 Eb66
Bánov CZ 137 Ha48
Bánov SK 145 Hb51
Banova Jaruga HR 152 Gc60
Bánovce nad Bebravou SK 137 Hb49
Banovci Dunav SRB 153 Jc61
Banovići BIH 153 Hc63
Bánréve H 146 Jb50
Bansha IRL 13 Ca24
Bansin D 120 Fb31
Bansjo MK 183 Ca75
Banská Bystrica SK 138 Hd49
Banská Stiavnica SK 146 Hc50
Banské SK 139 Jd48
Bansko BG 184 Cc74
Banstead GB 20 Fc29
Banteer IRL 12 Bc25
Banteln D 126 Db37
Bantheville F 24 Ja35
Bantry IRL 12 Bb26
Bantzenheim F 31 Kc39
Bañuelos de Bureba E 38 Dd58
Bañugues E 37 Cc53
Bānūži LV 106 Kd49
Banwell GB 19 Eb28
Banyalbufar E 56 Ha67
Banyoles E 49 Hb59
Banyuls-sur-Mer F 41 Hb58
Banzi I 162 Gb75
Banzkow D 119 Ea33
Bapaume F 23 Ha32
Bár H 153 Hc57
Bar MNE 163 Ja71
Bar UA 204 Eb15
Bâra RO 172 Ed58
Bara RO 174 Ca60
Bara S 110 Ed56
Barabany RUS 107 Mb50
Baraboi MD 173 Fa54
Baracak TR 191 Ed82
Bărăganu RO 177 Fa65
Bărăganu RO 181 Fc67
Baragem da Aguieira P 44 Ad63
Barağı TR 192 Ga84
Barago E 38 Da55
Barahona E 47 Ea62
Barajas E 46 Dc64
Barajas de Melo E 47 Ea65
Barakaldo E 38 Ea55
Baraklı TR 193 Gd87
Baranavičy BY 202 Ea13
Baránd H 147 Jd53
Barane KSV 178 Ad71
Baranivka UA 204 Eb15
Baranjsko Petrovo Selo HR 153 Hc59
Barano d'Ischia I 161 Fa75
Baranovka LV 107 Ld50
Baranów PL 129 Ha40
Baranów PL 130 Ja37
Baranów PL 131 Ka39
Baranowo PL 122 Jc31
Baranowo PL 122 Jc33
Baranowo PL 129 Gc36
Baranów Sandomierski PL 131 Jd42
Baranyajenő H 152 Hb57
Baraolt RO 176 Ea61
Baraque-Saint-Jean F 41 Ha52
Baraqueville F 41 Ha52
Bårared S 102 Ed52
Barásoain E 39 Ed57
Bărăşti RO 175 Db65
Bărăteaz RO 174 Bc60
Barbacena P 51 Bb68
Barbadillo E 45 Cb62
Barbadillo de Herreros E 46 Dd59
Barbadillo del Mercado E 46 Dd59
Barbadillo del Pez E 46 Dd59
Barbalimpia E 53 Eb66
Barban HR 151 Fa61
Barbantes E 36 Ba57
Barbarano Vicentino I 150 Dd60
Barbaros TR 185 Dd80
Barbaros TR 185 Ed78
Barbaros TR 191 Ea86
Barbarušince SRB 178 Bd71
Barbaste F 40 Fd52
Barbastro E 48 Fd59
Barbate E 59 Bd77
Bărbăteşti RO 175 Cd64
Bărbăteşti RO 175 Da63
Barbatovac SRB 178 Bb69
Barbâtre F 27 Ec43
Barbazan F 40 Ga56
Barbeitos E 37 Bd55
Bārbele LV 106 Kc52
Barber Booth GB 16 Ed22
Barberino di Mugello I 155 Dc64
Barberino Val d'Elsa I 155 Dc66
Barbezieux-Saint-Hilaire F 32 Fc48
Barbières F 35 Jc49
Barbing D 135 Eb48
Barbizon F 29 Ha38
Bärbo S 95 Gb45
Barboles E 47 Fa60
Barbonne-Fayel F 24 Hc37
Barbotan-les-Thermes F 40 Fc53
Barbu R N 93 Db46
Bărbuleţu RO 176 Dd64
Barbullush AL 163 Jb71
Barbuñales E 48 Fc59
Barby D 127 Eb38
Barca E 47 Ea61
Bârca RO 179 Cd67
Barca de Alva P 45 Bc62
Barcaggio F 154 Cc67
Barcaldine GB 6 Dc11
Bărcăneşti RO 176 Ec65
Barcani RO 176 Eb62
Barcarrota E 51 Bc70
Barcea RO 177 Fa62
Barcellona Pozzo di Gotto I 167 Fd84
Barcelona E 49 Ha61
Barcelonne-du-Gers F 40 Fc54
Barcelonnette F 43 Kb51
Barcelos P 44 Ad60
Bárcena de Ebro E 38 Db56
Bárcena del Monasterio E 37 Ca54
Bárcena de Pie de Concha E 38 Db55
Bárcena Mayor E 38 Db55
Barchem NL 125 Bd37
Barchín del Hoyo E 53 Eb67
Barčiai LT 114 Kd59
Barcial del Barco E 45 Cb59
Barciany PL 122 Jb30
Barcillonnette F 42 Jd51
Barcin PL 121 Ha35
Barcis I 150 Eb57
Barco P 44 Ba64
Barcones E 47 Ea61
Barcos P 44 Bb61
Barcs H 152 Ha58
Barcus F 39 Fb55
Barczewko PL 122 Ja31
Barczewo PL 122 Ja31
Bard I 148 Bd58
Bârda RO 174 Bd62
Bardakçı TR 192 Fb84
Bardakçı TR 193 Gd83
Bardakçılar TR 191 Ec81
Bardal N 70 Fa21
Bardallur E 47 Fa60
Bardar MD 173 Fc58
Bărdarski Geran BG 179 Da68
Barde DK 108 Da24
Bardejov SK 139 Jd46
Bardejovské Kúpele SK 139 Jd46
Bårdesø DK 109 Dd26
Bardi I 149 Cd62
Bardineto I 148 Bd63
Bard-le-Régulier F 30 Hd42
Bardney GB 17 Fc22
Bardo PL 137 Gc43
Bardolino I 149 Db59
Bardonecchia I 148 Ba60
Bardowick D 118 Dc33
Bardsea GB 11 Eb19
Bardsey GB 16 Fa20
Bardu bygdetun N 67 Gc12
Bardujord N 67 Gc12
Bare BIH 159 Hd65
Bare MNE 159 Jb68
Bare SRB 174 Bb66
Băreaneşti RO 176 Eb65
Bäreberg S 102 Ed47
Barèges F 40 Fd56
Bärenbad A 143 Ea54
Barenburg D 118 Cd35
Barendrecht NL 124 Ad37
Bärenstein D 128 Fa42
Bärenstein D 135 Ed43
Barentin F 23 Ga34
Barenton F 28 Fb38
Barevo BIH 152 Gd63
Bärfendal S 102 Eb46
Barfleur F 22 Fa34
Barford GB 17 Ga24
Barford Saint Martin GB 20 Ed29
Barga I 155 Da64
Bargas E 52 Db66
Bărgăuani RO 172 Ec58
Barge I 148 Bc61
Bargême F 43 Kb53
Bargemon F 43 Kb53
Bargen, Helmstadt- D 134 Cd46
Bargeshagen D 119 Eb31
Bargfeld-Stegen D 118 Dc32
Barghe I 149 Db59
Bărghis RO 175 Dc61
Bargłówka PL 137 Hb44
Bargłów Kościelny PL 123 Ka31
Bargoed GB 19 Ea27
Bargrennan GB 10 Dd16
Bargstedt D 118 Da33
Bargteheide D 118 Dc32
Bargullas AL 182 Ac77
Bar Hill GB 20 Fd25
Bari I 162 Gd74
Barić SRB 153 Jc62
Barić Draga HR 151 Fd63
Barice SRB 174 Bc62
Barilović HR 151 Fd60
Barinas E 55 Fa71
Båring DK 108 Dc26
Bari Sardo I 169 Cc78
Barisciano I 156 Ed70
Barisey-la-Côte F 25 Jc37
Barjac F 34 Hc51
Barjac F 34 Ja51
Bårjås S 72 Ha18
Barjols F 42 Ka54
Bark D 118 Dc31
Bărkač BG 180 Db69
Barkåker N 93 Dd43
Barkarö S 95 Gb43
Barkava LV 107 Lb50
Barkelsby D 108 Db29
Barkeryd S 103 Fc49
Barkestad N 66 Fc12
Barking GB 20 Fd28
Barklainiai LT 114 Kc55
Barkowo PL 120 Fd32
Barkowo PL 121 Gc32
Barkston GB 16 Fb23
Barkway GB 20 Fd26
Bârla RO 175 Dc66
Barla TR 193 Gd87
Bårlad RO 177 Fa60
Barleben D 127 Ea37
Bar-le-Duc F 24 Jb37
Barles F 42 Ka51
Barletta I 162 Gb73
Barlinek PL 120 Fd35
Barlingbo S 104 Ha49
Barlo D 125 Bd37
Barlow GB 16 Fa21
Barmash AL 182 Ad78
Barmouth GB 15 Dd24
Barmstedt D 118 Db32
Barna IRL 12 Bc21
Bârna RO 174 Ca61
Barnaderg IRL 8 Bd20
Barnard Castle GB 11 Ed18
Barnarp S 103 Fb49
Bärnau D 135 Eb45
Barnave F 35 Jc50
Barnay F 30 Hd42
Barne-Åsaka S 102 Ed47
Barneberg D 127 Dd37
Barnes GB 20 Fc28
Barnesmore IRL 9 Cb16
Barnetby le Wold GB 17 Fc21
Barneveld NL 116 Bb36
Barneville-Carteret F 22 Ed35
Barnewitz D 127 Ec36
Barney GB 17 Ga23
Barnim PL 120 Fc34
Bärnkopf A 144 Fc50
Barnoldswick GB 16 Ed20
Bărnova RO 173 Fa58
Barnówko PL 120 Fc35
Barnsley GB 16 Fa21
Barnsley GB 20 Ed27
Barnstädt D 127 Ea40
Barnstaple GB 19 Dd29
Barnstorf D 118 Cd35
Barntrup D 126 Cd38
Baron F 23 Ha36
Baroncea MD 173 Fb54
Baronissi I 161 Fc75
Baronville F 25 Ka36
Baroševac SRB 153 Jc63
Barösund FIN 98 Ka40
Barovo MK 183 Bd75
Barqueiro P 44 Ad65
Barqueiros P 44 Ac60
Barquilla de Pinares E 45 Cc65
Barr F 25 Kb37
Barracas E 54 Fb66
Barrachina E 47 Fa63
Barraco E 46 Da64
Barra de Mira P 44 Ac63
Barrado E 45 Cb65
Barraduff IRL 12 Bb25
Barrafranca I 167 Fa86
Barral (Castrelo de Miño) E 36 Ba57
Barrancos P 51 Bb71
Barranco Velho P 58 Ad74
Barranda E 61 Ec72
Barrax E 53 Eb69
Barrea I 161 Fa72
Barreiro P 50 Aa69
Barrême F 42 Ka52
Barret-le-Bas F 42 Jd51
Barrhead GB 10 Dd13
Barrhill GB 10 Dc16
Barriada de Jarana E 59 Bd76
Barriada Las Canteras E 61 Eb75
Barrière de Champlon B 132 Ba43
Barrigone IRL 12 Bc23
Barri Mar E 54 Fc67
Barrio de Nuestra Señora E 37 Cc57
Barrit DK 108 Dc25
Barro E 38 Da54
Barrô P 44 Ba61
Barroca P 44 Ba64
Barroças e Taias P 36 Ad58
Barros E 38 Db55
Barroselas P 44 Ac59
Barrosinha P 50 Ac70
Barrou F 29 Ga43
Barrowby GB 16 Fb23
Barrow-in-Furness GB 11 Eb19
Barrow-upon-Soar GB 16 Fa24
Barruç AL 178 Ad73
Barruecopardo E 45 Bd62
Barruelo de Santullán E 38 Db56
Barry GB 19 Ea28
Bârsa RO 170 Cb59
Bârsana RO 171 Db54
Bârsăneşti RO 176 Ec60
Barsanges F 33 Gd48
Bârsău de Sus RO 171 Cd55
Barsbüttel D 118 Dc32
Bårse DK 109 Eb27
Barsebäckshamm S 110 Ed55
Barsele S 72 Gc24
Bârseşti RO 176 Ec61
Barsinghausen D 126 Da36
Barsinghausen D 126 Da37
Barsk MNE 159 Jb67
Barßel D 117 Cb33
Barst F 25 Ka35
Barstyčiai LT 113 Jc53
Bar-sur-Aube F 30 Ja38
Bar-sur-Seine F 30 Hd39
Barsviken S 88 Gc33
Barszczewo PL 123 Kb33
Bārta LV 113 Jb53
Bartağ PL 122 Ja32
Bartenheim F 31 Kc40
Bartenstein D 134 Da46
Barth D 119 Ec30
Bartholomä D 134 Da48
Bartın TR 205 Fa20
Bartne PL 139 Jd45
Bartniki PL 130 Ja38
Bartninkai LT 114 Ka59
Bartołty Wielkie PL 122 Jb31
Barton GB 16 Ed24
Barton Mills GB 20 Fd25
Barton-upon-Humber GB 17 Fc21
Bartoszyce PL 122 Jb30
Barty PL 122 Hd31
Baru RO 175 Cc62
Baruchowo PL 130 Hc36
Barum D 118 Dc34
Barumini I 169 Ca78
Barun RUS 203 Ga14
Baruth/Mark D 128 Fa38
Barutin BG 184 Da75
Barva S 95 Gb43
Barvas GB 4 Da04
Barvaux B 124 Ba42
Barvaux-Condroz B 124 Ba42
Barver D 118 Cd35
Bårvik N 63 Hc06
Barvinkove UA 205 Fb15
Barwice PL 121 Gb32
Barwinek PL 139 Jd46
Barwino PL 121 Gc30
Barycz PL 139 Ka44
Barycz PL 139 Ka44
Baryš RUS 203 Fd10
Barysav BY 202 Eb12
Bârza RO 175 Da66
Barzago I 149 Cc58
Bârzava RO 174 Ca60
Barzdai LV 114 Kb58
Barzdžiūnai LT 123 Kc30
Bărzija BG 179 Cc69
Bărzina BG 179 Cd68
Barzio I 149 Cd58
Bås N 93 Da45
Basaid SRB 174 Bb61
Başalma MD 177 Fc61
Basarabeasca MD 177 Fd60
Basarabi RO 181 Fc67
Başarap TR 193 Gc86
Basarbovo BG 180 Ea68
Basardilla E 46 Db62
Basauri E 38 Ea55
Basavžže N 65 Kb06
Bâsca Chiojdului RO 176 Eb63
Başcalia MD 177 Fd60
Bàscara E 49 Hb59
Başçayır TR 192 Fa87
Baschi I 156 Ea69
Baschurch GB 15 Eb24
Basconcillos del Tozo E 38 Db57
Bascones de Ojeda E 38 Da57
Bascov RO 175 Dc64
Basdahl D 118 Da33
Basdorf D 119 Ed35
Basel CH 141 Bd52
Båseland N 93 Da46
Baselga di Piné I 149 Dc57
Baselice I 161 Fc73
Băseşti RO 171 Cd55
Başgöze TR 199 Hb88
Båsheim N 93 Dc41
Basi LV 105 Jb51
Başıbüyük TR 186 Fd78
Basicò I 167 Fc84
Basigo de Bakio E 38 Ea55
Basildon GB 20 Fd28
Basiliano I 150 Ec58
Basilique de Hennebont F 27 Ea40
Bašin SRB 174 Bb65
Basinge S 95 Gd55
Basingstoke GB 20 Fa29
Basırlar TR 193 Gc84
Bäsjösätern S 86 Fa38
Baška CZ 137 Hb46
Baška HR 151 Fc61
Båskas FIN 81 Ja30
Baskemölla S 111 Fb56
Baške Oštarije HR 151 Fd63
Başköy TR 191 Ed87
Başköy TR 192 Fc81
Başköy TR 192 Fd83
Başköy TR 193 Hb87
Båsksele S 79 Gb26
Bäsksjö S 79 Gb26
Başlamiş TR 192 Fa84
Başlar TR 199 Ha90
Baslow GB 16 Fa22
Başmakçı TR 199 Gb88
Bäsna S 95 Fd39
Basonys LT 114 Kc58
Başören TR 193 Gc82
Başören TR 193 Gc86
Başören TR 193 Gd81
Basovizza I 151 Fa59
Başpınar TR 199 Gb90
Bassac F 32 Fc47
Bassacutena I 168 Cb73
Bassano del Grappa I 150 Dd59
Basse D 119 Ec31
Bassella E 48 Gb59
Bassenthwale GB 11 Eb17
Bassevuovdde N 68 Jc11
Bassignac F 33 Ha48
Bassignac-le-Haut F 33 Gd49
Bassilac F 33 Ga49
Bassingham GB 16 Fb22
Bassou F 30 Hc40
Bassoues F 40 Fd54
Bassum D 118 Cd35
Bast FIN 81 Jb28
Båstad N 94 Eb42
Båstad S 110 Ed53
Baštanka UA 204 Ed16
Bastardo I 156 Eb68
Bastasi BIH 152 Gb63
Bästdal S 88 Gc35
Bastelica F 154 Cb70
Bastheim D 134 Db43
Bastia F 154 Cc68
Bastia Umbra I 156 Eb67
Båstlund DK 108 Da25
Bastnäs S 94 Ed41
Bastogne B 132 Ba43
Baston GB 17 Fc24
Bastorf D 119 Eb31
Bastuträsk S 80 Hb25
Bastuträsk S 80 Ha28
Bastuträsk by S 80 Hb25
Bastwick GB 17 Gb24
Baszków PL 129 Gd39
Bata BG 179 Da72
Bata BG 181 Ed72
Báta H 153 Hc57
Bata MNE 159 Hd69
Bata RO 174 Ca60
Batajnica SRB 153 Jc61
Batajsk RUS 205 Fc15
Batak BG 184 Da74
Batak BG 180 Dd69
Batakiai LT 113 Jd56
Batalha P 50 Ab66
Bátamonostor H 153 Hd57
Băţani RO 176 Ea60
Batanovci BG 179 Cb71
Batăr RO 170 Ca58
Bătarci RO 171 Cd54
Båtas S 79 Fd25
Bátaszék H 153 Hc57
Batea E 48 Fd62
Båteng N 64 Ka07
Baterno E 52 Cd69
Bath GB 19 Ec28
Bathgate GB 10 Ea13
Bathmen NL 117 Bc36
Batida H 146 Jc56
Batignano I 155 Dd68
Batıköy TR 197 Ec89
Batin BG 180 Ea68
Batina HR 153 Hc58
Batır MD 173 Fd59
Bátka SK 146 Jb50
Batković BIH 153 Hd62
Batlava KSV 178 Bb70
Batley GB 16 Ed20
Batnfjordsøra N 77 Da31
Batočina SRB 174 Bb66
Bátonyterenye H 146 Ja51
Batorz PL 131 Kb41
Batoş RO 171 Dc58
Bátovce SK 146 Hc50
Batovo BG 181 Fa70
Batowo PL 120 Fc34
Bătrâna RO 174 Cb61
Batrge SRB 178 Ad69
Batrina HR 152 Ha60
Båtsfjord N 65 Kc05
Batsí GR 190 Da87
Båtsjaur S 72 Gb21
Båtskärsnäs S 73 Jb21
Battaglia Terme I 150 Dd60
Battenberg D 126 Cc41
Bätterkinden CH 141 Bd53
Battipaglia I 161 Fc76
Battle GB 20 Fd30
Battonya H 147 Jd56
Batulci BG 179 Da70
Batuša SRB 174 Bc65
Båtvik S 73 Hc24
Bátya H 146 Hd56
Batyk H 145 Gd55
Batyrevo RUS 203 Fd09
Baud F 27 Ea40
Baudreville F 29 Gc38
Bauduen F 42 Ka53
Baugé F 28 Fc41
Baugy F 29 Ha42
Bauladu I 169 Bd77
Baulmes CH 141 Bb54
Bauma CH 142 Cc53
Baumbach, Ransbach- D 125 Ca42
Baumber GB 17 Fc22
Baume-les-Doubs F 31 Ka41
Baume-les-Messieurs F 31 Jc43
Baumholder D 133 Bd45
Baunatal D 126 Da40
Baunei I 169 Cc77
Bauņi LV 106 Kd47
Baurci MD 177 Fc61
Baurci-Moldoveni MD 177 Fb61
Baurene BG 179 Cd69
Bauska LV 106 Kc52
Bauţar RO 174 Cb62
Bautzen D 128 Fb41
Bavanište SRB 174 Bb63
Bavay F 24 Hc32
Bavella F 154 Cb72
Bavigne L 133 Bb44
Bavorov CZ 136 Fa48
Bawdeswell GB 17 Ga24
Bawdsey GB 21 Gb26
Bawinkel D 117 Cb35
Bawnboy IRL 9 Cb18
Bawtry GB 16 Fb21
Bayat TR 192 Ga87
Bayat TR 193 Gb83
Bayat TR 193 Gd84
Bayat TR 205 Fb20
Bayatbademler TR 199 Gc90
Bayburt TR 205 Ga19
Baye F 24 Hc37
Bayerbach D 135 Eb49
Bayerbach D 143 Ed50
Bayerisch Eisenstein D 135 Ed48
Bayeux F 22 Fb35
Bayındır TR 186 Ga79
Bayındır TR 191 Ed86
Bayındır TR 199 Gb91
Bayındır TR 199 Gc89
Bayır TR 197 Fa90
Bayır TR 197 Fa91
Bayırköy TR 185 Eb79
Bayırköy TR 186 Ga80
Bayırköy TR 187 Gb80
Bayırköy TR 197 Fa91
Bayo E 37 Cb54
Bayon F 25 Jd37
Bayonne F 39 Ed54
Bayons F 42 Ka51
Bayraktar TR 187 Gb78
Bayralar TR 198 Ga92
Bayramdere TR 185 Ed75
Bayramdere TR 186 Fb80
Bayramiç TR 191 Eb81
Bayramlı TR 185 Ec76
Bayramoğlu TR 186 Fd78
Bayramşah TR 192 Ga81
Bayramşah TR 192 Ga83
Bayreuth D 135 Ea45
Bayrischzell D 143 Ea52
Bayubas de Abajo E 47 Ea61
Baza E 61 Ea74
Băzăn BG 180 Ea68
Bazán E 52 Dc70
Bazarnye Mataki RUS 203 Ga09
Bazarnyi Karabulak RUS 203 Fd11
Bazas F 32 Fc51
Bazenheid CH 142 Cc53
Baziaş RO 174 Bc64
Bazicourt F 23 Ha35
Bazie AL 159 Ja70
Baziège F 40 Gc55
Bazna RO 175 Db60
Bazoches F 30 Hc41
Bazoches-les-Gallerandes F 29 Gd39
Bazoches-sur-Hoëne F 28 Fd38
Bazolles F 30 Hc42
Bazoques F 23 Ga36
Bazoş RO 174 Bd61
Bazouges-la-Perouse F 28 Ed38
Băzovec BG 179 Cd68
Bazsi H 145 Gd55
Bazzano I 149 Dc63
Beaconsfield GB 20 Fb28
Beal IRL 12 Bb23
Bealach an Doirín IRL 8 Bd19
Bealach Conglais IRL 13 Cc22
Bealach Féich IRL 9 Cb16
Bealaha IRL 12 Bb23
Bealalaw Bridge IRL 12 Ba25
Béal an Átha IRL 8 Bc18
Béal an Átha Móir IRL 9 Cb19
Béal an Mhuirthead IRL 8 Bb17
Béal Atha an Ghaorthaidh IRL 12 Bb26
Béal Átha hAmhnais IRL 8 Bd19
Béal Átha na Muice IRL 8 Bd19
Béal Átha na Sluaighe IRL 13 Ca21
Béal Atha Seanaidh IRL 8 Ca17
Béal Deirig IRL 8 Bc17
Bealdovuobmi FIN 68 Jb13
Bealnablath IRL 12 Bc26
Beaminster GB 19 Eb30
Beanntrai IRL 12 Bb26
Béard F 30 Hb43
Beardsen GB 10 Dd13
Beare Green GB 20 Fc29
Beariz E 36 Ba57
Bearna IRL 12 Bc21
Béar Tairbirt IRL 9 Cb18
Beas E 59 Bc73
Beasain E 39 Eb56
Beas de Segura E 53 Dd71
Beateberg S 103 Fb46
Beatenberg CH 141 Bd55
Beaucaire F 42 Jb53
Beaucamps-le-Vieux F 23 Gc33
Beauchamps F 22 Fa37
Beauchamps F 23 Gb33
Beauchastel F 34 Jb50
Beauche F 23 Ga37
Beauchêne F 22 Fb37
Beaufay F 28 Fd39
Beaufort F 35 Ka46
Beaufort IRL 12 Bb25
Beaufort L 133 Bb44
Beaugency F 29 Gc40
Beaujeu F 31 Jc41
Beaujeu F 34 Ja45
Beaujeu F 42 Ka51
Beaulard I 148 Bb60
Beaulieu F 23 Ga37
Beaulieu F 29 Ha41
Beaulieu GB 20 Fa30
Beaulieu-sur-Dordogne F 33 Gc50
Beauly GB 7 Dd08
Beaumaris GB 15 Dd22
Beaumesnil F 22 Fa37
Beaumesnil F 23 Ga36
Beaumetz-lès-Loges F 23 Ha32
Beaumont B 124 Ac42
Beaumont F 25 Jc36
Beaumont-de-Lomagne F 40 Gb53
Beaumont-du-Gâtinais F 29 Ha39
Beaumont-du-Périgord F 33 Ga50
Beaumont-en-Argonne F 24 Ja34
Beaumont-Hague F 22 Ed34
Beaumont-Hamel F 23 Ha33
Beaumont-la-Ronce F 29 Ga41
Beaumont-le-Roger F 23 Ga36
Beaumont-lès-Valence F 34 Jb50
Beaumont-sur-Oise F 23 Gd36
Beaumont-sur-Sarthe F 28 Fd39
Beaumont-sur-Vingeanne F 30 Jb41
Beaune F 30 Ja42
Beaune-la-Rolande F 29 Gd39
Beaupréau F 28 Fa42
Beauquesne F 23 Gd33
Beauraing B 132 Ad43
Beaurainville F 23 Gc31
Beauregard F 40 Gc52
Beaurepaire F 34 Jb48
Beaurières F 35 Jc50
Beauvais F 23 Gd35
Beauval F 23 Gd33
Beauvezer F 43 Kb52
Beauvoir-sur-Mer F 27 Ec43
Beauvoir-sur-Niort F 32 Fb46
Beauzac F 34 Hd48
Beauzée-sur-Aire F 24 Jb36
Bebares E 37 Ca54
Beba Veche RO 170 Bb59
Bebe LV 105 Jb52
Bebekli TR 192 Fc86
Bebertal D 127 Ea37

Betton – Blumau

Betton F 28 Ed39
Bettona I 156 Eb68
Bettws Cedewain GB 15 Ea24
Bettyhill GB 5 Ea04
Bettystown IRL 9 Cd20
Betws-y-Coed GB 15 Ea22
Betxí E 54 Fc66
Betz F 23 Ha36
Betzdorf D 125 Cb41
Betzenstein D 135 Dd45
Betzweiler-Wälde D 133 Cb49
Beugneux F 24 Hb35
Beuil F 43 Kc52
Beulah GB 15 Ea26
Beuna D 127 Eb40
Beuningen NL 125 Bb37
Beunza E 39 Ed56
Beura I 148 Ca57
Beuren D 126 Db40
Beurnevésin CH 141 Bc52
Beuron D 142 Cc51
Beutelsbach D 135 Ed49
Beuvron-en-Auge F 22 Fc36
Beuvry F 23 Ha31
Beuzec-Cap-Sizun F 27 Db39
Beuzeville F 22 Fd35
Bevagna I 156 Eb68
Bevensen D 126 Da36
Beverley GB 17 Fc20
Bevern D 126 Da38
Beverstedt D 118 Cd33
Beverungen D 126 Da39
Beverwijk NL 116 Ad35
Béville-le-Comte F 29 Gc38
Bevorchians I 143 Ec56
Bevtoft DK 108 Da27
Bewcastle GB 11 Ec16
Bexbach D 133 Bd46
Bexhill GB 20 Fd30
Beyağaç TR 198 Fc90
Beyazköy TR 186 Fa76
Beyçayırı TR 185 Ec80
Beyce TR 187 Gb80
Beyce TR 191 Ed83
Beycik TR 199 Gc92
Beyciler TR 186 Fb77
Beycuma TR 187 Hb77
Beydağ TR 192 Fa87
Beydili TR 187 Gd80
Beydili TR 199 Ha89
Beydilli TR 193 Gb86
Beyel TR 192 Fc82
Beyelli TR 192 Ga87
Beyerli TR 198 Fb88
Beykışla TR 193 Gd83
Beyköy TR 185 Eb78
Beyköy TR 192 Fa82
Beyköy TR 193 Gc84
Beyköy TR 193 Ha87
Beyköy TR 198 Ga90
Beyler TR 191 Eb86
Beylerbeyi TR 198 Fc88
Beylerli TR 198 Ga88
Beylikova TR 193 Ha82
Beymelek TR 199 Gb93
Beynac-et-Cazenac F 33 Gb50
Beynat F 33 Gc49
Beynes F 23 Gc37
Beyoba TR 185 Ec79
Beyoba TR 191 Ed85
Beyobası TR 198 Fc91
Beyoğlu TR 185 Ec78
Beyören TR 193 Gd83
Beypazarı TR 187 Hb80
Beyşehir TR 199 Hb88
Beyyayla TR 193 Gd81
Beyyazı TR 193 Gc85
Bežanicy RUS 202 Eb10
Bežanovo BG 179 Da70
Bežanovo BG 181 Fb69
Bežany RUS 99 Mb42
Bezas E 47 Ed65
Bezau A 142 Da53
Bézaudun-sur-Bîne F 35 Jc50
Bezdan SRB 153 Hd58
Bezdead RO 176 Dd63
Bezden BG 179 Cb70
Bezděz CZ 136 Fc43
Bezdonys LT 114 La57
Bèze F 30 Jb41
Bežeck RUS 202 Ed09
Bezenčuk RUS 203 Ga10
Béziers F 41 Hc55
Bezkese TR 198 Fc91
Bezledy PL 122 Ja30
Bezmer BG 181 Ed68
Bezno CZ 136 Fc43
Bez'va RUS 99 Ld44
Bezvěrov CZ 135 Ed45
Biała PL 120 Fd33
Biała PL 121 Gb34
Biała PL 129 Ha38
Biała PL 130 Hd38
Biała PL 131 Ka38
Biała PL 137 Gd43
Białaczów PL 130 Ja40
Biała Góra PL 121 Hb31
Biała Piska PL 123 Jd32
Biała Podlaska PL 131 Kb37
Biała Rawska PL 130 Ja38
Białaszewo PL 123 Ka32
Białawy Wielkie PL 129 Gc40
Białebłoto-Kobyla PL 122 Jc35
Białka PL 138 Ja46
Białobłoty PL 129 Ha38
Białobrzegi PL 123 Ka31
Białobrzegi PL 130 Jb36
Białobrzegi PL 130 Jb39
Białobrzegi PL 139 Kb43
Białogard PL 120 Ga31
Białogarda PL 121 Gd29
Białogóra PL 112 Gd58
Białogóry PL 123 Kb30
Białopole PL 131 Kd40
Białośliwie PL 121 Gc34
Białousy PL 123 Kb32
Białowąs PL 121 Gb32
Białowieża PL 123 Kc35
Białuty PL 122 Ja34
Biały Bór PL 121 Gc32
Biały Dunajec PL 138 Ja46
Białystok PL 123 Kb33
Biancavilla I 167 Fc85
Bianchi I 164 Gc80
Bianco I 164 Gb84
Biandrate I 148 Ca59
Biar E 55 Fb70
Biarritz F 39 Ed54
Biarrotte F 39 Fa54
Bias F 39 Fa52
Biasca CH 142 Cc56
Biatorbágy H 146 Hc53
Bibaktad N 64 Jc07
Bibbiano I 149 Da62
Bibbiena I 156 Dd65
Bibbona I 155 Da67
Biberach D 133 Ca49
Biberach an der Riß D 142 Da50
Biberbach D 134 Dc49
Biberist CH 141 Bd53
Bibertal D 142 Db50
Biberwier A 142 Dc53
Bibiana I 148 Bc61
Bibione I 150 Ec59
Biblis D 134 Cc45
Bibury GB 20 Ed27
Bicaj AL 178 Ad72
Bıçakçi TR 192 Fa87
Bicaz RO 171 Cd55
Bicaz RO 172 Eb58
Bicaz-Chei RO 172 Eb57
Bicazu Ardelean RO 172 Eb58
Biccari I 161 Fd73
Biçer TR 193 Hb82
Bicester GB 20 Fa27
Bichiş RO 171 Db59
Bichl D 143 Dd52
Bichlbach A 142 Dc53
Bickendorf D 133 Bc43
Bickenriede D 126 Dc40
Bicker GB 17 Fc23
Bickleigh GB 19 Ea30
Bickley Moss GB 15 Ec23
Bicorp E 54 Fb69
Bicos P 58 Ab72
Bicske H 146 Hc53
Bidalite S 111 Ga53
Biddenden GB 21 Ga29
Biddestone GB 19 Ec28
Biddinghuizen NL 116 Bb35
Biddulph GB 16 Ed22
Bideford GB 19 Dd29
Bidegyan E 39 Ec55
Bidingen D 142 Dc52
Bidjovagge N 63 Hd10
Bidonì I 169 Ca77
Bidovce SK 139 Jd48
Biduedo E 36 Ba57
Bie S 95 Ga44
Biebelried D 134 Db45
Bieberehren D 134 Db46
Biebergemünd D 134 Cd44
Biebersdorf D 128 Fa38
Biebertal D 126 Cc42
Biebesheim D 134 Cc45
Biecz PL 128 Fc39
Biecz PL 139 Jd45
Biedaszek PL 122 Hc33
Biedenkopf D 126 Cc41
Biederitz D 127 Ea37
Biedrusko PL 129 Gc36
Biel CH 141 Bc53
Biel E 39 Fa58
Bielanka PL 138 Ja46
Bielany-Żyłaki PL 131 Ka36
BielatalRosenthal D 128 Fa42
Bielawa PL 129 Gb42
Bielawy PL 128 Ga39
Bielawy PL 130 Hd37
Bielba (Herrerías) E 38 Db55
Bielcza PL 138 Jb44
Bielefeld D 126 Cc37
Bielica PL 122 Hd31
Bielice PL 122 Hc33
Biella I 148 Ca59
Bielland N 92 Cb46
Bielmonte I 148 Ca58
Bielsa E 40 Fd57
Bielsk PL 122 Hd35
Bielsko-Biała PL 138 Hc45
Bielsk Podlaski PL 123 Kb34
Bienenbüttel D 118 Dc34
Bieniów PL 128 Fd39
Bieńkowice PL 137 Hb44
Bienne CH 141 Bc53
Bienno I 149 Da58
Bienservida E 53 Ea71
Bientina I 155 Db65
Bienvenida E 51 Bd71
Bienvenida E 52 Cd70
Bierawa PL 137 Hb44
Bierdzany PL 129 Ha42
Bière CH 140 Ba55
Biere D 127 Ea38
Bierge E 48 Fc59
Biergenis S 71 Ga21
Bieringen D 134 Da46
Bierné F 28 Fb40
Biersted DK 100 Dc20
Biertan RO 175 Dc60
Bieruń PL 138 Hc44
Bieruń Str. PL 138 Hc44
Bierutów PL 129 Gd41
Bierwart B 124 Ad41
Bierzwienna Długa PL 129 Hb37
Bierzwnica PL 120 Ga32
Biesal PL 122 Ja32
Biescas E 40 Fc57
Biesenthal D 120 Fa35
Biesiekierz PL 120 Ga31
Biesles F 30 Jb39
Bieşti MD 173 Fd56
Bieszkowice PL 121 Ha29
Bietigheim D 133 Cb48
Bietigheim-Bissingen D 134 Cd48
Bieuzy-Lanvaux F 27 Ea40
Bièvre B 132 Ad43
Biez B 124 Ad41
Bieżuń PL 122 Hd34
Biga TR 185 Ec80
Bigadiç TR 192 Fa83
Bigalı TR 185 Ea80
Biganos F 32 Fa51
Bigaunciems LV 106 Ka50
Bigbury-on-Sea GB 19 Dd32
Bigganjarg N 65 Kb06
Biggar GB 11 Eb14
Biggleswade GB 20 Fc26
Bignan F 27 Eb40
Bignasco CH 141 Cb56
Bignor GB 20 Fb30
Bigny F 29 Gd43
Bigor MNE 159 Ja70
Bigorne P 44 Ba61
Bigüézal E 39 Fa57
Bihać BIH 151 Ga62
Biharia RO 170 Cb56
Biharkeresztes H 147 Ka53
Biharnagybajom H 147 Jd53
Bihireşti RO 172 Ed59
Bijela MNE 159 Hd69
Bijele Poljane MNE 159 Hd69
Bijeljani BIH 159 Hc67
Bijeljina BIH 153 Hd62
Bijelo Brdo HR 153 Hd59
Bijelo polje HR 153 Hd58
Bijelo Polje MNE 159 Jb67
Bikal H 152 Hb57
Bikavėnai LT 113 Jc56
Bikernieki LV 115 Lc53
Bikovo SRB 153 Ja58
Biksēre LV 107 Lb50
Biksti LV 105 Jd51
Bila Cerkva UA 204 Ec15
Bilalovac BIH 158 Hb64
Bílá Voda CZ 137 Gc43
Bilbao E 38 Ea55
Bilbo = Bilbao E 38 Ea55
Bilbor RO 172 Ea57
Bilčice CZ 137 Gd45
Bilciureşti RO 176 Ea65
Bilcza PL 130 Jb42
Bildsberg S 102 Fa48
Bildudalur IS 2 Ac02
Bileća BIH 159 Hc68
Bilecik TR 187 Gb80
Biled RO 174 Bc60
Bilelyeri TR 199 Gc91
Biłgoraj PL 131 Kb42
Bilhorod-Dnistrovs'kyj UA 204 Ec17
Biliat F 35 Jd45
Bilicenii Vechi MD 173 Fb56
Bilina CZ 136 Fa43
Bilišane HR 157 Ga64
Bilisht AL 182 Ba77
Biljača KSV 178 Bc72
Bilje HR 153 Hc59
Bilka BG 181 Ed71
Billdal S 102 Eb49
Billé F 28 Fa39
Billeberga S 110 Ed55
Billerbeck D 125 Ca37
Billericay GB 20 Fd27
Billesdon GB 16 Fb24
Billesholm S 110 Ed54
Billigheim D 134 Cd46
Billigheim-Ingenheim D 133 Cb47
Billingborough GB 17 Fc23
Billinge S 110 Fa55
Billingen N 85 Da34
Billingham GB 11 Fa17
Billinghay GB 17 Fc23
Billingsfors S 94 Ec45
Billingshurst GB 20 Fc30
Billnäs FIN 97 Jd40
Billom F 34 Hc47
Billsta S 80 Gd30
Billum DK 108 Cd25
Billund DK 108 Da25
Billy F 34 Hc45
Bilohors'k UA 205 Fa17
Bilokurakyne UA 203 Fb14
Bilopillja UA 202 Ed13
Bilovec CZ 137 Ha45
Bilovods'k UA 203 Fb14
Bilshausen D 126 Db39
Bilska LV 106 La48
Bilsko PL 138 Jb45
Bilto N 63 Hb10
Bilzingsleben D 127 Dd40
Bimeda E 37 Ca55
Biňa SK 146 Hc51
Binaced E 48 Fd60
Binarowa PL 138 Jc45
Binarville F 24 Ja35
Binas F 29 Gb40
Binasco I 149 Cc60
Binbrook GB 17 Fc21
Binche B 124 Ac42
Bińcze PL 121 Gc32
Bindalseidet N 70 Ed24
Bindslev DK 101 Dd19
Binéfar E 48 Fd60
Bingen D 133 Cb44
Bingen D 142 Cd50
Bingen N 93 Dc41
Bingen N 94 Eb42
Bingham GB 16 Fb23
Bingley GB 16 Ed20
Bingöl TR 205 Ga20
Bingsjö S 87 Fd38
Bingsta S 87 Fa21
Binibèquer Vell E 57 Ja66
Binic F 26 Eb37
Biniés E 39 Fb57
Binimel-là E 57 Ja65
Binissafullet E 57 Ja66
Binissalem E 57 Hb67
Binkos BG 180 Ea72
Binn CH 141 Ca56
Binn Éadair IRL 13 Da21
Binneberg S 102 Fa46
Binsfeld D 133 Bc44
Binswangen D 134 Dc49
Binz D 120 Fa30
Bioča MNE 159 Jb68
Bioče MNE 159 Ja69
Biograd na moru HR 157 Fd65
Biokovina BIH 152 Gd63
Bionaz I 148 Bc57
Biorine HR 158 Gc66
Biorra IRL 13 Ca22
Bioska SRB 159 Jb65
Biot F 43 Kc53
Biota E 39 Fa58
Bippen D 117 Cb35
Birboieni MD 173 Fb58
Birchiş RO 174 Cb60
Bircza PL 139 Kb45
Birdhill IRL 12 Bd23
Birdlip GB 20 Ed27
Birdsmoor Gate GB 19 Eb30
Birgi TR 192 Fa86
Birgi Novo I 166 Ea84
Birgland D 135 Ea46
Biri N 86 Ea38
Biriņi LV 106 Kc49
Biristrand N 86 Ea38
Birító H 146 Hc56
Birkeland N 92 Ca45
Birkeland N 92 Cc46
Birkeland N 93 Da46
Birkelse DK 100 Dc20
Birkenau D 134 Cc46
Birkende DK 109 Dd26
Birkenes N 93 Da46
Birkenfeld D 133 Bd45
Birkenfeld D 134 Cc48
Birkenfeld D 134 Da45
Birkenhead GB 15 Eb22
Birkenwerder D 127 Ed36
Birkerød DK 109 Ec25
Birkestrand N 64 Ka05
Birket DK 109 Ea28
Birkfeld A 144 Ga53
Birkungen D 126 Dc40
Birlădeni MD 173 Fa54
Birmingham GB 20 Ed25
Birnova MD 173 Fa53
Birónico CH 149 Cc57
Birr IRL 13 Ca22
Birsay GB 5 Eb02
Birstein D 134 Cd43
Birštonas LT 114 Kc58
Biruința MD 173 Fb55
Biruința MD 177 Fc61
Biržai LT 114 Kd53
Birzebbuga M 166 Eb88
Birzes LV 106 Kc52
Birzgale LV 106 Kc51
Birži LV 105 Jb51
Birži LV 106 La52
Birzuļi LV 106 La48
Bisaccia I 161 Fd74
Bisacquino I 166 Ec85
Biscarrosse F 32 Fa51
Biscarrosse-Plage F 32 Fa51
Bisceglie I 162 Gc73
Bischberg D 134 Dc45
Bischbrunn D 134 Da45
Bischheim F 25 Kc37
Bischoffen D 126 Cc42
Bischofsgrün D 135 Ea44
Bischofsheim D 133 Cb44
Bischofsheim D 134 Db43
Bischofshofen A 143 Ed53
Bischofsmais D 135 Ec48
Bischofsreut D 136 Fa48
Bischofswerda D 128 Fb41
Bischofswiesen D 143 Ec52
Bischofszell CH 142 Cd52
Bischwiller F 25 Kc36
Bisenti I 157 Fa69
Biser BG 185 Ea74
Biserci BG 180 Eb68
Bishop Auckland GB 11 Fa17
Bishop's Castle GB 15 Eb24
Bishop's Lydeard GB 19 Ea29
Bishop's Stortford GB 20 Fd27
Bishop's Waltham GB 20 Fa30
Bisiano F 154 Ca71
Bisignano I 164 Gb79
Bisingen D 142 Cc50
Bisisthal CH 142 Cc54
Bisko HR 158 Gc66
Biskopsbyn S 86 Fa38
Biškupci HR 152 Ha60
Biskupice PL 129 Ha41
Biskupice PL 131 Kb40
Biskupiec PL 122 Hc33
Biskupiec PL 122 Jb31
Biskupin PL 121 Gd35
Bislev DK 100 Dc21
Bisley GB 19 Ec27
Bislich D 125 Bc38
Bismark D 127 Ea36
Bismervik N 63 Hd05
Bismo N 85 Db34
Bisoca RO 176 Ec62
Bispberg S 95 Fd40
Bispgården S 79 Gb31
Bispingen D 118 Db34
Bissendorf D 126 Cc37
Bissendorf D 126 Cc37
Bisserup DK 109 Ea27
Bissingen D 134 Dc49
Bissingen, Bietigheim- D 134 Cd48
Bissjön S 80 Hc26
Bissone I 149 Cc58
Bissy-sur-Fley F 30 Ja44
Bistagno I 148 Ca62
Bistar SRB 179 Ca72
Bistarac BIH 153 Hc63
Bistra BG 180 Eb70
Bistra RO 171 Cd59
Bistra RO 171 Db54
Bistra SLO 151 Fb58
Bistražin KSV 178 Ad71
Bistrec BG 181 Ec73
Bistreț RO 179 Cd67
Bistrica BG 179 Cb73
Bistrica BG 179 Cc71
Bistrica BIH 152 Gd61
Bistrica BIH 152 Gd62
Bistrica BIH 158 Ha65
Bistrica BIH 159 Hc65
Bistrica MK 183 Bb76
Bistrica MNE 159 Ja68
Bistrica SRB 159 Jb66
Bistričak BIH 152 Hb63
Bistrița RO 171 Dc57
Bistrița Bârgăului RO 171 Dc57
Biszcza PL 131 Kb42
Bisztynek PL 122 Jb31
Bitburg D 133 Bc44
Bitche F 25 Kb35
Bitelić HR 158 Gc65
Bitem E 48 Ga63
Bitetto I 162 Gc74
Bitola MK 183 Bb76
Bitonto I 162 Gc74
Bitterfeld D 127 Eb39
Bitterna S 102 Ed47
Bitterstad N 66 Fc13
Bitti I 168 Cb75
Bitton GB 19 Ec28
Bitz D 142 Cc50
Biville F 22 Ed34
Bivio CH 142 Cd56
Bivolari RO 173 Fa56
Bivona I 166 Ec85
Bixad RO 176 Ea61
Bixter GB 5 Ed05
Bıyıklar TR 192 Fb84
Bıyıklı TR 197 Ed88
Bize H 145 Gd56
Bizeljsko SLO 151 Ga58
Bizeneuille F 33 Ha45
Bizovac HR 153 Hc59
Bizzarone I 148 Cb58
Bjæverskov DK 109 Eb26
Bjahoml' BY 202 Ea12
Bjala BG 180 Dd69
Bjala BG 180 Ea72
Bjala BG 181 Fa71
Bjala čerkva BG 184 Db74
Bjala Čerkva BG 180 Dc70
Bjala reka BG 184 Dc74
Bjala Reka BG 180 Dc70
Bjala Reka BG 181 Ec71
Bjala Slatina BG 179 Da69
Bjala Voda BG 180 Dc68
Bjälbo S 103 Fc47
Bjal izvor BG 184 Dc75
Bjal Izvor BG 180 Dd73
Bjal Kladenec BG 180 Ea73
Bjalo Pole BG 180 Dd73
Bjalyničy BY 202 Eb12
Bjännberg S 80 Hb29
Bjännfors S 80 Hc27
Bjår N 93 Db42
Bjäresjö S 110 Fa56
Bjärklunda S 102 Fa47
Bjarkøy N 66 Ga12
Bjärme S 87 Gb33
Bjar'movo RUS 107 Ma50
Bjärnum S 110 Fa54
Bjaroza BY 202 Ea13
Bjarozavka BY 202 Ea13
Bjärred S 110 Ed56
Bjärsjölagård S 110 Fa56
Bjärten S 80 Ha28
Bjärtrå S 80 Gc31
Bjästa S 80 Gd30
Bjela BIH 159 Hd66
Bjelahe KSV 178 Ad70
Bjelahe SRB 159 Jc68
Bjelajci BIH 152 Gc61
Bjelland N 92 Cb46
Bjelopérica SRB 159 Jb64
Bjelovar HR 152 Gc58
Bjerangen N 71 Fb19
Bjergby DK 100 Dc19
Bjergby DK 100 Da23
Bjerghuse DK 100 Cd23
Bjerka N 71 Fb21
Bjerkreim N 92 Ca45
Bjerkvik N 67 Gb13
Bjerre DK 101 Dd22
Bjerre DK 108 Dc25
Bjerreby DK 109 Dd28
Bjerregård DK 108 Cd24
Bjerregrav DK 100 Db22
Bjerringbro DK 100 Db23
Bjkörkö-Arholma S 96 Ha41
Bjoestrand N 92 Ca41
Bjølstad N 85 Dc35
Bjönsaberg S 87 Fb37
Bjørånes N 85 Ea36
Bjørbo S 95 Fc40
Björboholm S 102 Ec48
Bjordal N 84 Cb37
Bjørdal N 84 Cd34
Bjordal N 92 Cb45
Bjorelvnes N 62 Gc10
Bjørgan N 86 Ea32
Bjørgo N 85 Dc38
Bjørhusdalen N 78 Fa25
Björka S 87 Fc38
Björkås N 67 Gd12
Björkås S 71 Fd23
Björkbäcken S 71 Fd22
Björkberg S 73 Hc21
Björkberg S 80 Gc26
Björkberg S 87 Fc36
Björkboda FIN 97 Jc40
Björkborn S 95 Fc43
Björkbysätern S 94 Ed40
Björke N 84 Cc34
Björke S 96 Gc39
Björkebakken N 67 Gb11
Björkebol S 94 Ec43
Bjørkedal N 84 Cc34
Bjørkedal N 93 Da46
Bjørkekjær N 93 Db45
Bjørkelangen N 94 Eb41
Björketorp S 102 Ec50
Björkfors S 73 Jb21
Björkfors S 103 Ga48
Björkhöjden S 79 Ga30
Björkholmen S 72 Gd19
Björkland S 72 Gd23
Björklia N 77 Ea30
Björkliden S 67 Gd13
Björkliden S 72 Gb22
Björkliden S 73 Hb24
Björklinge S 96 Gc41
Björklund S 72 Gd23
Björklunda S 72 Gd20
Bjørkneset N 65 Kc08
Bjørkness N 94 Eb41
Björkö FIN 97 Hd40
Björkö FIN 97 Ja40
Björkö FIN 97 Ja41
Björkö S 103 Fc50
Björköby FIN 81 Hd30
Björköby S 103 Fc49
Björksele S 79 Gb28
Björksele S 80 Gd25
Björksjön S 80 Gc30
Björksta S 95 Gb42
Björkvattnet S 79 Fb26
Björkvik S 95 Gb45
Björlanda S 102 Eb49
Bjørlia N 78 Ed25
Bjørn N 70 Ed21
Björna S 80 Gd29
Bjørndalen N 78 Ec25
Björneborg S 95 Fb44
Bjørnenga N 63 Hd08
Bjørnenes N 66 Ga12
Bjørnerheim N 84 Cc35
Bjørnevatn N 65 Kd08
Bjørnhaugseter N 85 Dd36
Björnhult S 103 Ga50
Björnliden S 86 Ed34
Björnlunda S 96 Gc44
Björnrike S 87 Fb33
Bjørnset N 63 Ja08
Björnsjö S 80 Gd29
Bjørnskinn N 66 Fd12
Bjørnstad N 65 Kd07
Bjørnstad N 71 Fc18
Bjørnstad N 78 Fa25
Björnvik FIN 90 Kd38
Björsäter S 102 Fa46
Björsäter S 103 Ga47
Björsberg S 95 Fd39
Bjuråker S 87 Ga35
Bjurbäck S 102 Fa48
Bjurberget S 94 Ed39
Bjurfors S 80 Hc25
Bjurfors S 80 Hb26
Bjurholm S 80 Ha28
Bjurön S 81 Hd26
Bjursås S 95 Fd39
Bjursele S 80 Hb26
Bjursele S 80 Ha25
Bjurselet S 73 Hc24
Bjurström S 80 Hb25
Bjurtjärn S 95 Fb43
Bjurträsk S 72 Ha24
Bjurträsk S 73 Hd22
Bjurum S 102 Fa47
Bjurvattnet S 80 Ha28
Bjurvattnet S 80 Hb25
Bjuv S 110 Ed54
Blaby GB 16 Fa24
Blace BIH 158 Hb66
Blace HR 158 Ha68
Blace SRB 178 Bc69
Blachownia PL 130 Hc42
Black Bull IRL 13 Cd21
Blackburn GB 10 Ea13
Blackburn GB 15 Ec20
Blacke S 81 Hd26
Blackhall GB 11 Fa17
Blackhill GB 4 Da07
Blacklion IRL 9 Cb18
Blacklunans GB 7 Eb10
Blackmoor Gate GB 19 Dd29
Black Mount GB 7 Dd11
Black Notley GB 21 Ga27
Blackpool GB 15 Eb20
Blackridge GB 10 Ea13
Blacksnäs FIN 89 Hd32
Blacksta S 95 Gb45
Blackstad S 103 Ga49
Blackwater GB 20 Fa31
Blackwater IRL 13 Cd24
Blackwaterfoot GB 10 Db14
Blackwood GB 19 Ea27
Bladåker S 96 Gd41
Bladel NL 124 Ba39
Błądzim PL 121 Ha33
Blaenau Ffestiniog GB 15 Dd23
Blaenavon GB 19 Eb27
Blaengarw GB 19 Ea27
Blæsbjerg DK 101 Dd19
Blagaj BIH 152 Gb61
Blagaj BIH 158 Hb67
Blagdon GB 19 Eb28
Blăgeşti RO 172 Ec59
Blăgeşti RO 177 Fb61
Blagnac F 40 Gb54
Blagodarnyj RUS 205 Ga16
Blagoevgrad BG 179 Cb73
Blagoevo BG 180 Eb69
Blagojev Kamen SRB 174 Bd65
Blagon F 32 Fa50
Blåhøj DK 108 Da25
Blaibach D 135 Ec47
Blaichach D 142 Db52
Blaiken S 72 Gb24
Blaikliden S 71 Fd24
Blain F 28 Ed41
Blainville-Crevon F 23 Gb35
Blainville-sur-l'Eau F 25 Jd37
Blairgowrie GB 7 Eb11
Blaise F 30 Ja38
Blaisy-Bas F 30 Ja41
Blaj RO 175 Da60
Blajan F 40 Ga55
Blăjani RO 176 Ec63
Blăjel RO 175 Db60
Blăjeni RO 171 Cc59
Błąkały PL 123 Ka30
Blakeney GB 17 Ga23
Blakeney GB 19 Ec27
Blaker N 94 Eb41
Blakesley GB 20 Fa26
Blakstad N 77 Da31
Blakstad N 93 Da46
Blâmont F 25 Ka37
Blan F 41 Gd54
Blanca E 55 Ed72
Blancafort F 29 Ha41
Blancas E 47 Ed63
Blanchardstown IRL 13 Cd21
Blanchland GB 11 Ed17
Blancos E 36 Bb58
Blandford Forum GB 19 Ec30
Blandiana RO 175 Cd60
Blanes E 49 Hb60
Blaney GB 9 Cb17
Blangy-sur-Bresle F 23 Gc33
Blangy-sur-Ternoise F 23 Gd31
Blankaholm S 103 Gb49
Blankenau D 126 Da42
Blankenberg D 135 Ea43
Blankenberge B 124 Aa38
Blankenburg D 127 Dd38
Blankenfelde-Mahlow D 127 Ed37
Blankenhain D 127 Dd42
Blankenhain D 127 Eb42
Blankenheim D 125 Bc42
Blankenheim D 127 Ea39
Blankenrath D 133 Bd44
Blankensee D 119 Ed33
Blanquefort F 32 Fb50
Blans DK 108 Db28
Blansko CZ 137 Gc47
Blanzac F 32 Fd48
Blanzy F 30 Ja44
Blarnalearoch GB 4 Dc06
Blarney IRL 12 Bd25
Blaron F 43 Kb52
Blåskovo BG 181 Ed71
Blåsmark S 73 Hc23
Blåsut S 102 Ec47
Błaszki PL 129 Hb39
Blatna BIH 152 Gb61
Blatná CZ 136 Fa47
Blatné SK 145 Gd50
Blato HR 158 Gb68
Blato na Cetini HR 158 Gc66
Blatten CH 141 Bd56
Blatten CH 141 Ca56
Blattniksele S 72 Gc23
Blatzheim D 125 Bc41
Blaubeuren D 134 Da49
Blaufelden D 134 Da47
Blaustein D 134 Da49
Blauwe Hand NL 117 Bc35
Blauwhuis NL 116 Bb33
Blåvand DK 108 Cd26
Blåvik S 80 Gc25
Blåviksjön S 80 Gc25
Blavozy F 34 Hd49
Blaxton GB 16 Fb21
Blaye F 32 Fb49
Blaye F 41 Ha52
Blaye-les-Mines F 41 Gd53
Blaževo SRB 178 Bb69
Blāzma LV 105 Jc49
Błażowa PL 139 Ka44
Blažuj BIH 158 Hb65
Bleadon GB 19 Eb28
Bleckåsen S 79 Fb30
Bleckede D 119 Dd33
Blecket S 87 Fd38
Bled SLO 151 Fa57
Błędów PL 130 Jb38
Błędów PL 138 Hd43
Błędowo PL 121 Hb33
Bledzew PL 128 Fd36
Bleialf D 133 Bc43
Bleiburg A 144 Fc56
Bleicherode D 126 Dc40
Bleik N 66 Fd11
Bleiknesmo N 71 Fd18
Bleikvasslia N 71 Fb22
Blejeşti RO 176 Dd66
Blejoi RO 176 Ea64
Bleken S 102 Ec46
Blekendorf D 119 Dd30
Bleket S 102 Eb48
Blender D 118 Da34
Blendija SRB 178 Bd68
Bléneau F 29 Ha40
Błenna PL 129 Hb36
Blennerville IRL 12 Bb24
Blénod-lès-Toul F 25 Jc37
Blentarp S 110 Fa56
Blera I 156 Ea70
Blérancourt F 24 Hb34
Bléré F 29 Ga42
Blesa E 47 Fa62
Bleskestad N 92 Cc42
Blesle F 34 Hb48
Blessington IRL 13 Cd22
Bleşteni MD 173 Fa54
Blet F 29 Ha43
Bletchingdon GB 20 Fa27
Bletsoe GB 20 Fc26
Bletterans F 31 Jc43
Bleurville F 31 Jd39
Bleury F 30 Hb40
Blévaincourt F 31 Jc39
Blèves F 28 Fd38
Blewbury GB 20 Fa28
Blidari RO 171 Da54
Blīdene LV 105 Jd52
Blidö S 96 Ha42
Bliedersdorf D 118 Da33
Bliedersdorf D 118 Db33
Bliesbruck F 25 Kb35
Blieskastel D 133 Bd46
Blievenstorf D 119 Ea33
Bligny F 24 Hc35
Bligny F 30 Ja39
Bligny-sur-Ouche F 30 Ja42
Blijnii Hutor MD 173 Ga58
Bliksund N 93 Da47
Bliksvær N 66 Fb17
Blinisht AL 163 Jc71
Blinja HR 152 Gb60
Bliūdžiai LT 114 Ka56
Blizanów PL 129 Ha38
Blížejov CZ 135 Ec46
Bliznaci BG 181 Ec69
Bliznaci BG 181 Fa71
Blizne PL 139 Ka45
Bllacë AL 182 Ad74
Blockley GB 20 Ed26
Bloemendaal NL 116 Ad35
Blois F 29 Gb41
Blokhus DK 100 Dc20
Blokzijl NL 117 Bc34
Blombacka S 94 Fa43
Blomberg D 117 Cb32
Blomberg D 126 Cd38
Blome LV 106 La48
Blomhöjden S 79 Fc26
Blommenslyst DK 108 Dc26
Blomskog S 94 Ec44
Blomsøy N 70 Ed22
Blomstermåla S 103 Gb51
Blomvåg N 84 Bd38
Blond F 33 Gb46
Blönduós IS 2 Ad03
Błonie PL 129 Gc41
Błonie PL 130 Jb37
Bloška Polica SLO 151 Fb59
Blötberget S 95 Fc41
Błotnica Strzelecka PL 137 Hb43
Błotno PL 120 Fc32
Blovice CZ 135 Ed46
Blovstrød DK 109 Ec25
Blowatz D 119 Ea31
Bloxham GB 20 Fa26
Bludenz A 142 Da54
Bludov CZ 137 Gc45
Bludowo PL 122 Hd30
Blue Ball IRL 13 Cb21
Blueford IRL 12 Bc24
Blumau A 145 Gb53

Blumau – Bösdorf

Blumau I 143 Dd56
Blumberg D 141 Cb51
Blumberg, Ahrensfelde- D 128 Fa36
Blumenhagen D 120 Fa33
Blumenthal D 119 Ec34
Blyberg S 87 Fb37
Blynki RUS 99 Ld43
Blyth GB 11 Fa16
Blyth Bridge GB 11 Eb14
Bnin PL 129 Gc37
Bø N 62 Gc09
Bø N 66 Fc13
Bø N 66 Fd13
Bø N 77 Db31
Bø N 84 Ca36
Bø N 92 Ca43
Bø N 92 Cd45
Bø N 93 Db43
Bø N 93 Dc43
Bo S 95 Fd45
Bo'Ness GB 10 Ea13
Boadilla del Monte E 46 Db64
Boadilla de Rioseco E 37 Cd58
Boal E 37 Bd54
Boalt S 111 Fb53
Boan MNE 159 Ja68
Boario Terme I 149 Da58
Boat of Garten GB 7 Ea08
Boa Vista P 44 Ac65
Boba H 145 Gd54
Bobadilla del Campo E 46 Cd62
Bobadilla Estación E 60 Cd75
Bobâlna RO 171 Da57
Bobbau D 127 Eb39
Bobbio I 149 Cc61
Bobbio Pellice I 148 Bb61
Bobeica MD 173 Fc58
Bobenheim-Roxheim D 133 Cb45
Boberg S 79 Fd30
Bobicești RO 175 Da66
Bobigny F 23 Gd36
Böbing D 142 Dc52
Bobingen D 142 Dc50
Böbingen an der Rems D 134 Da48
Bobitz D 119 Ea32
Böblingen D 134 Cc48
Bobolice PL 121 Gb31
Boboševo BG 179 Cb73
Bobota HR 153 Hd60
Bobota RO 171 Cc56
Bobovdol BG 179 Cb72
Bobovište MNE 159 Ja70
Bobowa PL 138 Jc45
Bobowo PL 121 Hb31
Bobr BY 202 Eb12
Bobrețu RO 175 Da65
Bóbrka PL 139 Kb46
Bobrov RUS 203 Fb13
Bobrovec SK 138 Hd47
Bobrovycja UA 202 Ec14
Bobrowice PL 128 Fc38
Bobrówko PL 120 Fd35
Bobrówko PL 122 Jc32
Bobrowniki PL 122 Hc35
Bobrowniki PL 123 Kc33
Bobrowniki Wielkie PL 138 Jc44
Bobrynec' UA 204 Ed16
Boc MNE 159 Jc68
Boc MNE 178 Ad69
Bóč SK 145 Gd51
Boca de Huérgano E 37 Cd56
Bocairent E 55 Fb70
Bocale I 164 Ga84
Bocani MD 173 Fb56
Bočar SRB 153 Jb58
Bocca di l'Orù F 154 Cb72
Bocca di Piazza I 164 Gc80
Bocchigliero I 164 Gc79
Boceguillas E 46 Dc61
Böçen TR 192 Ga82
Bochnia PL 138 Jb44
Bocholt B 125 Bb39
Bocholt D 125 Bd38
Bochov CZ 135 Ed44
Bochum D 125 Ca39
Bocigas E 46 Da61
Bockara S 103 Ga50
Bockau D 135 Ec43
Bockenem D 126 Db38
Bockfliess A 145 Gc50
Bockhorn D 118 Cc33
Bockhorn D 143 Ea50
Bócki PL 123 Kb35
Böckstein A 143 Ec54
Bockträsk S 72 Gc23
Böckweiler D 133 Bd46
Bočna ob Dreti SLO 151 Fc57
Bocognano F 154 Cb70
Bócsa H 146 Ja56
Bocșa RO 171 Cd56
Bocșa RO 174 Bd62
Bocsig RO 170 Ca59
Boczów PL 128 Fc37
Bod RO 176 Ea62
Boda S 87 Fd38
Boda S 87 Gb32
Boda S 94 Ed43
Boda S 94 Ed43
Böda S 104 Gc50
Bodaczów PL 131 Kc41
Boda glasbruk S 103 Fd52
Bodajk H 145 Hb53
Bødal N 84 Cd35
Bodange B 132 Ba44
Bođani SRB 153 Hd60
Bodaño E 36 Ba56
Bodators S 103 Fc50
Bodbacka FIN 89 Hd32
Bodbyn S 80 Hb28
Boddam GB 5 Fa08
Boddensdorf A 144 Fa56
Boddum DK 100 Da22
Bodegraven NL 116 Ad36
Boden A 142 Db53
Boden D 125 Cb42
Boden S 73 Hd21
Bodenfelde D 126 Da39
Bodenheim D 133 Cb44
Bodenkirchen D 143 Eb50
Bodenmais D 135 Ed48
Bodenwerder D 126 Da38
Bodenwöhr D 135 Eb47
Bodești RO 172 Ec57
Bodfari GB 15 Ea22
Bodilsker DK 111 Fc58
Bodman D 142 Cc51
Bodmin GB 18 Db31
Bodnegg D 142 Da52
Bodö FIN 81 Jb28
Bodø N 66 Fc17
Bodoc RO 176 Ea61
Bodom N 78 Ec28
Bodonal de la Sierra E 51 Bc71
Bodonci SLO 145 Gb55
Bodorgan Station GB 15 Dd22
Bodrost BG 179 Cc73
Bodrum TR 197 Ec90
Bodsjö S 87 Fc32
Bodsjöedet S 78 Ed30
Bodträskfors S 73 Hc21
Bodyke IRL 12 Bd22
Bodzanów PL 130 Ja36
Bodzanowice PL 129 Hb41
Bodzechów PL 131 Jd41
Bodzentyn PL 130 Jc41
Bodzewo PL 129 Gc38
Boé F 40 Ga52
Boecillo E 46 Da60
Boedapest = Budapest H 146 Hd53
Boëge F 35 Ka45
Boekel NL 125 Bb38
Boekelo NL 117 Bd36
Boën F 34 Hd47
Boen N 93 Da47
Boeslunde DK 109 Ea27
Boeza E 37 Ca56
Bofara S 87 Ga37
Boffzen D 126 Da38
Bofin IRL 8 Ba19
Bofors S 95 Fc43
Boftsa N 64 Ka06
Bogács H 146 Jc51
Bogaczów PL 128 Fd38
Bogádmindszent H 152 Hb58
Bogan N 78 Ed25
Bøgard N 66 Fd11
Bogarra E 53 Eb70
Bogata RO 171 Db59
Bogați RO 176 Dd64
Bogatić SRB 153 Ja61
Bogatovo RUS 113 Jb58
Bogatovo RUS 122 Ja30
Bogatynia PL 128 Fc42
Boğazak TR 199 Ha91
Boğazcık TR 198 Ga92
Boğazi CY 206 Jd96
Boğaziçi TR 198 Ga88
Boğaziçi TR 199 Gb89
Boğaziği TR 198 Fd92
Boğazkale TR 205 Fb20
Boğazkent TR 193 Hb86
Boğazköy TR 186 Ga80
Boğazköy TR 192 Fc84
Bogdan BG 180 Db72
Bogdana RO 173 Fa59
Bogdanci BG 181 Ec69
Bogdanci MK 183 Ca76
Bogdand RO 171 Cd56
Bogdănești RO 172 Ec56
Bogdănești RO 176 Ec60
Bogdănești RO 177 Fa60
Bogdaniec PL 128 Fc36
Bogdănița RO 177 Fa60
Bogdanovca Nouă MD 177 Fd60
Bogdanovo BG 180 Ea73
Bogdanów PL 130 Hd40
Bogdan Vodă RO 171 Db55
Bogë AL 159 Jb69
Boge S 104 Ha49
Bogen D 135 Ec48
Bogen N 66 Fd15
Bogen N 67 Gb13
Bogen S 94 Ed41
Bogense DK 108 Dc26
Bogetići MNE 159 Hd69
Bogna IRL 9 Cc19
Boghenii Noi MD 173 Fb56
Boghești RO 177 Fa61
Boghiceni MD 173 Fc58
Bogliasco I 148 Cb63
Boglösa S 96 Gc43
Bognanco Fonti I 148 Ca57
Bognelv N 63 Hc08
Bognelvdalen N 63 Hc08
Bognes N 66 Ga14
Bogno CH 149 Cc57
Bognor Regis GB 20 Fb30
Bogny-sur-Meuse F 24 Ja33
Bogø By DK 109 Eb28
Bogodol BIH 158 Ha66
Bogojevac SRB 178 Bc69
Bogojevice SRB 178 Bd70
Bogojevo SRB 153 Hd59
Bogojina SLO 145 Gb56
Bogomila MK 183 Bb74
Bogomilovo BG 180 Dd73
Bogomolje HR 158 Gd67
Bogoria PL 130 Jc42
Bogorodick RUS 203 Fa11
Bogorodsk RUS 203 Fb09
Bogorovo BG 181 Ed68
Bogosavac SRB 153 Ja62
Bogoslov BG 179 Ca72
Bogova RO 174 Cb65
Bogovina SRB 178 Bd67
Böğrüdelik TR 193 Hb85
Bogsta S 96 Gc45
Bogstad N 84 Cc35
Bogsund N 92 Cb43
Bogučar RUS 203 Fc13
Boguchwałow PL 137 Ha44
Boguchwały PL 122 Hd31
Bogue GB 10 Dd16
Bogumiłów PL 129 Hb39
Bogumiłowice PL 130 Hc40
Boguszewo PL 121 Hb33
Boguszów-Gorce PL 129 Gb42
Bogutovac SRB 178 Ba67
Boguty-Pianki PL 123 Ka35
Bogyiszló H 146 Hc56
Bogzești MD 173 Fc56
Bohain-en-Vermandois F 24 Hb33
Bohan B 132 Ad44
Bohdalice CZ 137 Gc47
Bohdalov CZ 136 Ga46
Bohdašin CZ 137 Gb43
Boheden S 73 Ja20
Böheimkirchen A 144 Ga51
Boherboy IRL 12 Bc25
Boherlalan IRL 13 Ca23
Bohinjska Bistrica SLO 151 Fa57
Böhl-Iggelheim D 133 Cb46
Böhme D 118 Da35
Böhmenkirch D 134 Da49
Bohmte D 117 Cc36
Bohoduchiv UA 203 Fa14
Boholt RO 175 Cc60
Bohonal de Ibor E 51 Cb66
Böhönye H 145 Gd56
Bohot BG 180 Db69
Bohukaly PL 131 Kc36
Bohula MK 183 Bd75
Bohumín CZ 137 Hb45
Bohuňovice CZ 137 Gd46
Bohus S 102 Ec48
Bohuslav UA 204 Ec15
Bohutín CZ 136 Fa46
Boialvo P 44 Ad63
Boianu Mare RO 171 Cc56
Boiereni RO 171 Db56
Boiro E 36 Ac56
Boiry-Saint-Matin F 23 Ha32
Boiscommun F 29 Gd39
Bois-de-Céné F 28 Ed43
Bois-le-Roi F 29 Ha38
Boismont F 25 Jc34
Boișoara RO 175 Db62
Boisredon F 32 Fb48
Boisseron F 41 Hd53
Boisson F 42 Ja52
Boišta = Slepač most MNE 159 Jb67
Boisville F 29 Gc38
Boitzenburg D 120 Fa34
Boiu Mare RO 171 Da56
Bóixols E 48 Gb59
Boizenburg D 119 Dd33
Böja S 102 Fa46
Bojadła PL 128 Ga38
Bojadžik BG 180 Eb73
Bojančište MK 183 Bc75
Bojane MK 178 Bb73
Bojano I 161 Fb73
Bojanovo BG 180 Eb73
Bojanów PL 139 Ka43
Bojanowo PL 129 Gc39
Bojas LV 105 Jb52
Bojčinovci BG 179 Cc69
Bøjden DK 108 Dc27
Bojewyan GB 18 Cd32
Bojišta MK 182 Ba75
Bojka BG 180 Ea70
Bojkovice CZ 137 Ha48
Bojmie PL 131 Jd37
Bojná SK 137 Ha49
Bojnica BG 179 Cb67
Bojnice SK 137 Hb48
Bojnik SRB 178 Bc70
Bojszowy PL 138 Hc44
Bojtiken S 71 Fc23
Boka SRB 174 Bb62
Bókaháza H 145 Gd55
Bokel D 118 Cd33
Bokenäs S 102 Eb47
Bokinka Pańska PL 131 Kc37
Böklund D 108 Db29
Bokod H 145 Hb53
Boków PL 130 Jb40
Bokros H 146 Jb55
Böksholm S 103 Fc51
Boksjok N 64 Ka05
Boksjön S 71 Fd22
Bol HR 158 Gc67
Bol' SK 139 Ka49
Bolandoz F 31 Jd42
Bolaños de Calatrava E 52 Dc69
Bolaños de Campos E 45 Cc59
Bolayır TR 185 Eb79
Bolbec F 22 Fd34
Bölberget S 86 Fa34
Bolboși RO 175 Cc64
Bolca I 149 Dc59
Bölcske H 146 Hd55
Bolderaja LV 106 Kb50
Boldești-Grădiștea RO 176 Ec65
Boldești-Scăeni RO 176 Ea64
Boldogkőváralja H 147 Jd50
Boldon GB 11 Fa16
Boldu RO 176 Ed63
Boldur RO 174 Ca61
Boldurești MD 173 Fb57
Boldva H 146 Jc50
Böle FIN 98 Ka40
Bøle N 78 Eb26
Böle S 73 Hc23
Böle S 73 Hd21
Böle S 79 Fb30
Böle S 79 Gb31
Böle S 87 Fb33
Bolea E 39 Fb58
Boleč SRB 153 Jc62
Boleč SRB 174 Bb64
Bolemin PL 128 Fd36
Boleráz SK 145 Gd50
Bolesław PL 138 Hd43
Bolesławiec PL 128 Fd40
Bolesławiec PL 129 Ha40
Boleszkowice PL 128 Fc36
Boleszyn PL 122 Hd33
Bolewice PL 128 Ga37
Bolewicko PL 128 Ga37
Bolfan HR 152 Gc57
Bolfoss N 94 Eb41
Bolga N 70 Fa19
Bolgatovo RUS 107 Mb49
Bolgheri I 155 Db67
Bolhás H 152 Gd57
Bolhó H 152 Gd58
Bolhov RUS 202 Ed12
Bolhrad UA 204 Ec18
Boliden S 80 Hb25
Bolimów PL 130 Ja37
Bolinglanna IRL 8 Bb19
Bolintin-Deal RO 176 Ea66
Bolintin-Vale RO 176 Ea66
Boljanic BIH 152 Hb62
Boljanići MNE 159 Ja66
Boljarino BG 180 Dc73
Boljarovo BG 185 Ec74
Boljarsko BG 180 Eb73
Boljevac SRB 178 Bd67
Boljevci SRB 153 Jc62
Boljkovci SRB 159 Jc64
Bolkesjø N 93 Dc42
Bölkow D 119 Eb31
Bolków PL 128 Ga42
Boll, Bad D 134 Da49
Bollebygd S 102 Ec49
Bollendorf D 133 Bc44
Bollène F 42 Jb52
Bollermoen N 71 Fb21
Bollezeele F 21 Gd30
Bólliga E 47 Eb65
Bollnäs S 87 Ga37
Bollosetra N 63 Ja08
Bollsbyn S 94 Ec44
Bollstabruk S 80 Gc31
Bolluca TR 186 Fc77
Bollullos de la Mitación E 59 Bd74
Bollullos par del Condado E 59 Bc74
Bolman HR 153 Hc59
Bolmen S 102 Fa52
Bölmepınar TR 198 Ga90
Bolmsö S 102 Fa51
Bolnhurst GB 20 Fc26
Bolnuevo E 55 Ed74
Bologna I 149 Dc63
Bologne F 30 Jb39
Bolognetta I 166 Ed84
Bolognola I 156 Ec68
Bologoe RUS 202 Ec09
Bologovo RUS 202 Eb10
Bolohani MD 173 Fd56
Bolotana I 169 Ca76
Boloteşti RO 176 Ed62
Bolotovo RUS 107 Ma47
Bol'šaja Polja RUS 99 Lc42
Bol'šaja Poljana RUS 113 Jb59
Bol'šakovo RUS 113 Jc58
Bolsena I 156 Ea69
Bol'ševik RUS 203 Fd12
Bol'šie Berežki RUS 113 Jb57
Bol'šinka RUS 203 Fc14
Bol'šoe Zareč'e RUS 99 Mb41
Bol'šoj Borovnja RUS 99 Ld42
Bol'šoj Ižora RUS 99 Ma39
Bol'šoj Jamno RUS 99 Ld44
Bol'šoj Kolpany RUS 99 Mb40
Bol'šoj Kuzemkino RUS 99 Lc41
Bol'šoj L'zi RUS 99 Mb44
Bol'šoj Ozerticy RUS 99 Ma41
Bol'šoj Pustomerža RUS 99 Ld41
Bol'šoj Rožki RUS 99 Ld43
Bol'šoj Ruddilovo RUS 99 Ld40
Bol'šoj Sabicy RUS 99 Ma43
Bol'šoj Sabsk RUS 99 Ma42
Bol'šoj Selo RUS 113 Jd57
Bol'šoj Stremlenie RUS 99 Ld40
Bol'šoj Taglino RUS 99 Mb40
Bol'šoj Teškovo RUS 99 Ma40
Bol'šoj Vruda RUS 99 Ma41
Bol'šoj Zagorje RUS 107 Ma46
Bol'šoj Zahon'e RUS 99 Mb44
Bolsover GB 16 Fa22
Bolstad S 102 Ec46
Bolsward NL 116 Bb33
Bolszewo PL 121 Ha29
Boltaña E 40 Fd58
Boltenhagen D 119 Ea31
Boltigen CH 141 Bc55
Bolton GB 15 Ec21
Bolton Abbey GB 16 Ed20
Bolton-le-Sand GB 11 Ec19
Boltun MD 173 Fc58
Bolu TR 187 Hb79
Bölüceağac TR 198 Ga93
Bolungarvík IS 2 Ac02
Bolvadin TR 193 Gd85
Bolvașnița RO 174 Cb62
Bóly H 153 Hc58
Bolzano I 143 Dd56
Bomal B 124 Ba42
Bomarken S 94 Eb44
Bomba I 161 Fb71
Bombarral P 50 Aa67
Bominaco I 156 Ed70
Bomlitz D 118 Db35
Bømlo N 92 Bd41
Bompas F 41 Hb57
Bomporto I 149 Dc62
Bomsund S 79 Fd31
Bona F 30 Hc43
Bona S 103 Fc46
Bonac F 40 Gb56
Bönan S 96 Gc39
Bonanza E 59 Bd75
Boñar E 37 Cc56
Bonar Bridge GB 5 Ea06
Bonarcado I 169 Bd77
Bonares E 59 Bc74
Bonäs S 87 Fb38
Bonäset S 78 Fa30
Bonäset S 79 Fd28
Bonåsjøen N 66 Fd16
Bonawe GB 6 Dc11
Bonboillon F 31 Jc41
Boncath GB 14 Dc26
Bonchester Bridge GB 11 Ec15
Boncuklu TR 191 Ed83
Bończa PL 131 Kc40
Bondari RUS 107 Mb52
Bondary PL 123 Kc34
Bondeborg S 73 Ja21
Bondemon S 94 Eb45
Bondeno I 150 Dd61
Bonderup DK 100 Db21
Bondorf D 134 Cc49
Bondstorp S 103 Fb49
Bondyrz PL 131 Kc42
Bönebüttel D 118 Dc31
Bonefro I 161 Fc72
Bonelli I 150 Eb62
Bönen D 125 Cb39
Bones N 67 Gc13
Bonese D 119 Dd35
Bonete E 55 Ed70
Bönhamn S 80 Gd31
Bonhill GB 10 Dd13
Bonhomme F 31 Kb38
Boniches E 54 Ed66
Boniewo PL 129 Hb36
Bonifacio F 154 Cb72
Bonifato F 154 Ca69
Bonilla de la Sierra E 45 Cc64
Bonin PL 120 Fd34
Bonlieu F 31 Jd44
Bonn D 125 Bd41
Bonnat F 33 Gc45
Bonndorf D 141 Cb51
Bonne F 35 Ka45
Bonnebosq F 22 Fd36
Bønnerup Strand DK 101 Dd23
Bonnet DK 100 Cd22
Bonnétable F 28 Fd39
Bonneuil-Matours F 29 Ga44
Bonneval F 29 Gb39
Bonneval F 35 Kb47
Bonneval-en-Diois F 35 Jd50
Bonnevaux F 31 Jd43
Bonnevaux F 31 Ka44
Bonneville F 35 Ka45
Bonneville-la-Louvet F 22 Fd35
Bonnières-sur-Seine F 23 Gc36
Bonnieux F 42 Jc53
Bönnigheim D 134 Cd47
Bönningstedt D 118 Db32
Bonnyapuszta H 145 Ha56
Bonny-sur-Loire F 29 Ha41
Bono E 40 Ga58
Bono I 168 Cb76
Bonorva I 168 Ca76
Bonrepaux F 40 Gc53
Bons F 35 Ka45
Bonsecours F 23 Gb35
Bønsnes N 93 Dd41
Bønsvig DK 109 Eb27
Bontgoch Elerch GB 15 Dd24
Bonțida RO 171 Da57
Bonvilston GB 19 Ea28
Bőny H 145 Ha52
Bonyhád H 153 Hc57
Boo S 96 Gd43
Boock D 119 Ea35
Boolakennedy IRL 13 Ca24
Boos D 142 Db51
Boos F 23 Gb35
Boostedt D 118 Dc31
Bootle GB 11 Eb18
Bopfingen D 134 Db48
Boppard D 133 Ca43
Boquiñeni E 47 Fa60
Bor CZ 135 Ec46
Bor S 103 Fb51
Bor SRB 174 Ca66
Boraja HR 158 Gb66
Borås S 102 Ed49
Borăscu RO 175 Cc65
Borawe PL 122 Jc34
Borawskie PL 123 Ka30
Borba P 50 Ba69
Borca RO 172 Ea57
Borča SRB 153 Jc61
Borca di Cadore I 143 Eb56
Borcea RO 181 Fa67
Börcek TR 191 Ed83
Borchen D 126 Cd39
Borci BIH 152 Ha63
Borci BIH 158 Hb66
Borculo NL 125 Bd37
Bordalba E 47 Ec61
Børdalen N 78 Eb30
Bordány H 146 Jb56
Bordeaux F 32 Fb50
Bordeira P 58 Aa73
Bordei Verde RO 177 Fa64
Bordelum D 108 Da29
Bordères-Louron F 40 Fd57
Bordesholm D 118 Dc30
Bordessoule F 33 Gd45
Bordeşti RO 176 Ed62
Borðeyri IS 2 Ad03
Bordighera I 43 Kd52
Bording DK 108 Db24
Bordon GB 20 Fb29
Bords F 32 Fb47
Bordușani RO 177 Fa66
Bore I 149 Cd62
Borehamwood GB 20 Fc27
Borek PL 138 Jb44
Borek Wielkopolski PL 129 Gc38
Boreland GB 11 Eb15
Borello I 156 Ea64
Borensberg S 103 Fd46
Boretto I 149 Db61
Bore Verdalen N 92 Ca44
Borg N 66 Fb14
Borgå FIN 98 Kc39
Borgafjäll S 79 Fc25
Borgan N 78 Eb25
Borgarnes IS 2 Ac04
Borgata Marina I 164 Gc78
Borge N 93 Ea44
Borgen N 92 Cd43
Borgen S 80 Gc27
Borgentreich D 126 Da39
Börger D 117 Cb34
Börger D 117 Cb34
Borger NL 117 Bd34
Borger NL 117 Ca34
Borgetto I 166 Ec84
Borggård S 95 Fd45
Borghamn S 103 Fc47
Borghetto I 150 Ea63
Borghetto d'Arroscia I 148 Bd63
Borghetto di Vara I 149 Cd63
Borghetto Santo Spirito I 148 Bd63
Borgholm S 103 Gb52
Borgholzhausen D 126 Cc37
Borghorst D 125 Ca37
Borghusseter N 77 Dd33
Borgia I 164 Gc81
Borgloon B 124 Ba41
Børglum DK 100 Dc20
Borgo F 154 Cc69
Borgo a Mozzano I 155 Da64
Borgo Cortili I 150 Dd62
Borgoforte I 149 Db61
Borgofranco d'Ivrea I 148 Bd59
Borgo Grappa I 160 Ec73
Borgo Libertà I 161 Ga74
Borgomanero I 148 Ca58
Borgomasino I 148 Bd59
Borgonovo Ligure I 149 Cc63
Borgonovo Val Tidone I 149 Cc61
Borgo Piave I 160 Eb73
Borgorose I 156 Ec70
Borgo San Dalmazzo I 148 Bc63
Borgo San Giusto I 161 Fd73
Borgo San Lorenzo I 155 Dc64
Borgo San Michele I 160 Ec73
Borgo San Siro I 148 Cb60
Borgo Schisina I 167 Fd84
Borgo Segezia I 161 Fd73
Borgosesia I 148 Ca58
Borgo Tossignano I 150 Dd63
Borgo Val di Taro I 149 Cd62
Borgo Valsugana I 150 Dd58
Borgsdorf D 127 Ed36
Borgsjö S 80 Gc27
Borgsjö S 87 Ga33
Borgstena S 102 Ed48
Borgund N 85 Da37
Borgunda S 102 Fa47
Borgvattnet S 79 Fd30
Borgvik S 94 Ed43
Bori RUS 99 Ma43
Boriç AL 159 Jb70
Borika BG 179 Cd72
Borima BG 180 Db70
Borina SRB 153 Hd63
Borino BG 184 Da75
Borinskoe RUS 203 Fb12
Borisenki RUS 107 Ma51
Borisoglebsk RUS 203 Fc12
Borisovka RUS 203 Fa14
Borisovo BG 180 Eb68
Borisovo RUS 202 Ed08
Borisovo-Sudskoe RUS 202 Ec08
Borja E 47 Ed60
Børja N 94 Ec41
Borje HR 151 Ga62
Börjelsbyn S 73 Ja21
Börjelslandet S 73 Hd22
Borkan S 71 Fd24
Borkel NL 124 Ba39
Borken D 125 Bd38
Borken (Hessen) D 126 Cd41
Borkheide D 127 Ec37
Borki PL 131 Ka38
Borki PL 138 Jc43
Borki RUS 99 Ma39
Børkop DK 108 Db25
Borków PL 130 Jb42
Borkowo PL 123 Jd33
Borkum D 117 Bd32
Borlänge S 95 Fd40
Borlaug N 85 Da37
Borlești RO 172 Ec58
Børlja N 86 Ea32
Borlu TR 192 Fb85
Bormes-les-Mimosas F 43 Kb55
Bormida I 148 Ca63
Bormio I 142 Db56
Born D 119 Ec30
Born NL 125 Bb40
Born S 87 Fd38
Borna D 127 Ec41
Borna D 127 Ed40
Borne D 127 Ea38
Borne F 34 Hd49
Borne NL 117 Bd36
Borness GB 10 Dd17
Borne Sulinowo PL 121 Gb33
Bornheim D 125 Bd41
Bornhöved D 118 Dc31
Börnichen D 127 Ed42
Børnes N 64 Jc05
Borno I 149 Da58
Bornos E 59 Ca76
Börnsen D 118 Dc33
Bornstedt D 127 Ea39
Boroaia RO 172 Ec56
Borobia E 47 Ec60
Borod RO 171 Cc57
Borodino RUS 113 Jc59
Borodjanka UA 202 Ec14
Borogani MD 177 Fc60
Borohrádek CZ 136 Ga44
Boronów PL 130 Hc42
Borore I 169 Ca76
Boroseni Noi MD 173 Fa54
Boroșneu Mare RO 176 Eb61
Borotin CZ 136 Fc46
Borotno RUS 99 Mb45
Borova UA 203 Fb14
Borova Glava SRB 159 Jb65
Borová Lada CZ 136 Fa48
Borovan BG 179 Cd69
Borovany CZ 136 Fc48
Borovci BG 179 Cc69
Borovci HR 158 Ha67
Borovec BG 179 Cc73
Borovenka RUS 202 Ec09
Boroviči RUS 202 Ec09
Borovik HR 152 Hb60
Borovik RUS 99 Ld45
Borovnica BIH 152 Hb63
Borovnica SLO 151 Fb58
Borovnice CZ 137 Gb46
Borovno CZ 136 Fa46
Borovo BG 180 Ea69
Borovo HR 153 Hd60
Borovo Selo HR 153 Hd60
Borovsk RUS 202 Ed11
Borovye RUS 107 Mb52
Borów PL 129 Gc42
Brów PL 131 Jd41
Borowa PL 138 Jc43
Borowie PL 131 Jd37
Borowiec PL 128 Ga39
Borowina PL 128 Fd39
Borówno PL 121 Ha33
Borowno PL 130 Hc41
Borowo PL 121 Ha30
Borox E 46 Dc65
Borrby S 111 Fb56
Borrby strandbad S 111 Fb57
Borre N 93 Dd43
Borredà E 49 Gd59
Borres E 37 Ca54
Borrèze F 33 Gb50
Borriana E 54 Fc66
Börringe S 110 Fa56
Borriol E 54 Fc66
Borris DK 108 Da24
Borris IRL 13 Cc24
Borris in Ossory IRL 13 Cb22
Borrisokane IRL 13 Ca22
Borrisoleigh IRL 13 Ca23
Börrum S 103 Gb47
Borș RO 170 Ca56
Børsa N 77 Ea30
Borșa RO 171 Da57
Borșa RO 171 Dc55
Borsækoia N 92 Cd43
Borščiv UA 204 Ea16
Borsdorf D 127 Ec40
Borsec RO 172 Ea58
Børselv N 64 Jc06
Borsfa H 145 Gc56
Borsh AL 182 Ab78
Borsk PL 121 Gd31
Borskoe RUS 113 Jb59
Borský Mikuláš SK 137 Gd49
Borsodivánka H 146 Jc52
Borsodnádasd H 146 Jb51
Borsosgyőr H 145 Gd53
Borssele NL 124 Ab38
Börßum D 126 Dc37
Børsted DK 109 Eb27
Borstel D 118 Cd35
Börstig S 102 Fa48
Börstil S 96 Gd40
Bortan S 94 Ed41
Borth D 125 Bd38
Borth GB 15 Dd24
Bortigali I 169 Ca76
Bort-les-Orgues F 33 Ha48
Börtlüce TR 192 Fb85
Börtnan S 87 Fb32
Bortnen N 84 Cb34
Boruja PL 128 Ga37
Boruja Kościelna PL 128 Ga37
Borum DK 108 Dc24
Borup DK 100 Db21
Borup DK 109 Eb26
Boruszyn PL 121 Gb35
Borutta I 168 Ca75
Borve GB 4 Cd06
Borynja UA 204 Dd16
Boryspil' UA 202 Ec14
Boryszyn PL 128 Fd37
Borzechów PL 131 Ka40
Borzechowo PL 121 Ha31
Borzęcice PL 129 Gd38
Borzęciczki PL 129 Gd38
Borzecin PL 138 Jb44
Borzęcin Duży PL 130 Jb37
Borzna UA 202 Ec14
Borzonasca I 149 Cc63
Borzykowa PL 130 Hd41
Borzymy PL 123 Ka31
Borzysław PL 121 Gc31
Borzytuchom PL 121 Gc31
Bosa I 169 Bd76
Bosa Marina I 169 Bd76
Bosanci RO 172 Ec56
Bosanic HR 151 Fd60
Bosanka Kostajnica BIH 152 Gc60
Bosanki Dubočac BIH 152 Hb61
Bosanska Bojna BIH 151 Ga61
Bosanska Krupa BIH 152 Gb62
Bosanska Rača BIH 153 Ja61
Bosanski Brod BIH 152 Hb61
Bosanski Kobaš BIH 152 Ha61
Bosanski Petrovac BIH 152 Gb63
Bosansko Grahovo BIH 158 Gb64
Bošany SK 137 Hb49
Bősárkány H 145 Gd52
Bosau D 118 Dc31
Bosbury GB 15 Ec26
Boscamnant F 32 Fc49
Boșcana MD 173 Fd57
Boscastle GB 18 Db30
Bosco I 156 Eb67
Bosco/Gurin CH 141 Cb56
Bosco Chiesanuova I 149 Dc59
Bosco Marengo I 148 Cb61
Boscotrecase I 161 Fb75
Bösdorf D 118 Dc31

Bosebo – Brisley

Bosebo S 102 Fa50
Bosebyn S 94 Ed42
Bösel D 117 Cc34
Bösenbrunn D 135 Eb43
Bosherston GB 18 Db27
Bosilegrad SRB 179 Ca72
Bosiljevo HR 151 Fd60
Bosilkovci BG 180 Dd69
Bosjön S 95 Fb42
Boskic HR 152 Hb59
Boskoop NL 116 Ad36
Boškov CZ 137 Gd46
Boskovice CZ 137 Gc46
Bosley GB 16 Ed22
Bosna BG 181 Ec68
Bosna TR 185 Eb75
Bosnek BG 179 Cc72
Bošnjace SRB 178 Bd70
Bošnjaci HR 153 Hc61
Boșorod RO 175 Cc61
Bossbøen N 93 Da42
Bossbu N 92 Cc43
Bossea I 148 Bd63
Bossée F 29 Ga42
Bossolasco I 148 Bd62
Bossòst E 40 Ga57
Bostanci TR 185 Ed80
Bostandere TR 185 Ec80
Bostandere TR 199 Hb89
Boštanj SLO 151 Fd58
Bostanlı TR 185 Ec75
Bostanlı TR 193 Gc84
Bostanyeri TR 187 Ha78
Böste läge S 110 Ed57
Boston GB 17 Fc23
Bostrak N 93 Db44
Bošulja BG 179 Da73
Bosund FIN 81 Jb28
Bosundet S 79 Ga28
Bosut SRB 153 Ja61
Bosuta SRB 153 Jc63
Boswil CH 141 Cb53
Böszénfa H 152 Ha57
Boszkowo PL 129 Gb38
Bot E 48 Fd63
Bote S 80 Gc31
Botesdale GB 21 Ga25
Botești RO 172 Ec57
Boțești RO 173 Fb58
Botești RO 176 Dd64
Botevgrad BG 179 Cd70
Botevo BG 179 Cd68
Botevo BG 181 Fa70
Botfei RO 170 Cb58
Bothel D 118 Da34
Bothel GB 11 Eb17
Bothenheilingen D 126 Dc40
Boticas P 44 Bb59
Botilsäter S 94 Ed44
Botiz RO 171 Cd54
Botiza RO 171 Db55
Botley GB 20 Fa30
Botn N 62 Ha09
Botn N 67 Gb13
Botnărești MD 173 Fd58
Botne N 92 Ca44
Botne N 93 Dd43
Botnen N 84 Cc34
Botngård N 77 Dd28
Botnlia N 86 Ec32
Bótoa E 51 Bc68
Botoroaga RO 180 Dd67
Botorrita E 47 Fa61
Botoš SRB 153 Jc60
Botoš SRB 174 Bb62
Botoșana RO 172 Eb55
Botoșani RO 172 Ec55
Botrange B 125 Bb42
Botricello I 165 Gd81
Botsmark S 80 Hb27
Bottarone I 149 Cc60
Botteghelle I 167 Fb87
Botten S 94 Ed43
Bottesford GB 16 Fb23
Bottheim N 85 Dc34
Bottidda I 168 Ca76
Böttingen D 142 Cc50
Bottna S 102 Eb46
Bottnaryd S 102 Fa49
Bottrop D 125 Bd39
Bottsfjord N 63 Hd06
Botun MK 182 Ba75
Botunje SRB 174 Bb66
Boturić SRB 178 Bb68
Bötzingen D 141 Ca50
Bötzow D 127 Ed36
Bouaye F 28 Ed42
Bouça P 45 Bc60
Bouce F 22 Fc37
Bouchain F 24 Hb32
Bouçoães P 45 Bc59
Boucq F 25 Jc37
Boudin F 35 Ka46
Boudreville F 30 Ja39
Boudry CH 141 Bb54
Boueilho F 40 Fc54
Bouessay F 28 Fc40
Bouesse F 29 Gc44
Bouges-le-Château F 29 Gc43
Bouglainval F 29 Gb38
Bouguenais F 28 Ed42
Bouilland F 30 Ja42
Bouillargues F 42 Ja53
Bouillé-Ménard F 28 Fa40
Bouillon B 132 Ad43
Bouillon B 132 Ad44
Bouilly F 30 Hd39
Bouin F 27 Ec43
Boujailles F 31 Jd43
Boúka GR 188 Ad83
Boúka GR 194 Bb89
Bouladuff IRL 13 Ca23
Boulay-Moselle F 25 Jd35
Bouligneux F 34 Jb46
Bouligny F 25 Jc35
Bouloc F 41 Hb52
Boulogne-Billancourt F 23 Gd37
Boulogne-sur-Gesse F 40 Ga55
Boulogne-sur-Mer F 21 Gc30
Bouloire F 29 Ga40
Bouloz CH 141 Bb55
Bouniagues F 33 Ga50
Bouray sur-Juine F 29 Gd38
Bourbon-Lancy F 30 Hc44
Bourbon-l'Archambault F 30 Hb44
Bourbonne-les-Bains F 31 Jc39
Bourbourg F 21 Gd30
Bourbriac F 26 Ea38
Bourdeaux F 35 Jc50
Bourdeilles F 33 Ga48
Bourdon F 23 Gc33
Bourdons-sur-Rognon F 30 Jb39
Bouresse F 33 Ga45
Bourg F 32 Fb49
Bourg-Achard F 23 Ga35
Bourganeuf F 33 Gc46
Bourg-Archambault F 33 Gb45
Bourg-Argental F 34 Ja48
Bourg-Beaudouin F 23 Gb35
Bourg-Blanc F 26 Db38
Bourg-de-Péage F 34 Jb49
Bourg-des Comptes F 28 Ed40
Bourg-de-Visa F 40 Gb52
Bourg-d'Oueil F 40 Ga57
Bourg-en-Bresse F 34 Jb45
Bourges F 29 Gd43
Bourg-et-Comin F 24 Hc35
Bourg-Lastic F 33 Ha47
Bourg-Madame F 41 Gd58
Bourgneuf F 29 Gd42
Bourgneuf F 35 Ka47
Bourgneuf-en-Retz F 27 Ec43
Bourgogne F 24 Hd35
Bourgoin-Jallieu F 35 Jc47
Bourg-Saint-Andéol F 42 Jb51
Bourg-Saint-Maurice F 35 Kb47
Bourg-Saint Pierre CH 148 Bc57
Bourgthéroulde-Infreville F 23 Ga35
Bourgueil F 28 Fd42
Bourn GB 20 Fc26
Bournand F 28 Fd43
Bourne GB 17 Fc24
Bournemouth GB 20 Ed31
Bourneville F 23 Ga35
Bournezeau F 28 Fa44
Bournos F 40 Fc55
Bouro P 44 Ad59
Bourriot-Bergonce F 40 Fc52
Bourron F 29 Ha38
Bourtange NL 117 Ca34
Bourth F 23 Ga37
Bourton-on-the-Water GB 20 Ed27
Bousières F 31 Jd42
Boussac F 33 Gd45
Boussais F 28 Fc43
Boussens F 40 Gb56
Boussès F 40 Fd52
Boussière-Poitevine F 33 Ga45
Bouvières F 42 Jc51
Bouville F 29 Gd38
Bouvron F 28 Ed41
Bouxwiller F 25 Kb36
Bouy F 24 Hd36
Bouzas E 36 Ad57
Bouzonville F 25 Jd35
Bouzov CZ 137 Gc46
Bova I 164 Gb84
Bøvær N 62 Gb10
Bovalino I 164 Gb83
Bovalino Marina I 164 Gb84
Bovallstrand S 102 Eb46
Bova Marina I 164 Gb84
Bovan SRB 178 Bd68
Bovec SLO 150 Ed57
Bóveda E 36 Bc56
Bóveda E 38 Dd56
Bovegno I 149 Da58
Bovenau D 118 Db30
Bovenden D 126 Db39
Bovense DK 109 Dd26
Bøverdal N 85 Db35
Bøverfjord N 77 Db31
Boves F 23 Gd33
Boves I 148 Bc63
Bovey Tracey GB 19 Dd31
Boviel GB 9 Cd16
Bovigny B 133 Bb43
Bovik FIN 96 Hb40
Boviken S 80 Hc25
Bovingdon GB 20 Fb27
Bovino I 161 Fd74
Bøvlingbjerg DK 100 Cd23
Bovolone I 149 Dc60
Bovrup DK 108 Db28
Bowburn GB 11 Fa17
Bowes GB 11 Ed18
Bowmore GB 6 Da13
Bowness-on-Solway GB 11 Eb16
Box FIN 98 Kc39
Box GB 19 Ec28
Boxberg D 128 Fb40
Boxberg D 134 Da46
Boxford GB 20 Fa28
Boxholm S 103 Fc47
Boxmeer NL 125 Bb38
Boxtel NL 124 Ba38
Boyabat TR 205 Fb20
Boyalı TR 192 Fa84
Boyalı TR 199 Hb89
Boyalıca TR 186 Ga79
Boyalıca TR 192 Fc82
Boyalık TR 186 Fc77
Boyalılar TR 192 Fa85
Boyardville F 32 Fa46
Boyle IRL 8 Ca19
Bøylestad N 93 Da46
Boynanalar TR 191 Ed81
Boynes F 29 Gd39
Boynton GB 17 Fc19
Bøyum N 84 Cc36
Bozahlat TR 186 Fb80
Bozalan TR 191 Ec85
Bozan TR 193 Gb87
Bozan TR 193 Gd82
Božanka PL 121 Gc31
Bozarmut TR 187 Hb79
Bozarmut TR 197 Fa89
Božava HR 157 Fc64
Bozbelen TR 192 Fd82
Bozbük TR 192 Fb83
Bozburun TR 187 Gb78
Bozburun TR 197 Fa91
Bozcaada TR 191 Ea81
Bozcaarmut TR 192 Ga81
Bozcaatlı TR 192 Fc85
Bozdağ TR 192 Fa86
Bozdağ TR 192 Ga87
Bozdoğan TR 198 Fb88
Bożejewo PL 123 Jd33
Božejov CZ 136 Fd47
Bozel F 35 Kb47
Bozen I 143 Dd56
Božeń PL 129 Gb40
Bozen TR 192 Fb81
Božencite BG 180 Dd71
Bożepole Wielkopolski PL 121 Gd29
Božetići SRB 178 Ad67
Boževac SRB 174 Bc65
Bożewo PL 122 Hd35
Bozhane TR 184 Ed77
Bozhigrad AL 182 Ba77
Bozhüyük TR 193 Gc84
Bozhüyük TR 199 Gb91
Božica SRB 179 Ca71
Božice CZ 137 Gb48
Bozieni MD 173 Fc59
Bozieni RO 172 Ed58
Bozioru RO 176 Ec63
Bozkaya TR 199 Ha90
Bozkır TR 191 Ed86
Bozkurt TR 198 Ga88
Bozkuș TR 192 Ga85
Bozlar TR 185 Ed80
Bozören TR 191 Ed82
Bozouls F 33 Ha51
Bozova TR 199 Gb90
Bozovici RO 174 Ca64
Bozrük TR 197 Ec89
Bozsok H 145 Gb54
Boztepe TR 187 Gc79
Boztepe TR 199 Gd91
Boztepe TR 199 Hb92
Božurište BG 179 Cc71
Božurovo BG 180 Eb68
Božurovo BG 181 Fa69
Bozüyük TR 193 Gb81
Bozvelijsko BG 181 Ed71
Bozyaka TR 198 Fd91
Bozzecca I 149 Db58
Bozzolo I 149 Db61
Bra B 124 Ba42
Bra I 148 Bd61
Braaid GB 10 Dc19
Braak D 118 Dc32
Braås S 103 Fc51
Brabova RO 175 Cd66
Bracadale GB 4 Da08
Braccagni I 155 Db68
Bracciano I 160 Ea71
Bracebridge Heath GB 17 Fc22
Braćevac SRB 174 Cb66
Brach F 32 Fa49
Brachlewo PL 121 Hb32
Brachstedt D 127 Eb39
Bracht D 125 Bc39
Brachttal D 134 Cd43
Bracieux F 29 Gc41
Bracigliano I 161 Fc75
Bracigovo BG 184 Da74
Brackagh IRL 13 Cc21
Bräcke S 87 Fd32
Bräcke S 94 Ec44
Brackel D 118 Db33
Brackenheim D 134 Cd47
Brackley GB 20 Fa26
Bracknell GB 20 Fb28
Braco GB 7 Ea12
Brad RO 175 Cc60
Bradaiž LV 107 Ld51
Brădeanu RO 176 Ec65
Brădeni RO 175 Dc60
Bradesiai LT 115 Lb54
Brădești RO 175 Cd65
Brădești RO 176 Dd60
Bradfield GB 20 Fa28
Bradford GB 16 Ed20
Bradford-on-Avon GB 19 Ec28
Brådland N 92 Cb44
Brádno SK 138 Ja49
Bradu RO 175 Dc65
Brădulet RO 175 Dc63
Brădut RO 176 Ea60
Bradvari BG 181 Ed68
Bradwell-on-Sea GB 21 Ga27
Bradworthy GB 18 Dc30
Brae GB 5 Fa04
Brædstrup DK 108 Db24
Braemar GB 7 Eb09
Brændstrup DK 108 Da26
Brăești RO 172 Ec55
Brăești RO 172 Ed57
Brăești RO 176 Ec63
Braeswick GB 5 Ec02
Braga P 44 Ad60
Bragadiru RO 176 Ea66
Bragadiru RO 180 Dd68
Bragança P 45 Bd59
Bragayrac F 40 Gb54
Brăicău MD 173 Fb53
Braies I 143 Ea55
Brail CH 142 Da55
Brăila MD 173 Fd58
Brăila RO 177 Fb64
Brailes GB 20 Fa26
Brailovo MK 183 Bb74
Braine F 24 Hb35
Braintree GB 20 Fd27
Braives B 124 Ba41
Brajkovići BIH 158 Ha64
Brajkovići HR 151 Fa61
Brajkovići SRB 159 Jb64
Brake D 118 Cd33
Brakel D 126 Cd38
Brakel NL 124 Ba37
Bräkne-Hoby S 111 Fd54
Brålanda S 102 Ec46
Bralin PL 129 Ha40
Braljina SRB 178 Bc67
Brallo di Pregola I 149 Cc62
Brálos GR 189 Bd84
Braloștița RO 175 Cd65
Bram F 41 Gd55
Bramberg A 143 Eb54
Bramhope GB 16 Fa20
Brämhult S 102 Ed49
Bramming DK 108 Da26
Brampton GB 11 Ec16
Brampton GB 21 Gb25
Bramsche D 117 Cb36
Bramstedt D 118 Cd33
Bran RO 176 Dd62
Brånaberg S 71 Ga23
Brånäs S 94 Ed39
Braña Vieja E 38 Db56
Branč SK 145 Hb50
Branca I 156 Eb67
Brancaleone Marina I 164 Gb84
Br'ančaninovo RUS 107 Ma48
Brancaster GB 17 Ga23
Brânceni RO 180 Dd68
Brancion F 30 Ja44
Brâncovenești RO 171 Dc58
Brâncoveni RO 175 Db66
Brand A 142 Cd54
Brandal N 76 Cc32
Brändåsen S 86 Ed33
Brandasund N 84 Bd40
Brandberg A 143 Ea54
Brandbu N 85 Ea40
Brande DK 108 Da24
Brände S 80 Hc26
Brandenberg A 143 Ea53
Brandenburg D 127 Ec36
Brand-Erbisdorf D 127 Ed42
Branderup DK 108 Da27
Brandeso E 36 Ba55
Brandis D 127 Ec40
Brandlecht D 117 Ca36
Brando F 154 Cc68
Brandö FIN 97 Hd39
Brandomil E 36 Ac55
Brandon GB 11 Fa17
Brandon GB 21 Ga25
Brandön S 73 Ja22
Brändövik FIN 81 Hd30
Brandsby GB 16 Fb19
Brandshagen D 119 Ed30
Brandsøy N 84 Ca35
Brandstad N 77 Db32
Brandstorp S 103 Fb48
Brandsvoll N 92 Cd46
Brandval N 94 Ec40
Brandýs nad Labem-Stará Boleslav CZ 136 Fc44
Brănești RO 176 Dd64
Brănești RO 176 Eb66
Branica BG 185 Ea74
Branice PL 137 Ha44
Braničevo BG 181 Ed69
Braničevo SRB 174 Bc64
Braniewo PL 122 Hd30
Branik SLO 151 Fa58
Brănișca RO 175 Cc60
Branište BG 181 Fa69
Branistea RO 171 Db57
Braniștea RO 176 Dd65
Braniștea RO 176 Eb63
Brankovina SRB 153 Jb63
Branków PL 130 Jc38
Branná CZ 137 Gc44
Bränna S 94 Ec45
Brännåker S 79 Fd25
Brännan FIN 81 Jb29
Brännan N 78 Ec29
Brännan S 73 Hb23
Brännan S 73 Hd21
Brännäs S 73 Hb24
Brännås S 87 Ga34
Brannay F 30 Hb39
Brännberg S 73 Hc22
Branne F 32 Fc50
Brannenburg D 143 Ea52
Brännfors S 73 Hc24
Brännholmen S 72 Gd21
Brännkälen S 80 Hc25
Brännland S 80 Hb28
Brännland S 80 Ha28
Brännö S 102 Eb49
Brännvattnet S 80 Hb26
Brännvattnet S 80 Hc26
Brañosera E 38 Db56
Brańsk PL 123 Kb35
Bransles F 29 Ha39
Brańszczyk PL 122 Jc35
Brant Broughton GB 16 Fb23
Brantevik S 111 Fb56
Branti LV 106 La49
Brantice CZ 137 Gd44
Brantôme F 33 Ga48
Braset N 71 Fb19
Braskereidfoss N 94 Ec39
Braslav BY 202 Ea11
Brăšljanica BG 180 Db69
Brașov RO 176 Ea62
Brasparts F 26 Dc38
Brassac F 41 Ha54
Brasschaat B 124 Ad39
Brassempouy F 39 Fb54
Brassy F 30 Hd42
Brastad N 70 Ed22
Brastad S 102 Eb46
Brastavățu RO 180 Db67
Břasy CZ 136 Fa45
Brąszewice PL 129 Hb39
Braszowice PL 137 Gc43
Brataj AL 182 Ab78
Bratanica BG 179 Da73
Bratca RO 171 Cc57
Brateljevici BIH 159 Hc64
Brateș RO 176 Eb61
Bratian PL 122 Hd33
Bratislava SK 145 Gd51
Bratja Daskalovi BG 180 Dc73
Bratkowice PL 139 Ka44
Bratonci SLO 145 Gb56
Bratoszewice PL 130 Hd38
Bratovoești RO 175 Da66
Bratronice CZ 136 Fa44
Brattåker S 71 Ga24
Bråttas S 81 Hd26
Brattbäcken S 79 Fd27
Brattby S 71 Ga24
Brattby S 80 Hb28
Bratteborg S 103 Fb49
Bratten N 66 Fc17
Bratten S 80 Gd26
Brattfors S 80 Hb29
Brattfors S 95 Fb42
Bratthøvollseter N 77 Ea33
Brattli N 65 Kd08
Brattli N 67 Gc12
Brattmon S 94 Ed39
Bråttö FIN 96 Hc41
Bratto I 149 Da58
Bratton GB 19 Ec29
Brattsbäcken S 80 Ha28
Brattsele S 79 Gb28
Brattset N 77 Dc31
Brattvåg N 76 Cc32
Bratunac BIH 159 Ja64
Brătușeni MD 173 Fa54
Braubach D 133 Ca43
Braughing GB 20 Fc27
Braunau a.Inn A 143 Ec50
Braunfels D 126 Cc42
Braunlage D 126 Dc39
Bräunlingen D 141 Cb51
Braunsbach D 134 Da47
Braunsbedra D 127 Ea40
Braunschweig D 126 Dc37
Braunsdorf-Langhennersdorf D 127 Ed41
Braunton GB 19 Dd29
Brauteseter N 94 Eb41
Bravães P 44 Ad59
Bravnica BIH 152 Gd63
Bravuogn CH 142 Cd55
Bray IRL 13 Cd22
Bray Shop GB 18 Dc31
Bray-sur-Seine F 30 Hb38
Bray-sur-Somme F 23 Ha33
Braz A 142 Da54
Brazatortas E 52 Da70
Brazey-en-Plain F 30 Jb42
Brazi RO 176 Ea65
Brazii RO 170 Cb59
Brazii RO 176 Eb65
Brbinj HR 157 Fc64
Brčigovo BIH 159 Hd65
Brčko BIH 153 Hc61
Brdani SRB 159 Jc64
Brdovec HR 151 Ga58
Brdów PL 129 Hb37
Bré IRL 13 Cd22
Brea de Aragón E 47 Ed61
Breakish GB 4 Db08
Brean GB 19 Eb28
Breasclete GB 4 Da05
Breasta RO 175 Cd66
Bréau F 29 Ha38
Breaza RO 171 Dc58
Breaza RO 172 Ea55
Breaza RO 176 Ea63
Brebeni RO 175 Db66
Brebu RO 174 Ca62
Brebu RO 176 Ea64
Brebu Nou RO 174 Ca62
Brécey F 22 Fa37
Brechfa GB 15 Dd26
Brechin GB 7 Ec10
Brecht B 124 Ad39
Breckerfeld D 125 Ca40
Břeclav CZ 137 Gc49
Brecon GB 15 Ea26
Bred S 95 Gb42
Breda E 49 Ha60
Breda NL 124 Ad38
Bredablikk N 92 Cd45
Bredal DK 108 Db25
Bredared S 102 Ed48
Bredaryd S 102 Fa51
Bredballe DK 108 Db25
Bredbyn S 79 Fb29
Bredbyn S 80 Gd30
Breddin D 119 Eb35
Breddorf D 118 Da33
Bredebro DK 108 Da27
Bredenbury GB 15 Ec25
Bredene B 21 Ha29
Bredenfelde D 119 Ed33
Bredereiche D 119 Ed34
Bredestad S 103 Fc49
Bredevad DK 108 Da28
Bredgar GB 21 Ga29
Bredkälen S 79 Fd28
Bredon GB 20 Ed26
Bredsäter S 102 Fa46
Bredsättra S 103 Gb52
Bredsel S 73 Hb22
Bredsjö S 95 Fc42
Bredsjön S 87 Gb32
Bredstedt D 108 Da29
Bredsten DK 108 Db25
Bredstrup DK 108 Db26
Bredträsk S 80 Gd28
Bredvik S 80 Hb29
Bredviken S 73 Jb21
Bredwardine GB 15 Eb26
Bredynki PL 122 Jb31
Bree B 125 Bb40
Breg SLO 151 Fd58
Bregana HR 151 Ga58
Breganze I 150 Dd59
Bregare BG 179 Da68
Bregenz A 142 Da53
Breginj SLO 150 Ed57
Bregninge DK 108 Dc28
Bregninge DK 109 Dd28
Bregovo BG 174 Cb66
Bréhal F 22 Ed37
Bréhand F 26 Eb38
Bréhec-en-Plouha F 26 Eb37
Brehme D 126 Dc39
Brehna D 127 Eb39
Breibuktnes N 68 Hd11
Breidablik N 85 Da34
Breiðdalsvik IS 3 Bc06
Breidenbach D 126 Cc41
Breidenbach F 25 Kb35
Breidvik N 78 Eb28
Breidvik N 93 Da44
Breidvika N 66 Fc13
Breiholz D 118 Db30
Breil CH 142 Cc55
Breil F 28 Fd41
Breil-sur-Roya F 43 Kd52
Brein N 84 Cc35
Breisach D 141 Bd50
Breistein N 84 Ca39
Breitenaich A 144 Fa50
Breitenau A 144 Fb52
Breitenbach CH 141 Bd52
Breitenbach D 126 Da42
Breitenbach D 126 Da42
Breitenberg D 136 Fa49
Breitenbrunn A 145 Gc51
Breitenbrunn D 135 Ea48
Breitenbrunn D 135 Ec43
Breitenbrunn D 142 Db50
Breitenfelde D 119 Dd32
Breitenfurth bei Wien A 145 Gb51
Breitengüßbach D 134 Dc44
Breitenworbis D 126 Dc40
Breitscheid D 125 Cb42
Breitungen D 126 Db42
Breivik N 63 Hc06
Breivik N 64 Ka05
Breivik N 66 Ga12
Breivik N 66 Fd17
Breivik N 66 Ga11
Breivik N 92 Cb43
Breivikbotn N 63 Hd05
Breivikeidet N 62 Gd09
Breja RUS 99 Ma42
Brejning DK 108 Db25
Brejtovo RUS 202 Ed09
Brekka N 70 Fa22
Brekke N 84 Ca37
Brekken N 78 Eb29
Brekken N 86 Ec32
Brekkestø N 93 Da47
Brekkhus N 84 Cb38
Brekko N 92 Ca44
Brekkvasselv N 78 Fa25
Breklum D 108 Da29
Brekov SK 139 Ka48
Brekovo SRB 178 Ad67
Brekstad N 77 Dd29
Breland N 92 Cc45
Brembilla I 149 Cd58
Breme I 148 Cb60
Bremen D 118 Cd34
Bremen D 125 Cb39
Bremerhaven D 118 Cd32
Bremervörde D 118 Da33
Bremgarten CH 141 Cb53
Bremm D 133 Bd43
Bremnes N 66 Fd12
Bremnes N 92 Bd41
Bremsnes N 77 Da30
Brem-sur-Mer F 28 Ed44
Breń PL 120 Ga34
Brénaz F 35 Jd46
Brence E 36 Bc57
Brenderup DK 108 Dc26
Brenes E 59 Ca73
Brenesh AL 182 Ac75
Brenguļi LV 106 Kd48
Brenica BG 179 Da69
Brenica BG 181 Ec68
Brenish GB 4 Cd05
Brenna N 66 Fc14
Brenna PL 138 Hc45
Brennan N 78 Ec30
Brennberg D 135 Eb48
Brennbergbánya H 145 Gb52
Brennfjell N 62 Ha10
Brennsvik N 63 Ja06
Breno I 149 Da58
Brenod F 35 Jc46
Brensbach D 134 Cc45
Breńsk PL 121 Gc32
Brentonico I 149 Dc58
Brentwood GB 20 Fd28
Brény F 24 Hb35
Brenzett GB 21 Ga30
Brenzone I 149 Db59
Bres E 37 Bd54
Brescello I 149 Db61
Brescia I 149 Da59
Bresinchen D 128 Fc38
Breskens NL 124 Ab38
Breslau = Wrocław PL 129 Gc41
Bresles F 23 Gd35
Bressanone I 143 Dd55
Bressuire F 28 Fb43
Brest BG 180 Db68
Brest BY 202 Dd14
Brest F 26 Db38
Brest HR 151 Fa60
Brestak BG 181 Ed69
Brestanica SLO 151 Fd58
Breste BG 179 Da69
Brestova HR 151 Fb61
Brestovac SRB 174 Ca66
Brestovac SRB 178 Bd69
Brestovačka Banja SRB 174 Ca66
Brestovac Požeški HR 152 Ha60
Brestovăț RO 174 Ca60
Brestovec BG 180 Db69
Brestovene BG 180 Eb68
Brestovica BG 180 Db73
Brestovik SRB 174 Bb64
Brestovo BG 180 Dc70
Brețcu RO 176 Eb61
Bretea Română RO 175 Cc61
Breteau F 29 Ha40
Bretenoux F 33 Gc50
Breteuil F 23 Gd34
Breteuil-sur-Iton F 23 Ga37
Bretford GB 20 Fa25
Bretforton GB 20 Ed26
Brétignolles-sur-Mer F 28 Ed44
Bretigny-sur-Orge F 23 Gd37
Bretnig-Hauswalde D 128 Fb41
Bretoncelles F 29 Ga38
Bretstein A 144 Fb53
Bretten D 134 Cc47
Brettesnes N 66 Fc14
Bretteville-sur-Ay F 22 Ed35
Bretteville-sur-Laize F 22 Fc36
Bretzfeld D 134 Cd47
Breuil-Cervinia I 148 Bd57
Breuillet F 29 Gd38
Breuilpont F 23 Gb36
Breukelen NL 116 Ba36
Breum DK 100 Db22
Breuna D 126 Cd39
Breuvannes-en-Bassigny F 31 Jc39
Brevens bruk S 95 Fd45
Brevik N 93 Dc44
Brevik S 96 Gd43
Brevik S 96 Gd44
Brevik S 103 Fb46
Breza BIH 158 Hb64
Breza MK 178 Bc72
Brežani BG 183 Cb74
Brežđe SRB 153 Jb63
Breze BG 179 Cc70
Breze SLO 151 Fd57
Březí CZ 137 Gb49
Brežice SLO 151 Ga58
Brézins F 35 Jc48
Brezje pri Tržič SLO 151 Fb57
Breznica KSV 178 Bc71
Breznica PL 122 Jc30
Breznica Đakovačka HR 152 Hb60
Breznica Našička HR 152 Hb59
Březnice CZ 136 Fa46
Breznički Hum HR 152 Gb58
Breznik BG 179 Cb71
Breznița-Motru RO 175 Cc65
Březno CZ 136 Fc43
Brezno SK 138 Ja48
Brezno SLO 144 Fd56
Brezoaia MD 177 Ga60
Brezoi RO 175 Db63
Brezolles F 23 Gb37
Březolupy CZ 137 Gd47
Březová CZ 135 Ec44
Březová nad Svitavou CZ 137 Gb46
Brezová pod Bradlom SK 137 Gd49
Brezovica KSV 178 Ba72
Brezovica SK 138 Jc47
Brezovica SLO 151 Fb58
Brezovo BG 180 Dc73
Brezovo Polje BIH 153 Hd62
Brezovo Polje HR 152 Gb61
Brgat HR 158 Hb69
Briançon F 35 Kb49
Briare F 29 Ha41
Briatexte F 41 Gd54
Briatico I 164 Gb82
Bribir HR 157 Ga65
Briceni MD 172 Ed53
Briceni MD 173 Fb53
Bricherasio I 148 Bc61
Bricon F 30 Jb39
Bricquebec F 22 Ed35
Bricqueville F 22 Fb35
Bridaga LV 106 Kb48
Bride GB 10 Dd18
Bridel L 133 Bb45
Brideswell IRL 8 Ca20
Bridge End IRL 9 Cc15
Bridgend GB 19 Ea28
Bridgent GB 6 Da13
Bridge of Baldie GB 7 Dd11
Bridge of Ericht GB 7 Dd10
Bridge of Orchy GB 7 Dd11
Bridgetown IRL 13 Cc25
Bridgnorth GB 15 Ec24
Bridgwater GB 19 Eb29
Břdličná CZ 137 Gd45
Bridlington GB 17 Fc19
Bridport GB 19 Eb30
Briec F 27 Dc39
Brie-Comte-Robert F 23 Ha37
Brielle NL 124 Ac37
Brienne-le-Château F 30 Ja38
Briénon-sur-Armançon F 30 Hc39
Brienz CH 141 Ca55
Brienza I 161 Ga76
Brienzwiler CH 141 Ca55
Brieselang D 127 Ed36
Briesen D 128 Fb37
Brieskow-Finkenheerd D 128 Fb37
Brietlingen D 118 Dc33
Brieulles-sur-Bar F 24 Ja34
Brieva de Cameros E 47 Ea59
Brieves E 37 Ca54
Briey F 25 Jc35
Brig CH 141 Ca56
Brigachtal D 141 Cb51
Brigels CH 142 Cc55
Brigg GB 17 Fc21
Brighouse GB 16 Ed20
Brightlingsea GB 21 Ga27
Brighton GB 18 Db31
Brighton GB 20 Fc30
Brigi LV 107 Ma51
Brignais F 34 Jb47
Brignogan-Plage F 26 Dc37
Brignoles F 42 Ka54
Brignoud F 35 Jd48
Brig o'Turk GB 7 Dd12
Brigueuil F 33 Ga46
Brihuega E 47 Ea63
Brijesta HR 158 Ha68
Brik BIH 159 Hd65
Briksdal N 84 Cd35
Brillon-en-Barrois F 24 Jb37
Brilon D 126 Cc39
Brimfield GB 15 Ec25
Brimnes N 84 Cc39
Brinches P 50 Ba71
Brindisi I 162 Hb75
Bringetofta S 103 Fc50
Brinje HR 151 Fd61
Brinkum D 118 Cd34
Brinkworth GB 20 Ed28
Brinlack IRL 8 Ca15
Brinon-sur-Beuvron F 30 Hc42
Brinon-sur-Sauldre F 29 Gd41
Brintbodarna S 95 Fb39
Brînzeni MD 172 Ed54
Brînzenii Noi MD 173 Fc56
Brinzio I 148 Cb58
Brion F 29 Gc43
Briones E 38 Ea57
Brione Verzasca CH 141 Cb56
Brionne F 23 Ga36
Brion-près-Thouet F 28 Fc43
Brion-sur-Ource F 30 Ja39
Brioude F 34 Hc48
Brioux-sur-Boutonne F 32 Fc46
Briouze F 22 Fc37
Briscous F 39 Ed55
Brisighella I 156 Dd64
Brisley GB 17 Ga24

Brismene – Busachi

Brismene S 102 Fa48
Brissac-Quince F 28 Fc42
Brissago CH 148 Cb57
Bristen CH 141 Cb55
Bristol GB 19 Ec28
Briston GB 17 Ga23
Britiande P 44 Ba61
Brittas IRL 13 Cd22
Britten D 133 Bc45
Britvica BIH 158 Ha66
Britz D 120 Fa35
Brive-la-Gaillarde F 33 Gc49
Brives F 29 Ga40
Briviesca E 38 Dd57
Brivio I 149 Cd58
Brixen I 143 Dd55
Brixen im Thale A 143 Eb53
Brixham GB 19 Ea31
Brixlegg A 143 Ea53
Brize Norton GB 20 Fa27
Brjagovo BG 184 Dc74
Brjanka UA 205 Fb15
Brjansk RUS 202 Ed12
Brjastovec BG 181 Ed72
Brka BIH 153 Hc62
Brložnik BIH 159 Hd64
Brmyan GB 5 Ec02
Brna HR 158 Gc68
Brnaze HR 158 Gc66
Brněnec CZ 137 Gb46
Brnično CZ 137 Gc45
Brniště CZ 128 Fc42
Brnjica SRB 178 Ad68
Brno CZ 137 Gb47
Bro S 94 Ed44
Bro S 96 Gc43
Bro S 104 Ha49
Broad Chalke GB 20 Ed29
Broadford GB 4 Db08
Broadford IRL 12 Bc24
Broadford IRL 12 Bd22
Broad Haven GB 18 Db27
Broad Hinton GB 20 Ed28
Broad Oak GB 21 Ga30
Broadstairs GB 21 Gb28
Broadwas GB 15 Ec25
Broadway GB 19 Eb30
Broadway GB 20 Ed26
Broadwell Ho GB 11 Ed17
Broadwey GB 19 Ec31
Broadwindsor GB 19 Eb30
Brøager DK 108 Db28
Broaryd S 102 Ed51
Broby S 111 Fb54
Brobyværk DK 108 Dc27
Broćanac BIH 158 Ha66
Brocas F 39 Fb53
Brocēni LV 105 Jd52
Brochel GB 4 Db08
Brochów PL 130 Ja37
Bročice HR 152 Gc60
Brock D 125 Cb37
Brockel D 118 Da34
Bröckel D 126 Dc36
Brockenhurst GB 20 Ed30
Brockhagen D 126 Cc37
Broczyno PL 121 Gb33
Brod BIH 159 Hd66
Brod KSV 178 Ba73
Brod MK 183 Bb74
Brod MK 183 Bb76
Brod SRB 179 Ca70
Brodalen S 102 Eb46
Brodarevo SRB 159 Jb67
Brodce CZ 136 Fc44
Broddarp S 102 Fa48
Broddbo S 95 Ga41
Broddetorp S 102 Fa47
Brodec MK 178 Ba72
Brodec'ke UA 204 Eb15
Brodek u Přerova CZ 137 Gd46
Brodek u Prostějova CZ 137 Gc47
Brodenbach D 133 Ca43
Broderstorf D 119 Eb31
Broderup DK 108 Da28
Brodica SRB 174 Bd65
Brodick GB 10 Dc14
Brodie Castle GB 5 Eb07
Brodina RO 172 Ea55
Brodina de Jos RO 172 Ea55
Brod na Kupi HR 151 Fc60
Brodnica PL 122 Hc34
Brodowe Łąki PL 122 Jb33
Brodowo PL 129 Gd37
Brodski Stubnik HR 152 Ha61
Brody PL 128 Fc39
Brody PL 128 Fd38
Brody PL 130 Jb36
Brody UA 204 Ea15
Broglie F 23 Ga36
Brojce PL 120 Fd31
Brok PL 123 Jd35
Brokdorf D 118 Da31
Brokęcino PL 121 Gc33
Brokefjell N 93 Da43
Brokind S 103 Fd47
Brokke N 92 Cd44
Brokstedt D 118 Db31
Brolo I 167 Fc84
Bromarv FIN 97 Jc41
Bromberg A 145 Gb52
Bromberg = Bydgoszcz PL 122 Ha34
Brome D 127 Dd36
Brome GB 21 Gb25
Bromley GB 20 Fd28
Bromma N 85 Dc39
Brommösund S 94 Fa45
Bromnes N 62 Gd08
Bromölla S 111 Fb54
Brompton GB 17 Fc19
Brömsebro S 111 Ga54
Bromsgrove GB 20 Ed25
Bromskirchen D 126 Cc40
Bromyard GB 15 Ec26
Bron F 34 Jb47
Brönäs S 94 Ed39
Bronchales E 47 Ed64
Brøndby Strand DK 109 Ec26
Brønderslev DK 100 Dc20
Broni I 149 Cc61
Bronice PL 128 Fc39
Bronikowo PL 120 Ga34
Bronikowo PL 129 Gb38
Broniszew PL 130 Hc41
Bronken N 94 Eb39
Bronkow D 128 Fa39
Brönnestad S 110 Fa54
Brønnøysund N 70 Ed23
Bronowo PL 123 Jd33
Brøns DK 108 Da27
Bronte I 167 Fc85
Bronzani BIH 152 Gc62
Brook GB 20 Ed30
Brookhouse GB 11 Ec19
Broomfield GB 20 Fd27
Broomfield IRL 9 Cd19
Broomhaugh GB 11 Ed16
Broons F 26 Ec38
Brora GB 5 Ea06
Brørup DK 108 Da26
Brösarp S 111 Fb56
Broscauți RO 172 Ec54
Brossac F 32 Fc48
Brøstadbotn N 67 Gb11
Broșteni MD 173 Ga55
Broșteni RO 172 Ea57
Broșteni RO 175 Cc64
Broșteni RO 176 Ed62
Broszków PL 131 Jd37
Brotas P 50 Ad68
Broto E 40 Fc57
Brotråsk S 80 Hc26
Brottby S 96 Gd43
Brøttem N 77 Ea30
Brotterode D 126 Dc42
Brøttum N 86 Ea38
Brou F 29 Gb39
Brouage F 32 Fa47
Broué F 23 Gb37
Brough GB 11 Ec18
Brough Lodge GB 5 Fa03
Broughshane GB 9 Da16
Broughton GB 11 Eb17
Broughton GB 15 Eb22
Broughton GB 15 Ec20
Broughton GB 16 Fb21
Broughton GB 20 Fa29
Broughton Astley GB 16 Fa24
Broughton-in-Furness GB 11 Eb18
Broughton Poggs GB 20 Ed27
Broumov CZ 137 Gb43
Brousse-le-Château F 41 Ha53
Broussey-Raulecourt F 25 Jc36
Broutzéika GR 195 Bd87
Brouvelieures F 31 Ka38
Brouwershaven NL 124 Ac37
Brouzet-lès-Alès F 42 Ja52
Brovary UA 202 Ec14
Brovst DK 100 Db21
Brown Candover GB 20 Fa29
Brownhills GB 16 Ed24
Brownston GB 19 Dd32
Broxton GB 15 Eb23
Broye F 31 Jc41
Brozas E 51 Bc66
Brożec PL 129 Gc42
Brozolo I 148 Bd60
Brozzo I 149 Da58
Brseč HR 151 Fb61
Bršanavo HR 158 Gb66
Brtnice CZ 136 Ga47
Brtonigla HR 150 Ed60
Brú IS 2 Ad04
Brua N 86 Eb34
Bruay-la-Buissière F 23 Gd31
Bruay-sur-les-Eaux F 24 Hb31
Brubakk N 78 Eb30
Bruchhausen-Vilsen D 118 Cd35
Bruchköbel D 134 Cd43
Bruchmühlbach-Miesau D 133 Bd46
Bruchsal D 134 Cc47
Bruck A 143 Ec54
Brück D 127 Ec37
Bruck/Opf. D 135 Eb47
Bruck an der Leitha A 145 Gc51
Bruck an der Mur A 144 Fd53
Bruckberg D 134 Dc46
Bruckberg D 135 Ea49
Brücken D 133 Bd46
Brückl A 144 Fb55
Bruckmühl D 143 Ea52
Brucoli I 167 Fd86
Bruc-sur-Aff F 27 Ec40
Brudzeń Duży PL 122 Hc35
Brudzew PL 129 Hb37
Brudzowice PL 138 Hc43
Brue-Auriac F 42 Ka54
Brüel D 119 Ea32
Bruès E 36 Ba57
Bruff IRL 12 Bd24
Bruflat N 85 Dc38
Brugg CH 141 Ca52
Brugge B 124 Aa39
Brüggen D 125 Bc39
Brüggen D 126 Db37
Brugnato I 149 Cd63
Bruhagen N 77 Da31
Bruheim N 84 Cd35
Brühl D 125 Bd41
Brühl D 134 Cc46
Bruinisse NL 124 Ac37
Bruino I 148 Bc60
Bruino I 148 Bc60
Bruiu RO 175 Dc61
Bruksvallarna S 86 Ed32
Brullés E 38 Dc57
Brûlon F 28 Fc40
Brumath F 25 Kc36
Brumby D 127 Ea38
Brummen NL 125 Bc37
Brumov-Bylnice CZ 137 Ha48
Brumovice CZ 137 Gc48
Brumundal N 86 Ea38
Brunate I 149 Cc58
Brunau D 119 Ea35
Brunava LV 106 Kc52
Brundby DK 109 Dd25
Brune N 76 Cd33
Bruneck I 143 Ea55
Brunehamel F 24 Hd33
Brunella I 168 Cc75
Brünen D 125 Bd38
Brunet F 42 Ka53
Brunete E 46 Db64
Bruneval F 22 Fd34
Brunflo S 79 Fc31
Brunhosinho P 45 Bd61
Brunico I 143 Ea55
Bruniquel F 40 Gc53
Brunkeberg N 93 Da43
Brunmyrheden S 72 Gd23
Brunn D 119 Ed32
Brunn S 96 Ha43
Brunn S 102 Fa49
Brünn = Brno CZ 137 Gb47
Brunna S 96 Gc43
Brunnalm A 144 Fd53
Brunn an der Wild A 136 Fd49
Brunnen CH 141 Cb54
Brunnsberg S 87 Fb37
Brunnthal D 143 Ea51
Brunsbüttel D 118 Da31
Brunskog S 94 Ed42
Brunssum NL 125 Bb40
Brunswijk = Braunschweig D 126 Dc37
Bruntál CZ 137 Gd45
Bruree IRL 12 Bd24
Brus SRB 178 Bb68
Brusago I 150 Dd57
Brusand N 92 Ca45
Brušane HR 151 Fd63
Brusarci BG 179 Cc68
Brusasco I 148 Bd60
Brusen BG 179 Da71
Brüsewitz D 119 Ea32
Brushkuli AL 182 Ab74
Bruskowo Wielkopolski PL 121 Gc30
Brusnik SRB 174 Ca66
Brusník SK 146 Hd50
Brusno-kúpele SK 138 Hd48
Br'usovo RUS 113 Jd59
Brušperk CZ 137 Hb45
Brusque F 41 Hb53
Brussel B 124 Ac40
Brusson I 148 Bd58
Brüssow D 120 Fb33
Brusturi RO 170 Cb56
Brusturi-Drăgănești RO 172 Ec57
Brusturoasa RO 172 Eb59
Brusy PL 121 Gd32
Brutelles F 23 Gb32
Bruton GB 19 Ec29
Brutovce SK 138 Jc47
Bruttig-Fankel D 133 Bd43
Brutuļi LV 106 La48
Bruvik N 84 Cb39
Bruvno HR 151 Ga63
Bruvoll N 94 Eb40
Bruxelles B 124 Ac40
Bruyères F 31 Ka38
Bruyères-et-Montberault F 24 Hc34
Bruz F 28 Ed39
Bruzaholm S 103 Fd49
Bruzilas LV 105 Jd52
Bruzzano Zeffirio I 164 Gb84
Břvarty CZ 136 Fa43
Brvenica MK 178 Ba73
Brvenik SRB 178 Ba68
Brwinow PL 130 Jb37
Brydalen N 86 Eb34
Bryggesåk N 92 Cc46
Bryggja N 84 Cb34
Brylle DK 108 Dc27
Bryn N 93 Dd41
Brynamman GB 19 Dd27
Bryncethin GB 19 Ea28
Bryne N 92 Ca44
Bryngwran GB 14 Dc22
Bryngwyn GB 15 Eb26
Bryn-henllan GB 14 Db26
Brynica PL 129 Ha42
Brynje S 79 Fc31
Brynmawr GB 19 Eb27
Bryrup DK 108 Db24
Bryzgiel PL 123 Kb30
Brzączowice PL 138 Ja45
Brzan SRB 174 Bc66
Brza Palanka SRB 174 Cb65
Brzava MNE 159 Jb67
Brzeće SRB 178 Bb68
Brzechowo PL 122 Hd35
Brzeg PL 129 Gd42
Brzeg Dolny PL 129 Gc40
Brzeg Głogowski PL 128 Ga39
Brzemiona PL 121 Ha33
Brześce PL 130 Jc37
Brześć Kujawski PL 129 Hb36
Brzesko PL 138 Jb44
Brzeszcze PL 138 Hc44
Brzezie PL 121 Gc32
Brzezie PL 129 Ha38
Brzezina PL 120 Fd34
Brzezinki PL 129 Ha41
Brzeziny PL 120 Ga34
Brzeziny PL 129 Ha39
Brzeziny PL 130 Hd38
Brzeziny PL 139 Jd44
Brzeźnica PL 138 Hd44
Brzeźnica Krajeńska PL 121 Gb33
Brzeźnio PL 129 Hb39
Brzeźno PL 120 Ga32
Brzeźno PL 121 Hb34
Brzeźno PL 128 Fc37
Brzeźno PL 131 Kd40
Brzeźno Lęborskie PL 121 Gd29
Brzeźno Szlacheckie PL 121 Gc31
Brzezówka PL 138 Jc43
Brzohode SRB 174 Bc65
Brzostek PL 139 Jd44
Brzotín SK 138 Jb49
Brzoza PL 121 Ha34
Brzóza PL 130 Jc39
Brzóza Królewska PL 139 Ka43
Brzozie PL 122 Hd33
Brzozie Lubawskie PL 122 Hc33
Brzózka PL 128 Fc38
Brzozów PL 139 Ka45
Brzozowa PL 123 Kb32
Brzozowiec PL 128 Fd36
Brzozowo PL 122 Ja34
Brzozowo PL 123 Kb32
Brzuska PL 139 Kb45
Brzuze PL 122 Hc34
Bšezno CZ 135 Ed43
Bû F 23 Gb37
Bua S 102 Ec50
Buais F 28 Fb38
Buar S 94 Eb45
Buavåg N 92 Ca41
Buba RO 176 Ec63
Bubakken N 77 Ea33
Bubbio I 148 Ca62
Bubenreuth D 135 Dd46
Buberget S 80 Hb27
Bubiai LT 114 Ka54
Bublava CZ 135 Ec43
Bubnevo RUS 107 Ld48
Bubry F 27 Ea40
Bubuieci MD 173 Fd58
Bubwith GB 16 Fb20
Buc F 23 Gd37
Buča UA 202 Ec14
Bučač UA 204 Ea16
Bucak TR 197 Ed89
Bucak TR 198 Fc88
Bucak TR 199 Gc89
Bucak TR 199 Ha91
Bucakşeyhler TR 199 Ha91
Buccheri I 167 Fc87
Bucchianico I 157 Fa70
Buccino I 161 Fd75
Buccleuch GB 11 Eb15
Bucelas P 50 Aa68
Buceş RO 175 Cc60
Buch D 142 Db50
Buch D 143 Ea50
Buchanty GB 7 Ea11
Buchau, Bad D 142 Cd51
Buchbach D 143 Eb50
Buchdorf D 134 Dc48
Bucheben A 143 Ec54
Bucheloh D 127 Dd42
Büchen D 118 Dc33
Buchen D 134 Cd46
Buchenbach D 134 Da47
Büchenbach D 135 Dd47
Buchenberg D 142 Db52
Büchenbeuren D 133 Bd44
Buchholz D 118 Db33
Buchholz D 118 Db35
Buchholz D 127 Ed37
Buchholz (Westerwald) D 125 Ca41
Buchin RO 174 Ca62
Buchişu RO 179 Da67
Büchlberg D 135 Ed49
Buchloe D 142 Dc51
Buchlovice CZ 137 Gd48
Buchs CH 142 Cd54
Buchy F 23 Gb34
Bučin MK 183 Bb75
Bucine I 156 Dd66
Bučin Prohod BG 179 Cc70
Bučionys LT 114 Kd57
Bučište MK 178 Bd73
Bucium RO 171 Cd59
Buciumeni MD 173 Fa57
Buciumeni RO 176 Ed61
Buciumi RO 171 Cd57
Buciumoni RO 176 Dd64
Bučiūnai LT 114 Kb53
Buciuşca MD 173 Fd56
Bučje HR 152 Gd60
Bučje SRB 174 Ca66
Buckarby S 95 Gb41
Buckden GB 11 Ed19
Buckden GB 20 Fc25
Bückeburg D 126 Cd37
Bücken D 118 Da35
Buckfastleigh GB 19 Dd31
Buckhaven GB 7 Eb12
Buckie GB 5 Ec07
Buckingham GB 20 Fb26
Buckland GB 20 Fa27
Bucklay GB 15 Eb22
Buckminster GB 16 Fb24
Bucknell GB 15 Eb25
Buckow D 128 Fb36
Bucks Green GB 20 Fc29
Bucoşniţa RO 174 Cb62
Bucov RO 176 Eb64
Bucovăţ MD 173 Fc57
Bucovăţ RO 175 Cd66
Bucovica BIH 158 Gd66
Bučovice CZ 137 Gc47
Bucquoy F 23 Ha32
Bucsa H 147 Jd53
Bucşani RO 176 Ea64
Bucşani RO 176 Ea66
Bucureşci RO 175 Cc60
Bucureşti RO 176 Eb66
Bucuria MD 177 Fc61
Bucuru RO 175 Cd61
Bucy-lès-Pierrepont F 24 Hc34
Buczek PL 130 Hc39
Buczkowice PL 138 Hc45
Bud N 76 Cd31
Budachów PL 128 Fc37
Budačka Rijeka HR 151 Ga60
Budacu de Jos RO 171 Dc57
Budacu de Sus RO 171 Dc57
Budăi MD 173 Fc56
Budakdoğanca TR 185 Eb75
Budakeszi H 146 Hc53
Budaklar TR 187 Gc78
Budaklar TR 191 Ea82
Budaklar TR 192 Ga86
Budakovo MK 183 Bb76
Budanovci SRB 153 Jb61
Budaörs H 146 Hc53
Budapest H 146 Hd53
Búðardalur IS 2 Ac03
Budby GB 16 Fb22
Buddbyn S 73 Hd21
Büddenstedt D 127 Dd37
Buddusò I 168 Cb75
Bude GB 18 Dc30
Budeasa RO 175 Dc64
Budei MD 177 Fc62
Budel NL 125 Bb39
Büdelsdorf D 118 Db30
Budënnovsk RUS 205 Ga16
Budens P 58 Aa74
Büderich D 125 Bd38
Büdesheim D 133 Bc43
Budeşti MD 173 Fd58
Budeşti RO 171 Db55
Budeşti RO 171 Db58
Budeşti RO 175 Db64
Budeşti RO 180 Eb67
Budevo SRB 178 Ad68
Budia E 47 Ea64
Budila RO 176 Ea62
Budilovo RUS 99 Ma43
Budimci HR 152 Hb60
Budimír SK 139 Jd48
Budimlić Japra BIH 152 Gb62
Büdingen D 134 Cd43
Budišov CZ 136 Ga47
Budišov nad Budišovkou CZ 137 Gd45
Budkovce SK 139 Ka48
Budleigh Salterton GB 19 Ea31
Budmerice SK 145 Gd50
Budogošč' RUS 202 Eb08
Budoi RO 170 Cb56
Budomierz Duży PL 139 Kc43
Budoni I 168 Cc75
Budoviž RUS 107 Ld46
Budraičiai LT 114 Ka55
Budrio I 150 Dd63
Budry PL 122 Jc30
Budumirci MK 183 Bc76
Budureasa RO 171 Cc58
Buduslău RO 170 Cb55
Budva MNE 159 Hd70
Būdviečiai LT 113 Jc56
Būdviečiai LT 114 Ka59
Būdviečiai LT 114 Ka59
Būdvietis LV 114 Kb59
Budweis = České Budějovice CZ 136 Fb48
Budy PL 130 Hd36
Budyně CZ 136 Fb43
Budzeń PL 120 Fc33
Budziska PL 123 Jd30
Budzisz PL 122 Hc31
Budziszewice PL 130 Ja39
Budzyń PL 121 Gc35
Buenache de Alarcón E 53 Eb67
Buenache de la Sierra E 47 Ec65
Buenaventura E 46 Cd65
Buenavista de Valdavia E 38 Da57
Buendía E 47 Ea65
Buer D 126 Cc37
Buerås S 102 Eb50
Bueres E 37 Cd55
Bueu E 36 Ad57
Buftea RO 176 Ea66
Bugac H 146 Ja55
Bugarra E 54 Fb67
Buğdaylar TR 192 Fd85
Buğdaylı TR 186 Fa80
Buğdüz TR 193 Gd81
Buğdüz TR 199 Gb89
Bugeac MD 177 Fc60
Bugeat F 33 Gd47
Bügeniai LT 113 Jc53
Buggerru I 169 Bd79
Bughea de Jos RO 175 Dc63
Būginiai LT 114 Kd53
Buglose F 39 Fa54
Bugnara I 161 Fa71
Bugojno BIH 158 Ha64
Bugøyfjord N 65 Kc07
Bugøynes N 65 Kc07
Bugraz TR 186 Fd78
Buguchwała PL 139 Ka44
Bugul'ma RUS 203 Ga09
Bugurzyn PL 122 Ja34
Büğüş TR 197 Fa92
Bugyi H 146 Hd54
Buharkent TR 192 Fc87
Bühl D 133 Cb48
Bühlertal D 133 Cb48
Bühlertann D 134 Da47
Bühlerzell D 134 Da48
Buhoci RO 172 Ed59
Buhølen N 92 Cc47
Buholmen N 65 Kc07
Buhovci BG 181 Ec70
Buhovo BG 179 Cc71
Buhuşi RO 172 Ec59
Builth Wells GB 15 Ea26
Buinsk RUS 203 Fd09
Buirios Uí Chéin IRL 13 Ca22
Buironfosse F 24 Hc33
Buis-les-Baronnies F 42 Jc51
Buitenpost NL 117 Bc33
Buitrago del Lozoya E 46 Dc62
Buivydžiai LT 115 Lb57
Buj RUS 203 Fa08
Buják H 146 Ja51
Bujalance E 52 Da72
Bujanicy RUS 99 Ma40
Bujanovac KSV 178 Bc71
Bujaraloz E 48 Fc61
Buje HR 150 Ed60
Bujnovci BG 180 Ea71
Bujor MD 173 Fc58
Bujoreni RO 180 Dd67
Bujoru RO 180 Dd68
Buk H 145 Gc53
Buk PL 129 Gb37
Bukaiši LV 106 Jd50
Bukanovskaja RUS 203 Fc13
Bukas LV 106 Kd48
Bükdere TR 192 Fb82
Bükkábrány H 146 Jc51
Bukkemoen N 62 Gb10
Bükkösd H 152 Hb57
Büklüce TR 199 Ha91
Bukonys LT 114 Kc56
Bukorovac SRB 174 Bb66
Bukovac SRB 153 Hd59
Bukova Gora BIH 158 Gd66
Bukovec BG 179 Cb68
Bukovi SRB 159 Jb64
Bukovica HR 152 Ha59
Bukovica MNE 159 Ja67
Bukovica SLO 151 Fb57
Bukowa PL 131 Kb42
Bukowice PL 129 Gc40
Bukowiec PL 121 Ha33
Bukowiec PL 128 Ga37
Bukowina Tatrzańska PL 138 Ja46
Bukówko PL 120 Ga31
Bukownica PL 129 Ha40
Bukowno PL 138 Hd43
Bukowsko PL 139 Ka46
Buksnes N 66 Fd12
Bukta N 64 Jd05
Bukta N 78 Ea29
Buky UA 204 Ec15
Bülach CH 141 Cb52
Bulăieşti MD 173 Fd56
Bulair BG 181 Ed71
Bulanlak TR 205 Fd19
Bulărda MD 173 Fc57
Bulavėnai LT 114 Ka55
Bulboaca MD 173 Fa53
Bulboaca MD 173 Ga58
Bulboci MD 173 Fb54
Bulbucata RO 176 Ea66
Bulbuente E 47 Ed60
Buldan TR 192 Fc87
Bulduri LV 106 Kb50
Bulgar RUS 203 Fd09
Bulgiza AL 163 Jc72
Bulgiza AL 182 Ac74
Bulgurca TR 191 Ec87
Buli Potok SRB 178 Bd68
Bülkau D 118 Da32
Bulken N 84 Cb38
Bulkowo PL 130 Ja36
Bull N 92 Cc46
Bullas E 61 Ec72
Bullaun IRL 12 Bd21
Bulle CH 141 Bc55
Bullerup DK 109 Dd26
Büllingen B 125 Bc42
Bullmark S 80 Hc27
Bully-les-Mines F 23 Ha31
Bulnes E 38 Da55
Bulshizë AL 163 Jb71
Bultei I 168 Ca75
Bulz RO 171 Cc57
Bulzeşti RO 175 Da65
Bulzeştii de Sus RO 171 Cc59
Bumbăta MD 173 Fb57
Bumbeşti-Jiu RO 175 Cd63
Bumbeşti-Pitic RO 175 Da63
Buna BIH 158 Hb67
Bun an Phobail IRL 9 Cc15
Bunarkaig GB 6 Dc09
Bunbeg IRL 8 Ca15
Bunbrosna IRL 9 Cb20
Bunclody IRL 13 Cc23
Buncrana IRL 9 Cc15
Bun Cranncha IRL 9 Cc15
Bunde D 117 Ca33
Bünde D 126 Cd37
Bundenthal D 133 Ca47
Bun Dobhráin IRL 8 Ca17
Bundoran IRL 8 Ca17
Bundorf D 134 Dc44
Bunes N 65 Kb06
Bunessan GB 6 Da11
Buneşti RO 172 Ec56
Buneşti RO 175 Db63
Buneşti RO 176 Dd60
Buneşti-Avereşti RO 173 Fb59
Bungay GB 21 Gb25
Bunge S 104 Ha48
Bunić HR 151 Ga62
Bunila RO 175 Cc61
Bunka LV 105 Jb52
Bunkeflostrand S 110 Ed56
Bunken DK 101 Dd19
Bunkris S 86 Fa36
Bunmahon IRL 13 Cb25
Bun na hAbhna IRL 8 Bb18
Bunnahowen IRL 8 Bb18
Bun na Leaca IRL 8 Ca15
Bunnyconnellan IRL 8 Bd18
Buño E 36 Ad54
Buñol E 54 Fb68
Bunovo BG 179 Cd71
Bunschoten NL 116 Bb36
Bunteşti RO 170 Cb58
Buntingford GB 20 Fc26
Buntowo PL 121 Gc34
Buñuel E 47 Ed59
Bünüs TR 187 Hb78
Bunyola E 57 Hb67
Buochs CH 141 Cb54
Buoldavarre S 68 Hc18
Buonabitacolo I 161 Ga77
Buonalbergo I 161 Fc74
Buonconvento I 155 Dc67
Bur DK 100 Cd23
Burano I 150 Eb60
Burbach D 125 Cb41
Burbáguena E 47 Ed63
Burbia E 37 Bd56
Burbiškiai LV 114 Kb56
Burcei I 169 Cb79
Burcin TR 186 Ga80
Burdąg PL 122 Jb32
Burdnomohkki FIN 69 Ka13
Burdur TR 199 Gb88
Bureå S 72 Gc23
Bureå S 80 Hb25
Bureåborg S 80 Gc30
Burela E 36 Bc53
Burelles F 24 Hc33
Büren D 126 Cc39
Buren NL 117 Bc32
Buren NL 124 Ba37
Büren an der Aare CH 141 Bd53
Bures GB 21 Ga26
Burfjord N 63 Hc08
Burford GB 20 Ed27
Burg D 118 Da31
Burg D 127 Eb37
Burg D 128 Fb38
Burgas BG 181 Ed73
Burgau A 145 Gb54
Burgau D 134 Db49
Burg auf Fehmarn D 119 Ea30
Burgberg D 142 Db52
Burgbernheim D 134 Db46
Burgbrohl D 125 Bd42
Burgdorf CH 141 Bd54
Burgdorf D 126 Db36
Burgdorf D 126 Db37
Burgebrach D 134 Dc45
Bürgel D 127 Ea41
Burgess Hill GB 20 Fc30
Burghagel D 134 Db49
Burghammer D 128 Fb40
Burghaslach D 134 Dc45
Burghaun D 126 Da42
Burghausen D 127 Eb40
Burghausen D 143 Ec51
Burghead GB 5 Eb07
Burgheim D 134 Dc49
Burgh-Haamstede NL 124 Ab37
Burgh le Marsh GB 17 Fd22
Burgh Saint Peter GB 21 Gb25
Burgillos del Cerro E 51 Bc70
Burgio I 166 Ec85
Burgio I 167 Fc88
Burgkirchen A 143 Ec51
Burgkirchen D 143 Ec51
Burgkunstadt D 135 Dd44
Burg Lauenstein D 135 Dd43
Burglauer D 134 Db43
Burglengenfeld D 135 Ea47
Burgo E 36 Bb55
Burgo P 44 Ad62
Burgoberbach D 134 Dc47
Burgohondo E 46 Cd64
Burgos E 38 Dc58
Burgos I 168 Ca76
Burgpreppach D 134 Dc44
Burgsalach D 135 Dd48
Burgsinn D 134 Da44
Burgstädt D 127 Ec41
Bürgstadt D 134 Cd45
Burg Stargard D 119 Ed33
Burgsteinfurt D 125 Ca37
Burgsvik S 104 Gd51
Burgthann D 135 Dd47
Burgueira E 36 Ac58
Burguete E 39 Ed56
Burgui E 39 Fa57
Burguillos E 59 Ca73
Burguillos de Tajo E 52 Db66
Burgum NL 117 Bc33
Burgwald D 126 Cc41
Burgwedel D 126 Db36
Burgwindheim D 134 Dc45
Burhan TR 192 Fd82
Burhaniye TR 191 Ec82
Buriasco I 148 Bc61
Burie F 32 Fc47
Burila Mare RO 174 Cb65
Burja BG 180 Dc70
Burjassot E 54 Fb67
Burjuc RO 174 Cb60
Burk D 134 Db47
Burkal DK 108 Da28
Burkardroth D 134 Db43
Burkat PL 122 Ja33
Burkaty PL 122 Jb35
Burkhardtsdorf D 127 Ec42
Burlăceni MD 177 Fc62
Burlacu MD 177 Fc61
Burladingen D 142 Cc50
Burlăneşti MD 172 Ed54
Burley in Wharfedale GB 16 Ed20
Burlo D 125 Bd37
Burlton GB 15 Eb23
Burmahan TR 199 Ha90
Burness GB 5 Ed02
Burnham-on-Crouch GB 21 Ga27
Burnham-on-Sea GB 19 Eb29
Burnley GB 16 Ed20
Burntisland GB 11 Eb13
Buronzo I 148 Ca59
Burovac SRB 174 Bc65
Burow D 119 Ed32
Burøysund N 62 Gd07
Burrafirth GB 5 Fa03
Burravoe GB 5 Fa04
Burrel AL 163 Jc72
Burren IRL 12 Bc21
Burres E 36 Ba55
Burringham GB 16 Fb21
Burry Port GB 19 Dd27
Burs S 104 Ha50
Bursa TR 186 Fd80
Burscheid D 125 Bd40
Burscough GB 15 Eb21
Burseryd S 102 Fa51
Bursiljum S 80 Hc26
Bürstadt D 134 Cc45
Bursuc MD 173 Fc58
Burszewo PL 122 Jb31
Burtenbach D 142 Db50
Burtnieki LV 106 Kd48
Burton Agnes GB 17 Fc19
Burton Constable GB 17 Fc20
Burton-in-Kendal GB 11 Ec19
Burton Latimer GB 20 Fb25
Burtonport IRL 8 Ca15
Burton-upon-Stather GB 16 Fb21
Burton-upon-Trent GB 16 Fa23
Burträsk S 80 Hc26
Burujón E 52 Da66
Burvik S 81 Hd26
Burwash GB 20 Fd30
Burwell GB 17 Fd22
Burwell GB 20 Fd25
Burwick GB 5 Ec04
Bury GB 15 Ec21
Bury Saint Edmunds GB 21 Ga25
Burzenin PL 129 Hb40
Burzyn PL 123 Ka33
Busachi I 169 Ca77

Busalla – Cañaveral de León

Busalla I 148 Cb62
Busana I 149 Da63
Busano I 148 Bd59
Buşăuca MD 173 Fd56
Busca I 148 Bc62
Busche I 150 Ea58
Busdorf D 108 Db29
Buseck D 126 Cc42
Busemarke DK 109 Ec28
Busenberg D 133 Ca47
Busendorf D 134 Dc44
Bušetina HR 152 Gd58
Buševec HR 152 Gb59
Bushat AL 163 Jb71
Bushey GB 20 Fc27
Bushfield IRL 12 Bd23
Bushmills GB 9 Cd15
Busici MK 183 Bc74
Busigny F 24 Hb33
Buşila MD 173 Fb56
Busilovac SRB 178 Bc67
Bušince SK 146 Hd50
Bus'k UA 204 Ea15
Buske DK 109 Eb27
Buskhyttan S 103 Gb46
Busko-Zdrój PL 138 Jb43
Bušletić BIH 152 Hb62
Busño PL 131 Kd40
Busnovi HR 152 Ha60
Busot E 55 Fb71
Busovača BIH 158 Hb64
Bussac-Forêt F 32 Fc49
Bussang F 31 Ka39
Busséol F 34 Hb47
Busseto I 149 Da61
Bussière-Badil F 33 Ga47
Bussières F 24 Hb36
Büßleben D 127 Dd41
Bussö FIN 96 Hc40
Bussoleno I 148 Bb60
Busson F 30 Jb38
Bussum NL 116 Ba36
Bussy-le-Repos F 30 Hb39
Bustadmon S 78 Fa30
Bustares E 46 Dd62
Bustarviejo E 46 Dc63
Buşteni RO 176 Ea63
Bustidoño E 38 Db56
Bustillo de Páramo E 37 Cb57
Bustnes N 71 Fb20
Busto E 37 Ca53
Busto Arsizio I 148 Cb59
Buštranje SRB 178 Bd72
Bustuchin RO 175 Da64
Büsum D 118 Da30
Buszkowo PL 121 Gd33
Buszów PL 120 Fd35
Butan BG 179 Cd68
Butea RO 172 Ed57
Buţeni MD 173 Fc58
Buteni RO 170 Cb59
Butera I 167 Fa87
Bütgenbach B 125 Bb42
Butimanu RO 176 Ea65
Bütingė LT 113 Jb54
Butjadingen D 117 Cc32
Butkaičiai I LT 114 Ka56
Butkiškė LT 114 Ka55
Butkiškiai LT 114 Kc55
Butler's Bridge IRL 9 Cb19
Butlerstown IRL 12 Bc26
Butley GB 21 Gb26
Butniūnai LT 114 Kd53
Butoieşti RO 175 Cd65
Butovo BG 180 Dc70
Butrimonys LT 114 Kc59
Butrint AL 182 Ab79
Butron E 38 Ea55
Butryny PL 122 Ja32
Butryny PL 122 Ja32
Bütschwil CH 142 Cc53
Büttelborn D 134 Cc44
Buttenheim D 135 Dd45
Buttenwiesen D 134 Dc49
Buttevant IRL 12 Bd24
Buttington GB 15 Eb24
Buttlar D 126 Db42
Buttle S 104 Ha50
Buttlerstown IRL 13 Cb25
Buttstädt D 127 Ea41
Buttstedt D 126 Db40
Butuceni MD 173 Fd56
Buturlinovka RUS 203 Fb13
Buturugeni RO 176 Ea66
Butzbach D 134 Cc43
Bützow D 119 Eb32
Buurse NL 125 Bd37
Buvåg N 66 Fd14
Buvarp N 78 Eb27
Buvik N 77 Da32
Buvika N 70 Fa19
Buvika N 70 Fa20
Buvika N 77 Ea30
Buvika N 86 Ec34
Buxières-les-Mines F 30 Hb44
Buxtehude D 118 Db33
Buxton GB 16 Ed22
Buxy F 30 Ja43
Büyükalan TR 198 Ga90
Büyükanafarta TR 185 Ea80
Büyükbelen TR 192 Fa85
Büyükbelkıs TR 199 Ha91
Büyükçavuşlu TR 185 Ed76
Büyükçavuşlu TR 186 Fa77
Büyük Çekmece TR 186 Fc77
Büyükdağdere TR 192 Fb83
Büyükdöllük TR 185 Eb75
Büyükfındık TR 191 Ed82
Büyük Gökçeli TR 199 Gd88
Büyükhusum TR 191 Ea82
Büyükışıklar TR 191 Ed83
Büyükkale TR 191 Ed87
Büyükkalecik TR 193 Gc85
Büyükkaraağaç TR 198 Fb91
Büyükkarabağ TR 193 Ha85
Büyükkarıştıran TR 185 Ed77
Büyükkayalı TR 192 Fd86
Büyükkılıclı TR 186 Fb77
Büyükköy TR 199 Gb90
Büyükkumluca TR 199 Gd91
Büyükmandıra TR 185 Ec76
Büyükögünlü TR 185 Eb74
Büyükorhan TR 192 Fc82
Büyükoturak TR 193 Gb85
Büyükpınar TR 191 Ed81
Büyüksaka TR 193 Gb83
Büyükşapçı TR 191 Ec82
Büyüksöğle TR 199 Gb92
Büyüktekke TR 187 Ha77
Büyükyayla TR 193 Gc84
Büyükyenice TR 191 Ed83
Büyükyoncalı TR 186 Fa76
Buza RO 171 Db57
Buzançais F 29 Gb43
Buzancy F 24 Ja34
Buzău RO 176 Ec64
Buzescu RO 180 Dd67
Buzet HR 151 Fa60
Buziaş RO 174 Bd61
Buzica SK 138 Jc49
Bužim BIH 152 Gb61
Buzluca TR 193 Ha84
Buzoeşti RO 175 Dc65
Buzovgrad BG 180 Dd72
Buzsák H 145 Ha56
Bweeng IRL 12 Bc25
Bwlch GB 15 Ea26
Bwlchllan GB 15 Dd25
Bwlch-y-ffridd GB 15 Ea24
Bwlch-y-Sarnau GB 15 Ea25
By N 78 Ea28
By S 94 Ed42
By S 94 Ed44
By S 95 Ga41
Byans-sur-Doubs F 31 Jd42
Byarum S 103 Fb49
Byberget S 87 Fd33
Bybjerg DK 109 Eb25
Bychav BY 202 Eb12
Bychawa PL 131 Kb40
Bycina PL 137 Hb43
Byczki PL 130 Ja38
Byczyna PL 129 Ha41
Byczyna PL 138 Hd44
Bydalen S 79 Fb31
Bydgoszcz PL 121 Ha34
Bydlino PL 121 Gc29
Bye S 88 Gc33
Byford GB 15 Eb26
Bygdeå S 80 Hc27
Bygdeträsk S 80 Hc26
Bygdisheim N 85 Db36
Bygdsiljum S 80 Hc26
Bygget S 102 Ed52
Bygland N 92 Cd45
Byglandsfjord N 92 Cd45
Bykle N 92 Cd43
Byklestøylane N 92 Cd43
Bykovo RUS 203 Fd13
Bylchau GB 15 Ea22
Byluft N 65 Kb07
Byn S 94 Ed42
Byneset N 77 Ea30
Byremo N 92 Cc46
Byrkjedal N 92 Cb44
Byrkjelo N 84 Cc35
Byrness GB 11 Ec15
Byrudstua N 85 Ea40
Byrum DK 101 Ea20
Byšice CZ 136 Fc44
Byske S 73 Hc24
Byškovice CZ 137 Ha46
Bysław PL 121 Ha33
Byssträsk S 80 Ha27
Býšť CZ 136 Ga44
Bysting N 77 Dd29
Bystrá SK 138 Hd48
Bystré CZ 137 Gb46
Bystré SK 139 Jd47
Bystrecovo RUS 107 Ma47
Bystřice CZ 136 Fc46
Bystřice CZ 138 Hc46
Bystřice nad Pernštejnem CZ 137 Gb46
Bystřice pod Hostýnem CZ 137 Ha47
Bystrzyca PL 131 Ka41
Bystrzyca Kłodzka PL 137 Gc44
Byszyno PL 120 Ga31
Bytča SK 137 Hb47
Bytnica PL 128 Fd37
Bytom PL 138 Hc43
Bytom Odrzański PL 128 Ga39
Bytoń PL 129 Hb36
Bytów PL 121 Gd31
Bytyń PL 129 Gb36
Byvattnet S 80 Gc30
Byxelkrok S 104 Gc50
Bzenec CZ 137 Gd48
Bzovik SK 146 Hd50

C

Căbăieşti MD 173 Fb57
Cabaj-Cápor SK 145 Ha50
Cabaleiros (Tordoia) E 36 Ad54
Cabanac F 32 Fb51
Cabañaquinta (Aller) E 37 Cc55
Cabañas de la Dornilla E 37 Ca57
Cabanes E 54 Fd65
Cabañes de Esgueva E 46 Dc60
Cabanillas E 47 Ed59
Cabanillas de la Sierra E 46 Dc63
Čabar HR 151 Fc59
Cabasse F 42 Ka54
Cabdella E 40 Gb58
Cabeça de Carneiro P 50 Ba70
Cabeça Gorda P 50 Ad71
Cabeço de Vide P 50 Ba68
Cabella Ligure I 149 Cc62
Cabertarar TR 192 Fc86
Căbeşti RO 170 Cb57
Cabezabellosa E 45 Ca65
Cabeza del Buey E 52 Cc69
Cabeza la Vaca E 51 Bd71
Cabezamesada E 53 Dd66
Cabezarados E 52 Da69
Cabezarrubias E 52 Da70
Cabezas del Villar E 45 Cc63
Cabezas Rubias E 59 Bb72
Cabezón E 46 Da60
Cabezón de la Sal E 38 Db55
Cabezón de Liébana E 38 Da55
Cabezuela E 46 Db62
Cabezuela del Valle E 45 Cb65
Cabia E 38 Dc58
Čabiny SK 139 Ka47
Caboalles de Arriba E 37 Ca56
Cabourg F 22 Fc35
Cabra E 60 Cd74
Čabra KSV 178 Ba70
Cabrach GB 7 Ec08
Cabra del Santo Cristo E 60 Dc73
Cabra de Mora E 54 Fb65
Cabragh GB 9 Cc17
Cabrahigos E 59 Ca77
Cabras I 169 Bd77
Cabredo E 39 Eb57
Cabreiros E 36 Bb54
Cabrejas del Pinar E 47 Ea60
Cabrela P 50 Ac69
Cabrerets F 33 Gc51
Cabrières F 41 Hc54
Cabrillas E 45 Ca63
Cabruñana E 37 Cb54
Cabuna HR 152 Ha59
Cacabelos E 37 Bd57
Cacabezë AL 182 Ab75
Čačak SRB 159 Jc64
Caccamo I 166 Ed84
Caccuri I 165 Gd80
Cacela Velha P 58 Ba74
Cáceres E 51 Bd67
Čačersk BY 202 Ec13
Čačėvičy BY 202 Eb12
Cachafeiro E 36 Ba56
Cachão P 45 Bc60
Cachopo P 58 Ad73
Čachtice SK 137 Ha49
Cacia P 44 Ac62
Cacica RO 172 Eb55
Cacin E 60 Db75
Čačinci HR 152 Ha59
Căciulata RO 175 Db63
Cádabo (Baleira) E 36 Bc55
Cadafresnas E 37 Bd57
Cadagua E 38 Dd56
Cadalen F 41 Gd53
Cadalso de los Vidrios E 46 Da65
Cadaqués E 41 Hc58
Cadaval P 50 Ab67
Cadavedo E 37 Ca54
Čađavica BIH 152 Gd63
Čađavica HR 152 Ha59
Čađavica Gornja BIH 153 Hd62
Čadca SK 138 Hc46
Cadelbosco di Sopra I 149 Db62
Caden F 27 Ec41
Cadenabbia I 149 Cc57
Cadenberge D 118 Da32
Cadenet F 42 Jc53
Cádiar E 60 Dc76
Cadillac F 32 Fc51
Cadillon F 40 Fc54
Čadinje SRB 159 Jb66
Cadis F 41 Gd54
Cádiz E 59 Bd76
Cadolzburg D 134 Dc46
Cadouin F 33 Ga50
Cadreita E 47 Ed59
Cadzand NL 124 Ab38
Caen F 22 Fc36
Caerleon GB 19 Eb27
Caernarfon GB 15 Dd22
Caerphilly GB 19 Eb28
Caersws GB 15 Ea24
Čaevo RUS 202 Ed08
Ćafa MK 182 Ba74
Ćafe MNE 159 Ja69
Cagan Aman RUS 203 Ga14
Cagan-Nur RUS 203 Ga14
Caggiano I 161 Fd76
Çağıllar TR 192 Fc84
Çağış TR 192 Fa82
Cagitán E 61 Ec72
Çağlarca TR 199 Gc91
Çağlayık TR 185 Ed74
Cagli I 156 Eb66
Cagliari I 169 Ca80
Čaglin HR 152 Hb60
Çağman TR 199 Gb93
Cagnano Varano I 161 Ga72
Cagnes-sur-Mer F 43 Kc53
Cagnotte F 39 Fa54
Čagoda RUS 202 Ec08
Caher IRL 8 Bc20
Cahir IRL 13 Ca24
Caherdaniel IRL 12 Ba26
Cahersiveen IRL 12 Ba25
Cahors F 33 Gc51
Cahul MD 177 Fb61
Cahuzac-sur-Vére F 41 Gd53
Căianu RO 171 Da58
Căianu Mic RO 171 Db56
Caiazzo I 161 Fb74
Caín E 38 Da55
Căinari MD 173 Fd59
Căinarii Vechi MD 173 Fb54
Căineni RO 175 Db62
Căineni-Băi RO 176 Ed64
Caión E 36 Ad54
Čaira BG 179 Cd73
Cairaclia MD 177 Fc62
Cairnborrow GB 7 Ec08
Cairndow GB 6 Dc12
Cairnryan GB 10 Dc16
Cairo Montenotte I 148 Ca62
Caiseal IRL 13 Ca24
Caisleán an Bharraigh IRL 8 Bc19
Caisleán an Chomair IRL 13 Cb23
Caister-on-Sea GB 17 Gc24
Caistor GB 17 Fc21
Caivano I 161 Fb74
Cajarc F 33 Gc51
Cajba MD 173 Fa55
Čajetina SRB 159 Jb65
Čajić BIH 158 Gc65
Čajka BG 181 Fb70
Čajle MK 178 Ba73
Čajniče BIH 159 Hd66
Cajvana RO 172 Eb55
Čák H 145 Gb53
Çakallar TR 191 Ec86
Çakallar TR 191 Ed82
Čakany SK 145 Gd51
Çakılköyü TR 186 Fa79
Çakıllı TR 186 Fa76
Çakıllı TR 192 Fa83
Čakino RUS 203 Fc12
Çakır TR 191 Ed81
Çakır TR 198 Fd90
Çakırbeyli TR 197 Ed88
Çakırca TR 186 Ga79
Çakırdere TR 191 Ec82
Çakırlar TR 191 Ec83
Çakırlar TR 192 Fc85
Çakırlar TR 193 Hb87
Çakırlar TR 199 Gc91
Çakırözü TR 193 Gc86
Çakmak TR 191 Eb83
Çakmak TR 192 Fd82
Çakmak TR 192 Ga83
Çakmak TR 193 Hb84
Çakmak TR 198 Fb90
Čakovci HR 153 Hd60
Čakovec HR 152 Gb57
Çal TR 192 Fd87
Cala E 59 Bd72
Cala P 51 Bb69
Cala Antena E 57 Hc67
Calabernardo I 167 Fd88
Cala Blanca E 57 Ja66
Cala Blava E 57 Hb67
Calabritto I 161 Fd75
Călacea RO 170 Ca58
Calaceite E 48 Fc63
Calacuccia F 154 Cb69
Cala de Mijas E 60 Cd77
Cala d'Or E 57 Hc68
Cala en Porter E 57 Ja66
Calaf E 49 Gc60
Calafat RO 179 Cc67
Calafell E 49 Gc62
Cala Figuera E 57 Hc68
Calafindeşti RO 172 Eb55
Calafort Ros Láir IRL 13 Cd25
Calafuria I 155 Da66
Cala Galdana E 57 Ja66
Cala Gonone I 169 Cc76
Calahonda E 60 Cd77
Calahonda E 60 Dc76
Calahora de Boedo E 38 Db57
Calahorra E 39 Ec58
Calais F 21 Gc30
Cala Liberotto I 168 Cc76
Cala Llenya E 56 Gc69
Cala Llonga E 56 Gc69
Calalzo di Cadore I 143 Eb56
Cala Major E 57 Hb67
Calambrone I 155 Da65
Cala Mesquida E 57 Jb66
Cala Millor E 57 Hd67
Calamocha E 47 Ed63
Calamonaci I 166 Ec86
Calamonte E 51 Bd69
Cala Morell E 57 Ja65
Călan RO 175 Cc61
Calañas E 59 Bb72
Calanda E 48 Fc63
Calangianus I 168 Cb74
Cala Pi E 57 Hb68
Calapica BG 180 Db73
Cala Rajada E 57 Hd67
Călăraşi MD 173 Fc57
Călăraşi RO 171 Da59
Călăraşi RO 173 Fa56
Călăraşi RO 179 Da68
Călăraşi RO 181 Ed67
Cala Rossa F 154 Cb72
Cala Sant Vicenç E 56 Gc69
Cala Sant Vicenç E 57 Hc66
Calascibetta I 167 Fa85
Călăşeni MD 173 Fa55
Calasetta I 169 Bc80
Calasparra E 61 Ec72
Calatafimi-Segesta I 166 Eb84
Calatañazor E 47 Ea60
Calatayud E 47 Ed61
Călăţele RO 171 Cd58
Calaţii Bistriţei RO 171 Dc57
Calatorao E 47 Ed61
Cala Turqueta E 57 Ja66
Calau D 128 Fa39
Cala Vedella E 56 Gb69
Calbe D 127 Ea38
Calberlah D 126 Dc36
Calçakırlar TR 192 Fd87
Calcatoggio F 154 Ca70
Calcena E 47 Ec60
Çalcı TR 193 Ha81
Calcinelli I 156 Ec65
Calcio I 149 Cd59
Calco I 149 Cc58
Căldăraru RO 175 Dc66
Caldaro I 142 Dc56
Caldarola I 156 Ec67
Caldas da Felgueira P 44 Ba63
Caldas da Rainha P 50 Ab66
Caldas de Monchique P 58 Ab73
Caldas de Reis E 36 Ad56
Caldas de Vizela P 44 Ad60
Caldbeck GB 11 Eb17
Calde E 36 Bb55
Caldearenas E 39 Fb58
Caldebarcos E 36 Ac55
Caldelas E 36 Ad58
Caldelas P 44 Ad60
Caldelas P 44 Ad59
Calden D 126 Da39
Calderari I 167 Fb86
Çaldere TR 192 Fb82
Calder Mains GB 5 Eb04
Calders E 49 Gd60
Caldes de Boí E 40 Ga58
Caldes de Malavella E 49 Hb60
Caldes de Montbui E 49 Gd60
Caldirola I 149 Cc62
Caldueño E 38 Da54
Caleao E 37 Cc55
Caledon GB 9 Cd18
Calella E 49 Hb60
Calella de Palafrugell E 49 Hc60
Calenzana F 154 Ca69
Calera de León E 51 Bd71
Calera y Chozas E 52 Cd66
Caleruega E 46 Dc60
Caleruela E 52 Cc66
Cales de Mallorca E 57 Hc67
Calestano I 149 Da62
Calfa MD 173 Ga58
Calfsound GB 5 Ec02
Calgary GB 6 Da10
Çalı TR 186 Fc80
Çalıbahçe TR 191 Ec84
Càlig E 48 Fd64
Calignac F 40 Fd52
Călimăneşti RO 175 Db63
Călineşti MD 173 Fa56
Călineşti RO 171 Db55
Călineşti RO 175 Dc64
Călineşti RO 180 Dd67
Călineşti-Oaş RO 171 Da54
Çalışlar TR 193 Gc85
Calitri I 161 Fd75
Calizzano I 148 Bd63
Çalkara TR 193 Gc81
Çalkaya TR 193 Ha81
Çalkaya TR 199 Gd91
Çalköy TR 193 Gb84
Çalköy TR 193 Gb84
Callac F 26 Ea38
Callainn IRL 13 Cb24
Callan IRL 13 Cb24
Callander GB 7 Dd12
Callanish GB 4 Da05
Callantsoog NL 116 Ba34
Callas F 43 Kb53
Callelongue F 42 Jc55
Calliano I 148 Ca60
Calliano I 149 Dc58
Çallıca TR 199 Gb89
Çallıcaalan TR 187 Ha80
Callington GB 18 Dc31
Callosa d'En Sarrià E 55 Fc70
Callosa de Segura E 55 Fa72
Callow IRL 8 Bd19
Callús E 49 Gd60
Čalma SRB 153 Ja61
Călmăneşti RO 176 Ed61
Călmăţuiu RO 180 Dc67
Călmăţuiu de Sus RO 180 Dc67
Calne GB 20 Ed28
Calnegre y Los Curas E 55 Ed74
Călnic RO 175 Cc64
Călnic RO 175 Da61
Calolziocorte I 149 Cd58
Calonge E 49 Hc60
Calonge E 57 Hc68
Calonne-Ricouart F 23 Gd31
Calopăr RO 175 Cd66
Calp E 55 Fd70
Calpe E 55 Fd70
Caltabellotta I 166 Ec85
Caltagirone I 167 Fb87
Caltanissetta I 167 Fa86
Caltavuturo I 167 Fa85
Çaltepe TR 193 Ga89
Çaltepe TR 199 Ha90
Çaltı TR 193 Gb81
Çaltı TR 198 Ga88
Çaltıçukur TR 199 Hb91
Çaltıkkoru TR 191 Ec83
Çaltılıbük TR 192 Fc81
Caltojar E 47 Ea61
Călugăreni RO 180 Ea67
Caluso I 148 Bd59
Calvão P 44 Ac63
Calvarrasa de Abajo E 45 Cb62
Calvello I 161 Ga76
Calver GB 16 Fa22
Calvering GB 20 Fd26
Calverrasa de Arriba E 45 Cb62
Calvi F 154 Ca69
Calvià E 56 Ha67
Calviac F 33 Gd50
Calvi dell' Umbria I 156 Eb70
Calvine GB 7 Ea10
Calvinet F 33 Ha50
Calvini RO 176 Eb63
Calvisson F 42 Ja53
Calvos de Randín E 36 Ba58
Calw D 134 Cc48
Calzada de Bureba E 38 Dd57
Calzada de Calatrava E 52 Db70
Calzada del Coto E 37 Cd58
Calzada de los Molinos E 38 Da58
Calzada de Valdunciel E 45 Cb62
Calzadilla E 45 Bd65
Calzadilla de los Barros E 51 Bd71
Camaiore I 155 Da64
Çamalan TR 192 Fd82
Çamalan TR 193 Gd81
Camaldoli I 156 Dd65
Camaleño E 38 Da55
Çamaltı İskelesi TR 191 Eb86
Camañas E 47 Fa64
Camăr RO 171 Cc56
Camarasa E 48 Ga60
Çamarası TR 198 Fc88
Cămăraşu RO 171 Db58
Camarena E 46 Db65
Camarena de la Sierra E 47 Fa65
Camarenilla E 52 Db66
Camarès F 41 Hb53
Camaret-sur-Mer F 26 Db38
Camarinal E 59 Ca78
Camariñas E 36 Ac54
Camarles E 48 Ga63
Camarma de Esteruelas E 46 Dc64
Camarmeña E 38 Da55
Cămărzana RO 171 Da54
Camarzana de Tera E 45 Cb59
Camas E 59 Bd74
Camastra I 166 Ed86
Cambados E 36 Ad56
Cambas P 44 Ba65
Cambazlı TR 192 Fa85
Çambel TR 191 Ed86
Cambela E 36 Bc58
Cambeo E 36 Bb57
Camber GB 21 Ga30
Çambeyli TR 193 Gb85
Cambil E 60 Dc73
Camblesforth GB 16 Fb20
Cambo GB 11 Ed16
Cambo-les-Bains F 39 Ed55
Camborne GB 18 Da32
Cambra P 44 Ad62
Cambrai F 24 Hb32
Cambre E 36 Ba54
Cambres P 44 Ba61
Cambridge GB 20 Fd26
Cambrils E 48 Gb62
Cambs D 119 Ea32
Camburg D 127 Ea41
Çamcı TR 191 Ec82
Çamdere TR 192 Fd86
Çamdibi TR 192 Ga83
Camedo CH 148 Cb57
Camelford GB 18 Dc31
Çameli TR 198 Fd90
Camelle E 36 Ac54
Camenca MD 173 Fa55
Camenca MD 173 Fd54
Camerano I 156 Ed66
Camerata Cornello I 149 Cd58
Cameri I 148 Cb59
Camerino I 156 Ec67
Camerota I 161 Fd77
Çamiçi TR 191 Ec85
Çamiçi TR 197 Ed89
Camiers F 23 Gc31
Çamiliyayla TR 192 Ga82
Caminha P 36 Ac58
Caminomorisco E 45 Ca64
Caminreal E 47 Ed63
Çamırdık TR 192 Ga84
Camisano Vicentino I 150 Dd59
Çamızlar TR 198 Fd92
Çamkonak TR 187 Gc77
Çamköy TR 191 Ea81
Çamköy TR 197 Ed90
Çamköy TR 198 Ga90
Çamköy TR 199 Gd91
Çamlı TR 187 Ha78
Çamlı TR 191 Eb86
Çamlı TR 197 Fa90
Çamlıca TR 191 Ea81
Çamlıca TR 199 Hb88
Çamlıdere TR 199 Gc89
Çamlık TR 192 Fc83
Çamlık TR 197 Ec88
Çamlık TR 197 Ed90
Çamlık TR 199 Hb89
Çamlıkköy TR 191 Ec82
Çamlıköy TR 198 Fd92
Çamlitepe TR 199 Hb91
Cammarata I 166 Ed85
Camogli I 149 Cc63
Camolin IRL 13 Cd24
Camoluk TR 198 Fb89
Çamönü TR 192 Fa84
Camors F 27 Ea40
Camp IRL 12 Ba24
Campagna I 161 Fd75
Campagnano di Roma I 156 Ea70
Campagne F 39 Fb53
Campana I 165 Gd79
Campanario E 51 Cb69
Campanas E 39 Ed57
Campanet E 57 Hb66
Câmpani RO 171 Cc58
Campanillas E 60 Cd76
Campaspero E 46 Db61
Campbeltown GB 10 Db14
Campel F 27 Ec40
Campénéac F 27 Ec40
Câmpeni MD 177 Fc62
Câmpeni RO 171 Cd59
Camperduin NL 116 Ba34
Campia P 44 Ad62
Campi Bisenzio I 155 Dc65
Câmpie Turzii RO 171 Da59
Campiglia Marittima I 155 Da67
Campiglia Soana I 148 Bc59
Campigliatello Silano I 164 Gc80
Campigna I 156 Dd65
Campillo E 45 Cb60
Campillo E 47 Fa65
Campillo de Altobuey E 53 Ec67
Campillo de Arenas E 60 Db74
Campillo de Azaba E 45 Bd63
Campillo de Deleitosa E 51 Cb66
Campillo de Dueñas E 47 Ed63
Campillo de las Doblas E 53 Ec70
Campillo de Llerena E 51 Ca70
Campillos E 60 Cc75
Campillos Sierra E 47 Ec65
Câmpina RO 176 Ea64
Çampınar TR 191 Ed85
Câmpineanca RO 176 Ed62
Campisábalos E 46 Dd62
Campi Salentina I 162 Hb76
Campitello F 154 Cb69
Campitello di Fassa I 143 Dd56
Campitello Matese I 161 Fb73
Campli I 156 Ed69
Camplongo E 37 Cc56
Campo E 40 Fd58
Campo Arcis E 54 Fa68
Campobasso I 161 Fc72
Campobecerros E 36 Bc58
Campobello di Licata I 167 Fa86
Campobello di Mazara I 166 Eb85
Campo Blénio CH 142 Cc55
Campocologno CH 149 Da57
Campodarsego I 150 Ea59
Campo de Besteiros P 44 Ad63
Campo de Caso E 37 Cd55
Campo de Criptana E 53 Dd68
Campo del Hospital E 36 Bb53
Campo de San Pedro E 46 Dc61
Campo de Víboras P 45 Bd60
Campo di Giove I 161 Fa71
Campodimele I 160 Ed73
Campo do Gerês P 44 Ba59
Campodolcino I 142 Cd56
Campo Felice I 156 Ed70
Campofelice di Roccella I 167 Fa84
Campofiorito I 166 Ec85
Campofrío E 59 Bc72
Campogalliano I 149 Db62
Campohermoso E 61 Eb76
Campolasta I 143 Dd56
Campolattaro I 161 Fc73
Campoli Appennino I 160 Ed72
Campo Ligure I 148 Cb62
Campolongo E 36 Ba54
Campolongo Maggiore I 150 Ea60
Campo Lugar E 51 Cb68
Campo Maior P 51 Bb68
Campomarino I 161 Fc71
Campomarino I 162 Ha76
Camponaraya E 37 Bd57
Campora San Giovanni I 164 Gb81
Campo Real E 46 Dc65
Camporeale I 166 Ec84
Campo Redondo P 58 Ab72
Camporrells E 48 Ga59
Camporrobles E 54 Ed67
Campos E 57 Hc68
Camposampiero I 150 Ea59
Camposancos E 36 Ac58
Camposanto I 149 Dc62
Campo Staffi I 160 Ed71
Campotéjar E 60 Db74
Campo Tenese I 164 Gb78
Campotosto I 156 Ed69
Campo Tures I 143 Ea55
Campo Vallemaggia CH 141 Cb56
Campo Xestada E 36 Ad54
Camprodon E 41 Ha58
Camps-en-Amiénois F 23 Gc33
Camptown GB 11 Ec15
Câmpu lui Neag RO 175 Cc62
Câmpulung RO 175 Dc63
Câmpulung la Tisa RO 171 Db54
Câmpulung Moldovenesc RO 172 Ea56
Câmpuri RO 176 Ec61
Camrose GB 14 Db26
Çamsu TR 192 Ga85
Çamucu TR 191 Ed82
Camuñas E 52 Dc68
Çamurköy TR 198 Fd92
Çamurluk TR 187 Gd80
Çamyayla TR 193 Gb81
Çamyazı TR 192 Fd85
Çamyuva TR 192 Ga85
Çamyuva TR 199 Gc92
Çan TR 191 Ec81
Čaňa SK 139 Jd49
Canabal E 36 Bb57
Cañada E 55 Fa70
Cañada de la Cruz E 61 Eb72
Cañada del Hoyo E 53 Ec66
Cañada del Rosal E 60 Cc73
Cañadajuncosa E 53 Eb67
Cañada Vellida E 47 Fa64
Cañadillas E 60 Cd74
Čanak HR 151 Fd62
Çanakçı TR 192 Fc83
Çanakçı TR 192 Fc86
Çanakçı TR 199 Gd91
Çanakkale TR 185 Ea80
Çanaklı TR 199 Gc89
Canale I 148 Bd61
Canalejas del Arroyo E 47 Eb65
Canals E 54 Fb69
Canal San Bovo I 150 Dd57
Cañamares E 47 Eb64
Cañamares E 53 Ea70
Cañamero E 51 Cb67
Canaples F 23 Gd33
Canara E 61 Ec72
Canari F 154 Cc68
Canas de Senhorim P 44 Ba63
Cañaveral E 51 Bd66
Cañaveral de León E 51 Bc71

Castel San Pietro Terme – Chalais

Castel San Pietro Terme I 150 Dd63
Castelsantangelo sul Nera I 156 Ec68
Castel San Vincenzo I 161 Fa72
Castelsaraceno I 162 Gb77
Castelsardo I 168 Ca74
Castelsarrasin F 40 Gb53
Castelseprio I 148 Cb58
Castelserás E 48 Fc63
Casteltermini I 166 Ed86
Castelu RO 181 Fb67
Castelvecchio I 149 Dc59
Castelvecchio di Rocca Barbena I 148 Bd63
Castelvecchio Subequo I 160 Ed71
Castelvetrano I 166 Eb85
Castel Viscardo I 156 Ea68
Castel Volturno I 161 Fa74
Castenedolo I 149 Da59
Castéra-Verduzan F 40 Fd53
Castets F 39 Fa53
Castex F 40 Fd55
Casti CH 142 Cd55
Castiadas I 169 Cb80
Castiblanco de los Arroyos E 59 Ca73
Castiello de Jaca E 39 Fb57
Castigaleu E 48 Ga59
Castiglioncello I 155 Da66
Castiglione I 161 Fb71
Castiglione Chiavarese I 149 Cc63
Castiglione dei Pepoli I 155 Dc64
Castiglione del Lago I 156 Ea67
Castiglione della Pescaia I 155 Db68
Castiglione delle Stiviere I 149 Db60
Castiglione di Garfagnana I 155 Da64
Castiglione di Sicilia I 167 Fd84
Castiglione d'Orcia I 156 Dd68
Castiglione Olona I 148 Cb58
Castiglion Fiorentino I 156 Dd66
Castilblanco E 52 Cc68
Castil de Peones E 38 Dd58
Castilfabib E 47 Ed65
Castilfrío de la Sierra E 47 Eb60
Castiliscar E 39 Fa58
Castilléjar E 61 Ea73
Castillejo de Iniesta E 53 Ec67
Castillejo de Martín Viejo E 45 Bd63
Castillejo de Mesleón E 46 Dc61
Castillejo de Robledo E 46 Dc61
Castillo de Bayuela E 46 Cd65
Castillo de Garcimuñoz E 53 Eb67
Castillo de la Reina E 46 Dd59
Castillo de Locubín E 60 Db74
Castillon-du-Gard F 42 Ja53
Castillon-en-Couserans F 40 Gb56
Castillon-la-Bataille F 32 Fc50
Castillonnès F 33 Ga51
Castilruiz E 47 Ec60
Castino I 148 Ca62
Castione della Presolana I 149 Da58
Castions di Strada I 150 Ec58
Částkov CZ 135 Ec45
Castle Acre GB 17 Ga24
Castle Ashby GB 20 Fb25
Castlebaldwin IRL 8 Ca18
Castlebar IRL 8 Bc19
Castlebay GB 6 Cc09
Castlebellingham IRL 9 Cd19
Castleblayney IRL 9 Cd19
Castlebridge IRL 13 Cd24
Castle Bytham GB 17 Fc24
Castle Cary GB 19 Ec29
Castle Combe GB 19 Ec28
Castlecomer IRL 13 Cb23
Castlecove IRL 12 Ba26
Castlederg GB 9 Cb16
Castledermot IRL 13 Cc23
Castle Douglas GB 10 Ea16
Castlefinn IRL 9 Cb16
Castleford GB 16 Fa20
Castlegal IRL 8 Ca17
Castlehill IRL 8 Bb18
Castleisland IRL 12 Bb24
Castlejordan IRL 13 Cc21
Castlemaine IRL 12 Bb24
Castlemartin GB 18 Db27
Castlemartyr IRL 13 Ca26
Castlepollard IRL 9 Cb20
Castlerea IRL 8 Bd19
Castleton GB 16 Ed22
Castleton GB 19 Eb28
Castletown GB 5 Eb04
Castletown GB 10 Dc19
Castletown IRL 12 Bc24
Castletown IRL 13 Cb21
Castletown IRL 13 Cd23
Castletownbere IRL 12 Ba26
Castletownshead IRL 12 Bb27
Castlewellan GB 9 Da18
Casto I 149 Da59
Castranova RO 179 Da67
Castrejón E 45 Cc61
Castrejón de la Peña E 38 Da56
Castrelo do Val E 36 Bb58
Castrelos P 45 Bd59
Castres F 41 Gd54
Castres-Gironde F 32 Fb51
Castricum NL 116 Ad35
Castries F 41 Hd54
Castril E 61 Ea73
Castrillo de Cabezón E 38 Db58
Castrillo de Don Juan E 46 Db60
Castrillo de la Vega E 46 Dc60
Castrillo de Río Pisuerga E 38 Db57
Castrillo de Sepúlveda E 46 Dc61
Castrillo de Villavega E 38 Da57
Castrillo-Tejeriego E 46 Da60
Castriz E 36 Ad54
Castro E 36 Ba53
Castro E 36 Bb57
Castro E 36 Bc55
Castrobarto E 38 Dd56
Castrobol E 37 Cc58
Castrocalbón E 37 Cb58
Castro Caldelas E 36 Bc57
Castro (Carballedo) E 36 Bb57
Castrocaro Terme I 156 Ea64
Castrocontrigo E 37 Ca58
Castro Daire P 44 Ba62
Castro de Filabres E 61 Ea75
Castro de Fuentidueña E 46 Dc61
Castro dei Volsci I 160 Ed73
Castro del Río E 60 Cd73
Castro de Rei E 36 Bc54
Castro (Dozón) E 36 Ba56
Castrofilippo I 166 Ed86
Castrojeriz E 38 Db58
Castro Laboreiro P 36 Ba58
Castromao E 36 Bc58
Castro Marim P 58 Ba74
Castro Marina I 163 Hc77
Castromonte E 46 Cd60
Castronuevo E 45 Cc60
Castronuño E 45 Cc61
Castronuovo di San Andrea I 162 Gb77
Castronuovo di Sicilia I 166 Ed85
Castropol E 37 Bd54
Castrop-Rauxel D 125 Ca39
Castroreale I 167 Fd84
Castroreale Terme I 167 Fd84
Castro-Urdiales E 38 Dd55
Castrovega de Valmadrigal E 37 Cc58
Castroverde E 36 Bc55
Castro Verde P 58 Ac72
Castroverde de Campos E 45 Cc59
Castroverde de Cerrato E 46 Db60
Castroviejo E 38 Ea58
Castrovillari I 164 Gb78
Castuera E 51 Cb69
Caşunca MD 173 Fc55
Çat TR 205 Ga20
Cața RO 176 Dd60
Çatacık TR 187 Gd80
Cataeggio I 149 Cd57
Çatak TR 192 Fa86
Çatak TR 193 Gc87
Çataklı TR 186 Ga77
Çatalağil TR 186 Fc80
Çatalağzı TR 187 Hb76
Çatalca TR 186 Fb77
Çatalçam TR 192 Fb82
Catalina RO 176 Eb61
Çatalköprü TR 187 Gc78
Çatallar TR 199 Gb92
Çatallar TR 199 Gd90
Cataloi RO 177 Fc64
Çataltepe TR 186 Fd80
Catane RO 179 Cd67
Catania I 167 Fd86
Catanzaro I 164 Gc81
Catanzaro Marina I 164 Gc81
Catarroja E 54 Fb68
Câțcău RO 171 Da56
Căteasca RO 175 Dc65
Cățeleni MD 173 Fb58
Catenanuova I 167 Fc85
Cateraggio F 154 Cc70
Caterham GB 20 Fc29
Čatež SLO 151 Fc58
Cathair na Mart IRL 8 Bc19
Cathair Saidhbhín IRL 12 Ba25
Cati E 48 Fd64
Catignano I 157 Fa70
Cătina RO 171 Db58
Cătina RO 176 Eb63
Catívelos P 44 Ba63
Çatkuyu TR 193 Gc85
Catlowdy GB 11 Ec16
Catoira E 36 Ad56
Çatoluk TR 198 Ga93
Catral E 55 Fa72
Cattedrale di Anagni I 160 Ec72
Catterick Bridge GB 11 Fa18
Catterick Garrison GB 11 Ed18
Cattolica I 156 Eb65
Cattolica Eraclea I 166 Ec86
Cătunele RO 175 Cc64
Catus F 33 Gb51
Căuaş RO 171 Cc55
Caudebec-en-Caux F 23 Ga34
Caudebec-lès-Elbeuf F 23 Gb35
Caudecoste F 40 Ga52
Caudete E 55 Fa70
Caudete de las Fuentes E 54 Ed67
Caudiel E 54 Fb66
Caudiès-de-Fenouillèdes F 41 Ha57
Caudrot F 32 Fc51
Caudry F 24 Hb32
Caujac F 40 Gc55
Caulnes F 27 Ec39
Caulonia I 164 Gc83
Caumont F 40 Gb53
Caumont-l'Éventé F 22 Fb36
Caumont-sur-Durance F 42 Jb53
Caunes-Minervois F 41 Ha55
Cauro F 154 Ca71
Căuşeni MD 173 Ga59
Causeway IRL 12 Bb24
Çaush AL 182 Ab79
Caussade F 40 Gc52
Cautano I 161 Fb74
Cauterets F 40 Fc56
Cava d'Aliga I 167 Fc88
Cava de' Tirreni I 161 Fc75
Cavadineşti RO 177 Fb61
Cavagnac F 33 Gd51
Cavaillon F 42 Jc53
Cavalaire-sur-Mer F 43 Kb55
Cavaleiro P 58 Ab72
Cavalese I 150 Dd57
Cavalière F 43 Kb55
Cavallermaggiore I 148 Bc61
Cavallino I 150 Eb60
Cavan IRL 9 Cb19
Cavanagarvan IRL 9 Cc18
Căvăran RO 174 Ca61
Cavarzere I 150 Ea61
Cavazzo Carnico I 150 Ec57
Çavdar TR 197 Ed88
Çavdar TR 198 Fb89
Çavdarhisar TR 192 Ga84
Çavdır TR 198 Fd93
Çavdır TR 198 Ga90
Cave di Predil I 143 Ed56
Caveirac F 42 Ja53
Cavertitz D 127 Ed40
Cavezzo I 149 Dc61
Cavi I 149 Cc63
Cavignac F 32 Fc49
Čavle HR 151 Fb60
Cavnic RO 171 Db55
Cavo I 155 Da68
Cavour I 148 Bc61
Cavriglia I 156 Dd66
Cavtat HR 159 Hc69
Çavuşbaşı TR 186 Fd77
Çavuşçugöl TR 193 Hb86
Çavuşköy TR 185 Ec76
Çavuşköy TR 199 Gc93
Çavuşlu TR 187 Gb78
Cavusy BY 202 Ec12
Cawood GB 16 Fa20
Cawsand GB 18 Dc32
Cawston GB 17 Gb24
Caxarias P 50 Ac66
Caxton GB 20 Fc26
Çay TR 193 Gd86
Çayağazı TR 187 Ha77
Çayağzı TR 186 Fa79
Çayağzı TR 186 Fd77
Çayeli TR 205 Ga19
Cayeux-sur-Mer F 23 Gb32
Çayhisar TR 198 Fc91
Çayır TR 198 Fc90
Çayırgan TR 198 Fc89
Çayırhan TR 193 Hb81
Çayıroluk TR 192 Ga82
Çayıryaka TR 193 Gd86
Çayıryazı TR 193 Gd86
Çaykışla TR 192 Fc86
Çaykışla TR 193 Ha85
Çayköy TR 187 Gc79
Çayköy TR 193 Gc81
Çayköy TR 199 Gd88
Çaylakköy TR 187 Gd80
Çaylar TR 205 Ga20
Caylus F 40 Gc52
Caynham GB 15 Ec25
Çayören TR 192 Fd82
Çaypınar TR 192 Fa81
Çaypınar TR 192 Fa86
Cayres F 34 Hd50
Cayrols F 33 Gd50
Caythorpe GB 16 Fb23
Cazaclia MD 177 Fc61
Cazalegas E 46 Cd65
Cazalla de la Sierra E 59 Ca72
Cazals F 33 Gb51
Căzăneşti MD 173 Fc56
Căzăneşti RO 173 Fa58
Căzăneşti RO 175 Cc64
Căzăneşti RO 176 Ed66
Cazangic MD 173 Fc59
Cazanuecos E 37 Cb58
Cazaubon F 40 Fc53
Cazaux F 32 Fa51
Cazères F 40 Gb55
Cazes-Mondenard F 40 Gb52
Cazin BIH 151 Ga61
Čazma HR 152 Gc59
Cazorla E 61 Dd72
Cazouls-lès-Béziers F 41 Hb55
Cea E 37 Cd57
Ceadea E 45 Ca60
Ceadîr-Lunga MD 177 Fd61
Ceahlău RO 172 Eb57
Cealâd MD 177 Fc62
Ceamurlia de Jos RO 177 Fc65
Ceanannus Mór IRL 9 Cc20
Ceann Toirc IRL 12 Bc24
Ceanu Mare RO 171 Db58
Ceapach Choinn IRL 13 Ca25
Cea (San Cristóbal de Cea) E 36 Ba57
Ceatad RO 174 Bc60
Ceatalchioi RO 177 Fc64
Ceatharlach IRL 13 Cc23
Ceaucé F 28 Fb38
Ceauşu de Câmpie RO 171 Dc58
Cebara BIH 158 Gd66
Cebas E 61 Dd73
Cebeceiras de Basto P 44 Ba60
Cebeci TR 187 Gb77
Čeboksary RUS 203 Fc09
Cebolais de Cima P 50 Ba66
Cebolla E 52 Da66
Cebrail TR 193 Hb85
Cebreros E 46 Da64
Cebrones del Río E 37 Cb58
Čečava BIH 152 Ha62
Ceccano I 160 Ec72
Cece H 146 Hc55
Čečejovce SK 138 Jc49
Čečel'nyk UA 204 Ec16
Cecenowo PL 121 Gd29
Čechtice CZ 136 Fc46
Čechtín CZ 136 Ga47
Čechy pod Kosířem CZ 137 Gc46
Cecina I 155 Da66
Ceclavín E 51 Bc66
Cecos E 37 Bd55
Čečovice CZ 135 Ec46
Čedasai LT 114 La53
Cedegolo I 149 Da57
Cedeira E 36 Bb53
Cedillo E 51 Bb66
Cedrillas E 47 Fa64
Cedynia PL 120 Fb35
Cée E 36 Ac55
Cefa RO 170 Ca57
Cefalù I 167 Fa84
Ceggia I 150 Eb59
Cegléd H 146 Ja54
Ceglie Messapica I 162 Ha75
Cegłów PL 131 Jd37
Čegrane MK 178 Ba73
Cehal RO 171 Cc56
Cehăluţ RO 171 Cc55
Cehegín E 61 Ec72
Čehlare BG 180 Dc72
Čehov RUS 203 Fa11
Čehovo RUS 113 Ja59
Cehu Silvaniei RO 171 Cd56
Ceica RO 170 Cb57
Ceikiniai LT 115 Lc55
Ceilhes-et-Rocozels F 41 Hb53
Ceinos de Campos E 46 Cd59
Ceintrey F 25 Jd37
Ceira P 44 Ad64
Ceivães P 36 Ad58
Čejč CZ 137 Gc48
Čejkov SK 139 Ka49
Čejkovice CZ 137 Gc48
Cekcyn PL 121 Ha33
Çekerek TR 205 Fb20
Çekirdekli TR 192 Fa83
Čekiškė LV 114 Kb56
Čekonje MNE 159 Hd69
Ceków-Kolonia PL 129 Ha38
Cela E 36 Bc56
Celada E 37 Cb57
Celadas E 47 Fa64
Čelákovice CZ 136 Fc44
Celano I 160 Ed71
Celanova E 36 Ba58
Čelanovo RUS 107 Ma50
Čelarevo SRB 153 Ja60
Celaru RO 179 Da67
Celbowo PL 121 Ha29
Celbridge IRL 13 Cd21
Čelebić BIH 158 Gc65
Čelebići BIH 159 Hd66
Celeiro P 44 Ba60
Celepköy TR 186 Fb76
Celerina CH 142 Da56
Celestynów PL 130 Jc37
Čelić BIH 153 Hd62
Čelije SRB 153 Jc63
Çelikler TR 192 Fc83
Celina CZ 136 Fb46
Celina RUS 205 Fd15
Čelinac Donji BIH 152 Gd62
Celjachany BY 202 Ea13
Celje SLO 151 Fd57
Cella E 47 Ed64
Cellarhead GB 16 Ed23
Celldömölk H 145 Gd54
Celle D 126 Db36
Celle Ligure I 148 Ca63
Cellers E 48 Ga59
Celles B 124 Ad42
Celles-sur-Belle F 32 Fc45
Cellettes F 29 Gb41
Celliers F 35 Ka47
Cellino San Marco I 162 Hb76
Cellole I 161 Fa74
Celmenieki LV 105 Jc52
Celmini LV 106 Kb51
Čelopeč BG 179 Da71
Čelopeci MK 182 Ba74
Čelopek MK 178 Ba73
Celorico da Beira P 44 Bb63
Cel'ovce SK 139 Ka49
Celrà E 49 Hb59
Çeltek TR 199 Gb89
Çeltik TR 185 Eb78
Çeltik TR 186 Fb77
Çeltik TR 193 Hb84
Çeltikçi TR 186 Fa79
Çeltikçi TR 186 Ga80
Çeltikçi TR 199 Gc89
Çeltikçi TR 199 Ha91
Çeltikdere TR 187 Hb80
Cemalçavus TR 192 Fc85
Cembra I 149 Dc57
Cemerno BIH 159 Hc67
Čeminac HR 153 Hc59
Çemişgezek TR 205 Fd20
Cemke TR 186 Fd77
Cemmaes Road GB 15 Ea24
Cempi LV 106 Kd48
Cenac MD 177 Fc60
Cenad RO 170 Bb59
Cenade RO 175 Da60
Cenajo E 53 Ec71
Cenarth GB 14 Dc26
Cenas LV 106 Kb51
Cencenighe Agordino I 150 Ea57
Çendik TR 199 Gb88
Cenei RO 174 Bc60
Čenej SRB 153 Jb60
Çeneköy TR 185 Ec77
Cenes de la Vega E 60 Dc75
Ceneselli I 149 Dc61
Cénevières F 33 Gc51
Çengelli TR 185 Ed77
Çenger TR 198 Fd91
Çenger TR 199 Hb92
Cengio I 148 Bd62
Cenicero E 38 Ea58
Cenicientos E 46 Da65
Cenizate E 53 Ec68
Cenlle E 36 Ba57
Čenovan SLO 151 Fa58
Cenovo BG 180 Dd69
Censeau F 31 Jd43
Čenta SRB 153 Jc60
Centallo I 148 Bc62
Centelles E 49 Ha60
Cento I 149 Dc62
Centuri F 154 Cc67
Centuripe I 167 Fc85
Cepagatti I 157 Fa70
Cepăria MD 173 Fb55
Čepelare BG 184 Db75
Cepeleuţi MD 173 Fa53
Cépet F 40 Gc54
Čepić HR 151 Fa61
Čepigova MK 183 Bb75
Čepin HR 153 Hc59
Ceplenița RO 172 Ed56
Çepni TR 186 Fa80
Çepni TR 186 Fc80
Çepni TR 193 Gb85
Ceppo I 156 Ed69
Ceprano I 160 Ed73
Ceptura RO 176 Eb64
Cequeril E 36 Ad56
Čer MK 182 Ba75
Cerachovka BY 202 Ec13
Čeralije HR 152 Ha59
Cerami I 167 Fb85
Cerano I 148 Cb59
Ceranów PL 123 Jd35
Cérans-Foulletourte F 28 Fd40
Ceraso I 161 Fd77
Cerașu RO 176 Eb63
Cerăt RO 179 Cd67
Ceraukste LV 106 Kc52
Cëravë AL 182 Ad76
Cerbaia I 155 Dc65
Cerbăl RO 175 Cc61
Cerbère F 41 Hc58
Cercadillo E 47 Ea62
Cercal P 50 Ab67
Cercal P 58 Ab72
Čerčany CZ 136 Fc45
Cerceda E 36 Ba55
Cerceda E 46 Db63
Cercedilla E 46 Db63
Cercemaggiore I 161 Fc73
Cerchezu RO 181 Fb68
Cerchiara di Calabria I 164 Gc78
Cercs E 49 Gd59
Cercy-la-Tour F 30 Hc43
Cerda I 166 Ed84
Čerdakly RUS 203 Fd09
Cerdanyola E 49 Gd61
Cerdedelo E 36 Bc58
Cerdedo E 36 Ad56
Cerdeira P 45 Bc63
Cerdeirinhas P 44 Ba59
Cerdon F 29 Gd41
Céré F 29 Gc43
Cēre LV 105 Jd50
Cerea I 149 Dc60
Cereceda E 38 Dd57
Cerecinos de Campos E 45 Cc59
Cered H 146 Ja50
Cereglio I 149 Dc63
Čerëha RUS 107 Ma47
Cerekwica PL 121 Gd35
Cerekwica PL 129 Gb36
Cérences F 22 Fa37
Čerencovo RUS 202 Eb08
Cerentino CH 141 Cb56
Cerenzia I 165 Gd80
Cereo E 36 Ad54
Čerepovec RUS 202 Ed08
Čerepovo BG 185 Ea74
Ceres I 148 Bc60
Čereša BG 181 Ec71
Čereševo BG 180 Eb68
Ceresole Reale I 148 Bc59
Čerešovica BG 179 Cb69
Céreste F 42 Jd53
Céret F 41 Hb58
Čeretelevo BG 180 Db73
Čerević SRB 153 Ja60
Cerezal E 45 Ca64
Cerezal de Peñahorcada E 45 Bd61
Cerezo de Abajo E 46 Dc62
Cerezo de Riotirón E 38 Dd58
Cergău RO 175 Da60
Cergnago I 148 Cb60
Ceriana I 43 La52
Cerić HR 153 Hd60
Cëricë AL 182 Ac77
Cerignola I 161 Ga73
Cérilly F 29 Ha44
Cérilly F 30 Ja40
Čerin BIH 158 Ha67
Čerin SK 138 Hd49
Cerisiers F 30 Hb39
Cérisy-la-Forêt F 22 Fb36
Cerisy-la-Salle F 22 Fa36
Cerityaylası TR 193 Gb87
Cerizay F 28 Fb43
Cerjë AL 182 Ba77
Čerkaski BG 179 Cc69
Čerkasy UA 204 Ed15
Çerkeş TR 205 Fa20
Çerkeşli TR 186 Ga78
Çerkesli TR 187 Gb80
Čerkessk RUS 205 Fd17
Çerkezköy TR 186 Fa77
Çerkezmüsellim TR 185 Ec76
Cerkiewnik PL 122 Ja31
Cerklje SLO 151 Fb57
Cerklje ob Krki SLO 151 Fd58
Cerknica SLO 151 Fb59
Cerkno SLO 151 Fa57
Čerkovna BG 180 Eb70
Cērkste LV 106 Ka50
Cerkvenjak SLO 144 Ga56
Cerkwica PL 120 Fc31
Cerlina MD 173 Fc54
Čerma RUS 99 Lc43
Cermë e poshtëme AL 182 Ab75
Cermei RO 170 Ca58
Cermenate I 149 Cc58
Cermone I 156 Ec70
Čern' RUS 203 Fa12
Černa BG 181 Fa68
Cerna HR 153 Hc60
Cerna RO 177 Fb64
Cernache de Bonjardim P 44 Ad65
Černá Hora CZ 137 Gb47
Černaja Lahta RUS 99 Ma39
Cerna-Sat RO 174 Cb63
Cernat RO 176 Eb61
Cernătești RO 175 Cd65
Cernătești RO 176 Ec63
Černava RUS 203 Fa11
Černava RUS 203 Fa12
Cernavodă RO 181 Fb67
Čerņavskije LV 107 Ma52
Cernay F 31 Kb39
Cernay-la-Ville F 23 Gc37
Cerne Abbas GB 19 Ec30
Cernégula E 38 Dc57
Černeja RUS 107 Mb51
Cernele RO 175 Cd66
Cernești RO 171 Da55
Cerneux F 24 Hb37
Černëvo RUS 99 Ld44
Černica BG 181 Ec72
Cernica RO 176 Eb66
Černičevo BG 180 Db72
Černihiv UA 202 Ec14
Černik HR 152 Gd60
Černilov CZ 136 Ga44
Černi Osăm BG 180 Db71
Černi Rid BG 185 Ea75
Cernişoara RO 175 Da64
Cerniţa MD 173 Fc55
Černivci UA 204 Ea16
Černi Vit BG 179 Da71
Černi Vrăh BG 179 Cc68
Černjachiv UA 202 Eb14
Černjahovsk RUS 113 Jc59
Černjanka RUS 203 Fa13
Černjovo BG 179 Cd72
Černo RUS 99 Ld43
Cernobbio I 149 Cc58
Černochov CZ 136 Fa43
Černoe RUS 99 Mb41
Černogorovo BG 179 Da73
Černoleuca MD 173 Fa53
Černolik BG 181 Ed68
Černomorec BG 181 Fa73
Černoočene BG 184 Dc75
Černook BG 181 Ed70
Černookovo BG 181 Fb69
Černošice CZ 136 Fb45
Černošín CZ 135 Ec45
Černovice CZ 136 Fc47
Černovskoe RUS 99 Ld42
Cernoy-en-Berry F 29 Ha41
Černozemen BG 180 Db72
Cerny-en-Laonnois F 24 Hc35
Černyševskoe RUS 114 Ka58
Černyškovskij RUS 203 Fd14
Cerova SRB 179 Ca69
Cerovac HR 157 Ga64
Cerovac SRB 174 Bb66
Cerova Korija BG 180 Dd71
Cerovica SRB 178 Bd68
Cerovljani BIH 152 Gd61
Cerovlje HR 151 Fa60
Cerovo BG 179 Cc70
Cerovo BG 179 Cd72
Cerponzons E 36 Ad56
Cerqueto I 156 Ea68
Cerralbo E 45 Bd62
Cerredo E 37 Ca56
Cerredolo I 149 Db63
Cerreto d'Esi I 156 Ec67
Cerreto Sannita I 161 Fb73
Cerrigydrudion GB 15 Ea23
Cërrik AL 182 Ac75
Cerro al Volturno I 161 Fa72
Cerro Muriano E 60 Cd72
Čerskaja RUS 107 Ma47
Certaldo I 155 Dc66
Çerte TR 192 Ga83
Certeju de Sus RO 175 Cc60
Cerțeşti RO 177 Fa61
Certeze RO 171 Da54
Čertižné SK 139 Ka46
Čertkovo RUS 203 Fc14
Čertovidovo RUS 107 Ma48
Ceru-Băcăinţi RO 175 Cd60
Čerusti RUS 203 Fa10
Cervara di Roma I 160 Ec71
Cervaro I 161 Fa73
Cervatos de la Cueza E 38 Da58
Červen BG 184 Db74
Červen BG 180 Ea69
Červen' BY 202 Eb12
Červená CZ 136 Fb47
Çervenakë AL 182 Ad76
Červená Řečice CZ 136 Fd46
Červená Skalá SK 138 Jb48
Červena Voda BG 180 Ea68
Červená Voda CZ 137 Gc44
Červen Brjag BG 179 Da69
Červenci BG 181 Ed69
Cervenia RO 180 Dd68
Červený Kláštor SK 138 Jb46
Červený Kostelec CZ 136 Ga43
Cervera E 48 Gb60
Cervera de Buitrago E 46 Dc63
Cervera de Llano E 53 Eb66
Cervera del Maestrat E 48 Fd64
Cervera del Río Alhama E 47 Ec59
Cervera de Pisuerga E 38 Da56
Cervesina I 149 Cc60
Cerveteri I 160 Ea71
Cervia I 156 Eb64
Cervià de les Garrigues E 48 Ga61
Cervià de Ter E 49 Hb59
Cervico Navero E 46 Db59
Cervières F 35 Kb49
Cervignano di Friuli I 150 Ed59
Cervinara I 161 Fb74
Cervione F 154 Cc69
Cervo E 36 Bc53
Cervo I 43 La52
Cervon F 30 Hc42
Červonohrad UA 204 Dd15
Čërykav BY 202 Ec12
Cerzeto I 164 Gb79
Cesana Torinese I 148 Bb60
Cesarica HR 151 Fc63
Cesarò I 167 Fc85
Cesarowice PL 129 Gb41
Cescau F 39 Fb55
Cesena I 156 Ea64
Cesenatico I 156 Eb64
Cēsis LV 106 Kd49
Česká Bělá CZ 136 Ga46
Česká Kamenice CZ 128 Fb42
Česká Kubice CZ 135 Ec47
Česká Lípa CZ 128 Fb42
Česká Skalice CZ 136 Ga43
Česká Třebová CZ 137 Gb45
České Budějovice CZ 136 Fb48
České Velenice CZ 136 Fc49
Český Brod CZ 136 Fc44
Český Dub CZ 136 Fc43
Český Krumlov CZ 136 Fb49
Český Těšín CZ 137 Hb45
Çeşme TR 191 Ea86
Çeşmealtı TR 185 Ed80
Çeşmekolu TR 185 Ed76
Çeşmeköy TR 197 Ed88
Çeşmeköy TR 198 Ga93
Çeşmeli TR 186 Fa77
Cesole I 149 Db61
Cespedosa de Tormes E 45 Cb63
Cessenon F 41 Hb54
Cessières F 24 Hb34
Cestas F 32 Fb50
Čestice CZ 136 Fa47
Čestimensko BG 181 Ed68
Čestín CZ 136 Fd45
Čestobrodica SRB 159 Jb64
Cesuna I 150 Dd58
Cesvaine LV 107 Lb50
Cetara I 161 Fc75
Cetariu RO 170 Cb56
Cetate RO 171 Dc57
Cetate RO 175 Cc66
Cetatea de Baltă RO 175 Db60
Cetățeni RO 176 Dd63
Cetenov CZ 136 Fc43
Cetina E 47 Ec62
Çetince TR 193 Ha87
Cetingrad HR 151 Ga61
Cetinje MNE 159 Hd70
Četirci BG 179 Cb72
Cetireni MD 173 Fb57
Ceton F 29 Ga39
Cetona I 156 Dd68
Cetraro I 164 Gb79
Cetraro Marina I 164 Gb79
Céüse 2000 F 42 Jd51
Ceuta E 59 Cb79
Ceutí E 55 Ed72
Ceva I 148 Bd62
Cevico de la Torre E 46 Da59
Cevio CH 141 Cb56
Cevizli TR 193 Gd83
Cevizli TR 199 Hb90
Çevlik TR 199 Gb88
Čevo MNE 159 Hd69
Cewice PL 121 Gd30
Cewków PL 139 Kc43
Ceylanköy TR 198 Ga91
Ceyzériat F 35 Jc45
Cézens F 34 Hb49
Cezieni RO 175 Da66
Cezura E 38 Db56
Chaam NL 124 Ad38
Chabanais F 33 Ga47
Chabeuil F 34 Jb49
Chabielice PL 130 Hc40
Chablis F 30 Hc40
Chabrac F 33 Ga46
Chabreloche F 34 Hc46
Chabris F 29 Gc42
Chacim P 45 Bd60
Chaffayer F 35 Jd50
Chaffois F 31 Jd43
Chagny F 30 Ja43
Chailland F 28 Fb39
Chaillé-les-Marais F 32 Fa45
Chailley-Turny F 30 Hc39
Chailly-en-Bière F 29 Ha38
Chailly-en-Brie F 24 Hb37
Chailly-sur-Armançon F 30 Ja42
Chaintré F 34 Ja45
Chaintrix F 24 Hd36
Chakistra CY 206 Ja97
Chalabre F 41 Gd56
Chalais F 32 Fd49

Corral-Rubio – Czerwona Woda

Corral-Rubio E 55 Ed70
Corran GB 6 Dc10
Corrano F 154 Cb71
Corraree IRL 13 Ca21
Corre F 31 Jd39
Corredoiras E 36 Ba55
Correggio I 149 Db62
Correlha P 44 Ad59
Corrençon en-Vercors F 35 Jc49
Correpoco E 38 Db55
Corrèze F 33 Gc48
Corridonia I 156 Ed67
Corrie GB 10 Dc14
Corris GB 15 Dd24
Corrofin IRL 12 Bc22
Corrubedo E 36 Ac56
Corseul F 26 Ec38
Corsham GB 19 Ec28
Corsica F 154 Cb69
Corsicana F 154 Cc70
Corsock GB 10 Ea16
Corston GB 19 Ec28
Cortak TR 192 Fc85
Cortale I 164 Gc81
Čortanovci SRB 153 Jb60
Corte F 154 Cb69
Corte de Peleas E 51 Bc69
Corté Figueira P 58 Ad73
Cortegada E 36 Ba57
Cortegada E 36 Bb58
Cortegana E 59 Bc72
Cortelona I 149 Cc60
Cortemaggiore I 149 Cd61
Cortemilia I 148 Ca62
Corten MD 177 Fc61
Cortes E 47 Ed60
Cortés E 54 Fa67
Cortes de Aragón E 47 Fa63
Cortes de Arenoso E 54 Fb65
Cortes de Baza E 61 Ea73
Cortes de la Frontera E 59 Cb76
Cortes de Pallás E 54 Fa68
Corte Sines P 58 Ba72
Cortijada el Pilar E 61 Eb75
Cortijo de Garci-Gómez E 52 Da71
Cortijos Nuevos E 53 Ea71
Cortijos Nuevos del Campo E 61 Eb73
Cortina d'Ampezzo I 143 Ea56
Čortkiv UA 204 Ea16
Cortona I 156 Ea67
Coruche P 50 Ac68
Çoruk TR 191 Ec82
Çoruk TR 192 Fa84
Corullón E 37 Bd57
Çorum TR 205 Fb20
Coruña del Conde E 46 Dd60
Corund RO 172 Dd59
Corvara in Badia I 143 Ea56
Corvera E 55 Fa73
Corvera de Asturias E 37 Cb54
Corvillón E 36 Bb58
Corvite E 36 Bc54
Corwen GB 15 Ea23
Cosâmbeşti RO 176 Ed66
Cosăuţi MD 173 Fc54
Coşbuc RO 171 Dc56
Coşcalia MD 173 Ga59
Coşcodeni MD 173 Fb56
Coscojuela de Sobrarbe E 40 Fd58
Coşeiu RO 171 Cd56
Cosenza I 164 Gb80
Coşereni RO 176 Ec65
Coşerniţa MD 173 Fc55
Coşerniţa MD 173 Fd57
Coşeşti RO 175 Dc64
Cosgaya E 38 Da55
Cosham GB 20 Fa30
Ćosići BIH 158 Ha64
Coslada E 46 Dc64
Cosmeşti RO 176 Dd66
Cosmeşti RO 176 Ed61
Cosminele RO 176 Ea64
Cosne-Cours-sur-Loire F 29 Ha41
Cosne-d'Allier F 29 Ha44
Coşniţa MD 173 Fd57
Cosoleto I 164 Gb83
Coşoveni RO 175 Da66
Cossato I 148 Ca59
Cossé-le-Vivien F 28 Fb40
Cossoine I 168 Ca75
Cossonay CH 141 Bb55
Costache Negri RO 177 Fa62
Costa da Caparica P 50 Aa69
Costa de Canyamel E 57 Hd67
Costa de Lavos P 44 Ab64
Costa de Santo André P 50 Ab71
Costangalia MD 173 Fd59
Coştangalia MD 177 Fc61
Costa Nova E 55 Fd70
Costa Paraiso I 168 Ca74
Costaros F 34 Hd50
Costa Valle Imagna I 149 Cd58
Coşteiu RO 174 Ca61
Costelloe IRL 12 Bb21
Costeşeşti RO 175 Dc65
Costessey GB 17 Gb24
Costeşti MD 173 Fa55
Costeşti MD 173 Fd58
Coşteşti RO 173 Fa59
Costeşti RO 175 Da63
Costeşti RO 176 Ec64
Costigliole d'Asti I 148 Ca61
Costigliole Saluzzo I 148 Bc62
Costineşti RO 181 Fc68
Costişa RO 172 Ec58
Costuleni RO 173 Fb58
Coswig D 127 Ec38
Coswig D 128 Fa41
Coteala MD 172 Ed53
Coteana RO 175 Db66
Coteşti RO 176 Ed62
Cotgrave GB 16 Fb23
Cotherstone GB 11 Ed18
Cotihania MD 177 Fb61
Cotillas E 53 Ea71
Cotillo (Anievas) E 38 Dc55
Cotiujeni MD 172 Ed53
Cotiujenii Mari MD 173 Fc55
Cotiujenii Mici MD 173 Fc56
Cotmeana RO 175 Db64
Cotnari RO 172 Ed57
Cotofăneşti RO 176 Ed61
Coţofenii din Jos RO 175 Cd65
Cotova MD 173 Fb54
Cotovscoe MD 177 Fc61
Cotronei I 165 Gd80
Cottanello I 156 Eb70
Cottbus D 128 Fb39
Cotul Morii MD 173 Fb58
Coţuşca RO 172 Ed54
Cotu Văii RO 181 Fb68
Coubert F 23 Ha37
Coublanc F 31 Jc40
Coubon F 34 Hd49
Couches F 30 Ja43
Couço P 50 Ac68
Coucy-le-Château-Auffrique F 24 Hb34
Couddes F 29 Gb42
Coudekerque-Branche F 21 Gd30
Coudray F 28 Fb40
Coudrecieux F 29 Ga40
Coudron F 29 Gd43
Coudures F 39 Fb54
Couflens F 40 Gb57
Couhé F 32 Fd45
Couiza F 41 Ha56
Coulaines F 28 Fd39
Coulandon F 30 Hb44
Coulanges-lès-Nevers F 30 Hb43
Coulaures F 33 Gb48
Couleuvre F 30 Hb44
Coullons F 29 Ha41
Coulmier-le-Sec F 30 Ja40
Coulombiers F 32 Fd45
Coulombs F 23 Gc37
Coulomby F 23 Gc31
Coulommiers F 24 Hb37
Coulon F 32 Fb45
Coulonges-Cohan F 24 Hc35
Coulonges-sur-l'Autize F 32 Fb45
Couloutre F 30 Hb41
Coulport GB 6 Dc12
Coupar Angus GB 7 Eb11
Coupéville F 24 Ja36
Coupray F 30 Ja39
Couptrain F 28 Fc38
Courban F 30 Ja39
Courcelles F 31 Jd42
Courcelles-sur-Nied F 25 Jd35
Courcelles-sur-Seine F 23 Gb36
Courcemont F 28 Fd39
Courchevel F 35 Kb47
Cour-Cheverny F 29 Gb41
Courcité F 28 Fc39
Courcon F 32 Fb45
Cour-et-Buis F 34 Jb48
Courgains F 28 Fd39
Courgeon F 29 Ga38
Courgivaux F 24 Hb37
Courmayeur I 148 Bb58
Courmont F 24 Hc36
Courniou F 41 Ha54
Cournon-d'Auvergne F 34 Hb47
Courpalay F 23 Ha37
Courpière F 34 Hc47
Coursan F 41 Hb55
Coursegoules F 43 Kc53
Courseulles-sur-Mer F 22 Fc35
Cours-la Ville F 34 Ja46
Courson-les-Carrières F 30 Hc41
Courtacon F 24 Hb37
Courtalain F 29 Gb39
Courtenay F 30 Hb39
Courtenot F 30 Hd39
Courthézon F 42 Jb52
Courtivron F 30 Jb41
Courtomer F 22 Fd37
Courtown IRL 13 Cd24
Courville-sur-Eure F 29 Gb38
Cousolre F 24 Hc32
Coussac-Bonneval F 33 Gb48
Coussegrey F 30 Hd39
Coussey F 31 Jc38
Coustellet F 42 Jc53
Coustouges F 41 Ha58
Coutances F 22 Fa36
Couterne F 28 Fc38
Coutras F 32 Fc49
Couture-d'Argenson F 32 Fc46
Coutures F 28 Fc42
Couvron-et-Aumencourt F 24 Hb34
Couy F 29 Ha42
Covaleda E 47 Ea59
Covarrubias E 46 Dc59
Covas E 36 Bc53
Covas E 37 Bd57
Covas P 36 Ad58
Covas do Barroso P 44 Bb59
Covăsinţ RO 170 Ca59
Covasna RO 176 Eb61
Cove GB 4 Db06
Cove GB 19 Ea30
Covelo E 36 Ad57
Covelo P 44 Ad62
Çövenli TR 186 Fa76
Coventry GB 20 Fa25
Coverack GB 18 Db32
Coveş RO 175 Dc61
Covet E 48 Gb59
Covide P 44 Ba59
Covilhã P 44 Bb64
Covurlui MD 173 Fc59
Cowbit GB 17 Fc24
Cowbridge GB 19 Ea28
Cowdenbeath GB 7 Eb12
Cowes GB 20 Fa30
Cowfold GB 20 Fc30
Cowshill GB 11 Ed17
Cox E 55 Fa72
Cox F 40 Gb54
Coxwold GB 11 Fa19
Coy E 61 Ec72
Coylton GB 10 Dd14
Cózar E 53 Dd70
Cozes F 32 Fb48
Cozieni RO 176 Ec63
Cozma RO 171 Dc58
Cozmeşti RO 173 Fb58
Cozzano F 154 Cb71
Cozze I 162 Gd74
Crăcăoani RO 172 Ec57
Crăciunelu de Jos RO 175 Da60
Crăciuneşti RO 171 Dc59
Craco I 162 Gc76
Craidorolţ RO 171 Cc55
Crăieşti RO 171 Dc58
Craigavon GB 9 Cd18
Craigellachie GB 7 Eb08
Craighouse GB 6 Da13
Craigmalloch GB 10 Dd15
Craignure GB 6 Db11
Craigton GB 7 Eb11
Craig-y-nos GB 19 Ea27
Craik GB 11 Eb15
Crail GB 7 Ec12
Crailsheim D 134 Db47
Craiova RO 175 Cd66
Craiva RO 170 Ca58
Cramant F 24 Hc36
Cramlington GB 11 Fa16
Cramme D 126 Dc37
Cranborne GB 20 Ed30
Cranbrook GB 21 Ga29
Crançot F 31 Jc43
Cranford IRL 9 Cb15
Crângu RO 180 Dc68
Cranleigh GB 20 Fc29
Cranny IRL 12 Bc23
Crans CH 141 Bc56
Cranwell GB 17 Fc23
Cranworth GB 17 Ga24
Cranzahl D 135 Ec43
Craon F 28 Fb40
Craponne-sur-Arzon F 34 Hd48
Crask Inn GB 4 Dd05
Crasna RO 171 Cc56
Crasna RO 175 Cd63
Crăsnăşeni MD 173 Fc56
Crasnencoe MD 173 Fd55
Crasnoarmeiscoe MD 173 Fc58
Crasnogorca MD 173 Ga58
Craster GB 11 Fa15
Crathie GB 7 Eb09
Cratloe IRL 12 Bd23
Crato P 50 Ba67
Craughwell IRL 12 Bd21
Cravant F 29 Gc40
Cravant F 30 Hc40
Craveggia I 148 Cb57
Craven Arms GB 15 Eb25
Crawfordjohn GB 10 Ea14
Crawinkel D 126 Dc42
Crawley GB 20 Fc29
Crayford GB 20 Fd28
Creaca RO 171 Cd56
Creagorry GB 6 Cd07
Creaguaineach Lodge GB 7 Dd10
Crecente E 36 Ba58
Crécy-Couvé F 23 Gb37
Crécy-en-Ponthieu F 23 Gc32
Crécy-la-Chapelle F 23 Ha37
Crécy-s-Serre F 24 Hc34
Credenhill GB 15 Eb26
Crediton GB 19 Ea30
Creegh IRL 12 Bb22
Creeslough IRL 9 Cb15
Creevagh IRL 8 Bc18
Creeves IRL 12 Bc23
Cregenzán E 48 Fd59
Cregg IRL 12 Bc21
Creggan GB 9 Cc17
Creggs IRL 8 Ca20
Creglingen D 134 Db46
Creil F 23 Gd35
Crema I 149 Cd60
Cremenciug MD 173 Fb54
Cremenciug MD 173 Ga59
Crémenes E 37 Cd56
Crémieu F 35 Jc47
Cremona I 149 Da60
Créon F 32 Fc50
Crepaja SRB 153 Jc61
Crepaja SRB 174 Bb63
Crépey F 25 Jc37
Crépy F 24 Hb34
Crépy-en-Valois F 23 Ha35
Cres HR 151 Fb61
Crešan MK 178 Bc73
Crescentino I 148 Ca60
Crespino I 150 Ea61
Crespino del Lamone I 156 Dd64
Crespos E 46 Cd63
Cressage GB 15 Ec24
Cressanges F 34 Hb45
Cressensac F 33 Gc49
Cressia F 31 Jc44
Cressonsacq F 23 Gd35
Cresswell GB 11 Fa15
Crest F 34 Jb50
Cresta CH 142 Cd56
Cretas E 48 Fd63
Créteil F 23 Gd37
Creţeni RO 175 Da65
Creţeşti RO 173 Fb59
Creţoaia MD 173 Fd58
Creully F 22 Fb35
Creussen D 135 Ea45
Creutzwald F 25 Ka35
Creuzburg D 126 Db41
Crevacuore I 148 Ca58
Crevalcore I 149 Dc62
Crevant F 33 Gc45
Crevechamps F 25 Jd37
Crèvecœur-en-Auge F 22 Fd36
Crèvecœur-le-Grand F 23 Gd34
Crevedia RO 176 Ea65
Crevedia Mare RO 176 Ea66
Crevenicu RO 180 Dd67
Crevillente E 55 Fa72
Crevoladossola I 148 Ca57
Crévoux F 35 Kb50
Crewe GB 15 Ec22
Crewkerne GB 19 Eb30
Criales E 38 Dd56
Crianlarich GB 7 Dd11
Cribyn GB 15 Dd26
Cricău RO 175 Da60
Criccieth GB 15 Dd23
Criciova RO 174 Ca61
Crick GB 20 Fa25
Crickhowell GB 19 Eb27
Cricklade GB 20 Ed27
Cricova MD 173 Fd57
Crieff GB 7 Ea11
Criel-sur-Mer F 23 Gb33
Criewen D 120 Fb35
Crihana MD 173 Fd56
Crihana Veche MD 177 Fb62
Crikvenica HR 151 Fc61
Crillon F 23 Gc34
Crimmitschau D 127 Eb42
Crinan GB 6 Db12
Crinitz D 128 Fa39
Criquetot-l'Esneval F 22 Fd34
Crişan RO 177 Ga64
Crişcăuţi MD 173 Fb54
Crişcior RO 175 Cc60
Crişeni RO 171 Cd56
Crîsnai Vinogradari MD 173 Ga57
Crispiano I 162 Ha76
Crissolo I 148 Bb61
Cristeşti MD 173 Fc58
Cristeşti RO 171 Dc59
Cristeşti RO 172 Ec57
Cristian RO 175 Da61
Cristian RO 176 Dd62
Cristinacce F 154 Ca70
Cristineşti RO 172 Ec54
Criştioru de Jos RO 171 Cc59
Cristóbal E 45 Cb64
Cristo del Espíritu Santo E 52 Db68
Cristolţ RO 171 Da56
Cristopol' RUS 203 Ga08
Cristuru Secuiesc RO 176 Dd60
Criuleni MD 173 Fd57
Criva MD 172 Ed53
Crivina RO 174 Cb65
Crivitz D 119 Ea33
Crizbav RO 176 Dd61
Crkvice BIH 158 Hb64
Crkvice HR 158 Ha68
Crkvice MNE 159 Hd69
Crkvine MNE 159 Ja68
Crkvine SRB 178 Ad69
Crljivica BIH 152 Gb63
Crmljan KSV 178 Ad71
Crna Bara SRB 170 Bb59
Crnac HR 152 Hb59
Črna na Koroškem SLO 144 Fc56
Crna Trava SRB 179 Ca70
Crnča SRB 153 Ja63
Črniče SLO 151 Fa58
Crni Guber BIH 159 Ja64
Crnik MK 183 Cb74
Crni Kuk MNE 159 Hc68
Crni Padež HR 151 Fc62
Črni vrh SLO 151 Fa58
Crnjelovo BIH 153 Hd61
Crnokliště SRB 179 Ca69
Crnokrpe MNE 159 Jc68
Crnokrpe MNE 178 Ad69
Crnoljevo KSV 178 Ba71
Črnomelj SLO 151 Fd59
Črnova SLO 151 Fd57
Črnuče SLO 151 Fb58
Crock D 134 Dc43
Crockernwell GB 19 Dd30
Crocketford GB 10 Ea16
Crocq F 33 Gd46
Crocy F 22 Fc37
Crodo I 141 Ca56
Croes-goch GB 14 Db26
Crofty GB 19 Dd27
Croggan GB 6 Db11
Croick GB 4 Dd06
Crois Mhaoilíona IRL 8 Bc18
Croissilles F 23 Ha32
Croissy-sur-Selle F 23 Gd34
Croithlí IRL 8 Ca15
Crolly IRL 8 Ca15
Cromarty GB 5 Ea07
Cromer GB 17 Gb23
Cromoge IRL 13 Cb22
Cronat F 30 Hc44
Crook GB 11 Ed17
Crookedwood IRL 9 Cb20
Crookhaven IRL 12 Ba27
Crook of Devon GB 7 Eb12
Crookstown IRL 13 Cc22
Croom IRL 12 Bd23
Cropalati I 164 Gc79
Cropani I 165 Gd81
Cropani Marina I 165 Gd81
Crosby GB 10 Dc19
Cros-de-Cagnes F 43 Kc53
Cross IRL 8 Bc20
Cross IRL 12 Bb23
Crossakeel IRL 9 Cc20
Crossbost GB 4 Da05
Crossdoney IRL 9 Cb19
Crossens GB 15 Eb21
Crosses F 29 Ha43
Crossgar GB 9 Da18
Crossgare GB 9 Cd15
Cross Hands GB 19 Dd27
Crosshaven IRL 12 Bd26
Cross Inn GB 15 Dd25
Cross Keys IRL 9 Cc20
Cross Keys IRL 13 Cd21
Crossmaglen GB 9 Cd19
Crossmolina IRL 8 Bc18
Croston GB 15 Ec21
Crostwitz D 128 Fb41
Crotenay F 31 Jd43
Crotone I 165 Gd81
Crots F 35 Kb50
Crottendorf D 135 Ec43
Crouy F 24 Hb35
Crove IRL 8 Ca16
Crowborough GB 20 Fd29
Crowcombe GB 19 Ea29
Crow Hill GB 15 Ec26
Crowland GB 17 Fc24
Crowle GB 16 Fb21
Crowthorne GB 20 Fb28
Croxton GB 21 Ga25
Croxton Kerrial GB 16 Fb23
Croy GB 7 Ea08
Croyde GB 18 Dc29
Croydon GB 20 Fc28
Crozant F 33 Gc45
Crozon F 26 Db38
Črtil' RUS 203 Fb12
Cruas F 34 Jb50
Crucea RO 172 Ea56
Crucea RO 177 Fb66
Cruceni RO 174 Bd60
Cruces E 36 Bb55
Crucişor RO 171 Cd55
Crucoli I 165 Gd79
Cruden Bay GB 5 Ed08
Crudgington GB 15 Ec24
Crudwell GB 20 Ed27
Cruglic MD 173 Fd57
Crug-y-bar GB 15 Dd26
Cruis F 42 Jd52
Crulai F 23 Ga37
Crumlin GB 9 Da17
Cruseilles F 35 Jd45
Cruser I 150 Ea63
Cruşeţ RO 175 Cd65
Crusheen IRL 12 Bc22
Cruzamento de Pegões P 50 Ac69
Cruz da Légua P 50 Ab66
Cruz de João Mendes P 50 Ab71
Cruz do Incio E 36 Bc56
Cruzeşti MD 173 Fd58
Cruzy F 41 Hb55
Cruzy-le-Châtel F 30 Hd40
Crvena Luka HR 157 Fd65
Crvena Voda MK 178 Bb73
Crvenka SRB 153 Ja59
Crvica SRB 159 Ja64
Crynant GB 19 Dd27
Csabrendek H 145 Gd54
Csaholc H 147 Kc50
Csakvár H 145 Hb53
Csanádapáca H 147 Jd56
Csanádpalota H 153 Jc57
Csány H 146 Ja52
Csányoszró H 152 Ha58
Csánytelek H 146 Jb56
Csapod H 145 Gc53
Csaroda H 147 Kb50
Császár H 145 Hb53
Császártöltés H 146 Hd56
Csátalja H 153 Hd58
Csataszög H 146 Jb55
Csávoly H 153 Hd57
Csenger H 147 Kc51
Csép H 145 Hb53
Csépa H 146 Jb55
Csepreg H 145 Gc53
Cserebökény H 146 Jc55
Cserkeszőlő H 146 Jb55
Csernely H 146 Jb50
Cserszegtomaj H 145 Gd55
Csesznek H 145 Ha53
Csesztreg H 145 Gb56
Csobád H 146 Jc50
Csobaj H 147 Jd51
Csökmő H 147 Jd54
Csököly H 152 Ha57
Csömör H 146 Hd52
Csönge H 145 Gd53
Csongrád H 146 Jb55
Csonkahegyhát H 145 Gc55
Csorna H 145 Gd52
Csörnend H 145 Ha56
Csörötnek H 145 Gb55
Csorvás H 147 Jd55
Csót H 145 Ha53
Csurgó H 152 Gd57
Cuacos de Yuste E 45 Cb65
Cuadramón E 36 Bc54
Cualedro E 36 Bb58
Cuarte de Huerva E 47 Fa61
Cuba P 50 Ad71
Cubalhão P 36 Ba58
Cubel E 47 Ed62
Cubelles E 49 Gc62
Cubells E 48 Gb60
Cubilla E 47 Ea60
Cubillas de los Oteros E 37 Cc58
Cubillas de Rueda E 37 Cd57
Cubillejo de la Sierra E 47 Ec63
Cubillejo del Sitio E 47 Ec63
Cubillo E 38 Da56
Cubillos del Rojo E 38 Dc56
Cubla E 47 Fa65
Cubo de Benavente E 37 Ca58
Cubo de Bureba E 38 Dd57
Cubo de la Solana E 47 Eb61
Cubolta MD 173 Fb55
Çubukçular TR 198 Fd89
Çubukköy TR 187 Gd79
Çubuklu TR 198 Fc91
Cuca RO 175 Db64
Cuca RO 177 Fb62
Čučer MK 178 Bb72
Cucerdea RO 171 Db59
Čučerje HR 152 Gb58
Čuchny RUS 107 Mb49
Cuci RO 171 Db59
Cuckfield GB 20 Fc30
Čučkovo RUS 203 Fb11
Cucoara MD 177 Fb61
Cuconeştii Noi MD 173 Fa54
Cucq F 23 Gc31
Cucuron F 42 Jc53
Cucuruzeni MD 173 Fd56
Cucuteni RO 172 Ed57
Cudalbi RO 177 Fa62
Cuddington GB 15 Ec22
Cudhin AL 182 Ac74
Cudillero E 37 Cb54
Čudnići BIH 152 Ha63
Čudniv UA 204 Eb15
Čudovo RUS 202 Eb09
Cudrefin CH 141 Bc54
Cudworth GB 16 Fa21
Čudzin BY 202 Ea13
Cuéllar E 46 Da61
Cuenca E 53 Eb66
Cuenca de Campos E 46 Cd59
Cuers F 42 Ka55
Cuerva E 52 Da67
Cuevas Bajas E 60 Cd74
Cuevas de Almanzora E 61 Ec75
Cuevas de Almudén E 48 Fb63
Cuevas de Cañart E 48 Fb63
Cuevas del Becerro E 60 Cc75
Cuevas del Campo E 61 Dd73
Cuevas del Sil E 37 Ca56
Cuevas de San Clemente E 46 Dc59
Cuevas de San Marcos E 60 Cd74
Cuevas de Velasco E 47 Eb65
Cuevas Labradas E 47 Fa64
Cugand F 28 Fa43
Cuges-les-Pins F 42 Jd55
Cuggiono I 148 Cb59
Cugir RO 175 Cd61
Cuglieri I 169 Bd76
Cugnaux F 40 Gb54
Čuhloma RUS 203 Fa08
Cuhneşti MD 173 Fa56
Čuhujiv UA 203 Fa14
Cuhureşti de Jos MD 173 Fc55
Cuied RO 170 Ca59
Cuijk NL 125 Bb38
Cúil an tSúdaire IRL 13 Cc22
Cuillé F 28 Fa40
Cuiseaux F 31 Jc44
Cuisery F 30 Jb44
Cujmiru RO 175 Cc66
Čukojevac SRB 178 Bb67
Çukular TR 191 Ed82
Čukura BG 184 Da74
Çukurağıl TR 192 Fd85
Çukurca TR 192 Ga82
Çukurca TR 193 Gb85
Çukurhisar TR 193 Gc81
Çukurhisar TR 193 Gd81
Cukuriņi LV 115 Lb53
Çukurköy TR 185 Ec76
Çukurköy TR 186 Ga79
Çukurköy TR 198 Fd88
Çukurköy TR 199 Gd88
Çukurören TR 187 Hb78
Çukurören TR 192 Ga84
Çukurören TR 193 Hb81
Çukuröz TR 197 Fa90
Çukurpınar TR 185 Ed75
Çukuryurt TR 186 Fa76
Culan F 29 Gd44
Culciu Mare RO 171 Cd54
Culdaff IRL 9 Cc15
Culemborg NL 124 Ba37
Culine SRB 153 Hd63
Čuljkovic SRB 153 Ja62
Culkain GB 4 Dc05
Culla E 54 Fc65
Cullahill IRL 13 Cb23
Cúllar-Baza E 61 Ea74
Cullaville GB 9 Cd19
Culleens IRL 8 Bd18
Cullen GB 5 Ec07
Cullera E 54 Fc69
Cullompton GB 19 Ea30
Culmington GB 15 Eb25
Culmstock GB 19 Ea30
Culnacraig GB 4 Dc06
Culnaknock GB 4 Db07
Culoz F 35 Jd46
Culross GB 7 Eb12
Culswick GB 5 Ed05
Cumaalanı TR 198 Fd90
Cumalı TR 191 Ed86
Cumalıkızık TR 186 Fd80
Cumbernauld GB 10 Ea13
Cumbres de Enmedio E 51 Bc71
Cumbres Mayores E 51 Bc71
Cumhuriyet TR 186 Fd77
Cumiana I 148 Bc60
Čumić SRB 174 Bb66
Cuminestown GB 5 Ed08
Cumnock GB 10 Dd14
Cumnor GB 20 Fa27
Cumpăna RO 181 Fc67
Cunault F 28 Fc42
Cuneo I 148 Bc62
Cunewalde D 128 Fb41
Cunfin F 30 Ja39
Cungrea RO 175 Db65
Cunha P 36 Ad58
Cunicea MD 173 Fc55
Čuništa BIH 159 Hc64
Cunit E 49 Gc62
Cunlhat F 34 Hc47
Cunningburn GB 10 Db17
Cuntis E 36 Ad56
Cuon F 28 Fc41
Cuorgnè I 148 Bd59
Cupar GB 7 Eb12
Cupcini MD 173 Fa54
Cupcui MD 173 Fc59
Cupello I 161 Fc71
Cupoli I 157 Fa70
Cupra Marittima I 157 Fa68
Cupramontana I 156 Ec66
Ćuprija SRB 178 Bc67
Cupşeni RO 171 Db55
Curaglia CH 142 Cc55
Curăţele RO 170 Cb58
Curcani RO 181 Ec67
Curcay-sur-Dive F 28 Fc43
Čurek BG 179 Cd71
Curia P 44 Ad63
Curon Venosta I 142 Db55
Curracloe IRL 13 Cd24
Curreeny IRL 13 Ca23
Currelos E 36 Bb56
Curryglass IRL 12 Ba26
Cursdorf D 127 Dd42
Cursi I 163 Hc77
Curtea RO 174 Cb61
Curtea de Argeş RO 175 Dc63
Curţeşti RO 172 Ec55
Curticelle I 161 Fc75
Curtici RO 170 Bd59
Curtis E 36 Ba54
Curtişoara RO 175 Db65
Curtuişeni RO 170 Cb55
Čurug SRB 153 Jb59
Çürüttüm TR 193 Gc83
Cusano Mutri I 161 Fb73
Cuse F 31 Ka41
Cusercoli I 156 Ea64
Cusey F 30 Jb40
Cushendall IRL 9 Da15
Cushendun GB 9 Da15
Cuşmirca MD 173 Fd55
Cussac F 33 Ga47
Cussac-Fort-Médoc F 32 Fb49
Cussangy F 30 Hd39
Cusset F 34 Hc46
Cussey-les-Forges F 30 Jb40
Cussy-les-Forges F 30 Hd41
Custonaci I 166 Eb84
Cusy F 35 Jd46
Cut RO 175 Da61
Čuteevo RUS 203 Fd09
Cutigliano I 155 Db64
Cutnall Green GB 15 Ec25
Čutove UA 203 Fa14
Cutro I 165 Gd81
Cutrofiano I 163 Hc77
Çuvallı TR 198 Ga89
Cuxac-Carbadès F 41 Gd55
Cuxac-d'Aude F 41 Hb55
Cuxhaven D 118 Cd31
Cuzap RO 171 Cc56
Cuzăplac RO 171 Cd57
Cuza Vodă RO 177 Fa65
Cuza Vodă RO 181 Ed67
Cuzdrioara RO 171 Db57
Cuzmin MD 173 Fc54
Cuzorn F 33 Ga51
Cvikov CZ 128 Fc42
Cvitović HR 151 Ga61
Čvrstec HR 152 Gc58
Cwmafan GB 19 Dd27
Cwmbach GB 14 Dc26
Cwmbran GB 19 Eb27
Cwmcarn GB 19 Eb27
Cwmduad GB 14 Dc26
Cwmllynfell GB 19 Dd27
Cwmystwyth GB 15 Ea25
Cwrt-newydd GB 15 Dd26
Cybinka PL 128 Fc37
Cyców PL 131 Kc39
Cygany PL 131 Jd42
Čyhyryn UA 204 Ed15
Cymmer GB 19 Ea27
Cynghordy GB 15 Ea26
Cynwyd GB 15 Ea23
Cyprianka PL 122 Hc35
Cysoing F 24 Hb31
Czacz PL 129 Gb38
Czajków PL 129 Hb40
Czaplinek PL 121 Gb33
Czarna PL 138 Jc44
Czarna PL 139 Ka43
Czarna PL 139 Kb46
Czarna Białostocka PL 123 Kb33
Czarna Dąbrówka PL 121 Gd30
Czarna Sędziszowska PL 139 Jd44
Czarna Woda PL 121 Ha32
Czarne PL 121 Gc32
Czarnia PL 122 Jb33
Czarnków PL 121 Gb35
Czarnocin PL 120 Fc32
Czarnocin PL 130 Hd39
Czarnów PL 128 Fc36
Czarnowasy PL 129 Ha42
Czarnowo PL 121 Ha34
Czarnożyły PL 129 Hb40
Czarny Dunajec PL 138 Ja46
Czarny Las PL 129 Gd39
Czarny Las PL 130 Hc41
Czartajew PL 131 Kb36
Czastary PL 129 Hb40
Czchów PL 138 Jb45
Czechowice-Dziedzice PL 138 Hc45
Czechy PL 121 Gb32
Czekanów PL 129 Ha39
Czekarzewice PL 131 Jd40
Czekarzewice PL 131 Jd41
Czeladź PL 138 Hc43
Czemierniki PL 131 Kb38
Czempiń PL 129 Gc37
Czeremcha PL 123 Kc35
Czerkasy PL 131 Kd42
Czermin PL 129 Gd38
Czermnica PL 120 Fc32
Czermno PL 130 Ja41
Czermno PL 131 Kd41
Czerna PL 128 Fc39
Czerna PL 138 Hd44
Czernica PL 129 Gd41
Czernichów PL 138 Hd44
Czernięcin Poduchowny PL 131 Kb41
Czerniejewo PL 129 Gd36
Czerniewice PL 130 Ja39
Czernikowo PL 121 Hb35
Czernina PL 129 Gb39
Czersk PL 121 Ha32
Czersk PL 130 Jc38
Czerwieńsk PL 128 Fd38
Czerwin PL 123 Jd34
Czerwińsk nad Wisłą PL 130 Ja36
Czerwionka-Leszczyny PL 137 Hb44
Czerwonak PL 129 Gc36
Czerwona Woda PL 128 Fd41

Dialambí – Dörnholthausen

Dialambí GR 184 Dc77
Dialektó GR 182 Ba78
Diamante I 164 Ga79
Dianalund DK 109 Ea26
Diano d'Alba I 148 Bd62
Diano Marina I 43 La52
Diarville F 31 Jd38
Diásello GR 183 Bc80
Diavatá GR 183 Ca77
Diavolítsi GR 194 Bb88
Dibekdere TR 197 Ed89
Dibekören TR 187 Hb80
Dibič BG 181 Ec70
Dichiseni RO 181 Fa67
Dicmo HR 158 Gc66
Dicomano I 156 Dd65
Didam NL 125 Bc37
Diddlebury GB 15 Eb25
Didești RO 175 Dc66
Didieji Ibėnai LT 114 Kc57
Didim TR 197 Ec89
Didimótiho GR 185 Eb76
Didkiemis LT 113 Jc56
Didvyžiai LT 114 Ka58
Dídyma GR 195 Ca88
Didžiasalis LT 115 Lc55
Die F 35 Jc50
Dieburg D 134 Cc44
Diedorf D 142 Dc50
Diegliai LT 113 Jb56
Diego Álvaro E 45 Cc63
Diekholzen D 126 Db37
Diekirch L 133 Bb44
Diélette F 22 Ed34
Dielmissen D 126 Da38
Diemelstadt D 126 Cd39
Diemen NL 116 Ba35
Diémoz F 34 Jb47
Dienheim D 133 Cb45
Dienne F 33 Ha49
Dienstedt D 127 Dd42
Dienstedt-Hettstedt D 127 Dd42
Dienten am Hochkönig A 143 Ec53
Dienville F 30 Ja38
Diepenau D 126 Cd36
Diepenbeek B 124 Ba40
Diepenheim NL 117 Bd36
Diepenveen NL 117 Bc36
Diepholz D 117 Cc35
Dieppe F 23 Gb33
Diera-Zehren D 127 Ed41
Dierdorf D 125 Ca42
Dieren NL 125 Bc37
Dierhagen D 119 Ec30
Dierona CY 206 Jb97
Dierrey-Saint-Pierre F 30 Hc38
Diersbach A 143 Ed50
Dierzki PL 122 Jb32
Diesdorf D 119 Dd35
Dieskau D 127 Eb40
Diespeck D 134 Dc46
Dießen D 142 Dc51
Diessenhofen CH 142 Cc52
Diest B 124 Ad40
Diestedde D 126 Cc38
Dietachdorf A 144 Fb51
Dietenheim D 142 Da50
Dietenhofen D 134 Dc46
Dieterode D 126 Db40
Dietersburg D 143 Ec50
Dietersdorf D 127 Ec38
Dietfurt D 135 Ea48
Dietharz, Tambach- D 126 Dc42
Dietikon CH 141 Cb53
Dietkaušćizna LT 115 Lc55
Dietmannsried D 142 Db52
Dietramszell D 143 Dd52
Dietramszell D 143 Ea52
Dietzenbach D 134 Cc44
Dietzhölztal D 126 Cc41
Dieue F 24 Jb36
Dieulefit F 42 Jb51
Dieulouard F 25 Jd36
Dieupentale F 40 Gb53
Dieuze F 25 Ka36
Dievenišķės LT 115 Lb59
Diever NL 117 Bd34
Diez D 133 Cb43
Diezma E 60 Dc74
Differdange L 132 Ba45
Digaléto GR 188 Ac85
Digerberget S 87 Fc33
Digerberget S 87 Fc38
Digerberget S 94 Ed40
Digermulen N 66 Fc14
Dignac F 32 Fd48
Dignāja LV 107 Lb52
Dignano I 150 Ec58
Digne-les-Bains F 42 Ka52
Digny F 29 Gb38
Digoin F 30 Hd44
Diğrak TR 193 Hb87
Dijon F 30 Jb41
Dikanäs S 71 Ga24
Dikance KSV 178 Ba72
Díkea GR 185 Ea75
Dikenli TR 186 Ga78
Dikili TR 191 Eb84
Dikļi LV 106 Kd48
Dikmen TR 185 Ec80
Dikmen TR 187 Gd79
Dikmen TR 193 Ha83
Diksmuide B 21 Ha29
Dil TR 186 Fd78
Dilesi GR 189 Cb85
Dilináta GR 188 Ac85
Diljatyn UA 204 Ea16
Dillenburg D 126 Cc41
Dillingen D 133 Bc46
Dillingen a.d.Donau D 134 Db49
Dillnäs S 96 Gc44
Dillön S 94 Fa45
Dilofo GR 189 Bd81
Dílofos GR 185 Eb75
Dílos GR 196 Db89
Dilsen B 125 Bb40
Dimaro I 149 Dc57
Dimbo S 102 Fa47
Dímena GR 195 Ca87
Diminió GR 189 Bd86
Dimitrie Cantemir RO 173 Fb59
Dimitrievo BG 180 Dd73
Dimitrítsi GR 184 Cc77
Dimitrovgrad BG 185 Dd74
Dimitrovgrad RUS 203 Ga09
Dimitrovgrad SRB 179 Cb70
Dimitsána GR 194 Bb87
Dimmelsvik N 84 Cb40
Dimovo BG 179 Cb68
Dinami I 164 Gb82
Dinan F 26 Ec38
Dinant B 124 Ad42
Dınar TR 193 Gb87
Dinard F 26 Ec37
Dindarlı TR 192 Fc87
Dinek TR 193 Hb83
Dinekköyü TR 193 Ha81
Dinevo BG 185 Dd74
Dingden D 125 Bd38
Dingé F 28 Ed38
Dingelstädt D 126 Dc40
Dingelstedt D 127 Dd38
Dîngeni MD 173 Fa53
Dingle IRL 12 Ba24
Dingle S 102 Eb46
Dingolfing D 135 Eb49
Dingolshausen D 134 Db45
Dingtuna S 95 Ga43
Dingwall GB 4 Dd07
Diniaş RO 174 Bc61
Dinjiška HR 151 Fd63
Dinkelsbühl D 134 Db47
Dinkelscherben D 142 Db50
Dinklage D 117 Cc35
Dinnington GB 16 Fa22
Dinnyés H 146 Hc54
Dinsdurbe LV 105 Jb52
Dinslaken D 125 Bd38
Dinteloord NL 124 Ac38
Dinxperlo NL 125 Bd37
Diö S 103 Fb52
Diódia GR 194 Ba89
Diomídia GR 184 Db77
Díon GR 183 Bd79
Diónisos GR 189 Cc86
Diónissos GR 189 Ca84
Diorios CY 206 Ja96
Diors F 29 Gc43
Diosig RO 170 Cb56
Diósjenő H 146 Hc51
Dióskál H 145 Gd56
Dioşti RO 179 Da67
Diou F 30 Hc44
Dipevler TR 193 Gd85
Dipkarpaz = Rizokarpaso CY 206 Ka95
Dipótama GR 184 Da76
Dipotamiá GR 182 Ba77
Dipótamos GR 184 Da77
Dippach D 126 Db41
Dippach L 133 Bb45
Dippen GB 10 Db14
Dipperz D 126 Da42
Dippoldiswalde D 128 Fa42
Dipsizgöl TR 187 Ha79
Dırazali TR 186 Ga80
Dirdal N 92 Cb44
Direkli TR 199 Gc88
Dirgenler TR 198 Ga93
Dirksland NL 124 Ac37
Dirlewang D 142 Db51
Dirráhi GR 194 Bb88
Dirvonakiai LT 114 Kd53
Dirvonėnai LT 113 Jd54
Dischingen D 134 Db49
Disentis/ Mustér CH 141 Cb55
Dişli TR 193 Gd85
Diso I 163 Hc77
Dison B 125 Bb41
Dispilió GR 182 Ba78
Diss GB 21 Gb25
Dissen D 126 Cc37
Dissenchen D 128 Fb39
Distington GB 10 Ea17
Dístomo GR 189 Bd85
Dístos GR 189 Cc85
Dístrato GR 182 Ba79
Ditchling GB 20 Fc30
Ditfurt D 127 Dd38
Diträu RO 172 Ea58
Dittelbrunn D 134 Db44
Dittenheim D 134 Dc47
Dittmannsdorf D 127 Ec41
Ditton Priors GB 15 Ec24
Dituva LT 113 Jb55
Ditzingen D 134 Cc48
Diux A 144 Fc55
Divača SLO 151 Fa59
Divakë AL 182 Ab75
Divaráta GR 188 Ac84
Diva Slatina BG 179 Cb69
Divčevoto BG 179 Da71
Divci SRB 153 Jb63
Divčibare SRB 159 Jb64
Divčice CZ 136 Fb48
Divenskaja RUS 99 Mb41
Dives-sur-Mer F 22 Fc35
Diviaky SK 138 Hc48
Dividal N 67 Gd12
Divieto I 167 Fd83
Divin SK 138 Hd49
Divišov CZ 136 Fc45
Divlja BG 179 Ca71
Divljana SRB 179 Ca69
Divnoe RUS 205 Ga15
Divonne F 31 Jd44
Divotino BG 179 Cb71
Divri GR 189 Bd83
Divriği TR 205 Fd20
Divuša HR 152 Gb61
Dixmont F 30 Hb39
Dižstende LV 105 Jd50
Dizy F 24 Hc36
Djäkneboda S 80 Hc28
Djäkneböle S 80 Hb28
Djankovo BG 180 Eb69
Djärström FIN 96 Hc40
Djat'kovo RUS 202 Ed12
Djatlicy RUS 99 Ma40
Djenäs S 94 Fa43
Djulevo BG 181 Ed73
Djulino BG 181 Fa71
Djuni BG 181 Fa73
Djupdal N 93 Dc41
Djupdal S 79 Ga26
Djupfest N 77 Dd28
Djupfjord N 66 Fd13
Djupfors S 71 Ga22
Djúpivogur IS 3 Bb06
Djupsjö S 78 Fa29
Djupsjö S 80 Gc30
Djupslia N 85 Ea36
Djupträsk S 73 Hc21
Djupvik N 62 Ha09
Djupvika N 66 Fd17
Djupviken S 67 Gd13
Djupviken S 94 Ed44
Djura S 95 Fc39
Djurås S 95 Fc39
Djurdj HR 152 Gc57
Djurgården S 95 Fb44
Djurmo S 95 Fc39
Djurö S 96 Ha43
Djurröd S 110 Fa55
Djursdala S 103 Ga49
Dlhá Ves SK 138 Jb49
Długa Goślina PL 129 Gc36
Długie PL 120 Fd33
Długie PL 120 Ga35
Długie PL 122 Hc34
Długołęka PL 123 Ka33
Długołęka PL 129 Gc41
Długołęka PL 130 Hd37
Długopole-Zdrój PL 137 Gb44
Długosiodło PL 122 Jc35
Długoszyn PL 128 Fc36
Dłutów PL 130 Hd39
Dłutówka PL 122 Jc34
Dłutowo PL 122 Hd34
Dłużniewo PL 122 Ja35
Dmitrievka RUS 203 Fb12
Dmitriev-L'govskij RUS 202 Ed13
Dmitrov RUS 202 Ed10
Dmitrovo RUS 107 Mb51
Dmosin PL 130 Hd38
Dmusy PL 123 Jd32
Dmytrivka UA 202 Ed14
Dniprodzeržyns'k UA 205 Fa15
Dnipropetrovs'k UA 205 Fa15
Dniprorudne UA 205 Fa16
Dno RUS 202 Eb10
Doade E 36 Bc57
Doagh GB 9 Da17
Doba RO 171 Cc54
Dobârceni RO 172 Ed55
Dobârlău RO 176 Ea62
Dobbertin D 119 Eb32
Dobbiaco I 143 Eb55
Dobčice CZ 136 Fb48
Dobczyce PL 138 Ja45
Dobel D 133 Cb48
Dobele LV 106 Ka52
Döbeln D 127 Ed41
Doberlug-Kirchhain D 128 Fa39
Döbern D 128 Fc39
Dobersberg A 136 Fd48
Doberschütz D 127 Ec40
Dobiegniew PL 120 Ga35
Dobieszczyn PL 120 Fb33
Dobieszewo PL 121 Gc30
Dobl A 144 Fd55
Dobnište BG 184 Cc74
Dobo RUS 99 Ma42
Doboj BIH 152 Hc62
Doborovci BIH 153 Hc62
Doboz H 147 Jd55
Dobrá CZ 137 Hb46
Dobra PL 120 Fb33
Dobra PL 120 Fd33
Dobra PL 129 Hb38
Dobra PL 138 Jb45
Dobra PL 139 Kb43
Dobra PL 139 Kb45
Dobra RO 174 Cb60
Dobra SRB 174 Bd64
Dobra Gora MNE 159 Hd69
Dobrá Niva SK 138 Hd49
Dobřany CZ 135 Ed46
Dobrcane KSV 178 Bc71
Dobrcz PL 121 Ha34
Dobre PL 121 Hb35
Dobre PL 131 Jd36
Dobre Miasto PL 122 Ja31
Dobreni RO 172 Ec58
Dobreni RO 180 Eb67
Dobre Polje SRB 178 Bd67
Dobrești RO 170 Cb57
Dobrești RO 176 Dd63
Dobrești RO 176 Dd64
Dobrevo MK 178 Bd73
Dobri H 145 Gc56
Döbriach A 144 Fa55
Dobrič BG 185 Dd74
Dobrič BG 181 Fa69
Dobrica SRB 174 Bb62
Dobričevo SRB 174 Bc63
Dobřichovice CZ 136 Fb45
Dobri Do MK 178 Ba73
Dobri Do SRB 174 Bb65
Dobrilovina MNE 159 Ja67
Dobrin BG 181 Fa68
Dobrin RO 171 Cd56
Dobrinci SRB 153 Jb61
Dobrinj HR 151 Fc61
Dobrinka RUS 203 Fb12
Dobrino RUS 113 Ja58
Dobříš CZ 136 Fb45
Dobritz D 127 Eb38
Dobrjanka UA 202 Ec13
Dobrjatino RUS 203 Fb10
Dobrljin BIH 152 Gc61
Dobrna SLO 151 Fd57
Dobrnič SLO 151 Fc58
Dobrnja BIH 152 Gd62
Dobrnja BIH 153 Hc62
Dobrocin PL 122 Hd31
Dobrodzień PL 129 Hb42
Dobrogea Veche MD 173 Fb55
Dobroje Pole RUS 107 Mb47
Döbrököz H 145 Hb56
Dobromierz PL 129 Gb42
Dobromierz PL 130 Ja41
Dobromir BG 181 Ed71
Dobromir RO 181 Fa68
Dobromirci BG 184 Dc76
Dobromirka BG 180 Dc70
Dobromiru din Deal RO 181 Fa68
Dobromyl' UA 204 Dd15
Dobron PL 130 Hc39
Dobronín CZ 136 Ga46
Dobropillja UA 205 Fb15
Dobro Polje BIH 159 Hc66
Dobro selo HR 152 Gb63
Dobrošinci MK 183 Ca75
Dobrosławice PL 137 Ha44
Dobrosloveni RO 175 Db66
Dobrosołowo PL 129 Ha37
Dobrošte MK 178 Bb72
Dobroszyce PL 129 Gd40
Dobroteasa RO 175 Db65
Dobrotești RO 175 Dc66
Dobrotič BG 181 Ed70
Dobrotica BG 180 Eb70
Dobrotica BG 181 Ec68
Dobrotino BG 184 Cc75
Dobrovăț RO 173 Fa58
Dobrovice CZ 136 Fc43
Dobrovnik SLO 145 Gb56
Dobrovo SLO 150 Ed58
Dobrovol'sk RUS 113 Jd58
Dobruči RUS 99 Lc43
Dobrudžanka BG 181 Fa68
Dobrun BIH 159 Ja65
Dobrun RO 175 Da66
Dobruš BY 202 Ec13
Dobruševo MK 183 Bb75
Dobruška CZ 137 Gb44
Dobry Las PL 123 Jd33
Dobrzany PL 120 Fd33
Dobrzejewice PL 121 Hb34
Dobrzelin PL 130 Hd37
Dobrzeń Wielki PL 129 Ha42
Dobrzyca PL 129 Gd38
Dobrzyków PL 130 Hd36
Dobrzyniewo Duże PL 123 Kb33
Dobrzyń nad Wisłą PL 130 Hc36
Dobšiná SK 138 Jb48
Dobsza H 152 Ha58
Docelles F 31 Ka38
Docking GB 17 Ga23
Docksta S 80 Gd31
Dockweiler D 133 Bc43
Doclin RO 174 Bd62
Doddington GB 16 Fb22
Döderhult S 103 Gb50
Dodington GB 19 Ec28
Dodorga TR 193 Gb82
Dodro E 36 Ad56
Dodurgalar TR 198 Ga89
Doesburg NL 125 Bc37
Doetinchem NL 125 Bc37
Dofteana RO 176 Ec60
Doğal TR 192 Ga87
Doğanalanı TR 192 Fc81
Doğanay TR 193 Ha83
Doğanbaba TR 198 Ga89
Doğanbey TR 191 Eb87
Doğanbey TR 199 Hb88
Doğanbey TR 185 Ec76
Doğançam TR 192 Fb82
Doğançay TR 187 Gc79
Doğançayır TR 193 Gd82
Doğancık TR 193 Ha85
Doğancık TR 193 Ha86
Doğancıl TR 187 Gc79
Doğancılar TR 187 Gb78
Doğancılar TR 187 Gc78
Doğanhisar TR 193 Hb87
Doğankent TR 205 Fd19
Doğanlar TR 186 Fa79
Doğanlar TR 191 Ed81
Doğanlı TR 187 Ha78
Doğanlı TR 193 Gc86
Doğanoğlu TR 193 Ha82
Doganović KSV 178 Bb72
Doğanpınar TR 186 Fa80
Doğansu TR 193 Gb86
Doğanyurt TR 187 Hb80
Doğanyurt TR 193 Hb84
Döğer TR 193 Gc84
Doğla TR 186 Fb80
Dogliani I 148 Bd62
Doğluşah TR 193 Gb83
Dognecea RO 174 Bd62
Dogueno P 58 Ad73
Döğüşbelen TR 198 Fb91
Döhlau D 135 Ea44
Dohna D 128 Fa41
Dohren D 117 Cb35
Doibani MD 173 Ga57
Doicești RO 176 Dd64
Doina MD 177 Fc61
Doiráni GR 183 Ca76
Doiras E 37 Bd54
Doische B 132 Ac43
Dojeviće SRB 178 Ba69
Dojkinci SRB 179 Cb69
Dojrenci BG 180 Db70
Dokjovci BG 179 Ca71
Dokka N 85 Dd38
Dokkas S 68 Hc17
Dokkedal DK 101 Dd21
Dokkum NL 117 Bc32
Doksany CZ 136 Fb43
Doksy CZ 136 Fc43
Dokšycy BY 202 Ea12
Doktor-Josifovo BG 179 Cc68
Dokučajevs'k UA 205 Fb15
Dokumacılar TR 187 Hb80
Dokurcun TR 187 Gd79
Dokuz TR 187 Gc80
Dokuzdere TR 187 Gd78
Dolac KSV 178 Ba71
Dolancourt F 30 Ja38
Dolany CZ 135 Ed46
Dolay TR 187 Ha79
Dolaylar TR 192 Fa86
Dolbenmaen GB 15 Dd23
Dolcè I 149 Dc59
Dolceacqua I 43 Kd52
Dol-de-Bretagne F 28 Ed38
Dole BIH 153 Hd63
Dole F 31 Jc42
Dølemo N 93 Da45
Dolenci MK 182 Ba75
Dolenja Vas HR 151 Fa60
Dolenjske Toplice SLO 151 Fc59
Dolfor GB 15 Ea25
Dolgarrog GB 15 Ea22
Dolgellau GB 15 Dd24
Dołgie PL 120 Fc34
Dołgie PL 120 Ga33
Dolgorukovo RUS 113 Ja59
Dolgovka RUS 99 Mb42
Dolhan TR 185 Ec75
Dolhasca RO 172 Ec56
Dolhești RO 172 Ec56
Dolhești RO 173 Fb58
Dolianova I 169 Ca79
Dolice PL 120 Fd34
Dolici HR 158 Gb66
Doliești RO 172 Ed58
Dolíhi GR 183 Bc79
Dolina Volgyifolu SLO 145 Gb56
Doliwy PL 123 Jd30
Doljani BIH 158 Ha65
Doljani HR 152 Gb63
Dolla IRL 13 Ca23
Döllach im Mölltal A 143 Ec55
Dollar GB 7 Ea12
Dollart D 117 Ca33
Dolle D 127 Ea36
Dollern D 118 Db32
Dollerup D 108 Db28
Döllingen D 128 Fa40
Döllnitz D 127 Eb40
Dollnstein D 135 Dd48
Dolna MD 173 Fc57
Dolna Banja BG 179 Cd72
Dolna Dikanja BG 179 Cb72
Dolna Gradešnica BG 183 Cb74
Dolna Kamarci BG 179 Cd71
Dolná Krupa SK 145 Gd50
Dolná Mariková SK 137 Hb47
Dolna Mitropolija BG 180 Db69
Dolna Orjahovica BG 180 Dd70
Dolna Ribnica BG 183 Cb75
Dolná Strehová SK 146 Hd50
Dolna Verenica BG 179 Cc69
Dolneni MK 183 Bb75
Dolné Vestenice SK 137 Hb49
Dolní Benešov CZ 137 Ha45
Dolní Bousov CZ 136 Fd43
Dolní Břežany CZ 136 Fb45
Dolní Bukovsko CZ 136 Fb47
Dolni Čiflik BG 181 Fa71
Dolni Dăbnik BG 180 Db69
Dolní Dvořiště CZ 136 Fb49
Dolni Glavanak BG 185 Dd75
Dolní Kounice CZ 137 Gb48
Dolní Krupá CZ 136 Fc43
Dolni Lom BG 179 Cb68
Dolni Lukovit BG 179 Da69
Dolní Město CZ 136 Fd46
Dolní Němčí CZ 137 Gd48
Dolni Okol BG 179 Cc72
Dolní Újezd CZ 137 Gb45
Dolni Zemunik HR 157 Fd64
Dolno Ablanovo BG 180 Ea68
Dolno Botevo BG 185 Dd75
Dolno Cerovene BG 179 Cc68
Dolno Drjanovo BG 184 Cd75
Dolno Dupeni MK 182 Ba76
Dolno Levski BG 179 Da72
Dolno Paničerevo BG 180 Ea72
Dolno Sahrane BG 180 Dc72
Dolno Ujno BG 179 Ca72
Dolný Kubín SK 138 Hd47
Dolný Turček SK 138 Hc48
Dolo I 150 Ea60
Dolores E 55 Fb72
Dolovo SRB 174 Bb63
Dölsach A 143 Ec55
Dolscy RUS 107 Mb52
Dólsk PL 121 Ha33
Dólsk PL 129 Gc38
Dolsko SLO 151 Fc58
Dol. Suhor SLO 151 Fd59
Dolton GB 19 Dd30
Dołubowo PL 123 Kb35
Dołuje PL 120 Fb33
Dolus-d'Oléron F 32 Fa46
Dolyns'ka UA 204 Ed16
Dol. Žandov CZ 135 Ec44
Dolžanskaja RUS 205 Fb16
Dolžicy RUS 99 Ma44
Dölzig D 127 Eb40
Domaháza H 146 Jb50
Domaine-de-Méjanes F 42 Ja54
Doman RO 174 Ca62
Domănești RO 171 Cc54
Domaniç TR 192 Ga82
Domanice PL 129 Gb41
Domanice PL 131 Ka37
Domanico I 164 Gb80
Domaniewice PL 130 Hd38
Domaniewice PL 130 Ja39
Domaniki SK 146 Hc50
Domaniža SK 137 Hb48
Domanovići BIH 158 Hb67
Domanów PL 128 Ga42
Domaradz PL 121 Gc30
Domaradz PL 139 Ka45
Domarby FIN 97 Hb40
Domaševo BIH 159 Hc68
Domaškovicy RUS 99 Ma41
Domașnea RO 174 Cb63
Domaszków PL 137 Gc44
Domaszowice PL 129 Ha41
Domats F 30 Hb39
Domažlice CZ 135 Ec46
Domba N 84 Ca35
Dombaj RUS 205 Ga17
Dombås N 85 Dc34
Dombasle-sur-Meurthe F 25 Jd37
Dombay TR 185 Eb74
Dombaylı TR 192 Fb85
Dombegyház H 147 Jd56
Dombóvár H 145 Hb56
Dombrád H 147 Ka50
Dombresson CH 141 Bc53
Dombrot-le-Sec F 31 Jc39
Dombühl D 134 Db47
Domeikava LT 114 Kc57
Domène F 35 Jd48
Domeño E 54 Fa67
Domerat F 33 Ha45
Domersleben D 127 Ea37
Domèvre-sur-Vezouze F 25 Ka37
Dómez E 45 Ca60
Domfront F 28 Fb38
Domingo Pérez E 52 Da66
Domingo Pérez E 60 Dc74
Dominikowo PL 120 Ga34
Domino F 32 Ed46
Dominowo PL 129 Gd37
Dominteni MD 173 Fb55
Dömitz D 119 Ea34
Domljan BG 180 Db72
Dommartin-les-Cuiseaux F 31 Jc44
Domme F 33 Gb50
Dommitzsch D 127 Ec39
Domnești RO 175 Dc63
Domnitz D 127 Ea39
Domnovo RUS 113 Jb59
Domodedovo RUS 203 Fa10
Domodossola I 148 Ca57
Domokós GR 189 Bc82
Domorovce KSV 178 Bc71
Dömös H 146 Hc52
Domoszló H 146 Jb51
Domousnice CZ 136 Fc43
Dompaire F 31 Jd38
Dompierre-du-Chemin F 28 Fa39
Dompierre-sur-Besbre F 30 Hc44
Dompierre-sur-Mer F 32 Fa46
Dompierre-sur-Veyle F 34 Jb46
Domps F 33 Gc47
Domrémy-la-Pucelle F 31 Jc38
Dom Savica SLO 151 Fa57
Dömsöd H 146 Hd54
Domsten S 110 Ec54
Domsühl D 119 Eb33
Domurcalı TR 185 Ec75
Domus de Maria I 169 Bd80
Domusnovas I 169 Bd79
Domžale SLO 151 Fc57
Donabate IRL 13 Cd21
Donadea IRL 13 Cc21
Donagh GB 9 Cb18
Donaghadee GB 10 Db17
Donaghmore GB 9 Cd17
Don Álvaro E 51 Bd69
Doña Mencía E 60 Da73
Donaueschingen D 141 Cb51
Donaustauf D 135 Eb48
Donauwörth D 134 Dc49
Don Benito E 51 Ca69
Doncaster GB 16 Fa21
Donchery F 24 Ja34
Doncos E 36 Bc56
Don. Dubrave HR 151 Fd60
Donduran TR 197 Fa88
Dondurma TR 185 Eb80
Dondușeni MD 173 Fa54
Donec'k UA 205 Fb15
Donegal IRL 8 Ca16
Doneztebe E 39 Ed56
Dongen NL 124 Ba38
Donges F 27 Ec42
Dongio CH 142 Cc56
Dongo I 149 Cc57
Donici MD 173 Fc57
Donja Bačuga HR 152 Gb60
Donja Badanja SRB 153 Ja63
Donja Bebrina HR 152 Hb61
Donja Brela HR 158 Gd66
Donja Brezna MNE 159 Hd68
Donja Drežnica BIH 158 Ha66
Donja Gatnja KSV 178 Bb72
Donja Gorevnica SRB 159 Jc64
Donja Kržanja MNE 159 Ja69
Donja Kupčina HR 151 Ga59
Donja Lepenica BIH 152 Ha61
Donja Nevlja SRB 179 Cb70
Donja Sabanta SRB 174 Bb66
Donja Stubica HR 151 Ga58
Donja Suvaja HR 152 Gb63
Donja Tijarica HR 158 Gc66
Donja Toponica SRB 178 Bc69
Donja Vrijeska HR 152 Gd59
Donje Biljane HR 157 Fd64
Donje Crkvice MNE 159 Hc68
Donje Grančarevo BIH 159 Hc69
Donje Pazarište HR 151 Fd62
Donje Peulje BIH 158 Gc64
Donji Agići BIH 152 Gc61
Donji Aglarci MK 183 Bb76
Donji Andrijevci HR 152 Hb60
Donji Čaglić HR 152 Gd60
Donji Čičevo MK 183 Bc74
Donji Desinec HR 151 Ga59
Donji Dubovnik BIH 152 Gb62
Donji Dušnik SRB 178 Bd69
Donji Kamengrad BIH 152 Gc62
Donji Karin HR 157 Ga64
Donji Kazanci BIH 158 Gc64
Donji Krčin SRB 178 Bc67
Donji Krnjin KSV 178 Ba69
Donji Lapac HR 151 Ga63
Donji Lipovik MK 183 Ca75
Donji Livoč KSV 178 Bc71
Donji Macelj HR 151 Ga57
Donji Martijanec HR 152 Gc57
Donji Medum MNE 159 Ja69
Donji Miholjac HR 152 Hb59
Donji Milanova SRB 174 Ca65
Donji Mosti HR 152 Gc58
Donji Murici MNE 159 Ja70
Donji Rujani BIH 158 Gc65
Donji Sjeničak HR 151 Ga60
Donji Solnje MK 178 Bb73
Donji Srb HR 152 Gb63
Donji Stajevac SRB 178 Bd72
Donji Striževac SRB 179 Ca70
Donji Tovarnik SRB 153 Jb61
Donji Vakuf BIH 158 Ha64
Donji Vijačani BIH 152 Ha62
Donji Zirovac HR 152 Gb61
Donkerbroek NL 117 Bd34
Donnalucata I 167 Fb88
Donnemarie-Dontilly F 30 Hb38
Donnersbach A 144 Fb53
Donnersbachwald A 144 Fb53
Donnersdorf D 134 Db44
Donnerskirchen A 145 Gc52
Donohill IRL 13 Ca24
Donop D 126 Cd38
Donostia E 39 Ec55
Donoughmore IRL 12 Bc25
Donoúsa GR 196 Dc90
Donskoe RUS 205 Fd16
Donskoje RUS 113 Hd58
Donsö S 102 Eb49
Donta Deli HR 158 Hb68
Dontreix F 33 Ha46
Dontrien F 24 Hd35
Donyatt GB 19 Eb30
Donzac F 40 Ga52
Donzdorf D 134 Da49
Donzère F 42 Jb51
Donzy F 30 Hb42
Doocharry IRL 8 Ca16
Dooega IRL 8 Bb18
Doogary IRL 9 Cb19
Doogort IRL 8 Bb18
Doolin IRL 12 Bc22
Doon IRL 12 Bd23
Doorn NL 125 Bb37
Dopiewo PL 129 Gb37
Dor RUS 203 Fa08
Dora CY 206 Ja98
Dorålseter N 85 Dd34
Dörarp S 103 Fb51
Đorče Petrov MK 178 Bb73
Dorchester GB 19 Ec30
Dorchester GB 20 Fa27
Dørdal N 93 Dc44
Dordives F 29 Ha39
Dordrecht NL 124 Ad37
Dore-l'Eglise F 34 Hc48
Dorénaz CH 141 Bc56
Dörentrup D 126 Cd37
Dores GB 7 Dd08
Dorf A 143 Ed51
Dorfchemnitz D 127 Ed42
Dorfen D 143 Eb50
Dorfgastein A 143 Ec54
Dörfles-Esbach D 135 Dd43
Dörfli CH 141 Cb54
Dorf Mecklenburg D 119 Ea32
Dorfprozelten D 134 Cd45
Dorgali I 169 Cc76
Dorgoş RO 174 Ca60
Doria I 148 Cb62
Dorikó GR 185 Ea77
Dório GR 194 Ba88
Dorískos GR 185 Ea78
Dorking GB 20 Fc29
Dorkó H 147 Ka50
Dorkovo BG 179 Da73
Dormagen D 125 Bd40
Dormánd H 146 Jb52
Dormans F 24 Hc36
Dormansland GB 20 Fd29
Dor Mărunt RO 176 Ec66
Dormitz D 135 Dd46
Dörna D 126 Dc40
Dorna- Arini RO 172 Ea56
Dorna Candrenilor RO 172 Dd56
Dornas F 34 Ja50
Dornava SLO 144 Ga56
Dornberk SLO 151 Fa58
Dornbirn A 142 Da53
Dornburg D 125 Cb42
Dornburg D 127 Ea41
Dorndorf D 126 Db42
Dorndorf-Steudnitz D 127 Ea41
Dornecy F 30 Hc41
Dornes F 30 Hb44
Dornești RO 172 Eb55
Dornhan D 133 Cb49
Dörnholthausen D 125 Cb40

Dornie – East Haddon

Dornie GB 6 Dc08
Dornişoara RO 172 Dd57
Dornoch GB 5 Ea06
Dornstadt D 134 Da49
Dornstetten D 133 Cb49
Dornum D 117 Cb32
Dornumersiel D 117 Cb32
Dorobanţu RO 177 Fb65
Dorobenţu RO 181 Ec67
Dorog H 146 Hc52
Dorohoi RO 172 Ec54
Dorohusk PL 131 Kd40
Dorolţ RO 171 Cd54
Doroslovo SRB 153 Hd59
Dorotea S 79 Ga27
Doroţeaia MD 173 Ga57
Dörpen D 117 Ca34
Dorras N 63 Hc08
Dorrås N 78 Eb27
Dorrington GB 15 Eb24
Dorris S 79 Fd25
Dörrmoschel D 133 Ca45
Dorsten D 125 Bd38
Dortan F 35 Jc45
Dortmund D 125 Ca39
Dörtyol TR 191 Ed82
Doruchów PL 129 Ha40
Dorum D 118 Cd32
Dorupe LV 106 Ka52
Dörverden D 118 Da35
Dorvvinjargga N 64 Jc09
Dorweiler D 133 Ca43
Dörzbach D 134 Da46
Dos Aguas E 54 Fb68
Dosbarrios E 52 Dc66
Döşeme TR 187 Gb79
Dösemealtı TR 199 Gc91
Dos Hermanas E 59 Ca74
Dösjebro S 110 Ed55
Dospat BG 184 Da75
Dossenheim D 134 Cc46
Dos Torres E 52 Cc70
Døstrup DK 100 Dc22
Døstrup DK 108 Da27
Dotkomyrene N 65 Kb06
Dötlingen D 117 Cc34
Dotnuva LV 114 Kb56
Dotsikó GR 182 Ba79
Döttingen CH 141 Cb52
Douai F 23 Ha32
Douarnenez F 27 Dc39
Doubravčice CZ 136 Fc45
Douchy F 30 Hb40
Douchy-les-Mines F 24 Hb32
Doucier F 31 Jd44
Doudeville F 23 Ga34
Doue F 24 Hb37
Doué-la-Fontaine F 28 Fc42
Douglas GB 10 Dd19
Doulaincourt-Saucourt F 30 Jb38
Doulevant-le-Château F 30 Ja38
Doullens F 23 Gd32
Dounby GB 5 Ec02
Doune GB 7 Ea12
Dounoux F 31 Jd39
Dourdan F 29 Gd38
Dourgne F 41 Gd54
Douriez F 23 Gc32
Dournazac F 33 Ga47
Doussard F 35 Ka46
Douvaine F 35 Ka45
Douvres-la-Délivrande F 22 Fc35
Douzy F 24 Ja34
Dovadola I 156 Dd64
Dovatorovka RUS 113 Jc59
Dover GB 21 Gb29
Dovhe UA 204 Dd16
Døvik N 92 Cb43
Dovilai LT 113 Jb55
Døvling DK 108 Da24
Dovre N 85 Dc34
Dovreskogen N 85 Dc34
Dovsk BY 202 Eb13
Downham GB 20 Fd25
Downhill GB 9 Cd15
Downpatrick GB 9 Da18
Dowra IRL 8 Ca18
Dowsby GB 17 Fc23
Doxarás GR 182 Ba79
Doxarás GR 189 Bc81
Doxáto GR 184 Da77
Doyuran TR 191 Eb82
Dozulé F 22 Fc36
Dozza I 150 Dd63
Drabeši LV 106 Kd49
Drabiv UA 202 Ed14
Dråby DK 109 Dd24
Drača SRB 174 Bb66
Dračevo BIH 158 Hb68
Dračevo MK 178 Bc73
Drachselsried D 135 Ec48
Drachten NL 117 Bc33
Dračić SRB 153 Jb63
Drag N 66 Ga15
Drag N 78 Eb25
Draga Baščanska HR 151 Fc61
Dragacz PL 121 Hb33
Dragalina RO 176 Ed66
Dragalj MNE 159 Hd69
Dragaljevac BIH 153 Hd62
Dragalovci BIH 152 Ha62
Dragana BG 179 Da70
Drăgăneşti MD 173 Fc55
Drăgăneşti RO 170 Cb58
Drăgăneşti RO 176 Eb65
Drăgăneşti RO 177 Fa62
Drăgăneşti de Vede RO 180 Dc67
Drăgăneşti-Olt RO 180 Db67
Drăgăneşti-Vlaşca RO 180 Dd67
Draganići HR 151 Ga59
Draganovo BG 180 Dd70
Drăganu RO 175 Dc64
Dragaryd S 102 Fa52
Dragaš KSV 178 Ba72
Drăgăsani RO 175 Db65
Dragas Vojvoda BG 180 Dc68
Dragatuš SLO 151 Fd59
Drage D 118 Dc33
Drage HR 157 Ga65
Dragedal N 92 Cc47
Drăgeşti RO 170 Cb57
Drăghiceni RO 179 Da67
Dragičevo BG 179 Cc71
Draginac SRB 153 Ja63
Draginje SRB 153 Jb62
Draginovo BG 179 Cd73
Dragland N 66 Ga13
Draglica SRB 159 Jb66
Dragnic BIH 158 Gd64
Drago RO 171 Cd57
Dragobi AL 159 Jc69
Dragobrača SRB 174 Bb66
Dragočaj BIH 152 Gd62
Dragocvet SRB 174 Bc66
Dragodana RO 176 Dd65
Drăgoeşti RO 175 Db64
Dragoevo BG 181 Ec70
Dragoevo MK 183 Bd74
Dragógi GR 194 Bb88
Drăgoieşti RO 172 Eb56
Dragojčinci BG 179 Ca71
Dragojnovo BG 184 Dc74
Dragoman BG 179 Cb70
Dragomer SLO 151 Fb58
Dragomireşti RO 171 Dc55
Dragomireşti RO 172 Ec58
Dragomireşti RO 173 Fa59
Dragomireşti RO 176 Dd64
Dragomirovo BG 180 Dc69
Dragør DK 109 Ec26
Dragomireşti-Vale RO 176 Ea66
Dragoslavele RO 176 Dd63
Dragostunjë AL 182 Ad75
Dragoş Vodă RO 176 Ed66
Drăgoteşti RO 175 Cc64
Drăgoteşti RO 175 Da66
Dragotina HR 152 Gb60
Dragot-Sulovë AL 182 Ac76
Dragov Dol MK 183 Bb74
Dragovica Polje MNE 159 Ja68
Dragoviştica BG 179 Ca72
Dragsmark S 102 Eb47
Dragsvik FIN 97 Jd40
Dragsvik N 84 Cc36
Draguć HR 151 Fa60
Draguignan F 43 Kb54
Drăguşeni RO 172 Ec57
Drăguşeni RO 172 Ed54
Drăguşeni RO 177 Fa61
Drăguteşti RO 175 Cc64
Drahičyn BY 202 Ea14
Drahnsdorf D 128 Fa38
Drahonice CZ 136 Fa47
Drajna RO 176 Eb63
Draka BG 181 Ec73
Drakéi GR 197 Ea88
Drakenburg D 118 Da35
Drákia GR 189 Ca82
Drakótripa GR 188 Bb81
Drakovoúni GR 194 Bb87
Drakseník BIH 152 Gc60
Dralfa BG 180 Eb70
Dráma GR 184 Cd76
Drammen N 93 Dd42
Drămşa BG 179 Cc70
Drânceni RO 173 Fb58
Drangan IRL 13 Cb24
Drange N 92 Cb46
Drangedal N 93 Db44
Drangovo BG 180 Dc73
Drängsered S 102 Ed51
Drängsmark S 80 Hc25
Drangsnes IS 2 Ad03
Drangstedt D 118 Cd32
Drănic RO 179 Da67
Dransfeld D 126 Da39
Dranske D 119 Ed29
Drarović HR 152 Gd60
Draše HR 151 Ga58
Drasenhofen A 137 Gc49
Drăşliceni MD 173 Fd57
Drąsučiai LT 114 Ka54
Drávafok H 152 Ha58
Drávaszabolcs H 152 Hb58
Drávaszentes H 152 Gd58
Drávasztára H 152 Ha58
Draveil F 23 Gd37
Dravískos GR 184 Cd77
Dravograd SLO 144 Fc56
Dravovce SK 137 Ha49
Drawno PL 120 Ga34
Drawsko PL 120 Ga35
Drawsko Pomorskie PL 120 Ga33
Drążdżewo PL 122 Jb34
Draženov CZ 135 Ec46
Draževac SRB 153 Jc62
Dražgoše SLO 151 Fb57
Dražice HR 151 Fb60
Dražmirovac SRB 174 Bc66
Drebber D 117 Cc35
Drebkau D 128 Fb39
Dreenagh IRL 12 Ba23
Dreetz D 119 Ec35
Drégelypalánk H 146 Hd51
Dreieich D 134 Cc44
Dreierwalde D 117 Cb36
Dreis D 133 Bc44
Dreis-Brück D 133 Bc43
Dreißigacker D 126 Db42
Drejø By DK 108 Dc28
Drelnes DK 3 Ca07
Drelów PL 131 Kb37
Drem GB 11 Ec13
Dren BG 179 Cb72
Drena I 149 Dc58
Drenchia I 150 Ed57
Drenovac SRB 178 Bd71
Drenovci HR 153 Hd61
Drenovë AL 182 Ad77
Drenovec BG 179 Cb68
Drenovo MK 183 Bc75
Drenovstica MNE 159 Hd69
Drensteinfurt D 125 Cb38
Drenta BG 180 Ea71
Drépano GR 183 Bc78
Drépano GR 195 Bd88
Drepcăuţi MD 172 Ed53
Dresden D 128 Fa41
Drētun' BY 202 Eb11
Dretyń PL 121 Gc31
Dreux F 23 Gb37
Dřevčice CZ 136 Fb43
Drevdagen S 86 Ed35
Dreverna LT 113 Jb56
Dřevohostice CZ 137 Gd46
Drevsjø N 86 Ec35
Drevvatn N 70 Fa21
Drewitz D 127 Eb37
Drewnica PL 121 Hb30
Drezdenko PL 120 Ga35
Drežnica HR 151 Fd61
Drežnik SRB 159 Jb65
Drežnik Grad HR 151 Ga61
Dríalos GR 194 Bc91
Dricāni LV 107 Lc51
Dridu RO 176 Ed65
Driebergen-Rijsenburg NL 116 Ba36
Driebes E 46 Dd65
Driedorf D 125 Cb42
Drieliņi LV 106 Kc48
Drienov SK 139 Jd48
Driesum NL 117 Bc33
Drietoma SK 137 Ha48
Driffield GB 17 Fc20
Drimnin GB 6 Db10
Drimoleague IRL 12 Bb26
Drimónas GR 188 Bb84
Drimós GR 183 Ca77
Drimpton GB 19 Eb30
Drinagh IRL 13 Cd25
Drinic BIH 152 Gc63
Drinjača BIH 153 Hd63
Drinovci BIH 158 Gd67
Drionville F 23 Gc31
Driopída GR 195 Cd89
Drióvouno GR 183 Bb78
Drishtë AL 159 Jb70
Drizë AL 182 Aa76
Drizë AL 182 Ac76
Drjanovec BG 180 Ea69
Drjanovec BG 180 Eb69
Drjanovo BG 185 Ea74
Drjanovo BG 180 Dd71
Drlače SRB 159 Ja64
Drmno SRB 174 Bc64
Drniš HR 158 Gb65
Drnje HR 152 Gc57
Drnovice CZ 137 Gc47
Dro I 149 Dc58
Drøbak N 93 Ea42
Drobeta-Turnu Severin RO 174 Cb65
Drobin PL 122 Hd35
Drochia MD 173 Fb54
Drochia MD 173 Fb54
Drochow D 128 Fa39
Drochtersen D 118 Da32
Drogheda IRL 9 Cd20
Drogomin PL 128 Fc36
Drogosze PL 122 Jb30
Drohiczyn PL 131 Ka36
Drohobyč UA 204 Dd16
Droichead Átha IRL 9 Cd20
Droichead na Bandan IRL 12 Bc26
Droisy F 23 Gb37
Droitwich GB 20 Ed25
Drolshagen D 125 Cb40
Drołtowice PL 129 Gd40
Drom SRB 153 Jb58
Droman GB 4 Dc04
Dromcolliher IRL 12 Bc24
Dromina IRL 12 Bc24
Drommahane IRL 12 Bc25
Drömme S 80 Gd30
Dromod IRL 8 Ca19
Dromore GB 9 Cb17
Dromore GB 9 Da18
Dromore West IRL 8 Bd18
Dronero I 148 Bc62
Dronfield GB 16 Fa22
Dronninglund DK 101 Dd20
Dronningmølle DK 109 Ec25
Dronten NL 116 Bb35
Dropkovec HR 152 Gb58
Dropla BG 181 Fb69
Drosbacken S 86 Ed35
Drosendorf Stadt A 136 Ga48
Drosiá GR 189 Cb85
Droskovo RUS 203 Fa12
Drosopigí = Vourgareli GR 188 Ba81
Drossáto GR 183 Ca76
Drosseró GR 183 Bb78
Drosseró GR 183 Bd77
Drossopigí GR 183 Bb77
Drottninghaug N 76 Cd33
Drottningskär S 111 Fd54
Droué F 29 Gb39
Drouseia CY 206 Hd97
Drozdowo PL 121 Gb30
Drozdowo PL 123 Jd33
Drozdyn' UA 202 Ea14
Drożki PL 129 Ha41
Drübeck D 126 Dc38
Drugan BG 179 Cb72
Drugnia PL 130 Jb42
Drulingen F 25 Kb36
Drumbeg GB 4 Dc05
Drumcliff IRL 8 Ca17
Drumclog GB 10 Dd14
Drumcondra IRL 9 Cd19
Drume MNE 159 Ja70
Drumevo BG 181 Ed70
Drumfin IRL 8 Ca18
Drumfree IRL 9 Cc15
Drumgoft IRL 13 Cd22
Drumkeen IRL 9 Cb16
Drumkeeran IRL 8 Ca18
Drumlegagh GB 9 Cb17
Drumlish IRL 9 Cb19
Drummannon GB 9 Cd17
Drummore GB 10 Dc17
Drumnadrochit GB 7 Dd08
Drumnakilly GB 9 Cc17
Drumreagh IRL 8 Bb18
Drumrunie GB 4 Dc06
Drumsallie GB 6 Dc10
Drumshanbo IRL 8 Ca19
Drunen NL 124 Ba38
Druskininkai LT 123 Kc30
Drusti LV 106 La49
Druten NL 125 Bb37
Druva LV 105 Jd52
Druvas LV 105 Jd52
Druviena LV 107 Lb49
Druyes-les-Belles-Fontaine F 30 Hb41
Družba RUS 113 Jb59
Družba UA 202 Ed13
Družbice PL 130 Hd40
Družetić SRB 153 Jb63
Družetići SRB 159 Jc64
Družnaja Gorka RUS 99 Mb41
Drvar BIH 152 Gb63
Drvenik HR 158 Gd67
Drwalew PL 130 Jb38
Drwęczno PL 122 Hd31
Drybrook GB 19 Ec27
Drygały PL 123 Jd32
Drymen GB 7 Dd12
Dryszczów PL 131 Kd40
Drzązgowo PL 129 Gc37
Drzecin PL 128 Fc37
Drzewce PL 129 Ha37
Drzewce PL 129 Hb37
Drzewce PL 131 Ka39
Drzewiany PL 121 Gb31
Drzewica PL 130 Jb39
Držková CZ 137 Ha47
Drzonów PL 128 Fd38
Drzonowo PL 120 Ga31
Drzonowo PL 121 Gc32
Drzycim PL 121 Ha33
Duacı TR 199 Gc91
Duagh IRL 12 Bb24
Dualar TR 191 Ed83
Dualchi I 169 Ca76
Duas Igrejas P 45 Ca60
Dub SRB 159 Jb64
Dubá CZ 136 Fb43
Dubac HR 158 Hb69
Dubăsari MD 173 Fd57
Dubăsarii Vechi MD 173 Ga57
Duba Stonska HR 158 Ha68
Dubău MD 173 Ga56
Dub-Bor RUS 99 Ld45
Dubci HR 158 Gc66
Dubeni LV 105 Jb52
Dubeņi LV 105 Jb52
Dubeniniki PL 123 Ka30
Dubeşti RO 174 Ca60
Dubí CZ 128 Fa42
Dubicko CZ 137 Gc45
Dubicze Cerkiewne PL 123 Kc35
Dubienka PL 131 Kd40
Dubin PL 129 Gc39
Dubingiai LT 114 La56
Dubinné SK 139 Jd47
Dubiny PL 123 Kc34
Dub'jazy RUS 203 Fd08
Dubki RUS 107 Ma49
Dubleva LV 107 Lc49
Dublin IRL 13 Cd21
Dublovice CZ 136 Fb46
Dubna LV 115 Lc53
Dubna MD 173 Fc55
Dubna RUS 202 Ed10
Dubna RUS 203 Fa11
Dub nad Moravou CZ 137 Gd46
Dubňany CZ 137 Gc48
Dubné CZ 136 Fb48
Dubnica SRB 178 Bd71
Dubnica nad Váhom SK 137 Hb48
Dubník SK 145 Hb51
Dubno UA 204 Ea15
Dubočka SRB 174 Bd65
Duboštica BIH 153 Hc63
Dubova RO 174 Ca65
Dubovac KSV 178 Ba70
Dubovac SRB 174 Bc64
Dubovac Okučanski HR 152 Gd60
Dubovka RUS 203 Fd13
Dubovskoje RUS 113 Jd58
Dubovskoje RUS 205 Fd15
Dubovyj Ovrag RUS 203 Fd14
Dubranec HR 151 Ga59
Dubrava BIH 152 Ha62
Dubrava HR 152 Gb58
Dubrava HR 152 Gc58
Dubrava RUS 113 Jd59
Dubrave BIH 153 Hc62
Dubrave BIH 153 Hc63
Dubrave BIH 158 Gc64
Dubravica BIH 158 Hb64
Dubravica HR 151 Ga58
Dubravica SRB 174 Bc64
Dubravice BIH 153 Ja63
Dubravka HR 159 Hc69
Dubrivka UA 204 Eb15
Dubrovka RUS 107 Mb51
Dubrovka RUS 203 Fc12
Dubrovnik HR 158 Hb69
Dubrovno RUS 107 Mb46
Dubrovy RUS 107 Mb49
Dubrovycja UA 202 Ea14
Dubuļi LV 107 Ld52
Dubulti LV 106 La52
Ducaj AL 159 Jb70
Ducey F 28 Fa38
Duchally GB 4 Dd05
Duchcov CZ 136 Fa43
Ducherow D 120 Fa32
Duclair F 23 Ga35
Duda-Epureni RO 173 Fb59
Dudaklı TR 186 Fd80
Dudar H 145 Ha53
Duddington GB 16 Fb24
Dudelange L 133 Bb45
Dudeldorf D 133 Bc44
Düdenhofen D 133 Cb46
Düdenköy TR 198 Ga89
Düdenköy TR 199 Gb92
Duderstadt D 126 Db39
Dudeşti RO 177 Fa65
Dudeştii Vechi RO 170 Bb59
Đuđevo SRB 153 Jb60
Dudince SK 146 Hc50
Dudley GB 16 Ed24
Dudovica SRB 153 Jc63
Dueñas E 46 Da59
Duesund N 84 Ca37
Dufftown GB 7 Eb08
Duffus GB 5 Eb07
Duga Poljana SRB 178 Ad68
Duga Resa HR 151 Fd60
Düğer TR 199 Gb89
Duggendorf D 135 Ea47
Dugi Rat HR 158 Gc66
Dugo Selo HR 152 Gb59
Düğrek TR 198 Fb90
Düğüncüler TR 192 Fb83
Duhnen D 118 Cd31
Duhnovo RUS 107 Mb49
Duhovec BG 181 Ec69
Duhovnickoe RUS 203 Ga11
Duingen D 126 Da38
Duingt F 35 Ka46
Duinkerken = Dunkerque F 21 Gd29
Duino I 150 Ed59
Duirinish GB 4 Db08
Duisburg D 125 Bd39
Duiven NL 125 Bc37
Dukat AL 182 Aa78
Dukat SRB 178 Bd72
Dukla PL 139 Jd45
Dūkštas LT 115 Lb55
Dūkštos LT 114 La57
Dukuļava LV 107 Ld49
Dulceşti RO 172 Ed58
Dulcza Wielkia PL 138 Jc43
Duleek IRL 9 Cd20
Duljci BIH 152 Gd63
Dulje KSV 178 Ba71
Dullingham GB 20 Fd26
Dülmen D 125 Ca38
Dulovka RUS 107 Ma47
Dulovo BG 181 Ed68
Dulverton GB 19 Ea29
Duły PL 123 Jd30
Dumača SRB 153 Jb62
Dumanalanı TR 185 Ed80
Dumanlar TR 192 Fc85
Dumanlı TR 192 Fd86
Dumanlı TR 199 Ha89
Dumbarton GB 10 Dd13
Dumbleton GB 20 Ed26
Dumbrava RO 174 Ca61
Dumbrava RO 175 Cc65
Dumbrava RO 176 Eb65
Dumbrăveni RO 172 Ec55
Dumbrăveni RO 175 Dc60
Dumbrăveni RO 176 Ed62
Dumbrăveni RO 181 Fb68
Dumbrăviţa MD 173 Fb56
Dumbrăviţa RO 171 Da55
Dumbrăviţa RO 174 Ca60
Dumbrăviţa RO 176 Dd62
Dümenler TR 192 Ga85
Dumeşti RO 172 Ed58
Dumeşti RO 173 Fa57
Dumfries GB 10 Ea16
Dumha Eige IRL 8 Bb18
Dumitra RO 171 Dc57
Dumitreşti RO 176 Ec62
Dumluca TR 193 Ha82
Dumlupınar TR 193 Gb85
Dummerstorf D 119 Eb31
Dümpelfeld D 125 Bd42
Dümrek TR 191 Ea81
Dümrek TR 193 Hb81
Dümrek TR 193 Hb82
Duna N 78 Ec26
Dunafalva H 153 Hc57
Dunaff IRL 9 Cc15
Dunaföldvár H 146 Hc55
Dunaharaszti H 146 Hd53
Dunajivci UA 204 Eb16
Dunajská Lužná SK 145 Gd51
Dunajská Streda SK 145 Ha51
Dunakeszi H 146 Hd52
Dunakömlőd H 146 Hc55
Dunalka LV 105 Jb52
Dunapataj H 146 Hd56
Dunăreni RO 179 Cd67
Dūņas LV 107 Lb52
Dunaszekcső H 153 Hc57
Dunaszentbenedek H 146 Hd56
Dunaszentgyörgy H 146 Hc56
Dunatetétlen H 146 Hd55
Dunaújváros H 146 Hc54
Dunava LV 107 Lb52
Dunavăţu de Jos RO 177 Fd65
Dunavci BG 179 Cb67
Dunavci BG 180 Dc72
Dunavecse H 146 Hd55
Dunbar GB 11 Ec13
Dunblane GB 7 Ea12
Dunboyne IRL 13 Cd21
Dún Chaoin IRL 12 Ad24
Dunchurch GB 20 Fa25
Duncormick IRL 13 Cc25
Dundaga LV 105 Jc49
Dundalk IRL 9 Cd19
Dündarlı TR 191 Ec84
Dun Dealgan IRL 9 Cd19
Dundee GB 7 Ec11
Dunderland N 71 Fc20
Dunderrow IRL 12 Bc26
Dundonald GB 9 Da17
Dundonnell GB 4 Dc06
Dundrenan GB 10 Ea17
Dundrum IRL 13 Ca23
Dunecht GB 7 Ed09
Dunes F 40 Ga53
Dunfanaghy IRL 9 Cb15
Dunfermline GB 7 Eb12
Dungannon GB 9 Cd17
Dún Garbhán IRL 13 Ca25
Dungarvan IRL 13 Ca25
Dungiven GB 9 Cd16
Dunglow IRL 8 Ca15
Dungourney IRL 12 Bd25
Dunholme GB 17 Fc22
Dunières F 34 Ja48
Dunika LV 113 Jb53
Duninowo PL 121 Gb29
Dunje MK 183 Bc75
Dunjica MK 183 Bd75
Dunkeld GB 7 Eb11
Dunker S 95 Gb44
Dunkerque F 21 Gd29
Dunkerrin IRL 13 Ca22
Dunkeswell GB 19 Ea30
Dunkineely IRL 8 Ca17
Dünkirchen = Dunkerque F 21 Gd29
Dunkirk GB 19 Ec28
Duńkowice PL 139 Kc44
Dun Laoghaire IRL 13 Cd21
Dunlavin IRL 13 Cc22
Dunleer IRL 9 Cd20
Dun-le-Palestel F 33 Gc45
Dunlop GB 10 Dd14
Dún Manmhaí IRL 12 Bc26
Dunmanus IRL 12 Ba26
Dunmanway IRL 12 Bc26
Dún Mór IRL 8 Bd20
Dunmore GB 9 Da19
Dunmore IRL 8 Bd20
Dunmore East IRL 13 Cc25
Dunnamanagh GB 9 Cc16
Dunnamore GB 9 Cc17
Dun na nGall IRL 8 Ca16
Dunnet GB 5 Eb04
Dunningen D 141 Cb50
Dunoon GB 6 Dc13
Dunquin IRL 12 Ad24
Duns GB 11 Ed14
Dunscore GB 10 Ea16
Dünsen D 118 Cd34
Dunsford GB 19 Dd30
Dunshaughlin IRL 13 Cd21
Dunstable GB 20 Fb27
Dunster GB 19 Ea29
Dun-sur-Auron F 29 Ha43
Dun-sur-Meuse F 24 Jb34
Dunte LV 106 Kc49
Duntish GB 19 Ec30
Dunum D 117 Cb32
Dunure GB 10 Dc15
Dunvegan GB 4 Da07
Dupnica BG 179 Cb72
Durabeyler TR 192 Fc82
Durach D 142 Db52
Đurađ HR 152 Hb59
Durağan TR 205 Fb20
Durak TR 199 Hb89
Duraklar TR 187 Ha78
Đurakovac KSV 178 Ba70
Duran BG 181 Ec69
Durance F 40 Fd52
Durango E 39 Eb55
Durankulak BG 181 Fc69
Duras F 32 Fd51
Durasılar TR 192 Fb83
Durasıllı TR 192 Fb86
Durbach D 133 Ca49
Durban-Corbières F 41 Hb56
Durbe LV 105 Jb52
Durbuy B 124 Ba42
Dúrcal E 60 Db75
Durdat-Larequille F 33 Ha45
Đurđenovac HR 152 Hb59
Đurđevac HR 152 Gd58
Đurđevik BIH 153 Hc63
Đurđevo SRB 174 Bb65
Đurđin SRB 153 Ja58
Dūre LV 106 Kd48
Düren D 125 Bc41
Durfort F 41 Hd53
Durfort-Lacapelette F 40 Gb52
Durham GB 11 Fa17
Durhasan TR 192 Fc81
Durhasan TR 192 Fc84
Đurinci SRB 174 Bb64
Durlangen D 134 Da48
Durlas IRL 13 Ca23
Durleşti MD 173 Fd58
Đurmanec HR 151 Ga57
Durmersheim D 133 Cb47
Durness GB 4 Dd04
Durneşti RO 172 Ed55
Durnholz I 143 Dd55
Dürnkrut A 145 Gc50
Dürnstein A 144 Fb55
Dürnstein A 144 Fd50
Duronia I 161 Fb72
Dürrboden CH 142 Da55
Durrës AL 182 Ab74
Dürrhennersdorf D 128 Fc41
Durrington GB 20 Ed29
Dürröhrsdorf-Dittersbach D 128 Fb41
Durrow IRL 13 Cb23
Durrus IRL 12 Bb26
Dürrwangen D 134 Db47
Dursunbey TR 192 Fc82
Durtal F 28 Fc41
Duruelo de la Sierra E 47 Ea59
Durup DK 100 Da22
Dūrupe LV 105 Jc51
Dury F 23 Gd33
Dušanci BG 179 Da71
Dūseikiai LT 113 Jd54
Dusetos LT 115 Lb54
Dusina BIH 158 Hb65
Dušinci BG 179 Ca71
Dušmani MD 173 Fa55
Dusmenys LT 114 Kd59
Dusnok H 146 Hd56
Dusocin PL 121 Hb32
Düsseldorf D 125 Bd40
Dussen NL 124 Ba37
Dußlingen D 134 Cc49
Duston GB 20 Fb25
Duszniki PL 129 Gb36
Duszniki-Zdrój PL 137 Gb43
Dutağaç TR 198 Fb88
Duthil GB 7 Ea08
Dutka LV 106 Kd48
Dutluca TR 192 Fd82
Dutluca TR 192 Fd86
Dutluca TR 193 Gb82
Dutluca TR 198 Ga88
Dutovlje SLO 151 Fa59
Duvberg S 87 Fb34
Duved S 78 Ed30
Düverdüzü TR 187 Gd78
Düvertepe TR 192 Fb83
Düzağaç TR 193 Gb85
Düzağaz TR 199 Ha90
Duża Klonownica PL 131 Kb37
Düzce TR 187 Ha78
Duži BIH 158 Hb68
Dužica HR 152 Gb59
Düzkışla TR 193 Gb85
Düzköy TR 187 Gb78
Düzorman TR 185 Ed75
Düzova TR 186 Fa76
Duzy-le-Gros F 24 Hc34
Dvärsätt S 79 Fc30
Dve Mogili BG 180 Ea69
Dverberg N 66 Fd11
Dviete LV 115 Lb53
Dvor HR 152 Gb61
Dvor SLO 151 Fc59
Dvorčani LV 115 Ld53
Dvoriki RUS 203 Fa11
Dvorišće RUS 99 Ld42
Dvorišće RUS 107 Mb51
Dvory nad Žitavou SK 145 Hb51
Dvůr Králové nad Labem CZ 136 Ga43
Dwikozy PL 131 Jd41
Dwingeloo NL 117 Bd34
Dwórzno PL 122 Ja30
Dyan GB 9 Cd18
Dyblin PL 122 Hc35
Dybów PL 131 Jd36
Dyce GB 7 Ed09
Dydnia PL 139 Ka45
Dyffryn Ardudwy GB 15 Dd23
Dyfjord N 64 Jd04
Dygowo PL 120 Ga31
Dykan'ka UA 202 Ed14
Dyke GB 18 Dc29
Dykehead GB 7 Ec10
Dykends GB 7 Eb10
Dylewo PL 122 Jc33
Dylicy RUS 99 Mb40
Dylife GB 15 Ea24
Dymchurch GB 21 Ga29
Dymer UA 202 Ec14
Dymock GB 15 Ec26
Dymokury CZ 136 Fd44
Dynów PL 139 Ka44
Dyping N 66 Fd15
Dypvåg N 93 Db45
Dyranut N 84 Cd39
Dyrham GB 19 Ec28
Dyrkorn N 76 Cd33
Dyrnes N 77 Db29
Dyrøy N 67 Gb11
Dysberg S 87 Fb37
Dysbodarna S 86 Fa38
Dysna LT 115 Lc55
Dywity PL 122 Ja31
Džalil' RUS 203 Ga08
Džanići BIH 158 Hb65
Džankoj UA 205 Fa17
Dzbonie PL 122 Jb34
Džebel BG 184 Dc75
Dzedri LV 105 Jd50
Dzelda LV 105 Jc52
Dzelmes LV 106 Kd51
Dzelzava LV 107 Lb50
Dzeņi LV 106 La48
Džep SRB 178 Bd71
Džepište MK 182 Ad74
Džērbene LV 106 La49
Dzerjinscoe MD 173 Ga57
Dzeržinsk RUS 203 Fb09
Dzeržinskoje RUS 113 Jc58
Dziadkowice PL 123 Kb35
Dziadkowo PL 129 Gd39
Dziadowa Kłoda PL 129 Gd40
Działdowo PL 122 Ja33
Działoszyce PL 138 Jb43
Działoszyn PL 130 Hc41
Działyń PL 131 Kb38
Dziekanowice PL 138 Ja45
Dziektarzewo PL 122 Ja35
Dziemiany PL 121 Gd31
Dzierżązna PL 122 Ja35
Dzierżązno Wielkie PL 121 Gb35
Dzierzgoń PL 122 Hc31
Dzierzgowo PL 122 Jb34
Dzierzkowice Rynek PL 131 Ka41
Dzierżoniów PL 129 Gb42
Dzierżysław PL 137 Ha44
Dziesław PL 129 Gb40
Dzietrzychowo PL 122 Jb30
Dziewin PL 138 Jb44
Džigolj SRB 178 Bc69
Dzikowo PL 120 Fd35
Dzikowo PL 121 Gb34
Dzików Stary PL 139 Kc43
Dzirciems LV 105 Jd50
Dziwnów PL 120 Fc31
Dziwnówek PL 120 Fc31
Dzjaržynsk BY 202 Ea12
Dzjatlava BY 202 Ea13
Džuba RUS 205 Fc17
Džūkste LV 106 Ka51
Džuljunica BG 180 Ea70
Džurkovo BG 184 Db74
Džurovo BG 179 Da70
Džuryn UA 204 Eb16
Dźwierszno Wielkie PL 121 Gd34
Dźwierzno PL 121 Hb34
Dźwierzuty PL 122 Jb32
Dźwiżyno PL 120 Fd31

E

Ea E 39 Eb55
Éadan Doire IRL 13 Cc21
Eaglesfield GB 11 Eb16
Eaní GR 183 Bc79
Eanodat FIN 68 Ja13
Eántio GR 195 Cb87
Earby GB 16 Ed20
Earls Barton GB 20 Fb25
Earls Colne GB 21 Ga26
Earlsferry GB 7 Ec12
Earlston GB 11 Ec14
Easdale GB 6 Db11
Easington GB 11 Fa17
Easington GB 17 Fd21
Easington GB 20 Fb27
Easingwold GB 11 Fa19
Easky IRL 8 Bd18
Eastbourne GB 20 Fd30
East Brent GB 19 Eb29
Eastchurch GB 21 Ga28
Eastcote GB 20 Fc28
East Cowes GB 20 Fa30
East Dereham GB 17 Ga24
Eastergate GB 20 Fb30
East Grafton GB 20 Ed28
East Grinstead GB 20 Fc29
East Haddon GB 20 Fb25

East Hanningfield – Emersleben

East Hanningfield GB 21 Ga27
East Horsley GB 20 Fc29
East Ilsley GB 20 Fa28
East Kilbride GB 10 Dd13
East Leake GB 16 Fa23
Eastleigh GB 20 Fa30
East Linton GB 11 Ec13
East Morden GB 19 Ec30
East Norton GB 16 Fb24
Eastoft GB 16 Fb21
Easton GB 17 Gb24
Easton GB 19 Ec31
Easton Grey GB 19 Ec27
East Poringland GB 17 Gb24
East Portlemouth GB 19 Dd32
East Ravendale GB 17 Fc21
East Rudham GB 17 Ga24
East Tisted GB 20 Fb29
Eastville GB 17 Fd23
East Winch GB 17 Fd24
Eastwood GB 16 Fa23
Eatoševo BG 180 Dc71
Eaux-Bonnes F 40 Fc56
Eauze F 40 Fd53
Ebberup DK 108 Dc27
Ebbo FIN 98 Kc39
Ebbw Vale GB 19 Eb27
Ebchester GB 11 Ed17
Ebeleben D 126 Dc40
Ebeltoft DK 109 Dd24
Eben A 143 Ea53
Ebene Reichenau A 144 Fa55
Ebenfurt A 145 Gb52
Ebensee A 144 Fa52
Ebensfeld D 134 Dc44
Eberbach D 134 Cd46
Eberdingen D 134 Cc48
Ebergassing A 145 Gb51
Ebergötzen D 126 Db39
Eberhardzell D 142 Da51
Ebermannsdorf D 135 Ea47
Ebermannstadt D 135 Dd45
Ebern D 134 Dc44
Ebernburg D 133 Ca45
Eberndorf A 144 Fc56
Ebersbach D 127 Ed41
Ebersbach D 128 Fa40
Ebersbach D 128 Fc41
Ebersbach D 128 Fc41
Ebersbach D 134 Cd48
Ebersberg D 143 Ea51
Ebersburg D 134 Da43
Eberschwang A 143 Ed51
Ebersdorf D 135 Dd44
Ebersdorf, Saalburg- D 135 Ea43
Eberswalde D 120 Fa35
Ebnat-Kappel CH 142 Cc53
Eboli I 161 Fc76
Ebrach D 134 Dc45
Ebreichsdorf A 145 Gb51
Ebreuil F 34 Hb46
Ebsdorfergrund D 126 Cd42
Ebstorf D 118 Dc34
Ecaterinovca MD 173 Fd59
Écaussinnes-Lalaing B 124 Ac41
Eccles GB 11 Ec14
Eccleshall GB 15 Ec23
Eceabat TR 185 Ea80
Echalar E 39 Ed55
Echallens CH 141 Bb55
Echalot F 30 Ja41
Echarri- E 39 Ec56
Echassières F 34 Hb45
Echauri E 39 Ec57
Eching D 135 Ea49
Eching D 143 Ea50
Echiré F 32 Fc45
Echourgnac F 32 Fd49
Echt GB 7 Ed09
Echt NL 125 Bb40
Echteld NL 125 Bb37
Echterdingen, Leinfelden- D 134 Cd49
Echternach L 133 Bc44
Écija E 60 Cc73
Ecirli TR 199 Ha89
Ečka SRB 174 Bb62
Eckartsau A 145 Gc51
Eckartsberga D 127 Ea41
Eckental D 135 Dd46
Eckernförde D 108 Db29
Eckerö FIN 96 Hb40
Eckersdorf D 135 Dd45
Eckington GB 16 Fa22
Eclaron-Braucourt F 24 Ja37
Ecly F 24 Hd34
Écommoy F 28 Fd40
Ecouché F 22 Fc37
Ecouflant F 28 Fb41
Écouis F 23 Gb35
Ecoyeux F 32 Fb47
Ecques F 23 Gd31
Ecseg H 146 Ja51
Ecsegfalva H 147 Jd54
Ecueillé F 29 Gb43
Écury-sur-Coole F 24 Hd36
Ed S 79 Gb30
Ed S 94 Ec45
Eda S 94 Ec42
Eda Glasbruck S 94 Ec41
Edam NL 116 Ba35
Edane S 94 Ed42
Ēdas LV 105 Jc51
Eddelak D 118 Da31
Edderton GB 5 Ea07
Eddleston GB 11 Eb14
Ede NL 125 Bb37
Ede S 79 Fd29
Ede S 87 Ga33
Edebäck S 94 Fa41
Edebo S 96 Ha41
Edeby S 96 Ha41
Edefors S 73 Hc21
Edelaye By DK 108 Dc25
Edelény H 146 Jc50
Edelschrott A 144 Fc55
Edelsfeld D 135 Ea46
Edemissen D 126 Db38
Edemissen D 126 Dc36
Eden S 79 Gb29
Edenbridge GB 20 Fd29
Edenderry IRL 13 Cc21
Edenkoben D 133 Cb46
Edersleben D 127 Dd40
Edertal D 126 Cd40
Edesbyn S 87 Fd37
Edesheim D 133 Cb46
Édessa GR 183 Bc77
Edestad S 111 Fd54
Edevik S 78 Ed28
Edewecht D 117 Cc34
Edgbaston GB 20 Ed25
Edgeworthstown = Mostrim IRL 9 Cb20
Edhem S 103 Fb47
Edinburgh GB 11 Eb13
Edincik TR 186 Fa80
Edineț MD 173 Fa54
Edipsós GR 189 Ca83
Edırne TR 185 Eb75
Edith Weston GB 16 Fb24
Edlingham GB 11 Ed15
Edlitz A 145 Gb54
Edmundbyers GB 11 Ed17
Ēdole LV 105 Jb51
Edolo I 149 Da57
Edremit TR 191 Ec82
Edrželija MK 183 Bd74
Edsberg S 95 Fc44
Edsbro S 96 Ha41
Edsbruk S 103 Gb48
Edsele S 79 Ga30
Edshult S 103 Fd49
Edshultshall S 102 Eb47
Edsleskog S 94 Ec44
Edsta S 87 Gb35
Edsvalla S 94 Fa43
Edsvära S 102 Ed47
Edsvik FIN 89 Hd32
Edzell GB 7 Ec10
Eeklo B 124 Ab39
Eelde NL 117 Bd33
Eemshaven NL 117 Ca32
Eemsmond NL 117 Ca32
Eerbeek NL 125 Bc37
Eernegem B 21 Ha29
Eersel NL 124 Ba39
Efeköy TR 193 Gc86
Efendiköprüsü TR 192 Ga84
Efendili TR 192 Fb84
Eferding A 144 Fa50
Effelder D 135 Dd43
Effretikon CH 141 Cb53
Efimovskij RUS 202 Ec08
Efir TR 192 Fc83
Efkarpía GR 183 Ca76
Efkarpía GR 183 Ca77
Efkarpía GR 184 Cc77
Efláni TR 205 Fa20
Eforie Nord RO 181 Fc68
Eforie Sud RO 181 Fc68
Efremov RUS 203 Fa12
Efteløt N 93 Dc42
Eg DK 108 Da25
Egáleo GR 189 Cb86
Egáni GR 183 Bd80
Egby S 103 Gb52
Egebæk DK 108 Da27
Egebjerg DK 108 Dc25
Egebjerg DK 109 Eb25
Egeln D 127 Ea38
Egense DK 101 Dd21
Eger H 146 Jb51
Egerbakta H 146 Jb51
Eğerci TR 187 Hb77
Egeris DK 108 Da24
Egersund N 92 Ca45
Egeskov DK 108 Db26
Egestorf D 118 Db34
Egg A 142 Da53
Eggby S 102 Fa46
Eggebek D 108 Da29
Eggedal N 85 Dc40
Eggemoen N 65 Kd07
Eggenburg A 136 Ga49
Eggenfelden D 143 Ec50
Eggenstein-Leopoldshafen D 133 Cb47
Eggerding A 143 Ed50
Eggermühlen D 117 Cb35
Eggersdorf, Fredersdorf- D 128 Fa36
Eggesin D 120 Fb32
Eggingen D 141 Cb52
Eggiwil CH 141 Bd54
Eggkleiva N 77 Db30
Egglescliffe GB 11 Fa18
Egglham D 135 Ec49
Egglkofen D 143 Eb50
Eggolsheim D 135 Dd45
Eggstätt D 143 Eb51
Eggum N 66 Fb14
Egham GB 20 Fb28
Eghezée B 124 Ad41
Egiáli GR 196 Dd90
Egiertowo PL 121 Ha30
Egiés GR 194 Bc90
Egileta E 39 Eb57
Egilsstaðir IS 3 Bc05
Égina GR 195 Cb87
Eging am See D 135 Ed49
Egínio GR 183 Bd78
Égio GR 188 Bb85
Egíra GR 189 Bc85
Eğirdir TR 199 Gd88
Égiros GR 184 Dc77
Egkomi CY 206 Jd96
Églaine LV 115 Lb53
Égletons F 33 Gd48
Eğlikler TR 199 Hb88
Egling D 142 Dc50
Egling D 143 Dd51
Eglingham GB 11 Ed15
Eglisau CH 141 Cb52
Égliseneuve-d'Antraigues F 33 Ha48
Egloffstein D 135 Dd45
Eglwysfach GB 15 Dd24
Eglwyswrw GB 14 Dc26
Eğmir TR 191 Ec82
Egmond aan Zee NL 116 Ad34
Egna I 150 Dd57
Egnach CH 142 Cd52
Egor'e RUS 202 Ed11
Egoreni MD 173 Fc54
Egor'evsk RUS 203 Fa10
Egorlykskaja RUS 205 Fc16
Egorovca MD 173 Fb56
Eğrekli TR 198 Fc91
Egremont GB 10 Ea18
Égreville F 29 Ha39
Eğridere TR 192 Fb87
Eğrioğlu TR 187 Gc78
Eğriöz TR 192 Fd83
Eğriöz TR 192 Ga82
Egsmark DK 109 Dd24
Egton GB 11 Fb18
Egtved DK 108 Db26
Éguilles F 42 Jc54
Eguisheim F 31 Kb39
Eguzon F 33 Gc45
Egyed H 145 Gd53
Egyek H 146 Jc52
Egyházasradoc H 145 Gc54
Egyptinkorpi FIN 83 Lc27
Ehekirchen D 134 Dc49
Ehingen D 134 Dc47
Ehingen am Ries D 134 Dc48
Ehingen (Donau) D 142 Da50
Ehínos GR 184 Db76
Ehningen D 134 Cc48
Ehra-Lessien D 127 Dd36
Ehrang D 133 Bc44
Ehrenberg D 134 Db43
Ehrenburg D 118 Cd35
Ehrenfriedersdorf D 127 Ec42
Ehrenhain D 127 Ec41
Ehrenhausen A 144 Fd55
Ehrenkirchen D 141 Ca51
Ehringshausen D 126 Cc42
Ehrwald A 142 Dc53
Ehtamo FIN 89 Jb37
Eia N 92 Cb45
Eiane N 92 Cb44
Eibar E 39 Eb55
Eibau D 128 Fc41
Eibelstadt D 134 Db45
Eibenstock D 135 Ec43
Eibergen NL 125 Bd37
Eibiswald A 144 Fd56
Eiby N 63 Hd08
Eich D 133 Cb45
Eichenbarleben D 127 Ea37
Eichenbrunn A 137 Gb49
Eichendorf D 135 Ec49
Eichenzell D 134 Da43
Eichstätt D 135 Dd48
Eichstetten D 141 Ca50
Eichwalde D 128 Fa37
Eičiai LT 113 Jd57
Eicklingen D 126 Dc36
Eid N 77 Dc29
Eid N 77 Da32
Eid N 78 Ea28
Eidanger N 93 Dc44
Eidapere EST 98 Kc44
Eiðar IS 3 Bc05
Eidbukt N 66 Fd12
Eidbukta N 71 Fb19
Eide N 66 Fc14
Eide N 77 Da31
Eide N 84 Ca36
Eide N 84 Cc39
Eide N 92 Cb45
Eide N 93 Da47
Eidem N 70 Ec23
Eidesund N 92 Ca43
Eidet N 62 Gc10
Eidet N 65 Kd07
Eidet N 66 Ga14
Eidet N 77 Dd30
Eidet N 93 Db45
Eidevik N 84 Cb36
Eidfjord N 84 Cd39
Eiði DK 3 Ca06
Eidkjosen N 62 Gc09
Eidnes N 63 Ja04
Eidså N 76 Cb33
Eidsberg N 94 Eb43
Eidsborg N 93 Da42
Eidsdal N 76 Cd33
Eidsfoss N 93 Dd42
Eidskog N 94 Ec41
Eidslandet N 84 Cb38
Eidsnes N 63 Hd08
Eidsøra N 77 Db31
Eidsvåg N 77 Db32
Eidsvåg N 92 Ca41
Eidsvoll N 94 Eb40
Eidvågeid N 63 Hd06
Eiesland N 92 Cc45
Eige N 92 Ca45
Eigebrekk N 92 Cd47
Eigeland N 92 Ca44
Eigeland N 92 Ca45
Eigeltingen D 142 Cc51
Eigirdonys LT 114 Kd58
Eigirdžiai LT 113 Jd54
Eigirgala LT 114 Kc57
Eijsden NL 125 Bb41
Eik N 92 Ca43
Eik N 92 Cb45
Eikange N 84 Ca38
Eikåsgrend N 92 Cb46
Eikefjord N 84 Cb35
Eikeland N 92 Cb46
Eikeland N 92 Cd46
Eikeland N 93 Db45
Eikelandsosen N 84 Cb40
Eiken N 92 Cc46
Eikenes N 84 Ca36
Eikla EST 105 Jc46
Eiknes N 84 Cb40
Eilenburg D 127 Ec40
Èilgar RUS 205 Ga15
Eilsleben D 127 Dd37
Eime D 126 Db37
Eimen D 126 Db38
Eimisjärvi FIN 83 Ma30
Eimke D 118 Dc34
Eina N 85 Ea39
Einastrand N 85 Ea39
Einavoll N 85 Ea39
Einbeck D 126 Db38
Eindhoven NL 125 Bb39
Einhausen D 134 Cc45
Einola FIN 83 Lb28
Einsiedel D 127 Ec42
Einsiedeln CH 141 Cb54
Einville-au-Jaurd F 25 Jd37
Eisden B 125 Bb40
Eisenach D 126 Db41
Eisenbach D 141 Cb51
Eisenberg D 127 Ea41
Eisenberg D 133 Cb45
Eisenerz A 144 Fc53
Eisenheim D 134 Db45
Eisenhüttenstadt D 128 Fc37
Eisenkappel A 144 Fb56
Eisenstadt A 145 Gb52
Eisentratten A 143 Ed55
Eisfeld D 134 Dc43
Eisgarn A 136 Fd48
Eišiškės LT 114 La59
Eisķene LV 105 Jb50
Eisma EST 98 Kd41
Eitensheim D 135 Dd48
Eiterfeld D 126 Da42
Eitorf D 125 Ca41
Eitrheimsnes N 84 Cc40
Eitting D 143 Ea50
Eivere EST 98 Kd43
Eivindvik N 84 Ca37
Eivissa E 56 Gc69
Eixo P 44 Ac62
Ejby DK 108 Dc26
Ejby DK 109 Eb26
Ejea de los Caballeros E 47 Fa59
Ejheden S 87 Fd37
Ejsing DK 100 Da22
Ejsk RUS 205 Fb16
Ejstrupholm DK 108 Db24
Ejulve E 48 Fb63
Ek S 102 Fa46
Ekängen S 103 Fd46
Ekaterinovka RUS 203 Fa12
Ekaterinovka RUS 203 Fc12
Ekby S 102 Fa46
Eke S 104 Ha50
Ekeberga S 103 Fd52
Ekeby S 96 Gd41
Ekeby S 96 Gc44
Ekeby S 103 Fc47
Ekeby S 104 Ha49
Ekeby S 110 Ed55
Ekeby-Almby S 95 Fd44
Ekebyborna S 103 Fd46
Ekedalen S 102 Fa47
Ekenäs FIN 97 Jd40
Ekenässjön S 103 Fc50
Eker S 95 Fc44
Ekerö S 96 Gd44
Ekeskog S 103 Fb46
Eket S 110 Ed54
Eketånga S 102 Ed52
Ekfors S 73 Jb20
Ekimovići RUS 202 Ec12
Ekinhisar TR 193 Gb86
Ekinli TR 186 Fb80
Ekinli TR 187 Gc79
Ekkerøy N 65 Kc06
Eknäs FIN 97 Jc40
Ekne N 78 Eb29
Ekola FIN 81 Jb30
Ekorrsele S 80 Ha26
Ekorrträsk S 80 Ha26
Ekså N 92 Cd45
Ekshärad S 94 Fa41
Ekşidere TR 191 Ed81
Ekşi Gediz TR 192 Fd84
Ekşili TR 199 Gc90
Eksingedal N 84 Cb38
Eksjö S 103 Fc49
Ekskogen S 96 Gd42
Eksta S 104 Gd50
Ekträsk S 80 Hb26
Ekzarh Antimovo BG 181 Ec72
Ekzarh Josif BG 180 Ea69
Elabuga RUS 203 Ga08
Elafohóri GR 184 Da77
Elafohóri GR 185 Ea76
Elafónissos GR 195 Bd91
Elafótopos GR 182 Ad79
El Álamo E 46 Db65
El Álamo E 59 Bd73
El Álamo E 59 Cb73
El Algar E 55 Fa73
El Aljibe y las Brencas de Sicilia E 61 Ec73
El Alquián E 61 Eb76
Elämäjärvi FIN 82 Kb28
Elan' RUS 203 Fd12
El Ángel E 60 Cc77
Elan'-Kolenovskij RUS 203 Fc13
Elantxobe E 39 Eb55
El Arahal E 59 Cb74
El Arenal E 45 Cc65
Elassóna GR 183 Bc80
El Astillero E 38 Dc55
Eláta GR 191 Dd86
Eláti GR 183 Bc79
Elati GR 188 Bb81
Elátia GR 189 Bd84
Elat'ma RUS 203 Fb10
Elatohóri GR 182 Ba79
Elatohóri GR 183 Bd78
Élatos GR 182 Ba79
Elatoú GR 188 Bb84
El Azagador E 54 Fa67
El Ballestero E 53 Ea70
El Barco de Ávila E 45 Cb64
Elbasan AL 182 Ac75
Elbasan TR 186 Fb77
El Batán E 45 Bd65
El Baúl E 61 Dd74
El Bayo E 47 Fa59
Elbe D 126 Dc37
El Bercial E 52 Cc66
Elbeuf F 23 Ga35
Elbeyli TR 186 Ga79
Elbingerode D 126 Dc38
Elbląg PL 122 Hc30
El Bocal E 47 Ed59
El Bodón E 45 Bd64
El Bonillo E 53 Ea69
El Bosque E 59 Cb76
El'brus RUS 205 Ga17
Elbtal D 125 Cb42
El Bujeo E 59 Ca78
El Bullaque E 52 Da68
Elburg NL 117 Bc35
El Burgo E 60 Cc76
El Burgo de Ebro E 48 Fb61
El Burgo de Osma E 46 Dd60
El Burgo Ranero E 37 Cd57
El Buste E 47 Ed60
El Cabaco E 45 Ca63
El Cabo de Gata E 61 Eb76
El Calonge E 59 Cb73
El Campamento E 59 Cb78
el Campello E 55 Fb71
El Campillo E 53 Dd71
El Campillo E 53 Ea71
El Campillo de la Jara E 52 Cc67
El Campo de Peñaranda E 45 Cc62
El Cañavate E 53 Eb67
El Cardoso de la Sierra E 46 Dc62
El Carpio E 60 Cd72
El Carpio de Tajo E 52 Da66
El Casar de Escalona E 46 Da65
El Casar de Talamanca E 46 Dc63
El Castaño E 59 Ca77
El Castellar E 47 Fa65
El Castillo de las Guardas E 59 Bd73
El Centenillo E 52 Db71
El Cerro de Andévalo E 59 Bb72
El Chaparral E 60 Cd77
Elche E 55 Fb71
Elche de la Sierra E 53 Eb71
Elchesheim-Illingen D 133 Cb47
Elchingen D 134 Da49
Elciego E 39 Eb58
Elçili TR 185 Eb76
Elcóaz E 39 Fa57
El Cobo E 61 Ec72
el Cogul E 48 Ga61
El Collado E 54 Fa66
El Colmenar E 59 Cb76
El Colmenar E 59 Cb77
El Colorado E 59 Bd77
El Corchuelo E 59 Bc74
El Coronil E 59 Ca75
El Crucero E 37 Ca54
El Cuartón E 59 Ca78
El Cubillo de Uceda E 46 Dc63
El Cubo de Don Sancho E 45 Ca62
El Cubo de la Tierra del Vino E 45 Cb61
El Cuervo E 59 Bd75
Elda E 55 Fa71
Elda N 66 Ga12
Eldalen N 92 Cd46
Eldek TR 192 Fa85
Eldena D 119 Ea34
Eldforsen S 95 Fb40
Eldingen D 118 Dc35
Eldsberga S 110 Ed53
Eléa GR 195 Bd90
Elec RUS 203 Fa12
Eledio CY 206 Hd98
Elefsína GR 189 Cb86
Elefthério GR 189 Bd81
Elefthero GR 182 Ad79
Eleftherohóri GR 183 Bb79
Eleftheroúpoli GR 184 Da77
Eleja LV 106 Kb52
El Ejido E 61 Dd76
Elek H 147 Jd56
Èlektostal' RUS 203 Fa10
Elektrėnai LT 114 Kd58
Elemir SRB 153 Jc59
Elemno RUS 99 Ma43
Elena BG 180 Ea71
Elenovo BG 180 Ea73
Eleófito GR 188 Ba83
Eleohóri GR 184 Cd77
Eleohóri GR 194 Bb89
Eleón GR 184 Cc76
Eleón GR 189 Bc84
Eleoússa GR 182 Ad80
El Escorial E 46 Db64
Elešnica BG 184 Cc74
El Espinar E 46 Da63
Elfershausen D 134 Db44
Elford GB 16 Ed24
El Frago E 39 Fa58
El Frasno E 47 Ed61
Elgå N 86 Ec34
Elganowo PL 121 Ha31
El Gargantón E 52 Da69
El Garrobo E 59 Bb73
El Gastor E 59 Cb76
Elgg CH 142 Cc52
Elgin GB 5 Eb07
Elgiszewo PL 121 Hb34
Elgoibar E 39 Eb55
Elgol GB 6 Db09
El Grado E 48 Fd59
El Granado E 58 Ba73
el Grau de Castelló E 54 Fc66
el Grau de Gandia E 54 Fc69
Elgsmyra N 86 Ec36
Elgsnes N 66 Ga12
El Guijar E 46 Db62
El Guijo E 52 Cd70
Elham GB 21 Gb29
El Haza del Riego E 61 Ea75
El Herrumblar E 54 Ed68
El Higuerón E 60 Cc72
El Hijate E 61 Ea74
Elhovka RUS 203 Ga09
Elhovo BG 180 Dd73
Elhovo BG 180 Eb73
El Hoyo E 52 Db71
El Hoyo de Pinares E 46 Da64
Eliá GR 194 Ba88
Elijärven kaivos FIN 74 Jc21
Elíka GR 195 Bd91
Elikónas GR 189 Bd85
Elimäki FIN 90 Kd37
Elincourt-Sainte-Marguerite F 23 Ha34
Elinókastro GR 183 Bb80
Elin Pelin BG 179 Cd71
Elionka RUS 202 Ec13
Elisejna BG 179 Cc70
Èlista RUS 205 Ga15
Elizarovo RUS 107 Ld46
Elizavetino RUS 99 Mb40
Elizondo E 39 Ed56
El Jardín E 53 Eb70
El Jardón E 60 Cd73
Eljaröd S 111 Fb56
El Jautor E 59 Ca77
Ełk PL 123 Jd31
Elkeland N 92 Cc46
Elkenroth D 125 Cb41
Elkšņi LV 106 La52
Elkšņukrogs LV 106 La52
Elkstone GB 20 Ed27
Ellamaa EST 98 Ka43
El Lance de la Virgen E 61 Dd76
Ellastone GB 16 Ed23
Elleholm S 111 Fc54
Ellenberg D 134 Db48
Ellen's Green GB 20 Fc29
El Lentiscal E 59 Ca78
Ellerau D 118 Db32
Ellesmere GB 15 Eb23
Ellesmere Port GB 15 Eb22
Ellewoutsdijk NL 124 Ab38
Ellhofen D 134 Cd47
Elliant F 27 Dd39
Ellidshøj DK 100 Dc21
Elling DK 101 Dd19
Ellingen D 134 Dc47
Ellinikó GR 189 Cb83
Ellinikó GR 189 Bc86
Ellinikó GR 194 Bb87
Ellinikó GR 194 Bc87
Ellinikó GR 195 Bd91
Ellinikó GR 195 Cb87
El Llano (San Tirso de Abres) E 37 Bd54
Ellmau A 143 Eb53
Ellon GB 5 Ed08
Ellös S 102 Eb47
Ellrich D 126 Dc39
Ellwangen D 142 Da51
Ellwangen/Jagst D 134 Db48
Elm CH 142 Cc54
Elmabağı TR 192 Fa86
Elmacık TR 185 Ed74
Elmacık TR 199 Gb89
El Maderal E 45 Cb61
El Madroño E 59 Bc73
Elmalı TR 185 Ec78
Elmalı TR 186 Fd77
Elmalı TR 187 Gb79
Elmalı TR 198 Ga91
El Manantial E 59 Bd76
Elmas I 169 Ca79
el Masnou E 49 Ha61
Elmdon GB 20 Fd26
Elmelunde DK 109 Ec28
Elmen A 142 Db53
Elmenhorst D 118 Dc32
Elmenhorst D 119 Eb31
Elmley Castle GB 20 Ed26
El Molar E 46 Dc63
el Molar E 48 Ga62
El Molar E 61 Dd72
El Molinillo E 52 Da67
El Moncayo E 55 Fb72
El Moral E 61 Eb72
Elmore GB 19 Ec27
el Morell E 48 Gb62
Elmshorn D 118 Db32
Elmstein D 133 Ca46
El Musel E 37 Cc54
Elne F 41 Hb57
Elnesvågen N 76 Cd31
El Niño E 55 Ed72
El'nja RUS 202 Ec11
Elopía GR 189 Ca85
Elorrio E 39 Eb56
Élos GR 200 Ca95
Előszállás H 146 Hc55
Eloúnta GR 201 Dc96
Eloyes F 31 Ka39
el Palmar E 54 Fc68
El Palmar E 55 Fa72
El Palmar de Troya E 59 Ca75
El Parador de las Hortichuelas E 61 Ea76
El Paraíso E 60 Cc77
El Pardo E 46 Dc64
el Pas de la Casa AND 40 Gc58
el Pas de la Casa AND 40 Gc58
El Pedernoso E 53 Ea67
El Pedregal E 47 Ed63
El Pedroso E 37 Cc54
El Pedroso E 59 Ca72
El Pedroso de la Armuña E 45 Cc62
El Peral E 53 Ec67
El Perdigón E 45 Cb61
el Perelló E 48 Ga63
el Perelló E 54 Fc68
Elphin GB 4 Dc06
Elphin IRL 8 Ca19
el Pla de Santa Maria E 48 Gb61
El Picazo E 53 Eb68
el Pi de Sant Just E 49 Gc59
El Pilar de la Horadada E 55 Fb73
el Pinell de Brai E 48 Ga63
El Piñero E 45 Cc61
El Pintado E 59 Ca72
el Poblenou del Delta E 48 Ga64
El Pobo E 47 Fa64
El Pobo de Dueñas E 47 Ed63
el Pont d'Armentera E 49 Gc61
el Pont de Suert E 40 Ga58
el Pont de Vilomara E 49 Gd60
El Portal E 59 Bd76
el Port de Borriana E 54 Fc66
el Port de la Selva E 41 Hc58
el Port de Sagunt E 54 Fc67
El Portil E 59 Bb74
El Pozo de los Frailes E 61 Eb76
El Priorato E 59 Cb73
El Provencio E 53 Ea68
El Puente del Arzobispo E 52 Cc66
El Puente del Río E 61 Dd76
El Puente (Guriezo) E 38 Dd55
El Puerto E 37 Cb55
El Puerto E 51 Bc71
El Puerto de Santa María E 59 Bd76
El Pulpillo E 55 Ed70
El Puntal E 37 Cd54
El Real de la Jara E 59 Bd72
El Real de San Vicente E 46 Cd65
El Rincón E 61 Ec74
El Robledo E 52 Da68
El Rocío E 59 Bc74
el Rodriguillo E 55 Fa71
El Romeral E 52 Dc67
El Rompido E 59 Bb74
El Ronquillo E 59 Bd72
El Royo E 47 Ea60
El Rubio E 60 Cc74
El Sabinar E 47 Fa59
El Sabinar E 61 Eb72
el Sahuco E 61 Ea74
el Saler E 54 Fc68
El Salobral E 53 Ec69
El Saltador E 61 Ec74
El Santiscal E 59 Ca76
els Arcs E 48 Fd61
El Saucejo E 60 Cc75
Elsazı TR 199 Gd89
Elsdon GB 11 Ed15
Elsdorf D 118 Da33
Elsdorf D 125 Bc40
Elsdorf-Westermühlen D 118 Db30
Elsenborn B 125 Bb42
Elsenfeld D 134 Cd45
Elsenham GB 20 Fd27
el Serrat AND 40 Gc57
el Serrat AND 40 Gc57
Elsfjord N 71 Fb21
Elsfleth D 118 Cd33
els Hostalets d'en Bas E 49 Ha59
Elšica BG 179 Da72
Elsing D 127 Ec39
Elsing GB 17 Ga24
Elsinvaara FIN 83 Lc25
el Soleràs E 48 Ga61
Elspeet NL 116 Bb36
els Prats de Rei E 49 Gc60
Elsrickle GB 11 Eb14
Elst NL 125 Bb37
Elstad N 78 Ed26
Elstal D 127 Ed36
Elsted GB 20 Fb29
Elster D 127 Ec38
Elstertrebnitz D 127 Eb41
Elsterwerda D 128 Fa40
Elstow GB 20 Fc26
Elstra D 128 Fb41
Eltendorf A 145 Gb55
Eltham GB 20 Fd28
El Tiemblo E 46 Da64
El Toboso E 53 Dd67
Elton IRL 12 Bd24
Èl'ton RUS 203 Ga13
El Torno E 59 Bd76
El Toro E 54 Fa66
El Toro E 54 Fb66
El Tricheto E 52 Da68
El Trobal E 59 Ca75
El Tumbalejo E 59 Bc73
Eltvik N 76 Ca33
Eltville D 133 Cb44
Elva EST 106 La46
Elva I 148 Bb62
El Vacar E 60 Cc72
Elvanfoot GB 10 Ea15
Elvas P 51 Bb68
Elvåsen N 78 Ec25
Elvdal N 86 Ec36
Elve N 92 Cb46
Elvebakken N 62 Gd08
Elvebakken N 63 Hd08
Elveden GB 21 Ga25
Elvedjupkroken N 64 Ka06
Elvegården N 67 Gb14
El Vellón E 46 Dc63
Elvemund N 64 Jc09
Elven F 27 Eb40
el Vendrell E 49 Gc62
Elvenes N 65 Kd07
Elvenes N 66 Fc12
Elvenheim N 65 La07
El Ventorillo E 38 Db56
Elverum N 67 Gc11
Elverum N 86 Eb38
Elvestad N 93 Ea42
Elvevollen N 62 Ha10
El Villar de Arnedo E 39 Ec58
el Vilosell E 48 Gb61
Elviria E 60 Cc77
El Viso E 52 Cc70
El Viso del Alcor E 59 Ca74
Elvkroken N 66 Fd16
Elvran N 78 Eb30
Elwick GB 11 Fa17
Elworthy GB 19 Ea29
Elx E 55 Fb71
Elxleben D 127 Dd41
Ely GB 20 Fd25
Elz D 133 Cb43
Elzach D 141 Ca50
Elze D 126 Db37
Elztal D 134 Cd46
Emagny F 31 Jc41
Emanville F 23 Ga36
Embid E 47 Ec63
Embid de Ariza E 47 Ec61
Émbonas GR 197 Ed93
Embório GR 183 Bb78
Embório GR 196 Db92
Emborió GR 197 Eb90
Emborió GR 197 Ec92
Emboriós GR 197 Ed92
Embrach CH 141 Cb52
Embrun F 35 Kb50
Embsen D 118 Dc34
Embūte LV 105 Jc52
Embun E 39 Fb57
Emburga LV 106 Kb52
Emden D 117 Ca33
Emecik TR 197 Ed91
Emerando E 38 Ea55
Emersleben D 127 Dd38

Emet – Fåker

Emet TR 192 Fd83
Emincik TR 187 Hb80
Emiralem TR 191 Ec85
Emirdağ TR 193 Ha84
Emirhisa TR 192 Ga86
Emirhisar TR 193 Gb86
Emirköy TR 192 Fd82
Emirler TR 192 Fb83
Emirler TR 198 Ga91
Emiryakup TR 185 Ec77
Emkendorf D 118 Db30
Emlichheim D 117 Bd35
Emly IRL 12 Bd24
Emmaboda S 111 Fd53
Emmaljunga S 110 Fa53
Emmaste EST 97 Jc45
Emmeloord NL 117 Bc34
Emmelsbüll-Horsbüll D 108 Cd28
Emmelshausen D 133 Ca43
Emmen NL 117 Ca34
Emmendingen D 141 Ca50
Emmer-Compascuum NL 117 Ca34
Emmerich D 125 Bc37
Emmerik = Emmerich D 125 Bc37
Emmerthal D 126 Da37
Emmerting D 143 Ec51
Emmingen-Liptingen D 142 Cc51
Emmoo IRL 8 Ca20
Emo IRL 13 Cb22
Emőd H 146 Jc51
Emoniemi FIN 82 Kb28
Empa CY 206 Hd98
Empessós GR 188 Ba82
Empfingen D 134 Cc49
Empo FIN 97 Jb39
Empoli I 155 Db65
Empuriabrava E 41 Hc58
Emre TR 186 Fb80
Emre TR 192 Fb85
Emremsultan TR 193 Ha81
Emsbüren D 117 Ca36
Emsdetten D 125 Cb37
Emsfors S 103 Gb51
Emskirchen D 134 Dc46
Emstek D 117 Cc35
Emtinghausen D 118 Cd34
Emyvale IRL 9 Cc18
Ena E 39 Fb58
Enafors S 78 Ed30
Enäjärvi FIN 90 La37
Enåker S 95 Gb41
Enånger S 87 Gb36
Enarsvedjan S 79 Fb29
Enåsa S 95 Fb45
Encekler TR 192 Fb85
Encima-Angulo E 38 Dd56
Encinas E 46 Dc61
Encinas de Abajo E 45 Cc62
Encinas de Esgueva E 46 Db60
Encinasola E 51 Bc71
Encinasola de los Comendadores E 45 Bd62
Encinas Reales E 60 Cd74
Encío E 38 Dd57
Enciso E 47 Eb59
Encs H 147 Jd50
Endach A 143 Eb53
Endingen CH 141 Cb52
Endingen D 141 Ca50
Endla EST 98 La44
Endon GB 16 Ed23
Endre S 104 Ha49
Endriejavas LT 113 Jc55
Endrinal E 45 Cb63
Endrup DK 108 Da26
Enebakk N 93 Ea42
Enego I 150 Dd58
Enerhodar UA 205 Fa16
Eneryda S 103 Fb52
Enez TR 185 Ea78
Enfesta E 36 Ad56
Engan N 70 Ed21
Engarés GR 196 Db90
Engdal N 77 Dc30
Enge N 77 Dc30
Engelberg CH 141 Cb55
Engelhartszell A 144 Fa50
Engeln D 118 Cd35
Engels RUS 203 Fd12
Engelsberg D 143 Eb51
Engelsbrand D 134 Cc48
Engelskirchen D 125 Ca41
Engelst DK 100 Db21
Engelsviken N 93 Ea43
Engelthal D 135 Dd46
Engen D 142 Cc51
Engene N 93 Da46
Engenes N 67 Gb12
Enger D 126 Cc37
Enger N 85 Dd39
Engerdal N 86 Ec35
Engerneset N 86 Ec36
Engesland N 93 Da46
Engesvang DK 108 Db24
Enghien B 124 Ab41
Engi CH 142 Cc54
Engilli TR 193 Ha86
Engis B 124 Ba41
Englancourt F 24 Hc33
Englefontaine F 24 Hc32
Engstingen D 134 Cd49
Engstlenalp CH 141 Cb55
Enguera E 54 Fb69
Enguídanos E 54 Ed67
Engure LV 106 Ka50
Engürücük TR 186 Fd80
Engvik N 62 Gc08
Engvoll N 85 Ea34
Enica BG 179 Da69
Enichioi MD 177 Fc60
Enina BG 180 Dd72
Eningen D 134 Cd49
Enisala RO 177 Fc65
Enix E 61 Ea76
Enkenbach-Alsenborn D 133 Ca46
Enkhausen D 126 Cc40
Enkhuizen NL 116 Bb34
Enklinge FIN 97 Hd40
Enköping S 95 Gb42
Enköpings-Näs S 95 Gb43
Enmo N 86 Ea32
Enna I 167 Fa86
Enneberg I 143 Ea56
Ennepetal D 125 Ca39
Enney CH 141 Bc55
Ennezat F 34 Hb46
Ennigerloh D 125 Cb38
Enningdal N 94 Eb44
Ennis IRL 12 Bc22
Enniscorthy IRL 13 Cc24
Enniskean IRL 12 Bc26
Enniskerry IRL 13 Cd22
Enniskillen GB 9 Cb18
Ennistimon IRL 12 Bc22
Enns A 144 Fb51
Ennyinen FIN 97 Ja39
Eno FIN 83 Ld30
Enodden N 78 Ea31
Enokunta FIN 89 Jd35
Enonkoski FIN 91 Lc32
Enonkylä FIN 82 Kc25
Enonlahti FIN 82 La30
Enontekiö FIN 68 Ja13
Ens NL 117 Bc35
Enschede NL 117 Bd36
Ensdorf D 135 Ea47
Ense D 125 Cb39
Ensen S 87 Fd38
Ensisheim F 31 Kb39
Enskogen S 87 Fd35
Enstone GB 20 Fa26
Enter NL 117 Bd36
Entlebuch CH 141 Ca54
Entracque I 148 Bc63
Entradas P 58 Ad72
Entrages F 42 Ka52
Entraigues F 29 Gc43
Entraigues F 35 Jd49
Entrains-sur-Nohain F 30 Hb41
Entrambasmestas E 38 Dc55
Entrammes F 28 Fb40
Entraunes F 43 Kb51
Entraygues-sur-Truyère F 33 Ha51
Entrecasteaux F 42 Ka54
Entrechaux F 42 Jc52
Entrena E 39 Eb58
Entre-os-Rios P 44 Ad61
Entrevaux F 43 Kb52
Entrín Bajo E 51 Bc69
Entroncamento P 50 Ac66
Entuğrulköy TR 193 Hb83
Entzheim F 25 Kc37
Envendos P 50 Ba66
Envermeu F 23 Gb33
Envernallas E 37 Bd55
Enviken S 95 Fd39
Enville GB 15 Ec25
Enying H 145 Hb55
Enzenkirchen A 144 Fa50
Enzersdorf im Thale A 137 Gb49
Enzesfeld A 145 Gb52
Enzinger Boden A 143 Eb54
Enzklösterle D 133 Cb48
Eochaill IRL 13 Ca26
Čohkkiras S 67 Hb15
Epagny F 24 Hb35
Epagny F 30 Jb41
Epaignes F 22 Fd35
Epáno Fellós GR 190 Da87
Epanomí GR 183 Ca78
Epaux-Bézu F 24 Hb36
Epe NL 117 Bc36
Épehy F 24 Hb33
Épernay F 24 Hc36
Epernon F 29 Gc38
Epfig F 31 Kb38
Epieds F 24 Hb36
Epierre F 35 Ka47
Epikopí GR 195 Ca89
Épila E 47 Fa61
Épinal F 31 Jd38
Epineuil-le-Fleuriel F 29 Ha44
Epiry F 30 Hc42
Episcopia I 162 Gb77
Episkopí CY 206 Ja98
Episkopí GR 188 Bb83
Episkopí GR 200 Cc95
Episkopí GR 200 Da96
Epitálio GR 194 Ba87
Epizon F 30 Jb38
Époisses F 30 Hd41
Epoo FIN 98 Kc39
Epoye F 24 Hd35
Eppan I 142 Dc56
Eppelborn D 133 Bd46
Eppenbrunn D 133 Ca47
Eppendorf D 127 Ed42
Eppe-Sauvage F 24 Hd32
Epping GB 20 Fd27
Eppingen D 134 Cc47
Eppstein D 134 Cc44
Epsom GB 20 Fc28
Eptagoneia CY 206 Jb97
Eptahóri GR 182 Ba78
Eptakomi CY 206 Jd95
Eptálofos GR 183 Cb76
Eptálofos GR 189 Bd84
Epuisay F 29 Ga40
Epureni RO 177 Fb60
Epworth GB 16 Fb21
Équeurdreville-Hainneville F 22 Ed34
Equihen-Plage F 23 Gb31
Equi Terme I 155 Da64
Eraclea I 150 Eb59
Eraclea Mare I 150 Ec59
Erahtur RUS 203 Fb10
Eräjärvi FIN 90 Ka35
Eräjärvi FIN 91 Lc34
Eranova I 164 Gb83
Eräslahti FIN 90 Ka34
Erastvere EST 107 Lb46
Eratiní GR 189 Bc85
Erátira GR 183 Bb78
Erba I 149 Cc58
Erbaa TR 205 Fc20
Erbach D 134 Cd45
Erbach D 142 Da50
Erbajolo F 154 Cb70
Erbalunga F 154 Cc68
Erbedeiro E 36 Bb57
Erbendorf D 135 Eb45
Ērberge LV 106 Kd52
Erbes-Büdesheim D 133 Cb45
Erbiceni RO 173 Fa57
Ercheu F 23 Ha34
Erchie I 162 Hb76
Ercolano I 161 Fb75
Ercsi H 146 Hc54
Erd H 146 Hc53
Erdal N 63 Ja06
Erdal N 84 Cd34
Erdal N 84 Cb35
Erdeborn D 127 Ea40
Erdek TR 186 Fa79
Erdelek TR 198 Ga91
Erdemli TR 187 Gb79
Erden BG 179 Cc69
Erdeven F 27 Ea41
Erdevik SRB 153 Ja61
Erding D 143 Ea50
Erdington GB 16 Ed24
Erdőbénye H 147 Jd50
Erdoğlu TR 187 Gc79
Erdut HR 153 Hd59
Erdweg D 143 Dd50
Eréac F 27 Ec39
Erecek TR 191 Ea82
Ereğli TR 187 Ha77
Erehnovo RUS 107 Ld46
Ereira P 50 Ab67
Eremitu RO 172 Dd58
Erenköy TR 193 Gb82
Erenler TR 186 Ga77
Eresfjord N 77 Db32
Eressós GR 191 Dd83
Erétria GR 189 Bd82
Erétria GR 189 Cc85
Erezée B 124 Ba42
Erfde D 118 Da30
Erfjord N 92 Cb42
Erftstadt D 125 Bd41
Erfurt D 127 Dd41
Ērgeme LV 106 La47
Ergersheim D 134 Db46
Ergili TR 186 Fa80
Ērgli LV 106 La50
Ergolding D 135 Eb49
Ergoldsbach D 135 Eb49
Ergué-Gabéric F 27 Dc39
Eriboll GB 4 Dd04
Erice I 166 Ea84
Erice TR 192 Ga86
Ericeira P 50 Aa68
Ericek TR 186 Fd80
Ericek TR 187 Gd80
Erikler TR 185 Ec75
Erikli TR 185 Eb78
Erikli TR 186 Fa80
Erikli TR 193 Gb81
Erikoussa GR 182 Aa79
Eriksberg S 71 Fd24
Eriksberg S 102 Eb47
Erikslund S 87 Ga33
Eriksmåla S 103 Fd52
Eriksrud N 85 Ea39
Erikstad N 66 Fd13
Erikstad S 102 Ec46
Ering D 143 Ed50
Eringsboda S 111 Fd53
Ēriškiai LT 114 Kc55
Eriskirch D 142 Cd52
Eriswell GB 20 Fd25
Eriswil CH 141 Ca54
Erithrés GR 189 Ca86
Erka N 85 Db34
Erkelenz D 125 Bc40
Erkheikki S 68 Ja17
Erkheim D 142 Db51
Erkner D 128 Fa36
Erla E 47 Fa59
Erlabrunn D 134 Da45
Erlach A 145 Gb52
Erlangen D 135 Dd46
Erlau D 127 Ec41
Erlbach D 143 Ec50
Erle D 125 Bd38
Erlėnai LT 113 Jb54
Erlenbach D 134 Cd45
Erlenbach D 134 Cd47
Erlensee D 134 Cd44
Erligheim D 134 Cd47
Erlinsbach CH 141 Ca53
Erlsbach A 143 Eb55
Erm NL 117 Bd35
Ermakiá GR 183 Bc78
Ermakovo RUS 122 Jb30
Ermakovo RUS 203 Ga09
Erma reka BG 184 Db76
Ermatingen CH 142 Cc52
Ermelo NL 116 Bb36
Ermelo P 44 Ba60
Ermenonville F 23 Ha36
Ermesinde P 44 Ad61
Ermida P 44 Ac63
Ermidas-Aldeia P 50 Ac71
Ermióni GR 195 Ca88
Ermiš RUS 203 Fb10
Ermita de Carrión E 51 Bb68
Ermita del Ramonete E 55 Ed74
Ermoclia MD 173 Ga59
Ermoúpoli GR 196 Da89
Ermsleben D 127 Dd39
Ermua E 39 Eb55
Erndtebrück D 126 Cc41
Ernée F 28 Fb39
Ernei RO 171 Dc59
Ernestinovo HR 153 Hc60
Ernsgaden D 135 Ea49
Ernstbrunn A 137 Gb49
Erolzheim D 142 Da51
Erôme F 34 Jb49
Erp NL 125 Bb38
Erpingham GB 17 Gb23
Erquy F 26 Eb37
Erriff Bridge IRL 8 Bb19
Erril IRL 13 Cb23
Errindlev DK 109 Ea29
Erritsø DK 108 Db26
Erro E 39 Ed56
Errol GB 7 Eb11
Erschwil CH 141 Bd53
Érsekcsanád H 153 Hd57
Ersekë AL 182 Ad78
Érsekvadkert H 146 Hd51
Ersfjordbotn N 62 Gc09
Erši RUS 202 Ed11
Erska S 102 Ec47
Erslev DK 100 Da21
Ersmark S 72 Gb24
Ersmark S 80 Hc25
Ersmark S 80 Hb28
Ersnäs S 73 Hd22
Eršovo RUS 107 Ld46
Erstein F 25 Kc37
Erstfeld CH 141 Cb55
Ersvika N 66 Fc17
Ertingen D 142 Cd50
Erto I 150 Eb57
Ertsjärv S 73 Hd19
Ertuğrul TR 185 Ed76
Ertuğrul TR 186 Fc80
Ertuğrul TR 191 Ed82
Ertuğrul TR 192 Fc87
Ervalla S 95 Fd43
Ervasti FIN 75 Kc22
Ervauville F 29 Ha39
Ervedal P 50 Ba68
Ervedosa do Douro P 44 Bb61
Ervelä FIN 97 Jd40
Ervenik HR 157 Ga64
Ervidel P 50 Ad71
Ervik N 76 Ca33
Ervita EST 98 Kd43
Ervy-le-Châtel F 30 Hc39
Erwitte D 126 Cc39
Erwood GB 15 Ea26
Erxleben D 127 Dd37
Erzgrube D 133 Cb49
Erzincan TR 205 Fd20
Erzurum TR 205 Ga20
Eržvilkas LT 114 Ka56
Esadiye TR 186 Fd79
Esanos E 38 Da55
Esatlar TR 192 Ga83
Esbjerg DK 108 Cd26
Esbo FIN 98 Kb39
Esbønderup DK 109 Ec24
Escairón (Saviñao) E 36 Bb56
Escalada E 38 Dc56
Escalaplano I 169 Cb78
Escalhão P 45 Bc62
Escalles F 21 Gc30
Escalona E 40 Fd58
Escalona E 46 Da65
Escalona del Prado E 46 Db62
Escalonilla E 52 Da66
Escalos de Baixo P 44 Bb65
Escalos de Cima P 44 Bb65
Escamplero E 37 Cb54
Escañuela E 52 Da72
es Capdellà E 56 Ha67
Escarabote E 36 Ac56
Escariche E 46 Dd64
Escároz E 39 Fa56
Escarrilla E 40 Fc57
es Castell E 57 Jb66
Escatalens F 40 Gb53
Escatrón E 48 Fc62
Eschach D 134 Da48
Eschau D 134 Cd45
Eschborn D 134 Cc44
Escheburg D 118 Dc33
Eschede D 118 Dc35
Eschenau A 144 Fd51
Eschenbach D 135 Ea45
Eschenburg D 126 Cc41
Eschenfelden D 135 Ea46
Eschenlohe D 143 Dd52
Eschershausen D 126 Da38
Eschlkam D 135 Ec47
Esch-s.-Alz. L 133 Bb45
Esch-sur-Sûre L 133 Bb44
Eschwege D 126 Db40
Eschweiler D 125 Bc41
Escombreras E 55 Fa74
Escorihuela E 47 Fa64
Escos F 39 Fa55
Escot F 39 Fb56
Escouloubre F 41 Gd57
Escource F 39 Fa52
Escrennes F 29 Gd39
es Cubells E 56 Gb69
Escucha E 48 Fb63
Escudeiros P 44 Ad60
Escuderos E 46 Db59
Escurial E 51 Ca68
Escusa P 50 Ad67
Esechioi RO 181 Ed68
Eşelek TR 185 Ec80
Eşeler TR 192 Fa82
Eşelnița RO 174 Ca64
Esen BG 181 Ec71
Eşen TR 192 Fd82
Eşen TR 198 Fd92
Esenbağ TR 192 Fc83
Esence TR 186 Fc80
Esence TR 193 Gd82
Esendere TR 193 Gc87
Esenkaya TR 198 Fb89
Esenköy TR 187 Gc80
Esenköy TR 198 Fb88
Esenköy TR 198 Fd92
Esenler TR 185 Ed77
Esenli TR 192 Fa82
Esens D 117 Cb32
Esenyazı TR 192 Fb86
Esenyurt TR 186 Fc77
Esgos E 36 Bb57
es Grau E 57 Jb66
Esguevillas de Esgueva E 46 Da60
Esher GB 20 Fc28
Esh Winning GB 11 Fa17
Eskdale Green GB 11 Eb18
Eskdalemuir GB 11 Eb15
Eskebjerg DK 109 Ea25
Eskelhem S 104 Ga49
Eskiakören TR 193 Ha84
Eskiçine TR 197 Fa89
Eskidanişment TR 192 Fd81
Eskifjörður IS 3 Bc05
Eskihisar TR 197 Fa89
Eskikaraağaç TR 186 Fc80
Eskiler TR 193 Ha87
Eskilsäter S 94 Ed45
Eskilstrup DK 109 Eb28
Eskilstuna S 95 Gb43
Eskin TR 192 Fc85
Eskipazar TR 205 Fa20
Eskişehir TR 193 Gc82
Eskisığırcı TR 186 Fa80
Eskiyayla TR 187 Gb79
Eskola FIN 81 Jd27
Eskragh GB 9 Cc17
Esku EST 98 Kd44
Eslared S 102 Fa52
Eslarn D 135 Eb46
Eslida E 54 Fc66
es Llombards E 57 Hc68
Eslohe D 125 Cb40
Eslöv S 110 Ed55
Esmared S 102 Ed52
Esme TR 192 Fc86
es Mercadal E 57 Ja65
es Migjorn Gran E 57 Ja66
es Molinar E 57 Hb67
Esmoriz P 44 Ac61
Esna EST 98 Kd43
Esnandes F 32 Fa45
Esneux B 124 Ba42
Esnouveaux F 30 Jb39
Espadañedo E 37 Ca58
Espalion F 33 Ha51
Esparragal E 61 Ec74
Esparragalejo E 51 Bd68
Esparragosa de la Serena E 51 Cb70
Esparreguera E 49 Gd61
Esparron F 42 Jd54
Esparron-de-Verdon F 42 Ka53
Espås N 77 Ea30
Espe DK 108 Dc27
Espe N 84 Cc40
Espejo E 38 Ea56
Espejo E 60 Cd73
Espel NL 116 Bb34
Espeland N 84 Ca39
Espeland N 92 Cb45
Espeli N 92 Cd45
Espelkamp D 126 Cd36
Espeluche F 42 Jb51
Espenau D 126 Da40
Espera E 59 Ca75
Esperança P 51 Bb68
Espéraza F 41 Gd56
Esperia I 160 Ed73
Esperstedt D 127 Dd40
Espetøl N 93 Da44
Espevær N 92 Bd41
Espezel F 41 Gd57
Espiel E 52 Cc71
Espinama E 38 Da55
Espiñaredo E 36 Bb53
Espinasses F 42 Ka51
Espinhal P 44 Ad65
Espinho P 44 Ac61
Espinilla E 38 Db56
Espinosa de Cerrato E 46 Db59
Espinosa de Cervera E 46 Dc59
Espinosa de Henares E 46 Dd63
Espinosa de los Monteros E 38 Dc56
Espinoso del Rey E 52 Cd67
Espírito Santo P 58 Ba73
Esplantas F 34 Hc50
Esplús E 48 Fd60
Espoey F 40 Fc55
Espolla E 41 Hb58
Espoo FIN 98 Kb39
Esporles E 57 Hb67
es Port E 57 Hb68
Esposende P 44 Ac59
Esprels F 31 Jd40
es Pujols E 56 Gc70
Esquedas E 48 Fb59
Esquivias E 46 Db65
Esrange S 67 Hb15
Esrum DK 109 Ec24
Essay F 28 Fd38
Esse FIN 81 Jb29
Esselbach D 134 Da45
Essen B 124 Ad38
Essen D 117 Cb35
Essen D 125 Bd39
Essenbach D 135 Eb49
Essenniki RUS 107 Mb50
Essentuki RUS 205 Ga17
Essertaux F 23 Gd34
Essertenne F 31 Jc41
Essimi GR 185 Dd77
Essing D 135 Ea48
Essingen D 134 Da48
Esslingen D 134 Cd48
Essômes-sur-Marne F 24 Hb36
Essoyes F 30 Ja39
Essunga S 102 Ed47
Essvik S 88 Gc33
Establet F 42 Jc51
Estação de Ourique P 58 Ac72
Estacas E 36 Ad57
Estación de Cártama E 60 Cd76
Estación de Páramo E 37 Ca56
Estación de Salinas E 60 Da75
Estadilla E 48 Fd59
Estagel F 41 Ha57
Estaing F 33 Ha51
Estaires F 23 Ha31
Estang F 40 Fc53
Estarreja P 44 Ac62
Estavayer-le-Lac CH 141 Bb54
Este I 150 Dd60
Estedt D 127 Ea36
Estela P 44 Ac60
Estella E 39 Ec57
Estellencs E 56 Ha67
Estenfeld D 134 Db45
Esteng F 43 Kb51
Estepa E 60 Cc74
Estépar E 38 Dc58
Estepona E 59 Cb77
Estercuel E 48 Fb63
Esternay F 24 Hc37
Esternberg A 135 Ed49
Esterri d'Àneu E 40 Gb57
Estersmark S 80 Hc26
Esterwegen D 117 Cb34
Esterzili I 169 Cb78
Estiche de Cinca E 48 Fd60
Estissac F 30 Hc38
Estivella E 54 Fc67
Estorf D 118 Da32
Estorf D 126 Da36
Estoril P 50 Aa68
Estorninhos P 58 Ad74
Estrées-Saint-Denis F 23 Ha35
Estrée-Wamin F 23 Gd32
Estreito P 44 Ba65
Estremera E 46 Dd65
Estremoz P 50 Ba69
Estrup DK 109 Eb26
Estry F 22 Fb37
Estuna S 96 Ha42
Estvad DK 100 Da22
Esztergom H 146 Hc52
Étain F 25 Jc35
Etais F 30 Ja40
Etalans F 31 Jd42
Etalle B 132 Ba44
Étampes F 29 Gd38
Étang-sur-Arroux F 30 Hd43
Étaples F 23 Gc31
Etauliers F 32 Fb49
Etel F 27 Ea41
Eteläinen FIN 90 Ka37
Eteläkylä FIN 90 Kd34
Etelälahti FIN 82 Ka27
Etelä-Niskamäki FIN 90 Kd32
Eteläpää FIN 89 Hd33
Etelä Varisala FIN 97 Ja39
Etelhem S 104 Ha50
Eterna E 38 Dd58
Etevaux F 30 Jb41
Etili TR 191 Ec81
Etival F 31 Jd44
Etival-Clairefontaine F 31 Ka38
Etne N 92 Cb41
Étoges F 24 Hc36
Etoile-Rhône F 34 Jb50
Etola FIN 90 Kb37
Etolikó GR 188 Ba84
Etouy F 23 Gd35
Étréaupont F 24 Hc33
Etréchy F 29 Gd38
Etrembières F 35 Jd45
Etrépagny F 23 Gc35
Étretat F 22 Fd34
Étreux F 24 Hc33
Etrœungt F 24 Hc33
Etropole BG 179 Cd71
Etroubles I 148 Bc58
Etsaut F 39 Fb56
Ettelbruck L 133 Bb44
Ettenheim D 141 Ca50
Etten-Leur NL 124 Ad38
Ettiswil CH 141 Ca53
Ettlingen D 133 Cb48
Ettrickbridge GB 11 Eb14
Ettringen D 142 Dc51
Etu-Ikola FIN 90 Kc33
Etulia MD 177 Fc63
Etusson F 28 Fb43
Etuz F 31 Jd41
Etxano E 38 Ea55
Etzen A 136 Fc49
Etzenricht D 135 Eb46
Eu F 23 Gb33
Euerbach D 134 Db44
Euerdorf D 134 Db44
Eugénie-les-Bains F 40 Fc54
Eulatal D 127 Ec41
Eupen B 125 Bb41
Eura FIN 89 Jb37
Eurajoki FIN 89 Ja37
Euratsfeld A 144 Fc51
Eursinge NL 117 Bd34
Euskirchen D 125 Bd42
Eußenheim D 134 Da44
Euston GB 21 Ga25
Euthal CH 142 Cc54
Eutin D 119 Dd31
Euzet F 42 Ja52
Evaillé F 29 Ga40
Eväjärvi FIN 90 Ka34
Evangelismós GR 183 Bd80
Evangelismós GR 194 Ba89
Evangelístria GR 189 Ca85
Evanger N 84 Cb38
Evanton GB 5 Ea07
Evaux-les-Bains F 33 Ha45
Evciler TR 185 Ed75
Evciler TR 191 Eb81
Evciler TR 191 Ed82
Evciler TR 191 Ed83
Evciler TR 192 Ga87
Evdilos GR 196 Dd88
Ēvele LV 106 Kd48
Evelix GB 5 Ea06
Evenhus N 78 Ea29
Evenskjer N 66 Ga13
Evenstad N 86 Eb36
Evercreech GB 19 Ec29
Everleigh GB 20 Ed29
Everöd S 111 Fb55
Eversley GB 20 Fb28
Everswinkel D 125 Cb38
Evertsberg S 87 Fb37
Evesham GB 20 Ed26
Évian-les-Bains F 31 Ka44
Evijärvi FIN 81 Jc29
Evillers F 31 Jd42
Evinohóri GR 188 Ba85
Evisa F 154 Ca70
Evitskog FIN 98 Ka40
Evja N 66 Fc17
Evje N 92 Cd45
Evkafteke TR 191 Ed84
Evlalo GR 184 Db77
Evlanovo RUS 203 Fa12
Évora P 50 Ad69
Évora Monte P 50 Ba69
Evran F 26 Ec38
Evrecy F 22 Fb36
Evrencik TR 186 Fa75
Evrensekiz TR 185 Ed76
Evreşe TR 185 Ec78
Évreux F 23 Gb36
Evrieu F 35 Jc47
Evriguet F 27 Ec39
Évron F 28 Fc39
Évry F 23 Gd37
Evrychou CY 206 Ja97
Ewell GB 20 Fc28
Examília GR 195 Bd87
Exaplátanos GR 183 Bd76
Éxarhos GR 189 Ca84
Exbourne GB 19 Dd30
Excideuil F 33 Gb48
Exeter GB 19 Ea30
Exford GB 19 Ea29
Exilles I 148 Bb60
Exloo NL 117 Ca34
Exmes F 22 Fd37
Exmouth GB 19 Ea31
Exogí GR 188 Ac84
Exohí GR 182 Ad79
Exohí GR 184 Cd75
Exohí GR 184 Db77
Éxo Moulianá GR 201 Dc96
Éxo Nímfio GR 194 Bc91
Extertal D 126 Cd37
Extremo P 36 Ad58
Eyam GB 16 Ed22
Eydehavn N 93 Db46
Eydelstedt D 118 Cd35
Eydemir TR 193 Gb84
Eye GB 17 Fc24
Eye GB 21 Gb25
Eyerci TR 186 Fc80
Eyeries IRL 12 Ba26
Eygalières F 42 Jb53
Eygliers F 43 Kb50
Eygluy-Esculin F 35 Jc50
Eyguians F 42 Jd51
Eyguières F 42 Jb53
Eygurande F 33 Ha47
Eygurande-et-Gardedeuil F 32 Fd49
Eymet F 32 Fd51
Eymir TR 187 Ha80
Eymoutiers F 33 Gc47
Eynez TR 191 Ed84
Eyrarbakki IS 2 Ac05
Eyrecourt IRL 13 Ca21
Eyrein F 33 Gd48
Eystrup D 118 Da35
Eyübler TR 193 Gd87
Ezaro E 36 Ac55
Ezcaray E 38 Ea58
Ezcurra E 39 Ec56
Eze F 43 Kd53
Ezerče BG 180 Eb69
Ezere LV 113 Jd53
Ezerec BG 181 Fc69
Ezerėlis LT 114 Kb57
Ezeriş RO 174 Ca62
Ezermala LV 107 Ld51
Ezernieki LV 107 Ld52
Ezerovo BG 181 Fa70
Eziler TR 192 Fc87
Ezine TR 191 Ea81
Ezy-sur-Eure F 23 Gb37

F

Faaborg DK 108 Dc27
Faak am See A 144 Fa56
Fabara E 48 Fd62
Fabas F 40 Ga55
Fabas F 40 Gb56
Fabbrica Curone I 149 Cc61
Fåberg N 84 Cd35
Fåberg N 85 Ea37
Fabero E 37 Bd56
Fábiánsebestyén H 146 Jc55
Fäboda FIN 81 Jb28
Fäbodliden S 80 Gc26
Fåborg DK 108 Dc27
Fabrègues F 41 Hd54
Fabrezan F 41 Ha56
Fabriano I 156 Ec67
Fabrica di Roma I 156 Ea70
Fabro Scalo I 156 Ea68
Făcăeni RO 177 Fa66
Facho P 50 Ab66
Facinas E 59 Ca78
Fadd H 146 Hc56
Fadón E 45 Cb61
Faedis I 150 Ed57
Faenza I 150 Dd63
Færvik N 93 Db46
Faeto I 161 Fd73
Fafe P 44 Ba60
Fafleralp CH 141 Bd56
Fagagna I 150 Ec57
Făgăraş RO 175 Dc61
Fågelberget S 79 Fc27
Fågelfors S 103 Ga51
Fågelmara S 111 Ga54
Fågelsjö S 87 Fc35
Fågelsta S 79 Ga27
Fågelsta S 103 Fc46
Fågelsundet S 96 Gd39
Fågeltofta S 111 Fb56
Fagerås S 94 Fa43
Fagerdal S 79 Fd29
Fagerhaug N 64 Jb04
Fagerhaug N 77 Dd32
Fagerhult S 94 Eb45
Fagerhult S 102 Ec46
Fagerhult S 103 Fb48
Fagerhult S 103 Fd51
Fagermoen N 71 Fb21
Fagernes N 62 Gd10
Fagernes N 67 Gb13
Fagernes N 85 Dc38
Fagersanna S 103 Fb46
Fagersta S 95 Fd41
Fagerstrand N 93 Ea42
Fagertun N 67 Gc12
Fagervik FIN 98 Ka40
Fagervik N 78 Eb28
Fagervika N 70 Fa21
Fagerviken S 96 Gc39
Fäget RO 174 Cb60
Făgețelu RO 175 Db65
Faggeby S 95 Ga40
Faggen A 142 Db54
Fåglavik S 102 Ed47
Fåglum S 102 Ed47
Fagnano Castello I 164 Gb79
Fågre S 103 Fb46
Fagurhólsmýri IS 2 Ba06
Fahan IRL 9 Cc15
Fahrenbach D 134 Cd46
Fahrenkrug D 118 Dc31
Fahrenwalde D 120 Fb33
Fahrenzhausen D 143 Dd50
Fährhafen Sassnitz D 120 Fa30
Fahrland D 127 Ed36
Fahrwangen CH 141 Ca53
Fai della Paganella I 149 Dc57
Faido CH 141 Cb56
Fain-lès-Montbard F 30 Hd41
Fairbourne GB 15 Dd24
Fairford GB 20 Ed27
Fairlight GB 21 Ga30
Fairy Cross GB 18 Dc29
Fajsławice PL 131 Kb40
Fajsz H 146 Hc56
Fakenham GB 17 Ga23
Fåker S 79 Fc31

Fakija – Fobello

Fakija BG 181 Ec73
Fakılı TR 192 Fd85
Fakovići BIH 159 Ja64
Faksdal N 78 Eb26
Fakse DK 109 Eb27
Fakse Ladeplads DK 109 Eb27
Falaise F 22 Fc37
Fálana GR 183 Bd80
Fålasjö S 80 Gc31
Falcade I 150 Ea57
Falces E 39 Ec58
Falciano del Massico I 161 Fa74
Fălciu RO 177 Fb60
Fălcoiu RO 175 Db66
Falconara I 167 Fa87
Falconara Marittima I 156 Ed66
Falcone I 167 Fc84
Faldsled DK 108 Dc27
Falerna I 164 Gb81
Falerna Marina I 164 Gb81
Falerum S 103 Ga47
Fălești MD 173 Fa56
Faleștii Noi MD 173 Fb56
Falfield GB 19 Ec27
Falileevo RUS 99 Ld41
Faliráki GR 197 Fa93
Falkelva N 66 Ga15
Falkenberg D 120 Fa35
Falkenberg D 127 Ed39
Falkenberg D 143 Ec50
Falkenberg S 102 Ec52
Falkenhagen D 128 Fb37
Falkenhain D 127 Ec40
Falkensee D 127 Ed36
Falkenstein D 135 Eb43
Falkenstein D 135 Eb48
Falkenthal D 119 Ed35
Falkerslev DK 109 Eb28
Falkirk GB 10 Ea13
Falköping S 102 Fa47
Fałków PL 130 Ja40
Falla S 103 Fd46
Fållen S 103 Fb52
Falleron F 28 Ed43
Fallet N 85 Dd34
Fallford GB 11 Eb16
Fällfors S 73 Hc24
Fallingbostel D 118 Db35
Fälloheden S 72 Gd22
Fallon F 31 Ka41
Fällträsk S 73 Hd22
Falmouth GB 18 Db32
Falnes N 92 Bd43
Falset E 48 Ga62
Falsnes N 62 Ha10
Falsterbo S 110 Ed57
Fălticeni RO 172 Ec56
Falträsk S 80 Gd25
Falun S 95 Fd39
Famagusta = Ammochostos CY 206 Jd96
Fambach D 126 Db42
Fameck F 25 Jd35
Fana N 84 Ca39
Fanagmore GB 4 Dc04
Fanano I 155 Db64
Fanári GR 184 Dc77
Fanari GR 188 Bb81
Fandrup DK 100 Db22
Fane I 149 Dc59
Fångåmon S 78 Fa31
Fangel DK 108 Dc27
Fanjeaux F 41 Gd55
Fanlo E 40 Fc57
Fannerup DK 101 Dd23
Fänneslunda S 102 Ed48
Fannrem N 77 Dd30
Fano I 156 Ec65
Fanore IRL 12 Bc21
Fanós GR 183 Bd76
Fänsta S 87 Ga33
Fântânele RO 170 Bd59
Fântânele RO 171 Dc59
Fântânele RO 172 Ec56
Fântânele RO 175 Cd66
Fanthyttan S 95 Fc42
Fantoft N 84 Ca39
Fao E 36 Ba55
Fărăgău RO 171 Dc58
Fara in Sabina I 156 Eb70
Faramontanos de Tábara E 45 Cb59
Fara Novarese I 148 Ca59
Faraoani RO 176 Ed60
Fara San Martino I 161 Fa71
Farasdués E 47 Fa59
Fărău RO 171 Db59
Fårberget S 80 Ha27
Fårbo S 103 Gb50
Fărcas RO 175 Cd65
Fărcașa RO 171 Da55
Farcașa RO 172 Eb57
Fărcașele RO 180 Db67
Fărcășești RO 175 Cc64
Farchant D 142 Dc53
Fărdea RO 174 Ca61
Fardella I 162 Gb77
Fardhem S 104 Gd50
Färdkällan S 86 Ed37
Fardrum IRL 13 Ca21
Fåred S 95 Fb45
Fareham GB 20 Fa30
Faremoutiers F 23 Ha37
Fårentuna S 96 Gc43
Farés GR 194 Bb89
Farestad N 92 Cc47
Fårevejle DK 109 Ea25
Fårevejle Stationsby DK 109 Ea25
Farfa I 156 Eb70
Färgaryd S 102 Fa51
Färgelanda S 102 Ec46
Fargues-Saint-Hilaire F 32 Fb50
Fargues-sur-Ourbise F 40 Fd52
Farhult S 110 Ec54
Färila S 87 Fd35
Faringdon GB 20 Ed27
Faringe S 96 Gd41
Färingtofta S 110 Fa54
Farini d'Olmo I 149 Cd62
Fariza E 45 Ca61
Färjestaden S 103 Gb52
Farkadóna GR 189 Bc81
Farkaševac HR 152 Gc58
Farkasfa H 145 Gb55
Farkazdin SRB 153 Jc60
Farkazdin SRB 174 Bb62
Farlete E 48 Fb60
Fărliug RO 174 Ca62
Färlöv S 111 Fb54
Farmakas CY 206 Jb97
Farmakonissi GR 197 Eb89
Farmborough GB 19 Ec28
Farmtown GB 7 Ec08
Färna S 95 Ga42
Farná SK 145 Hb51
Farnanes Cross Roads IRL 12 Bc26
Färnäs S 87 Fc38
Farnborough GB 20 Fb29
Farnborough GB 20 Fd28
Farnese I 156 Dd69
Farnham GB 20 Fb29
Färnigen CH 141 Cb55
Farnstädt D 127 Ea40
Farnworth GB 15 Ec21
Faro P 58 Ad74
Fårö S 104 Hb48
Fårösund S 104 Hb48
Farra d'Alpago I 150 Eb57
Farranfore IRL 12 Bb24
Farre DK 108 Dc24
Farre DK 108 Db25
Fársala GR 189 Bd82
Farsø DK 100 Db22
Farstad N 77 Da31
Farstorp S 110 Fa54
Farstrup DK 100 Db21
Farsund N 92 Cb47
Fârţăneşti RO 177 Fb62
Fărtăţeşti RO 175 Da64
Farum DK 109 Ec25
Fårup DK 100 Dc23
Fårvang DK 100 Dc23
Faryny PL 122 Jc32
Fasana I 165 Gd80
Fasano I 162 Ha75
Fasgar E 37 Ca56
Fasillar TR 199 Hb88
Fáskrúðsfjörður IS 3 Bc05
Fasnacloich GB 6 Dc11
Faßberg D 118 Dc35
Fässjödal S 87 Fd34
Faster DK 108 Da24
Fasterholt DK 108 Da24
Fasterna S 96 Gd42
Fastias E 37 Ca54
Fastiv UA 204 Ec15
Fasty PL 123 Kb33
Fatež RUS 203 Fa13
Fátima P 50 Ac66
Fatjas S 73 Hb19
Fatmomakke S 71 Fd24
Fatnica BIH 159 Hc68
Fatsa TR 205 Fc19
Fättjaur S 71 Fd24
Faucogney-et-la-Mer F 31 Ka39
Faugères F 41 Hb54
Fauguerolles F 32 Fd51
Fauldhouse GB 10 Ea13
Faulenrost D 119 Ec32
Faulquemont F 25 Ka35
Fauquembergues F 23 Gd31
Faura E 54 Fc67
Făurei RO 172 Ec58
Făurei RO 176 Ed64
Făurei RO 181 Ec67
Făurei RO 181 Fa68
Făureşti RO 175 Da65
Fausing DK 100 Dc23
Fauske N 66 Fd17
Faustynowo PL 129 Gb38
Fauville-en-Caux F 23 Ga34
Faux F 33 Ga50
Faux F 34 Hc51
Favaios P 44 Bb61
Fåvang N 85 Dd36
Fåvangfjellet N 85 Ea36
Favara E 54 Fc69
Favara I 166 Ed86
Faverges F 35 Ka46
Faverney F 31 Jd40
Faverolles F 23 Ga36
Faverolles F 23 Gc37
Faversham GB 21 Ga29
Favignana I 166 Ea84
Favone F 154 Cb72
Favrholt DK 108 Db24
Fawley GB 20 Fa30
Fay-aux-Loges F 29 Gd40
Fay-de-Bretagne F 28 Ed41
Fayence F 43 Kb53
Fayet F 41 Hb53
Fayl-Billot F 31 Jc40
Fayón E 48 Fd62
Fay-sur-Lignon F 34 Ja49
Fažana HR 151 Fa61
Fazlıca TR 191 Ec82
Feakle IRL 12 Bd22
Fearnan GB 7 Ea11
Fearn Lodge GB 5 Ea06
Feas E 36 Bb53
Fécamp F 22 Fd34
Feces de Abaixo P 44 Bb59
Feckenham GB 20 Ed25
Feda N 92 Cb46
Fedamore IRL 12 Bd23
Federi RO 175 Cd62
Fedje N 84 Bd37
Fedkovščyna RUS 99 Ld43
Fëdorovka RUS 205 Fb15
Fedosino RUS 107 Ma48
Fedotovo RUS 113 Jb59
Fegen S 102 Ed51
Fegyvernek H 146 Jc53
Fehérgyarmat H 147 Kc50
Fehmarn D 119 Ea30
Fehrbellin D 119 Ec35
Fehring A 144 Ga55
Feichten A 142 Dc54
Feignies F 24 Hc32
Feilitz D 135 Ea43
Feimaņi LV 107 Lc52
Feins F 28 Ed38
Feira do Monte E 36 Bc54
Feiring N 85 Ea40
Feiring N 94 Eb39
Feistritz im Rosental A 144 Fb56
Feiteira P 58 Ad74
Feketić SRB 153 Ja59
Felanitx E 57 Hc67
Felchow D 120 Fb34
Felcsút H 146 Hc53
Feldafing D 143 Dd51
Feld am See A 144 Fa55
Feldatal D 126 Cd42
Feldbach A 144 Ga55
Feldbach F 31 Kb40
Feldballe DK 101 Dd23
Feldberg D 119 Ed33
Feldberger Seenlandschaft D 119 Ed33
Feldborg DK 100 Da23
Felde D 118 Db30
Feldioara RO 176 Ea61
Feldkirch A 142 Cd53
Feldkirchen D 135 Eb48
Feldkirchen D 143 Ea51
Feldkirchen in Kärnten A 144 Fa56
Feldkirchen-Westerham D 143 Ea51
Feldru RO 171 Dc56
Feleacu RO 171 Da58
Felechosa E 37 Cc55
Feletto I 148 Bd59
Felgueiras P 44 Ba60
Feliceni RO 176 Dd60
Felina I 149 Da63
Felindre GB 15 Eb25
Felindre GB 19 Dd27
Félines-Minervois F 41 Ha55
Félines-Termenès F 41 Ha56
Felinfach GB 15 Ea26
Felino I 149 Da62
Felitto I 161 Fd76
Félix E 61 Ea76
Felixdorf A 145 Gb52
Felixstowe GB 21 Gb26
Felizli TR 187 Gc78
Felizzano I 148 Ca61
Fell A 143 Ed54
Fellabær IS 3 Bc05
Fellbach D 134 Cd48
Fellegrenda N 93 Db44
Fellering F 31 Kb39
Felletin F 33 Gd46
Fellí GR 183 Bb79
Fellingfors N 70 Fa23
Fellingsbro S 95 Fd43
Felm D 118 Dc30
Felmín E 37 Cc56
Felnac RO 170 Bd59
Felnémet H 146 Jb51
Felsberg D 126 Da40
Felsőcsatar H 145 Gb54
Felsőkörtvélyes H 146 Hc55
Felsőnyárád H 146 Jc50
Felsőnyék H 145 Hb55
Felsősima H 147 Ka51
Felsőszolnok H 145 Gb55
Felsőtárkány H 146 Jb51
Felsővadász H 146 Jc50
Felsőzsolca H 146 Jc50
Felsted GB 20 Fd27
Feltham GB 20 Fc28
Felton GB 15 Ec26
Feltre I 150 Ea58
Femanger N 84 Cb40
Femsjö S 102 Fa52
Femundssundet N 86 Ec35
Fenagh IRL 9 Cb19
Fendeille F 41 Gd55
Fene E 36 Ba53
Fenerköy TR 186 Fb77
Fenes N 66 Fb17
Fénétrange F 25 Ka36
Feneu F 28 Fb41
Fengersfors S 94 Ec45
Fenioux F 28 Fb44
Fenioux F 32 Fb47
Fenit IRL 12 Ba24
Fennagh IRL 13 Cc23
Fensmark DK 109 Eb27
Fenstad N 94 Eb40
Fenstanton GB 20 Fc25
Fensterbach D 135 Eb46
Fenwick GB 10 Dd14
Fenwick GB 11 Ed14
Feodosija UA 205 Fb17
Feohanagh IRL 12 Bc24
Féole F 28 Fa44
Feolin Ferry GB 6 Da13
Feragen N 86 Ec33
Ferapontievca MD 177 Fd60
Ferbane IRL 13 Ca21
Ferdinandovac HR 152 Gd58
Ferdinandshof D 120 Fa32
Fère-Champenoise F 24 Hc37
Fère-en-Tardenois F 24 Hb35
Ferendia RO 174 Bd62
Ferentillo I 156 Eb69
Ferentino I 160 Ec72
Féres GR 185 Ea78
Férez E 53 Ec71
Feria E 51 Bc70
Feričanci HR 152 Hb59
Ferla I 167 Fc87
Ferlach A 144 Fb56
Fermignano I 156 Eb65
Fermo I 156 Ed67
Fermoselle E 45 Ca61
Fermoy IRL 12 Bd25
Fernáncaballero E 52 Db68
Fernán-Núñez E 60 Cd73
Ferndown GB 20 Ed30
Ferness GB 7 Ea08
Ferney-Voltaire F 35 Jd45
Fernhurst GB 20 Fb29
Ferns IRL 13 Cd24
Fernwald D 126 Cc42
Ferovac HR 152 Ha60
Ferpècle CH 148 Bd57
Ferraj AL 182 Ac74
Ferrandina I 162 Gc76
Ferrão Ferro P 50 Aa69
Ferrara I 150 Dd62
Ferrara di Monte Baldo I 149 Db59
Ferrazzano I 161 Fc73
Ferreira E 36 Bb55
Ferreira do Alentejo P 50 Ad71
Ferreira do Zêzere P 50 Ad66
Ferreira (Valadouro) E 36 Bc53
Ferreiros E 36 Bc55
Ferreras de Abajo E 45 Cb59
Ferreras de Arriba E 45 Ca59
Ferreries E 57 Ja66
Ferreruela de Huerva E 47 Fa62
Ferret CH 148 Bc57
Ferrette F 31 Kb40
Ferreux F 30 Hc38
Ferriere I 149 Cc62
Ferrières F 41 Ha54
Ferrières-en-Brie F 23 Ha37
Ferrières-en-Gâtinais F 29 Ha39
Ferrières-Saint-Mary F 34 Hb49
Ferrières-sur-Sichon F 34 Hc46
Ferring DK 100 Cd22
Ferritslev DK 109 Dd27
Ferrol E 36 Ba53
Ferry Bridge IRL 12 Bc23
Ferryhill GB 11 Fa17
Fertilia I 168 Bd75
Fertőd H 145 Gc52
Fertőrakos H 145 Gc52
Fertőszentmiklós H 145 Gc53
Fervaques F 22 Fd36
Ferwerd NL 117 Bc32
Fessenheim F 31 Kc39
Feştelița MD 173 Ga59
Festøy N 76 Cc33
Festvåg N 66 Fc17
Feteşti MD 172 Ed54
Feteşti RO 177 Fa66
Feteşti-Gară RO 177 Fa66
Fethard IRL 13 Ca24
Fethard IRL 13 Cc25
Fethiye TR 186 Ga80
Fethiye TR 193 Gc83
Fethiye TR 198 Fc92
Fetsund N 94 Eb41
Fettercairn GB 7 Ec10
Fettwell GB 20 Fd25
Feucht D 135 Dd46
Feuchtwangen D 134 Db47
Feudingen D 126 Cc41
Feuerleiten A 143 Ec54
Feugarolles F 40 Fd52
Feuges F 30 Hd38
Feuquières F 23 Gc34
Feuquières-en-Vimeu F 23 Gc33
Feurs F 34 Hd47
Fevik N 93 Da46
Fevral'skoje RUS 113 Jd58
Fevzipaşa TR 186 Fb80
Fevziye TR 187 Gb79
Feytiat F 33 Gb47
Ffestiniog GB 15 Dd23
Ffostrasol GB 14 Dc26
Fiane N 93 Db46
Fiano I 148 Bc60
Fiaschetti I 150 Eb58
Fibiş RO 174 Bd60
Ficarazzi I 166 Ed84
Ficarolo I 150 Dd61
Fichtelberg D 135 Ea44
Fichtenau D 134 Db47
Fichtenberg D 127 Ed40
Fichtenberg D 134 Da48
Ficulle I 156 Ea68
Fiddleton GB 11 Eb15
Fiddown IRL 13 Cb24
Fide S 104 Gd51
Fidenza I 149 Da61
Fidjastølen N 92 Cb44
Fidjeland N 92 Cc44
Fidjetun N 93 Da46
Fieberbrunn A 143 Eb53
Fielbmatgiedde N 64 Jc08
Fieni RO 176 Dd64
Fienvillers F 23 Gd32
Fier AL 182 Ab76
Fiera di Primiero I 150 Ea57
Fierbinți-Târg RO 176 Eb65
Fier Shegan AL 182 Ab76
Fierzë AL 159 Jc70
Fiesch CH 141 Ca56
Fiesole I 155 Dc65
Figaredo E 37 Cc55
Figari F 154 Cb72
Figeac F 33 Gd51
Figeholm S 103 Gb50
Figgjo N 92 Ca44
Figiás GR 190 Cd86
Figliere I 148 Bb62
Figline Valdarno I 155 Dc66
Figueira da Foz P 44 Ab64
Figueira de Castelo Rodrigo P 45 Bc62
Figueira dos Cavaleiros P 50 Ac71
Figueiró dos Vinhos P 44 Ad65
Figueras E 37 Bd53
Figueres E 41 Hb58
Figuerola d' Orcau E 48 Gb59
Figueroles E 54 Fc65
Fijnaart NL 124 Ad38
Fiksdal N 76 Cd32
Filadélfi GR 184 Cc77
Filadelfia I 164 Gb82
Filain F 31 Jd41
Filakí GR 189 Bd82
Filákio GR 185 Ea75
Fil'akovo SK 146 Ja50
Filatova Gora RUS 107 Ld47
Filderstadt D 134 Cd49
Fildu de Jos RO 171 Cd57
Fildu de Sus RO 171 Cd57
Filettino I 160 Ec71
Filevo BG 184 Dc74
Filey GB 17 Fc19
Filí GR 189 Cb86
Filia GR 188 Bb86
Filía GR 189 Bc82
Filiaşi RO 175 Cd65
Filiátes GR 182 Ac80
Filiatrá GR 194 Ba88
Filicudi Porto I 167 Fb82
Filinskoe RUS 203 Fb10
Filipeni MD 177 Fc60
Filipeni RO 172 Ed59
Filipeşti RO 172 Ed59
Filipeşti de Pădure RO 176 Ea64
Filipeşti de Târg RO 176 Ea64
Filipi GR 184 Da77
Filipiáda GR 188 Ad82
Filipovci BG 179 Cb70
Filipów PL 123 Ka30
Filippovka RUS 113 Jb59
Filipstad S 95 Fb42
Filiriá GR 183 Bd77
Fillan N 77 Dc29
Fillières F 25 Jc34
Fillingsnes N 77 Dc29
Fillingtveit N 93 Da46
Fillira GR 185 Dd77
Fillo GR 189 Bc81
Film S 96 Gd40
Filótas GR 183 Bb77
Filóti GR 196 Db90
Filottrano I 156 Ed66
Filsbäck S 102 Fa46
Filskov DK 108 Da25
Filsnes N 76 Cc32
Filsum D 117 Cb33
Filzmoos A 143 Ed53
Finale Emilia I 149 Dc62
Finale Ligure I 148 Ca63
Finaña E 61 Dd75
Finbo FIN 96 Hc40
Finby FIN 97 Jc40
Finchingfield GB 20 Fd26
Finchley GB 20 Fc28
Finderup DK 100 Db23
Finderup DK 108 Cd24
Findhorn GB 5 Eb07
Fındıcak TR 186 Fd80
Fındıklı TR 185 Eb79
Findochty GB 5 Ec07
Findon GB 20 Fc30
Finedal N 63 Hd05
Finhan F 40 Gb53
Finikas GR 196 Da89
Finike TR 199 Gb93
Finikoúnda GR 194 Ba90
Finiq AL 182 Ab79
Finiş RO 170 Cb58
Finja S 110 Fa54
Finkenstein A 144 Fa56
Finmere GB 20 Fa26
Finnäs FIN 81 Jb28
Finnasand N 92 Ca43
Finnbacka S 87 Fd38
Finnea IRL 9 Cb20
Finneby S 87 Fd34
Finneidfjord N 71 Fb21
Finnentrop D 125 Cb40
Finnerödja S 95 Fb45
Finnes N 63 Ja04
Finnes N 71 Fb18
Finnfjordeidet N 67 Gc11
Finnforsfallet S 80 Hb25
Finngruvan S 95 Fb39
Finnhöle S 95 Gb40
Finning D 142 Dc51
Finnisglin IRL 8 Bb20
Finnkroken N 62 Gd09
Finnliden S 73 Hb23
Finnøya N 66 Fd15
Finnsäter S 79 Fb29
Finnsjå N 63 Hd08
Finnsnes N 67 Gc11
Finnsta S 87 Ga33
Finnstad N 78 Ec28
Finnstad N 86 Eb34
Finnstuga S 87 Fd37
Finntorp S 94 Ec43
Finnträsk S 73 Hc24
Finnvelta N 94 Ec40
Finnvollan N 78 Fa25
Finny IRL 8 Bc20
Fino Mornasco I 149 Cc58
Finowfurt D 120 Fa35
Fins F 23 Ha33
Finse N 84 Cd39
Finsjö S 103 Ga51
Finsland N 92 Cd46
Finspång S 103 Fd46
Finsterau D 135 Ed48
Finsterwalde D 128 Fa39
Finstown GB 5 Ec03
Finström FIN 96 Hc40
Finta RO 176 Ea65
Fintel D 118 Db34
Fintinița MD 173 Fb54
Fintona GB 9 Cc17
Fintown IRL 8 Ca16
Finvik N 63 Hd05
Finvoy GB 9 Cd16
Fiodh Ard IRL 13 Ca24
Fiolleda E 36 Bb56
Fionnaithe IRL 8 Bc20
Fionnay CH 148 Bc57
Fionnphort GB 6 Da11
Fiorenzuola d'Arda I 149 Cd61
Firenze I 155 Dc65
Firenzuola I 155 Dc64
Firiteaz RO 174 Bd60
Firiza RO 171 Da55
Firkeel IRL 12 Ba26
Firlădeni MD 173 Fc59
Firlădeni MD 173 Ga59
Firlej PL 131 Ka39
Firminy F 34 Ja48
Firmo I 164 Gb78
Firoga PL 121 Ha30
Firovo RUS 202 Ec09
Fischach D 142 Dc50
Fischamend A 145 Gc51
Fischbach A 144 Ga53
Fischbach D 133 Bd45
Fischbach D 133 Ca47
Fischbachau D 143 Ea52
Fischen D 142 Db53
Fischering A 144 Fc55
Fishbourne GB 20 Fb30
Fishburn GB 11 Fa17
Fishguard GB 14 Db26
Fishsätra S 96 Gd43
Fiskå N 76 Cb33
Fiskå N 92 Bd42
Fiskárdo GR 188 Ac84
Fiskarheden S 86 Fa38
Fiskari FIN 97 Jd40
Fiskars FIN 97 Jd40
Fiskavaig GB 4 Da08
Fiskebäckskil S 102 Eb47
Fiskebøl N 66 Fc13
Fiskefjord N 66 Ga13
Fiskenes N 66 Ga11
Fisketjønnbu N 92 Ca44
Fiskevik N 63 Ja06
Fiskevollen N 86 Eb35
Fiskö FIN 97 Hd39
Fiskum N 93 Dc42
Fislisbach CH 141 Cb53
Fismes F 24 Hc35
Fiss A 142 Db54
Fister N 92 Cb43
Fisterra E 36 Ac55
Fistéus E 36 Bc57
Fıstıklı TR 186 Fc79
Fitá GR 191 Dd85
Fitero E 47 Ec59
Fithi GR 195 Bd87
Fities GR 188 Ad83
Fitionești RO 176 Ed61
Fitjar N 84 Ca40
Fitou F 41 Hb56
Fittja S 96 Gc42
Fittleton GB 20 Ed29
Fiuggi I 160 Ec72
Fiumata I 156 Ec70
Fiumefreddo Bruzio I 164 Gb80
Fiumefreddo di Sicilia I 167 Fd85
Fiumicello-San Venere I 164 Ga78
Fiumicino I 160 Ea72
Fiveally IRL 13 Ca22
Five Ashes GB 20 Fd30
Fivelanes GB 18 Dc31
Fivemiletown GB 9 Cc18
Five Oaks GB 20 Fc29
Fivizzano I 149 Da63
Fivlered S 102 Fa48
Fixin F 30 Jb42
Fizeşu Gherlii RO 171 Db57
Fjær N 66 Fc16
Fjæra N 92 Cb41
Fjærland N 84 Cc36
Fjågesund N 93 Db43
Fjäl S 79 Fc30
Fjälbyn S 81 Hd26
Fjälkinge S 111 Fb54
Fjällåsen S 67 Ha16
Fjällbacka S 102 Ea46
Fjällbonäs S 72 Ha22
Fjällgården S 87 Fb33
Fjällnäs S 72 Gc22
Fjällnäs S 86 Ec32
Fjällsjönäs S 71 Ga23
Fjaltring DK 100 Cd22
Fjärås S 102 Ec50
Fjärdhundra S 95 Gb42
Fjelberg N 92 Ca41
Fjelde DK 109 Eb29
Fjell N 78 Eb26
Fjell N 84 Ca39
Fjellbu N 67 Gb14
Fjellbu N 85 Dc38
Fjellbygda N 86 Eb37
Fjelldal N 66 Ga13
Fjellerad DK 100 Dc21
Fjellerup DK 101 Dd23
Fjellheim N 85 Db38
Fjellkjøsa N 77 Dd30
Fjellså N 92 Cb46
Fjellstad N 67 Gc12
Fjellstrand N 93 Ea42
Fjelltoten N 94 Eb41
Fjelsø DK 100 Db22
Fjelsted DK 108 Dc26
Fjelstervang DK 108 Da24
Fjelstrup DK 108 Db27
Fjerritslev DK 100 Db21
Fjølvika N 70 Ec24
Fjon N 84 Cb37
Fjordgård N 62 Gb10
Fjotland N 92 Cc45
Fjugesta S 95 Fc44
Flåbygd N 93 Db43
Flacà E 49 Hb59
Flachau A 143 Ed53
Flachslanden D 134 Dc46
Fläckebo S 95 Ga42
Fladan FIN 89 Hd34
Fladbury GB 20 Ed26
Flade DK 100 Da21
Fladungen D 134 Db43
Flagy F 29 Ha38
Flaine F 35 Kb45
Flaka FIN 96 Hc41
Flakaberg S 73 Hd19
Flakaträsk S 72 Gb23
Flakaträsk S 80 Gd27
Flakeberg S 102 Ed47
Flakk N 78 Ea29
Flakkstadvåg N 67 Gb11
Flaknan N 78 Eb31
Flakstad N 66 Fa14
Flåm N 84 Cd38
Flămânzi RO 172 Ed56
Flamatt CH 141 Bc54
Flamborough GB 17 Fc19
Flambouréssi GR 183 Bb80
Flámbouro GR 183 Bb77
Flámbouro GR 184 Cc77
Flammerans F 31 Jc42
Flammerécourt F 30 Jb38
Flammersfeld D 125 Ca42
Flamoudi CY 206 Jc96
Flamouriá GR 183 Bc77
Flámpoura GR 188 Bb86
Flamstead GB 20 Fc27
Flärke S 80 Ha29
Flarken S 80 Hc27
Flash GB 16 Ed22
Flassans-sur-Issole F 42 Ka54
Flatdal N 93 Db42
Flateby N 93 Ea42
Flateland N 92 Cd43
Flateland N 93 Da45
Flåten N 63 Hb08
Flaten N 93 Da45
Flåtestøa N 86 Eb37
Flatøydegard N 85 Dc38
Flatraket N 84 Ca34
Flåtsbo S 87 Fd37
Flått N 78 Ed26
Flattach A 143 Ec55
Flattnitz A 144 Fa55
Flatvoll N 62 Gc10
Flauenskjold DK 101 Dd20
Flaugeac F 32 Fd50
Flavigny-sur-Ozerain F 30 Ja41
Flavin F 41 Ha52
Flavy-le Martel F 24 Hb34
Flawil CH 142 Cc53
Flayat F 33 Ha47
Flayosc F 43 Kb54
Flechtdorf D 126 Cd40
Flechtingen D 127 Dd37
Fleckeby D 108 Db29
Fleet GB 20 Fb29
Fleetmark D 119 Ea35
Fleetwood GB 15 Eb20
Fleines N 66 Fc13
Flekke N 84 Ca36
Flekkefjord N 92 Cb46
Flem N 76 Cc32
Flemløse DK 108 Dc27
Flemma N 77 Db31
Flen S 95 Gb44
Flen S 95 Fc40
Flensburg D 108 Db28
Flensungen D 126 Cd42
Fleres I 143 Dd55
Fleringe S 104 Ha48
Flerohopp S 103 Ga52
Flers F 22 Fb37
Flesberg N 93 Dc41
Flesnes N 66 Fd13
Flessau D 119 Ea35
Fleurance F 40 Ga53
Fleuré F 33 Ga45
Fleurier CH 141 Bb54
Fleurville F 30 Jb44
Fleury F 41 Hb55
Fleury-la-Vallée F 30 Hb40
Fleury-les-Aubrais F 29 Gc40
Fleury-sur-Andelle F 23 Gb35
Fléville F 24 Ja35
Fleys F 30 Hc40
Flieden D 134 Da43
Flikka N 92 Cb46
Flims CH 142 Cc55
Flimwell GB 20 Fd29
Flines-les-Raches F 24 Hb31
Flint GB 15 Eb22
Flintbek D 118 Dc30
Flintnes N 63 Hd08
Flirey F 25 Jc36
Flirsch A 142 Db54
Flisa N 94 Ec39
Flisberget N 86 Ec38
Flisby S 103 Fc49
Fliseryd S 103 Ga51
Flistad S 103 Fd46
Flisy PL 131 Kb42
Flitwick GB 20 Fc26
Flix E 48 Ga62
Flixecourt F 23 Gd33
Flixton GB 21 Gb25
Flize F 24 Ja34
Flø N 76 Cc32
Flo N 84 Cd34
Flo S 102 Ec47
Floby S 102 Fa47
Floda S 80 Hb26
Floda S 95 Ga44
Floda S 95 Fc40
Floda S 95 Fd40
Floda S 102 Ec48
Flodigarry GB 4 Da07
Flogny-la-Chapelle F 30 Hc39
Flöha D 127 Ed42
Floh-Seligenthal D 126 Dc42
Flon S 86 Ed32
Flor S 87 Fc34
Florac F 34 Hc51
Florange F 25 Jd35
Flor da Rosa P 50 Ba67
Florence = Firenze I 155 Dc65
Floreni MD 173 Fd58
Florensac F 41 Hc55
Florenville B 132 Ad44
Florenz = Firenze I 155 Dc65
Flores de Ávila E 46 Cd62
Floresta I 167 Fc84
Floreşti MD 173 Fc55
Floreşti RO 171 Da58
Floreşti RO 176 Ea64
Floreşti RO 177 Fc64
Floreşti-Stoeneşti RO 176 Ea66
Flória GR 200 Cb95
Floriáda GR 188 Ba82
Floridia I 167 Fd87
Flórina GR 183 Bb77
Florinas I 168 Bd75
Floriţoaia Veche MD 173 Fb57
Flornes N 78 Eb30
Florø N 84 Ca35
Flörsbachtal D 134 Cd44
Flörsheim D 133 Cb44
Flörsheim-Dalsheim D 133 Cb45
Florstadt D 134 Cc43
Florvåg N 84 Ca39
Florynka PL 138 Jc46
Floß D 135 Eb45
Flossenbürg D 135 Eb45
Flosta N 93 Db46
Flostrand N 70 Fa20
Flöthe D 126 Dc37
Flötningen S 86 Ec35
Fluberg N 85 Dd38
Flúðir IS 2 Ac05
Flüelen CH 141 Cb54
Flühli CH 141 Ca54
Flumet F 35 Ka46
Flumini I 169 Cb80
Fluminimaggiore I 169 Bd79
Flums CH 142 Cd54
Fluorn-Winzeln D 141 Cb50
Fluren S 87 Ga36
Flurkmark S 80 Hb28
Flutbukt N 63 Ja06
Flyggsjö S 80 Ha29
Flygsandsvær N 84 Ca40
Flygsfors S 103 Ga52
Flyinge S 110 Fa55
Flykälen S 79 Fc28
Flymen S 111 Ga53
Flyn S 79 Ga29
Flytåsen S 87 Fd37
Fobello I 148 Ca58

Foča – Furset

Foča BIH 159 Hd66
Foça TR 191 Eb85
Focene I 160 Ea72
Fochabers GB 5 Ec07
Fockbek D 118 Db30
Focşani RO 176 Ed62
Focuri RO 172 Ed57
Fódele GR 200 Da95
Foeni RO 174 Bc61
Fogdö S 95 Gb43
Foggia I 161 Ga73
Föglö FIN 96 Hc41
Fohnsdorf A 144 Fc54
Föhren D 133 Bc44
Foiano della Chiana I 156 Dd67
Foiano di Val Fortore I 161 Fc73
Foieni RO 171 Cc54
Foissiat F 34 Jb45
Foix F 40 Gc56
Fojnica BIH 158 Hb64
Fojnica BIH 159 Hc67
Fokino RUS 202 Ed12
Fokovci SLO 145 Gb55
Føland N 92 Cc46
Folby DK 100 Dc23
Földeák H 146 Jc56
Foldereid N 78 Ed25
Földes H 147 Jd53
Foldingbro DK 108 Da26
Fole S 104 Ha49
Folégandros GR 196 Da91
Folelli F 154 Cc69
Folgaria I 149 Dc58
Folgarida I 149 Dc57
Folgensbourg F 31 Kc40
Folgosinho P 44 Bb63
Folgoso E 36 Ba56
Folgoso de la Ribera E 37 Ca57
Folgoso do Courel E 36 Bc56
Folgueiro E 36 Bc53
Foliá GR 184 Cd77
Foligno I 156 Eb68
Føling N 78 Ec27
Folkestad N 76 Cc33
Folkestone GB 21 Gb29
Folkingham GB 17 Fc23
Folladal N 78 Eb28
Follafoss N 78 Eb28
Folldal N 85 Dd34
Følle DK 101 Dd23
Follebu N 85 Dd37
Follina I 150 Ea58
Follingbo S 104 Ha49
Föllinge S 79 Fc29
Follonica I 155 Db68
Fölsbyn S 94 Ec43
Folsztyn PL 121 Gb35
Folteşti RO 177 Fb62
Folusz PL 139 Jd45
Folven N 84 Cd34
Folwarki PL 130 Hd41
Fombellida E 38 Db56
Fominki RUS 203 Fb09
Fompedraza E 46 Db61
Fon N 93 Dd43
Foncebadón E 37 Ca57
Foncine-le-Bas F 31 Jd44
Foncquevillers F 23 Ha32
Fondi I 160 Ed73
Fondo I 142 Dc56
Fondón E 61 Dd75
Föne S 87 Ga35
Fönebo S 87 Gb35
Fonelas E 60 Dc74
Fonfría E 36 Bc56
Fonfría E 45 Ca60
Fonn N 84 Cc35
Fonni I 169 Cb77
Fonollosa E 49 Gc60
Fons F 42 Ja53
Fonsorbes F 40 Gb54
Fontainebleau F 29 Ha38
Fontaine-Chalendray F 32 Fc46
Fontaine-de-Vaucluse F 42 Jc53
Fontaine-Française F 30 Jb41
Fontaine-la-Gaillarde F 30 Hb39
Fontaine-le-Bourg F 23 Gb34
Fontaine-le-Dun F 23 Ga34
Fontaine-les-Grès F 30 Hc38
Fontaines-en-Duesmois F 30 Ja40
Fontaine-sur-Coole F 24 Hd37
Fontainhas P 44 Ac60
Fontainhas P 50 Ab70
Fontan F 43 Kd52
Fontanamare I 169 Bd79
Fontanar E 46 Dd63
Fontanar E 61 Dd73
Fontanarejo E 52 Da68
Fontanars dels Alforins E 55 Fb70
Fontane Bianche I 167 Fd87
Fontanelice I 150 Dd63
Fontanella I 155 Db65
Fontanellato I 149 Da61
Fontanelle I 150 Eb58
Fontanes-du Causse F 33 Gc51
Fontanières F 33 Ha46
Fontanigorda I 149 Cc62
Fontaniva I 150 Dd59
Fontanosas E 52 Cd69
Fontdepou E 48 Ga59
Fonteblanda I 155 Dc69
Fontecchio I 156 Ed70
Fontecha E 37 Cc57
Fonte da Telha P 50 Aa69
Fontenai-les-Louvets F 28 Fc38
Fontenay-le-Comte F 32 Fb45
Fontenay-le-Marmion F 22 Fc36
Fontenay-Trésigny F 23 Ha37
Fontenelle-en-Brie F 24 Hb36
Fontet F 32 Fc51
Fontette F 30 Ja39
Fontevraud-l'Abbaye F 28 Fd42
Fontibre E 38 Db56
Fontioso E 46 Dc59
Fontiveros E 46 Cd62
Font-Romeu F 41 Gd58
Fontstown IRL 13 Cc22
Fontvieille F 42 Jb53
Fonyód H 145 Ha55
Fonz E 48 Fd59
Fonzaso I 150 Ea58
Foppiano I 141 Ca56
Foppolo I 149 Cd57
Föra S 103 Gb51
Forăşti RO 172 Ec56
Forbach D 133 Cb48
Forbach F 25 Ka35
Förby FIN 97 Jc40
Forcall E 48 Fc64
Forcalqueiret F 42 Ka54
Forcalquier F 42 Jd52
Forcarei E 36 Ba56
Forchheim D 135 Dd45
Forchtenberg D 134 Da47
Ford GB 6 Db12
Ford GB 11 Ed14
Ford GB 20 Ed26
Førde N 84 Cb36
Førde N 84 Cc35
Førde N 92 Ca41
Förderstedt D 127 Ea38
Førdesfjorden N 92 Ca42
Fordham GB 20 Fd25
Fordingbridge GB 20 Ed30
Fordongianus I 169 Ca77
Fordoun GB 7 Ed10
Fordstown IRL 9 Cc20
Fore N 71 Fb18
Forenza I 161 Ga75
Forestburn Gate GB 11 Ed15
Forest Green GB 20 Fc29
Forest-Montiers F 23 Gc32
Forest Row GB 20 Fd29
Forfar GB 7 Ec11
Forgés F 33 Gc49
Forges-les-Eaux F 23 Gb34
Foria I 161 Fd77
Forio I 161 Fa75
Förkärla S 111 Fd54
Förlanda S 102 Ec50
Forlev DK 109 Ea27
Forlì I 156 Ea64
Forlimpopoli I 156 Ea64
Formazza I 141 Ca56
Formby GB 15 Eb21
Formentor E 57 Hc66
Formerie F 23 Gc34
Formia I 160 Ed73
Formiche Alto E 47 Fa65
Formicola I 161 Fb74
Formigara I 149 Cd60
Formigine I 149 Db62
Formigliana I 148 Ca59
Formignana I 150 Ea62
Formigny F 22 Fb35
Formiguères F 41 Gd57
Formofoss N 78 Ed27
Fornalhas Novas P 58 Ac72
Fornåsa S 103 Fd46
Fornazzo I 167 Fd85
Forneby S 95 Gb41
Fornelli I 168 Bd74
Fornells E 57 Ja65
Fornelos E 36 Ad58
Fornelos P 44 Ad59
Fornelos de Montes E 36 Ad57
Fornes N 67 Gb12
Forneset N 62 Ha09
Forni Avoltri I 143 Ec56
Forni di Sopra I 143 Eb56
Forni di Sotto I 150 Eb57
Forno I 148 Bc60
Forno I 148 Ca57
Forno Alpi Graie I 148 Bc59
Forno di Zoldo I 150 Ea57
Fornoli I 155 Db64
Fornos de Algodres P 44 Bb63
Fornovo di Taro I 149 Da62
Foros da Fonte de Pau P 50 Ac68
Foros de Vale de Figueira P 50 Ac69
Foros do Arrão P 50 Ad67
Foros do Cortiço P 50 Ad69
Forotic RO 174 Bd62
Forøya N 70 Fa19
Forráskút H 146 Jb56
Forres GB 5 Eb07
Forronda E 38 Ea56
Fors S 80 Gd30
Fors S 95 Ga41
Fors S 102 Ec47
Forsa N 66 Ga14
Forsa S 87 Gb35
Forsand N 92 Cb44
Forsås S 79 Gb30
Forsbacka S 80 Hb25
Forsbacka S 87 Gb37
Forsbacka S 95 Gb39
Forsby FIN 81 Jb29
Forsby FIN 90 Kd38
Forsby S 103 Fb47
Forsby Koskenkyla FIN 90 Kc38
Forsen N 71 Fb21
Forserum S 103 Fb49
Forset N 85 Dd37
Forshaga S 94 Fa43
Forshälla S 102 Eb47
Forshed S 73 Hd20
Forsheda S 102 Fa51
Forshem S 102 Fa46
Forsholm S 80 Ha25
Forsinard GB 5 Ea05
Forsland N 70 Fa20
Förslöv S 110 Ed53
Forsmark S 71 Fd23
Forsmark S 96 Gd40
Forsmo S 79 Gb30
Forsmo S 79 Gb29
Forsmoen N 70 Fa21
Forsnäs S 72 Gd20
Forsnäs S 72 Gb22
Forsnäs S 73 Hd21
Forsnäs S 73 Hc20
Forsnäs S 79 Gb27
Forsnes N 77 Db29
Forsøl N 63 Ja05
Forssa FIN 89 Jd38
Forssa S 95 Gb45
Forssjö S 95 Ga45
Forst D 128 Fc39
Forst D 134 Cc47
Forstau A 143 Ed53
Forstern D 143 Ea51
Forstinning D 143 Ea51
Forsträskhed S 73 Hd21
Forsvik S 72 Gb24
Forsvik S 103 Fb46
Fortan F 29 Ga40
Fortanete E 48 Fb64
Fort Augustus GB 7 Dd09
Forte dei Marmi I 155 Da64
Fortezza I 143 Dd55
Forth GB 10 Ea13
Förtha D 126 Db41
Fortino I 161 Ga77
Fort-Mahon-Plage F 23 Gb32
Forton GB 15 Ec24
Fortrose GB 5 Ea07
Fortun N 85 Da36
Fortuna E 55 Fa72
Fortunago I 149 Cc61
Fortuneswell GB 19 Ec31
Fort William GB 6 Dc10
Forvika N 70 Ed22
Forza d'Agrò I 167 Fd84
Forzo I 148 Bc59
Fos F 40 Ga56
Fösked S 94 Fa42
Foskros S 86 Ed34
Foskvallen S 86 Ed35
Fosnavåg N 76 Cb33
Fosnes N 78 Ec25
Foss S 102 Eb46
Fossacesia I 157 Fb70
Fossacesia Marina I 157 Fb70
Fossano I 148 Bc62
Fossato di Vico I 156 Eb67
Fossato Ionico I 164 Ga84
Fossbakken N 67 Gc12
Fossbua N 67 Ha12
Fosse N 84 Cb39
Fossegården N 85 Ea37
Fossemagne F 33 Gb49
Fossen N 84 Cd36
Fosser N 94 Eb42
Fosses F 23 Gd36
Fosses-la-Ville B 124 Ad42
Fossestrand N 64 Jb07
Fosshaug N 67 Gc12
Fossheim N 62 Ha10
Fossheim N 65 Kc09
Fossheim N 85 Db35
Fossholm N 64 Ka07
Fossli N 84 Cd39
Fossmoen N 78 Fa25
Fossombrone I 156 Eb65
Fos-sur-Mer F 42 Jb54
Fót H 146 Hd52
Fotheringhay GB 17 Fc24
Fotiní GR 183 Bb77
Fotinovo BG 184 Da74
Fotlandsvåg N 84 Ca38
Fotolívos GR 184 Cd77
Fouesnant F 27 Dc40
Fougeré F 28 Fc41
Fougères F 28 Fa38
Fougères-sur-Bièvre F 29 Gb41
Fougerolles F 31 Jd39
Fougerolles-du-Plessis F 28 Fb38
Fouilloy F 23 Gc34
Foulain F 30 Jb39
Foulayronnes F 40 Ga52
Fouligny F 25 Jd35
Foulsham GB 17 Ga24
Foulum DK 100 Db23
Fountain Cross IRL 12 Bc22
Fountainhal GB 11 Ec14
Fouquerolles F 23 Gd35
Fouras F 32 Fa46
Fourcamont F 23 Gb33
Fourcès F 40 Fd53
Fourchambault F 30 Hb43
Four Crosses GB 15 Eb24
Fourfourás GR 200 Cd96
Fourka GR 182 Ad78
Fourmies F 24 Hc33
Four Mile House IRL 8 Ca20
Fourná GR 188 Bb82
Fournaudin F 30 Hc39
Fournels F 34 Hb50
Fournés GR 200 Cb95
Fournet F 31 Kb42
Fourni GR 197 Ea88
Fourques F 41 Hb57
Fours F 30 Hc43
Fousing Kirkeby DK 100 Cd23
Foussais F 28 Fb44
Foústani GR 183 Bd76
Fovrfeld DK 108 Cd26
Fowey GB 18 Dc31
Fownhope GB 15 Ec26
Foxford IRL 8 Bc18
Foxhall IRL 8 Bc20
Foxo E 36 Ba56
Foxup GB 11 Ed19
Foynes IRL 12 Bc23
Foz E 36 Bc53
Foz de Arouce P 44 Ad64
Foz de Odeleite P 58 Ba73
Foz do Arelho P 50 Aa66
Foz Giraldo P 44 Ba65
Frabosa Soprana I 148 Bd63
Frącki PL 123 Kb30
Fraddon GB 18 Db31
Frades de la Sierra E 45 Cb63
Fraga E 48 Fd61
Fragagnano I 162 Ha76
Fragistra GR 188 Bb83
Frahier-et-Châtebier F 31 Ka40
Frailes E 60 Db74
Frais F 31 Kb40
Fraisse-sur-Agout F 41 Hb54
Fraize F 31 Kb38
Framlev DK 108 Dc24
Framlingham GB 21 Gb25
Frammersbach D 134 Da44
Främmestad S 102 Ed47
Framnäs S 72 Ha19
Frampol PL 131 Kb42
Framura I 149 Cc63
França P 45 Bb59
Francaltreff F 25 Ka36
Francardo F 154 Cb69
Francavilla al Mare I 157 Fb70
Francavilla di Sicilia I 167 Fd84
Francavilla Fontana I 162 Ha76
Francavilla sul Sinni I 162 Gb77
Francescas F 40 Fd53
Francești RO 175 Db64
Franciszkowo PL 122 Hd34
Francofonte I 167 Fc87
Francolise I 161 Fa74
Francorchamps B 125 Bb42
Francos E 46 Dd61
Francova Lhota CZ 137 Ha47
Frändefors S 102 Ec46
Franeker NL 116 Bb33
Franekeradeel NL 116 Bb33
Fránga GR 188 Ba85
Frangádes GR 182 Ad80
Frangouléika GR 188 Ba84
Frangy F 35 Jd46
Frankenau D 126 Cd40
Frankenberg D 126 Cd41
Frankenberg D 127 Ed42
Frankenburg A 143 Ed51
Frankenförde D 127 Ed38
Frankenhardt D 134 Da47
Frankenmarkt A 143 Ed51
Frankenstein D 133 Cb46
Frankenthal D 133 Cb46
Frankfurt am Main D 134 Cc44
Frankfurt (Oder) D 128 Fb37
Frankleben D 127 Ea40
Franknowo PL 122 Ja31
Frankrike S 78 Fa29
Frånö S 80 Gc31
Franqueville F 40 Ga56
Františkovy Lázně CZ 135 Eb44
Franzburg D 119 Ed31
Franzensfeste I 143 Dd55
Frascati I 160 Eb72
Frascineto I 164 Gb78
Frasdorf D 143 Eb52
Fraserburgh GB 5 Ed07
Fra'shër AL 182 Ac78
Frasin MD 173 Fa54
Frasin RO 172 Eb56
Frăsinet RO 181 Ec67
Frasne F 31 Jd43
Frassene I 150 Ea57
Frassinoro I 149 Db63
Frasso Telesino I 161 Fb74
Frastanz A 142 Cd54
Frata RO 171 Db58
Frătăuţii Noi RO 172 Eb54
Frataţii Vechi RO 172 Eb54
Fratel P 50 Ba66
Frăteşti RO 180 Ea67
Frátsia GR 195 Bd92
Frattamaggiore I 161 Fb74
Fratta Polesine I 150 Dd61
Frauenau D 135 Ed48
Frauenfeld CH 142 Cc52
Frauenhain D 127 Ed40
Frauenkirch CH 142 Cd55
Frauenkirchen A 145 Gc52
Frauensee D 126 Db41
Frauenstein D 128 Fa42
Frauenwald D 126 Dc42
Fraugde DK 109 Dd27
Fraunberg D 143 Ea50
Frayssinet-le-Gélat F 33 Gb51
Frecăţei RO 177 Fb65
Frecăţei RO 177 Fc64
Frechen D 125 Bd41
Frechilla E 37 Cd58
Freckenhorst D 125 Cb38
Freckleben D 127 Ea39
Freckleton GB 15 Eb20
Frécourt F 31 Jc39
Freden D 126 Db38
Fredenbeck D 118 Da32
Fredensborg DK 109 Ec25
Fredericia DK 108 Db26
Frederiks DK 100 Db23
Frederiksberg DK 109 Ec26
Frederiksberg DK 109 Ea26
Frederikshavn DK 101 Dd20
Frederikssund DK 109 Eb25
Frederiksværk DK 109 Eb25
Fredersdorf-Eggersdorf D 128 Fa36
Frednowy PL 122 Hd32
Fredrika S 80 Gd28
Fredriksberg S 95 Fb41
Fredriksli N 77 Dd30
Fredrikstad N 93 Ea44
Fredriksten N 94 Eb44
Fredropol PL 139 Kb45
Fredros S 94 Ed41
Fredsberg S 95 Fb45
Fredvang N 66 Fa14
Freeland GB 20 Fa27
Freemount IRL 12 Bc24
Freethorpe GB 17 Gb24
Fregenal de la Sierra E 51 Bc71
Fregene I 160 Ea71
Fréhel F 26 Ec37
Frei N 77 Da31
Freiamt D 141 Ca50
Freibach A 144 Fb56
Freiberg D 127 Ed42
Freiberg (Neckar) D 134 Cd48
Freiburg D 118 Da31
Freiburg D 141 Ca51
Freidorf RO 174 Bc61
Freiensteinau D 134 Da43
Freienwill D 108 Db29
Freigericht D 134 Cd44
Freihung D 135 Ea46
Freila E 61 Dd74
Freilassing D 143 Ec52
Freisen D 133 Bd45
Freising D 143 Ea50
Freissinières F 35 Kb50
Freistadt A 144 Fb50
Freistatt D 118 Cd35
Freiston GB 17 Fd23
Freital D 128 Fa41
Freixedas P 45 Bc63
Freixeiro E 36 Bc57
Freixianda P 44 Ac65
Freixo de Espada à Cinta P 45 Bd61
Fréjairolles F 41 Gd53
Frejlev DK 100 Dc21
Frejlev DK 109 Eb29
Fréjus F 43 Kb54
Fremdingen D 134 Db48
Frenchpark IRL 8 Ca19
Frencq F 23 Gc31
Frende P 44 Ba61
Frenelle F 31 Jd38
Frenelles F 23 Gb35
Frensdorf D 134 Dc45
Frensham GB 20 Fb29
Frenštát pod Radhoštěm CZ 137 Hb46
Freren D 117 Cb36
Freshford IRL 13 Cb23
Freshwater GB 20 Fa31
Fresnay-sur-Sarthe F 28 Fd39
Fresneda E 38 Dd58
Fresneda E 53 Eb66
Fresnedillas E 46 Db64
Fresnedo de Valdellorma E 37 Cd56
Fresnedoso de Ibor E 51 Cb66
Fresne-Léguillon F 23 Gc35
Fresne-Saint-Mamès F 31 Jc41
Fresnes-au-Mont F 24 Jb36
Fresnes-en-Woëvre F 25 Jc35
Fresnes-sur-Apance F 31 Jc39
Fresnes-sur-les-Eaux F 24 Hb31
Fresno-Alhándiga E 45 Cb63
Fresno de Cantespino E 46 Dc61
Fresno de Caracena E 46 Dd61
Fresno de la Ribera E 45 Cc60
Fresno de la Vega E 37 Cc58
Fresno de Sayago E 45 Cb61
Fresno el Viejo E 45 Cc61
Fresnoy-en-Bassigny F 31 Jc39
Fresnoy-Folny F 23 Gb33
Fresnoyrand F 24 Hb33
Fresselines F 33 Gc45
Fressingfield GB 21 Gb25
Fresvik N 84 Cd37
Freswick GB 5 Ec04
Fretigney-et-Velloreille F 31 Jd41
Frétigny F 29 Ga38
Frettes F 31 Jc40
Fretzdorf D 119 Ec34
Freudenberg D 125 Cb41
Freudenberg D 134 Cd45
Freudenberg D 135 Ea46
Freudenstadt D 133 Cb49
Freudental D 134 Cc47
Frévent F 23 Gd32
Freyburg D 127 Ea40
Freyenstein D 119 Ec34
Freyming-Merlebach F 25 Ka35
Freystadt D 135 Dd47
Freyung D 135 Ed49
Frí GR 201 Eb95
Frías E 38 Dd57
Frías de Albarracín E 47 Ed65
Fribourg CH 141 Bc54
Frick CH 141 Ca52
Frička SK 138 Jc46
Frickenhausen D 134 Db45
Frickhofen D 125 Cb42
Frickingen D 142 Cd51
Fričovce SK 138 Jc47
Fridafors S 111 Fc53
Fridaythorpe GB 16 Fb19
Fridene S 103 Fb47
Fridhem S 102 Ed47
Fridingen D 142 Cc51
Fridlevstad S 111 Fd54
Fridolfing D 143 Ec51
Friedberg A 144 Ga53
Friedberg D 134 Cc43
Friedberg D 142 Dc50
Friedburg A 143 Ed51
Friedeburg D 117 Cc32
Friedenfels D 135 Eb45
Friedenweiler D 141 Cb51
Friedersdorf D 127 Eb39
Friedersdorf D 128 Fa37
Friedewald D 126 Db41
Friedland D 120 Fa32
Friedland D 126 Db40
Friedland D 128 Fb38
Friedrichroda D 126 Dc41
Friedrichsbrunn D 127 Dd39
Friedrichsdorf D 134 Cc43
Friedrichshafen D 142 Cd52
Friedrichshain D 128 Fb39
Friedrichskoog D 118 Da31
Friedrichsruhe D 119 Eb33
Friedrichstadt D 118 Da30
Friedrichsthal D 119 Ed35
Friedrichsthal D 133 Bd46
Friedrichswalde D 120 Fa34
Friel S 102 Ed46
Frielendorf D 126 Da41
Friera E 37 Bd57
Friesach A 144 Fb55
Friesack D 119 Ec35
Friesenheim D 133 Ca49
Friesenried D 142 Db51
Friesoythe D 117 Cb34
Frifelt DK 108 Da27
Friggesund S 87 Ga35
Frigiliana E 60 Db76
Frigole I 163 Hc76
Frihetsli N 67 Ha12
Frilford GB 20 Fa27
Friligiánika GR 195 Bd92
Frillesås S 102 Ec50
Frimley GB 20 Fb29
Frinnaryd S 103 Fc48
Frinton-on-Sea GB 21 Gb27
Friockheim GB 7 Ec11
Friol E 36 Bb55
Frisange L 133 Bb45
Friskney GB 17 Fd23
Fristad S 102 Ed48
Frithville GB 17 Fc23
Fritsla S 102 Ed49
Fritzlar D 126 Cd40
Friville-Escarbotin F 23 Gb33
Frjanovo RUS 203 Fa10
Froan N 77 Dd28
Fröderyd S 103 Fc50
Frödinge S 103 Ga49
Frodisia CY 206 Hd97
Frogn N 93 Ea42
Frogner N 93 Ea41
Frogner (Oslo) N 93 Ea41
Frohburg D 127 Ec41
Frohen-le-Grand F 23 Gd32
Frohnleiten A 144 Fd54
Froissy F 23 Gd34
Fröjel S 104 Gd50
Fröjered S 103 Fb47
Froland N 93 Da46
Frolovo RUS 203 Fd13
Frombork PL 122 Hc30
Frome GB 19 Ec29
Fromentel F 22 Fc37
Fromentine F 27 Ec43
Frómista E 38 Da58
Fröndenberg D 125 Cb39
Fronhausen D 126 Cc42
Fronreute D 142 Cd51
Front I 148 Bd59
Fronteira P 50 Ba68
Frontenard F 30 Jb43
Frontenay-Rohan-Rohan F 32 Fb45
Frontenex F 35 Ka47
Frontenhausen D 135 Eb49
Frontignan F 41 Hd54
Fronton F 40 Gb53
Frørup DK 109 Dd27
Frose D 127 Ea38
Fröseke S 103 Ga51
Frosinone I 160 Ed72
Frøskeland N 66 Fc12
Fröskog S 94 Ec45
Frøslev DK 100 Da21
Fröslunda S 96 Gc42
Frösö S 79 Fc31
Frosolone I 161 Fb72
Frossay F 27 Ec42
Frosta N 78 Eb29
Frösthult S 95 Gb42
Frostkåge S 80 Hc25
Frøstrup DK 100 Db21
Frösunda S 96 Gd42
Frösve S 103 Fb46
Frötuna S 96 Ha42
Frouard F 25 Jd36
Froussioúna GR 194 Bc87
Frövi S 95 Fd43
Frövifors S 95 Fd43
Froxfield GB 20 Ed28
Frøyset N 84 Ca37
Frøysnes N 92 Cd44
Frufällan S 102 Ed49
Fruges F 23 Gd31
Frula E 48 Fb60
Frumoasa MD 173 Fc57
Frumoasa RO 172 Ea59
Frumoasa RO 180 Dd68
Frumosu RO 172 Ea55
Frumuşani RO 180 Eb67
Frumuşica MD 173 Fb55
Frumuşica MD 177 Fc61
Frumuşica RO 172 Ed56
Frumuşiţa RO 177 Fb62
Fruniz E 38 Ea55
Frunză MD 173 Fa53
Frunzivka UA 204 Ec16
Frúrio GR 183 Bc79
Frutak MNE 159 Hd69
Frutigen CH 141 Bd55
Fruzenskoe RUS 113 Jc59
Frýdek-Místek CZ 137 Hb45
Frýdlant CZ 128 Fc42
Frýdlant nad Ostravicí CZ 137 Hb46
Fryele S 103 Fb50
Frygnowo PL 122 Hd33
Frykerud S 94 Ed43
Fryksände S 94 Ed41
Fryksås S 87 Fc37
Frymburk CZ 136 Fb49
Fryšták CZ 137 Ha47
Frysztak PL 139 Jd44
Fterë AL 182 Ab78
Fuans F 31 Ka42
Fubine I 148 Ca61
Fucecchio I 155 Db65
Fuchsmühl D 135 Eb45
Fuchsstadt D 134 Da44
Fuchstal D 142 Dc51
Füchtorf D 125 Cb37
Fuencaliente E 52 Da71
Fuendejalón E 47 Ed60
Fuendetodos E 47 Fa61
Fuengirola E 60 Cd77
Fuenlabrada E 46 Db65
Fuenlabrada de los Montes E 52 Cd68
Fuensalida E 46 Da65
Fuensanta E 53 Eb68
Fuensanta E 61 Ec73
Fuensanta de Martos E 60 Db73
Fuente-Álamo E 55 Fa73
Fuente-Álamo E 55 Ed70
Fuentealbilla E 54 Ed68
Fuentearmegil E 46 Dd60
Fuente-Blanca E 55 Fa71
Fuentecaliente de Lucio E 38 Db57
Fuente Carreteros E 60 Cc73
Fuentecén E 46 Dc60
Fuente Dé E 38 Da55
Fuente de Cantos E 51 Bd71
Fuente del Arco E 51 Ca71
Fuente del Maestre E 51 Bd70
Fuente del Pino E 55 Ed71
Fuente de Pedro Naharro E 53 Dd66
Fuente de Piedra E 60 Cd75
Fuente de Reina E 54 Fb66
Fuente el Fresno E 52 Db68
Fuente el Olmo de Íscar E 46 Da61
Fuente el Saz de Jarama E 46 Dc64
Fuente el Sol E 46 Cd62
Fuente Encalada E 37 Cb58
Fuenteheridos E 59 Bc72
Fuentelapeña E 45 Cc61
Fuentelcésped E 46 Dc60
Fuentelespino deHaro E 53 Ea67
Fuentelespino de Moya E 54 Ed66
Fuentelmonje E 47 Eb61
Fuentelsaz E 47 Ec62
Fuentemilanos E 46 Db63
Fuente Obejuna E 51 Cb71
Fuente Palmera E 60 Cc73
Fuentepelayo E 46 Db62
Fuentepinilla E 47 Ea61
Fuenterrebollo E 46 Db61
Fuenterrobles E 54 Ed67
Fuentes E 53 Ec66
Fuentesaúco E 45 Cc61
Fuentesaúco de Fuentidueña E 46 Db61
Fuentes Claras E 47 Ed63
Fuentes de Andalucia E 59 Cb73
Fuentes de Béjar E 45 Cb64
Fuentes de Carbajal E 37 Cc58
Fuentes de Cesna E 60 Da74
Fuentes de Ebro E 48 Fb61
Fuentes de León E 51 Bc71
Fuentes de Nava E 46 Da59
Fuentes de Oñoro E 45 Bc63
Fuentes de Ropel E 45 Cc59
Fuentes de Valdepero E 46 Da59
Fuentespalda E 48 Fd63
Fuentespina E 46 Dc60
Fuente Tójar E 60 Da74
Fuentidueña E 46 Db61
Fuentidueña E 60 Db73
Fuentidueña de Tajo E 46 Dd65
Fuerte del Rey E 60 Db72
Fuestrup D 125 Cb37
Fügen A 143 Ea53
Fugleberg N 67 Gb12
Fuglebjerg DK 109 Ea27
Fuglestad N 92 Ca45
Fuglsø DK 109 Dd24
Fuglstad N 70 Ed24
Fuhrberg D 126 Db36
Fulacık TR 186 Ga79
Fulda D 126 Da42
Fülesd H 147 Kc50
Fulga RO 176 Eb65
Fulgatore I 166 Eb84
Fullerton GB 20 Fa29
Fullestad S 102 Ed48
Fullösa S 102 Fa46
Fulnek CZ 137 Ha45
Fulnetby GB 17 Fc22
Fülöpjakab H 146 Ja55
Fülöpszállás H 146 Hd55
Fulpmes A 143 Dd54
Fulunäs S 86 Ed37
Fumay F 24 Ja33
Fumel F 33 Gb51
Funäsdalen S 86 Ed33
Funbo S 96 Gd42
Funchal P
Fundão P 44 Bb64
Fundata RO 176 Dd63
Fundeni RO 176 Eb66
Fundeni RO 177 Fa62
Fundres I 143 Ea55
Fundulea RO 176 Eb66
Fundu Moldovei RO 172 Ea56
Fundurii Noi MD 173 Fa55
Fundurii Vechi MD 173 Fb55
Funes E 39 Ec58
Fünfstetten D 134 Dc48
Funtana HR 150 Ed61
Funzie GB 5 Fa03
Furadouro P 44 Ac62
Furco E 36 Bb56
Furculeşti RO 180 Dc68
Furen BG 179 Cd69
Fürfeld D 133 Ca45
Fürged H 145 Hb55
Furingstad S 103 Ga46
Furiz E 38 Ea55
Furlo I 156 Eb66
Furmanov RUS 203 Fa09
Furmanovo RUS 113 Jd59
Furore I 161 Fb76
Furset N 77 Da31

Gonnosfanadiga – Grenči

Gonnosfanadiga I 169 Bd79
Gonnosnò I 169 Ca78
Gonsans F 31 Jd42
Gontán E 36 Bc54
Gönü TR 186 Fb80
Gönyű H 145 Ha52
Gonzaga I 149 Db61
Gonzar E 36 Bb56
Gooderstone GB 17 Ga24
Goodwick GB 14 Db26
Goole GB 16 Fb21
Goor NL 117 Bd36
Gopegi E 38 Ea56
Goppenstein CH 141 Bd56
Göppingen D 134 Da49
Gor E 61 Dd74
Gora HR 152 Gb60
Góra PL 122 Ja35
Góra PL 129 Gb39
Gora RUS 107 Ma47
Gora Bobyli RUS 107 Mb47
Gorafe E 61 Dd74
Gorai RUS 107 Ma49
Gorainiai LT 113 Jc56
Goraiolo I 155 Db64
Goraj PL 131 Kb41
Gorajec-Zagroble PL 131 Kb42
Góra Kalwaria PL 130 Jc37
Goran BG 180 Db70
Goráni GR 194 Bc89
Goransko MNE 159 Hd67
Góra Puławska PL 131 Jd39
Góra Świętej Anny PL 137 Ha43
Gorawino PL 120 Fd31
Goražde BIH 159 Hd65
Gorban RO 173 Fb58
Gorbănești RO 172 Ed55
Görbeháza H 147 Jd51
Gorbovo RUS 107 Ld47
Gorbunova Gora RUS 107 Ld48
Görcsöny H 152 Hb58
Gorczenica PL 122 Hc34
Gördalen S 86 Ed36
Gordaliza del Pino E 37 Cd58
Gordes F 42 Jc53
Gördes TR 192 Fb84
Gordinești MD 173 Fa54
Gørding DK 108 Da26
Gordoa E 39 Eb56
Gordoe RUS 113 Jb59
Gordola CH 148 Cb57
Gordon GB 11 Ec14
Gordona I 142 Cc56
Gordoncillo E 37 Cc58
Gördsbyn S 94 Ed42
Gorelki RUS 203 Fa11
Gorelovo RUS 99 Mb39
Gorenja Kanomlja SLO 151 Fa58
Gorenja Trebuša SLO 151 Fa58
Gorenja vas SLO 151 Fb58
Gorey GBJ 26 Ec36
Gorey IRL 13 Cd23
Gorgast D 128 Fb36
Görgeteg H 152 Gd57
Gorgogiri GR 188 Bb81
Gorgoglione I 162 Gb76
Gorgonzola I 149 Cc59
Gorgopotamos GR 189 Bc83
Gorgota RO 176 Eb65
Gorica BG 180 Ea70
Gorica BG 181 Ed72
Gorica BG 181 Fa71
Gorica BIH 158 Gd64
Gorica BIH 158 Gd66
Gorica BIH 159 Hc69
Gorica HR 157 Fd64
Goricë AL 182 Ba76
Goriče SLO 151 Fb57
Goricy RUS 202 Ed09
Gorinchem NL 124 Ba37
Goring GB 20 Fa28
Gorino I 150 Eb62
Goritsá GR 194 Bc89
Goritz D 119 Ec31
Gorizia I 150 Ed58
Gorjačevo RUS 107 Mb50
Gorjačij Ključ RUS 205 Fc17
Gorjani SRB 159 Jb65
Gorjão P 50 Ad67
Gorka RUS 99 Lc44
Gorka RUS 99 Ma42
Górki PL 130 Hc36
Górki PL 138 Jc43
Gorki RUS 99 Mb40
Gorki RUS 99 Mb40
Gorki RUS 107 Mb47
Górki Noteckie PL 120 Fd35
Gørlev DK 109 Ea26
Gorlice PL 138 Jc45
Görlitz D 128 Fc41
Gørløse DK 109 Ec25
Görmar D 126 Dc40
Gormaz E 46 Dd61
Görmin D 119 Ed31
Gorna Bešovica BG 179 Cd70
Gorna Graštica BG 179 Cb72
Gorna Kremena BG 179 Cd70
Gorna Lipnica BG 180 Dd70
Gorna Mitropolija BG 180 Db69
Gorna Orjahovica BG 180 Dd70
Gorna Rosica BG 180 Dc71
Gorna Studena BG 180 Dd69
Gornau D 127 Ed42
Gornești RO 171 Dc58
Gornet RO 176 Eb64
Gornet Cricov RO 176 Eb64
Gorni Cibăr BG 179 Cd68
Gorni Dăbnik BG 179 Da69
Gorni Lom BG 179 Cb68
Gorni Okol BG 179 Cc72
Gornja Badanja SRB 153 Ja62
Gornja Belica MK 183 Bb74
Gornja Bistra HR 151 Ga58
Gornjackij RUS 203 Fc14
Gornja Deržnica BIH 158 Ha66
Gornja Golubinja BIH 152 Hb63
Gornja Grabovica BIH 158 Ha66
Gornja Klina KSV 178 Ba70
Gornja Lisina SRB 179 Ca71
Gornja Ljubovida SRB 153 Ja63
Gornja Ljuta BIH 159 Hc66
Gornjane SRB 174 Ca66
Gornja Ploča HR 151 Ga63
Gornja Radgona SLO 144 Ga56
Gornja Rogatica SRB 153 Ja58
Gornja Sabanta SRB 174 Bb66
Gornja Stubica HR 151 Ga58
Gornja Suvaja BIH 152 Gb62
Gornja Trepča MNE 159 Hd68
Gornja Trešnjevica SRB 153 Jc63
Gornja Tuzla BIH 153 Hc62
Gornja Vranjska SRB 153 Jb62
Gornje Dubočke MNE 159 Hc68
Gornje Jelenje HR 151 Fc60
Gornje Komarevo HR 152 Gb60
Gornje Lopiže SRB 159 Jb66
Gornje Lopiže SRB 178 Ad68
Gornje Ratkovo BIH 152 Gc63
Gornje Taborište HR 151 Ga60
Gornje Vinovo HR 158 Gb65
Gornje Vratno HR 152 Gb57
Gornje Zuniče SRB 179 Ca68
Gornji Banjani SRB 159 Jc64
Gornji Čevljanovići BIH 159 Hc64
Gornji Dolac HR 158 Gc66
Gornji Dolič SLO 151 Fd57
Gornji Grad SLO 151 Fc57
Gornji Humac HR 158 Gc67
Gornji Jabolčište MK 183 Bb74
Gornji Kamengrad BIH 152 Gc62
Gornji Kokoti MNE 159 Ja70
Gornji Kraljevec HR 152 Gb57
Gornji Krušje MK 182 Ba75
Gornji Lapac HR 152 Gb63
Gornji Lukavac BIH 159 Hc67
Gornji Malovan BIH 158 Gd65
Gornji Miklouš HR 152 Gc59
Gornji Milanovac SRB 159 Jc64
Gornji Muć HR 158 Gc66
Gornji Nemzi MK 178 Bb73
Gornji Orizari MK 183 Bc74
Gornji Podgradci BIH 152 Gd61
Gornji Rajić HR 152 Gd60
Gornji Ribnik BIH 152 Gc63
Gornji Stepos SRB 178 Bc68
Gornji Vakuf = Uskoplje BIH 158 Ha65
Górno PL 130 Jb41
Gorno Botevo BG 180 Dd73
Gorno Izvorovo BG 180 Dd72
Gorno Kamarci BG 179 Cd71
Gorno Novo Selo BG 180 Dc72
Gorno Ozirovo BG 179 Cc69
Gornyj RUS 203 Ga11
Goro I 150 Ea62
Gorobinci MK 178 Bc73
Gorodec RUS 99 Mb44
Gorodec RUS 203 Fb09
Gorodenka EST 99 Lc42
Gorodišče RUS 203 Fd11
Gorodkovo RUS 113 Jc57
Gorodovikovsk RUS 205 Fd16
Górowo Iławeckie PL 122 Ja30
Gor. Primišlje HR 151 Fd61
Gorran Heaven GB 18 Db32
Gorre F 33 Gb47
Gorredijk NL 117 Bc34
Gorron F 28 Fb38
Görsbach D 127 Dd40
Görsdorf D 127 Ed38
Goršečnoe RUS 203 Fa13
Gorseinon GB 19 Dd27
Gorsk PL 121 Ha34
Gorska poljana BG 185 Ec74
Gorski izvor BG 184 Dc74
Gorsko Kosovo BG 180 Dc70
Gorsko Novo Selo BG 180 Ea70
Gorsko Slivovo BG 180 Dc70
Gørslev DK 109 Eb26
Gorssel NL 117 Bc36
Gort IRL 12 Bd22
Gortaclare GB 9 Cc17
Gortahork IRL 9 Cb15
Gort an Choirce IRL 9 Cb15
Gorteen IRL 8 Bd19
Gortin GB 9 Cc16
Gortipohl A 142 Da54
Gortmore IRL 8 Bb20
Gortymadden IRL 12 Bd21
Goruia RO 174 Bd63
Gorun BG 181 Fc69
Gorv N 84 Cb35
Görvik S 79 Fd29
Görwihl D 141 Ca52
Gorzanów PL 137 Gb43
Görzig D 127 Eb39
Görzke D 128 Fb37
Görzke D 127 Eb37
Gorzkowice PL 130 Hd40
Gorzków-Osada PL 131 Kc40
Górzna PL 121 Gc33
Górzno PL 122 Hd34
Górzno PL 129 Ha39
Górzno PL 131 Jd38
Gorzów Śląski PL 129 Hb41
Gorzów Wielkopolski PL 128 Fd36
Gorzupia PL 128 Fd39
Górzyca PL 120 Fd31
Górzyca PL 128 Fc36
Gorzyce PL 131 Jd42
Gorzyce PL 137 Hb45
Górzyn PL 128 Fc39
Gorzyń PL 128 Ga36
Goržžam N 64 Jd07
Gosaldo I 150 Ea57
Gosau A 143 Ed53
Gosberton GB 17 Fc23
Göschenen CH 141 Cb55
Göscheneralp CH 141 Cb55
Gościcino PL 121 Ha29
Gościęcin PL 137 Ha44
Gościeradów PL 131 Ka41
Gościkowo Jordanowo PL 128 Fd37
Gościm PL 120 Ga35
Gościno PL 120 Fd31
Gościsław PL 129 Gb41
Gościszewo PL 121 Hb31
Gościszów PL 128 Fd41
Gosdorf A 144 Ga55
Goseck D 127 Ea41
Gosen-Neu Zittau D 128 Fa37
Gosforth GB 10 Ea18
Gosheim D 142 Cc50
Goslar D 126 Dc38
Gosławice PL 129 Ha37
Goślice PL 130 Hd36
Gospić HR 151 Fd63
Gospodinci BG 184 Cd75
Gospođinci SRB 153 Jb60
Gospori LV 107 Lb52
Gosport GB 20 Fa30
Gossa D 127 Ec39
Gössäter S 102 Fa46
Gossau CH 142 Cd53
Gössel A 144 Fa52
Gössenheim D 134 Da44
Gossensass I 143 Dd55
Gösslunda S 102 Ed46
Gößnitz D 127 Eb42
Gößweinstein D 135 Dd45
Gostavățu RO 180 Db67
Gosticy RUS 99 Lc42
Gostifisht AL 182 Ad78
Gostilica BG 180 Dd70
Gostilicy RUS 99 Ma40
Gostilja BG 179 Da68
Gostiņi LV 106 La51
Gostinja BG 180 Db70
Gostinu RO 180 Ea67
Gostivar MK 178 Ba73
Göstling an der Ybbs A 144 Fc52
Gostomia PL 121 Gb34
Gostun SRB 159 Jb67
Gostycyn PL 121 Gd33
Gostyń PL 129 Gc38
Gostynin PL 130 Hd36
Goszcz PL 129 Gd40
Goszczanów PL 129 Hb39
Goszczanówko PL 128 Fd36
Goszczyn PL 130 Jb38
Goszczyna PL 129 Gc42
Göta S 102 Ec47
Göteborg S 102 Eb49
Götene S 102 Fa46
Gotești MD 177 Fb61
Göteve S 102 Fa47
Gotha D 126 Dc41
Gotham GB 16 Fa23
Gothem S 104 Ha49
Götlunda S 95 Fd43
Gotlybiškiai LT 114 Ka57
Gotovuša MNE 159 Ja66
Gottböle FIN 89 Hd33
Gottby FIN 96 Hb41
Göttersdorf D 135 Ec49
Gotteszell D 135 Ec48
Gottfrieding D 135 Eb49
Göttingen D 126 Db39
Gottlob RO 174 Bb60
Gottmadingen D 142 Cc52
Gottne S 80 Gd30
Gottow D 127 Ed38
Gottröra S 96 Gd42
Gøttrup DK 100 Db21
Gottsdorf A 144 Fa50
Gottskär S 102 Eb50
Götzendorf an der Leitha A 145 Gc51
Götzis A 142 Cd53
Gouarec F 27 Ea39
Gouda NL 116 Ad36
Goudargues F 42 Ja52
Goudhurst GB 20 Fd29
Gouesnou F 26 Db38
Goulémi GR 189 Ca84
Goulven F 26 Dc37
Gouménissa GR 183 Bd77
Goúmero GR 188 Ba86
Gourdon F 33 Gb50
Gourdon F 43 Kc53
Gourgançon F 24 Hc37
Gourgé F 28 Fc44
Gouriá GR 188 Ba84
Gourin F 27 Dd39
Gournay-en-Bray F 23 Gc35
Goúrnes GR 200 Da95
Gournier F 35 Ka50
Gourock GB 6 Dc13
Gourri CY 206 Jb97
Gourville F 32 Fc47
Goussainville F 23 Gd36
Gouveia P 44 Bb63
Goúves GR 189 Cb83
Goúves GR 195 Bd90
Gouvia GR 182 Ab80
Gouvy B 133 Bb43
Gouzeaucourt F 24 Hb33
Gouzon F 33 Gd45
Goveđari HR 158 Ha68
Goven F 28 Ed39
Governolo I 149 Dc61
Gowarczów PL 130 Jb40
Gowidlino PL 121 Gd30
Goworowo PL 122 Jc34
Gowran IRL 13 Cc23
Göykaya TR 186 Fa75
Göynük TR 187 Gd80
Göynük TR 193 Gd85
Göynük TR 199 Gc92
Göynükbelen TR 192 Fd81
Gózd PL 130 Jc39
Gozdnica PL 128 Fc40
Gozdowice PL 120 Fb35
Gözler TR 192 Fd87
Gozon = Luanco E 37 Cc53
Gözpınar TR 193 Hb86
Gozzano I 148 Ca58
Graal-Müritz D 119 Eb30
Graauw NL 124 Ac39
Grab BIH 159 Hc67
Grab BIH 159 Hc69
Grab MNE 159 Jb67
Grab PL 129 Gd38
Grabarka PL 131 Kb36
Grabbskog FIN 97 Jd40
Grabe D 126 Dc40
Gräben D 127 Ec37
Graben-Neudorf D 133 Cb47
Grabenstätt D 143 Eb52
Grabica PL 130 Hd39
Grabice PL 128 Fc38
Grabjan AL 182 Ab76
Grabnik PL 123 Jd31
Gråbo S 102 Ec48
Graboszyce PL 138 Hd45
Grabovac HR 151 Ga61
Grabovac HR 153 Hc59
Grabovac HR 158 Gd66
Grabovac SRB 153 Jb62
Grabovci SRB 153 Jb62
Grabovica SRB 174 Cb65
Grabovnica SRB 178 Bc69
Grabow D 119 Ea34
Grabow D 127 Eb37
Grabów PL 130 Hc37
Grabowhöfe D 119 Ec33
Grabowiec PL 123 Kb35
Grabowiec PL 131 Kd41
Grabówka PL 123 Kb33
Grabów nad Prosną PL 129 Ha39
Grabownica Starzeńska PL 139 Ka45
Grabowno PL 121 Gc34
Grabowno Wielkie PL 129 Gd40
Grabowo PL 121 Gc35
Grabowo PL 122 Jb31
Grabowo PL 123 Jd30
Grabowo-Skorupki PL 122 Jb33
Grabowskie PL 123 Jd32
Grabupiai LT 113 Jc56
Gračac HR 157 Ga64
Gračanica BIH 152 Hb62
Gračanica BIH 153 Hd63
Gračanica BIH 158 Ha64
Gračanica BIH 158 Ha65
Gračanica SRB 159 Jb66
Graçay F 29 Gc42
Gracciano I 156 Dd67
Gracen AL 182 Ac75
Gračenica HR 152 Gc59
Gračevka RUS 205 Fd16
Grächen CH 141 Bd56
Gračišće HR 151 Fa60
Gracze PL 129 Gd42
Gradac BIH 158 Hb68
Gradac HR 158 Ha67
Gradac MNE 159 Hd69
Gradac MNE 159 Ja66
Gradac SLO 151 Fd59
Gradac SRB 178 Ba68
Gradačac BIH 153 Hc61
Gradara I 156 Eb65
Graddis N 71 Fd19
Gräddö S 96 Ha42
Gradec BG 179 Cb67
Gradec BG 180 Eb71
Gradec HR 152 Gb58
Gradec MK 183 Bd75
Gradec MK 183 Ca74
Gradefes E 37 Cd57
Grades A 144 Fb55
Gradešnica BG 179 Cd69
Gradešnica MK 183 Bc76
Gradevo BG 183 Cb74
Gradina BG 180 Dd70
Grădinari RO 174 Bd63
Grădinari RO 175 Db65
Gradinarovo BG 181 Ed70
Grădinița MD 173 Ga59
Gradisca d'Isonzo I 150 Ed58
Gradiška BIH 152 Gd61
Gradište BG 180 Dc69
Gradište BG 180 Dc70
Gradište HR 153 Hc61
Gradište MD 173 Fd59
Gradište MK 178 Bc73
Gradište SRB 179 Ca68
Gradište SRB 179 Ca69
Grădiștea RO 175 Da64
Grădistea RO 176 Eb65
Grădistea RO 176 Ed63
Grădiștea RO 180 Eb67
Grădiștea RO 181 Ed67
Grădiștea de Munte RO 175 Cd61
Gradki PL 122 Ja31
Gradna SRB 178 Ba68
Gradnica BG 180 Dc71
Grado E 37 Cb54
Grado I 150 Ed59
Grådö S 95 Gb40
Gradojević SRB 153 Ja62
Gradoli I 156 Dd69
Gradsko MK 183 Bc74
Gradskovo SRB 179 Ca67
Grad Straža SLO 151 Fc59
Grady PL 137 Gd43
Grądy-Woniecko PL 123 Ka33
Graena E 60 Dc74
Græsted DK 109 Ec24
Gräfelfing D 143 Dd51
Grafenau D 135 Ed48
Gräfenberg D 135 Dd46
Grafengehaig D 135 Ea44
Gräfenhainichen D 127 Ec39
Grafenhausen D 141 Cb51
Gräfenroda D 126 Dc42
Grafenstein A 144 Fb56
Gräfenthal D 135 Dd43
Gräfentonna D 126 Dc41
Grafenwiesen D 135 Ec47
Grafenwöhr D 135 Ea45
Grafhorst D 127 Dd36
Graf-Ignatievo BG 180 Db73
Gräfinau-Angstedt D 127 Dd42
Grafing D 143 Ea51
Grafling D 135 Ec48
Grafrath D 143 Dd51
Gräfsnäs S 102 Ec48
Gräftåvallen S 79 Fb31
Graglia I 148 Bd59
Gragnague F 40 Gc54
Gragnano I 161 Fb75
Grahovo MNE 159 Hd69
Grahovo SLO 151 Fa57
Grahovo SLO 151 Fb59
Graig na Manach IRL 13 Cc24
Graigue Hill IRL 13 Cc23
Graiguenamanagh IRL 13 Cc24
Grain GB 21 Ga28
Grainet D 136 Fa49
Grainville-Langannerie F 22 Fc36
Graja de Iniesta E 53 Ec67
Grajal de Campos E 37 Cd58
Grajduri RO 173 Fa58
Grajewo PL 123 Ka32
Grajvoron RUS 203 Fa14
Gralewo PL 122 Ja35
Gralhos P 44 Bb59
Gralhos P 45 Bd60
Gralla A 144 Fd55
Gram DK 108 Da27
Gramada BG 179 Cb67
Gramais A 142 Db53
Gramastetten A 144 Fb50
Gramat F 33 Gc50
Gramatikó GR 189 Bc82
Gramatikó GR 189 Cc86
Gramatikovo BG 186 Fa74
Gramatsneusiedl A 145 Gb51
Grambow D 120 Fb33
Graméni GR 184 Cd76
Graméno GR 188 Ad80
Grămești RO 172 Eb55
Gramatten A 136 Fd48
Grammendorf D 119 Ed31
Gramméni Oxiá GR 188 Bb83
Grammichele I 167 Fb87
Grámmos GR 182 Ad78
Gramont F 40 Ga53
Gramsdale GB 6 Cd07
Gramsh AL 182 Ac76
Gramsh AL 182 Ac77
Gramsh i Lushnjes AL 182 Ab75
Gramzda LV 113 Jb53
Gramzow D 120 Fb34
Gran N 85 Ea40
Granabeg IRL 13 Cd22
Granada E 60 Db75
Granaione I 155 Dc68
Gran Alacant E 55 Fb72
Granard IRL 9 Cb20
Gránard IRL 9 Cb20
Granås S 71 Fd22
Granåsen N 86 Ec36
Granåsen S 79 Gb28
Granátula de Calatrava E 52 Db70
Granberg S 73 Hb23
Granberget S 72 Gc23
Granberget S 79 Gb27
Granbergsträsk S 73 Hb24
Granbo S 79 Fc30
Granboda FIN 96 Hc41
Granby GB 16 Fb23
Grand F 30 Jb38
Grandas de Salime E 37 Bd55
Grand-Auverne F 28 Fa41
Grand-Bornand F 35 Ka46
Grandcamp-Maisy F 22 Fa35
Grand-Champ F 27 Eb40
Grandchamps F 30 Hb40
Grandcour CH 141 Bc54
Grand-Couronne F 23 Ga35
Grand Crohot Océan F 32 Fa50
Grandecourt F 31 Jc40
Grandes E 46 Cd63
Grandfontaine F 25 Kb37
Grand-Fort-Philippe F 21 Gc30
Grand-Fougeray F 28 Ed40
Grand Halleux B 125 Bb42
Grândola P 50 Ab70
Grandpré F 24 Ja35
Grandrieu F 34 Hc50
Grand-Rullecourt F 23 Gd32
Grandson CH 141 Bb54
Grandtully GB 7 Ea10
Grand-Vabre F 33 Ha51
Grandvelle-et-le-Perrenot F 31 Jd41
Grandvillars F 31 Kb40
Grandvilliers F 23 Gc34
Grane F 34 Jb50
Grane N 70 Fa23
Grañén E 48 Fc60
Grañena E 60 Db73
Grangärde S 95 Fc40
Grangärdes Hästberg S 95 Fc40
Grange IRL 13 Ca25
Grangeford IRL 13 Cc23
Grange-le-Bocage F 30 Hb38
Grangemouth GB 10 Ea13
Grängesberg S 95 Fc41
Granges-sur-Aube F 24 Hc37
Granges-sur-Vologne F 31 Ka38
Grängshyttan S 95 Fc42
Grängsjö S 87 Gb36
Granheim N 92 Cd44
Granhult S 68 Hc17
Granica BG 179 Ca72
Granica SRB 159 Ja66
Grăniceri RO 170 Bd58
Granicești RO 172 Eb55
Gränichen CH 141 Ca53
Granieri I 167 Fb87
Graninge S 79 Gb31
Granit BG 180 Dc73
Granitis GR 184 Cd76
Granitola Torretta I 166 Eb85
Granitsa GR 188 Ba82
Granitsopoúla GR 182 Ac80
Granja P 51 Bb70
Granja de Moreruela E 45 Cb59
Granja de Torrehermosa E 51 Cb71
Grankulla FIN 98 Kb39
Grankullavik S 104 Gc50
Granliden S 79 Ga25
Granmoen N 70 Fa21
Gränna S 103 Fb48
Grannäs S 71 Ga24
Grannäs S 72 Gb22
Granne PL 123 Ka35
Grannes N 71 Fb23
Granö S 80 Ha27
Granollers E 49 Ha61
Granowo PL 129 Gb37
Grañs E 36 Bb53
Grans F 42 Jc54
Gransee D 119 Ed35
Gränsfors S 87 Gb34
Gränsgård S 72 Gc23
Gransha GB 10 Db16
Gransherad N 93 Db42
Gransholm S 103 Fc52
Gransjö S 72 Gd24
Gransjö S 73 Hc21
Gransjøbergstra N 86 Eb37
Gränsjön S 94 Ec42
Grantham GB 16 Fb23
Grantown-on-Spey GB 7 Eb08
Granträsk S 73 Hc22
Granträsk S 80 Gd27
Gränträskmark S 73 Hc23
Grantshouse GB 11 Ed13
Granucillo E 45 Cb59
Granum S 111 Fc54
Granusjön S 86 Fa36
Granvik S 103 Fc46
Granvika N 85 Ea35
Granville F 22 Ed37
Granvin N 84 Cc39
Granzin D 119 Eb33
Grapska BIH 152 Hb62
Grasbakken N 65 Kb07
Grasberg D 118 Cd34
Gräsbrickan S 86 Ed38
Graševo BG 184 Cd74
Gräsgård S 111 Gb54
Grasleben D 127 Dd37
Gräsmark S 94 Ed41
Grasmere GB 11 Eb18
Gräsmyr S 80 Hb28
Gräsö S 96 Gd40
Grassano I 162 Gb75
Grassau D 127 Ed39
Grassau D 143 Eb52
Grasse F 43 Kc53
Grassington GB 11 Ed19
Grässjön S 87 Fd32
Gråsten DK 108 Db28
Grästorp S 102 Ed47
Gratallops E 48 Ga62
Gråtånes N 71 Fc18
Gratangsbotn N 67 Gb13
Gråtanliden S 79 Gb25
Gratens F 40 Gb55
Gratentour F 40 Gc54
Gratia RO 176 Dd66
Grătiești MD 173 Fd58
Gratkorn A 144 Fd54
Gråträsk S 72 Ha23
Gratteri I 167 Fa84
Grattersdorf D 135 Ed49
Gratwein A 144 Fd54
Grauballe DK 108 Db24
Grau-d'Agde F 41 Hc55
Graulhet F 41 Gd54
Graulinster L 133 Bb44
Graun im Vinschgau I 142 Db55
Graupa D 128 Fa41
Graus E 48 Fd59
Grava S 94 Fa43
Grávalos E 47 Ec59
Gravås S 94 Ed42
Grávavencsellő H 147 Ka50
Gravberget N 86 Ec38
Gravdal N 66 Fb14
Grave NL 125 Bb38
Gräve S 95 Fc44
Gravedona I 149 Cc57
Graveley GB 20 Fc25
Gravelines F 21 Gd30
Gravellona Toce I 148 Ca57
Gravenhage, 's- NL 116 Ad36
Gravens DK 108 Db26
Grävenwiesbach D 134 Cc43
Grāveri LV 115 Ld53
Gravesend GB 20 Fd28
Graveson F 42 Jb53
Graviá GR 189 Bc84
Gravigny F 23 Gb36
Gravina di Puglia I 162 Gc75
Gravmark S 80 Hb27
Gravoúna GR 184 Da77
Gravvik N 78 Ec25
Gray F 31 Jc41
Grays GB 20 Fd28
Graz A 144 Fd54
Grazalema E 59 Cb76
Grążawy PL 122 Hd33
Graziškiai LT 114 Ka59
Grazzanise I 161 Fa74
Grazzano Visconti I 149 Cd61
Grčarice SLO 151 Fc59
Grčina KSV 178 Ad71
Grdelica SRB 178 Bd70
Greaca RO 180 Eb67
Greåker N 93 Ea44
Great Ayton GB 11 Fb18
Great Bentley GB 21 Ga27
Great Bircham GB 17 Ga23
Great Cornard GB 21 Ga26
Great Cubley GB 16 Ed23
Great Dalby GB 16 Fb24
Great Dunmow GB 20 Fd27
Great Eccleston GB 15 Eb20
Great Ellingham GB 17 Ga24
Great Glen GB 16 Fb24
Great Grimsby GB 17 Fc21
Great Hanwood GB 15 Eb24
Great Harwood GB 15 Ec20
Great Hockham GB 21 Ga25
Great Horkesley GB 21 Ga26
Great Langton GB 11 Fa18
Great Malvern GB 15 Ec26
Great Milton GB 20 Fa27
Great Ponton GB 16 Fb23
Great Shefford GB 20 Fa28
Great Smeaton GB 11 Fa18
Great Snoring GB 17 Ga23
Greatstone-on-Sea GB 21 Ga30
Great Tew GB 20 Fa26
Great Torrington GB 19 Dd29
Great Totham GB 21 Ga27
Great Wakering GB 21 Ga28
Great Yarmouth GB 17 Gc24
Great Yeldham GB 20 Fd26
Grebănu RO 176 Ed63
Grebbestad S 94 Ea45
Grebci BIH 158 Hb68
Grebenac SRB 174 Bc63
Grebenau D 126 Da42
Grebenhain D 134 Cd43
Grebenișu de Câmpie RO 171 Db58
Grebenstein D 126 Da39
Grebin D 118 Dc30
Grębków PL 131 Ka36
Greblești MD 173 Fc57
Grebneva LV 107 Ld50
Grebo S 103 Ga47
Grębocin PL 121 Hb34
Grębów PL 131 Jd42
Grečanica KSV 178 Bb71
Greccio I 156 Eb70
Grecești RO 175 Cc65
Greci I 161 Fd73
Greci RO 175 Cc65
Greci RO 177 Fb64
Gredelj BIH 159 Hc67
Greding D 135 Dd48
Gredstedbro DK 108 Da26
Greencastle GB 9 Da19
Greencastle IRL 9 Cd15
Greenfield GB 15 Eb22
Green Hammerton GB 11 Fa19
Green Hammerton GB 16 Fa20
Greenhead GB 11 Ec16
Greenlaw GB 11 Ec14
Greenock GB 6 Dc13
Greenodd GB 11 Eb19
Greenway GB 19 Ea31
Greenwich GB 20 Fc28
Greetland GB 16 Ed21
Greetsiel D 117 Ca32
Greffen D 126 Cc37
Grefrath D 125 Bc39
Gregurovec HR 152 Gb58
Greifenberg D 120 Fa34
Greifenburg A 143 Ed55
Greifswald D 119 Ed31
Grein A 144 Fc51
Greipstad N 62 Gc10
Greipstad N 92 Cd47
Greiskani LV 107 Ld51
Greith A 144 Fd52
Greiz D 127 Eb42
Gremersdorf D 119 Dd30
Gremjač'e RUS 203 Fb13
Grenaa DK 101 Dd23
Grenaa Strand DK 101 Ea23
Grenade F 40 Gb54
Grenade-sur-l'Adour F 39 Fb54
Grenant F 31 Jc40
Grenås S 79 Fd29
Grenchen CH 141 Bd53
Grenči LV 105 Jd51

Grenctāle – Gutowiec

Grenctāle LV 114 Kc53
Grendavė LT 114 Kd58
Grenivík IS 2 Ba03
Grenoble F 35 Jd48
Grense Jakobselv N 65 Kd07
Grentzingen F 31 Kb40
Grenzhausen, Höhr- D 125 Ca42
Gréolières F 43 Kc53
Gréoux-les-Bains F 42 Jd53
Greppin D 127 Eb39
Gresse-en-Vercors F 35 Jc49
Gressoney-La-Trinité I 148 Bd58
Gressoney-Saint-Jean I 148 Bd58
Gressvik N 93 Ea44
Grésy-sur-Isère F 35 Ka47
Gretna GB 11 Eb16
Grettstadt D 134 Db44
Greußen D 127 Dd40
Grevbäck S 103 Fb47
Greve DK 109 Ec26
Greve in Chianti I 155 Dc66
Greven D 125 Cb37
Grevená GR 183 Bb79
Grevenbroich D 125 Bc40
Greveníti GR 182 Ba80
Grevenmacher L 133 Bc45
Grevesmühlen D 119 Ea32
Greve Strand DK 109 Ec26
Grevie S 110 Ed53
Grevnäs FIN 90 Kc38
Greyabbey GB 10 Db17
Greysteel GB 9 Cc15
Greystoke GB 11 Eb17
Greystone GB 9 Cd17
Greystones IRL 13 Da22
Grézels F 33 Gb51
Grez-en-Bouère F 28 Fb40
Grèzes F 33 Gc51
Grezzana I 149 Dc59
Grgar SLO 151 Fa58
Grgurevci SRB 153 Ja61
Grgurnica MK 178 Bb73
Gribanovskij RUS 203 Fc12
Gribuli RUS 107 Ld48
Gridino RUS 99 Ld45
Grieben D 127 Eb36
Griebenow D 119 Ed31
Griem'aćje RUS 113 Jc58
Gries A 142 Dc54
Griesalp CH 141 Bd55
Gries am Brenner A 143 Dd54
Griesbach, Bad Peterstal- D 133 Cb49
Griesheim D 134 Cc45
Gries im Sellrain A 142 Dc54
Grieskirchen A 144 Fa50
Griesstätt D 143 Eb51
Griffen A 144 Fc56
Grigale LV 114 Kd53
Grigiškes LT 114 La58
Grignan F 42 Jb51
Grignani I 166 Ea85
Grignasco I 148 Ca58
Grigno I 150 Dd58
Grignols F 33 Ga49
Grignols F 40 Fc52
Grigor'evskoe RUS 203 Fb08
Grigorievca MD 173 Ga59
Grigoriopol MD 173 Ga57
Grijota E 46 Da59
Grijpskerk NL 117 Bd33
Griki LV 105 Jc51
Gríkos GR 197 Ea89
Grillby S 96 Gc42
Grilli I 155 Db68
Grillos GR 194 Ba87
Grimaldi I 164 Gb80
Grimăncăuţi MD 172 Ed53
Grimaud F 43 Kb54
Grimbråten S 94 Ed44
Grimdalen N 93 Da43
Grimentz CH 141 Bd56
Grimeton S 102 Ec51
Grimma D 127 Ec40
Grimmen D 119 Ed31
Grimmenstein A 145 Gb53
Grimmialp CH 141 Bd55
Grimnäs S 87 Fd32
Grimo N 84 Cc39
Grimsås S 102 Fa50
Grímsey IS 3 Bb03
Grimslöv S 103 Fc52
Grímsstaðir IS 3 Bb04
Grimstad N 93 Da46
Grimston GB 17 Fd24
Grimstorp S 103 Fc49
Grimstrup DK 108 Da26
Grimzdai LT 113 Jc55
Grinăuţi MD 173 Fb55
Grinăuţi-Raia MD 173 Fa53
Grindavík IS 2 Ab05
Grinde N 84 Cc37
Grindelwald CH 141 Ca55
Grinder N 94 Ec40
Grindheim N 92 Cb41
Grindheim N 92 Cc46
Grindholmen FIN 81 Jb29
Grindjorda N 67 Gb14
Grindon GB 16 Ed23
Grindsted DK 108 Da25
Grindu RO 176 Ec65
Grindu RO 177 Fb63
Gringley on the Hill GB 16 Fb21
Griniai LT 114 Ka55
Grinkiškis LV 114 Kb55
Grinneröd S 102 Eb47
Griñón E 46 Db65
Grinstad S 102 Ec46
Grinţieş RO 172 Eb57
Grip N 77 Da30
Gripenberg S 103 Fc48
Grisi I 166 Ec84
Grisignano di Zocco I 150 Dd60
Griškabūdis LV 114 Kb58
Grisolia I 164 Ga78
Grisolles F 40 Gb53
Grisselören FIN 81 Ja29
Grisslehamn S 96 Ha41
Griva LV 115 Lc53
Grivaši LV 105 Jd52
Grivenskaja RUS 205 Fc16
Griviţa RO 176 Ed65
Griviţa RO 177 Fa61
Griviţa RO 177 Fa62
Grizáno GR 189 Bc81
Grizebeck GB 11 Eb19
Grizic HR 152 Ha60
Grizzana Morandi I 149 Dc63
Grjadišče RUS 99 Ld45
Grjady RUS 202 Eb09
Grjazi RUS 203 Fb12
Grjazovec RUS 203 Fa08
Grljan SRB 179 Ca67
Grøa N 77 Dc32
Gröbers D 127 Eb40
Grobiņa LV 105 Jb52
Grobla PL 138 Jb44
Grobla PL 139 Kb43
Gröbming A 144 Fa53
Gröbzig D 127 Ea39
Grocka SRB 174 Bb64
Grodås N 84 Cc34
Gródek PL 121 Gb33
Gródek PL 123 Kc33
Gródek PL 131 Ka36
Gródek PL 131 Kd42
Gródek nad Dunajcem PL 138 Jc45
Gröden D 128 Fa40
Gröding A 143 Ec52
Grödinge S 96 Gd44
Gröditsch D 128 Fa38
Gröditz D 127 Ed40
Gródki PL 122 Hd33
Gródki PL 131 Kb41
Grodków PL 129 Gd42
Grodziczno PL 122 Hd33
Grodziec PL 128 Ga41
Grodziec PL 129 Ha38
Grodziec PL 129 Hb42
Grodziec PL 138 Hc45
Grodzisk PL 123 Jd34
Grodzisk PL 123 Ka35
Grodzisk Mazowiecki PL 130 Jb37
Grodzisko PL 123 Jd30
Grodzisko PL 139 Kb43
Grodzisk Wielkopolski PL 129 Gb37
Grodziszcze PL 129 Gb42
Groeningen NL 125 Bc38
Groenlo NL 125 Bd37
Groesbeek NL 125 Bb38
Grogan IRL 13 Cb21
Grohotno BG 184 Da75
Groitzsch D 127 Eb41
Groix F 27 Dd41
Grojdibodu RO 179 Da68
Grójec PL 129 Gd37
Grójec PL 130 Jb38
Grolanda S 102 Fa48
Grom PL 122 Jb32
Gromada PL 131 Kb42
Gromadka PL 128 Ga40
Gromadno PL 121 Gd34
Gromandcyzna PL 123 Ka29
Gromiljak BIH 158 Hb64
Grömitz D 119 Dd31
Gromnik PL 138 Jc45
Gromo I 149 Da58
Gromovo RUS 113 Jb58
Gron F 30 Hb39
Grøna N 85 Db35
Grönahög S 102 Fa49
Gronau (Leine) D 126 Db37
Gronau (Westfalen) D 117 Ca36
Grønbæk DK 100 Db23
Grønbjerg DK 108 Cd24
Grønbjerg DK 108 Da25
Grönbo S 73 Hb24
Grönbo S 95 Fd43
Grønbua N 85 Db35
Grøndal N 84 Cb35
Gröndal S 71 Fc22
Grondola I 149 Cd63
Grönenbach D 142 Db51
Grönfjäll S 71 Fd24
Grong N 78 Ed26
Grönhögen S 111 Gb54
Grønhøj DK 100 Db23
Gröningen D 127 Dd38
Groningen NL 117 Bd33
Grønlia N 78 Ea28
Grönliden S 80 Hb25
Grønnemose DK 108 Dc26
Grono CH 149 Cc57
Gronów PL 128 Fc36
Gronowo PL 122 Hd30
Gronowo Elbląskie PL 122 Hc31
Grönskara S 103 Fd51
Grönskåra S 103 Ga51
Grönwohld D 118 Dc32
Grootegast NL 117 Bd33
Gropello Cairoli I 148 Cb60
Gropen S 95 Fc44
Gropeni RO 177 Fa64
Gropniţa RO 173 Fa57
Gropparello I 149 Cd61
Grornv HR 151 Fb62
Grosbliederstroff F 25 Ka35
Grosbous L 133 Bb44
Grosbreuil F 28 Ed44
Groscavallo I 148 Bc59
Grosebay GB 4 Da06
Groşi RO 171 Da55
Grosio I 149 Da57
Grošnica SRB 174 Bb66
Großaitingen D 142 Dc50
Großalmerode D 126 Db40
Großalsleben D 127 Dd38
Groß Ammensleben D 127 Ea37
Großarl A 143 Ed54
Großbeeren D 127 Ed37
Groß-Bieberau D 134 Cc45
Großbodungen D 126 Dc39
Großbothen D 127 Ec41
Großbottwar D 134 Cd47
Großbreitenbach D 127 Dd42
Großburgwedel D 126 Db36
Groß Dölln D 120 Fa35
Großdubrau D 128 Fb40
Großefehn D 117 Cb33
Großeibstadt D 134 Dc43
Grosselfingen D 142 Cc50
Großenaspe D 118 Db31
Großenbrode D 119 Dd30
Großenehrich D 126 Dc40
Großenhain D 128 Fa40
Großenkneten D 117 Cc34
Großenlüder D 126 Da42
Großenlüder D 126 Da42
Großenlupnitz D 126 Dc41
Großensee D 118 Dc32
Großenseebach D 134 Dc46
Großenwiehe D 108 Da29
Grossenzersdorf A 145 Gb51
Grossepeterdorf A 145 Gb54
Großerlach D 134 Cd47
Grosseto I 155 Dc68
Grosseto Prugna F 154 Ca71
Großfurra D 126 Dc40
Groß Gaglow D 128 Fb39
Groß Garz D 119 Ea35
Groß-Gerau D 134 Cc44
Großgerungs A 136 Fc49
Groß Glienicke D 127 Ed36
Großglobnitz A 136 Fd49
Großgörschen D 127 Eb40
Groß Grönau D 119 Dd32
Großhabersdorf D 134 Dc46
Großhansdorf D 118 Dc32
Großharthau D 128 Fb41
Großhartmannsdorf D 127 Ed42
Großheide D 117 Cb32
Großheirath D 135 Dd44
Großhennersdorf D 128 Fc41
Großheubach D 134 Cd45
Großhöchstetten CH 141 Bd54
Groß Ippener D 118 Cd34
Großkarolinenfeld D 143 Ea52
Groß Kiesow D 120 Fa31
Groß Kölzig D 128 Fc39
Groß Köris D 128 Fa37
Großkoschen D 128 Fb40
Groß Kreutz D 127 Ec37
Großkugel D 127 Eb40
Großlangheim D 134 Db45
Großlehna D 127 Eb40
Groß Leine D 128 Fb38
Großlittgen D 133 Bc44
Großlohra D 126 Dc40
Groß Miltzow D 120 Fa33
Groß Muckrow D 128 Fb38
Grossmugl A 145 Gb50
Groß Mühlingen D 127 Ea38
Groß Naundorf D 127 Ed39
Groß Oesingen D 126 Dc36
Großostheim D 134 Cd44
Grossouvre F 30 Hb43
Groß Pankow D 119 Eb34
Großpertholz A 136 Fc49
Groß Pösna D 127 Ec40
Großpostwitz D 128 Fb41
Groß Quenstedt D 127 Dd38
Großraming A 144 Fb52
Großräschen D 128 Fa39
Großreifling A 144 Fc52
Großrinderfeld D 134 Da45
Groß Rodensleben D 127 Ea37
Groß-Rohrheim D 134 Cc45
Großröhrsdorf D 128 Fa41
Groß Rosenburg D 127 Eb38
Groß-Sankt-Florian A 144 Fd55
Groß Särchen D 128 Fb40
Groß Schacksdorf D 128 Fc39
Großschirma D 127 Ed41
Großschönau D 128 Fc42
Groß Schönebeck D 120 Fa35
Groß Schwechten D 127 Ea36
Großschweidnitz D 128 Fc41
Gross-Schweinparth A 145 Gc50
Groß-Siegharts A 136 Fd49
Großsölk A 144 Fa53
Großsolt D 108 Db29
Großsteinberg D 127 Ec40
Großthiemig D 128 Fa40
Großtreben D 127 Ed39
Groß Twülpstedt D 127 Dd36
Groß-Umstadt D 134 Cc45
Großwallstadt D 134 Cd45
Groß Warnow D 119 Ea34
Grossweikersdorf A 144 Ga50
Großweitzschen D 127 Ed41
Groß Wokern D 119 Ec32
Großwudicke D 127 Eb36
Groß Ziescht D 128 Fa38
Grostenquin F 25 Ka36
Grosuplje SLO 151 Fc58
Grøtavær N 66 Ga12
Grotle LV 107 Lb49
Grotle N 84 Ca34
Grotli N 85 Da34
Grötlingbo S 104 Ha51
Grøtnes N 63 Hd06
Grøtnesdalen N 62 Gd09
Grotniki PL 130 Hc38
Grotów PL 120 Ga35
Grötsch D 128 Fb39
Grottaglie I 162 Ha76
Grottaminarda I 161 Fc74
Grottammare I 157 Fa68
Grotte I 166 Ed86
Grotte di Castro I 156 Dd69
Grotteria I 164 Gb83
Grotte Santo Stefano I 156 Ea69
Grottole I 162 Gc76
Grötvågen N 77 Dc30
Grou NL 117 Bc33
Grov N 67 Gb13
Grova N 93 Db43
Grozas LV 107 Lc51
Grozdjovo BG 181 Ed71
Grozeşti RO 173 Fb58
Grozeşti RO 175 Cd65
Grožnjan HR 151 Fa60
Grua N 85 Ea40
Grub D 135 Dd44
Grubben N 71 Fb22
Grubbenvorst NL 125 Bc39
Grubišno Polje HR 152 Gd59
Gruczno PL 121 Ha33
Gruda HR 159 Hc69
Gruda Donja BIH 159 Hc68
Grude BIH 158 Ha66
Grudusk PL 122 Ja34
Grudziądz PL 121 Hb33
Grues F 32 Fa45
Gruffy F 35 Jd46
Gruia RO 174 Cb66
Gruissan F 41 Hb56
Gruissan-Plage F 41 Hb56
Gruiu RO 176 Eb65
Grumăzeşti RO 172 Ec57
Grumento Nova I 161 Ga77
Grumo Appula I 162 Gc74
Grums S 94 Ed43
Grünau im Almtal A 144 Fa52
Grünbach D 135 Eb43
Grünbach am Schneeberg A 144 Ga52
Grünberg D 126 Cd42
Grünberg PL 128 Fd38
Grünburg A 144 Fb51
Grundarfjörður IS 2 Ab03
Grundfors S 71 Fc24
Grundfors S 80 Gc25
Grundforsen S 86 Ed37
Grundsel S 73 Hb22
Grundsjö S 79 Ga28
Grundsjö S 79 Gb25
Grundsjön S 87 Fd33
Grundsund S 102 Eb47
Grundsunda FIN 96 Hc40
Grundsunda S 80 Ha30
Grundtjärn S 79 Gb29
Grundträsk S 72 Ha23
Grundträsk S 72 Ha24
Grundträsk S 73 Hd20
Grundträsk S 73 Hb24
Grundvattnet S 73 Hb22
Grundzāle LV 106 La48
Grüneberg D 119 Ed35
Grunewald D 125 Bc38
Grünewalde D 128 Fa40
Grungedal N 92 Cd42
Grünhain D 135 Ec43
Grünheide D 128 Fa37
Grunnerud S 94 Eb44
Grunnfjord N 62 Gd08
Grunnfjordbotn N 66 Ga15
Grünsfeld D 134 Da46
Grünstadt D 133 Cb45
Grüntal D 120 Fa35
Grünwald D 143 Dd51
Grunwald PL 122 Hd33
Grupčin MK 178 Bb73
Grury F 30 Hd44
Grüsch CH 142 Cd54
Grūšlaukė LT 113 Jb54
Gruszeczka PL 129 Gc40
Gruszka PL 130 Ja41
Gruta PL 121 Hb33
Grūtas LT 123 Kc30
Gruvbyn S 87 Fc35
Gruyères CH 141 Bc55
Gruža SRB 174 Bb66
Gruzdiškė LT 114 Ka56
Gruzdžiai LT 114 Ka53
Grybėnai LT 115 Lb55
Grybów PL 138 Jc45
Grycksbro S 95 Fd39
Gryfice PL 120 Fd32
Gryfino PL 120 Fb34
Gryfów Śląski PL 128 Fd41
Grykë AL 182 Aa76
Gryllefjord N 62 Gb10
Grymyr N 85 Dd40
Grynberget S 79 Gb27
Gryt S 95 Gb44
Gryt S 103 Gb47
Gryta N 77 Dc29
Gryta S 96 Gc42
Grytåa N 70 Ed22
Gryteryd S 102 Ed51
Grytgöl S 95 Fd45
Grythyttan S 95 Fc42
Grytnäs S 95 Ga41
Grytsjö S 79 Fd25
Gryttjom S 96 Gc40
Gryzavino RUS 107 Ma48
Gryzy PL 123 Jd30
Gryżyce PL 129 Gb40
Gryżyna PL 129 Gb38
Grza SRB 178 Bd67
Grzebienisko PL 129 Gb37
Grzechotki PL 122 Hd30
Grzęda PL 122 Jb30
Grzegorzew PL 129 Hb37
Grzegrzółki PL 122 Jb32
Grzmiąca PL 121 Gb32
Grzybiany PL 129 Gb41
Grzybno PL 120 Fc35
Grzybno PL 122 Hc33
Grzybowo PL 129 Gd37
Grzymałków PL 130 Jb41
Grzymiszew PL 129 Hb38
Grzywna Biskupia PL 121 Hb34
Gschnitz A 143 Dd54
Gschwandt A 144 Fa51
Gschwend D 134 Da48
Gstaad CH 141 Bc55
Gsteig CH 141 Bc56
Guadahortuna E 60 Dc74
Guadalajara E 46 Dd64
Guadalaviar E 47 Ec65
Guadalcanal E 51 Ca71
Guadalcázar E 60 Cc73
Guadalix de la Sierra E 46 Dc63
Guadalmedina E 60 Cd76
Guadalmez E 52 Cc70
Guadalupe E 52 Cc67
Guadalupe E 61 Eb73
Guadamur E 52 Db66
Guadarrama E 46 Db63
Guadassuar E 54 Fb69
Guadiana del Caudillo E 51 Bc68
Guadix E 61 Dd74
Guadramil P 45 Bd59
Guagnano I 162 Hb76
Guagno F 154 Cb70
Guaire IRL 13 Cd23
Guájar-Faragüit E 60 Db76
Gualachulain GB 6 Dc11
Gualdo Tadino I 156 Eb67
Gualöv S 111 Fb54
Gualtieri I 149 Db61
Guarcino I 160 Ec72
Guarda CH 142 Da55
Guarda P 44 Bb63
Guardalfiera I 161 Fc72
Guardamar del Segura E 55 Fb72
Guardapasso I 160 Ea72
Guardavalle I 164 Gc82
Guardea I 156 Ea69
Guàrdia de Tremp E 48 Ga59
Guardiagrele I 157 Fb70
Guardia Lombardi I 161 Fd75
Guardia Perticara I 162 Gb76
Guardia Piemontese Marina I 164 Gb79
Guardiaregia I 161 Fb73
Guardia Sanframondi I 161 Fb73
Guardias Viejas E 61 Dd76
Guardiola de Berguedà E 49 Gd59
Guardiola de Font-rubí E 49 Gc61
Guardo E 38 Da56
Guareña E 51 Ca69
Guaro E 60 Cc76
Guarromán E 52 Db71
Guasila I 169 Ca78
Guastalla I 149 Db61
Guaza de Campos E 37 Cd58
Gubanicy RUS 99 Ma40
Gubavac MNE 159 Jb67
Gubbhögen S 79 Fd27
Gubbio I 156 Eb67
Gubbmyran S 86 Fa37
Gubbträsk S 72 Gc24
Guben D 128 Fc38
Gubeš BG 179 Cb70
Gubin PL 128 Fc38
Gubkin RUS 203 Fa13
Guča SRB 178 Ad67
Guča Gora BIH 158 Ha64
Gücenoluk TR 193 Gc83
Güçlüköy TR 199 Hb91
Gudai LT 113 Jc57
Gúdar E 48 Fb64
Gudbjerg DK 109 Dd27
Guddal N 84 Cb36
Guddalbru N 92 Cb45
Gudeliai LT 123 Kc30
Gudeliai LV 114 Kb59
Gudenieki LV 105 Jb51
Gudensberg D 126 Da40
Guderup DK 108 Db28
Gudhjem DK 111 Fc57
Gudin N 78 Ec27
Gudinge S 96 Gd39
Gudkaimis LT 114 Ka58
Gudme DK 109 Dd27
Gudmindrup DK 109 Ea25
Gudmont-Villiers F 30 Jb38
Gudmundrå S 80 Gc31
Gudmuntorp S 110 Fa55
Gudow D 119 Dd33
Gudowo PL 120 Ga33
Gudum DK 100 Cd22
Gudumholm DK 100 Dc21
Gudurica SRB 174 Bd62
Gudvangen N 84 Cc38
Gudžiūnai LV 114 Kb55
Guebwiller F 31 Kb39
Güéjar Sierra E 60 Dc75
Guémar F 31 Kb38
Guémené-Penfao F 28 Ec41
Guémené-sur-Scorff F 27 Ea39
Guengat F 27 Dc39
Guenrout F 27 Ec41
Guer F 27 Ec40
Guérande F 27 Eb42
Guéret F 33 Gc46
Guérigny F 30 Hb42
Guernica = Gernika E 38 Ea55
Güesa E 39 Fa57
Gües-d'Oloron F 39 Fb55
Gueugnon F 30 Hd44
Güevejar E 60 Db74
Gugalj SRB 159 Jc64
Gugeşti RO 176 Ed62
Güglingen D 134 Cc47
Guglionesi I 161 Fc71
Gugney-aux-Aulx F 31 Jd38
Gugny PL 123 Ka33
Gugutka BG 185 Ea76
Guhttás S 68 Hd13
Guia P 44 Ac65
Guichen F 28 Ed40
Guidizzolo I 149 Db60
Guidonia-Montecelio I 160 Eb71
Guiglia I 149 Db63
Guignen F 28 Ed40
Guignes F 23 Ha37
Guijo de Coria E 45 Bd65
Guijosa E 47 Ea62
Guijuelo E 45 Cb63
Guildford GB 20 Fb29
Guilheta P 44 Ac59
Guillar E 36 Ba56
Guillaumes F 43 Kb52
Guillena E 59 Bd73
Guillestre F 35 Kb50
Guillos F 32 Fb51
Guilsfield GB 15 Eb24
Guilvinec F 27 Dc40
Guimarães P 44 Ad60
Guimiliau F 26 Dc38
Guines F 21 Gc30
Guingamp F 26 Ea38
Guipavas F 26 Dc38
Guipry F 28 Ed40
Guipy F 30 Hc42
Guisando E 45 Cc65
Guisborough GB 11 Fb18
Guiscard F 23 Ha34
Guiscriff F 27 Dd39
Guise F 24 Hc33
Guissona E 48 Gb60
Guist GB 17 Ga24
Guitalens F 41 Gd54
Guiting Power GB 20 Ed26
Guitiriz E 36 Bb54
Guitres F 32 Fc49
Guizan E 36 Ad57
Gujan-Mestras F 32 Fa51
Gukovo RUS 205 Fc15
Gulbene LV 107 Lb49
Gulbēris LV 106 La50
Gulbji LV 105 Ja51
Gülçayır TR 193 Ha83
Gulcz PL 121 Gb35
Güldalı TR 199 Ha89
Guldborg DK 109 Eb28
Güldibi TR 187 Gd78
Guldrupe S 104 Ha50
Gulen N 84 Ca37
Gulgofjorden N 65 Kb05
Gulholmen N 66 Fd13
Guljanci BG 180 Db68
Gul'kevici RUS 205 Fd16
Gülköy TR 199 Gb88
Gulla N 77 Dc31
Gullabo S 111 Ga53
Gulladuff GB 9 Cd16
Gullan GB 11 Ec13
Gullaskruv S 103 Fd52
Gullberg S 103 Fd47
Gullbrandstorp S 102 Ed52
Gulleråsen S 87 Fd38
Gullered S 102 Fa49
Gullesfjordbotn N 66 Fd13
Gullgammen N 64 Jb04
Gullhaug N 93 Dd43
Gullholmen N 64 Ka05
Gullholmen S 102 Eb47
Gullön S 72 Gd22
Gullringen S 103 Fd49
Gullsby S 94 Ed41
Gullspång S 95 Fb45
Gulltjärn S 80 Hb27
Gullträsk S 73 Hc20
Güllü TR 192 Fd86
Güllübahçe TR 197 Ec88
Güllüce TR 192 Fb81
Güllük TR 197 Ed90
Gullvik S 80 Gd30
Gülpınarı TR 191 Ea82
Gulsele S 79 Gb28
Gulsrud N 93 Dd41
Gulstøa N 84 Ca34
Gulsvik N 85 Dc40
Gumboda S 73 Hb24
Gumboda S 80 Hc27
Gumbodahamn S 80 Hc27
Gümele TR 192 Ga84
Gümeli TR 191 Ec83
Gumiel de Hizán E 46 Dc60
Gumiel de Mercado E 46 Dc60
Gumlösa S 111 Fb54
Gummark S 80 Hc25
Gummersbach D 125 Ca40
Gumowo PL 122 Ja35
Gumpelstadt D 126 Db42
Gumpersdorf D 143 Ec50
Gumpoldskirchen A 145 Gb51
Gumtow D 119 Eb35
Gümülceli TR 191 Ed85
Gümüldür TR 191 Eb87
Gümüşçay TR 185 Ec80
Gümüşdamla TR 199 Hb90
Gümüşhane TR 205 Fd19
Gümüşlük TR 197 Ec90
Gümüşoluk TR 187 Gd78
Gümüşova TR 187 Gd78
Gümüşpınar TR 186 Fb77
Gümüşpınar TR 192 Fc81
Gümüşsu TR 193 Gb87
Gümüşsuyu TR 186 Fa77
Gümüşyaka TR 199 Gb91
Gümüşyeni TR 192 Ga82
Günaydın TR 192 Fa81
Guncati SRB 153 Jc62
Gundelfingen D 134 Db49
Gundelfingen D 141 Ca50
Gundelsheim D 134 Cd47
Gundelsheim D 134 Dc45
Gundertshausen A 143 Ec51
Gunderup DK 108 Cd25
Gündoğan TR 185 Ed80
Gündoğan TR 197 Ec90
Gündoğdu TR 185 Ec80
Gündoğdu TR 185 Ed79
Gündoğdu TR 186 Fd80
Gündüzler TR 193 Gd81
Gündüzlü TR 185 Ed77
Günekestane TR 192 Ga81
Güneli TR 193 Gd82
Güneşli TR 192 Fb84
Güneşlı TR 199 Gc92
Güney TR 192 Fc83
Güney TR 192 Fc86
Güney TR 192 Fc87
Güney TR 198 Fc89
Güney TR 198 Ga89
Güneyce TR 199 Gd88
Güneykaya TR 199 Hb91
Güneykent TR 193 Gc87
Güneyköy TR 193 Gb85
Güneyköy TR 193 Gd84
Güngören TR 192 Fc81
Güngörmez TR 186 Fa76
Güngörmez TR 186 Fb80
Gunhåberget S 94 Fa39
Günlüce TR 192 Fd83
Günlük TR 197 Ed89
Günlükbaşı TR 198 Fd92
Gunnarn S 80 Gc25
Gunnarnes N 63 Ja05
Gunnarp S 102 Ed51
Gunnarsbyn S 73 Hd21
Gunnarsjö S 102 Ec50
Gunnarskog S 94 Ed42
Gunnarskulla FIN 98 Kb40
Gunnarsnäs S 94 Ec45
Gunnarvattnet S 79 Fb27
Gunnebo S 103 Gb49
Gunnfarnes N 66 Ga11
Gunnilbo S 95 Ga42
Gunnislake GB 18 Dc31
Günseck A 145 Gb53
Gunskirchen A 144 Fa51
Gunsta S 96 Gd42
Günstedt D 127 Dd40
Gunten CH 141 Bd55
Guntersblum D 133 Cb45
Gunter's Bridge GB 20 Fb30
Guntersdorf A 136 Ga49
Günthersleben D 126 Dc41
Gunthorpe GB 16 Fb23
Guntín de Pallares E 36 Bb55
Günyarık TR 193 Gb81
Günyüzü TR 193 Hb83
Günzburg D 134 Db49
Gunzenhausen D 134 Dc47
Guovdageaidnu N 68 Hd11
Gura Bicului MD 173 Ga58
Gura Camencii MD 173 Fc55
Gura Foii RO 176 Dd65
Gürağaç TR 192 Fd82
Gura Galbenei MD 173 Fc59
Gura Haitii RO 172 Dd57
Gurahonţ RO 170 Cb59
Gura Humorului RO 172 Eb56
Gurakuq AL 182 Ac75
Gura Ocniţei RO 176 Dd64
Gura Râului RO 175 Da61
Gurasada RO 174 Cb60
Gura Şuţii RO 176 Dd65
Gura Teghii RO 176 Eb63
Gura Vadului RO 176 Eb64
Gura Văii RO 174 Cb64
Gura Văii RO 176 Ec60
Gurb E 49 Gd59
Gurba RO 170 Ca58
Gurbăneşti RO 176 Ec66
Gürceğiz TR 197 Ed90
Güre TR 191 Eb82
Güre TR 192 Fd85
Güre TR 198 Fb89
Gürece TR 197 Ec90
Güreci TR 185 Ec79
Gur'evsk RUS 113 Ja58
Gurghiu RO 171 Dc58
Gurgljat BG 179 Cb71
Gur i Bardha AL 182 Ac74
Gur i Zi AL 163 Jb71
Gurk A 144 Fb55
Gurkovo BG 180 Db72
Gurkovo BG 181 Fb69
Gürle TR 191 Ec85
Gürlek TR 192 Ga85
Gurnos GB 19 Dd27
Gürpınar TR 186 Fc78
Gürpınar TR 192 Ga86
Gurrë AL 182 Ac75
Gurre DK 109 Ec24
Gurrea de Gállego E 48 Fb59
Gurr'e madhë AL 182 Ac74
Gursken N 76 Cb33
Gürsöğüt TR 193 Hb81
Gürsü TR 186 Fd80
Gurteen IRL 8 Ca18
Gurteen IRL 12 Bd21
Gurten A 143 Ed50
Gurunhuel F 26 Ea38
Gurviksdalen N 77 Dc28
Gusborn D 119 Dd34
Gušće HR 152 Gc60
Güsen D 127 Eb37
Gusendo de los Oteros E 37 Cc58
Gusev RUS 113 Jd59
Guševac SRB 179 Ca69
Gusevo RUS 107 Mb51
Gusevo RUS 113 Jc59
Gus'-Hrustal'nyj RUS 203 Fa10
Gusinje MNE 159 Jb69
Gusmar AL 182 Ab78
Guşoeni RO 175 Da65
Gusow D 128 Fb36
Guspini I 169 Bd78
Gusselby S 95 Fd42
Gusselfeld D 119 Ea35
Güssing A 145 Gb54
Gusswerk A 144 Fd52
Gustav Adolf S 95 Fb41
Gustav Adolf S 103 Fb48
Gustavsberg S 80 Ha25
Gustavsberg S 96 Gd43
Gustavsfors S 94 Fa41
Gustavsfors S 94 Ec44
Güsten D 127 Ea38
Guštirna HR 158 Gb66
Güstrow D 119 Eb32
Gusum S 103 Gb47
Gusvattnet S 79 Fb26
Gus'-Železnyj RUS 203 Fb10
Gutach D 141 Ca50
Gutach D 141 Cb50
Gutar E 61 Dd72
Gutau A 144 Fb50
Gutcher GB 5 Fa03
Gutenbrunn A 144 Fd50
Gutenstein A 144 Ga52
Gutenstetten D 134 Dc46
Gutenswegen D 127 Ea37
Gutenzell D 142 Da50
Güterfelde D 127 Ed37
Gütersloh D 126 Cc38
Gutorfölde H 145 Gc56
Gutowiec PL 121 Gd32

Gúttamási – Harville

Gúttamási H 145 Hb54
Guttannen CH 141 Ca55
Guttaring A 144 Fb55
Gützkow D 119 Ed31
Guvåg N 66 Fc13
Güveçlik TR 198 Fc88
Güvem TR 192 Fb81
Güvemalanı TR 185 Ed80
Güvençetmi TR 192 Fa82
Güvendik TR 191 Eb86
Güvendik TR 193 Hb87
Güvenir TR 198 Fb89
Güvercinlik TR 197 Ed90
Güves GR 201 Db95
Guxhagen D 126 Da40
Guxinde E 36 Ba58
Guyancourt F 23 Gd37
Guyhirn GB 17 Fd24
Güzelbağ TR 199 Hb91
Güzelbahçe TR 191 Eb86
Güzelçamlı TR 197 Ec88
Güzelce TR 186 Fb78
Güzelköy TR 185 Ed78
Güzeloba TR 199 Gd91
Güzelpınar TR 192 Fd87
Güzelsu TR 199 Hb91
Güzelyurt = Morfou CY 206 Ja96
Guzmán E 46 Db60
Gvardejskoe RUS 113 Ja59
Gvarv N 93 Db43
Gvodz MNE 159 Hd68
Gvozd HR 151 Ga60
Gvozdansko HR 152 Gb61
Gwalchmai GB 15 Dd22
Gwardejsk RUS 113 Jb59
Gwbert GB 14 Dc26
Gwda Wielka PL 121 Gc32
Gweek GB 18 Da32
Gwieździn PL 121 Gc32
Gwizdały PL 130 Jc36
Gwizdanów PL 129 Gb40
Gwyddgrug GB 15 Dd26
Gwytherin GB 15 Ea22
Gy F 31 Jc41
Gya N 92 Cb45
Gyál H 146 Hd53
Gyarmat H 145 Gd53
Gyékényes H 152 Gd57
Gyenesdiás H 145 Gd55
Gyé-sur-Seine F 30 Hd39
Gyhum D 118 Da33
Gyl N 77 Db31
Gyland N 92 Cb46
Gyliai LT 114 Ka56
Gyljen S 73 Ja20
Gylling DK 108 Dc25
Gyltvika N 66 Fd17
Gymnich D 125 Bd41
Gyoma H 146 Jc54
Gyomaendrőd H 146 Jc54
Gyömrő H 146 Hd53
Gyón H 146 Hd54
Gyöngyös H 146 Ja52
Gyöngyöspata H 146 Ja52
Gyönk H 146 Hc56
Győr H 145 Ha52
Györgytarló H 147 Ka50
Győrszemere H 145 Ha53
Győrzsentiván H 145 Ha52
Győrtelek H 147 Kb51
Győrvár H 145 Gc55
Gypsou CY 206 Jc96
Gysinge S 95 Gb40
Gyttorp S 95 Fc43
Gyula H 147 Jd55
Gyulafirátót H 145 Ha54
Gyulaj H 145 Hb56
Gžatsk RUS 202 Ed11
Gziq AL 163 Jc71
Gzy PL 122 Jb35

H

Haabneeme EST 98 Kb42
Haabsaare EST 107 Lb47
Häädemeeste EST 106 Kb47
Haag A 144 Fa51
Haag A 144 Fb51
Haag D 143 Eb51
Haag a.d.Amper D 143 Ea50
Haajainen FIN 82 Kc28
Haaksbergen NL 125 Bd37
Haan D 125 Bd40
Haanja EST 107 Lc47
Haapaharju FIN 82 La29
Haapajärvi FIN 82 Ka28
Haapajärvi FIN 82 Kd27
Haapajärvi FIN 91 Lc36
Haapajoki FIN 81 Jd25
Haapa Kimola FIN 90 Kd37
Haapakoski FIN 81 Jc31
Haapakoski FIN 90 Kd32
Haapakumpu FIN 69 Kc16
Haapakylä FIN 81 Jc29
Haapakylä FIN 82 Kc31
Haapala FIN 74 Kb22
Haapala FIN 81 Jc28
Haapala FIN 90 La37
Haapalahti FIN 64 Ka10
Haapalahti FIN 83 Ld29
Haapalankylä FIN 90 Kc32
Haapaluoma FIN 89 Jc32
Haapamäki FIN 82 La29
Haapamäki FIN 82 Kb28
Haapamäki FIN 83 Lb31
Haapamäki FIN 90 Ka33
Haapaniemi FIN 91 Lb32
Haapasaari FIN 98 La39
Haapasalmi FIN 91 Ld32
Haapavaara FIN 91 Ma32
Haapavesi FIN 82 Ka26
Haapimaa FIN 89 Jc35
Haapola FIN 75 La24
Haapovaara FIN 83 Mb30
Haapsalu EST 98 Ka44
Haar D 143 Ea51
Haarajärvenkylä FIN 81 Jc31
Haarajoki FIN 90 Kd33
Haarajoki FIN 90 Kb38
Haarala FIN 82 Kc30
Haarala FIN 90 Kb32
Haaraoja FIN 82 Kb25
Haarasajo FIN 74 Jc19
Haarbach D 143 Ed50
Haarbrück D 126 Da39
Haarby DK 108 Dc27
Haarjärvi FIN 97 Jd39
Haarlem NL 116 Ad35
Haaroinen FIN 89 Jc38
Haataja FIN 75 Kd19
Haatajankylä FIN 83 Lc25
Haavisto FIN 81 Jc28
Haavisto FIN 90 Kb33
Haavisto FIN 98 Ka39
Habaja EST 98 Kc43
Habartice CZ 128 Fc41
Habartov CZ 135 Ec44
Habas F 39 Fa54
Habay-la-Neuve B 132 Ba44
Häbbersliden S 73 Hb24
Habère-Poche F 35 Ka45
Habernau A 144 Fa52
Habichtswald D 126 Da40
Habipler TR 186 Fc77
Habkern CH 141 Bd55
Hablingbo S 104 Gd50
Habo S 103 Fb48
Håbol S 94 Ec45
Håbo-Tibble kyrkby S 96 Gc43
Habry CZ 136 Fd45
Habura SK 139 Ka46
Håby S 102 Eb46
Hacet TR 192 Fa83
Hachenburg D 125 Cb42
Hacıali TR 192 Fb81
Hacıaliler TR 192 Ga84
Hacıbekir TR 199 Gb90
Hacıbekir TR 192 Ga83
Hacıbeyli TR 193 Gb84
Hacıbozlar TR 191 Ec83
Hacıdanişment TR 185 Ec74
Hacienda 2 Mares E 55 Fb73
Hacıeyüblü TR 198 Fc88
Hacıfakılı TR 185 Ed75
Hacıfakılı TR 193 Hb85
Hacıgelen TR 185 Eb80
Hacıhaliller TR 191 Ed85
Hacıhıdır TR 192 Fa85
Hacıhıdırlar TR 198 Fc88
Hacıhüseyinler TR 191 Eb83
Hacıkasım TR 191 Eb81
Hacıköseli TR 192 Fb85
Hacıköy TR 185 Eb77
Hacılar TR 193 Gd87
Hacılar TR 199 Gb89
Hacılebbeleni TR 197 Fa88
Hacılı TR 185 Ec77
Hacinas E 46 Dd59
Hacıömer TR 205 Ga20
Hacıömerli TR 191 Ec84
Hacıpehlivan TR 185 Ed80
Hacıranmanlı TR 191 Ed85
Hacısungur TR 185 Ec77
Hacıtufan TR 192 Fc86
Hacıveliler TR 191 Eb83
Hacıvelioba TR 191 Ed81
Hacıyakup TR 187 Gd78
Hacıyeri TR 187 Ha78
Hacıyusuflar TR 198 Ga91
Hackås S 79 Fc31
Hacketstown IRL 13 Cd23
Hacksjö S 79 Gb26
Hacksta S 96 Gc43
Håcksvik S 102 Ed50
Hackvad S 95 Fc44
Haczów PL 139 Ka45
Hadamar D 125 Cb42
Hädanberg S 80 Gd29
Hădărăuţi MD 173 Fa53
Hadbjerg DK 100 Dc23
Haddal N 76 Cb33
Haddeland N 92 Cc45
Haddenham GB 20 Fb27
Haddenham GB 20 Fd25
Haddington GB 11 Ec13
Hadersdorf am Kamp A 144 Ga50
Haderslev DK 108 Db27
Haderup DK 100 Da23
Hadım TR 192 Ga87
Hadjač UA 202 Ed14
Hadleigh GB 21 Ga26
Hadle Szklarskie PL 139 Ka44
Hadmersleben D 127 Dd38
Hadol F 31 Ka39
Hadsel N 66 Fc13
Hadsten DK 100 Dc23
Hadsund DK 100 Dc22
Hadsund Syd DK 100 Dc22
Hægebostad N 92 Cc46
Hægebostad N 92 Cc47
Hægeland N 92 Cd46
Haelen NL 125 Bb39
Hærland N 94 Eb43
Haeska EST 98 Ka44
Haeska EST 105 Jc46
Håkøybotn N 62 Gc09
Hafenlohr D 134 Da45
Hafik TR 205 Fc20
Hafling I 142 Dc56
Hafnarfjörður IS 2 Ac04
Hafnir IS 2 Ab04
Hafslo N 84 Cd36
Hafslund N 93 Ea44
Hafsmo N 77 Dd30
Haga N 94 Eb41
Haga S 96 Gc42
Haganj HR 152 Gc58
Hagaström S 95 Gb39
Hagbøen N 77 Db32
Hagby S 96 Gc42
Hagby S 111 Ga53
Hage D 117 Cb32
Hage N 78 Ea31
Hagebro DK 100 Da23
Hagebyhöga S 103 Fc46
Hagelberg S 103 Fb47
Hagen D 118 Cd33
Hagen D 125 Ca39
Hagen D 125 Cb37
Hagenbach D 133 Cb47
Hagenburg D 126 Da36
Hagenow D 119 Dd33
Hageri EST 98 Kb43
Hagestad N 93 Da46
Hagetmau F 39 Fb54
Hagfors S 94 Fa41
Häggås S 79 Ga27
Häggdånger S 88 Gc33
Häggeby S 96 Gc42
Häggemåla S 103 Ga51
Häggenås S 79 Fc30
Häggesled S 102 Ed47
Häggnäs S 80 Hb27
Häggnäset S 79 Fb27
Häggsjön S 78 Ed29
Häggsjövik S 79 Fb28
Häggum S 102 Fa47
Häggvik S 80 Gd31
Håghig RO 176 Ea61
Håle-Täng S 102 Ed47
Hagimus MD 173 Ga59
Häglinge S 110 Fa55
Hagondange F 25 Jd35
Hagota RO 172 Ea58
Hagshult S 103 Fb50
Hagudi EST 98 Kb43
Haguenau F 25 Kc36
Hahausen D 126 Db38
Håhellarhytta N 92 Cc44
Håheller N 92 Cb44
Hahmajärvi FIN 90 Kb35
Hahnbach D 135 Ea46
Hahnstätten D 133 Cb43
Hahót H 145 Gc56
Haibach D 134 Cd44
Haibach D 135 Ec48
Haidmühle D 136 Fa49
Haiger D 125 Cb42
Haigerloch D 134 Cc49
Häijää FIN 89 Jc35
Haikáli GR 188 Ba85
Haikkaanlahti FIN 91 Lb35
Haillainville F 31 Ka38
Hailsham GB 20 Fd30
Hailuoto FIN 74 Jd24
Haimburg A 144 Fc56
Haimhausen D 143 Dd50
Haiming A 142 Dc54
Haiming D 143 Ec50
Haimoo FIN 98 Ka39
Haina D 126 Cd41
Hainburg D 134 Cd44
Hainburg an der Donau A 145 Gc51
Hainfeld A 144 Ga51
Hainford GB 17 Gb24
Hainichen D 127 Ed41
Hainneville, Équeurdreville-F 22 Ed34
Hainsfarth D 134 Dc48
Hainton GB 17 Fc22
Hairlach A 142 Dc54
Haiterbach D 134 Cc49
Hajala FIN 97 Jc39
Hajdúböszörmény H 147 Ka52
Hajdučica SRB 174 Bc62
Hajdúdorog H 147 Ka51
Hajdúhadház H 147 Ka52
Hajdúnánás H 147 Jd51
Hajdúsámson H 147 Ka52
Hajdúszoboszló H 147 Jd52
Hajdúszovát H 147 Ka53
Hajdúvid H 147 Ka51
Hajmel AL 163 Jb71
Hajnáčka SK 146 Ja50
Hajnówka PL 123 Kc34
Hajom S 102 Ec50
Hajós H 146 Hd56
Hajredin BG 179 Cd68
Hajsyn UA 204 Ec15
Håkafot S 79 Fc27
Håkantorp S 102 Fa47
Hakarp S 103 Fb49
Hakenstedt D 127 Dd37
Hakerud S 102 Ec46
Hakjala EST 105 Jc46
Hakkas S 73 Hc18
Hakkenpää FIN 97 Ja39
Häkkilä FIN 82 Kb31
Häkkilä FIN 90 Kd33
Häkkiskylä FIN 90 Ka33
Hakkstabben N 63 Hd07
Håkmark S 80 Hb28
Håknäs S 80 Hb29
Hakojärvi FIN 89 Jd32
Hakokylä FIN 75 La24
Hakola FIN 82 La25
Hakola FIN 82 Kb30
Hakomäki FIN 89 Jd32
Håkøybotn N 62 Gc09
Håksberg S 95 Fd41
Hakuni FIN 89 Ja32
Hakvåg N 66 Fd15
Håkvika N 67 Gb13
Halaç TR 199 Gb93
Halaçar TR 193 Gb85
Hålaforsen S 79 Gb29
Halahora de Sus MD 173 Fa54
Halalca TR 192 Fa82
Håland N 92 Ca45
Håland N 92 Cb46
Håland N 92 Cc47
Hålanda S 102 Ec48
Halándri GR 189 Cc86
Halandrítsa GR 188 Bb85
Hålandsdal N 84 Cb40
Halapić BIH 158 Gc64
Halaštra GR 183 Ca78
Halászi H 145 Gd52
Hălăuceşti RO 172 Ed57
Halbe D 128 Fa38
Halbenrain A 144 Ga55
Hålberg S 72 Ha23
Halberstadt D 127 Dd38
Halbjerg DK 101 Dd20
Halblech D 142 Dc52
Hälchiu RO 176 Ea62
Hald DK 100 Db22
Hald DK 100 Dc22
Haldagerlille DK 109 Ea27
Halden N 94 Eb44
Haldensleben D 127 Ea37
Haldenwang D 142 Db52
Haldern D 125 Bc38
Haldrup DK 108 Dc25
Halen B 124 Ba40
Halenbeck D 119 Eb34
Halenkov CZ 137 Hb47
Halenkovice CZ 137 Gd47
Halesowen GB 20 Ed25
Halesworth GB 21 Gb25
Halfing D 143 Eb51
Halford GB 20 Ed26
Halhalca TR 186 Ga80
Halhjem N 84 Ca40
Halič UA 204 Ea16
Halidiye TR 187 Gb80
Halifax GB 16 Ed20
Halíki GR 182 Ba80
Halikko FIN 97 Jc39
Haliliağa TR 191 Eb81
Halilbağı TR 193 Ha82
Halitpaşa TR 191 Ed85
Haljala EST 98 La42
Häljarp S 110 Ed55
Halk DK 108 Db27
Hálki GR 189 Bd81
Hálki GR 191 Dd86
Hálki GR 197 Ed93
Halkia FIN 90 Kc38
Halkida GR 189 Cb85
Halkidó GR 183 Ca77
Halkio GR 189 Bd86
Halkirk GB 5 Eb04
Halkivaha FIN 89 Jc37
Halkokari FIN 74 Jd23
Halkokumpu FIN 90 Kd33
Halkosaari FIN 81 Jb31
Hall S 104 Ha48
Hälla S 79 Gb28
Halla-aho FIN 82 Kd26
Halla-aho FIN 90 La33
Hallabro S 111 Fc53
Hällabrottet S 95 Fd44
Hallaç TR 193 Gc86
Hallaçlar TR 191 Ec82
Hallaçlar TR 197 Fa88
Hallaçlı TR 186 Fa76
Hållan S 79 Fb29
Halland GB 20 Fd30
Hallaperä FIN 82 Kc28
Hallapuro FIN 81 Jd30
Hallaryd S 110 Fa53
Hallaryd S 111 Fc54
Hällbacken S 72 Gb20
Hällberga S 95 Gb43
Hallbergmoos D 143 Ea50
Hällbo S 87 Ga37
Hällbybrunn S 95 Ga43
Halle B 124 Ac41
Halle D 126 Cc37
Halle D 126 Da38
Hälleberga S 103 Fd52
Hällefors S 95 Fc42
Hälleforsnäs S 95 Gb44
Hallein A 143 Ec52
Hällekis S 102 Fa46
Hallen S 79 Fb31
Hallenberg D 126 Cc40
Hallenberg, Steinbach- D 126 Dc42
Hallencourt F 23 Gc33
Hallerndorf D 134 Dc45
Halle (Saale) D 127 Eb40
Hällesåker S 102 Ec49
Hällesjö S 79 Ga31
Hällestad S 103 Fd46
Hällestad S 102 Fa48
Hällestrand S 93 Ea44
Hällestrom S 73 Hd23
Hällevadsholm S 102 Eb46
Hällevik S 111 Fc55
Hälleviksstrand S 102 Eb47
Hall Green GB 20 Ed25
Hall-Håxåsen S 79 Fd29
Halli FIN 90 Ka34
Hallila FIN 90 Kc36
Hallingby N 85 Dd40
Hallingeberg S 103 Ga48
Hällingsjö S 102 Ec49
Hällinmäki FIN 90 La33
Hall in Tirol A 143 Dd53
Halliste EST 106 Kd46
Hällnäs S 72 Gc20
Hällnäs S 80 Ha27
Hällnäs S 96 Gd39
Hallormsstaður IS 3 Bb05
Hallsberg S 95 Fc44
Hallschlag D 125 Bc42
Hallsta S 87 Fd33
Hällsta S 95 Ga44
Hällstad S 102 Fa48
Hallstadt D 134 Dc45
Hallstahammar S 95 Ga43
Hallstatt A 144 Fa53
Hällstavik S 96 Ha41
Halltal A 143 Dd53
Hallthwaites GB 11 Eb19
Hälltorp S 111 Ga53
Hällvattnet S 79 Ga28
Hällvik S 72 Gc21
Hällviken S 79 Fd29
Hälmägel RO 171 Cc59
Hälmagiu RO 171 Cc59
Halmäsd RO 171 Cc56
Halmeniemi FIN 90 La35
Halmeu RO 171 Cd54
Halmstad S 102 Ed52
Halna S 103 Fb46
Halosenkylä FIN 90 La34
Halosenniemi FIN 74 Jd23
Hals DK 101 Dd21
Halsa N 77 Db31
Hal'šany BY 202 Ea12
Halsbrücke D 127 Ed41
Halsen N 70 Ed23
Hälsingfors S 80 Ha27
Hålsjö S 87 Gb35
Hälsö S 102 Eb49
Halsskov DK 109 Ea27
Halstead GB 21 Ga26
Halsted DK 109 Ea28
Halstenbek D 118 Db32
Halsteren NL 124 Ac38
Halsua FIN 81 Jd29
Halsvik N 84 Ca37
Haltern D 125 Ca38
Haltie FIN 90 Ka36
Halttula FIN 91 Lb33
Haltwhistle GB 11 Ec16
Haluna FIN 82 La29
Halvari FIN 69 Jd17
Halvarsgårdarna S 95 Fd40
Halver D 125 Ca40
Halvorstorp S 102 Ec47
Halvrimmen DK 100 Db21
Halwell GB 19 Dd31
Halwill GB 18 Dc30
Halže CZ 135 Ec45
Ham F 23 Ha34
Hämäläinen FIN 90 La36
Hamamdere TR 192 Fc85
Hamamkarahisar TR 193 Hb83
Hamamköy TR 192 Fa87
Hamamüstü TR 187 Gd79
Hamar N 86 Eb38
Hambergen D 118 Cd33
Hambledon GB 20 Fa30
Hambleton GB 16 Fa20
Hambrücken D 133 Cb47
Hambühren D 126 Db36
Hamburg D 118 Db32
Hamburgsund S 102 Ea46
Hambye F 22 Fa36
Hamcearca RO 177 Fc64
Hamdibey TR 186 Fa75
Hamdibey TR 191 Ec81
Hamdorf D 118 Db30
Hämeenkoski FIN 90 Kb37
Hämeenkylä FIN 83 Lb26
Hämeenkyrö FIN 89 Jc35
Hämeenlinna FIN 90 Ka37
Hameln D 126 Da37
Hamersleben D 127 Dd38
Hamidiye TR 185 Ea80
Hamidiye TR 185 Eb77
Hamidiye TR 186 Fa75
Hamidiye TR 186 Fd80
Hamidiye TR 187 Gb80
Hamidiye TR 192 Fa83
Hamidiye TR 192 Fb85
Hamidiye TR 192 Ga81
Hamidiye TR 193 Gd82
Hamidiye TR 193 Gd85
Hamidiye TR 193 Ha84
Hamidiye TR 193 Hb81
Hamilton GB 10 Ea13
Hamina FIN 90 La38
Hamit TR 198 Fb91
Hamitabat TR 192 Ga82
Hamitler TR 193 Hb87
Hamitli TR 185 Eb76
Hamlot N 66 Fd14
Hamm D 125 Ca41
Hamm D 134 Cc45
Hamm/ Westf. D 125 Cb38
Hammah D 118 Da32
Hammar N 78 Eb28
Hammar S 95 Fc45
Hammar S 111 Fb54
Hammarby S 95 Gb39
Hammarby S 96 Gc43
Hammarland FIN 96 Hb40
Hammarnäs S 79 Fb31
Hammarnes N 64 Jd06
Hammarö S 94 Fa43
Hammarslund S 111 Fb55
Hammarstrand S 79 Ga31
Hammarvika N 77 Dc29
Hammaslahti FIN 83 Ld31
Hammel DK 100 Dc23
Hammelburg D 134 Da44
Hammelev DK 108 Db27
Hammelspring D 119 Ed34
Hammenhög S 111 Fb56
Hammer DK 108 Db25
Hammer N 78 Eb29
Hammer N 78 Ec26
Hammer N 78 Ec27
Hammerdal S 79 Fd29
Hammerfest N 63 Hd06
Hämmern D 135 Dd43
Hammershøj DK 100 Dc23
Hammerum DK 108 Da24
Hamminkeln D 125 Bd38
Hamn N 70 Ed22
Hamna N 77 Dc29
Hamnavoe GB 5 Fa05
Hamnbukt N 64 Jb07
Hamneda S 102 Fa52
Hamneidet N 63 Hb08
Hamnes N 66 Ga13
Hamnes N 70 Ed22
Hamnes N 78 Eb26
Hamnøy N 66 Fa15
Hamnsund N 76 Cc32
Hamnvågnes N 62 Gd10
Hamnvik N 67 Gb12
Hamoir B 124 Ba42
Hamois B 124 Ad42
Håmojåkk S 67 Ha17
Hamolovo RUS 99 Lc40
Hamont B 125 Bb39
Hámor H 146 Jc50
Hampen DK 108 Db24
Hampetorp S 95 Fd44
Hampovica HR 152 Gd58
Hampstead GB 20 Fc28
Hamra S 86 Ec33
Hamra S 87 Fc36
Hamra S 104 Gd51
Hamrånge S 87 Gb38
Hamrångefjärden S 87 Gb38
Hamre N 84 Ca38
Hamre N 92 Cd47
Hamre S 87 Ga36
Hamremoen N 85 Dc40
Hamstreet GB 21 Ga29
Hamsund N 66 Fd14
Hamula FIN 82 Kb29
Hamula FIN 82 Kc30
Hamyški RUS 205 Fd17
Hamzabey TR 185 Ed76
Hamzabey TR 186 Ga80
Hamzabeyli TR 185 Eb74
Hamzali MK 183 Ca75
Hamzalı TR 186 Fd79
Hamzalı TR 198 Fb88
Hån S 95 Fb41
Han TR 193 Gd84
Hana N 65 Kb06
Hanadal N 64 Ka06
Hanak TR 205 Ga18
Hånanbihen F 22 Ec38
Hanaskog S 111 Fb54
Han Asparuhovo BG 180 Ea72
Hanau D 134 Cd44
Hanbury GB 20 Ed25
Hanbury GB 20 Ed25
Hancăuţi MD 173 Fa54
Hancavičy BY 202 Ea13
Handbjerg DK 100 Da23
Handegg CH 141 Ca55
Hadeland N 92 Cb45
Handeloh D 118 Db33
Handenberg A 143 Ec51
Händene S 102 Fa47
Handest DK 100 Dc22
Handewitt D 108 Da28
Handley GB 15 Eb22
Handlová SK 138 Hc49
Handnes N 70 Fa21
Handog S 79 Fc30
Handöl S 78 Ed30
Handrás GR 201 Dd96
Handrup D 117 Cb35
Handstein N 70 Fa20
Hanebo S 87 Gb37
Hanekamhaug N 77 Da32
Hanerau-Hademarschen D 118 Da30
Hånes N 92 Cd47
Hanestad N 85 Ea35
Hăneşti RO 172 Ed55
Hang N 85 Fb46
Han Garaučića MNE 159 Jb68
Hangaskylä FIN 89 Ja32
Hangastenmaa FIN 90 La34
Hangelsberg D 128 Fa37
Hänger S 103 Fb51
Hangö FIN 97 Jc41
Hångstad S 94 Ec42
Hangu RO 172 Eb57
Hangvar S 104 Ha48
Hanhals S 102 Ec50
Hanhijärvi FIN 91 Lc36
Hanhimaa FIN 68 Jc14
Hanhisalo FIN 81 Jd28
Hanho FIN 89 Jd34
Haniá GR 200 Cb94
Hånick S 87 Gb35
Hänigsen D 126 Db36
Hanikase EST 107 Lc46
Haniótis GR 184 Cc80
Hankamäki FIN 82 Kd31
Hankamäki FIN 83 Lb28
Hankasalmen asema FIN 90 Kc32
Hankasalmi FIN 90 Kc32
Hankavaara FIN 91 Lc32
Hanken S 103 Fb46
Hankensbüttel D 118 Dc35
Han Knežica BIH 152 Gc61
Hanko FIN 97 Jc41
Hanmer GB 15 Eb23
Hanna PL 131 Kc38
Hannäs S 103 Ga47
Hannemyr N 93 Db45
Hännilä FIN 91 Lc35
Hannington GB 20 Ed27
Hannover D 126 Db36
Hannoversch Münden D 126 Da40
Hannukainen FIN 68 Jb16
Hannut B 124 Ad41
Hanoğlu TR 192 Ga85
Hanovo BG 180 Eb73
Hanøy N 66 Fd13
Hanpaşa TR 192 Fa84
Han Pijesak BIH 159 Hd64
Hansca MD 173 Fd58
Hansjö S 87 Fc37
Hańsk PL 131 Kc39
Hansnes N 62 Gd08
Hanstedt D 118 Db33
Hanstedt D 118 Dc34
Hanstholm DK 100 Da20
Hanstorf D 119 Eb31
Han-sur-Lesse B 132 Ad43
Han-sur-Nied F 25 Jd36
Häntälä FIN 97 Jd39
Hantos H 146 Hc54
Hanušovce nad Topl'ou SK 139 Jd47
Hanušovice CZ 137 Gc44
Hanyatak TR 187 Gc79
Hanyeri TR 192 Fd86
Haparanda S 74 Jc21
Haparanda hamn S 74 Jc21
Hapert NL 124 Ba39
Happakylä FIN 98 Ka39
Häppälä FIN 90 Kc33
Happurg D 135 Dd46
Hapträsk S 73 Hb21
Hapua FIN 89 Jb35
Hara S 79 Fc31
Haraba MD 173 Fd55
Harad S 95 Gb43
Haradok BY 202 Eb11
Harads S 73 Hc21
Häradsbäck S 111 Fb53
Häradsbygden S 95 Fc39
Häradshammer S 103 Gb46
Haradzišča BY 202 Ea13
Haragiş MD 177 Fc60
Harákas GR 195 Bd90
Harákas GR 200 Da96
Haraker S 95 Ga42
Haráki GR 197 Fa93
Haraldseng N 63 Hc06
Haraldshaugen N 92 Bd42
Harasiuki PL 131 Kb42
Harău RO 175 Cc61
Haravgí GR 183 Bc78
Harbach A 136 Fc49
Harbak N 78 Ea27
Hårberg N 77 Dd29
Härbergsdalen S 79 Fc26
Harbke D 127 Dd37
Harbo S 96 Gc41
Harbølle DK 109 Eb28
Harboøre DK 100 Cd22
Harborg N 86 Eb32
Harburg D 134 Dc48
Harby GB 16 Fb23
Harcılar TR 192 Fb82
Harcourt F 23 Ga36
Hardegg A 136 Ga48
Hardegsen D 126 Db39
Hardelot-Plage F 23 Gb31
Hardemo S 95 Fc44
Hardenberg NL 117 Bd35
Hardenberg, Nörten- D 126 Db39
Harderwijk NL 116 Bb36
Hardeshøj DK 108 Db28
Hardheim D 134 Da46
Hardinghen F 21 Gc30
Hardom FIN 90 Kd38
Hareid N 76 Cc33
Haren NL 117 Bd33
Haren (Ems) D 117 Ca35
Harestad S 102 Eb48
Harestua N 85 Ea40
Harewood GB 16 Fa20
Harg S 96 Gd40
Harghita-Băi RO 176 Ea60
Hargimont B 132 Ba43
Hargla EST 107 Lb48
Hargnies F 24 Ja32
Hargrave GB 20 Fc25
Hargrave Green GB 21 Ga26
Hargshamn S 96 Gd41
Harhala FIN 90 Ka36
Hariéssa GR 183 Bc77
Harije SLO 151 Fb59
Harivaara FIN 83 Lc29
Härja S 103 Fb48
Harjakangas FIN 89 Ja35
Harjakoski FIN 89 Jb35
Harjankylä FIN 89 Ja32
Härjåsjön S 87 Fb35
Harjavalta FIN 89 Jb36
Härjevad S 102 Ed47
Harju FIN 75 Kc24
Harju FIN 82 La28
Harjula FIN 74 Ka21
Harjula FIN 82 Kd26
Harjunmaa FIN 90 Kd34
Harjunpää FIN 89 Ja36
Harjunsalmi FIN 90 Kb34
Harju-Risti EST 98 Ka43
Härkäjoki FIN 69 Kb16
Harkány H 152 Hb58
Härkäpää FIN 98 Kd39
Härkeberga S 96 Gc42
Harken DK 100 Dc20
Härkki FIN 91 Lc32
Harkmark N 92 Cd47
Härkmeri FIN 89 Hd34
Härkmyran S 73 Hc19
Harku EST 98 Kb42
Hârlău RO 172 Ed56
Harlaug N 85 Dc35
Harlech GB 15 Dd23
Harlesiel D 117 Cc32
Harleston GB 21 Gb25
Hårlev DK 109 Ec27
Harlingen NL 116 Bb33
Harlösa S 110 Fa56
Harlow GB 20 Fd27
Harmaalanranta FIN 82 Kb29
Harmaasalo FIN 83 Lc30
Härman RO 176 Ea62
Harmancık TR 192 Fd82
Harmancık TR 192 Fd82
Harmanec SK 138 Hc48
Harmånger S 87 Gb35
Harmanköy TR 193 Gc81
Härmänkylä FIN 83 Lb25
Harmanli BG 185 Ea74
Harmanlı TR 185 Eb77
Harmanlı TR 186 Fb80
Harmanlı TR 198 Ga89
Härmänmäki FIN 82 La25
Harmannsdorf A 145 Gb50
Harmanören TR 199 Gd88
Harmaţca MD 173 Fd56
Harmica HR 151 Ga58
Harmoinen FIN 90 Kb35
Härna S 102 Ed48
Harndrup DK 108 Dc26
Harnes F 23 Ha31
Härnösand S 88 Gc32
Haro E 38 Ea57
Harola FIN 89 Jb37
Háromfa H 152 Gd57
Haroúda GR 194 Bb90
Haroué F 25 Jd37
Härpe FIN 98 Kd39
Harpefoss N 85 Db36
Harpenden GB 20 Fc27
Harplinge S 102 Ed52
Harpstedt D 118 Cd34
Harpswell GB 16 Fb22
Harra D 135 Ea43
Harrå S 67 Ha16
Harrachov CZ 128 Fd42
Harrachsthal A 144 Fc50
Harre DK 100 Da22
Harrejaur S 73 Hb19
Harres DK 108 Da27
Harrested DK 109 Ea27
Harridslev DK 100 Dc23
Harrislee D 108 Db28
Harritslev DK 108 Dc26
Harrogate GB 16 Fa20
Harrow GB 20 Fc28
Harrsele S 80 Ha28
Harrsjö S 71 Ga24
Harrsjö S 79 Fd26
Harrsjön S 79 Fd27
Harrström FIN 89 Hd32
Harrvik S 71 Ga24
Harrviken S 73 Ja22
Härryda S 102 Ec49
Harsa S 87 Ga36
Harsängen S 102 Ec46
Harsány H 146 Jc51
Harsefeld D 118 Da33
Harseni RO 176 Dd61
Hârseşti RO 175 Dc65
Harsewinkel D 126 Cc37
Harskamp NL 116 Bb36
Harsleben D 127 Dd38
Hârşova RO 177 Fb65
Harsovo BG 181 Ec69
Harsovo BG 181 Ed69
Harsprånget S 72 Ha18
Hårstad N 62 Gc10
Harstad N 66 Ga12
Harsum D 126 Db37
Harsvika N 78 Ea27
Harsz PL 122 Jc30
Harta H 146 Hd55
Harta PL 139 Ka44
Hartaanselkä FIN 82 Ka25
Hartberg A 144 Ga54
Hårte S 88 Gc35
Hartenholm D 118 Dc31
Hartennes F 24 Hb35
Hartenstein D 127 Ec42
Hartenstein D 135 Ea46
Hartfield GB 20 Fd29
Harth D 126 Cc39
Hartha D 127 Ec41
Hartheim D 141 Bd51
Hârtieşti RO 176 Dd64
Hartington GB 16 Ed22
Hartland GB 18 Dc29
Hartlebury GB 15 Ec25
Hartlepool GB 11 Fa17
Hartley GB 20 Fd28
Hartmanice CZ 135 Ed47
Hartmanndorf A 144 Ga54
Hartmannsdorf D 127 Ec42
Hartola FIN 90 Kc35
Hartola FIN 90 Kd36
Hartpury GB 15 Ec26
Hårup DK 100 Dc23
Harvaluoto FIN 97 Jb39
Harvanmäki FIN 82 Kd28
Harvasstua N 71 Fc24
Harviala FIN 90 Ka37
Harville F 25 Jc35

Harwell – Hiirijärvi

Harwell GB 20 Fa28
Harwich GB 21 Gb26
Harworth GB 16 Fb21
Harzgerode D 127 Dd39
Hasanağa TR 185 Eb75
Hasanağa TR 186 Fc80
Hasanbey TR 185 Ed80
Hasanbey TR 187 Gc78
Håsand N 66 Fc16
Hasandede TR 192 Ga87
Hasanköy TR 192 Ga85
Hasanlar TR 191 Ec85
Hasanlar TR 192 Fd83
Hasanlı TR 186 Ga78
Hasanpaşa TR 198 Ga90
Hasbergen D 125 Cb37
Hasborn D 133 Bd44
Hasdümen TR 199 Gd90
Haselbach D 135 Ec48
Haselbourg F 25 Kb36
Häselgehr A 142 Db53
Haselund D 108 Da29
Haselünne D 117 Cb35
Hasfjord N 63 Hc06
Hasgebe TR 199 Gd90
Håsjö S 79 Ga31
Haskovo BG 185 Dd74
Hasköy TR 185 Ea78
Hasköy TR 185 Ec75
Hasköy TR 192 Fd86
Hasla N 93 Da46
Haslach D 141 Ca50
Haslach an der Mühl A 136 Fa49
Hasle CH 141 Bd54
Hasle DK 111 Fc57
Haslemere GB 20 Fb29
Haslemoen N 94 Ec39
Haslev DK 109 Eb27
Haslingden GB 15 Ec20
Hasloch D 134 Da45
Hasloh D 118 Db32
Haslöv S 110 Ed56
Hasmark DK 109 Dd26
Hășmaș RO 170 Cb58
Hăsnăşenii Mari MD 173 Fb55
Hăsnăşenii Noi MD 173 Fb55
Hasparren F 39 Fa55
Haßbergen D 118 Da35
Hassel D 118 Da35
Hassel S 87 Gb34
Hassela S 87 Gb34
Hasselfelde D 127 Dd39
Hasselfors S 95 Fc44
Hasselösund S 102 Ea47
Hasselroth D 134 Cd44
Hasselt B 124 Ba40
Hasselt NL 117 Bc35
Haßfurt D 134 Dc44
Hassi FIN 90 Kb34
Hässjö S 88 Gc33
Hasslarp S 110 Ed54
Hassle S 95 Fb45
Haßleben D 120 Fa34
Hässleholm S 110 Fa54
Hasslö S 111 Fd54
Haßloch D 133 Cb46
Hasslösa S 102 Fa46
Haßmersheim D 134 Cd46
Håstad N 78 Eb26
Hästbacka FIN 81 Jc29
Hästbo S 95 Gb39
Hästbo S 95 Ga40
Haste D 126 Da36
Hästhagen S 96 Gd43
Hästholmen S 103 Fc47
Hastiere-Lavaux B 124 Ad42
Hastings GB 21 Ga30
Hästö FIN 97 Jc40
Hästveda S 111 Fb54
Håsum DK 100 Da22
Hasvik N 63 Hc06
Hațeg RO 175 Cc61
Hatfield GB 15 Ec25
Hatfield GB 16 Fb21
Hatfield GB 20 Fc27
Hatfield Heath GB 20 Fd27
Hatfield Peverel GB 21 Ga27
Hatherleigh GB 19 Dd30
Hathersage GB 16 Fa22
Hätila FIN 90 Ka37
Hatipkışla TR 197 Ed89
Hatıplar TR 191 Ed84
Hatlestrand N 84 Cb40
Hatlinghus N 78 Ec27
Hatrik N 84 Ca40
Hatsola FIN 90 La33
Hattem NL 117 Bc35
Hatten D 117 Cc34
Hatten F 25 Kc36
Hattersheim D 134 Cc44
Hattert D 125 Cb42
Hattevik N 77 Dc29
Hattfjelldal N 71 Fb23
Hatting DK 108 Db25
Hattingen D 125 Ca39
Hattorf D 126 Db39
Håttorp S 95 Fb45
Hattstedt D 108 Da29
Hattula FIN 90 Ka37
Hattusaari FIN 83 Lc28
Hattuselkonen FIN 83 Ld27
Hatu EST 98 Ka43
Hatulanmäki FIN 82 Kd26
Hatun TR 191 Ed83
Håtuna S 96 Gc42
Hatunkylä FIN 83 Ld28
Hatvan H 146 Ja52
Hatvanpuszta H 146 Hc55
Hatzfeld D 126 Cc41
Haubourdin F 23 Ha31
Haudainville F 24 Jb35
Hauenstein D 133 Ca47
Haug N 67 Gb11
Haug N 85 Da36
Haug N 93 Dd42
Haugastøl N 85 Da39
Hauge N 65 Kc09
Hauge N 84 Cd37
Hauge N 92 Cb46
Haugen N 92 Cc44
Haugesund N 92 Bd42
Haugeveit N 92 Cd44
Haugfoss N 93 Da43
Haughom N 92 Cb45
Haugland N 70 Fa20
Haugli N 67 Gc12
Haugnes N 62 Ha08
Haugsdorf A 136 Ga49
Haugsvik N 84 Cc38
Hauho FIN 90 Ka36
Hauhuu FIN 89 Jd33
Haukanmaa FIN 90 Kc33
Haukedal N 84 Cc36
Haukeligrend N 92 Cd41
Haukeliseter N 92 Cc41
Haukijärvi FIN 75 Kd22
Haukijärvi FIN 89 Jc35
Haukilahti FIN 83 Lb25
Haukilahti FIN 91 Lc35
Haukiniemi FIN 91 Lc32
Haukipudas FIN 74 Ka23
Haukitaipale FIN 74 Ka20
Haukivaara FIN 83 Ma30
Haukivuori FIN 90 La33
Haukkilahti FIN 81 Jd29
Hauklappi FIN 91 Lc34
Hauknes N 71 Fb20
Hauneck D 126 Da41
Haunetal D 126 Da42
Haunia FIN 89 Jb35
Haunsheim D 134 Db49
Hauptstuhl D 133 Ca46
Haurida S 103 Fc48
Haurukylä FIN 74 Ka24
Haus N 84 Ca39
Hausach D 141 Cb50
Hausen D 134 Db45
Hausen D 135 Ea48
Hausen D 141 Ca52
Häusern D 141 Ca51
Hausham D 143 Ea52
Hausjärvi FIN 90 Kb38
Hausmannstätten A 144 Fd55
Haustreisa N 70 Fa23
Hausvik N 92 Cc47
Hauta-Aho FIN 83 Lb31
Hautajärvi FIN 74 Kd18
Hautajoki FIN 82 Kb27
Hautajoki FIN 82 Kc28
Hautakylä FIN 81 Jd31
Hautaranta FIN 75 La19
Haut-Asco F 154 Cb69
Hautefort F 33 Gb49
Hauteluce F 35 Ka46
Haute-Nendaz CH 141 Bc56
Hauterives F 34 Jb48
Hauteville-Lompnès F 35 Jc46
Hauteville-Plage F 22 Ed36
Hautjärvi FIN 90 Kc38
Hautmont F 24 Hc32
Hautolahti FIN 82 Kc30
Hautvillers F 24 Hc36
Hauzenberg D 136 Fa49
Havaj SK 139 Ka46
Havant GB 20 Fb30
Havari GR 188 Ba86
Havârna RO 172 Ec54
Håvberget S 95 Fc40
Havbro DK 100 Db22
Havdáta GR 188 Ab85
Havdhem S 104 Gd51
Havdrup DK 109 Eb26
Håve S 94 Eb45
Havelange B 124 Ba42
Havelberg D 119 Eb35
Havelte NL 117 Bc34
Havenbuurt NL 116 Ba35
Haverdal S 102 Ec52
Haverdalsstrand S 102 Ec52
Haverfordwest GB 18 Db27
Haverhill GB 20 Fd26
Haverö S 87 Fc33
Häverö S 96 Ha41
Haversin B 124 Ad42
Haverslev DK 100 Dc22
Håverud S 94 Ec45
Havířov CZ 137 Hb45
Havixbeck D 125 Ca37
Hävla S 95 Ga45
Havlíčkův Brod CZ 136 Ga46
Havnbjerg DK 108 Db27
Havndal DK 100 Dc22
Havneby DK 108 Cd27
Havnemark DK 109 Dd26
Havnsø DK 109 Ea25
Havnstrup DK 108 Da24
Havøysund N 63 Ja04
Havraň CZ 136 Fa43
Havran TR 191 Ec82
Håvre S 87 Fd35
Havrebjerg DK 109 Ea26
Havrylivka UA 205 Fb15
Havsa TR 185 Ec76
Havsnäs S 79 Fd28
Havstensund S 94 Ea45
Havumäki FIN 90 Kc33
Havusalmi FIN 82 Kb30
Havusalmi FIN 90 Kc32
Havvness N 62 Ha09
Havza TR 205 Fb20
Hawes GB 11 Ed18
Hawick GB 11 Ec15
Hawkhurst GB 20 Fd29
Hawkinge GB 21 Gb29
Hawkshead GB 11 Eb18
Hawsker GB 11 Fb18
Haxey GB 16 Fb21
Hayalli TR 192 Fb86
Hayange F 25 Jc35
Haydar TR 185 Ec80
Haydarköy TR 192 Fa81
Haydarlı TR 193 Gc87
Haydaroba TR 191 Ed81
Haydere TR 198 Fb89
Haydon Bridge GB 11 Ed16
Hayes GB 20 Fc28
Hayfield GB 16 Ed22
Häyhtiönmaa FIN 89 Jb36
Hayingen D 142 Cd50
Hayle GB 18 Da32
Haymana TR 193 Gc83
Hay-on-Wye GB 15 Eb26
Hayrabolu TR 185 Ec77
Hayriye TR 186 Fc79
Hayriye TR 198 Ga88
Hayscastle GB 14 Db26
Haywards Heath GB 20 Fc30
Haza del Lino E 60 Dc76
Hazebrouck F 21 Gd30
Hazelbank GB 10 Ea14
Hazinedar TR 185 Ec76
Hazırlar TR 198 Fd93
Hažlín SK 139 Jd46
Hazlov CZ 135 Eb44
Heacham GB 17 Fd23
Headcorn GB 21 Ga29
Headford IRL 8 Bc20
Headley GB 20 Fb29
Heager DK 108 Cd24
Heanor GB 16 Fa23
Heath End GB 20 Fa28
Heather GB 16 Fa24
Heathfield GB 20 Fd30
Heath Hayes GB 16 Ed24
Heber D 118 Db34
Heberg S 102 Ec52
Hebertsfelden D 143 Ec50
Hebnes N 92 Cb42
Heby S 95 Gb41
Hèches F 40 Fd56
Hechingen D 142 Cc50
Hecho E 39 Fb57
Hechtel-Eksel B 124 Ba40
Hechthausen D 118 Da32
Heciul Nou MD 173 Fb55
Heckelberg D 120 Fa35
Heckfield GB 20 Fb28
Heckington GB 17 Fc23
Hecklingen D 127 Ea38
Hed S 95 Fd42
Heda S 103 Fc47
Hedalen N 85 Dc39
Hedared S 102 Ed48
Hedås S 94 Fa43
Hedben Bridge GB 16 Ed20
Hedberg S 72 Gd23
Hedby S 95 Fc39
Hedbyn S 95 Fd41
Heddal N 93 Db42
Hedderen N 92 Cd44
Hédé F 28 Ed39
Hede S 86 Fa33
Hede S 95 Ga40
Hede S 95 Gb41
Hede S 102 Eb46
Hedegård DK 108 Db25
Hedehusene DK 109 Ec26
Hedekas S 102 Eb46
Hedemora S 95 Ga40
Heden DK 108 Dc27
Heden S 73 Hd22
Heden S 86 Ed35
Heden S 87 Fb37
Hedenäset S 73 Jb20
Hedenstad N 93 Dc42
Hedensted DK 108 Db25
Hedersleben D 127 Dd38
Hedersleben D 127 Ea39
Hedesunda S 95 Gb40
Hedeviken S 86 Fa33
Hedon GB 17 Fc20
Hedon GB 17 Fc21
Hedrum N 93 Dd44
Hedwiżyn PL 131 Kb42
Hee DK 108 Cd24
Heede D 117 Ca34
Heek D 125 Ca37
Heel NL 125 Bb40
Heemsen D 118 Da35
Heemskerk NL 116 Ad35
Heemstede NL 116 Ad35
Heerbrugg CH 142 Cd53
Heerde NL 117 Bc36
Heere D 126 Dc37
Heerenveen NL 117 Bc34
Heerhugowaard NL 116 Ba34
Heerlen NL 125 Bb41
Heers B 124 Ba41
Heesch NL 125 Bb38
Heeslingen D 118 Da33
Heestrand S 102 Ea46
Heeten NL 117 Bc36
Heeze NL 125 Bb39
Hegge N 85 Dc37
Heggelia N 67 Gc11
Heggen N 93 Dd41
Heggenes N 67 Gd11
Heggheim N 84 Cb36
Heggmoen N 66 Fc17
Heglesvollen N 78 Ec29
Hegra N 78 Eb30
Hegyeshalom H 145 Gd51
Hegyfalu H 145 Gc53
Hegyhátsál H 145 Gc55
Hegykő H 145 Gc53
Hegyköszég H 145 Gc54
Hehlen D 126 Da38
Heia N 67 Gd11
Heia N 78 Ed27
Heidal N 85 Dc35
Heide D 118 Da30
Heideck D 135 Dd47
Heidelberg D 134 Cc46
Heiden D 125 Bd38
Heidenau D 118 Db33
Heidenau D 128 Fa41
Heidenheim D 134 Db49
Heidenheim D 134 Dc48
Heidenreichstein A 136 Fd48
Heidenrod D 133 Cb43
Heiderscheid L 133 Bb44
Heidersdorf D 127 Ed42
Heidgraben D 118 Db32
Heigrestad N 92 Ca45
Heikendorf D 118 Dc30
Heikinkylä FIN 90 Kd38
Heikkil N 68 Hd11
Heikkilä FIN 75 La19
Heikkilä FIN 75 Kd21
Heikkilä FIN 81 Jc29
Heikkilä FIN 82 Kb28
Heikkilä FIN 83 Lb25
Heikkilä FIN 89 Ja33
Heikkilä FIN 89 Jb37
Heikkurila FIN 91 Lb33
Heikola FIN 89 Ja38
Heilbronn D 134 Cd47
Heilevong N 84 Cb35
Heiligenberg D 142 Cd52
Heiligenblut A 143 Ec54
Heiligendamm D 119 Eb31
Heiligenfelde D 119 Ea35
Heiligengrabe D 119 Ec34
Heiligenhafen D 119 Dd30
Heiligenhaus D 125 Bd39
Heiligenkreuz A 144 Ga55
Heiligenkreuz A 145 Gb51
Heiligenkreuz im Lafnitztal A 145 Gb55
Heiligenstadt D 126 Db40
Heiligenstadt D 135 Dd45
Heiligenthal D 127 Ea39
Heiligerlee NL 117 Ca33
Heilitz-le-Maurupt F 24 Ja37
Heiloo NL 116 Ba35
Heilsbronn D 134 Dc47
Heim N 77 Dc30
Heimbuchenthal D 134 Cd45
Heimburg D 127 Dd38
Heimdal N 62 Gd10
Heimdal N 77 Ea30
Heimenkirch D 142 Da52
Heimertingen D 142 Db51
Heimola FIN 69 Kb15
Heimsheim D 134 Cc48
Heimsnes N 78 Ed25
Heinäaho FIN 83 Ma30
Heinade D 126 Da38
Heinajoki FIN 90 Kb37
Heinälahti FIN 83 Lb25
Heinämaa FIN 90 Kc37
Heinämäki FIN 82 Kc29
Heinämäki FIN 82 La25
Heinäperä FIN 89 Jd32
Heinävaara FIN 83 Ld30
Heinävesi FIN 83 Lb31
Heinebach D 126 Da41
Heinersdorf D 128 Fb36
Heinijärvi FIN 74 Ka24
Heinijoki FIN 89 Jb38
Heinikoski FIN 74 Jd22
Heinilä FIN 89 Ja35
Heiningen D 126 Dc37
Heiniranta FIN 82 Kd26
Heinisuo FIN 74 Kb20
Heinlahti FIN 90 La38
Heino NL 117 Bc35
Heinola FIN 90 Kd36
Heinolanperä FIN 82 Ka25
Heinoniemi FIN 91 Ld32
Heinoo FIN 89 Jc36
Heinsberg D 125 Bc40
Heinsen D 126 Da38
Heistad N 93 Dc44
Heiste EST 97 Jc44
Heitersheim D 141 Bd51
Heiterwang A 142 Dc53
Heituinlahti FIN 90 La36
Hejde S 104 Gd50
Hejls DK 108 Db26
Hejlsminde DK 108 Db26
Hejnice CZ 128 Fd42
Hejnsvig DK 108 Da25
Hejnum S 104 Ha49
Hejőbába H 146 Jc51
Hejsager DK 108 Db27
Hekimdağ TR 193 Gc81
Heksem N 78 Eb31
Hel PL 121 Hb29
Helbra D 127 Ea39
Heldburg, Bad Colberg- D 134 Dc43
Helden NL 125 Bb39
Heldrungen D 127 Dd40
Helechal E 51 Cb70
Helechosa E 52 Cd68
Helegiu RO 176 Ec60
Helenelund FIN 89 Hd32
Helensburgh GB 10 Dd13
Helfenberg A 136 Fb49
Helgarö S 95 Gb43
Helgatun N 84 Cc38
Helgen N 93 Dc43
Helgeroa N 93 Dc44
Helgerød N 93 Dd44
Helgesta S 95 Gb44
Helgheim N 84 Cc35
Helgøy N 62 Gd08
Helgøy N 85 Ea39
Helgøysund N 92 Ca43
Helgum S 79 Gb31
Heli N 93 Ea43
Helidóni GR 194 Ba87
Heligfjäll S 79 Ga25
Héliopolis F 43 Kb55
Hell N 78 Eb30
Hella IS 2 Ac05
Hella N 84 Cc36
Hellamaa EST 97 Jd44
Hellamaa EST 97 Jd45
Helland N 66 Ga15
Helland N 77 Dc30
Hellandsbygd N 92 Cb41
Hellanmaa FIN 81 Jb30
Helle N 92 Cb44
Helle N 92 Cd44
Hellebæk DK 109 Ec24
Hellefjord N 63 Hd06
Helleland N 92 Ca45
Hellendoorn NL 117 Bd36
Hellenthal D 125 Bc42
Hellesøy N 84 Bd38
Hellesvikan N 77 Dc28
Hellesylt N 84 Cd34
Hellevad DK 108 Da27
Hellevik N 84 Ca36
Hellevoetsluis NL 124 Ac37
Helligvær N 66 Fb17
Hellimer F 25 Ka36
Hellín E 53 Ec71
Hellissandur IS 2 Ab03
Hellmobotn N 66 Ga15
Hellmonsödt A 144 Fb50
Hellnar IS 2 Ab03
Hellnes N 63 Hb08
Hellsö FIN 97 Hd41
Helmbrechts D 135 Ea44
Helme EST 106 La46
Helminghausen D 126 Cd39
Helmlüla EST 98 Ka45
Helmond NL 125 Bb38
Helmsdale GB 5 Eb06
Helmsley GB 16 Fb19
Helmstadt D 134 Da45
Helmstadt-Bargen D 134 Cd46
Helmstedt D 127 Dd37
Helnæs By DK 108 Dc27
Helnessund N 66 Fc16
Hel'pa SK 138 Ja48
Helpfau-Uttendorf A 143 Ed51
Helppi FIN 68 Jc17
Helsa D 126 Da40
Helsby GB 15 Ec22
Helse D 118 Da31
Helshan AL 178 Ad72
Helsingborg S 110 Ec54
Helsingby FIN 81 Ja31
Helsinge DK 109 Ec24
Helsingfors FIN 98 Kb39
Helsingør DK 109 Ec24
Helsinki FIN 97 Ja39
Helsinki FIN 98 Kb39
Helstad N 70 Ed24
Helston GB 18 Da32
Heltermaa EST 97 Jd44
Helvacı TR 191 Ec85
Hem N 93 Dd43
Hemau D 135 Ea48
Hemavan S 71 Fc22
Hemden D 125 Bd37
Hemeiuș RO 172 Ed59
Hemel Hempstead GB 20 Fc27
Hemer D 125 Cb39
Hemfjällstangen S 86 Fa38
Hemfurth D 126 Cd40
Hemhofen D 134 Dc45
Héming F 25 Ka37
Hemingbrough GB 16 Fb20
Hemling S 80 Gd29
Hemmesjö S 103 Fc52
Hemmesta S 96 Ha43
Hemmet DK 108 Cd25
Hemmingen D 126 Db37
Hemmingen D 134 Cc48
Hemmingen S 80 Ha25
Hemmingsjord N 67 Gc11
Hemmingsmark S 73 Hc23
Hemmingstedt D 118 Da30
Hemmonranta FIN 82 La30
Hemmoor D 118 Da32
Hemnes N 94 Eb42
Hemnesberget N 71 Fb21
Hemsbach D 134 Cc45
Hemse S 104 Ha50
Hemsedal N 85 Db38
Hemsjö S 102 Ec48
Hemslingen D 118 Db34
Hemsö S 88 Gd32
Hemyock GB 19 Ea30
Hen N 85 Dd40
Henån S 102 Eb47
Henarejos E 54 Ed66
Hencida H 147 Ka53
Henclová SK 138 Jb48
Hendaye F 39 Ec55
Hendek TR 187 Gd78
Hendungen D 134 Db43
Henfield GB 20 Fc30
Henfort GB 18 Dc30
Henfort GB 18 Dc30
Hengelo NL 117 Bd36
Hengelo NL 125 Bc37
Hengersberg D 135 Ec49
Hengevelde NL 117 Bd36
Heni N 93 Ea41
Heničes'k UA 205 Fa17
Hénin-Beaumont F 23 Ha31
Henley GB 20 Ed25
Henley-on-Thames GB 20 Fb28
Henllys GB 19 Eb27
Hennan S 87 Ga34
Hennebont F 27 Ea40
Hennef D 125 Ca41
Henne Stationsby DK 108 Cd25
Henne Strand DK 108 Cd25
Hennickendorf D 128 Fa36
Hennigsdorf D 127 Ed36
Henning N 78 Ec28
Henningen D 119 Dd35
Henningskälen S 79 Fc28
Henningsvær N 66 Fb14
Hennstedt D 118 Da30
Henrichemont F 29 Ha42
Henriksdal FIN 89 Hd34
Henryków PL 129 Gc42
Henrykowo PL 122 Hd30
Hensås N 85 Db37
Henstedt-Ulzburg D 118 Db32
Henstridge GB 19 Ec30
Hentorp S 102 Fa47
Hentula FIN 91 Lb35
Heol Senni GB 15 Ea26
Hepberg D 135 Dd48
Hepojoki FIN 97 Jc39
Hepola FIN 74 Jc21
Heppenheim D 134 Cc45
Herad N 85 Dc38
Herad N 92 Cb47
Heradsbygd N 86 Eb38
Herajärvi FIN 83 Ma30
Herajoki FIN 83 Ld29
Herajoki FIN 90 Kb38
Heraklion = Iráklio GR 200 Da95
Herakulma FIN 90 Ka34
Herálec CZ 136 Fd46
Herand N 84 Cc39
Heraniemi FIN 83 Ld29
Herăști RO 180 Eb67
Herbault F 29 Gb41
Herbeli AL 182 Ad74
Herbern D 125 Cb38
Herbertingen D 142 Cd51
Herbertstown IRL 12 Bd23
Herbeumont B 132 Ad44
Herbignac F 27 Ec41
Herbisse F 24 Hd37
Herbitzheim F 25 Kb35
Herbolzheim D 141 Ca50
Herborn D 126 Cc42
Herbrechtingen D 134 Db49
Herbsleben D 126 Dc41
Herbstein D 126 Cd42
Herby PL 130 Hc42
Herceg-Novi MNE 159 Hc69
Hercegovac HR 152 Gd59
Hercegszántó H 153 Hc58
Herdal N 76 Cd33
Herdecke D 125 Ca39
Herdla N 84 Bd38
Herdorf D 125 Cb41
Herdwangen-Schönach D 142 Cd51
Hereclean RO 171 Cd56
Hereford GB 15 Eb26
Héreg H 145 Hb52
Hereke TR 186 Ga78
Herencia E 52 Dd68
Herencsény H 146 Hd51
Herend H 145 Ha54
Herentals B 124 Ad39
Herépian F 41 Hb54
Herfølge DK 109 Eb26
Herford D 126 Cd37
Herguijuela E 51 Cb67
Héric F 28 Ed41
Héricourt F 31 Ka40
Héricourt-en-Caux F 23 Ga34
Hérimoncourt F 31 Kb41
Heringen D 126 Db41
Heringsdorf D 119 Dd30
Heringsdorf D 120 Fb31
Heriot GB 11 Ec13
Herisau CH 142 Cd53
Hérisson F 29 Ha44
Herjangen N 67 Gb13
Herk-de-Stad B 124 Ba40
Herl'any SK 139 Jd48
Herleshausen D 126 Db41
Herlev DK 109 Ec25
Herlies F 23 Ha31
Herlufmagle DK 109 Eb27
Herm F 39 Fa53
Hermagor A 143 Ed56
Hermannsburg D 118 Db35
Heřmanova Hut' CZ 135 Ed46
Heřmanovice CZ 137 Gd44
Hermanowice PL 139 Kc45
Hermansverk N 84 Cd37
Heřmanův Městec CZ 136 Ga45
Hermaringen D 134 Db49
Hérmedes de Cerrato E 46 Db60
Herment F 33 Ha47
Hermes F 23 Gd35
Hermeskeil D 133 Bd45
Hermsdorf D 127 Ea42
Hermsdorf D 128 Fa40
Hermsdorf D 128 Fa42
Hernádkécs H 147 Jd50
Hernádnémeti H 146 Jc51
Hernani E 39 Ec55
Hernansancho E 46 Cd63
Herne D 125 Ca39
Herne Bay GB 21 Gb28
Herning DK 108 Da24
Herold D 127 Ec42
Heroldsbach D 134 Dc45
Heroldsberg D 135 Dd46
Herongen D 125 Bc39
Herónia GR 189 Bd85
Herónissos GR 195 Cd90
Herøyholmen N 70 Ed21
Herpont F 24 Ja36
Herråkra S 103 Fd52
Herrala FIN 90 Kc37
Herräng S 96 Ha41
Herraskylä FIN 89 Jd33
Herrberga S 103 Fd47
Herre N 93 Dc44
Herrefoss N 93 Da46
Herrenberg D 134 Cc49
Herrera E 60 Cc74
Herrera de Alcántara E 51 Bb66
Herrera del Duque E 52 Cc68
Herrera de los Navarros E 47 Fa62
Herrera de Pisuerga E 38 Db57
Herrere F 39 Fb56
Herreros de Jamuz E 37 Cb58
Herreros de Suso E 46 Cd63
Herreruela E 51 Bc67
Herreruela de Castillería E 38 Db56
Herrestad S 102 Eb47
Herrestrup DK 109 Eb25
Herrieden D 134 Db47
Herrischried D 141 Ca52
Herrljunga S 102 Ed48
Herrngiersdorf D 135 Eb49
Herrnhut D 128 Fc41
Herrö S 87 Fb34
Herröskaten FIN 96 Hc41
Herrsching D 143 Dd51
Herrskog S 80 Gc31
Herrstein D 133 Bd45
Herrup DK 100 Da23
Herry F 30 Hb42
Hersbruck D 135 Dd46
Herschbach D 125 Ca42
Herscheid D 125 Cb40
Herselt B 124 Ad40
Hérso GR 183 Ca76
Herstadberg S 103 Ga46
Hersvik N 84 Ca36
Herten D 125 Ca38
Hertford GB 20 Fc27
Hertnik SK 139 Jd47
Hertsånger S 80 Hc27
Herttuansaari FIN 91 Ld33
Herukka FIN 74 Ka23
Hervanta FIN 89 Jd36
Hervás E 45 Cb64
Herve B 125 Bb41
Herveland N 92 Cb46
Herves E 36 Ba54
Hervik N 92 Ca42
Herxheim D 133 Cb47
Herzberg D 119 Ed35
Herzberg D 127 Ed39
Herzberg am Harz D 126 Dc39
Herzebrock-Clarholz D 126 Cc38
Herzfeld D 126 Cc38
Herzfelde D 128 Fa36
Herzhorn D 118 Db32
Herzlake D 117 Cb35
Herzogenaurach D 134 Dc46
Herzogenbuchsee CH 141 Bd53
Herzogenburg A 144 Ga50
Herzogenrath D 125 Bb41
Herzsprung D 119 Ec34
Hesby N 92 Ca43
Hesdin F 23 Gc32
Hesel D 117 Cb33
Heskestad N 92 Cb45
Hesnæs DK 109 Eb28
Hespe D 126 Cd36
Hesperange L 133 Bb45
Hesselager DK 109 Dd27
Hesselbjerg DK 100 Da21
Hessellund DK 100 Db23
Hessen D 126 Dc38
Hesseng N 65 Kd07
Hessfjord N 62 Gd08
Hessisch Lichtenau D 126 Da40
Hessisch Oldendorf D 126 Da37
Hessvik N 84 Cb40
Hestad N 84 Cb36
Hestad N 92 Cb45
Hesteneset N 64 Jb09
Hestenesøyri N 84 Cc34
Hestmona N 70 Fa20
Hestnes N 64 Jb06
Hestnes N 66 Ga14
Heston GB 20 Fc28
Hestra S 102 Fa50
Hestra S 103 Fc48
Hestvika N 63 Hb08
Hestvika N 77 Dc29
Hetekylä FIN 74 Kb23
Hetényegyháza H 146 Ja55
Hetes H 145 Ha56
Hethpool GB 11 Ed14
Hetin SRB 174 Bc61
Hetta FIN 68 Ja13
Hettange-Grande F 25 Jd34
Hettensen D 126 Db39
Hetton-le-Hole GB 11 Fa17
Hettstedt D 127 Ea39
Hettstedt, Dienstedt- D 127 Dd42
Hetvebely H 152 Hb57
Hetzbach D 134 Cd45
Hetzerath D 133 Bc44
Heubach D 134 Da48
Heuchelheim D 126 Cc42
Heuchin F 23 Gd31
Heuchlingen D 134 Da48
Heudeber D 127 Dd38
Heumen NL 125 Bb38
Heusden NL 124 Ba38
Heusden-Zolder B 124 Ba40
Heusenstamm D 134 Cc44
Heustreu D 134 Db43
Heves H 146 Jb52
Hevilliers F 24 Jb37
Hevingham GB 17 Gb24
Héviz H 145 Gd55
Hevlín CZ 137 Gb49
Hevosmäki FIN 82 Kd28
Hevosoja FIN 90 Ka38
Hevosoja FIN 90 La36
Hevossuo FIN 90 Kd37
Hewas Water GB 18 Db32
Hexham GB 11 Ed16
Heybeli TR 199 Gc89
Heybrook Bay GB 19 Dd32
Heyerode D 126 Db40
Heygendorf D 127 Dd40
Heyrieux F 34 Jb47
Heysham GB 11 Eb19
Heytesbury GB 19 Ec29
Hickling GB 16 Fb23
Hickling Green GB 17 Gb24
Hickstead GB 20 Fc30
Hida RO 171 Cd57
Hidas H 153 Hc57
Hidasnémeti H 139 Jd49
Hiddenhausen D 126 Cd37
Hidinge S 95 Fc44
Hıdırdivani TR 192 Fc84
Hıdırköylü TR 197 Ed88
Hidișelu de Sus RO 170 Cb57
Hieflau A 144 Fc53
Hiekkaniemi FIN 75 Kc24
Hiendelaencina E 46 Dd62
Hierden NL 116 Bb36
Hiersac F 32 Fc47
Hietakylä FIN 82 La31
Hietalanperä FIN 82 Ka26
Hietana FIN 90 Kd37
Hietanen FIN 90 La34
Hietaniemi FIN 69 Kd15
Hietaniemi FIN 90 Kd35
Hietaperä FIN 83 Lb25
Hietaranta FIN 75 La21
Hietoinen FIN 90 Kb37
Higham GB 21 Ga26
Higham Ferrers GB 20 Fb25
Highampton GB 19 Dd30
High Bentham GB 11 Ec19
Highbridge GB 19 Eb29
Highclere GB 20 Fa28
High Easter GB 20 Fd27
High Ercall GB 15 Ec24
Higher Town GB 18 Cc32
High Halden GB 21 Ga29
High Hesket GB 11 Ec17
Highworth GB 20 Ed27
High Wycombe GB 20 Fb27
Higuera de Arjona E 60 Db72
Higuera de Calatrava E 60 Da73
Higuera de las Dueñas E 46 Da65
Higuera de la Serena E 51 Ca70
Higuera de la Sierra E 59 Bd72
Higuera de Llerena E 51 Ca70
Higuera de Vargas E 51 Bb70
Higuera la Real E 51 Bc71
Higueruela E 54 Ed69
Higueruelas E 54 Fa67
Hihnavaara FIN 69 Kc15
Hiidenkylä FIN 82 Kb28
Hiidenlahti FIN 83 Lb30
Hiidensaari FIN 90 Kd36
Hiirijärvi FIN 89 Jb36

Hiirola – Horodyszcze

Hiirola FIN 90 La34
Hiisi FIN 82 La27
Hiisijärvi FIN 82 La25
Hiitelä FIN 90 Kc37
Hiittinen FIN 97 Jc41
Hijar E 48 Fb62
Hijdieni MD 173 Fa55
Hijosa E 38 Db57
Hikiä FIN 90 Kb38
Hilchenbach D 125 Cb41
Hildburghausen D 134 Dc43
Hilden D 125 Bd40
Hilders D 126 Db42
Hildesheim D 126 Db37
Hildre N 76 Cc32
Hilgermissen D 118 Da35
Hilgertshausen D 143 Dd50
Hiliódendro GR 182 Ba78
Hiliomódi GR 195 Bd87
Hilișeu-Horia RO 172 Ec54
Hiliuți MD 173 Fa55
Hiliuți MD 173 Fb56
Hill GB 19 Ec27
Hilla FIN 98 Ka40
Hillared S 102 Ed49
Hille D 126 Cd36
Hille S 95 Gb39
Hillegom NL 116 Ad35
Hillerød DK 109 Ec25
Hillersboda S 95 Ga39
Hillerse D 126 Dc36
Hillerslev DK 100 Da21
Hillerslev DK 108 Dc27
Hillerstorp S 102 Fa50
Hillesheim D 133 Bc43
Hilleshög S 96 Gc43
Hillesøy N 62 Gc10
Hillestad N 93 Dd43
Hillested DK 109 Ea29
Hillhead GB 10 Dd16
Hilliä FIN 81 Jc27
Hilliä FIN 90 Kb36
Hillington GB 17 Ga24
Hillion F 26 Eb38
Hillmersdorf D 128 Fa39
Hillo FIN 90 La38
Hill of Fearn GB 5 Ea07
Hillosensalmi FIN 90 Kd36
Hillringsberg S 94 Ed43
Hillsand S 79 Fd28
Hillsborough GB 9 Da18
Hillswick GB 5 Ed04
Hilltown GB 9 Da18
Hilmiye TR 192 Ga81
Hilok RUS 99 Ma42
Hilovo RUS 107 Mb46
Hilpoltstein D 135 Dd47
Hilsenheim F 31 Kc38
Hiltenfingen D 142 Dc50
Hilter D 126 Cc37
Hiltpoltstein D 135 Dd46
Hiltula FIN 91 Lb33
Hiltulanlahti FIN 82 La30
Hiltunen FIN 75 Lb20
Hiltusen vaara FIN 75 La22
Hilvarenbeek NL 124 Ba38
Hilversum NL 116 Ba36
Hilzingen D 142 Cc51
Himalansaari FIN 90 La35
Himanka FIN 81 Jc27
Himankakylä FIN 81 Jc27
Himarë AL 182 Ab78
Himaros GR 183 Cb76
Himbergen D 119 Dd34
Himesháza H 153 Hc57
Himki RUS 202 Ed10
Himmelberg A 144 Fa55
Himmelkron D 135 Ea44
Himmelpforten D 118 Da32
Himmelstadt D 134 Da44
Himmeta S 95 Ga43
Himmetoğlu TR 187 Hb76
Hinbjørgen N 78 Eb31
Hincăuți MD 173 Fa53
Hincești MD 173 Fc58
Hinckley GB 16 Fa24
Hindår FIN 98 Kc39
Hindås S 102 Ec49
Hindelang, Bad D 142 Db53
Hindeloopen NL 116 Bb34
Hindersby FIN 90 Kd38
Hindersön S 73 Ja22
Hindhead GB 20 Fb29
Hindsby FIN 98 Kc39
Hindsig DK 108 Cd25
Hınıs TR 205 Ga20
Hinișeni MD 173 Fc56
Hinka GR 182 Ad80
Hinna N 92 Ca44
Hinnerjoki FIN 89 Jb37
Hinnerup DK 100 Dc23
Hinneryd S 110 Fa53
Hinojal E 51 Bd66
Hinojales E 51 Bc71
Hinojar E 55 Ed73
Hinojares E 61 Dd73
Hinojos E 59 Bd74
Hinojosa de la Sierra E 47 Ea60
Hinojosa del Duque E 52 Cc70
Hinojosa del Valle E 51 Bd70
Hinojosas de Calatrava E 52 Da70
Hinova RO 174 Cb65
Hinsala FIN 89 Jd36
Hinstock GB 15 Ec23
Hinte D 117 Ca32
Hinterbichl A 143 Eb54
Hinterrhein CH 142 Cc56
Hinterriß A 143 Dd53
Hintersee A 143 Ed52
Hintersee D 120 Fb33
Hinterstoder A 144 Fb52
Hintertux A 143 Dd54
Hinterweidenthal D 133 Ca47
Hinterzarten D 141 Ca51
Hinthaara FIN 98 Kc39
Hinwil CH 142 Cc53
Hio E 36 Ac57
Hióna GR 188 Ba86
Hios GR 191 Dd86
Hippolytushoef NL 116 Ba34
Hipstedt D 118 Da33
Hîrbovaț MD 173 Ga58
Hircești MD 173 Fb56
Hird H 152 Hb57
Hirel F 28 Ed38
Hirjău MD 173 Fd55
Hırka TR 198 Fc89
Hırkalı TR 192 Fb84
Hırkatepe TR 187 Hb80
Hirla EST 98 La43
Hirova MD 173 Fc56
Hirsala FIN 98 Kb40
Hirschaid D 134 Dc45
Hirschau A 142 Da53
Hirschau D 135 Ea46
Hirschbach D 135 Ea46
Hirschberg D 134 Cc46
Hirschegg A 142 Da53
Hirschegg-Rein A 144 Fc55
Hirschfeld D 128 Fa40
Hirschfelde D 128 Fc42
Hirschhorn D 134 Cc46
Hirsijärvi FIN 74 Kb24
Hirsikangas FIN 83 Lb27
Hirsilä FIN 90 Ka34
Hirsingue F 31 Kb40
Hirsjärvi FIN 89 Jd38
Hirson F 24 Hc33
Hirtolahti FIN 90 Ka35
Hirtop MD 173 Fc59
Hirtop MD 173 Ga57
Hirtopul Mare MD 173 Fd57
Hirtshals DK 100 Dc19
Hirtzfelden F 31 Kc39
Hirvaanmäki FIN 82 Kb31
Hirvälä FIN 97 Jd39
Hirvas FIN 74 Jd19
Hirvaskoski FIN 75 Kc22
Hirvasniemi FIN 74 Ka24
Hirvassalmi FIN 69 Jd12
Hirvasvaara FIN 74 Kd18
Hirvelä FIN 83 Lc25
Hirvelä FIN 90 La37
Hirveläpää FIN 89 Ja32
Hirvenlahti FIN 90 Kd34
Hirvensalmi FIN 90 Kd34
Hirviäkuru FIN 69 Ka16
Hirvihaara FIN 90 Kb38
Hirvijärvi FIN 82 Kd27
Hirvijärvi FIN 82 Kd30
Hirvijärvi FIN 89 Ja34
Hirvijärvi FIN 90 Ka38
Hirvijärvi S 73 Ja19
Hirvijoki FIN 81 Jc31
Hirvikangas FIN 90 Kb32
Hirvikoski FIN 90 Kd38
Hirvikylä FIN 90 Ka32
Hirvilahti FIN 82 Kd30
Hirvimäki FIN 90 Kb33
Hirviperä FIN 89 Jc34
Hirvipohja FIN 90 Kc34
Hirvisalo FIN 90 Kd36
Hirvivaara FIN 75 Lb24
Hirvlax FIN 81 Ja29
Hirwaun GB 19 Ea27
Hirzenhain D 134 Cd43
Hisar TR 198 Fd90
Hisar TR 199 Gc89
Hisaralan TR 192 Fb83
Hisarardı TR 197 Fa89
Hisarcık TR 192 Fd83
Hisarja BG 180 Db72
Hisarköy TR 193 Ha84
Hisarlık TR 187 Gb80
Hisarönü Köy TR 198 Fd92
Hischberg D 135 Ea43
Hishult S 110 Fa53
Hisingen S 102 Eb49
Hiski RUS 99 Lb40
Hislaviči RUS 202 Ec12
Hisøy N 93 Da46
Hissjön S 80 Hb28
Histijanovo BG 180 Dd73
Hita E 46 Dd63
Hitcham GB 21 Ga26
Hitchin GB 20 Fc26
Hitiaș RO 174 Bd61
Hitis FIN 97 Jc41
Hitovo BG 181 Fa68
Hitra N 77 Dc29
Hittarp S 110 Ec54
Hittisau A 142 Da53
Hitzacker D 119 Dd34
Hitzhofen D 135 Dd48
Hiukamaa FIN 89 Jd33
Hiukkaa FIN 90 Ka34
Hiukkajoki FIN 91 Ld33
Hızırkahya TR 199 Gb93
Hjäggsjö S 80 Hb28
Hjallerup DK 100 Dc20
Hjällstad S 94 Ed39
Hjälmseryd S 103 Fc50
Hjälmsjö S 110 Ed54
Hjälsta S 96 Gc42
Hjälstad S 103 Fb46
Hjältevad S 103 Fd49
Hjärnarp S 110 Ed53
Hjärsås S 111 Fb54
Hjartdal N 93 Db42
Hjärtum S 102 Ec47
Hjarup DK 108 Db26
Hjelle N 84 Cc34
Hjelle N 85 Da36
Hjellestad N 84 Ca39
Hjelm DK 109 Eb28
Hjelmeland N 92 Cb43
Hjelmset N 70 Ed24
Hjelset N 77 Da31
Hjemås N 66 Fd17
Hjerkinn N 85 Dd34
Hjerm DK 100 Da23
Hjerpsted DK 108 Cd27
Hjerting DK 108 Cd26
Hjo S 103 Fb47
Hjøllund DK 108 Db24
Hjordkær DK 108 Db27
Hjørring DK 100 Dc19
Hjortdal DK 100 Db20
Hjorte DK 108 Dc26
Hjorted S 103 Ga49
Hjorteset N 84 Cb35
Hjortkvarn S 95 Fd45
Hjortsberga S 103 Fb52
Hjortshøj DK 100 Dc23
Hjulsbro S 103 Fd47
Hjulsjö S 95 Fc42
Hlebine HR 152 Gc57
Hlevacha UA 202 Ec14
Hligeni MD 173 Fd55
Hlina MD 172 Ed53
Hlinaia MD 173 Fa54
Hlinaia MD 173 Ga57
Hlinky CZ 135 Ec44
Hlinsko CZ 136 Ga45
Hlipiceni RO 172 Ed56
Hljabovo BG 185 Ea74
Hlobyne UA 204 Ed15
Hlohovec SK 145 Ha50
Hlubočky CZ 137 Gd46
Hluboká nad Vltavou CZ 136 Fb48
Hluchiv UA 202 Ed13
Hlučín CZ 137 Ha45
Hluk CZ 137 Gd48
Hlusk BY 202 Eb13
Hlybokae BY 202 Ea11
Hniezdne SK 138 Jb46
Hnilec SK 138 Jb48
Hnivan' UA 204 Eb15
Hnjótur IS 2 Ab02
Hnojník CZ 137 Hb45
Hnúšťa SK 138 Ja49
Hobeck D 127 Eb38
Hõbesalu EST 98 Ka45
Hobița RO 175 Cc62
Hobol H 152 Ha58
Hobro DK 100 Dc22
Hocaköy TR 187 Gb78
Hocaköy TR 187 Hb78
Hocalar TR 193 Gb86
Hocalı TR 199 Hb91
Hocaş TR 187 Hb80
Hoceni RO 173 Fb59
Höchberg D 134 Da45
Hochburg A 143 Ec51
Hochdonn D 118 Da31
Höchenschwand D 141 Ca51
Hochfinstermünz A 142 Db55
Hochgurgl A 142 Dc55
Hochheim D 133 Cb44
Höchheim D 134 Dc43
Hochnaukirchen A 145 Gb53
Hochspeyer D 133 Ca46
Höchst CH 142 Cd53
Höchst D 134 Cd45
Hochstadt D 133 Cb46
Höchstädt D 134 Db49
Höchstadt D 134 Dc45
Höchstädt D 135 Ea44
Höchstädt D 135 Eb44
Hochwolkersdorf A 145 Gb52
Hoçisht AL 182 Ba77
Hockenheim D 134 Cc46
Hockley Heath GB 20 Ed25
Hoczew PL 139 Kb46
Hodac RO 172 Dd58
Hodal N 86 Eb33
Hodász H 147 Kb51
Hodde DK 108 Da25
Hoddesdon GB 20 Fc27
Hoddevika N 76 Ca33
Hodejov SK 146 Ja50
Hodenhagen D 118 Da35
Hodkovice nad Mohelkou CZ 128 Fc42
Hódmezővásárhely H 146 Jb56
Hodnanes N 92 Ca41
Hodnet GB 15 Ec23
Hodod RO 171 Cd56
Hodøl N 86 Ec33
Hodonín CZ 137 Gd48
Hodoš SLO 145 Gb55
Hodoșa RO 171 Dc59
Hodošan HR 152 Gc57
Hodrua-Hámre SK 146 Hc50
Hodsager DK 100 Da23
Hodslavice CZ 137 Ha46
Hodul TR 185 Ed80
Hoegaarden B 124 Ad41
Hoek NL 124 Ab38
Hoek van Holland NL 116 Ac36
Hoenderloo NL 117 Bc36
Hoeselt B 124 Ba41
Hoetmar D 125 Cb38
Hof D 135 Ea43
Hof N 93 Dd42
Hof N 93 Dd43
Hofbieber D 126 Da42
Höfen A 142 Db53
Höfen D 134 Cc48
Höfer D 118 Dc35
Hoff N 76 Cc32
Hoffen F 25 Kc36
Hofgeismar D 126 Da39
Hofheim D 134 Cc44
Hofheim D 134 Dc44
Hofkirchen A 144 Fa51
Hofkirchen D 135 Ed49
Hofkirchen im Traunkreis A 144 Fb51
Hofles N 78 Ec25
Höfn IS 3 Bb06
Hofors S 95 Ga39
Hofsós IS 2 Ba03
Hofsøy N 67 Gb11
Hofstad N 78 Ea27
Hofstätten A 144 Ga54
Hofstetten D 142 Dc51
Hofsvík IS 2 Ac04
Hög S 87 Gb35
Höga S 102 Eb48
Höganäs S 110 Ec54
Högås S 80 Gc26
Högås S 102 Eb47
Högbo S 95 Gb39
Högbränna S 72 Gc23
Högbränna S 72 Ha23
Högby S 104 Gc51
Högdal S 93 Ea44
Høgebru N 84 Cd36
Högen S 94 Eb45
Högerund S 94 Ed43
Høgeset N 85 Da37
Högfors S 95 Fc41
Högfors S 95 Ga41
Höggais FIN 97 Jb40
Höggeröd S 102 Eb47
Högheden S 73 Hb24
Hoghilag RO 175 Dc60
Hoghiz RO 176 Dd61
Høgild DK 108 Da24
Hogland RUS 98 La39
Högland S 79 Fd26
Högland S 80 Ha29
Högland S 87 Gb35
Höglekardalen S 79 Fb31
Höglunda S 79 Fd31
Högnabba FIN 81 Jc29
Hogne B 124 Ba42
Hognes N 78 Ed25
Högsåra FIN 97 Jb41
Högsäter S 102 Ec46
Högsätter S 94 Ec42
Högsbo S 95 Gb41
Högsby S 103 Ga51
Högsjö S 88 Gc32
Högsjö S 95 Fd44
Högsön S 73 Ja21
Hogstad S 103 Fc47
Høgstadgård N 67 Gd12
Högstena S 102 Fa47
Högträsk S 73 Hb19
Högvålen S 86 Ed34
Högvalta S 94 Ed42
Hőgyész H 146 Hc56
Hohberg D 133 Ca49
Hohburg D 127 Ec40
Hoheleye D 126 Cc40
Hohen D 128 Fa36
Hohenahr D 126 Cc42
Hohenaspe D 118 Db31
Hohenau A 137 Gc49
Hohenau D 135 Ed48
Hohenberg A 144 Ga52
Hohenberg D 135 Eb44
Hohenbocka D 128 Fa40
Hohenbrunn D 143 Ea51
Hohenbucko D 127 Ed39
Hohenems A 142 Cd53
Hohenfels D 135 Ea47
Hohenfurch D 142 Dc51
Hohengörsdorf D 127 Ed38
Hohenhameln D 126 Db37
Höhenkirchen D 143 Ea51
Hohenleipisch D 128 Fa40
Hohenleuben D 127 Eb42
Hohenlinden D 143 Ea51
Hohenlobese D 127 Eb37
Hohenlockstedt D 118 Db31
Hohenmocker D 119 Ed32
Hohenmölsen D 127 Eb41
Hohennauen D 127 Eb36
Hohen Neuendorf D 127 Ed36
Hohenpolding D 143 Eb50
Hohenroth D 134 Db43
Hohensaaten D 120 Fb35
Hohenseeden D 127 Eb37
Hohenseefeld D 127 Ed38
Hohenselchow D 120 Fb34
Hohen Sprenz D 119 Eb31
Hohenstein D 133 Cb43
Hohenstein D 142 Cd50
Hohenstein-Ernstthal D 127 Ec42
Hohentauern A 144 Fb53
Hohentengen D 142 Cd51
Hohenthann D 135 Eb49
Hohen Wangelin D 119 Ec32
Hohenwarsleben D 127 Ea37
Hohenwart D 135 Dd49
Hohenwarth A 144 Ga50
Hohenwarth D 135 Ec47
Hohenwestedt D 118 Db31
Hohenziatz D 127 Eb37
Hohn D 118 Db30
Hohne D 126 Dc36
Höhnhart A 143 Ed51
Höhnhart A 143 Ed52
Höhnstedt D 127 Ea39
Hohnstein D 128 Fb41
Hohnstorf D 118 Dc33
Hoho FIN 90 Kc32
Höhr-Grenzhausen D 125 Ca42
Hohwacht D 119 Dd30
Høiby DK 109 Eb25
Hoikankylä FIN 82 Kd31
Hoikka FIN 75 La24
Hoilola FIN 83 Ma31
Hoisko FIN 81 Jd30
Højby DK 109 Dd27
Højen DK 101 Dd19
Højer DK 108 Cd28
Højerup DK 109 Ec27
Højmark DK 108 Cd24
Højslev DK 100 Db22
Højslev Stationsby DK 100 Db22
Hojsova Stráž CZ 135 Ed47
Hok S 103 Fb50
Hökåsen S 95 Gb42
Hökhuvud S 96 Gd40
Hokka FIN 90 Kd33
Hokkåsen N 94 Ec40
Hokkaskylä FIN 89 Jd33
Hokksund N 93 Dd42
Hokland N 66 Ga12
Hökmark S 81 Hd26
Hökön S 111 Fb53
Hököpinge S 110 Ed56
Hokstad N 78 Eb28
Hökvattnet S 79 Fc28
Hol N 77 Dd31
Hol N 85 Da39
Holand N 66 Fc14
Holand N 79 Fb26
Holandsvika N 70 Fa21
Holapantörmä FIN 75 Kc23
Hola Prystan' UA 204 Ed17
Hólar IS 2 Ba03
Holasovice CZ 137 Ha44
Holbæk DK 101 Dd22
Holbæk DK 109 Eb25
Holbeach GB 17 Fd24
Holbeach Saint Matthew GB 17 Fd23
Holboca RO 173 Fa57
Holbøl DK 108 Db28
Holdenstedt D 127 Ea40
Holdorf D 117 Cc35
Holdre EST 106 Kd47
Høle N 92 Ca44
Hole N 93 Dd41
Hole S 94 Fa41
Holeby DK 109 Ea29
Hølen N 93 Ea43
Holercani MD 173 Fd57
Holešov CZ 137 Gd47
Holevik N 84 Ca35
Holford GB 19 Ea29
Holguera E 45 Bd65
Holíč SK 137 Gd49
Holice CZ 136 Ga44
Holice SK 145 Gd51
Hölick S 88 Gc36
Holiseva FIN 90 Ka34
Holja FIN 90 Ka36
Höljäkka FIN 83 Lc28
Höljes S 86 Ed38
Holkestad N 66 Fc15
Holkonkylä FIN 89 Jd32
Holla N 77 Dc30
Hollabrunn A 136 Ga49
Hollád H 145 Gd56
Hollandstoun GB 5 Ed02
Hollange B 132 Ba44
Holle D 126 Db37
Holleben D 127 Ea40
Høllen N 92 Cd47
Hollenfels L 133 Bb44
Hollenstedt D 118 Db33
Hollerath D 125 Bc42
Hollern-Twielenfleth D 118 Db32
Hollersbach A 143 Eb54
Hollfeld D 135 Dd45
Hollingsholm N 76 Cd31
Hollóháza H 139 Jd49
Hollókő H 146 Ja51
Hollola FIN 90 Kc37
Hollolan FIN 90 Kb37
Hollstadt D 134 Db43
Hollum NL 117 Bc32
Höllviken S 110 Ed57
Hollybush GB 10 Dd15
Hollyford IRL 13 Ca23
Hollyfort IRL 13 Cd23
Hollymount IRL 8 Bc20
Hollywood IRL 13 Cd22
Holm D 118 Db32
Holm DK 108 Db27
Holm FIN 81 Jb28
Holm N 66 Fd12
Holm N 70 Ed24
Holm N 77 Da32
Holm N 93 Ea44
Holm RUS 202 Eb10
Holm S 87 Gb32
Holm S 94 Ec45
Holm S 96 Gc42
Holma FIN 90 Ka35
Hólmavík IS 2 Ad03
Holme S 79 Gb30
Holmedal N 92 Cb41
Holmedal S 94 Ec43
Holmegil N 94 Eb44
Holmen N 70 Fa23
Holmenkollen N 93 Ea41
Holme-Olstrup DK 109 Eb27
Holme-on-Spalding-Moor GB 16 Fb20
Holmes Chapel GB 15 Ec22
Holmestad S 102 Fa46
Holmestrand N 93 Dd43
Holmfirth GB 16 Ed21
Holmfors S 72 Gc24
Holmfors S 73 Hb23
Holmfors S 73 Hc24
Holmisperä FIN 82 Ka29
Holmmo N 78 Fa25
Holmön S 80 Hc28
Holmøyane N 84 Cc34
Holmsbu N 93 Dd42
Holmsjö S 72 Gd24
Holmsjö S 79 Fd31
Holmsjö S 80 Gc29
Holmsjö S 103 Ga52
Holmsjö S 111 Fd53
Holmskij RUS 205 Fc17
Holmstrand N 64 Jb09
Holmsund S 80 Hc29
Holmsvattnet S 80 Hc26
Holmsveden S 87 Gb37
Holmträsk S 73 Hc23
Holmträsk S 80 Hb25
Holmträsk S 80 Ha26
Holmträsk S 80 Gc28
Holmudden S 104 Hb48
Holmvassdalen N 70 Fa23
Holm-Žirkovskij RUS 202 Ec11
Hölö S 96 Gc44
Holod RO 170 Cb57
Holoșnița MD 173 Fc54
Holøydal N 86 Eb34
Holsbybrunn S 103 Fd50
Holsen N 84 Cc36
Holsljunga S 102 Ed50
Holstad N 78 Eb27
Holstebro DK 100 Da23
Holsted DK 108 Da26
Holsted Stationsby DK 108 Da26
Holstinmäki FIN 74 Ka23
Holsworthy GB 18 Dc30
Holt GB 17 Ga23
Holt N 93 Db45
Holtdalsvollen N 78 Eb31
Holte N 78 Ea31
Holten NL 117 Bd36
Holtet DK 101 Dd21
Holtgast D 117 Cb32
Holt Heath GB 15 Ec25
Holtsee D 118 Db30
Holtslåtten N 94 Eb39
Holum N 92 Cc47
Holungen D 126 Dc39
Holven N 84 Cc39
Holvika N 78 Eb26
Holwerd NL 117 Bc32
Holy Cross IRL 13 Ca23
Holyhead GB 14 Dc22
Holýšov CZ 135 Ed46
Holywell GB 15 Eb22
Holywell GB 19 Eb30
Holywood GB 9 Da17
Holzbach D 133 Ca44
Holzdorf D 127 Ed39
Holzgerlingen D 134 Cc49
Holzhausen D 133 Cb43
Holzheim D 134 Db49
Holzkirchen D 143 Ea52
Holzminden D 126 Da38
Holzthaleben D 126 Dc40
Holzweiler D 125 Bc40
Holzweißig D 127 Eb39
Holzwickede D 125 Ca39
Hömb S 103 Fb47
Homberg (Efze) D 126 Da41
Homberg (Ohm) D 126 Cd42
Homborsund N 93 Da47
Hombourg-Budange F 25 Jd35
Hombourg-Haut F 25 Ka35
Hombukt N 63 Hc08
Homburg am Main D 134 Da45
Homburg (Saar) D 133 Bd46
Homel' BY 202 Ec13
Homeshi AL 182 Ad74
Homme N 92 Cd46
Homme N 92 Cd46
Hommelstø N 70 Ed23
Hommelvik N 78 Eb30
Hommerts NL 116 Bb34
Homocea RO 176 Ed61
Homokszentgyörgy H 152 Ha57
Homoroade RO 171 Cd55
Homorod RO 176 Dd61
Hompland N 92 Cb45
Homps F 41 Ha55
Homrogd H 146 Jc50
Homstad N 78 Ec26
Homstean N 92 Cd46
Homutovka RUS 202 Ed13
Hømvejle DK 108 Da26
Hømyrfors S 73 Jb21
Honaz TR 198 Fd88
Honderribia E 39 Ec55
Hondelange B 132 Ba45
Hondón de las Nieves E 55 Fa71
Hondón de los Frailes E 55 Fa71
Hondschoote F 21 Gd30
Hønefoss N 85 Dd40
Honfleur F 22 Fd35
Høng DK 109 Ea26
Hongisto FIN 90 Ka38
Hongset N 70 Ed23
Hónikas GR 195 Bd87
Honing GB 17 Gb24
Honiton GB 19 Ea30
Honkajärvi FIN 89 Ja34
Honkajoki FIN 89 Jb34
Honkakoski FIN 82 Kd28
Honkakoski FIN 89 Ja35
Honkakylä FIN 89 Jb32
Honkalahti FIN 91 Lc35
Honkamäki FIN 83 Lb31
Honkamukka FIN 69 Kd15
Honkaperä FIN 82 Kb26
Honkaperä FIN 82 Kb28
Honkaranta FIN 82 Ka29
Honkilahti FIN 89 Jb37
Honkola FIN 82 Kb31
Honkola FIN 89 Jd37
Hønning DK 108 Da27
Honningsvåg N 64 Jc04
Hönö S 102 Eb49
Honrubia E 53 Eb67
Hønseby N 63 Hd06
Hontalbilla E 46 Db61
Hontanares E 46 Cd65
Hontanaya E 53 Ea67
Hontangas E 46 Dc60
Hontianske Nemce SK 146 Hc50
Hontoria del Pinar E 46 Dd60
Hoofddorp NL 116 Ad35
Hoofdplaat NL 124 Ab38
Hoogerheide NL 124 Ac38
Hoogersmilde NL 117 Bd34
Hoogeveen NL 117 Bd35
Hoogezand-Sappemeer NL 117 Ca33
Hooge Zwaluwe NL 124 Ad37
Hooghalen NL 117 Bd34
Hoogkarspel NL 116 Ba34
Hoogkerk NL 117 Bd33
Hoogstade B 21 Ha30
Hoogstede D 117 Ca35
Hoogstraten B 124 Ad38
Hook GB 20 Fb29
Hook Norten GB 20 Fa26
Hooksiel D 117 Cc32
Höör S 110 Fa55
Hoorn NL 116 Ba34
Hopa TR 205 Ga19
Hopârta RO 171 Da59
Hope GB 4 Dd04
Hope GB 15 Eb22
Hope GB 19 Dd32
Hope N 93 Db45
Hope Bowdler GB 15 Eb24
Hopen N 66 Fc14
Hopen N 66 Fd15
Hopen N 77 Db29
Hopfgarten A 143 Ea53
Hopfgarten A 143 Eb55
Höpfingen D 134 Cd46
Hôpital-Camfrout F 26 Dc38
Hopovo SRB 153 Jb60
Hoppegarten D 128 Fa36
Hoppula FIN 74 Kb19
Hopseidet N 64 Ka05
Hopsten D 117 Cb36
Hopsu FIN 90 Kb34
Hopton GB 17 Gc24
Hopton Wafers GB 15 Ec25
Hoptrup DK 108 Db27
Hóra GR 194 Ba89
Hóra GR 196 Db91
Hóra GR 197 Eb88
Horam GB 20 Fd30
Horasan TR 205 Ga19
Horasanlı TR 198 Fc89
Hóra Sfakíon GR 200 Cc95
Hora Svatého Kateřiny CZ 135 Ed43
Hora Svaté Šebestiána CZ 135 Ed43
Horaždovice CZ 136 Fa47
Horb am Neckar D 134 Cc49
Horbelev DK 109 Eb28
Horbury GB 16 Fa21
Hørby DK 100 Dc22
Hørby DK 101 Dd20
Hörby S 110 Fa55
Horcajada de la Torre E 53 Ea66
Horcajode las Torres E 46 Cd62
Horcajo de los Montes E 52 Cd68
Horcajo de Santiago E 53 Dd66
Horcajo Medianero E 45 Cc63
Horche E 46 Dd64
Horda S 103 Fb51
Hörda S 103 Fb51
Hordabø N 84 Ca38
Hordáki GR 200 Cc94
Hörden D 126 Dc39
Hordorf D 127 Dd38
Hørdum DK 100 Db21
Høre N 85 Db37
Horea RO 171 Cc59
Horeb GB 14 Dc26
Höreda S 103 Fc49
Horeftó GR 189 Ca81
Horémis GR 194 Bb88
Horești MD 173 Fa56
Horești MD 173 Fd58
Horezu RO 175 Da63
Horgau D 142 Dc50
Horgen CH 141 Cb53
Horgenzell D 142 Cd51
Hörgertshausen D 135 Ea49
Horgești RO 176 Ed60
Horgevik N 93 Da43
Horgheim N 77 Da33
Horgoš SRB 153 Jb57
Horhausen D 125 Ca42
Höri CH 141 Cb52
Horia RO 172 Ed58
Horia RO 177 Fb66
Horia RO 177 Fc64
Hořice CZ 136 Ga43
Hořice na Šumavě CZ 136 Fb49
Horigio GR 183 Ca76
Hořiněves CZ 136 Ga44
Horió GR 197 Eb90
Horistí GR 184 Cd76
Hörja S 110 Fa54
Horka D 128 Fc40
Horki BY 202 Eb12
Hörkkölä FIN 91 Lc35
Horlești RO 173 Fa57
Horley GB 20 Fc29
Horlivka UA 205 Fb15
Hörlösa S 103 Gb51
Hormakumpu FIN 68 Jc15
Hormanloukko FIN 81 Jb31
Hormigos E 46 Da65
Horn A 136 Ga49
Horn N 70 Ed23
Horn N 70 Fa21
Horn S 103 Fb46
Horn S 103 Ga48
Horna E 55 Ed70
Hornachos E 51 Ca70
Hornachuelos E 60 Cc72
Horná Súča SK 137 Ha48
Horn-Bad Meinberg D 126 Cd38
Hornbæk DK 109 Ec24
Hornberg D 141 Cb50
Hornberga S 87 Fc37
Hornburg D 126 Dc38
Horncastle GB 17 Fc22
Horndal S 95 Ga40
Horne DK 100 Dc19
Horne DK 108 Dc27
Hörnebo S 103 Fb47
Horneburg D 118 Db33
Hörnefors S 80 Hb29
Horné Motešice SK 137 Hb48
Horné Mýto SK 145 Ha51
Hornesund N 92 Cd46
Horní Bečva CZ 137 Hb46
Horní Benešov CZ 137 Gd45
Horní Blatná CZ 135 Ec43
Horní Bříza CZ 135 Ed45
Horní Cerekev CZ 136 Fd47
Horní Jelení CZ 136 Ga44
Horní Jiřetín CZ 135 Ed43
Horní Kněžeklady CZ 136 Fb47
Horní Kruty CZ 136 Fc45
Horní Lideč CZ 137 Ha47
Hornillatorre E 38 Dc56
Hornillos de Cerrato E 46 Db59
Hornindal N 84 Cc34
Horning DK 108 Dc24
Horning GB 17 Gb24
Horninglow GB 16 Ed23
Hornio FIN 89 Jc36
Horní Planá CZ 136 Fa49
Horní Slavkov CZ 135 Ec44
Horní Vltavice CZ 136 Fa48
Hornmyr S 80 Gd26
Hornnes N 92 Cd45
Hornoy-le-Bourg F 23 Gc33
Hornsea GB 17 Fc20
Hornsjø N 85 Ea37
Hörnsjö S 80 Ha28
Hornslet DK 100 Dc23
Hornstein A 145 Gb52
Hornsträsk S 73 Hb24
Hornsyld DK 108 Dc25
Hörnum D 108 Cd28
Hornum DK 100 Db21
Horný Tisovník SK 146 Hd50
Horoatu Crasnei RO 171 Cc56
Horochiv UA 204 Ea15
Horodca MD 173 Fc58
Horodenka UA 204 Ea16
Horodiște MD 173 Fa55
Horodiște MD 173 Fb54
Horodiște MD 173 Fc57
Horodiște MD 173 Fd56
Horodło PL 131 Kd40
Horodnic RO 172 Eb55
Horodniceni RO 172 Eb56
Horodnja UA 202 Ec13
Horodnycja UA 202 Eb14
Horodok UA 204 Ea15
Horodyšče UA 204 Ec15
Horodyszcze PL 131 Kb38

Horonkylä – Impalata

Horonkylä FIN 82 Kc30
Horonkylä FIN 89 Ja32
Horoszki Duże PL 131 Kb36
Hořovice CZ 136 Fa45
Hořovičky CZ 135 Ed44
Horoz TR 198 Ga89
Horrabridge GB 19 Dd31
Horred S 102 Ec50
Hörröd S 111 Fb55
Horrskog S 95 Gb40
Horsdal N 71 Fb18
Horse and Jockey IRL 13 Ca23
Horseleap IRL 13 Cb21
Horsens DK 108 Dc25
Horsham GB 20 Fc29
Hørsholm DK 109 Ec25
Horslunde DK 109 Ea28
Horsmanaho FIN 83 Lc30
Hörsne S 104 Ha49
Horšovský Týn CZ 135 Ec46
Horst D 118 Db32
Horst NL 125 Bc39
Hörstel D 117 Cb36
Horstmar D 125 Ca37
Horstwalde D 127 Ed38
Horsunlu TR 198 Fb88
Hort H 146 Ja52
Horta de Sant Joan E 48 Fd63
Hortas E 36 Ba55
Hortáta GR 188 Ac83
Hørte N 93 Da46
Horten N 93 Dd43
Hortes F 31 Jc40
Hortezuela E 47 Ea61
Hortiátis GR 183 Cb78
Hortigüela E 46 Dd59
Hortlax S 73 Hd23
Hortobágy H 147 Jd52
Horton GB 20 Ed30
Horton GB 20 Fb26
Horton-cum-Studley GB 20 Fa27
Horton in Ribbledale GB 11 Ec19
Hörup D 108 Da28
Hørup DK 108 Dc28
Hørve DK 109 Ea25
Horven N 78 Ec25
Hörvik S 111 Fc54
Horwich GB 15 Ec21
Horyniec PL 139 Kc43
Horyszów Ruski PL 131 Kd41
Horzamalayaka TR 192 Fb86
Horzum TR 192 Fa86
Horzumenbelli TR 192 Fb86
Hoşafoglu TR 187 Ha78
Hosanger N 84 Ca38
Hösbach D 134 Cd44
Hosby DK 108 Dc25
Hoscheid L 133 Bb44
Hosena D 128 Fa40
Hosenfeld D 134 Da43
Hoset N 66 Fc17
Hoset N 77 Da31
Hosiári GR 194 Bc90
Hosingen L 133 Bb43
Hosio FIN 74 Ka21
Hoslemo N 92 Cd42
Hospice de France F 40 Ga57
Hospital E 36 Bc56
Hospital E 40 Fd58
Hospital IRL 12 Bd24
Hospital de Órbigo E 37 Cb57
Hossa FIN 75 Lb21
Hossegor F 39 Ed54
Hössjö S 80 Hb28
Hössjön S 79 Fd28
Hössna S 102 Fa48
Hosszúhetény H 152 Hb57
Hosszúpályi H 147 Ka53
Hosszúpereszteg H 145 Gc54
Hostal de Ispiés E 40 Fc58
Hostalric E 49 Hb60
Hostens F 32 Fb51
Hostěradice CZ 137 Gb48
Hostikka FIN 91 Lb37
Hostinné CZ 136 Ga43
Hostivice CZ 136 Fb44
Hošťka CZ 136 Fb43
Hostomice CZ 136 Fa45
Höstoppen S 79 Fd28
Hostouň CZ 135 Ec46
Hostrupskov DK 108 Db27
Hotanlı TR 186 Fb80
Hotarele RO 180 Eb67
Hotaşlar TR 192 Fa82
Hotedršica SLO 151 Fa58
Hötensleben D 127 Dd37
Hoticy RUS 107 Ld46
Hoting S 79 Ga27
Hotneža RUS 99 Ma42
Hotnica BG 180 Dd70
Hotolisht AL 182 Ad75
Hotonj BIH 158 Hb68
Hotton B 124 Ba42
Hötzelsdorf A 136 Ga49
Hou DK 101 Dd21
Hou DK 108 Dc25
Houdain F 23 Gd31
Houdan F 23 Gc37
Houdelaincourt F 24 Jb37
Houeillès F 40 Fd52
Houetteville F 23 Gb36
Houffalize B 133 Bb43
Houghton-le-Spring GB 11 Fa17
Houhajärvi FIN 89 Jc36
Houlbjerg DK 100 Dc23
Houlgate F 22 Fc35
Houliarádes GR 182 Ad80
Houmnikó GR 184 Cc77
Hourtin F 32 Fa49
Hourtin-Plage F 32 Fa49
Houssay F 28 Fb40
Housukoski FIN 90 Ka32
Houten NL 124 Ba37
Houthalen-Helchteren B 124 Ba40
Houtsala FIN 97 Ja40
Houtskär FIN 97 Ja40
Houyet B 132 Ad43
Hov N 62 Gd09
Hov N 66 Ga13
Hov N 78 Eb26
Hov N 85 Dd39
Hov S 103 Fc47
Hov S 110 Ed53
Hova S 95 Fb45
Høvåg N 93 Da47
Hovås S 102 Eb49
Hovborg DK 108 Da26
Hovda N 92 Cb43
Hovden N 66 Fc12
Hove GB 20 Fc30
Hove N 84 Cb35
Hovedgård DK 108 Dc24
Hövej H 145 Gc53
Hövelhof D 126 Cd38
Hoven DK 108 Da25
Hovenäset S 102 Ea46
Hovet N 85 Da39
Hovězí CZ 137 Ha47
Hovi FIN 82 La30
Hovid S 88 Gc33
Hovika N 78 Ec26
Höviken S 94 Ed41
Höviksnäs S 102 Eb48
Hovin N 78 Ea31
Hovin N 93 Db41
Hovin N 93 Ea42
Hovinmäki FIN 90 La34
Hovinsalo FIN 90 Kd33
Hovland N 92 Cb45
Hovmantorp S 103 Fd52
Hovorany CZ 137 Gc48
Hovsherad N 92 Cb45
Hovslätt S 103 Fb49
Hovslund Stationsby DK 108 Db27
Hovsta S 95 Fd43
Hovsund N 66 Fb14
Hovsvågen N 70 Ed21
Howden GB 16 Fb20
Howmore GB 6 Cd08
Hownam GB 11 Ec15
Howth IRL 13 Da21
Höxter D 126 Da38
Hoya D 118 Da35
Hoya de Santa Maria E 59 Bd72
Hoya-Gonzalo E 54 Ed69
Høyanger N 84 Cb36
Høydalsmo N 93 Da42
Hoyerswerda D 128 Fb40
Høyholm N 70 Ed22
Høyjord N 93 Db43
Höykkylä FIN 81 Jc30
Höylä FIN 83 Lb28
Hoylake GB 15 Eb21
Høylandet N 78 Ed26
Hoyland Nether GB 16 Fa21
Hoym D 127 Dd38
Hoyocasero E 46 Cd64
Hoyo de Manzanares E 46 Db64
Hoyos E 45 Bd64
Höytiä FIN 90 Kb32
Høyvik N 63 Hc06
Høyvik N 84 Ca35
Hoz E 40 Fc57
Hozabejas E 38 Dc57
Hrabrovo RUS 113 Ja58
Hrabušice SK 138 Jb48
Hrabyně CZ 137 Ha45
Hradčany CZ 136 Fc43
Hradec Králové CZ 136 Ga44
Hradec nad Moravicí CZ 137 Ha45
Hradec nad Svitavou CZ 137 Gb46
Hrádek CZ 136 Fa46
Hrádek CZ 137 Gb49
Hrádek nad Nisou CZ 128 Fc42
Hradyz'k UA 204 Ed15
Hrafnagil IS 2 Ba04
Hrafnseyri IS 2 Ac02
Hráni GR 194 Bb88
Hranice CZ 135 Eb43
Hranice CZ 137 Ha46
Hraničné SK 138 Jc46
Hranovnica SK 138 Jb48
Hrastelnica HR 152 Gb60
Hrastje HR 152 Gb58
Hrastnik SLO 151 Fd57
Hrebenne PL 139 Kd43
Hrebinka UA 202 Ed14
Hredino RUS 99 Mb45
Hřensko CZ 128 Fb42
Hrhov SK 138 Jc49
Hrib-Loški Potok SLO 151 Fb59
Hriňová SK 138 Hd49
Hrísafa GR 194 Bc89
Hrísey IS 2 Ba03
Hříškov CZ 136 Fa44
Hrisópetra GR 183 Cb77
Hrisóstomos GR 196 Dd88
Hrissí GR 201 Db97
Hrissó GR 184 Cc76
Hrissoúpoli GR 184 Db77
Hrissovitsi GR 194 Bb87
Hristiáni GR 194 Ba88
Hristós GR 196 Dd88
Hristovaia MD 173 Fd54
Hrnjadi BIH 152 Gb63
Hrochův Týnec CZ 136 Ga45
Hrodna BY 202 Dd13
Hrómio GR 183 Bb79
Hrónia GR 189 Cb84
Hronov CZ 137 Gb43
Hronský Beňadik SK 146 Hc50
Hrostovice SK 139 Ka47
Hrotovice CZ 136 Ga48
Hroznětin CZ 135 Ec44
Hrtkovci SRB 153 Jb61
Hrubieszów PL 131 Kd41
Hrubov SK 139 Ka47
Hrud PL 131 Kb37
Hrușca MD 173 Fc54
Hrušica SLO 144 Fa56
Hrušica SLO 151 Fa58
Hrușova MD 173 Fd57
Hruštin SK 138 Hd47
Hrušuvacha UA 203 Fa14
Hrvaćani BIH 152 Ha62
Hrvace HR 158 Gc65
Hrvatska Dubica HR 152 Gc60
Hrvatska Kostajnica HR 152 Gc60
Hrženica HR 152 Gc57
Huaröd S 111 Fb55
Hubbo S 95 Gb42
Huben A 143 Eb55
Huby PL 129 Gb36
Hubynycha UA 205 Fa15
Huchet F 39 Ed53
Hückelhoven D 125 Bc40
Hückeswagen D 125 Ca40
Hucknall GB 16 Fa23
Hucqueliers F 23 Gc31
Huddersfield GB 16 Ed21
Huddunge S 95 Gb41
Hüde D 117 Cc36
Hude D 118 Cd34
Hudene S 102 Ed48
Hudënisht AL 182 Ad76
Hudești RO 172 Ec54
Hudiksvall S 87 Gb35
Huedin RO 171 Cd57
Huélago E 60 Dc74
Huélamo E 47 Ec65
Huelgoat F 26 Dd38
Huelma E 60 Dc73
Huelva E 59 Bb74
Huéneja E 61 Dd75
Huércal-Overa E 61 Ec74
Huércanos E 38 Ea58
Huergas E 37 Cb56
Huergas E 37 Cc56
Huérmeces E 38 Dc57
Huerta de Arriba E 46 Dd59
Huerta de la Obispalía E 53 Eb66
Huerta del Rey E 46 Dd60
Huerta de Valdecarábanos E 52 Dc66
Huertahernado E 47 Eb63
Huérteles E 47 Eb59
Huerto E 48 Fc60
Huesa E 61 Dd73
Huesa del Común E 47 Fa63
Huesca E 48 Fc59
Huéscar E 61 Ea73
Huete E 47 Ea65
Huétor Santillán E 60 Dc75
Huétor Tajar E 60 Da75
Hüfingen D 141 Cb51
Hugh Town GB 18 Cc32
Hugla N 70 Fa21
Hugley GB 15 Ec24
Huglfing D 143 Dd52
Huğlu TR 199 Hb89
Huhmarkoski FIN 81 Jc30
Huhtaa FIN 89 Jc36
Huhtala FIN 74 Jd21
Huhtalanniemi FIN 74 Jd18
Huhtamo FIN 89 Jc37
Huhtapuhto FIN 81 Jd27
Huhti FIN 89 Jd37
Huhtia FIN 90 Kb33
Huhtijärvi FIN 90 Ka33
Huhtilampi FIN 83 Ma31
Huhus FIN 83 Ma29
Huikkola FIN 83 Ma31
Huilliécourt F 31 Jc39
Huisheim D 134 Dc48
Huissen NL 125 Bc37
Huissinkylä FIN 81 Jb31
Huittinen FIN 89 Jc37
Huizen NL 116 Ba36
Hujakkala FIN 91 Lb37
Hujansalo FIN 90 Kd36
Hukanmaa S 68 Hd16
Hukkajärvi FIN 83 Ld25
Hukkala FIN 83 Lc30
Hukkala FIN 89 Jc32
Hulby DK 109 Ea27
Hulderbu N 85 Dc34
Hulín CZ 137 Gd47
Huljajpole UA 205 Fb15
Huljen S 87 Gb34
Hullbridge GB 21 Ga27
Hüllhorst D 126 Cd36
Hullo EST 97 Jd44
Hülsede D 126 Da37
Hulsig DK 101 Dd19
Hulst NL 124 Ac39
Hult S 95 Fb44
Hult S 103 Fd49
Hultafors S 102 Ed49
Hulterstad S 111 Gb53
Hultsfred S 103 Ga50
Hultsjö S 103 Fc50
Hulubești RO 176 Dd64
Huluboaia MD 177 Fc61
Hum BIH 159 Hd66
Hum HR 151 Fa60
Humada E 38 Db57
Humaloja FIN 82 Ka26
Humanby GB 17 Fc19
Humanes E 46 Dd63
Humberston GB 17 Fc21
Humble GB 11 Ec13
Humble DK 109 Dd28
Humenné SK 139 Ka47
Humes-Jorquenay F 30 Jb39
Humilladero E 60 Cd75
Humla S 102 Fa48
Humlebæk DK 109 Ec25
Humljani HR 152 Ha59
Humlum DK 100 Da22
Hummelholm S 80 Ha29
Hummelo NL 125 Bc37
Hummelsta S 95 Gb42
Hummelvik N 63 Hc07
Hummersö FIN 96 Hc41
Hummovaara FIN 91 Ld32
Hummuli EST 106 La47
Humpolec CZ 136 Fd46
Humppi FIN 82 Ka31
Humppila FIN 89 Jd37
Hunawihr F 31 Kb38
Hundåla N 70 Fa22
Hundberg N 62 Gd10
Hundberg S 72 Gd23
Hundborg DK 100 Da21
Hundeidvik N 76 Cc33
Hundelev DK 100 Dc20
Hundeluft D 127 Eb38
Hunderdorf D 135 Ec48
Hundeshagen D 126 Db40
Hundested DK 109 Eb25
Hundholmen N 66 Ga14
Hundisburg D 127 Ea37
Hundorp N 85 Dd36
Hundred House GB 15 Ea25
Hundsangen D 125 Cb42
Hundsbach D 133 Ca45
Hundsjö S 80 Ha29
Hundsjön S 73 Hd21
Hundslund DK 108 Dc25
Hundsnes N 76 Cb33
Hundvin N 84 Ca38
Hune DK 100 Dc20
Hunedoara RO 175 Cc61
Hünfeld D 126 Da42
Hunge S 87 Fc32
Hungen D 134 Cd43
Hungerford GB 20 Fa28
Hunnebostrand S 102 Ea46
Hunnefossen N 92 Ca46
Hunnestad S 102 Ec51
Hunspach F 25 Kc35
Hunstanton GB 17 Fd23
Huntingdon GB 20 Fc25
Huntley GB 19 Ec27
Huntly GB 7 Ec08
Hünxe D 125 Bd38
Huopana FIN 82 Kb30
Huopanankoski FIN 82 Kb30
Huparlac F 33 Ha50
Huppy F 23 Gc33
Hüpstedt D 126 Dc40
Hurbanovo SK 145 Hb52
Hurdal N 85 Ea40
Hurdegrave NL 117 Bc33
Hurezani RO 175 Cd64
Huriel F 33 Ha45
Hurissalo FIN 91 Lb34
Hurlers Cross IRL 12 Bc23
Hurliness GB 5 Eb03
Hurones E 38 Dc58
Hurskaala FIN 90 La32
Hurstbourne Priors GB 20 Fa29
Hurstbourne Tarrant GB 20 Fa29
Hurst Green GB 20 Fd30
Hurşunlu TR 193 Hb85
Hürtgenwald D 125 Bc41
Hürth D 125 Bd41
Hurttala FIN 91 Lb37
Huruiești RO 176 Ed60
Huruksela FIN 90 La38
Hurum N 93 Dd42
Hurup DK 100 Cd22
Huruslahti FIN 90 La32
Hurva S 110 Fa55
Hurworth-on-Tees GB 11 Fa18
Hurzuf UA 205 Fa18
Husa N 84 Cb40
Husa S 78 Fa30
Husaby S 102 Fa46
Húsafell IS 2 Ac04
Husasău de Tinca RO 170 Ca57
Húsavík IS 3 Bb03
Husbondliden S 80 Gd25
Husby D 108 Db28
Husby DK 100 Cd23
Husby N 70 Fa21
Husby S 95 Ga40
Husby-Ärlinghundra S 96 Gd42
Husby-Rekarne S 95 Ga43
Husby-Sjuhundra S 96 Ha42
Husby-Sjutolft S 96 Gc42
Hüseyin TR 199 Gb92
Hüseyinpaşalar TR 191 Ec82
Hushinish GB 4 Cd06
Huși RO 173 Fb59
Husinec CZ 136 Fa48
Huskvarna S 103 Fb49
Huslenky CZ 137 Ha47
Husnes N 92 Ca41
Husnicicara RO 175 Cc64
Husøy N 62 Gb10
Hustad N 76 Cd31
Hustopeče CZ 137 Gc48
Husula FIN 90 La38
Husula FIN 91 Lb36
Husum D 108 Da29
Husum D 126 Da36
Husum S 80 Ha30
Husum-Ballum DK 108 Cd27
Husvika N 70 Ed22
Huszlew PL 131 Kb37
Hutovo BIH 158 Hb68
Hüttenberg A 144 Fb55
Hüttenberg D 126 Cc42
Hüttenrode D 127 Dd39
Hütthurm D 135 Ed49
Hüttlingen D 134 Db48
Hutton Sessay GB 11 Fa19
Hüttschlag A 143 Ed54
Huttukylä FIN 74 Ka23
Huttula FIN 90 Ka33
Huttwil CH 141 Ca54
Huuhilo FIN 90 La36
Huuhilonkylä FIN 83 Lb25
Huuhkala FIN 69 Ka11
Huukki S 68 Jb16
Huutijärvi FIN 89 Jd35
Huutokoski FIN 83 Lc29
Huutokoski FIN 90 La32
Huutoperä FIN 82 Kb28
Huuttila FIN 90 Kd35
Huuvari FIN 90 Kc38
Huwniki PL 139 Kb45
Huy B 124 Ba41
Hüyük TR 199 Hb88
Hüyüklü TR 193 Ha87
Huzenbach D 133 Cb49
Hvåle N 85 Db40
Hvaler N 93 Ea44
Hvalpsund DK 100 Db22
Hvalvík DK 3 Ca06
Hvalynsk RUS 203 Ga11
Hvam DK 100 Db23
Hvam Mejeriby DK 100 Da23
Hvammstangi IS 2 Ad03
Hvam Stationsby DK 100 Db22
Hvanneyri IS 2 Ac04
Hvar HR 158 Gc67
Hvarnes N 93 Dd43
Hvastoviči RUS 202 Ed12
Hveragerði IS 2 Ac05
Hvidbjerg DK 100 Da22
Hvide Sande DK 108 Cd24
Hvilson DK 100 Db22
Hvirring DK 108 Db25
Hvitsten N 93 Ea42
Hvittingfoss N 93 Dd43
Hvitträsk FIN 98 Kb40
Hvojna BG 184 Db74
Hvolsvöllur IS 2 Ac05
Hvornum DK 100 Dc22
Hvorostjanka RUS 203 Ga10
Hvorslev DK 100 Dc23
Hybo S 87 Ga35
Hycklinge S 103 Ga48
Hyde GB 16 Ed21
Hyen N 84 Cb35
Hyenville F 22 Fa36
Hyères F 42 Ka55
Hyères-Plage F 42 Ka55
Hyet F 31 Jd41
Hylestad N 92 Cd44
Hylke DK 108 Dc24
Hylla N 78 Eb28
Hyllestad N 84 Ca36
Hyllested Skovgårde DK 109 Dd24
Hyllinge DK 109 Eb27
Hyltebruk S 102 Ed51
Hyltinge S 95 Gb44
Hymont F 31 Jd38
Hynish GB 9 Da14
Hynnekle N 93 Da45
Hyönölä FIN 98 Ka39
Hyötyy FIN 90 La33
Hyrkäs FIN 74 Kb24
Hyrkkälä FIN 91 Lb35
Hyrkkölä FIN 98 Ka39
Hyrsyla FIN 98 Ka39
Hyrvälä FIN 90 Ka37
Hyry FIN 74 Ka22
Hyrylä FIN 98 Kb39
Hyrynsalmi FIN 75 La24
Hysgjokaj AL 182 Ab76
Hysnes N 77 Dd29
Hyssna S 102 Ec49
Hythe GB 20 Fa30
Hythe GB 21 Gb29
Hytölä FIN 82 Kc31
Hytti FIN 91 Lc36
Hyttikoski FIN 82 Kb25
Hyväniemi FIN 75 Kd19
Hyvikkälä FIN 90 Ka37
Hyvinkää FIN 90 Kb38
Hyvölänranta FIN 82 Kb26
Hyvönmäki FIN 91 Ld32
Hyynilä FIN 89 Jc35
Hyypiö FIN 74 Kb18
Hyyppä FIN 89 Ja33
Hyyrylä FIN 90 Ka34
Hyytiälä FIN 90 Ka34
Hyżne PL 139 Ka44

I

Ia GR 196 Db92
Iabloana MD 173 Fa55
Iacobeni RO 172 Ea56
Iacobeni RO 175 Dc60
Ialoveni MD 173 Fd58
Ialpugeni MD 173 Fc59
Iam RO 174 Bd63
Iana RO 177 Fa60
Ianca RO 177 Fa64
Ianca RO 179 Da68
Iancu Jianu RO 175 Da65
Ianoșda RO 170 Ca57
Iare RO 171 Da58
Iargara MD 177 Fc60
Iarova MD 173 Fb53
Iași RO 173 Fa57
Iasmos GR 184 Dc77
Ibahernando E 51 Ca67
Iballë AL 159 Jc70
Ibănești RO 172 Dd58
Ibănești RO 172 Ec54
Ibarra E 39 Ec56
Ibbenbüren D 117 Cb36
Ibdes E 47 Ec62
Ibeas de Juarros E 38 Dc58
İbecik TR 198 Fd90
Ibi E 55 Fb70
İbirler TR 192 Fa82
Ibiza E 56 Gc69
İbradı TR 199 Hb90
Ibramowice PL 138 Ja43
Ibrány H 147 Ka50
İbrikbaba TR 185 Eb79
İbriktepe TR 185 Eb77
Ibros E 52 Dc72
Ibstone GB 20 Fb27
İçdedeler TR 187 Gc79
Ičera BG 180 Eb72
Ichalia GR 189 Bc81
Ichenhausen D 142 Db50
Ichenheim D 133 Ca49
Ichtershausen D 127 Dd41
İçikler TR 192 Fb85
İçikli TR 193 Gc86
Icking D 143 Dd51
Icklingham GB 21 Ga25
Icksjö S 87 Fc38
Iclănzel RO 171 Db59
Iclod RO 171 Da57
İçmeler TR 197 Fa91
Ičnja UA 202 Ec14
Icoana RO 175 Db66
Icușești RO 172 Ed58
Idala S 102 Ec50
Idala S 110 Fa56
Idanha-a-Nova P 44 Bb65
Idar-Oberstein D 133 Bd45
Idbacka S 79 Gb26
Idd N 94 Eb44
Ideciu de Jos RO 171 Dc58
Iden D 119 Eb35
Iden GB 21 Ga30
Ideņa LV 107 Lc50
Idenor S 87 Gb36
Idivuoma S 68 Hd13
Idkerberget S 95 Fd40
Idom DK 100 Cd23
Idoméni GR 183 Ca76
Idoš SRB 174 Bb60
İdra GR 195 Cb88
Idre S 86 Ed35
Idrica RUS 107 Mb51
Idrija RUS 107 Mb51
Idrija SLO 151 Fa58
İdrisyayla TR 193 Gc83
Idro I 149 Db58
Idrsko SLO 150 Ed57
Idstein D 133 Cb43
Idus LV 106 Kc47
Idvattnet S 79 Gb26
Idvor SRB 153 Jc60
Idvor SRB 174 Bb62
Idzików PL 137 Gc44
Iecava LV 106 Kb52
Iecelnieki LV 107 Lc50
Iedera RO 176 Ea64
Ieper B 21 Ha30
Iepurești RO 180 Ea67
Ierápetra GR 201 Dc96
Ieras LV 105 Jc51
Ieriķi LV 106 Kd49
Ierissós GR 184 Cd79
Iernut RO 171 Db59
Ieropigí GR 182 Ba77
Ieud RO 171 Db55
Iezărenii Vechi MD 173 Fb56
Ifac E 55 Fd70
Iffeldorf D 143 Dd52
Iffendic F 27 Ec39
Iffezheim D 133 Cb48
Iffigenalp CH 141 Bc56
Ifield GB 20 Fc29
Ig SLO 151 Fb58
Igaküla EST 97 Jd45
Igal H 145 Ha56
Igalo MNE 159 Hc69
Igar H 146 Hc55
Igate LV 106 Kc49
Iğdeci TR 199 Gc88
Iğdecik TR 192 Fb85
Iğdecik TR 192 Fb87
İğdecik TR 193 Hb82
Iğdır TR 186 Fd80
Igé F 34 Ja45
Igea E 47 Ec59
Igea Marina I 156 Eb64
Igel D 133 Bc45
Igelfors S 95 Fd45
Igelstorp S 103 Fb47
Igensdorf D 135 Dd46
Igerøy N 70 Ed22
Igersheim D 134 Da46
Iggaldas N 64 Jb07
Iggensbach D 135 Ed49
Iggesund S 87 Gb36
Iggön S 88 Gc38
Ighișu Nou RO 175 Db60
Ighiu RO 175 Cd60
Ightham GB 20 Fd29
Iglarevo KSV 178 Ba71
Iglesiarrubia E 46 Dc59
Iglesias E 38 Db58
Iglesias I 169 Bd79
Igliauka LV 114 Kb58
Iglika BG 181 Ec69
Iglišķēliai LV 114 Kb58
Igls A 143 Dd54
Ignaberga S 110 Fa54
Ignalina LT 115 Lb55
Ignatei MD 173 Fc56
İğneada TR 186 Fa75
İğneler TR 185 Ed76
Ignești RO 170 Cb59
Igny-Comblizy F 24 Hc36
Igoldy F 39 Fa55
Igołomia PL 138 Ja44
Igomel' RUS 99 Ma44
Igoumenítsa GR 182 Ac80
Igrane HR 158 Gd67
Igrejinha P 50 Ad69
Igualada E 49 Gc61
Igualeja E 60 Cc76
Igüeña E 37 Ca56
Ihamäki FIN 89 Jd38
Ihamaniemi FIN 91 Lc32
Ihamaru EST 107 Lb46
Ihari FIN 90 Ka36
Iharos H 152 Gd57
Iharosberény H 152 Gd57
Ihasalu EST 98 Kc42
Ihaste EST 99 Lb45
Ihastjärvi FIN 90 La33
Ihlienworth D 118 Cd32
Ihlow D 117 Cb33
Ihode FIN 89 Ja37
Iholdy F 39 Fa55
Ihotunlahti FIN 82 Kd28
Ihova SLO 144 Ga56
Ihrlerstein D 135 Ea48
İhsaniye TR 186 Fc79
İhsaniye TR 186 Ga79
İhsaniye TR 193 Gc83
İhsaniye TR 193 Gc84
İhsaniye TR 199 Gd91
Ii FIN 74 Ka23
Iidır TR 191 Ea86
Iigaste EST 106 La47
Iijärvi FIN 64 Ka09
Iiksenvaara FIN 83 Ld30
Iinattijärvi FIN 75 Kc22
Iinattiniemi FIN 75 Kc22
Iiroonranta FIN 81 Jd31
Iisalmi FIN 82 Kd28
Iisinki FIN 74 Jd18
Iisvesi FIN 82 Kd31
Iitin FIN 90 Kd37
Iittala FIN 90 Ka37
IJmuiden NL 116 Ad35
IJsselmuiden NL 117 Bc35
IJsselstein NL 124 Ba37
IJzendijke NL 124 Ab38
Ikaalinen FIN 89 Jc35
Ikast DK 108 Db24
Ikervár H 145 Gc54
İkibaşlı TR 192 Fd83
İkizce TR 198 Fd93
İkizdere TR 191 Ed87
Ikkala FIN 89 Jd33
Ikkala FIN 98 Ka39
Ikkeläjärvi FIN 89 Jb33
Ikla EST 106 Kb47
Ikornnes N 76 Cc33
Ikosenniemi FIN 74 Kb22
İkramiye TR 187 Gb79
Ikrény H 145 Gd52
Ikšķile LV 106 Kc51
Ilandža SRB 174 Bc62
Ilanz CH 142 Cc55
Ilava SK 137 Hb48
Iława PL 122 Hc32
Ilberstedt D 127 Ea38
Ilbro DK 100 Dc20
il Castagno I 155 Db66
Ilche E 48 Fd59
Ilchester GB 19 Eb30
Ileana RO 176 Ec66
Ileanda RO 171 Da56
Île de Fédrun F 27 Ec42
Ilenuța MD 173 Fb56
Il'eši RUS 99 Ma41
Ilfeld D 126 Dc39
Ilford GB 20 Fd28
Ilfracombe GB 19 Dd29
Ilgardere TR 185 Eb80
Ilgaz TR 205 Fb20
Ilgın TR 193 Hb87
Ilgižiai LV 114 Kb56
Ilguva LV 114 Kb57
Ílhavo P 44 Ac63
Ilia GR 189 Ca83
Ilia RO 175 Cc60
Iliç TR 205 Fd20
Ilıca TR 191 Ea86
Ilıca TR 192 Fa81
Ilıcabaşı TR 193 Gd83
Ilıcak TR 186 Fa80
Ilıcaköy TR 199 Ha91
Ilıcaksu TR 192 Ga82
Ilıcasu TR 192 Fd84
Ilidža BIH 159 Hc65
Ilija Bláskovo BG 181 Ec70
Ilijaš BIH 159 Hc64
Ilijno BG 180 Eb70
Il'ino RUS 202 Eb11
Il'insko-Zaborskoe RUS 203 Fb08
Iliókastro GR 195 Ca88
Iliokómi GR 184 Cd77
Ilirska Bistrica SLO 151 Fb59
Il'jinskoje RUS 113 Jd59
Il'jušino RUS 113 Jd59
Ilkestone GB 16 Fa23
Ilkkurşunköy TR 192 Fa87
Ilkley GB 16 Ed20
Illana E 47 Ea65
Illano E 37 Bd54
Illar E 61 Ea76
Illasi I 149 Dc59
Illby FIN 90 Kb38
Illerrieden D 142 Da50
Illertissen D 142 Da50
Illescas E 46 Db65
Ille-sur-Têt F 41 Ha57
Illičivs'k UA 204 Ec17
Illiers-Combray F 29 Gb39
Illingen D 133 Bd46
Illingen D 134 Cc48
Illkirch-Graffenstaden F 25 Kc37
Illmensee D 142 Cd51
Illmitz A 145 Gc52
Illo FIN 89 Jc36
Illo FIN 97 Jc40
Illois F 23 Gc34
Íllora E 60 Db74
Illschwang D 135 Ea46
Illueca E 47 Ed61
Illuka EST 99 Lb42
Illzach F 31 Kb39
Ilmajoki FIN 89 Jb32
Ilmenau D 127 Dd42
Il'men' Suvorovskij RUS 203 Fd14
Ilmington GB 20 Ed26
Ilminster GB 19 Eb30
Ilmjärve EST 107 Lb47
Ilmoila FIN 90 Ka36
Ilmola FIN 74 Jc21
Ilmolahti FIN 82 Kb30
Il'mova Gora RUS 107 Mb49
Ilok HR 153 Ja60
Ilola FIN 90 Kc38
Ilomäki FIN 82 Kc31
Ilomäki FIN 89 Jd33
Ilomantsi FIN 83 Ma30
Iloren TR 193 Hb82
Ilosjoki FIN 82 Kb29
Ilovăt RO 174 Cb64
Ilovice BIH 159 Hc65
Ilovita RO 174 Cb64
Iłów PL 130 Ja36
Iłowa PL 128 Fd40
Iłowo PL 121 Gd33
Iłowo-Osada PL 122 Ja34
Ilsbo S 87 Gb35
Ilsede D 126 Dc37
Ilsenburg D 126 Dc38
Ilseng N 86 Eb38
Ilsfeld D 134 Cd47
Ilshofen D 134 Da47
Ilskov DK 100 Da23
Ilttula FIN 97 Jc39
Ilūkste LV 115 Lb53
Ilumäe EST 98 Kd41
Ilva Mare RO 172 Dd56
Ilva Mică RO 171 Dc56
Ilvesjoki FIN 89 Jb33
Ilyas TR 199 Gb88
İlyasbey TR 187 Gb80
İlyaslı TR 192 Fd85
İlyaslar TR 191 Ed84
İlyaslar TR 192 Fb83
İlyaslar TR 193 Hb87
İlyaspaşa TR 193 Hb84
Iłża PL 130 Jc40
Ilzene LV 107 Lb48
İmamlar TR 198 Fd90
Imatra FIN 91 Lc35
Imatrankoski FIN 91 Lc35
Imavere EST 98 Kd44
Imbarė LT 113 Jb54
Imbradas LT 115 Lb54
İmbros GR 200 Cc95
İmecik TR 199 Gb91
Imeciksusuzu TR 199 Gb91
Imel' SK 145 Hb51
Imenicy RUS 99 Mb42
Imeno SLO 151 Ga57
Imer I 150 Ea57
Imeros GR 184 Dc77
Imielin PL 138 Hc44
Imirizaldu E 39 Fa57
Imjärvi FIN 90 Kd36
Immeln S 111 Fb54
Immendingen D 142 Cc51
Immenhausen D 126 Da39
Immenreuth D 135 Ea45
Immenstaad D 142 Cd52
Immenstadt D 142 Db52
Immilä FIN 90 Kc37
Immingham GB 17 Fc21
Immolanmäki FIN 91 Lb32
Imola I 150 Dd63
Imón E 47 Ea62
Imotski HR 158 Gd66
Impalata I 162 Ha75

Jasa Tornič – Kąkolewnica Wschodnia

Jasa Tornič SRB 174 Bc61
Jašćera RUS 99 Mb41
Jasenak HR 151 Fc60
Jasenica BIH 152 Gb62
Jasenica SRB 174 Ca66
Jasenice HR 157 Ga64
Jasenie SK 138 Hd48
Jasenik HR 152 Gd58
Jasenkovo BG 181 Ec69
Jasenovac HR 152 Gc60
Jasenovec BG 181 Ec69
Jasenovo SRB 174 Bc63
Jasenovo SRB 178 Ad67
Jasenskaja RUS 205 Fc16
Jasień PL 121 Gd30
Jasień PL 121 Hb30
Jasień PL 128 Fc39
Jasienica PL 120 Fb33
Jasienica PL 128 Fc38
Jasienica PL 130 Jc36
Jasienica PL 138 Hc45
Jasienica Dolna PL 137 Gd43
Jasienie PL 129 Ha41
Jasieniec PL 130 Jb38
Jasika SRB 178 Bc68
Jasikovo SRB 174 Bd66
Jasionka PL 139 Ka43
Jasionna PL 121 Gb35
Jasionna PL 130 Hd38
Jasionów PL 138 Ja46
Jasionówka PL 123 Kb32
Jasionowo PL 123 Ka30
Jašiūnai LT 114 La58
Jaškul' RUS 205 Ga15
Jaślany PL 139 Jd43
Jasło PL 139 Jd45
Jasná SK 138 Hd48
Jasnaja Poljana RUS 113 Jd59
Jasna Poljana BG 181 Fa73
Jasnoe RUS 113 Jc57
Jasnogorsk RUS 203 Fa11
Jasov SK 138 Jc48
Jásova SK 145 Hb51
Jastarnia PL 121 Hb29
Jastkowice PL 131 Ka42
Jastrebarsko HR 151 Ga59
Jastrebino RUS 99 Ma41
Jastrowie PL 121 Gc33
Jastrząb PL 130 Jc40
Jastrząbka PL 122 Jc34
Jastrzębia PL 130 Jc39
Jastrzębia PL 138 Jc45
Jastrzębia Góra PL 112 Ha58
Jastrzębie-Zdrój PL 137 Hb45
Jaświły PL 123 Kb32
Jasynuvata UA 205 Fb15
Jászalsószentgyörgy H 146 Jb53
Jászapáti H 146 Jb53
Jászárokszállás H 146 Ja52
Jászberény H 146 Ja53
Jaszczołty PL 123 Ka35
Jászfényszaru H 146 Ja52
Jászkarajenő H 146 Jb54
Jászkisér H 146 Jb53
Jászladány H 146 Jb53
Jaszów PL 137 Gd43
Jászszentandrás H 146 Jb52
Jászszentlászló H 146 Ja56
Jät S 103 Fc52
Játar E 60 Db75
Jatko FIN 75 Kc22
Jättendal S 87 Gb35
Jättensö S 87 Ga33
Jättölä FIN 98 Ka39
Jatwież PL 123 Kb32
Jatznick D 120 Fa33
Jauge F 32 Fb51
Jauhojärvi FIN 68 Jc16
Jauja E 60 Cd74
Jaulín E 47 Fa61
Jaulnay F 28 Fd43
Jaun CH 141 Bc55
Jaunaglona LV 107 Lc52
Jaunalūksne LV 107 Lc48
Jaunanna LV 107 Lc49
Jaunauce LV 105 Jd52
Jaunbērze LV 106 Ka51
Jaunciems LV 105 Jc48
Jaunciems LV 105 Jd49
Jaundziras LV 105 Jd51
Jaungulbene LV 107 Lb49
Jauniūnai LT 114 La57
Jaunjelgava LV 106 Kd51
Jaunjērcēni LV 106 Kd48
Jaunkalsnava LV 106 La51
Jaunlaicene LV 107 Lb48
Jaunlutriņi LV 105 Jc51
Jaunmuiža LV 105 Jc51
Jaunpasts LV 105 Jd50
Jaunpiebalga LV 106 La49
Jaunpils LV 106 Ka51
Jaunsaras E 39 Ec56
Jaunsāti LV 105 Jd51
Jaunsaule LV 106 Kc52
Jaunsmiltene LV 106 La48
Jaunsvirlauka LV 106 Kb52
Jaurakkajärvi FIN 75 Kc23
Jausa EST 97 Jc45
Jausiers F 43 Kb51
Javarus FIN 69 Kb17
Jávea E 55 Fd70
Jävenitz D 127 Ea36
Javerlhac-et-la-Chapelle-Saint-Robert F 33 Ga48
Javgur MD 173 Fc59
Javier E 39 Fa57
Javierre E 40 Fc58
Javorani BIH 152 Gd62
Javorec BG 180 Dc71
Javorina SK 138 Ja47
Javoriv UA 204 Dd15
Javorná CZ 135 Ec44
Javorná CZ 135 Ed47
Javornic HR 151 Fd61
Javorník CZ 137 Gc43
Jävre S 73 Hd24
Javron F 28 Fc38
Jawor PL 129 Gb41
Jaworki PL 138 Jb46
Jawornik PL 138 Ja45
Jaworowice PL 139 Kb45
Jaworze PL 138 Hc45
Jaworzno PL 129 Hb41
Jaworzno PL 138 Hd44
Jaworzyna Śląska PL 129 Gb42
Jayena E 60 Db75
Jaywick GB 21 Gb27
Jaz MNE 159 Hd70
Jazente P 44 Ba61
Jeantes F 24 Hc33
Jebel RO 174 Bc61
Jedburgh GB 11 Ec15
Jedlicze PL 139 Jd45
Jedlina-Zdrój PL 129 Gb42
Jedlińsk PL 130 Jc39
Jedlnia-Letnisko PL 130 Jc39
Jednorożec PL 122 Jb34
Jedovnice CZ 137 Gc47
Jędrychowo PL 122 Hc32
Jędrychowo PL 122 Hd30
Jędrzejów PL 130 Ja42
Jędrzychowice PL 129 Gb39
Jédula E 59 Ca76
Jedwabne PL 123 Jd33
Jedwabno PL 122 Jb32
Jeesiö FIN 69 Jd15
Jeesiöjärvi FIN 69 Jd15
Jegălia RO 181 Fa67
Jegerup DK 108 Db27
Jeggau D 127 Dd36
Jegind DK 100 Da22
Jegłownik PL 122 Hc31
Jégun F 40 Fd54
Jegunovce MK 178 Bb72
Jēkabpils LV 106 La52
Jeksen DK 108 Dc24
Jektvika N 70 Fa19
Jektvika N 70 Fa19
Jelaci SRB 178 Bb68
Jelah BIH 152 Hb62
Jelanec' UA 204 Ed16
Jelašca BIH 159 Hc66
Jelašnica SRB 174 Ca66
Jelcz-Laskowice PL 129 Gd41
Jelen Do SRB 159 Jc64
Jelenec SK 145 Hb50
Jelenia Gora PL 128 Ga42
Jeleniewo PL 123 Ka30
Jelenin PL 128 Fd39
Jelenino PL 121 Gb32
Jelesejevići SRB 159 Jb64
Jelésnia PL 138 Hd46
Jelgava LV 106 Kb51
Jelgavkrasti LV 106 Kc49
Jelling DK 108 Db25
Jel'niki RUS 113 Jc58
Jelonki PL 123 Jd34
Jelovac SRB 174 Bd66
Jelovoje RUS 113 Jd58
Jełowa PL 129 Ha42
Jels DK 108 Da26
Jelsa HR 158 Gc67
Jelsa N 92 Cb42
Jelšane SLO 151 Fb60
Jelšava SK 138 Jb49
Jelsi I 161 Fc73
Jemelle B 132 Ba43
Jemenovci SRB 174 Bc62
Jemenuño E 46 Da62
Jemeppe-sur-Meuse B 124 Ad42
Jemgum D 117 Cb33
Jemielnica PL 137 Hb43
Jemielno PL 129 Gb39
Jena D 127 Ea41
Jenakijeve UA 205 Fb15
Jenaz CH 142 Cd54
Jenbach A 143 Ea53
Jenikowo PL 120 Fd33
Jenlain F 24 Hb32
Jennersdorf A 145 Gb55
Jenny S 103 Gb49
Jensåsvoll N 86 Ec32
Jenstad N 77 Dc33
Jenzat F 34 Hb45
Jeppo FIN 81 Jb29
Jeprca SLO 151 Fb57
Jepua FIN 81 Jb29
Jerez de La Frontera E 59 Bd76
Jerez del Marquesado E 61 Dd75
Jerez de los Caballeros E 51 Bc70
Jergucat AL 182 Ac79
Jérica E 54 Fb66
Jerichow D 127 Eb36
Jerka PL 129 Gc38
Jerlev DK 108 Db25
Jerli Perlez KSV 178 Bb71
Jerpåsen N 71 Fb23
Jerrettspass GB 9 Cd18
Jersika LV 107 Lb52
Jerslev DK 100 Dc20
Jeršov RUS 203 Ga11
Jeršovo RUS 113 Jb58
Jerte E 45 Cb65
Jerup DK 101 Dd19
Jerxheim D 127 Dd37
Jerzens A 142 Dc54
Jerzmanowa PL 128 Ga39
Jerzmanowice PL 138 Hd44
Jerzu I 169 Cb78
Jerzwałd PL 122 Hc32
Jesberg D 126 Cd41
Jesenice CZ 135 Ed44
Jesenice CZ 136 Fb45
Jesenice SLO 144 Fa56
Jeseník CZ 137 Gd44
Jeserig D 127 Ec37
Jesewitz D 127 Ec40
Jesi I 156 Ec66
Jesolo I 150 Eb59
Jésonville F 31 Jd39
Jessen D 127 Ed39
Jessheim N 94 Eb41
Jeßnitz D 127 Eb39
Jesteburg D 118 Db33
Jestetten D 141 Cb52
Jestřebí CZ 136 Fc43
Jeti EST 106 La47
Jettingen D 134 Cc49
Jettingen-Scheppach D 142 Db50
Jetzendorf D 143 Dd50
Jeugny F 30 Hd39
Jeumont F 24 Hc32
Jeurre F 31 Jc44
Jevenstedt D 118 Db30
Jever D 117 Cc32
Jevíčko CZ 137 Gc46
Jevišovice CZ 136 Ga48
Jevnaker N 85 Dd40
Jevpatorija UA 205 Fa17
Jevreni MD 173 Fd57
Jeże PL 123 Jd32
Jezera BIH 152 Ha63
Jezerane HR 151 Fd61
Jezerce KSV 178 Bb71
Jezero BIH 152 Gd63
Ježević HR 158 Gc65
Ježevo HR 152 Gb59
Jeżewo PL 121 Hb33
Jeżewo PL 122 Hd35
Jeziorany PL 122 Ja31
Jeziora Wielkie PL 129 Ha36
Jeziorki Wałeckie PL 120 Ga34
Jeziorko PL 123 Jd33
Jeziorowice PL 130 Hd42
Jeziorsko PL 129 Hb38
Jeziory Wielkie PL 129 Gc37
Jeziorzany PL 131 Ka39
Jeżów PL 130 Ja38
Jeżowe PL 139 Ka43
Jiana RO 174 Cb65
Jiana Mare RO 174 Cb65
Jibert RO 176 Dd61
Jibou RO 171 Cd56
Jichișu de Jos RO 171 Da57
Jičín CZ 136 Fd43
Jičíněves CZ 136 Fd43
Jidvei RO 175 Db60
Jieríjärvi S 73 Ja18
Jieznas LT 114 Kc58
Jihlava CZ 136 Fd47
Jijila RO 177 Fb63
Jijona E 55 Fb71
Jilava RO 176 Ea66
Jilavele RO 176 Ec65
Jilemnice CZ 136 Fd43
Jilové CZ 128 Fb42
Jilové u Prahy CZ 136 Fb45
Jiltjaur S 72 Gb23
Jimbolia RO 174 Bb60
Jimena E 60 Dc73
Jimena de la Frontera E 59 Cb77
Jiménez de Jamuz E 37 Cb58
Jimramov CZ 137 Gb46
Jina RO 175 Da61
Jince CZ 136 Fa45
Jindřichov CZ 137 Gd44
Jindřichovice CZ 135 Ec44
Jindřichovice pod Smrkem CZ 128 Fd41
Jindřichův Hradec CZ 136 Fc48
Jinošov CZ 137 Gb47
Jirkov CZ 135 Ed43
Jirlău RO 176 Ed64
Jistebnice CZ 136 Fb46
Jitia RO 176 Ec62
Jivjany CZ 135 Ec46
Joachimsthal D 120 Fa35
Joakim-Gruevo BG 180 Db73
João Serra P 58 Ad72
Joarilla de las Matas E 37 Cd58
Jobbágyi H 146 Ja52
Jochberg A 143 Eb53
Jocketa D 135 Eb43
Jockfall S 73 Ja19
Jockgrim D 133 Cb47
Jódar E 60 Dc73
Jodeliszki PL 123 Kb30
Jodłowa PL 139 Jd44
Jodłownik PL 138 Jb45
Jodoigne B 124 Ad41
Jõelähtme EST 98 Kc42
Joensuu FIN 83 Ld30
Joesjö S 71 Fc22
Jõgeva EST 98 La44
Johampolis LT 114 Ka55
Johannesfors S 80 Hc28
Johann-Georgenstadt D 135 Ec43
Johannishus S 111 Fd54
Johanniskirchen D 135 Ec49
Johanniskreuz D 133 Ca46
Johansfors S 102 Ed52
Johansfors S 103 Fd52
John o'Groats GB 5 Ec04
Johnsbach A 144 Fb53
John's Cross GB 20 Fd30
Johnshaven GB 7 Ed10
Johnstone GB 10 Dd13
Johnstown IRL 13 Cb23
Johnstown IRL 13 Cd23
Johovac BIH 152 Hb62
Johovac BIH 153 Hd62
Jöhstadt D 135 Ed43
Jõhvi EST 99 Lb42
Joigny F 30 Hb39
Joinville F 30 Jb38
Joița RO 176 Ea66
Jokela FIN 74 Ka19
Jokela FIN 82 Kc27
Jokela FIN 90 Kb38
Jøkelfjord N 63 Hc08
Jokihaara FIN 89 Jb35
Jokihaara FIN 90 Kb32
Jokijärvi FIN 75 Kd21
Jokijärvi FIN 82 Kc30
Joki-Kokko FIN 74 Kb23
Jokikunta FIN 98 Ka39
Jokikylä FIN 74 Ka23
Jokikylä FIN 75 La24
Jokikylä FIN 81 Jd27
Jokikylä FIN 81 Jc29
Jokikylä FIN 81 Ja31
Jokikylä FIN 82 Kb27
Jokikylä FIN 82 Ka25
Jokikylä FIN 89 Jc33
Jokina Čuprija SRB 159 Jb65
Jokiniemi FIN 90 Ka38
Jokioinen FIN 89 Jd38
Jokiperä FIN 81 Ja31
Jokipii FIN 89 Jb32
Jokisalo FIN 81 Ja31
Jokivarsi FIN 81 Jd31
Jokivarsi FIN 89 Jb34
Jokivarsi FIN 89 Jc32
Jokkikylä FIN 83 Lb27
Jokkmokk S 72 Ha19
Jokūbavas LT 113 Jb55
Jola E 51 Bb67
Jolanda di Savoia I 150 Ea61
Jolda P 44 Ad59
Jolkka FIN 81 Jc28
Jølle N 92 Cb47
Jöllen S 87 Fb37
Joloskylä FIN 74 Kb23
Jølstad N 86 Ea38
Joltai MD 177 Fd61
Jomala FIN 96 Hc40
Jomås N 93 Da45
Jonai LV 114 Kb59
Jönåker S 95 Gb45
Jonasvollen N 86 Ec34
Jonava LT 114 Kc57
Joncherey F 31 Kb40
Jonchery F 30 Jb39
Jonchery-sur-Vesle F 24 Hc35
Joncy F 30 Ja44
Jondal N 84 Cb39
Jondalen N 93 Dc42
Joniec PL 122 Ja35
Joniškis LT 114 Kb53
Joniškis LT 115 Lb56
Joniškėlis LT 114 Kc53
Jonkeri FIN 83 Lc26
Jönköping S 103 Fb49
Jonkovo BG 181 Ec69
Jonkowe PL 122 Ja31
Jonku FIN 75 Kc22
Jonquières F 42 Jb52
Jonsa FIN 82 La28
Jonsberg S 103 Gb46
Jonsdorf D 128 Fc42
Jonsered S 102 Ec49
Jönshyttan S 95 Fc42
Jønsrud N 86 Eb38
Jonsrud N 94 Eb39
Jonstorp S 110 Ec54
Jonvelle F 31 Jc39
Jonzac F 32 Fc48
Jonzier F 35 Jd45
Jõpiste EST 97 Jd45
Joppolo I 164 Ga82
Jora de Mijloc MD 173 Fd56
Jorăști RO 177 Fb61
Jordankino BG 179 Cd71
Jordanów PL 138 Ja45
Jordanów Śląski PL 129 Gc42
Jordbro S 96 Gd44
Jördenstorf D 119 Ec32
Jordet N 86 Ec36
Jordløse DK 108 Dc27
Jorgastak N 64 Jc10
Jõrgeveste EST 106 La47
Jork D 118 Db33
Jörlanda S 102 Eb48
Jørlunde DK 109 Ec25
Jormasjokisuu FIN 82 La26
Jormlien S 79 Fb25
Jormua FIN 82 Kd25
Jormvattnet S 79 Fb26
Jörn S 73 Hb24
Jornini LV 105 Jc49
Joroinen FIN 90 La32
Jørpeland N 92 Ca44
Jorquera E 54 Ed69
Jørstad N 78 Ed27
Jørstad N 92 Ca43
Jørstadmoen N 85 Ea37
Jørundland N 93 Da44
Jorvas FIN 98 Kb40
Jošanica BIH 159 Hc65
Jošanica KSV 178 Ba70
Jošanica SRB 178 Bd67
Jošanička Banja SRB 178 Ba68
Joseni RO 172 Ea58
Josenii Bârgăului RO 171 Dc57
Joševa SRB 153 Ja62
Josipdol HR 151 Fd61
Josipovac HR 153 Hc59
Joškar-Ola RUS 203 Fc08
Joskaudai LT 113 Jb54
Josnes F 29 Gc40
Jøsok N 76 Cb33
Jossa D 134 Da43
Jössefors S 94 Ec42
Josselin F 27 Eb40
Jøssenøya N 77 Dc29
Jossgrund D 134 Da44
Jøssund N 78 Eb27
Jostaji LV 105 Jd51
Jósvafő H 138 Jb49
Josvainiai LT 114 Kb56
Jotainiai LT 114 Kc55
Jou P 44 Bb60
Joudeikiai LT 114 Ka53
Joué-Etiau F 28 Fb42
Joué-lès-Tours F 29 Ga42
Joué-sur-Erdre F 28 Fa41
Jouet-sur-l'Aubois F 30 Hb43
Jõuga EST 99 Lb42
Jougne F 31 Ka43
Jouhenvaara FIN 91 Ld32
Jouhet F 33 Ga45
Joux F 33 Gd48
Joukio FIN 91 Ld34
Joukokylä FIN 75 Kd23
Jouques F 42 Jd53
Joure NL 117 Bc34
Journy F 21 Gc30
Joutenniva FIN 82 Ka27
Joutsa FIN 90 Kc34
Joutsenkylä FIN 75 La20
Joutsenlampi FIN 90 Kc34
Joutseno FIN 91 Lc36
Joutsijärvi FIN 74 Kc18
Joutsjärvi FIN 90 Kd35
Joux-la-Ville F 30 Hc41
Jouy-le-Châtel F 24 Hb37
Jouy-le-Potier F 29 Gc40
Jovkovo BG 181 Fb68
Jovnes N 93 Db45
Jovsa SK 139 Ka48
Joyeuse F 34 Ja51
Józefów PL 130 Jc37
Józefów PL 131 Jd41
Józefów PL 131 Kc42
Józsa H 147 Ka52
Juankoski FIN 83 Lb29
Juan-les-Pins F 43 Kc53
Jübar D 119 Dd35
Jübek D 108 Db29
Jublains F 28 Fb39
Jubrique E 59 Cb76
Jučaičiai LT 113 Jd56
Juchavičy BY 202 Ea11
Jüchen D 125 Bc40
Juchnowiec Dolny PL 123 Kb34
Juchowo PL 121 Gb32
Jüchsen D 134 Dc43
Jucu RO 171 Da58
Judaberg N 92 Ca43
Jūdaži LV 106 Kb50
Judelnik BG 180 Eb68
Judenau A 144 Ga50
Judenburg A 144 Fc54
Judin RUS 203 Fc14
Judino RUS 107 Ma48
Judino RUS 113 Jc59
Judinsalo FIN 90 Kb34
Judrėnai LT 113 Jc55
Juelsminde DK 108 Dc25
Juf CH 142 Cd56
Juggijaur S 72 Ha19
Jugon-les-Lacs F 26 Ec38
Jugorje SLO 151 Fd59
Jugureni RO 176 Eb64
Jugy F 30 Jb44
Juhnov RUS 202 Ed11
Juhonpieti S 68 Ja17
Juhtimäki FIN 89 Jc34
Juigné-des-Moutiers F 28 Fa41
Juillac F 33 Gb48
Juilly F 23 Ha36
Juist D 117 Ca32
Jukajärvi FIN 91 Lc34
Jukeronperä FIN 82 Kb26
Jukkasjärvi S 67 Hb15
Juknaičiai LT 113 Jc56
Juksjaur S 71 Fd22
Juktån S 72 Gc24
Jule N 79 Fb27
Julianadorp NL 116 Ba34
Julianstown IRL 9 Cd20
Jülich D 125 Bc41
Julita S 95 Ga44
Jullouville F 22 Ed37
Julnes N 78 Ec28
Julo FIN 83 Ld28
Jumaliskylä FIN 75 Lb24
Jumeaux F 34 Hc48
Jumesniemi FIN 89 Jc35
Jumilhac-le-Grand F 33 Gb48
Jumilla E 55 Ed71
Juminda EST 98 Kc41
Juminen FIN 82 La28
Jumisko FIN 75 Kc19
Jumkil S 96 Gc41
Jumo FIN 97 Ja39
Jumprava LV 106 Kd51
Jumurda LV 106 La50
Juncosa E 48 Ga61
Jundola BG 179 Cd73
Juneda E 48 Ga61
Jung S 102 Ed47
Jungėnai LV 114 Kb59
Jungingen D 142 Cc50
Junglinster L 133 Bb44
Jungsund FIN 81 Hd30
Junik KSV 178 Ad71
Junik SRB 159 Jc69
Juniskär S 88 Gc33
Juniville F 24 Hd35
Junkerdal N 71 Fd18
Junkerdal turistcenter N 71 Fd19
Junkovac SRB 174 Bb65
Junnikkala FIN 91 Lc35
Junnonoja FIN 89 Jb34
Junnonperä FIN 81 Jd27
Junosando S 68 Hd16
Junqueira P 44 Ad62
Junquera de Tera E 45 Ca59
Junsele S 79 Gb29
Juntinaapa FIN 69 Ka16
Juntinvaara FIN 83 Lc25
Juntusranta FIN 75 Lb22
Juodaičiai LV 114 Kb56
Juodainiai LT 113 Jd55
Juodeikiai LT 113 Jb54
Juodkrantė LT 113 Jb56
Juodpėnai LT 114 Kd54
Juodupė LT 114 La53
Juojärvi FIN 83 Lc31
Juoksengi S 73 Jb19
Juoksenki FIN 73 Jb19
Juokslahti FIN 90 Kb34
Juokuanvaara FIN 74 Jd21
Juonto FIN 83 Lb25
Juopuli FIN 74 Kb23
Juorkuna FIN 75 Kc23
Juornaankylä FIN 90 Kc38
Juostininkai LT 114 Kd55
Juotasjärvi FIN 74 Kb19
Juper BG 180 Eb68
Jupilles F 28 Fd40
Jupiter RO 181 Fc68
Jupiterle B 124 Ba41
Jura MD 173 Fd56
Jurata PL 121 Hb29
Jurbarkas LT 114 Ka57
Juré F 34 Hd46
Jūrė LV 114 Kb58
Jūrė LV 114 Kb58
Jur'evec RUS 203 Fb08
Jur'ev-Pol'skij RUS 203 Fa09
Jurgelionys LT 115 Lb59
Jurgežeriai LV 114 Kb59
Jurgi LV 105 Jd51
Jüri EST 98 Kb42
Jurignac F 32 Fc48
Jurilovca RO 177 Fd65
Jur'jivka UA 205 Fa15
Jūrkalne LV 105 Jb51
Jurki PL 122 Hd31
Jurklošter SLO 151 Fd58
Jurkowice PL 130 Jc42
Jurkowo Węgorzewskie PL 123 Jd30
Jūrmala LV 106 Kb50
Jūrmalciems LV 113 Ja53
Jurmo FIN 97 Hd39
Jurmo FIN 97 Ja41
Jurmu FIN 75 Kd21
Juromenha P 51 Bb69
Jurovo RUS 203 Fb08
Jurowce PL 123 Kb33
Juršići HR 151 Fa61
Juršinci SLO 144 Ga56
Jursla S 103 Ga46
Jurva FIN 89 Ja32
Jurvala FIN 91 Lb36
Jurvansalo FIN 82 Kb30
Juseu E 48 Fd59
Juškino RUS 99 Lc44
Juškovo RUS 107 Ld48
Jussac F 33 Ha49
Jussey F 31 Jc40
Jussy-Champagne F 29 Ha43
Jussy-le-Chaudrier F 30 Hb42
Justa RUS 203 Ga14
Justøy N 93 Da47
Juszkowy Gród PL 123 Kc34
Juta H 145 Ha56
Jüterbog D 127 Ed38
Jutigny F 30 Hb38
Jutis S 72 Gb20
Jutrosin PL 129 Gc39
Jutsajaure S 72 Ha18
Juttila FIN 90 Ka36
Juttuanvaara FIN 83 Lc25
Juuansaari FIN 83 Ma29
Juujärvi FIN 74 Kb19
Juuka FIN 83 Lc28
Juuma FIN 74 La18
Juupajoki FIN 90 Ka34
Juupakylä FIN 89 Jc32
Juurikka FIN 83 Lb31
Juurikka FIN 91 Ma32
Juurikkalahti FIN 82 La26
Juurikkamäki FIN 83 Lb30
Juurikkasalmi FIN 91 Ld32
Juurikorpi FIN 90 La38
Juuru EST 98 Kc43
Juurussuo FIN 74 Ka24
Juutinen FIN 82 Kc26
Juva FIN 89 Jb38
Juva FIN 91 Lb33
Juvigné F 28 Fa39
Juvigny-en-Perthois F 24 Jb37
Juvigny-le-Tertre F 22 Fa37
Juvola FIN 91 Lc32
Juvre DK 108 Cd27
Juža RUS 203 Fb09
Juzanvigny F 30 Ja38
Juzennecourt F 30 Ja39
Juzet-d'Izaut F 40 Ga56
Jūžintai LT 114 La54
Južnoukrajins'k UA 204 Ec16
Južnyj RUS 113 Ja59
Južnyj RUS 205 Ga15
Jyderup DK 109 Ea26
Jylhä FIN 82 Kc29
Jylhämä FIN 82 Kc25
Jyllinge DK 109 Eb25
Jyllinkoski FIN 89 Jb34
Jyllintaival FIN 89 Jb32
Jyrinki FIN 81 Jd27
Jyrkänkoski FIN 75 La19
Jyrkkä FIN 82 Kd27
Jyry FIN 81 Ja31
Jyväskylä FIN 90 Kb33
Jyväskylän maalaiskunta FIN 90 Kb32
Jzobil'nyj RUS 205 Fd16

K

Kaagjärve EST 106 La47
Kaagvere EST 99 Lb45
Kaagvere EST 107 Lb46
Kaakamo FIN 74 Jc21
Kaalasjärvi S 67 Ha15
Kaali EST 105 Jc46
Kaali EST 105 Jd46
Kaamanen FIN 64 Ka10
Kaamasjoki FIN 64 Ka10
Kaamasmukka FIN 64 Jd09
Kaanaa FIN 89 Jd34
Kaanaa FIN 90 Kb38
Kaanaa FIN 97 Jb39
Käännänmäki FIN 82 Ka28
Kaansoo EST 98 Kc45
Kääntöjärvi S 68 Hc16
Kääpa EST 107 Lc47
Kaarakkala FIN 82 Kd27
Kaarela FIN 74 Ka23
Kaarepere EST 98 La44
Kaaresuvanto FIN 68 Hd13
Kääriälä FIN 90 La34
Kääriänperä FIN 74 Kb23
Kaarina FIN 97 Jb39
Kaarlela FIN 81 Jb28
Kaarma EST 105 Jc46
Kaarnalampi FIN 83 Lc30
Kaarnevaara S 68 Ja15
Kaarnijärvi FIN 74 Kb19
Kaaro FIN 89 Ja37
Kaarßen D 119 Dd34
Kaarst D 125 Bd40
Kaartilankoski FIN 91 Lb34
Kaarto FIN 69 Jd16
Kaartotienperä FIN 74 Jd23
Kaartunen FIN 81 Jc30
Kaasmarkku FIN 89 Ja36
Kaavere EST 98 Kd45
Kaavi FIN 83 Lb29
Kaba H 147 Jd53
Kabaağaç TR 198 Fc88
Kabaca TR 187 Ha80
Kabakça TR 186 Fb77
Kabaklar TR 192 Ga85
Kabaklı TR 192 Fd83
Kabakoz TR 186 Ga77
Kabakoz TR 192 Fb84
Kabakum TR 191 Eb83
Kabala EST 98 Kd44
Kabalak TR 178 Ha78
Kabalar TR 192 Fd87
Kabalı TR 191 Ed81
Kabalı TR 205 Fb19
Kabasekı TR 198 Ga92
Kabböle FIN 98 Kd39
Kåbdalis S 73 Hb21
Kabeliai LT 123 Kd30
Kabelvåg N 66 Fc14
Kaberneeme EST 98 Kc42
Kabile BG 180 Eb72
Kabile LV 105 Jc51
Kablešovo BG 181 Ed72
Kabli EST 106 Kb47
Kabmasmohkki FIN 64 Jd09
Kabriste EST 106 Kb46
Kač SRB 153 Jb60
Kačanik KSV 178 Bb72
Kačanovo RUS 107 Ld48
Kačarevo SRB 174 Bb63
Kacelovo BG 180 Ea69
Kačerginė LV 114 Kb57
Kačergiškė LT 115 Lc55
Kaceřov CZ 135 Ed45
Kachovka UA 205 Fa16
Kacice PL 122 Jb35
Kačikol KSV 178 Bb70
Kącłowa PL 138 Jc45
Kácov CZ 136 Fc45
Kaczanowo PL 129 Gd37
Kaczkowo PL 129 Gb39
Kaczorów PL 128 Ga42
Kaczory PL 121 Gc34
Kadaga LV 106 Kc50
Kadaň CZ 135 Ed43
Kadıdondurma TR 185 Eb77
Kadijača KSV 178 Ba69
Kadiķi LV 106 Kb51
Kadıköy TR 185 Ec78
Kadıköy TR 186 Fa76
Kadıköy TR 186 Fd79
Kadıköy TR 187 Ha80
Kadıköy TR 191 Ec83
Kadıköy TR 191 Ed81
Kadıköy TR 193 Gd85
Kadıköy TR 197 Fa89
Kadıköya TR 192 Fa83
Kadıköy = Evreşe TR 185 Ec78
Kadıkuyusu TR 193 Gd84
Kadılar TR 185 Eb80
Kadılar TR 193 Gc87
Kadılı TR 186 Ga78
Kadıncık TR 193 Hb83
Kadıovacık TR 191 Ea86
Kadirler TR 198 Ga93
Kadłub PL 129 Hb42
Kadłubówka PL 123 Kb35
Kadłub Turawski PL 129 Ha42
Kadrifakovo MK 183 Bd74
Kadrina EST 98 Kd42
Kadriye TR 185 Ec76
Kaduj RUS 202 Ed08
Kädva EST 98 Kc44
Kadyj RUS 203 Fb08
Kadymka RUS 113 Jd59
Kadzidło PL 122 Jc33
Kædeby DK 109 Dd28
Kaelase EST 98 Kb45
Käenkoski FIN 83 Ma29
Kafacakaplancık TR 197 Fa89
Kåfjord N 62 Ha09
Kåfjord N 64 Jc05
Kåfjordbotn N 63 Hb10
Kåfjorddalen N 63 Hb10
Kağan TR 191 Ed85
Kåge S 80 Hc25
Kågeröd S 110 Ed55
Kaharlyk UA 204 Ec15
Kähkölä FIN 83 Lc26
Kahl D 134 Cd44
Kahla D 127 Ea42
Kähtävä FIN 81 Jd27
Kahya TR 198 Fc92
Kaidankylä FIN 89 Jd34
Kaihlasjärvi FIN 75 Kc23
Kaikino RUS 99 Lc41
Käikul S 73 Hb20
Käina EST 97 Jc44
Kainach A 144 Fc54
Kainasto FIN 81 Jb31
Kainasto FIN 89 Ja32
Kaindorf A 144 Ga54
Kainu FIN 81 Jc29
Kainulasjärvi S 73 Hd18
Kainuunkylä FIN 73 Jb20
Kainuunmäki FIN 82 Kd27
Kaipiainen FIN 90 La37
Kaipola FIN 90 Kb34
Kairahta FIN 90 Kc33
Kairala FIN 69 Kb16
Kairala FIN 75 Kd20
Kairėnai LV 114 Kb55
Kairiai LT 114 Kb54
Kairiai LT 113 Jb55
Kairila FIN 89 Jb35
Kairiškiai LT 113 Jd53
Kaisepakte S 67 Gd14
Kaisers A 142 Db54
Kaisersbach D 134 Da48
Kaisersesch D 133 Bd43
Kaiserslautern D 133 Ca46
Kaisheim D 134 Dc48
Kaišiadorys LT 114 Kd57
Kaitainen FIN 90 La33
Kaitainsalmi FIN 82 La26
Kaitajärvi FIN 74 Jc19
Kaitsor FIN 81 Ja30
Kaitum S 67 Ha16
Kaiu EST 98 Kc43
Kaivanto FIN 82 Kc25
Kaive LV 105 Jd50
Kaive LV 106 La50
Kaivola FIN 89 Ja38
Kaivomäki FIN 90 La33
Kajaani FIN 82 Kd26
Kajala FIN 97 Jb39
Kajan AL 182 Ab76
Kajánújfalu H 146 Jc55
Kajbolovo RUS 99 Lc40
Kajbolovo RUS 99 Ld40
Kajdacs H 146 Hc56
Kajnardža BG 181 Fa68
Kajoo FIN 83 Lb29
Kájov CZ 136 Fb49
Kajsackoe RUS 203 Ga12
Kakalétri GR 194 Bb88
Kakanj BIH 158 Hb64
Kakasd H 153 Hc57
Kakavija AL 182 Ac79
Käkelä FIN 75 La23
Kakerbeck D 127 Ea36
Kaki GR 195 Cb87
Käkilahti FIN 82 Kc26
Kakkisenvaara FIN 83 Ld28
Kaklık TR 198 Fd88
Kakmuži MNE 159 Ja67
Kąkol PL 121 Hb34
Kąkolewnica Wschodnia PL 131 Kb37

Kakolewnica Wschodnia – Karjalaisenniemi

Kakolewnica Wschodnia PL 131 Kb37
Kąkolewo PL 129 Gb38
Kakopetria CY 206 Ja97
Kakóvatos GR 194 Ba87
Kakskerta FIN 97 Jb39
Kakslauttanen FIN 69 Ka12
Kakuåsen S 79 Fc29
Kál H 146 Jb52
Kälä FIN 90 Kc34
Kalabakbaşı TR 191 Ec81
Kålaboda S 80 Hc26
Kalač RUS 203 Fc13
Kalace MNE 159 Jc68
Kalace MNE 178 Ad70
Kalač-na-Donu RUS 203 Fd14
Kalafat TR 191 Ea81
Kalafati SRB 159 Ja66
Kalaja FIN 82 Ka28
Kalajoki FIN 81 Jc26
Kalak N 64 Jd05
Kalakoski FIN 89 Jc32
Kalamáfka GR 201 Db96
Kalamáki GR 188 Ac86
Kalamáki GR 189 Ca81
Kalamákia GR 189 Cc83
Kalamariá GR 183 Ca78
Kalamark S 73 Hc23
Kalamáta GR 194 Bb89
Kalambáka GR 183 Bb80
Kalambáki GR 184 Cd77
Kalamítsi GR 184 Cd80
Kálamos GR 188 Ad83
Kálamos GR 189 Cc85
Kalamotí GR 191 Db86
Kalamotó GR 183 Cb78
Kalana EST 97 Jb44
Kalana EST 98 La44
Kalančak UA 205 Fa17
Kalándra GR 183 Cb80
Kalá Nerá GR 189 Ca82
Kalanos GR 188 Bb86
Kalanti FIN 89 Ja38
Kalapódi GR 189 Ca84
Kälarne S 79 Ga31
Kálathos GR 197 Fa93
Kalavárda GR 197 Ed93
Kalavasos CY 206 Jb98
Kalávrita GR 188 Bb86
Kalax FIN 89 Hd32
Kalbach D 134 Da43
Kalbe D 127 Ea36
Kalbensteinberg D 134 Dc47
Kalburcu TR 186 Ga78
Kalburcu TR 192 Fa82
Kalce SLO 151 Fb58
Kalčevo BG 180 Eb73
Kalchreuth D 135 Dd46
Káld H 145 Gd54
Kaldal N 79 Fb26
Kaldenkirchen D 125 Bc39
Kaldfarnes N 67 Gb11
Kaldfjord N 62 Gc09
Kaldvika N 66 Ga14
Kale TR 198 Fc89
Kalealtı TR 185 Eb78
Kale = Demre TR 199 Gb93
Kaledibi TR 205 Ga19
Kalefeld D 126 Db38
Kalekovec BG 180 Db73
Kaleköy TR 185 Dd80
Kaleköy TR 198 Ga93
Kalela FIN 89 Jb38
Kalemköy TR 197 Fa90
Kälen S 73 Hc24
Kalenci SRB 153 Jc62
Kalenik BG 180 Db70
Kaléntzi GR 188 Ad81
Kaléntzi GR 188 Bb86
Kalérgo GR 190 Cd86
Kalesi EST 98 Kc42
Kalesija BIH 153 Hd63
Kalesninkai LT 114 Kc59
Kalesninkai LT 114 La59
Kaleste EST 97 Jb44
Kalēti LV 113 Jb53
Kaletnik PL 123 Kb30
Kalety PL 138 Hc43
Kaleüçağız TR 198 Ga93
Kaleva FIN 97 Jc39
Kalfaköy TR 192 Fb81
Kalho FIN 90 Kc35
Kalí GR 183 Bd77
Kali HR 157 Fd64
Kalídona GR 194 Ba87
Kalífitos GR 184 Da76
Kalimanci BG 181 Fa70
Kálimnos GR 197 Eb90
Kalina FIN 83 Ld28
Kalınağılköyü TR 197 Fa90
Kalınharman TR 192 Fc85
Kalinina RUS 203 Fb08
Kaliningrad RUS 113 Ja58
Kalininsk RUS 203 Fd12
Kalininskoe RUS 113 Jd59
Kalinkavičy BY 202 Eb13
Kalınkoz TR 198 Fd90
Kalinovik BIH 159 Hc66
Kalinovka RUS 113 Jc58
Kalinovo SK 146 Ja50
Kalinowa PL 129 Hb39
Kalinówka Kościelna PL 123 Kb32
Kalinowo PL 123 Ka31
Kalipéfki GR 183 Bd80
Kaliroí GR 182 Ba80
Kaliska PL 121 Ha31
Kalisko PL 130 Hd40
Kališta MK 182 Ad75
Kalisty PL 122 Hd31
Kalisz PL 121 Gd31
Kalisz PL 129 Ha39
Kaliszki PL 123 Jd32
Kalisz Pomorski PL 120 Ga34
Kalithéa GR 183 Cb80
Kalithía GR 184 Cd76
Kalīti LV 105 Jc50
Kalitino RUS 99 Mb41
Kalivári GR 190 Da87
Kalíves GR 184 Da78
Kalíves GR 200 Cc95
Kalívia GR 188 Ba84
Kalívia GR 194 Bc90
Kalí Vríssi GR 184 Cd76
Kalix S 73 Jb21
Kalixforsbron S 67 Ha15
Kaljazin RUS 202 Ed09
Kaljord N 66 Fd13
Kaljunen FIN 91 Ld34
Kalkan TR 198 Fd93
Kalkanlı TR 193 Gd82
Kalkar D 125 Bc38
Kalkhorst D 119 Dd31
Kalķi LV 105 Jc49
Kalkım TR 191 Ec81
Kalkkiainen FIN 69 Kc17
Kalkkikangas FIN 68 Jb16
Kalkkimaa FIN 74 Jc21
Kalkkinen FIN 90 Kc36
Kalkstein A 143 Eb55
Kalkstrand FIN 98 Kc39
Kalkūne LV 115 Lc53
Kall D 125 Bc42
Kall S 78 Fa30
Källa S 104 Gc51
Kalland N 92 Cd46
Kållands-Åsaka S 102 Ed46
Kallarberg N 93 Da45
Källarbo S 95 Fd40
Kallaste EST 99 Lb44
Kallax S 73 Hd22
Källbäcken S 95 Fc40
Källbomark S 73 Hc24
Källby FIN 81 Jb29
Källby S 102 Fa46
Källered S 102 Ec49
Kallernäs S 95 Fd42
Kållerstad S 102 Fa51
Kalletal D 126 Cd37
Källfallet S 95 Fd42
Kallham A 144 Fa50
Kallholen S 87 Fc37
Kalli EST 98 Ka45
Kallimassiá GR 191 Dd86
Kallinge S 111 Fd54
Kallio FIN 83 Lb26
Kallio FIN 89 Jd34
Kállio GR 189 Bc84
Kalliojoki FIN 83 Lc25
Kalliokylä FIN 82 Kc28
Kalliola FIN 90 Kc36
Kallioluoma FIN 75 Lb20
Kalliomäki FIN 82 Kd27
Kallislahti FIN 91 Lc33
Kallithéa GR 183 Bc80
Kallithéa GR 189 Cb85
Kallithéa GR 194 Ba89
Kallithéa GR 194 Bc89
Kallithéa GR 197 Ea88
Kallíthiro GR 188 Bb82
Kallivere RUS 99 Lc41
Kallmet AL 163 Jb71
Kallmora S 87 Fc37
Kallmünz D 135 Ea47
Kallo FIN 68 Jc16
Kálló H 146 Hd52
Källö-Knippla S 102 Eb49
Kallön S 72 Gc22
Kalloní GR 191 Ea83
Kalloní GR 195 Ca88
Kállósemjén H 147 Ka51
Kall-Rör S 78 Fa29
Källsjö S 102 Ec50
Källsjön S 87 Ga38
Kallträsk FIN 89 Ja34
Källunga S 102 Ed48
Källunge S 104 Ha49
Källvik S 103 Gb48
Kallviken S 81 Hd26
Kalmaküla EST 99 Lb43
Kalmar S 96 Gc43
Kalmar S 103 Gb52
Kalmari FIN 82 Ka31
Kalmonmäki FIN 82 La27
Kalmthout B 124 Ad38
Kalmykovskij RUS 203 Fd14
Kalna SRB 179 Ca69
Kalna SRB 179 Ca70
Kalnaberže LT 114 Kc56
Kalnamuiža LV 105 Jc52
Kálna nad Hronom SK 145 Hb50
Kalná Roztoka SK 139 Kb47
Kalnbirze LV 107 Lb51
Kalncempji LV 107 Lb48
Kalnciems LV 106 Ka51
Kalniena LV 107 Lc49
Kalnik PL 122 Hd31
Kalniški LV 113 Jb53
Kalniškiai LT 113 Jb54
Kalnovo BG 181 Ec71
Kalnujai LT 114 Ka56
Kalócfa H 145 Gc55
Kalo Chorio CY 206 Ja96
Kalo Chorio CY 206 Ja97
Kalo Chorio CY 206 Jb97
Kalo Chorio CY 206 Jc97
Kalocsa H 146 Hd56
Kalofer BG 180 Dc72
Kalógiri GR 188 Bb81
Kalógria GR 188 Ba85
Kalóhio GR 183 Bb79
Kalohóri GR 182 Ba78
Kaló Horió GR 201 Dc96
Kaló Horió GR 201 Dd96
Kaloí Liménes GR 200 Cd96
Kalojan BG 181 Ed69
Kalojanovec BG 180 Dd73
Kalojanovo BG 180 Db73
Kalojanovo BG 180 Eb72
Kalókastro GR 183 Cb77
Kälom S 79 Fb30
Kalonéri GR 183 Bb78
Kaló Neró GR 194 Ba88
Kaloní GR 196 Db88
Kalopanagiotis CY 206 Ja97
Kalopsida CY 206 Jc96
Kalopsida CY 206 Jc97
Kalotina BG 179 Cb70
Kaloúsi GR 188 Bb86
Káloz H 146 Hc55
Kaložicy RUS 99 Ma41
Kalpáki GR 182 Ad79
Kalpio FIN 75 Kd24
Kals A 143 Eb54
Kalsdorf bei Graz A 144 Fd55
Kälsjärv S 73 Jb21
Kalsko PL 128 Fd36
Kaltanėnai LT 115 Lb56
Kaltbrunn CH 142 Cc53
Kaltenbach A 143 Ea53
Kaltenbrunn A 142 Dc54
Kaltene LV 105 Jd49
Kaltenkirchen D 118 Db32
Kaltennordheim D 126 Db42
Kaltensundheim D 126 Db42
Kaltental D 142 Dc51
Kaltern I 142 Dc56
Kaltesluokta S 67 Gd17
Kaltinėnai LT 113 Jd55
Kaltsila FIN 89 Jc36
Kalttonen FIN 82 Kc29
Kaluđerovići SRB 159 Ja66
Kaluđerovo SRB 174 Bd63
Kaludra MNE 159 Jb68
Kaluga RUS 202 Ed11
Kalugerovc BG 179 Da72
Kalugerovo BG 179 Cd70
Kalundborg DK 109 Ea25
Kalupe LV 115 Lc53
Kaluš UA 204 Ea16
Kałuszyn PL 131 Jd37
Kalužskoe RUS 113 Jc58
Kalv S 102 Ed50
Kalvåg N 84 Ca34
Kalvarija LV 114 Kb59
Kalvatn N 84 Cc34
Kalvbäcken S 80 Gc28
Kalvehave DK 109 Eb28
Kalvene LV 105 Jb52
Kälvene S 102 Fa48
Kalvi EST 98 La41
Kälviä FIN 81 Jc28
Kalviai LT 114 Kc58
Kalvitsa FIN 90 La33
Kalvjärv S 73 Ja20
Kalvola FIN 90 Ka37
Kalvslund DK 108 Da26
Kalvträsk S 80 Hb25
Kalwang A 144 Fc53
Kalwaria Zebrzydowska PL 138 Hd45
Kalwy PL 129 Gb37
Kalynivka UA 204 Eb15
Kám H 145 Gc54
Kamajai LT 114 La54
Kämäränkylä FIN 83 Lc25
Kamärde LV 114 Kc53
Kamáres GR 188 Bb85
Kamáres GR 195 Cd90
Kamáres GR 200 Cd96
Kamári GR 196 Db92
Kamarino RUS 99 Mb45
Kamariótissa GR 184 Dc79
Kamarítsa GR 189 Cb84
Kamaroúla GR 188 Ba84
Kambánis GR 183 Ca77
Kambí GR 188 Ad81
Kambiá GR 191 Dd85
Kambja EST 107 Lb46
Kambo N 93 Ea43
Kámbos GR 188 Ba83
Kámbos GR 188 Ba86
Kámbos GR 188 Bb84
Kámbos GR 194 Bb89
Kámbos GR 196 Dd88
Kámbos GR 197 Ea89
Kámbos GR 197 Eb88
Kámbos GR 200 Ca95
Kamčija BG 181 Fa71
Kamçılı TR 192 Fa81
Kamen BG 180 Ea70
Kamen BG 180 Eb72
Kamen D 125 Cb39
Kamenar BG 181 Fa70
Kaména Voúrla GR 189 Bd84
Kamen Brjag BG 181 Fc70
Kamenec BG 180 Dc69
Kamenec RUS 99 Ld43
Kamenica BIH 152 Gb63
Kamenica BIH 152 Hb63
Kamenica BIH 159 Ja64
Kamenica MK 179 Ca73
Kamenica SK 138 Jc47
Kamenica SRB 178 Ba67
Kamenica SRB 178 Bd69
Kamenica SRB 179 Ca68
Kamenica nad Cirochou SK 139 Ka47
Kamenicë AL 182 Ad77
Kamenice CZ 136 Fc45
Kamenice nad Lipou CZ 136 Fc47
Kamenjane MK 178 Ba73
Kamenka RUS 99 Ld43
Kamenka RUS 107 Ld46
Kamenka RUS 203 Fb13
Kamenka RUS 203 Fc11
Kamennogorsk RUS 202 Ea08
Kamennyj Konec RUS 99 Lc43
Kamenný Přívoz CZ 136 Fb45
Kameno BG 181 Ed72
Kameno Pole BG 179 Cd69
Kamenovo BG 180 Eb68
Kamenskij RUS 203 Fd12
Kamenski Vučjak HR 152 Ha60
Kamensko BIH 153 Hc63
Kamensko HR 152 Ha60
Kamensko HR 158 Gd66
Kamenskoe RUS 113 Jc59
Kamensk-Šahtinskij RUS 203 Fc14
Kamenz D 128 Fb40
Kames GB 6 Dc13
Kameškovo RUS 203 Fa09
Kamičak BIH 152 Gc62
Kamień PL 122 Jc32
Kamień PL 128 Fc36
Kamień PL 129 Ha38
Kamień PL 130 Ja39
Kamień PL 131 Jd40
Kamień PL 131 Kd40
Kamień PL 139 Ka43
Kamienica PL 121 Gc35
Kamienica PL 128 Fd42
Kamienica PL 138 Jb46
Kamienica Dolna PL 139 Jd44
Kamieniec PL 122 Hc32
Kamieniec PL 129 Gb37
Kamieniec Ząbkowicki PL 137 Gc43
Kamienka SK 138 Jb46
Kamień Krajeński PL 121 Gd33
Kamienna Góra PL 128 Ga42
Kamiennik PL 137 Gc43
Kamiennik Wielkopolski PL 122 Hc30
Kamień Pomorski PL 120 Fc31
Kamieńsk PL 130 Hd40
Kamilski Dol BG 185 Ea75
Kamin'-Kašyrs'kyj UA 202 Ea14
Kamion PL 130 Ja38
Kamionek Wielki PL 122 Jc30
Kamionka PL 131 Ka39
Kamionka Wielka PL 138 Jc46
Kamionna PL 128 Ga36
Kamışlı TR 187 Gc79
Kam'janec-Podil's'kyj UA 204 Eb16
Kam'janiec BY 202 Dd13
Kam'janka UA 204 Ed15
Kamjanka-Buz'ka UA 204 Ea15
Kamlunge S 73 Ja21
Kämmäkkä FIN 89 Jc36
Kammela FIN 89 Hd38
Kammeltal D 142 Db50
Kämmenniemi FIN 89 Jd35
Kammerstein D 134 Dc47
Kamminke D 120 Fb32
Kammlach D 142 Db51
Kamnik AL 182 Ad78
Kamnik SLO 151 Fc57
Kamniška Bistrica SLO 151 Fb57
Kamorūnai LT 114 Kd59
Kamøyvær N 64 Jc04
Kampen D 108 Cd28
Kampen NL 117 Bc35
Kampertal A 144 Fb52
Kampevoll N 67 Gb11
Kampia CY 206 Jb97
Kampinkylä FIN 89 Ja32
Kampinos PL 130 Ja37
Kamp-Lintfort D 125 Bc39
Kampor HR 151 Fc62
Kampos CY 206 Ja97
Kamsdorf D 127 Dd42
Kamsjö S 80 Hb27
Kamskoe Ust'e RUS 203 Fd09
Kamula FIN 82 Kb27
Kamyk PL 130 Hc41
Kamýk nad Vltavou CZ 136 Fb46
Kamyšin RUS 203 Fd13
Kanaküla EST 106 Kc46
Kanal SLO 150 Ed58
Kanala FIN 81 Jd29
Kanála GR 195 Cd89
Kanáli GR 182 Ab80
Kanáli GR 188 Ac82
Kanália GR 189 Ca81
Kanan S 71 Fd23
Kanaš RUS 113 Jc57
Kanaš RUS 113 Jc58
Kanaš RUS 203 Fd09
Kanatádika GR 189 Ca83
Kanatlarci MK 183 Bb75
Kańczuga PL 139 Kb44
Kandakjulja RUS 99 Ld39
Kandakopšino RUS 99 Mb40
Kándanos GR 200 Cb95
Kandava LV 105 Jd50
Kandel D 133 Cb47
Kandergrund CH 141 Bd55
Kandern D 141 Bd51
Kandersteg CH 141 Bd55
Kandestederne DK 101 Dd19
Kándia GR 195 Bd88
Kandila GR 194 Bc87
Kandıra TR 187 Gb77
Kandle EST 98 Kd41
Kandyty PL 122 Ja30
Kanepi EST 107 Lb46
Kånešštohpu FIN 64 Jd08
Kanevskaja RUS 205 Fc16
Kanfanar HR 151 Fa61
Kangarisi LV 106 Kc50
Kangas FIN 81 Jd26
Kangas FIN 81 Jb30
Kangas FIN 81 Jb31
Kangasaho FIN 82 Ka31
Kangasala FIN 89 Jd35
Kangasalan asema FIN 89 Jd35
Kangashäkki FIN 90 Kb32
Kangaskylä FIN 82 Kc25
Kangaskylä FIN 82 Kb26
Kangaskylä FIN 82 Ka28
Kangaskylä FIN 82 Ka29
Kangaslahti FIN 82 La28
Kangaslampi FIN 91 Lb32
Kangasniemi FIN 90 Kd33
Kangasoja FIN 81 Jd28
Kangasperä FIN 82 Kc25
Kangasvieri FIN 81 Jd29
Kangos S 68 Hd16
Kangosjärvi FIN 68 Ja15
Kania PL 120 Fd33
Kania PL 121 Ha35
Kanigowo PL 122 Ja33
Kaniów PL 128 Fc38
Kaniv UA 204 Ec15
Kanjiža SRB 153 Jb57
Kankaanpää FIN 89 Jb35
Kankaanpää FIN 89 Jb37
Kankaanpää FIN 90 Ka33
Kankainen FIN 90 Kd32
Kankainen FIN 90 Kc33
Kankari FIN 82 Kc25
Kankberg S 80 Hb25
Kankböle FIN 90 Kc38
Kankkula FIN 82 Kd29
Kånna S 102 Fa52
Kannas FIN 91 Ld34
Kannawurf D 127 Dd40
Kannonkoski FIN 82 Ka30
Kannonsaha FIN 82 Ka30
Kannus FIN 81 Jc27
Kannusjärvi FIN 90 La37
Kannuskoski FIN 90 La36
Kansız TR 192 Fb81
Kanstad N 66 Fd13
Kantala FIN 90 La33
Kantara CY 206 Jd96
Kanteenmaa FIN 89 Jc37
Kantele FIN 90 Kc38
Kantemirovka RUS 203 Fb14
Kantii FIN 89 Jb34
Kantinieki LV 107 Lc51
Kantküla EST 98 La44
Kantojärvi FIN 74 Jc21
Kantojoki FIN 75 La19
Kantokylä FIN 81 Jd27
Kantola FIN 74 Jd22
Kantomaanpää FIN 73 Jb19
Kantoperä FIN 89 Jc33
Kántorjánosi H 147 Kb51
Kantornes N 62 Gd10
Kantou CY 206 Ja98
Kantsjö S 80 Gd29
Kanturk IRL 12 Bc24
Kánya H 145 Hb55
Kányavár H 145 Gc56
Kaolinovo BG 181 Ed69
Kaona SRB 178 Ba67
Kaonik SRB 178 Bc68
Kapaklı TR 186 Fa76
Kapaklı TR 186 Fc79
Kapaklı TR 191 Ed84
Kapaklı TR 193 Hb87
Kapanbelem TR 185 Ec80
Kapandríti GR 189 Cc86
Kapanlar TR 193 Gb81
Kaparéli GR 189 Ca85
Kaparéli GR 194 Bc87
Kapčiamiestis LT 123 Kc30
Kapee FIN 89 Jd34
Kapela HR 152 Gc58
Kapellen A 144 Ga52
Kapellen B 124 Ac39
Kapellen D 125 Bc38
Kapelln A 144 Ga50
Kapera EST 107 Lc47
Kāpessils LV 107 Ld50
Kapfenberg A 144 Fd53
Kápi GR 191 Ea83
Kapice PL 123 Ka32
Kapıkaya TR 191 Ec84
Kapıkaya TR 192 Fd84
Kapıkaya TR 193 Gd81
Kapiņi LV 107 Ld52
Kāpinovo BG 181 Fb69
Kapitan Andeevo BG 185 Ea75
Kapitan-Dimitrievo BG 179 Da73
Kapitan Dimitrovo BG 181 Fa68
Kapitan Petko BG 181 Ec69
Kapız TR 198 Fc90
Kapłan PL 123 Ka35
Kaplangı TR 192 Ga85
Kaplice CZ 136 Fb49
Kapljuh BIH 152 Gb63
Kapolcs H 145 Ha55
Kápolna H 146 Jb52
Kápolnásnyék H 146 Hc54
Kapolypuszta H 145 Ha55
Kaposfüred H 145 Ha56
Kaposgyarmat H 152 Ha57
Kaposmérő H 152 Ha57
Kaposszekcső H 152 Hb57
Kaposvár H 152 Ha57
Kapp N 85 Ea39
Kappel D 133 Bd44
Kappel D 133 Ca44
Kappel DK 109 Dd28
Kappel Grafenhausen D 141 Ca50
Kappeln D 108 Dc29
Kappelrodeck D 133 Cb49
Kappelshamn S 104 Ha48
Kappelskär S 96 Ha42
Kappl A 142 Db54
Käpponis S 73 Hb20
Kaprije HR 157 Ga66
Kaprun A 143 Ec54
Kapsajoki FIN 68 Jc14
Kapsáli GR 195 Bd92
Kapsalos CY 206 Jc96
Kapsēde LV 105 Ja52
Kapshtica AL 182 Ba77
Káptalanfa H 145 Gd54
Káptalantóti H 145 Ha55
Kaptol HR 152 Ha60
Kapūne LV 107 Lc50
Kapušany SK 139 Jd47
Kapuvár H 145 Gc53
Käpysalo FIN 82 Kd30
Karáad H 145 Ha55
Karaadilli TR 193 Gc86
Karaağa TR 193 Hb87
Karaağaç TR 185 Eb75
Karaağaç TR 185 Ed76
Karaağaç TR 186 Fc77
Karaağaç TR 187 Gc77
Karaağaç TR 187 Ha80
Karaağaç TR 191 Eb82
Karaağaç TR 192 Fa83
Karaağaç TR 192 Ga84
Karaağaç TR 193 Gb84
Karaağaçlı TR 191 Ed85
Karaahmetler TR 198 Fb88
Karaahmetler TR 199 Gd90
Karaahmetli TR 186 Ga79
Karaali TR 199 Hb88
Karaaliler TR 199 Gc89
Karaatlı TR 197 Ed88
Karabahadır TR 186 Ga80
Karabayır TR 198 Fd91
Karabedirler TR 192 Ga86
Karabeyler TR 192 Fc85
Karabeyli TR 185 Ed76
Karabeyli TR 186 Ga77
Karabeyli TR 192 Fd85
Karabiga TR 185 Ed79
Karaböğürtlen TR 198 Fb90
Karabucak TR 199 Ha90
Karabük TR 199 Hb90
Karabük TR 205 Fa20
Karabulut TR 193 Ha86
Karabunar BG 179 Da73
Karabürçek TR 185 Ec77
Karaburun TR 186 Fc76
Karaburun TR 191 Ea81
Karaburun TR 191 Ea85
Karaby S 102 Ed46
Karacaağaç TR 197 Fa90
Karacaahmet TR 192 Fd86
Karacaahmet TR 193 Hb82
Karacaali TR 186 Fd79
Karacaali TR 192 Fb87
Karacabey TR 186 Fb80
Karacadağ TR 186 Fa74
Karačaevsk RUS 205 Ga17
Karacahisar TR 192 Ga84
Karacahisar TR 192 Ga85
Karacahisar TR 199 Ha88
Karacaibrahim TR 192 Fb85
Karacakılavuz TR 185 Ed77
Karacaköy TR 186 Fb76
Karacaköy TR 186 Ga77
Karacaköy TR 197 Fa91
Karacalar TR 191 Ed83
Karacalar TR 192 Fb83
Karacalar TR 199 Hb91
Karaçalı TR 185 Ed78
Karacalı TR 186 Fa80
Karaçalı TR 187 Gc77
Karaçaltı TR 192 Fb82
Karaçam TR 191 Ed83
Karaçam TR 198 Fc90
Karacaoğlan TR 185 Ec76
Karacaören TR 193 Gc86
Karacaören TR 193 Gc87
Karacaören TR 193 Gd82
Karacaören TR 193 Hb83
Karacaören TR 197 Fa88
Karacaören TR 198 Fb88
Karacaören TR 198 Fc91
Karacaören TR 199 Gb89
Karacaören TR 199 Gd89
Karacaşehir TR 193 Gc82
Karacaşehir TR 193 Gc84
Karacasu TR 187 Hb79
Karacasu TR 198 Fb88
Karaçepiş TR 191 Ed82
Karačev RUS 202 Ed12
Karácsond H 146 Jb52
Karaçulha TR 198 Fd92
Karaçulha TR 198 Ga91
Karadağ TR 198 Ga93
Karadat TR 193 Hb82
Karadayı TR 199 Gd91
Karadere TR 185 Ed74
Karadere TR 187 Gc78
Karadere TR 187 Gd79
Karadere TR 191 Ec82
Karadere TR 191 Ed84
Karadiken TR 187 Gc78
Karadiken TR 198 Fc90
Karadiken TR 199 Gd89
Karadirek TR 193 Gb86
Karadordevo SRB 153 Ja60
Karageorgievo BG 181 Ed72
Karagöl TR 198 Fc89
Karagöllü TR 186 Ga78
Karagöz TR 192 Fb82
Karahacılı TR 192 Ga87
Karahacılı TR 193 Gb87
Karahallı TR 192 Ga86
Karahamza TR 185 Ec75
Karahasantaşı TR 198 Ga91
Karahıdırlı TR 191 Ec84
Karahisar TR 185 Eb78
Karahisar TR 198 Fc89
Karahisargölcük TR 193 Ha81
Karahka FIN 74 Ka21
Karahka FIN 74 Kb23
Karahüyük TR 193 Ha86
Karahüyük TR 198 Fd89
Karainebeyli TR 185 Ea79
Karakadı TR 192 Ga81
Karakavur TR 187 Hb77
Karakaya TR 192 Fa82
Karakaya TR 192 Fa83
Karakaya TR 192 Fd87
Karakaya TR 193 Ha83
Karakaya TR 197 Ed89
Karakiraz TR 186 Fd77
Karakışla TR 199 Hb90
Karako H 145 Gd54
Karakoca TR 186 Fb80
Karakoçan TR 205 Ga20
Karakólithos GR 189 Bd85
Karaköse TR 193 Gb85
Karaköy TR 187 Hb80
Karaköy TR 191 Ec84
Karaköy TR 191 Ed86
Karaköy TR 192 Fa85
Karaköy TR 192 Fc81
Karaköy TR 192 Fc87
Karaköy TR 197 Ed91
Karaköy TR 198 Fc89
Karaköy TR 199 Gb91
Karaköy TR 199 Gd90
Karakür TR 192 Fd85
Karakütük TR 199 Gd90
Karakuyu TR 191 Ec87
Karakuyu TR 199 Gc90
Karakuzu TR 191 Ec85
Karala EST 105 Jb46
Karalaks N 64 Jb08
Karališkiai LT 114 Ka57
Karališkiai LT 114 La56
Karalkreslis LT 114 Ka59
Karamanca TR 192 Fd84
Karamanci BG 184 Dc74
Karamandere TR 186 Fb76
Karamanlar TR 199 Hb92
Karamanlı TR 198 Ga89
Karamanovo BG 180 Dd69
Karamehmet TR 186 Fa76
Karamık TR 198 Ga92
Karamıkkaracaören TR 193 Gd86
Karamürsel TR 186 Ga79
Karamyševo RUS 107 Ma46
Karamyševo RUS 113 Jd59
Karancslapujtő H 146 Ja50
Karancsság H 146 Ja51
Karankamäki FIN 82 Kc27
Karanovo BG 180 Ea72
Karaoğlanlı TR 191 Ed85
Karaören TR 193 Gc83
Karaorman TR 192 Fb81
Karaot TR 199 Gc90
Karaova TR 197 Ed90
Karaöz TR 199 Gc93
Karapazar TR 193 Gc82
Karapelit BG 181 Fa69
Karapınar TR 192 Fb82
Karapınar TR 193 Ha85
Karapınar TR 199 Gb89
Karapınar TR 199 Gc89
Karapürçek TR 187 Gc79
Karapürçek TR 192 Fb81
Kararkút H 152 Ha57
Karasandıklı TR 193 Gb86
Kárášjohka N 64 Jc09
Karasjok N 64 Jc09
Karasu TR 187 Gd77
Kárász H 152 Hb57
Karataş TR 192 Fb85
Karatas TR 199 Gc90
Karatepe TR 185 Ea80
Karatepe TR 193 Gd82
Karats S 72 Gd19
Karaurgan TR 205 Ga19
Karavas CY 206 Jb96
Karavás GR 195 Bd91
Karaveliler TR 191 Ec83
Karaveliler TR 199 Gc90
Karavelovo BG 180 Db72
Karavóstamo GR 196 Dd88
Karavostasi CY 206 Ja96
Karavostásis GR 196 Da91
Karavukovo SRB 153 Hd59
Karayakup TR 192 Fa85
Karayakuplu TR 186 Ga78
Karayayla TR 198 Fc89
Karayokuş TR 193 Ha85
Karbach D 134 Da45
Karbasan TR 192 Fd83
Karbasan TR 192 Ga87
Karben D 134 Cc45
Karbenning S 95 Ga41
Karbinci MK 183 Bd74
Kårböle S 87 Fd35
Karbowo PL 122 Hc33
Karbow-Vietlübbe D 119 Eb33
Karby DK 100 Da22
Karby S 96 Gd43
Karca TR 197 Fa90
Karcag H 146 Jc53
Karcsa H 147 Ka50
Karczew PL 130 Jc37
Karczmiska PL 131 Jd40
Karczmy PL 130 Hc39
Karczyn PL 129 Gc42
Kärda S 103 Fb51
Kardakáta GR 188 Ab84
Kardam BG 181 Fb69
Kardamás GR 188 Ad86
Kardámena GR 197 Ec91
Kardámila GR 191 Dd85
Kardamíli GR 194 Bb89
Kardašova Řečice CZ 136 Fc47
Kärde EST 98 La44
Kardis S 68 Jb17
Karditsa GR 188 Bb81
Kärdla EST 97 Jc44
Kardos H 146 Jc55
Kărdžali BG 184 Dc75
Kareby S 102 Eb48
Karegašnjarga FIN 64 Jc09
Kårehamn S 103 Gb51
Kåremo S 103 Gb52
Karepa EST 98 La41
Karés GR 200 Cc95
Karesuando S 68 Hd13
Kärevere EST 98 Kd44
Kärevere EST 98 La45
Kärevete EST 98 Kd43
Kargalı TR 186 Ga78
Kargalı TR 193 Hb85
Kargalı TR 198 Ga90
Kargalıhanbaba TR 187 Gc78
Kargersee I 143 Dd56
Kargı TR 193 Hb81
Kargı TR 197 Fa89
Kargı TR 198 Fc91
Kargı TR 199 Gd90
Kargı TR 205 Fb20
Kargılı TR 192 Fd82
Kargılı TR 199 Gc91
Kargın TR 192 Fa85
Kargın TR 199 Gc90
Kargınkürü TR 198 Fc91
Kargów PL 130 Jc42
Kargowa PL 128 Ga38
Kargula EST 107 Lb47
Karhe FIN 89 Jc35
Karhi FIN 81 Jc27
Karhila FIN 90 Ka32
Karhujärvi FIN 74 Kd18
Karhukangas FIN 82 Ka26
Karhula FIN 89 Jc38
Karhula FIN 90 La38
Karhunkylä FIN 89 Jd33
Karhunoja FIN 89 Jc38
Karhunpää FIN 83 Lb27
Karhusjärvi FIN 91 Lc36
Karhuvaara FIN 75 Kd22
Karhuvaara FIN 75 Lb24
Kari FIN 83 Lb28
Kariá GR 188 Ac83
Kariá GR 189 Bc86
Kariá GR 194 Bc87
Kariani GR 184 Cd78
Karidiá GR 183 Bc77
Karidohóri GR 184 Cc76
Kariés GR 182 Ba77
Kariés GR 184 Cd79
Kariés GR 194 Ba88
Kariés GR 194 Bc88
Karigasniemi FIN 64 Jc09
Karihaugen N 66 Ga14
Karijoki FIN 89 Ja33
Karilatsi EST 107 Lb46
Karinainen FIN 89 Jc38
Karıncalı TR 192 Fc81
Karine TR 197 Ec88
Käringön S 102 Ea47
Karinkanta FIN 74 Jd24
Kariótes GR 188 Ac83
Kariótissa GR 183 Bd77
Kariovoúni GR 194 Bc90
Karırçeşme TR 192 Fb81
Karis FIN 97 Jd40
Karise DK 109 Ec27
Karisjärvi FIN 98 Ka39
Káristos GR 195 Cd87
Karítena GR 194 Bb87
Karítsa GR 188 Bb83
Karja EST 97 Jc45
Karjaa FIN 97 Jd40
Karjala FIN 89 Jb38
Karjalaisenniemi FIN 75 Kd19

Karjalan – Kičenica

Karjalan FIN 89 Jb38
Karjalankylä FIN 74 Ka22
Karjalanvaara FIN 74 Kb19
Karjalohja FIN 97 Jd40
Karjatnurme EST 106 Kd47
Kärjenkoski FIN 89 Ja34
Kärjenniemi FIN 89 Jd36
Karjula FIN 89 Jd34
Karjulanmäki FIN 81 Jd28
Karkaloú GR 194 Bb87
Karkažiškė LT 115 Lb57
Karkeamaa FIN 90 La33
Kärkelä FIN 97 Jd39
Karken D 125 Bb40
Kārķi LV 106 Kd47
Karkın TR 193 Ha82
Karkinágri GR 196 Dd88
Kärkkäälä FIN 82 Kc31
Karkkila FIN 90 Ka38
Karkku FIN 89 Jc36
Karkkula FIN 90 Kc37
Karklampi FIN 90 Kb35
Kärklax FIN 81 Ja30
Karklėnai LT 113 Jd55
Karkliniai LV 114 Kb59
Kärkna EST 99 Lb45
Kärkölä FIN 90 Kb37
Kärkölä FIN 90 Ka38
Karksi EST 106 Kd46
Karksi-Nuia EST 106 Kd46
Karkučiai LT 114 Kd58
Kärla EST 105 Jc46
Karlanda S 94 Ec43
Karlbo S 95 Ga41
Karlby FIN 97 Hd41
Karleby FIN 81 Jb28
Karleby FIN 81 Jb28
Karleby S 102 Fa46
Karlewo PL 122 Hd35
Karl Gustav S 102 Ec50
Karlholmsbruk S 96 Gc39
Kārļi LV 106 Kc51
Kārļi LV 106 Kd49
Karlık TR 191 Ed81
Karlino PL 120 Ga31
Karlıova TR 205 Ga20
Karlivka UA 203 Fa14
Karlobag HR 151 Fc63
Karlovac HR 151 Ga60
Karlovássi GR 197 Eb88
Karlova Studánka CZ 137 Gd44
Karlovčić SRB 153 Jb61
Karlovice CZ 137 Gd44
Karlovka RUS 203 Ga11
Karlovo BG 180 Db72
Karlovy Vary CZ 135 Ec44
Karłów PL 137 Gb43
Karłowice PL 129 Gd42
Karlsbäck S 80 Gd28
Karlsbad D 133 Cb48
Karlsbad = Karlovy Vary CZ 135 Ec44
Karlsberg S 87 Fd36
Karlsborg S 103 Fb47
Karlsborg S 73 Jb21
Karlsborg S 103 Fc46
Karlsburg D 120 Fa31
Karlsby S 103 Fc46
Karlsfeld D 143 Dd50
Karlshagen D 120 Fa31
Karlshamn S 111 Fc54
Karlshuld D 135 Dd49
Karlskoga S 95 Fc43
Karlskrona S 111 Fd54
Karlslunda S 111 Ga53
Karlslunde Strand DK 109 Ec26
Karlsøy N 62 Ha08
Karlsruhe D 133 Cb47
Karlstad N 67 Gc11
Karlstad S 94 Fa43
Karlstadt D 134 Da44
Karlstein A 136 Fd48
Karlstift A 136 Fc49
Karlstorp S 103 Fd50
Karmacs H 145 Gd55
Karmannsbo S 95 Fd42
Karmas S 67 Gd17
Karmėlava LT 114 Kc57
Karmin PL 129 Gb38
Kärna FIN 81 Jc30
Kärnä FIN 82 Kb29
Kärna S 102 Eb48
Karnabrunn A 145 Gb50
Kărnare BG 180 Db71
Kärne S 95 Fc43
Karnezéika GR 195 Ca88
Karnice PL 120 Fc31
Karniewo PL 122 Jb35
Karnjarga N 64 Jd07
Karnkowo PL 122 Hc35
Karnobat BG 181 Ec72
Karojba HR 151 Fa60
Karolewo PL 121 Ha33
Karonsbo S 80 Gd26
Karoševina SRB 159 Ja66
Karoussádes GR 182 Aa79
Karow D 119 Eb33
Karpacz PL 128 Ga42
Kärpänkylä FIN 75 Lb20
Karpássi GR 184 Dc80
Karpbukt N 65 Kd07
Karpenísi GR 188 Bb83
Karperí GR 183 Cb76
Karperö FIN 81 Hd30
Karperó GR 183 Bb79
Kárpi GR 183 Bd76
Karpicko PL 128 Ga37
Karpinvaara FIN 75 La24
Karpowicze PL 123 Kb32
Kärppälä FIN 89 Jc36
Kärppäsuo FIN 74 Ka22
Karpuzlu TR 197 Ed89
Kärra FIN 97 Jb40
Kärråkra S 102 Fa48
Kärrbäck S 95 Gb41
Kärrbackstrand S 86 Ed38
Kärrbo S 95 Fd42
Kärrbo S 95 Gb43
Karrebæksminde DK 109 Eb27
Karrsjö S 80 Gd29
Karsak TR 186 Fd80
Karsakiškis LT 114 Kc54
Kärsämä FIN 82 Ka25
Kärsämäki FIN 82 Kb27
Karsanlahti FIN 82 La28
Kārsava LV 107 Ld50
Karsbach D 134 Da44
Karsdorf D 127 Ea40
Karsibór PL 120 Fb32
Karsikas FIN 82 Ka27
Karsikko FIN 74 Jd22
Karsikkovaara FIN 82 Kd26
Karsin PL 121 Gd31
Karşıyaka TR 186 Fa79
Karsjö S 87 Ga36
Karskog FIN 98 Ka40
Kårsta S 96 Gd42
Karstädt D 119 Ea34
Kärstna EST 106 Kd46
Karstula FIN 82 Ka31
Karsun RUS 203 Fd10
Kartalkaya TR 187 Hb79
Kartalpınar TR 199 Gc89
Kartena LT 113 Jb54
Karterés GR 183 Cb77
Karterés GR 183 Cb77
Kartéri GR 188 Ac81
Kårtjevuolle sameviste S 67 Gc15
Kartno PL 120 Fc34
Karttiperä FIN 89 Jc34
Karttula FIN 82 Kd30
Kartuzy PL 121 Ha30
Käru EST 98 Ka45
Käru EST 98 Kc44
Karula EST 106 La47
Karulõpe EST 98 La41
Karuna FIN 97 Jc40
Karungi S 73 Jb20
Karunki FIN 74 Jc20
Karup DK 100 Db23
Karvala FIN 81 Jc30
Karvasalmi FIN 82 Kd29
Kärväskylä FIN 82 Kb29
Karvia FIN 89 Jb33
Karviankylä FIN 89 Jb33
Karvila FIN 91 Lc32
Karviná CZ 137 Hb45
Karvio FIN 83 Lb31
Karvoskylä FIN 82 Ka27
Karvys LT 114 La57
Karwia PL 112 Ha58
Karwica PL 122 Jc32
Karwin PL 120 Ga31
Karwowo-Wszebory PL 123 Jd33
Karyağmaz TR 192 Fc82
Karzec PL 129 Gc39
Kås DK 100 Dc20
Kaş TR 198 Ga93
Kåsa N 77 Dc32
Kasaba TR 198 Ga93
Kasaböle FIN 89 Hd34
Kasala FIN 89 Hd34
Kašalj SRB 178 Ba69
Kasapa SRB 153 Jb63
Kašary RUS 203 Fc14
Kascjukovičy BY 202 Ec12
Kascjukovka BY 202 Ec13
Kåseberga S 111 Fb57
Kasejovice CZ 136 Fa46
Kasendorf D 135 Dd44
Kasepää EST 99 Lb44
Kasfjord N 66 Ga12
Kaşıkçı TR 185 Ec77
Kaşıkçı TR 191 Ec84
Kaşıkçı TR 192 Fb84
Kaşıkçışeyhler TR 187 Gc79
Kasımlar TR 187 Gb80
Kasımlar TR 199 Ha89
Kasimov RUS 203 Fb10
Kašin RUS 202 Ed09
Kašina HR 152 Gb58
Kasina Wielka PL 138 Ja45
Kasiniemi FIN 90 Kb35
Kasinka Mała PL 138 Ja45
Kaširskoe RUS 113 Ja58
Kåskats S 73 Hb19
Kaskii FIN 91 Lb33
Kaskinen FIN 89 Hd33
Kaskö FIN 89 Hd33
Kas'kovo RUS 99 Ma40
Käsma FIN 75 La20
Käsmänlatva FIN 69 Kd17
Käsmu EST 98 Kd41
Kasnäs FIN 97 Jb41
Káspakas GR 190 Db81
Kašperské Hory CZ 135 Ed47
Kaspičan BG 181 Ed70
Kassa S 68 Jb17
Kassari EST 97 Jd45
Kassari saar EST 97 Jd45
Kasseedorf D 119 Dd31
Kassel D 126 Da40
Kassiópi GR 182 Ab79
Kassjö S 80 Hb28
Kastamonu TR 205 Fa20
Kastanées GR 183 Ca76
Kastaneri GR 183 Bd76
Kastaniá GR 182 Ad78
Kastaniá GR 182 Ba80
Kastaniá GR 183 Bc78
Kastaniá GR 188 Bb82
Kastaniá GR 189 Bc83
Kastaniá GR 189 Bc86
Kastaniés GR 185 Eb75
Kastaniótissa GR 189 Ca83
Kastanítsa GR 194 Bc88
Kastanófito GR 182 Ba78
Kastav HR 151 Fb60
Kastel HR 150 Ed60
Kastéla GR 189 Cb85
Kaštela HR 158 Gb66
Kastelev DK 109 Eb28
Kastéli GR 201 Db96
Kastellaun D 133 Ca44
Kastélli GR 189 Bc84
Kastelruth I 143 Dd56
Kastelyosdombó H 152 Ha58
Kaštel Žegarski HR 157 Ga64
Kasterlee B 124 Ad39
Kastl D 143 Ec51
Kastlösa S 111 Gb53
Kastneshamn N 67 Gb12
Kastoriá GR 182 Ba77
Kastós GR 188 Ad84
Kastráki GR 189 Bd86
Kastraki GR 196 Db90
Kastre EST 99 Lb45
Kastrí GR 182 Ac80
Kastrí GR 189 Bd81
Kastrí GR 194 Bc88
Kastrí GR 200 Cb97
Kastria GR 188 Bb86
Kastrítsa GR 182 Ad80
Kástro GR 188 Ad86
Kástro GR 189 Ca85
Kástro GR 196 Da90
Kastrosikiá GR 188 Ac82
Kastrup DK 109 Eb28
Kašučiai LT 113 Jb54
Kasukkala FIN 91 Lc36
Kaszaper H 147 Jd56
Kasztanowo PL 122 Hd31
Kaszyce PL 129 Gc40
Katafigio GR 183 Bc79
Katáfito GR 184 Cc76
Katahás GR 183 Bd78
Katajamäki FIN 83 Lb28
Katajamäki FIN 90 La32
Katákolo GR 194 Ad87
Kåtaliden S 72 Gc23
Kataloinen FIN 90 Kb37
Katalónia GR 183 Bd78
Katänjoki FIN 81 Jc31
Katápola GR 196 Dc91
Kåtaselet S 73 Hb23
Katastári GR 188 Ac86
Katauskiai LT 114 Ka55
Kåtaviken S 71 Fc21
Kateczyn PL 122 Jb32
Kateríni GR 183 Bd79
Katerma FIN 83 Lb26
Katesbridge GB 9 Da18
Kathení GR 189 Cc85
Kathikas CY 206 Hd97
Katići SRB 178 Ad67
Kåtilla S 87 Fb37
Katina BG 179 Cc71
Katinac HR 152 Gd59
Katinhänta FIN 89 Ja38
Kätkäsuvanto FIN 68 Ja14
Kätkävaara FIN 74 Jd20
Kätkesuando S 68 Ja14
Katko FIN 89 Jb34
Katlanovska Banja MK 178 Bc73
Katlenburg-Lindau D 126 Db39
Katleši LV 107 Ld48
Káto Ahaía GR 188 Ba85
Káto Alepohóri GR 189 Ca86
Káto Almirí GR 195 Ca87
Káto Asítes GR 200 Da96
Káto Asséa GR 194 Bc88
KatoDeftera CY 206 Jb97
Káto Dikomo CY 206 Jb96
Káto Doliană GR 195 Bd88
Káto Figália GR 194 Ba88
Káto Gialia CY 206 Hd97
Káto Glikóvrisi GR 195 Bd90
Katohí GR 188 Ba84
Káto Horió GR 201 Dc96
Káto Hrisovitsa GR 188 Bb84
Káto Kastaniá GR 195 Bd91
Káto Kastrítsi GR 188 Bb85
Katokopia CY 206 Ja96
Káto Koutrafas CY 206 Ja97
Káto Lapsista GR 182 Ad80
Káto Makrinoú GR 188 Ba84
Káto Meriá GR 195 Cd88
Káto Moni CY 206 Jb97
Káto Mousounitsa GR 189 Bc84
Káto Nevrokópi GR 184 Cd76
Káto Polemidia CY 206 Ja98
Káto Pyrgos CY 206 Ja96
Káto Samikó GR 194 Ba87
Káto Sotiritsa GR 189 Ca81
Káto Soúnio GR 195 Cc88
Katosranta FIN 75 La21
Káto Tarsós GR 189 Bc86
Káto Theodoráki GR 183 Cb76
Káto Tritos GR 191 Ea83
Katoúna GR 188 Ad83
Káto Vérmio GR 183 Bc78
Káto Vlassia GR 188 Bb86
Kátó Vrontoú GR 184 Cc76
Katowice PL 138 Hc44
Káto Zákros GR 201 Dd96
Katriņa LV 106 La50
Katrineholm S 95 Ga45
Katsarós GR 194 Bb88
Katsch an der Mur A 144 Fb54
Katsikás GR 182 Ad80
Katsimbalis GR 194 Bb88
Kattarp S 110 Ed54
Kattavia GR 197 Ed94
Kättbo S 87 Fb38
Kattelus FIN 89 Jd32
Katterat N 67 Gc13
Katterjåkk S 67 Gc13
Katthammarsvik S 104 Ha50
Kattilainen FIN 91 Lb38
Kattilakoski FIN 81 Jc29
Kattilasaari S 73 Jb21
Kattisavan S 80 Gc25
Kattisberg S 80 Ha25
Kattlunds S 104 Ha51
Kattowitz = Katowice PL 138 Hc44
Kattuvuoma S 67 Ha14
Katunci BG 184 Cc75
Katund i Ri AL 182 Ab74
Katunica BG 180 Db73
Katusice CZ 136 Fc43
Katvari LV 106 Kc48
Katwijk aan Zee NL 116 Ad36
Kąty PL 123 Jd33
Katy PL 131 Ka42
Katyčiai LT 113 Jc56
Katymár H 153 Hd58
Kąty Rybackie PL 122 Hc30
Katy Wrocławskie PL 129 Gc41
Katzenelnbogen D 133 Cb43
Katzhütte D 135 Dd43
Kaub D 133 Ca44
Kaufbeuren D 142 Db51
Kaufering D 142 Dc51
Kaufungen D 126 Da40
Kauhajärvi FIN 81 Jc30
Kauhajärvi FIN 89 Jb33
Kauhajoki FIN 89 Ja33
Kauhanoja FIN 89 Jc38
Kauhava FIN 81 Jb30
Kauhee FIN 83 Ld29
Kauk- FIN 98 Kb40
Kaukalampi FIN 90 Kc38
Kaukas FIN 90 Kb38
Kaukassalo FIN 97 Jc40
Kaukela FIN 90 Kb35
Kauklainen FIN 89 Ja37
Kaukola FIN 97 Jd39
Kaukolikai LT 113 Jc53
Kaukonen FIN 68 Jc16
Kauksi EST 99 Lb43
Kaukuri FIN 97 Jd40
Kaulaci LV 105 Jd51
Kaulakiai LT 114 Ka56
Kaulinranta FIN 73 Jb19
Kaulio FIN 90 La36
Kaunas LT 114 Kc57
Kaunata LV 107 Ld52
Kaunatava LT 113 Jd54
Kauniainen FIN 98 Kb39
Kaunisjoensuu S 68 Jb16
Kaunisvaara S 68 Ja16
Kaunitz D 126 Cc38
Kaupanger N 84 Cd37
Kauppila FIN 90 Kd32
Kauppilanmäki FIN 82 Kd27
Kaupuži LV 107 Ld50
Kaurajärvi FIN 81 Jb30
Kauria FIN 90 La35
Kaurissalo FIN 97 Ja39
Kauronkylä FIN 83 Lc25
Kauša LV 107 Lc52
Kausala FIN 90 Kd37
Kausen D 125 Cb41
Kausland N 84 Bd39
Kaustajärvi FIN 83 Ma31
Kaustari FIN 81 Jb28
Kaustinen FIN 81 Jc29
Kautokeino N 68 Hd11
Kauttua FIN 89 Jb37
Kautzen A 136 Fd48
Kauvatsa FIN 89 Jb36
Káva H 146 Ja53
Kavacık TR 185 Eb77
Kavacık TR 192 Fb82
Kavacık TR 193 Gc81
Kavacık TR 199 Gb88
Kavadarci MK 183 Bd75
Kavajë AL 182 Ab75
Kavak TR 205 Fc20
Kavakarası TR 198 Fc91
Kavakçalı TR 198 Fb90
Kavakdere TR 185 Ed75
Kavakdere TR 198 Ga91
Kavakköy TR 185 Ec79
Kavakköy TR 193 Hb81
Kavaklı TR 185 Eb77
Kavaklı TR 185 Ec75
Kavaklı TR 186 Fb77
Kavaklı TR 186 Fc78
Kavaklı TR 186 Ga80
Kavaklı TR 192 Ga81
Kavaklı TR 198 Fb88
Kavaklıdere TR 198 Fb89
Kavala FIN 90 Ka34
Kavála GR 184 Da77
Kavarna BG 181 Fb70
Kavarskas LT 114 Kd55
Kavelstorf D 119 Eb31
Kåvenvallen S 86 Ed33
Kavgacılar TR 199 Gd91
Kavlac BG 180 Ea70
Kävlinge S 110 Ed55
Kavos GR 188 Ab81
Kavoúsi GR 201 Dc96
Kavşıt TR 197 Fa88
Kavslunde DK 108 Db26
Kawęczyn PL 129 Hb38
Kawice PL 129 Gb40
Kaxås S 79 Fb30
Kaxholmen S 103 Fb48
Kayaağıl TR 192 Fd85
Kayabaşı TR 186 Fc77
Kayabaşı TR 192 Fb81
Kayabaşı TR 197 Ed89
Kayabaşı TR 198 Fd92
Kayabaşı TR 198 Ga91
Kayabaşı TR 199 Ha89
Kayabükü TR 193 Hb81
Kayabükü TR 197 Ed89
Kayacık TR 186 Fd80
Kayacık TR 192 Fa84
Kayacık TR 198 Fc91
Kayadibi TR 191 Ec85
Kayaışık TR 192 Fc84
Kayakalan TR 192 Fa85
Kayakent TR 193 Hb83
Kayaköy TR 191 Ed87
Kayaköy TR 198 Fc92
Kayalar TR 191 Ed81
Kayalar TR 199 Ha89
Kayalı TR 185 Ec75
Kayalı TR 192 Fc86
Kayalı TR 199 Gb90
Kayalıdere TR 192 Fc83
Kayalıoğlu TR 191 Ed84
Kayapa TR 185 Eb75
Kayapa TR 186 Fc80
Kayapa TR 191 Ed82
Kayapınar TR 191 Ea85
Kayapınar TR 191 Ed81
Kayapınar TR 198 Fc89
Kayı TR 185 Ed77
Kayı TR 193 Gd83
Kayı TR 193 Ha81
Kayıköy TR 199 Gc88
Kayış TR 199 Gc89
Kayışlar TR 191 Ed84
Käylä FIN 74 La18
Käymäjärvi S 68 Ja16
Kaymakçı TR 192 Fa87
Kaymakoba TR 186 Fc80
Kaymaz TR 187 Gb78
Kaymaz TR 193 Ha83
Kayna D 127 Eb41
Kaynaklar TR 191 Ec86
Kaynarca TR 187 Gc78
Kaynaşlı TR 187 Ha78
Käyppälä FIN 81 Ja31
Käyrämö FIN 69 Ka17
Kayran TR 192 Fb87
Kaysersberg F 31 Kb38
Kazačka RUS 203 Fc12
Kazan' RUS 203 Fd08
Kažani MK 182 Ba76
Kazanka UA 204 Ed16
Kazanlăk BG 180 Dd72
Kazanów PL 130 Jc40
Kazanskaja RUS 203 Fc13
Kazdanga LV 105 Jb52
Kaziċene BG 179 Cc71
Kazıklı TR 186 Fd80
Kazimierza Wielka PL 138 Jb43
Kazimierz Biskupi PL 129 Ha37
Kazimierz Dolny PL 131 Jd40
Kazimierzewo PL 121 Hb35
Kazimierzewo PL 122 Hc30
Kazımpaşa TR 187 Gc78
Kazincbarcika H 146 Jc50
Kazitiškis LT 115 Lb55
Kazivera CY 206 Ja96
Kazliškis LT 114 La53
Kazlų Rūda LV 114 Kb58
Kaźmierz PL 129 Gb36
Kaznějov CZ 135 Ed45
Kcynia PL 121 Gd35
Kdyně CZ 135 Ec47
Keadew IRL 8 Ca18
Keady GB 9 Cd18
Keal GB 17 Fd22
Kealkil IRL 12 Bb26
Keava EST 98 Kc44
Keb RUS 107 Ma46
Kecel H 146 Hd56
Kecerovce SK 139 Jd48
Keçiborlu TR 199 Gc88
Keçidere TR 192 Fb82
Keçiler TR 193 Gb84
Kecskemét H 146 Ja55
Kėdainiai LT 114 Kc56
Kédros GR 189 Bc82
Kędrzyno PL 120 Fd31
Kędzierzyn-Koźle PL 137 Ha43
Keeagh IRL 12 Bc21
Keeken D 125 Bc37
Keel IRL 8 Bb18
Keelby GB 17 Fc21
Keeni EST 106 La47
Kefalári GR 189 Bc86
Kéfalos GR 197 Eb91
Kefalóvrisso GR 183 Bc80
Kefenrod D 134 Cd43
Kefermarkt A 144 Fb50
Kefferhausen D 126 Db40
Kefken TR 187 Gb77
Keflavík IS 2 Ab04
Ķegums LV 106 Kc51
Kegworth GB 16 Fa23
Kehidakustány H 145 Gd55
Kehl D 133 Ca49
Kehra EST 98 Kc42
Kehrigk D 128 Fa37
Kehrókambos GR 184 Da76
Kehtna EST 98 Kc44
Keighley GB 16 Ed20
Keihärinkoski FIN 82 Kb30
Keihäskoski FIN 89 Jb38
Keihäsniemi FIN 90 Kb34
Keikyä FIN 89 Jb36
Keila EST 98 Kb42
Keila-Joa EST 98 Kb42
Keillmore GB 6 Db13
Keimola FIN 98 Kb39
Keinäsperä FIN 75 Kc23
Keinojärvi FIN 65 Kb10
Keino sameviste S 67 Gd17
Keinovuopio S 67 Hb12
Keinton Mandeville GB 19 Eb29
Ķeipene LV 106 Kd50
Keisala FIN 81 Jd31
Keistiö FIN 97 Ja40
Keitele FIN 82 Kc29
Keitelepohja FIN 82 Kb29
Keith GB 7 Ec08
Keitjärvi FIN 90 La37
Keituri FIN 90 Kc37
Ķekava LV 106 Kb51
Kéked H 139 Jd49
Kekkilä FIN 82 Kb31
Kekkonen FIN 89 Jd34
Kelankylä FIN 74 Kb21
Kelberg D 133 Bd43
Kelbra D 127 Dd40
Kelč CZ 137 Ha46
Kelchsau A 143 Ea53
Këlcyrë AL 182 Ac78
Keld GB 11 Ed18
Keldbylille DK 109 Ec28
Keldernæs DK 109 Ea28
Keldinge FIN 97 Jb40
Kelebija SRB 153 Ja57
Keléd H 145 Gd54
Kelekci TR 198 Fd90
Kelemér H 146 Jb50
Keler TR 191 Ec87
Keles TR 192 Fd81
Kelheim D 135 Ea48
Kéli GR 183 Bb77
Kelionkangas FIN 90 Kb33
Kelkheim D 134 Cc44
Kelkit TR 205 Fd20
Kelkkala FIN 97 Jd40
Kellahti FIN 89 Ja35
Kellaki CY 206 Jb97
Kellenhusen D 119 Dd30
Kellerberg A 144 Fa56
Kellia CY 206 Jc97
Kelling GB 17 Gb23
Kellinghusen D 118 Db31
Kello FIN 74 Ka23
Kellokoski FIN 90 Kb38
Kelloniemi FIN 74 Kc18
Kellosalmi FIN 90 Kb35
Kelloselkä FIN 69 Kd17
Kells IRL 9 Cc20
Kells IRL 12 Ba25
Kellybray GB 18 Dc31
Kelmė LT 114 Ka55
Kelmis B 125 Bb41
Kelokedara CY 206 Hd98
Kelontekemä FIN 69 Jd15
Kelottijärvi FIN 68 Hc13
Kelovaara FIN 68 Ja14
Kelsale GB 21 Gb25
Kelsall GB 15 Ec22
Kelso GB 11 Ec14
Kelstrup DK 108 Db27
Keltakangas FIN 90 La37
Keltaniemi FIN 90 Kc36
Keltiäinen FIN 89 Jd38
Keltti FIN 90 Kd37
Kelty GB 7 Eb12
Kelujärvi FIN 69 Ka15
Kelvä FIN 83 Ld29
Kelvedon GB 21 Ga27
Kemah TR 205 Fd20
Kemaliye TR 187 Gb79
Kemaliye TR 192 Fb86
Kemaller TR 185 Ed77
Kemaller TR 187 Gc79
Kemallı TR 191 Ea81
Kemalpaşa TR 191 Ec86
Kemalpaşa TR 205 Ga18
Ķemari LV 106 La51
Kematen A 144 Fc51
Kemberg D 127 Ec39
Kemble GB 20 Ed27
Kemecse H 147 Ka50
Kemence H 146 Hc51
Kemeneshőgyész H 145 Gd53
Kemer TR 185 Ec79
Kemer TR 192 Fa85
Kemer TR 198 Ga93
Kemer TR 199 Gb89
Kemer TR 199 Gc92
Kemerburgaz TR 186 Fc77
Kemerdamları TR 192 Fa85
Kemerdamları TR 193 Gd87
Kemerkasım TR 187 Ha78
Kémes H 152 Hb58
Kemeten A 145 Gb54
Kemi FIN 74 Jc21
Kemie FIN 83 Ma31
Kemihaara FIN 69 Kc13
Kemijärvi FIN 74 Kb18
Kemiklidere TR 191 Ed85
Kemilä FIN 75 La20
Keminmaa FIN 74 Jc21
Keminperä FIN 75 La21
Kemiö FIN 97 Jc40
Kemlja RUS 203 Fc10
Kemmel B 21 Ha30
Kemnath D 135 Ea45
Kemnay GB 7 Ed09
Kemnitz D 120 Fa31
Kemnitz D 127 Ed37
Kempele FIN 74 Ka24
Kempen D 125 Bc39
Kempenich D 125 Bd42
Kempsey GB 15 Ec26
Kempston GB 20 Fc26
Kempten CH 142 Cc53
Kempten D 142 Db52
Kemtau D 127 Ec42
Kena LT 115 Lb58
Kendal GB 11 Ec18
Kenderes H 146 Jc53
Kendice SK 139 Jd48
Kéndro GR 188 Ba86
Kéndro GR 194 Bb89
Kenestupa FIN 64 Jd08
Kenfig GB 19 Dd28
Kenger TR 197 Fa88
Kengis S 68 Ja17
Kengyel H 146 Jb54
Kenilworth GB 20 Fa25
Kenknock GB 7 Dd11
Kenmare IRL 12 Bb25
Neidín IRL 12 Bb25
Kenmore GB 7 Ea11
Kenn GB 19 Ea31
Kennää FIN 82 Kb30
Kennacraig GB 6 Db13
Kenninghall GB 21 Ga25
Kenraalinkylä FIN 83 Ma31
Kentisbury Ford GB 19 Dd29
Kentmere GB 11 Ec18
Kentrikó GR 183 Ca76
Kéntro GR 183 Bb79
Kenttan N 64 Jc09
Kenyeri H 145 Gd53
Kenzingen D 141 Ca50
Kepaliai LT 114 Kb53
Kepekler TR 192 Fb82
Kepen TR 193 Ha83
Kepenekli TR 185 Ed77
Kepezbeleni TR 199 Hb91
Kępice PL 121 Gc30
Kępno PL 129 Ha40
Kepsut TR 192 Fa82
Kerälä FIN 82 Ka25
Keramídi GR 189 Ca81
Kéramos GR 191 Dd85
Keramotí GR 184 Db77
Keränen FIN 75 Kd19
Keräntöjärvi S 68 Ja15
Kerasohóri GR 188 Bb82
Kerasóna GR 188 Ad81
Keräs-Sieppi FIN 68 Jb14
Kerássovo GR 182 Ac79
Keratea GR 195 Cc87
Keratókambos GR 201 Db96
Kerauzern F 26 Ea37
Kerava FIN 98 Kb39
Keravere EST 98 Ka44
Kerbanlar TR 187 Hb80
Kerč UA 205 Fb17
Kerecsend H 146 Jb52
Kereka BG 180 Dd70
Kerekegyháza H 146 Ja55
Kereki H 145 Ha55
Keremköy TR 191 Eb83
Kerepestarcsa H 146 Hd52
Kergrist-Moëlou F 26 Ea38
Kergu EST 98 Kc45
Kerí GR 188 Ac86
Kérien F 26 Ea38
Kerimäki FIN 91 Ld33
Kerimler TR 192 Fc87
Keriniemi FIN 91 Lb34
Kerisalo FIN 91 Lb32
Kérity F 27 Dc40
Kerkafalva H 145 Gb55
Kerken D 125 Bc39
Kerkíni GR 183 Cb76
Kerkíra GR 182 Ab80
Kerkkoo FIN 90 Kc38
Kerkliņi LV 105 Jd52
Kerko FIN 90 Kc38
Kerkola FIN 89 Jd38
Kerkonkoski FIN 82 Kc31
Kerkow D 120 Fa34
Kerkrade NL 125 Bb41
Kerma FIN 83 Lc31
Kermen BG 180 Ea72
Kernascléden F 27 Ea39
Kernavė LT 114 Kd57
Kernhof A 144 Fd52
Kernovo RUS 99 Ld40
Kerns CH 141 Ca54
Kernu EST 98 Kb43
Kéros GR 196 Dc90
Kerpe TR 187 Gb77
Kerpen D 125 Bc41
Kerpen (Eifel) D 133 Bc43
Kerpiçlik TR 191 Ed86
Kerpiçlik TR 192 Fc84
Kerpini GR 188 Bb86
Kerry GB 15 Eb24
Kersalu EST 98 Ka42
Kersilö FIN 69 Ka15
Kersleti EST 97 Jd44
Kerstovo RUS 99 Ld41
Kerstovo RUS 99 Ld41
Kerteminde DK 109 Dd26
Kertészsziget H 147 Jd54
Kértezi GR 188 Bb86
Kerthpulë AL 163 Jb71
Kertil TR 192 Fa83
Kerttuankylä FIN 81 Jc29
Keryneia CY 206 Jb96
Kerzers CH 141 Bc54
Kesälahti FIN 91 Ld33
Kesämäki FIN 82 La29
Keşan TR 185 Eb78
Kesäpuro FIN 64 Ka07
Kesarevo BG 180 Ea70
Kesasjärv S 73 Hd20
Kesčiai LT 113 Jd56
Kesecik TR 199 Hb89
Keselyüs H 153 Hc57
Kesenler TR 193 Gc83
Kesh GB 9 Cb17
Kesh IRL 8 Ca18
Keshcarigan IRL 8 Ca19
Kesik TR 191 Eb85
Keskijärvi FIN 83 Ld30
Keskikylä FIN 74 Ka22
Keskikylä FIN 74 Jd24
Keskikylä FIN 74 Ka24
Keskikylä FIN 81 Jd31
Keskikylä FIN 81 Jd26
Keskikylä FIN 89 Jb33
Keskikylä FIN 91 Lb33
Keskin TR 193 Gc81
Keskinen FIN 75 Lb24
Keski-Nurmo FIN 81 Jb31
Keski-Palokka FIN 90 Kb32
Keskipiiri FIN 74 Ka24
Keskisaari FIN 91 Lb32
Keski-Valli FIN 89 Jb32
Keski-Vuokko FIN 83 Lb28
Kesme TR 199 Ha89
Kesnacken S 94 Ec44
Kęsowo PL 121 Gd33
Kessel NL 125 Bc39
Kesselfall A 143 Ec54
Kesselinkylä FIN 83 Lc26
Kesselsdorf D 128 Fa41
Kessingland GB 21 Gc25
Kessock GB 7 Ea08
Kestad S 102 Fa46
Kestanelik TR 186 Fb77
Kestanepınarı TR 187 Gd78
Kestel TR 192 Fd84
Ķesterciems LV 106 Ka50
Kesteren NL 125 Bb37
Kesteri LV 113 Jb53
Kesti FIN 89 Ja32
Kestilä FIN 74 Jd23
Kestilä FIN 82 Kb26
Kesusmaa FIN 91 Ld33
Keswick GB 11 Eb17
Keszthely H 145 Gd55
Ketčenery RUS 203 Ga14
Kétegyháza H 147 Jd56
Ketelhaven NL 117 Bc35
Ketendere TR 192 Fb87
Ketenova TR 192 Fb87
Kéthely H 145 Gd56
Ketola FIN 74 Kb18
Ketomella FIN 68 Jb13
Kétpó H 146 Jc54
Keträvaara FIN 75 La22
Kętrzyn PL 122 Jc30
Ketsch D 134 Cc46
Kettenkamp D 117 Cb35
Kettering GB 20 Fb25
Kettilsbyn S 94 Ed44
Kettinge DK 109 Eb29
Kettletoft GB 5 Ed02
Kettlewell GB 11 Ed19
Kéttornyúlak H 145 Gd54
Kettula FIN 97 Jd39
Ketūnai LT 113 Jc53
Keturkaimis LT 114 Ka58
Keturvalakiai LV 114 Kb59
Kéty H 146 Hc56
Kęty PL 138 Hd45
Ketzin D 127 Ec36
Ketzür D 127 Ec36
Keula D 126 Dc40
Keula D 126 Dc40
Keuruu FIN 90 Ka33
Keväjärvi FIN 69 Kb11
Kevastu EST 99 Lb45
Kevelaer D 125 Bc38
Kevele LV 105 Jd52
Kevermes H 147 Jd56
Kevi SRB 153 Jb58
Kewstoke GB 19 Eb28
Kexby GB 16 Fb22
Keynsham GB 19 Ec28
Keyritty FIN 82 La28
Keyston GB 20 Fc25
Keyworth GB 16 Fb23
Kežmarok SK 138 Jb47
Kiaby S 111 Fb54
Kiados CY 206 Jc96
Kiannanniemi FIN 75 La22
Kiáto GR 189 Bd86
Kiaunoriai LT 114 Ka55
Kibæk DK 108 Da24
Kiberg N 62 Gc09
Kiberg N 65 Kd05
Kıbrıscık TR 187 Hb80
Kiburi LV 113 Jb53
Kiby N 65 Kc06
Kibyšiai LT 123 Kc30
Kičenica BG 180 Eb69

Klenovica – Korita

Klenovica HR 151 Fc61
Kleosin PL 123 Kb33
Kleppe N 85 Dc35
Kleppe N 92 Ca44
Kleppenes N 84 Cb34
Kleppestø N 84 Ca39
Klępsk PL 128 Ga38
Klepstad N 66 Fb14
Klėriškės LT 114 Kd58
Kleśno PL 120 Ga35
Kleszczele PL 123 Kb35
Kleszczewo PL 129 Gc37
Kleszczów PL 130 Hc40
Kleszczów PL 137 Hb43
Kleszewo PL 122 Jb35
Klėtiškė LT 113 Jd55
Kletnja RUS 202 Ec12
Kletno PL 137 Gc44
Kletskij RUS 203 Fd13
Klettgau D 141 Cb52
Klettwitz D 128 Fa39
Kleve D 125 Bc38
Kleven N 92 Cc47
Klevmarken S 94 Eb45
Klevshult S 103 Fb50
Klewianka PL 123 Ka32
Klewki PL 122 Ja32
Klezeno RUS 107 Lc47
Kličav BY 202 Eb12
Kličevac SRB 174 Bc64
Kliczków PL 128 Fd40
Klidí GR 183 Bb77
Klidí GR 183 Ca78
Klieken D 127 Eb38
Kliening A 144 Fc55
Klietz D 127 Eb36
Kligene LV 106 Kd50
Klíma GR 183 Bb78
Klíma GR 189 Cc83
Klimaszewnica PL 123 Ka32
Klimatáki GR 182 Ba79
Klimatiá GR 182 Ab79
Klimavičy BY 202 Ec12
Kliment BG 181 Ec69
Klimkovice CZ 137 Ha45
Klimontów PL 131 Jd42
Klimontów PL 138 Jb43
Klimovo RUS 107 Ma47
Klimovo RUS 202 Ec13
Klimovsk RUS 202 Ed10
Klimpfjäll S 71 Fc24
Klin RUS 202 Ed10
Klina KSV 178 Ba70
Klincovka RUS 113 Ja58
Klincovka RUS 203 Ga11
Klincy RUS 202 Ec13
Klindiá GR 188 Ba86
Klinga N 78 Ec26
Klingenbach A 145 Gb52
Klingenberg D 134 Cd45
Klingenmünster D 133 Cb47
Klingenthal D 135 Eb43
Klingersel S 73 Hc20
Klingnau CH 141 Cb52
Kliniča Sela HR 151 Ga59
Klink D 119 Ec33
Klinkby DK 100 Cd22
Klinó GR 182 Ba80
Klintebjerg DK 109 Dd26
Klintehamn S 104 Gd50
Klippan S 110 Ed54
Klippen S 71 Fc22
Klippen S 80 Gc28
Klippinge DK 109 Ec27
Klirou CY 206 Jb97
Klis HR 158 Gc66
Klisa HR 153 Hd59
Klisino PL 137 Ha44
Klissoúra GR 183 Bb78
Klissoúra GR 188 Ad81
Klisura BG 179 Cc72
Klisura BG 179 Da71
Klisura SRB 179 Ca71
Klisurica BG 179 Cc68
Klitmøller DK 100 Da21
Klitoría GR 188 Bb86
Klitten D 128 Fc40
Klitten S 87 Fb37
Klivi LV 106 Kc52
Kljajićevo SRB 153 Hd58
Kljasino RUS 99 Ma40
Kljavino RUS 203 Ga09
Ključ BIH 152 Gc63
Klo N 66 Fd12
Klobouky u Brna CZ 137 Gc48
Kłobuck PL 130 Hc41
Klobuk BIH 158 Ha67
Klobuky CZ 136 Fa44
Klöch A 144 Ga55
Klockestrand S 88 Gc32
Klockrike S 103 Fd46
Klockträsk S 73 Hb24
Kłoczew PL 131 Jd38
Kłodawa PL 120 Fd35
Kłodawa PL 130 Hc37
Klöden D 127 Ec39
Kłodzko PL 137 Gc43
Kløfta N 93 Ea41
Klokk N 76 Cd32
Klokkarvik N 84 Ca39
Klokkarvollen N 62 Ha08
Klokkerholm DK 100 Dc20
Klokočevac SRB 174 Ca65
Klokočevci HR 152 Hb59
Klokočov SK 137 Hb46
Klokotnica BG 185 Dd74
Kłomnice PL 130 Hd41
Klonowa PL 129 Hb40
Klooga EST 98 Ka43
Kloogaranna EST 98 Ka42
Klopicy RUS 99 Ma40
Kłopoty-Stanisławy PL 123 Kb35
Klos AL 182 Ac74
Klosi AL 163 Jc72
Kloštar HR 152 Gd58
Kloštar Ivanic HR 152 Gb59
Kloster DK 108 Cd24
Klosterfelde D 120 Fa35
Klosterhaar NL 117 Bd35
Klösterle A 142 Da54
Klosterlechfeld D 142 Dc50
Klostermansfeld D 127 Ea39
Klosterneuburg A 145 Gb50
Klosters CH 142 Da55
Kloster Zinna D 127 Ed38
Kloten CH 141 Cb53
Kloten S 95 Fd42
Klötze D 127 Dd36
Klovainiai LT 114 Kb54
Klovborg DK 108 Db24
Klövedal S 102 Eb48
Klöverfors S 73 Hc24
Klöverträsk S 73 Hc22
Kløvimoen N 71 Fb23
Klövsjö S 87 Fb33
Kløvstad N 86 Eb37
Klubben N 65 Kc06
Klubben N 84 Ca34
Klubbfors S 73 Hc24
Klubbukt N 63 Ja06
Klubbvik N 65 Kb06
Kluczbork PL 129 Ha41
Klucze PL 138 Hd43
Kluczewo PL 120 Ga32
Kluczewsko PL 130 Ja41
Kluki PL 121 Gc29
Klukowa Huta PL 121 Gd30
Klukowicze PL 131 Kb36
Klukowo PL 122 Jb35
Klukowo PL 123 Ka35
Kluksdal N 78 Ec30
Klund N 94 Eb43
Klundert NL 124 Ad38
Klungland N 92 Ca45
Klupe BIH 152 Ha62
Kluse D 117 Ca34
Kl'ušov SK 139 Jd47
Klüsserath D 133 Bc44
Klusy PL 123 Jd31
Klutmark S 80 Hc25
Klutsjön S 86 Ed34
Klütz D 119 Ea31
Klwów PL 130 Jb39
Klykoliai LT 113 Jd53
Kłyżów PL 131 Ka42
Knaben N 92 Cc45
Knaften S 80 Gd26
Knäm S 94 Ea45
Knaphill GB 20 Fb29
Knappenrode D 128 Fb40
Knapphus N 92 Ca42
Knapstad N 93 Ea42
Knapton GB 16 Fb19
Knäred S 110 Fa53
Knaresborough GB 11 Fa19
Knarvik N 84 Ca38
Knätte S 102 Fa48
Knebel DK 109 Dd24
Kneesall GB 16 Fb22
Kneese D 119 Dd32
Kneesworth GB 20 Fc26
Knesebeck D 118 Dc35
Kneža BG 179 Da69
Knežak SLO 151 Fb59
Kneževici Sušica SRB 159 Jb65
Kneževi Vinogradi HR 153 Hc59
Kneževo HR 153 Hc58
Knězice CZ 136 Fd44
Knežina BIH 159 Hd64
Kněžmost CZ 136 Fc43
Knić SRB 174 Bb66
Knićanin SRB 153 Jc60
Knídi GR 183 Bb79
Knighton GB 15 Eb25
Knight's Town IRL 12 Ad25
Knin HR 158 Gb64
Knislinge S 111 Fb54
Knista S 95 Fc44
Knittelfeld A 144 Fc54
Knittlingen D 134 Cc47
Knivert LV 105 Jb52
Kniveton GB 16 Ed23
Knivsta S 96 Gc42
Knjaževac SRB 179 Ca68
Knjazevo RUS 107 Mb51
Knjaževo RUS 203 Fb08
Knjažica RUS 99 Ma45
Knock IRL 8 Bd19
Knock IRL 12 Bb23
Knockalough IRL 12 Bc23
Knockaunalour IRL 12 Bd25
Knockaunnaglashy IRL 12 Ba24
Knockbrandon IRL 13 Cd23
Knockcroghery IRL 8 Ca20
Knockdrin IRL 9 Cb20
Knockeen Cross Roads IRL 12 Bd24
Knockferry IRL 8 Bc20
Knockin GB 15 Eb23
Knocknabul Cross IRL 12 Bb24
Knocknagashel IRL 12 Bb24
Knocks IRL 12 Bc26
Knocktopher IRL 13 Cb24
Knockvicar IRL 8 Ca19
Knodara CY 206 Jc96
Knokke-Heist B 124 Aa38
Knopkägra FIN 97 Jc40
Knoppe S 87 Gb34
Knorydy PL 123 Kb35
Knottingley GB 16 Fa20
Knowehead GB 10 Dd15
Knowl Hill GB 20 Fb28
Knudby DK 100 Db22
Knudshoved DK 109 Dd27
Knurów PL 137 Hb44
Knurowiec PL 122 Jc35
Knutby S 96 Gd41
Knutsford GB 15 Ec22
Knutsvik N 92 Cb43
Knyszyn PL 123 Ka33
Koactarla TR 185 Ed74
Kobaklar TR 192 Fb84
Kobarid SLO 150 Ed57
Kobbevåg N 62 Gd10
Kobbevåg N 63 Hc06
Kobbfoss N 65 Kc09
Kobela EST 107 Lb47
Købelev DK 109 Ea28
Kobeljaky UA 204 Ed15
København DK 109 Ec26
Kobeřice CZ 137 Ha45
Kobern-Gondorf D 133 Ca43
Kobiele Wielkie PL 130 Hd41
Kobiljane BG 184 Dc75
Kobilje SLO 145 Gb56
Kobiór PL 138 Hc44
Kobišnica SRB 174 Cb66
Koblenz D 133 Ca43
Kobona RUS 202 Eb08
Koboža RUS 202 Ec08
Kobrinskoe RUS 99 Mb40
Kobryn BY 202 Dd14
Kobyla Góra PL 129 Ha40
Kobylanka PL 120 Fc33
Kobylin PL 123 Jd33
Kobylin PL 129 Gc39
Kobylin-Borzymy PL 123 Ka34
Kobyłka PL 130 Jc36
Kobylnica PL 121 Gc30
Kobylniki PL 129 Gb36
Kobylniki PL 130 Ja36
Koca Ahmetler TR 199 Gd90
Kocaali TR 185 Ec79
Kocaali TR 187 Gd78
Kocaaliler TR 199 Gd90
Kocaavşar TR 191 Ed82
Kocabaş TR 198 Fd88
Kocabey TR 192 Fb83
Kocaçeşme TR 185 Eb78
Kocadağ TR 191 Ec82
Kocadağ TR 199 Gd90
Kocadere TR 198 Fd88
Kocadöngel TR 187 Gc78
Kocaelı TR 187 Gb78
Kocagöl TR 186 Fa80
Kocagöl TR 193 Gb86
Kocahıdır TR 185 Ea78
Kocaiskan TR 192 Fa83
Koçak TR 192 Ga86
Koçak TR 193 Gb83
Kocakanğan TR 192 Fa84
Kocakaymaz TR 187 Gb78
Kocakovacık TR 192 Fd81
Kocalar TR 185 Eb80
Kočane SRB 178 Bb69
Kočani MK 179 Ca73
Kocaoba TR 191 Ed82
Kocaöz TR 193 Gd85
Kocapınar TR 191 Ed81
Kocapınar TR 187 Gd78
Koçarlı TR 197 Ed88
Kocatepe TR 193 Hb87
Kocayaka TR 192 Ga87
Kocayazı TR 185 Ec74
Koçbeyli TR 193 Gd86
Koceljevo SRB 153 Jb63
Kočėnai LT 106 Kd52
Kočerin BIH 158 Ha66
Kočerinovo BG 179 Cb73
Kočetovka RUS 203 Fb12
Kočevje SLO 151 Fc59
Kočevska Reka SLO 151 Fc59
Kochanowice PL 129 Hb42
Kochcice PL 129 Hb42
Kochel am See D 143 Dd52
Kochfidisch A 145 Gb54
Kochowo PL 129 Ha37
Kocień Wielkie PL 121 Gb35
Kocierzew PL 130 Ja37
Kočilar MK 183 Bc74
Kociołek Szlachecki PL 122 Jc32
Kock PL 131 Ka38
Kočkarlej RUS 203 Fd10
Kočmar BG 181 Ed69
Kočov CZ 135 Ec45
Kočovo BG 181 Ec70
Kocs H 145 Hb52
Kocsér H 146 Jb54
Kocsola H 145 Hb56
Kocsord H 147 Kb51
Kocsújfalu H 146 Jc52
Kocular TR 199 Ha88
Koçyazı TR 193 Hb85
Koczała PL 121 Gc32
Kodal N 93 Dd44
Kodavere EST 99 Lb44
Kode S 102 Eb48
Kodeń PL 131 Kc37
Kodeniec PL 131 Kb38
Kodersdorf D 128 Fc41
Kodesjärvi FIN 89 Ja34
Kodiksami FIN 89 Ja37
Kodisjoki FIN 89 Ja37
Köditz D 135 Ea43
Kodjala FIN 89 Ja38
Kodrąb PL 130 Hd41
Kodyma UA 204 Ec16
Kodžadžik MK 182 Ad74
Koekelare B 21 Ha29
Kœnigsmacker F 25 Jd34
Koersel B 124 Ba40
Koeru EST 98 Kd43
Koetschette L 132 Ba44
Kœtzingue F 31 Kc40
Kofçaz TR 185 Ec74
Kofinou CY 206 Jb97
Köflach A 144 Fc54
Köfles A 142 Dc54
Kog SLO 145 Gb56
Køge DK 109 Ec26
Kogula EST 105 Jc46
Koguva EST 97 Jd45
Kohila EST 98 Kb43
Köhkörö FIN 89 Jc35
Kohlberg D 135 Eb46
Köhlen D 118 Cd32
Kohma RUS 203 Fa09
Kohmu FIN 82 Kb31
Kohren-Sahlis D 127 Ec41
Kohtla-Järve EST 99 Lb41
Kohtla Nõmme EST 99 Lb42
Koigi EST 98 Kd43
Koigi EST 98 Kd44
Koijärvi FIN 89 Jd37
Koikkala FIN 91 Lb34
Koikküla EST 106 La47
Koili CY 206 Hd97
Koilovci BG 180 Db69
Kõima EST 106 Kb46
Koimäki FIN 90 Kd32
Koimla EST 105 Jc47
Köinge S 102 Ec51
Koirakoski FIN 82 La28
Koirasalmi FIN 82 Ka29
Koiravaara FIN 75 La21
Koisjärvi FIN 98 Ka39
Koisko SLO 150 Ed58
Koitila FIN 75 Kd21
Koitsanlahti FIN 91 Ld34
Koivisto FIN 90 Kb32
Koivistonpää FIN 73 Jb19
Koivu FIN 74 Jd20
Koivujärvi FIN 82 Kc28
Koivukylä FIN 82 Kd26
Koivulahti FIN 81 Ja30
Koivumäki FIN 81 Jd30
Koivumäki FIN 82 La29
Koivumäki FIN 89 Jb33
Koivuniemi FIN 74 Ka21
Kojanlahti FIN 83 Lb30
Kojdalen N 86 Ec32
Kojetín CZ 137 Gd47
Kojnare BG 179 Da69
Kojola FIN 81 Jb31
Kojola FIN 82 Ka28
Kojonperä FIN 89 Jc37
Kóka H 146 Ja53
Kokála GR 194 Bc91
Kokanin PL 129 Ha38
Kokar FIN 97 Hd41
Kokava nad Rimavicou SK 138 Ja49
Köke TR 193 Gd87
Kokelv N 63 Ja06
Kokemäki FIN 89 Jb36
Kokin Brod SRB 159 Jb66
Kokíni GR 182 Ab80
Kokiniá GR 182 Ac80
Kokiniá GR 183 Cb76
Kokinolithári GR 182 Ac80
Kokinombléa GR 189 Cb83
Kokinopilós GR 183 Bd79
Kokinvaara FIN 83 Ma30
Kokkári GR 197 Eb88
Kokkila FIN 90 Jc39
Kokkila FIN 97 Jc39
Kókkino Neró GR 183 Ca80
Kokkinotrimithia CY 206 Jb96
Kokkokylä FIN 74 Kb21
Kokkola FIN 75 Lb24
Kokkola FIN 81 Jb28
Kokkola FIN 90 Ka35
Kokkolahti FIN 91 Lc32
Kokkoniemi FIN 75 Lb22
Kokkosenlahti FIN 90 La34
Kokkovaara FIN 68 Jc16
Koklë AL 182 Ac76
Köklot FIN 81 Hd30
Koknese LV 106 Kd51
Koknese LV 106 La51
Kokonkylä FIN 90 Kd33
Kokonniemi FIN 75 Lb24
Kokonvaara FIN 83 Lc30
Kokora EST 99 Lb44
Kokořín CZ 136 Fb43
Kokory CZ 137 Gd46
Kokošinje MK 178 Bd73
Kokotí GR 189 Bd83
Kökpınar TR 205 Ga20
Kokrica SLO 151 Fb57
Koksijde-Bad B 21 Gd29
Kokšino RUS 107 Ma49
Koktebel' UA 205 Fb17
Kokträsk S 72 Gd23
Kola BIH 152 Gd62
Kola FIN 81 Jc28
Köla S 94 Ec42
Kölaby S 102 Fa48
Kołacin PL 130 Hd38
Kołacze PL 131 Kc39
Kołaczkowo PL 129 Gd37
Kołaczyce PL 139 Jd45
Kolak TR 198 Fd90
Koláka GR 189 Ca84
Kołaki Kościelne PL 123 Ka34
Koland N 92 Cd45
Kolankaya TR 192 Fc86
Kolarci BG 181 Fa68
Kolari FIN 68 Jb16
Kolari SRB 174 Bb64
Kolárovice SK 137 Hb47
Kolarovo BG 180 Dd73
Kolarovo BG 181 Ec68
Kolárovo SK 145 Ha51
Kolås N 76 Cc33
Kolåsen S 78 Fa29
Kolašin MNE 159 Jb68
Kolatovo BG 183 Cb75
Kolbäck S 95 Ga43
Kolbermoor D 143 Ea52
Kołbiel PL 130 Jc37
Kolbnitz A 143 Ed55
Kolbu N 85 Ea39
Kolbudy Grn. PL 121 Ha30
Kolbulia N 86 Eb38
Kolbuszowa PL 139 Jd43
Kølby DK 100 Db21
Kolby DK 109 Dd25
Kolby Kås DK 109 Dd25
Kol'čugino RUS 203 Fa10
Kołczewo PL 120 Fc31
Kołczygłowy PL 121 Gc30
Koldby DK 100 Da21
Koldere TR 191 Ed85
Kolding DK 108 Db26
Kołdrąb PL 121 Gd35
Koler S 73 Hb23
Kölesd H 146 Hc56
Koleška BIH 159 Hc67
Kolešovice CZ 136 Fa44
Kolga-Jaani EST 98 Kd45
Kolgaküla EST 98 Kd42
Kolgomp'a RUS 99 Ld40
Kolhiki GR 183 Bb77
Kolhikó GR 183 Cb77
Kolho FIN 90 Ka33
Koli FIN 83 Lc29
Kolimbári GR 200 Cb94
Kolímbia GR 197 Fa93
Kolín CZ 136 Fd45
Kolind DK 101 Dd23
Kolindrós GR 183 Bd78
Kolinec CZ 135 Ed47
Kölingared S 102 Fa48
Koliseva FIN 90 Kd37
Kolitzheim D 134 Db45
Kõljala EST 105 Jd46
Koljane HR 158 Gc65
Kolka LV 105 Jc48
Kolkær DK 108 Da24
Kolkanlahti FIN 82 Ka31
Kolkja EST 99 Lb44
Kolkku FIN 82 Kb29
Kolko FIN 97 Ja39
Kolkonjärvi FIN 75 La21
Kolkonpää FIN 91 Lb33
Kolkontaipale FIN 91 Lb33
Kolkwitz D 128 Fb39
Kolky UA 202 Ea14
Kollaja FIN 74 Kb22
Kölleda D 127 Dd40
Kollersdorf A 144 Ga50
Kollerud S 94 Ed40
Kollerup DK 100 Db21
Kölliken CH 141 Ca53
Kollines GR 194 Bc88
Kollinmäki FIN 89 Jb33
Kollinperä FIN 90 Ka32
Kollmar D 118 Db32
Kollnburg D 135 Ec48
Kölln-Reisiek D 118 Db32
Kollum NL 117 Bc33
Kollund DK 108 Db28
Kollungeröd S 102 Eb47
Kolma FIN 90 La32
Kolmården S 103 Ga46
Kolmjärv S 73 Hd20
Kolm-Saigurn A 143 Ec54
Köln D 125 Bd41
Kolno PL 122 Jb31
Kolno PL 123 Jd33
Kolo BIH 158 Gd65
Koło PL 129 Hb37
Kołobrzeg PL 120 Fd31
Kołodzież PL 123 Ka33
Kologrivo RUS 99 Ld42
Kolokolčovka RUS 203 Fd12
Kolokolovo RUS 99 Lc44
Kolomna RUS 203 Fa10
Kolomyja UA 204 Ea16
Kolonia AL 182 Ab78
Kolonowskie PL 129 Hb42
Kolossi CY 206 Ja98
Koloveč CZ 135 Ed46
Kolpino RUS 107 Lc46
Kolpino RUS 202 Eb08
Kolpny RUS 203 Fa12
Kolppi FIN 81 Jb29
Kolrep D 119 Eb34
Kolsätter S 87 Fc34
Kolsillre S 87 Fd33
Kölsjön S 87 Ga34
Kolsko PL 128 Ga38
Kolsva S 95 Ga43
Kolta SK 145 Hb51
Kolu FIN 81 Jd31
Kolumna PL 130 Hc39
Kolunić BIH 152 Gb63
Koluszki PL 130 Hd38
Kolut SRB 153 Hd58
Koluvere EST 98 Ka44
Kolvereid N 78 Ec25
Kolvik N 64 Jb07
Kolyčivka UA 202 Ec14
Kolyšlej RUS 203 Fc11
Komádi H 147 Ka54
Komagfjord N 63 Hd07
Komagvær N 65 Kd06
Komagvik N 62 Gd08
Komańcza PL 139 Ka46
Kómanos GR 183 Bc78
Komar BIH 158 Ha64
Kómara GR 185 Ea75
Komarani SRB 178 Ad68
Komarevo BG 180 Db69
Komarno MNE 159 Ja70
Komárno SK 145 Hb52
Komárom H 145 Hb52
Komárov CZ 136 Fa45
Komarówka Podlaska PL 131 Kb38
Komarów-Osada PL 131 Kc41
Koma tou Gialou CY 206 Jd95
Kombóti GR 188 Ad82
Kombsija AL 182 Ac74
Kombuļi LV 115 Ld53
Komen SLO 151 Fa59
Komi CY 206 Jd96
Komi FIN 89 Jc35
Kómi GR 189 Bc86
Komin HR 158 Ha68
Kominternivs'ke UA 204 Ec17
Kómito GR 190 Cd86
Komiža HR 158 Gb68
Komjatice SK 145 Hb51
Kömlő H 146 Jb52
Komló H 152 Hb57
Kommerniemi FIN 91 Lc33
Komnes N 93 Dd43
Komniná GR 183 Bc77
Komniná GR 184 Db76
Komninádes GR 182 Ba77
Komorane KSV 178 Ba71
Komorniki PL 129 Gc37
Komorowo PL 122 Jc35
Komorowo PL 129 Gc40
Komorowo PL 129 Gd36
Komorze PL 129 Gd37
Komorzno PL 129 Ha41
Komosomol'sk RUS 203 Fa09
Komossa FIN 81 Jb30
Komoštica BG 179 Cc68
Komotiní GR 184 Dc77
Kompakka FIN 83 Ld31
Kompelusvaara S 68 Hd17
Kompina PL 130 Ja37
Komprachcice PL 129 Ha42
Kõmsi EST 98 Ka45
Komsi FIN 89 Ja33
Komsomol'sk RUS 113 Hd59
Komsomol'sk RUS 113 Ja59
Komsomol'skij RUS 203 Fc10
Komsomol'sk Zappvednik RUS 113 Ja59
Komu FIN 82 Kb28
Komula FIN 82 La26
Komunari BG 181 Ed71
Komuniga BG 184 Dc74
Kömürcü TR 192 Fa84
Kömürköy TR 186 Fa75
Kömür Limanı TR 185 Ed78
Konak BG 180 Eb70
Konak SRB 174 Bc62
Konak TR 198 Fd89
Konakkale TR 193 Hb87
Konaklı TR 199 Hb92
Konakovo RUS 202 Ed10
Konakpınar TR 192 Fa83
Konare BG 180 Ea72
Konare BG 181 Fb69
Konarevo SRB 178 Ba67
Konarı TR 193 Hb86
Konary PL 130 Jc38
Konarzewo PL 129 Gb37
Konarzyce PL 123 Jd33
Konarzyny PL 121 Gd32
Konäs S 78 Fa29
Končanica HR 152 Gd59
Konče MK 183 Bd75
Kończewice PL 121 Hb34
Kondiás GR 190 Db81
Kondofrej BG 179 Cb72
Kondolovo BG 186 Fa74
Kondopoúli GR 190 Dc81
Kondorfa H 145 Gb55
Kondoros H 146 Jc55
Kondratovo RUS 107 Ma47
Kondratów PL 128 Ga41
Kondratowice PL 129 Gc42
Kondrić HR 152 Hb60
Kondrovo RUS 202 Ed11
Køng DK 109 Eb27
Konga S 111 Fd53
Köngäs FIN 64 Jd07
Köngäs FIN 68 Jc14
Köngäs FIN 69 Ka14
Köngäs FIN 69 Kb17
Kongasmäki FIN 75 Kd24
Kongens Lyngby DK 109 Ec25
Kongerslev DK 100 Dc21
Konginkangas FIN 82 Kb31
Kongsberg N 93 Dc42
Kongselva N 66 Fd13
Kongsfjord N 65 Kb04
Kongshavn N 93 Db46
Kongsli N 67 Gd11
Kongsmark DK 108 Cd27
Kongsmoen N 78 Ed25
Kongsvika N 66 Ga13
Kongsvinger N 94 Ec40
Koņi LV 106 Kd47
Koniaków PL 138 Hc46
Konice CZ 137 Gc46
Koniecpol PL 130 Hd42
Konieczna PL 139 Jd46
Koniewo PL 120 Fc32
Königerode D 127 Dd39
Königgrätz = Hradec Králové CZ 136 Ga44
Königheim D 134 Da45
Königsaue D 127 Ea38
Königsbach-Stein D 134 Cc47
Königsberg D 134 Dc44
Königsbronn D 134 Db48
Königsbrück D 128 Fa40
Königsbrunn D 142 Dc50
Königsdorf D 143 Dd52
Königsee D 127 Dd42
Königsfeld D 135 Dd45
Königsfeld D 141 Cb50
Königshain-Wiederau D 127 Ec41
Königshofen D 134 Da46
Königslutter D 127 Dd37
Königsmoos D 135 Dd49
Königstein D 128 Fb42
Königstein D 134 Cc43
Königstein D 135 Ea46
Königswartha D 128 Fb40
Königswiesen A 144 Fc50
Königswinter D 125 Bd41
Königs Wusterhausen D 128 Fa37
Konin PL 129 Ha37
Konina PL 138 Ja46
Koņinciems LV 105 Jb51
Konispol AL 182 Ab80
Kónitsa GR 182 Ad79
Köniz CH 141 Bd54
Konjavo BG 179 Cb72
Konjic BIH 158 Hb66
Konjsko BIH 158 Ha66
Konjsko BIH 159 Hc69
Konjsko SRB 178 Ba68
Konju EST 99 Lc41
Konjuh KSV 178 Bb71
Konjuhe MNE 159 Jb68
Konnekoski FIN 82 Kd31
Könnern D 127 Ea39
Konnersreuth D 135 Eb44
Konnerud N 93 Dd42
Konnevesi FIN 82 Kc31
Könni FIN 81 Jb31
Konnovo RUS 99 Lc40
Kõnnu EST 98 Kc44
Kõnnu EST 105 Jd46
Konnunsuo FIN 91 Lc36
Konnuslahti FIN 82 La31
Konohovicy RUS 99 Ma41
Könölä FIN 74 Jc20
Konopiska PL 130 Hc42
Konopište MK 183 Bd75
Konopki PL 122 Ja34
Konopnica PL 130 Hc40
Konotop PL 120 Ga33
Konotop PL 128 Ga38
Konotop UA 202 Ed14
Konradsreuth D 135 Ea44
Końskie PL 130 Jb40
Konsko MK 183 Bd76
Końskowola PL 131 Ka39
Konsmo N 92 Cc46
Konstancin-Jeziorna PL 130 Jc37
Konstantin BG 180 Ea71
Konstantinova LV 107 Ld52
Konstantinovka RUS 113 Ja58
Konstantinovsk RUS 205 Fc15
Konstantinovy Lázně CZ 135 Ec45
Konstantynów PL 131 Kb36
Konstantynów Łódzki PL 130 Hc39
Konstanz D 142 Cc52
Kontea CY 206 Jc97
Kontemenos CY 206 Jb96
Kontiainen FIN 81 Jc30
Kontiainen FIN 89 Jc32
Kontinjoki FIN 82 Kd26
Kontiolahti FIN 83 Ld30
Kontiomäki FIN 82 La25
Kontioranta FIN 83 Ld30
Kontiovaara FIN 83 Ma29
Kontiovaara FIN 83 Ld28
Kontkala FIN 83 Lc30
Konttajärvi FIN 74 Jc18
Konttimäki FIN 83 Lb29
Konttimäki FIN 83 Lb30
Konttimäki FIN 90 Ka32
Kontu FIN 91 Lc36
Konuklu TR 187 Gc78
Konuralp TR 187 Ha78
Konuš BG 185 Dd74
Kóny H 145 Gd52
Konz D 133 Bc45
Konzell D 135 Ec48
Kõo EST 98 Kd44
Koobassaare EST 107 Lb47
Koonga EST 98 Kb45
Kooraste EST 107 Lb46
Koorküla EST 106 La47
Köörtilä FIN 89 Ja35
Koosa EST 99 Lb44
Kootwijk NL 116 Bb36
Kopáni GR 188 Ad81
Kopanica PL 128 Ga38
Kopanie PL 129 Gd42
Koparnes N 76 Cb33
Kópasker IS 3 Bb03
Kópavogur IS 2 Ac05
Kopciówka PL 123 Kb32
Kopdarbs LV 105 Ja52
Kopenhagen = København DK 109 Ec26
Koper SLO 151 Fa59
Kopervik N 92 Bd42
Kopfing A 144 Fa50
Kopice PL 120 Fc32
Kopice PL 129 Gd42
Kopidlno CZ 136 Fd44
Kopilovci BG 179 Cb69
Köping S 95 Ga43
Köpingebro S 110 Fa56
Köpingsvik S 103 Gb52
Kopisk PL 123 Kb33
Koplik i Poshtëm AL 159 Ja70
Köpmanholm S 96 Ha42
Köpmanholmen S 80 Gd31
Kopor'e RUS 99 Ld40
Koporic'e KSV 178 Bb69
Koposperä FIN 82 Ka27
Koppang N 86 Eb36
Koppangen N 62 Ha09
Kopparåsen S 67 Gc13
Kopparberg S 95 Fc42
Koppardal N 70 Ed21
Kopparmora S 96 Ha43
Koppelo FIN 69 Kb11
Koppelo FIN 83 Lb27
Kopperå N 78 Ec30
Koppom S 94 Ec42
Koprivec BG 180 Ea69
Koprivlen BG 184 Cd75
Koprivna SLO 144 Fc56
Koprivnica HR 152 Gc57
Kopřivnice CZ 137 Ha46
Koprivštica BG 179 Da72
Köprübaşı TR 187 Gd78
Köprübaşı TR 192 Fb85
Köprücek TR 187 Gc80
Köprühisar TR 186 Ga80
Köprüören TR 192 Ga82
Koprzywnica PL 131 Jd42
Kopsa FIN 81 Jd25
Kopstad N 93 Dd43
Kõpu EST 97 Jc44
Kõpu EST 106 Kd46
Kopyčynci UA 204 Ea16
Korablino RUS 203 Fb11
Koračica SRB 174 Bb65
Koraj BIH 153 Hd62
Koraşı TR 193 Hb86
Korb D 134 Cd48
Korbach D 126 Cd40
Korbenići RUS 202 Ec08
Korbevac SRB 178 Bd71
Korbielów PL 138 Hd46
Korbøl N 71 Fc18
Korbovo SRB 174 Cb65
Korčanica BIH 152 Gb62
Korçë AL 182 Ad77
Korčevka RUS 203 Fd10
Korčula HR 158 Gd68
Korczew PL 131 Ka36
Korczyna PL 139 Ka45
Kordel D 133 Bc44
Korec' UA 202 Eb14
Köreken TR 192 Ga83
Korenevo RUS 202 Ed13
Korenica HR 151 Ga62
Korenica KSV 178 Ad71
Korenica SRB 159 Jc69
Korenovsk RUS 205 Fc16
Korentokylä FIN 75 Kc22
Korentovaara FIN 83 Mb29
Körez TR 192 Fc85
Korfantów PL 137 Gd43
Körfez TR 186 Ga78
Kórfos GR 195 Ca87
Korfovoúni GR 188 Ad81
Korfu = Kérkira GR 182 Ab80
Korgen N 71 Fb21
Korģene LV 106 Kc48
Körgepalu EST 107 Lb47
Körgessaare EST 97 Jc44
Korhasan TR 193 Ha83
Korholanmäki FIN 82 Kd31
Korhosenniemi FIN 75 Kd20
Korhoskylä FIN 81 Jd27
Korhoskylä FIN 89 Jc33
Koria FIN 90 Kd37
Korifási GR 194 Ba89
Korifi GR 182 Ba79
Korifi GR 188 Ba81
Korinós GR 183 Bd79
Korinth DK 108 Dc27
Korinth = Kórinthos GR 189 Bd86
Kórinthos GR 189 Bd86
Koriseva FIN 83 Lc28
Korissía GR 195 Cd88
Korissós GR 183 Bb78
Korita BIH 158 Gb64
Korita BIH 159 Hc67
Korita HR 152 Gd60
Korita HR 158 Ha69
Korita MNE 159 Jb69

Kysucké Nové Mesto – Lampinsaari

Kysucké Nové Mesto SK 138 Hc47
Kysucký Lieskovec SK 138 Hc47
Kytäjä FIN 90 Kb38
Kythrea CY 206 Jc96
Kytkylehto FIN 82 La25
Kytö FIN 97 Jc39
Kytökylä FIN 82 Ka26
Kytömäki FIN 75 Kd24
Kyyjärvi FIN 81 Jd30
Kyynämöinen FIN 90 Kb32
Kyynärö FIN 90 Ka35
Kyyrönniemi FIN 91 Ld32

L

Laa an der Thaya A 137 Gb49
Laaber D 135 Ea48
La Acenuela E 60 Cc74
La Adrada E 46 Da64
Laafeld A 144 Ga56
Laage D 119 Ec31
Laagri EST 98 Kb42
Laaja FIN 75 La23
Laajala FIN 68 Jb16
Laajaranta FIN 82 Kb31
Laajoki FIN 89 Jb38
Laakajärvi FIN 82 La27
Laakirchen A 144 Fa51
La Alameda E 52 Db70
La Alberca E 45 Ca64
La Alberca de Záncara E 53 Ea67
La Albergueria de Argañán E 45 Bc64
La Albuera E 51 Bc69
La Aldea del Obispo E 51 Ca67
La Aldea del Portillo de Busto E 38 Dd57
La Aldehuela E 45 Cc64
La Alfahuara E 61 Eb73
La Algaba E 59 Ca73
La Algaida E 59 Bd75
La Aliseda de Tormes E 45 Cc64
La Aljorra E 55 Fa73
La Almarcha E 53 Eb67
La Almolda E 48 Fc61
La Almunia de Doña Godina E 47 Ed61
Laamala FIN 91 Lc35
Laanila FIN 69 Ka12
Lääniste EST 99 Lb45
La Antilla E 58 Ba74
Laapinjärvi FIN 90 Kd38
Laar D 117 Bd35
Laarne B 124 Ab39
Laas D 127 Ed40
Laas I 142 Db56
Laasala FIN 81 Jd31
La Atalaya E 55 Ed74
Laatre EST 106 Kd47
Laatre EST 106 La47
Laatzen D 126 Db37
La Aulaga E 59 Bd73
Laax CH 142 Cc55
La Azohia E 55 Fa74
Labacolla E 36 Ad55
la Bade F 33 Ha49
Labadžiai LV 114 Kb57
Labalme F 35 Jc45
la Balme-de-Sillingy F 35 Jd46
La Baña E 37 Bd58
La Bañeza E 37 Cb58
Labanoras LT 115 Lb56
La Barca de la Florida E 59 Bd76
La Barca de la Florida E 59 Ca76
Labarces E 38 Db55
Labardžiai LT 113 Jc55
la Barre-en-Ouche F 23 Ga36
La Barrela E 36 Bb56
la Barthe-de-Neste F 40 Fd56
Labasheeda IRL 12 Bc23
la Bassée F 23 Ha31
la Bastide F 43 Kb53
Labastide-Beauvoir F 40 Gc54
Labastide-Clairence F 39 Fa55
Labastide-d'Armagnac F 40 Fc53
la Bastide-de-Lordat F 40 Gc56
la Bastide-des-Jourdans F 42 Jd53
Labastide-Murat F 33 Gc51
la Bastide-Puylaurent F 34 Hd51
Labastide-Rouairoux F 41 Ha54
Labastide-Saint-Pierre F 40 Gb53
la Bathie F 35 Ka47
la Bâtie-Neuve F 35 Ka50
Labatlan H 146 Hc52
la Baule F 27 Ec42
La Bazana E 51 Bc71
la Bazoche-Gouet F 29 Ga39
la Bazoge F 28 Fd39
l'Abbaye F 41 Hd52
Labby FIN 90 Kd38
Läbbyn S 94 Ec43
Labeaume F 34 Ja51
Łabędnik PL 122 Jb30
Łabędzie PL 120 Ga32
Labège F 40 Gc54
la Bégude-Blanche F 42 Ka52
Laben A 144 Ga51
Labenne F 39 Ed54
Labenne-Océan F 39 Ed54
Labenz D 118 Dc32
la Bérade F 35 Ka49
Laberg N 67 Gc12
Laberget N 67 Gb13
la Bernerie-en-Retz F 27 Ec43
Laberweinting D 135 Eb49
l'Aber-Wrac'h F 26 Db37
Labin HR 151 Fa61
Labinsk RUS 205 Fd17
la Bisbal de Falset E 48 Ga62
la Bisbal del Penedès E 49 Gc62
la Bisbal d'Empordà E 49 Hb59
Łabiszyn PL 121 Ha35
Lablachère F 34 Ja51
Labljane KSV 178 Bb71
La Bobadilla E 60 Da73
la Bocca F 43 Kc54
Lábod H 152 Gd57
Laboe D 118 Dc30
la Boissière F 22 Fd36
la Bonneville-sur-Iton F 23 Gb36
Laborel F 42 Jd51
la Borne F 29 Ha42
La Bouëxière F 28 Fa39
Labouheyre F 39 Fa52
la Bouille F 23 Ga35
la Bourboule F 33 Ha47
Laboutarie F 41 Gd53
la Boutière F 35 Jd48
Labovë AL 182 Ac78
La Bóveda de Toro E 45 Cc61
Łabowa PL 138 Jc46
Labrags LV 105 Jb51
l'Abre F 33 Ga47
la Brède F 32 Fb51
la Bresse F 31 Ka39
la Brévine CH 141 Bb54
la Bridoire F 35 Jd47
la Brillanne F 42 Jd52
Labrit F 39 Fb52
Labrousse F 33 Gb46
Labroye F 23 Gc32
la Bruffière F 28 Fa43
Labruguière F 41 Gd54
La Bruyère B 124 Ad41
l'Absie F 28 Fb44
Labuť CZ 135 Ec45
Labudnjača SRB 153 Hd59
Labuerda E 40 Fd58
Labūnava LT 114 Kc56
Łabunie PL 131 Kc41
Labuništa MK 182 Ad75
la Burbanche F 35 Jc46
la Bussière F 29 Ha40
la Butte F 28 Fc43
Lac AL 163 Jb72
La Cabrera E 46 Dc63
la Caillère F 28 Fb44
La Calahorra E 61 Dd75
La Calera E 38 Dd55
la Caletta I 168 Cc75
la Caletta I 169 Bc80
la Calmet F 42 Ja53
La Calzada de Oropesa E 52 Cc66
La Campana E 59 Cb73
La Cañada E 46 Da64
La Cañada de Cañepla E 61 Eb73
La Cañada de San Urbano E 61 Ea76
La Cañada de Verich E 48 Fc63
Lacanau F 32 Fa50
Lacanau-Océan F 32 Fa49
la Canourgue F 34 Hb51
la Capelle F 24 Hc33
la Capelle F 34 Hc51
la Capelle-lès-Boulogne F 23 Gc31
Lacapelle-Marival F 33 Gd50
Lacapelle-Viescamp F 33 Gd50
Lačarak SRB 153 Ja61
La Cardenchosa E 51 Cb71
La Cardenchosa E 51 Cb71
La Caridad E 37 Bd53
La Carlota E 60 Cc73
La Carolina E 52 Db71
La Carrasca E 60 Da74
La Carrasca E 60 Db73
La Casicas E 53 Eb71
la Cassa I 148 Bc60
Lacaune F 41 Ha54
La Cavada E 38 Dc55
la Cavalerie F 41 Hb53
Lacave F 33 Gc50
Lacco Ameno I 161 Fa75
Lac de Tignes F 35 Kb47
Lacedonia I 161 Fd74
Lacelle F 33 Gc47
la Celle-Dunoise F 33 Gc45
la Celle-en-Morvan F 30 Hd43
la Cellera de Ter E 49 Ha59
la Celle-Saint-Avant F 29 Ga43
La Cerca E 38 Dd56
La Cerollera E 48 Fc63
La Cervera E 54 Fa66
Laces I 142 Dc56
Łacha PL 122 Jc32
la Chaise-Dieu F 34 Hc48
la Chaize F 28 Fa44
la Chaize-Giraud F 28 Ed44
la Chambre F 35 Ka48
la Champenoise F 29 Gc43
Lachamp Raphaël F 34 Ja50
la Chapelaude F 33 Ha45
La Chapelle F 24 Ja33
la Chapelle F 35 Ka47
la-Chapelle-au-Riboul F 28 Fc38
la Chapelle-aux-Chasses F 30 Hc44
Lachapelle-aux-Pots F 23 Gc35
la Chapelle-Bertrand F 28 Fc44
la Chapelle-Bouëxic F 28 Ed40
la Chapelle-d'Angillon F 29 Gd42
la Chapelle-du-Bois F 29 Ga39
la Chapelle-du-Chêne F 28 Fb39
la Chapelle-du-Noyer F 29 Gb39
la Chapelle-en-Valgaudemar F 35 Ka49
la Chapelle-en-Vercors F 35 Jc49
la Chapelle-Faucher F 33 Ga48
La Chapelle-Glain F 28 Fa41
la Chapelle-la-Reine F 29 Ha38
la Chapelle-Laurent F 34 Hb49
la Chapelle-Montreuil F 28 Fd44
la Chapelle-Rainsoui F 28 Fb39
la Chapelle-Saint-André F 30 Hb41
la Chapelle-Saint-Géraud F 33 Gd49
la Chapelle-Saint-Laurent F 28 Fb44
la Chapelle-Saint-Quillain F 31 Jc41
Lachapelle-sous-Rougemont F 31 Kb40
la Chapelle-Vendômoise F 29 Gb41
la Chapelle Verlain F 33 Ga48
la Chapelle-Vicomtesse F 29 Gb40
la Chapelle-Yvon F 22 Fd36
la Chapelotte F 29 Ha42
Láchar E 60 Db75
la Charce F 42 Jc51
la Charité-sur-Loire F 30 Hb42
la Chartre-sur-le-Loir F 29 Ga40
la Châtaigneraie F 28 Fb44
la Châtelaine F 31 Jd43
la Châtre F 29 Gd44
la Châtre-Langlin F 33 Gb45
la Chaudière F 35 Jc50
la Chaume F 28 Ed44
La Chaux-de-Fonds CH 141 Bb53
la Chavade F 34 Hd50
Lachen CH 142 Cc53
Lachendorf D 126 Dc36
la Cheppe F 24 Hd36
la Chèze F 27 Eb39
Lachowo PL 123 Jd32
La Cierva E 53 Ec66
Laçin TR 193 Gd81
la Ciotat F 42 Jd55
Lack GB 9 Cb17
Łąck PL 130 Hd36
Läčkalns LV 106 La52
Läckeby S 103 Ga52
Łącko PL 138 Jb46
la Clayette F 34 Ja45
la Clisse F 32 Fb47
la Clusaz F 35 Ka46
la Cluse F 35 Jc45
la Cluse F 35 Jd50
la Cluse-et-Mijoux F 31 Ka43
La Codoñera E 48 Fc63
La Codosera E 51 Bb67
la Combe F 35 Jc47
La Concha E 38 Dc55
Laconi I 169 Ca77
La Contienda E 51 Bb71
La Copa E 61 Ec72
la Coquille F 33 Gb48
La Coronada E 51 Cb69
La Coronada E 51 Cb71
La Corte E 59 Bc72
La Coruña E 36 Ba54
La Costana E 38 Db56
la Côte-Saint-André F 35 Jc48
la Cotinière F 32 Fa46
la Couarde-sur-Mer F 32 Ed46
la Couronne F 32 Fd47
Lacourt F 40 Gb56
la Courtine F 33 Gd47
la Couvertoirade F 41 Hc53
La Coveta Fumada E 55 Fc71
Lacq F 39 Fb55
la Crèche F 32 Fc45
la Crocina I 156 Dd66
Lacroix F 23 Ha35
la Croix-aux-Bois F 24 Ja34
la Croix-aux-Bois F 24 Ja35
la Croix-Avranchin F 28 Fa38
Lacroix-Barrez F 33 Ha50
La Croixille F 28 Fa39
La Croix-Laurent F 28 Ed41
Lacroix-sur-Meuse F 24 Jb36
la Croix-Valmer F 43 Kb55
La Crosetta I 150 Eb58
La Cuesta E 46 Db62
La Cumbre E 51 Ca67
La Cure F 31 Jd44
Lacu Roşu RO 172 Ea58
Lacu Sărat RO 177 Fb64
Lacu Sinaia RO 176 Ec64
Łączki Brzeskie PL 139 Jd43
Łączna PL 130 Jb41
Łącznik PL 137 Ha43
Łączno PL 122 Hd31
Lad H 152 Ha57
Ład PL 129 Ha37
Ladapeyre F 33 Gd45
Ladbergen D 125 Cb37
Ladby DK 109 Dd26
Läde LV 106 Kc49
Läde S 87 Fb38
Ladeburg D 128 Fa36
Lądek-Zdrój PL 137 Gc43
Ladelund D 108 Da28
Ladenburg D 134 Cc46
Ladendorf A 137 Gb49
La Derrasa E 36 Bb57
Lădeşti RO 175 Da64
Ladezers LV 106 Kc49
Ládi GR 185 Ea76
Ladignac F 33 Gb47
Ladino RUS 107 Mb49
Ladispoli I 160 Ea71
Ladoeiro P 44 Bb65
Ladon F 29 Ha39
la Douze F 33 Ga49
Ladovo RUS 107 Mb47
la Drée F 30 Ja43
La Duquesa E 59 Cb77
Laduškin RUS 113 Hd59
Laduz F 30 Hb40
Ladybank GB 7 Eb12
Ladyżyn UA 204 Ec16
Ładzice PL 130 Hd41
Læborg DK 108 Da26
Lædre N 92 Ca46
Laekvere EST 98 La43
La Encinilla E 59 Ca75
Laer D 125 Ca37
Láerma GR 197 Ed93
La Ermita E 61 Eb74
Laerru I 168 Ca74
La Espina E 37 Ca54
La Espina E 37 Cd56
La Estación E 59 Ca73
La Estrella E 52 Cc66
Laeva EST 98 La45
Lævvajokgiedde N 64 Jd07
La Farga de Moles E 40 Gc58
La Fatarella E 48 Ga62
la Faurie F 35 Jd50
la Favière F 43 Kb51
La Feclaz F 35 Jd47
La Felguera = Langreo E 37 Cc55
La Felipa E 53 Ec69
la Fère F 24 Hb34
la Ferière-en-Parthenay F 28 Fc44
la Ferrière F 28 Fa44
la Ferrière F 35 Ka48
la Ferrière-aux-Étangs F 22 Fb37
la-Ferrière-sur-Risle F 23 Ga36
la Ferté F 30 Ja44
la Ferté-Alais F 29 Gd38
la Ferté-Bernard F 29 Ga39
la Ferté-Frênel F 22 Fd37
la Ferté-Gaucher F 24 Hb37
la Ferté-Imbault F 29 Gc42
la Ferté-Loupière F 30 Hb40
La Ferté-Macé F 28 Fc38
la Ferté-Milon F 24 Hb36
La Ferté-Saint-Aubin F 29 Gc40
la Ferté-Saint-Cyr F 29 Gc41
la Ferté-sous-Jouarre F 24 Hb36
Laferté-sur-Amance F 31 Jc40
Laferté-sur-Aube F 30 Ja39
la Ferté-Vidame F 29 Ga38
Lafeuillade-en-Vézie F 33 Ha50
La Feuillie F 23 Gb35
La Figal E 37 Ca54
Navia E 37 Ca54
Lafitte F 40 Gb53
Lafka GR 194 Bc87
Láfkos GR 189 Cb82
la Flèche F 28 Fc41
La Florida E 37 Ca54
la Flotte F 32 Fa46
la Foia E 55 Fb72
la Fontaine-Saint-Martin F 28 Fd40
la Font de la Figuera E 55 Fa70
la Font d'en Carròs E 54 Fc69
la Force F 32 Fd50
la Forêt-Fouesnant F 27 Dc40
la Forêt-Sainte-Croix F 29 Gd38
la Forêt-sur-Sèvre F 28 Fb44
la Forie F 34 Hc47
Laforsen S 87 Fd35
la Fouillade F 41 Gd52
la Fourche F 30 Ja44
la Foux-d'Allos F 43 Kb51
La Franca E 38 Da54
Lafrançaise F 40 Gb52
la Freissinouse F 35 Jd50
La Fresneda E 48 Fd63
la Frette F 35 Jc48
La Frontera E 47 Eb64
La Frua I 141 Ca56
La Fuencubierta E 60 Cc73
La Fuente de San Esteban E 45 Ca63
la Fuliola E 48 Gb60
Łag PL 121 Ha32
La Gacilly F 27 Ec40
La Galera E 48 Ga64
La Gallega E 46 Dd59
Lagan S 103 Fb52
Laganás GR 188 Ac86
La Ganchosa E 59 Ca72
Lagar E 37 Bd54
la Garde F 34 Hc50
la Garde F 42 Ka55
la Garde-Adhémar F 42 Jb51
la Garde-Freinet F 43 Kb54
la Garde-Guérin F 34 Hd51
Lagarelhos P 44 Bb59
La Garganta E 37 Bd54
La Garganta E 45 Cb64
La Garovilla E 51 Bd69
la Garriga E 49 Ha60
Lagartera E 52 Cc66
la Gaubretière F 28 Fa43
Lagavara GB 9 Da15
Lagdei I 149 Cd63
Lage D 117 Ca36
Lage D 126 Cd37
Lagedi EST 98 Kc42
Lage Mierde NL 124 Ba39
Lägerdorf D 118 Db31
Laget N 93 Db45
Lagg GB 6 Db13
Lagga S 96 Gd42
Laggan GB 7 Ea09
Laggars FIN 81 Ja29
Laggerberg S 87 Gb33
Laghy IRL 8 Ca17
Łagiewnik PL 129 Gc39
Łagiewniki PL 129 Gc42
Laginá GR 183 Cb77
La Gineta E 53 Ec69
La Gironda E 59 Ca75
la Giustiniana I 160 Ea71
Lagje AL 182 Ac74
Laglio I 149 Cc58
Lagnieu F 35 Jc46
Lagnö S 103 Gb47
Lagny F 23 Ha34
Lagny-sur-Marne F 23 Ha37
Lago I 164 Gb80
Lagoa P 58 Ab74
Lagoa (Campo Lameiro) E 36 Ad56
Łagoda PL 128 Fd38
la Godivelle F 34 Hb48
Lagolovo RUS 99 Mb40
Lagonegro I 161 Ga77
Lágos GR 184 Dc77
Lagos P 58 Ab74
Lagosanto I 150 Ea62
la Goutelle F 33 Ha47
Łagów PL 128 Fd37
Łagów PL 130 Jc41
Lagrán E 39 Eb57
La Granada de Riotinto E 59 Bc72
la Granadella E 48 Ga61
la Grand-Combe F 41 Hd52
la Grand-Croix F 34 Ja47
la Grande-Motte F 41 Hd54
la Grande-Motte F 42 Ja54
la Granja d'Escarp E 48 Fd61
La Granjuela E 51 Cb71
Lagrasse F 41 Ha56
la Grave F 29 Ha44
la Grave F 35 Ka49
la Gravelle F 28 Fd38
la Grolle F 28 Ed44
Lägsta S 80 Gc28
Laguardia E 39 Eb57
La Guardia E 52 Dc66
La Guardia de Jaén E 60 Db73
Laguarta E 40 Fc58
Laguépie F 41 Gd52
la Guerche-de-Bretagne F 28 Fa40
la Guerche-sur-l'Aubois F 30 Hb43
la Guérinière F 27 Ec43
Lagueruela E 47 Fa62
La Guijarrosa E 60 Cc73
Laguiole F 34 Hb50
Laguna de Contreras E 46 Db61
Laguna de Duero E 46 Da60
Laguna del Maquesado E 47 Ec65
Laguna de Negrillos E 37 Cc58
Laguna de Somoza E 37 Ca57
Laguna Rodrigo E 46 Da62
Lagunilla E 45 Ca64
Lagzdene LV 105 Jb50
La Haba E 51 Ca69
Lahanás GR 183 Cb77
Lahaniá GR 197 Ed94
Lahardaun IRL 8 Bc18
Laharie F 39 Fa53
La Haye-du-Puits F 22 Ed35
la Haye-Pesnel F 22 Fa37
Lähden D 117 Cb35
Lahdenkylä FIN 89 Jd33
Lahdenkylä FIN 90 Ka34
Lahdenkylä FIN 90 Kb34
Lahdenperä FIN 82 Kd28
Lahdenperä FIN 82 Ka30
Lahdenpohja FIN 90 Kb36
Lahdentaus FIN 91 Ld32
Lahe EST 98 Kd41
Lahe EST 107 Lb46
Lahenpää S 73 Ja18
La Herguijuela E 45 Cc64
la Hérie-la-Viéville F 24 Hc33
la Herlière F 23 Gd32
La Hermida E 38 Da55
La Herradura E 60 Db76
La Herrera E 53 Eb69
La Herrería E 60 Cc73
Laheycourt F 24 Ja36
La Higuera E 55 Ed70
Lahinch IRL 12 Bc22
La Hinojosa E 53 Eb67
Lahišyn BY 202 Ea13
Lahm D 135 Dd44
Lahnajärvi FIN 97 Jd39
Lahnajärvi S 73 Hd18
Lahnakoski FIN 81 Jc28
Lahnalahti FIN 90 La32
Lahnanen FIN 82 Kb27
Lahnasjärvi FIN 82 Kd26
Lahnstein A 144 Fa52
Lahnstein D 133 Ca43
Lahntal D 126 Cc41
Laholm S 110 Ed53
Laholuoma FIN 89 Jb34
La Horcajada E 45 Cc64
La Horra E 46 Dc60
Lahovaara FIN 83 Lb28
La Hoya E 55 Ed73
Lahr D 133 Ca49
Lahstedt D 126 Dc37
Lähte EST 99 Lb45
Lähteenkylä FIN 89 Jb37
Lahti FIN 89 Ja38
Lahti FIN 90 Kc37
lahti FIN 98 Kb40
Lahtiranta FIN 81 Jd25
Lähtru EST 98 Ka44
la Hutte F 28 Fd39
Lai CH 142 Cd55
Laichingen D 134 Da49
Laičiai LT 114 La55
Laide GB 4 Dc06
Laidi LV 105 Jc52
Laidinmäki FIN 82 Kd28
Laidze LV 105 Jd50
l'Aigle F 23 Ga37
La Iglesuela E 46 Cd65
La Iglesuela del Cid E 48 Fc64
Laigné F 28 Fb40
Laignes F 30 Hd40
Laigueglia I 149 Ca63
l'Aiguillon-sur-Mer F 32 Fa45
Laihia FIN 81 Ja31
Laikko FIN 91 Ld34
Laikšės LT 114 Ka55
Laiksjö S 79 Ga27
Laikülä EST 98 Ka44
Lailiás GR 184 Cc76
Lailly-en-Val F 29 Gc40
Laimbach am Ostrong A 144 Fd50
Laimetsa EST 98 Kd44
Laimjala EST 105 Jd46
Laimoluokta sameviste S 67 Ha14
Laimont F 24 Ja36
la Ina E 59 Bd76
Lainach A 143 Ec55
Lainate I 149 Cc59
Lainejaur S 72 Gd24
Lainio S 68 Hd15
Lair GB 6 Dc08
Laisbäck S 72 Gb24
La Isla E 37 Cd54
Laissac F 34 Hb51
Láista GR 182 Ad79
Laisvall S 72 Gb21
Laisvalls by S 72 Gb21
Laitamaa S 68 Hd17
Laitasaari FIN 74 Ka24
Laiterla FIN 97 Jc40
Laitiainen FIN 89 Jd38
Laitikkala FIN 90 Ka36
Laitila FIN 89 Ja38
Laitineva FIN 82 Kb25
Laitse EST 98 Kb43
Laiuse EST 98 La44
Laiva sameviste S 71 Fd21
Laives F 30 Jb44
Laives I 143 Dd56
Laize-la-Ville F 22 Fc36
Laižuva LT 113 Jd53
la Jana E 48 Fd64
la Javie F 42 Ka52
Lajkovac SRB 153 Jc63
la Jonchère-Saint-Maurice F 33 Gc46
la Jonquera E 41 Hb58
Lajoskomárom H 145 Hb55
Lajosmizse H 146 Ja54
Lajunlahti FIN 83 Lb31
Láka GR 188 Ab81
Lakaluoma FIN 81 Jc31
Lakaniemi FIN 81 Jc30
Łąka Prudnicka PL 137 Gd43
Lakasjö S 80 Gc28
Lakatnik BG 179 Cc70
Lakaträsk S 73 Hc20
Lakavica MK 178 Ba73
Lakavica MK 183 Bd74
Lakenheath GB 20 Fd25
Läki BG 184 Db74
Laki MK 183 Ca74
Łąkie PL 121 Gc33
Lakinsk RUS 203 Fa10
Lakitelek H 146 Jb55
Lakki GR 197 Eb90
Lákki GR 200 Cb95
Lakkia CY 206 Jb97
Lákkoma GR 184 Dc79
Laknasi AL 182 Ab74
Lakócsa H 152 Ha58
Lakolk DK 108 Cd27
Łakorz PL 122 Hc33
Lakså N 66 Fd15
Laksåvik N 77 Dc29
Lakselv N 64 Jb07
Lakselv bukt N 62 Gd10
Laksfors N 70 Fa23
Lakshola N 66 Fd17
Laksnes N 64 Jd07
Laksvatn N 62 Gd10
Łąkta PL 129 Gc39
Laktaši BIH 152 Gd61
Låktatjåkka S 67 Gc13
Lakyle IRL 12 Bb23
Lalacelle F 28 Fc38
Lalandelle F 23 Gc35
La Lantejuela E 59 Cb74
La Lapa E 51 Bd70
Lălapaşa TR 185 Eb75
Lalar AL 182 Ab76
Lálas GR 194 Ba87
la Latette F 31 Jd43
l'Albagés E 48 Ga61
l'Albaron F 42 Ja54
Lalbenque F 40 Gc52
l'Albi E 48 Gb61
l'Albufereta E 55 Fb71
l'Alcora E 54 Fc66
l'Alcúdia E 54 Fb68
l'Alcúdia de Crespins E 54 Fb69
l'Alcúdia de Veo E 54 Fc66
La Lechère I 148 Bc57
Lalendorf D 119 Ec32
Lalevade-d'Ardèche F 34 Ja50
Lalić SRB 153 Ja59
la Lima I 155 Db64
Lalín E 36 Ba56
Lalinde F 33 Ga50
La Línea de la Concepción E 59 Cb78
la Llacuna E 49 Gc61
Lalleu F 28 Ed40
Lalling D 135 Ed48
Lalm N 85 Dc35
l'Almadrava E 48 Ga63
Lalœuf F 25 Jd37
La Lomba E 38 Db56
la Londe-les-Maures F 42 Ka55
Laloşu RO 175 Da65
la Loupe F 29 Gb38
Lalouvesc F 34 Ja49
La Louvière B 124 Ac41
Lalova MD 173 Fd56
Lalsi EST 98 La45
l'Alpe-d'Huez F 35 Ka49
l'Altet E 55 Fb71
Lalueza E 48 Fc60
La Luisiana E 59 Cb73
Laluque F 39 Fa53
Lam D 135 Ec47
la Maçana AND 40 Gc57
La Maçana AND 40 Gc57
la Machine F 30 Hc43
La Maddalena I 168 Cb73
Lama dei Peligni I 161 Fa71
La Madelaine F 22 Fa35
La Madeleine-Bouvet F 29 Ga38
La Magdalena E 37 Cb56
Lamaids F 33 Ha45
la Main F 31 Ka42
la Malène F 41 Hc52
la Malmaison F 24 Hc34
Lamalonga E 37 Bd58
Lamalou-les-Bains F 41 Hb54
Lama Mocogno I 149 Db63
Lamandia I 162 Ha74
Lamanère F 41 Ha58
La Manga del Mar Menor E 55 Fb73
La Marañosa E 46 Dc65
Lamarche F 31 Jc39
La Marea E 37 Cc55
Lamargelle F 30 Ja41
la Marina E 55 Fb72
la Marolle-en-Sologne F 29 Gc41
Lamarque F 32 Fb49
la Martella I 162 Gc75
la Martyre F 26 Dc38
La Masadera E 48 Fc60
Lamas de Olo P 44 Ba60
Lamas de Podence P 45 Bc60
Lamas do Vouga P 44 Ad63
Lamastre F 34 Ja49
La Mata E 52 Da66
La Mata de Monteagudo E 37 Cd56
Lambach A 144 Fa51
Lamballe F 26 Eb38
Lamberhurst GB 20 Fd29
Lambesc F 42 Jc53
Lámbia GR 188 Bb86
Łambinowice PL 137 Gd43
Lambley GB 11 Ec16
Lambókambos GR 195 Bd90
Lamborn S 87 Fd38
Lambourn GB 20 Fa28
Lambrecht D 133 Cb46
Lambrechten A 143 Ed50
Lambsheim D 133 Cb46
Lamego P 44 Ba61
La Meilleraye-de-Bretagne F 28 Fa41
La Melgosa E 53 Eb66
l'Amelie-sur-Mer F 32 Fa48
La Membrolle-sur-Longuenée F 28 Fb41
Lamerdingen D 142 Dc51
la Merlatière F 28 Fa44
l'Ametlla del Vallès E 49 Ha60
l'Ametlla de Mar E 48 Ga63
Lamezia Terme I 164 Gc81
Lamía GR 189 Bd83
la Milesse F 28 Fd39
Lamington GB 10 Ea14
Lamlash GB 10 Dc14
Lammasperä FIN 90 Ka33
Lammela FIN 89 Ja35
Lammersdorf D 125 Bc41
Lammhult S 103 Fc51
Lammi FIN 81 Jc30
Lammi FIN 90 Kb37
Lamminaho FIN 82 Kb28
Lamminkoski FIN 89 Jc34
Lamminkylä FIN 75 La22
Lamminkylä FIN 82 La25
Lamminkylä FIN 83 Ld31
Lamminmaa FIN 89 Jb32
Lamminmäki FIN 90 Kd32
Lamminperä FIN 74 Ka22
Lammu FIN 83 Lc31
Lamnay F 29 Ga39
La Mojonera E 61 Ea76
la Môle F 43 Kb55
La Molina E 41 Gd58
Lamone CH 149 Cc57
la Mongie F 40 Fd56
Lamontgie F 34 Hc48
La Montiela E 60 Cc73
La Morera E 51 Bc70
Lamosa E 36 Ad57
la Mothe-Achard F 28 Ed44
la Mothe-Saint-Héray F 32 Fc45
la Motte F 23 Ha35
La Motte F 27 Eb39
la Motte F 42 Ka51
Lamotte-Beuvron F 29 Gd41
la Motte-Bourbon F 28 Fc43
la Motte-Chalancon F 42 Jc51
la Motte-d'Aigues F 42 Jd53
la Motte-Saint-Martin F 35 Jd49
Lamotte-Warfusée F 23 Ha33
Lamovita BIH 152 Gc62
Lampaanjärvi FIN 82 Kc29
Lampaluoto FIN 89 Ja35
Lampaul-Guimiliau F 26 Dc38
Lampaul-Plouarzel F 26 Db38
Lampeland N 93 Dc41
Lamperila FIN 82 Kd30
Lampertheim D 134 Cc45
Lampertswalde D 128 Fa40
Lampeter GB 15 Dd26
Lampinsaari FIN 82 Ka26

Lampiselkä – Launkalne

Lampiselkä FIN 69 Ka16
l'Ampolla E 48 Ga63
Lamport GB 20 Fb25
Lampovo RUS 99 Mb41
Lamppi FIN 89 Ja35
Lamsfeld D 128 Fb38
Lamspringe D 126 Db38
Lamstedt D 118 Da32
Lamu FIN 82 Kb26
La Mudarra E 46 Cd60
La Muela E 47 Ea60
La Muela E 47 Fa61
Lamujoki FIN 82 Kb26
la Mure F 35 Jd49
Lamure-sur-Azergues F 34 Ja46
Lamvik N 63 Hd07
Lana I 142 Dc56
Lanabregas AL 182 Ac74
Lanabukt N 65 Kd07
Lanaja E 48 Fc60
Lanaken B 125 Bb40
la Napoule F 43 Kc54
Lanarce F 34 Hd50
Lanark GB 10 Ea14
La Nava E 59 Bc72
La Nava de Ricomalillo E 52 Cd67
La Nava de Santiago E 51 Bd68
Lancaster GB 11 Ec19
Lanciano I 157 Fb70
Lanciego E 39 Eb57
Lancin F 35 Jc47
Lančiūnava LT 114 Kc56
Lanckorona PL 138 Ja45
Lançon-Provence F 42 Jc54
Lańcucka PL 139 Kb43
Łańcut PL 139 Ka44
Landa S 102 Ec50
Landau a.d. Isar D 135 Ec49
Landau in der Pfalz D 133 Cb47
Landaul F 27 Ea40
Landaville-la-Haut F 31 Jc38
Landbobyn S 95 Fb39
Lande N 70 Fa24
Landéan F 28 Fa38
Landeck A 142 Db54
Landeleau F 27 Dd39
Landen B 124 Ad41
Landepereuse F 23 Ga36
Landerneau F 26 Dc38
Landerum NL 116 Bb32
Landeryd S 102 Ed51
Landeryd S 103 Fd47
Landesbergen D 126 Da36
Landet DK 109 Dd28
Landete E 54 Ed66
Landévant F 27 Ea40
Landévennec F 26 Dc38
Landford GB 20 Ed30
Landgraaf NL 125 Bb40
Landiras F 32 Fb51
Landivisiau F 26 Dc38
Landivy F 28 Fa38
Landkey GB 19 Dd29
Landkirchen D 119 Ea30
Landl A 143 Ea53
Landön S 79 Fb29
Landön S 111 Fb55
Landos F 34 Hd50
Landouzy-la-Ville F 24 Hc33
Landquart CH 142 Cd54
Landrecies F 24 Hc32
Landres F 25 Jc35
Landriano I 149 Cc60
Landsberg D 127 Eb39
Landsberg = Gorzów Wielkopolski PL 128 Fd36
Landsberg a. Lech D 142 Dc51
Landsbro S 103 Fc50
Landscheid D 133 Bc44
Landsee A 145 Gb53
Landshut D 135 Eb49
Landskrona S 110 Ed55
Landsmarkakap N 93 Db43
Landsmeer NL 116 Ba35
Landstuhl D 133 Ca46
Landudec F 27 Dc39
Landvetter S 102 Ec49
Landvik N 93 Da46
Landze LV 105 Jb50
Låne N 84 Cc36
Lane End GB 20 Fb28
Lanersbach A 143 Ea54
Lane-Ryr S 102 Ec46
Lanesborough IRL 8 Ca20
Lanestosa E 38 Dd55
la Neuville-en-Tourne-à-Fuy F 24 Hd35
Langå DK 100 Dc23
Langa E 46 Cd62
Långå S 86 Fa33
Langáda GR 191 Dd85
Langadás GR 183 Cb77
Langa de Duero E 46 Dd60
Langádia GR 194 Bb87
Långalma S 96 Gd40
Långåminne FIN 81 Ja31
Langangen N 93 Dc44
Långared S 102 Ec48
Långaryd S 102 Fa51
Långås S 102 Ec51
Långasjö S 111 Fd53
Langau A 136 Ga49
Långbäcken S 80 Gc27
Långban S 95 Fb42
Långbo S 87 Ga36
Långby S 87 Gb35
Langdal N 77 Da33
Langdon Beck GB 11 Ed17
Langdorf D 135 Ed48
Langeac F 34 Hc49
Langeais F 28 Fd42
Langebæk DK 109 Eb28
Langedijk NL 116 Ba34
Langegg A 136 Fc49
Langeid N 92 Cd44
Längelmäki FIN 90 Ka34
Langeln D 126 Dc38
Langelsheim D 126 Dc38
Långemåla S 103 Ga51
Langemark B 21 Ha30
Langen D 117 Cb35
Langen D 118 Cd32
Langen D 134 Cc44
Langenaltheim D 134 Dc48
Langenargen D 142 Cd52
Langenäs S 94 Ed41
Langenau D 127 Ed42
Langenau D 134 Db49
Langenbach D 143 Ea50
Langenberg D 127 Ec42
Langenberg/Westf. D 126 Cc38
Langenbernsdorf D 127 Eb42
Langenburg D 134 Da47
Langendernbach D 125 Cb42
Langeneichstädt D 127 Ea40
Langenenslingen D 142 Cd50
Langenes N 66 Fc12
Längenfeld A 142 Dc54
Langenfeld D 125 Bd40
Langenhagen D 126 Db36
Langenhahn D 125 Cb42
Langenhoe GB 21 Ga27
Langenhorn D 108 Da29
Langenleuba-Niederhain D 127 Ec41
Langenleuba-Oberhain D 127 Ec41
Langenlois A 144 Ga50
Langenlonsheim D 133 Ca44
Langennerie F 29 Ga41
Langenneufnach D 142 Db50
Langenpreising D 143 Ea50
Langen-Selbold D 134 Cd43
Langenthal CH 141 Bd53
Langenwang A 144 Ga53
Langenweddingen D 127 Ea38
Langenwetzendorf D 127 Eb42
Langenwolmsdorf D 128 Fb41
Langenzenn D 134 Dc46
Langeoog D 117 Cb31
Langerringen D 142 Dc51
Langerwehe D 125 Bc41
Langeskov DK 109 Dd27
Langesund N 93 Dc44
Langevåg N 76 Cc32
Langevåg N 92 Bd41
Langewiesen D 127 Dd42
Langey F 29 Gb39
Langfjord N 63 Hc08
Langfjordbotn N 65 Kd08
Langfjordhamn N 63 Hc08
Langfjordnes N 64 Ka05
Långforsselet S 73 Ja19
Langfurth D 134 Db47
Langgöns D 126 Cc42
Langhagen D 119 Ec32
Långhed S 87 Ga37
Långhem S 102 Ed49
Langhirano I 149 Da62
Langholm GB 11 Eb16
Langhus N 93 Ea42
Långjum S 102 Ed47
Langleeford GB 11 Ed14
Langli N 65 Kd08
Langlingen D 126 Dc36
Långlöt S 103 Gb52
Långnäs FIN 96 Hc41
Långnäs S 73 Hc23
Långnäs S 95 Ga39
Langnau im Emmental CH 141 Bd54
Langnes N 63 Ja06
Langø DK 109 Dd28
Langogne F 34 Hd50
Langoiran F 32 Fc51
Langon F 32 Fc51
Langonnet F 27 Dd39
Langør DK 109 Dd25
Langosco I 148 Ca60
Langport GB 19 Eb29
Langquaid D 135 Ea48
Langreo E 37 Cc55
Langres F 30 Jb40
Langrick GB 17 Fc23
Långron S 80 Ha30
Langschlag A 136 Fc49
Långsel S 73 Hd20
Långsele S 79 Gb31
Långsele S 80 Gd27
Långselet S 80 Hb25
Langserud S 94 Ed44
Langset N 94 Eb40
Langseter N 94 Eb42
Långshyttan S 95 Ga40
Långsjöby S 72 Gb24
Långsjön S 73 Hc21
Langslett N 63 Hb09
Langstrand N 63 Hd06
Langstrand N 64 Jc05
Långstranda N 78 Ea28
Langtoft GB 17 Fc19
Långtora S 96 Gc42
Långträsk S 72 Ha24
Långträsk S 73 Hb23
Långträsk S 80 Ha26
Languidic F 27 Ea40
Langvad N 71 Fd18
Langvågen N 66 Ga14
Langvatn N 71 Fb20
Långvattnet S 80 Hb25
Långvattnet S 80 Gc28
Långvik FIN 98 Kb40
Langvik N 85 Ea37
Långvik S 96 Ha44
Långviken S 72 Gc22
Långviken S 80 Hc25
Långviksmon S 80 Gd29
Langvind S 87 Gb36
Långvinds bruk S 87 Gb36
Langwathby GB 11 Ec17
Langwedel D 118 Da34
Langweid D 134 Dc49
Langwies CH 142 Cd55
Langwyfan GB 15 Ea22
Lanhélin F 28 Ed38
Lanheses P 44 Ad59
Lanhouarneau F 26 Dc37
Łanięta PL 122 Jb34
Łaniewo PL 122 Ja31
Lanilar GB 15 Dd25
Lanildut F 26 Db38
Lanjarón E 60 Dc76
Lankamaa FIN 90 Kc32
Lankas LV 105 Jb52
Lanke D 120 Fa35
Lankeliškiai LT 114 Ka59
Łankiejmy PL 122 Jb30
Lankila FIN 90 La37
Lankojärvi FIN 74 Jc18
Lankoori FIN 89 Ja36
Lankosi FIN 89 Ja35
Lanloup F 26 Ea37
Lanmeur F 26 Dd37
Lanna S 95 Fc44
Lanna S 95 Gb44
Länna S 96 Gd42
Länna S 96 Ha42
Lanna S 102 Fa50
Lännäs S 95 Fd44
Lannavaara S 68 Hc14
Lannéanou F 26 Dd38
Lannemezan F 40 Fd56
Lanneray F 29 Gb39
Lannevesi FIN 82 Kb31
Lannilis F 26 Db37
Lannion F 26 Ea37
la Nocle-Maulaix F 30 Hc43
Lanouaille F 33 Gb48
Lansån S 73 Hd19
Lans-en-Vercors F 35 Jc49
Länsi-Aure FIN 89 Jc34
Länsi-Kalmari FIN 82 Ka31
Länsikoski FIN 74 Jc21
Länsikylä FIN 81 Jc31
Länsiranta FIN 64 Ka10
Länsiranta FIN 81 Jc31
Länsi-Saamainen FIN 82 La31
Länsi-Teisko FIN 89 Jd35
Länsi-Vuokka FIN 83 Lb28
Lansjärv S 73 Hd19
Lanškroun CZ 137 Gb45
Lanslebourg-Mont-Cenis F 35 Kb48
Lanslevillard F 35 Kb48
Lanta F 40 Gc54
Lantadilla E 38 Db58
Lantenay F 30 Ja41
Lanterot F 31 Ka40
Lantjärv S 73 Jb21
Lantosque F 43 Kd52
Lantsch CH 142 Cd55
la Nucia E 55 Fc70
Lanuéjols F 41 Hc52
La Nuez de Arriba E 38 Dc57
Lanusei I 169 Cb77
Lanuvio I 160 Eb72
Lanvellec F 26 Dd37
Lanvéoc F 26 Db38
Lanvollon F 26 Ea37
Lány CZ 136 Fa44
Łany PL 137 Ha44
Lánycsók H 153 Hc58
Lanz D 119 Ea34
Lanza E 36 Ba55
Lanzahita E 46 Cd65
Lanzas Agudas E 38 Dd55
Lanžhot CZ 137 Gc49
Lanzo d'Intelvi I 149 Cc57
Lanzós E 36 Bb54
Lanzo Torinese I 148 Bc59
Lanzuela E 47 Fa62
Lao EST 106 Kb46
Laon F 24 Hc34
Laons F 23 Gb37
La Orbada E 45 Cc62
La Paca E 61 Ec73
la Pacaudière F 34 Hd45
Łapafö H 145 Hb56
Lapajärvi FIN 69 Kc17
Lapalisse F 34 Hc45
La Palma E 55 Fa73
La Palma del Condado E 59 Bc73
la Palmyre F 32 Fa47
la Palud-sur-Verdon F 42 Ka53
Lapan AL 182 Ac77
Lapan F 29 Gd43
la Panadella E 49 Gc61
Łapanów PL 138 Jb45
La Paquelais F 28 Ed42
Laparade F 40 Fd52
La Paradilla E 46 Db64
La Paraya E 37 Cc55
La Parra E 51 Bc70
La Parra de las Vegas E 53 Eb66
La Parte de Sotoscueva E 38 Dc56
Lápas GR 188 Ba85
La Pava E 61 Eb72
Łapczyca PL 138 Jb44
La Peña E 45 Bd61
La Peral E 37 Cb54
La Peraleja E 47 Ea65
Laperdiguera E 48 Fc59
Lapės LT 114 Kc57
La Pescia I 161 Ga73
La Pesga E 45 Ca64
La Pesquera E 54 Ed67
la Petite-Pierre F 25 Kb36
la Petrizia I 164 Gc81
Lapeyrade F 40 Fc53
la Peyrade F 41 Hd54
Lapeyrouse F 34 Hb45
La Peza E 60 Dc74
la Pezade F 41 Hc53
Lapford GB 19 Dd30
la Piarre F 42 Jd51
la Pierre-Percée F 30 Hb44
Lapijoki FIN 89 Ja37
La Pinilla E 55 Ed73
Lapinkangas FIN 74 Ka24
Lapinkylä FIN 90 Kd38
Lapinkylä FIN 98 Ka39
Lapinlahti FIN 82 Kd28
Lapinsaari FIN 89 Jb32
Lapinsalo FIN 82 Kc27
Lapiosalmi FIN 75 Kc20
Lapiovaara FIN 83 Ma29
Lapithos CY 206 Jb96
Lapjärvi FIN 91 Lb37
la Plagne F 35 Kb47
la Plaine F 28 Fb43
la Plaine-sur-Mer F 27 Ec42
la Planchette F 35 Ka48
La Plaza (Teverga) E 37 Cb55
Lapleau F 33 Gd48
Laplume F 40 Ga52
Lapmežciems LV 106 Ka50
La Pobla de Benifassà E 48 Fd64
la Pobla de Cérvoles E 48 Gb61
la Pobla de Lillet E 41 Gd58
la Pobla de Massaluca E 48 Fd62
la Pobla de Montornès E 49 Gc62
la Pobla de Segur E 48 Gb59
la Pobla de Vallbona E 54 Fb67
la Pobla Llarga E 54 Fb69
la Pobla Tornesa E 54 Fc66
La Pobleta de Andilla E 54 Fa66
La Pola de Gordón E 37 Cc56
la Porta F 154 Cc69
La Portellada E 48 Fd63
La Portera E 54 Fa68
Lapoș RO 176 Eb64
Lapouyade F 32 Fc49
La Póveda de Soria E 47 Eb59
Lapovo SRB 174 Bc66
Lappach I 143 Ea55
Lappago I 143 Ea55
Lappajärvi FIN 81 Jc30
Läppäkoski FIN 90 Kb37
Lappberg S 67 Ha16
Lappböle FIN 98 Ka39
Lappea FIN 68 Jb17
Lappeenranta FIN 91 Lb36
Lappers FIN 98 Ka40
Lappersdorf D 135 Eb48
Lappetelä FIN 82 Kd29
Lappfjärd FIN 89 Hd33
Lappfors FIN 81 Jb29
Lappi FIN 75 La22
Lappi FIN 89 Jd33
Lappi FIN 89 Ja37
Lappila FIN 90 Kb37
Lappineva FIN 89 Jc34
Lappo FIN 97 Hd40
Lappohja FIN 97 Jd41
Lappoluobbal N 63 Ja10
Lappträsk FIN 90 Kd38
Lappträsk S 73 Jb21
Lappvattnet S 80 Hc26
Lappvik FIN 97 Jd41
la Praye F 30 Hd44
la Preste F 41 Ha58
la Primaube F 41 Ha52
Lâpseki TR 185 Eb79
Läpsi FIN 83 Ld28
Lapta = Lapithos CY 206 Jb96
Laptevo RUS 107 Mb50
Laptovicy RUS 99 Lc43
Lapua FIN 81 Jb31
La Puebla de Almoradiel E 53 Dd67
La Puebla de Castro E 48 Fd59
La Puebla de Cazalla E 59 Cb74
La Puebla de Hijar E 48 Fb62
La Puebla de los Infantes E 59 Cb72
La Puebla del Río E 59 Bd74
La Puebla de Montalbán E 52 Da66
La Puebla de Valdavia E 38 Da57
La Puebla de Valverde E 47 Fa65
La Pueblanueva E 52 Cd66
la Puerta de Segura E 53 Ea71
Lăpugiu de Jos RO 174 Cb60
La Punt-Chamues-ch CH 142 Da55
Lăpuș RO 171 Db56
Lăpușata RO 175 Da64
Lăpușna MD 173 Fc58
Lăpușna RO 172 Db58
Lăpușnicel RO 174 Ca63
la Puye F 29 Ga44
Lapväärtti FIN 89 Hd33
Łapy PL 123 Kb34
L'Aquila I 156 Ed70
la Quintaine F 41 Ha53
La Rábita E 60 Dc76
Laracha E 36 Ad54
Lara de los Infantes E 46 Dd59
la Rades E 46 Dc62
Laragh IRL 13 Cd22
Laragne-Montéglin F 42 Jd51
la Raille F 35 Kb50
La Rambla E 60 Cd73
La Rasa E 46 Dd61
Larbert GB 10 Ea13
l'Arboç E 49 Gc62
l'Arbresle F 34 Ja46
Lärbro S 104 Ha48
Larce MK 178 Bb73
Larceveau F 39 Fa55
Larchant F 29 Ha38
Larche F 33 Gb49
Lårdal N 93 Da43
Lardaro I 149 Db58
Larderello I 155 Db67
Lardero E 39 Eb58
Lárdos GR 197 Fa93
Lardosa P 44 Bb65
Lardy F 29 Gd38
La Reale I 168 Bd73
Laredo E 38 Dd54
La Redondela E 58 Ba74
La Regla E 37 Ca55
Laren NL 116 Ba36
Laren NL 117 Bc36
la Réole F 32 Fc51
Larer CH 142 Da55
La Revilla E 38 Db55
Larg GB 5 Ea06
Larga MD 172 Ed53
Largentière F 34 Ja51
l'Argentière-la Bessée F 35 Kb49
Largoward GB 7 Ec12
Largs GB 6 Dc13
Largu RO 176 Ed64
Lărguța MD 177 Fc60
la Riba E 48 Gb62
La Riba de Escalote E 47 Ea61
Lárimna GR 189 Cb84
Larino I 161 Fc72
Larinsaari FIN 83 Lc29
Lario E 37 Cd56
Lárissa GR 189 Bd81
La Riva E 38 Dc56
la Rivière-Thibouville F 23 Ga36
Larkhall GB 10 Ea14
Larkhill GB 20 Ed29
Larkollen N 93 Ea43
Larmor-Plage F 27 Ea40
Larnaka CY 206 Jc97
Larne GB 9 Da16
la Robine F 42 Ka52
La Robla E 37 Cc56
La Roca de la Sierra E 51 Bc68
la Roca del Vallès E 49 Ha61
la Rocca I 167 Fc84
la Rochebeaucourt-et-Argentine F 32 Fd48
La-Roche-Bernard F 27 Ec41
la Roche-Chalais F 32 Fc49
la Roche-de Rame F 35 Kb50
la Roche-Derrien F 26 Ea37
la Roche-des-Arnauds F 35 Jd50
la Roche-en-Ardenne B 132 Ba43
la Rochefoucauld F 32 Fd47
la Roche-Guyon F 23 Gc36
la Rochelle F 32 Fa46
Larochemillay F 30 Hd43
la Roche-Morey F 31 Jc40
la Roche-Posay F 29 Ga44
la Rochepot F 30 Ja43
la Roche-sur-Foron F 35 Ka45
la Roche-sur-Yon F 28 Ed44
la Rochette F 35 Ka47
la Rochette F 43 Kc52
Larochette L 133 Bb44
La Roda E 37 Bd53
La Roda E 53 Eb68
La Roda de Andalucía E 60 Cd75
la Roë F 28 Fa40
Laroles E 61 Dd75
la Romagne F 28 Fa43
La Romana E 55 Fa71
la Romieu F 40 Ga53
Larón E 37 Ca55
la Ronde F 32 Fb45
Laroquebrou F 33 Gd50
la Roquebrussane F 42 Ka54
la Roque-d'Anthéron F 42 Jc53
Laroque-de-Fa F 41 Ha56
Laroque-d'Olmes F 41 Gd56
la Roque-Gageac F 33 Gb50
la Roque-sur-Cèze F 42 Ja52
Laroque-Timbaut F 40 Ga52
La Rösa CH 142 Da56
la Rosière 1850 F 35 Kb47
Larouco E 36 Bc57
Larrabetzu E 38 Ea55
Larraga E 39 Ec57
Larraínzar E 39 Ed56
Larraona E 39 Eb57
Larrazet F 40 Gb53
Larressingle F 40 Fd53
Larroque F 40 Ga55
Larroque F 40 Gc53
Larseng N 62 Gc10
Larsmo FIN 81 Jb28
Larsnes N 76 Cb33
La Rubia E 47 Eb60
Laruns F 39 Fb56
Larva E 61 Dd73
Larvik N 93 Dd44
Las PL 138 Hd45
Lasa I 142 Db56
Las Alcantarillas E 59 Ca75
Las Aljabaras E 60 Cc72
la Salle F 31 Ka38
Lasalle F 41 Hd52
la Salle-de-Vihiers F 28 Fb42
Las Almontarás E 61 Ea73
la Salvetat-Peyralès F 41 Gd52
la Salvetat-Saint-Gilles F 40 Gb54
la Salvetat-sur-Agout F 41 Ha54
La Salzedella E 48 Fd64
Läsänkoski FIN 90 Kd33
La Santa Espina E 46 Cd60
la Sarraz CH 141 Bb55
La Sauceda E 59 Ca76
La Sauceda E 59 Ca77
la Saulce F 42 Ka51
la-Saulsotte F 30 Hb38
la Sauve F 32 Fc50
la Sauvetat-du-Dropt F 32 Fd51
Las Berlanas E 46 Cd63
Låsby DK 108 Dc24
Las Cabezas de San Juan E 59 Ca75
Las Casas de Xilxes E 54 Fc67
Las Cobatillas E 61 Eb73
Lascuarre E 48 Ga59
Las Cuevas E 54 Ed67
Las Cuevas de los Medinas E 61 Eb76
Las Cuevas de Soria E 47 Ea60
La Seca E 46 Cd61
La Secada E 37 Cc54
La Secuita E 48 Gb62
la Selle-sur-le-Bied F 29 Ha39
La Selva del Camp E 48 Gb62
la Selve F 41 Ha52
Las Encarnaciones E 59 Cb75
La Sénia E 48 Fd64
Lásenice CZ 136 Fc48
La Serna E 38 Da58
la Serre F 33 Gd48
la Seu d'Urgell E 40 Gc58
la Seyne-sur-Mer F 42 Ka55
Las Fraguas E 38 Db55
Lasham GB 20 Fa29
Las Herast E 38 Da56
Las Herencias E 52 Cd66
Las Herrerías E 58 Ba73
Lasila EST 98 Kd42
Łasin PL 122 Hc33
Las Infantas E 60 Db72
Lasinia HR 151 Ga59
Las Jarillas E 59 Ca72
Łask PL 130 Hc39
Laska PL 121 Gd31
Łaskarzew PL 131 Jd38
Laski PL 121 Gb31
Laski PL 122 Jc33
Laskino RUS 113 Ja59
Łasko PL 120 Ga34
Laško SLO 151 Fd57
Laskowa PL 138 Jb45
Laskowice PL 123 Ka33
Laskowice PL 137 Ha43
Laskowiec PL 121 Ha33
Las Labores E 52 Dc68
Las Lagunillas E 60 Da74
Laslea RO 175 Dc60
Las Majadas E 47 Ec65
Las Mellizas E 60 Cd76
Las Mesas E 53 Ea68
Las Minas E 53 Ec71
Las Navas E 60 Da74
Las Navas de la Concepción E 59 Cb72
Las Navas del Marqués E 46 Da64
Las Negras E 61 Eb76
Las Nogueras E 54 Fa67
La Solana E 53 Dd69
La Solana E 53 Eb70
la Source F 29 Gc40
la Souterraine F 33 Gc45
Lasovo SRB 179 Ca67
Lasowice PL 129 Gd40
Lasówka PL 137 Gb44
Las Pachecas E 53 Dd69
Las Pajanosas E 59 Bb73
Laspaúles E 40 Ga58
Las Pedroñeras E 53 Ea68
Las Pedrosas E 47 Fa59
La Spezia I 155 Cd64
Las Planas E 48 Fc63
Las Quintanillas E 38 Dc58
Las Rozas E 46 Db64
Lassa CY 206 Hd97
Låssa S 96 Gc43
Lassahn D 119 Dd32
Las Salas E 37 Cd56
Lassan D 120 Fa31
Lassay-les-Châteaux F 28 Fb38
Lassee A 145 Gc50
Lassemoen N 78 Ed26
Lasseube F 39 Fb55
Lassigny F 23 Ha34
Lassila FIN 89 Jb35
Lassila FIN 89 Jc33
Lassnitz bei Murau A 144 Fb54
Låstad S 102 Fa46
Lastak sameviste S 72 Gc18
la Sterza I 155 Db66
Lastic F 33 Ha47
Las Torrecillas E 51 Bc69
Las Torres de Aliste E 45 Ca59
Las Torres de Cotillas E 55 Ed72
Lastovo HR 158 Gd68
Lastra a Signa I 155 Dc65
Lastras de Cuéllar E 46 Db61
Lastres E 37 Cd54
Lästringe S 96 Gc45
Lastrup D 117 Cb35
Lastulahti FIN 82 La29
Las Uces E 45 Bd62
la Suze-sur-Sarthe F 28 Fd40
Lasva EST 107 Lc47
Las Veguillas E 45 Cb63
las Ventanas E 55 Ed72
Las Ventas con Peña Aguilera E 52 Da67
Las Ventas de Retamosa E 46 Db65
Las Ventas de San Julián E 45 Cc65
Las Viñas E 61 Dd74
Las Virtudes E 52 Dc70
Lašva BIH 158 Hb64
Łaszczów PL 131 Kd42
Laszki PL 139 Kc44
la Tannière F 28 Fa38
Latasa E 39 Ec56
La Tercia E 53 Ec71
la Terrasse-sur Dorlay F 34 Ja48
Laterza I 162 Gd76
la Teste F 32 Fa51
Lathen D 117 Ca34
Latheron GB 5 Eb05
la Thuile I 148 Bb58
Lathus F 33 Ga45
Latiano I 162 Hb76
Latikberg S 79 Gb26
Latillé F 28 Fd44
Latina I 160 Eb73
Latisana I 150 Ec59
Látky SK 138 Ja49
La Toba E 47 Ec65
Latomaa FIN 89 Jc36
Latorpsbruk S 95 Fc44
La Torre E 54 Ed67
La Torre de Cabdella E 40 Gb58
La Torre de Esteban Hambrán E 46 Da65
la Torre de Fontaubella E 48 Ga62
La Torre del Cap E 54 Fc68
la Torre de l'Espanyol E 48 Ga62
La Torre dels Beltrans E 54 Fc65
La Torre d'En Besora E 54 Fc65
La Torresaviñán E 47 Ea63
Latoszyn PL 139 Jd44
Latoue F 40 Ga56
la Tour-Blanche F 32 Fd48
la Tour-d'Aigues F 42 Jd53
la Tour-d'Auvergne F 33 Ha48
Latour-de-Carol F 41 Gd58
la Tour-du-Pin F 35 Jc47
la Tour-Fondue F 42 Ka55
la Toussuire F 35 Ka48
Latovainio FIN 89 Jd37
Latowicz PL 131 Jd37
la Tranche-sur-Mer F 32 Ed45
Latrány H 145 Ha55
la Tremblade F 32 Fa47
Latresne F 32 Fb50
la Trimouille F 33 Gb45
La Trinité-Porhoët F 27 Eb39
Latronico I 162 Gb77
Latronquière F 33 Gd50
Latsch I 142 Dc56
Latteluokta S 67 Ha14
Latterbach CH 141 Bd55
Lattern N 63 Hb09
Lattervik N 62 Ha09
Lattin IRL 12 Bd24
Lattomeri FIN 89 Ja36
Lattrop NL 117 Ca36
Lattuna FIN 69 Kc14
la Turballe F 27 Eb42
la Turbie F 43 Kd53
Latva FIN 75 Kc21
Latva FIN 75 Kd24
Latva FIN 82 Ka26
Latvajärvenperä FIN 75 Kd22
Latvalampi FIN 83 Lc31
Latvaset FIN 82 Ka28
Lau S 104 Ha50
Laubach D 126 Cd42
Lauben D 142 Db51
Laubere LV 106 Kd50
Laubert F 34 Hc51
Laubrières F 28 Fa40
Laubusch D 128 Fb40
Laucesa LV 115 Lc54
Laucha D 127 Ea40
Lauchhammer D 128 Fa40
Lauchheim D 134 Db48
Laučiai LT 113 Jc56
Lauda-Königshofen D 134 Da46
Laudal N 92 Cc46
Laudenbach D 134 Cc45
Lauder GB 11 Ec14
Lauderi LV 107 Ma51
Laudio E 38 Ea55
Laudiškiai LV 114 Kb55
Ļaudona LV 107 Lb51
Laudun F 42 Jb52
Lauenau D 126 Da37
Lauenberg D 126 Db38
Lauenbrück D 118 Db34
Lauenburg D 118 Dc33
Lauenen CH 141 Bc56
Lauenförde D 126 Da39
Lauf D 135 Dd46
Laufach D 134 Cd44
Laufen CH 141 Bd52
Laufen D 143 Ec51
Laufenburg CH 141 Ca52
Laufenburg D 141 Ca52
Lauffen D 134 Cd47
Laugaland N 92 Cb43
Laugaliai LT 113 Jb55
Laugar IS 3 Bb04
Laugarbakki IS 2 Ad03
Laugarvatn IS 2 Ac05
Laugharne GB 18 Dc27
Laugnac F 40 Ga52
Lauhala FIN 89 Jb34
Lauhkea FIN 75 Kc20
Lauingen (Donau) D 134 Db49
Laujar de Andarax E 61 Dd75
Laujuzan F 40 Fc53
Lauka EST 97 Jc44
Laukaa FIN 90 Kc32
Laukansaari FIN 91 Ld33
Laukeland N 84 Cb36
Lauker S 72 Ha22
Laukgaļi LV 113 Jb53
Laukka-aho FIN 83 Lb30
Laukkala FIN 82 Kc29
Laukkala FIN 91 Lb36
Laukkuluspa S 67 Ha15
Laukna EST 98 Kb44
Laukoski FIN 98 Kc39
Lauko Soda LT 113 Jc54
Lauksargiai LT 113 Jd57
Lauksundskardet N 62 Ha08
Laukuva LT 113 Jd55
Laukvik N 62 Gd08
Laukvik N 62 Gc09
Laukvik N 62 Gb10
Laukvik N 63 Hd07
Laukvik N 64 Jd04
Laukvika N 66 Fc14
Laukviken N 66 Fc16
Laukžemė LT 113 Jb54
La Uña E 37 Cd55
Launac F 40 Gb54
Launaguet F 40 Gc54
Launceston GB 18 Dc31
Laundos P 44 Ac60
La Unión E 55 Fa74
La Unión de Campos E 45 Cc59
Launkalne LV 106 La49

le Raincy – Lindsdal

le Raincy F 23 Ha36
Lerbäck S 95 Fc45
Lerberget S 110 Ec54
Lerbo S 95 Ga40
Lerbo S 95 Ga45
Lercara Friddi I 166 Ed85
Lerdal S 94 Eb45
Lerdala S 102 Fa46
L'Eree GBG 26 Eb35
le Relecq-Kerhuon F 26 Dc38
le Reposoir F 35 Ka45
Lerești RO 176 Dd63
le Revest-les-Eaux F 42 Ka55
Lerga E 39 Ed57
Lerheim N 77 Da32
Lerici I 155 Cd64
Lerín E 39 Ec58
le Rival F 35 Jc48
Lerkehaug N 78 Ec28
Lerma E 46 Dc59
Lerma I 148 Cb62
Lerm-et-Musset F 40 Fc52
Lermontovo RUS 203 Fc11
Lermoos A 142 Dc53
le Roc-Saint-André F 27 Eb40
le Rouget F 33 Gd50
Lérouville F 24 Jb36
le Roux F 35 Kb49
le Rozier-Peyreleau F 41 Hb52
Lerrain F 31 Jd38
Lerum S 102 Ec49
le Russey F 31 Ka42
Lerwick GB 5 Fa05
Les E 40 Ga57
Leș RO 170 Ca57
les 4 Routes F 34 Hb47
les Abrets F 35 Jc47
les Aix-d'Angillon F 29 Ha42
Lešak KSV 178 Ba69
le Sambuc F 42 Jb54
les Ancizes-Comps F 33 Ha46
les Andelys F 23 Gb35
les Angles F 41 Gd57
Lešani MK 182 Ba75
le Sap F 22 Fd37
les Arcs F 35 Kb47
les Arcs F 43 Kb54
les Arques F 33 Gb51
les Aspres F 23 Ga37
les Auberts F 35 Ka50
les Autels-Villevillon F 29 Ga39
le Sauze F 42 Ka51
le Sauze F 43 Kb51
les Avellanes E 48 Ga60
les Baux-de-Provence F 42 Jb53
les Bertins F 30 Hb42
les Bézards F 29 Ha40
les-Bordes F 29 Gd40
les Bordes F 30 Hb39
les Borges Blanques E 48 Ga61
les Borges del Camp E 48 Gb62
les Bourdelins F 29 Ha43
Lesbury GB 11 Fa15
les Cabannes F 40 Gc57
les Cabòries E 49 Gd61
l'Escala E 49 Hc59
les Cammazes F 41 Gd55
les Camposines E 48 Ga62
Lescar F 39 Fb55
l'Escarène F 43 Kd52
les Cars F 33 Gb47
Lesce SLO 151 Fa57
les Cerqueux F 28 Fb43
les Chaises F 23 Gc37
Les-Champs-de-Losques F 22 Fa36
les Chapieux F 35 Kb46
les Chênes-Secs F 28 Fb39
Lescheraines F 35 Jd47
les-Choux F 29 Ha40
Lesčiai LV 114 Kb56
les Claux F 35 Kb50
les Clayes-sous-Bois F 23 Gc37
Lescoff F 27 Db39
Lesconil F 27 Dc40
les Contamines-Montjoie F 35 Kb46
les Coves de Vinromà E 54 Fd65
Lescun F 39 Fb56
Lescure-d'Albigeois F 41 Gd53
les Deux-Alpes F 35 Ka49
les Eaux-Chaudes F 39 Fb56
les Écharmeaux F 34 Ja45
les Echelles F 35 Jd48
les Ecrennes F 29 Ha38
le Sel-de-Bretagne F 28 Ed40
Lesencetomaj H 145 Gd55
le Sentier CH 140 Ba55
les Epesses F 28 Fb43
le Sépey CH 141 Bc56
Les Epioux B 132 Ad44
les Essarts F 28 Fa44
les Estables F 34 Hd50
les Étangs F 25 Jd35
les Eyzies-de-Tayac F 33 Gb50
les Fabres F 35 Kb50
les Fins F 31 Ka42
les Forges F 30 Hd40
les Genets F 33 Gc45
les Gets F 35 Ka45
les Grandes-Chapelles F 30 Hd38
Les Hautes-Rivières F 24 Ja33
les Hayons F 23 Gb34
les Herbiers F 28 Fa43
les Hermaux F 34 Hb51
les Hermites F 29 Ga41
les Hôpitaux-Neufs F 31 Ka43
Lesičeri BG 180 Dd70
Lesičovo BG 179 Da72
Lesidren BG 179 Da70
les Iffs F 28 Ed39
Lesina I 161 Fd71
les Islettes F 24 Ja35
les Issambres F 43 Kb54
Lesja N 85 Dc34
Lesjaskog N 77 Db33
Lesjaverk N 85 Db34
Lešje SRB 178 Bc67
Lesjöfors S 95 Fb41
Lesjötorp S 79 Ga28
Leskelä FIN 82 Kb26
Leskelänkylä FIN 82 Kc31
Lesko PL 139 Kb46
Leskova SRB 178 Ad69
Leskovac SRB 178 Bd70
Leskova dolina SLO 151 Fb59
Leskovec BG 179 Da68
Leskovec CZ 137 Gd45
Leskovec pri Krškem SLO 151 Fd58
Leskovic AL 182 Ad78
Leskovo BG 181 Fa69
les Llosses E 49 Gd59
les Lucs-sur-Boulogne F 28 Ed43
les Mages F 42 Ja52
les Maisons Blanches F 32 Fd46
les Mares F 23 Ga37
les Martys F 41 Ha55
les Matelles F 41 Hd53
les Mées F 42 Ka52
les Menuires F 35 Ka48
les Minières F 32 Fd45
Lesmont F 30 Hd38
les Moulins CH 141 Bc55
les Moulins F 34 Hd46
les Moussières F 35 Jd45
les Moutiers F 27 Ec43
Les Mureaux F 23 Gc36
Lesná CZ 135 Ec45
Leśna PL 128 Fd41
Leśna Podlaska PL 131 Kb37
les Nègres F 32 Fd46
Lesneven F 26 Dc37
Lesní Albrechtice CZ 137 Ha45
Leśnica PL 137 Ha43
Lešnica SRB 153 Ja62
Leśniewo PL 121 Ha29
Leśniewo PL 122 Jc30
Leśniów PL 128 Fd38
Leśniowice PL 131 Kc40
Lesnoe RUS 202 Ec09
Lesnoj RUS 113 Ja57
Lesnoj RUS 113 Ja59
Lesnoje RUS 113 Ja58
Lesnoje RUS 113 Jc58
Lesnoje RUS 113 Jd57
les Nonières F 35 Jd50
Lesnovo BG 179 Cd71
Lesnovo MK 178 Bd73
le Soler F 41 Hb57
les Ollières-sur-Eyrieux F 34 Ja50
le Somail F 41 Hb55
les Ormes F 29 Ga43
les Orres F 35 Kb50
le Souquet F 39 Fa53
les Ourgneaux F 30 Hc43
les Paccots CH 141 Bc55
les Palmeres E 54 Fc68
Lesparre-Médoc F 32 Fa48
Lesperon F 39 Fa53
l'Esperou F 41 Hc52
Lespezi RO 172 Ec56
les Pieux F 22 Ed35
les Placeaux F 30 Hb40
les Planches-en-Montagne F 31 Jd43
les Planes d'Hostoles E 49 Ha59
les Plans CH 141 Bc56
l'Espluga de Francolí E 48 Gb61
les Ponts-de-Cé F 28 Fb41
les-Ponts-de-Martel CH 141 Bb54
les Portes-en-Ré F 32 Ed45
les Pujols F 40 Gc56
Les Quatre-Chemins B 132 Ad44
les Riceys F 30 Hd39
les Rosaires F 26 Eb38
les Rotes E 55 Fd70
les Rouges-Eaux F 31 Ka38
les Rousses F 31 Jd44
Les Sables-d'Olonne F 28 Ed44
Lessach A 144 Fa54
les Saisies F 35 Ka46
les Salles-du-Gardon F 41 Hd52
Lessay F 22 Ed36
les Scaffarels F 43 Kb52
Lessebo S 103 Fd52
les Sièges F 30 Hc39
Lessíni GR 188 Ad84
Lessolo I 148 Bd59
l'Estany E 49 Gd60
l'Estaque F 42 Jc54
Lestards F 33 Gc48
l'Estartit E 49 Hc59
Lestelle-Bétharram F 40 Fc56
Lestene LV 106 Ka51
les Ternes F 34 Hb49
Lesterps F 33 Ga46
les Thilliers-en-Vexin F 23 Gc35
les Thons-le-Grand F 31 Jc39
les Thuiles F 43 Kb51
Lestijärvi FIN 81 Jd29
Lestkov CZ 135 Ec45
les Touches F 28 Fa41
l'Estréchure F 41 Hd52
les Trois-Moutiers F 28 Fd43
Leşu RO 171 Dc56
les Ulis F 23 Gd37
Lesura BG 179 Cd69
les Useres E 54 Fc65
les Vanels F 41 Hc52
les Vans F 34 Hd51
les Verchers-sur-Layon F 28 Fc42
les Verrières CH 141 Bb54
les Vignes F 41 Hb52
Leswalt GB 10 Dc16
Leszcz PL 122 Hd33
Leszcze PL 138 Jb43
Łeszkowy PL 121 Hb30
Leszno PL 128 Fd40
Leszno PL 129 Gb38
Leszno PL 130 Jb37
Lesznowola PL 130 Jb38
Letafors S 94 Ed39
Létavértes H 147 Ka53
Letca RO 171 Da56
Letcani RO 173 Fa57
Letca Nouă RO 180 Ea67
Letchworth Garden City GB 20 Fc26
Letea RO 177 Ga64
le Teil F 42 Jb51
le Teilleul F 28 Fb38
le Temple F 29 Ga40
le Temple F 23 Ha35
Le Temple-de-Bretagne F 28 Ed42
Letenye H 145 Gc56
Letham GB 7 Eb12
le Theil F 22 Fa34
le Theil F 29 Ga39
le Thillot F 31 Ka39
le Tholy F 31 Ka39
le Thor F 42 Jb53
le Thoronet F 42 Ka54
le Thour F 24 Hd34
Letino I 161 Fb73
Letiny CZ 135 Ed46
Letipea EST 98 La41
l'Etivaz CH 141 Bc56
Letkés H 146 Hc51
Letku FIN 89 Jd38
Letnica BG 180 Dc70
Letohrad CZ 137 Gb44
Letoianni I 167 Fd84
le Touquet-Paris-Plage F 23 Gb31
Le-Tour-du-Parc F 27 Eb41
le Touvet F 35 Jd48
Letovice CZ 137 Gb46
Łętowice PL 138 Jc44
Le Trait F 23 Ga35
le Transloy F 23 Ha33
Le Tréport F 23 Gb33
le Trivalou F 41 Gd53
le Trois Epis F 31 Kb38
le Tronquay F 23 Gb35
Letsbo S 87 Ga35
Letschin D 128 Fb36
Letterbreen GB 9 Cb18
Letterfrack IRL 8 Bb20
Letterkelly IRL 12 Bc22
Letterkenny IRL 9 Cb16
Lettermullan IRL 12 Bb21
Letur E 53 Eb71
Letuš SLO 151 Fc57
Letux E 48 Fb62
Letyčiv UA 204 Eb15
Letzlingen D 127 Ea36
Leu RO 175 Da66
Leubingen D 127 Dd40
Leubnitz D 127 Eb42
Leubsdorf D 127 Ed42
Leucate-Plage F 41 Hb56
Leuchars GB 7 Ec11
Leuchey F 30 Jb40
Leuchtenberg D 135 Eb46
Leuglay F 30 Ja40
Leugny F 30 Hb40
Leuhu FIN 82 Kb31
Leuk CH 141 Bd56
Leukerbad CH 141 Bd56
Leun D 126 Cc42
Leuna D 127 Eb40
Leunovo MK 182 Ba74
Leupoldsgrün D 135 Ea43
Leupoldstein D 135 Dd45
Leușeni MD 173 Fb58
Leușeni MD 173 Fc56
Leussow D 119 Ea33
Leutasch A 142 Dc53
Leutenbach D 134 Cd48
Leutenberg D 135 Ea43
Leutershausen D 134 Db47
Leutesdorf D 125 Ca42
Leutkirch D 142 Da51
Leutschach A 144 Fd56
Leuven B 124 Ad40
Leuze B 124 Ad41
le Val F 42 Ka54
Levala EST 98 La42
le Val-André F 26 Eb38
le Val d'Ajol F 31 Ka39
Levänen FIN 91 Lb35
Levang N 70 Fa21
Levang N 93 Dc45
Levanger N 78 Eb29
Levanjska Varoš HR 152 Hb60
Levanpelto FIN 89 Jb36
Levanto FIN 90 Kc38
Levanto I 149 Cc63
Levanzo I 166 Ea84
Levar S 80 Ha29
Leväranta FIN 69 Kb17
Leväsjoki FIN 89 Ja35
Leväslahti FIN 90 Ka35
le Vast F 22 Fa34
Levdun N 63 Ja07
Leveäselkä FIN 74 Kb18
Levécourt F 31 Jc39
Leveld N 85 Db38
Leven GB 7 Ec12
Leven GB 17 Fc20
Levens GB 11 Ec19
Levenwick GB 5 Fa06
Leverano I 162 Hb76
Leverburgh GB 4 Cd06
Leverbyn S 94 Ec43
le Verdon-sur-Mer F 32 Fa48
Leverkusen D 125 Bd40
Levern D 117 Cc36
le Vernet F 42 Ka51
Lever-Tara MNE 159 Ja67
Levet F 29 Gd43
le Veudre F 30 Hb44
Levice SK 146 Hc50
Levico Terme I 149 Dc58
Levide S 104 Gd50
Levídi GR 194 Bc87
Levie F 154 Cb71
Levier F 31 Jd42
le Vigan F 41 Hc53
Lévignac F 40 Gb54
Levignac-de-Guyenne F 32 Fd51
Lévignacq F 39 Fa53
Lévignen F 23 Ha35
Levijoki FIN 81 Jd30
le Vilhain F 29 Ha44
le Ville I 156 Ea66
Levinovac HR 152 Ha59
Levitha GR 197 Ea90
le Vivier-sur-Mer F 28 Ed38
Levka BG 185 Ea74
Levkaditi GR 189 Bc84
Levoberežnoje RUS 113 Jb57
Levoča SK 138 Jb47
Levočské Kúpele SK 138 Jb47
Levring DK 100 Db23
Levroux F 29 Gc43
Levski BG 180 Dc69
Levski BG 181 Fa70
le Wast F 21 Gc30
Lewdown GB 18 Dc30
Lewes GB 20 Fd30
Lewice PL 128 Ga36
Lewin Brzeski PL 129 Gd42
Leyburn GB 11 Ed18
Leyland GB 15 Ec20
Leyr F 25 Jd36
Leysdown-on-Sea GB 21 Ga28
Leyton GB 20 Fc28
Leżajsk PL 139 Kb43
Lézan F 41 Hd52
Lézan F 41 Hd53
Lézardrieux F 26 Ea37
Lézat F 31 Jd44
Lézat-sur-Lezé F 40 Gb55
Lezay F 32 Fc45
Lezhë AL 163 Jb71
Lézignan-Corbières F 41 Hb55
Lězna BY 202 Eb11
Lezník CZ 137 Gb45
Leźno PL 121 Ha30
Lezoux F 34 Hc47
Lezuza E 53 Eb69
Lezzeno I 149 Cc58
Lgiń PL 129 Gb38
Lgota PL 138 Hd44
L'gov RUS 202 Ed13
l'Haÿ-les-Roses F 23 Gd37
Lhenice CZ 136 Fb48
l'Herbaudière F 27 Ec43
l'Herbergement F 28 Fa43
l'Hermenault F 28 Fb44
l'Hermitage F 28 Ed39
l'Hermitage-Lorge F 26 Eb38
l'Homy-Plage F 39 Ed53
l'Hôpital d'Orion F 39 Fb55
l'Hôpital-Saint-Blaise F 39 Fb55
l'Hospitalet F 41 Gd57
l'Hospitalet F 42 Jd52
L'Hospitalet de Llobregat E 49 Ha61
Lhuis F 35 Jc47
Lhuître F 24 Hd37
Li N 92 Cc47
Liá GR 182 Ac80
Lia N 62 Gd10
Lia N 67 Gb12
Lia N 85 Dd36
Liabygda N 76 Cd33
Liancourt F 23 Gd35
Lianokládi GR 189 Bc83
Liared S 102 Fa48
Liart F 24 Hd33
Liatorp S 103 Fb52
Lībagi LV 105 Jd50
Libáň CZ 136 Fd43
Libanja SLO 145 Gb56
Libardón E 37 Cd54
Libatse EST 98 Kb45
Libberton GB 10 Ea14
Libčeves CZ 136 Fa43
Libciems LV 105 Jb50
Liběchov CZ 136 Fb43
Libeliče SLO 144 Fc56
Liber E 37 Bd56
Liberec CZ 128 Fc42
Liběšice CZ 136 Fb43
Libeznice CZ 136 Fb44
Libhošť CZ 137 Ha46
Libiąż PL 138 Hd44
Libice nad Cidlinou CZ 136 Fd44
Lībieši LV 114 Kc53
Libin B 132 Ad43
Libina CZ 137 Gc45
Liblar D 125 Bd41
Libočany CZ 135 Ed44
Libochovice CZ 136 Fa43
Libofshë AL 182 Ab76
Libohovë AL 182 Ac79
Libos F 33 Ga51
Libouchec CZ 128 Fa42
Libourne F 32 Fc50
Libramont-Chevigny B 132 Ba43
Librari I 162 Ha76
Librazhd AL 182 Ac75
Libřice CZ 136 Ga44
Librilla E 55 Ed73
Libros E 47 Ed65
Libušín CZ 136 Fa44
Libusza PL 138 Jc45
Lič HR 151 Fc60
Licata I 167 Fa87
Lice TR 205 Ga20
Licenza I 160 Ec71
Liceras E 46 Dd61
Lich D 126 Cc42
Lichères-Aigremont F 30 Hc40
Lichfield GB 16 Ed24
Lichnov CZ 137 Gd44
Lichnowy PL 121 Hb31
Lichtaart B 124 Ad39
Lichtajny PL 122 Hd32
Lichtenau A 144 Fd50
Lichtenau D 126 Cd39
Lichtenau D 134 Dc47
Lichtenberg D 135 Ea43
Lichtenborn D 133 Bb43
Lichtenegg A 145 Gb53
Lichtenfels D 126 Cd40
Lichtenfels D 135 Dd44
Lichtensteig CH 142 Cc53
Lichtenstein D 127 Ec42
Lichtenstein D 134 Cd49
Lichtentanne D 127 Eb42
Lichtenvoorde NL 125 Bd37
Lichterfelde D 120 Fa35
Lichtervelde B 21 Ha29
Liči LV 105 Jc50
Licince SK 138 Jb49
Lička Kaldrma HR 158 Gb64
Lickershamn S 104 Ha48
Lički RUS 99 Ld42
Lički Osik HR 151 Fd63
Lički Ribnik HR 151 Fd63
Ličko Lešće HR 151 Fd62
Licodia Eubea I 167 Fc87
Licola Mare I 161 Fa75
Ličo Petrovo Selo HR 151 Ga62
Licques F 21 Gc30
Licurici RO 175 Cd64
Licze PL 122 Hc32
Lid S 94 Fa42
Lid S 95 Gb45
Lida BY 202 Ea12
Lidar N 85 Dc37
Liden S 79 Ga25
Liden S 87 Gb32
Lidhult S 102 Fa52
Lidingö S 96 Gd43
Lidköping S 102 Ed46
Lido I 150 Eb60
Lido Adriano I 150 Ea63
Lido Arenella I 167 Fd87
Lido Azzurro I 162 Gd76
Lido degli Estensi I 150 Ea62
Lido degli Scacchi I 150 Ea62
Lido delle Nazioni I 150 Ea62
Lido di Camaiore I 155 Da64
Lido di Capo Portiere I 160 Eb73
Lido di Casalbordino I 157 Fb70
Lido di Castel Fusano I 160 Ea72
Lido di Classe I 150 Ea63
Lido di Dante I 150 Ea63
Lido di Fermo I 157 Fa67
Lido di Foce Verde I 160 Eb73
Lido di Jesolo I 150 Eb59
Lido di Metaponto I 162 Gd76
Lido di Noto I 167 Fd88
Lido di Ostia I 160 Ea72
Lido di Pittulongu I 168 Cc74
Lido di Plaia I 167 Fd86
Lido di Policoro I 162 Gc77
Lido di Pomposa I 150 Ea62
Lido di Portonuovo I 162 Gb72
Lido di Rivoli I 161 Ga73
Lido di Savio I 150 Ea63
Lido di Siponto I 161 Ga72
Lido di Spina I 150 Ea62
Lido di Squillace I 164 Gc82
Lido di Volano I 150 Ea62
Lidón E 47 Fa63
Lido Ponticello I 166 Ea85
Lido Riccio I 157 Fb70
Lidoriki GR 189 Bc84
Lido Sant'Angelo I 164 Gc79
Lido Specchiolla I 162 Hb75
Lidsjöberg S 79 Fd27
Lidsjön S 80 Hb26
Lidzbark PL 122 Hd33
Lidzbark Warmiński PL 122 Ja30
Liebenau A 144 Fc50
Liebenau D 118 Da35
Liebenau D 126 Da39
Liebenburg D 126 Dc38
Liebenfels A 144 Fb55
Liebenwalde D 119 Ed35
Lieberose D 128 Fb38
Liebertwolkwitz D 127 Ec40
Liebling RO 174 Bd61
Liedakka S 68 Hc13
Liedakkala FIN 74 Jc21
Liede LV 106 La50
Liédena E 39 Fa57
Liedenpohja FIN 89 Jc32
Liedikas LV 105 Jb50
Liège B 124 Ba41
Liegi LV 105 Jb52
Liegnitz = Legnica PL 128 Ga41
Lieko FIN 74 Jd20
Liekokylä FIN 74 Kb21
Lieksa FIN 83 Ld28
Lielahti FIN 97 Jb40
Lielā Pikova LV 107 Ma51
Lielauce LV 105 Jd52
Lielax FIN 97 Jb40
Lielciecere LV 105 Jd52
Lielie Andžani LV 107 Ma52
Lielirbe LV 105 Jc49
Lielsātiķi LV 105 Jd51
Lielsesava LV 106 Kb52
Lielstraupe LV 106 Kc49
Lielvārde LV 106 Kc51
Lielvirbi LV 105 Jd50
Lien S 94 Ec42
Liencres E 38 Dc54
Lienen D 125 Cb37
Lienz A 143 Ec55
Liepa LV 106 Kd49
Liepāja LV 105 Ja52
Liepas LV 106 Kb52
Liepen D 120 Fa32
Liepene LV 105 Jb49
Liepkalne LV 106 La50
Lieplaukė LT 113 Jc54
Liepna LV 107 Lc48
Lieponys LT 114 Kd59
Lier B 124 Ad39
Lierbyen N 93 Dd42
Lierena E 51 Ca71
Lierfoss N 94 Eb41
Liérganes E 38 Dc55
Lierneux B 125 Bb42
Liernais F 30 Hd42
Liernolles F 34 Hc45
Lierville F 23 Gc36
Liesborn D 126 Cc38
Lieshout NL 125 Bb38
Liesjärvi FIN 89 Jd38
Liesjärvi FIN 90 Ka32
Lieskau D 127 Ea39
Liesniemi FIN 97 Jc39
Lieso FIN 90 Kb36
Liesse-Notre-Dame F 24 Hc34
Liessies F 24 Hc32
Liestal CH 141 Bd52
Liești RO 177 Fa62
Lietavská Lúčka SK 138 Hc47
Lietekylä FIN 75 La24
Lieto FIN 97 Jb39
Liétor E 53 Ec71
Lietsa FIN 90 Ka38
Liettik S 67 Gd16
Lieurac F 40 Gc56
Lieurey F 22 Fd35
Lievestuore FIN 90 Kc32
Lievikoski FIN 89 Jb36
Liévin F 23 Ha31
Lievio FIN 98 Ka39
Lievisenmäki FIN 82 La27
Lieviskä FIN 91 Lc34
Lievoperä FIN 82 Kb26
Liezen A 144 Fb53
Liffol-le-Grand F 31 Jc38
Liffré F 28 Ed39
Lifjell N 93 Db43
Lifton GB 18 Dc31
Ligardes F 40 Fd53
Ligardes F 40 Ga53
Ligatne LV 106 Kd49
Ligciems LV 105 Jd50
Ligerí GR 183 Bb78
Liggavägen S 72 Ha19
Ligiá GR 188 Ac82
Lignano Riviera I 150 Ec59
Lignano Sabbiadoro I 150 Ec59
Lignières F 29 Gd44
Lignières-de-Touraine F 28 Fd42
Lignières-Sonneville F 32 Fc48
Lignol-le-Château F 30 Ja39
Ligny-en-Barrois F 24 Jb37
Ligny-le-Châtel F 30 Hc40
Ligny-le-Ribault F 29 Gc41
Ligonchio I 149 Da63
Ligórtinos GR 200 Da96
Ligota PL 129 Gc40
Ligota PL 129 Gd39
Ligota Prószkowska PL 137 Ha43
Ligourió GR 195 Ca87
Ligowo PL 122 Hc35
Ligueil F 29 Ga43
Ligugé F 32 Fd45
Lihás GR 189 Ca83
Lihjamo FIN 90 Ka32
Lihme DK 100 Da22
Lihoslavl' RUS 202 Ed10
Lihovskoj RUS 205 Fc15
Lihula EST 98 Ka45
Liiansaari FIN 91 Lb35
Liikasenvaara FIN 74 La18
Liikavaara S 68 Hc17
Liikkala FIN 90 La37
Liimala EST 99 Lb41
Liimattala FIN 82 Kb31
Liinamaa FIN 81 Jb30
Liitonjoki FIN 82 Kb29
Liitsola FIN 89 Jc37
Liittoperä FIN 82 Kb28
Liiva EST 97 Jd45
Liivi EST 98 Ka44
Liješće BIH 152 Hb61
Lijeska BIH 159 Ja65
Lijeva Rijeka MNE 159 Ja69
Lijevi Dubravčak HR 152 Gb59
Likančiai LT 114 La54
Likėnai LT 114 Kc53
Likenäs S 94 Ed39
Likiškės LT 114 Kc59
Likodra SRB 153 Ja63
Likoporiá GR 189 Bc86
Likósoura GR 194 Bb88
Likostomo GR 184 Da77
Likovskoe RUS 99 Ld42
Liksna LV 115 Lb53
Likummuiža LV 106 La51
Liland N 66 Fd12
Liland N 66 Ga13
Lilaste LV 106 Kb50
l'Île-Bouchard F 28 Fd43
Lilienfeld A 144 Ga51
Lilienthal D 118 Cd34
Liljak BG 180 Eb70
Liljanovo BG 184 Cc75
Liljedal S 94 Ed44
Liljendal FIN 90 Kd38
Liljendal S 95 Fb41
Lilkovo BG 184 Db74
Lillå S 73 Hb20
Lilla Edet S 102 Ec47
Lillåfors S 73 Hc20
Lilla Lappträsk S 73 Ja21
Lilla Moberget S 86 Ed37
Lillån S 95 Fd44
Lillbo S 87 Ga35
Lillby FIN 81 Jb29
Lille F 23 Ha31
Lillebekken N 65 Kc08
Lillebonne F 22 Fd35
Lillebukt N 63 Hc07
Lilledalen N 64 Jb06
Lillefjord N 63 Ja05
Lillegården N 93 Dc44
Lillehammer N 85 Ea37
Lille Lerresfjord N 63 Hd07
Lille Molvik N 64 Ka05
Lillers F 23 Gd31
Lillesand N 93 Da47
Lille Skensved DK 109 Eb26
Lillestrøm N 93 Ea41
Lillevorde DK 100 Dc21
Lillhärad S 95 Ga42
Lillhärdal S 87 Fb35
Lillholmsjö S 79 Fb29
Lillholmträsk S 72 Ha24
Lilli EST 106 Kd47
Lillkågeträsk S 73 Hc24
Lillkyrka S 95 Fd44
Lillkyrka S 96 Gc43
Lillkyrka S 103 Ga46
Lillo E 53 Dd67
Lillögda S 80 Gc27
Lillpite S 73 Hc23
Lillsele S 79 Gb29
Lillsele S 80 Ha26
Lillskog S 87 Fd36
Lillskogshöiden S 94 Ed40
Lillträsk S 73 Hc22
Lillträsk S 73 Hb23
Lima S 86 Fa38
Limanáki GR 188 Ba85
Limáni Litohórou GR 183 Bd79
Limannvika N 79 Fb26
Limanowa PL 138 Jb45
Limanu RO 181 Fc68
Limavady GB 9 Cd15
Limbach D 133 Bc45
Limbach D 134 Cd46
Limbach-Oberfrohna D 127 Ec42
Limbaži LV 106 Kc48
Limbenii Noi MD 173 Fa55
Limbenii Vechi MD 173 Fa55
Limbourg B 125 Bb41
Limburg D 133 Cb43
Limedsforsen S 86 Fa38
Limenária GR 184 Da78
Liménas Géraka GR 195 Bd90
Liménas Hersonissou GR 201 Db95
Limerick IRL 12 Bd23
Limerzel F 27 Ec41
Limes B 132 Ba44
Limingen N 79 Fb26
Limingoån S 73 Ja18
Liminka FIN 74 Ka24
Liminkajärvi S 73 Ja18
Liminkakylä FIN 81 Jd26
Liminpuro FIN 82 Kc25
Limmared S 102 Fa49
Límnes GR 195 Bd87
Límnes GR 201 Db96
Límni GR 189 Cb84
Límni GR 194 Bc87
Limniá GR 184 Da77
Limnitis CY 206 Ja96
Limnitsa GR 188 Bb84
Límni Vouliagménis GR 189 Bd86
Limnohóri GR 183 Bb77
Limnohóri GR 183 Cb76
Limoges F 33 Gb47
Limogne-en-Quercy F 33 Gc51
Limoise F 30 Hb44
Limone Piemonte I 148 Bc63
Limones E 60 Db74
Limone sul Garda I 149 Db58
Limours-en-Hurepoix F 23 Gd37
Limoux F 41 Gd56
Limpley Stoke GB 19 Ec28
Limpuero E 38 Dd55
Lin AL 182 Ad76
Linå DK 108 Db24
Lina älv S 67 Hb17
Linanäs S 96 Ha43
Linards F 33 Gc47
Linarejos E 45 Ca59
Linares E 37 Ca55
Linares E 60 Db72
Linares de Mora E 54 Fb65
Linares de Riofrío E 45 Cb63
Linariá GR 190 Da84
Lincoln GB 17 Fc22
Lind DK 108 Da24
Linda D 127 Ea42
Lindale GB 11 Eb19
Lindärva S 102 Ed46
Lindås N 84 Ca38
Lindås S 111 Fd53
Lindau D 118 Db30
Lindau D 127 Eb38
Lindau D 142 Cd52
Lindau, Katlenburg- D 126 Db39
Lindberg S 95 Fc39
Lindberg S 102 Ec51
Lindby S 96 Gc43
Linde DK 100 Da23
Linde DK 100 Dc23
Linde LV 106 Kd51
Linde S 104 Ha50
Lindefallet S 87 Gb36
Lindefjell N 92 Cc45
Lindelse DK 109 Dd28
Linden A 144 Fc50
Linden D 126 Cc42
Lindenberg D 128 Fa36
Lindenberg D 142 Da52
Lindenfels D 134 Cc45
Linderås S 103 Fc48
Linderhof D 142 Dc52
Lindern D 117 Cb34
Linderöd S 110 Fa55
Lindesberg S 95 Fd43
Lindesnäs S 95 Fc40
Lindesnes N 92 Cc47
Lindewitt D 108 Da29
Lindfors S 95 Fb43
Lindholm DK 100 Dc21
Lindholm, Risum- D 108 Da28
Lindholmen S 96 Gd42
Lindhorst D 126 Da36
Lindi EST 106 Kb46
Lindkoski FIN 90 Kd38
Lindlar D 125 Ca40
Lindö S 103 Ga46
Lindome S 102 Ec49
Lindön S 94 Ea45
Lindos GR 197 Fa93
Lindoso P 44 Bb59
Lindow D 119 Ed35
Lindsberg S 87 Fc37
Lindsdal S 103 Ga52

Looe – Luzaga

Looe GB 18 Dc31
Loon op Zand NL 124 Ba38
Loon-Plage F 21 Gd30
Lööpõllu EST 105 Jc47
Loos F 23 Ha31
Loosdorf A 144 Fd51
Loosdrecht NL 116 Ba36
Loose D 108 Db29
Lopadea Nouă RO 171 Da59
Lopar HR 151 Fc62
Lopare BIH 153 Hd62
Lopătari RO 176 Ec63
Lopatica MK 183 Bb75
Lopatino RUS 107 Ma47
Lopatino RUS 203 Fd11
Łopatki PL 122 Hc33
Lopatnic MD 172 Ed54
Lopatovo RUS 107 Ma46
Lopcombe Corner GB 20 Ed29
Lõpe EST 98 Ka45
Lopera E 52 Da72
Łopiennik PL 131 Kc40
Loppa N 63 Hb07
Loppersum NL 117 Ca33
Loppi FIN 90 Ka38
Loppula FIN 74 Ka23
Lopud HR 158 Hb69
Lopuhinka RUS 99 Ma40
Łopuszna PL 138 Ja46
Łopuszno PL 130 Ja41
Loqueffret F 26 Dd38
Lora de Estepa E 60 Cc74
Lora del Río E 59 Cb73
Loranca de Tajuña E 46 Dd64
Lorbé E 36 Ba54
Lörby S 111 Fc54
Lorca E 61 Ec73
Lorch D 133 Ca44
Lorch D 134 Da48
Lorcha E 55 Fc70
Lordolo P 44 Ad61
Lordosa P 44 Ba62
Lørenfallet N 94 Eb41
Lorentzer F 25 Kb36
Lorenzago di Cadore I 143 Eb56
Lorenzana E 37 Cc57
Lorenzana I 155 Da66
Loreo I 150 Ea61
Loreto I 156 Ed66
Loreto Aprutino I 157 Fa70
Lórév H 146 Hc54
Lorgues F 43 Kb54
Lorguichon F 22 Fc36
Lorica I 164 Gc80
Lorient F 27 Ea40
Loriga P 44 Ba64
Loriguilla E 54 Fa67
Lőrinci H 146 Ja52
Loriol-sur-Drôme F 34 Jb50
Lormaison F 23 Gd35
Lormes F 30 Hc42
Loro Ciuffenna I 156 Dd66
Lorquí E 55 Ed72
Lörrach D 141 Bd52
Lorrez-le-Bocage F 29 Ha39
Lorris F 29 Ha40
Lorsch D 134 Cc45
Lørslev DK 100 Dc20
Lorton GB 11 Eb17
Lorup D 117 Cb34
l'Orxa E 55 Fc70
Lörzweiler D 133 Cb44
Loś PL 130 Jb38
Los S 87 Fd35
Losa del Obispo E 54 Fa67
Los Alares E 52 Cd67
Los Alazdres E 60 Da75
Los Alcázares E 55 Fa73
Los Algarbes E 60 Cc73
Los Arcos E 39 Eb57
Losar de la Vera E 45 Cb65
Los Arejos E 61 Ec74
Los Arenales E 59 Cb74
Los Ausines E 38 Dc58
Los Badalejos E 59 Ca77
Los Barrios E 59 Ca78
Los Barrios de Luna E 37 Cb56
Los Bayos E 37 Cb56
Los Belmontes E 53 Eb71
Los Belones E 55 Fb74
Los Blázquez E 51 Cb70
Los Caños E 59 Bd77
Los Castaños E 61 Eb75
Los Centenaros E 61 Ea72
Los Cerezos E 54 Fa66
Los Cerralbos E 52 Da66
Los Clementes E 61 Dd76
Los Corrales E 60 Cc75
Los Corrales de Buelna E 38 Db55
Los Cortijos de Arriba E 52 Db68
Loscos E 47 Fa62
Los Dolores E 55 Fa73
Losenstein A 144 Fb52
Los Escoriales E 52 Db71
Los Estrechos E 61 Ec74
Løsetdalen N 86 Ec36
Łosewo PL 123 Jd33
Los Gallardos E 61 Ec75
Los Guadalperales E 51 Cb68
Los Guiraos E 61 Eb74
Losheim am See D 133 Bc45
Los Hinojoso E 53 Ea67
Losi RUS 107 Ma49
Łosice PL 131 Kb36
Losicy RUS 99 Ma44
Losilla E 54 Fa66
Łosinka PL 123 Kc34
Łosino PL 121 Gc30
Los Isidros E 54 Ed68
Los Jinetes E 59 Ca73
Loskeran IRL 13 Ca25
Loškovicy RUS 99 Ma40
Los Lobos E 61 Ec74
Los Maldonados E 55 Ed73
Los Molares E 59 Ca74
Los Molinos E 46 Db63
Los Monteros E 60 Cc77
Los Montesinos E 55 Fb72
Los Morones E 60 Dc76
Los Navalmorales E 52 Cd66
Los Navalucillos E 52 Cd67
Los Nietos E 55 Fb73
Løsning DK 108 Db25
Los Nogueroners E 60 Da73
Los Ojuelos E 59 Cb74
Losomäki FIN 83 Lb29
Losovaara FIN 75 Kd23
Los Palacios y Villafranca E 59 Ca74
Los Pastores E 59 Cb78
l'Ospedale F 154 Cb72
Los Pedrones E 54 Fa68
Los Piedros E 60 Cd74
Los Pozuelos de Calatrava E 52 Da69
Los Rábanos E 47 Eb60
Los Rosales E 59 Ca73
Los Ruices E 54 Ed67
Lossa D 127 Ea40
Los Santos E 45 Cb63
Los Santos de Maimona E 51 Bd70
Loßburg D 133 Cb49
Losse F 40 Fc52
Losser NL 117 Ca36
Losset IRL 9 Cb15
Lossiemouth GB 5 Eb07
Los Silos E 59 Bc72
Lößnitz D 135 Ec43
Los Tablones E 60 Dc76
Lostallo CH 142 Cc56
Loštice CZ 137 Gc45
Los Tonosas E 61 Eb74
Los Tuelas E 55 Ed73
Lostwithiel GB 18 Dc31
Los Villaesteres E 45 Cc60
Los Villares E 60 Db73
Los Villares E 60 Da74
Los Yébenes E 52 Db67
Los Yesos E 61 Eb75
Löt S 96 Gc43
Löt S 103 Gb51
Lote N 84 Cc34
Løten N 86 Eb38
Lothmore GB 5 Eb06
Lotlax FIN 81 Ja30
Lotorp S 95 Ga45
Lotošino RUS 202 Ed10
Lotovicy RUS 107 Mb50
Lotte D 117 Cb36
Lottefors S 87 Ga36
Löttorp S 104 Gc51
Lottum NL 125 Bb39
Łotyń PL 121 Gc33
Lotzorai I 169 Cc77
Louans F 29 Ga42
Louargat F 26 Ea38
Loubillé F 32 Fc46
Loučeň CZ 136 Fc44
Louchats F 32 Fb51
Loučka CZ 137 Ha46
Loučná Hora CZ 136 Fd44
Loučná nad Desnou CZ 137 Gc44
Loudéac F 27 Eb39
Loudun F 28 Fd43
Loué F 28 Fc40
Loue FIN 74 Jd20
Louejärvi FIN 74 Jd19
Louejoki FIN 74 Jd19
Loughanavally IRL 9 Cb20
Loughborough GB 16 Fa24
Lougher IRL 12 Ba24
Loughglinn IRL 8 Bd19
Lough Gowna IRL 9 Cb19
Loughlinstown IRL 13 Cd22
Loughmoe IRL 13 Ca23
Loughrea IRL 12 Bd21
Loughton GB 20 Fd27
Lougratte F 33 Ga51
Loúha GR 188 Ac86
Louhans F 30 Jb44
Louhioja FIN 83 Ld29
Louhivaara FIN 83 Ma28
Louisburgh IRL 8 Bb19
Loukás GR 194 Bc87
Loukee FIN 90 La33
Loukinainen FIN 97 Jb39
Loukissia GR 189 Cb85
Loukkojärvi FIN 74 Ka23
Loukunvaara FIN 91 Ma32
Loukusa FIN 75 Kd21
Loulans F 31 Jd41
Loulay F 32 Fb46
Loulé P 58 Ac74
Lõunaküla EST 98 Kb42
Lounovice CZ 136 Fc46
Louny CZ 136 Fa43
Lourdes F 40 Fc56
Louredo P 44 Ad61
Loures P 50 Aa68
Louriçal P 44 Ac64
Lourinhã P 50 Aa67
Lourmarin F 42 Jc53
Louro E 36 Ac55
Louro P 44 Ad60
Loúros GR 188 Ad82
Lourosa P 44 Ad61
Loury F 29 Gd39
Lousã P 44 Ad64
Lousa P 45 Bc61
Lousada E 36 Bb55
Lousada P 44 Ad60
Louth GB 17 Fd22
Louth IRL 9 Cd19
Loutrá GR 184 Cc76
Loutrá GR 184 Cc80
Loutrá GR 191 Ea84
Loutrá GR 194 Bb87
Loutrá GR 195 Cd88
Loutrá Edipsoú GR 189 Ca83
Loutrá Eleftherón GR 184 Cd78
Loutrá Ipátis GR 189 Bc83
Loutráki GR 183 Bc76
Loutráki GR 188 Ad83
Loutráki GR 189 Ca86
Loutra Kilínis GR 188 Ad86
Loutrá Smokóvou GR 189 Bc82
Loutrá Thermopilón GR 189 Bd83
Loutró GR 183 Bd78
Loutró GR 200 Cb95
Loutropigí GR 189 Bc82
Loutrópoli Thermís GR 191 Ea83
Loutrós GR 185 Ea78
Loútsa GR 188 Ac81
Loútsa GR 195 Cc87
Louvankylä FIN 89 Ja33
Louverné F 28 Fb39
Louvie-Juzon F 40 Fc56
Louviers F 23 Gb36
Louvigné-de-Bais F 28 Fa39
Louvigné-du-Desert F 28 Fa38
Louvois F 24 Hd36
Louvroil F 24 Hc32
Louze F 30 Ja38
Lovagny F 35 Jd46
Lövånger S 81 Hd26
Lovas HR 153 Hd60
Lövås S 80 Gd27
Lovasberény H 146 Hc53
Lövåsen S 79 Ga30
Lovászhetény H 153 Hc57
Lovászi H 145 Gc56
Lovászpatona H 145 Ha53
Lövberg S 71 Fc24
Lövberga S 79 Fd28
Lövberget S 95 Fc40
Lovćenac SRB 153 Ja59
Lovčić HR 152 Ha60
Loveč BG 180 Db70
Lovec BG 180 Dd73
Lovečkovice CZ 136 Fb43
Løvel DK 100 Db22
Lovelhe P 36 Ad58
Lovere I 149 Da58
Lövestad S 110 Fa56
Loviisa FIN 90 Kd38
Lovik N 66 Fd12
Løvik N 76 Cd31
Lovikka S 68 Hd16
Lovinac HR 151 Ga63
Lovinobaňa SK 146 Ja50
Lovisa FIN 90 Kd38
Lovište HR 158 Gd68
Lövliden S 79 Ga26
Lövnäs S 72 Gc20
Lövnäs S 79 Ga25
Lövnäs S 80 Gc27
Lövnäs S 86 Fa37
Lövnäsvallen S 86 Fa35
Lovni Dol BG 180 Dc71
Lövö H 145 Gc53
Lovoleto I 150 Dd62
Lovosice CZ 136 Fa43
Lovran HR 151 Fb60
Lovreč HR 151 Fa61
Lovreć HR 158 Gd66
Lovrenc na Pohorju SLO 144 Fd56
Lovrin RO 174 Bc60
Lovrup DK 108 Da27
Lövsjö S 79 Fd25
Lövsjön S 95 Fc40
Løvskal DK 100 Dc23
Lövstabruk S 96 Gd40
Lövstalöt S 96 Gc41
Lövstrand S 79 Ga27
Lovund N 70 Ed20
Lövvik S 79 Ga27
Łowcza PL 139 Kc43
Löwenberg D 119 Ed35
Löwenberger Land D 119 Ed35
Lower Beeding GB 20 Fc29
Lower Boddington GB 20 Fa26
Lower Cam GB 19 Ec27
Lower Diabaig GB 4 Db07
Lower Killeyan GB 9 Da14
Lowestoft GB 21 Gc25
Lowgill GB 11 Ec19
Łowicz PL 130 Hd37
Łowicz Wałecki PL 120 Ga33
Low Row GB 11 Ec16
Łowyń PL 128 Ga36
Loxstedt D 118 Cd33
Loyers GB 7 Dd08
Loyettes F 35 Jc46
Löytänä FIN 82 Kb29
Löytö FIN 90 La34
Löytökylä FIN 74 Kb23
Löytölä FIN 83 Lb25
Löytövaara FIN 75 Kd20
Löytty FIN 90 Kd37
Löyttymäki FIN 90 Kb37
Lož SLO 151 Fb59
Lozarevo BG 181 Ec72
Lozari F 154 Cb68
Lozen B 125 Bb39
Lozen BG 179 Cc71
Lozenec BG 181 Ec72
Lozenec BG 181 Fa68
Lozhan AL 182 Ad77
Lozica BG 180 Dc69
Łozina PL 129 Gc40
Lozna RO 171 Da56
Lozna SRB 178 Bb67
Loznica BG 180 Eb70
Loznica BG 181 Fa68
Łoźnica PL 120 Fc32
Loznica SRB 153 Ja62
Łoznik PL 122 Ja30
Lozorno SK 145 Gc50
Lozova MD 173 Fc57
Lozova UA 205 Fa15
Lozovac HR 157 Ga65
Lozovik SRB 174 Bc65
Lozovik SRB 174 Bc66
Lozoya E 46 Dc62
Lozoyuela E 46 Dc63
Lozzo di Cadore I 143 Eb56
Luaces E 36 Bc55
Luanco (Gozon) E 37 Cc53
Luaras AL 182 Ad78
Luarca E 37 Ca54
Lubaczów PL 139 Kc43
Lubań PL 128 Fd41
Lubāna LV 107 Lb50
Lubanie PL 121 Hb35
Lubanowo PL 120 Fc34
Lübars D 127 Eb37
Lubartów PL 131 Kb39
Lubasz PL 121 Gb35
Lubatowa PL 139 Ka45
Lubawa PL 122 Hd33
Lubawka PL 128 Ga42
Lübbecke D 126 Cd36
Lübben/Spreewald D 128 Fa38
Lübbenau/Spreewald D 128 Fa38
Lübbow D 119 Dd35
Lubcroy GB 4 Dd06
Lubczyna PL 120 Fc33
Lübeck D 119 Dd32
Lubenec CZ 135 Ed44
Lubenia PL 139 Ka44
Lubersac F 33 Gb48
Lubes LV 105 Jd49
Lubián E 37 Bd58
Łubianka PL 120 Fd35
Łubianka PL 121 Hb34
Lubiatów PL 128 Fd38
Lubiatowo PL 120 Fc34
Lubiaż PL 129 Gb40
Lubichowo PL 121 Ha32
Lubicz PL 121 Hb34
Lubiec PL 130 Jb37
Lubień PL 128 Fc37
Lubień PL 138 Ja45
Lubień Kujawski PL 130 Hc36
Lubieszewo PL 120 Ga33
Lubiewo PL 121 Ha33
Lubiewo Zalesie PL 120 Fb32
Lubimec RUS 99 Lc43
Lubin PL 120 Fb32
Lubin PL 129 Gb40
Lubiń PL 129 Gc38
Lubiń PL 129 Ha36
Lubin-Kościelny PL 123 Kb35
Lubiny PL 129 Ha38
Lubjaniki RUS 203 Fb10
Lubla PL 139 Jd45
Lublewo Gdańskie PL 121 Ha30
Lublin PL 131 Kb40
Lubliniec PL 129 Hb42
Lubliniec PL 139 Kc43
Lubmin D 120 Fa31
Lubnia PL 121 Gd31
Lubniany PL 129 Ha42
Lubnice PL 129 Ha41
Lubnice PL 138 Jc43
Lubniewice PL 128 Fd36
Lubno PL 120 Fc35
Lubno PL 121 Gb33
Lubno PL 121 Gc31
Lubno PL 130 Hc37
Lubny UA 202 Ed14
L'ubochňa SK 138 Hd47
Lubochnia PL 130 Ja39
Lubomierz PL 128 Fd41
Lubomierz PL 138 Ja45
Lubomino PL 122 Ja31
Luboń PL 129 Gc37
Luboradz PL 129 Gb41
Luborzyca PL 138 Ja44
Lubostroń PL 121 Ha35
Lubosz PL 128 Ga36
L'ubotín SK 138 Jc47
Lubotyń PL 129 Hb36
Lubowidz PL 122 Hd34
Łubowo PL 121 Gb33
Łubowo PL 129 Gd36
Lubraniec PL 129 Hb36
Lubrín E 61 Eb75
Lubrza PL 128 Fd37
Lubrza PL 137 Gd43
Lubsko PL 128 Fc39
Lübstorf D 119 Ea32
Lubstów PL 129 Hb37
Lubsza PL 129 Gd41
Lübtheen D 119 Dd33
Lubuczewo PL 121 Gc29
Luby CZ 135 Eb44
Łuby PL 121 Ha32
Lubycza Królewska PL 131 Kd42
Lübz D 119 Eb33
Lubzina PL 139 Jd44
Luc F 34 Hd50
Luc F 41 Ha52
Luca Cernii de Jos RO 174 Cb61
Lucainena de las Torres E 61 Eb75
Lucan IRL 13 Cd21
Lucaph MD 177 Fc61
Lúcar E 61 Ea74
Lucareț RO 174 Bd60
Lučatin SK 138 Hd48
Luçay-le-Mâle F 29 Gb42
Lucca I 155 Da65
Lucena E 60 Cd74
Lucena del Puerto E 59 Bc74
Lucenay-le-Duc F 30 Ja41
Luc-en-Diois F 35 Jc50
Lučenec SK 146 Ja50
Luceni E 47 Fa60
Lucens CH 141 Bb55
Lucenza E 36 Bb58
Luče ob Savinji SLO 151 Fc57
Lucera I 161 Fd73
Lucéram F 43 Kd52
Lucey F 35 Jd46
Luché-Pringé F 28 Fd41
Lucheux F 23 Gd32
Lüchow D 119 Dd35
Luchów PL 139 Kb43
Luchy F 23 Gd34
Luciana E 52 Da69
Lučica SRB 174 Bc64
Lucień PL 130 Hd36
Lucieni RO 176 Dd65
Lucignano I 156 Dd67
Lucignano d' Arbia I 155 Dc67
Lucillos E 52 Cd66
Lučine SLO 151 Fb58
Lucito I 161 Fc72
Luciu RO 176 Ed64
Luciu RO 177 Fa65
Luc'k UA 204 Ea15
Lucka D 127 Eb41
Luckau D 128 Fa38
Luckenbach D 125 Cb42
Luckenwalde D 127 Ed38
Lucker GB 11 Fa14
Lucksta S 87 Gb34
Lückstedt D 119 Ea35
Lúčky SK 138 Hd47
Lucmau F 40 Fc52
Luco dei Marsi I 160 Ed71
Luçon F 32 Fa45
Luc-sur-Mer F 22 Fc35
Ludanice SK 137 Hb49
Ludborough GB 17 Fc21
Ludbreg HR 152 Gc57
Lüdelsen D 119 Dd35
Lüdenhausen D 126 Cd37
Lüdenscheid D 125 Ca40
Lüder D 118 Dc35
Lüderitz D 127 Ea36
Lüderode, Weißenborn- D 126 Dc39
Lüdersdorf D 119 Dd32
Ludești RO 176 Dd64
Ludford GB 17 Fc22
Ludgershall GB 20 Ed29
Ludgershall GB 20 Fb27
Ludgo S 96 Gc45
Ludiente E 54 Fc66
Lüdinghausen D 125 Ca38
Ludlow GB 15 Eb25
Ludogorci BG 181 Ec69
Ludomy PL 121 Gc35
Ludoș RO 175 Da61
Luduș RO 171 Db59
Ludvigsborg S 110 Fa55
Ludvika S 95 Fd41
Ludwigsburg D 134 Cd48
Ludwigsfelde D 127 Ed37
Ludwigshafen D 142 Cc51
Ludwigshafen a. Rh. D 133 Cb46
Ludwigslust D 119 Ea33
Ludwigsstadt D 135 Dd43
Ludwigswinkel D 133 Ca47
Ludwin PL 131 Kb39
Ludza LV 107 Ld51
Lüe F 39 Fa52
Luesia E 39 Fa58
Luesma E 47 Fa62
Lueta RO 176 Ea60
Lug BIH 159 Hc68
Lug HR 153 Hc59
Luga RUS 107 Mb46
Luga RUS 99 Mb43
Luga RUS 202 Ea09
Lugagnano Val d'Arda I 149 Cd61
Lugán E 37 Cc56
Lugano CH 149 Cc57
Lugasu de Jos RO 170 Cb57
Lugaži LV 106 La47
Lügde D 126 Da38
Lüge D 119 Ea35
Lugendorf A 144 Fd50
Ługi PL 122 Hd34
Luglon F 39 Fb53
Lugnano in Teverina I 156 Ea69
Lugnås S 102 Fa46
Lugnvik S 80 Gc31
Lugny F 30 Jb44
Lugo E 36 Bb55
Lugo I 149 Db63
Lugo I 150 Ea63
Lugo de Llanera E 37 Cc54
Lugoj RO 174 Ca61
Lugomerci SRB 153 Hd59
Lugones E 37 Cb54
Lugovoe RUS 113 Ja59
Lugovskoe RUS 99 Ma42
Lugros E 60 Dc75
Lugton GB 10 Dd13
Luh RUS 203 Fb09
Luhačovice CZ 137 Ha47
Luhalahti FIN 89 Jc35
Luhamaa EST 107 Lc47
Luhanka FIN 90 Kc34
Luhans'k UA 203 Fb14
Luhe-Wildenau D 135 Eb46
Lühmannsdorf D 120 Fa31
Luhovicy RUS 203 Fa10
Luhtaanmaa FIN 90 Kc36
Luhtanen FIN 90 Kd35
Luhtapohja FIN 83 Ma30
Luhtikylä FIN 90 Kc37
Luib GB 4 Db08
Luica RO 181 Ec67
Luidja EST 97 Jc44
Luige EST 98 Kb42
Luigny F 29 Gb39
Luik = Liège B 124 Ba41
Luikonlahti FIN 83 Lb30
Luimneach IRL 12 Bd23
Luino I 148 Cb57
Luintra (Nogueira de Ramuín) E 36 Bb57
Luiro FIN 69 Kb16
Luisant F 29 Gb38
Luisenthal D 126 Dc42
Luizi Călugăra RO 172 Ed59
Lújar E 60 Dc76
Luka BIH 158 Hb66
Luka HR 157 Fd65
Luka SRB 174 Ca66
Lukač HR 152 Gd58
Luka nad Jihlavou CZ 136 Ga47
Lukanja SLO 144 Fd56
Luka Pokupska HR 151 Ga59
Lukare SRB 178 Ba69
Lukaši RUS 99 Mb40
Lukavac BIH 153 Hc62
Lukavci SLO 145 Gb56
Lukavec CZ 136 Fc46
Łukawiec PL 139 Kc43
Luke MK 179 Ca72
Lukeswell IRL 13 Cb24
Lukićevo SRB 153 Jc60
Lukićevo SRB 174 Bb62
Lukinić Brdo HR 151 Ga59
Lukkaroistenperä FIN 81 Jd25
Luknės LT 113 Jb53
Lukojanov RUS 203 Fc10
Lukovica SLO 151 Fc57
Lukovica SRB 174 Bc66
Lukovit BG 179 Da70
Lukovnikovo RUS 202 Ec10
Lukovo BG 179 Cc71
Lukovo HR 151 Fc62
Lukovo MK 182 Ad75
Lukovo MNE 159 Hd68
Lukovo SRB 178 Bb69
Lukovo SRB 178 Bd67
Lukovo Šugarje HR 151 Fd63
Łuków PL 131 Ka37
Łukowa PL 130 Jb42
Łukowa PL 131 Kc42
Łukowica PL 138 Jb45
Łukowisko PL 131 Kb37
Łukowo PL 122 Jb35
Łukowo PL 129 Gc36
Lukšiai LT 114 Ka57
Lukštai LT 114 La53
Łukta PL 122 Hd32
Luktvatnet N 70 Fa21
Lula I 168 Cb75
Luleå S 73 Hd22
Lüleburgaz TR 185 Ed76
Lüllemäe EST 106 La47
Lullymore IRL 13 Cc21
Łułowo PL 121 Gd33
Lümanda EST 105 Jb46
Lumasi AL 182 Ac76
Lumbarda HR 158 Gd68
Lumbier E 39 Ed57
Lumbrales E 45 Bd62
Lumbrein CH 142 Cc55
Lumbres F 23 Gd31
Lumby DK 108 Dc26
Lumes F 24 Ja33
Lumezzane I 149 Da59
Lumijoki FIN 74 Ka24
Lumikylä FIN 82 Kd25
Lumimetsä FIN 82 Ka26
Lumina RO 181 Fc67
Lumio F 154 Ca69
Lummelunda S 104 Ha49
Lummen B 124 Ba40
Lummukka FIN 81 Jc30
Lumparland FIN 96 Hc41
Lumpiaque E 47 Ed60
Lumpzig D 127 Eb41
Lumsås DK 109 Ea25
Lumsheden S 95 Ga39
Lun HR 151 Fc62
Luna E 47 Fa59
Lunano I 156 Eb65
Lunas F 41 Hc54
Lunca RO 170 Cb58
Lunca RO 171 Dc58
Lunca RO 172 Ed56
Lunca RO 175 Cc60
Lunca RO 180 Dc68
Lunca Banului RO 173 Fb59
Lunca Bradului RO 172 Dd58
Lunca Corbului RO 175 Dc65
Lunca de Jos RO 172 Eb59
Lunca de Sus RO 172 Eb59
Lunca Ilvei RO 172 Dd56
Lunca Mureșului RO 171 Da59
Luncavița RO 174 Ca63
Luncavița RO 177 Fb63
Luncoiu de Jos RO 175 Cc60
Lund DK 108 Db25
Lund N 78 Ec25
Lund N 92 Cb46
Lund S 110 Fa56
Lunda S 96 Gd42
Lundamo N 78 Ea31
Lundbjörken S 95 Fc39
Lundby DK 100 Db21
Lundby DK 109 Dd28
Lundby DK 109 Eb27
Lundby S 95 Ga43
Lunde DK 108 Cd25
Lunde DK 108 Dc26
Lunde N 67 Gc12
Lunde N 84 Cd34
Lunde N 85 Dd38
Lunde N 93 Db43
Lunde S 88 Gc32
Lundeborg DK 109 Dd27
Lundebyvollen N 86 Ec38
Lunden D 118 Da30
Lunden N 93 Db45
Lundenes N 66 Ga12
Lundersæter N 94 Ec40
Lunderskov DK 108 Db26
Lundsbrunn S 102 Fa46
Lundsjön S 79 Fc29
Lüneburg D 118 Dc34
Lunel F 42 Ja54
Lünen D 125 Ca38
Lunestedt D 118 Cd33
Lunéville F 25 Jd37
Lunevščina RUS 99 Lc44
Lunga MD 173 Fd57
Lungeni RO 172 Ed57
Lungern CH 141 Ca55
Lungești RO 175 Da65
Lungön S 88 Gd32
Lungro I 164 Gb78
Lungsjön S 79 Ga30
Lungsund S 95 Fb43
Lungulețu RO 176 Ea65
Lunha MD 173 Fc55
Luninec BY 202 Ea13
Lunino RUS 113 Jd58
Lunino RUS 203 Fc10
Lunkkaus FIN 69 Kc16
Lünne D 117 Ca36
Lunneborg N 67 Gc11
Lunner N 85 Ea40
Lunning GB 5 Fa04
Lunow D 120 Fb35
Lunteren NL 116 Bb36
Lunz am See A 144 Fc52
Lunzenau D 127 Ec41
Luoba LT 113 Jc53
Luode FIN 89 Jc34
Luoftjok N 64 Ka06
Luogosanto I 168 Cb74
Luohua FIN 82 Ka25
Luohuan Ylipää FIN 82 Ka25
Luoke LT 113 Jd54
Luoma FIN 89 Jc32
Luoma-aho FIN 81 Jc30
Luomala FIN 82 Kb30
Luomankylä FIN 89 Ja33
Luonaala FIN 81 Ja31
Luonetjärvi FIN 90 Kb32
Luopa FIN 89 Jb32
Luopajärvi FIN 89 Jb32
Luopioinen FIN 90 Ka36
Luosto FIN 69 Kb16
Luosu FIN 68 Jb16
Luotakko FIN 82 Kb27
Luoto FIN 81 Jb28
Luotojärvi FIN 91 Lc32
Luotola FIN 91 Lb37
Luotolahti FIN 90 La35
Lupac RO 174 Ca62
Lupara I 161 Ga73
Łupawa PL 121 Gd30
Lupėnai LT 113 Jc57
Lupeni RO 172 Dd59
Lupeni RO 175 Cd62
Lupersat F 33 Gd46
Lupiac F 40 Fd54
Lupiana E 46 Dd64
Lupiñén E 48 Fb59
Łupków PL 139 Ka46
Luplanté F 29 Gb39
Lupogav HR 151 Fa60
Luppa D 127 Ec40
Luppoperä FIN 75 Kc23
Lupșa RO 171 Cd59
Lupșanu RO 176 Ec66
Lüptitz D 127 Ec40
Luque E 60 Da73
Luquín E 39 Ec57
Lur S 94 Eb45
Luras I 168 Cb74
Lurcy-Lévis F 30 Hb44
Lure F 31 Ka40
Lurgan GB 9 Cd17
Luri F 154 Cc68
Lurøy N 70 Fa20
Lurs F 42 Jd52
Lury-sur-Arnon F 29 Gd42
Lusanger F 28 Ed41
Lūšė LT 113 Jc53
Lüsen I 143 Ea55
Lüsens A 142 Dc54
Lusevera I 150 Ed57
Lushnjë AL 182 Ab76
Lusi FIN 90 Kc35
Lusiana I 150 Dd58
Lusignan F 32 Fd45
Lusigny F 30 Hc44
Lusigny-sur-Barse F 30 Hd38
Lusina PL 129 Gb41
Lusk IRL 13 Cd21
Luskovicy RUS 99 Mb40
Lus-la-Croix-Haute F 35 Jd50
Luso P 44 Ad63
Luson I 143 Ea55
Luspebryggan S 72 Ha18
Luspeholmen S 72 Gb24
Luss GB 7 Dd12
Lussac F 32 Fc50
Lussac-les-Châteaux F 33 Ga45
Lussac-les-Eglises F 33 Gb45
Lussan F 42 Ja52
Lussat F 33 Gd45
Lusta GB 4 Da07
Lustenau A 142 Cd53
Lustila FIN 89 Jc33
Łuszczów PL 131 Kb39
Łuszkowo PL 121 Ha33
Luszyn PL 130 Hd37
Lutago I 143 Ea55
Lutcza PL 139 Ka45
Lutepää LV 107 Ld46
Lütersheim D 126 Cd40
Lütfiye TR 186 Ga79
Lütfiye TR 191 Ed85
Luthenay-Uxeloup F 30 Hb43
Luthern-Bad CH 141 Ca54
Lutherstadt Eisleben D 127 Ea39
Lutherstadt Wittenberg D 127 Ec38
Lutin CZ 137 Gc46
Lütjenburg D 119 Dd30
Lütjensee D 118 Dc32
Lutocin PL 122 Hd34
Lutol Suchy PL 128 Ga37
Lutomiersk PL 130 Hc39
Luton GB 20 Fc27
Lütow D 120 Fa31
Lutowiska PL 139 Kb46
Lutówko PL 121 Gd33
Lutriņi LV 105 Jd51
Lutry PL 122 Jb31
Lütschental CH 141 Ca55
Lutsi N 92 Ca44
Lutta FIN 89 Ja37
Luttach I 143 Ea55
Lütte D 127 Ec37
Lutter am Barenberge D 126 Dc38
Lutterworth GB 20 Fa25
Lüttich = Liège B 124 Ba41
Lutuhyne UA 205 Fb15
Lututów PL 129 Hb40
Lutynia PL 129 Gc41
Lützelbach D 134 Cd45
Lützen D 127 Eb40
Lutzerath D 133 Bd43
Lutzkampen D 133 Bb43
Lutzmannsburg A 145 Gc53
Lützow D 119 Dd32
Luujoki FIN 74 Jd21
Luukkola FIN 91 Lb35
Luukkonen FIN 91 Lb34
Luumäen kirkonkylä FIN 91 Lb36
Luumäki FIN 91 Lb36
Luupujoki FIN 82 Kc28
Luupuvesi FIN 82 Kc27
Luusniemi FIN 90 Kd33
Luusua FIN 74 Kb18
Luutalahti FIN 83 Ma31
Luutsniku EST 107 Lc47
Luvelahti FIN 82 Kd30
Luvia FIN 89 Ja36
Luvos S 72 Gd19
Luxaondo E 38 Ea56
Luxembourg L 133 Bb45
Luxeuil-les-Bains F 31 Jd40
Luxey F 39 Fb52
Luyando E 38 Ea56
Luyères F 30 Hd38
Luynes F 29 Ga42
Luz P 50 Ba70
Luzaga E 47 Eb63

Luzaide-Valcarlos - Mandelbachtal

Luzaide-Valcarlos E 39 Ed56
Lužani HR 152 Ha61
Luzarches F 23 Gd36
Luz de Tavira P 58 Ad74
Luže CZ 136 Ga45
Luzech F 33 Gb51
Luzern CH 141 Ca54
Luzianes P 58 Ab72
Lužice CZ 137 Gc48
Lužicy RUS 99 Ld40
Luz i Madh AL 182 Ab75
Luzino PL 121 Ha29
Luzki PL 131 Kb36
Lužki RUS 113 Jc59
Lužná CZ 136 Fa44
Lūžņa LV 105 Jb49
Łużna PL 138 Jc45
Luz-Saint-Sauveur F 40 Fc57
Luzy F 30 Hd43
Luzzara I 149 Db61
Luzzi I 164 Gb79
L'viv UA 204 Dd15
L'vovskoe RUS 113 Jc59
Lwówek PL 128 Ga36
Lwówek Śląski PL 128 Fd41
Lybiskiai LT 113 Jd56
Lybster GB 5 Eb05
Lychen D 119 Ed34
Lycke S 102 Eb48
Lyckeby S 111 Fd54
Lycksaberg S 72 Gc24
Lycksele S 80 Gd26
Lydbury North GB 15 Eb25
Lydd GB 21 Ga30
Lydersholm DK 108 Da28
Lydney GB 19 Ec27
Lyduokiai LT 114 Kd56
Lyduvėnai LT 114 Ka55
Lye S 104 Ha50
Lygna N 85 Ea40
Lygudai LT 114 Ka54
Lygumai LT 114 Kb54
Lykling N 92 Bd41
Lyly FIN 90 Ka34
Lylykylä FIN 75 Kd23
Lyman UA 203 Fa14
Lyme Regis GB 19 Eb30
Lyminge GB 21 Gb29
Lymington GB 20 Fa30
Lymm GB 15 Ec22
Lympia CY 206 Jc97
Lympne GB 21 Ga29
Łyna PL 122 Ja33
Lyndby DK 109 Eb26
Lyndhurst GB 20 Ed30
Lyndlich GB 19 Ec30
Lyne DK 108 Cd25
Lyne GB 11 Eb14
Lyneham GB 20 Ed28
Lyness GB 5 Ec03
Lyngby DK 100 Cd21
Lyngby DK 101 Dd23
Lyngdal N 92 Cc47
Lyngdal N 93 Dc41
Lynge DK 109 Ec25
Lyngerup DK 109 Eb25
Lyngmoen N 66 Fc15
Lyngså DK 101 Dd20
Lyngseidet N 62 Ha10
Lyngsjö S 111 Fb55
Lyngstad N 77 Da31
Lyngvoll N 84 Cd34
Lyniew PL 131 Kc38
Lynmouth GB 19 Dd29
Lynton GB 19 Dd29
Lyø By DK 108 Dc27
Lyoffans F 31 Ka40
Lyökki FIN 89 Hd38
Lyon F 34 Jb47
Lyons-la-Forêt F 23 Gb35
Lyöttilä FIN 90 Kd37
Lypci UA 203 Fa14
Lypova Dolyna UA 202 Ed14
Lyrestad S 95 Fb45
Łysaków PL 130 Ja42
Lysá nad Labem CZ 136 Fc44
Lysá pod Makytou SK 137 Hb47
Łysa Polana PL 138 Ja47
Łyse PL 122 Jc33
Lyse S 102 Eb47
Lysebotn N 92 Cb44
Lysekil S 102 Eb47
Lysi CY 206 Jc97
Lysice CZ 137 Gb46
Lyski PL 137 Hb44
Lyskovo RUS 203 Fc09
Lysnes N 62 Gc10
Lyšnicy RUS 99 Mb44
Lyso CY 206 Hd97
Łysomice PL 121 Hb34
Łysów PL 131 Ka36
Lysøysundet N 77 Dd28
Lyss CH 141 Bc53
Lystbæk DK 100 Cd23
Lysthaugen N 78 Ec29
Lystrup DK 108 Dc24
Lystrup Strand DK 101 Dd23
Lysvik S 94 Fa41
Lysvoll N 66 Ga14
Lysyčans'k UA 203 Fb14
Lysye Gory RUS 203 Fd12
Łyszkowice PL 130 Hd38
Lytham GB 15 Eb20
Lytham Saint Anne's GB 15 Eb20
Lythrodontas CY 206 Jb97
Lyttylä FIN 89 Ja35

M

Maakeski FIN 90 Kb36
Maalahti FIN 81 Hd31
Maalismaa FIN 74 Ka23
Maam Cross IRL 8 Bb20
Maaninka FIN 82 Kd29
Maaninkavaara FIN 74 Kd18
Maanselkä FIN 82 La27
Maaralanperä FIN 82 Kb27
Maardu EST 98 Kc42
Maarheeze NL 125 Bb39
Maaria FIN 97 Jb39
Maarianhamina FIN 96 Hc41
Maarianvaara FIN 83 Lb30
Maaritsa EST 107 Lb46
Maarja EST 99 Lb44
Maarn NL 116 Bb36
Maarssen NL 116 Ba36
Maas IRL 8 Ca16
Maasbracht NL 125 Bb40
Maasbree NL 125 Bc39
Maaseik B 125 Bb40
Maasmechelen B 125 Bb40
Maassluis NL 124 Ac37
Maastricht NL 125 Bb41
Määttälä FIN 81 Jd28
Määttälänvaara FIN 75 La19
Maavehmaa FIN 90 Kb37
Maavesi FIN 90 La32
Maavuskylä FIN 90 La32
Mablethorpe GB 17 Fd22
Macael E 61 Eb74
Maçaínhas P 44 Bb64
Maçanet de Cabreneys E 41 Hb58
Maçanet de la Selva E 49 Hb60
Mação P 50 Ad66
Măcăreuca MD 173 Fb54
Macau F 32 Fb49
Maccagno I 148 Cb57
Macchiascandona I 155 Db68
Macclesfield GB 16 Ed22
Macduff GB 5 Ed07
Mače HR 152 Gb58
Mace IRL 8 Bc19
Macea RO 170 Bd58
Maceda E 36 Bb57
Macedo de Cavaleiros P 45 Bc60
Maceira E 36 Ad57
Macerata I 156 Ed67
Macerata Feltria I 156 Eb65
Măceşu de Jos RO 179 Cd67
Măceşu de Sus RO 179 Cd67
Mac Gregor's Corner GB 9 Da16
Long Bennington GB 16 Fb23
Machault F 24 Hd35
Mâche CH 148 Bc57
Machecoul F 28 Ed43
Machern D 127 Ec40
Machliny PL 121 Gb33
Machocice Kapitulne PL 130 Jb41
Machowa PL 138 Jc44
Machrihanish GB 10 Db14
Machynlleth GB 15 Dd24
Mącice PL 122 Jb33
Maciejów PL 129 Hb41
Maciejowice PL 131 Jd38
Măcin RO 177 Fb64
Macinaggio F 154 Cc67
Macisvenda E 55 Fa71
Măciuca RO 175 Da64
Mackan GB 9 Cb18
Mačkovac BIH 153 Hc63
Mačkovci SLO 145 Gb55
Maćkowa Ruda PL 123 Kb30
Maclas F 34 Ja48
Maclodio I 149 Da59
Macomer I 169 Ca76
Mâcon F 34 Jb45
Macotera E 45 Cc63
Macqueville F 32 Fc47
Macroom IRL 12 Bc25
Macugnaga I 148 Bd57
Macure HR 157 Ga64
Maczków PL 128 Fc37
Mád H 147 Jd50
Madan BG 179 Cc68
Madan BG 184 Db75
Mädängsholm S 103 Fb47
Madara BG 181 Ec70
Madaras H 153 Hd57
Mădăraş RO 170 Ca57
Madariaga E 39 Eb55
Maddalena Spiaggia, la I 169 Ca80
Maddaloni I 161 Fb74
Made NL 124 Ad38
Madekoski FIN 74 Ka24
Madeley GB 15 Ec23
Maden TR 205 Ga19
Maderuelo E 46 Dc61
Madesimo I 142 Cd56
Madetkoski FIN 69 Ka14
Madières F 41 Hc53
Madiran F 40 Fc54
Madise EST 98 Ka43
Madiswil CH 141 Bd53
Madla N 92 Ca44
Madliena LV 106 Kd50
Madona LV 107 Lb50
Madonna di Campiglio I 149 Dc57
Madonna di Senales I 142 Dc55
Madonna di Tirano I 149 Da57
Madosca H 146 Hd55
Madra CH 142 Cc56
Mădrec BG 185 Ea74
Madrid E 46 Dc64
Madridejos E 52 Dc67
Madrigal de las Altas Torres E 46 Cd62
Madrigal de la Vera E 45 Cc65
Madrigalejo E 51 Cb68
Madrigalejo del Monte E 46 Dc59
Madrigueras E 53 Ec68
Mădrino BG 181 Ec72
Madrona E 46 Db63
Madroñera E 51 Cb67
Madsøygrenda N 70 Ec24
Mădulari RO 175 Da65
Madžarovo BG 185 Dd75
Madžiūnai LT 114 La58
Mäebe EST 105 Jc47
Mæbø N 92 Cd47
Mæl N 93 Db41
Maël-Carhaix F 26 Ea38
Mælen N 78 Ea28
Maella E 48 Fd62
Maello E 46 Da63
Mælum N 93 Dc44
Maenclochog GB 14 Dc26
Mäentaka FIN 97 Jc39
Maerdy GB 15 Ea23
Mære N 78 Ec28
Măerişte RO 171 Cc56
Maesteg GB 19 Ea27
Maestrello I 156 Ea67
Maestu E 39 Eb57
Mäetaguse EST 99 Lb42
Maevka RUS 113 Jc58
Mafalda I 161 Fc71
Maffe B 124 Ba42
Maffiotto I 148 Bc60
Mafra P 50 Aa68
Magacela E 51 Cb69
Magallón E 47 Ed60
Magaluf E 57 Hb67
Magaña E 47 Eb60
Maganey IRL 13 Cc23
Mağara TR 187 Gc78
Mağaraları TR 191 Ec82
Măgari EST 98 Ka44
Magasa I 149 Db58
Magašici BIH 153 Ja63
Magaz E 46 Da59
Magdala D 127 Ea41
Magdeburg D 127 Ea37
Magenta I 148 Cb59
Magerholm N 76 Cc32
Magerøystua N 64 Jb04
Magescq F 39 Fa54
Măgeşti RO 171 Cc57
Magganári GR 196 Db91
Maggia CH 141 Cb56
Maghanlawaun IRL 12 Ba25
Maghera GB 9 Cd16
Magherabane IRL 9 Cc15
Magherafelt GB 9 Cd16
Magheralin GB 9 Da17
Magheramason GB 9 Cc16
Magheramorne GB 9 Da16
Magherani RO 171 Dc59
Măgheruş RO 172 Dd58
Maghull GB 15 Eb21
Magione I 156 Ea67
Măgireşti RO 172 Ec59
Maglaj BIH 152 Hb63
Maglavit RO 179 Cc67
Maglebrænde DK 109 Eb28
Magleby DK 109 Ec28
Maglehem S 111 Fb55
Maglehøj Strand DK 109 Ea29
Mäglen BG 181 Ed72
Magliano de'Marsi I 160 Ed71
Magliano in Toscana I 155 Dc69
Magliano Sabina I 156 Eb70
Maglić SRB 153 Ja60
Maglic SRB 178 Ba67
Maglie I 163 Hc77
Magliž BG 180 Dd72
Magnac-Bourg F 33 Gb47
Magnac-Laval F 33 Gb45
Magnano I 148 Bd59
Magnant F 30 Hd39
Magnat-l'Etrange F 33 Gd47
Magnières F 25 Ka37
Magnillseter N 77 Ea33
Magnor N 94 Ec41
Magnuszew PL 130 Jc38
Magnuszowice PL 129 Gd42
Magny-Cours F 30 Hb43
Magny-en-Vexin F 23 Gc36
Mágocs H 152 Hb57
Magra S 102 Ed47
Magreglio I 149 Cc58
Magstadt D 134 Cc48
Magueija P 44 Ba61
Maguelone F 41 Hd54
Maguilla E 51 Ca71
Maguiresbridge GB 9 Cb18
Magūnai LT 115 Lb57
Măgura RO 172 Ed59
Măgura RO 176 Ec63
Măgura RO 180 Dd67
Măgura RO 181 Fb68
Măgura Ilvei RO 172 Dd56
Măgurele MD 173 Fb56
Măgurele RO 176 Eb64
Măgureni RO 176 Ea64
Măgureni RO 177 Fb65
Măguri-Răcătău RO 171 Cd58
Magyarbóly H 153 Hc58
Magyarkeszi H 145 Hb55
Magyarmecske H 152 Hb58
Magyarszék H 152 Hb57
Magyarszentmiklós H 145 Gc56
Magyarszombatfa H 145 Gb55
Mahala MNE 159 Ja70
Mahdalynivka UA 205 Fa15
Maherádo GR 188 Ac86
Mahično HR 151 Fd59
Mahide E 45 Ca59
Mahilëv BY 202 Eb12
Mahlow, Blankenfelde- D 127 Ed37
Mahlu FIN 82 Ka31
Mahlwinkel D 127 Ea36
Mahmudia RO 177 Fd64
Mahmudiye TR 186 Ga80
Mahmudiye TR 191 Ea81
Mahmudiye TR 191 Ec83
Mahmudiye TR 192 Fb82
Mahmudiye TR 193 Gd83
Mahmutbey TR 186 Fc77
Mahmutköy TR 185 Eb78
Mahmutlar TR 199 Gd88
Mahmut Şevket Paşa TR 186 Fd77
Mahmut Şevket Paşa TR 186 Fd77
Mahnala FIN 89 Jc35
Mahnovka RUS 107 Mb47
Maholič BG 181 Ec71
Mahón E 57 Jb66
Mahon Bridge IRL 13 Cb25
Mahora E 53 Ec68
Mahovo HR 152 Gb59
Mahramlı TR 185 Ec78
Mähring D 135 Eb45
Mahtra EST 98 Kc43
Mahu EST 98 La41
Maia P 44 Ad61
Maiac MD 173 Ga57
Maials E 48 Ga61
Măicăneşti RO 177 Fa63
Maîche F 31 Ka41
Maida I 164 Gc81
Maida Marina I 164 Gb81
Maiden Bradley GB 19 Ec29
Maidenhead GB 20 Fb28
Maiden Newton GB 19 Eb30
Maidstone GB 20 Fd29
Maienfeld CH 142 Cd54
Maiern I 143 Dd55
Maieru RO 171 Dc56
Măieruş RO 176 Ea61
Maigh Chromtha IRL 12 Bc25
Maigh Cuilinn IRL 12 Bc21
Maigh Nuad IRL 13 Cd21
Maignelay-Montigny F 23 Gd34
Maijanen FIN 68 Jc17
Maijanen FIN 68 Jc17
Maikammer D 133 Cb46
Mailand = Milano I 149 Cc59
Mailat RO 174 Bc60
Maillas F 40 Fc52
Maillé F 32 Fb45
Mailley-et-Chazelot F 31 Jd41
Maillezais F 32 Fb45
Mailly-le-Camp F 24 Hd37
Mailly-Maillet F 23 Gd33
Mainar E 47 Ed62
Mainbernheim D 134 Db45
Mainbressy F 24 Hd34
Mainburg D 135 Ea49
Mainhardt D 134 Da47
Mainiemi FIN 90 Kd34
Mainistir Fhear Maí IRL 12 Bd25
Mainistir Laoise IRL 13 Cb22
Mainistir na Búille IRL 8 Ca19
Mainistir na Corann IRL 12 Bd26
Mainleus D 135 Dd44
Mainsat F 33 Ha46
Mainstockheim D 134 Db45
Mainstone GB 15 Eb24
Maintal D 134 Cc44
Maintenay F 23 Gc32
Maintenon F 29 Gc38
Mainua FIN 82 Kd26
Mainvilliers F 29 Gb38
Mainz D 133 Cb44
Maiori I 161 Fb76
Mairago I 149 Cd60
Mairena del Alcor E 59 Ca74
Maisach D 143 Dd50
Maisey-le-Duc F 30 Ja40
Maišiagala LT 114 La57
Maison-Neuve F 34 Ja51
Maison Pieraggi F 154 Cb70
Maison-Rouge F 30 Hb38
Maisons F 41 Ha56
Maisons-Laffitte F 23 Gd36
Maissau A 136 Ga49
Maisse F 29 Gd38
Maissin B 132 Ad43
Máistir Gaoithe IRL 12 Ba25
Maitenbeth D 143 Ea51
Maitoinen FIN 90 Kb38
Maivala FIN 75 Lb19
Maivala FIN 90 La34
Maizières F 22 Fc36
Maizières-lès-Vic F 25 Ka36
Maja HR 152 Gb60
Majadahonda E 46 Db64
Majadas E 45 Cb65
Majaelrayo E 46 Dd62
Majak Oktjabrja RUS 203 Ga13
Majakovo RUS 99 Mb45
Majakovske RUS 113 Jd59
Majaneque E 60 Cc72
Majava FIN 75 Kd20
Majavaoja FIN 68 Jb14
Majavatn N 70 Fa24
Majbølle DK 109 Eb28
Majdan PL 123 Jd35
Majdan RUS 203 Fd09
Majdan SK 138 Jc47
Majdan UA 204 Dd16
Majdan Królewski PL 139 Jd43
Majdan Nepryski PL 131 Kc42
Majdanpek SRB 174 Bd65
Majdan Radliński PL 131 Ka40
Majdan Sieniawski PL 139 Kb43
Majdan Stary PL 131 Kb42
Majilovac SRB 174 Bc64
Majkop RUS 205 Fd17
Majków PL 130 Jb40
Majori LV 106 Kb50
Majorskij RUS 205 Fd15
Majs H 153 Hc58
Majskoe RUS 113 Jd58
Majšperk SLO 151 Ga57
Majtum S 72 Ha20
Makariopolsko BG 181 Ec70
Makarovo RUS 203 Fc12
Makarska HR 158 Gd67
Makce SRB 174 Bc64
Mäkelä FIN 75 La19
Mäkelänperä FIN 89 Jc33
Mäkiänen FIN 89 Jc38
Makijivka UA 205 Fb15
Mäkikylä FIN 82 Kd29
Mäkipää FIN 82 Kb29
Makirráhi GR 189 Bc82
Makita EST 107 Lb46
Mäkitalo FIN 68 Jc16
Makkarkoski FIN 89 Jb38
Mäkkikylä FIN 89 Jd32
Mäkkikylä FIN 90 Kb33
Makkola FIN 90 Kc33
Makkola FIN 91 Lc33
Makkum NL 116 Bb33
Maklár H 146 Jb52
Makljenovac BIH 152 Hb62
Makmūnai LT 114 Kc59
Makó H 153 Jc57
Mąkoszyce PL 129 Gd41
Makov SK 137 Hb47
Makovac KSV 178 Bb70
Makovce SK 139 Ka46
Makovo BG 180 Eb70
Makovo MK 183 Bb76
Maków PL 130 Ja38
Maków PL 138 Ja43
Mąkowarsko PL 121 Gd33
Makowiska PL 121 Ha34
Makowiska PL 130 Hc41
Makowlany PL 123 Kb32
Maków Mazowiecki PL 122 Jb35
Makowo PL 122 Hd32
Maków Podhalanski PL 138 Hd45
Makrakómi GR 189 Bc83
Makreš Donji KSV 178 Bc71
Mákri GR 185 Dd78
Makríamos GR 184 Db78
Makrigialós GR 201 Dc96
Makrihóri GR 184 Da77
Makrihóri GR 189 Bc81
Makrinitsa GR 189 Ca82
Makriplágio GR 184 Da76
Makrirráhi GR 189 Ca82
Makrohóri GR 183 Bd78
Makrolívado GR 189 Bd83
Makrygialos GR 183 Ca78
Mäksa EST 99 Lb45
Maksamaa FIN 81 Ja30
Maksatiha RUS 202 Ed09
Makşempınar TR 186 Fc80
Maksniemi FIN 74 Jd21
Maksutlu TR 186 Fa77
Mäksy FIN 81 Jd30
Maksymilianowo PL 121 Ha34
Maksymilianowo PL 129 Gb37
Makušino RUS 107 Ma50
Makuži LV 107 Lc51
Mala IRL 12 Bc25
Malå S 72 Gd24
Malá E 60 Db75
Mala Bosna SRB 153 Ja57
Mala Buna HR 152 Gb59
Mala Čista HR 157 Ga65
Malacky SK 145 Gc50
Malá Domaša SK 139 Ka47
Maladzečna BY 202 Ea12
Malaf'evka RUS 99 Ld43
Málaga E 60 Cd76
Málaga del Fresno E 46 Dd63
Malagón E 52 Db68
Malagrotta I 160 Ea71
Malaguilla E 46 Dd63
Malahide IRL 13 Cd21
Malahvianvaara FIN 75 Lc23
Malaia RO 175 Da63
Mălăieşti MD 173 Fc56
Mălăieşti MD 173 Ga58
Mălăieşti RO 175 Cc62
Malaincourt F 31 Jc38
Malainn Bhig IRL 8 Bd16
Malaja Višera RUS 202 Eb09
Mala Kapela HR 151 Fd61
Malakása GR 189 Cc86
Malakássi GR 182 Ba80
Malăk izvor BG 185 Dd75
Mala Kladuša BIH 151 Ga61
Mălak Porovec BG 181 Ec68
Mălak Preslavec BG 181 Ec67
Malalbergo I 150 Dd62
Malá Morávka CZ 137 Gd45
Malandrino GR 189 Bc84
Mälång S 79 Fc31
Malangen N 62 Gc10
Malangseidet N 62 Gd10
Malanów PL 129 Hb38
Malarhusen S 111 Fb57
Malarrif IS 2 Ab03
Malaryta BY 202 Dd14
Mäläskä FIN 82 Kb25
Mala Subotica HR 152 Gc57
Małaszewicze PL 131 Kc37
Malaucène F 42 Jc52
Malåvännäs S 72 Gd24
Mala Vyska UA 204 Ed15
Mała Wieś PL 130 Ja36
Mała Wieś PL 130 Jb38
Malax FIN 81 Hd31
Malbekkvatnet N 65 Kc08
Malborghetto I 143 Ed56
Malbork PL 121 Hb31
Malborn D 133 Bd45
Malbouzon F 34 Hb50
Malbuisson F 31 Ka43
Mälby S 95 Ga41
Malča SRB 178 Bd69
Malcesine I 149 Db58
Mal'cevo RUS 113 Jc59
Malchin D 119 Ec32
Malching D 143 Ed50
Malchow D 119 Ec33
Malčice SK 139 Ka49
Malcoci MD 173 Fc58
Malcocinado E 51 Ca71
Malcontenta I 150 Ea60
Malcov SK 138 Jc46
Maldan TR 191 Ec84
Măldăreşti RO 175 Da63
Maldon GB 21 Ga27
Małdyty PL 122 Hd31
Måle DK 109 Dd26
Malé I 142 Dc56
Malechowo PL 121 Gb30
Male Drage HR 151 Fc60
Małe Gacno PL 121 Ha32
Malème GR 200 Cb94
Malente D 119 Dd30
Malente D 119 Dd30
Male Pijace SRB 153 Jb57
Mälerås S 103 Fc52
Máles GR 201 Db96
Malesco I 148 Cb57
Malesherbes F 29 Gd38
Malesina GR 189 Ca84
Malešov CZ 136 Fd45
Malestroit F 27 Ec40
Malesze PL 123 Kb34
Malevo BG 185 Dd74
Malexander S 103 Fd48
Malfa I 167 Fc82
Malga Ciapela I 143 Ea56
Malgaçmustafa TR 192 Fa87
Malgersdorf D 135 Ec49
Malgovik S 79 Ga26
Malgrat de Mar E 49 Hb60
Malhada Sorda P 45 Bc63
Malham GB 11 Ed19
Māļi LV 106 La50
Malia CY 206 Ja98
Mália GR 201 Db96
Malicorne-sur-Sarthe F 28 Fc40
Maliena LV 107 Lc48
Mali Iđoš SRB 153 Ja59
Mali Izvor SRB 179 Ca68
Malijai F 42 Ka52
Mali Konjari MK 183 Bb75
Malilanniemi FIN 75 Lb24
Målilla S 103 Ga50
Mali Lošinj HR 151 Fb63
Malin IRL 9 Cc15
Malina BG 181 Fb69
Malin Beg IRL 8 Bd16
Málinec SK 138 Ja49
Malingsbo S 95 Fd41
Mălini RO 172 Eb56
Maliniec PL 129 Ha37
Malinniki PL 123 Kb35
Maļinovka LV 115 Lc53
Malinovka RUS 113 Jb58
Malinovka RUS 113 Jc58
Malinovo BG 180 Dc70
Malinovscoe MD 173 Fa55
Malinska HR 151 Fb61
Mali Ostros MNE 163 Ja71
Mali Požarevac SRB 174 Bb64
Maliq AL 182 Ad77
Malisensuo FIN 75 Kd22
Mališevo RUS 99 Ld45
Maliskylä FIN 82 Ka27
Mali Stapar SRB 153 Hd59
Mali Štupelj KSV 178 Ad70
Mali Štupelj SRB 159 Jc68
Maliuc RO 177 Fd64
Mali Vranjska SRB 153 Jb62
Malix CH 142 Cd55
Mali Zam SRB 174 Bd62
Maljala FIN 91 Lb34
Maljamäki FIN 97 Jc39
Maljasalmi FIN 83 Lb30
Maljasset F 35 Kb50
Maljiševo KSV 178 Ba71
Maljkovo HR 158 Gc65
Malkar TR 185 Ec78
Małkinia Górna PL 123 Jd35
Malki Văršec BG 180 Dc70
Malki Voden BG 185 Ea75
Malkkila FIN 91 Lb32
Malkoca TR 192 Fa85
Malkoçlar TR 185 Ec74
Malko gradište BG 185 Ea75
Malko Tărnovo BG 185 Ed74
Mal'kovo RUS 107 Mb51
Malko Vranovo BG 180 Eb68
Małkowice PL 139 Kb44
Mallaig GB 6 Db09
Mälläinen FIN 89 Jc37
Mallemort F 42 Jc53
Mallén E 47 Ed60
Mallersdorf-Pfaffenberg D 135 Eb49
Malles Venosta I 142 Db55
Mallıca TR 193 Gd84
Malling DK 108 Dc24
Malliß D 119 Ea34
Mallnitz A 143 Ec55
Mallow IRL 12 Bc25
Mallusjoki FIN 90 Kc38
Mallwyd GB 15 Ea24
Malm N 78 Eb28
Malmbäck S 103 Fb49
Malmberget S 67 Hb17
Malme N 77 Da31
Malmedy B 125 Bb42
Malmesbury GB 20 Ed28
Malmi FIN 98 Kb39
Malmivaara S 67 Hb17
Malmköping S 95 Gb44
Malmö S 110 Ed56
Malmön S 102 Eb47
Malmslätt S 103 Fd46
Malmuiža LV 107 Lb49
Malmyž RUS 203 Fd08
Malnaş RO 176 Ea61
Malnate I 148 Cb58
Malnava LV 107 Ld50
Malnes N 77 Dc29
Malo I 150 Dd59
Maloarhangel'sk RUS 203 Fa12
Mal'oe Stremlenie RUS 99 Ld40
Małogoszcz PL 130 Ja41
Maloja CH 142 Cd56
Malojaroslavec RUS 202 Ed11
Malo Konare BG 179 Da73
Malo-les-Bains F 21 Gd29
Malo Malovo BG 179 Cb70
Małomice PL 128 Fd39
Malomir BG 180 Eb73
Malomirovo BG 185 Eb74
Malomožajskoe RUS 113 Jd58
Malónas GR 197 Fa93
Malonno I 149 Da57
Malonty CZ 136 Fb49
Malorad BG 179 Cd69
Malo Selo HR 151 Fc60
Malo Tičevo BIH 158 Gc64
Malounta CY 206 Jb97
Måløv DK 109 Ec25
Malovăt RO 174 Cb64
Malo Vukovje HR 152 Gc59
Małowidz PL 122 Jb33
Måløy N 84 Ca34
Malpaas GB 15 Eb23
Malpaga I 149 Cd59
Malpartida de Cáceres E 51 Bd67
Malpartida de Plasencia E 45 Ca65
Malpensado P 58 Ab72
Malpica de Arba E 39 Fa58
Malpica de Bergantiños E 36 Ad54
Malpica de Tajo E 52 Da66
Malpica do Tejo P 51 Bb66
Mālpils LV 106 Kd50
Malsätra S 96 Gd41
Malsch D 133 Cb48
Malschwitz D 128 Fb41
Målselv N 67 Gc11
Malsfeld D 126 Da41
Malšice CZ 136 Fb47
Mals im Vinschgau I 142 Db55
Malšín CZ 136 Fb49
Malsjö S 94 Ed43
Malsjöbodarna S 87 Fd33
Målsryd S 102 Ed49
Målsta S 79 Fc31
Malsta S 96 Ha42
Malta A 143 Ed55
Malta LV 107 Lc52
Maltarina BIH 158 Hb68
Maltat F 30 Hc44
Maltaverne F 29 Ha42
Maltby GB 16 Fa21
Maltby le Marsh GB 17 Fd22
Maltepe TR 185 Eb77
Maltepe TR 185 Ec80
Maltepe TR 191 Eb85
Malters CH 141 Ca54
Malton GB 16 Fb19
Maltträsk S 80 Ha26
Malu cu Flori RO 176 Dd63
Maluenda E 47 Ed62
Małujowice PL 129 Gd42
Malu Mare RO 175 Da66
Malung S 94 Fa39
Malungen N 94 Eb39
Malungen S 87 Gb34
Malungsfors S 94 Fa39
Mālupe LV 107 Lc48
Mălureni RO 175 Dc64
Măluşteni RO 177 Fb60
Małuszów PL 128 Fd37
Maluszyn PL 130 Hd41
Malva E 45 Cc60
Malvaglia CH 142 Cc56
Malvaste EST 97 Jc44
Malveira P 50 Aa68
Malvinavas LT 115 Lb55
Malyj Sabsk RUS 99 Ma42
Malyn UA 202 Eb14
Mały Płock PL 123 Jd33
Malyševo RUS 203 Fb10
Mamadys RUS 203 Ga08
Mamaia RO 181 Fc67
Mamatlar TR 187 Hb78
Mambrilla de Castrejón E 46 Db60
Mambrillas de Lara E 46 Dd59
Mamer L 133 Bb45
Mamers F 28 Fd38
Mametz F 23 Ha33
Maminas AL 182 Ab74
Mamirolle F 31 Jd42
Mammendorf D 143 Dd50
Mamming D 135 Ec49
Mammola I 164 Gb83
Mamoiada I 169 Cb76
Mamone I 168 Cb75
Mamonovo RUS 113 Hb59
Mamuras AL 163 Jb72
Mamykovo RUS 203 Ga09
Måmyra N 78 Ea27
Maňa SK 145 Hb51
Manacor E 57 Hc67
Manamansalo FIN 82 Kc25
Manán E 36 Bc55
Mañaria E 39 Eb55
Manarola I 155 Cd64
Manasia RO 176 Ec65
Manasterz PL 139 Kb44
Manastir BG 181 Ed70
Manastir BG 184 Db75
Manastir BG 185 Dd74
Manastır TR 198 Fd90
Mănăstirea RO 181 Ec67
Mănăstirea Caşin RO 176 Ec60
Mănăstirea Humorului RO 172 Eb56
Mănăstirea Neamţ RO 172 Eb57
Mănăstireni RO 171 Cd58
Manastirica SRB 174 Bb65
Mănăştiur RO 174 Ca60
Mănăştur RO 174 Bc60
Manavgat TR 199 Ha91
Mancera de Arriba E 45 Cc63
Mancha Real E 60 Db73
Manchecourt F 29 Gd39
Manchester GB 15 Ec21
Manching D 135 Dd49
Manchita E 51 Ca69
Manciano I 155 Dc69
Manciet F 40 Fd53
Mancılık TR 191 Ed81
Mandal N 92 Cc47
Mandanici I 167 Fd84
Mandas I 169 Ca78
Mandatoriccio I 165 Gd79
Mandayona E 47 Ea63
Mandelbachtal D 133 Bd46

Mandelieu-la Napoule – Massoult

Mandelieu-la Napoule F 43 Kc53
Mandello del Lario I 149 Cc58
Mandelsloh D 126 Da36
Mander NL 117 Bd36
Manderfeld B 125 Bc42
Manderscheid D 133 Bc43
Mandeure F 31 Ka41
Mandø DK 108 Cd26
Mándok H 139 Kb49
Mándra GR 184 Db77
Mándra GR 185 Ea76
Mándra GR 189 Cb86
Mândra RO 176 Dd61
Mandráki GR 197 Eb92
Mandre HR 151 Fc63
Mandria CY 206 Ja97
Mandrica BG 185 Ea76
Mandrikó GR 197 Ed93
Manduria I 162 Hb76
Mane F 40 Gb56
Mane F 42 Jd52
Manea GB 20 Fd25
Manebach D 126 Dc42
Măneciu RO 176 Ea63
Manent-Montaine F 40 Ga55
Manerba del Garda I 149 Db59
Manerbio I 149 Da60
Måneset N 78 Ec25
Mănești RO 176 Dd64
Mănești RO 176 Ea65
Manětín CZ 135 Ed45
Manevyči UA 202 Ea14
Mánfa H 152 Hb57
Manfredonia I 161 Ga72
Mangalia RO 181 Fc68
Manganeses de la Lampreana E 45 Cb60
Manganeses de la Polvorosa E 45 Cb59
Manganitis GR 196 Dd88
Mångbyn S 81 Hd26
Mangen N 94 Eb41
Manger N 84 Ca38
Mangskog S 94 Ed42
Mangualde P 44 Ba63
Manhay B 124 Ba42
Máni GR 185 Eb76
Maniago I 150 Eb57
Maniáki GR 183 Bc77
Manieczki PL 129 Gc38
Manikūnai LT 114 Kc53
Manilva E 59 Cb77
Maninghem F 23 Gc31
Manısa TR 191 Ed85
Manises E 54 Fb67
Manjärv S 73 Hb22
Manjärvträsk S 73 Hb23
Manjaur S 80 Ha25
Manjinac SRB 179 Ca68
Mank A 144 Fd51
Mankaičai LT 113 Jd56
Mankala FIN 90 Kd37
Månkarbo S 96 Gc40
Mańki PL 122 Ja32
Mankila FIN 82 Ka25
Mankūnai LT 114 Ka56
Manlleu E 49 Ha59
Manna DK 100 Dc20
Männamaa EST 97 Jc44
Mannersdorf Leithagebirge A 145 Gc51
Mannestad N 85 Ea40
Mannheim D 134 Cc46
Männikkö S 68 Hd17
Männiku EST 98 Kb42
Männiku EST 98 Kc44
Mannila FIN 89 Jb37
Manningtree GB 21 Ga26
Männistönpää FIN 68 Jb17
Mănoilești MD 173 Fb57
Manole BG 180 Db73
Manoleasa RO 172 Ed54
Manolovo BG 180 Dc72
Mañón E 36 Bb53
Manonville F 25 Jc36
Manoppello I 157 Fa70
Manorbier GB 18 Dc27
Manorhamilton IRL 8 Ca18
Manosque F 42 Jd53
Manowo PL 121 Gb31
Manresa E 49 Gd60
Månsåsen S 79 Fb31
Månsberg S 79 Ga27
Manschnow D 128 Fb36
Mansfeld D 127 Ea39
Mansfield GB 16 Fa22
Mansigné F 28 Fd40
Mansilla E 47 Ea59
Mansilla de las Mulas E 37 Cc57
Mansilla de las Mulas E 38 Dc58
Mansilla del Páramo E 37 Cb57
Manskivi FIN 90 Kb36
Mansle F 32 Fd47
Mansoniemi FIN 89 Jc34
Månsted S 102 Fa49
Månsträsk S 72 Gd23
Mansuè I 150 Eb58
Manta MD 177 Fb62
Mantamádos GR 191 Ea83
Mantasiá GR 189 Bd82
Manteigas P 44 Bb63
Mantel D 135 Eb46
Mantes-la-Jolie F 23 Gc36
Mantes-la-Ville F 23 Gc36
Mantet F 41 Ha58
Manthelan F 29 Ga42
Manthiréa GR 194 Bc88
Mantila FIN 89 Jb32
Mantiloperä FIN 89 Jd33
Mäntlahti FIN 91 Lb38
Måntorp S 79 Ga27
Mantorp S 103 Fd47
Mantoúdi GR 189 Cb84
Mantova I 149 Db60
Mäntsälä FIN 90 Kc38
Mänttä FIN 90 Ka33
Mantua = Mantova I 149 Db60
Manturovo RUS 203 Fb08
Mantviliškis LV 114 Kb55
Mäntyharju FIN 90 Kd35
Mäntyjärvi FIN 74 Jd18
Mäntyjärvi FIN 75 Kc20
Mäntyjärvi FIN 83 Lb29
Mäntylä FIN 82 Kc30
Mäntylahti FIN 82 Kd29
Mäntylänperä FIN 81 Jd25
Mäntyluoto FIN 89 Ja35
Mäntyvaara FIN 73 Jb19
Mäntyvaara FIN 83 Lc30
Mäntyvaara S 73 Hc18
Manuden GB 20 Fd27
Manuel E 54 Fb69
Manyas TR 192 Fa81
Mânzălești RO 176 Ec63
Manzanal del Puerto E 37 Ca57
Manzanares E 52 Dc69
Manzanares el Real E 46 Db63
Manzaneda E 36 Bc57
Manzaneda E 37 Ca58
Manzanedo E 38 Dc56
Manzaneque E 52 Db67
Manzanera E 54 Fa66
Manzano I 150 Ed58
Manzat F 34 Hb46
Manziana I 160 Ea71
Manziat F 34 Jb45
Mäo EST 98 Kd44
Maó E 57 Jb66
Maoča BIH 153 Hc62
Maothail IRL 9 Cb19
Maqellarë AL 182 Ad74
Maqueda E 46 Da65
Mar P 44 Ac59
Mara I 168 Bd76
Marac F 30 Jb39
Maracalagonis I 169 Ca79
Maracena E 60 Db75
Mărăcineni RO 175 Dc64
Mărăcineni RO 176 Ec64
Marainviller F 25 Ka37
Maramonovca MD 173 Fb54
Maranchón E 47 Eb62
Mărăndeni MD 173 Fb56
Maranello I 149 Db62
Maraneve I 167 Fc85
Maranhão P 50 Ad68
Marano di Napoli I 161 Fa75
Marano Lagunare I 150 Ec59
Marans F 32 Fa45
Maranville F 30 Ja39
Mărășești RO 176 Ed61
Marásia GR 185 Eb75
Mărașu RO 177 Fb65
Maratea I 164 Ga78
Marathiás GR 188 Bb85
Marathókambos GR 197 Eb88
Marathónas GR 189 Cc86
Marathópoli GR 194 Ba89
Marathoússa GR 184 Cc78
Marathovounos CY 206 Jc96
Marault F 30 Jb39
Maraye-en-Othe F 30 Hc39
Marazion GB 18 Da32
Marbach A 144 Fd51
Marbach A 144 Fd51
Marbach D 134 Cd48
Marbäck S 102 Fa49
Marbäck S 103 Fc48
Mårbacka S 94 Fa42
Mårbacken S 94 Ed41
Marbella E 60 Cc77
Marboué F 29 Gb39
Marboz F 34 Jb45
Marburg D 126 Cc41
Marburg = Maribor SLO 144 Ga56
Marby S 79 Fb31
Marca RO 171 Cc56
Marçà E 48 Ga62
Marcali H 145 Gd56
Marcaltő H 145 Gd53
Marčana HR 151 Fa61
Marcaria I 149 Db60
Mărcăuți MD 173 Fa53
Mărcăuți MD 173 Fd57
Marcé F 28 Fc41
Marceddì I 169 Bd78
Marcelová SK 145 Hb52
Marcena I 142 Dc56
Marcenat F 34 Hb48
Marčevo BG 179 Cc68
March D 141 Ca50
March GB 17 Fd24
Marchagaz E 45 Ca64
Marchais F 24 Hc34
Marchamalo E 46 Dd64
Marche-en-Famenne B 132 Ba43
Marchegg A 145 Gc50
Marchenilla E 59 Cb77
Marchenoir F 29 Gb40
Marcheprime F 32 Fb50
Marchiennes F 24 Hb31
Marchin B 124 Ba42
Marchtrenk A 144 Fa51
Marchwiel GB 15 Eb23
Marciac F 40 Fd54
Marciana I 155 Cd68
Marciana Marina I 155 Cd68
Marcianise I 161 Fb74
Marciena LV 107 Lb50
Marcigny F 34 Hd45
Marcilla E 39 Ec58
Marcillac-la-Croisille F 33 Gd48
Marcillac-Vallon F 33 Ha51
Marcillat-en-Combraille F 33 Ha46
Marcilliy-sur-Eure F 23 Gb37
Marcilloles F 34 Jb48
Marcilly-en-Gault F 29 Gc41
Marcilly-en-Villette F 29 Gd40
Marcilly-le-Hayer F 30 Hc38
Marcilly-sur-Seine F 24 Hc37
Marcinkonys LT 123 Kd30
Marcinkowice PL 129 Gd41
Marcinkowice PL 138 Jb45
Marcinowice PL 129 Gb42
Marciszów PL 128 Ga42
Marck F 21 Gc30
Marckolsheim F 31 Kc38
Marco E 36 Bb55
Marco de Canaveses P 44 Ba61
Marcoing F 24 Hb32
Mărculești MD 173 Fc55
Mărculești MD 173 Fc55
Mårdaklev S 102 Ed50
Mardal N 70 Ed23
Mardalen N 77 Db33
Mar de Cristal E 55 Fb74
Marden GB 20 Fd29
Mardilly F 22 Fd37
Mårdsel S 73 Hc20
Mårdsele S 80 Ha26
Mårdsjö S 79 Ga27
Mårdsjö S 79 Fd30
Mårdsund S 79 Fb30
Måre DK 109 Dd27
Marebbe I 143 Ea56
Maredret B 124 Ad42
Mårem N 93 Db41
Marennes F 32 Fa47
Marentes E 37 Bd55
Maresfield GB 20 Fd30
Marettimo I 166 Dd84
Mareuil F 32 Fd48
Mareuil-en-Brie F 24 Hc36
Mareuil-sur-Arnon F 29 Gd43
Mareuil-sur-Lay F 28 Fa44
Mareuil-sur-Ourcq F 24 Hb36
Mar'evka RUS 203 Ga10
Marevo RUS 202 Eb10
Marezige SLO 151 Fa60
Marfa M 166 Eb87
Marga RO 174 Cb62
Margam GB 19 Dd27
Mărgăritești RO 176 Ec63
Margariti GR 188 Ac81
Margaritove RUS 205 Fc16
Margate GB 21 Gb28
Mărgău RO 171 Cc58
Margaux F 32 Fb49
Margecany SK 138 Jc48
Margès F 34 Jb49
Margetshöchheim D 134 Da45
Margherita di Savoia I 162 Gb73
Marghita RO 170 Cb56
Margina RO 174 Cb60
Marginea RO 172 Eb55
Mărgineni RO 172 Ec58
Mărgineni RO 172 Ed59
Margolles E 37 Cd54
Margon F 29 Ga38
Margone I 148 Bc60
Margonin PL 121 Gc35
Margraten NL 125 Bb41
Margretetorp S 110 Ed53
Marguerittes F 42 Ja53
Margueron F 32 Fd50
Margut F 24 Jb34
Marham GB 17 Fd24
Marhaň SK 139 Jd47
Marhanec' UA 205 Fa16
Marholm GB 17 Fc24
Mari CY 206 Jb98
Maria E 61 Eb73
Maria Alm A 143 Ec53
Maria de Huerva E 47 Fa61
Maria de la Salut E 57 Hc67
Maria Elend A 144 Fa56
Mariager DK 100 Dc22
Marialva P 45 Bc62
Mariana E 47 Eb65
Marianca de Jos MD 177 Ga60
Maria Neustift A 144 Fc51
Mariannelund S 103 Fd49
Marianopoli I 167 Fa85
Marianowo PL 120 Fd33
Mariánské Lázně CZ 135 Ec45
Maria Saal A 144 Fb56
Maria Schmolln A 143 Ed51
Maria Wörth A 144 Fb56
Mariazell A 144 Fd52
Maribáñez E 59 Ca74
Maribo DK 109 Ea29
Maribor SLO 144 Ga56
Marieberg S 95 Fd44
Marieby S 79 Fc31
Mariefred S 96 Gc44
Mariehamn FIN 96 Hc41
Marieholm S 102 Fa50
Marieholm S 110 Ed55
Marielund N 64 Ka06
Marielund S 72 Gc22
Marielund S 96 Gd42
Marielyst DK 109 Eb29
Marienbad = Mariánské Lázně CZ 135 Ec45
Mariënbad = Mariánské Lázně CZ 135 Ec45
Marienbaum D 125 Bc38
Marienberg D 127 Ed42
Mariënberg NL 117 Bd35
Marienfließ D 119 Eb33
Marienhafe D 117 Cb32
Marienhagen D 126 Da37
Marienheide D 125 Ca40
Marienmünster D 126 Da38
Mariental D 127 Dd37
Marienwerder D 120 Fa35
Mariés GR 184 Da78
Mariestad S 102 Fa46
Marifjora N 84 Cd36
Marigenta E 59 Bc73
Marigliano I 161 Fb75
Marignac F 32 Fb48
Marignane F 42 Jc54
Marigné F 28 Fb40
Marigny F 22 Fa36
Marigny-en-Orxois F 24 Hb36
Marigny-le Châtel F 30 Hc38
Marijampolė LV 114 Kb59
Marija na Muri HR 152 Gc57
Marijskoje RUS 113 Ja59
Marikostenovo BG 184 Cc75
Marín E 36 Ad57
Marina GR 183 Bc77
Marina HR 158 Gb66
Marina di Alberese I 155 Db69
Marina di Amendolara I 164 Gc78
Marina di Andora I 43 La52
Marina di Arbus I 169 Bd78
Marina di Ascea I 161 Fd77
Marina di Belmonte I 164 Gb80
Marina di Belvedere I 164 Ga79
Marina di Bibbona I 155 Da67
Marina di Camerota I 164 Fd78
Marina di Campo I 155 Da68
Marina di Caronia I 167 Fb84
Marina di Carrara I 155 Cd64
Marina di Castagneto-Donoratico I 155 Da67
Marina di Caulonia I 164 Gc83
Marina di Cecina I 155 Da66
Marina di Chieuti I 161 Fd71
Marina di Fuscaldo I 164 Gb79
Marina di Gairo I 169 Cc78
Marina di Ginosa I 162 Gd76
Marina di Gioia Tauro I 164 Ga83
Marina di Gioiosa Jonica I 164 Gc83
Marina di Grosseto I 155 Db68
Marina di Lago di Patria I 161 Fa75
Marina di Leuca I 165 Hc78
Marina di lu Impostu I 168 Cc74
Marina di Massa I 155 Da64
Marina di Minturno I 160 Ed74
Marina di Modica I 167 Fc88
Marina di Montemarciano I 156 Ed66
Marina di Montenero I 161 Fc71
Marina di Novaglie I 165 Hc78
Marina di Nova Siri I 162 Gc77
Marina di Orosei I 169 Cc76
Marina di Ostuni I 162 Ha75
Marina di Palma I 166 Ed87
Marina di Pescia Romana I 155 Dc70
Marina di Pietrasanta I 155 Da64
Marina di Pisa I 155 Da65
Marina di Pisciotta I 161 Fd77
Marina di Pulsano I 162 Ha76
Marina di Ragusa I 167 Fb88
Marina di Ravenna I 150 Ea63
Marina di San Vito I 157 Fb70
Marina di Sibari I 164 Gc78
Marina di Sorso I 168 Bd74
Marina di Strongoli I 165 Gd80
Marina di Torre Grande I 169 Bd77
Marina di Zambrone I 164 Gb82
Marinaleda E 60 Cc74
Marina Palmense I 157 Fa67
Marina Romea I 150 Ea63
Marina Schiavonea I 164 Gc79
Marina Serra I 165 Hc78
Marina Velca I 156 Dd70
Marinbrod HR 152 Gb60
Marine d'Albo F 154 Cc68
Marine de Sisco F 154 Cc68
Marinella I 166 Eb85
Marineo I 166 Ec84
Marines E 54 Fb67
Marines F 23 Gc36
Maringues F 34 Hc46
Marinha das Ondas P 44 Ac64
Marinha Grande P 44 Ab65
Marini I 165 Hc78
Marinka BG 181 Ed73
Marinkainen FIN 81 Jc27
Marino I 160 Eb72
Mar'insko RUS 99 Ld43
Mariotto I 162 Gc74
Maripérez E 53 Eb69
Marișel RO 171 Cd58
Marișelu RO 171 Dc57
Maritsá GR 197 Fa93
Mariupol' UA 205 Fb16
Marjaliza E 52 Db67
Märjamaa EST 98 Kb44
Marjan BG 180 Ea71
Marjanci HR 152 Hb59
Marjaniemi FIN 74 Jd24
Marjokylä FIN 75 Lc23
Marjoniemi FIN 90 Kc36
Marjoperä FIN 81 Jd30
Marjovaara FIN 83 Ma30
Marjusaari FIN 81 Jd29
Mark S 79 Ga26
Marka N 71 Fb18
Marka S 102 Fa47
Märkalne LV 107 Lc48
Markaryd S 110 Fa53
Markby FIN 81 Jb29
Mark Cross GB 20 Fd29
Markdorf D 142 Cd52
Markelo NL 117 Bd36
Market Bosworth GB 16 Fa24
Market Deeping GB 17 Fc24
Market Drayton GB 15 Ec23
Market Harborough GB 20 Fb25
Markethill GB 9 Cd18
Market Rasen GB 17 Fc22
Market Weighton GB 16 Fb20
Markfield GB 16 Fa24
Markgröningen D 134 Cd48
Markhausen D 117 Cb34
Marki PL 130 Jb36
Markina-Xemein E 39 Eb55
Märkisch-Buchholz D 128 Fa38
Markitta S 68 Hc17
Markivka UA 203 Fb14
Markkina FIN 68 Hd13
Markkleeberg D 127 Eb40
Markkula FIN 81 Jd27
Marklkofen D 135 Eb49
Marklohe D 118 Da35
Marklowice PL 137 Hb44
Marknesse NL 117 Bc34
Markneukirchen D 135 Eb43
Marko CY 206 Jc97
Markoldendorf D 126 Db38
Markop N 63 Ja06
Markópoulo GR 195 Cc87
Markovac SRB 174 Bb65
Markovac SRB 174 Bc65
Markovac SRB 174 Bd63
Markovo BG 180 Db73
Markovo BG 181 Ed70
Markovščina SLO 151 Fa59
Markov Sušica MK 178 Bb73
Markowa PL 139 Ka44
Markowice PL 121 Ha35
Markowo PL 122 Hd31
Markranstädt D 127 Eb40
Markszewo PL 122 Jb32
Marksuhl D 126 Db41
Markt Allhau A 145 Gb54
Marktbergel D 134 Db46
Markt Berolzheim D 134 Dc48
Markt Bibart D 134 Db45
Marktbreit D 134 Db45
Markt Einersheim D 134 Db45
Markt Erlbach D 134 Dc46
Marktgraitz D 135 Dd44
Marktheidenfeld D 134 Da45
Markt Indersdorf D 143 Dd50
Marktjärn S 87 Ga32
Marktl D 143 Ec50
Marktleugast D 135 Ea44
Marktleuthen D 135 Eb44
Markt Nordheim D 134 Db46
Marktoberdorf D 142 Db52
Marktoffingen D 134 Db48
Markt Piesting A 145 Gb52
Marktredwitz D 135 Eb45
Markt Rettenbach D 142 Db51
Marktrodach D 135 Dd44
Markt Sankt Florian A 144 Fb51
Markt Sankt Martin A 145 Gb53
Marktschorgast D 135 Ea44
Markt Schwaben D 143 Ea51
Marktsteft D 134 Db45
Marktzeuln D 135 Dd44
Markušica HR 153 Hc60
Markušovce SK 138 Jb48
Markutiškiai LT 114 Kc56
Markvarec CZ 136 Fd48
Marl D 125 Ca38
Marlborough GB 20 Ed28
Marle F 24 Hc34
Marlenheim F 25 Kb37
Marlishausen D 127 Dd42
Marloes GB 18 Db27
Marlow D 119 Ec31
Marlow GB 20 Fb28
Marly F 25 Jd35
Marly-Gomont F 24 Hc33
Marma S 96 Gc40
Marmagne F 30 Ja43
Marmande F 32 Fd51
Mármara GR 196 Db90
Marmara TR 185 Ed79
Marmaracık TR 186 Fa77
Marmaraereğlisi TR 186 Fa78
Marmári GR 190 Cd86
Marmári GR 197 Ec91
Marmaris TR 197 Fa91
Mármaro GR 191 Dd85
Marmav S 87 Gb37
Marmelete P 58 Ab73
Marmolejo E 52 Da72
Marmorbyn S 95 Ga44
Marmore I 156 Eb69
Marmoutier F 25 Kb36
Marnand CH 141 Bb54
Marnäs S 87 Fd38
Marnay F 31 Jc41
Marne D 118 Da31
Mårnes N 71 Fb18
Marnheim D 133 Cb45
Marnitz D 119 Eb33
Marnoch GB 7 Ec08
Maro E 60 Db76
Marœuil F 23 Ha32
Maroilles F 24 Hc32
Marola I 149 Da63
Maroldsweisach D 134 Dc44
Marolles-les-Braults F 28 Fd39
Maron F 25 Jd37
Maroñas E 36 Ac55
Marónia GR 184 Dc77
Maroslele H 153 Jc57
Marostica I 150 Dd59
Marotta I 156 Ec65
Maroufenha P 58 Ab72
Marovac KSV 178 Bc71
Marpingen D 133 Bd46
Marple GB 16 Ed21
Marpod RO 175 Db61
Marquartstein D 143 Eb52
Marquion F 23 Ha32
Marquise F 21 Gc30
Marradi I 156 Dd64
Marrasjärvi FIN 69 Jd17
Marraskoski FIN 74 Jd18
Marrault F 30 Hd41
Marrazes P 44 Ab65
Marrebæk DK 109 Eb29
Marroquin-Encina Hermosa E 60 Db73
Marroule F 33 Gd51
Marrubiu I 169 Bd78
Marrum NL 117 Bc32
Marrupe E 46 Cd65
Marsaglia I 149 Cc62
Marsais F 32 Fb46
Marsala I 166 Ea85
Maršal'skoe RUS 113 Ja58
Marșani RO 175 Db67
Maršavicy RUS 107 Mb48
Marsberg D 126 Cd39
Marschacht D 118 Dc33
Marsciano I 156 Ea68
Marsden GB 16 Ed21
Marseillan F 41 Hc55
Marseillan-Plage F 41 Hc55
Marseille F 42 Jc55
Marseille-en-Beauvaisis F 23 Gc34
Marsh GB 19 Eb30
Marshfield GB 19 Ec28
Marsh Gibbon GB 20 Fb27
Marsia I 156 Ed68
Marsiconuovo I 161 Ga76
Marsicovetere I 161 Ga76
Marsiliana I 155 Dc69
Marsjärv S 73 Hd19
Marske-by-the-Sea GB 11 Fb18
Mars-la-Tour F 25 Jc35
Mårslet DK 108 Dc24
Mårsliden S 71 Fd24
Mārsnēni LV 106 Kd48
Marson F 24 Hd36
Marssac-sur-Tarn F 41 Gd53
Marssum NL 117 Bc33
Märsta S 96 Gd42
Marstal DK 109 Dd28
Marston GB 16 Fb23
Marston Magna GB 19 Ec29
Marstrand S 102 Eb48
Marstrup DK 108 Db27
Marsvinsholm S 110 Fa56
Märsylä FIN 81 Jc27
Marszów PL 128 Fd39
Marta I 156 Dd69
Martainville F 23 Gb35
Martanesh AL 182 Ac74
Martano I 163 Hc77
Martebo S 104 Ha49
Martel F 33 Gc50
Martelange B 132 Ba44
Mártély H 146 Jb56
Marten BG 180 Ea68
Mårtensboda S 80 Hc26
Martfeld D 118 Da35
Martfű H 146 Jb54
Mártha GR 201 Db96
Marthon F 32 Fd47
Martiago E 45 Bd64
Martignas-sur-Jalle F 32 Fb50
Martigné F 28 Fb39
Martigné-Briand F 28 Fc42
Martigné-Ferchaud F 28 Fa40
Martigny CH 148 Bc57
Martigny-le-Comte F 30 Ja44
Martigny-les-Bains F 31 Jc39
Martigny-lès-Gerbonvaux F 31 Jc38
Martigues F 42 Jc54
Martilla FIN 97 Jc39
Martim Longo P 58 Ad73
Martin SK 138 Hc47
Martina CH 142 Db55
Martina Franca I 162 Ha75
Martiñán E 36 Bc54
Martin Brod BIH 152 Gb63
Martinci SRB 153 Ja61
Martinci Čepinski HR 153 Hc59
Martin de la Jara E 60 Cc75
Martín del Río E 47 Fa63
Martin de Yeltes E 45 Ca63
Martin Drove End GB 20 Ed30
Martinești RO 175 Cd61
Martinet E 40 Gc58
Martingança P 44 Ab65
Mărtiniș RO 176 Dd60
Martín Muñoz de las Posadas E 46 Da62
Martinniemi FIN 74 Jd23
Martíno GR 189 Ca84
Martinsberg A 144 Fd50
Martinšćica HR 151 Fb62
Martinsheim D 134 Db46
Martinsicuro I 157 Fa68
Martinskj HR 151 Fa61
Martinstown GB 9 Da16
Martizay F 29 Gb44
Martletwy GB 18 Db27
Martley GB 15 Ec25
Martna EST 98 Ka44
Martock GB 19 Eb30
Martofte DK 109 Dd26
Martonoš SRB 153 Jb57
Martonvaara FIN 83 Lc29
Martonvásár H 146 Hc53
Martorell E 49 Gd61
Martos E 60 Db73
Martragny F 22 Fb35
Martron F 32 Fc49
Mårtsbo S 96 Gc39
Mårtsviken S 86 Fa38
Martti FIN 69 Kc15
Marttila FIN 90 Kc37
Marttila FIN 98 Ka39
Martužāni LV 107 Ld50
Maruflar TR 191 Ec84
Marugán E 46 Da63
Maruggio I 162 Ha76
Marum NL 117 Bd33
Marum S 102 Fa47
Marunowo PL 121 Gb35
Mărunței RO 175 Db66
Mārupe LV 106 Kb51
Maruševec HR 152 Gb57
Maruszów PL 131 Jd40
Marvão P 51 Bb67
Marvejols F 34 Hc51
Marvik N 92 Cb42
Marville F 24 Jb34
Marwałd PL 122 Hd33
Marwitz D 127 Ed36
Marxzell D 133 Cb48
Märy FIN 97 Jc39
Marybank GB 4 Dd07
Maryfield GB 5 Fa05
Marykirk GB 7 Ec10
Marynowy PL 121 Hb30
Marypark GB 7 Eb08
Maryport GB 10 Ea17
Mary Tavy GB 19 Dd31
Marzabotto I 149 Dc63
Marzahna D 127 Ec38
Marzamemi I 167 Fd88
Marzán E 37 Cb56
Marzęcice PL 122 Hc33
Marzell D 141 Bd51
Marzell D 141 Ca51
Marzewo PL 122 Hd31
Marzoa E 36 Ba55
Marzocca I 156 Ed66
Masa E 38 Dc57
Masahoca TR 191 Ed83
Masari CY 206 Ja96
Masarolis I 150 Ed57
Masboquera E 48 Ga63
Mascali I 167 Fd85
Mascalucia I 167 Fc85
Mascaraque E 52 Db66
Mas-Carbadès F 41 Ha55
Mas de Barberans E 48 Fd63
Mas de las Matas E 48 Fc63
Masegosa E 47 Ec64
Masegoso E 53 Eb70
Masegoso de Tajuña E 47 Ea63
Maselheim D 142 Da50
Måsenes N 64 Jc06
Maser I 150 Ea58
Masera I 148 Ca57
Masevaux F 31 Kb40
Masfjorden N 84 Ca38
Mas-Grenier F 40 Gb53
Masham GB 11 Fa19
Maside E 36 Ba57
Masi Måze N 63 Ja10
Maskaur S 72 Gc22
Maskjok N 64 Ka06
Masku FIN 97 Jb39
Maslacq F 39 Fb55
Maslarevo BG 180 Dd69
Masléon F 33 Gc47
Maslinica HR 158 Gb67
Masloc RO 174 Bd60
Maslovare BIH 152 Ha63
Masłowice PL 130 Hd41
Masłowo PL 129 Gc38
Mas-Neuf-sur-Orb F 41 Hb53
Maso FIN 82 Kb31
Maso Corto I 142 Dc55
Masoúri GR 197 Eb90
Måsøy N 64 Jb04
Masquefa E 49 Gd61
Massa I 155 Da64
Massa d'Albe I 160 Ed71
Massa Finalese I 149 Dc61
Massa Fiscaglia I 150 Ea62
Massafra I 162 Gd76
Massagette F 33 Ha47
Massais F 28 Fc43
Massa Lombarda I 150 Dd63
Massa Lubrense I 161 Fb76
Massamagrell E 54 Fc67
Massa Marittima I 155 Db67
Massa Martana I 156 Eb68
Massarosa I 155 Da65
Massat F 40 Gb56
Massay F 29 Gd42
Maßbach D 134 Db44
Massenbachhausen D 134 Cd47
Masserano I 148 Ca59
Masserberg D 135 Dd43
Masseret F 33 Gc48
Masseria I 143 Dd55
Masseria Airili I 161 Fd73
Masseria Anzani I 162 Gb73
Masseria Candelaro I 161 Ga72
Masseria Cangiulli I 162 Gc75
Masseria Monaco Cappelli I 161 Ga72
Masseria Montanaro I 162 Gd75
Masseria Motta Panetteria I 161 Fd72
Masseria Petrulli I 161 Fd72
Masseria Stimpato I 167 Fc86
Masseube F 40 Ga55
Massford GB 9 Da18
Massiac F 34 Hb48
Massiaru EST 106 Kc47
Massignac F 33 Ga47
Massing D 143 Ec50
Massoult F 30 Ja40

Massu – Metamórfosi

Massu EST 98 Ka45
Măstăcani RO 177 Fb62
Mästerby S 104 Gd50
Masterelv N 63 Ja06
Mastergeehy IRL 12 Ba25
Masterud N 94 Ec41
Mas Thibert F 42 Jb54
Mastholte D 126 Cc38
Mastihári GR 197 Eb91
Mästocka S 110 Ed53
Masty BY 202 Dd13
Masua I 169 Bd79
Masugnsbyn S 68 Hd16
Mašun SLO 151 Fb59
Måsvik N 62 Gc08
Maszewko PL 121 Gd29
Maszewo PL 120 Fc33
Maszewo PL 128 Fc38
Mata E 38 Db55
Mata E 38 Dc57
Mata P 50 Ac66
Matabuena E 46 Dc62
Mata de Alcántara E 51 Bc66
Matala FIN 74 Jd21
Mátala GR 200 Cd96
Matalalahti FIN 82 Kd28
Matalascañas E 59 Bc75
Matalebreras E 47 Ec60
Matallana E 37 Cc58
Matamala de Almazán E 47 Ea61
Matamorisca E 38 Db56
Matamorosa E 38 Db56
Matanza E 37 Cc58
Mataporquera E 38 Db56
Matapozuelos E 46 Cd61
Matara FIN 83 Lb28
Matarága GR 188 Ba84
Mataramäki FIN 90 Kd32
Mataránga GR 189 Bc81
Mataró E 49 Ha61
Mataruge MNE 159 Ja67
Mataruška Banja SRB 178 Ba67
Mătăsari RO 175 Cc64
Mätäsvaara FIN 83 Lc28
Mątawy PL 121 Hb33
Matca RO 177 Fa62
Matching Green GB 20 Fd27
Matcze PL 131 Kd40
Mateeşti RO 175 Da63
Matei RO 171 Db57
Matejče MK 178 Bc72
Matelica I 156 Ec67
Matera I 162 Gc75
Materija SLO 151 Fa59
Mateševo MNE 159 Jb68
Mátészalka H 147 Kb51
Mateus P 44 Bb61
Matfors S 87 Gb33
Matha F 32 Fc47
Mathi I 148 Bc59
Mathiatis CY 206 Jb97
Mathieu F 22 Fc35
Mathildedal FIN 97 Jc40
Mathopen N 84 Ca39
Matienzo E 38 Dd55
Matignon F 26 Ec38
Matigny F 23 Ha33
Matilda FIN 97 Jc40
Matilla de los Caños del Río E 45 Cb63
Matinella I 161 Fd76
Matiši LV 106 Kd48
Matka MK 178 Bb73
Matkaniva FIN 82 Ka26
Matkavaara FIN 75 La24
Matku FIN 89 Jd37
Matkule LV 105 Jd51
Matlaukys LT 114 Ka59
Matlock GB 16 Fa22
Mătnica BG 181 Ec70
Mato E 36 Bb54
Matojärvi S 73 Jb20
Matos P 50 Ad71
Matosinhos P 44 Ac61
Matour F 34 Ja45
Mátraderecske H 146 Jb51
Mátrafüred H 146 Ja52
Mátraterenye H 146 Ja51
Matre N 92 Cb41
Matrei A 143 Eb54
Matrei am Brenner A 143 Dd54
Matrei in Osttirol A 143 Eb55
Matrice I 161 Fc72
Matrosovo RUS 113 Ja58
Matrosovo RUS 113 Jb57
Matsalu EST 98 Ka45
Matsdal S 71 Fd23
Matsi EST 106 Ka46
Matsoúki GR 188 Ba83
Matteröd S 110 Fa54
Mattersburg A 145 Gb52
Mattila FIN 89 Jb33
Mattila FIN 90 Kc38
Mattila FIN 91 Lc34
Mattilanmäki FIN 69 Kc17
Mattilanperä FIN 81 Jd25
Mattinata I 162 Gb72
Mattinen FIN 89 Ja38
Mattisudden S 72 Ha19
Mattmar S 79 Fb30
Mattnäs FIN 97 Ja40
Mattsee A 143 Ec51
Mattsund S 73 Hd22
Matuizos LT 114 Kd59
Matveev Kurgan RUS 205 Fc15
Mátyásdomb H 145 Hb55
Matzaccara I 169 Bd80
Maubeuge F 24 Hc32
Mauborget CH 141 Bb54
Maubourguet F 40 Fd55
Maubuisson F 32 Fa49
Mauchline GB 10 Dd14
Mauerkirchen A 143 Ed51
Mauern D 135 Ea49
Maughold GB 10 Dd18
Mauguio F 41 Hd54
Maukkula FIN 83 Ma30
Maula FIN 74 Jc21
Maulbronn D 134 Cc47
Maulburg D 141 Ca52
Maulde F 24 Hb31
Maule F 23 Gc37
Mauléon F 28 Fb43
Mauléon-Barousse F 40 Ga56
Mauléon-Licharre F 39 Fa55
Maulévrier F 28 Fb43
Mauls I 143 Dd55
Maumusson F 28 Fa41
Maunola FIN 91 Lb35
Maunu S 68 Hd13
Maunujärvi FIN 69 Jd16
Maunula FIN 74 Ka22
Mauperthuis F 23 Ha37
Mauprévoir F 33 Ga46
Maura N 85 Ea40
Maurach A 143 Ed54
Maure-de-Bretagne F 27 Ec40
Mauriac F 33 Gd49
Maurnes N 66 Fd12
Mauron F 27 Ec39
Maurrin F 40 Fc53
Maurs F 33 Gd50
Maurstad N 84 Cb34
Mauru FIN 74 Ka20
Mauručiai LT 114 Kc58
Mauruciems LV 105 Jb49
Maurumaa FIN 89 Ja38
Maurvangen N 85 Db36
Maury F 41 Ha57
Maussane F 42 Jb53
Mauterndorf A 144 Fa54
Mautern in Steiermark A 144 Fc53
Mauth D 136 Fa48
Mauthausen A 144 Fb50
Mauthen, Kötschach- A 143 Ec56
Mauvezin F 40 Fd56
Mauvezin F 40 Ga54
Mauvoisin CH 148 Bc57
Mauzé-sur-le-Mignon F 32 Fb46
Mevagissey GB 18 Db32
Mavas sameviste S 71 Ga18
Mavikent TR 199 Gc93
Mavranéi GR 182 Ba79
Mavréli GR 183 Bc80
Mavrodin RO 180 Dd67
Mavrohóri GR 183 Bb78
Mavromáta GR 188 Bb82
Mavromáti GR 188 Bb81
Mavromáti GR 194 Bb88
Mavrommáti GR 189 Ca85
Mavronéri GR 183 Ca77
Mavropigí GR 183 Bb78
Mavroúda GR 184 Cc77
Mavrovi Anovi MK 182 Ba74
Mavrovo MK 182 Ba74
Mavrovoúni GR 189 Bc81
Mavrovoúni GR 194 Bc90
Maxdorf D 133 Cb46
Maxent F 27 Ec40
Maxey-sur-Meuse F 31 Jc38
Maxey-sur-Vaise F 25 Jc37
Maxhütte-Haidhof D 135 Eb47
Maxieira P 50 Ad66
Măxineni RO 177 Fa63
Maxmo FIN 81 Ja30
Mayalde E 45 Cb61
Maybole GB 10 Dc15
Mayen D 133 Bd43
May-en-Multien F 23 Ha36
Mayenne F 28 Fb39
Mayerling A 145 Gb51
Mayet F 28 Fd40
Mayfield GB 16 Ed23
Mayfield GB 20 Fd30
Maynooth IRL 13 Cd21
Mayobridge GB 9 Da18
Mayorga E 37 Cc58
Mäyränperä FIN 82 Ka26
Mayreville F 41 Gd55
Mayrhofen A 143 Ea54
Mäyry FIN 81 Jc31
Máza H 152 Hb57
Mazagón E 59 Bb74
Mazaleón E 48 Fd62
Mazamet F 41 Ha54
Mazan-l'Abbaye F 34 Hd50
Mazara del Vallo I 166 Ea85
Mazarambroz E 52 Db67
Mazarete E 47 Eb63
Mazargan F 24 Hd35
Mazarrón E 55 Ed74
Mazarulleque E 47 Ea65
Mazaterón E 47 Ec61
Mazé F 28 Fc41
Mažeikiai LT 113 Jd53
Mazeley F 31 Jd38
Maženiai LT 114 Kc55
Mazères F 40 Gc55
Mazerny F 24 Hd34
Mazgramzda LV 113 Jb53
Mazières-en-Gâtine F 28 Fc44
Mazières-lès-Metz F 25 Jd35
Mazıköy TR 197 Ed90
Mazille F 34 Ja45
Mazilmaja LV 105 Jb52
Mazin HR 151 Ga63
Mazirbe LV 105 Jc48
Mažonai LT 113 Jd56
Mazotos CY 206 Jc98
Mazsalaca LV 106 Kc47
Mażucie PL 123 Jd30
Mažučište MK 183 Bb75
Mazuela E 38 Dc58
Mažurani HR 151 Fd63
Mazury PL 123 Ka34
Mazury PL 139 Ka43
Mazy B 124 Ad41
Mazyr BY 202 Eb13
Mazzarino I 167 Fa86
Mazzarò I 167 Fd85
Mazzarrà Sant'Andrea I 167 Fd84
Mcensk RUS 203 Fa12
Mchowo PL 122 Jb34
Mchy PL 129 Gc38
Mda RUS 99 Lc45
Mdzewo PL 122 Ja34
Méailles F 43 Kb52
Mealhada P 44 Ad63
Mealsgate GB 11 Eb17
Meana Sardo I 169 Ca77
Méaudre F 35 Jc49
Meaulne F 29 Ha44
Meaux F 23 Ha36
Meauzac F 40 Gb53
Mébecq F 29 Gb44
Mecca I 148 Bc59
Mechelen B 124 Ac40
Mechernich D 125 Bc42
Měcholupy CZ 135 Ed44
Mechowo PL 120 Fc32
Mecidiye TR 185 Eb78
Mecidiye TR 191 Ed84
Mecidiye TR 192 Fa82
Mecidiye TR 193 Gb84
Męcikał PL 121 Gd32
Měčín CZ 135 Ed46
Męcina PL 138 Jb45
Męcinka PL 128 Ga41
Mecitözü TR 205 Fb20
Mečka BG 180 Db69
Mečka BG 180 Ea68
Meckenbeuren D 142 Cd52
Meckenheim D 125 Bd42
Meckenheim/Pfalz D 133 Cb46
Meckesheim D 134 Cc46
Meco E 46 Dd64
Mecseknádasd H 153 Hc57
Męczki PL 123 Ka33
Meda I 149 Cc58
Meda SRB 174 Bc61
Meda P 45 Bc62
Medak HR 151 Fd63
Medåker S 95 Fd43
Medas BIH 153 Hd63
Medaši BIH 153 Ja61
Médavy F 22 Fd37
Medbourne GB 16 Fb24
Medby N 66 Fd12
Medby N 67 Gb11
Meddon GB 18 Dc30
Mede I 148 Cb60
Medebach D 126 Cc40
Međeđa BIH 159 Ja65
Medeikiai LT 114 Kd53
Medeiros E 44 Bb59
Medelås S 80 Gc25
Medelim P 44 Bb65
Medellín E 51 Ca69
Medelplana S 102 Fa46
Medemblik NL 116 Ba34
Medena-Selišta BIH 158 Gc64
Medeni Poljani BG 184 Cd74
Meden Kladenec BG 180 Eb73
Medeno polje BIH 152 Gb63
Medesano I 149 Da62
Medet TR 198 Fc89
Medevi S 103 Fc46
Medgidia RO 181 Fb67
Medgyesegyháza H 147 Jd56
Medhamn S 95 Fb44
Mediana E 48 Fb61
Mediaş RO 175 Db60
Medicina I 150 Dd63
Médière F 31 Ka41
Medieşu Aurit RO 171 Cd54
Medinaceli E 47 Eb62
Medina de las Torres E 51 Bd70
Medina del Campo E 46 Cd61
Medina de Pomar E 38 Dd56
Medina de Rioseco E 46 Cd59
Medina Sidonia E 59 Bd77
Medinci HR 152 Ha59
Medingėnai LT 113 Jc55
Medininkai LT 115 Lb58
Medinyà E 49 Hb59
Mediona E 49 Gc61
Medīševa LV 107 Ld50
Medjuhana SRB 178 Bc69
Medkovec BG 179 Cc68
Medle S 80 Hc25
Medņi LV 107 Lc49
Medovo BG 181 Ed72
Medovo BG 181 Fa69
Médréac F 27 Ec39
Mędrzechów PL 138 Jc43
Medskogen S 86 Ed33
Medstugan S 78 Ed29
Medulin HR 151 Fa62
Medumi LV 115 Lb54
Meduno I 150 Ec57
Međurečje SRB 178 Ad67
Međurić HR 152 Gc60
Međurječje MNE 159 Ja68
Meduši, Star. RUS 99 Ma40
Međuvođe BIH 152 Gc61
Medvedja SRB 174 Bc66
Medvedja SRB 178 Bc70
Medveď'ov SK 145 Ha52
Medveja HR 151 Fb60
Medveja MD 172 Ed53
Medvenka RUS 203 Fa13
Medvida HR 157 Ga64
Medvode SLO 151 Fb57
Medyka PL 139 Kc44
Medynia Głogowska PL 139 Ka43
Medze LV 105 Ja52
Medzev SK 138 Jc48
Medzilaborce SK 139 Ka46
Medžitlija MK 183 Bb76
Meeder D 134 Dc43
Meek N 77 Da31
Meenlaragh IRL 8 Ca15
Meerane D 127 Eb42
Meerapalu EST 99 Lc45
Meerbusch D 125 Bd39
Meerhout B 124 Ba39
Meerkerk NL 124 Ba37
Meerle B 124 Ad38
Meersburg D 142 Cd52
Meeth GB 19 Dd30
Meeuwen-Gruitrode B 124 Ba40
Mefjordvær N 62 Gb10
Méga Dério GR 185 Ea76
Méga Eleftherohóri GR 183 Bc80
Méga Kefalóvriso GR 188 Bb81
Megála GR 188 Bb81
Megáli Kápsi GR 188 Bb83
Megáli Panagía GR 184 Cc78
Megáli Stérna GR 183 Ca76
Megáli Vríssi GR 183 Ca76
Megalóhari GR 188 Ba82
Megalohóri GR 188 Bb81
Megalohóri GR 195 Ca88
Megálo Horió GR 197 Eb89
Megálo Horió GR 197 Ec92
Mégalo Livádi GR 195 Cd89
Megalópoli GR 194 Bb88
Méga Peristéri GR 182 Ba80
Mégara GR 189 Ca86
Megården N 66 Fd17
Mégaro GR 182 Ba79
Méga Spíleo GR 189 Bc86
Megeces E 46 Da61
Megève F 35 Ka46
Meggenhofen A 144 Fa51
Megísti GR 198 Ga93
Megrunn N 85 Dc36
Megyaszó H 147 Jd50
Mehadia RO 174 Cb64
Mehadica RO 174 Ca63
Mehamn N 64 Ka04
Mehedeby S 96 Gc40
Mehikoorma EST 99 Lc45
Mehlis, Zella- D 126 Dc42
Mehmed Paša = Sokolovici BIH 159 Hd64
Mehmetalanı TR 191 Ec82
Mehren D 133 Bd43
Mehring D 133 Bc44
Mehring D 143 Ec51
Mehringen D 127 Ea39
Mehrnbach A 143 Ed51
Mehrstetten D 142 Cd50
Mehtäkylä FIN 81 Jc26
Mehtäperä FIN 81 Jd27
Mehun-sur-Yèvre F 29 Gd42
Meiåvollen N 86 Eb32
Meiden CH 141 Bd56
Meidrim GB 14 Dc26
Meifod GB 15 Eb24
Meijel NL 125 Bb39
Meijerinkylä FIN 82 Ka25
Meilán E 36 Bc54
Meilen CH 141 Cb53
Meillant F 29 Ha44
Meillerie F 31 Kb44
Meillers F 30 Hb44
Meilūnai LT 114 Kd56
Meimoa P 45 Bc64
Meina I 148 Cb58
Meine D 126 Dc36
Meineringhausen D 126 Cd40
Meinersen D 126 Dc36
Meinerzhagen D 125 Ca40
Meinhard D 126 Db40
Meiningen D 126 Dc42
Meinkenbracht D 125 Cb40
Meira E 36 Bc54
Meirāni LV 107 Lb50
Meirás E 36 Ba53
Meiringen CH 141 Ca55
Meisburg D 133 Bc43
Meisenheim D 133 Ca45
Meisingset N 77 Db31
Meißen D 127 Ed41
Meißner D 126 Db40
Meitene LV 106 Kb52
Meitingen D 134 Dc49
Meixdevant-Virton B 132 Ba45
Meixedo P 44 Bb59
Meixide P 44 Bb59
Mejlby DK 100 Dc23
Mejorada E 46 Cd65
Mejrup Kirkeby DK 100 Da23
Męka PL 129 Hb39
Mekece TR 187 Gb79
Mekényes H 145 Hb56
Mekinjar HR 151 Ga63
Mekrijärvi FIN 83 Ma29
Mel I 150 Ea58
Mel N 84 Cc36
Melá GR 190 Da84
Melaje SRB 178 Ad69
Melalahti FIN 82 La30
Melalahti FIN 82 Kd25
Mélambes GR 200 Cd96
Meland N 63 Hd06
Meland N 84 Ca38
Melaniós GR 191 Dd85
Melánthio GR 182 Ba78
Melás GR 182 Ba77
Melates GR 188 Ad82
Melay F 34 Hd45
Melbārži LV 106 La49
Melbeck D 118 Dc34
Melbourn GB 20 Fd26
Melbourne GB 16 Fa23
Melbu N 66 Fc13
Melby DK 109 Eb25
Melč CZ 137 Ha45
Melchsee Frutt CH 141 Ca55
Meldal N 77 Dd31
Meldola I 156 Ea64
Meldorf D 118 Da31
Meldzere LV 105 Jc52
Melegnano I 149 Cc60
Melekçeoruç TR 187 Gb79
Melen N 78 Ec26
Melenci SRB 153 Jc59
Melendugno I 163 Hc77
Melenki RUS 203 Fb10
Meleski EST 98 La45
Melesse F 28 Ed39
Meleti I 149 Cd60
Meletovo RUS 107 Ma46
Melfi I 161 Ga74
Melfjorden N 71 Fb20
Melfort GB 6 Db12
Melgaço P 36 Ba58
Melgar de Arriba E 37 Cd58
Melgar de Fernamental E 38 Db58
Melgar de Yuso E 38 Db58
Melgarve GB 7 Dd09
Melholt DK 101 Dd21
Melhus N 77 Ea30
Meliana E 54 Fc67
Mélida E 39 Ed58
Melide CH 148 Cb58
Melide E 36 Ba55
Melides P 50 Ab70
Meligalás GR 194 Bb88
Melíki GR 183 Bb78
Melilli I 167 Fd87
Melineşti RO 175 Cd65
Meling N 92 Ca44
Melini CY 206 Jb97
Mélisey F 31 Ka40
Mélissa GR 189 Bd81
Melissa I 165 Gd81
Melissohóri GR 183 Ca77
Melissohóri GR 189 Ca85
Melissópetra GR 182 Ad79
Melissótopos GR 183 Bb77
Melissourgós GR 184 Cc78
Melíti GR 183 Bb77
Melitopol' UA 205 Fa16
Melito Porto Salvo I 164 Ga84
Melívia GR 183 Ca80
Melívia GR 184 Db76
Melk A 144 Fd51
Melkarlia N 71 Fb23
Melkas LV 106 Kc47
Melkkola FIN 91 Lb36
Melkoniemi FIN 91 Ld34
Melksham GB 19 Ec28
Mellanjärvi FIN 74 Jc19
Mellakoski FIN 74 Jc19
Mellanfjärden S 88 Gc35
Mellansel S 80 Gd30
Mellansjö S 80 Ha28
Mellanström S 72 Gc22
Mellanzos E 37 Cc57
Mellau A 142 Da53
Mellby S 102 Ed46
Mellby S 103 Fc49
Mellbystrand S 110 Ed53
Melle D 126 Cc37
Melle F 32 Fc45
Melle I 148 Bc62
Mellen D 119 Ea34
Mellensee D 127 Ed37
Mellerud S 94 Ec45
Mellilä FIN 89 Jc38
Mellin D 127 Dd36
Mellinghausen D 118 Cd35
Mellingsmoen N 70 Fa24
Mellionnec F 27 Ea39
Mello F 23 Gd35
Mellomstrand N 92 Ca45
Mellösa S 95 Gb44
Mellrichstadt D 134 Db43
Melmerby GB 11 Ec17
Melnica MK 183 Bc74
Melnica SRB 174 Bd65
Melnice HR 151 Fc61
Mělnické Vtelno CZ 136 Fc43
Mel'nicy RUS 99 Ld45
Melnik BG 184 Cc75
Mělník CZ 136 Fb43
Mel'nikovo RUS 113 Ja58
Melnrage LT 113 Jb55
Melnsils LV 105 Jc48
Melón E 36 Ba57
Melouseia CY 206 Jc97
Meløysund N 71 Fb19
Meløyvær N 66 Ga11
Melrand F 27 Ea39
Melres P 44 Ad61
Melrose GB 11 Ec14
Mels CH 142 Cd54
Melsomvik N 93 Dd44
Melsted DK 111 Fc57
Melsträsk S 73 Hb24
Melsungen D 126 Da40
Melsvik N 63 Hd08
Meltaus FIN 69 Jd17
Meltham GB 16 Ed21
Melton Mowbray GB 16 Fb24
Meltosjärvi FIN 74 Jc19
Melun F 29 Ha38
Melvaig GB 4 Db06
Melvich GB 5 Ea04
Mélykút H 153 Ja57
Melzo I 149 Cc59
Memaliaj AL 182 Ab78
Membrilla E 52 Dc69
Membrillar E 38 Da57
Membrío E 51 Bc66
Memeceler TR 187 Gc80
Mēmele LV 106 Kd52
Memer F 41 Gd52
Memleben D 127 Ea40
Memmelsdorf D 134 Dc45
Memmingen D 142 Db51
Memória P 44 Ac65
Memucaj AL 182 Ab77
Mena UA 202 Ec13
Menaggio I 149 Cc57
Menai Bridge GB 15 Dd22
Mėnaičiai LV 114 Kb55
Menaldum NL 117 Bc33
Menàrguens E 48 Ga60
Menasalbas E 52 Da67
Menat F 34 Hb46
Menata I 150 Ea62
Menaza E 38 Db56
Menčiai LT 113 Jd53
Mencshely H 145 Ha55
Mendavia E 39 Eb58
Mende F 34 Hc51
Mendeleevsk RUS 203 Ga08
Menden D 125 Cb39
Mendenítsa GR 189 Bd84
Menderes TR 191 Ec86
Mendicino I 164 Gb80
Mendig D 133 Bd43
Mendiga P 50 Ab66
Mendigorría E 39 Ec57
Mendola I 166 Eb84
Ménéac F 27 Eb39
Menée F 35 Jc50
Menemen TR 191 Ec85
Menen B 21 Ha30
Menen B 124 Aa40
Meneou CY 206 Jc97
Ménerbes F 42 Jc53
Menesjärvi FIN 69 Jd11
Menestreau-en-Villette F 29 Gd40
Menetés GR 201 Eb95
Menetou-Salon F 29 Ha42
Ménétréol-sur-Sauldre F 29 Gd41
Menfi I 166 Eb85
Mengamuñoz E 46 Cd64
Mengara I 156 Eb67
Mengele LV 106 Kd51
Mengen D 142 Cd51
Mengen TR 205 Fa20
Mengerskirchen D 125 Cb42
Mengeš SLO 151 Fb57
Mengibar E 60 Db72
Mengiševo BG 180 Eb71
Mengkofen D 135 Eb49
Menidi GR 188 Ad82
Ménigoute F 32 Fc45
Ménil F 28 Fb40
Ménil-la-Tour F 25 Jc36
Menisjavri FIN 69 Jd11
Menkijärvi FIN 81 Jc31
Mennetou-sur-Cher F 29 Gc42
Mennogeia CY 206 Jb97
Menonen FIN 89 Jd37
Menouille F 31 Jc44
Mens F 35 Jd50
Menslage D 117 Cb35
Mensträsk S 72 Ha24
Menstrup DK 109 Ea27
Mentana I 160 Eb71
Menteroda D 126 Dc40
Menteş TR 191 Eb86
Menteş TR 193 Gb86
Menteşe TR 192 Fd81
Menteşe TR 198 Fb89
Menton F 43 Kd53
Mentoulles I 148 Bb60
Méntrida E 46 Da65
Menz D 119 Ed34
Menzelinsk RUS 203 Ga08
Meopham GB 20 Fd28
Méounes-les-Montrieux F 42 Ka55
Mepal GB 20 Fd25
Meppel NL 117 Bc35
Meppen D 117 Ca35
Mequinenza E 48 Fd61
Mer F 29 Gc41
Mera E 36 Bb53
Mera RO 176 Ed62
Meråker N 78 Ec30
Meran I 142 Dc55
Merano I 142 Dc55
Merás E 37 Ca54
Merasjärvi S 68 Hc16
Merate I 149 Cc58
Mercadillo E 38 Dd55
Mercadillo E 45 Cc63
Mercatello I 156 Eb68
Mercatello sul Metauro I 156 Ea66
Mercatino Conca I 156 Eb65
Mercato I 161 Fc75
Mercato San Severino I 161 Fc75
Mercato Saraceno I 156 Ea65
Merćez SRB 178 Bb69
Merching D 142 Dc50
Mercœur F 33 Gd49
Mercogliano I 161 Fc75
Mercues F 33 Gb51
Mercurey F 30 Ja43
Merdanja BG 180 Ea70
Merdare KSV 178 Bb70
Merdrignac F 27 Ec39
Mere GB 19 Ec29
Meré E 37 Cd54
Merefa UA 203 Fa14
Merei RO 176 Ec64
Meremäe EST 107 Lc47
Merendero E 36 Bb54
Mereni MD 173 Fc59
Mereni MD 173 Fd58
Mereni RO 180 Dd67
Mereni RO 181 Fb68
Merenlahti FIN 91 Lb36
Mereşeni MD 173 Fc59
Mereşti RO 176 Ea60
Mereworth GB 20 Fd29
Mergenli TR 198 Fb91
Merghndeal RO 175 Dc61
Mergozzo I 148 Ca57
Mēri LV 106 La48
Méribel F 35 Kb47
Meriç TR 185 Eb77
Meriçler TR 197 Ed89
Meričleri BG 180 Db73
Mérida E 51 Bd69
Mérignac F 32 Fb50
Mérignac F 32 Fc47
Mérignac F 32 Fc48
Mérihas GR 195 Cd89
Merijärvi FIN 81 Jd26
Merikarvia FIN 89 Ja35
Meriläinen FIN 81 Jd29
Merilänranta FIN 83 Ld28
Merimasku FIN 97 Ja39
Meřín CZ 136 Ga47
Mérindol F 42 Jc53
Mering D 142 Dc50
Meri-Pori FIN 89 Ja36
Merişani RO 175 Dc64
Mérk H 147 Kb51
Merkebekk N 93 Db44
Merkem B 21 Ha30
Merkendorf D 134 Dc47
Merkeşler TR 187 Hb78
Merkinė LT 123 Kc30
Merklín CZ 135 Ed46
Merklingen D 134 Da49
Merlevenez F 27 Ea40
Merlimont F 23 Gc31
Merlimont-Plage F 23 Gb31
Merlines F 33 Ha47
Mern DK 109 Eb28
Mernieki LV 106 Kb47
Mernye H 145 Ha56
Merone I 149 Cc58
Merošina SRB 178 Bb69
Merriott GB 19 Eb30
Merry-Sec F 30 Hc40
Mersch L 133 Bb44
Merschwitz D 127 Ed40
Merseburg D 127 Eb40
Mērsrags LV 105 Jd49
Mers-sur-Indre F 29 Gc44
Merstham GB 20 Fc29
Merstola FIN 89 Jb36
Mertajärvi S 68 Hd13
Mertala FIN 91 Lc33
Merthyr Cynog GB 15 Ea26
Merthyr Tydfil GB 19 Ea27
Merthyr Vale GB 19 Ea27
Mertingen D 134 Dc49
Mértola P 58 Ba72
Méru F 23 Gd35
Merufe P 36 Ad58
Mervans F 30 Jb43
Mervent F 28 Fb44
Merville F 23 Ha31
Méry-sur-Seine F 30 Hc38
Merza E 36 Ba56
Merzdorf D 127 Ed38
Merzen D 117 Cb36
Merzenich D 125 Bc41
Merzhausen D 141 Ca51
Merzifon TR 205 Fb20
Merzig (Saar) D 133 Bc45
Mesagne I 162 Hb76
Mesanagrós GR 197 Ed94
Mésandans F 31 Ka41
Mesão Frio P 44 Ba61
Mesariá GR 190 Da87
Mesas de Ibor E 51 Cb66
Meschede D 126 Cc40
Meschers-sur-Gironde F 32 Fa48
Mešeišta MK 182 Ba75
Meselefors S 79 Gb26
Meşelik TR 193 Hb85
Meşelik TR 197 Ed90
Meşendorf RO 176 Dd60
Meşeni MD 173 Fc56
Mesenikólas GR 188 Bb81
Meseşenii de Jos RO 171 Cd56
Meshaw GB 19 Dd29
Mesia E 36 Ba55
Mesiano I 164 Gb82
Mesić SRB 174 Bd63
Mesići BIH 159 Hd65
Mesihovina BIH 158 Gd66
Mesinge DK 109 Dd26
Meškalaukis LT 114 Kc54
Meskenvaara FIN 83 Ma30
Meškinė LT 113 Jc56
Mesklá GR 200 Cb95
Meškučiai LT 114 Kd59
Meškuičiai LT 114 Kb53
Meslan F 27 Dd39
Meslay-du-Maine F 28 Fb40
Meslon F 29 Ha44
Mesnali N 85 Ea37
Mešnik SRB 159 Jb65
Mesnil-Saint-Père F 30 Hd38
Mesnil-Sellières F 30 Hd38
Mesocco CH 142 Cc56
Mesogi CY 206 Hd98
Mesohóri GR 183 Bb76
Mesohóri GR 183 Bc80
Mesohóri GR 189 Bc82
Mesohóri GR 194 Bb89
Mesohória GR 190 Cd86
Mesola I 150 Ea61
Mesón do Vento E 36 Ba54
Mesones E 46 Dc63
Mesópirgos GR 188 Ba82
Mesopotamiá GR 182 Ba77
Mesopótamo GR 188 Ac81
Mesoraca I 165 Gd81
Mesorópi GR 184 Cd77
Mesóvouno GR 183 Bc77
Mespelbrunn D 134 Cd44
Mesquer F 27 Eb41
Messac F 28 Ed40
Messancy B 132 Ba45
Messanges F 39 Ed53
Messanges-Plage F 39 Ed53
Messaure S 73 Hb19
Meßdorf D 119 Ea35
Messeix F 33 Ha47
Messejana P 58 Ac72
Messelt N 86 Eb36
Méssi GR 184 Dc77
Messigny-et-Vantoux F 30 Jb41
Messina I 164 Ga83
Messingen D 117 Ca36
Messingham GB 16 Fb21
Messini GR 194 Bb89
Messinó GR 189 Bc86
Meßkirch D 142 Cc51
Messlingen S 86 Ed32
Messohóri GR 201 Eb95
Messolóngi GR 188 Ba84
Messongí GR 182 Ab80
Meßstetten D 142 Cc50
Mesta BG 184 Cc74
Mestá GR 191 Dd86
Mestanza E 52 Db70
Mestas E 37 Ca55
Městečko Trnávka CZ 137 Gc46
Městec Králové CZ 136 Fd44
Mestervik N 62 Gd10
Mésti GR 185 Dd77
Meštica BG 179 Cb71
Mestilä FIN 89 Jb37
Mestlin D 119 Eb33
Město Albrechtice CZ 137 Gd44
Město Libavá CZ 137 Gd45
Město Touškov CZ 135 Ed45
Mestre I 150 Ea60
Mesudiye TR 186 Fc80
Mesum D 117 Ca36
Mesutlar TR 199 Hb88
Mesvres F 30 Hd43
Mesztegnyő H 145 Gd56
Meta I 161 Fb75
Metajna HR 151 Fc63
Metallikó GR 183 Ca76
Metamórfosi GR 183 Bb78
Metamórfosi GR 189 Bc81
Metamórfosi GR 194 Ba89

Metamorfósi – Mo

Metamorfósi GR 195 Bd90
Metamórfossi GR 183 Ca76
Metamórfossi GR 184 Cc79
Metangitsi GR 184 Cc79
Meţaparks LV 106 Kb50
Metaurilia I 156 Ec65
Metaxádes GR 185 Ea76
Metaxás GR 183 Bc79
Metelen D 125 Ca37
Meteliai LT 114 Kc59
Meteş RO 175 Cd60
Méthamis F 42 Jc52
Méthana GR 195 Ca88
Metheringham GB 17 Fc22
Methil GB 7 Eb12
Methlick GB 5 Ed08
Methóni GR 194 Ba89
Methven GB 7 Ea11
Methwold GB 20 Fd25
Metković HR 158 Ha68
Metlič SRB 153 Ja62
Metličina BG 181 Ed69
Metlika SLO 151 Fd59
Metnitz A 144 Fb55
Mętno PL 120 Fb35
Metodievo BG 181 Ec70
Metóhi GR 189 Cb84
Metóhi GR 189 Cc84
Metovnica SRB 179 Ca67
Mętów PL 131 Kb40
Metsäkansa FIN 89 Jd36
Metsäkantano FIN 83 Lb27
Metsäkylä FIN 75 Kd22
Metsäkylä FIN 90 La37
Metsälä FIN 75 Kc21
Metsälä FIN 89 Ja34
Metsämaa FIN 89 Jc37
Metsä-Muuronen FIN 91 Lb37
Metsküla EST 97 Jc45
Metslawier NL 117 Bc32
Métsovo GR 182 Ba80
Mettä Dokkas S 68 Hc17
Mettäjärvi S 74 Jb18
Mettälä FIN 90 Kd37
Metten D 135 Ec48
Mettenheim D 133 Cb45
Mettenheim D 143 Eb50
Mettersdorf am Saßbach A 144 Ga55
Mettevoll N 63 Hb08
Mettingen D 117 Cb36
Mettlach D 133 Bc45
Mettlen CH 141 Ca54
Mettmann D 125 Bd40
Mettmenstetten CH 141 Cb53
Metveit N 93 Da46
Metz F 25 Jd35
Metzeral F 31 Kb39
Metzervisse F 25 Jd35
Metzingen D 134 Cd49
Meucon F 27 Eb40
Meulan F 23 Gc36
Meung-sur-Loire F 29 Gc40
Meursault F 30 Ja43
Meuse F 31 Jc39
Meuselwitz D 127 Eb41
Meussia F 31 Jc44
Meuzac F 33 Gb48
Mevassvika N 78 Ed26
Meximieux F 34 Jb46
Mey GB 5 Eb04
Meydancik TR 205 Ga18
Meyenburg D 118 Cd33
Meyenburg D 119 Eb33
Meymac F 33 Gd48
Meyrargues F 42 Jd53
Meyrueis F 41 Hc52
Meysee F 34 Jb50
Meysey Hampton GB 20 Ed27
Meyssac F 33 Gc49
Meyzieu F 34 Jb47
Mézapos GR 194 Bb91
Mežāre LV 107 Lb51
Mežatites LV 107 Lb51
Mežda BG 180 Ea73
Mežden BG 181 Ed68
Mezdra BG 179 Cd70
Meždureč'e RUS 113 Jc59
Meždurečje RUS 113 Jd58
Mèze F 41 Hc54
Mezek BG 185 Ea75
Meženin PL 123 Ka34
Mézeray F 28 Fc40
Mézérial F 34 Jb45
Mežica SLO 144 Fc56
Mézidon-Canon F 22 Fc36
Mézières-en-Brenne F 29 Gb43
Mézières-sur-Issoire F 33 Ga46
Mézilhac F 34 Ja50
Mézilles F 30 Hb40
Mezimĕstí CZ 137 Gb43
Mézin F 40 Fd53
Mezit TR 192 Ga81
Mezitler TR 192 Fb82
Mezőberény H 147 Jd55
Mezőcsát H 146 Jc51
Mezőfalva H 146 Hc55
Mezőhegyes H 147 Jd56
Mezőhék H 146 Jb54
Mezőkeresztes H 146 Jc51
Mezőkomárom H 145 Hb55
Mezőkovácsháza H 147 Jd56
Mezőkövesd H 146 Jc51
Mezőladany H 147 Kb50
Mezőörs H 145 Ha53
Mézos F 39 Fa52
Mézos F 39 Fa53
Mezőszilas H 146 Hc55
Mežotne LV 106 Kb52
Mezőtúr H 146 Jc54
Meževidi LV 107 Ld50
Mezzana I 149 Db57
Mezzano I 150 Ea63
Mezzojuso I 166 Ed85
Mezzoldo I 149 Cd57
Mezzolombardo I 149 Dc57
Mgarr M 166 Ea87
Miączyn PL 131 Kd41
Miajadas E 51 Ca68
Mialet F 33 Ga48
Mialet F 41 Hd52
Miały PL 120 Ga35
Mianowice PL 121 Gc30
Miasteczko Krajeńskie PL 121 Gc34
Miasteczko Śląskie PL 138 Hc43
Miastko PL 121 Gc31
Miastków Kościelny PL 131 Jd38
Miastkowo PL 123 Jd33
Miavaig GB 4 Cd05
Miazzina I 148 Cb57
Mica RO 171 Db57
Mica RO 171 Db59
Micaičiai LT 114 Ka54
Micăsasa RO 175 Db60
Micereces de Tera E 45 Cb59
Miceşti RO 175 Da60
Miceşti RO 175 Dc64
Miceştii de Câmpie RO 171 Db58
Michaelchurch Escley GB 15 Eb26
Michaelnbach A 144 Fa50
Michajlovskoe RUS 203 Fc09
Michal'any SK 139 Ka49
Michalin PL 121 Hb35
Michałkowo PL 122 Jb30
Michalová SK 138 Ja48
Michalovce SK 139 Ka48
Michałów PL 131 Kd42
Michałów PL 138 Jb43
Michałowice PL 129 Gd42
Michałowice PL 138 Ja44
Michałowo PL 123 Kc33
Michelau D 134 Db45
Michelbach A 144 Ga51
Michelbach D 134 Da47
Micheldorf in Oberösterreich A 144 Fb52
Michelfeld D 134 Da47
Michelsdorf D 127 Ec37
Michelsneukirchen D 135 Eb47
Michelstadt D 134 Cd45
Michendorf D 127 Ed37
Michery F 30 Hb38
Michnowce PL 123 Kb30
Michorzewo PL 129 Gb37
Michów PL 131 Ka39
Mičiči SRB 153 Ja63
Micılar TR 192 Fb82
Mickai LT 113 Jb55
Mickelsträsk S 80 Hb27
Mickhausen D 142 Dc50
Mickleton GB 11 Ed17
Micleşti MD 173 Fd57
Micleşti RO 173 Fb58
Micula RO 171 Cd54
Mičurin BG 186 Fa74
Mičurinsk RUS 203 Fb12
Midbea GB 5 Ec02
Middelbeers NL 124 Ba38
Middelburg NL 124 Ab38
Middelfart DK 108 Db26
Middelharnis NL 124 Ac37
Middelkerke B 21 Ha29
Middels D 117 Cb32
Middelstum NL 117 Bd33
Middenbeemster NL 116 Ba35
Middenmeer NL 116 Ba34
Middleham GB 11 Ed19
Middlemarsh GB 19 Ec30
Middle Rasen GB 17 Fc22
Middlesbrough GB 11 Fa18
Middleton GB 21 Gb25
Middleton in Teesdale GB 11 Ed17
Middleton-on-Sea GB 20 Fb30
Middleton-on-the-Wolds GB 16 Fb20
Middletown GB 9 Cc18
Middletown GB 15 Eb24
Middle Wallop GB 20 Ed29
Middlewich GB 15 Ec22
Midgeholme GB 11 Ec16
Midhurst GB 20 Fb30
Midıklı TR 192 Fc85
Midleton IRL 12 Bd26
Midlum D 108 Cd28
Midlum D 118 Cd32
Midrevaux F 31 Jc38
Midskog S 79 Fd30
Midsomer Norton GB 19 Ec29
Midsund N 76 Cd32
Midtgård N 65 Kd07
Midtre Fingervatn N 64 Ka06
Midtskogberget N 86 Ec37
Mid Yell GB 5 Fa03
Miechów PL 128 Fd36
Miechów PL 138 Ja43
Miechów-Charsznica PL 138 Ja43
Miechucino PL 121 Ha30
Miecze PL 123 Ka32
Miedes E 47 Ed62
Miedes de Atienza E 47 Ea62
Miedzichowo PL 128 Ga37
Miedzna PL 131 Jd36
Miedźno PL 130 Hc41
Międzybórz PL 129 Gd40
Międzybrodzie Bialskie PL 138 Hc45
Międzychód PL 128 Ga36
Międzygórze PL 137 Gc44
Międzyleś PL 131 Kc37
Międzylesie PL 137 Gc44
Międzyrzec Podlaski PL 131 Kb37
Międzyrzecz PL 128 Fd36
Międzywodzie PL 120 Fc31
Międzyzdroje PL 120 Fb32
Miegėnai LT 114 Kc55
Miehikkälä FIN 91 Lb37
Miehlen D 133 Ca43
Miejsce Piastowe PL 139 Ka45
Miejska Górka PL 129 Gc39
Miekak S 72 Gb18
Miękinia PL 129 Gc41
Miekojärvi S 73 Ja20
Miękowo PL 120 Fc33
Mielagėnai LT 115 Lc55
Miélan F 40 Fd55
Mielec PL 139 Jd43
Mielęcin PL 121 Gb34
Mielęcin PL 130 Hc36
Mielenko Drawskie PL 120 Ga33
Mieleszyn PL 129 Gd36
Mielnik PL 131 Kb36
Mielno PL 120 Fd33
Mielno PL 120 Ga30
Mielno PL 128 Fc39
Mielno PL 129 Gd36
Mieluskylä FIN 82 Ka26
Mielżyn PL 129 Gd37
Mieming A 142 Dc53
Miemo I 155 Db66
Mień PL 123 Ka35
Miera E 37 Cc55
Mieraslompolo FIN 64 Ka08
Mierašluobbal FIN 64 Ka08
Miercurea-Ciuc RO 176 Ea60
Miercurea Nirajului RO 171 Dc59
Miercurea Sibiului RO 175 Da61
Mierczany PL 128 Fc37
Mieres E 37 Cc55
Mieres E 49 Hb59
Miereszyn PL 121 Ha30
Mierlo NL 125 Bb39
Mierojokka N 68 Hd11
Mieroszów PL 129 Gb42
Miersig RO 170 Ca57
Mieruniszki PL 123 Ka30
Mierzawa PL 130 Ja42
Mierzęcice PL 138 Hc43
Mierzyno PL 121 Gd29
Miesbach D 143 Ea52
Mieścisko PL 121 Gd35
Miesenbach A 144 Ga53
Miesenbach D 133 Ca46
Mieslahti FIN 82 Kd25
Mieste D 127 Dd36
Miesterhorst D 127 Dd36
Mieszków PL 129 Gd38
Mieszkowice PL 120 Fb35
Mietków PL 129 Gc42
Mietoinen FIN 97 Jb39
Miettinen FIN 89 Jc34
Mieza E 45 Bd61
Mieżaičiai LV 114 Kb55
Mieżiškiai LT 114 Kd55
Mifol AL 182 Aa77
Migennes F 30 Hc39
Migliarino I 150 Ea62
Migliarino I 155 Da65
Miglionico I 162 Gc76
Mignano Monte Lungo I 161 Fa73
Migné F 29 Gb44
Mignères F 29 Ha39
Miguel Esteban E 53 Dd67
Miguelturra E 52 Db69
Mihăeşti RO 175 Dc64
Mihăeşti RO 180 Dc67
Mihai Bravu RO 177 Fc65
Mihai Bravu RO 180 Ea67
Mihai Eminescu RO 172 Ec55
Mihăileni MD 173 Fa54
Mihăileni MD 173 Fa54
Mihăileni RO 172 Ea59
Mihăileni RO 172 Eb54
Mihăileni RO 175 Db61
Mihăileşti RO 176 Ea66
Mihăileşti RO 176 Ec65
Mihail Kogălniceanu RO 173 Fa57
Mihail Kogălniceanu RO 177 Fa65
Mihail Kogălniceanu RO 177 Fc64
Mihail Kogălniceanu RO 181 Fc67
Mihailovca MD 173 Fc56
Mihailovca MD 173 Fd55
Mihailovca MD 173 Fd56
Mihailovca MD 173 Fd59
Mihai Viteazu RO 171 Da59
Mihai Viteazu RO 177 Fc66
Mihajlov RUS 203 Fa11
Mihajlovac SRB 174 Bb64
Mihajlovac SRB 174 Cb65
Mihajlovka RUS 203 Fd13
Mihajlovo BG 179 Cd68
Mihajlovo BG 180 Dd73
Mihajlovo RUS 113 Jd58
Mihajlovo SRB 174 Bb61
Mihajlovskoe RUS 107 Mb49
Mihălăşeni MD 173 Fa53
Mihălăşeni RO 172 Ed55
Mihald H 145 Gd56
Mihalgazi TR 193 Gc81
Mihalıççık TR 193 Ha81
Mihalkovo BG 184 Da74
Mihalţ RO 175 Da60
Mihályfa H 145 Gd55
Mihas GR 188 Bb86
Miheşu de Câmpie RO 171 Db58
Mihkil EST 98 Kb45
Mihla D 126 Dc41
Mihnevo RUS 203 Fa10
Miholjska HR 158 Ha69
Mihovljan HR 151 Ga57
Miikkula FIN 91 Lc33
Miiluranta FIN 82 Kb27
Mijanès F 41 Gd57
Mijares E 46 Cd64
Mijas E 60 Cd76
Mijdrecht NL 116 Ba36
Mijoska SRB 159 Jb66
Mijoux F 31 Jd44
Mikaševičy BY 202 Eb13
Mikaszówka PL 123 Kb31
Mike H 152 Ha57
Miķeļtornis LV 105 Jc49
Míki GR 184 Db76
Mikicin PL 123 Kb32
Mikínes GR 195 Bd87
Mikitamäe EST 107 Lc46
Mikkanen FIN 90 Kd35
Mikkelbostad N 67 Gb12
Mikkeli FIN 90 La34
Mikkelsnes N 65 Kc08
Mikkelvik N 62 Gd08
Mikkola FIN 69 Jd15
Mikkolanniemi FIN 91 Ld33
Miklavž na Dr. p. SLO 144 Ga56
Mikleuš HR 152 Ha59
Mikniūnai LT 114 Kb53
Mikołajki PL 122 Jc31
Mikołajki Pomorskie PL 122 Hc31
Mikolin PL 129 Gd42
Mikoliškiai LT 113 Jb55
Mikołów PL 138 Hc44
Míkonos GR 196 Db89
Mikorowo PL 121 Gd30
Mikorzyn PL 129 Ha40
Mikre BG 180 Db70
Mikrí Vólvi GR 184 Cc78
Mikró Dério GR 185 Ea76
Mikrókambos GR 183 Ca77
Mikrolímni GR 182 Ba77
Mikrolívado GR 182 Ba79
Mikromiliá GR 184 Cd75
Mikró Monastíri GR 183 Bd77
Mikró Perivoláki GR 189 Bd81
Mikrópoli GR 184 Cd76
Mikstat PL 129 Ha39
Mikulov CZ 137 Gd49
Mikulovice CZ 137 Gd44
Mikytai LV 114 Kb57
Miladinovci MK 178 Bc73
Miłakowo PL 122 Hd31
Milano E 45 Bd62
Milano I 149 Cc59
Milano Marittima I 150 Ea63
Milanovo BG 179 Cc70
Milanovo BG 181 Ec70
Milanovo SRB 178 Bd70
Milanów PL 131 Kb38
Milanówek PL 130 Jb37
Milaş RO 171 Dc58
Milas TR 197 Ed89
Milašaičiai LV 114 Kb56
Milašiūnai LT 114 Kb56
Milatkoviće SRB 178 Ba68
Milatos GR 201 Db95
Milazzo I 167 Fd83
Milborne Saint Andrew GB 19 Ec30
Milcoiu RO 175 Db64
Milcov RO 175 Db66
Milcovul RO 176 Ed62
Mildenberg D 119 Ed35
Mildenhall GB 20 Fd25
Mildı TR 192 Fd87
Mildstedt D 108 Da29
Miléa GR 182 Ba80
Miléa GR 183 Bc79
Mileanca RO 172 Ed54
Milehouse IRL 13 Cc24
Milejczyce PL 123 Kb35
Milejów-Wieś PL 131 Kb40
Milena I 166 Ed86
Mileševo SRB 153 Jb58
Milešov CZ 136 Fb46
Milešov CZ 136 Fa43
Mileşti MD 173 Fb57
Mileştii Mici MD 173 Fd58
Milestone IRL 13 Ca23
Mileszewy PL 122 Hc33
Miletićevo SRB 174 Bc62
Miletín CZ 136 Ga43
Miletkovo MK 183 Bd75
Mileto I 164 Gb82
Milevsko CZ 136 Fb46
Milewo Gałązki PL 123 Jd32
Milford GB 20 Fb29
Milford Haven GB 18 Db27
Milhars F 41 Gd52
Mili GR 195 Bd88
Miliá GR 185 Ea75
Miliá GR 194 Bc87
Miliá GR 194 Bc90
Milianni I 167 Fa84
Milice PL 137 Ha44
Milići BIH 159 Hd64
Milíčín CZ 136 Fc46
Miličinica SRB 153 Jb63
Milicz PL 129 Gd39
Miliés GR 189 Ca82
Milín CZ 136 Fa46
Milína GR 189 Cb82
Milino MK 183 Bc74
Miliotádes GR 182 Ad80
Milis I 169 Bd77
Milişăuţi RO 172 Eb55
Militello in Val di Catania I 167 Fc86
Militsa GR 194 Ba89
Miljana HR 151 Ga58
Miljen BIH 159 Hd66
Miljević SRB 174 Bd64
Miljevina BIH 159 Hc66
Miljkovac SRB 178 Bd68
Miljutino RUS 99 Mb44
Miłki PL 122 Jc31
Milkjovci BG 179 Cb71
Milkovica BG 180 Db68
Millancay F 29 Gc41
Millares E 54 Fb68
Millas F 41 Ha57
Millau F 41 Hb52
Millerovo RUS 203 Fc14
Millesimo I 148 Bd63
Millesvik S 94 Ed45
Millevaches F 33 Gd47
Millford IRL 9 Cb15
Mill Hill GB 20 Fc27
Millinge DK 108 Dc27
Millingen aan de Rijn NL 125 Bc37
Millisle GB 10 Db17
Millom GB 11 Eb19
Millport GB 6 Dc13
Mill-Sint Hubert NL 125 Bb38
Millstatt A 143 Ed55
Millstreet IRL 12 Bc25
Millstreet IRL 13 Ca25
Milltown GB 11 Eb16
Milltown GB 19 Dd29
Milltown IRL 8 Bd20
Milltown IRL 12 Bb24
Milltown Malbay IRL 12 Bb22
Milly-la-Forêt F 29 Gd38
Milly-le-Meugnon F 28 Fc42
Milmarcos E 47 Ec62
Milmersdorf D 120 Fa34
Milna HR 158 Gb68
Milnathort GB 7 Eb12
Milngavie GB 10 Dd13
Milnthorpe GB 11 Ec19
Milo I 167 Fd85
Miločaj SRB 178 Ba67
Miločer MNE 159 Hd70
Miłocice PL 121 Gc31
Miłogórze PL 122 Ja31
Miłomłyn PL 122 Hd32
Miłoradz PL 121 Hb31
Miloşeşti RO 176 Ed65
Miloševa Kula SRB 174 Ca66
Milošev Do SRB 159 Jb66
Miloševo SRB 174 Cb66
Miłosław PL 129 Gd37
Mílos = Pláka GR 195 Cd91
Milot AL 163 Jb72
Milotice CZ 137 Gd48
Milovaig GB 4 Da07
Milow D 127 Eb36
Milówka PL 138 Hc46
Mils bei Imst A 142 Db54
Miltach D 135 Ec47
Milte D 125 Cb37
Miltenberg D 134 Cd45
Miltern D 127 Eb36
Milton GB 5 Ea07
Milton GB 7 Dd08
Milton Abbas GB 19 Ec30
Milton Abbot GB 18 Dc31
Milton Keynes GB 20 Fb26
Miltzow D 119 Ed31
Milutinovac SRB 174 Cb65
Milverton GB 19 Ea29
Milwich GB 16 Ed23
Milžavėnai LT 114 Ka56
Milżyn PL 129 Hb36
Mimizan F 39 Fa52
Mimizan-Plage F 39 Fa52
Mimoň CZ 136 Fc43
Mína GR 194 Bc91
Mina da Juliana P 50 Ad71
Mina de São Domingos P 58 Ba72
Miñagón E 37 Bd54
Minard GB 6 Dc12
Minare TR 198 Fd92
Minas de Riotinto E 59 Bc72
Minaya E 53 Eb68
Mincenii de Jos MD 173 Fd56
Minchinhampton GB 19 Ec27
Minde P 50 Ac66
Mindelheim D 142 Db51
Mindelo P 44 Ac60
Mindelstetten D 135 Ea48
Minden D 126 Cd36
Mindic MD 173 Fb54
Mindja BG 180 Ea71
Mindreşti MD 173 Fc56
Mindszent H 146 Jb56
Mindtangen N 70 Ed22
Minehead GB 19 Ea29
Mineo I 167 Fc86
Mineralni bani BG 184 Dc74
Mineral'nye Vody RUS 205 Ga16
Minerbe I 149 Dc60
Minerbio I 150 Dd62
Minerve F 41 Ha55
Minervino Murge I 162 Gb74
Minety GB 20 Ed27
Minfeld D 133 Cb47
Minfford GB 15 Dd24
Mingajny PL 122 Hd30
Mingajny PL 122 Ja30
Mingir MD 173 Fc59
Minglanilla E 54 Ed67
Mingorría E 46 Cd63
Minićevo SRB 179 Ca68
Minija LT 113 Jb56
Mining A 143 Ed50
Miniszków PL 130 Ja40
Minkiö FIN 89 Jd38
Minkowskie PL 129 Gd41
Minnetler TR 191 Ed82
Minnetler TR 192 Fc84
Miño de Medinaceli E 47 Eb62
Miño de San Esteban E 46 Dd61
Miñol E 36 Ba54
Minot F 30 Ja40
Miňovce SK 139 Jd47
Minsk BY 202 Ea12
Mińsk Mazowiecki PL 130 Jc37
Minster GB 21 Ga28
Minster GB 21 Gb28
Minster Lovell GB 20 Fa27
Mintia RO 175 Cc60
Mintiu Gherlii RO 171 Db57
Mintlaw GB 5 Ed08
Mintraching D 135 Eb48
Minturno I 160 Ed73
Mioarele RO 176 Dd63
Miočinovići HR 152 Gb60
Miodnica PL 128 Fd39
Miokovci SRB 159 Jc64
Miomo F 154 Cc68
Mionica SRB 153 Jb63
Mions F 34 Jb47
Mios F 32 Fa51
Mioska MNE 159 Ja68
Miotek PL 138 Hc43
Mioveni RO 175 Dc64
Mira E 54 Ed67
Mira GR 188 Bb85
Míra GR 189 Bd81
Mira I 150 Ea60
Mira P 44 Ac63
Mirabeau F 42 Jd53
Mirabel E 51 Ca66
Mirabel F 34 Ja50
Mirabel F 34 Jb50
Mirabel F 40 Gc52
Mirabel-aux-Baronnies F 42 Jc51
Mirabella Eclano I 161 Fc74
Mirabella Imbaccari I 167 Fb86
Mirachowo PL 121 Ha30
Miradoux F 40 Ga53
Miraflores de la Sierra E 46 Dc63
Miralrío E 47 Ea63
Miramar F 43 Kc54
Miramar P 44 Ac61
Miramare I 156 Eb64
Miramas F 42 Jb54
Mirambeau F 32 Fb48
Mirambel E 48 Fc64
Miramont-de-Guyenne F 32 Fd51
Miranda de Arga E 39 Ec58
Miranda de Ebro E 38 Ea57
Miranda del Castañar E 45 Ca64
Miranda do Corvo P 44 Ad64
Miranda do Douro P 45 Ca60
Mirande F 40 Fd54
Mirandela P 45 Bc60
Mirandilla E 51 Bd68
Mirandola I 149 Dc61
Mirandol-Bourgnounac F 41 Gd52
Miranje HR 157 Ga65
Mirano I 150 Ea59
Mirantes de Luna E 37 Cb56
Miraš KSV 178 Bb71
Mirăslău RO 171 Da59
Miraumont F 23 Ha32
Miravci MK 183 Bd75
Miravet E 48 Ga62
Miravete E 48 Fb64
Mircea Vodă RO 176 Ed64
Mircea Vodă RO 181 Fb67
Mirceşti RO 172 Ed57
Mircze PL 131 Kd41
Miré F 28 Fb40
Mirebeau F 28 Fd44
Mirebeau-sur-Bèze F 30 Jb41
Mirebel F 31 Jc43
Mirecourt F 31 Jd38
Miren SLO 150 Ed58
Mirepoix F 41 Gd56
Míres GR 200 Cd96
Mireşti MD 173 Fc58
Mireşu Mare RO 171 Da55
Mireval F 41 Hd54
Miribel F 34 Jb46
Miričina BIH 153 Hc62
Mírina GR 190 Db81
Miriokéfala GR 200 Cc95
Mirkovo BG 179 Cd71
Mirmande F 34 Jb50
Mirna SLO 151 Fc58
Mirocin PL 128 Fd39
Mirojedy RUS 107 Ma51
Mironeasa RO 173 Fa58
Mirones E 38 Dc55
Miroševce SRB 178 Bd70
Miroşi RO 175 Dc66
Miroslav CZ 137 Gb48
Miroslava RO 173 Fa57
Miroslavas LT 114 Kc59
Mirosławiec PL 120 Ga33
Miroslovești RO 172 Ec57
Mirošov CZ 136 Fa46
Mirostowice PL 128 Fc39
Mirotice CZ 136 Fa47
Mirovci BG 181 Ed69
Mirovec BG 181 Ec70
Mirovice CZ 136 Fa46
Mirović Zagora HR 158 Gb65
Mirovo BG 179 Ca72
Mirovo BG 180 Ea70
Mirow D 119 Ec34
Mirów PL 130 Hd42
Mirów PL 130 Jc40
Mirşid RO 171 Cd56
Mirsína GR 183 Bb79
Mirsíni GR 194 Bc90
Mirsk PL 128 Fd41
Mirto I 165 Gd79
Mirtos GR 201 Db96
Mirzec PL 130 Jc40
Misa LV 106 Kc52
Misano Adriatico I 156 Eb64
Mişca RO 170 Ca58
Mischii RO 175 Da66
Misefa H 145 Gc55
Miškelovo RUS 99 Ma39
Misi FIN 74 Kb18
Misilmeri I 166 Ec84
Mišinci BIH 152 Hb61
Mišiniai LV 123 Kb30
Miske H 146 Hd56
Miskolc H 146 Jc50
Miskolctapolca H 146 Jc51
Mislîče SLO 151 Fa59
Mislina HR 158 Ha68
Mislinja SLO 144 Fd56
Mišnjak HR 151 Fc62
Missanello I 162 Gb77
Missen D 142 Da52
Missenträsk S 72 Ha24
Missery F 30 Hd42
Missillac F 27 Ec41
Misso EST 107 Lc47
Mistegná GR 191 Ea83
Mistelbach A 137 Gb49
Mistelbach D 135 Ea45
Mistelgau D 135 Dd45
Misten N 66 Fc17
Misterbianco I 167 Fc86
Misterdalsetra N 86 Eb35
Misterhult S 103 Gb50
Mistrás GR 194 Bc89
Mistretta I 167 Fb84
Mistrós GR 189 Cc85
Mišučiai LT 113 Jd56
Misurina I 143 Eb56
Misvær N 71 Fc18
Misvak TR 191 Ea82
Misy-sur-Yonne F 30 Hb38
Miszewo PL 121 Ha30
Miszewo Murowane PL 130 Hd36
Mitáto GR 201 Dd96
Mitcham GB 20 Fc28
Mitchell GB 18 Db31
Mitchelstown IRL 12 Bd24
Míthimna GR 191 Ea83
Mítikas GR 188 Ac82
Mítikas GR 188 Ad83
Mitilíni GR 191 Ea83
Mitilinií GR 197 Eb88
Mitkovcy RUS 107 Ld47
Mitlo HR 158 Gb66
Mitoc RO 172 Ed54
Mitocu Dragomirnei RO 172 Ec55
Mitragalys LT 114 La53
Mitrašinci MK 183 Ca74
Mitreni RO 181 Ec67
Mitrofanovka RUS 203 Fb14
Mitrópoli GR 188 Bb81
Mitrova Reka SRB 178 Ba68
Mitrovica SRB 153 Ja61
Mitrovići BIH 152 Hb63
Mitrovo SRB 178 Bb68
Mitry-Mory F 23 Ha36
Mitsero CY 206 Jb97
Mittådalen S 86 Ed32
Mittelbach D 127 Ec42
Mittelberg A 142 Da53
Mittelberg A 142 Dc55
Mittelbiberach D 142 Da51
Mitteldorf an der Raab A 144 Ga54
Mitteleschenbach D 134 Dc47
Mittelherwigsdorf D 128 Fc42
Mittelsinn D 134 Da44
Mittelurbach D 142 Da51
Mittenaar D 126 Cc42
Mittenwald D 143 Dd53
Mittenwalde D 120 Fa34
Mittenwalde D 128 Fa37
Mitterbach am Erlaufsee A 144 Fd52
Mitterfels D 135 Ec48
Mitterkirchen im Machland A 144 Fc51
Mittersheim F 25 Ka36
Mittersill A 143 Eb54
Mitterskirchen D 143 Ec50
Mitterteich D 135 Eb45
Mitterweissenbach A 144 Fa52
Mittet N 77 Da32
Mittewald an der Drau A 143 Eb55
Mittliden S 79 Fb25
Mittweida D 127 Ec41
Mittweide D 128 Fb38
Mitwitz D 135 Dd44
Mizija BG 179 Cd68
Mizil RO 176 Eb64
Mjadzel BY 202 Ea12
Mjakiševo RUS 107 Mb50
Mjaksa RUS 202 Ed08
Mjåland N 92 Cb44
Mjåland N 93 Da45
Mjäldrunga S 102 Ed48
Mjällby S 111 Fc54
Mjällom S 80 Gd31
Mjåvatn N 93 Db45
Mjåvatn N 93 Da46
Mjelde N 66 Fc15
Mjell N 84 Cc36
Mjels DK 108 Db27
Mjöbäck S 102 Ed50
Mjöhult S 110 Ec54
Mjölby S 103 Fd47
Mjölkberg S 72 Gc22
Mjölkvattnet S 78 Fa28
Mjølvik N 62 Gc08
Mjømna N 84 Ca37
Mjönäs S 94 Fa42
Mjøndalen N 93 Dd42
Mjønes N 77 Dd29
Mjørlund N 85 Ea39
Mjösjöby S 83 Gd28
Mjösund FIN 97 Jb40
Mladá Boleslav CZ 136 Fc43
Mladá Vožice CZ 136 Fc46
Mladé Buky CZ 136 Ga43
Mladen BG 180 Dc70
Mladenovac SRB 174 Bb65
Mladenovo SRB 153 Hd60
Mladikovina BIH 152 Ha63
Mladinovo BG 185 Ea74
Mlado MK 178 Bc72
Mladotice CZ 135 Ed45
Mladovo BG 180 Ea72
Mláka CZ 136 Fc48
Mlanča SRB 178 Ba68
Mława PL 122 Ja34
Mlebniko RUS 203 Fd08
Mlečevo BG 180 Dc71
Mlečino BG 184 Dc75
Mleczno PL 129 Gb40
Mlekarevo BG 180 Ea73
Mlik AL 182 Ab75
Mlini HR 159 Hc69
Mliništa BIH 158 Gc64
Mljetičak MNE 159 Ja68
Młock PL 122 Ja35
Młodasko PL 129 Gb36
Młodoszowice PL 129 Gd42
Młodzawy PL 138 Jb43
Młodzianów PL 129 Gd39
Młodzieszyn PL 130 Ja37
Młogoszyn PL 130 Hd37
Mlynary PL 122 Hd30
Mlynarze PL 122 Jc34
Mlyniv UA 204 Ea15
Mlýny CZ 136 Fc47
Mnich CZ 136 Fc47
Mnichov CZ 135 Ec44
Mnichovice CZ 136 Fc45
Mnichovo Hradiště CZ 136 Fc43
Mnichów PL 130 Jb42
Mnin PL 130 Ja41
Mniów PL 130 Jb41
Mníšek nad Hnilcom SK 138 Jc48
Mniszew PL 130 Jc38
Mo N 70 Ed23
Mo N 76 Cd33
Mo N 77 Dc31
Mo N 84 Cb38

Mo N 92 Cd42
Mo N 93 Db45
Mo N 94 Eb40
Mo N 94 Eb42
Mo S 79 Gb30
Mo S 79 Gb29
Mo S 80 Gd30
Mo S 87 Gb37
Mo S 94 Ed44
Mo S 94 Eb45
Moacşa RO 176 Eb61
Moaña E 36 Ad57
Moara RO 172 Eb56
Moara de Piatră MD 173 Fb55
Moara Nouă MD 173 Fb57
Moara Vlăsiei RO 176 Eb65
Moate IRL 13 Cb21
Moçan AL 182 Ad76
Mocejón E 52 Db66
Močenok SK 145 Ha50
Mochau D 127 Ed41
Móchlos GR 201 Dc96
Mochowo PL 122 Hd35
Mochrum GB 10 Dd17
Mochy PL 129 Gb38
Močidlec CZ 135 Ed44
Mociu RO 171 Db58
Mockai LV 114 Kb59
Möckern D 127 Eb37
Mockfjärd S 95 Fc40
Möckmühl D 134 Cd46
Mockrehna D 127 Ec40
Mockträsk S 73 Hd22
Moclin E 60 Db74
Moclinejo E 60 Da76
Mocra MD 173 Fd56
Mocsa H 145 Hb52
Mőcsény H 153 Hc57
Moczydły-Kukiłki PL 123 Ka35
Modane F 35 Kb48
Modave B 124 Ba42
Modbury GB 19 Dd32
Modelu RO 181 Ed67
Modena I 149 Db62
Möderbrugg A 144 Fb54
Moderki PL 123 Ka35
Moderówka PL 139 Jd45
Módi GR 189 Bd84
Modica I 167 Fc88
Modigliana I 156 Dd64
Modliborzyce PL 131 Ka41
Mödling A 145 Gb51
Modliszewko PL 129 Gd36
Modlna PL 130 Hc38
Modolicy RUS 99 Mb44
Modolo I 169 Bd76
Modra SK 145 Gd50
Modran BIH 152 Hb61
Modrany SK 145 Hb52
Modrava CZ 135 Ed48
Modrej SLO 151 Fa57
Modriach A 144 Fc55
Modriča BIH 152 Hb61
Modrica SRB 178 Bc68
Mõdriku EST 98 La42
Modrovka SK 137 Ha49
Modruš HR 151 Fd61
Modrý Kameň SK 146 Hd50
Modrze PL 129 Gb37
Modrzejowice PL 130 Jc40
Modrzewie PL 120 Fc33
Modugno I 162 Gc74
Moeche E 36 Bb53
Moëlan-sur-Mer F 27 Dd40
Moelfre GB 15 Dd21
Moelv N 86 Ea38
Moen N 67 Gc11
Moen N 78 Eb29
Moena I 143 Dd56
Moerdijk NL 124 Ad37
Moergestel NL 124 Ba38
Moers D 125 Bd39
Mofalla S 103 Fb47
Moffat GB 11 Eb15
Mofreita P 45 Bd59
Moftinu Mic RO 171 Cc55
Mogadouro P 45 Bd61
Mogata S 103 Gb46
Møgeltønder DK 108 Da28
Mogenstrup DK 100 Da23
Mogenstrup DK 109 Eb27
Mogente E 55 Fb70
Moggio I 149 Cd58
Moggio Udinese I 143 Ed56
Mögglingen D 134 Da48
Mogielnica PL 130 Jb39
Mogila BG 181 Ed70
Mogila MK 183 Bb76
Mogilany PL 138 Ja45
Mogili RUS 107 Ma51
Mogilište BG 181 Fb69
Mogilno PL 129 Ha36
Moglia I 149 Db61
Mogliano I 156 Ed67
Mogliano Veneto I 150 Ea59
Möglingen D 134 Cd48
Mogón E 61 Dd72
Mogor E 36 Ad57
Mogorić HR 151 Ga63
Mogoro I 169 Bd78
Mogoşani RO 176 Dd65
Mogoşeşti RO 173 Fa58
Mogoşeşti-Siret RO 172 Ed57
Mogosoaia RO 176 Ea66
Mogro E 38 Dc54
Moguer E 59 Bb74
Mogutovo RUS 99 Ma45
Mohács H 153 Hc58
Moharras E 53 Eb68
Moheda S 103 Fc51
Mohedas E 45 Ca64
Mohedas de la Jara E 52 Cc67
Mohelnice CZ 137 Gc45
Mohelno CZ 137 Gb48
Mohil IRL 13 Cb23
Mohill IRL 9 Cb19
Möhkö FIN 83 Mb30
Möhlau D 127 Eb39
Möhnesee D 125 Cb39
Möhnesee D 126 Cc39
Moholm S 103 Fb46
Mohon F 27 Eb39
Mohora H 146 Hd51
Mohorn D 127 Ed41
Mohós GR 201 Db96
Mohrkirch D 108 Db29
Mohtola FIN 90 La32
Mohyliv-Podil's'kyj UA 204 Eb16
Moi N 92 Cb45
Moià E 49 Gd60
Moie I 156 Ec66
Moikipää FIN 81 Hd31
Moilala FIN 90 La33
Moimenta da Beira P 44 Bb62
Moineşti RO 172 Ec59
Moinniemi FIN 91 Lc33
Moinsalmi FIN 91 Ld33
Móinteach Milic IRL 13 Cb22
Mo i Rana N 71 Fb20
Moirans F 35 Jc48
Moirans-en-Montagne F 31 Jc44
Moirax F 40 Ga52
Moircy B 132 Ba43
Mõisaküla EST 98 Ka45
Mõisaküla EST 106 Kc46
Moisburg D 118 Db33
Moisei RO 171 Dc55
Moisio FIN 90 La34
Moisiovaara FIN 75 Lb24
Moissac F 40 Gb52
Moissac-Bellevue F 42 Ka53
Moissey F 31 Jc42
Moisson F 23 Gc36
Moisund N 92 Cd46
Moisy F 29 Gb40
Moita F 154 Cc70
Moita P 50 Ab69
Moitaselkä FIN 69 Kc17
Moixent E 55 Fb70
Möja S 96 Ha43
Mojácar E 61 Ec75
Mojados E 46 Da61
Mojęcice PL 129 Gb40
Mojeciu RO 176 Dd62
Mojkovac MNE 159 Jb68
Mojstrana SLO 144 Fa56
Møkland N 66 Fc12
Möklinta S 95 Gb41
Mokliště MK 183 Bd75
Mokobody PL 131 Jd36
Mokolai LV 114 Kb58
Mokra Gora SRB 159 Ja65
Mokre PL 121 Ha32
Mokre PL 129 Gb37
Mokren BG 180 Eb72
Mokreni MK 183 Bb74
Mokreš BG 179 Cc68
Mokrin SRB 153 Jc58
Mokrin SRB 174 Bb60
Mokro BIH 159 Hc65
Mokro MNE 159 Jb69
Mokronog SLO 151 Fd58
Mokronoge BIH 152 Gc63
Mokronoge BIH 158 Gd65
Mokro Polje HR 158 Gb64
Mokrous RUS 203 Ga11
Mokrzesz PL 130 Hd42
Mokrzyska PL 138 Jb44
Mokšan RUS 203 Fc11
Moksi FIN 90 Kb33
Møkster N 84 Bd40
Mol B 124 Ba39
Mol SRB 153 Jb58
Mola di Bari I 162 Gd74
Molái GR 195 Bd90
Molainiai LT 114 Kc54
Moland N 66 Fb14
Moland N 93 Da42
Molare I 148 Ca62
Molas F 40 Ga55
Molbergen D 117 Cb34
Mølby DK 108 Db26
Mold GB 15 Eb22
Moldava CZ 128 Fa42
Moldava nad Bodvou SK 138 Jc49
Mołdawin PL 120 Fd32
Molde N 76 Cd32
Moldova Nouă RO 174 Bd64
Moldova-Sulița RO 172 Dd55
Moldova Veche RO 174 Bd64
Moldoveneşti RO 171 Da59
Moldoveni RO 172 Ec58
Moldovița RO 172 Ea55
Møldrup DK 100 Db22
Moldusen N 94 Ed40
Moldvik N 66 Ga12
Moledo do Minho P 36 Ac58
Moleno CH 142 Cc56
Moléson CH 141 Bc55
Moleşti MD 173 Fd59
Molėtai LT 114 La56
Molezuelas de la Carballeda E 37 Ca58
Molfetta I 162 Gc74
Molfsee D 118 Dc30
Móli GR 183 Bd80
Moliden S 80 Gd30
Moliens-Dreuil F 23 Gc33
Molières F 40 Gb52
Moliets-et-Maa F 39 Ed53
Moliets-Plage F 39 Ed53
Molin SRB 153 Jc59
Molin SRB 174 Bb61
Molina I 150 Dd57
Molina Aterno I 160 Ed71
Molina de Aragon E 47 Ec63
Molina de Segura E 55 Fa72
Molinella I 150 Dd62
Molineuf F 29 Gb41
Molinges F 35 Jd45
Molinicos E 53 Eb71
Molinos E 36 Ac54
Molinos E 48 Fb63
Molinos de Duero E 47 Ea60
Molins del Rei E 49 Gd61
Moliterno I 161 Ga77
Molitg-les-Bains F 41 Ha57
Molkojärvi FIN 69 Jd16
Molkom S 94 Fa43
Molla S 102 Ed48
Mollafeneri TR 186 Ga78
Mollagjesh AL 182 Ac75
Molland N 93 Da46
Mollans-sur-Ouvèze F 42 Jc52
Mollaoğlu TR 193 Gc82
Mollas AL 182 Ac76
Mollasüleymanlı TR 192 Fc86
Möllbrücke A 143 Ed55
Mölle S 110 Ec54
Möllenhagen D 119 Ed33
Mollerussa E 48 Ga60
Mollet del Vallès E 49 Ha61
Mollia I 148 Ca58
Mollières F 43 Kc51
Mollina E 60 Cd75
Mollis CH 142 Cc54
Mölln A 144 Fb52
Mölln D 119 Dd32
Mollösund S 102 Eb48
Mölltorp S 103 Fb46
Mølna N 78 Eb29
Mölnbo S 96 Gc44
Mølnbukt N 77 Dd29
Mölndal S 102 Eb49
Mölnebo S 102 Eb48
Mölnlycke S 102 Ec49
Molochişul Mare MD 173 Fd55
Moločišče RUS 107 Mb47
Molodi RUS 99 Ld45
Molodi RUS 107 Ma46
Mołodycz PL 139 Kc43
Molompize F 34 Hb49
Mólos GR 189 Bd83
Moloskovicy RUS 99 Ma41
Molovata MD 173 Fd57
Molovata Nouă MD 173 Fd57
Moloy F 30 Jb41
Moložva RUS 107 Ld46
Molpe FIN 81 Hd31
Molsheim F 25 Kb37
Moltajny PL 122 Jb30
Moltjorda N 71 Fc18
Mołtowo PL 120 Ga31
Moltrasio I 149 Cc58
Moltustranda N 76 Cb33
Molunat HR 159 Hc69
Molvero I 149 Dc57
Molvizar E 60 Db76
Mólyvos = Míthimna GR 191 Ea83
Molzbichl A 143 Ed55
Momán E 36 Bb54
Momarken N 94 Eb43
Mombaldone I 148 Ca62
Mombaroccio I 156 Ec65
Mombaruzzo I 148 Ca61
Mömbris D 134 Cd44
Mombuey E 45 Ca59
Momčilgrad BG 184 Dc75
Momino BG 180 Eb70
Momino Selo BG 180 Db73
Momin Sbor BG 180 Dd70
Mömlingen D 134 Cd45
Mommark DK 108 Dc28
Mommila FIN 90 Kb37
Momoty Górne PL 131 Kb42
Momrak N 93 Da44
Momuy F 39 Fb54
Mon CH 142 Cd55
Mon S 79 Fb26
Monå FIN 81 Ja29
Monachil E 60 Dc75
Monaghan IRL 9 Cc18
Monahiti GR 182 Ba79
Monar Lodge GB 6 Dc08
Monäs FIN 81 Ja29
Monasterace Marina I 164 Gc83
Monasterevin IRL 13 Cc22
Monasterio de la Sierra E 46 Dd59
Monasterio del Coto E 37 Bd55
Monasterio de Rodilla E 38 Dd58
Monastir I 169 Ca79
Monastiráki GR 184 Cd76
Monastiráki GR 188 Ad83
Monastyrek RUS 99 Ld42
Monastyrščina RUS 202 Ec12
Monastyryšče UA 204 Ec15
Monastyrys'ka UA 204 Ea16
Monbahus F 33 Ga51
Monbiel CH 142 Da55
Moncada E 54 Fc67
Moncalieri I 148 Bd60
Moncalvillo E 46 Dd59
Moncalvillo del Huete E 47 Ea65
Moncalvo I 148 Ca60
Monção P 36 Ad58
Moncarapacho P 58 Ad74
Moncel-sur-Seille F 25 Jd36
Mönchberg D 134 Cd45
Mönchdorf A 144 Fc50
Mönchengladbach D 125 Bc40
Mönchhof A 145 Gc52
Mönchholzhausen D 127 Dd41
Monchio delle Corti I 149 Da63
Monchique P 58 Ab73
Mönchkirchen A 144 Ga53
Mönchsdeggingen D 134 Dc48
Mönchsroth D 134 Db48
Monclar F 33 Ga51
Monclar-de-Quercy F 40 Gc53
Moncofa E 54 Fc66
Moncontour F 26 Eb38
Moncontour F 28 Fc43
Moncoutant F 28 Fb44
Monda E 60 Cc76
Mondaino I 156 Eb65
Mondariz E 36 Ad57
Mondavio I 156 Ec66
Mondéjar E 46 Dd65
Mondello, Partanna- I 166 Ec83
Mondim da Beira P 44 Ba61
Mondim de Basto P 44 Ba60
Mondolfo I 156 Ec65
Mondoñedo E 36 Bc54
Mondonville F 40 Gb54
Mondorf-les-Bains L 25 Jd34
Mondorf-les-Bains L 133 Bb45
Mondoubleau F 29 Ga40
Mondovì I 148 Bd62
Mondragon F 42 Jb52
Mondragone I 161 Fa74
Mondreganes E 37 Cd57
Mondriz E 36 Bc55
Mondsee A 143 Ed52
Möne S 102 Fa48
Moneasa RO 170 Cb58
Moneen IRL 8 Bd20
Moneglia I 149 Cc63
Monegrillo E 48 Fb61
Monein F 39 Fb55
Monemvassiá GR 195 Bd90
Moneo E 38 Dd56
Mones E 37 Ca54
Monesi I 148 Bc63
Monesiglio I 148 Bd62
Monesma y Cajigar E 48 Ga59
Monesterio E 51 Bd71
Monestier-de-Clermont F 35 Jd49
Monestiés F 41 Gd52
Moneteau F 30 Hc40
Moneva E 47 Fa62
Moneygall IRL 13 Ca22
Moneygold IRL 8 Ca17
Moneymore GB 9 Cd17
Moneyneany GB 9 Cd16
Moneyslane GB 9 Da18
Monfalcone I 150 Ed59
Monfarracinos E 45 Cb60
Monfero E 36 Bb54
Monflanquin F 33 Ga51
Monflorite E 48 Fc59
Monforte P 51 Bb68
Monforte d'Alba I 148 Bd62
Monforte del Cid E 55 Fb71
Monforte de Lemos E 36 Bb57
Monforte San Giorgio I 167 Fd84
Monghidoro I 155 Dc64
Mongiana I 164 Gc82
Mongiardino Ligure I 148 Cb62
Mongstad N 84 Ca37
Monguelfo I 143 Ea55
Monguilhem F 40 Fc53
Monheim D 134 Dc48
Monheim am Rhein D 125 Bd40
Moniaive GB 10 Ea15
Moniatis CY 206 Ja97
Mon-Idée F 24 Hd33
Monifieth GB 7 Ec11
Moninmäki FIN 82 La31
Möniste EST 107 Lb48
Monistrol-d'Allier F 34 Hc49
Monistrol de Montserrat E 49 Gd61
Monistrol-sur-Loire F 34 Hd48
Mönkeberg D 118 Dc30
Monk Fryston GB 16 Fa20
Mońki PL 123 Ka32
Monleras E 45 Ca61
Monlezun-d'Armagnac F 40 Fc53
Monlong F 40 Ga55
Monmouth GB 19 Eb27
Monnai F 22 Fd37
Monnaie F 29 Ga41
Monnerville F 29 Gd38
Mönni FIN 83 Ld30
Monni FIN 90 Kb38
Monnickendam NL 116 Ba35
Monninkylä FIN 90 Kc38
Monnoinen FIN 97 Jb39
Monodéndri GR 182 Ad79
Monódrio GR 189 Cc85
Monolithio GR 188 Ad81
Monólithos GR 196 Db92
Monólithos GR 197 Ed93
Monopoli I 162 Ha74
Monor H 146 Hd53
Monor RO 171 Dc57
Monoskylä FIN 89 Jd33
Monóspita GR 183 Bd77
Monostorapáti H 145 Ha55
Monóvar E 55 Fa71
Monpazier F 33 Ga51
Monreal D 133 Bd43
Monreal de Ariza E 47 Ec62
Monreal del Campo E 47 Ed63
Monreale I 166 Ec84
Monroy E 51 Ca66
Monroyo E 48 Fc63
Mons B 124 Ab41
Mons F 43 Kb53
Monsanto P 45 Bc65
Monsaraz P 50 Ba70
Monschau D 125 Bc42
Monsegur F 32 Fd51
Monselice I 150 Dd60
Monsheim D 133 Cb45
Mönsheim D 134 Cd48
Monsiega N 92 Cc44
Monsols F 34 Ja45
Mønsted DK 100 Db23
Monster NL 116 Ac36
Mönsterås S 103 Gb51
Monsummano Terme I 155 Db65
Montà I 148 Bd61
Montabaur D 125 Cb42
Montady F 41 Hb55
Montagna I 150 Dd60
Montagnac F 41 Hc54
Montagnac-d'Auberoche F 33 Gb49
Montagne F 35 Jc49
Montagnol F 41 Hb53
Montagny F 34 Hd46
Montaigu F 28 Fa43
Montaigu-de-Quercy F 40 Gb52
Montaiguët-en-Forez F 34 Hc45
Montaigu-les-Bois F 22 Fa37
Montaigut F 33 Ha45
Montaigut-le-Blanc F 33 Gc46
Montaigut-sur-Save F 40 Gb54
Montainville F 29 Gc39
Montaivo P 58 Ba72
Montalba-le-Château F 41 Ha57
Montalbán E 48 Fb63
Montalbán de Córdoba E 60 Cd73
Montalbanejo E 53 Ea67
Montalbano I 162 Ha75
Montalbano Elicona I 167 Fc84
Montalbano Jonico I 162 Gc77
Montalbo E 53 Ea66
Montalcino I 155 Dc67
Montaldo di Cosola I 149 Cc62
Montale I 155 Dc64
Montalegre P 44 Bb59
Montalieu-Vercieu F 35 Jc46
Montalivet-les-Bains F 32 Fa48
Montallegro I 166 Ec86
Montalto delle Marche I 156 Ed68
Montalto di Castro I 156 Dd70
Montalto Marina I 156 Dd70
Montalto Pavese I 149 Cc61
Montalto Uffugo I 164 Gb79
Montalvão P 50 Ba66
Montalvos E 53 Ec68
Montamarta E 45 Cb60
Montamy F 22 Fb36
Montán E 54 Fb66
Montana BG 179 Cc69
Montana CH 141 Bd56
Montañana E 48 Fb60
Montanaro I 148 Bd60
Montánchez E 51 Ca68
Montanejos E 54 Fb66
Montaner F 40 Fc55
Montano Antilia I 161 Fd77
Montans F 41 Gd53
Montargil P 50 Ad68
Montargis F 29 Ha39
Montargull E 48 Gb59
Montari FIN 90 Kc37
Montastruc-la-Coceillère F 40 Gc54
Montauban F 40 Gb53
Montauban-de-Bretagne F 27 Ec39
Montaud F 35 Jc48
Montazzoli I 161 Fb71
Montbard F 30 Hd41
Montbarrey F 31 Jc42
Montbazens F 33 Gd51
Montbazon F 29 Ga42
Montbéliard F 31 Ka40
Montbenidorm E 55 Fc71
Montbeugny F 30 Hc44
Montbizot F 28 Fd39
Montblanc E 48 Gb61
Montbovon CH 141 Bc55
Montbozon F 31 Jd41
Montbrand F 35 Jd50
Montbrió del Camp E 48 Gb62
Montbrison F 34 Hd47
Montbron F 33 Ga47
Montbrun-les-Bains F 42 Jc52
Montceau-les-Mines F 30 Ja44
Montceaux-les-Provins F 24 Hb37
Montcenis F 30 Ja43
Montchanin F 30 Ja43
Montchevrier F 33 Gc45
Montcornet F 24 Hc34
Montcresson F 29 Ha40
Montcuq F 40 Gb52
Montdardier F 41 Hc53
Mont-Dauphin F 35 Kb50
Mont-de-Marsan F 39 Fb53
Montdidier F 23 Gd34
Mont-Dol F 28 Ed38
Monteagudo E 47 Ed59
Monteagudo de las Salinas E 53 Ec66
Monteagudo de las Vicarias E 47 Eb61
Montealegre E 46 Cd59
Montealegre del Castillo E 55 Ed70
Montebello Vicentino I 150 Dd59
Montebelluna I 150 Ea59
Montebourg F 22 Fa35
Montebruno I 149 Cc62
Monte Buono I 156 Ea67
Montecalvo Irpino I 161 Fc74
Monte-Carlo MC 43 Kd53
Montecarotto I 156 Ec66
Montecastrilli I 156 Eb69
Montecatini Terme I 155 Db65
Montecchio I 156 Eb65
Montecchio Emilia I 149 Da62
Montecchio Maggiore I 150 Dd59
Monte Cerignone I 156 Eb65
Montech F 40 Gb53
Montechiarugolo I 149 Da62
Monteciccardo I 156 Eb65
Monte Claro P 50 Ba66
Montecorto E 59 Cb76
Montecorvino Rovella I 161 Fc75
Monte da Pedra P 50 Ba67
Monte das Flores P 50 Ad69
Monte de Baixo Grande P 58 Ba73
Monte de Goula P 44 Ba65
Montederramo E 36 Bb57
Montedor P 44 Ac59
Montedoro I 166 Ed86
Monte do Trigo P 50 Ba70
Monte Estremo F 154 Ca69
Montefalco I 156 Eb68
Montefalcone di Val Fortore I 161 Fc73
Montefalcone nel Sannio I 161 Fc71
Montefiascone I 156 Ea69
Monte Fidalgo P 50 Ba66
Montefiore Conca I 156 Eb65
Montefiore dell'Aso I 156 Ed68
Montefiorino I 149 Db63
Monteforte Cilento I 161 Fd76
Monteforte da Beira P 51 Bb66
Monteforte Irpino I 161 Fc75
Montefortino I 156 Ed68
Montefrío E 60 Da74
Montefurado E 36 Bc57
Montegil E 59 Cb75
Montegiordano Marina I 162 Gc77
Montegiorgio I 156 Ed67
Monte Gordo P 44 Ba65
Monte Gordo P 58 Ba74
Montegrotto Terme I 150 Dd60
Montehermoso E 45 Bd65
Montejaque E 59 Cb76
Montejicar E 60 Dc74
Montejo de Bricia E 38 Dc56
Montejo de la Sierra E 46 Dc62
Montejo de la Vega E 46 Dc61
Montejos del Camino E 37 Cc57
Montelanico I 160 Ec72
Montel-de-Gelat F 33 Ha46
Monteleone di Puglia I 161 Fd74
Monteleone di Spoleto I 156 Ec69
Monteleone d'Orvieto I 156 Ea68
Monteleone Rocca Doria I 168 Bd75
Montelepre I 166 Ec84
Montélimar F 42 Jb51
Montella I 161 Fc75
Montellano E 59 Cb75
Montellier F 34 Jb46
Monte Isola I 149 Da58
Montelungo I 149 Cd63
Montelupo Fiorentino I 155 Dc65
Montelupone I 156 Ed67
Montemaggiore Belsito I 166 Ed85
Montemagno I 148 Ca61
Montemarano I 161 Fc75
Montemarcello I 155 Cd64
Montemassi I 155 Db68
Montemayor E 60 Cd73
Montemayor del Río E 45 Cb64
Montemayor de Pililla E 46 Da61
Montemerano I 155 Dc69
Montemesola I 162 Ha76
Montemiletto I 161 Fc74
Montemilone I 162 Gb74
Montemolín E 51 Bd71
Montemonaco I 156 Ed68
Montemor-o-Novo P 50 Ad69
Montemor-o-Velho P 44 Ac64
Montemurro I 162 Gb77
Montendre F 32 Fc49
Montenegro de Cameros E 47 Ea59
Montenero I 155 Da66
Montenero di Bisaccia I 161 Fc71
Montenerodomo I 161 Fb71
Monteneuf F 27 Ec40
Monte Novo P 50 Ab70
Montepaone Lido I 164 Gc82
Montepescali I 155 Dc68
Monte Petrosu I 168 Cc74
Montepiano I 155 Dc64
Montepulciano I 156 Dd67
Monterchi I 156 Ea66
Monterde de Albarracín E 47 Ed64
Monte Real P 44 Ab65
Montereale I 156 Ec69
Montereale Valcellina I 150 Eb57
Montereau F 29 Ha38
Montereau F 29 Ha40
Monte Redondo P 44 Ac65
Monterenzio I 149 Dc63
Monteriggioni I 155 Dc66
Monte Romano I 156 Dd70
Monteroni d'Arbia I 155 Dc67
Monterosi I 156 Ea70
Monterosso al Mare I 155 Cd64
Monterosso Almo I 167 Fc87
Monterosso Calabro I 164 Gb82
Monterotondo I 160 Eb71
Monterotondo Marittimo I 155 Db67
Monterroso E 36 Bb56
Monterrubio de la Serena E 51 Cb70
Monterrubio de la Sierra E 45 Cb63
Montesa E 54 Fb69
Montesalgueiro E 36 Ba54
Monte San Biagio I 160 Ed73
Monte San Giusto I 156 Ed67
Monte San Maria Tiberina I 156 Ea66
Montesano Salentino I 163 Hc77
Montesano sulla Marcellana I 161 Ga77
Monte San Savino I 156 Dd67
Monte Sant'Angelo I 162 Gb72
Monte San Vito I 156 Ec66
Montesarchio I 161 Fb74
Montescaglioso I 162 Gc76
Montesclaros E 46 Cd65
Montesilvano Marina I 157 Fa69
Montespertoli I 155 Dc65
Montespluga I 142 Cc56
Montesquieu-Volvestre F 40 Gb55
Montesquieux F 40 Gb52
Montesquiou F 40 Fd54
Montestruc-sur-Gers F 40 Ga54
Monteux F 42 Jb52
Montevago I 166 Eb85
Montevarchi I 156 Dd66
Montevecchio I 169 Bd78
Monteveglio I 149 Dc63
Monteverde I 161 Ga74
Montevil P 50 Ab70
Montezemolo I 148 Bd62
Montfalcó Murallat E 49 Gc60
Montfaucon CH 141 Bc53
Montfaucon F 28 Fa43
Montfaucon-d'Argonne F 24 Jb35
Montfaucon-en-Velay F 34 Ja49
Montferrand-du-Périgord F 33 Ga50
Montferrat F 43 Kb53
Montfleur F 35 Jc45
Montfoort NL 116 Ba36
Montfort F 40 Ga53
Montfort NL 125 Bb40
Montfort-en-Chalosse F 39 Fb54
Montfort-l'Amaury F 23 Gc37
Montfort-sur-Meu F 28 Ed39
Montfort-sur-Risle F 23 Ga35
Montfranc F 41 Ha53
Montfrin F 42 Jb53
Montfront-le-Gesnois F 28 Fd39
Montgarri E 40 Gb57
Montgeron F 23 Gd37
Montgerval F 28 Ed39
Montgomery GB 15 Eb24
Montgueux F 30 Hc38
Montguyon F 32 Fc49
Monthermé F 24 Ja33
Monthey CH 141 Bb56
Monthois F 24 Ja35
Monthureux-sur-Saône F 31 Jd39
Monti I 168 Cb74
Montiano E 38 Dd56
Montiano I 155 Dc69
Monticchio Bagni I 161 Ga74
Monticelli I 162 Ha75
Monticelli d'Ongina I 149 Cd61
Monticelli Terme I 149 Da62
Montichiari I 149 Da60
Monticiano I 155 Dc67
Montiel E 53 Dd70
Montier-en-Der F 30 Ja38
Montieri I 155 Db67
Montiers-sur-Saulx F 24 Jb37
Montiglio I 148 Bd60
Montignac F 33 Gb49
Montignac-le-Coq F 32 Fd48
Montignac-sur-Charente F 32 Fd47
Montigny F 25 Ka37
Montigny F 29 Ha42
Montigny-la-Resle F 30 Hc40
Montigny-le Chartif F 29 Gb39
Montigny-Lencoup F 30 Hb38
Montigny-le-Roi = Val-de-Meuse F 31 Jc39
Montigny-lès-Metz F 25 Jd35
Montigny-sur-Aube F 30 Ja39
Montigny-sur-Loing F 29 Ha38
Montijo E 51 Bc69
Montijo P 50 Ab69
Montilla E 60 Cd73
Montilly F 30 Hb44
Montivilliers F 22 Fd34
Montjay F 42 Jd51
Montjean F 28 Fb40
Montjean F 32 Fd46
Montjean-sur-Loire F 28 Fb42
Montlaur F 41 Ha56
Mont-lès-Lamarche F 31 Jc39
Montlieu-la-Garde F 32 Fc49
Montlivault F 29 Gb41
Mont-Louis F 41 Gd58
Montlouis-sur-Loire F 29 Ga42
Montluçon F 33 Ha45
Montluel F 34 Jb46
Montmajor E 49 Gc59
Montmarault F 34 Hb45
Montmaur F 35 Jd50
Montmaurin F 40 Ga55
Montmédy F 24 Jb34
Montmelian F 35 Jd47

Montmerle-sur-Saône – Muro

Montmerle-sur-Saône F 34 Jb46
Montmesa E 48 Fb59
Montmeyan F 42 Ka53
Montmeyran F 34 Jb50
Montmirail F 24 Hb36
Montmirail F 29 Ga39
Montmirat F 41 Hd53
Montmoreau-Saint-Cybard F 32 Fd48
Montmorency F 23 Gd36
Montmorillon F 33 Ga45
Montmort-Lucy F 24 Hc36
Montmoyen F 30 Ja40
Mont-Notre-Dame F 24 Hb35
Montodine I 149 Cd60
Montoggio I 148 Cb62
Montoir-de-Bretagne F 27 Ec42
Montoire-sur-le-Loir F 29 Ga40
Montoison F 34 Jb50
Montoito P 50 Ba70
Montón E 47 Ed62
Montone I 156 Ea66
Montorio E 38 Dc57
Montorio al Vomano I 156 Ed69
Montoro E 52 Da72
Montouto P 45 Bc59
Montowo PL 122 Hd33
Montpascal F 35 Ka48
Montpellier F 41 Hd54
Montpezat-de-Quercy F 40 Gc52
Montpezat-sous-Bauzon F 34 Ja50
Montpon-Ménestérol F 32 Fd50
Montpont-en-Bresse F 30 Jb44
Mont-ral E 48 Gb62
Montréal F 40 Fd53
Montréal F 41 Gd55
Montredon-Labessonnie F 41 Ha54
Montréjeau F 40 Ga56
Montrésor F 29 Gb42
Montresta I 168 Bd76
Montret F 30 Jb44
Montreuil F 23 Gc31
Montreuil-aux-Lions F 24 Hb36
Montreuil-Bellay F 28 Fc42
Montreuil-l'Argillé F 22 Fd36
Montreux CH 141 Bb55
Montrevel-en-Bresse F 34 Jb45
Montrichard F 29 Gb42
Montricoux F 40 Gc53
Montrigaud F 34 Jb48
Mont-roig del Camp E 48 Gb62
Montrond-le-Château F 31 Jd42
Montrond-les-Bains F 34 Hd47
Montrose GB 7 Ec10
Montroy E 54 Fb68
Monts F 29 Ga42
Mont-Saint-Aignan F 23 Gb35
Mont-Saint-Léger F 31 Jc40
Mont-Saint-Michel F 22 Ed37
Montsalvy F 33 Ha50
Montsapey F 35 Ka47
Montsauche-les-Settons F 30 Hd42
Montsaunès F 40 Gb56
Montségur F 41 Gd56
Montségur-sur-Lauzon F 42 Jb51
Montseny E 49 Ha60
Monts-sur-Guesnes F 28 Fd43
Montsûrs F 28 Fb39
Montsurvent F 22 Ed36
Montuenga E 46 Da62
Montuenga de Soria E 47 Eb62
Montuïri E 57 Hc67
Monturque E 60 Cd74
Montvert F 33 Gd49
Monza I 149 Cc59
Monzón E 48 Fd60
Monzón de Campos E 46 Da59
Mooncoin IRL 13 Cb24
Moone IRL 13 Cc22
Moorenweis D 142 Dc50
Moormerland D 117 Cb33
Moorrege D 118 Db32
Moortown GB 17 Fc21
Moos D 142 Cc52
Moosbach D 135 Eb46
Moosburg a.d.Isar D 143 Ea50
Moosdorf A 143 Ec51
Moosinning D 143 Ea50
Mooste EST 107 Lc46
Moosthenning D 135 Eb49
Mór H 145 Hb53
Mora E 52 Db67
Mora P 50 Ad68
Mora S 87 Fc38
Moraby S 95 Fd40
Moracz PL 120 Fc32
Móra d'Ebre E 48 Ga62
Mora de Rubielos E 54 Fb65
Moradillo de Roa E 46 Dc61
Morąg PL 122 Hd31
Mórahalom H 153 Jb57
Moraice MNE 159 Hd67
Moraines F 24 Hc37
Moraira E 55 Fd70
Morais P 45 Bd60
Morakovo MNE 159 Ja69
Morakowo PL 121 Gd35
Móra la Nova E 48 Ga62
Moral de Calatrava E 52 Dc69
Moraleda de Zafayona E 60 Db75
Moraleja E 45 Bd65
Moraleja del Vino E 45 Cb60
Moraleja de Sayago E 45 Cb61
Morales E 37 Cb57
Morales de Campos E 46 Cd59
Morales del Vino E 45 Cb61
Morales de Rey E 45 Cb59
Morales de Toro E 45 Cc60
Morales de Valverde E 45 Cb59
Moralina E 45 Ca60
Moralzarzal E 46 Db63
Moramochi RUS 107 Mb49
Morancelle E 36 Ac55
Moräng S 72 Ha23
Morannes F 28 Fc40
Morano Calabro I 164 Gb78
Mora-Noret S 87 Fc38
Morar GB 6 Db09
Morărești RO 175 Db64
Mörarp S 110 Ed54
Morás E 36 Bc53
Morasverdes E 45 Ca63
Morata de Jalón E 47 Ed61
Morata de Jiloca E 47 Ed62
Moratade Tajuña E 46 Dc65
Moratalla E 60 Cc72
Moratalla E 61 Ec72
Morava BG 180 Dc69
Morava SLO 151 Fc59
Moravany SK 139 Ka48
Moravče SLO 151 Fc57
Moravče SLO 151 Fc58
Moravci SLO 145 Gb56
Moravec CZ 137 Gb46
Moravița RO 174 Bc62
Moravka BG 180 Eb70
Morávka CZ 137 Hb46
Moravská Nova Ves CZ 137 Gc49
Moravská Třebová CZ 137 Gc45
Moravské Budějovice CZ 136 Ga48
Moravské Lieskové SK 137 Ha48
Moravský Beroun CZ 137 Gd45
Moravský Krumlov CZ 137 Gb48
Morawica PL 130 Jb42
Morawin PL 129 Ha38
Morbach D 133 Bd44
Mörbacka S 94 Ed39
Morbegno I 149 Cd57
Morbier F 31 Jd44
Mörbisch am See A 145 Gc52
Mörbylånga S 111 Gb53
Morcenx F 39 Fa53
Morciano di Romagna I 156 Eb65
Morcillo E 45 Bd65
Morcone I 161 Fc73
Morcote CH 148 Cb58
Morcuera E 46 Dd61
Mordanga LV 105 Jc50
Mordelles F 28 Ed39
Mordiford GB 15 Ec26
Mordoğan TR 191 Eb85
Mordovo RUS 203 Fb12
Mordovskoe RUS 113 Jb58
Mordy PL 131 Ka36
More LV 106 Kd50
Mor'e RUS 202 Eb08
Moreanes P 58 Ba72
Morebattle GB 11 Ec14
Morecambe GB 11 Eb19
Moreda E 60 Dc74
Moreda de Aller E 37 Cc55
Morée F 29 Gb40
Moreiras E 36 Bb58
Mörel CH 141 Ca56
Morella E 48 Fc64
Moreni RO 176 Ea64
Mores I 168 Ca75
Moresco I 156 Ed67
Morestel F 35 Jc47
Moretonhampstead GB 19 Dd31
Moreton-in-Marsh GB 20 Ed26
Moreton Say GB 15 Ec23
Moret-sur-Loing F 29 Ha38
Moretta I 148 Bc61
Moreuil F 23 Gd34
Morez F 31 Jd44
Morfasso I 149 Cd62
Mörfelden D 134 Cc44
Mórfio GR 188 Ac81
Morfjorden N 66 Fc14
Morfou CY 206 Ja96
Morfovoúni GR 188 Bb81
Morgan's Vale GB 20 Ed30
Morgårdshammar S 95 Fd41
Morgat F 27 Db39
Morgenröthe-Rautenkranz D 135 Ec43
Morges CH 141 Bb55
Morgex I 148 Bb58
Morgins CH 141 Bb56
Morgny F 23 Gc35
Morgongåva S 95 Gb41
Morgos RO 171 Cd59
Morgowniki PL 123 Jd33
Morhange F 25 Ka36
Morhet B 132 Ba43
Mori I 149 Dc58
Mória GR 191 Ea83
Moriani-Plage F 154 Cc69
Mórichida H 145 Gd53
Moricone I 160 Eb71
Morienval F 23 Ha35
Moriers F 29 Gb39
Moriles E 60 Cd74
Morillas E 38 Ea56
Morina KSV 178 Ad71
Morina SRB 159 Jc69
Moringen D 126 Db39
Moripen N 93 Da45
Moritz D 127 Eb38
Moritzburg D 128 Fa41
Morjärv S 73 Ja21
Mork N 85 Da34
Morkarla S 96 Gd41
Mørke DK 101 Dd23
Mørkedal N 77 Db30
Morki RUS 203 Fd08
Morkkaperä FIN 69 Kb17
Mörkö S 96 Gc44
Morkov CZ 137 Ha46
Mørkøv DK 109 Ea26
Morkovice-Slížany CZ 137 Gd47
Mörkret S 86 Ed36
Mørkri N 85 Da36
Mørkveden N 66 Fa15
Morl D 127 Eb39
Morla E 37 Ca58
Morlaàs F 40 Fc55
Morlac F 29 Gd44
Morlaix F 26 Dd37
Morlanne F 39 Fb54
Mörlenbach D 134 Cc45
Morles D 126 Da42
Morley F 24 Jb37
Morley GB 16 Fa20
Mörlunda S 103 Ga50
Mormanno I 164 Gb78
Mormoiron F 42 Jc52
Mormont B 124 Ba42
Mornant F 34 Ja47
Mornas F 42 Jb52
Mornay-Berry F 29 Ha43
Mornay-sur-Allier F 30 Hb43
Mörnsheim D 134 Dc48
Moroeni RO 176 Dd63
Mörön S 73 Hd23
Morón de Almazán E 47 Eb61
Morón de la Frontera E 59 Cb75
Moros E 47 Ec61
Morosaglia F 154 Cb69
Morottaja FIN 74 Kd18
Morović SRB 153 Hd61
Morøya N 66 Fc15
Morozeni MD 173 Fc57
Morozovo RUS 99 Ma41
Morozovsk RUS 203 Fc14
Morozzo I 148 Bc62
Morpeth GB 11 Fa16
Mørriaunet N 78 Ea28
Morro d'Alba I 156 Ec66
Morrone del Sannio I 161 Fc72
Mörrum S 111 Fc54
Morrvollen N 78 Ea28
Morsains F 24 Hb37
Moršansk RUS 203 Fb11
Mörsbach D 125 Cb41
Morschen D 126 Da41
Morschheim D 133 Cb45
Mörsil S 78 Fa30
Morskoga krog S 95 Fd42
Morskoj RUS 113 Ja57
Mörskom FIN 90 Kc38
Morsleben D 127 Dd37
Morsovo RUS 203 Fb11
Morsum D 118 Da34
Mørsvik N 66 Fd16
Mortagne-au-Perche F 29 Ga38
Mortagne-sur-Gironde F 32 Fb48
Mortagne-sur-Sèvre F 28 Fa43
Mortágua P 44 Ad63
Mortain F 22 Fb37
Mortaizé F 28 Fd43
Mortara I 148 Cb60
Mortavika N 92 Ca43
Mörtberg S 73 Hc20
Mortcerf F 23 Ha37
Morteau F 31 Ka42
Mortegliano I 150 Ec58
Mortelle I 164 Ga83
Mortemart F 33 Ga46
Mortemer F 23 Gb34
Morteni RO 176 Dd65
Mortensnes N 63 Hd07
Mortensnes N 65 Kb06
Mörtfors S 103 Gb49
Mörtnäs S 96 Ha43
Mortola I 43 Kd53
Mortorp S 111 Ga53
Mortrée F 22 Fd37
Mörtschach A 143 Ec55
Mörtsjön S 79 Fc29
Mörttjärn S 72 Ha24
Morud DK 108 Dc26
Morunglav RO 175 Da66
Morup S 102 Ec51
Morup Mølle DK 100 Cd21
Morvich GB 6 Dc08
Morvillars F 31 Kb40
Morwenstow GB 18 Dc30
Moryń PL 120 Fb35
Morzeszczyn PL 121 Hb32
Morzine F 35 Kb45
Morzyczyn PL 120 Fc33
Mos E 36 Ad57
Mosal'sk RUS 202 Ed11
Moșana MD 173 Fb53
Mosås S 95 Fd44
Mosätt S 87 Fb34
Mosbach D 134 Cd46
Mosbekk N 94 Ec41
Mosbjerg DK 101 Dd19
Mosby N 92 Cd47
Moščenice HR 151 Fb60
Moščenička Draga HR 151 Fb60
Moschendorf A 145 Gb54
Mościska PL 131 Kd40
Mościsko PL 129 Gb42
Moscoso E 36 Ad57
Moscovei MD 177 Fc61
Mosculdy F 39 Fa55
Moseby DK 100 Dc20
Mosėdis LT 113 Jb53
Mösel A 144 Fb55
Mosel D 127 Eb42
Möser D 127 Ea37
Moșești RO 176 Ed64
Mosfellsbær IS 2 Ac04
Mosfiloti CY 206 Jb97
Moshófito GR 188 Ba81
Moshohóri GR 183 Bd79
Moshohóri GR 189 Bd83
Moshopótamos GR 183 Bd78
Mosina PL 129 Gc37
Mosiny PL 121 Gc33
Mosjö S 80 Gc30
Mosjøen N 70 Fa22
Moškanjci SLO 151 Ga57
Moskaret N 85 Ea34
Mosko BIH 159 Hc68
Moskoaia RO 175 Dc64
Moskog N 84 Cb36
Moskojärvi S 68 Hc16
Moskorzew PL 130 Ja42
Moskosel S 72 Ha22
Moskuvaara FIN 69 Ka15
Moskva RUS 202 Ed10
Moslavina Podravska H 152 Hb58
Mosles F 22 Fb35
Moșna RO 173 Fb58
Moșna RO 175 Db60
Moșnița RO 174 Bd61
Mosonmagyaróvár H 145 Gd52
Mošorin SRB 153 Jb60
Mošovce SK 138 Hc48
Mosqueruela E 54 Fb65
Moss N 93 Ea43
Mossala FIN 97 Ja40
Mossat GB 7 Ec09
Mossautal D 134 Cc45
Mosset F 41 Ha57
Mössingen D 134 Cc49
Mösslacher A 143 Ed56
Mosstodloch GB 5 Eb07
Møsstrand N 93 Da41
Most BG 185 Dd75
Most CZ 136 Fa43
Mostar BIH 158 Hb67
Moste SLO 144 Fb56
Moste SLO 151 Fb57
Mosteiro P 44 Bb62
Mostek CZ 136 Ga43
Moșteni RO 180 Dd67
Moster N 92 Ca41
Mosterhamn N 92 Ca41
Mostervika N 78 Ea27
Mosti N 66 Fc17
Mostki PL 128 Fd37
Mostki PL 130 Jc42
Mostkowo PL 122 Hd31
Móstoles E 46 Db65
Mostová SK 145 Ha51
Mostovoje RUS 113 Jc57
Mostovskoj RUS 205 Fd17
Mostowo PL 121 Gb31
Mostrim IRL 9 Cb20
Mosty PL 120 Fc33
Mosty PL 131 Kc38
Mosty u Jablunkova CZ 138 Hc46
Mošune HR 151 Fc61
Mosvik N 78 Eb28
Moszczanka PL 131 Jd39
Moszczanka PL 137 Gd44
Moszczenica PL 130 Hd39
Mota de Altarejos E 53 Eb66
Mota del Cuervo E 53 Ea67
Mota del Marqués E 46 Cd60
Moțăieni RO 176 Dd64
Motala S 103 Fc46
Motarzyno PL 121 Gc30
Motăței RO 175 Cc66
Moțca RO 172 Ec57
Motherwell GB 10 Ea13
Möthlow D 127 Ec36
Motike BIH 158 Gc64
Motilla del Palancar E 53 Ec67
Motilleja E 53 Ec68
Mötingselberget S 79 Gb25
Motkowice PL 130 Jb42
Motnik SLO 151 Fc57
Motoșeni RO 177 Fa60
Motovun HR 151 Fa60
Motril E 60 Dc76
Motru RO 175 Cc64
Motta I 150 Dd59
Motta di Livenza I 150 Eb59
Motta Montecorvino I 161 Fd73
Motteggiana I 149 Db61
Mottisfont GB 20 Fa29
Mottola I 162 Gd75
Möttönen FIN 81 Jd30
Motycz PL 131 Ka40
Mötzing D 135 Eb48
Mou DK 100 Dc21
Mouchamps F 28 Fa44
Mouchan F 40 Fd53
Mouchard F 31 Jc42
Moudon CH 141 Bb55
Moúdros GR 190 Dc81
Mougins F 43 Kc53
Mougon F 32 Fc45
Mouhijärvi FIN 89 Jc35
Mouhu FIN 90 Kd35
Mouilleron-en-Pareds F 28 Fb44
Moulay F 28 Fb39
Mouliherne F 28 Fd41
Moulins F 28 Fa40
Moulins F 30 Hb44
Moulins-Engilbert F 30 Hc43
Moulins-la-Marche F 22 Fd37
Moulismes F 33 Ga45
Moulle F 21 Gd30
Moulsoe GB 20 Fb26
Moult F 22 Fc36
Mountain Ash GB 19 Ea27
Mount Bellew IRL 8 Bd20
Mountbenger GB 11 Eb14
Mountcollins IRL 12 Bc24
Mount Garret IRL 13 Cc24
Mount Hamilton GB 9 Cc16
Mountmellick IRL 13 Cb22
Mount Nuggent IRL 9 Cc19
Mountrath IRL 13 Cb22
Mount Talbot IRL 8 Ca20
Mount Uniacke IRL 13 Ca25
Moura P 50 Ba71
Mourão P 51 Bb70
Moure P 44 Ad59
Mourentán E 36 Ad58
Mourenx F 39 Fb55
Mourèze F 41 Hc54
Mouriès F 42 Jb53
Mouriés GR 183 Ca76
Mouriscas P 50 Ad66
Mourmelon-le-Grand F 24 Hd35
Mourniés GR 200 Cb95
Mourujärvi FIN 74 Kd18
Mourulle E 36 Bb56
Mousehole GB 18 Da32
Mousoulita CY 206 Jc96
Moussac F 42 Ja53
Moussey F 25 Ka37
Moustéru F 26 Ea38
Moustey F 39 Fb52
Moustiers-Sainte-Marie F 42 Ka53
Moutfort L 133 Bb45
Mouthe F 31 Jd43
Mouthier-Haute-Pierre F 31 Jd42
Moutier CH 141 Bd53
Moutier-d'Ahun F 33 Gd46
Moûtiers F 35 Ka47
Moutiers-au-Perche F 29 Ga38
Moutiers-les-Mauxfaits F 32 Ed45
Moutiers-sur-le-Lay F 28 Fa44
Moutsoúna GR 196 Dc90
Moux-en-Morvan F 30 Hd42
Mouy F 23 Gd35
Mouzáki GR 188 Ba86
Mouzáki GR 188 Bb81
Mouzáki GR 194 Ba89
Mouzon F 24 Ja34
Movattnet S 80 Gd29
Movila RO 177 Fa66
Movila Banului RO 176 Ec64
Movila Miresii RO 177 Fa64
Movileni RO 172 Ed57
Movileni RO 173 Fa57
Movileni RO 175 Db66
Movileni RO 177 Fa62
Movilița RO 176 Eb65
Movilița RO 176 Ed61
Moville IRL 9 Cc15
Movriki GR 189 Cb85
Moy GB 9 Cd17
Moyarget GB 9 Da15
Moyasta IRL 12 Bb23
Moyaux F 22 Fd36
Moycullen IRL 12 Bc21
Moy-de-l'Aisne F 24 Hb34
Moyenvic F 25 Ka36
Moyeuvre F 25 Jc35
Möykky FIN 89 Ja33
Möykkylänperä FIN 82 Kc26
Möykkyperä FIN 81 Jd25
Moylgrove GB 14 Dc26
Moylough IRL 8 Bd20
Moymore IRL 12 Bd22
Moyne IRL 13 Cd23
Moyuela E 47 Fa62
Moyvalle IRL 13 Cc21
Moyvore IRL 9 Cb20
Mozac F 34 Hb46
Mozăceni RO 176 Dd65
Možajsk RUS 202 Ed10
Mózar E 45 Cb59
Mozárbez E 45 Cb62
Mozelj SLO 151 Fc59
Možga RUS 203 Ga08
Mozgovo SRB 178 Bd68
Mozirje SLO 151 Fc57
Mozoncillo E 46 Db62
Mozuli RUS 107 Ma50
Mozyr RUS 113 Jc59
Mozzanica I 149 Cd59
Mozzate I 148 Cb58
Mozzecane I 149 Db60
Mračaj BIH 158 Ha65
Mrągowo PL 122 Jb31
Mrakovica BIH 152 Gc61
Mramor BG 185 Eb74
Mramor BIH 158 Hb68
Mramor SRB 178 Bd69
Mramorak SRB 174 Bc63
Mratinje MNE 159 Hd67
Mrežičko MK 183 Bc76
Mrežničko HR 151 Fd60
Mrkalji BIH 159 Hd64
Mrkonjić Grad BIH 152 Gd63
Mrkopalj HR 151 Fc60
Mrmoš SRB 178 Bb68
Mrocza PL 121 Gd34
Mroczeń PL 129 Ha40
Mroczno PL 122 Hd33
Mrozy PL 131 Jd37
Mrsać SRB 178 Ba67
Mrzen MK 183 Bc75
Mrzezino PL 121 Ha29
Mrzeżyno PL 120 Fd31
Mrzli Studenec SLO 151 Fa57
Mrzygłód PL 139 Kb45
Mšcice PL 120 Ga31
Mścichy PL 123 Ka32
Mscislav BY 202 Ec12
Mšec CZ 136 Fa44
Mšené Lázně CZ 136 Fb43
Mšeno CZ 136 Fc43
Mšinskaja RUS 99 Mb42
Mstyczów PL 130 Ja42
Mszana Dolna PL 138 Ja45
Mszanna PL 131 Kb37
Mszczonów PL 130 Jb38
Mtež RUS 107 Lc46
Muccia I 156 Ec67
Much D 125 Ca41
Muchalls GB 7 Ed09
Mucharz PL 138 Hd45
Mücheln D 127 Ea40
Muchówka PL 138 Jb45
Much Wenlock GB 15 Ec24
Mučibaba KSV 178 Bc72
Mučibaba SRB 179 Ca68
Mučići HR 151 Fb60
Mucientes E 46 Cd60
Mücka D 128 Fc40
Muckamore GB 9 Da17
Mučkapskij RUS 203 Fc12
Mücke D 126 Cd42
Muckross IRL 12 Bb25
Muda P 50 Ab71
Mudanya TR 186 Fc80
Mudaralı TR 186 Ga78
Mudau D 134 Cd46
Müden D 118 Db35
Mudiste EST 98 Kd45
Mudurnu TR 187 Ha79
Muel E 47 Fa61
Muelas de los Caballeros E 37 Ca58
Muelas del Pan E 45 Cb60
Muereasca RO 175 Db63
Müezzinler TR 187 Gc78
Müezzinler TR 199 Gd89
Muff IRL 9 Cc15
Muga de Sayago E 45 Ca61
Mugaire E 39 Ed56
Mugardos E 36 Ba53
Muge P 50 Ab67
Mügeln D 127 Ed38
Mügeln D 127 Ed40
Mugeni RO 176 Dd60
Muggensturm D 133 Cb48
Muggia I 151 Fa59
Muğla TR 198 Fb90
Müglitztal D 128 Fa42
Mugnano del Cardinale I 161 Fc75
Mugron F 39 Fb54
Muhi H 146 Jc51
Mühlacker D 134 Cc48
Mühlanger D 127 Ec38
Mühlau D 127 Ec42
Mühlbeck D 127 Eb39
Mühlberg D 127 Ed40
Mühldorf A 144 Fd50
Mühldorf a.Inn D 143 Eb50
Mühlenbach am Hochkönig A 143 Ec53
Mühlen-Eichsen D 119 Ea32
Mühlenthal D 135 Eb43
Mühlhausen D 126 Dc40
Mühlhausen D 134 Dc45
Mühlhausen D 134 Dc49
Mühlhausen D 135 Dd47
Mühlhausen/Kraichgau D 134 Cc47
Mühlhausen = Mulhouse F 31 Kb40
Mühlheim A 143 Ed50
Mühlheim D 134 Cc44
Mühlheim D 142 Cc51
Mühlhofen D 142 Cd52
Mühltal A 143 Dd54
Mühltal D 134 Cc45
Mühltroff D 135 Ea43
Muhos FIN 74 Kb24
Muhovo BG 179 Cd72
Muhr A 143 Ed54
Muhr am See D 134 Dc47
Muides-sur-Loire F 29 Gc41
Muikirk GB 10 Ea14
Muimenta E 36 Ba56
Muíña E 36 Bc55
Muinchille IRL 9 Cc19
Muineachán IRL 9 Cc18
Muine Bheag IRL 13 Cc23
Muir of Ord GB 7 Dd08
Muittari FIN 82 Ka31
Mujdić BIH 158 Gd64
Mujejärvi FIN 83 Lc26
Mukačeve UA 204 Dd16
Mukašov CZ 136 Fc45
Mukate KSV 178 Bb71
Mukkajärvi FIN 74 Jd18
Mukkajärvi S 73 Ja19
Mukkala FIN 69 Kb15
Mukkala FIN 69 Kd16
Mukkavaara FIN 69 Kc16
Mukkurasoja FIN 64 Jc10
Muktupāveli LV 107 Lb52
Mula E 55 Ed72
Mularinperä FIN 75 Kc20
Mulbarton GB 17 Gb24
Mulben GB 7 Ec08
Mulda D 127 Ed42
Mulegns CH 142 Cd56
Mules I 143 Dd55
Mulfingen D 134 Dd46
Mülheim an der Ruhr D 125 Bd39
Mulhouse F 31 Kb40
Mulino di Arzachena I 168 Cb74
Muljava SLO 151 Fc58
Muljula FIN 91 Ld32
Mülkköy TR 193 Hb82
Mullach Íde IRL 13 Cd21
Mullagh IRL 13 Cd21
Mullardoch House GB 6 Dc08
Mullerup DK 109 Ea26
Müllheim CH 142 Cc52
Müllheim D 141 Bd51
Mullhyttan S 95 Fc44
Mullinahone IRL 13 Cb24
Mullinavat IRL 13 Cb24
Mullingar IRL 9 Cb20
Mullion GB 18 Da32
Müllrose D 128 Fb37
Mullsjö S 80 Hb29
Mullsjö S 102 Fa48
Mulrany IRL 8 Bb19
Mulsanne F 28 Fd40
Mulseryd S 102 Fa49
Mulstranda N 66 Fc17
Mulstrup DK 109 Eb26
Multeddu I 168 Ca74
Multia FIN 90 Ka32
Multiperä FIN 75 Lb20
Multrå S 80 Gc31
Mumby GB 17 Fd22
Mumcuköy TR 192 Fb83
Mumor H 145 Gc56
Munaðarnes IS 2 Ad02
Munakka FIN 81 Jb31
Muñana E 46 Cd63
Münchberg D 135 Ea44
Müncheberg D 128 Fb36
München D 143 Dd51
Münchenbernsdorf D 127 Ea42
Münchhausen D 126 Cc41
Münchsmünster D 135 Ea49
Münchsteinach D 134 Dc45
Münchwilen CH 142 Cc52
Muncurlu TR 187 Ha78
Mundaka E 38 Ea55
Mundão P 44 Ba62
Munderfing A 143 Ed51
Munderkingen D 142 Da50
Mundesley GB 17 Gb23
Mundford GB 17 Ga24
Mundheim N 84 Cb40
Mundolsheim F 25 Kc37
Munébrega E 47 Ec62
Munera E 53 Ea69
Mungia E 38 Ea55
Mungret IRL 12 Bd23
Muņi LV 105 Jc49
Münichreit A 144 Fd50
Muñico E 46 Cd63
Muniesa E 48 Fb62
Munina Wielkie PL 139 Kb44
Muniskiai LV 114 Kb57
Munka-Ljungby S 110 Ed54
Munkbysjön S 87 Ga33
Munkebo DK 109 Dd26
Munkedal S 102 Eb46
Munken N 77 Dd29
Munkflohögen S 79 Fc29
Munkfors S 94 Fa42
Munkla N 67 Gb14
Munknes N 65 Kc08
Munksund S 73 Hd23
Munktorp S 95 Ga43
Munkviken S 81 Hd26
Münnerstadt D 134 Db43
Munningen D 134 Dc48
Muñogalindo E 46 Cd63
Muñopedro E 46 Da63
Munsala FIN 81 Ja29
Münsing D 143 Dd51
Münsingen CH 141 Bd54
Münsingen D 134 Cd49
Munsö S 96 Gc43
Münster CH 141 Ca56
Munster D 118 Db34
Münster D 125 Cb37
Münster D 134 Cc44
Munster F 25 Ka36
Munster F 31 Kb39
Münster/Lech D 134 Dc49
Münstermaifeld D 133 Ca43
Münstertal D 141 Ca51
Muntele Băișorii RO 171 Cd58
Muntele Cacovei RO 171 Cd59
Munteni RO 177 Fa61
Munteni Buzău RO 176 Ec65
Muntenii de Jos RO 173 Fa59
Muntraching D 142 Dc51
Muntzenheim F 31 Kc38
Münzenberg D 134 Cc43
Münzkirchen A 143 Ed50
Muodoslompolo S 68 Ja14
Muonio FIN 68 Ja14
Muonionalusta S 68 Ja14
Muoniovaara S 68 Ja14
Muorjevaara S 67 Hb17
Muotathal CH 141 Cb54
Muotkajärvi FIN 68 Ja13
Muotkanruoktu FIN 64 Jd10
Muotkavaara FIN 68 Jb15
Muradelle E 36 Bb56
Muradiye TR 191 Ec85
Muradiyesarnıç TR 192 Fb81
Murakka FIN 90 Kc35
Muráň SK 138 Ja48
Murāni LV 107 Lc51
Murani RO 174 Bd60
Murano I 150 Eb60
Muraste EST 98 Kb42
Murat F 34 Hb49
Muratátka H 145 Gc56
Muratbağı TR 193 Ha87
Muratbey TR 187 Ha79
Murati EST 107 Lc47
Muratlar TR 191 Eb81
Muratlı TR 185 Ed77
Muratlı TR 192 Ga85
Murato F 154 Cb69
Murat-sur-Vèbre F 41 Hb54
Murau A 144 Fb54
Muravera I 169 Cb79
Muravka LV 115 Lc53
Murazzano I 148 Bd62
Murça P 44 Bb60
Murchin D 120 Fa32
Murcia E 55 Fa72
Murcki PL 138 Hc44
Murczyn PL 121 Gd35
Mur-de-Barrez F 33 Ha50
Mur-de-Bretagne F 27 Ea39
Mur-de-Sologne F 29 Gc41
Mureck A 144 Ga56
Mürefte TR 185 Ec78
Mureno BG 179 Cb71
Mures E 60 Db74
Muret F 40 Gb55
Murg D 141 Ca52
Murgaševo MK 183 Bb75
Murgași RO 175 Da65
Murgeni RO 177 Fb60
Murgenthal CH 141 Ca53
Murgești RO 176 Ec63
Murgia E 38 Ea56
Muri CH 141 Cb53
Muriedas E 38 Dc54
Murigan AL 163 Ja71
Murighiol RO 177 Fd64
Murillo de Río Leza E 39 Eb58
Murillo el Fruto E 39 Ed58
Murino MNE 159 Jb68
Murizë AL 182 Ac74
Murjek S 73 Hc19
Mürlenbach D 133 Bc43
Murley GB 9 Cc17
Murmastiene LV 107 Lb51
Mürmuiža LV 106 Kd48
Murnau am Staffelsee D 143 Dd52
Mürnieki LV 106 La50
Mürnieki LV 107 Lb51
Muro E 57 Hc67
Muro F 154 Cb69

Muro – Nejdek

Muro P 44 Ad60
Muro de Aguas E 47 Ec59
Muro del Alcoy E 55 Fb70
Murol F 34 Hb47
Murole FIN 89 Jd34
Muro Leccese I 163 Hc77
Muro Lucano I 161 Fd75
Murom RUS 203 Fb10
Muromskoe RUS 113 Ja58
Muron F 32 Fb46
Murony H 147 Jd55
Muros E 36 Ac55
Murovicy RUS 107 Ld46
Murów PL 129 Ha42
Murowana Goślina PL 129 Gc36
Mürren CH 141 Bd55
Murrhardt D 134 Da48
Murronkylä FIN 74 Kb24
Murs F 42 Jc53
Mursal TR 198 Ga92
Mursalevo BG 179 Cb73
Mursallı TR 185 Ec78
Mursallı TR 197 Ed88
Mürseller TR 192 Fd81
Mürseller TR 199 Gb89
Mûrs-Erigné F 28 Fb42
Murska Sobota SLO 145 Gb56
Mursko Središće HR 145 Gb56
Mursley GB 20 Fb26
Murtamo FIN 89 Ja37
Murtas E 61 Dd76
Murten CH 141 Bc54
Murter HR 157 Ga65
Murtino MK 183 Ca75
Murto FIN 74 Ka24
Murtoi FIN 83 Ma31
Murtoinen FIN 90 Kd32
Murtolahti FIN 82 La29
Murtomäki FIN 82 Kd26
Murtomäki FIN 82 Kc28
Murton GB 11 Fa17
Murtoranta FIN 83 Ld28
Murtosa P 44 Ac62
Murtovaara FIN 75 Lc24
Murtovaara FIN 75 La20
Murtovaara FIN 83 Lc27
Muruvik N 78 Eb30
Murvica HR 157 Fd64
Murviel-lès-Béziers F 41 Hb54
Mürzsteg A 144 Fd52
Murzynko PL 121 Hb35
Murzynowo PL 128 Fd36
Mürzzuschlag A 144 Ga53
Muş TR 205 Ga20
Muša RUS 203 Fd08
Musaca TR 192 Fa84
Musaitu MD 177 Fc62
Musaköy TR 192 Ga83
Musalar TR 192 Fd83
Musamaa FIN 81 Jc30
Muşăteşti RO 175 Dc63
Müsch D 125 Bd42
Müschenbach D 125 Cb42
Muselievo BG 180 Dc68
Müsellim TR 185 Ed76
Muşeniţa RO 172 Eb54
Muşeteşti RO 175 Cd63
Musetrene N 85 Dc36
Musina BG 180 Dd70
Musken N 66 Ga15
Muskö S 96 Gd44
Muslu TR 187 Hb76
Musninkai LT 114 Kd57
Musorka RUS 203 Ga10
Mušovića Rijeka MNE 159 Jb68
Musqetë AL 182 Ac75
Mussalo FIN 90 La38
Musselburgh GB 11 Eb13
Musselkanaal NL 117 Ca34
Mussidan F 32 Fd49
Mussomeli I 166 Ed85
Mussy-sur-Seine F 30 Ja39
Mustadfors S 94 Ec45
Mustafakemalpaşa TR 192 Fb81
Müstair CH 142 Db56
Mustajärvi FIN 89 Jb33
Mustajärvi FIN 89 Jd34
Mustajoki FIN 89 Jb35
Mustalahti FIN 90 Ka34
Mustalammi FIN 89 Jd39
Mustamaa FIN 81 Jd29
Mustamaa FIN 82 Kb25
Mustansalo FIN 82 La31
Mustasaari FIN 81 Ja30
Mustaskulma FIN 90 Ka35
Mustavaara FIN 75 La22
Mustavaara FIN 75 Kc20
Musteaţa MD 173 Fa56
Müstecep TR 185 Ec78
Mustikkaperä FIN 82 Ka30
Mustila FIN 90 Kd37
Mustinlahti FIN 83 Lb30
Mustinmäki FIN 82 La31
Mustinsalo FIN 91 Lb32
Mustio FIN 98 Ka40
Mustjala EST 105 Jc46
Mustla EST 106 La46
Mustola FIN 69 Kb11
Mustolanmäki FIN 82 Kd31
Mustolanmäki FIN 82 La28
Mustvee EST 99 Lb43
Musulcali TR 191 Ed85
Musut SRB 179 Ca71
Mušutište KSV 178 Ba72
Muszaki PL 122 Ja33
Muszyna PL 138 Jc46
Muta SLO 144 Fd56
Mutala FIN 89 Jd35
Mutalahti FIN 83 Mb30
Mutapohja FIN 82 Kb31
Mutěnice CZ 137 Gc48
Muthill GB 7 Ea12
Mutka FIN 74 Jd20
Mutlangen D 134 Da48
Mutlu TR 191 Eb83
Mutluca TR 197 Ed90
Muttalip TR 193 Gc81
Mutterberg-Alm A 142 Dc54
Mutters A 143 Dd54
Mutterstadt D 133 Cb46
Mutxamel E 55 Fb71
Mutzig F 25 Kb37
Mützlitz D 127 Ec36
Mutzschen D 127 Ec40
Muurame FIN 90 Kb33
Muurasjärvi FIN 82 Ka28
Muurikkala FIN 91 Lb37
Muurla FIN 97 Jd39
Muurola FIN 74 Jd19
Muurola FIN 91 Lb37
Muuruvesi FIN 82 La29
Muuskonkangas FIN 74 Kb18
Müüsleri EST 98 Kd43
Muvga EST 98 Kb42
Muxía E 36 Ac54
Muzga BG 180 Dc71
Muzillac F 27 Eb41
Muzinë AL 182 Ac79
Mužla SK 146 Hc52
Mužlja SRB 153 Jc60
Mužlja SRB 174 Bb62
Muzzana del Turgnano I 150 Ec58
Mybster GB 5 Eb04
Mychajlivka UA 205 Fa16
Mycielin PL 129 Ha38
Myckelgensjö S 80 Gc29
Myckle S 80 Hc25
Myckleby S 102 Eb47
Myckling S 80 Gd30
Myczków PL 139 Kb46
Myddfai GB 15 Dd26
Mydland N 92 Cb45
Mydroilyn GB 15 Dd25
Myggenäs S 102 Eb48
Myhinpää FIN 82 Kd31
Myjava SK 137 Gd49
Mykanów PL 130 Hc41
Myking N 84 Ca38
Mykland N 93 Da45
Myklebostad N 66 Ga13
Myklebostad N 66 Fc16
Myklebostad N 92 Cd45
Myklebust N 84 Ca35
Myklenes N 67 Gb11
Myklestøyl N 92 Cd44
Mykolajiv UA 204 Dd15
Mykolajiv UA 204 Fd16
Mykolajivka UA 205 Fa17
Mylau D 135 Eb43
Myllperä FIN 90 Ka33
Myllyaho FIN 82 Ka29
Mylly-Karttu FIN 89 Jc34
Myllykoski FIN 81 Jb31
Myllykoski FIN 90 La37
Myllykselä FIN 90 Kb36
Myllykylä FIN 89 Jb32
Myllykylä FIN 89 Jd38
Myllykylä FIN 90 Ka35
Myllykylä FIN 98 Ka39
Myllylahti FIN 75 Lb23
Myllymaa FIN 89 Jc36
Myllymäki FIN 89 Jd32
Myllypohja FIN 90 Kc37
Mylopótamos GR 195 Bd92
Mylund DK 100 Dc20
Mynämäki FIN 89 Jb38
Mynterlä FIN 98 Ka39
Myntillä FIN 90 Kd35
Myon F 31 Jd42
Myöntäjä FIN 89 Jb35
Myr N 66 Fd16
Myra S 87 Gb35
Myran N 78 Ea29
Myrane N 92 Ca45
Myrås S 72 Gc22
Myrbacka S 72 Gd21
Myrbakken N 64 Ka06
Myre N 66 Fd11
Myre N 66 Fc12
Myreng N 85 Dc36
Myresjö S 103 Fc50
Myrhaug N 67 Gd11
Myrheden S 73 Hb21
Myrheden S 73 Hb23
Myrholen S 95 Fc40
Myrhorod UA 202 Ed14
Myrkdalen N 84 Cc38
Myrkky FIN 89 Ja33
Myrland N 66 Fd12
Myrland N 66 Fa14
Myrlandshaugen N 67 Gb12
Myrmoen N 86 Ec32
Myrnes N 63 Hc07
Myronivka UA 204 Ec15
Myrorna S 80 Hc28
Myrset N 64 Jb06
Myrset N 78 Ed27
Myrskylä FIN 90 Kc38
Myrtou CY 206 Ja96
Myrvika N 78 Ec26
Myrviken S 79 Fb31
Mysen N 94 Eb43
Myshall IRL 13 Cc23
Myślachowice PL 138 Hd44
Myślenice PL 138 Ja45
Myślibórz PL 120 Fc35
Myślibórz PL 128 Ga41
Myślice PL 122 Hc31
Myślina PL 129 Hb42
Mysłowice PL 138 Hc44
Mysovka RUS 113 Jb57
Myssjö S 79 Fb31
Mystki PL 120 Fc35
Myszków PL 130 Hd42
Myszyniec PL 122 Jc33
Mytišči RUS 202 Ed10
Mýtna SK 138 Hd49
Mýto CZ 136 Fa45
Mýto pod Ďumbierom SK 138 Ja48
Mzurki PL 130 Hd40

N

Naakenavuoma FIN 68 Jc15
Naaldwijk NL 116 Ac36
Naamanka FIN 75 Kc21
Naamijoki FIN 74 Jb18
Naantali FIN 97 Jb39
Naappila FIN 90 Ka35
Naapurinvaara FIN 82 La26
Naarajärvi FIN 83 Ld28
Naarajärvi FIN 90 Kd32
Naarajoki FIN 81 Ja31
Naaranlahti FIN 91 Ld33
Naarden NL 116 Ba36
Näärinki FIN 90 La33
Naarminkylä FIN 89 Jc33
Naartijärvi S 73 Jb21
Naarva FIN 83 Ma28
Naas IRL 13 Cc22
Näätämö FIN 65 Kc08
Näätänmaa FIN 83 Lb31
Näätävaara FIN 75 Lb23
Naatule FIN 89 Jc37
Nabbelund S 104 Gc50
Nabburg D 135 Eb46
Naberežny Čelny RUS 203 Ga08
Naburn GB 16 Fb20
Nabuvoll N 86 Eb33
Nacak TR 185 Ec76
Na Cealla Beaga IRL 8 Ca16
Načeradec CZ 136 Fc46
Nachamps F 32 Fb46
Náchod CZ 137 Gb43
Nachrodt-Wiblingwerde D 125 Ca39
Nacimiento E 61 Ea75
Nacina Ves SK 139 Ka48
Näckådalen S 87 Fb37
Nackenheim D 133 Cb44
Naclaw PL 121 Gb31
Na Clocha Liatha IRL 13 Da22
Nacpolsk PL 130 Ja36
Nad IRL 12 Bc25
Nadalj SRB 153 Jb59
Nadarevo BG 181 Ec70
Nadarzyce PL 121 Gb33
Nadarzyn PL 130 Jb37
Nadăş RO 170 Ca59
Nádasd H 145 Gc55
Nádasdladány H 145 Hb54
Nadbory PL 123 Ka33
Naddvik N 85 Da37
Nådendal = Naantali FIN 97 Jb39
Nadeş RO 175 Dc60
Nadezdino RUS 122 Ja30
Nădlac RO 170 Bc59
Nădrag RO 174 Ca61
Nadrljan SRB 153 Jb58
Nádudvar H 147 Jd53
Nadușita MD 173 Fb54
Nadvirna UA 204 Ea16
Năeni RO 176 Ec64
Nærbø N 92 Ca45
Nærestad N 93 Db45
Nærøy N 78 Eb25
Nærøy N 84 Cc37
Nærsnes N 93 Dd42
Næs DK 109 Eb28
Næsbjerg DK 108 Da25
Næstved DK 109 Eb27
Näfels CH 142 Cc54
Nafizpaşa TR 192 Ga81
Náfpaktos GR 188 Bb85
Náfplio GR 195 Bd88
Nafría de Llana E 47 Ea60
Nag N 92 Ca43
Nagajbakovo RUS 203 Ga08
Nagele NL 116 Bb35
Naggen S 87 Ga34
Naglarby S 95 Fd40
Naglestad N 92 Cc46
Nagli LV 107 Lb52
Nagli LV 107 Lc51
Nagłowice PL 130 Ja42
Nagold D 134 Cc49
Nagore E 39 Ed57
Nagor'e RUS 202 Ed09
Nagórki PL 130 Hc37
Nagoszewo PL 123 Jd35
Nago-Torbole I 149 Dc58
Nagu FIN 97 Jb40
Nagyalásony H 145 Gd54
Nagyatád H 152 Gd57
Nagybajom H 152 Ha57
Nagybaracska H 153 Hd58
Nagyberki H 152 Hb57
Nagybörzsöny H 146 Hc51
Nagycenk H 145 Gc53
Nagydobos H 147 Kb50
Nagydorog H 146 Hc56
Nagyecsed H 147 Kb51
Nagyfüged H 146 Jb52
Nagyhalász H 147 Ka50
Nagyharsany H 153 Hc58
Nagyigmánd H 145 Hb52
Nagyiván H 146 Jc52
Nagykálló H 147 Ka51
Nagykamarás H 147 Jd56
Nagykanizsa H 145 Gc56
Nagykáta H 146 Ja53
Nagykereki H 147 Ka53
Nagykónyi H 145 Hb56
Nagykőrös H 146 Ja54
Nagylak H 153 Jc57
Nagylengyel H 145 Gc55
Nagylóc H 146 Ja51
Nagymágocs H 146 Jc56
Nagymányok H 153 Hc57
Nagymaros H 146 Hc52
Nagynyárád H 153 Hc58
Nagyoroszi H 146 Hd51
Nagypeterd H 152 Ha58
Nagyrábé H 147 Jd53
Nagyrécse H 145 Gd56
Nagyszékely H 146 Hc56
Nagyszénás H 146 Jc55
Nagyvázsony H 145 Ha55
Nagyvenyim H 146 Hc55
Naha EST 99 Lc45
Naharros E 53 Ea66
Nahe D 118 Dc32
Nahimovo RUS 113 Jb58
Nahkela FIN 98 Kb39
Nahkiaisoja FIN 74 Jc20
Nahrendorf D 119 Dd34
Nahwinden D 127 Dd42
Naidaş RO 174 Bd64
Naila D 135 Ea43
Nailloux F 40 Gc55
Nailly F 30 Hb39
Nailsea GB 19 Eb28
Nailstone GB 16 Fa24
Nailsworth GB 19 Ec27
Naipköy TR 185 Ed78
Nairn GB 5 Ea07
Naisjärv S 73 Hd19
Naitisuanto S 67 Hb16
Naiviai LT 114 Kd54
Naizin F 27 Eb39
Najac F 41 Gd52
Najdenovo BG 180 Dc73
Nájera E 38 Ea58
Nakielno PL 121 Gb34
Nakkilä FIN 68 Ja12
Nakkaş TR 186 Fc77
Nakkeri FIN 90 Kb34
Nakkeslett N 62 Gd07
Nakkila FIN 89 Jb36
Naklik PL 139 Kb43
Nakło PL 130 Hd42
Nakło PL 137 Ha43
Naklo SLO 151 Fb57
Nakło nad Notecią PL 121 Gd34
Nakolec MK 182 Ba76
Nakomiady PL 122 Jc31
Nakovo SRB 153 Jc58
Nakovo SRB 174 Bb60
Nakskov DK 109 Ea28
Nalbant RO 177 Fc64
Nalbantlar TR 197 Ed88
Nal'čik RUS 205 Ga17
Nalda E 39 Eb58
Nälden S 79 Fb30
Naldöken TR 191 Ec86
Nałęczów PL 131 Ka40
Naleda E 36 Bc55
Nálepkovo SK 138 Jc48
Nalınlar TR 192 Fc81
Näljänka FIN 75 Kd22
Nalkki FIN 75 Kd24
Nallıdere TR 193 Ha81
Nalliers F 32 Fa45
Nallıhan TR 187 Ha80
Nalzen F 40 Gc56
Nalžovské Hory CZ 135 Ed47
Námata GR 189 Bd81
Namazgâh TR 191 Ec81
Nambroca E 52 Db66
Namdalseid N 78 Eb27
Nämdö S 96 Ha44
Namen = Namur B 124 Ad42
Náměšť nad Oslavou CZ 137 Gb47
Náměšť na Hané CZ 137 Gc46
Námestovo SK 138 Hd46
Namiķi LV 105 Jd52
Namna N 94 Ec39
Nămoloasa RO 177 Fa63
Nampcel F 24 Hb34
Nämpnäs FIN 89 Hd32
Nampont F 23 Gc32
Namsos N 78 Ec26
Namsskogan N 78 Fa25
Namsvatn N 79 Fb25
Namur B 124 Ad42
Namysłów PL 129 Gd41
Nana RO 181 Ec67
Nançay F 29 Gd42
Nanclares de la Oca E 38 Ea56
Nancras F 32 Fb47
Nancray F 31 Jd41
Nancy F 25 Jd37
Nandlstadt D 135 Ea49
Nănești RO 177 Fa63
Nangis F 30 Hb38
Nannerch GB 15 Eb22
Nanov RO 180 Dd67
Nans-les-Pins F 42 Jd54
Nans-sous-Sainte-Anne F 31 Jd42
Nant F 41 Hc53
Nant-ddu GB 19 Ea27
Nanterre F 23 Gd37
Nantes F 28 Ed42
Nantes P 44 Bb59
Nanteuil-en-Vallée F 32 Fd46
Nanteuil-la-Forêt F 24 Hc36
Nanteuil-le-Haudouin F 23 Ha36
Nantgaredig GB 15 Dd26
Nantiat F 33 Gb46
Nanton F 30 Jb44
Nantua F 35 Jc45
Nantwich GB 15 Ec23
Nantyffyllon GB 19 Ea27
Nantyglo GB 19 Eb27
Nant-y-moel GB 19 Ea27
Naours F 23 Gd33
Náousa GR 196 Db90
Náoussa GR 183 Bc77
Năpădeni MD 173 Fb56
Năpadova MD 173 Fc54
Nåpågard N 93 Db41
Napajedla CZ 137 Gd47
Napierki PL 122 Ja33
Napiwoda PL 122 Ja33
Napkor H 147 Ka51
Napoli I 161 Fb75
Năpradea RO 171 Cd56
Napton GB 20 Fa25
Náquera E 54 Fb67
När S 104 Ha50
Narač BY 202 Ea12
Nárad SK 145 Ha52
Nárai H 145 Gc54
Narberth GB 18 Dc27
Narbolia I 169 Bd77
Narbonne F 41 Hb55
Narbonne-Plage F 41 Hb55
Narcao I 169 Bd80
Narcy F 30 Hb42
Nard HR 153 Hc59
Nardevitz D 120 Fa29
Nardò I 162 Hb77
Narečenski bani BG 184 Db74
Narew PL 123 Kc34
Narewka PL 123 Kc34
Närhilä FIN 82 Kc31
Narila FIN 90 La33
Narinceli TR 192 Fc86
Nariņciems LV 105 Jd50
Narjoki FIN 89 Ja37
Narjordet N 86 Eb33
Narkaus FIN 74 Ka19
Narken S 73 Ja18
Narlı TR 185 Ed79
Narlı TR 193 Hb81
Narman TR 205 Ga19
Narni I 156 Eb69
Naro I 166 Ed86
Narodowy PL 137 Gb43
Naro-Fominsk RUS 202 Ed10
Narol PL 131 Kc42
Narón E 36 Bb56
Narost PL 120 Fb35
Narovlja BY 202 Eb13
Närpes FIN 89 Hd33
Närpiö FIN 89 Hd33
Narros del Castillo E 46 Cd63
Närsäkkälä FIN 91 Ma32
Narsdorf D 127 Ec41
Närsen S 95 Fb40
Narta AL 182 Aa77
Narta HR 152 Gc58
Nartkala RUS 205 Ga17
Nārtuna S 96 Gd42
Narty PL 122 Jb32
Nāruja RO 176 Ec62
Nārunga S 102 Ed48
Naruska FIN 69 Kd16
Naruszewo PL 130 Ja36
Narva EST 99 Lc41
Narva FIN 89 Jd36
Närvä FIN 90 Kb35
Narva-Jõesuu EST 99 Lc41
Närvijoki FIN 89 Ja32
Narvik N 67 Gb13
Naryškino RUS 202 Ed12
Narzole I 148 Bd62
Näs N 93 Db44
Näs S 79 Fc31
Näs S 95 Fc40
Näs S 102 Ec48
Näs S 104 Gd51
Naşa TR 192 Fc84
Näsåker S 79 Gb30
Năsăud RO 171 Dc56
Nasavrky CZ 136 Ga45
Nasbinals F 34 Hb50
Näs bruk S 95 Gb41
Na Sceiri IRL 9 Da20
Naseby GB 20 Fb25
Našec KSV 178 Ba72
Näset FIN 81 Hd31
Näset S 79 Fd26
Näset S 87 Fc37
Näset S 87 Fd33
Näset S 87 Ga33
Näshult S 103 Fd50
Näshulta S 95 Ga44
Našice HR 152 Hb59
Nasiedle PL 137 Ha44
Nasielsk PL 130 Jb36
Näsinge S 94 Eb44
Näske S 80 Gd31
Näskott S 79 Fb30
Näsland S 80 Ha28
Näsliden S 72 Ha24
Naso I 167 Fc84
Nasrettinhoca TR 193 Hb83
Nassau D 133 Ca43
Nassenfels D 135 Dd48
Nassenheide D 119 Ed35
Nassereith A 142 Dc53
Nässja S 103 Fc46
Nässjö S 79 Ga29
Nässjö S 103 Fc49
Nässuma EST 105 Jd46
Nässvallen S 87 Fb33
Nästansjö S 79 Ga25
Nastätten D 133 Cb43
Nastazin PL 120 Fd33
Nästebacka S 94 Ec43
Nästi FIN 89 Ja38
Nästola FIN 90 Kc37
Nästurelu RO 180 Dd68
Näsum S 111 Fb54
Nasutów PL 131 Ka39
Nasuty PL 123 Jd30
Nasva EST 105 Jc47
Näsviken S 79 Fd28
Näsviken S 87 Gb35
Natalinci SRB 174 Bb65
Natile Nuovo I 164 Gb83
Natkiškiai LT 113 Jc57
Natoye B 124 Ad42
Nattavaara S 73 Hc19
Nattavaara by S 73 Hc18
Natternbach A 144 Fa50
Nattheim D 134 Db49
Nättraby S 111 Fd54
Nattvatn N 64 Jc09
Naturno I 142 Dc55
Naturns I 142 Dc55
Naucelle F 41 Ha52
Naudaskalns LV 107 Lc49
Nauders A 142 Db55
Naudite LV 106 Ka52
Nauen D 127 Ec36
Nauendorf D 127 Eb39
Nauheim D 134 Cc44
Naujadvaris LT 114 La59
Naujakiemis LT 114 La58
Naujamiestis LT 114 Kc55
Naujasėdžiai LT 114 La59
Naujasis Obelynas LT 113 Jd56
Naujasodė LT 114 La53
Naujasodis LT 123 Kc30
Naujas Strūnaitis LT 115 Lb56
Naujene LV 115 Lc53
Naujieji Verkiai LT 114 La57
Naujoji Akmenė LT 113 Jd53
Naujoji Ūta LT 114 Kc58
Naujoji Vilnia LT 114 La58
Naukšēni LV 106 Kd47
Naul IRL 9 Cd20
Naulaperä FIN 75 Kd23
Naum S 102 Ed47
Naumburg D 126 Cd40
Naumburg D 127 Ea41
Naumovskij RUS 205 Fd15
Naundorf D 127 Ec40
Naundorf D 127 Ed40
Naunhof D 127 Ec40
Naurisvaara FIN 83 Mb29
Naurstad N 66 Fc17
Naustbukt N 62 Gc09
Naustdal N 84 Cb35
Naustvika N 77 Db33
Nautijaur S 72 Gd18
Nautsund N 84 Ca36
Nauviale F 33 Ha51
Nauvo FIN 97 Jb40
Nava E 37 Cc54
Näva S 94 Ec42
Navacepeda de Tormes E 45 Cc64
Navacepedilla de Corneja E 45 Cc64
Navacerrada E 46 Db63
Navacerrada E 52 Da69
Navaconcejo E 45 Cb65
Nava de Abajo E 53 Ec70
Nava de Arévalo E 46 Cd62
Nava de Campana E 53 Ec71
Nava de la Asunción E 46 Da62
Nava del Rey E 46 Cd61
Nava de Roa E 46 Db60
Navahermosa E 52 Da67
Navahrudak BY 202 Ea13
Naval E 48 Fd59
Navalacuz E 46 Cd64
Navalagamella E 46 Db64
Navalcaballo E 47 Eb60
Navalcán E 45 Cc65
Navalcarnero E 46 Db65
Navalcuervo E 51 Cb71
Navaleno E 47 Ea60
Navalguijo E 45 Cb64
Navalilla E 46 Db61
Navalmanzano E 46 Db62
Navalmoral E 46 Cd64
Navalmoral de la Mata E 51 Cb66
Navalón de Arriba E 54 Fa69
Navalonguilla E 45 Cb64
Navalperal de Pinares E 46 Da64
Navaluenga E 46 Cd64
Navalvillar de Pela E 51 Cb68
Navamorcuende E 46 Cd65
Navan IRL 9 Cd20
Navapolack BY 202 Eb11
Navarcles E 49 Gd60
Navardún E 39 Fa58
Navarrenx F 39 Fb55
Navarrés E 54 Fb69
Navarrete E 39 Eb58
Navarrete del Río E 47 Fa63
Navarrevisca E 46 Cd64
Navàs E 49 Gd60
Navascués E 39 Fa57
Navas de Estena E 52 Da67
Navas de Jorquera E 53 Ec68
Navas del Madroño E 51 Bd66
Navas del Rey E 46 Da64
Navas de Oro E 46 Da62
Navas de San Antonio E 46 Da63
Navas de San Juan E 52 Dc72
Navasëlki BY 202 Eb13
Navašino RUS 203 Fb10
Navata E 41 Hb58
Navatalgordo E 46 Cd64
Navatrasierra E 52 Cc67
Nave I 149 Da59
Nävekvarn S 103 Gb46
Navelgas E 37 Ca54
Navelli I 156 Ed70
Navelsaker N 84 Cc34
Nävelsjö S 103 Fc50
Navenby GB 17 Fc23
Näveråsen FIN 89 Hd32
Nave Redonda P 58 Ab73
Näverkärret S 95 Fd42
Naveros E 59 Bd77
Näversjöberg S 79 Fc30
Naverstad S 94 Eb45
Navès E 49 Gc59
Navia E 37 Ca53
Navia de Suarna E 37 Bd55
Navilly F 30 Jb43
Năvirneţ MD 173 Fa56
Navit N 63 Hc09
Nävlinge S 110 Fa54
Navlja RUS 202 Ed12
Navlus N 78 Ed27
Năvodari RO 180 Dc68
Năvodari RO 181 Fc67
Navolok RUS 107 Ma49
Navoloki RUS 203 Fa09
Nävragöl S 111 Fd53
Návsí CZ 138 Hc46
Nawcz PL 121 Gd29
Nawiady PL 122 Jc32
Nawojowa PL 138 Jc46
Na Xamena E 56 Gc69
Náxos GR 196 Db90
Nay F 40 Fc56
Nayland GB 21 Ga26
Nažadovo RUS 99 Mb44
Nazaré P 50 Ab66
Nazarje SLO 151 Fd57
Nazilli TR 198 Fb88
Ndermenas AL 182 Aa76
Ndreja AL 159 Jb70
Ndroq AL 182 Ab74
Néa Aghíalos GR 189 Ca82
Néa Alikarnassós GR 200 Da95
Néa Apolonía GR 184 Cc78
Néa Artáki GR 189 Cb85
Nea Dimmata CY 206 Hd97
Néa Éfessos GR 183 Bd79
Néa Epídavros GR 195 Ca87
Néa Filadélfia GR 183 Ca77
Néa Filadélfia GR 189 Cc86
Néa Fókea GR 183 Cb79
Néa Hilí GR 185 Dd78
Neahtšil FIN 68 Ja12
Néa Ionía GR 189 Ca82
Nea Iraklitsa GR 184 Da77
Néa Kalikrátia GR 183 Cb79
Néa Karváli GR 184 Da77
Néa Kerasoús GR 188 Ad82
Néa Kerdília GR 184 Cc77
Néa Kíos GR 195 Bd87
Nealstown IRL 13 Cb22
Néa Mákri GR 189 Cc86
Néa Mesimvría GR 183 Ca77
Néa Messángala GR 183 Ca80
Néa Mihanióna GR 183 Ca78
Néa Moudania GR 183 Cb79
Néa Nikópolis GR 183 Bb78
Neap GB 5 Fa04
Néa Péla GR 183 Bd77
Neapel = Napoli I 161 Fb75
Néa Péramos GR 184 Da77
Néa Péramos GR 189 Cb86
Néa Pétra GR 184 Cc77
Néa Plágia GR 183 Cb79
Neápoli GR 183 Bb78
Neápoli GR 195 Bd91
Neápoli GR 201 Db96
Néa Potídea GR 183 Cb79
Néa Róda GR 184 Cd79
Néa Sánda GR 185 Dd77
Néa Silata GR 183 Cb79
Néa Stíra GR 190 Cd86
Néa Ténedos GR 183 Cb79
Neath GB 19 Dd27
Néa Tirintha GR 195 Bd87
Néa Triglia GR 183 Cb79
Neaua RO 171 Dc59
Néa Víssa GR 185 Eb75
Néa Zíhni GR 184 Cd77
Néa Zoí GR 183 Bc77
Nebel D 108 Cd29
Nebenstedt D 119 Dd34
Nebiler TR 191 Eb83
Nebiler TR 199 Gb91
Nebiler TR 199 Gd91
Nebljusi HR 151 Ga62
Nebolči RUS 202 Ec08
Nebra D 127 Ea40
Nebreda E 46 Dc59
Nečemice CZ 136 Fa44
Nechanice CZ 136 Ga44
Necipköy TR 192 Fa81
Neckarbischofsheim D 134 Cc46
Neckargemünd D 134 Cc46
Neckargerach D 134 Cd46
Neckarsteinach D 134 Cc46
Neckarsulm D 134 Cd47
Neckartailfingen D 134 Cd49
Neckarzimmern D 134 Cd46
Neckenmarkt A 145 Gb53
Necmiyeköy TR 186 Ga80
Necşeşti RO 175 Dc66
Nečtiny CZ 135 Ed45
Nécy F 22 Fc37
Neda E 36 Ba53
Néda GR 194 Bb88
Nedansjö S 87 Gb33
Neded SK 145 Ha51
Nedelino BG 184 Dc76
Nedelišće HR 152 Gb57
Nederby DK 100 Db21
Neder Hvam DK 100 Db23
Nedervetil FIN 81 Jc28
Neder Vindinge DK 109 Eb28
Nederweert NL 125 Bb39
Nedingė LT 114 Kd59
Nedjalsko BG 181 Ec73
Nedlitz D 127 Eb38
Nedrabø N 92 Ca45
Nedre Bäck S 81 Hd26
Nedreberg N 86 Eb38
Nedre Flåsjön S 73 Hd21
Nedre Gärdsjö S 87 Fd38
Nedre Jervan N 77 Ea30
Nedre Kuouka S 73 Hb19
Nedre Maudal N 92 Cb44
Nedrenes N 64 Jc09
Nedre Parakka S 68 Hc16
Nedre Saxnäs S 72 Gb23
Nedre Soppero S 68 Hc14
Nedre Tväråsel S 73 Hc22
Nedre Vojakkala S 74 Jc21
Neðribær IS 2 Ac02
Nedryhajliv UA 202 Ed14
Nedstrand N 92 Ca42
Nedvědice CZ 137 Gb46
Nędza PL 137 Hb44
Neede NL 125 Bd37
Needham Market GB 21 Ga26
Neēlovo RUS 107 Ld47
Neerijnen NL 124 Ba37
Neeroeteren B 125 Bb40
Neerpelt B 124 Ba39
Nées Kariés GR 189 Bd81
Neftenbach CH 141 Cb52
Nefyn GB 14 Dc23
Negádes GR 182 Ad79
Negoi RO 179 Cc67
Negomir RO 175 Cc64
Negorci MK 183 Bd76
Negotin SRB 174 Cb66
Negotino MK 183 Bd75
Negovanovci BG 174 Cb66
Negraşi RO 175 Dc65
Negrea MD 173 Fc58
Negreira E 36 Ad55
Nègrepelisse F 40 Gc53
Negreşti RO 173 Fa58
Negreşti RO 181 Fb68
Negreşti-Oaş RO 171 Da54
Negri RO 172 Ed59
Négrondes F 33 Ga48
Negru Vodă RO 181 Fb68
Negureni MD 173 Fc56
Nehaevskij RUS 203 Fc13
Neheim D 125 Cb39
Nehoiu RO 176 Eb63
Nehringen D 119 Ed31
Nehrybka PL 139 Kb45
Nehvonniemi FIN 83 Mb30
Neiden N 65 Kc08
Neikovo BG 180 Eb71
Neikšāni LV 107 Ma52
Neila E 47 Ea59
Neißeaue D 128 Fc40
Neistenkangas S 74 Jb18
Neitaskaite S 73 Hd19
Neittävä FIN 82 Kc25
Neja RUS 203 Fb08
Nejdek CZ 135 Ec43

Nivala – Nufăru

Nivala FIN 82 Ka27
Nivankylä FIN 74 Jd18
Nivelles B 124 Ac41
Nivenskoe RUS 113 Ja59
Nivjanin BG 179 Cd69
Nivnice CZ 137 Ha48
Niwica PL 128 Fc39
Niwiska PL 128 Fd39
Niwiska PL 139 Jd43
Niyazcar TR 198 Ga89
Nižbor CZ 136 Fa45
Niziny PL 130 Jc42
Nižná SK 138 Hd47
Nižná Boca SK 138 Ja48
Nižna Polianka SK 139 Jd46
Nižná Slaná SK 138 Jb48
Nižnekamsk RUS 203 Ga08
Nižnij Novgorod RUS 203 Fb09
Nižný Hrabovec SK 139 Ka48
Nizovicy RUS 99 Ld45
Nizy-le-Comte F 24 Hc34
Nižyn UA 202 Ec14
Nizza Monferrato I 148 Ca61
Nizza = Nice F 43 Kd53
Njakaure S 73 Hb21
Njallavárri S 68 Hc17
Njallejaur S 72 Ha22
Njasviž BY 202 Ea13
Njavve S 72 Gc18
Njegoševo SRB 153 Ja58
Njegovuda MNE 159 Ja67
Njellim FIN 69 Kb11
Njetsavare S 73 Hb19
Njivice HR 151 Fb61
Njuorggam FIN 64 Ka07
Njurunda S 88 Gc34
Njurundabommen S 88 Gc34
Njutånger S 87 Gb36
No DK 108 Cd24
Noailhac F 41 Ha54
Noailles F 23 Gd35
Noailly F 34 Hd45
Noale I 150 Ea59
Noalejo E 60 Db74
Noasca I 148 Bc59
Nöbbele S 103 Fc52
Nöbbele S 103 Fc52
Nöbbelöv S 111 Fb55
Nobber IRL 9 Cd20
Nöbdenitz D 127 Eb42
Nobitz D 127 Ec41
Noblejas E 52 Dc66
Noćaj SRB 153 Ja61
Nocé F 29 Ga38
Noceda E 37 Ca56
Nocedo de Curueño E 37 Cc56
Nocedo do Val E 36 Bb58
Nocelleto I 161 Fa74
Nocera Inferiore I 161 Fb75
Nocera Terinese I 164 Gb81
Nocera Umbra I 156 Eb67
Noceto I 149 Da61
Nochowo PL 129 Gc38
Noci I 162 Gd75
Nociglia I 163 Hc77
Nociunai LT 114 Kb53
Nociūnai LT 114 Kc56
Nocrich RO 175 Db61
Nodanö S 95 Ga41
Nodar E 36 Bb55
Nødebo DK 109 Ec25
Nodeland N 92 Cd47
Nödinge-Nol S 102 Ec48
Nods F 31 Ka42
Noé F 40 Gb55
Noepoli I 162 Gb77
Nœux-les-Mines F 23 Ha31
Noevci BG 179 Cb71
Noez E 52 Da66
Nofuentes E 38 Dd56
Nogale LV 105 Jd49
Nogales E 51 Bc70
Nogara I 149 Dc60
Nogarejas E 37 Ca58
Nogaro F 40 Fc54
Nogawczyce PL 137 Hb43
Nogent F 30 Jb39
Nogent-le-Roi F 23 Gc37
Nogent-le-Rotrou F 29 Ga38
Nogent-sur-Aube F 30 Hd38
Nogent-sur-Marne F 23 Gd37
Nogent-sur-Seine F 30 Hb38
Nogent-sur-Vernisson F 29 Ha40
Nogersund S 111 Fc55
Nogheredo I 150 Eb58
Nõgiaru EST 98 La45
Noginsk RUS 203 Fa10
Nogna F 31 Jc44
Nógrádmegyer H 146 Ja51
Nogueira E 36 Ba57
Nogueira de Ramuín E 36 Bb57
Noguera E 47 Ed64
Nogueruelas E 54 Fb65
Nohant-en-Graçay F 29 Gc42
Nohant-Vic F 29 Gd44
Nohèdes F 41 Ha57
Nohfelden D 133 Bd45
Nohn D 133 Bc43
Nohra D 126 Dc40
Nohutalan TR 191 Ea86
Noia E 36 Ac56
Noicattaro I 162 Gd74
Noidanpola FIN 68 Ja14
Noidans-le-Ferroux F 31 Jd40
Noirefontaine F 31 Ka41
Noirétable F 34 Hc47
Noirlieu F 28 Fc43
Noirmoutier-en-l'Île F 27 Ec43
Nois E 36 Bc53
Noiseux B 124 Ba42
Noja E 38 Dd54
Nojewo PL 129 Gb36
Nojorid RO 170 Ca57
Nokia FIN 89 Jd36
Nokka FIN 90 Kc34
Nokkamäki FIN 82 La28
Nokkosmäenkulma FIN 89 Ja34
Nola I 161 Fb75
Nolay E 47 Eb61
Nolay F 30 Ja43
Noli I 148 Ca63
Nolimo FIN 74 Kc18
Nomansland GB 19 Ea30
Nömba EST 97 Jc44
Nombela E 46 Da65
Nomeland N 92 Cd44
Nomeny F 25 Jd36
Nomexy F 31 Jd38
Nomí GR 189 Bc81
Nómia GR 195 Bd91
Nõmme EST 98 Kb42
Nõmmküla EST 97 Jd45
Nomparedes E 47 Eb61
Nonancourt F 23 Gb37
Nonant-le-Pin F 22 Fd37
Nonantola I 149 Dc62
Nonaspe E 48 Fd62
None I 148 Bc61
Nonnweiler D 133 Bd45
Nõnova EST 107 Lc47
Nontron F 33 Ga48
Nonvilliers F 29 Gb38
Nonza F 154 Cc68
Nõo EST 99 Lb45
Noordbeemster NL 116 Ba35
Noordwijk aan Zee NL 116 Ad36
Noordwijkerhout NL 116 Ad36
Noormarkku FIN 89 Ja35
Nopala FIN 91 Lb37
Nopankylä FIN 89 Ja32
Noposenaho FIN 81 Jd30
Noppikoski S 87 Fc36
Noppo FIN 90 Kb38
Nor N 84 Cc34
Nor N 94 Ec40
Nor S 87 Fd32
Nor S 94 Fa43
Nora S 87 Gb33
Nora S 88 Gd32
Nora S 95 Fc43
Nora S 95 Gb41
Norageliai LT 114 Kc59
Nøragger DK 100 Db22
Noragugume I 169 Ca76
Norberg S 95 Ga41
Norbo S 95 Fd40
Norcia I 156 Ec68
Nordagutu N 93 Dc43
Nordanå S 110 Ed53
Nordanåker S 79 Ga30
Nordanås S 71 Ga23
Nordanås S 72 Gd22
Nordanås S 80 Gd27
Nordanholen S 95 Fc40
Nordankäl S 79 Ga29
Nordansjö S 79 Ga25
Nordarnøy N 66 Fb17
Nordausques F 21 Gc30
Nordbakk N 78 Fa26
Nordberg N 85 Db34
Nordbø N 93 Da47
Nordborg DK 108 Db27
Nordby DK 108 Cd26
Nordby DK 109 Dd25
Nordby N 86 Eb37
Nordby N 93 Ea41
Nordby N 93 Ea42
Norddal N 84 Cb35
Norddeich D 117 Ca32
Norddorf D 108 Cd28
Nordeidet N 64 Jb06
Nordelph GB 17 Fd24
Norden D 117 Ca32
Norden S 72 Ha21
Nordendorf D 134 Dc49
Nordenham D 118 Cd32
Nordenskov DK 108 Da25
Norderåsen S 79 Fc30
Norderhov N 93 Dd41
Norderney D 117 Ca31
Norderön S 79 Fb31
Norderstedt D 118 Db32
Nord-Etnedal N 85 Dc37
Nordfjord N 66 Fd17
Nordfjordbotn N 67 Gd11
Nordfjordeid N 84 Cc34
Nordfjorden N 70 Fa20
Nord-Flatanger N 78 Eb26
Nord-Fogn N 92 Ca43
Nordfold N 66 Fd16
Nord-Gutvika N 70 Ec24
Nordhalben D 135 Ea43
Nordhallen S 78 Ed30
Nordhamna N 63 Ja05
Nordhastedt D 118 Da30
Nordhausen D 126 Dc39
Nordheim D 134 Cd47
Nordheim vor der Rhön D 134 Db43
Nordhella N 62 Gd09
Nordholz D 118 Cd32
Nordhorn D 117 Ca36
Nordhorsfjord N 70 Ec24
Nordhus N 63 Hd08
Nordingrå S 80 Gd31
Nordkirchen D 125 Ca38
Nordkisa N 94 Eb40
Nordkjosbotn N 67 Gd11
Nordkroken S 102 Ec47
Nordland N 66 Fa16
Nordleda D 118 Cd32
Nord-Leirvåg N 65 Kc07
Nordli N 71 Fb23
Nördlingen D 134 Db48
Nordmaling S 80 Ha29
Nordmannset N 64 Jc04
Nordmannset N 64 Jb06
Nordmannvik N 62 Ha09
Nordmark S 95 Fb42
Nordmela N 66 Fd11
Nordnes N 71 Fd18
Nordnesøya N 70 Ed19
Nordomsjön S 86 Fa35
Nordøyvågen N 70 Ed21
Nordre Gavesluft N 64 Ka05
Nordre Osen N 86 Ec37
Nordrollnes N 67 Gb12
Nord-Sel N 85 Dc35
Nordseter N 85 Ea37
Nordsinni N 85 Dd38
Nordsjö S 79 Ga29
Nordsjö S 87 Ga36
Nordskjørin N 78 Ea27
Nordskov DK 109 Dd26
Nord-Statland N 78 Eb26
Nordstemmen D 126 Db37
Nordstrand D 108 Da29
Nordstrand N 62 Gc10
Nordstrand N 76 Cc32
Nord-Værnes N 70 Fa19
Nordvågen N 64 Jc04
Nordvik FIN 97 Jc40
Nordvik N 65 Kd08
Nordvik N 70 Ed21
Nordvik N 77 Dc31
Nordvika N 77 Db29
Nordwalde D 125 Ca37
Nore N 85 Db40
Nore S 87 Ga35
Norem N 78 Eb28
Noreña E 37 Cc54
Noresund N 85 Dc40
Noret S 81 Hd27
Norfjärden S 88 Gc34
Norg NL 117 Bd33
Norges-la-Ville F 30 Jb41
Norgravsjö S 80 Gd28
Nørhå DK 100 Da21
Norham GB 11 Ed14
Norheimsund N 84 Cb39
Norinkylä FIN 89 Ja32
Norje S 111 Fc54
Norma I 160 Ec72
Normandy GB 20 Fb29
Normanton GB 16 Fa21
Normée F 24 Hd37
Normlösa S 103 Fd47
Norn S 95 Fd40
Nornäs S 86 Fa36
Norola FIN 90 La34
Noroy-le-Bourg F 31 Jd40
Norra Åsum S 111 Fb55
Norra Avradsberg S 94 Fa40
Norra Björke S 102 Ec47
Norra Bredåker S 73 Hc21
Norra Fågelås S 103 Fb47
Norra Fårträsk S 72 Gd24
Norra Finnskoga S 86 Ed38
Norra Fjällnäs S 71 Fd22
Norrahammar S 103 Fb49
Norra Härene S 102 Ed46
Norra Hjulbäck S 95 Fc39
Norra Holmnäs S 72 Ha22
Norra Kedum S 102 Ed46
Norråker S 79 Gb25
Norråker S 79 Fd26
Norrala S 87 Gb37
Norra Latikberg S 79 Gb26
Norra Löten S 86 Ed38
Norra Lundby S 102 Fa47
Norra Mellby S 110 Fa54
Norra Möckleby S 103 Gb52
Norrånös S 79 Ga29
Norra Ny S 94 Fa40
Norra Örnäs S 72 Gb23
Norra Prästholm S 73 Hd21
Norra Rörum S 110 Fa55
Norra Sandby S 110 Fa54
Norra Sandsjö S 103 Fc50
Norra Skärvången S 79 Fb29
Norra Stensund S 72 Gb23
Norra Sunderbyn S 73 Hd22
Norra Ullerud S 94 Fa43
Norra Umstrand S 71 Ga24
Norra Unnaryd S 102 Fa49
Norra Vallgrund FIN 81 Hd30
Norra Vånga S 102 Fa47
Norra Vi S 103 Fd48
Norra Volgsjöfors S 79 Gb26
Norrback FIN 89 Ja32
Norrbäck S 80 Gc25
Norrberg S 72 Gb24
Norrbo S 87 Gb35
Norrboda FIN 96 Hc40
Norrboda S 87 Fd37
Norrboda S 96 Gd39
Norrby FIN 81 Jb28
Norrby S 80 Hb26
Norrby S 95 Gb41
Norrbyås S 95 Fd44
Norrbyberg S 80 Gd25
Norrbyn S 80 Hb29
Norrdal S 72 Gb24
Nørre Aaby DK 108 Dc26
Nørre Alslev DK 109 Eb28
Nørre Bork DK 108 Cd25
Nørre Broby DK 108 Dc27
Nørreby DK 109 Ea28
Nørre Halne DK 100 Dc20
Nørre Havrvig DK 108 Cd24
Nørre Herlev DK 109 Ec25
Nørre Jernløse DK 109 Eb26
Nørre Knudstrup DK 100 Db23
Nørre Kongerslev DK 100 Dc21
Nørre Lyndelse DK 108 Dc27
Nørre Lyngby DK 100 Dc20
Nørre Nebel DK 108 Cd25
Nørre Snede DK 108 Db24
Nørresundby DK 100 Dc21
Nørre Vejrup DK 108 Da26
Nørre Vilstrup DK 108 Db25
Nørre Vissing DK 108 Dc24
Nørre Vorupør DK 100 Cd21
Norrfjärden S 73 Hd23
Norrfjärden S 80 Hc28
Norrflärke S 80 Ha30
Norrfors S 80 Gd27
Norrfors S 80 Ha28
Norrgårdssälen S 86 Fa38
Norrhed S 73 Hc20
Norrhult S 103 Fd51
Norrliån S 73 Hd20
Norrköping S 103 Ga46
Norrlanda S 104 Ha49
Norrlångträsk S 73 Hc24
Norrmjöle S 80 Hb29
Norrnäs FIN 89 Hd32
Norrnäs S 79 Ga28
Norrsjön S 79 Fd26
Norrskedika S 96 Gd40
Norrsundet S 87 Gb38
Norrtälje S 96 Ha42
Norrtannflo S 79 Gb30
Norrvik S 80 Gc26
Nors DK 100 Da21
Norsholm S 103 Ga46
Norsjö S 80 Ha25
Norsjövallen S 80 Ha25
Norskbukta N 65 Kc07
Norsminde DK 108 Dc24
Nörten-Hardenberg D 126 Db39
Northallerton GB 11 Fa18
Northam GB 18 Dc29
Northampton GB 20 Fb25
North Berwick GB 11 Ec13
Northchapel GB 20 Fb29
North Charlton GB 11 Fa15
North Dalton GB 16 Fb20
Northeim D 126 Db39
North Ferriby GB 17 Fc20
North Ferriby GB 17 Fc21
North Grimston GB 16 Fb19
Northiam GB 21 Ga30
North Kilworth GB 20 Fa25
Northleach GB 20 Ed27
North Molton GB 19 Dd29
North Petherton GB 19 Eb29
North Somercotes GB 17 Fd21
North Tawton GB 19 Dd30
North Thoresby GB 17 Fc21
North Tidworth GB 20 Ed29
Northton GB 4 Cd06
Northwall GB 5 Ed02
North Walsham GB 17 Gb23
North Weald Bassett GB 20 Fd27
Northwich GB 15 Ec22
Northwood GB 15 Eb23
North Wootton GB 17 Fd24
Nortmoor D 117 Cb33
Norton GB 16 Fb19
Nortorf D 118 Db30
Nortrh Creake GB 17 Ga23
Nortrup D 117 Cb35
Nort-sur-Erdre F 28 Ed41
Noruliai LT 123 Kd30
Norum N 84 Cd37
Norum S 102 Eb48
Norup DK 100 Dc22
Norup DK 108 Dc26
Norvaišiai LT 114 La54
Norvajärvi FIN 74 Jd18
Norvalahti FIN 74 Jd18
Nörvenich D 125 Bc41
Norwich GB 17 Gb24
Norwick GB 5 Fa03
Nosivka UA 202 Ec14
Noskovo RUS 107 Ma46
Nosków PL 129 Gd38
Noşlac RO 171 Da59
Nosovo RUS 107 Ld49
Nøss N 66 Fd11
Nossa Senhora da Graça do Divor P 50 Ad69
Nossa Senhora das Neves P 50 Ad71
Nossa Senhora da Torega P 50 Ad70
Nossa Senhora de Machede P 50 Ba69
Nossebro S 102 Ed47
Nössemark S 94 Eb44
Nossen D 127 Ed41
Nossendorf D 119 Ed31
Nösslinge S 102 Ec50
Noss Mayo GB 19 Dd32
Nösund S 102 Eb47
Noszolop H 145 Gd54
Notaresco I 157 Fa69
Notėnai LT 113 Jc54
Nótia GR 183 Bd76
Nötö FIN 97 Ja41
Noto I 167 Fc88
Notodden N 93 Dc42
Notre-Dame-de-Gravenchon F 23 Ga35
Notre-Dame-de-Monts F 27 Ec43
Notre Dame du Laus F 35 Ka50
Nötsch A 143 Ed56
Nottage GB 19 Dd28
Nottebäck S 103 Fd51
Nottingham GB 16 Fa23
Nöttja S 102 Fa52
Nottuln D 125 Ca37
Nouaillé-Maupertuis F 32 Fd45
Nouan-le-Fuzellier F 29 Gd41
Nouans-les-Fontaines F 29 Gb42
Nouart F 24 Ja34
Nousiainen FIN 97 Jb39
Nousionmäki FIN 82 La29
Nousu FIN 69 Kd16
Nouvelle F 29 Ha44
Nouvion F 23 Gc32
Nouzonville F 24 Ja33
Nõva EST 98 Ka43
Nova H 145 Gc56
Nová Baňa SK 146 Hc50
Nova Borova UA 202 Eb14
Nova Breznica MK 178 Bb73
Nová Bystrica SK 138 Hc47
Nová Bystřice CZ 136 Fd48
Novačane BG 180 Dc69
Novačene BG 179 Cd70
Nova Černa BG 180 Eb68
Novaci MK 183 Bb76
Novaci RO 175 Cd63
Nova Crnja SRB 153 Jc59
Nova Crnja SRB 174 Bb61
Nová Dubnica SK 137 Hb48
Novafeltria I 156 Ea65
Nova Gorica SLO 150 Ed58
Nova Gradiška HR 152 Gd60
Novaja Bur'a RUS 99 Ma40
Novaja Derevnja RUS 113 Jb58
Novaja Kališče RUS 99 Ma39
Novaja Ladoga RUS 202 Eb08
Novajidrány H 139 Jd49
Nova Kachovka UA 205 Fa16
Nova Kamena BG 181 Ed69
Nova Kapela HR 152 Ha60
Nova Kasaba BIH 159 Hd64
Nová Kelča SK 139 Ka47
Novakovo BG 184 Dc74
Nováky SK 137 Hb49
Novalaise F 35 Jd47
Novales E 48 Fc59
Novalesa I 148 Bb60
Nova Levante I 143 Dd56
Novalja HR 151 Fc63
Novallas E 47 Ed59
Novalukoml' BY 202 Eb12
Nova Mahala BG 184 Da74
Nova Nadežda BG 185 Dd74
Nova Odesa UA 204 Ed16
Nová Paka CZ 136 Fd43
Nová Pec CZ 136 Fa49
Novara I 148 Cb59
Nova-Rača HR 152 Gc59
Novara di Sicilia I 167 Fd84
Nová Říše CZ 136 Fd48
Nová Sedlica SK 139 Kb47
Nova Šipka BG 181 Ed71
Nova Siri I 162 Gc77
Novate Mezzola I 149 Cd57
Nova Topola BIH 152 Gd61
Nova Ušycja UA 204 Eb16
Nova Varoš SRB 159 Jb66
Nova vas SLO 151 Fb59
Nová Ves CZ 136 Fb44
Nová Ves nad Žitavou SK 145 Hb50
Nová Viska CZ 135 Ed43
Nova Vodolaha UA 203 Fa14
Nova Zagora BG 180 Ea72
Nove I 150 Dd59
Nové Heřminovy CZ 137 Gd44
Nové Hrady CZ 136 Fc49
Nové Hrady CZ 137 Gb45
Novelda E 55 Fb71
Novelda del Guadiana E 51 Bc68
Novellara I 149 Db61
Nové Město nad Metují CZ 137 Gb43
Nové Mesto nad Vahom SK 137 Ha49
Nové Město na Moravě CZ 136 Ga46
Nové Město pod Smrkem CZ 128 Fd42
Nové Mitrovice CZ 136 Fa46
Noventa Vicentino I 150 Dd60
Noves F 42 Jb53
Novés E 46 Da65
Nove Sady SK 145 Ha50
Nové Strašecí CZ 136 Fa44
Nové Veselí CZ 136 Ga46
Nové Zámky SK 145 Hb51
Novgorod RUS 202 Eb09
Novgorodka RUS 107 Ma49
Novgorodskoje RUS 113 Ja58
Novgrad BG 180 Dd69
Novhorodka UA 204 Ed15
Novhorod-Sivers'kyj UA 202 Ed13
Novi Bečej SRB 153 Jb59
Novi Beograd SRB 153 Jc61
Novi Bilokorovyči UA 202 Eb14
Novi di Modena I 149 Db61
Novi Dojran MK 183 Ca76
Noviercas E 47 Ec60
Novi Glog SRB 178 Bd72
Novi Grad BIH 152 Gb61
Novi Grad BIH 152 Hb61
Novigrad HR 150 Ed60
Novigrad HR 157 Ga64
Novigrad-Podravski HR 152 Gc58
Novi Han BG 179 Cd71
Novi Iskăr BG 179 Cc71
Nøvik N 78 Eb28
Novi Karlovci SRB 153 Jc61
Novi Kneževac SRB 153 Jb57
Novi Korito SRB 179 Ca68
Novi Kozarci SRB 153 Jc58
Novi Kozarci SRB 174 Bb60
Novi Kozjak SRB 174 Bb62
Novi Ligure I 148 Cb61
Noville B 132 Ba43
Novi Marof HR 152 Gb57
Novion-Porcien F 24 Hd34
Novi Pazar BG 181 Ed70
Novi Pazar SRB 178 Ba69
Novi Sad SRB 153 Jb60
Novi Sanžary UA 204 Ed15
Novi Šeher BIH 152 Hb63
Novi Selo SRB 174 Bc65
Novi Slankamen SRB 153 Jc60
Novi Travnik BIH 158 Ha64
Novi Varoš HR 152 Gd61
Novi Vinodolski HR 151 Fc61
Novi Žednik SRB 153 Ja58
Novoaleksandrovsk RUS 205 Fd16
Novoanninskij RUS 203 Fc13
Novoarchanhel's'k UA 204 Ec15
Novoazovs'k UA 205 Fb16
Novo-Bobrujsk RUS 113 Jb59
Novo Brdo KSV 178 Bc71
Novočeboksarsk RUS 203 Fc09
Novočerkassk RUS 205 Fc15
Novocimljanskaja RUS 203 Fd14
Novofedorivka UA 204 Ed17
Novohrad-Volyns'kyj UA 202 Eb14
Novokašpirskij RUS 203 Ga10
Novokolhoznoe RUS 113 Jc57
Novokubansk RUS 205 Fd16
Novokujbyševsk RUS 203 Ga10
Novo Mesto SLO 151 Fd59
Novomičurinsk RUS 203 Fa11
Novomihajlovskij RUS 205 Fc17
Novo Miloševo SRB 153 Jc58
Novo Miloševo SRB 174 Bb60
Novomoskovsk RUS 203 Fa11
Novomoskovs'k UA 205 Fa15
Novomykolajivka UA 204 Ed17
Novomykolajivka UA 205 Fa15
Novomyrhorod UA 204 Ed15
Novonikolaevskij RUS 203 Fc13
Novonikol'skoe RUS 107 Ma47
Novooleksijivka UA 205 Fa17
Novo Orahovo SRB 153 Ja58
Novo Paničarovo BG 181 Ed73
Novopavlovsk RUS 205 Ga17
Novopokrovka UA 205 Fa15
Novopokrovskaja RUS 205 Fd16
Novopskov UA 203 Fb14
Novorossijsk RUS 205 Fc17
Novoržev RUS 202 Eb10
Novosad SK 139 Ka49
Novošahtinsk RUS 205 Fc15
Novo Sancti Petri E 59 Bd77
Novosedly nad Nežárkou CZ 136 Fc48
Novosel BG 181 Ec70
Novoselci BG 181 Ed73
Novosel'e RUS 99 Ld43
Novosel'e RUS 99 Ma45
Novosel'e RUS 99 Ma45
Novosel'e RUS 99 Mb44
Novosel'e RUS 99 Mb45
Novoselec BG 180 Ea73
Novoselija BIH 152 Gd62
Novoselivs'ke UA 205 Fa17
Novo Selo BG 174 Cb66
Novo Selo BG 179 Ca73
Novo Selo BG 179 Cd72
Novo Selo BG 180 Dd70
Novo Selo BG 180 Eb68
Novo selo BG 185 Ea75
Novo Selo BIH 152 Hb61
Novo Selo MK 183 Ca75
Novo Selo SRB 153 Ja62
Novo Selo SRB 178 Bb67
Novosokol'niki RUS 202 Eb10
Novostroevo RUS 113 Jc59
Novotroickoe RUS 203 Fc10
Novotrojic'ke UA 205 Fa17
Novotulka RUS 203 Ga12
Novoukrajinka UA 204 Ed16
Novouljanovsk RUS 203 Fd10
Novouzensk RUS 203 Ga12
Novovolyns'k UA 204 Dd15
Novo Zvečevo HR 152 Ha59
Novska HR 152 Gd60
Nový Bor CZ 128 Fb42
Nový Bydžov CZ 136 Fd44
Nový Dvůr CZ 137 Ha45
Nový Dvůr PL 128 Ga40
Novyj Oskol RUS 203 Fb13
Novyj Buh UA 204 Ed16
Nový Jičín CZ 137 Ha46
Novyj Izborsk RUS 107 Ld47
Novyj Usitva RUS 107 Ld48
Nový Knín CZ 136 Fb45
Nový Malín CZ 137 Gc45
Nový Rychnov CZ 136 Fd47
Nowa Brzeźnica PL 130 Hc41
Nowa Cerekwia PL 137 Ha44
Nowa Dęba PL 139 Jd43
Nowa Huta PL 138 Ja44
Nowa Karczma PL 121 Ha31
Nowa Rozedranka PL 123 Kb32
Nowa Ruda PL 137 Gb43
Nowa Sarzyna PL 139 Ka43
Nowa Słupia PL 130 Jc41
Nowa Sól PL 128 Ga39
Nowa Somianka PL 130 Jc36
Nowa Sucha PL 130 Ja37
Nowa Wieś PL 122 Jc34
Nowa Wieś Ełcka PL 123 Jd31
Nowa Wieś Lęborska PL 121 Gd29
Nowa Wieś Wielka PL 121 Ha35
Nowa Wola PL 123 Kc34
Nowe Berezowo PL 123 Kc34
Nowe Brzesko PL 138 Jb44
Nowe Dwór PL 122 Hd30
Nowe Kiejkuty PL 122 Jb32
Nowe Kościelnica PL 121 Hb30
Nowe Laski PL 120 Ga33
Nowe Ludzicko PL 120 Ga32
Nowe Miasteczko PL 128 Ga39
Nowe Miasto PL 122 Jb35
Nowe Miasto Lubawskie PL 122 Hd33
Nowe Miasto nad Pilicą PL 130 Jb39
Nowe Ostrowy PL 130 Hc37
Nowe Piekuty PL 123 Ka34
Nowe Skalmierzyce PL 129 Ha39
Nowe Warpno PL 120 Fb32
Nowe Witki PL 122 Jb30
Nowica PL 122 Hd30
Nowinka PL 123 Ka31
Nowiny Kasjerskie PL 123 Kb33
Nowiny Wielkie PL 128 Fc36
Nowodwór PL 131 Ka38
Nowogard PL 120 Fd32
Nowogród PL 123 Jd33
Nowogród Bobrzański PL 128 Fd39
Nowogrodziec PL 128 Fd41
Nowo Miasto nad Wartą PL 129 Gd38
Nowosady PL 123 Kc34
Nowosielce PL 139 Ka45
Nowosielec PL 131 Ka42
Nowosiółki PL 123 Kc33
Nowosiółki PL 131 Kc40
Nowosiółki PL 131 Kd42
Nowy Duninów PL 130 Hc36
Nowy Dwór PL 123 Kb31
Nowy Dwór Gdański PL 122 Hc30
Nowy Dwór Mazowiecki PL 130 Jb36
Nowy Gaj PL 130 Hc37
Nowy Jaromierz PL 128 Ga38
Nowy Kawęczyn PL 130 Ja38
Nowy Korczyn PL 138 Jb43
Nowy Kościoł PL 128 Ga41
Nowy Lubiel PL 122 Jc35
Nowy Orzechów PL 131 Kb39
Nowy Sącz PL 138 Jb45
Nowy Staw PL 121 Hb31
Nowy Targ PL 138 Ja46
Nowy Tomyśl PL 128 Ga37
Nowy Wiśnicz PL 138 Jb44
Nowy Wołkusz PL 123 Kb31
Nowy Żmigród PL 139 Jd45
Noyant F 28 Fd41
Noyant-de-Touraine F 29 Ga43
Noyant-la-Plaine F 28 Fc42
Noyelles-sur-Mer F 23 Gc32
Noyen-sur-Seine F 30 Hb38
Noyers F 30 Hd40
Noyers F 42 Jd52
Noyers-Saint-Martin F 23 Gd34
Noyon F 23 Ha34
Nozay F 28 Ed41
Nozdra MNE 159 Hd68
Nozdrzec PL 139 Ka45
Nozelos P 45 Bc61
Nozeroy F 31 Jd43
Nozières F 34 Ja49
N. Sedlo CZ 135 Ec44
Nuarbe E 39 Eb56
Nuars F 30 Hc41
Nuasjärvi FIN 74 Jc18
Nucăreni MD 173 Fc56
Nucet RO 171 Cc58
Nucet RO 176 Dd65
Nuci RO 176 Eb65
Nucşoara RO 175 Dc63
Nudersdorf D 127 Ec38
Nüdlingen D 134 Db44
Nudol' RUS 202 Ed10
Nueil-les Aubiers F 28 Fb43
Nuenen NL 125 Bb38
Nueno E 39 Fb58
Nueva E 37 Cd54
Nueva Andalucía E 60 Cc77
Nueva Carteya E 60 Cd73
Nueva Jarilla E 59 Bd76
Nuévalos E 47 Ec62
Nuevo Baztán E 46 Dd64
Nufăru RO 177 Fd64

Nuh – Ollikkala

Nuh TR 193 Gc85
Nuhören TR 193 Gb84
Nuiasodis LT 115 Lb54
Nuijamaa FIN 91 Lc36
Nuin E 39 Ed56
Nuisement-sur-Coole F 24 Hd36
Nuits F 30 Hd40
Nuits-Saint-Georges F 30 Jb42
Nukari FIN 90 Kb38
Nukkumajoki FIN 69 Ka11
Nukši LV 107 Ld51
Nuksujärvi S 68 Hd16
Nuksujärvi S 73 Ja18
Nuland N 92 Cb46
Nule I 168 Cb75
Nules E 54 Fc66
Nulvi I 168 Ca74
Numana I 156 Ed66
Numanoluk TR 193 Gc83
Numansdorp NL 124 Ad37
Nümbrecht D 125 Ca41
Numerne LV 107 Ld50
Numijoki FIN 81 Jd30
Nummela FIN 89 Jd38
Nummela FIN 98 Ka39
Nummenkylä FIN 90 Ka37
Nummenpää FIN 98 Kb39
Nummi FIN 97 Jb39
Nummi FIN 98 Ka39
Nummijärvi FIN 89 Jb33
Nummikoski FIN 89 Jb33
Nummilahti FIN 89 Jb33
Numminen FIN 90 Kc38
Nünchritz D 127 Ed40
Nuneaton GB 16 Fa24
Nunnanen FIN 68 Jb13
Nunnanlahti FIN 83 Lc28
Nunney GB 19 Ec29
Nunspeet NL 116 Bb36
Nunton GB 20 Ed29
Nuojua FIN 82 Kc25
Nuolijärvi FIN 83 Lb27
Nuomininkai LT 113 Jd55
Nuoramoinen FIN 90 Kc35
Nuorgam FIN 64 Ka07
Nuoritta FIN 74 Kb23
Nuoro I 169 Cb76
Nuorpinniemi FIN 64 Jc08
Nuortikon S 73 Hb18
Nuorunka FIN 75 Kc21
Nuottikylä FIN 75 La24
Nuottiranta FIN 83 Lc29
Núpsstaður IS 2 Ba06
Nur PL 123 Ka35
Nurachi I 169 Bd77
Nuragus I 169 Ca78
Nurallao I 169 Ca78
Nuraminis I 169 Ca79
Nureci I 169 Ca78
Nuribey TR 193 Gc85
Nuriye TR 191 Ed85
Nurlat RUS 203 Ga09
Nurmaa FIN 90 Kd35
Nurme EST 98 Kb45
Nurmes FIN 83 Lb27
Nurmeslahti FIN 82 La28
Nurmesperä FIN 82 Kb27
Nurmi FIN 89 Jd36
Nurmi LV 106 Kd47
Nurmijärvi FIN 83 Lc27
Nurmijärvi FIN 98 Kb39
Nurmo FIN 81 Jb31
Nurmsi EST 98 Kd44
Nurmuiža LV 105 Jd50
Nürnberg D 135 Dd46
Nurney IRL 13 Cc22
Nurrasuanto S 68 Hd16
Nurri I 169 Cb78
Nürtingen D 134 Cd49
Nurzec PL 123 Kb35
Nurzec-Stacja PL 131 Kb36
Nus I 148 Bc58
Nusco I 161 Fd75
Nuşeni RO 171 Db57
Nuşfalau RO 171 Cc56
Nusfjord N 66 Fa15
Nüshetiye TR 186 Ga80
Nusnäs S 87 Fc38
Nusplingen D 142 Cc50
Nusratlı TR 185 Ed78
Nusret TR 192 Fa82
Nussdorf A 143 Ed52
Nußdorf D 143 Eb52
Nußloch D 134 Cc46
Nuthetal D 127 Ed37
Nutley GB 20 Fd29
Nuttuperä FIN 82 Kb27
Nuulanki S 68 Hd14
Nuupas FIN 74 Ka20
Nuutajärvi FIN 89 Jd37
Nuutila FIN 82 Kb25
Nuutilanmäki FIN 90 La33
Nuttila FIN 89 Jd33
Nuvvos FIN 64 Jc08
Nuvvus FIN 64 Jc08
Ny S 94 Ec42
Nyåker S 80 Ha28
Nyåker S 80 Gc29
Nyárlőrinc H 146 Ja55
Nya Storbäcken S 80 Hc27
Nyberg S 80 Ha25
Nybergsund N 86 Ec36
Nyborg DK 109 Dd27
Nyborg N 65 Kb06
Nyborg N 79 Fb28
Nyborg S 73 Jb21
Nybro S 103 Ga52
Nybrostrand S 110 Fa57
Nybrott N 63 Hd08
Nyby FIN 81 Hd31
Nyby N 64 Jb07
Nyby S 79 Fd30
Nybyn S 73 Hc23
Nybyn S 73 Ja20
Nydala S 103 Fb50
Nyékládháza H 146 Jc51
Nyergesujfalu H 146 Hc52
Nygård N 67 Gc11
Nygård N 67 Gb13
Nygarden N 85 Ea35
Nyhammar S 95 Fc40
Nyhamnsläge S 110 Ec54
Nyheim N 65 Kd08
Nyhem S 87 Fd32
Ny Højen DK 108 Db25
Nyhyttan S 95 Fc42
Nýidalur IS 2 Ba05
Nyíkarász H 147 Kb50
Nyírábrány H 147 Kb52
Nyíracsád H 147 Kb52
Nyírád H 145 Gd54
Nyíradony H 147 Ka52
Nyírbátor H 147 Kb51
Nyírbéltek H 147 Kb52
Nyírbogát H 147 Kb51
Nyíregyháza H 147 Ka51
Nyírgyulaj H 147 Kb51
Nyírkáta H 147 Kb51
Nyírlugos H 147 Kb52
Nyírmada H 147 Kb50
Nyírmeggyes H 147 Kb51
Nyírtelek H 147 Ka51
Nyírtura H 147 Ka51
Nykälä FIN 90 Kd33
Nykarleby FIN 81 Ja29
Nyker DK 111 Fc57
Nykil S 103 Fd47
Nykirke N 85 Dd38
Nykirke N 93 Dd41
Nykirke N 93 Dd43
Nykøbing Falster DK 109 Eb29
Nykøbing M DK 100 Da21
Nykøbing S DK 109 Eb25
Nykøbing Strandhuse DK 109 Eb29
Nyköping S 95 Gb45
Nykroppa S 95 Fb42
Nyksund N 66 Fc12
Nykvarn S 96 Gc44
Nykyrka S 102 Fa48
Nyland S 79 Gb26
Nyland S 79 Fc30
Nyland S 80 Gc31
Nyland S 80 Ha29
Nyland S 80 Hb29
Nyland S 87 Gb33
Nylars DK 111 Fc58
Nyliden S 72 Gc22
Nyliden S 80 Gd29
Nyliden S 80 Ha27
Nyluspen S 79 Gb25
Nymburk CZ 136 Fc44
Nymindegab DK 108 Cd25
Nymo N 62 Ha08
Nymoen N 62 Gb10
Nynäshamn S 96 Gd45
Nyneset N 78 Ed26
Ny Nørup DK 108 Db25
Nyon CH 140 Ba55
Nyons F 42 Jc51
Nyord DK 109 Eb28
Nýřany CZ 135 Ed46
Nyröla FIN 90 Kb32
Nýrsko CZ 135 Ed47
Nyrud N 65 Kc09
Nysa PL 137 Gd43
Nysäter S 94 Ed44
Nysätern S 86 Fa33
Nysätra S 96 Gc42
Nysele S 80 Ha27
Nyseter N 85 Db34
Nyskoga S 94 Ed40
Nystadt = Uusikaupunki FIN 89 Ja38
Nysted DK 109 Eb29
Nystrand S 73 Hc22
Nystu Trønnes N 86 Eb36
Nysund S 95 Fb44
Nytjärn S 80 Gc28
Nytorp S 68 Hd17
Nyträsk S 73 Hb24
Nytrøa N 77 Ea33
Nyúl H 145 Ha53
Nyvall S 72 Ha23
Nyvoll N 63 Hd07
Nyvollen N 78 Ec29
Nyystölä FIN 90 Kb36
Nyžni Sirohozy UA 205 Fa16
Nyžni Torhaji UA 205 Fa16
Nyžn'ohirs'kyj UA 205 Fa17

O

Oaivos N 68 Hd11
Oakford GB 19 Ea30
Oakham GB 16 Fb24
Oakington GB 20 Fd25
Oakley GB 20 Fa29
Oakley GB 20 Fb27
Oalahti FIN 83 Lc31
Oancea RO 177 Fb61
Oanes N 92 Ca44
Oarda RO 175 Da60
Oarja RO 175 Dc65
Oarța de Jos RO 171 Cd55
Óassi GR 189 Bc86
Obalj BIH 159 Hc66
Oban GB 6 Db11
O Barco E 37 Bd57
Obârșia RO 179 Da67
Obârșia-Cloșani RO 174 Cb63
Obbekær DK 108 Da26
Obbnäs FIN 98 Ka40
Obbola S 80 Hb29
Obdach A 144 Fc54
Obecnice CZ 136 Fa46
Obedinenie BG 180 Dd69
Obejo E 60 Cc72
Obeliai LT 114 La53
Oberammergau D 142 Dc52
Oberasbach D 134 Dc46
Oberau A 143 Ea53
Oberau D 142 Dc53
Oberaudorf D 143 Eb52
Oberaula D 126 Da41
Oberaurach D 134 Dc45
Oberbeisheim D 126 Da41
Oberbergkirchen D 143 Eb50
Obercunnersdorf D 128 Fc41
Oberdachstetten D 134 Db46
Oberderdingen D 134 Cc47
Oberding D 143 Ea50
Oberdorla D 126 Dc40
Oberdrauburg A 143 Ec55
Oberei CH 141 Bd54
Obereisesheim D 134 Cd47
Oberelsbach D 134 Db43
Obergrafendorf A 144 Fd51
Obergünzburg D 142 Db51
Obergurgl A 142 Dc55
Oberhaching D 143 Dd51
Oberhaid D 134 Dc45
Oberharmersbach D 133 Cb49
Oberhausen D 125 Bd39
Oberheldrungen D 127 Dd40
Oberhof D 126 Dc42
Oberhofen CH 141 Bd55
Oberhoffen F 25 Kc36
Oberkail D 133 Bc43
Oberkappel A 136 Fa49
Oberkirch D 133 Ca49
Oberkirchen D 126 Cc40
Oberkochen D 134 Dd48
Oberkotzau D 135 Ea44
Oberlödla D 127 Eb41
Oberlungwitz D 127 Ec42
Obermaßfeld-Grimmenthal D 134 Dc43
Obermehler D 126 Dc40
Ober-Mörlen D 134 Cc43
Obermoschel D 133 Ca45
Obernai F 25 Kb37
Obernberg A 143 Ed50
Obernberg am Brenner A 143 Dd54
Obernbreit D 134 Db45
Obernburg D 134 Cd45
Oberndorf D 118 Da32
Oberndorf am Neckar D 141 Cb50
Oberndorf an der Melk A 144 Fd51
Oberndorf bei Salzburg A 143 Ec51
Obernheim D 142 Cc50
Obernholz D 118 Dc35
Obernkirchen D 126 Da37
Obernzell D 136 Fa49
Obernzenn D 134 Db46
Oberostendorf D 142 Dc51
Oberpframmern D 143 Ea51
Oberpleis D 125 Ca41
Oberpullendorf A 145 Gb53
Ober-Ramstadt D 134 Cc45
Oberreute D 142 Da52
Oberrickenbach CH 141 Cb54
Oberried CH 141 Ca55
Oberried D 141 Ca51
Oberriet CH 142 Cd53
Oberröblingen D 127 Dd40
Oberrot D 134 Da47
Oberscheinfeld D 134 Db45
Oberschleißheim D 143 Dd50
Oberschöna D 127 Ed42
Oberschwarzach D 134 Db45
Obersiggenthal CH 141 Cb52
Obersontheim D 134 Da47
Oberstadion D 142 Da50
Oberstadtfeld D 133 Bc43
Oberstaufen D 142 Da52
Oberstdorf D 142 Db53
Obersteigen F 25 Kb37
Obersteinbach F 25 Kc35
Oberstenfeld D 134 Cd47
Oberstreu D 134 Db43
Obersulm D 134 Cd47
Obertauern A 143 Ed54
Obertaufkirchen D 143 Eb50
Oberthal D 133 Bd45
Oberthulba D 134 Db44
Obertiefenbach D 125 Cb42
Obertilliach A 143 Eb55
Obertraubling D 135 Eb48
Obertraun A 144 Fa53
Oberturm am See A 143 Ec51
Oberursel D 134 Cc43
Obervellach A 143 Ed55
Oberviechtach D 135 Eb46
Oberwald CH 141 Ca55
Oberwart A 145 Gb54
Oberweis D 133 Bc44
Oberweissbach A 143 Ec53
Oberweißbach D 127 Dd42
Oberwesel D 133 Ca43
Oberweser D 126 Da39
Oberwiesenthal D 135 Ec43
Oberwölz A 144 Fb54
Oberzeiring A 144 Fb54
Obhausen D 127 Ea40
Óbidos P 50 Ab67
Obiedzino PL 123 Jd33
Obileni MD 173 Fb58
Obilić KSV 178 Bb70
Obing D 143 Eb51
Obinitsa EST 107 Lc47
Obiža RUS 107 Ld46
Objat F 33 Gb49
Objazda PL 121 Gc29
Objezierze PL 129 Gc36
Öblarn A 144 Fa53
Obljaj HR 152 Gb60
Obninsk RUS 202 Ed11
Obnova BG 180 Dc69
Öbög H 146 Jb54
Oboga RO 175 Da66
Obojan' RUS 203 Fa13
Obolon' UA 204 Ed15
Obón E 48 Fb63
Oborci BIH 158 Ha64
Oborin SK 139 Ka49
Oborište BG 179 Da72
Oborište BG 181 Fa69
Oborniki PL 129 Gc36
Oborniki Śląskie PL 129 Gc40
Obornjača SRB 153 Jb58
Oborowo PL 121 Hb35
Obory CZ 136 Fb46
Oborzany PL 120 Fc35
Obra PL 128 Ga38
Obreja RO 174 Cb62
Obrenovac SRB 153 Jc62
Obretenik BG 180 Ea69
Obrež HR 151 Ga59
Obrež SRB 153 Jb62
Obrigheim D 134 Cd46
Obrnice CZ 136 Fa43
Obročište BG 181 Fb70
Obrov SLO 151 Fa59
Obrovac HR 157 Ga64
Obrovac SRB 153 Ja60
Obrovac Sinjski HR 158 Gc65
Obršani MK 183 Bb75
Obrtići BIH 159 Hd65
Obryte PL 122 Jc35
Obrytki PL 123 Jd33
Obrzycko PL 129 Gb36
Obšistvi CZ 136 Fb44
Obsza PL 139 Kc43
Obudovac BIH 153 Hc61
Øby DK 100 Cd23
Obzor BG 181 Fa72
Očakiv UA 204 Ed17
Ocaklar TR 186 Fa79
Ocaklı TR 185 Eb79
Ocaña E 52 Dc66
Ocana F 154 Ca71
O Canizo E 36 Bc58
Occhiobello I 150 Dd61
Occold GB 21 Gb25
Ocentejo E 47 Eb63
Očeretuvate UA 205 Fa16
Očevlja BIH 159 Hc64
Ocharán E 38 Dd55
Ochiltree GB 10 Dd14
Ochiul Alb MD 173 Fb54
Ochiul Roș MD 173 Fd59
Ochla PL 128 Fd38
Ochojec PL 137 Hb44
Ochsenfurt D 134 Db45
Ochsenhausen D 142 Da51
Ochtendung D 133 Ca43
Ochtrup D 117 Ca36
Ochtyrka UA 202 Ed14
Ocieka PL 139 Jd43
Ocieseki PL 130 Jc42
Ockelbo S 87 Gb38
Ockholm D 108 Da29
Ockle GB 6 Db10
Ockley GB 20 Fc29
Ocksjön S 87 Fc32
Ocland RO 176 Dd60
Ocna de Fier RO 174 Ca62
Ocna Dejului RO 171 Da57
Ocna Mureș RO 171 Da59
Ocna Sibiului RO 175 Db61
Ocna Șugatag RO 171 Db55
Ocnele Mari RO 175 Db64
Ocnița MD 173 Fa53
Ocnița MD 173 Fc54
Ocnița RO 176 Dd64
Ocoale RO 171 Cc58
Ocolina MD 173 Fc54
Ocoliș RO 171 Cd59
Ocón E 39 Eb58
Očová SK 138 Hd49
Ocrkavlje BIH 159 Hc66
Ócsa H 146 Hd53
Ócsárd H 152 Hb58
Öcsény H 153 Hc57
Öcsöd H 146 Jc54
Octeville, Cherbourg F 22 Ed34
Octeville-sur-Mer F 22 Fd34
Octon F 41 Hc54
Ocypel PL 121 Ha32
Öd S 79 Fc31
Od S 102 Ed48
Odăile RO 176 Ec63
Ödåkra S 110 Ed54
Odals verk N 94 Ec40
Ödängla S 103 Gb51
Odărne BG 180 Dc69
Odby DK 100 Da22
Odda N 84 Cc40
Odde DK 101 Dd22
Odden N 62 Ha09
Odden N 70 Ed23
Odden N 86 Eb36
Odden Færgehavn DK 109 Ea25
Oddense DK 100 Da22
Odder DK 108 Dc24
Oddernes N 92 Cd47
Oddesund Nord DK 100 Da22
Oddesund Syd DK 100 Da22
Ödeborg S 102 Ec46
Ödeby S 95 Fd43
Odeceixe P 58 Ab73
Odelzhausen D 143 Dd50
Odemira P 58 Ab72
Ödemiș TR 192 Fa86
Odèn E 49 Gc59
Ódena E 49 Gc61
Ödenäs S 102 Ec48
Odensåker S 103 Fb46
Odensala S 96 Gd42
Odensbacken S 95 Fd44
Odense DK 108 Dc26
Odensjö S 102 Fa52
Odensjö S 103 Fb49
Odensvi S 95 Ga43
Odensvi S 103 Ga48
Oderberg D 120 Fb35
Oderljunga S 110 Fa54
Oderwitz D 128 Fc42
Oderzo I 150 Eb59
Odesa UA 204 Ec17
Ödeshög S 103 Fc47
Ödestugu S 103 Fb49
Odiáxere P 58 Ab74
Odiham GB 20 Fb29
Odincovo RUS 202 Ed10
Ødis DK 108 Db26
Odivelas P 50 Ac71
Ödkarby FIN 96 Hc40
Odnes N 85 Dd38
Odobasca RO 176 Ed62
Odobești RO 176 Dd65
Odobești RO 176 Ed62
Odolanów PL 129 Gd39
Odolena Voda CZ 136 Fb44
Odón E 47 Ed63
Odoorn NL 117 Ca34
Odoreu RO 171 Cd54
Odorheiu Secuiesc RO 176 Dd60
Odos F 40 Fd55
Odou CY 206 Jb97
Odrinci BG 181 Fa69
Odrowąż PL 130 Jb40
Odry CZ 137 Ha46
Odry PL 121 Ha31
Odrzykoń PL 139 Jd45
Odrzywół PL 130 Jb39
Ödskölt S 94 Ec45
Ödsmål S 102 Eb46
Ödsmål S 102 Eb47
Ødsted DK 108 Db25
Ødum DK 100 Dc23
Odžaci SRB 153 Hd59
Odžak BIH 152 Hb61
Odžak BIH 158 Hb67
Odžak MNE 159 Ja67
Odziena LV 106 La51
Oebisfelde D 127 Dd36
Oed A 144 Fc51
Oederan D 127 Ed42
Oederquart D 118 Da32
Oeffelt NL 125 Bb38
Oegstgeest NL 116 Ad36
Oehna D 127 Ed38
Oeiras P 50 Aa69
Öekény H 146 Hd54
Oelde D 126 Cc38
Oelsig D 127 Ed39
Oelsnitz D 127 Ec42
Oelsnitz D 135 Eb43
Oencia E 37 Bd57
Oensingen CH 141 Bd53
Oerel D 118 Da33
Oerlenbach D 134 Db44
Oerlinghausen D 126 Cd38
Oestrich-Winkel D 133 Cb44
Oettingen D 134 Dc48
Oetz A 142 Dc54
Oetzen D 119 Dd34
Œuf-en-Ternois F 23 Gd32
Oeversee D 108 Db29
Ofatinți MD 173 Fd56
Ofena I 157 Fa70
Offenau D 134 Cd47
Offenbach D 134 Cc44
Offenbach an der Queich D 133 Cb47
Offenbach-Hundheim D 133 Ca45
Offenberg D 135 Ec48
Offenburg D 133 Ca49
Offenhausen D 135 Dd46
Offerdal S 79 Fb30
Offersøya N 66 Fd14
Offida I 156 Ed68
Offingen D 134 Db49
Offne S 79 Fb30
Offranville F 23 Ga33
Oftedal N 92 Cb45
Ofterdingen D 134 Cc49
Oftringen CH 141 Ca53
Ogardy PL 120 Fd35
Ogbourne Saint George GB 20 Ed28
Øgelund DK 108 Da25
Ogéviller F 25 Ka37
Öggestorp S 103 Fb49
Oggevatn N 92 Cd46
Oggiono I 149 Cc58
Oglaine LV 106 Kb52
Oğlananasi TR 191 Ec86
Ogliastro Cilento I 161 Fc76
Ogliastro Marina I 161 Fc77
Öglunda S 102 Fa46
Ögmen TR 191 Ec81
Ogmore-by-Sea GB 19 Ea28
Ogna N 92 Ca45
Ognina I 167 Fd87
Ognjanovo BG 181 Fa68
Ognjanovo BG 184 Cd75
Ogoja BG 179 Cc70
Ogonki PL 122 Jc30
Ogonnelloe IRL 12 Bd22
Ogošte KSV 178 Bc71
Ogra CY 206 Ja96
Ogra RO 171 Db59
Ogre LV 106 Kc51
Ogreskalns LV 106 Kd50
Ogrezeni RO 176 Ea66
Ogródek PL 123 Jd31
Ogrodniczki PL 123 Kb33
Ogrodniki PL 123 Jd35
Ogrodniki PL 123 Kb30
Ogrodzieniec PL 138 Hd43
Ogrosen D 128 Fa39
O Grove E 36 Ac56
Ogulin HR 151 Fd60
Oğulpaşa TR 187 Gb79
Ohaba RO 175 Da60
Ohaba Lungă RO 174 Ca60
Ohanes E 61 Ea75
Ohenmäki FIN 82 Kd28
Ohey B 124 Ad42
Ohiró GR 184 Cd76
Ohkola FIN 90 Kb38
Ohlstadt D 143 Dd52
Öhningen D 142 Cc52
Ohotnoe RUS 113 Jc58
Ohrdruf D 126 Dc42
Ohrid MK 182 Ba75
Ohrikylä FIN 89 Ja33
Öhringen D 134 Cd47
Ohtaanniemi FIN 83 Lb30
Ohtanajärvi S 73 Ja18
Ohtinen FIN 89 Jd37
Ohtola FIN 89 Jd33
Ohtsejohka FIN 64 Jd07
Oiă P 44 Ac63
Oidrema EST 98 Ka45
Oijärvi FIN 74 Ka21
Oijusluoma FIN 75 La20
Oikarainen FIN 74 Ka19
Oileán Ciarraí IRL 12 Bb24
Oilgate IRL 13 Cc24
Oilgate IRL 13 Cd24
Oimbra E 44 Bb59
Oinaala FIN 90 Ka37
Oinacu RO 180 Ea68
Oinas FIN 69 Kb17
Oinasjärvi FIN 82 Kd27
Oinasjärvi FIN 97 Jd39
Oingt F 34 Ja46
Oinoskylä FIN 82 Ka30
Oinville F 23 Gc36
Oion E 39 Eb58
Oiron F 27 Fc43
Oirschot NL 124 Ba38
Ois E 36 Ba54
Øisang N 93 Db45
Oiselay-et-Grachaux F 31 Jd41
Oisemont F 23 Gc33
Oissel F 23 Gb35
Oisterwijk NL 124 Ba38
Oisu EST 98 Kd44
Õisu EST 106 Kd46
Oitti FIN 90 Kb37
Oittila FIN 90 Kc33
Oituz RO 176 Ec60
Oiu EST 98 La45
Oivu FIN 81 Jb28
Oix E 41 Ha58
Öja FIN 81 Jb28
Öja S 95 Ga44
Öja S 103 Fc52
Öja S 104 Gd51
Öjaby S 103 Fc52
Ojakkala FIN 98 Ka39
Ojakylä FIN 74 Jd24
Ojakylä FIN 74 Ka23
Ojakylä FIN 81 Jd27
Ojakylä FIN 82 Ka26
Ojakylä FIN 82 Ka27
Ojala FIN 81 Jc30
Ojalehto FIN 82 Ka27
Ojanperä FIN 82 Ka27
Ojanperä FIN 82 Kc26
Öjarn S 79 Fc28
Ojasoo EST 98 Kc43
Ojców PL 138 Ja44
Ojdula RO 176 Eb61
Öje S 88 Gc33
Öje S 95 Fb39
Öjebyn S 73 Hc23
Ojedo E 38 Da55
Ojén E 60 Cc77
Öjenäs S 94 Fa41
Ojinești MD 173 Fc57
Ojos Negros E 47 Ed63
Ojrzeń PL 122 Ja35
Ojuelos Altos E 51 Cb71
Öjvasseln S 86 Fa35
Okainiai LT 114 Kc56
Okalewko PL 122 Hd34
Okalewo PL 122 Hd34
Okány H 147 Jd54
Okartowo PL 122 Jc31
Okçu TR 193 Ha82
Okcyn PL 131 Kc37
Økdal N 78 Ea31
Okehampton GB 19 Dd30
Okeroinen FIN 90 Kc37
Okkelberg N 78 Eb29
Okkenhaug N 78 Ec29
Oklaj HR 158 Gb65
Okletac SRB 159 Ja64
Oključina HR 158 Gb68
Oklubalı TR 193 Gb82
Ökna S 103 Fd50
Okoč SK 145 Ha51
Okół PL 131 Jd41
Okoli HR 152 Gc59
Okome S 102 Ed51
Okonek PL 121 Gc33
Okonin PL 121 Hb33
Okop BG 180 Eb73
Okopy PL 131 Kd40
Okorág H 152 Ha58
Okorš BG 181 Ec68
Okovcy RUS 202 Ec10
Okřišky CZ 136 Ga47
Okrouhlice CZ 136 Fd46
Okruglica HR 151 Fd60
Okrúhle SK 139 Jd47
Okrzeja PL 131 Ka38
Oksa PL 130 Ja42
Oksajärvi S 68 Hd15
Oksakoski FIN 81 Jd29
Oksava FIN 82 Ka27
Oksbøl DK 108 Cd25
Oksby DK 108 Cd25
Okseidet N 68 Hd11
Øksendalen N 70 Fa22
Øksendalsøra N 77 Db32
Øksendalssetra N 85 Ea36
Øksfjord N 63 Hc07
Øksfjordbotn N 63 Hc08
Okskulma FIN 90 Kb34
Øksna N 86 Eb38
Øksnes N 78 Ec27
Øksneshavn N 66 Fd14
Øksninga N 78 Ec25
Okstad N 78 Eb30
Okstveit N 92 Cb41
Oksvoll N 77 Dd28
Okt'abr'skoje RUS 113 Jb59
Oktjabr'sk RUS 203 Ga10
Oktjabr'skij RUS 203 Fd14
Oktoniá GR 190 Cd85
Okučani HR 152 Gd60
Okuklje HR 158 Ha69
Okulice PL 138 Jb44
Okulovka RUS 202 Ec09
Okuniew PL 130 Jc36
Okuninka PL 131 Kc39
Okurçalar TR 199 Hb92
Öküzler TR 198 Fc90
Ólafsfjörður IS 2 Ba03
Ólafsvík IS 2 Ab03
Olagüe E 39 Ed56
Olaine LV 106 Kb51
Olalla E 47 Fa63
Oland N 93 Da45
Oland N 93 Db45
Olanes N 63 Hd07
Olang I 143 Ea55
Olanu RO 175 Db64
Olargues F 41 Hb54
Olari FIN 98 Kb40
Olari RO 170 Bd59
Oława PL 129 Gd41
Olazagutía E 39 Eb56
Olba E 54 Fb65
Olbernhau D 127 Ed42
Olbia I 168 Cb74
Olbięcin PL 131 Ka41
Olbramovice CZ 136 Fc46
Olbramovice CZ 137 Gb48
Olcea RO 170 Ca58
Olching D 143 Dd50
Ol'chovka RUS 113 Jb58
Old GB 20 Fb25
Oldcastle IRL 9 Cc20
Old Castleton GB 11 Ec15
Old Deer GB 5 Ed08
Olde DK 108 Dc28
Oldeberkoop NL 117 Bc34
Oldeboorn NL 117 Bc33
Oldebroek NL 117 Bc35
Oldeide N 84 Ca34
Oldekerk NL 117 Bd33
Oldemarkt NL 117 Bc34
Olden N 84 Cd34
Olden S 78 Fa29
Oldenburg D 117 Cc34
Oldenburg in Holstein D 119 Dd30
Oldendorf D 118 Da32
Oldenswort D 118 Da30
Oldenzaal NL 117 Bd36
Oldenzaal NL 117 Cc34
Olderdalen N 62 Ha09
Olderfjord N 64 Jb06
Oldernes N 63 Ja06
Olderneset N 64 Ka07
Oldervik N 62 Gd09
Oldervik N 64 Jd06
Oldervika N 70 Fa20
Oldham GB 16 Ed21
Oldhamstocks GB 11 Ec13
Old Head IRL 12 Bd26
Oldisleben D 127 Dd40
Old Lake GB 17 Fd23
Oldmeldrum GB 5 Ed08
Old Radnor GB 15 Eb25
Oldřichovice CZ 137 Hb46
Oldrões P 44 Ad61
Old Sodbury GB 19 Ec28
Old Somerby GB 16 Fb23
Old Warden GB 20 Fc26
Oldways End GB 19 Ea29
Olea E 38 Db56
Oleby S 94 Ed41
Olecko PL 123 Ka30
Olędy PL 123 Ka35
Oleggio I 148 Cb59
Oleiros E 36 Ac56
Oleiros P 44 Ad64
Oleksandrija UA 204 Ed15
Oleksandrivka UA 204 Ed15
Oleksandrivka UA 204 Ed15
Oleksandrivka UA 204 Ed17
Oleksandrivka UA 205 Fb15
Olelas E 36 Ba58
Olen B 124 Ad39
Ølen N 92 Ca42
Olenino RUS 202 Ec10
Olenivka UA 204 Ed17
Oleri LV 106 Kd47
Olesa de Montserrat E 49 Gd61
Olešná CZ 136 Fa45
Oleśnica PL 129 Gd40
Oleśnica PL 138 Jc43
Olešnice CZ 137 Gb46
Oleśniczka PL 129 Gd41
Olesno PL 129 Hb41
Olesno PL 138 Jc43
Oleszno PL 130 Ja41
Oleszyce PL 139 Kc43
Oletta F 154 Cc69
Olette F 41 Ha57
Olevs'k UA 202 Eb14
Olfen D 125 Ca38
Olgiate Comasco I 149 Cc58
Ol'gino RUS 99 Mb39
Ølgod DK 108 Da25
Olhalvo P 50 Ab67
Ølhammaren N 78 Ec26
Olhão P 58 Ad74
Olhava FIN 74 Jd22
Ol'hi RUS 203 Fb11
Ølholm DK 108 Db25
Ol'hovatka RUS 113 Jd59
Ol'hovatka RUS 203 Fb13
Ol'hovka RUS 203 Fd13
Olib HR 151 Fc63
Oliena I 169 Cb76
Oliete E 48 Fb63
Olímbi GR 191 Dd86
Olímbia GR 194 Ba87
Ólimbos GR 197 Eb94
Olimp RO 181 Fc68
Olimpiáda GR 184 Cc78
Oliņas LV 106 La48
Olingdal S 87 Fb35
Olișcani MD 173 Fd55
Olite E 39 Ed58
Oliva E 54 Fc69
Oliva de la Frontera E 51 Bc71
Oliva de Mérida E 51 Ca69
Oliva de Plasencia E 45 Ca65
Olivadi I 164 Gc82
Olivares E 59 Bd73
Olivares de Júcar E 53 Eb67
Oliveira de Azeméis P 44 Ad62
Oliveira de Barreiros P 44 Ba63
Oliveira do Bairro P 44 Ad63
Oliveira do Douro P 44 Ba61
Oliveira do Hospital P 44 Ba64
Olivenza E 51 Bb69
Olivet F 29 Gc40
Olivone CH 142 Cc56
Öljehult S 111 Fc53
Ol'ka SK 139 Ka47
Olkamangi S 74 Jb18
Olkijoki FIN 81 Jd25
Olkiluoto FIN 89 Ja37
Olkkajärvi FIN 74 Ka18
Olkkala FIN 98 Ka39
Olkkola FIN 82 Ka27
Olkusz PL 138 Hd43
Ollaberry GB 5 Fa04
Ollala FIN 82 Ka26
Ollebacken S 79 Fc29
Ollerías E 38 Ea56
Olleros de Pisuerga E 38 Db57
Ollerton GB 16 Fb22
Ollerup DK 109 Dd27
Olleta E 39 Ed57
Olliergues F 34 Hc47
Ollikkala FIN 90 La35

Ollikkala – Ostende

Ollikkala FIN 91 Lb33
Ollila FIN 89 Jc38
Olliilanvaara FIN 74 Jd18
Ollioules F 42 Jd55
Öllölä FIN 83 Ma31
Ollomont I 148 Bc57
Ollon CH 141 Bc56
Olloniego E 37 Cc55
Ölmbratorp S 95 Fd43
Ölme S 95 Fb43
Olmeda de la Cuesta E 47 Eb65
Olmeda del Rey E 53 Ec66
Olmedilla de Alarcón E 53 Eb67
Olmedillo de Roa E 46 Db60
Olmedo E 46 Da61
Olmedo I 168 Bd75
Olmeto F 154 Ca71
Ölmevalla S 102 Ec50
Ölmhult S 95 Fb43
Olmi-Capella F 154 Cb69
Olmillos de Castro E 45 Cb60
Olmillos de Sasamón E 38 Db58
Olmo al Brembo I 149 Cd58
Olmos P 45 Bd60
Olmos de la Picaza E 38 Db58
Olmos de Ojeda E 38 Da57
Olmos de Pisuerga E 38 Db57
Ölmstad S 103 Fb48
Olmütz = Olomouc CZ 137 Gd46
Olney GB 20 Fb26
Ołobok PL 129 Ha39
Olocau E 54 Fb67
Olocau del Rey E 48 Fc64
Olofsfors S 80 Ha29
Olofstorp S 102 Ec48
Olofström S 111 Fc54
Olombrada E 46 Db61
Olomouc CZ 137 Gd46
Olonne-sur-Mer F 28 Ed44
Olonzac F 41 Ha55
Oloron-Sainte-Marie F 39 Fb55
Olosig RO 170 Cb56
Olost E 49 Gd59
Olot E 49 Ha59
Olovi CZ 135 Ec44
Olovo BIH 159 Hc64
Olpe D 125 Cb39
Olpe D 125 Cb40
Ol'ša RUS 202 Ec11
Olsberg D 126 Cc40
Olsbrücken D 133 Ca45
Olsbu N 93 Da45
Olseröd S 111 Fb55
Ölserud S 94 Ed44
Olsewo Węrorzewskie PL 122 Jc30
Olshammar S 95 Fc45
Olší CZ 137 Gb46
Olsker DK 111 Fc57
Olsøy N 78 Ea29
Ölsremma S 102 Fa49
Olst NL 117 Bc36
Ølsted DK 108 Dc25
Ølsted DK 109 Eb25
Ølstrup DK 108 Cd24
Ølstykke DK 109 Eb25
Olsvika N 70 Ed24
Olszamy PL 130 Jb38
Olszanica PL 139 Kb46
Olszanka PL 123 Ka30
Olszanka PL 129 Gd42
Olszanka PL 131 Ka37
Olszany PL 139 Kb45
Olszewka PL 122 Jb33
Olszewnica PL 131 Ka37
Olszewo-Borki PL 122 Jc34
Olsztyn PL 122 Ja32
Olsztyn PL 130 Hc42
Olsztynek PL 122 Ja32
Olszyn PL 131 Kc37
Olszyna PL 128 Fc39
Olszyna PL 128 Fd41
Olszyny PL 122 Jb32
Oltedal N 92 Ca44
Olten CH 141 Ca53
Oltenești RO 173 Fb59
Olteni RO 180 Dd67
Oltenița RO 181 Ec67
Oltesvig N 92 Cb44
Oltina RO 181 Fa67
Oltre il Colle I 149 Cd58
Oltu TR 205 Ga19
Olukbaşı TR 198 Fb89
Olukbaşı TR 198 Fd90
Oluku TR 193 Gb81
Olula del Río E 61 Eb74
Olur TR 205 Ga19
Olustvere EST 98 Kd45
Olvan E 49 Gd59
Olvasjärvi FIN 75 Kc23
Ølve N 84 Ca40
Olveda E 36 Bb56
Ölvega E 47 Ec60
Olveiroa E 36 Ac55
Olvera E 59 Cb75
Ólvio GR 184 Db77
Ólynthos GR 183 Cb79
Olzai I 169 Ca76
Olzheim D 133 Bc43
Omagh GB 9 Cc17
Omali GR 182 Ba78
Omaló GR 183 Bd77
Oman BG 181 Ec73
Omarčevo BG 180 Ea72
Omarska BIH 152 Gc62
Ómassa H 146 Jb50
Omblèze F 35 Jc49
Ömböly H 147 Kb51
Omeath IRL 9 Cd19
Omedu EST 99 Lb44
Omegna I 148 Ca58
Ömen TR 186 Fc77
Omeñaca E 47 Eb60
Ömerköy TR 192 Fa81
Ömerler TR 192 Ga82
Ömerler TR 193 Hb82
Ömerler Bölüğü TR 197 Fa89
Ömeroba TR 185 Ec74
Omiš HR 158 Gc66
Omišalj HR 151 Fb61
Ommen NL 117 Bd35
Ommunddalen N 78 Ea28
Omø DK 109 Ea27
Omodos CY 206 Ja97
Omoljica SRB 174 Bb64
Omont F 24 Ja34
Omonville-la-Rogue F 22 Ed34
Omor RO 174 Bd62
Omorani MK 183 Bc74
Omorfohóri GR 189 Bd81
Ömossa FIN 89 Ja34
Omsjö S 79 Gb29
Omurlar TR 192 Fc84
Omurtag BG 180 Eb70
Omvriaki GR 189 Bc82
Øn N 84 Ca36
Ön S 73 Hc23
Ön S 79 Gb30
On S 79 Fd28
Oña E 38 Dd57
Ona N 76 Cd31
Onaç TR 199 Gc88
Onali FIN 90 Kc36
Onarheim N 84 Ca40
Oñati E 39 Eb56
Oncești RO 172 Ed59
Onda E 54 Fc66
Ondara E 55 Fc70
Ondarroa E 39 Eb55
Ondić HR 151 Ga63
Ondres F 39 Ed54
Ondrovo RUS 99 Mb40
Önerler TR 186 Fa77
Onesse-et-Laharie F 39 Fa53
Onești MD 173 Fc57
Onești MD 173 Fc58
Onești RO 176 Ec60
Onet-le-Château F 33 Ha51
Oniceni RO 172 Ed58
Onich GB 6 Dc10
Onifai I 168 Cc76
Oniferi I 169 Cb76
Onil E 55 Fb70
Onițcani MD 173 Fd57
Onkamaa FIN 91 Lb37
Onkamo FIN 69 Kd17
Onkamo FIN 74 Ka23
Onkamo FIN 83 Ld31
Onkemäki FIN 89 Jd36
Onkijoki FIN 89 Jc37
Onkiniemi FIN 90 Kc35
Onnaing F 24 Hb32
Önneköp S 110 Fa55
Önnestad S 111 Fb54
Önningeby FIN 96 Hc41
Onno I 149 Cc58
Onoz F 31 Jc44
Onsares E 53 Ea71
Onsbjerg DK 109 Dd25
Onsevig DK 109 Ea28
Onsey N 93 Ea44
Onslunda S 111 Fb56
Onstwedde NL 117 Ca34
Ontika EST 99 Lb41
Ontinar del Salz E 48 Fb59
Ontiñena E 48 Fd60
Ontinyent E 55 Fb70
Ontojoki FIN 83 Lb26
Ontón E 38 Dd55
Onttola FIN 83 Ld30
Ontur E 55 Ed70
Onum S 102 Ed47
Onuškis LT 114 Kd58
Onuškis LT 114 La53
Onville F 25 Jc36
Onzain F 29 Gb41
Onzonilla E 37 Cc57
Oola IRL 12 Bd23
Oonga EST 98 Ka44
Oonurme EST 99 Lb43
Oostburg NL 124 Ab38
Oost-Cappel F 21 Gd30
Oostduinkerke-Bad B 21 Ha29
Oostende B 21 Ha29
Oosterend NL 116 Ba33
Oosterend NL 116 Bb32
Oosterhesselen NL 117 Bd35
Oosterhout NL 124 Ad38
Oosterwolde NL 117 Bd34
Oosterzee NL 117 Bc34
Oosthuizen NL 116 Ba35
Oostkapelle NL 124 Ab38
Oostmalle B 124 Ad39
Oost-Souburg NL 124 Ab38
Oostvleteren B 21 Ha30
Oost-Vlieland NL 116 Bb32
Oostvoorne NL 124 Ac37
Ootmarsum NL 117 Bd36
Opaci MD 173 Ga59
Opaka BG 180 Ea69
Opalenica PL 129 Gb37
Opalenie PL 121 Hb32
Opaleniec PL 122 Jb33
Opaljenik SRB 178 Ad67
Opan BG 180 Dd73
Opařany CZ 136 Fb47
Opařić SRB 178 Bb67
Opatija HR 151 Fb60
Opatinec HR 152 Gb59
Opatov CZ 137 Gb45
Opatovac HR 153 Hd60
Opatovice nad Labem CZ 136 Ga44
Opatów PL 129 Ha40
Opatów PL 130 Hc41
Opatów PL 131 Jd41
Opatówek PL 129 Ha39
Opatowiec PL 138 Jb43
Opava CZ 137 Ha45
Opawica PL 137 Gd44
Ope S 79 Fc31
O Pedrouzo (O Pino) E 36 Ba55
Opglabeek B 125 Bb40
Ophemert NL 125 Bb37
Opi I 161 Fa72
Opinan GB 4 Dc06
O Pindo E 36 Ac55
Opinogóra PL 122 Jb34
Opišnja UA 202 Ed14
Opitter B 125 Bb40
Oploo NL 125 Bb38
Oplotnica SLO 151 Fd57
Opocka RUS 107 Mb50
Opočka RUS 202 Ea10
Opočno CZ 137 Gb44
Opoczno PL 130 Ja40
Opole PL 129 Ha42
Opol'e RUS 99 Ld41
Opole Lubelskie PL 131 Jd40
Opolno-Zdrój PL 128 Fc42
Oporelu RO 175 Db65
Oporów PL 130 Hd37
Opovo SRB 153 Jc61
Opovo SRB 174 Bb63
Oppach D 128 Fb41
Oppala S 95 Gb39
Oppdal N 77 Dd32
Oppdal N 78 Ec26
Oppdalen N 85 Ea40
Oppdøl N 77 Db32
Oppeano I 149 Dc60
Oppeby S 103 Ga48
Oppède-le-Vieux F 42 Jc53
Oppegård N 93 Ea42
Oppegard N 94 Eb39
Oppenau D 133 Cb49
Oppenberg A 144 Fb53
Oppenheim D 133 Cb45
Oppenwehe D 117 Cc36
Oppenweiler D 134 Cd48
Opphaug N 77 Dd29
Oppheim N 84 Cc38
Opphus N 86 Eb37
Oppido Lucano I 162 Gb75
Oppido Mamertina I 164 Gb83
Oppmanna S 111 Fb54
Opponitz A 144 Fc52
Oppsal N 92 Ca44
Oppstryn N 84 Cd34
Oppurg D 127 Ea42
Oprișor RO 175 Cc66
Oprtalj Pórtole HR 151 Fa60
Opshaugvik N 76 Cd33
Optași-Măgura RO 175 Db65
Optedal N 92 Cc47
Ópusztaszer H 146 Jb56
Opuzen HR 158 Ha68
Oquillas E 46 Dc60
Ör S 102 Ec46
Ör S 103 Fc51
Ör H 147 Kb51
Ora CY 206 Jb97
Ora I 150 Dd57
Øra N 63 Hb07
Öra S 102 Fa48
Orac MD 173 Fc59
Orada P 50 Ba71
Orada P 50 Ba68
Oradea RO 170 Cb56
Oradour-Saint-Genest F 33 Gb45
Oradour-sur-Glane F 33 Gb46
Orah BIH 159 Hc68
Orahova BIH 152 Gd61
Orahovac KSV 178 Ba71
Orahovac MNE 159 Hd69
Orahov Do BIH 158 Hb68
Orahovica BIH 153 Hc62
Orahovica BIH 153 Hc63
Orahovica HR 152 Ha59
Orahovičko Polje BIH 152 Ha63
Orahovlje BIH 158 Ha67
Oraison F 42 Ka52
Orajärvi FIN 74 Jb18
Orakylä FIN 69 Ka16
Orange F 42 Jb52
Orani I 169 Cb76
Oranienbaum D 127 Eb39
Oranienburg D 119 Ed35
Oranmore IRL 12 Bc21
Orašac HR 158 Hb69
Orašac SRB 174 Bb65
Orašac SRB 178 Bd69
Orasi MNE 159 Hd69
Orašje BIH 153 Hc61
Orăștie RO 175 Cd61
Orăștioara de Sus RO 175 Cd61
Orașu Nou RO 171 Da54
Orava EST 107 Lc46
Orava FIN 81 Jc30
Oravainen FIN 81 Ja30
Oravais FIN 81 Ja30
Oravala FIN 90 Kd36
Öravan S 80 Gc26
Oravasaari FIN 90 Kc33
Oravi FIN 91 Lb32
Oravica SRB 178 Bd70
Oravice SK 138 Ja47
Oravijoki FIN 82 Kd27
Oravikoski FIN 82 La31
Oravisalo FIN 83 Ld31
Oravița RO 174 Bd63
Oravivaara FIN 75 La24
Oravská Lesná SK 138 Hd46
Oravská Polhora SK 138 Hd46
Oravské Veselé SK 138 Hd46
Oravský Podzámok SK 138 Hd47
Orba E 55 Fc70
Orbacém E 44 Ac59
Ørbæk DK 109 Dd27
Orbais-l'Abbaye F 24 Hc36
Orbassano I 148 Bc60
Orbe CH 141 Bb54
Orbeasca RO 180 Dd67
Orbec F 22 Fd36
Orbeni RO 176 Ed60
Örberga S 103 Fc46
Orbetello I 155 Dc69
Orbigny F 29 Gb42
Ørby DK 108 Db27
Ørby DK 109 Dd24
Örbyhus S 96 Gc40
Orca P 44 Bb65
Orcau E 48 Gb59
Orce E 61 Ea73
Orcera E 53 Ea71
Orchamps F 31 Jc42
Orchies F 24 Hb31
Orchowo PL 129 Ha36
Orcières F 35 Ka50
Orcival F 34 Hb47
Ordaca TR 185 Eb80
Ordan-Larroque F 40 Fd54
Ordășei MD 173 Fc56
Ordejón de Arriba E 38 Db57
Ordes E 36 Ba55
Ørding DK 100 Da22
Ordizia E 39 Ec56
Ordona I 161 Ga73
Ordu TR 205 Fc19
Orduña E 38 Ea56
Ordžonikidze UA 205 Fa16
Ordžonikidzevskij RUS 205 Ga17
Øre N 77 Da31
Öre S 80 Hb29
Ore S 87 Fd37
Orea E 47 Ec64
Orebić HR 158 Gd68
Örebro S 95 Fd44
Oredež RUS 202 Eb09
Öregcsertő H 146 Hd56
Öregrund S 96 Gd40
Orehova RUS 107 Ma47
Orehovec HR 152 Gb58
Orehovec MK 183 Bc75
Orehoved DK 109 Eb28
Orehovica BG 180 Db68
Orehoviči RUS 107 Ma47
Orehovno RUS 99 Ma44
Orehovo BG 184 Db74
Orehovo-Zuevo RUS 203 Fa10
Orei GR 189 Ca83
Orel RUS 99 Lc43
Orel RUS 202 Ed12
Orellana de la Sierra E 51 Cb68
Orellana la Vieja E 51 Cb68
Ören TR 191 Ec82
Ören TR 192 Fa81
Ören TR 192 Ga84
Ören TR 197 Fa90
Ören TR 198 Fd90
Ören TR 198 Fd90
Ören TR 198 Fd91
Oreña E 38 Db54
Örencik TR 186 Fb76
Örencik TR 187 Gc79
Örencik TR 187 Hb76
Örencik TR 191 Ec81
Örencik TR 192 Ga83
Örenkaya TR 193 Gb86
Örenköy TR 192 Fc82
Örenköy TR 193 Ha87
Örenköy TR 193 Hb85
Orense E 36 Bb57
Oréo GR 184 Db76
Oreókastro GR 183 Ca77
Öreryd S 102 Fa50
Oreš BG 180 Dc69
Orešak BG 180 Db71
Orešak BG 181 Fa70
Orešan BG 185 Dd75
Orešec BG 185 Ea75
Orestiáda GR 185 Eb76
Öreström S 80 Ha28
Oresvika N 70 Fa20
Oreye B 124 Ba41
Öreyköy TR 185 Ec77
Orezu RO 176 Ec66
Orford GB 21 Gb26
Orfű H 152 Hb57
Orgáni GR 185 Dd76
Organyà E 48 Gb59
Orgaz E 52 Db67
Orgelet F 31 Jc44
Orgères-en-Beauce F 29 Gc39
Órgiva E 60 Dc76
Orglandes F 22 Fa35
Orgnac-l'Aven F 34 Ja51
Orgnac-sur-Vézère F 33 Gc48
Orgon F 42 Jb53
Orgosolo I 169 Cb76
Orgovány H 146 Ja55
Orhaneli TR 192 Fc81
Orhangazi TR 186 Fd79
Orhaniye TR 185 Eb78
Orhaniye TR 186 Fd80
Orhaniye TR 186 Ga79
Orhaniye TR 187 Gb78
Orhaniye TR 193 Ha82
Orhanlar TR 191 Ed81
Orhanlı TR 186 Fd78
Orhanlı TR 198 Ga89
Orhei MD 173 Fd57
Orhomenós GR 189 Ca85
Oria E 61 Eb74
Oria I 162 Hb76
Orichiv UA 205 Fa16
Origny-en-Thiérache F 24 Hc33
Origny-Sainte-Benoite F 24 Hb33
Orihuela E 55 Fa72
Orihuela del Tremedal E 47 Ed64
Orijahovo BG 179 Da68
Orikon AL 182 Aa77
Orillena E 48 Fc60
Orimattila FIN 90 Kc37
Oriniemi FIN 83 Lc29
Oriniemi FIN 89 Jc37
Oriní Meligoú GR 195 Bd88
Oriñón E 38 Dd55
Orio E 39 Ec55
Ório GR 189 Cc85
Oriola P 50 Ad70
Oriolo I 162 Gc77
Oripää FIN 89 Jc38
Orisberg FIN 81 Jb31
Orismala FIN 81 Ja31
Orisoain E 39 Ed57
Orissaare EST 97 Jd45
Oristano I 169 Bd77
Orivesi FIN 89 Jc37
Öriszentpéter H 145 Gb55
Oriveden asema FIN 90 Ka35
Orivesi FIN 90 Ka35
Orizare BG 181 Fa72
Orizovo BG 180 Dc73
Orjahovec BG 184 Db75
Orjaku EST 97 Jc45
Orjal E 36 Ba55
Orjanovo BG 185 Ea74
Ørje N 94 Eb43
Orkanger N 77 Dd30
Örkelljunga S 110 Ed54
Orkesta S 96 Gd42
Orkland N 77 Dd30
Orla PL 123 Kb35
Orlamünde D 127 Ea42
Orlane KSV 178 Bc70
Orlat RO 175 Da61
Orlea RO 180 Db68
Orléans F 29 Gc40
Örlemiş TR 191 Ec84
Orlești RO 175 Db64
Orljak BG 181 Ed69
Orljane BG 180 Db70
Orljevo SRB 174 Bc65
Orlová CZ 137 Hb45
Orlova Mogila BG 181 Fa69
Orlovat SRB 153 Jc60
Orlovat SRB 174 Bb62
Orlov dol BG 185 Ea74
Orlovec BG 180 Eb69
Orlov Gaj RUS 203 Ga12
Orlovskij RUS 205 Fd15
Orłowo PL 123 Jd30
Orłowo PL 123 Jd32
Orly F 23 Gd37
Orly RUS 99 Lc41
Orma GR 183 Bc76
Ormaiztegi E 39 Eb56
Ormanköy TR 191 Ed86
Ormanlı TR 186 Fb76
Ormanlı TR 187 Hb77
Ormaryd S 103 Fc49
Ormea I 148 Bd63
Ormelet N 93 Dd44
Ormelle I 150 Eb59
Ormemyr N 93 Db42
Orméni GR 185 Ea75
Ormeniș RO 176 Ea61
Orménykút H 146 Jc55
Örmepınar TR 198 Fb89
Ormesberga S 103 Fc51
Ormesby Saint Margaret GB 17 Gc24
Ormideia CY 206 Jc97
Ormília GR 184 Cc79
Ormont D 125 Bc42
Órmos GR 183 Ca78
Órmos Korthíou GR 190 Da87
Órmos Panagías GR 184 Cc79
Órmos Panórmou GR 196 Db88
Órmos Prínou GR 184 Da78
Ormož SLO 152 Gb57
Ormskirk GB 15 Eb21
Ormstad N 94 Eb41
Ornans F 31 Jd42
Ornäs S 95 Fd40
Örnäsudden S 72 Gb23
Ornavasso I 148 Ca57
Ornbau D 134 Dc47
Örnberg FIN 81 Ja30
Ørnes N 71 Fb18
Orneta PL 122 Hd31
Ørnhøj DK 100 Da23
Ornö S 96 Ha44
Örnsköldsvik S 80 Gd30
Ørnvika N 70 Fa20
Orodel RO 175 Cc66
Oroftiana RO 172 Ec54
Orolik HR 153 Hd60
Oron-la-Ville CH 141 Bb55
Orońsko PL 130 Jc40
Oropa I 148 Bd58
Oropesa E 52 Cc66
Oropós GR 189 Cc85
Ororbia E 39 Ec57
Oros H 147 Ka51
Orosei I 169 Cc76
Orosháza H 146 Jc56
Oroszlány H 145 Hb53
Oroszló H 152 Hb57
Orotelli I 169 Ca76
Orozko E 38 Ea56
Orpesa E 54 Fd66
Orphir GB 5 Ec03
Orpierre F 42 Jd51
Orp-Jauche B 124 Ad41
Orrbyn S 73 Hd21
Orre N 92 Ca44
Orrefors S 103 Ga52
Orrestad N 92 Cb46
Orrfors S 73 Ja19
Orria I 161 Fd77
Orriols E 49 Hb59
Orrliden S 86 Ed37
Orrmo S 87 Fb35
Orroli I 169 Cb78
Orrträsk S 73 Ja21
Orrviken S 79 Fb31
Orša BY 202 Eb12
Orsa S 87 Fc37
Orsala S 95 Fb40
Orsan F 29 Gd44
Orsans F 31 Ka41
Orsara di Puglia I 161 Fd73
Örsås S 102 Ed50
Örsåsen S 95 Fb39
Orsay F 23 Gd37
Örsbäck S 80 Hb29
Orscholz D 133 Bc45
Örserum S 103 Fc48
Orsingen D 142 Cc51
Örsjö S 103 Ga52
Ørslev DK 109 Ea26
Ørslev DK 109 Eb28
Örslösa S 102 Ed46
Orsmaal B 124 Ad41
Ørsnes N 76 Cd32
Orsoia BG 179 Cc68
Orsomarso I 164 Gb78
Orșova RO 174 Cb64
Orsoy D 125 Bd39
Ørsta N 76 Cc33
Ørsted DK 101 Dd23
Ørsted DK 108 Dc27
Örsundsbro S 96 Gc42
Orsy PL 122 Ja30
Ort A 143 Ed50
Orta TR 198 Fd91
Ortaburun TR 187 Gb78
Ortaca TR 192 Ga81
Ortaca TR 193 Gc81
Ortaca TR 198 Fc91
Ortacı TR 192 Fc83
Ortakarabağ TR 193 Ha85
Ortakent TR 197 Ec90
Ortaklar TR 193 Hb82
Ortaklar TR 197 Ed88
Ortaköy TR 185 Ec79
Ortaköy TR 187 Gd78
Ortaköy TR 187 Gd79
Ortaköy TR 187 Gd79
Ortaköy TR 191 Ec87
Ortaköy TR 192 Fb85
Ortaköy TR 192 Fd87
Ortaköy TR 192 Ga85
Ortaköy TR 193 Ha83
Ortaköy TR 193 Ha86
Ortaköy TR 197 Eb89
Ortaköy TR 198 Fb90
Ortaköy TR 198 Fc89
Ortaköy TR 205 Ga19
Ortamandıra TR 192 Fa82
Orta Nova I 161 Ga73
Ortaoba TR 191 Ed81
Orta San Giulio I 148 Ca58
Ortasarıbey TR 186 Fb80
Ortayazı TR 193 Gc87
Orte I 156 Ea69
Orten N 76 Cd31
Ortenberg D 133 Ca49
Ortenberg D 134 Cd43
Ortenburg D 135 Ed49
Orth an der Donau A 145 Gc51
Orthez F 39 Fb54
Orthovoúni GR 183 Bb80
Ortigosa E 47 Ea59
Ortigosa P 44 Ac65
Ortigosa de Rioalmar E 46 Cd63
Ortigueira E 36 Bb53
Ortiguera E 37 Bd53
Ortihovo RUS 107 Ld48
Ørting DK 108 Dc25
Ortisei I 143 Dd56
Orțișoara RO 174 Bd60
Ortnevik N 84 Cb37
Orto F 154 Ca70
Örtomta S 103 Ga46
Orton GB 11 Ec18
Ortona I 157 Fb70
Ortrand D 128 Fa40
Örträsk S 80 Ha27
Ortschwaben CH 141 Bd54
Ortucchio I 160 Ed71
Ortueri I 169 Ca77
Örtülü TR 191 Ec84
Örtülü TR 198 Fb89
Örtülüce TR 185 Ec79
Ortved DK 109 Eb26
Ortwig D 128 Fb36
Oru EST 99 Lc41
Öru EST 106 La47
Orubica HR 152 Ha61
Oruçoğlu TR 186 Ga77
Örüculer TR 192 Fb84
Ørum DK 100 Db23
Ørum DK 101 Dd23
Orune I 168 Cb76
Orusco E 46 Dd65
Orval F 29 Ha44
Orvault F 28 Ed42
Ørvella N 93 Db42
Orvelte NL 117 Bd34
Orvieto I 156 Ea69
Örviken S 80 Hc25
Orville F 30 Jb41
Orvilliers-Saint-Julien F 30 Hc38
Orvinio I 160 Ec71
Orwell GB 20 Fc26
Orzechowo PL 121 Hb34
Orzechowo PL 122 Ja31
Orzechowo PL 129 Gd37
Orzesze PL 138 Hc44
Orzinuovi I 149 Cd59
Orživ UA 202 Ea14
Orżycja UA 204 Ed15
Orzyny PL 122 Jb32
Orzysz PL 123 Jd31
Os N 66 Fc16
Os N 84 Ca40
Os N 86 Eb33
Os N 94 Eb43
Os S 103 Fb51
Ósa GR 183 Cb77
Osa N 84 Cd39
Osa de la Vega E 53 Ea67
Osamaniye TR 193 Gd83
Osani F 154 Ca69
Osbakk N 71 Fc18
Øsby DK 108 Db27
Osby S 111 Fb53
Oščadnica SK 138 Hc46
Oscaig GB 4 Db08
Oschatz D 127 Ed40
Oschersleben D 127 Dd38
Oschiri I 168 Cb75
Osdorf D 118 Dc30
Øse DK 108 Db25
Øse N 67 Gb13
Øse N 92 Cd44
Osečina SRB 153 Ja63
Osečišće RUS 107 Mb46
Osečná CZ 128 Fc42
Oseid N 93 Db44
O Seixo (Tomiño) E 36 Ac58
Oseja de Sajambre E 37 Cd55
Osek CZ 136 Fa43
Osekovo HR 152 Gc59
Osen N 77 Db32
Osen N 78 Ea27
Osen N 84 Cb36
Osenec BG 180 Eb69
Osenovlag BG 179 Cc70
Oșești RO 173 Fa59
Oset E 54 Fb66
Oset N 86 Eb38
Osetno PL 129 Gb39
Ősi H 145 Hb54
Osica de Sus RO 175 Db66
Osidda I 168 Cb75
Osie PL 121 Ha32
Osiec PL 129 Hb42
Osięciny PL 129 Hb36
Osieck PL 130 Jc37
Osieczna PL 121 Ha32
Osieczna PL 129 Gb38
Osiecznica PL 128 Fc38
Osieczno PL 120 Ga35
Osiek PL 121 Ha32
Osiek PL 121 Hb35
Osiek PL 122 Hc34
Osiek PL 122 Hd31
Osiek PL 131 Jd42
Osiek PL 138 Hd44
Osiek Drawski PL 120 Ga33
Osieki PL 120 Ga30
Osiek Jasielski PL 139 Jd45
Osiek nad Notecią PL 121 Gc34
Osielsko PL 121 Ha34
Osiglia I 148 Bd63
Osijek HR 153 Hd60
Osikovica BG 179 Da70
Osilnica SLO 151 Fc59
Osilo I 168 Ca74
Osimo I 156 Ed66
Osinja BIH 152 Hb62
Osinki PL 123 Ka30
Osinkino RUS 107 Mb48
Osinoviči RUS 107 Ma47
Osinovka RUS 113 Jb58
Osinów PL 120 Fb35
Osiny PL 130 Jc40
Osiny PL 131 Jd38
Osipaonica SRB 174 Bc64
Osišče RUS 99 Ld42
Osivica BIH 152 Ha62
Osjaków PL 130 Hc40
Osječenica MNE 159 Hd69
Oskal N 68 Ja12
Oskar S 111 Ga53
Oskarshamn S 103 Gb50
Oskarström S 102 Ed52
Os'kino RUS 203 Fb13
Oskola FIN 83 Ma31
Oskowo PL 121 Gd30
Öskü H 145 Hb54
Osľany SK 137 Hb49
Ošlejas LV 106 Ka51
Osli H 145 Gd52
Ošlje HR 158 Ha68
Oslo N 93 Ea41
Oslon F 30 Jb43
Øsløs DK 100 Db21
Osloß D 126 Dc36
Osma E 46 Dd61
Osma FIN 64 Jd07
Osma N 77 Db30
Osman TR 193 Gd81
Osmancalı TR 191 Ec85
Osmancık TR 185 Ed76
Osmancık TR 205 Fb20
Osmaneli TR 187 Gb80
Osmangazi TR 186 Fd80
Osmaniye TR 186 Ga80
Osmaniye TR 191 Ed86
Osmaniye TR 192 Fa82
Osmaniye TR 192 Fb86
Osmaniye TR 192 Fc81
Osmaniye TR 192 Fc83
Osmaniye TR 193 Gb82
Osmaniye TR 193 Gd81
Osmaniye TR 197 Fa91
Osmaniye TR 198 Fb91
Osmankalfalar TR 198 Ga90
Osmanlar TR 192 Fb83
Osmanlı TR 185 Ec75
Osmanville F 22 Fa35
Osmaslar TR 191 Ed82
Osmery F 29 Ha43
Osmington GB 19 Ec31
Os'mino RUS 99 Ma42
Os'mino RUS 202 Ea09
Ösmo S 96 Gd44
Osmotherley GB 11 Fa18
Osnabrück D 117 Cc36
Osne-le-Val F 24 Jb37
Ośno PL 122 Hc32
Ośno Lubuskie PL 128 Fc36
Osny F 23 Gc36
Osoblaha CZ 137 Ha44
Osogna CH 142 Cc56
Osoppo I 150 Ec57
Osor E 49 Hb60
Osor HR 151 Fb62
Osorhei RO 170 Cb56
Osorno la Mayor E 38 Db58
Osowa PL 123 Ka30
Osøyro N 84 Ca40
Osøyvollen N 86 Ea32
Os Peares E 36 Bb57
Ospedaletti I 43 La52
Ospedaletto I 156 Ea68
Ospitale di Cadore I 150 Eb57
Ospitaletto I 149 Da59
Oss NL 125 Bb38
Ossa de Montiel E 53 Ea69
Össeby-Garn S 96 Gd43
Osses F 39 Fa55
Ossett GB 16 Fa21
Ossi I 168 Bd75
Ossiach A 144 Fa56
Össjö S 110 Ed54
Oßling D 128 Fb40
Oßmannstedt D 127 Ea41
Osso E 48 Fd60
Östa S 95 Gb41
Ostabat F 39 Fa55
Östanå S 111 Fb54
Östanbäck S 80 Hc25
Östanberg FIN 97 Jc41
Östanbo S 87 Gb37
Östanfjärden S 73 Ja21
Östansjö S 72 Gd21
Östansjö S 87 Fb35
Östansjö S 95 Fc44
Östanskär S 87 Gb33
Ostarije HR 151 Fd60
Ostaškov RUS 202 Ec10
Ostaszewo PL 121 Hb30
Ostatija SRB 178 Ba68
Östavall S 87 Fd33
Östavik S 87 Fd37
Ostbevern D 125 Cb37
Östbirk DK 108 Db24
Östbjörka S 87 Fc38
Østby N 78 Ec31
Østby N 86 Ed37
Osted DK 109 Eb26
Osteel D 117 Cb32
Ostellato I 150 Ea62
Osten D 118 Da32
Ostende = Oostende B 21 Ha29

Pilchowice – Pojatno

Pilchowice PL 128 Ga41
Pilchowice PL 137 Hb44
Pilchowo PL 120 Fb33
Pile PL 121 Gb33
Piléa GR 185 Ea77
Pilés GR 201 Eb95
Pilgersdorf A 145 Gb53
Pilgrims Hatch GB 20 Fd27
Pilgrimstad S 79 Fc31
Pili GR 189 Cb86
Pili GR 197 Ec91
Pilica PL 138 Hd43
Pilica SRB 159 Ja64
Pilio GR 189 Cb84
Pilis H 146 Ja53
Pilis LT 114 Ka57
Pilistvere EST 98 Kd44
Pilisvörösvár H 146 Hc52
Piliuona LT 114 Kc58
Pilka EST 99 Lb45
Piłka PL 120 Ga35
Pillapalu EST 98 Kc42
Piller A 142 Db54
Pillerton Priors GB 20 Fa26
Pillon F 24 Jb34
Pillon F 24 Jb35
Pilníkov CZ 136 Ga43
Pilning GB 19 Ec28
Pilona PL 122 Hc31
Pilos GR 194 Ba89
Pilpala FIN 90 Ka38
Pilsach D 135 Dd47
Pilsblidene LV 105 Jd52
Pilsen = Plzeň CZ 135 Ed45
Pilskalne LV 114 Kd53
Pilskalne LV 115 Lb53
Pilskalns LV 107 Lb49
Pilštanj SLO 151 Fd58
Pilsting D 135 Ec49
Pilszcz PL 137 Ha44
Piltene LV 105 Jb50
Pilträsk S 73 Hb22
Pilu RO 170 Bd58
Pilvingiai LT 114 Kd59
Pilviškiai LV 114 Kb58
Pilzno PL 139 Jd44
Pimelles F 30 Hd40
Pimenikó GR 185 Eb76
Piña de Campos E 38 Da58
Pina de Ebro E 48 Fb61
Piñar E 60 Dc74
Pınarbaşı TR 185 Ed76
Pınarbaşı TR 191 Ea81
Pınarbaşı TR 191 Eb81
Pınarbaşı TR 199 Gb89
Pınarca TR 186 Fa76
Pınarcık TR 192 Fd81
Pınarcık TR 197 Ed89
Pinar de los Franceses E 59 Bd77
Pinarejo E 53 Eb67
Pinarejos E 46 Da61
Pinarella I 156 Eb64
Pinarello F 154 Cb72
Pınargözü TR 199 Gd90
Pinar Hermoso E 61 Ec72
Pınarhisar TR 185 Ed75
Pınarlar TR 198 Fd89
Pınarlı TR 187 Gb77
Pınarlı TR 191 Ed87
Pınarlıbelen TR 197 Ed90
Pınarlık TR 198 Fd88
Pincehely H 145 Hb55
Pinchbeck GB 17 Fc24
Pinczów PL 130 Jb42
Pindari LV 105 Jd49
Pindères F 40 Fd52
Pindstrup DK 101 Dd23
Pineda de Gigüela E 47 Ea65
Pineda de la Sierra E 38 Dd58
Pineda de Mar E 49 Hb60
Pinedo E 54 Fc68
Piñeira E 36 Bb57
Piñeiro E 36 Ad57
Pinela P 45 Bd60
Pinelo P 45 Bd60
Pinerolo I 148 Bc61
Pineto I 157 Fa69
Piney F 30 Hd38
Pingeyri IS 2 Ac02
Pinhal Novo P 50 Ab69
Pinhão P 44 Bb61
Pinheiro P 44 Ad61
Pinheiro P 44 Ad59
Pinheiro P 50 Ab69
Pinhel P 45 Bc62
Piniava LT 114 Kc54
Pinilla E 53 Ea70
Pinilla E 55 Ed70
Pinilla de Toro E 45 Cc60
Pinilla-Trasmonte E 46 Dc60
Pinipaju FIN 97 Ja39
Pinjainen FIN 97 Jd40
Pinkafeld A 145 Gb53
Pinkamindszent H 145 Gb54
Pinmore Mains GB 10 Dc15
Pinneberg D 118 Db32
Pinnow D 128 Fb38
Pino E 38 Dd57
Pino F 154 Cc68
Pino del Río E 38 Da57
Pino do Val E 36 Ac55
Pino Lago Maggiore I 148 Cb57
Pinols F 34 Hc49
Piñor E 36 Ba57
Pinoso E 55 Fa71
Pinos-Puente E 60 Db74
Pino Torinese I 148 Bd60
Pinseque E 47 Fa60
Pinsiö FIN 89 Jc35
Pinsk BY 202 Ea14
Pinsoro E 47 Ed59
Pinsot F 35 Jd48
Pintado P 50 Ac66
Pintamo FIN 75 Kc22
Pintic RO 171 Da57
Pinto E 46 Dc65
Pinwherry GB 10 Dc15
Pinzano al Tagliamento I 150 Ec57
Pînzareni MD 173 Fa56
Pinzolo I 149 Db57
Pinzón E 59 Bd74
Piobbico I 156 Eb66
Piolenc F 42 Jb52
Pioltello I 149 Cc59
Piombino I 155 Da68
Pionerskij RUS 113 Hd58
Pionki PL 130 Jc39
Pionsat F 33 Ha46
Pioppi I 161 Fd77
Pioppo I 166 Ec84
Pioraco I 156 Ec67
Piorna E 45 Cb65
Piors Hardwick GB 20 Fa26
Piorunkowice PL 137 Gd43
Piossasco I 148 Bc60
Piotrkosice PL 129 Gc39
Piotrków PL 131 Kb40
Piotrkowice PL 130 Jb42
Piotrków Kujawski PL 129 Hb36
Piotrków Trybunalski PL 130 Hd40
Piotrowice PL 130 Jc37
Piotrowiec PL 122 Hd30
Piotrowo PL 121 Gb35
Piotta CH 141 Cb56
Piove di Sacco I 150 Ea60
Piovene I 150 Dd59
Piovera I 148 Cb61
Pipaón E 38 Ea57
Pipirig RO 172 Eb57
Pipriac F 27 Ec40
Piqerasi AL 182 Ab79
Pir RO 171 Cc55
Pirá GR 189 Bc84
Piragi RUS 107 Ld49
Piran SLO 150 Ed59
Pirane KSV 178 Ba72
Piras I 168 Cb75
Piräus = Pireás GR 195 Cb87
Pirčiupiai LT 114 La59
Pirdop BG 179 Da71
Pireás GR 195 Cb87
Pireveliler TR 191 Ec83
Pirgadikia GR 184 Cc79
Pirgí GR 182 Ab80
Pírgi GR 183 Bc77
Pírgi GR 184 Cd76
Pirgí GR 191 Dd86
Pírgos GR 182 Ad78
Pírgos GR 189 Ca84
Pírgos GR 194 Ba87
Pírgos GR 194 Ba89
Pírgos GR 194 Bb90
Pírgos GR 197 Eb88
Pírgos GR 200 Da96
Pírgos Diroú GR 194 Bb90
Pirgovo BG 180 Ed68
Piriac-sur-Mer F 27 Eb42
Piricse H 147 Kb51
Pirilä FIN 91 Lb33
Pirin BG 184 Cc75
Pirinçci TR 186 Fc77
Piringsdorf A 145 Gb53
Pirita MD 173 Fd58
Pirjolteni MD 173 Fc57
Pirjota MD 173 Fa55
Pirk D 135 Eb46
Pirki BY 202 Ec14
Pirkkala FIN 89 Jd36
Pirlibey TR 198 Fb88
Pirliţa MD 173 Fb55
Pirliţa MD 173 Fb57
Pirliţa MD 173 Fc54
Pirmasens D 133 Ca46
Pirnar (Varinçe) TR 185 Eb78
Pirnesperä FIN 82 Ka26
Pirnmill GB 10 Db14
Pirok MK 178 Ba73
Pirot SRB 179 Ca69
Pirou F 22 Ed36
Pirovac HR 157 Ga65
Pirsógiani GR 182 Ad78
Pirsu EST 98 Kd42
Pirtó H 146 Ja56
Pirttijärvi FIN 89 Ja35
Pirttikoski FIN 74 Kb19
Pirttikoski FIN 81 Jd26
Pirttikoski FIN 89 Jd37
Pirttikylä FIN 89 Hd32
Pirttikylä FIN 89 Jc33
Pirttimäki FIN 82 La26
Pirttimäki FIN 82 Kc27
Pirttimäki FIN 82 Kd30
Pirttimäki FIN 82 Kc31
Pirttimäki FIN 83 Lb28
Pirttivaara FIN 75 Lb22
Pirttivuopio S 67 Gd15
Pišť CZ 137 Hb45
Pisa FIN 74 Jd19
Pisa I 155 Da65
Pisanec BG 180 Eb69
Pisanica PL 123 Ka31
Pisankoski FIN 83 Lb29
Pisany F 32 Fb47
Pisarovina HR 151 Ga59
Pisarovo BG 179 Da69
Pisarzowa PL 138 Jb45
Pisarzowice PL 128 Fd41
Piscărești MD 173 Fd55
Pischeldorf A 144 Fb56
Pischelsdorf A 143 Ec51
Pischelsdorf in der Steiermark A 144 Ga54
Pișchia RO 174 Bd60
Pisciotta I 161 Fd77
Pięcolt RO 170 Cb55
Piscu RO 177 Fa63
Pisculeț RO 179 Cc67
Piscu Mare RO 175 Db63
Piscu Vechi RO 179 Cc67
Písečné CZ 136 Fd48
Písek CZ 136 Fb47
Pishill GB 20 Fb28
Piski PL 123 Jd34
Piskokéfalo GR 201 Dd96
Piskorowice PL 139 Kb43
Piskorzyna PL 129 Gb40
Piskupat AL 182 Ad76
Pisogne I 149 Da58
Píso Livádi GR 196 Db90
Pisseloup F 31 Jc40
Píssia GR 189 Ca86
Pissignano I 156 Eb68
Pissiniemi S 68 Ja15
Pissodéri GR 182 Ba77
Pissónas GR 189 Cc85
Pissos F 39 Fb52
Pissouri CY 206 Ja98
Pisticci I 162 Gc76
Pisto FIN 75 La21
Pistoia I 155 Db64
Pistruieni MD 173 Fc56
Pisz PL 122 Jc32
Piszczac PL 131 Kc37
Pitäjänmäki FIN 82 Kb28
Pitälvbron S 72 Ha21
Pitämävaara FIN 83 Lc25
Pitcape GB 7 Ec08
Piteå S 73 Hd23
Piteå havsbad S 73 Hd23
Pitelino RUS 203 Fb10
Pitești RO 175 Dc64
Pithagório GR 197 Eb88
Píthio GR 183 Bc79
Píthio GR 185 Eb76
Pithiviers F 29 Gd39
Pitigliano I 156 Dd69
Pitillas E 39 Ed58
Pitítsa GR 188 Bb85
Pitiús GR 191 Dd85
Pitkäjärvi FIN 89 Jd38
Pitkäjärvi FIN 90 Ka35
Pitkäkoski FIN 82 Kd28
Pitkäkoski FIN 91 Lb37
Pitkälä FIN 91 Lc33
Pitkälahti FIN 90 La34
Pitkäluoto FIN 89 Ja38
Pitkämäki FIN 82 Kc27
Pitkäsenkylä FIN 81 Jc26
Pitlochry GB 7 Ea10
Pitmedden GB 5 Ed08
Pitomača HR 152 Gd58
Pitrags LV 105 Jc48
Pitres E 60 Dc76
Pitscottie GB 7 Ec12
Pittentrail GB 5 Ea06
Pitvaros H 146 Jc56
Piúgos E 36 Bc55
Pivašiūnai LT 114 Kd59
Pivca SLO 151 Fb59
Pivnice SRB 153 Ja59
Pivniceni MD 173 Fa54
Pivniczna-Zdrój PL 138 Jc46
Piyade TR 192 Fb82
Pizarra E 60 Cd76
Pižma RUS 203 Fc08
Pizzighettone I 149 Cd60
Pizzo I 164 Gb82
Pizzoferrato I 161 Fb71
Pizzolato I 166 Ea85
Pizzoli I 156 Ec70
Pizzolungo I 166 Ea84
Pjantbo S 95 Fd41
Pjasăčevo BG 185 Dd74
Pjasăčevo BG 185 Ea74
Pjatčino RUS 99 Ld40
Pjatidorožnoje RUS 113 Hd59
Pjatigorsk RUS 205 Ga17
Pjätteryd S 103 Fb52
P'jatychatky UA 204 Ed15
Pjelax FIN 89 Hd33
Pjenovac BIH 159 Hd64
Pjesker S 72 Ha23
Pjezgë AL 182 Ab74
Plaani EST 107 Lc47
Plabennec F 26 Dc38
Placios de la Sierra E 46 Dd59
Plačkovci BG 180 Dd71
Plaffeien CH 141 Bc55
Plage de Tahiti F 43 Kb55
Plagiá GR 183 Ca76
Plagiá GR 185 Dd77
Plaidt D 125 Ca42
Plăieștii de Jos RO 176 Eb60
Plăieștii de Sus RO 176 Eb60
Plaigne F 40 Gc55
Plaimpied-Givaudins F 29 Ha43
Plaisance F 33 Ga45
Plaisance F 40 Fd54
Plaisance F 41 Ha53
Plaisance-du-Toulouse F 40 Gb54
Plaisians F 42 Jc52
Plaissan F 41 Hc54
Pláka GR 184 Dc80
Pláka GR 195 Bd89
Pláka GR 195 Cd91
Plakanciems LV 106 Kb51
Plake MK 182 Ba75
Plakiás GR 200 Cc96
Plakotí GR 182 Ac80
Plakovo BG 180 Dd71
Plan E 40 Fd57
Plana BIH 159 Hc68
Planá CZ 135 Ec45
Plána GR 184 Cc79
Planá nad Lužnicí CZ 136 Fc47
Plancher-les-Mines F 31 Ka40
Planchez F 30 Hd42
Plancios I 143 Ea56
Plancoët F 26 Ec38
Plancy-l'Abbaye F 24 Hc37
Plan-d'Aups-Sainte-Baume F 42 Jd54
Plan-de-Baix F 35 Jc50
Plan-de-la-Tour F 43 Kb54
Plandište SRB 174 Bc62
Plan-du-Var F 43 Kc52
Planegg D 143 Dd51
Planeja KSV 178 Ba72
Plāņi LV 106 La48
Plánice CZ 135 Ed47
Planina SLO 144 Fa56
Planina SLO 151 Fb58
Planina SLO 151 Fc57
Planina pri Sevnici SLO 151 Fd58
Planinica SRB 179 Ca67
Planitéro GR 188 Bb86
Planjane HR 158 Gb65
Plankenfels D 135 Dd45
Plankstadt D 134 Cc46
Planoles E 41 Gd58
Planty F 30 Hc38
Plasencia E 45 Ca65
Plasenzuela E 51 Ca67
Plaški HR 151 Fd61
Plaškiai LT 113 Jc57
Plašnica MK 182 Ba74
Plášťovce SK 146 Hc50
Plassac F 32 Fb48
Plassen N 86 Ed37
Plăstina BG 180 Eb71
Plasy CZ 135 Ed45
Plat HR 159 Hc69
Platací I 164 Gc78
Platamona Lido I 168 Bd74
Platamónas GR 183 Bd80
Platamónas GR 184 Da77
Platána GR 194 Bc88
Platanákia GR 183 Cb76
Plataniá GR 189 Cb83
Platánia GR 194 Ba88
Platania I 164 Gb81
Plataniás GR 200 Cb94
Platanias GR 200 Cd95
Platanissos CY 206 Jd95
Platanistós GR 195 Cd87
Plátanos GR 188 Bb83
Plátanos GR 189 Bd82
Plátanos GR 194 Ba87
Plátanos GR 194 Bc90
Plátanos GR 200 Ca94
Plătărești RO 176 Eb66
Platariá GR 182 Ac80
Plate D 119 Ea33
Plateau-d'Assy F 35 Kb46
Plateés GR 189 Ca86
Plateliai LT 113 Jc54
Platerów PL 131 Kb36
Platerówka PL 128 Fd41
Platí GR 182 Ba76
Platí GR 183 Bd77
Pláti GR 185 Ea75
Platí GR 190 Db81
Pláti GR 194 Ba88
Plati I 164 Gb83
Platiána GR 194 Ba87
Platičevo SRB 153 Jb61
Platíkambos GR 189 Bd81
Platischis I 150 Ed57
Platís Gialós GR 196 Da90
Platís Gialós GR 196 Db89
Platišino RUS 107 Ma49
Platja d'Aro E 49 Hc60
Platja d'en Bossa E 56 Gc69
Platja de Nules E 54 Fc66
Platone LV 106 Kb52
Plátsa GR 194 Bb90
Plattling D 135 Ec49
Plau D 119 Eb33
Plaudren F 27 Eb40
Plaue D 126 Dc42
Plauen D 135 Eb43
Plaupe LV 106 Kc50
Plauru RO 177 Fd63
Plav MNE 159 Jc69
Plava KSV 178 Ba72
Plavča HR 151 Fd61
Plave SLO 150 Ed58
Plaveč SK 138 Jc47
Plavecký Mikuláš SK 137 Gd49
Plavējai LT 115 Lb54
Pļaviņas LV 106 La51
Plavna SRB 153 Hd60
Plavna SRB 174 Ca66
Plavnica MNE 159 Ja70
Plavnica SK 138 Jc47
Plavno HR 158 Gb64
Plavno RUS 113 Jd59
Plavsk RUS 203 Fa11
Playa Bella E 60 Cc77
Playa Serena E 61 Ea76
Playing Place GB 18 Db32
Plažane SRB 174 Bc66
Płazów PL 139 Kc43
Płazowo PL 121 Ha33
Pleaux F 33 Gd49
Plech D 135 Dd46
Plédéliac F 26 Ec38
Pleine-Fougères F 28 Ed38
Pleinfeld D 134 Dc47
Pleiskirchen D 143 Eb50
Plélan-le-Grand F 27 Ec39
Plélan-le-Petit F 26 Ec38
Plémet F 27 Eb39
Plénée-Jugon F 26 Ec38
Pléneuf-Val-André F 26 Eb38
Plenița RO 175 Cc66
Plenoy F 31 Jc39
Plentzia E 38 Ea55
Plérin F 26 Eb38
Pleš SK 146 Ja50
Pleščanicy BY 202 Ea12
Pleşcuţa RO 170 Cb59
Pleşeni MD 177 Fc60
Plešin SRB 178 Ba68
Plešivec SK 138 Jb49
Pleslin-Trigavou F 26 Ec38
Plesná CZ 135 Eb44
Pleśna PL 138 Jc44
Plessa D 128 Fa40
Plessala F 27 Eb39
Plessé F 28 Ed41
Pléssio GR 182 Ac80
Plestin-les-Grèves F 26 Dd37
Pleszew PL 129 Ha38
Pleternica HR 152 Ha60
Plettenberg D 125 Cb40
Pleumartin F 29 Ga44
Pleumeur-Bodou F 26 Dd37
Pleurs F 24 Hc37
Pleven BG 180 Db69
Pleyben F 27 Dc39
Pleyber-Christ F 26 Dd38
Pleystein D 135 Eb46
Pliego E 55 Ed73
Plienciems LV 106 Ka50
Pliešovce SK 146 Hd50
Pliezhausen D 134 Cd49
Plikáti GR 182 Ad78
Plikiai LT 113 Jb55
Plikiai LV 114 Kb56
Plintini LV 105 Jc49
Pliska BG 181 Ed70
Plítra GR 195 Bd90
Plittersdorf D 133 Cb48
Plitvice HR 151 Ga62
Plitvička Jezera HR 151 Ga62
Plitvički Ljeskovac HR 151 Ga62
Pljevlja MNE 159 Ja66
Pljussa RUS 99 Mb44
Pljussa RUS 202 Ea09
Pllanë AL 163 Jb72
Ploaghe I 168 Ca75
Ploçë AL 182 Ab77
Ploče HR 158 Ha68
Plochingen D 134 Cd48
Pločica SRB 174 Bb64
Płociczno PL 121 Gd33
Płociczno PL 123 Ka30
Płock PL 130 Hd36
Ploemeur F 27 Dd40
Ploërdut F 27 Ea39
Ploërmel F 27 Ec40
Plœuc-sur-Lié F 26 Eb38
Ploiești RO 176 Ea64
Plokščiai LT 114 Ka57
Plomári GR 191 Ea84
Plombières-les-Bains F 31 Ka39
Plomeur F 27 Dc40
Plomin HR 151 Fb61
Plomion F 24 Hc33
Plomodiern F 27 Dc39
Plön D 118 Dc31
Plonéour-Lanvern F 27 Dc40
Plonévez-Porzay F 27 Dc39
Płoniawy-Bramura PL 122 Jb34
Płońsk PL 122 Ja35
Płońsko PL 120 Fd34
Plop MD 173 Fb54
Plop MD 173 Ga59
Plopana RO 172 Ed59
Plopeni RO 176 Ea64
Plopeni RO 181 Fb68
Plopi MD 173 Fd55
Plopi MD 177 Fb60
Plopi RO 175 Cc65
Plopii-Slăvitești RO 180 Db67
Plopiș RO 171 Cc56
Plopșoru RO 175 Cd64
Plopu RO 176 Eb64
Plosca RO 180 Dc67
Ploscoș RO 171 Da58
Ploski PL 123 Kb34
Płoskinia PL 122 Hd30
Ploskoš' RUS 202 Eb10
Płośnica PL 122 Hd33
Ploștina RO 175 Cc64
Plothen D 127 Ea42
Plötitz D 127 Ed40
Płotno PL 120 Fd34
Płoty PL 120 Fd32
Plötzkau D 127 Ea39
Plouaret F 26 Dd37
Plouarzel F 26 Db38
Plouay F 27 Ea40
Ploubalay F 26 Ec38
Ploudalmézeau F 26 Db37
Plouégat-Moysan F 26 Dd37
Plouescat F 26 Dc37
Plouezoch F 26 Dd37
Plougasnou F 26 Dd37
Plougastel-Daoulas F 26 Dc38
Plougonvelin F 26 Db38
Plougonven F 26 Dd38
Plougonver F 26 Ea38
Plougrescant F 26 Ea37
Plouguenast F 27 Eb39
Plouguerneau F 26 Db37
Plouguernevel F 27 Ea39
Plouha F 26 Eb37
Plouharnel F 27 Ea41
Ploumanach F 26 Dd37
Plounéour-Menez F 26 Dd38
Plounéventer F 26 Dc38
Plounévez-du-Faou F 27 Dd39
Plounévez-Quintin F 26 Ea38
Plourac'h F 26 Dd38
Plouray F 27 Ea39
Plouvorn F 26 Dc37
Plouzané F 26 Db38
Plovdiv BG 180 Db73
Płowce PL 129 Hb36
Plowęż PL 122 Hc33
Plozévet F 27 Db39
Plūči LV 105 Jc51
Plugari RO 172 Ed56
Plugawice PL 129 Ha40
Plumbridge GB 9 Cc16
Plumelec F 27 Eb40
Pluméliau F 27 Ea40
Plumieux F 27 Eb39
Plumlov CZ 137 Gc46
Plumpton GB 11 Ec17
Plungė LT 113 Jc54
Pluszkiejmy PL 123 Jd30
Plutiškės LV 114 Kb58
Pluty PL 122 Ja30
Pluty PL 123 Ka33
Plutyczе PL 123 Kb34
Pluviers F 33 Ga47
Pluvigner F 27 Ea40
Plužine BIH 159 Hc67
Plužine MNE 159 Hd67
Płużnica PL 121 Hb33
Plymouth GB 18 Dc31
Plympton GB 19 Dd31
Płytnica PL 121 Gc34
Plzeň CZ 135 Ed45
Pnevo RUS 99 Lc45
Pniewo PL 120 Fb34
Pniewo PL 120 Fd32
Pniewo PL 122 Jc35
Pniewo-Czeruchy PL 122 Ja34
Pniewy PL 129 Gb36
Pniewy PL 130 Jb38
Poarta Albă RO 181 Fc67
Pobeda BG 180 Db69
Pobeda BG 181 Fa69
Pobedino RUS 114 Ka58
Poberežje RUS 113 Ja59
Pobes E 38 Ea57
Poběžovice CZ 135 Ec46
Pobiedziska PL 129 Gc36
Pobierowo PL 120 Fc31
Pobikry PL 123 Ka35
Pobit Kamăk BG 180 Eb69
Población de Cerrato E 46 Da60
Pobladura de la Sierra E 37 Ca57
Pobladura del Valle E 37 Cb58
Pobladura de Pelayo García E 37 Cc58
Poblete E 52 Db69
Poboleda E 48 Ga62
Pobórka PL 121 Gc34
Poboru RO 175 Db65
Počátky CZ 136 Fd47
Poceirão P 50 Ab69
Počep RUS 202 Ed12
Pöchlarn A 144 Fd51
Pociems LV 106 Kc48
Pocinho P 45 Bc61
Počinok RUS 202 Ec12
Pocinovice CZ 135 Ed47
Počitelj BIH 158 Hb67
Pociumbeni MD 173 Fa55
Pociūnėliai LV 114 Kb55
Pockar FIN 90 Kd38
Pockau D 127 Ed42
Pöcking D 143 Dd51
Pocking D 143 Ed50
Pocklington GB 16 Fb20
Pöckstein Zwischenwässern A 144 Fb55
Poćkuny PL 123 Kb30
Pocol I 143 Ea56
Pocola RO 170 Cb58
Poços P 58 Ad72
Pocrovca MD 173 Fb53
Pocsaj H 147 Ka53
Poćuta SRB 153 Jb63
Poczesna PL 130 Hc42
Podajva BG 181 Ec69
Podanin PL 121 Gc35
Podareš MK 183 Ca74
Podari RO 175 Cd66
Podbanské SK 138 Ja47
Podberez'e RUS 202 Eb09
Podberez'e RUS 202 Eb10
Podberezje RUS 107 Ma48
Podbořanský Rohozec CZ 135 Ed44
Podbořany CZ 135 Ed44
Podborov'e RUS 99 Lc45
Podborov'e RUS 107 Ma46
Podborov'e RUS 202 Ea10
Podborski Batinjani HR 152 Gd59
Podbožur MNE 159 Hd68
Podbrdo SLO 151 Fa57
Podbrezová SK 138 Hd48
Podčetrtek SLO 151 Ga57
Poddębice PL 130 Hc38
Poddor'e RUS 202 Eb10
Poddubje RUS 107 Ma46
Poděbrady CZ 136 Fd44
Podedwórze PL 131 Kc38
Podelzig D 128 Fb36
Podem BG 180 Db69
Podenii Noi RO 176 Eb64
Podersdorf am See A 145 Gc52
Podes E 37 Cb53
Podgajci Posavski HR 153 Hd61
Podgaje PL 121 Gc33
Podgora HR 158 Gd67
Podgora SLO 144 Fc56
Podgorač HR 152 Hb60
Podgorac SRB 178 Bd67
Podgoreni MD 173 Fd56
Podgorenskij RUS 203 Fb13
Podgori AL 182 Ad76
Podgorica MNE 159 Ja69
Podgorica SLO 151 Fb58
Podgorje SLO 144 Fc56
Podgórze PL 123 Jd34
Podgrab BIH 159 Hd65
Podgrad SLO 151 Fa60
Podgrade BIH 158 Ha65
Podgraj SLO 151 Fa58
Podhorod' SK 139 Kb48
Podhum BIH 158 Gd65
Podhum BIH 158 Hb65
Podhum MNE 159 Ja70
Podil UA 202 Ed14
Podivín CZ 137 Gc48
Podklastorze PL 130 Ja40
Podkoren SLO 144 Fa56
Podkova BG 184 Dc76
Podkowa Leśna PL 130 Jb37
Podkrajewo PL 122 Ja34
Podkrepa BG 185 Dd74
Podkum SLO 151 Fc58
Podlapača HR 151 Ga63
Podlesnoje RUS 203 Fd11
Podłęż PL 130 Jc38
Podlipje RUS 107 Mb50
Podlipovo RUS 113 Jc59
Podljubelj SLO 151 Fb57
Podlož'e RUS 99 Mb45
Podmilačje BIH 152 Gd63
Podmogile RUS 107 Ma47
Podmol MK 183 Bb75
Podmolje MK 182 Ba75
Podnanos SLO 151 Fa59
Podnovlje BIH 152 Hb61
Podoima MD 173 Fd55
Podoleš'e RUS 99 Lc43
Podoleš'e RUS 99 Ld43
Podolinec SK 138 Jb47
Podol Mali HR 151 Fb62
Podol'sk RUS 202 Ed10
Podoubowek PL 123 Ka30
Podpeč SLO 151 Fb58
Podplat SLO 151 Ga57
Podpreska SLO 151 Fc59
Podrašnica BIH 152 Gd63
Podravska Slatina HR 152 Ha59
Podromanija BIH 159 Hd65
Podróżna PL 121 Gc34
Põdruse EST 98 La42
Podrute HR 152 Gb57
Podsevy RUS 107 Mb46
Podsnežnoe RUS 203 Fd11
Podsreda SLO 151 Ga58
Podstráni CZ 135 Ec44
Podsuchi RUS 107 Mb47
Podsused HR 151 Ga58
Podturen HR 145 Gc56
Podturn SLO 151 Fc59
Podu Iloaiei RO 173 Fa57
Podujevo KSV 178 Bb70
Poduri RO 172 Ec59
Podu Turcului RO 177 Fa60
Podvelež BIH 158 Hb67
Podvinje HR 152 Hb60
Podvis BG 181 Ec71
Podwilcze PL 120 Ga32
Poelkapelle B 21 Ha30
Poeni RO 176 Dd66
Poenița MD 173 Fb53
Poffabro I 150 Ec57
Pogăceaua RO 171 Db58
Pogana RO 177 Fa60
Pogănești MD 173 Fb59
Poganovci HR 153 Hc59
Pogányszentpéter H 152 Gb57
Pogar BIH 159 Hc64
Pogar RUS 202 Ed13
Poggendorf D 119 Ed31
Poggiardo I 163 Hc77
Poggibonsi I 155 Dc66
Poggio a Caiano I 155 Dc65
Poggio Imperiale I 161 Fd72
Poggio Mirteto I 156 Eb70
Poggio Moiano I 156 Eb70
Poggio Renatico I 150 Dd62
Poggio Rusco I 149 Dc61
Pöggstal A 144 Fd50
Pogno I 148 Ca58
Pogny F 24 Hd36
Pogoanele RO 176 Ed65
Pogódki PL 121 Ha31
Pogonianí GR 182 Ac79
Pogorzel PL 123 Jd30
Pogorzela PL 129 Gc38
Pogorzelice PL 121 Gd30
Pogradec AL 182 Ad76
Pograničnoje RUS 113 Hd59
Pograničnoje RUS 122 Jc30
Pogrodzie PL 122 Hc30
Pogubie-Średnie PL 122 Jc32
Pohja FIN 82 Kb29
Pohja FIN 90 Ka35
Pohja FIN 97 Jd40
Pohjajoki FIN 82 Kd25
Pohjajoki FIN 89 Ja35
Pöhjaküla EST 98 Kb42
Pohja-Lankila FIN 91 Lc34
Pohjansaha FIN 89 Ja35
Pohjaranta FIN 89 Hd34
Pohjaslahti FIN 74 Kb19
Pohjaslahti FIN 89 Jd33
Pohjavaara FIN 82 La25
Pohjois-Haatala FIN 82 Kd29
Pohjois-li FIN 74 Ka22
Pohjoiskylä FIN 89 Ja32
Pohjoiskylä FIN 91 Lb32
Pohjoislahti FIN 89 Jc32
Pohjola FIN 90 Kc35
Pohjosjärvi FIN 90 Ka33
Pöhl D 135 Eb43
Pohlheim D 126 Cc42
Pohoarna MD 173 Fc55
Pohodlí CZ 137 Gb45
Pohorela SK 138 Ja48
Pohořelice CZ 137 Gb48
Pohoří na Šumavě CZ 136 Fc49
Pohorniceni MD 173 Fd57
Pohorská Ves CZ 136 Fc49
Pohoskylä FIN 90 Kd33
Pohrebyšče UA 204 Eb15
Pohtola FIN 89 Jd35
Poian RO 176 Eb61
Poiana MD 173 Fd55
Poiana RO 171 Da59
Poiana RO 176 Ea65
Poiana Blenchii RO 171 Da56
Poiana Câmpina RO 176 Ea64
Poiana Cristei RO 176 Ed62
Poiana Lacului RO 175 Dc65
Poiana Largului RO 172 Eb57
Poiana Mare RO 179 Cc67
Poiana Mărului RO 174 Cb62
Poiana Mărului RO 176 Dd62
Poiana Sărată RO 176 Ec60
Poiana Sibiului RO 175 Da61
Poiana Stampei RO 172 Dd56
Poiana Teiului RO 172 Eb57
Poiana Vadului RO 171 Cc59
Poibrene BG 179 Cd72
Pöide EST 97 Jd45
Poienari RO 172 Ed58
Poienarii Burchil RO 176 Ea65
Poienarii de Argeș RO 175 Db64
Poienarii de Muscel RO 175 Dc63
Poienești RO 173 Fa59
Poieni RO 171 Cc57
Poienile de Sub Munte RO 171 Dc55
Poienile Izei RO 171 Db55
Poigny-la-Forêt F 23 Gc37
Poijula FIN 75 Kc22
Poikajärvi FIN 74 Jd18
Poikelus FIN 89 Jd34
Poikkijärvi S 67 Hb15
Poikko FIN 97 Jb39
Poikmetsä FIN 90 Kb37
Põikva EST 98 Kc44
Poillé-sur-Vègre F 28 Fc40
Poilley F 28 Fa38
Poirino I 148 Bd61
Poisieux F 29 Gd43
Poisson F 34 Hd45
Poissons F 30 Jb38
Poissy F 23 Gd36
Poisvilliers F 29 Gb38
Poitiers F 28 Fd44
Poitschach A 144 Fa55
Poix-de-Picardie F 23 Gc34
Poix-Terron F 24 Ja34
Pojan AL 182 Aa76
Pojan AL 182 Ad77
Pojanluoma FIN 89 Jb32
Pojăreni MD 173 Fc58
Pojatno HR 151 Ga58

Poyaz – Putlitz

Poyaz TR 186 Fd77
Pöylä FIN 97 Jc39
Poynton GB 16 Ed22
Poyntz Pass GB 9 Cd18
Poyols F 35 Jc50
Poyra TR 193 Gb81
Poyralı TR 185 Ed75
Poyraz TR 192 Fa85
Poyrazcık TR 191 Ec84
Poyrazdamları TR 192 Fa85
Poyrazlı TR 185 Ed79
Pöyry FIN 90 Kd34
Poysdorf A 137 Gc49
Pöytiö FIN 97 Jd39
Pöytyä FIN 89 Jc38
Poza de la Sal E 38 Dd57
Pozal de Gallinas E 46 Cd61
Požarevac SRB 174 Bc64
Požarnica BIH 153 Hd63
Pozdeň CZ 136 Fa44
Pozdišovce SK 139 Ka48
Pozedrze PL 122 Jc30
Požega HR 152 Ha60
Požega SRB 159 Jb65
Požeranje KSV 178 Bb72
Požerė LT 113 Jd55
Pozières F 23 Ha33
Poznań PL 129 Gc37
Pozo Alcón E 61 Dd73
Pozoantiguo E 45 Cc60
Pozoblanco E 52 Cd71
Pozo-Cañada E 53 Ec70
Pozo de Guadalajara E 46 Dd64
Pozo de la Serna E 53 Dd70
Pozohondo E 53 Ec70
Pozo-Lorente E 54 Ed69
Pozondón E 47 Ed64
Pozořice CZ 137 Gc47
Pozorrubio E 53 Dd66
Poźrzadło Wielkie PL 120 Ga33
Pozuelo E 53 Eb70
Pozuelo de Alarcón E 46 Db64
Pozuelo de Aragón E 47 Ed60
Pozuelo de Calatrava E 52 Db69
Pozuelo del Páramo E 37 Cb58
Pozuelo de Zarzón E 45 Bd65
Pozza I 149 Db62
Pozza di Fassa I 143 Dd56
Pozzallo I 167 Fc88
Pozzillo I 167 Fd85
Pozzomaggiore I 168 Bd76
Pozzo San Nicola I 168 Bd74
Pozzuoli I 161 Fa75
Pozzuolo I 156 Dd67
Praag = Praha CZ 136 Fb44
Praaga EST 99 Lc45
Prabuty PL 122 Hc32
Prača BIH 159 Hd65
Prachatice CZ 136 Fa48
Prackenbach D 135 Ec48
Pračno HR 152 Gb60
Prada E 37 Bd57
Prádanos de Ojeda E 38 Db57
Pradelles F 34 Hd50
Pradelles-Cabardès F 41 Ha55
Prádena E 46 Dc62
Prades E 48 Gb62
Prades F 41 Ha57
Pradła PL 130 Hd42
Pradleves I 148 Bb62
Prado E 36 Ba56
Prado E 36 Ad57
Prado E 37 Cd54
Prado E 45 Cc59
Prado P 44 Ad59
Prado del Rey E 59 Ca76
Pradoluengo E 38 Dd58
Prads F 43 Kb51
Præstbro DK 101 Dd20
Præsteskov DK 109 Ec27
Præstø DK 109 Eb27
Prag = Praha CZ 136 Fb44
Pragelato I 148 Bb60
Prags I 143 Ea55
Praha CZ 136 Fb44
Prahecq F 32 Fc45
Prahovo SRB 174 Cb66
Praia a Mare I 164 Ga78
Praia da Areia Branca P 50 Aa67
Praia da Barra P 44 Ac62
Praia da Rocha P 58 Ab74
Praia das Maçãs P 50 Aa68
Praia da Tocha P 44 Ac63
Praia da Vagueira P 44 Ac63
Praia da Vieira P 44 Ab65
Praia de Esmoriz P 44 Ac61
Praia de Mira P 44 Ac63
Praia de Ofir P 44 Ac60
Praia de Quiaios P 44 Ab64
Praia de Santa Cruz P 50 Aa67
Praiano I 161 Fb76
Praid RO 172 Dd59
Prăjeni RO 172 Ed56
Prakovce SK 138 Jc48
Pralea RO 176 Ec61
Pralognan F 35 Kb47
Pralormo I 148 Bd61
Pra-Loup F 43 Kb51
Pram A 144 Fa50
Prámanda GR 188 Ba81
Prameny CZ 135 Ec44
Pramet A 143 Ed51
Pramort D 119 Ed30
Pramouton F 35 Kb50
Praniūnai LT 114 Kc59
Pranjani SRB 159 Jc64
Prapatnica HR 158 Gb66
Prapymas LT 113 Jc55
Prasés GR 200 Cb95
Prašice SK 137 Hb49
Prasiés GR 200 Cd95
Praslay F 30 Jb40
Praslovo RUS 122 Jc30
Prässebo S 102 Ec47
Prássino GR 194 Bb87
Prastavoniai LV 114 Kb55
Prastio CY 206 Ja98
Prastio CY 206 Jc96
Prästkulla FIN 97 Jd40
Prästö FIN 96 Hc40
Praszka PL 129 Hb41
Prat F 40 Gb56
Prata Sannita I 161 Fa73
Pratau D 127 Ec38
Prat-de-Chest F 41 Hb55
Prat de Comte E 48 Fd63
Pratella I 161 Fa73
Prati di Tivo I 156 Ed69
Prato CH 141 Cb56
Prato I 155 Dc65
Prato all'Isarco I 143 Dd56
Prato di Resia I 150 Ed57
Pratola Peligna I 161 Fa71
Pratola Serra I 161 Fc74
Prato Nevoso I 148 Bd63
Pratorotondo I 148 Bb62
Prats de Lluçanès E 49 Gd59
Prats-de-Mollo-la-Preste F 41 Ha58
Prats-du-Périgord F 33 Gb51
Pratteln CH 141 Bd52
Prauliena LV 107 Lb50
Pravda BG 181 Ec68
Pravdino RUS 113 Jd58
Pravdinsk RUS 113 Jb59
Pravec BG 179 Cd71
Praves E 38 Dc54
Pravia E 37 Cb54
Pravieniškės LT 114 Kc57
Pravini LV 106 Ka51
Pravište BG 180 Db73
Prayssac F 33 Gb51
Prayssas F 40 Ga52
Praz I 148 Bc58
Praze-an-Beeble GB 18 Da32
Praznice HR 158 Gc67
Prazzo I 148 Bb62
Prčanj MNE 159 Hd69
Préaux F 23 Gb35
Prebitz D 135 Ea45
Prebold SLO 151 Fd57
Přebuz CZ 135 Ec43
Prečec HR 152 Gb59
Préchac F 40 Fc52
Preci I 156 Ec68
Précigné F 28 Fc40
Prečistoe RUS 202 Ec11
Prečistoe RUS 203 Fa08
Précy-sous-Thil F 30 Hd41
Précy-sur-Oise F 23 Gd35
Predajane SRB 178 Bd70
Predappio I 156 Ea64
Predazzo I 150 Dd57
Predeal RO 176 Ea62
Predeal-Sărari RO 176 Eb64
Predești RO 175 Cd66
Predești RO 175 Db64
Preding A 144 Fd55
Predjama SLO 151 Fa59
Predlitz A 144 Fa54
Predmeja SLO 151 Fa58
Predosa I 148 Cb61
Predošćica HR 151 Fb61
Pré-en-Pail F 28 Fc38
Prees GB 15 Ec23
Preetz D 118 Dc30
Préfailles F 27 Ec42
Prefontaines F 29 Ha39
Pregarten A 144 Fb50
Pregrada HR 151 Ga57
Preila LT 113 Jb56
Preiļi LV 107 Lc52
Preitenegg A 144 Fc55
Preiviiki FIN 89 Ja36
Préjano E 47 Eb59
Prejtowo PL 122 Ja32
Prejmer RO 176 Ea62
Prekaja BIH 158 Gc64
Preko HR 157 Fd64
Prekopčelica SRB 178 Bc70
Prélenfrey F 35 Jd49
Preljina SRB 159 Jc64
Prelog HR 152 Gc57
Prelošćica HR 152 Gb60
Přelouč CZ 136 Fd45
Prem SLO 151 Fb59
Premana I 149 Cd57
Premantura HR 151 Fa62
Premeno I 148 Cb57
Prémery F 30 Hb42
Premià de Mar E 49 Ha61
Premilcuore I 156 Dd64
Premnitz D 127 Eb36
Prémont F 24 Hb33
Premuda HR 151 Fb63
Prenčov SK 146 Hc50
Prendeignes F 33 Gd50
Prendwick GB 11 Ed15
Prenika MK 182 Ba74
Prénouvellon F 29 Gc40
Prenzlau D 120 Fa34
Prepelița MD 173 Fc56
Přerov CZ 137 Gd46
Prerow D 119 Ec30
Pré-Saint-Didier I 148 Bb58
Prescot GB 15 Eb21
Presedo E 36 Ba54
Preseľany SK 145 Hb50
Preselec BG 180 Eb70
Preselenci BG 181 Fb69
Presencio E 38 Dc58
Preševo KSV 178 Bc72
Preshkëp AL 182 Aa77
Presicce I 165 Hc78
Presjaka MNE 159 Hd68
Presly F 29 Gd42
Prešov SK 139 Jd47
Pressac F 33 Ga46
Pressath D 135 Ea45
Pressbaum A 144 Ga51
Preßburg = Bratislava SK 145 Gd51
Presseck D 135 Ea44
Pressgutz A 144 Ga54
Pressig D 135 Dd43
Prestatyn GB 15 Ea22
Prestbakken N 67 Gc12
Presteid N 66 Fd15
Presteigne GB 15 Eb25
Prestelvbakken N 64 Jd06
Prestesætra N 78 Ed27
Prestfoss N 93 Dc41
Přeštice CZ 135 Ed46
Preston GB 15 Ec20
Preston GB 19 Ec31
Preston GB 21 Gb29
Preston Capes GB 20 Fa26
Prestranek SLO 151 Fb59
Prestwick GB 10 Dd14
Prestwood GB 20 Fb27
Pretoro I 157 Fa70
Prettin D 127 Ec39
Pretzfeld D 135 Dd45
Pretzsch D 127 Ec39
Preuilly-sur-Claise F 29 Ga43
Preußisch Oldendorf D 117 Cc36
Preutești RO 172 Ec56
Prevala BG 179 Cb68
Prevalje SLO 144 Fc56
Prevediños E 36 Ba55
Prévenchères F 34 Hd51
Préveranges F 33 Gd45
Préveza GR 188 Ac82
Prey F 23 Gb36
Prezë AL 182 Ab74
Prezëe Madhe AL 182 Ab75
Prez-v.-N. CH 141 Bc54
Prhovo SRB 153 Jb61
Priaranza del Bierzo E 37 Bd57
Priatu I 168 Cb74
Pribelja BIH 158 Gd64
Pribeta SK 145 Hb51
Pribinić BIH 152 Ha62
Priboieni RO 175 Dc64
Priboj BIH 153 Hd62
Priboj SRB 178 Bd71
Pribojska Goleša SRB 159 Ja66
Příbor CZ 137 Ha46
Pribovce SK 138 Hc48
Příbram CZ 136 Fa46
Pribrežnoje RUS 113 Ja59
Pribude HR 158 Gb65
Pribylina SK 138 Ja47
Přibyslav CZ 136 Ga46
Pričaly RUS 113 Jb57
Priceaca RO 175 Db65
Pri Cerkvi Strugah SLO 151 Fc59
Pričević SRB 153 Jb63
Prichsenstadt D 134 Db45
Pridnieki LV 105 Jc50
Pridvorci BIH 158 Hb67
Pridvorica SRB 174 Bb65
Pridvorje HR 159 Hc69
Priedaine LV 106 Kb50
Priego E 47 Eb64
Priego de Córdoba E 60 Da74
Priekulė LT 113 Jb56
Priekule LV 113 Jb53
Priekuļi LV 106 Kd49
Prien D 143 Eb52
Prienai LT 114 Kc58
Priescas E 37 Cd55
Priesendorf D 134 Dc45
Prievidza SK 138 Hc48
Prignano Cilento I 161 Fd76
Prigor RO 174 Ca64
Prigoria RO 175 Da63
Prigorica SLO 151 Fc59
Prigradica HR 158 Gc68
Pripalu EST 106 La46
Prijeboj HR 151 Ga62
Prijedor BIH 152 Gc61
Prijepolje SRB 159 Jb66
Prijutnoe RUS 205 Ga15
Prikra SK 139 Ka46
Prikraj HR 152 Gb58
Prikula BIH 158 Gd65
Prikuļi LV 107 Lc52
Prilep BG 181 Ec71
Prilep MK 183 Bb75
Prilike SRB 178 Ad67
Prima Porta I 160 Eb71
Přimda CZ 135 Ec46
Primel-Trégastel F 26 Dd37
Primolano I 150 Dd58
Primorje RUS 113 Hd58
Primorsk RUS 113 Hd58
Primorsk RUS 202 Ea08
Primorsk RUS 203 Fd13
Primorsko BG 181 Fa73
Primorsko-Ahtarsk RUS 205 Fc16
Primorskoje Novoje RUS 113 Hd59
Primošten HR 157 Ga66
Primstal D 133 Bd45
Princetown GB 19 Dd31
Principina a Mare I 155 Db69
Prínos GR 184 Da78
Prínos GR 188 Bb81
Priodrožnoje RUS 113 Jc58
Prioiro E 36 Ba53
Prióliithos GR 188 Bb86
Priolo I 167 Fb87
Priolo Gargallo I 167 Fd87
Prioro E 37 Cd56
Priozer'e RUS 113 Jc57
Pripiceni-Răzeși MD 173 Fd56
Priponești RO 177 Fa61
Prisad BG 181 Ed73
Prisad MK 183 Bc75
Prisches F 24 Hc32
Prisdorf D 118 Db32
Priselci BG 181 Fa71
Prisjan SRB 179 Ca70
Prisoja MNE 159 Jb68
Prisoje BIH 158 Gd65
Prissac F 29 Gb44
Pristeg HR 157 Ga65
Priština KSV 178 Bb71
Pristoe BG 181 Ed69
Prittitz D 127 Ea41
Prittriching D 142 Dc50
Pritzerbe D 127 Ec36
Pritzier D 119 Dd33
Pritzwalk D 119 Eb34
Privas F 34 Ja50
Priverno I 160 Ec73
Privlaka HR 153 Hd60
Privlaka HR 157 Fd64
Privol'noe RUS 113 Jc58
Privolžsk RUS 203 Fa09
Privuž RUS 99 Ld44
Prižba HR 158 Gc68
Priziac F 27 Ea39
Prizna HR 151 Fc63
Prizren KSV 178 Ba72
Prizzi I 166 Ec85
Prjamicyno RUS 203 Fa13
Prkosi BIH 152 Gb63
Prnjavor BIH 152 Ha62
Prnjavor SRB 153 Ja62
Proaza E 37 Cb55
Probota RO 172 Ec56
Probota RO 173 Fa57
Probsteierhagen D 118 Dc30
Probstzella D 135 Dd43
Probuda BG 181 Ec70
Probus GB 18 Db32
Procchio I 155 Da68
Próchnowo PL 121 Gc35
Prochod BG 181 Ec73
Prochowice PL 129 Gb40
Procida I 161 Fa75
Prodan AL 182 Ad78
Prodănești MD 173 Fc55
Prodo I 156 Ea68
Prodromi CY 206 Hd97
Prodromos CY 206 Ja97
Pródromos GR 188 Ad84
Pródromos GR 189 Ca85
Produlești RO 176 Dd65
Proença-a-Nova P 44 Ba65
Proença-a-Velha P 44 Bb65
Profesor Iširkovo BG 181 Ed68
Profítis GR 183 Cb78
Profítis Ilías GR 200 Da96
Progër AL 182 Ba77
Progresu RO 176 Eb66
Prohladnoe RUS 113 Jb57
Prohn D 119 Ed30
Próhoma GR 183 Ca77
Prohor Pćinski SRB 178 Bd72
Prokópi GR 189 Cb84
Prokuplje SRB 178 Bc69
Prolaz BG 180 Eb70
Proletarij RUS 202 Eb09
Proletarsk RUS 205 Fd15
Prolog HR 158 Ha67
Prolom SRB 178 Bc69
Prómahi GR 183 Bc76
Promahónas GR 184 Cc75
Promíri GR 189 Cb82
Promna PL 130 Jb38
Promnik PL 130 Jb41
Proniewicze PL 123 Kb34
Pronin RUS 203 Fc14
Pronsfeld D 133 Bc43
Pronstorf D 118 Dc31
Propriano F 154 Ca71
Proseč CZ 137 Gb45
Prosek AL 163 Jc71
Prösen D 128 Fa40
Prosenik BG 181 Ed72
Prosenjakovci SLO 145 Gb55
Prosienica PL 123 Jd34
Prosiměřice CZ 137 Gb48
Prosjek BIH 159 Ja65
Prosperous IRL 13 Cc21
Prossedi I 160 Ec73
Prosselsheim D 134 Db45
Prossotsáni GR 184 Cd76
Prostějov CZ 137 Gc46
Prostki PL 123 Ka32
Prostorno BG 180 Eb69
Prószków PL 137 Ha43
Proszowice PL 138 Jb44
Proszówki PL 138 Jb44
Próti GR 184 Cd77
Protići BIH 152 Gd63
Protivanov CZ 137 Gc46
Protivín CZ 136 Fb47
Protokklísi GR 185 Ea76
Prottes A 145 Gc50
Prötzel D 128 Fa36
Proussós GR 188 Bb83
Provadija BG 181 Ed70
Provadura E 36 Bb56
Provåker S 80 Ha28
Provatás GR 184 Cc76
Provató GR 185 Ea77
Provenchères F 31 Kb38
Provins F 30 Hb38
Provištip MK 178 Bd73
Provița de Sus RO 176 Ea64
Provo SRB 153 Jb62
Prozor HR 151 Fd62
Prozor = Rama BIH 158 Ha65
Prožura HR 158 Ha69
Prrenjas AL 182 Ad76
Pruchnik PL 139 Kb44
Prudentov RUS 203 Ga13
Prudhoe GB 11 Ed16
Prudnik PL 137 Gd43
Prudy RUS 113 Ja58
Prudziszki PL 123 Ka30
Prügy H 147 Jd50
Prüm D 133 Bc43
Pruna E 59 Cb75
Prundeni RO 175 Db65
Prundu RO 180 Eb67
Prundu Bârgăului RO 171 Dc57
Prunelli di Fiumorbo F 154 Cb70
Prunete F 154 Cc70
Prunetta I 155 Db64
Pruniers-en-Sologne F 29 Gc42
Prunișor RO 175 Cc65
Prunkila FIN 97 Jc39
Prusac BIH 158 Ha64
Prusak PL 129 Hb40
Prušće PL 121 Gc35
Prūšeliai LT 114 Kd54
Prusice PL 129 Gc40
Prūšiši LV 107 Lb50
Pruské SK 137 Hb48
Pruszcz PL 121 Gd33
Pruszcz PL 121 Ha33
Pruszcz Gdański PL 121 Hb30
Pruszków PL 130 Jb37
Pruszyn PL 131 Ka37
Pruteni MD 173 Fa56
Pružany BY 202 Dd13
Pružicy RUS 99 Ma41
Pružina SK 137 Hb48
Pryazovs'ke UA 205 Fa16
Pryłęk PL 139 Jd43
Pryluky UA 202 Ed14
Prymors'k UA 205 Fb16
Przasnysz PL 122 Jb34
Przebród PL 123 Ka30
Przechlewo PL 121 Gc32
Przechów PL 137 Gd43
Przeciszów PL 138 Hd44
Przecław PL 120 Fb33
Przecław PL 139 Jd43
Przecławice PL 129 Gc41
Przeczów PL 129 Gd41
Przedbórz PL 130 Ja41
Przedbórz PL 139 Jd43
Przedecz PL 130 Hc37
Przedświt PL 122 Jc35
Przegędza PL 137 Hb44
Przekolno PL 120 Fd34
Przełęk PL 137 Gd43
Przelewice PL 120 Fc34
Przemęt PL 129 Gb38
Przemiarowo PL 122 Jb35
Przemków PL 128 Ga40
Przemocze PL 120 Fc33
Przemyśl PL 139 Kb44
Przerośl PL 123 Ka30
Przerzeczyn-Zdrój PL 129 Gc42
Przesmyki PL 131 Ka36
Przewłoka PL 121 Gc29
Przewłoka PL 131 Kb38
Przeworno PL 129 Gc42
Przeworsk PL 139 Kb44
Przewóz PL 128 Fc40
Przewóz PL 129 Hb36
Przewrotne PL 139 Ka43
Przezmark PL 122 Hc31
Przine Zdralovac BIH 158 Gc64
Przodkowo PL 121 Ha30
Przybiernów PL 120 Fc32
Przyborowice PL 130 Ja36
Przybychowo PL 121 Gb35
Przybysławice PL 131 Ka39
Przydonica PL 138 Jc45
Przygodzice PL 129 Ha39
Przyjezierze PL 129 Ha36
Przykona PL 129 Hb38
Przyłęg PL 120 Fd35
Przyłęki PL 121 Ha34
Przylep PL 128 Fd38
Przyłubie PL 121 Ha34
Przyrów PL 130 Hd42
Przystajń PL 129 Hb41
Przystawka PL 123 Kb32
Przystawy PL 121 Gb30
Przyszów PL 131 Ka42
Przytoczna PL 128 Ga36
Przytoczno PL 131 Ka38
Przytyk PL 130 Jb39
Przywidz PL 121 Ha30
Przywory PL 137 Ha43
Przywóz PL 129 Hb41
Psača MK 178 Bd73
Psahná GR 189 Cb84
Psará GR 190 Dc85
Psarádes GR 182 Ba76
Psári GR 189 Bc86
Psary PL 130 Hc42
Psáthi GR 195 Cd90
Psáthi GR 196 Db91
Psebaj RUS 205 Fd17
Psérimos GR 197 Ec91
Psihikó GR 184 Cc77
Psínthos GR 197 Fa93
Pskov RUS 107 Ma46
Pskov RUS 202 Ea10
Pskovskoje RUS 113 Jd59
Psovlky CZ 136 Fa44
Pstrągowa PL 139 Jd44
Pszczew PL 128 Ga36
Pszczółki PL 121 Hb31
Pszczyna PL 138 Hc44
Pszów PL 137 Hb44
Pteléa GR 184 Da76
Pteleós GR 189 Ca83
Pteriá GR 182 Ba77
Ptolemaïda GR 183 Bb78
Ptuj SLO 151 Ga57
Ptujska Gora SLO 151 Ga57
Pūces LV 105 Jd51
Pučež RUS 203 Fb09
Puchaczów PL 131 Kb39
Puchały Stare PL 123 Kb35
Püchau D 127 Ec40
Puchberg am Schneeberg A 144 Ga52
Pucheni RO 176 Dd63
Pucherii Mari RO 176 Eb65
Püchersreuth D 135 Eb45
Puchheim A 144 Fa51
Puchheim D 143 Dd51
Púchov SK 137 Hb47
Pucioasa RO 176 Dd64
Pučišća HR 158 Gc67
Puck PL 121 Ha29
Puckakaun IRL 13 Ca22
Puçol E 54 Fc67
Puczniew PL 130 Hc38
Pudas FIN 69 Ka14
Pudas S 73 Jb19
Pudasjärvi FIN 75 Kc22
Puddletown GB 19 Ec30
Puderbach D 125 Ca42
Pudinava LV 107 Lc50
Pudob SLO 151 Fb59
Pudost' RUS 99 Mb40
Puebla de Albortón E 47 Fa61
Puebla de Alcocer E 52 Cc69
Puebla de Alfindén E 48 Fb61
Puebla de Almenara E 53 Ea66
Puebla de Brollón E 36 Bc57
Puebla de Don Fadrique E 61 Ea72
Puebla de Don Rodrigo E 52 Cd68
Puebla de Guzmán E 59 Bb73
Puebla de la Calzada E 51 Bc69
Puebla de la Reina E 51 Ca69
Puebla de la Sierra E 46 Dc62
Puebla de Lillo E 37 Cd56
Puebla del Maestre E 51 Ca71
Puebla del Príncipe E 53 Dd70
Puebla del Prior E 51 Bd70
Puebla del Salvador E 53 Ec67
Puebla de Obando E 51 Bc68
Puebla de Sanabria E 37 Bd58
Puebla de Sancho Pérez E 51 Bd70
Puebla de San Julián (Láncara) E 36 Bc56
Puebla de San Miguel E 54 Fa66
Puebla de Trives E 36 Bc57
Puebla de Vallés E 46 Dd63
Puente Almuhey E 37 Cd56
Puente Arce E 38 Dc54
Puente de Domingo Flórez E 37 Bd57
Puente de Génave E 53 Ea71
Puente de los Fierros E 37 Cc55
Puente de Montañana E 48 Ga59
Puente de Sanabria E 37 Bd58
Puente de San Martín E 37 Cb54
Puente de Vadillos E 47 Eb64
Puentedey E 38 Dc56
Puentedura E 46 Dc59
Puente-Genil E 60 Cd74
Puente la Reina E 39 Ec57
Puente la Reina de Jaca E 39 Fb58
Puentelarrá E 38 Ea57
Puentenansa (Rionansa) E 38 Db55
Puente Pumar E 38 Db55
Puente Viesgo E 38 Dc55
Puertas E 45 Ca62
Puerto de Conil E 59 Bd77
Puerto de Mazarrón E 55 Ed74
Puerto de Santa Cruz E 51 Ca67
Puerto de San Vicente E 52 Cc67
Puerto de Vega E 37 Ca53
Puerto Hurraco E 51 Cb70
Puerto-Lápice E 52 Dc68
Puertollano E 52 Da70
Puerto Lumbreras E 61 Ec74
Puertomingalvo E 54 Fb65
Puerto Real E 59 Bd76
Puerto Rey E 52 Cc67
Puerto Seguro E 45 Bd62
Puerto Serrano E 59 Cb75
Pueyo de Fañanás E 48 Fc59
Pufești RO 176 Ed61
Pugačev RUS 203 Ga11
Pugačevo RUS 113 Jd59
Puget-Théniers F 43 Kc52
Puget-Ville F 42 Ka54
Pugieu F 35 Jc46
Pugnac F 32 Fb49
Pugnochiuso I 162 Gb72
Puhăceni MD 173 Ga58
Puhar-Onkimaa FIN 90 Kc38
Puhja EST 98 La45
Puhoi MD 173 Fd58
Puhos FIN 75 Kd22
Puhos FIN 91 Ld32
Puhovac BIH 158 Hb64
Puhtaleiva EST 99 Lb45
Pui RO 175 Cc62
Puianello I 149 Db62
Puiatu EST 98 Kd45
Puicheric F 41 Ha55
Puiești RO 176 Ed63
Puiești RO 177 Fa60
Puig E 54 Fc67
Puigcerdà E 41 Gd58
Puigpunyent E 57 Hb67
Puig-reig E 49 Gd59
Puijas LV 105 Jd52
Puikule LV 106 Kc48
Puise EST 98 Ka44
Puiseaux F 29 Gd39
Puissalicon F 41 Hc54
Puisserguier F 41 Hb55
Puivert F 41 Gd56
Puka EST 106 La46
Pukalaidun FIN 89 Jc37
Pukanec SK 146 Hc50
Pukara FIN 89 Jc34
Pukara FIN 89 Jc35
Pukaro FIN 90 Kd38
Pukavik S 111 Fc54
Pukë AL 163 Jb71
Pukiš BIH 153 Hd62
Pukkila FIN 90 Kc38
Pula HR 151 Fa62
Pula I 169 Ca80
Pulaj AL 163 Ja71
Puławy PL 131 Jd39
Pulborough GB 20 Fc30
Pulfero I 150 Ed57
Pulgar E 52 Da67
Pulham Market GB 21 Gb25
Pulheim D 125 Bd40
Puliciano I 156 Dd66
Pulju FIN 68 Jc13
Pulkarne LV 106 Kb51
Pulkau A 136 Ga49
Pulkkala FIN 97 Jb40
Pulkkaviita FIN 69 Kd16
Pulkkila FIN 82 Kb26
Pulkkila FIN 90 Kc36
Pulkkinen FIN 81 Jc29
Pulkonkoski FIN 82 Kd29
Pulkovo RUS 99 Mb39
Pullach D 143 Dd51
Pullar TR 192 Ga83
Pullenreuth D 135 Eb45
Pullenried D 135 Eb46
Pulpí E 61 Ec74
Pulsa FIN 91 Lb36
Pulsano I 162 Ha76
Pulsen D 127 Ed40
Pulsnitz D 128 Fa41
Pulsujärvi S 67 Hb13
Pułtusk PL 122 Jb35
Pülümür TR 205 Ga20
Pulversheim F 31 Kb39
Pumpėnai LT 114 Kc54
Pumpula FIN 91 Lb36
Pumsaint GB 15 Dd26
Puņas LV 105 Jc49
Punat HR 151 Fc61
Puncești RO 173 Fa59
Pundrovka RUS 107 Mb49
Pundsvika N 66 Ga13
Punduri RUS 107 Ld49
Punghina RO 175 Cc66
Pungsetrene N 85 Dd35
Punia LT 114 Kc59
Punkaharju FIN 91 Ld33
Punsk PL 123 Kb30
Punta Ala I 155 Db68
Punta di San Vigilio I 149 Db59
Punta Križa HR 151 Fb62
Punta Marina I 150 Ea63
Punta Prima E 57 Jb66
Puntari FIN 90 Ka35
Punta Sabbioni I 150 Eb60
Punta Secca I 167 Fb88
Punta skala HR 157 Fd64
Punta Umbría E 59 Bb74
Puoddopohki FIN 64 Jd08
Puokio FIN 75 Kc24
Puolakkavaara FIN 69 Ka15
Puolanka FIN 75 Kd23
Puoltikasvaara S 68 Hc16
Puoltsa S 67 Ha15
Puottaure S 73 Hb20
Pupāji LV 107 Lc52
Pupnat HR 158 Gd68
Puraći BIH 152 Ha61
Puračić BIH 153 Hc63
Puralankylä FIN 82 Ka30
Purani RO 180 Dd67
Puraperä FIN 82 Ka28
Puras FIN 75 Lb23
Purchena E 61 Eb74
Purda PL 122 Ja32
Purdoški RUS 203 Fc10
Pūre LV 105 Jd50
Purgatorio I 166 Eb84
Purila EST 98 Kb43
Purini LV 106 Kb52
Puriton GB 19 Eb29
Purkersdorf A 145 Gb51
Purkjaur S 72 Ha19
Pürksi EST 98 Ka44
Purmerend NL 116 Ba35
Purmo FIN 81 Jb29
Purmojärvi FIN 81 Jc30
Purmsati LV 113 Jb53
Purnu S 73 Hc18
Purnumukka FIN 69 Ka13
Purnuvaara FIN 75 Kd20
Purnuvaara S 68 Hc17
Purola Svartbäck FIN 90 La38
Puromäki FIN 83 Lc31
Puronkylä FIN 82 Kc30
Purontaka FIN 81 Jd28
Puroranta FIN 82 Kc25
Pürsünler TR 192 Fb83
Purtovaara FIN 83 Ma31
Purtse EST 99 Lb42
Purunpää FIN 97 Jb41
Purvėnai LT 114 La59
Purveniai LT 113 Jd53
Purviniškė LV 114 Kb58
Puryševo RUS 107 Mb50
Puša LV 107 Ld52
Pusaankylä FIN 89 Jd32
Pušalotas LT 114 Kc54
Puškarevo RUS 113 Jb59
Puski EST 97 Jc44
Puškino RUS 203 Ga12
Puškinskie Gory RUS 107 Mb49
Puškinskie Gory RUS 202 Ea10
Pušmucova LV 107 Ld50
Pusnė LT 114 La56
Püspökladány H 147 Jd53
Pussay F 29 Gc38
Püssi EST 99 Lb42
Pustec AL 182 Ba76
Pustelnik PL 130 Jc38
Pusterwald A 144 Fb54
Pustevny CZ 137 Hb46
Pustoe Voskresen'e RUS 107 Ma49
Pustoška RUS 99 Ma42
Pustoška RUS 202 Eb11
Pustoški RUS 107 Ma49
Pustritz A 144 Fc55
Pustynia PL 139 Jd44
Pustynki RUS 107 Mb47
Pusula FIN 98 Ka39
Puszcza Mariańska PL 130 Ja38
Puszczykowo PL 129 Gc37
Pusztacsalád H 145 Gc53
Pusztakovácsi H 145 Ha56
Pusztamiske H 145 Gd54
Pusztaszabolcs H 146 Hc54
Pusztaszentlászló H 145 Gc56
Pusztavám H 145 Hb53
Putaja FIN 89 Jb36
Putanges F 22 Fc37
Putbus D 120 Fa30
Putgarten D 120 Fa29
Putignano I 162 Gd75
Putikko FIN 91 Ld33
Putinci SRB 153 Jb61
Putineiu RO 180 Dc68
Putineiu RO 180 Ea68
Putkela FIN 83 Ma30
Putkilahti FIN 90 Kc34
Putkivaara FIN 74 Kb19
Putla EST 105 Jc46
Putlitz D 119 Eb34

Putna - Rathen

Putna RO 172 Ea55
Putnok H 146 Jb50
Putte NL 124 Ac38
Puttelange-aux-Lacs F 25 Ka35
Putten NL 116 Bb36
Puttenham GB 20 Fb29
Puttgarden D 119 Ea29
Püttlingen D 133 Bc46
Putula FIN 90 Kb36
Putyvl' UA 202 Ed13
Putzu'Idu I 169 Bd77
Puujaa FIN 90 Kb37
Puukari FIN 83 Lb27
Puukkoinen FIN 90 Kb34
Puukkokumpu FIN 74 Jd21
Puukonsaari FIN 90 Kd34
Puulansalmi FIN 90 Kd34
Puumala FIN 91 Lb34
Puuppola FIN 90 Kb32
Puurmani EST 98 La44
Puurtila FIN 90 La32
Puurtturinjärvi FIN 74 Kb24
Putikkala FIN 90 Ka36
Putossalmi FIN 82 La30
Putteenperä FIN 74 Jd21
Puycasquier F 40 Ga54
Puydrouard F 32 Fb46
Puy-Guillaume F 34 Hc46
Puylagarde F 40 Gc52
Puylaroque F 40 Gc52
Puylaurens F 41 Gd54
Puy-l'Evêque F 33 Gb51
Puymiclan F 32 Fd51
Puymirol F 40 Ga52
Puyôo F 39 Fa54
Puy-Saint-Martin F 34 Jb50
Puy-Saint-Vincent F 35 Ka49
Puzači RUS 203 Fa13
Puzenieki LV 105 Jc50
Pwllheli GB 14 Dc23
Pyecombe GB 20 Fc30
Pyhäjärvi FIN 69 Jd11
Pyhäjärvi FIN 69 Kb16
Pyhäjärvi FIN 82 Kb28
Pyhäjoki FIN 81 Jc26
Pyhäjoki FIN 89 Jb37
Pyhäkoski FIN 90 Kd35
Pyhäkylä FIN 75 La22
Pyhälahti FIN 82 Kc31
Pyhältö FIN 90 La37
Pyhämaa FIN 89 Ja38
Pyhänkoski FIN 81 Jd26
Pyhänsivu FIN 74 Kb24
Pyhäntä FIN 82 Kb26
Pyhäntaka FIN 90 Kc36
Pyhäranta FIN 89 Ja38
Pyhäsalmi FIN 82 Kb28
Pyhäselkä FIN 83 Ld31
Pyhe FIN 97 Ja39
Pyhtää FIN 90 Kd38
Pykkvibær IS 2 Ac05
Pyla CY 206 Jc97
Pyla-sur-Mer F 32 Fa51
Pyle GB 19 Ea28
Pyli GR 188 Bb81
Pylkönmäki FIN 82 Ka31
Pylvänälä FIN 90 Kd33
Pylväsperä FIN 81 Jd27
Pyntäinen FIN 89 Ja34
Pyöli FIN 89 Jd38
Pyöree FIN 82 Kd27
Pyöreinen FIN 82 La29
Pyörni FIN 89 Ja32
Pyrbaum D 135 Dd47
Pyrénées 2000 F 41 Gd58
Pyrga CY 206 Jb97
Pyrga CY 206 Jc96
Pyrill IS 2 Ac04
Pyrjatyn UA 202 Ed14
Pyrzowice PL 138 Hc43
Pyrzyce PL 120 Fc34
Pyskowice PL 137 Hb43
Pyssykangas FIN 89 Ja36
Pyssyperä FIN 75 Kd23
Pystyoja FIN 64 Jc10
Pysznica PL 131 Ka42
Pytalovo RUS 107 Ld49
Pytalovo (Abrene) RUS 202 Ea10
Pytkynharju FIN 75 Kc21
Pytten N 92 Cc44
Pyttis FIN 90 Kd38
Pyydyskylä FIN 82 Kc31
Pyydysmäki FIN 89 Jd34
Pyykkölänvaara FIN 75 La24
Pyyli FIN 91 Lc32
Pyyrinlahti FIN 82 Kb31
Pyzdry PL 129 Gd37

Q

Qafë-Murrë AL 163 Jc72
Qafëzez AL 182 Ad77
Qarrishtë AL 182 Ad75
Qinam AL 182 Ab74
Qormi M 166 Eb88
Quafmollë AL 182 Ac74
Quaglietta I 161 Fd75
Quainton GB 20 Fb27
Quakenbrück D 117 Cc35
Qualiano I 161 Fa75
Quarff GB 5 Fa05
Quarnbek D 118 Dc30
Quarona I 148 Ca58
Quarré-les-Tombes F 30 Hd41
Quarteira P 58 Ac74
Quarto d'Altino I 150 Eb59
Quartu San Elena I 169 Ca79
Quasano I 162 Gc74
Quattro Venti, i I 161 Fb73
Quebradas P 50 Ab67
Quecedo E 38 Dd56
Quédillac F 27 Ec39
Quedlinburg D 127 Dd38
Queidersbach D 133 Ca46
Queiruga E 36 Ac56
Quelaines F 28 Fb40
Quellendorf D 127 Eb39
Quemada E 46 Dc60
Quemigny-Poisot F 30 Ja42
Quend F 23 Gc32
Quenstedt D 127 Ea39
Queralbs E 41 Gd58
Querceta I 155 Da64
Quercianella I 155 Da66
Querenhorst D 127 Dd37
Querfurt D 127 Ea40
Quero E 53 Dd67
Querol E 49 Gc61
Querrin IRL 12 Bb23
Quers F 31 Ka40
Quesada E 61 Dd73
Quessoy F 26 Eb38
Questembert F 27 Eb41
Quettehou F 22 Fa34
Quettetot F 22 Ed35
Queudes F 24 Hc37
Quevauvillers F 23 Gd33
Quevert F 26 Ec38
Quiaios P 44 Ac64
Quiberon F 27 Ea41
Quickborn D 118 Db32
Quiddelbach D 133 Bd43
Quigley's Point IRL 9 Cc15
Quillan F 41 Gd56
Quilly F 27 Ec41
Quilty IRL 12 Bb22
Quimper F 27 Dc39
Quimperlé F 27 Dd40
Quin IRL 12 Bc22
Quincoces de Yuso E 38 Dd56
Quindós E 37 Bd56
Quinéville F 22 Fa35
Quingey F 31 Jd42
Quiñonería E 47 Ec61
Quinsac F 32 Fb50
Quinson F 42 Ka53
Quinta do Lago P 58 Ac74
Quintana E 37 Ca55
Quintana E 37 Cc54
Quintana de Castillo E 37 Cb57
Quintana de la Serena E 51 Cb69
Quintana del Marco E 37 Cb58
Quintana del Puente E 46 Db59
Quintanadueñas E 38 Dc58
Quintanaélez E 38 Dd57
Quintana-Martín Galíndez E 38 Dd57
Quintanapalla E 38 Dc58
Quintanar de la Orden E 53 Dd67
Quintanar de la Sierra E 46 Dd59
Quintanar del Rey E 53 Ec68
Quintana Redonda E 47 Ea60
Quintanilla de Arriba E 46 Db60
Quintanilla de Flórez E 37 Cb58
Quintanilla del Agua E 46 Dc59
Quintanilla de la Mata E 46 Dc59
Quintanilla del Coco E 46 Dc59
Quintanilla del Molar E 45 Cc59
Quintanilla de Losada E 37 Ca58
Quintanilla de los Oteros E 37 Cc58
Quintanilla de Onésimo E 46 Da60
Quintanilla de Pienza E 38 Dd56
Quintanilla de Trigueros E 46 Da59
Quintanilla-Pedro Abarca E 38 Dc57
Quintanilla San García E 38 Dd57
Quintanilla-Sobresierra E 38 Dc57
Quintela E 37 Bd56
Quintela de Leirado E 36 Ba58
Quintes E 37 Cc54
Quint-Fonsegrives F 40 Gc54
Quintin F 26 Eb38
Quintinilla Rucandio E 38 Dc56
Quinto E 48 Fb61
Quintos P 50 Ad71
Quinto Vercellese I 148 Ca59
Quinzano d'Oglio I 149 Da60
Quiroga E 36 Bc57
Quirra I 169 Cb79
Quismondo E 46 Da65
Quissac F 41 Hd53
Quistello I 149 Dc61
Quistinic F 27 Ea40
Quittebeuf F 23 Ga36
Quitzdorf am See D 128 Fc40
Qukës AL 182 Ad75
Qundle GB 20 Fc25

R

Rå S 79 Gb30
Råå S 110 Ed55
Raab A 144 Fa50
Raabs an der Thaya A 136 Fd48
Raahe FIN 81 Jd25
Raajärvi FIN 74 Kb18
Raakku FIN 74 Kc18
Rääkkylä FIN 83 Ld31
Raalte NL 117 Bc36
Raanujärvi FIN 74 Jc18
Raappananmäki FIN 82 Kd25
Raappanansuo FIN 75 Kd21
Raasdorf A 145 Gb50
Raasiku EST 98 Kc42
Raasinkorpi FIN 89 Jb38
Raatala FIN 97 Jc39
Raate FIN 75 Lb23
Raatevaara FIN 83 Ma31
Raattama FIN 68 Jb14
Raatti FIN 82 La29
Rab HR 151 Fc62
Rabac HR 151 Fb61
Rabaçal P 44 Bb62
Rábade E 36 Bb55
Rábafüzes H 145 Gb55
Răbăgani RO 170 Cb58
Rábahidvég H 145 Gc54
Rabal E 36 Bc57
Rabanal de Camino E 37 Ca57
Rábano E 46 Db61
Rábano de Sanabria E 37 Bd58
Rábasömjen H 145 Gc54
Rabastens F 40 Gc53
Rabat M 166 Eb88
Rabatamasi H 145 Gd53
Raba Wyżna PL 138 Ja46
Rabenau D 126 Cd42
Rabenau D 128 Fa41
Rabensberg A 137 Gc49
Rabenstein A 144 Fd51
Råberg S 80 Gc26
Rabí CZ 136 Fa47
Rąbino PL 120 Ga32
Rabiša BG 179 Cb68
Rabka-Zdrój PL 138 Ja46
Rabouillet F 41 Ha57
Rabrovo BG 179 Cb67
Rabrovo SRB 174 Bd64
Rabštejn nad St. CZ 135 Ed44
Rabsztyn PL 138 Hd43
Råby-Rekarne S 95 Ga43
Råby-Rönö S 95 Gb45
Rača SK 145 Gd51
Rača SRB 174 Bb65
Rača SRB 178 Bc70
Răcăciuni RO 176 Ed60
Racale I 165 Hc78
Rácalmás H 146 Hc54
Racalmuto I 166 Ed86
Răcari RO 176 Ea65
Răcăria MD 173 Fa55
Răcășdia RO 174 Bd63
Racconigi I 148 Bc61
Raccuia I 167 Fc84
Rače SLO 144 Ga56
Rachanie PL 131 Kd42
Rachecourt-sur-Marne F 24 Jb37
Răchitoasa RO 177 Fa60
Răchitova RO 175 Cc61
Rachiv UA 204 Ea16
Raciąż PL 121 Gd32
Raciąż PL 122 Ja35
Raciążek PL 121 Hb35
Raciborsko PL 138 Ja44
Racibórz PL 137 Hb44
Raciechowice PL 138 Ja45
Račinovci HR 153 Hd61
Račišće HR 158 Gd68
Răciu RO 171 Db58
Răciula MD 173 Fc57
Račja Vas HR 151 Fa60
Rackeby S 102 Ed46
Ráckeve H 146 Hc54
Racków PL 129 Gb41
Racksund S 72 Gc21
Rackwitz D 127 Eb40
Racławice PL 138 Ja43
Racławice Śląskie PL 137 Ha43
Răcoasa RO 176 Ed61
Racoș RO 176 Dd61
Racot PL 129 Gb38
Racova RO 172 Ec59
Racovăț MD 173 Fc54
Racovița RO 175 Db62
Racovița RO 175 Db62
Racovița RO 177 Fa63
Racovițeni RO 176 Ec63
Răculești MD 173 Fd57
Rączki PL 122 Ja33
Råda S 94 Ed41
Råda S 102 Ed46
Radakowice PL 129 Gc41
Radalj SRB 153 Hd63
Rådanefors S 102 Ec46
Radanje MK 183 Bd74
Radanovo BG 180 Dd70
Radapole LV 107 Lc51
Rădășeni RO 172 Eb56
Radaškovičy BY 202 Ea12
Rădăuți RO 172 Eb55
Rădăuți-Prut RO 172 Ed54
Radawie PL 129 Hb42
Radawnica PL 121 Gc33
Radbruch D 118 Dc33
Radbyn S 102 Fa46
Radcliffe GB 15 Ec21
Radda in Chianti I 155 Dc66
Raddestorf D 126 Cd36
Raddon F 31 Ka39
Raddusa I 167 Fb86
Råde N 93 Ea43
Radeberg D 128 Fa41
Radebeul D 128 Fa41
Radeburg D 128 Fa40
Radeburg D 128 Fa41
Radeče SLO 151 Fd58
Radechiv UA 204 Ea15
Radęcin PL 120 Ga34
Radecki BG 180 Ea73
Radecznica PL 131 Kb41
Radefeld D 127 Eb40
Radegast D 119 Eb31
Radegast D 127 Eb39
Radenci SLO 145 Gb56
Rădeni MD 173 Fc57
Rădenii Vechi MD 173 Fb57
Radenthein A 144 Fa55
Rădești RO 171 Da59
Radevo BG 180 Ea73
Radevo KSV 178 Bb71
Radevormwald D 125 Ca40
Radgoszcz PL 138 Jc43
Radhimë AL 182 Aa77
Radibor D 128 Fb41
Radičevicevo SRB 153 Jb59
Radići BIH 152 Gd63
Radicofani I 156 Dd68
Radicondoli I 155 Db67
Radievo BG 180 Ea72
Radijovce MK 178 Ba73
Radilovo BG 179 Da73
Radis D 127 Ec39
Radizel SLO 144 Ga56
Radków PL 130 Ja42
Radków PL 137 Gb43
Radkowice PL 130 Jc41
Radlett GB 20 Fc27
Radlin PL 129 Gd38
Radlje ob Dravi SLO 144 Fd56
Radljevo SRB 153 Jc63
Radłów PL 129 Hb41
Radłów PL 138 Jc44
Radmansö S 96 Ha42
Radmer an der Hasel A 144 Fc53
Radmirje SLO 151 Fc57
Radnejaur S 72 Gc21
Radnevo BG 180 Ea73
Radnica PL 128 Fd38
Radnice CZ 136 Fa45
Rădoaia MD 173 Fb55
Radohova BIH 152 Ha63
Rădoiești RO 180 Dc67
Radojevo SRB 174 Bc60
Radojewice PL 121 Hb35
Radolfzell D 142 Cc52
Radom PL 130 Jc39
Rådom S 94 Ed41
Radomice PL 122 Hc35
Radomicko PL 128 Fc38
Radomicko PL 129 Gb38
Radomierzyce PL 128 Fc41
Radomin PL 122 Hc34
Radomir BG 179 Cb71
Radomirci BG 179 Da69
Radomirești RO 180 Db67
Radomno PL 122 Hc33
Radomsko PL 130 Hd41
Radomyšl CZ 136 Fa47
Radomyšl' UA 202 Eb14
Radomyśl n. Sanem PL 131 Ka42
Radomyśl Wielki PL 138 Jc43
Radonice CZ 135 Ed44
Radošice CZ 136 Fa46
Radošina SK 137 Ha49
Radošovce SK 137 Gd49
Radostowo PL 122 Ja31
Radoszewice PL 130 Hc40
Radoszki PL 122 Hd33
Radoszyce PL 130 Ja41
Radoszyn PL 128 Fd37
Radovac KSV 178 Ad70
Radovac SRB 159 Jc68
Radovan RO 175 Cd66
Radovanu RO 180 Eb67
Radovče MNE 159 Ja69
Radovec BG 185 Eb74
Radovel' RUS 99 Lc42
Radovesice CZ 136 Fb43
Radovići MNE 159 Hd70
Radoviš MK 183 Ca74
Radovljica SLO 151 Fb57
Radowo Wielkie PL 120 Fd32
Radozda MK 182 Ad75
Radstadt A 143 Ed53
Radsted DK 109 Eb29
Răducăneni RO 173 Fb58
Radučić HR 158 Gb64
Raduil BG 179 Cd72
Radujevac SRB 174 Cb66
Rădulenii Vechi MD 173 Fc55
Raduń PL 120 Fd34
Radunci BG 180 Dd72
Radu Negru RO 181 Ed67
Raduša MK 178 Bb72
Raduszec PL 128 Fd38
Radvaň nad Laborcom SK 139 Ka47
Radviliškis LT 114 Kb54
Radwanice PL 128 Ga39
Radwanów PL 128 Fd39
Radymno PL 139 Kb44
Radzanów PL 122 Ja34
Radzanów PL 130 Jb39
Radzanowo PL 130 Hd36
Radzewice PL 129 Gc37
Radzice Duże PL 130 Ja39
Radzieje PL 122 Jc30
Radziejów PL 129 Hb36
Radziejowice PL 130 Jb37
Radziemice PL 138 Ja43
Radziki Duże PL 122 Hc34
Radzików PL 128 Fc37
Radzików Wielki PL 131 Ka37
Radziłów PL 123 Ka33
Radzinciems LV 106 Ka50
Radzionków PL 138 Hc43
Radziszewo PL 120 Fb34
Radziwie PL 130 Hd36
Radziwiłłówka PL 131 Kb36
Radzymin PL 130 Jc36
Radzyń Chełmiński PL 121 Hb33
Radzyń Podlaski PL 131 Ka38
Raec MK 183 Bc75
Ræhr DK 100 Da20
Rækker Mølle DK 108 Da24
Raelingen N 93 Ea41
Rae na nDoirí IRL 12 Bb25
Raeren B 125 Bb41
Raesfeld D 125 Bd38
Rafelbuñol E 54 Fc67
Rafelbunyol E 54 Fc67
Raffadali I 166 Ed86
Rafína GR 189 Cc86
Răfov RO 176 Eb65
Rafsbotn N 63 Hd08
Raftópoulo GR 188 Ba82
Raftsjöhöjden S 79 Fc29
Ragaciems LV 106 Ka50
Ragály H 138 Jb49
Ragana LV 106 Kc49
Rågeleje DK 109 Ec24
Rägelin D 119 Ec35
Rågård S 94 Ec45
Raghly IRL 8 Bd17
Rågländа S 94 Ed44
Ragnabo S 111 Ga53
Ragnitz A 144 Ga55
Ragösen D 127 Ec37
Ragow D 128 Fb37
Ragozino RUS 107 Ma48
Raguhn D 127 Eb39
Ragunda S 79 Ga31
Ragusa I 167 Fc87
Raguva LT 114 Kd55
Raguvėlė LT 114 Kd55
Raguviškiai LT 113 Jb55
Ragvaldsnäs S 88 Gc34
Rahačov BY 202 Eb13
Rahan IRL 13 Cb21
Raharney IRL 9 Cc20
Rahden D 126 Cd36
Ráhes GR 189 Bd83
Ráhes GR 194 Bb87
Raheste EST 106 Ka46
Rahikka FIN 89 Ja33
Rahja FIN 81 Jc27
Rahkee FIN 83 Ld29
Rahkio FIN 89 Jc38
Rahkla EST 98 La43
Rahkmala FIN 89 Ja38
Rahkonen FIN 81 Jd28
Rahman RO 177 Fb65
Rahmanca TR 185 Eb76
Rahmanlar TR 192 Fc85
Raholanvaara FIN 83 Lb29
Råholt N 94 Eb40
Rahoúla GR 188 Bb82
Rahoúla GR 189 Bc81
Rahula FIN 90 La34
Rahumäe EST 107 Lc46
Raiano I 161 Fa71
Raič HR 152 Gc58
Raikkala FIN 89 Jb37
Raikküla EST 98 Kb44
Raikuu FIN 91 Ld32
Räimä FIN 82 La30
Raimonda P 44 Ad60
Rain D 134 Dc49
Rain D 135 Eb48
Rainbach im Mühlkreis A 136 Fb49
Rain in Taufers I 143 Ea55
Raipole LV 107 Ma51
Raippaluoto FIN 81 Hd30
Raippo FIN 91 Lb36
Raisälä FIN 74 Kc18
Raisälänmäki FIN 82 Ka28
Raisdorf D 118 Dc30
Raisio FIN 97 Jb39
Raiskio FIN 74 Ka20
Raiskio FIN 83 Lb26
Raiskums LV 106 Kd49
Raistakka FIN 75 Kc19
Raisting D 142 Dc51
Raitaperä FIN 81 Jd31
Raitenbuch D 135 Dd48
Raitenhaslach D 143 Ec51
Raitoo FIN 89 Jd37
Raivala FIN 89 Jb34
Rajac SRB 178 Ba67
Raja-Jooseppi FIN 69 Kb12
Rajala FIN 69 Jd15
Rajamäenkylä FIN 89 Ja33
Rajamäki FIN 90 Kb38
Rajaniemi FIN 90 Kd34
Rajanovci BG 179 Ca68
Rajastrand S 79 Fd26
Rajavaara FIN 91 Ld33
Rajcë AL 182 Ad75
Rajčinovica Banja SRB 178 Ba69
Rajcza PL 138 Hc46
Rajec SK 138 Hc47
Rájec-Jestřebí CZ 137 Gc47
Rajecké Teplice SK 138 Hc47
Rajec Poduchowny PL 130 Jc39
Rajgród PL 123 Ka31
Rajhrad CZ 137 Gc48
Rajince KSV 178 Bc72
Rajka H 145 Gd51
Rajkova moglia BG 185 Eb75
Rajković SRB 153 Jb63
Rajkovo BG 184 Db75
Rajkowy PL 121 Hb31
Rajnino BG 181 Ec68
Raka SLO 151 Fd58
Rakaca H 138 Jc49
Rakalj HR 151 Fa61
Rakamaz H 147 Jd50
Rakek SLO 151 Fb59
Rakeluft N 63 Hd07
Rakić BIH 153 Ja62
Rakita BG 179 Da69
Rakitna SLO 151 Fb58
Rakitnica BG 180 Dd73
Rakitnica BIH 159 Hc65
Rakitnica HR 152 Gc58
Rakitovica HR 152 Hb59
Rakitovo BG 184 Cd74
Rakke EST 98 La43
Rakkestad N 94 Eb43
Raklinovo BG 181 Ec72
Rákóczifalva H 146 Jb54
Rakoniewice PL 129 Gb37
Rákos H 146 Jc56
Rakoš KSV 178 Ba70
Rakoszyce PL 129 Gb41
Rakova Bara SRB 174 Bd65
Rakovica BG 179 Ca67
Rakovica HR 151 Ga61
Rakovník CZ 136 Fa44
Rakovo BG 180 Eb71
Rakovski BG 180 Dc73
Rakow D 119 Ed31
Raków PL 130 Jc42
Rakowo Piskie PL 123 Jd32
Rāksala LV 107 Lb51
Ráksi H 145 Ha56
Råkvågen N 78 Ea28
Rakvere EST 98 La42
Ralewice PL 129 Hb39
Ralingen D 133 Bc44
Ralja SRB 174 Bb64
Ralja SRB 174 Bb64
Raljin SRB 179 Ca70
Raljovo BG 180 Db69
Rälla S 103 Gb52
Ram SRB 174 Bc64
Rama BIH 158 Ha65
Ramacastañas E 46 Cd65
Ramacca I 167 Fc86
Rämälä FIN 89 Jd32
Rämälä FIN 90 La34
Ramales de la Victoria E 38 Dd55
Ramallosa (Teo) E 36 Ad55
Ramasaig GB 4 Da08
Ramatuelle F 43 Kb55
Rămăzan MD 173 Fa55
Ramberg N 66 Fa14
Rambervillers F 31 Ka38
Rambin D 119 Ed30
Rambjørgheia N 92 Cb45
Rambo S 80 Ha27
Rambouillet F 23 Gc37
Ramdala S 111 Ga54
Rameški RUS 202 Ed09
Râmeț RO 171 Da59
Ramfjordnes N 62 Gd10
Rámia GR 188 Ba81
Ramingstein A 144 Fa54
Ramirás E 36 Ba58
Ramji LV 106 Kd48
Ramkvilla S 103 Fc51
Ramljane HR 158 Gb65
Ramløse DK 109 Eb24
Ramma EST 98 Kd43
Ramme DK 100 Cd22
Rämmen S 95 Fb41
Ramna RO 174 Bd62
Ramnäs S 95 Ga42
Rämne S 94 Eb45
Ramnes N 93 Dd43
Râmnicelu RO 176 Ed63
Râmnicelu RO 177 Fa63
Râmnicu de Sus RO 177 Fc66
Râmnicu Sărat RO 176 Ed63
Râmnicu Vâlcea RO 175 Db63
Ramonai LT 114 Kd54
Ramosch CH 142 Db55
Ramså N 66 Ga11
Ramsau D 143 Ec53
Ramsau am Dachstein A 144 Fa53
Ramsbeck D 126 Cc40
Ramsbottom GB 15 Ec21
Ramsbury GB 20 Ed28
Ramsdorf D 125 Bd37
Ramsei CH 141 Bd54
Ramsele S 79 Ga29
Ramsele S 80 Ha28
Ramsey GB 10 Dd18
Ramsey GB 20 Fc25
Ramsey GB 21 Gb26
Ramsey Saint Mary's GB 20 Fc25
Ramsgate GB 21 Gb28
Rämshyttan S 95 Fd40
Ramsi EST 106 Kd46
Ramsjö S 87 Fd34
Ramsli N 92 Cb45
Rämsöö FIN 89 Jc36
Ramsta S 96 Gc42
Ramstad N 78 Eb25
Ramstein-Miesenbach D 133 Ca46
Ramsthal D 134 Db44
Ramsund N 66 Ga13
Ramsvika N 78 Ec26
Ramten DK 101 Dd23
Rāmuļi LV 106 Kd49
Ramundberget S 86 Ed32
Ramundeboda S 95 Fc45
Ramvik S 88 Gc32
Ramygala LT 114 Kc55
Raná CZ 136 Fa43
Ranalt A 142 Dc54
Rånäsudden S 73 Ja21
Rancon F 33 Gb46
Randaberg N 92 Ca43
Randalstown GB 9 Da16
Randan F 34 Hc46
Randanne F 34 Hb47
Randaträsk S 73 Hc20
Randazzo I 167 Fc84
Randbøldal DK 108 Db25
Rånddalen S 86 Fa34
Randebygd N 84 Cc34
Randegg A 144 Fc51
Randen N 85 Dc35
Randers DK 100 Dc23
Randersacker D 134 Db45
Randerup DK 108 Da27
Randesund N 92 Cd47
Randijaur S 72 Ha19
Randonnai F 23 Ga37
Randsverk N 85 Dc35
Randvere EST 98 Kb42
Rånea S 73 Hd21
Ranemsletta N 78 Ec26
Rânes F 22 Fc37
Rang-du-Fliers F 23 Gc32
Rångedala S 102 Ed49
Rangendingen D 134 Cc49
Rangersdorf A 143 Ec55
Rangsby FIN 89 Hd32
Rangsdorf D 127 Ed37
Rangstrup DK 108 Da27
Ranhados P 44 Bb62
Ranheim N 77 Ea30
Rani list BG 184 Dc75
Ranis D 127 Ea42
Ranizów PL 139 Ka43
Ranka LV 106 La49
Rankinen FIN 82 Ka25
Rankweil A 142 Cd53
Ranna EST 99 Lb44
Rannametsa EST 106 Kb46
Rannamõisa EST 98 Kb42
Rannankulma FIN 89 Jb37
Rannankylä FIN 81 Jd31
Rannankylä FIN 82 Kb27
Rannanmäki FIN 89 Jb38
Rannanpohjukka FIN 91 Ma32
Rånnaväg S 102 Fa49
Rännelanda S 102 Ec46
Rännelslöv S 110 Ed53
Rännö S 87 Gb33
Rannoch Station GB 7 Dd10
Rannsundet S 86 Fa33
Rannu EST 106 La46
Rannungen D 134 Db44
Rånön S 73 Ja22
Ranovac SRB 174 Bc65
Ranrupt F 31 Kb38
Ransäter S 94 Fa42
Ransbach-Baumbach D 125 Ca42
Ransby S 94 Ed39
Ransbysätter S 94 Fa41
Ransjö S 87 Fb34
Rańsk PL 122 Jb32
Ranskill GB 16 Fb22
Ransta S 95 Gb42
Ranstadt D 134 Cd43
Rantajärvi S 74 Jb18
Rantakunta FIN 89 Jc33
Rantakylä FIN 82 Ka31
Rantakylä FIN 83 Lc29
Rantakylä FIN 90 La34
Rantala FIN 81 Jd31
Rantasalmen asema FIN 91 Lb33
Rantasalmi FIN 91 Lb32
Ranta-Töysä FIN 89 Jc32
Rante E 36 Bb57
Rantrum D 108 Da29
Rantsila FIN 82 Ka25
Ranttila FIN 64 Jc10
Rantum D 108 Cd28
Ranty PL 123 Jd31
Rantzausminde DK 109 Dd28
Ranua FIN 74 Kb20
Ranum DK 100 Db21
Ranzig D 128 Fb38
Rao E 37 Bd55
Raon-l'Etape F 31 Ka38
Raossi I 149 Dc58
Rapa PL 123 Jd30
Râpa RO 170 Cb57
Rapajin Dol HR 151 Fd61
Rapala FIN 90 Kb35
Rapallo I 149 Cc63
Rapattila FIN 91 Lc36
Rapëza AL 182 Ab76
Raphoe IRL 9 Cb16
Rapice PL 128 Fc38
Räpina EST 107 Lc46
Rapla EST 98 Kb43
Rapness GB 5 Ec02
Rapolano Terme I 156 Dd67
Rapolla I 161 Ga74
Rapoltu Mare RO 175 Cc61
Raposa P 50 Ac68
Rapotín CZ 137 Gc45
Rapovce SK 146 Ja50
Rapperswil CH 142 Cc53
Rappin D 119 Ed30
Räpplinge S 103 Gb52
Rappottenstein A 144 Fc50
Rappvika N 63 Hb08
Rapsáni GR 183 Bd80
Rapuli FIN 83 Lb27
Rårup DK 109 Ea28
Ras SRB 178 Ad68
Raša HR 151 Fa61
Rasal E 39 Fb58
Räsälä FIN 82 La30
Räsälänlahti FIN 82 La30
Rasbokil S 96 Gd41
Rașca RO 172 Eb56
Rascafría E 46 Db63
Rașcov MD 173 Fd55
Rasdel BG 185 Eb74
Rasdorf D 126 Db42
Raseljke BIH 158 Gd66
Raseiniai LT 114 Ka56
Rasharkin GB 9 Cd16
Rashedoge IRL 9 Cb16
Rasi FIN 90 La36
Rašica SLO 151 Fc58
Rasimäki FIN 82 La28
Rasimäki FIN 83 Lb29
Rasimbegov MK 183 Bc75
Rasina EST 99 Lc45
Rășinari RO 175 Da61
Rasines E 38 Dd55
Rasinkylä FIN 75 Kd24
Rasisalo FIN 83 Ld31
Rasivaara FIN 83 Ma30
Rasivaara FIN 83 Ld31
Rasivaara FIN 83 Ld31
Råsjö S 87 Fd33
Raška SRB 178 Ba68
Rask Mølle DK 108 Db25
Raškovo BG 179 Cd70
Raslavice SK 139 Jd47
Rășmirești RO 180 Dd67
Rasná CZ 136 Fd47
Rašnevo RUS 107 Ma47
Râșnov RO 176 Dd62
Rasova RO 181 Fb67
Rasovo BG 179 Cc68
Raspilla E 53 Eb71
Răspopeni MD 173 Fc55
Rasquera E 48 Ga63
Rassach A 144 Fd55
Rassina I 156 Dd65
Rasskazovo RUS 203 Fc12
Rast RO 179 Cc67
Rastatt D 133 Cb48
Rasted DK 100 Dc23
Rastede D 118 Cc33
Rastenberg D 127 Ea41
Rastenfeld A 136 Fd49
Rasteš MK 183 Bb74
Rasti FIN 68 Jc15
Rasti FIN 91 Ld32
Rastina SRB 153 Hd58
Rastinkylä FIN 83 Lc26
Răstolița RO 172 Dd57
Rastovac MNE 159 Hd68
Rastovica MK 183 Bb75
Rastow D 119 Ea33
Råstrand S 72 Gc24
Răsuceni RO 180 Ea67
Rasueros E 46 Cd62
Raszków PL 129 Gd39
Raszkówka PL 129 Gb40
Raszujka PL 122 Jb33
Raszyn PL 130 Jb37
Ratan S 80 Hc28
Rätan S 87 Fc33
Ratasjärvi FIN 73 Jb19
Ratby GB 16 Fa24
Ratčino RUS 99 Ma40
Rateče SLO 144 Fa56
Ratekau D 119 Dd31
Ratevo MK 183 Cb74
Rathangan IRL 13 Cc21
Rath Cairn IRL 12 Bc23
Rathcoole IRL 13 Cd21
Rathcormack IRL 12 Bd25
Rathcroghan IRL 8 Ca19
Rathdangan IRL 13 Cd23
Rathdowney IRL 13 Cb23
Ráth Droma IRL 13 Cd23
Rathdrum IRL 13 Cd23
Rathen D 128 Fb41
Rathen GB 5 Ed07

Rijen – Rosoman

Rijen NL 124 Ad38
Rijnwarden NL 125 Bc37
Rijsbergen NL 124 Ad38
Rijsel = Lille F 23 Ha31
Rijssen NL 117 Bd36
Rijswijk NL 116 Ad36
Rikkaranta FIN 83 Lb30
Riksgränsen S 67 Gc13
Rikstad N 77 Dd31
Riksu EST 105 Jc47
Rila BG 179 Cb73
Rilax FIN 97 Jc41
Rilci BG 181 Fa69
Rilievo I 166 Ea84
Rillé F 28 Fd41
Rillo E 47 Fa63
Rilly-la-Montagne F 24 Hc35
Rima San Giuseppe I 148 Bd58
Rimasco I 148 Ca58
Rimaucourt F 30 Jb38
Rimavska Baňa SK 138 Ja49
Rimavska Seč SK 146 Jb50
Rimavská Sobota SK 146 Ja50
Rimbach D 134 Cc45
Rimbach D 135 Ec47
Rimbo S 96 Gd42
Rimella I 148 Ca57
Rimetea RO 171 Da59
Rimforsa S 103 Fd47
Rimicāni LV 107 Lb52
Rimini I 156 Eb64
Rimmi EST 107 Lb47
Rimmi FIN 81 Jb28
Rimmilä FIN 90 Ka37
Rimminjoki FIN 82 Kc30
Rimmu EST 106 Kd46
Rimnieki LV 105 Jc50
Rímnio GR 183 Bc79
Římov CZ 136 Fb48
Rimpar D 134 Da45
Rimpelä FIN 69 Jd15
Rimpilänniemi FIN 82 Kd26
Rimše LT 115 Lc54
Rimske Toplice SLO 151 Fd58
Rimsting D 143 Eb52
Rinchnach D 135 Ed48
Rincón de la Victoria E 60 Da76
Rinda LV 105 Jb49
Rindal N 77 Dc31
Rindbø N 66 Fd14
Rindby DK 108 Cd26
Rinde N 84 Cc37
Rindsholm DK 100 Db23
Rinella I 167 Fc82
Ringaliai LT 113 Jd56
Ringamåla S 111 Fc53
Ringarum S 103 Gb47
Ringaskiddy IRL 12 Bd26
Ringe D 117 Ca35
Ringe DK 109 Dd27
Ringebu N 85 Dd36
Ringelai D 135 Ed49
Ringgau D 126 Db41
Ringkøbing DK 108 Cd24
Ringleben D 127 Dd40
Ringnäs S 86 Fa37
Ringsend GB 9 Cd15
Ringsta S 79 Fc30
Ringsted DK 109 Eb26
Ringvattnet S 79 Fd27
Ringvoll N 93 Ea43
Ringwood GB 20 Ed30
Rinkaby S 95 Fd44
Rinkaby S 111 Fb55
Rinkabyholm S 103 Ga52
Rinkenæs DK 108 Db28
Rinkilä FIN 91 Lc33
Rinlo E 37 Bd53
Rinn A 143 Dd54
Rinna S 103 Fc47
Rinøya N 66 Fd14
Rinsumageest NL 117 Bc33
Rintala FIN 81 Jb30
Rintatalo FIN 81 Jb29
Rinteln D 126 Cd37
Rinyabesenyő H 152 Ha57
Rinyaszentkirály H 152 Gd57
Rio GR 188 Bb85
Riocorvo E 38 Db55
Rio de Onor P 45 Bd59
Río de Trueba E 38 Dc55
Riodeva E 47 Fa65
Rio Frio P 45 Bd59
Rio Frio P 50 Ab69
Riofrío E 37 Cb57
Riofrío E 46 Cd64
Riofrío de Aliste E 45 Ca59
Riofrío del Llano E 47 Ea62
Riola I 149 Dc63
Riola Sardo I 169 Bd77
Riolobos E 45 Bd65
Riolo Terme I 150 Dd63
Riom F 34 Hb46
Riomaggiore I 155 Cd64
Rio Maior P 50 Ab67
Riomalo de Arriba E 45 Ca64
Rio Marina I 155 Da68
Rio Mau P 44 Ac60
Riom-ès-Montagnes F 33 Ha48
Rion-des-Landes F 39 Fa53
Rionegro del Puente E 45 Ca59
Rionero in Vulture I 161 Ga75
Rionero Sannitico I 161 Fa72
Riópar E 53 Eb71
Rioscuro E 37 Ca56
Rioseco E 47 Ea60
Rioseco de Tapia E 37 Cb56
Ríoseco (Sobrescobio) E 37 Cc55
Riotord F 34 Ja48
Rioux F 32 Fb47
Rioveggio I 149 Dc63
Rioxuán E 36 Bc55
Rioz F 31 Jd41
Ripakluokta S 67 Gd17
Ripanj SRB 153 Jc62
Ripanj SRB 174 Bb64
Riparbella I 155 Da66
Ripatransone I 157 Fa68
Ripats S 73 Hb18
Ripatti FIN 90 Kd34
Ripiceni RO 172 Ed55
Ripky UA 202 Ec13
Ripley GB 16 Fa24
Ripoll E 49 Gd59
Ripollet E 49 Gd61
Ripon GB 11 Fa19
Riposto I 167 Fd85
Ripponden GB 16 Ed21
Rips NL 125 Bb38
Ripsa S 95 Gb45
Riquewihr F 31 Kb38
Riš BG 181 Ec71
Risan MNE 159 Hd69
Risåsen S 86 Ed33
Risbäck S 79 Fd26
Risbäck S 80 Gd29
Risberg S 80 Hb25
Risberg S 86 Fa38
Risberget N 94 Ec40
Risböle S 81 Hd26
Risby GB 21 Ga25
Risca GB 19 Eb27
Rişca RO 171 Cd58
Rişcani MD 173 Fa55
Riscle F 40 Fc54
Risco E 52 Cc69
Rişcova MD 173 Fd57
Risdal N 93 Da45
Risdal N 92 Cc46
Rise N 66 Fc12
Rise N 77 Dd33
Riseberga S 110 Ed54
Risede S 79 Fc27
Riseley GB 20 Fc25
Risholen S 95 Fd39
Risinge S 103 Ga46
Risipeni MD 173 Fa56
Risis FIN 97 Ja40
Riska N 92 Ca44
Risliden S 80 Hb25
Risliden S 80 Ha25
Risnabben S 73 Hb23
Risnes N 92 Cc45
Rišňovce SK 145 Ha50
Risögrund S 73 Jb21
Risør N 93 Db45
Risoul 1850 F 35 Kb50
Risøy N 62 Gc08
Risøyhamn N 66 Fd12
Rissa N 78 Ea29
Rissna S 79 Fd31
Riste FIN 89 Jb36
Ristee FIN 83 Ma31
Risteli FIN 83 Lb26
Risti EST 98 Ka44
Ristiina FIN 90 La35
Ristijärvi FIN 82 La25
Ristijärvi FIN 90 Ka34
Ristiküla EST 106 Kc46
Ristilä FIN 75 Kc19
Ristilä FIN 90 Kc32
Ristilampi FIN 69 Ka17
Ristimäki FIN 90 Kc32
Ristinen FIN 82 Kd29
Ristinge DK 109 Dd28
Ristinkylä FIN 83 Lc31
Ristonmännikkö FIN 69 Ka16
Ristovac KSV 178 Bc71
Risträsk S 79 Gb25
Risudden S 79 Ga28
Risulahti FIN 91 Lb34
Risum-Lindholm D 108 Da28
Risuperä FIN 75 Kd20
Risuperä FIN 82 Ka30
Risvolvollen N 78 Ec29
Ritabulli LV 106 Kb50
Ritamäki FIN 81 Jb31
Rite LV 114 La53
Ritini GR 183 Bd79
Ritola FIN 81 Jd31
Ritoniemi FIN 82 La30
Ritopek SRB 174 Bb64
Ritsem S 67 Gb16
Ritten I 143 Dd56
Ritterhude D 118 Cd34
Ritupe RUS 107 Ma49
Ritvala FIN 90 Ka36
Ritzleben D 119 Ea35
Riudarenes E 49 Hb60
Riudoms E 48 Gb62
Riumar E 48 Ga63
Riutta FIN 81 Jd28
Riutta FIN 83 Ld29
Riutta FIN 89 Ja35
Riuttala FIN 82 Kd30
Riuttala FIN 89 Jb35
Riuttanen FIN 89 Jc34
Riutula FIN 69 Ka11
Riva E 38 Dd55
Riva LV 105 Jb51
Riva-Bella F 22 Fc35
Riva dei Tessali I 162 Gd76
Riva del Garda I 149 Db58
Riva di Solto I 149 Da58
Riva di Tures I 143 Ea55
Rivanazzano I 148 Cb61
Rivarbukt N 63 Hd08
Rivarolo Canavese I 148 Bd59
Rivarolo Mantovano I 149 Da61
Rivas E 47 Fa59
Riva SanVitale I 149 Cc58
Rivas de Tereso E 38 Ea57
Rive-de-Gier F 34 Ja47
Rivello I 161 Ga77
Rivergaro I 149 Cd61
Riverstick IRL 12 Bd26
Riverstown IRL 12 Bd25
Riverville IRL 12 Bb24
Rives F 35 Jc48
Rivesaltes F 41 Hb57
Rivignano I 150 Ec58
Rivinperä FIN 82 Kb26
Rivio GR 188 Ba83
Rivisondoli I 161 Fa71
Rivne UA 202 Ea14
Rivne UA 204 Ed16
Rivoli I 148 Bc60
Rivolta d'Adda I 149 Cd59
Rixö S 102 Eb47
Riza GR 188 Bb85
Rižana SLO 151 Fa59
Rizário GR 183 Bc77
Rize TR 205 Ga19
Rizenbach CH 141 Bc54
Rízes GR 194 Bc88
Rízia GR 185 Eb75
Rizokarpaso CY 206 Ka95
Rizoma GR 183 Bb80
Rizómilos GR 189 Ca81
Rjabinovka RUS 113 Ja59
Rjabovskij RUS 203 Fc13
Rjahovo BG 180 Eb68
Rjånes N 76 Cb33
Rjasino RUS 107 Mb50
Rjazan' RUS 203 Fa11
Rjazanka RUS 203 Fc12
Rjažsk RUS 203 Fb11
Rjukan N 93 Db41
Rø DK 111 Fc57
Rö S 88 Gc32
Rö S 96 Gd42
Roa E 46 Db60
Roa N 85 Ea40
Roade GB 20 Fb26
Roager DK 108 Da27
Roaillan F 32 Fc51
Roald N 76 Cc32
Roan N 78 Ea27
Roana I 150 Dd58
Roanne F 34 Hd46
Roaschia I 148 Bc63
Roasjö S 102 Ed49
Roata de Jos RO 176 Dd66
Roavvegiedde N 64 Jd07
Roavvesávu FIN 64 Jc09
Röbäck S 80 Hb28
Robakowo PL 121 Hb33
Robănești RO 175 Da66
Robbio I 148 Cb60
Robeasca RO 176 Ed64
Robecco d'Oglio I 149 Da60
Röbel D 119 Ec33
Røberg N 78 Ea29
Roberton GB 11 Ec15
Robertsfors S 80 Hc27
Robertsholm S 95 Ga39
Robertville B 125 Bb42
Robeži LV 105 Jb50
Robežnieki LV 115 Ld53
Robič SLO 150 Ed57
Robilante I 148 Bc63
Robin Hood's Bay GB 17 Fc18
Robledillo de Trujillo E 51 Ca68
Robledo E 37 Bd57
Robledo E 53 Ea70
Robledo de Chavela E 46 Da64
Robledo del Buey E 52 Cd67
Robledo del Mazo E 52 Cd67
Robledollano E 51 Cb67
Robles de la Valcueva E 37 Cc56
Röblingen D 127 Ea40
Robliza de Cojos E 45 Cb62
Robregordo E 46 Dc62
Robres E 48 Fb60
Robres del Castillo E 39 Eb58
Robru N 85 Db38
Roc HR 151 Fa60
Rocafort de Queralt E 48 Gb61
Roca Llisa E 56 Gc69
Rocamadour F 33 Gc50
Roca Vecchia I 163 Hc76
Roccabianca I 149 Da61
Roccadaspide I 161 Fd76
Rocca di Cambio I 156 Ed70
Rocca di Mezzo I 156 Ed70
Rocca di Neto I 165 Gd80
Rocca di Papa I 160 Eb72
Roccaforte del Greco I 164 Gb84
Roccagorga I 160 Ec73
Rocca Imperiale I 162 Gc77
Roccalbegna I 155 Dc68
Roccalumera I 167 Fd84
Roccamandolfi I 161 Fb73
Roccamena I 166 Ec85
Roccamonfina I 161 Fa73
Roccanova I 162 Gb77
Roccapalumba I 166 Ed85
Rocca Pietore I 143 Ea56
Rocca Priora I 156 Ed66
Roccaraso I 161 Fa72
Rocca San Casciano I 156 Dd64
Roccasecca I 160 Ed72
Rocca Sinibalda I 156 Ec70
Roccastrada I 155 Dc67
Roccatederighi I 155 Db67
Roccaverano I 148 Ca62
Roccella Jonica I 164 Gc83
Rocchetta San Antonio I 161 Fd74
Rochdale GB 16 Ed21
Roche E 59 Bd77
Roche GB 18 Db31
Rochechouart F 33 Ga47
Rochecolombe F 34 Ja51
Rochefort B 132 Ad43
Rochefort F 32 Fa46
Rochefort-en-Terre F 27 Ec40
Rochefort-Montagne F 33 Ha47
Rochegude F 42 Jb52
Rochehaut B 132 Ad44
Rochemaure F 42 Jb51
Rocheservière F 28 Ed43
Rochester GB 11 Ed15
Rochester GB 20 Fd28
Rochetaillée F 35 Jd49
Rochetaillée-sur-Saône F 34 Jb46
Rochfortbridge IRL 13 Cb21
Rochlitz D 127 Ec41
Rochnia PL 122 Ja34
Rociana del Condado E 59 Bc74
Rociu RO 175 Dc65
Rock GB 18 Db31
Rockanje NL 124 Ac37
Rockchapel IRL 12 Bc24
Rockcorry IRL 9 Cc18
Rockenhausen D 133 Ca45
Rockhammar S 95 Fd43
Rockhill IRL 12 Bd24
Rockneby S 103 Gb52
Röcknitz-Böhlitz D 127 Ec40
Rockolding D 135 Ea49
Ročov CZ 136 Fa44
Rocroi F 24 Hd33
Rodach, Bad D 134 Dc43
Roda de Isábena E 40 Ga58
Roda de Ter E 49 Ha59
Rodaki PL 138 Hd43
Rodalben D 133 Ca46
Rodaljice HR 157 Ga64
Rodalquilar E 61 Eb76
Rödålund S 80 Hb27
Rödånäs S 80 Hb27
Rödåsel S 80 Hb27
Rodavgí GR 188 Ad81
Rødberg N 85 Db40
Rødbergshamn N 62 Gc10
Rödbo S 102 Eb48
Rødby DK 109 Ea29
Rødbyhavn DK 109 Ea29
Rødding DK 100 Da22
Rødding DK 100 Db23
Rødding DK 108 Da26
Røddinge DK 109 Eb28
Rodeberg D 126 Db40
Rödeby S 111 Fd54
Rode Heath GB 15 Ec22
Rodeiro E 36 Ba56
Rødekro DK 108 Db27
Rodel GB 4 Cd06
Roden NL 117 Bd33
Rodenbach D 134 Cd44
Rodenberg D 126 Da36
Rodenkirchen D 118 Cd33
Rödental D 135 Dd43
Rödermark D 134 Cc44
Rödermark D 134 Cd44
Rodersdorf D 135 Eb43
Rodewald D 118 Da35
Rodewisch D 135 Eb43
Rodewitz D 128 Fc41
Rodez F 33 Ha51
Rodgau D 134 Cc44
Rødhus Klit DK 100 Db20
Rodiá GR 182 Ba79
Rodiá GR 183 Bd80
Rodiá GR 189 Bc85
Rodiá GR 194 Ba88
Rodi-Fiesso CH 141 Cb56
Rodi Garganico I 161 Ga71
Roding D 135 Eb47
Rödingersdorf A 136 Ga49
Rödinghausen D 126 Cc37
Rödingträsk S 80 Gd26
Roditsa GR 189 Bd83
Rødkærsbro DK 100 Db23
Rodleben D 127 Eb38
Rodna RO 172 Dd56
Rodniki RUS 203 Fa09
Rodohóri GR 183 Bc77
Rodolivos GR 184 Cd77
Rödön S 79 Fb30
Rodonyà E 49 Gc62
Rodópoli GR 183 Cb76
Rodopós GR 200 Cb94
Ródos GR 197 Fa92
Rodováni GR 200 Cb95
Rødøy N 70 Fa19
Rodrażew PL 129 Gd39
Rodrigas (Riotorto) E 36 Bc54
Rødsand N 67 Gb11
Rødseidet N 78 Ec25
Rødsjøen N 78 Ea28
Rødskov DK 101 Dd23
Rødvig DK 109 Ec27
Rodzone PL 122 Hd33
Roela EST 98 La42
Røen N 77 Dc31
Roermond NL 125 Bb40
Roeselare B 21 Ha30
Roeselare B 124 Aa39
Roești RO 175 Da64
Roetgen D 125 Bb41
Roffiac F 34 Hb49
Röfors S 95 Fc45
Róg PL 122 Jb33
Rog S 95 Fd39
Rogač HR 158 Gb67
Rogačevka RUS 203 Fb13
Rogačica KSV 178 Bc71
Rogačica SRB 159 Jb64
Rogaieni MD 173 Fc55
Rogajny PL 122 Hd31
Rogale PL 123 Jd30
Rogalice PL 129 Gd41
Rogalin PL 129 Gc37
Rogart GB 5 Ea06
Rogäsen D 127 Eb37
Rogaška Slatina SLO 151 Ga57
Rogatec SLO 151 Ga57
Rogatica BIH 159 Hd65
Rogätz D 127 Ea37
Roggel NL 125 Bb39
Roggenburg D 142 Db50
Roggendorf D 119 Dd32
Roggentin D 119 Ed33
Roggiano Gravina I 164 Gb79
Roghi MD 173 Fd57
Roghudi I 164 Gb84
Rogil P 58 Ab73
Rogliano F 154 Cc67
Rogliano I 164 Gc80
Rognan N 71 Fd18
Rogne N 85 Dc37
Rognes F 42 Jc53
Rognmo N 67 Gc11
Rognskog N 77 Dd31
Rogny-les-Sept-Écluses F 29 Ha40
Rogoš BG 180 Db73
Rogovka LV 107 Ld50
Rogovo RUS 107 Ma47
Rogów PL 130 Hd38
Rogowo PL 121 Gd35
Rogowo PL 122 Hc34
Rogóż PL 122 Ja30
Rogoz RO 171 Db56
Rogozče BG 184 Dc76
Rogozina BG 181 Fb69
Rogoznica HR 157 Ga66
Rogożnica PL 129 Gd41
Rogożniczka PL 131 Kb37
Rogoźnik PL 129 Gb41
Rogoźno PL 121 Gc35
Rogoźno PL 121 Hb33
Rogóźno PL 130 Hd37
Rogslösa S 103 Fc47
Rogsta S 87 Gb35
Roguszyn PL 131 Jd36
Rohan F 27 Eb39
Rohia RO 171 Db56
Röhlingen D 134 Db48
Rohovládova Bělá CZ 136 Ga44
Rohozná CZ 137 Gb46
Rohožník SK 145 Gd50
Rohr D 126 Dc42
Rohr D 134 Dc47
Rohr D 135 Ea49
Rohrau A 145 Gc51
Rohrbach D 135 Dd49
Rohrbach an der Gölsen A 144 Ga51
Rohrbach an der Lafnitz A 144 Ga53
Rohrbach in Oberösterreich A 136 Fa49
Rohrbach-lès-Bitche F 25 Kb35
Rohrberg D 119 Dd35
Rohr im Gebirge A 144 Ga52
Röhrnbach D 135 Ed49
Röhrsdorf D 127 Ec42
Rohuküla EST 97 Jd44
Rohuneeme EST 98 Kb42
Rois E 36 Ad56
Roisel F 23 Ha33
Roismala FIN 89 Jc36
Roissy F 23 Ha37
Roitegi E 39 Eb57
Roitzsch D 127 Eb39
Roiu EST 99 Lb45
Roizy F 24 Hd34
Roja LV 105 Jd49
Rojales E 55 Fb72
Rojão P 44 Ad63
Röjdåfors S 94 Ed40
Rojewice PL 121 Ha35
Rojewo PL 121 Ha35
Rojiște RO 179 Da67
Röjnoret S 80 Hb25
Röka S 72 Gd24
Rokai LT 114 Kc57
Rokansalo FIN 91 Lb34
Röke S 110 Fa54
Røkenes N 66 Fd12
Røkenes N 67 Gb12
Rokiciny PL 130 Hd39
Rokietnica PL 129 Gc36
Rökiö FIN 81 Ja30
Rokiškis LT 114 La53
Rokitki PL 128 Ga40
Rokitnica PL 139 Kb44
Rokitno PL 131 Kc37
Rokity PL 121 Gd30
Rokkala FIN 91 Ma32
Rokkamäki FIN 90 Kc32
Rokke N 94 Eb44
Røkkum N 77 Db31
Roknäs S 73 Hc23
Rokua FIN 82 Kb25
Rokycany CZ 136 Fa46
Rokytne UA 202 Eb14
Rokytnice nad Jizerou CZ 128 Fd42
Rokytnice v. Orl. horách CZ 137 Gb44
Rolampont F 30 Jb39
Rölanda S 94 Eb45
Rolandstorp S 79 Fb26
Rold DK 100 Dc22
Røldal N 92 Cc41
Roldán E 55 Fa73
Rolde NL 117 Bd34
Role PL 121 Gc31
Rolfs S 73 Ja21
Rolfstorp S 102 Ec51
Rollag N 93 Dc41
Rollamienta E 47 Eb59
Rollán E 45 Cb62
Röllbach D 134 Cd45
Rolle CH 140 Ba55
Rollshausen D 126 Db39
Rolsberga S 110 Fa55
Rolsted DK 109 Dd27
Rolvenden GB 21 Ga29
Rolvsnes N 92 Ca41
Rom F 32 Fd45
Roma I 160 Eb71
Roma RO 172 Ec55
Romagnano Sesia I 148 Ca58
Romakkajärvi FIN 74 Jc18
Romakloster S 104 Ha49
Roman BG 179 Cd70
Roman RO 172 Ed58
Românași RO 171 Cd57
Romancos E 47 Ea63
Romănești RO 173 Fa55
Romănești RO 173 Fa57
Români RO 172 Ec58
Români de Sus RO 175 Da63
Romanija BIH 159 Hc65
Romanillos de Medinaceli E 47 Ea62
Romankovka RUS 99 Mb40
Romano di Lombardia I 149 Cd59
Romanów PL 131 Kc38
Romanówka PL 123 Kb32
Romanowo Górne PL 121 Gb35
Romanshorn CH 142 Cd52
Romans-sur-Isère F 34 Jb49
Romanu RO 177 Fa63
Romanyà de la Selva E 49 Hb60
Rombak N 67 Gc13
Rombas F 25 Jd35
Rombiolo I 164 Gb82
Romeán E 36 Bc55
Romelanda S 102 Ec48
Romenay F 30 Jb44
Romeny-sur-Marne F 24 Hb36
Rome = Roma I 160 Eb71
Römerstein D 134 Cd49
Rometta I 167 Fd84
Romeu P 45 Bc60
Romfartuna S 95 Gb42
Romfo N 77 Dc32
Romford GB 20 Fd28
Romhány H 146 Hd51
Römhild D 134 Dc43
Romilly-sur-Seine F 30 Hc38
Romme S 95 Fd40
Rommele S 102 Ec47
Rommerskirchen D 125 Bd40
Romny UA 202 Ed14
Romodan UA 202 Ed14
Romont CH 141 Bb55
Romorantin-Lanthenay F 29 Gc42
Romos RO 175 Cd61
Romoşel RO 175 Cd61
Romppala FIN 83 Ld29
Romrod D 126 Cd42
Romsey GB 20 Fa30
Romsila FIN 97 Jd39
Rømskog N 94 Eb42
Romstad N 78 Ec27
Romuli RO 171 Dc55
Romund N 85 Dc35
Røn N 85 Dc37
Rona de Jos RO 171 Db54
Rona de Sus RO 171 Db54
Ronäs S 71 Fc22
Rønbjerg DK 100 Da22
Roncal E 39 Fa57
Roncegno I 150 Dd58
Ronce-les-Bains F 32 Fa47
Roncesvalles E 39 Ed56
Ronchamp F 31 Ka40
Ronchi di Legionari I 150 Ed58
Ronciglione I 156 Ea70
Roncobello I 149 Cd58
Ronco Canavese I 148 Bc59
Ronco Scrivia I 148 Cb62
Ronda E 59 Cb76
Rondablikk N 85 Dd35
Rønde DK 101 Dd23
Rondissone I 148 Bd60
Rone S 104 Ha50
Ronehamn S 104 Ha50
Rones N 78 Eb28
Rong N 84 Cc39
Rongesund N 84 Bd38
Rõngu EST 106 La46
Ronkaisperä FIN 82 Ka27
Ronkala FIN 91 Lb33
Rönkhausen D 125 Cb40
Rönkönlehto FIN 82 La26
Rönkönvaara FIN 83 Lc31
Rönnäs FIN 98 Kd39
Rönnäs S 79 Ga25
Rönnbäcken S 71 Fd23
Rønne DK 111 Fc58
Ronneburg D 127 Eb42
Ronneburg D 134 Cd43
Ronneby S 111 Fd54
Ronneby hamn S 111 Fd54
Rønnede DK 109 Eb27
Ronnenberg D 126 Da36
Rønnes N 93 Da46
Rönneshytta S 95 Fc45
Rönnfällan S 80 Ha25
Rönnholm FIN 81 Hd31
Rönnholm S 80 Ha29
Rönninge S 96 Gc44
Rønningen N 67 Gc12
Rönnliden S 72 Ha23
Rönnöfors S 79 Fb29
Rönnskär S 80 Hc25
Rönnynkylä FIN 82 Kb29
Rönnynranta FIN 75 Kd19
Rönö S 103 Gb46
Ronquières B 124 Ac41
Ronsberg D 142 Db51
Ronse B 124 Ab40
Ronshausen D 126 Db41
Ronzone I 142 Dc56
Roobaka EST 97 Jd45
Roobe EST 106 La47
Roodeschool NL 117 Ca32
Röölä FIN 97 Jb39
Roonah Quay IRL 8 Bb19
Roosendaal NL 124 Ad38
Roosinpohja FIN 90 Ka33
Roosky IRL 8 Bd19
Roosky IRL 8 Ca17
Roosky IRL 8 Ca19
Rooslepa EST 97 Jd43
Roosna-Alliku EST 98 Kd43
Ropa PL 138 Jc45
Ropaži LV 106 Kc50
Ropczyce PL 139 Jd44
Ropefield IRL 8 Bd18
Ropeid N 92 Cb42
Roperuelos del Páramo E 37 Cb58
Ropinsalmi FIN 68 Hc12
Ropley GB 20 Fa29
Ropotovo MK 183 Bb75
Roppe F 31 Kb40
Ropša RUS 99 Mb40
Ropsley GB 17 Fc23
Ropso RUS 99 Lc41
Roquebillière F 43 Kd52
Roquebrun F 41 Hb54
Roquebrune-sur-Argens F 43 Kb54
Roquecourbe F 41 Gd54
Roquefort F 40 Fc53
Roquefort-sur-Soulzon F 41 Hb53
Roquesteron F 43 Kc52
Roquetas de Mar E 61 Ea76
Roquetes E 48 Ga63
Røra N 78 Eb28
Röra S 102 Eb47
Rörbäck S 73 Ja21
Rörbäcksnäs S 86 Ed37
Rørbæk DK 100 Dc22
Rørby DK 109 Ea26
Rore BIH 158 Gc64
Rørholt DK 101 Dd21
Rørholt N 93 Dc44
Rørnes N 62 Ha09
Rörö S 102 Eb49
Rörön S 87 Fc32
Røros N 86 Eb32
Rørøya N 70 Ed22
Rorschach CH 142 Cd53
Rørstad N 66 Fd16
Rörum S 111 Fb56
Rörvattnet S 79 Fb28
Rørvig DK 109 Eb25
Rørvik N 78 Eb25
Rørvik N 78 Ea29
Rörvik S 103 Fc50
Rørvika N 66 Ga13
Rørvika N 66 Ga14
Ros' BY 202 Dd13
Ros E 38 Dc58
Rösa D 127 Ec39
Rosà I 150 Dd59
Rosal E 36 Ac58
Rošal' RUS 203 Fa10
Rosala FIN 97 Jc41
Rosal de la Frontera E 51 Bb71
Rosalejo E 45 Cc65
Rosans F 42 Jc51
Rosapenna IRL 9 Cb15
Rosapineta I 150 Eb61
Rosário P 51 Bb69
Rosarno I 164 Gb82
Rosbach vor der Höhe D 134 Cc43
Roscales E 38 Da56
Roşcani MD 173 Fc57
Roşcani RO 174 Cb61
Roscanvel F 26 Db38
Rosche D 119 Dd34
Rosciano I 156 Ec65
Roščino RUS 202 Ea08
Rościszewo PL 122 Hd35
Roscoff F 26 Dc37
Ros Comáin IRL 8 Ca20
Roscommon IRL 8 Ca20
Ros Cré IRL 13 Ca22
Roscrea IRL 13 Ca22
Roščyno RUS 113 Jb59
Rosdorf D 126 Db39
Rose I 164 Gb80
Rosebush GB 14 Dc26
Rosedale Abbey GB 11 Fb18
Rosegreen IRL 13 Ca24
Rosehearty GB 5 Ed07
Roseldorf A 136 Ga49
Rosell E 48 Fd64
Roselle I 155 Dc68
Rosen BG 181 Ed73
Rosenberg D 134 Cd46
Rosenberg D 134 Da47
Rosenbergergut D 136 Fa49
Rosendahl D 125 Ca37
Rosendal FIN 97 Jc40
Rosendal N 78 Ed25
Rosendal N 84 Cb40
Rosenfeld D 142 Cc50
Rosenfors S 103 Ga50
Rosengarten D 118 Db33
Rosengarten D 134 Da47
Rosenheim D 143 Eb52
Rosenow D 119 Ed32
Rosenthal D 126 Cd41
Rosenthal D 128 Fb40
Rosentorp S 87 Fc37
Roses E 41 Hc58
Roseți RO 181 Ed67
Roseto Capo Spulico I 164 Gc78
Roseto degli Abruzzi I 157 Fa69
Roseto Valfortore I 161 Fd73
Rosetti, C.A. RO 176 Ed64
Rosetti, C.A. RO 177 Ga64
Rosheim F 25 Kb37
Rosia I 155 Dc67
Roșia RO 170 Cb57
Roșia RO 175 Db61
Roșia de Amaradia RO 175 Da63
Roșia de Secaș RO 175 Da60
Roșia Montană RO 171 Cd59
Roșia Nouă RO 174 Cb60
Rosica BG 181 Fa68
Rosice CZ 137 Gb47
Rosières F 34 Ja51
Rosières-aux-Salines F 25 Jd37
Rosières-en-Blois F 25 Jc37
Rosieres-en-Santerre F 23 Ha33
Roșiești RO 177 Fb60
Rosignano Marittima I 155 Da66
Rosignano Solvay I 155 Da66
Roșiile RO 175 Da64
Roșiori RO 170 Cb56
Roșiori RO 172 Ed59
Roșiori RO 176 Ed65
Roșiori de Vede RO 180 Dc67
Rositz D 127 Eb41
Roskhill GB 4 Da08
Roskilde DK 109 Eb26
Roskovec AL 182 Ab76
Roskow D 127 Ec36
Roslags-Bro S 96 Ha42
Roslags-Kulla S 96 Ha43
Ros Láir IRL 13 Cd25
Röslau D 135 Ea44
Roslavl' RUS 202 Ec12
Roslev DK 100 Da22
Rosli N 85 Dc35
Rosliston GB 16 Ed24
Rosmalen NL 124 Ba38
Rosmaninhal P 51 Bb66
Ros Mhic Thriúin IRL 13 Cc24
Rosmult IRL 13 Ca23
Rosnay F 29 Gb44
Rosnay-l'Hôpital F 30 Ja38
Rosnowo PL 121 Gb31
Rosochate Kościelne PL 123 Ka34
Rosolina I 150 Ea61
Rosolina Mare I 150 Eb61
Rosolini I 167 Fc88
Rosoman MK 183 Bc75

Rosoy – Sabaudia

Rosoy F 30 Hb39
Rosporden F 27 Dd39
Rossa CH 142 Cc56
Rossåga N 71 Fb21
Rossano I 164 Gc79
Rossano Stazione I 164 Gc79
Rossau D 127 Ed41
Roßbach D 127 Ea40
Roßbach D 135 Ec49
Rössbyn S 94 Ec43
Rosscahill IRL 8 Bc20
Rosscarbery IRL 12 Bc26
Roßdorf D 126 Db42
Roßdorf D 127 Eb36
Roßdorf D 134 Cc45
Rosseland N 92 Cd45
Rosses Point IRL 8 Bd18
Rossett GB 15 Eb22
Rossevatn N 92 Cc45
Rossfjord N 62 Gc10
Rossgeir IRL 9 Cc16
Rossglass GB 9 Da18
Roßhaupten D 142 Dc52
Rossiglione I 148 Cb62
Rossignol F 33 Ga49
Rossinver IRL 8 Ca17
Rossio ao Sul do Tejo P 50 Ad66
Roßla D 127 Dd40
Rossland N 84 Ca38
Rosslare IRL 13 Cd25
Rosslare Harbour IRL 13 Cd25
Roßlau, Dessau- D 127 Eb38
Roßleben D 127 Ea40
Rossnowlagh IRL 8 Ca17
Rossön S 79 Ga28
Ross-on-Wye GB 15 Ec26
Rossoš' RUS 203 Fb13
Rossosz PL 131 Kb37
Rossoszyca PL 129 Hb39
Roßtal D 134 Dc46
Røssvassbukta N 71 Fb22
Rossvika N 70 Ec24
Rossvoll N 67 Gc11
Roßwein D 127 Ed41
Rostadalen N 67 Ha11
Röstånga S 110 Ed55
Rostock D 119 Eb31
Rostov RUS 203 Fa09
Rostov- na-Donu RUS 205 Fc15
Rostrenen F 27 Ea39
Rostrevor GB 9 Da19
Röström S 79 Ga27
Rostudel F 27 Db39
Rosturk IRL 8 Bb19
Rostuša MK 182 Ad74
Røstvollen N 86 Ec34
Roşu MD 177 Fb61
Rösvattnet S 80 Gc29
Rosvik N 66 Fd17
Rosvik S 73 Hd23
Roszczyce PL 121 Gd29
Roszki PL 129 Gd39
Roszki-Wodzki PL 123 Ka34
Rot S 87 Fb37
Rota E 59 Bc76
Rota Greca I 164 Gb79
Rot am See D 134 Db47
Rot an der Rot D 142 Da51
Rotari MD 173 Fd54
Rotava CZ 135 Ec44
Rotberget N 94 Ed39
Rotebro S 96 Gd43
Rotella I 156 Ed68
Rotello I 161 Fc72
Rotenburg an der Fulda D 126 Da41
Rotenburg (Wümme) D 118 Da34
Rotgülden A 143 Ed54
Roth D 135 Dd47
Rotha D 127 Dd39
Rötha D 127 Eb41
Roth an der Our D 133 Bb44
Rothemühl D 120 Fa33
Röthenbach D 135 Dd46
Röthenbach D 142 Da52
Röthenbach im Emmental CH 141 Bd54
Rothenbuch D 134 Cd44
Rothenburg D 127 Ea39
Rothenburg D 128 Fc40
Rothenburg ob der Tauber D 134 Db46
Rothenfels D 134 Da45
Rothenschirmbach D 127 Ea40
Rotherham GB 16 Fa21
Rothes GB 7 Eb08
Rothesay GB 6 Dc13
Rothiesholm GB 5 Ec02
Röthlein D 134 Db44
Rothleiten A 144 Fd54
Rothwell GB 16 Fa20
Rothwell GB 20 Fb25
Rotimlja BIH 158 Hb67
Rotiojoki FIN 82 Kc27
Rotkreuz CH 141 Cb54
Rotnäset S 79 Fd26
Rotonda I 164 Gb78
Rotondella I 162 Gc77
Rótova E 54 Fc69
Rotsjö S 87 Fd32
Rotsund N 62 Ha09
Rotta D 127 Ec39
Rottach-Egern D 143 Ea52
Rott a. Inn D 143 Eb51
Røttangan N 66 Fd15
Röttenbach D 134 Dc45
Röttenbach D 134 Dc47
Rottenbuch D 142 Dc52
Rottenburg D 135 Ea49
Rottenburg am Neckar D 134 Cc49
Rottendorf D 134 Db45
Rottenmann A 144 Fb53
Rotterdam NL 124 Ad37
Rotthalmünster D 143 Ed50
Rottingdean GB 20 Fc30
Röttingen D 134 Da46
Röttle S 103 Fb48
Rottleberode D 127 Dd39
Rottmersleben D 127 Ea37
Rottne S 103 Fc51
Rottneros S 94 Ed42
Rottofreno I 149 Cd61
Rottum NL 117 Bc34
Rottweil D 141 Cb50
Rotunda MD 173 Fa54
Rotunda RO 180 Db67
Roturas E 51 Cb67
Rotvik N 67 Gb12
Rötviken S 79 Fb28
Rotvoll N 78 Ec30
Rötz D 135 Eb47
Rouaine F 43 Kb52
Roubaix F 24 Hb31
Rouchovany CZ 136 Ga48
Roudnice CZ 136 Fb43
Roudouallec F 27 Dd39
Rouen F 23 Gb35
Rouffach F 31 Kb39
Rõuge EST 107 Lb47
Rouge F 28 Ed40
Rougemont F 31 Jd41
Roughburn GB 7 Dd10
Rouillac F 32 Fc47
Rouillé F 32 Fd45
Roujan F 41 Hc54
Roukala FIN 81 Jc27
Roulans F 31 Jd41
Roullet-Saint-Estèphe F 32 Fd48
Roumazières-Loubert F 33 Ga47
Roundstone IRL 8 Bb20
Roundwood IRL 13 Cd22
Roupy F 24 Hb33
Rouravaara FIN 68 Jc14
Rouravaara FIN 68 Jc14
Rousínov CZ 137 Gc47
Roússa GR 185 Ea76
Roussac F 33 Gb46
Rousset-les-Vignes F 42 Jc51
Roussillon F 34 Jb48
Roussillon F 42 Jc53
Roust DK 108 Da26
Rouvray F 30 Hd41
Rouvres-sur-Aube F 30 Jd40
Rouvroy-sur-Audry F 24 Hd33
Rouy F 30 Hc43
Rovačko Trebaljevo MNE 159 Jb68
Rovakka S 74 Jb18
Rovala FIN 74 Kb18
Rovale I 164 Gc80
Rovaniemen maalaiskunta FIN 74 Ka18
Rovaniemi FIN 74 Jd19
Rovanpää FIN 69 Jd15
Rovasenda I 148 Ca59
Rovastinaho FIN 74 Ka20
Rovato I 149 Da59
Rovde N 76 Cb33
Roveň SK 139 Ka47
Roven'ki RUS 203 Fb14
Roverbella I 149 Db60
Rovere I 156 Ed70
Roveredo in Piano I 150 Eb58
Rovereto I 149 Dc58
Roveré Veronese I 149 Dc59
Rövershagen D 119 Eb31
Roverud N 94 Ec40
Rovetta I 149 Da58
Roviés GR 189 Ca84
Rovigo I 150 Dd61
Rovik N 77 Da32
Rovinari RO 175 Cc64
Rovine BIH 152 Gd61
Rovinj HR 150 Ed61
Rovišće HR 152 Gc58
Rovisuvanto FIN 64 Jc09
Rovné CZ 137 Gb46
Rovnoe RUS 203 Fd12
Rovnoje RUS 113 Jb59
Rovon F 35 Jc48
Rovtarica SLO 151 Fa57
Rów PL 120 Fc35
Rowde GB 20 Ed28
Rowland's Gill GB 11 Ed16
Rowsley GB 16 Fa22
Rowy PL 121 Gc29
Roxenbaden S 103 Fd46
Roxförde D 127 Ea36
Roya F 43 Kc51
Royal Leamington Spa GB 20 Fa25
Royal Tunbridge Wells GB 20 Fd29
Royan F 32 Fa47
Royat F 34 Hb47
Roybon F 35 Jc48
Roybridge GB 7 Dd10
Røydland N 92 Cc46
Roydon GB 21 Ga25
Roye F 23 Ha34
Røyelelva N 63 Hb09
Royère-de-Vienne F 33 Gc47
Røyken N 93 Dd42
Röykkä FIN 98 Kb39
Röylä FIN 98 Ka39
Røynestøl N 92 Cd44
Royos E 61 Eb73
Røyrmarka N 70 Ed23
Røyrneset N 64 Jc09
Røyrvik N 78 Fa25
Royston GB 16 Fa21
Royston GB 20 Fc26
Royton GB 16 Ed21
Röyttä FIN 74 Jc21
Røytvoll N 70 Ed24
Royuela E 47 Ed65
Roza BG 180 Eb73
Rozadas E 37 Bd54
Rozadas E 37 Cc54
Rozadio E 38 Db55
Rožaj MNE 159 Jc68
Rožaj MNE 178 Ad70
Rozalimas LT 114 Kb54
Różan PL 122 Jc34
Różaniec PL 139 Kb43
Różanka PL 137 Gb44
Różanki PL 120 Fd35
Różanna PL 121 Ha33
Różańsko PL 120 Fc35
Rožanstvo SRB 178 Ad67
Rozavlea RO 171 Db55
Róża Wielka PL 121 Gb34
Rozay-en-Brie F 23 Ha37
Roždalovice CZ 136 Fd44
Roždestveno RUS 99 Mb41
Rozdil'na UA 204 Ec17
Rozdol'ne UA 205 Fa17
Rozelieures F 25 Jd37
Roželov CZ 136 Fa46
Rožencovo RUS 203 Fc08
Rožēni LV 106 Kc47
Rożental PL 122 Hd32
Rozgarty PL 121 Hb34
Rozier-Côtes-d'Aurec F 34 Hd48
Rózinowo PL 122 Hc35
Rozivka UA 205 Fb16
Rozkopaczew PL 131 Kb39
Rozkoš CZ 136 Ga48
Rožmberk nad Vltavou CZ 136 Fb49
Rožmitál pod Tr. CZ 136 Fa46
Rožňava SK 138 Jb49
Rożniatow PL 129 Hb38
Roznov RO 172 Ec58
Rožnov'e RUS 99 Ma42
Rožnov pod Radhoštěm CZ 137 Hb46
Roznów PL 138 Jb45
Rożnowice PL 138 Jc45
Rożnowo PL 129 Gc36
Rozogi PL 122 Jc32
Rožok RUS 203 Fb09
Rozovec BG 180 Dc72
Rozoy-sur-Serre F 24 Hd34
Rozprza PL 130 Hd40
Rozsály H 147 Kc51
Roztoki Górne PL 106 Kb47
Roztoky CZ 136 Fb44
Rožula LV 106 Kc49
Rozvadov CZ 135 Ec46
Różyńsk Wielki PL 123 Jd32
Różyńsk Wlk. PL 123 Jd30
Rožyšče UA 202 Ea14
Rrogozhinë AL 182 Ab75
Rsavci SRB 178 Bb67
Rsovci SRB 179 Cb69
Rtiščevo RUS 203 Fc11
Rtyně v Podkrkonoší CZ 136 Ga43
Rua P 44 Bb62
Ruanes E 51 Ca67
Ruba BY 202 Eb11
Ruba LV 113 Jd53
Rubāni LV 107 Lc50
Rubbåsen N 67 Gb11
Rubbestad N 67 Gb11
Rubbestadneset N 92 Ca41
Rubcovščina RUS 99 Lc43
Rübeland D 127 Dd39
Rubene LV 106 Kd48
Rubeņi LV 115 Lb53
Rubeži MNE 159 Hd68
Rubí E 49 Gd61
Rubia E 37 Bd57
Rubián E 36 Bc56
Rubiás E 36 Bc55
Rubiás E 36 Bc58
Rubielos Bajos E 53 Ec68
Rubielos de la Cérida E 47 Fa63
Rubielos de Mora E 54 Fb65
Rubiera I 149 Db62
Rubigen CH 141 Bd54
Rubikai LT 113 Jc53
Rubikiai LT 114 La55
Rubkow D 120 Fa31
Rublacedo de Abajo E 38 Dc57
Rublenița MD 173 Fc54
Rubno Wielkopolski PL 122 Hc30
Rubuliai LT 113 Jb54
Rucăr RO 176 Dd63
Rucava LV 113 Jb54
Ruchna PL 131 Jd36
Ruč'i RUS 99 Ld40
Ruciane-Nida PL 122 Jc32
Ruciūnai LT 114 Kc56
Ruč'ji RUS 107 Ma48
Rückersdorf D 135 Dd46
Rucphen NL 124 Ad38
Rud N 93 Dd41
Rud S 94 Fa43
Ruda PL 123 Jd32
Ruda PL 123 Ka32
Ruda PL 131 Jd38
Ruda S 103 Ga51
Rudabánya H 146 Jc50
Ruda-Huta PL 131 Kc39
Rudaičai LT 113 Jc54
Rūdaičiai LT 113 Jb54
Rudakovo RUS 113 Jc58
Ruda Maleniecka PL 130 Ja40
Rudamina LT 114 La58
Rudamina LV 114 Kb59
Ruda nad Moravou CZ 137 Gc45
Rudanmaa FIN 89 Jb35
Rudare SRB 178 Bc69
Rudăria RO 174 Ca64
Ruda Różaniecka PL 139 Kc43
Ruda Śląska PL 138 Hc44
Rudawka PL 123 Kb31
Rudbarži LV 105 Jc52
Rüddingshausen D 126 Cd42
Rude DK 109 Ea27
Rude HR 151 Ga59
Rude LV 105 Jd49
Rude LV 113 Ja53
Ruden A 144 Fc56
Rudersberg D 134 Cd48
Rüdersdorf D 128 Fa36
Rüdershausen D 126 Db39
Ruderting D 135 Ed49
Rüdesheim D 133 Cb44
Rudgalviai LT 113 Jc55
Rudi MD 173 Fb53
Rudíkov CZ 136 Ga47
Rudiliai LT 114 Kd54
Rudilla E 47 Fa63
Rudina HR 151 Fb61
Rüdingsdorf D 128 Fa38
Rudinice MNE 159 Hd67
Rudinka HR 151 Fd62
Rudinovka RUS 107 Ma50
Rūdiškes LT 114 Kd58
Rudiškiai LT 114 Ka53
Rudka PL 122 Jb32
Rudka PL 123 Ka35
Rudka PL 131 Kd39
Rudkøbing DK 109 Dd28
Rudky UA 204 Dd15
Rhuddlan GB 15 Ea22
Rudlaukis LT 113 Jc56
Rudná CZ 136 Fb45
Rudna PL 129 Gb40
Rudn'a RUS 107 Mb51
Rudna S 73 Hb18
Rudna Glava SRB 174 Ca65
Rudňany SK 138 Jc48
Rudna Wielka PL 129 Gb39
Rudnia LT 123 Kd30
Rudnica MNE 159 Ja66
Rudnica PL 128 Fd36
Rudnica SRB 178 Ba68
Rudnik BG 181 Ed72
Rudnik BG 181 Fa71
Rudnik CZ 136 Ga43
Rudnik KSV 178 Ba70
Rudnik PL 121 Hb33
Rudnik PL 130 Jc41
Rudnik PL 131 Ka42
Rudnik PL 131 Kb41
Rudnik PL 137 Hb44
Rudnik SRB 159 Jc64
Rudniki PL 129 Hb41
Rūdninkai LT 114 La59
Rüdnitz D 120 Fa35
Rudnja RUS 202 Eb11
Rudno PL 121 Hb31
Rudno PL 129 Gb40
Rudno PL 131 Ka39
Rudno PL 131 Kb38
Rudno PL 137 Hb43
Rudno RUS 99 Ld43
Rudno SLO 151 Fb57
Rudno SRB 178 Ba68
Rudo BIH 159 Ja65
Rudolfov CZ 136 Fb48
Rudolstadt D 127 Dd42
Rudopolje Bruvanjsko HR 151 Ga63
Rudovci SRB 153 Jc63
Rudovoe RUS 107 Ld48
Rudozem BG 184 Db75
Rudshøgda N 86 Ea38
Rudsjön S 79 Ga28
Rudskoga S 95 Fb44
Rudstorp S 94 Fa42
Ruds Vedby DK 109 Ea26
Rudupiai LT 113 Jd54
Rudy PL 137 Hb44
Rudzāti LV 107 Lb52
Rudžiai LT 114 Kc56
Rudzica PL 138 Hc45
Rudziczka PL 137 Gd43
Rudzienice PL 122 Hd32
Rudzienko PL 130 Jc37
Rudzienko PL 131 Jd36
Rudziši LV 107 Ld52
Rue F 23 Gc32
Ruecas E 51 Ca68
Rueda E 46 Cd61
Rueda de Jalón E 47 Fa60
Rueda de Pisuerga E 38 Da56
Ruelle-sur-Touvre F 32 Fd47
Ruen BG 181 Ed72
Ruerrero E 38 Dc56
Ruesta E 39 Fa57
Ruffano I 163 Hc77
Ruffec F 32 Fd46
Ruffieu F 35 Jc46
Ruffieux F 35 Jd46
Rufford GB 15 Eb21
Rufina I 156 Dd65
Rugāji LV 107 Lc49
Rūgaliai LT 113 Jb56
Rugby GB 20 Fa25
Rugeley GB 16 Ed24
Rugendorf D 135 Dd44
Rugince MK 178 Bd72
Rugineşti RO 172 Eb58
Rugineşti RO 176 Ed61
Ruginoasa RO 172 Ed57
Rügland D 134 Dc46
Rugles F 23 Ga37
Rugsund N 84 Cb34
Rugunj RUS 202 Eb08
Ruha FIN 81 Jb31
Ruhala FIN 89 Jd34
Ruhan' RUS 202 Ec12
Ruhla D 126 Dc41
Ruhland D 128 Fa40
Ruhmannsfelden D 135 Ec48
Ruhnu EST 105 Jd48
Ruhovaara FIN 83 Mb31
Ruhpolding D 143 Eb52
Ruhstorf D 143 Ed50
Ruhwarden D 117 Cc32
Ruidera E 53 Dd69
Ruila EST 98 Kb43
Ruinas I 169 Ca77
Ruinen NL 117 Bd34
Ruissalo FIN 97 Jb39
Rujevac HR 152 Gb61
Rūjiena LV 106 Kd47
Rujišta BIH 158 Hb66
Rujno BG 181 Ec68
Ruka FIN 75 La19
Rukainiai LT 115 Lb58
Rukajärvi FIN 75 La19
Rukavac HR 158 Gb68
Rukla LT 114 Kc57
Rukmaņi LV 107 Ld52
Rukovo RUS 107 Mb52
Ruleva LV 107 Ma52
Rullbo S 87 Fc35
Rulli EST 106 La46
Rully F 23 Ha35
Rülzheim D 133 Cb47
Rum H 145 Gc54
Ruma SRB 153 Jb61
Rumar FIN 97 Ja40
Rumboci BIH 158 Ha65
Rumburgh GB 21 Gb25
Rumburk CZ 128 Fb42
Rumelifeneri TR 186 Fd77
Rumenka SRB 153 Jb60
Rumford GB 18 Db31
Rumia PL 121 Ha29
Rumian PL 122 Hd33
Rumigny F 24 Hd33
Rumilly F 35 Jd46
Rumilly-lès-Vaudes F 30 Hd39
Rümlang CH 141 Cb52
Rumney GB 19 Eb28
Rummu EST 98 Ka43
Rummukka FIN 90 La32
Rumo FIN 82 La27
Rumont F 24 Jb36
Rumpani LV 107 Lb48
Rumšiškės LT 114 Kc57
Rumskulla S 103 Fd49
Rumy PL 122 Jb32
Runcorn GB 15 Ec22
Runcu RO 175 Cc63
Runcu RO 175 Db63
Runcu RO 176 Dd63
Rundāni LV 107 Ma52
Runde N 76 Cb32
Rundfloen N 86 Ed38
Rundhaug N 67 Gd11
Rundhaugen N 71 Fc20
Runding D 135 Ec47
Rundvik S 80 Ha29
Runemo S 87 Ga37
Rungsted DK 109 Ec25
Runhällen S 95 Gb41
Runnabackan IRL 8 Ca20
Runni FIN 82 Kc28
Runów PL 130 Jb37
Runowo PL 122 Ja30
Runsten S 103 Gb52
Runtaleave GB 7 Eb10
Runtuna S 95 Gb45
Ruodusniemi S 68 Hd13
Ruohokangas FIN 69 Kb12
Ruokola FIN 74 Ka21
Ruokalahti FIN 83 Ld31
Ruokee FIN 91 Lc33
Ruokojärvi FIN 68 Jc17
Ruokojärvi FIN 91 Lc33
Ruokojärvi S 73 Ja19
Ruokokoski FIN 90 La32
Ruokola FIN 91 Lc36
Ruokolahti FIN 91 Lc35
Ruokolahti FIN 91 Ld33
Ruokotaipale FIN 91 Lb35
Ruokto S 67 Gd17
Ruolahti FIN 90 Kb35
Ruomi FIN 91 Lb36
Ruoms F 34 Ja51
Ruona FIN 81 Jc31
Ruona FIN 89 Ja37
Ruonlahti FIN 97 Jc39
Ruopsa FIN 74 Kb18
Ruorasmäki FIN 90 Kd34
Ruosniemi FIN 89 Ja36
Ruotaanmäki FIN 82 Kc28
Ruoti I 161 Ga75
Ruotinkylä FIN 82 Kb31
Ruotsalo FIN 81 Jb28
Ruotsinkylä Svenskby FIN 90 Kd38
Ruotsinpyhtää FIN 90 Kd38
Ruottisenharju FIN 75 Kc22
Ruovesi FIN 89 Jd34
Rupa HR 151 Fb60
Rupe HR 157 Ga65
Rupea RO 176 Dd61
Rupit E 49 Ha59
Rupperswil CH 141 Ca53
Ruppertshofen D 134 Da48
Ruppichteroth D 125 Ca41
Ruppovaara FIN 91 Ma32
Ruprechtov CZ 137 Gc47
Rupsa FIN 83 Lb29
Rupt-sur-Moselle F 31 Ka39
Rus RO 171 Da56
Rusalja BG 180 Dd70
Rusalka BG 181 Fc70
Rusănești RO 180 Db67
Rušanj SRB 153 Jc62
Rusca Montană RO 174 Cb61
Ruscova RO 171 Dc55
Rusdal N 92 Cb45
Ruse BG 180 Ea68
Ruše SLO 144 Fd56
Rusele S 80 Gc25
Ruşeni MD 173 Fa54
Ruşeţu RO 176 Ed64
Rusfors S 80 Gd25
Rush IRL 13 Da21
Rushaugen N 66 Ga13
Rushden GB 20 Fb25
Rusi FIN 90 Kc34
Rusiec PL 130 Hc40
Ruşii-Munţi RO 171 Dc58
Rusinovo MK 183 Ca74
Rusinów PL 128 Fd39
Rusinów PL 130 Jb39
Rusinowo PL 120 Fd32
Rusinowo PL 121 Gb34
Rusjaci MK 183 Bb74
Ruska Bela BG 179 Cd70
Ruské SK 139 Kb47
Ruskeala FIN 90 Kc35
Ruski Bród PL 130 Jb40
Ruski Krstur SRB 153 Ja59
Ruskington GB 17 Fc23
Rusko FIN 97 Jb39
Rusko Selo SRB 174 Bb60
Rusksand S 79 Gb29
Rusksele S 80 Gd25
Ruskträsk S 80 Gd25
Ruskulla FIN 97 Jc40
Ruskulova LV 107 Ld50
Rusnė LT 113 Jb56
Rusokastro BG 181 Ed73
Rusovce SK 145 Gd51
Russånes N 71 Fd18
Russar N 85 Db35
Rüsselsheim D 134 Cc44
Russeluft N 63 Hd08
Russelv N 62 Ha08
Russenes N 64 Jb06
Russi I 150 Ea63
Russka RUS 99 Lc42
Russkij Kameškir RUS 203 Fd11
Russkoje RUS 113 Hd58
Russko-Vysockoe RUS 99 Mb40
Russliseter N 85 Dc36
Rust A 145 Gc52
Rust D 141 Ca50
Rustefjelbma N 64 Ka06
Rustrel F 42 Jd53
Rusvekk N 94 Ec40
Ruswil CH 141 Ca54
Ruszów PL 128 Fd40
Rutakoski FIN 90 Kc32
Rutalahti FIN 90 Kc33
Rutalahti FIN 90 Kc36
Rutava FIN 89 Jc37
Rute E 60 Da74
Rute S 104 Ha48
Rüthen D 126 Cc39
Rutherglen GB 10 Dd13
Ruthin GB 15 Eb22
Rüthnick D 119 Ed35
Ruthwell GB 11 Eb16
Rüti CH 142 Cc53
Rutigliano I 162 Gd74
Rutino I 161 Fc77
Rutka-Tartak PL 123 Ka29
Rutki-Kossaki PL 123 Ka34
Rutledal N 84 Ca37
Ruto FIN 81 Ja31
Rutoši SRB 159 Jb66
Rutten NL 116 Bb34
Rutvik S 73 Hd22
Rutwica PL 121 Gb34
Ruuhijärvi FIN 74 Jc18
Ruuhijärvi FIN 90 Kc36
Ruuhilampi FIN 82 La31
Ruuhilampi FIN 90 Kd35
Ruuhimäki FIN 90 Kc33
Ruukki FIN 81 Jd25
Ruunaa FIN 83 Ld27
Ruurlo NL 125 Bd37
Ruusa EST 107 Lc46
Ruuskankylä FIN 82 Ka27
Ruusmäe EST 107 Lc47
Ruutana FIN 82 Kc28
Ruutana FIN 89 Jd35
Ruuvaoja FIN 69 Kc14
Ruvanaho FIN 74 Kd18
Ruvaslahti FIN 83 Lc29
Ruvo del Monte I 161 Ga75
Ruvo di Puglia I 162 Gc74
Ruynes-en-Margeride F 34 Hb49
Ruyuela de Río Franco E 46 Db59
Ruza RUS 202 Ed10
Ruzaevka RUS 203 Fc10
Ružany BY 202 Ea13
Ruzgai LT 113 Jc53
Ružić HR 158 Gb65
Ružica BG 181 Ed69
Ružina LV 107 Lc51
Ružinci BG 179 Cb68
Ružomberok SK 138 Hd47
Ruzsa H 153 Ja57
Ry DK 108 Dc24
Ryå DK 100 Dc20
Rya N 86 Ec35
Ryba RUS 113 Jb57
Rybaki PL 121 Ha30
Rybaki PL 128 Fc38
Rybany SK 137 Hb49
Rybczewice PL 131 Kb40
Rybienko Leśne PL 122 Jc35
Rybinsk RUS 202 Ed09
Rybna PL 138 Hd44
Rybnica Leśna PL 129 Gb42
Rybnik PL 123 Kb33
Rybnik PL 137 Hb44
Rybník CZ 135 Ec46
Rybno PL 122 Hd33
Rybno PL 122 Jb32
Rybno PL 130 Ja37
Rybnoe RUS 203 Fa11
Ryboły PL 123 Kb34
Rybotycze PL 139 Kb45
Rychliki PL 122 Hc31
Rychłocice PL 130 Hc40
Rychnov CZ 128 Fd42
Rychnov nad Kněžnou CZ 137 Gb44
Rychnów PL 129 Ha41
Rychnowo PL 122 Hd32
Rychnowy PL 121 Gd32
Rychtal PL 129 Ha41
Rychtářov CZ 137 Gc47
Rychwał PL 129 Ha38
Ryczów PL 138 Hd44
Ryczywół PL 121 Gc35
Ryczywół PL 130 Jc38
Ryd S 111 Fc53
Ryda S 102 Ed47
Rydaholm S 103 Fb51
Rydal S 102 Ed49
Rydbo S 96 Gd43
Rydboholm S 102 Ed49
Ryde GB 20 Fa30
Rydet S 102 Eb50
Rydland N 85 Ea35
Rydöbruk S 102 Ed51
Rydsgård S 110 Fa56
Rydsnäs S 103 Fd49
Rydułtowy PL 137 Hb44
Rydzewo PL 120 Ga33
Rydzewo PL 122 Jc34
Rydzewo-Świątki PL 123 Jc34
Rydzyna PL 129 Gb39
Rye F 31 Jc43
Rye GB 21 Ga30
Rye N 77 Ea30
Ryen N 92 Cd47
Ryfoss N 85 Db37
Rygge N 93 Ea43
Ryglice PL 138 Jc44
Ryhälä FIN 91 Lb34
Ryhälänmäki FIN 82 Kd27
Ryhäntä FIN 82 La25
Ryjewo PL 121 Hb31
Rykantai LT 114 La58
Rykene N 93 Da46
Ryki PL 131 Jd38
Ryliškiai LT 123 Kc30
Ryl'sk RUS 202 Ed13
Rymań PL 120 Fd31
Rymanów PL 139 Ka45
Rymanów-Zdrój PL 139 Ka45
Rýmařov CZ 137 Gd45
Rymättylä FIN 97 Jb39
Ryn PL 122 Jc31
Rynarcice PL 129 Gb40
Rynarcice PL 137 Gd43
Rynarzewo PL 121 Gd34
Rynie PL 123 Ka30
Rynkänpuoli FIN 74 Kb20
Rynkeby DK 109 Dd26
Rynoltice CZ 128 Fc42
Ryńsk PL 121 Hb34
Ryomgård DK 101 Dd23
Ryönä FIN 82 La30
Ryönänjoki FIN 82 Kc28
Rypefjord N 63 Hd06
Rypin PL 122 Hc34
Rysjedalsvika N 84 Ca36
Ryškėnai LT 113 Jc54
Ryslinge DK 109 Dd27
Ryssby S 103 Fb52
Ryssdal N 84 Cc35
Rystad S 103 Fd46
Rysum D 117 Ca33
Ryszewo PL 129 Gd36
Rytel PL 121 Gd32
Rytilahti FIN 74 Kc18
Rytinki FIN 75 Kc21
Rytky FIN 82 Kc28
Rytky FIN 82 Kd30
Rytkynperä FIN 82 Ka26
Rytro PL 138 Jb46
Rytterne S 95 Ga43
Ryttylä FIN 90 Kb37
Rytwiany PL 130 Jc42
Rywałd PL 122 Hc33
Rywociny PL 122 Ja34
Ryžoviště CZ 137 Gd45
Rząśnik PL 122 Jc35
Rzęczkowo PL 121 Ha34
Rzecznica PL 121 Gc32
Rzeczniów PL 130 Jc40
Rzeczyca PL 130 Ja39
Rzeczyca PL 131 Kb37
Rzeczyca Ziemiańska PL 131 Ka41
Rzęgnowo PL 122 Jb34
Rzejowice PL 130 Hd41
Rzekuń PL 122 Jc34
Rzemień PL 139 Jd43
Rzepedź PL 139 Ka46
Rzepin PL 128 Fc37
Rzepin PL 130 Jc41
Rzerzęczyce PL 130 Hd41
Rzeszów PL 139 Ka44
Ržev RUS 202 Ec10
Rževskoe RUS 113 Jc57
Rzewnie PL 122 Jc35
Rzezawa PL 138 Jb44
Rzgów PL 129 Ha37
Rzgów PL 130 Hd39
Rzucewo PL 121 Ha29
Rzuchów PL 137 Hb44
Rzuców PL 130 Jb40
Ržyščiv UA 204 Ec15

S

Saá E 36 Bc56
Saadet TR 192 Ga81
Sääksjärvi FIN 81 Jd30
Sääksjärvi FIN 89 Jb36
Sääksjärvi FIN 90 Kc38
Sääkskoski FIN 89 Jb36
Sääksmäki FIN 89 Jd36
Saal D 119 Ec30
Saalahti FIN 90 Kb34
Saal an der Donau D 135 Ea48
Saal an der Saale D 134 Db43
Saalbach A 143 Eb53
Saalburg-Ebersdorf D 135 Ea43
Saales F 31 Kb38
Saalfeld D 127 Dd42
Saalfelden am Steinernen Meer A 143 Ec53
Saalow D 127 Ed37
Säämälä FIN 91 Lb36
Saanen CH 141 Bc55
Säänjärvi FIN 91 Lb36
Saara D 127 Eb41
Saaramaa FIN 90 La37
Saarbrücken D 133 Bd46
Saarburg D 133 Bc45
Saare EST 99 Lb44
Sääre EST 105 Jc48
Sääre EST 106 Kb46
Saareküla EST 105 Jd46
Saarela FIN 82 Kc29
Saarela FIN 83 Lc26
Saaren kirkonkylä FIN 91 Ld33
Saarenkylä FIN 74 Ka19
Saarenkylä FIN 82 Ka29
Saarenmaa FIN 89 Ja36
Säärenperä FIN 74 Jd24
Saarensalmi FIN 83 Lb25
Saarepeedi EST 98 Kd45
Saaresmäki FIN 82 Kc26
Saari FIN 90 Kc38
Saari FIN 91 Ld33
Saariharju FIN 74 Kb20
Saarijärvi FIN 82 Kb31
Saarijärvi FIN 89 Jb36
Saari-Kämä FIN 74 Ka19
Saarikas FIN 82 Kc31
Saarikko FIN 89 Jd38
Saarikoski FIN 67 Hb12
Saarikoski FIN 82 Ka25
Saarikoski FIN 89 Ja35
Saarikylä FIN 75 La22
Saarikylät FIN 89 Jd36
Saarinen FIN 82 Kd25
Saario FIN 83 Ma31
Saaripudas FIN 68 Jb16
Saariselkä FIN 69 Ka12
Saarivaara FIN 75 Lb24
Saarivaara FIN 83 Lc30
Saarivaara FIN 83 Ma31
Saarlouis D 133 Bc46
Saarwellingen D 133 Bc46
Saas Almagell CH 148 Bd57
Saas Fee CH 148 Bd57
Saas Grund CH 148 Bd57
Sääskijärvi FIN 74 Kb20
Sääskiniemi FIN 82 La28
Sääskjärvi FIN 90 Kd37
Saastna EST 98 Ka45
Saatağacı TR 185 Eb77
Säätse LV 107 Ld46
Šabac SRB 153 Jb62
Sabadell E 49 Gd61
Şabanözü TR 205 Fa20
Šabany RUS 107 Ma48
Săbăoani RO 172 Ed58
Sabarat F 40 Gb56
Sabaudia I 160 Ec73

Sabbioneta – Saint-Just-en-Chevalet

Sabbioneta I 149 Db61
Sabero E 37 Cd56
Sab Gregório P 36 Ba58
Sabile LV 105 Jd50
Sabiñánigo E 40 Fc58
Sabinares E 53 Ea69
Sabinov SK 138 Jc47
Sabiote E 52 Dc72
Šabla BG 181 Fc69
Sables-d'Or-les-Pins F 26 Ec37
Sablé-sur-Sarthe F 28 Fc40
Sabnie PL 131 Ka36
Såböle S 78 Fa30
Saborsko HR 151 Fd61
Säbrå S 88 Gc32
Sabres F 39 Fb52
Sabro DK 108 Dc24
Sabrosa P 44 Bb61
Sabugal P 45 Bc64
Sabugeiro P 44 Ba63
Sabuncupınar TR 193 Gb82
Säby S 95 Ga43
Säby S 103 Fc48
Säbyggeby S 87 Gb38
Šaca SK 139 Jd49
sa Cabaneta E 57 Hb67
Săcădat RO 170 Cb57
Săcădate RO 175 Db61
Saçaklı TR 191 Eb81
Săcălaşeni RO 171 Da55
Săcălaz RO 174 Bc60
sa Calobra E 57 Hb66
sa Canal E 56 Gc70
Sacañet E 54 Fb66
Săcăşeni RO 171 Cc55
Sacavém P 50 Aa68
Sacecorbo E 47 Eb63
Saceda E 37 Ca57
Sacedón E 47 Ea64
Săcel RO 171 Dc55
Săcel RO 175 Dc60
Săcele RO 176 Ea62
Săcele RO 177 Fc66
Săcelu RO 175 Cd63
Săceni RO 175 Dc66
Saceruela E 52 Cd69
Sachsen D 134 Dc47
Sachsenbrunn D 135 Dd43
Sachsenburg A 143 Ed55
Sachsenhagen D 126 Da36
Sachsenheim D 134 Cd48
Sacile I 150 Eb58
Šack BY 202 Ea13
Šack RUS 203 Fb11
Šac'k UA 202 Dd14
Saclas F 29 Gd38
Sacos E 36 Ad56
Sacoşu Turcesc RO 174 Bd61
Sacquenay F 30 Jb41
Sacramenia E 46 Db61
Sacu RO 174 Ca61
Săcueni RO 170 Cb56
Săcuieu RO 171 Cc57
Sada E 36 Ba54
Sádaba E 39 Ed58
Sadaclia MD 177 Fd60
Sadala EST 98 La43
Sadali I 169 Cb78
Sadelkow D 120 Fa33
Sadîc MD 177 Fc60
Sădievo BG 180 Ea72
Sadıkhacı TR 199 Hb88
Sadıkkırı TR 193 Gb84
Sadikov Bunar SRB 179 Ca69
Sadina BG 180 Eb69
Sadjem S 73 Hc18
Sadki PL 121 Gd34
Sadkowice PL 130 Jb38
Sadkowice PL 131 Jd40
Sadlinki PL 121 Hb32
Sadłowo PL 122 Hc34
Sadova MD 173 Fc57
Sadova RO 172 Ea56
Sadova RO 179 Da67
Sadovec BG 179 Da69
Sadovo BG 180 Db73
Sadovo BG 181 Fa71
Sadovoe MD 173 Fb55
Sadovoe RUS 113 Jc59
Sadovoe RUS 113 Jd58
Sadovoe RUS 113 Jd59
Sadovoe RUS 203 Ga14
Sądów PL 128 Fc37
Sadów PL 130 Hc42
Sadowne PL 123 Jd35
Sadu RO 175 Db62
Sädvaluspen S 71 Ga20
Sady PL 130 Jb39
Sæbe N 84 Cd37
Sæbø N 76 Cc33
Sæbø N 84 Ca38
Sæbøvik N 92 Ca41
Sæby DK 101 Dd20
Sæby DK 109 Ea26
Sædballe DK 109 Dd28
Săedinenie BG 180 Db73
Săedinenie BG 180 Dc73
Săedinenie BG 181 Ec71
Saelices E 53 Ea66
Saelices de Mayorga E 37 Cd58
Sælvig DK 109 Dd25
Saerbeck D 125 Cb37
Særslev DK 108 Dc26
Sæteråsen N 78 Eb28
Sætervika N 78 Ea26
Sætra N 62 Gb10
Sætran N 78 Ed26
Sætre N 86 Ec38
Sætre N 86 Eb37
Saeul L 133 Bb44
Sævareid N 84 Cb40
Sævråsvåg N 84 Ca38
Safa TR 192 Ga81
Safaalan TR 186 Fb76
Safara P 51 Bb71
Säffle S 94 Ed44
Saffré F 28 Ed41
Saffron Walden GB 20 Fd26
Safien-Platz CH 142 Cc55
Safonovo RUS 202 Ec11
Šafov CZ 136 Ga48
Safranbolu TR 205 Fa20
Säfsnäs S 95 Fb41
Sâg RO 171 Cc57
Şag RO 174 Bc61
Sagadi EST 98 Kd41
Sagaidac MD 173 Fd59
Sagallos E 45 Ca59
Sağancı TR 191 Ec84
Sagard D 120 Fa30
Sagbakken N 86 Ec37
Săgeata RO 176 Ed64
Sageika GR 188 Ba85
Sågen S 95 Fb40
Sagfjorden N 66 Fd16
Saggrenda N 93 Dc42
Sağılar TR 192 Fc81
Sağırlar TR 192 Fb83
Sagmoen N 71 Ga18
Sågmyra S 95 Fd39
Sagna RO 172 Ed58
Sągnity PL 122 Ja30
Sagone F 154 Ca70
Sagra E 55 Fc70
Sagrado I 150 Ed58
Sağrak TR 199 Gd89
Sagres P 58 Aa74
Sağtamtaş TR 185 Ec78
Şagu RO 174 Bd60
Sagunt E 54 Fc67
Sagunto E 54 Fc67
Sagvåg N 92 Ca41
Ságvar H 145 Hb55
Sahagún E 37 Cd58
Sahalahti FIN 90 Ka35
Sahankylä FIN 89 Jb33
Saharna Nouă MD 173 Fd56
Sahăteni RO 176 Ec64
Sahavaara S 68 Ja16
Sahechores E 37 Cd57
Sahilkent TR 199 Gb93
Şahin TR 185 Ec77
Şahin TR 192 Ga83
Şahinli TR 185 Eb80
Şahinyurdu TR 186 Fd79
Sahloinen FIN 90 Kb33
Şahmelek TR 186 Fb80
Şahmelek TR 187 Gb79
Sahrajärvi FIN 90 Ka32
Sahryń PL 131 Kd41
Šahty RUS 205 Fc15
Sahune F 42 Jc51
Šahun'ja RUS 203 Fc08
Šahy SK 146 Hc51
Saignelègiers CH 141 Bc53
Saignes F 33 Ha48
Saignon F 42 Jc53
Saija FIN 69 Kd16
Säijä FIN 89 Jd36
Saijanlahti FIN 83 Lb31
Saikari FIN 82 Kd30
Säikkä FIN 75 Kd20
Saikkola FIN 91 Lb35
Sailer TR 192 Fb87
Saillagouse F 41 Gd58
Saillans F 35 Jc50
Saimaanharju FIN 91 Lb35
Säimen FIN 91 Lc32
Sains-en-Amiénois F 23 Gd33
Sains-Richaumont F 24 Hc33
Saint Abbs GB 11 Ed13
Saint-Affrique F 41 Hb53
Saint-Agil F 29 Ga39
Saint-Agnan F 30 Hd44
Saint Agnes GB 18 Da31
Saint-Agrève F 34 Ja49
Saint-Aignan F 29 Gb42
Saint-Aignan F 40 Gb53
Saint-Aignan-le-Jaillard F 29 Gd40
Saint-Aignan-sur-Roë F 28 Fa40
Saint-Aigulin F 32 Fc49
Saint-Alban F 26 Eb38
Saint Albans GB 20 Fc27
Saint-Alban-sur-Limagnole F 34 Hc50
Saint-Allouestre F 27 Eb40
Saint-Amand-de-Coly F 33 Gb49
Saint-Amand-en-Puisaye F 30 Hb41
Saint-Amandin F 33 Ha48
Saint-Amand-les-Eaux F 24 Hb31
Saint-Amand-Longpré F 29 Gb41
Saint-Amand-Montrond F 29 Ha44
Saint-Amand-sur-Fion F 24 Ja37
Saint-Amans F 34 Hc50
Saint-Amans-de-Mounis F 41 Hb54
Saint-Amans-des-Cots F 33 Ha50
Saint-Amans-Soult F 41 Ha54
Saint-Amant-Roche-Savine F 34 Hc47
Saint-Amant-Tallende F 34 Hb47
Saint-Ambroix F 42 Ja52
Saint-Amé F 31 Ka39
Saint-Amour F 31 Jc44
Saint-Andiol F 42 Jb53
Saint-André-de-Corcy F 34 Jb46
Saint-André-de-Cubzac F 32 Fb50
Saint-André-de-l'Eure F 23 Gb37
Saint-André-de-Sangonis F 41 Hc54
Saint-André-de-Valborgne F 41 Hd52
Saint-André-les-Alpes F 43 Kb52
Saint Andrews GB 7 Ec12
Saint-Angeau F 32 Fd47
Saint-Angel F 33 Gd48
Saint Ann's GB 11 Eb15
Saint-Anne GBA 26 Ec34
Saint-Anthème F 34 Hd47
Saint-Antoine F 154 Cb70
Saint-Antoine l'Abbaye F 35 Jc48
Saint-Antoine-sur-l'Isle F 32 Fd49
Saint-Antonin-Noble-Val F 40 Gc52
Saint-Antonius B 124 Ad39
Saint-Août F 29 Gd44
Saint-Apollinaire F 30 Jb41
Saint-Apollinaire F 35 Ka50
Saint-Arcons-d'Allier F 34 Hc49
Saint-Arnoult-des-Bois F 29 Gb38
Saint Arvans GB 19 Eb27
Saint Asaph GB 15 Ea22
Saint-Astier F 33 Ga49
Saint Athan GB 19 Ea28
Saint-Auban F 42 Ka52
Saint-Auban F 43 Kb53
Saint-Auban-sur-l'Ouvèze F 42 Jc51
Saint Aubin CH 141 Bb54
Saint Aubin CH 141 Bc54
Saint-Aubin F 30 Jb42
Saint-Aubin F 39 Fb54
Saint-Aubin d'Aubigné F 28 Ed39
Saint-Aubin-des-Châteaux F 28 Ed40
Saint-Aubin-des-Coudrais F 29 Ga39
Saint-Aubin-du-Cormier F 28 Fa39
Saint-Aubin-lès-Elbeuf F 23 Ga35
Saint-Aubin-sur-Aire F 24 Jb37
Saint-Aubin-sur-Loire F 30 Hc44
Saint-Aubin-sur-Mer F 22 Fc35
Saint-Augustin F 33 Gc48
Saint-Augustin-des-Bois F 28 Fb41
Saint-Aulaye F 32 Fd49
Saint Austell GB 18 Db31
Saint-Avit F 33 Ha46
Saint-Avit-de-Tardes F 33 Gd46
Saint-Avold F 25 Ka35
Saint-Aygulf F 43 Kb54
Saint-Barthélemy F 27 Ea40
Saint-Barthélémy-d'Anjou F 28 Fb41
Saint-Barthélemy-le-Plain F 34 Jb49
Saint-Baudille-et-Pipet F 35 Jd50
Saint-Bauzille-de-Montmel F 41 Hd53
Saint-Bauzille-de-Putois F 41 Hd53
Saint-Beat F 40 Ga56
Saint-Beauzély F 41 Hb52
Saint-Beauzire F 34 Hb48
Saint Bees GB 10 Ea18
Saint-Benin-d'Azy F 30 Hb43
Saint-Benoit F 35 Jc47
Saint-Benoit-des-Ondes F 22 Ed37
Saint-Benoit-du-Sault F 33 Gb45
Saint-Benoit-en-Woëvre F 25 Jc36
Saint-Benoit-sur-Loire F 29 Gd40
Saint-Bernard F 35 Jd48
Saint-Berthevin F 28 Fb39
Saint-Bertrand-de-Comminges F 40 Ga56
Saint-Blaise-la-Roche F 25 Kb37
Saint-Blimont F 23 Gc32
Saint-Blin F 30 Jb38
Saint-Bonnet F 35 Ka50
Saint-Bonnet-de-Joux F 30 Ja44
Saint-Bonnet-le-Château F 34 Hd48
Saint-Bonnet-le-Froid F 34 Ja49
Saint Boswells GB 11 Ec14
Saint-Brelade GBJ 26 Ec36
Saint-Brévin-les-Pins F 27 Ec42
Saint Briavels GB 19 Ec27
Saint-Brice-Courcelles F 24 Hc35
Saint-Brice-en-Cógles F 28 Fa38
Saint Brides GB 18 Db27
Saint-Brieuc F 26 Eb38
Saint-Bris-le-Vineux F 30 Hc40
Saint-Brisson F 30 Hd42
Saint Buryan GB 18 Da32
Saint-Calais F 29 Ga40
Saint-Cannat F 42 Jc54
Saint-Caprais F 29 Gd43
Saint-Capraise-de-Lalinde F 33 Ga50
Saint-Cast-le-Guildo F 26 Ec37
Saint Catherines GB 6 Dc12
Saint-Céneri-le-Gérei F 28 Fc38
Saint-Céré F 33 Gd50
Saint Cergue CH 140 Ba55
Saint-Cernin F 33 Ha49
Saint-Cernin-de-l'Herm F 33 Gb51
Saint-Chamant F 33 Gd49
Saint-Chamas F 42 Jc54
Saint-Chamond F 34 Ja48
Saint-Chaptes F 42 Ja53
Saint-Chély-d'Apcher F 34 Hc50
Saint-Chély-d'Aubrac F 34 Hb51
Saint-Chéron F 29 Gd38
Saint-Chinian F 41 Hb55
Saint-Christol F 42 Jd52
Saint-Christol-lès-Alès F 41 Hd52
Saint-Christoly-Médoc F 32 Fb48
Saint-Christophe-de-Double F 32 Fc49
Saint-Christophe-du-Ligneron F 28 Ed43
Saint-Christophe-en-Brionnais F 34 Hd45
Saint-Christophe-en-Oisans F 35 Ka49
Saint-Ciers-Champagne F 32 Fc48
Saint-Ciers-du-Taillon F 32 Fb49
Saint-Cirgues-de-Jordanne F 33 Ha49
Saint-Cirgues-en-Montagne F 34 Hd50
Saint-Cirq-Lapopie F 33 Gc51
Saint-Clair-sur-Epte F 23 Gc36
Saint-Clar F 40 Ga53
Saint-Clar-de-Rivière F 40 Gb55
Saint-Claude F 31 Jd44
Saint-Claud-sur-le-Son F 32 Fd47
Saint Clears GB 18 Dc27
Saint-Clement F 30 Hb39
Saint-Clément F 33 Gc48
Saint-Clément-des-Baleines F 32 Ed45
Saint-Clément-sur-Durance F 35 Kb50
Saint-Clet F 26 Ea37
Saint-Cloud F 29 Gb39
Saint-Colombier F 27 Eb41
Saint Columb Major GB 18 Db31
Saint Combs GB 5 Ed07
Saint-Côme-d'Olt F 34 Hb51
Saint-Cosme-en-Vairais F 28 Fd39
Saint-Crepin F 23 Gd35
Saint-Cyprien F 33 Gb50
Saint-Cyprien F 34 Hd47
Saint-Cyprien F 41 Hb57
Saint-Cyprien-Plage F 41 Hb57
Saint-Cyr-en-Val F 29 Gc40
Saint-Cyr-les-Colons F 30 Hc40
Saint Cyrus GB 7 Ed10
Saint-Dalmas-de-Tende F 43 Kd52
Saint-Dalmas-le-Selvage F 43 Kb51
Saint David's GB 14 Db26
Saint-Denis F 23 Gd36
Saint-Denis-de-Gastines F 28 Fb38
Saint-Denis-de-l'Hotel F 29 Gd40
Saint-Denis-de-Pile F 32 Fc50
Saint-Denis-d'Oléron F 32 Ed46
Saint-Denis-d'Orques F 28 Fc39
Saint Dennis GB 18 Db31
Saint-Denoual F 26 Ec38
Saint-Désiré F 29 Ha44
Saint-Didier-en-Velay F 34 Ja48
Saint-Dié-des-Vosges F 31 Ka38
Saint-Dier-d'Auvergne F 34 Hc47
Saint-Disdier F 35 Jd50
Saint-Dizier F 24 Ja37
Saint-Dizier-Leyrenne F 33 Gc46
Saint-Dolay F 27 Ec41
Saint-Domineuc F 28 Ed38
Saint-Donat-sur-l'Herbasse F 34 Jb49
Saint-Doulchard F 29 Gd42
Saint-Dyé-sur-Loire F 29 Gc41
Sainte-Anne-d'Auray F 27 Ea40
Sainte-Bazeille F 32 Fd51
Sainte-Cécile-d'Andorge F 41 Hd52
Sainte-Cécile-les-Vignes F 42 Jb52
Sainte-Colombe F 23 Ga36
Sainte-Colombe F 30 Hb42
Sainte Croix CH 141 Bb54
Sainte-Croix F 35 Jc50
Sainte-Croix-de-Verdon F 42 Ka53
Sainte-Croix-du-Mont F 32 Fc51
Sainte-Croix-en-Plaine F 31 Kb39
Sainte-Croix-Volvestre F 40 Gb56
Sainte-Engrace F 39 Fb56
Sainte-Enimie F 34 Hc51
Sainte-Eulalie F 34 Hd50
Sainte-Eulalie-d'Olt F 34 Hb51
Sainte-Eulalie-en-Royans F 35 Jc49
Sainte-Féréole F 33 Gc49
Sainte-Feyre F 33 Gd46
Sainte-Fortunade F 33 Gc49
Sainte-Foy de Morlaàs F 40 Fc55
Sainte-Foy-la-Grande F 32 Fd50
Sainte-Foy-l'Argentière F 34 Ja47
Sainte-Foy-Tarentaise F 35 Kb47
Sainte-Gauburge-Sainte-Colombe F 22 Fd37
Sainte-Geneviève des-Bois F 23 Gd37
Sainte-Geneviève-des Bois F 29 Ha40
Sainte-Geneviève-sur-Argence F 33 Ha50
Saint-Egrève F 35 Jd48
Sainte-Hélène F 32 Fb50
Sainte-Hermine F 28 Fa44
Sainte-Jalle F 42 Jc51
Sainte-Livrade-sur-Lot F 40 Ga52
Saint-Elix-Theux F 40 Fd55
Saint-Eloy-les-Mines F 33 Ha45
Sainte-Lucie-de-Porto-Vecchio F 154 Cb72
Sainte-Lucie-de-Tallano F 154 Cb71
Sainte-Marie F 34 Hb50
Sainte-Marie-aux-Mines F 31 Kb38
Sainte-Marie-de-Campan F 40 Fd56
Sainte-Marie-de-Ré F 32 Fa46
Sainte-Marie-du-Ménez-Hom F 27 Dc39
Sainte-Marie-du-Mont F 22 Fa35
Sainte-Maure-de-Touraine F 29 Ga43
Sainte-Maxime F 43 Kb54
Sainte-Menehould F 24 Ja36
Sainte-Mère F 40 Ga53
Sainte-Mère-Église F 22 Fa35
Saint-Emiland F 30 Ja43
Saint-Émilion F 32 Fc50
Sainte-Montaine F 29 Gd41
Sainteny F 22 Fa35
Sainte-Odile F 25 Kb37
Saint-Epain F 29 Ga42
Sainte-Pazanne F 28 Ed42
Sainte-Erme-Outre-et-Ramecourt F 24 Hc34
Saintes F 32 Fb47
Sainte-Sabine F 30 Ja42
Sainte-Savine F 30 Hd38
Sainte-Scolasse-sur-Sarthe F 28 Fd38
Sainte-Sévère-sur-Indre F 29 Gd44
Sainte-Sigolene F 34 Ja48
Saintes-Maries-de-la-Mer F 42 Ja54
Saint-Esteban F 39 Fa55
Saint-Estèphe F 32 Fb49
Saint-Estève F 41 Hb57
Saint-Estève F 42 Jc52
Sainte-Suzanne F 28 Fc39
Sainte-Thorette F 29 Gd42
Saint-Etienne F 34 Ja48
Saint-Etienne-de-Baïgorry F 39 Ed55
Saint-Etienne-de-Cuines F 35 Ka48
Saint-Etienne-de-Fursac F 33 Gc46
Saint-Etienne-de-Montluc F 28 Ed42
Saint-Etienne-de-Saint-Geoirs F 35 Jc48
Saint-Etienne-des-Sorts F 42 Jb52
Saint-Étienne-de-Tinée F 43 Kc51
Saint-Etienne-du-Bois F 35 Jc45
Saint-Etienne-du-Rouvray F 23 Gb35
Saint-Etienne-en-Dévoluy F 35 Jd50
Saint-Etienne-Estréchoux F 41 Hb54
Saint-Etienne-les-Orgues F 42 Jd52
Sainte-Vertu F 30 Hc40
Saint-Evroult-Notre-Dame-du-Bois F 22 Fd37
Saint-Fargeau F 30 Hb41
Saint-Félicien F 34 Ja49
Saint-Félix F 32 Fb46
Saint-Félix-de-Reillac F 33 Ga49
Saint-Félix-de-Sorgues F 41 Hb53
Saint-Félix-de-Villadeix F 33 Ga50
Saint-Félix-Lauragais F 41 Gd55
Saint Fergus GB 5 Fa08
Saint-Ferme F 32 Fd51
Saintfield GB 9 Da18
Saint Fillans GB 7 Ea11
Saint-Firmin F 35 Ka50
Saint-Florent F 154 Cb68
Saint-Florent-des-Bois F 28 Fa44
Saint-Florentin F 30 Hc39
Saint-Florent-le-Vieil F 28 Fa42
Saint-Florent-sur-Cher F 29 Gd43
Saint-Flour F 34 Hb49
Saint-Flovier F 29 Gb43
Saint-Folquin F 21 Gd30
Saint-Fort-sur-Gironde F 32 Fb48
Saint-Fort-sur-le-Né F 32 Fc48
Saint-Fraigne F 32 Fc46
Saint-Fraimbault F 28 Fb38
Saint-Front-sur-Lémance F 33 Gb51
Saint-Fulgent F 28 Fa43
Saint-Galmier F 34 Ja47
Saint-Gatien-des-Bois F 22 Fd35
Saint-Gaudens F 40 Ga56
Saint-Gaultier F 29 Gb44
Saint-Gély-du-Fesc F 41 Hd54
Saint-Genest-Malifaux F 34 Ja48
Saint-Geneviève F 23 Gd35
Saint-Gengoux-le-National F 30 Ja44
Saint-Geniès F 33 Gb49
Saint-Genies-de-Saintonge F 32 Fb48
Saint-Geniès-des-Mourgues F 41 Hd54
Saint-Geniez-d'Olt F 34 Hb51
Saint-Génis-des Fontaines F 41 Hb57
Saint-Genis-Laval F 34 Jb47
Saint-Genis-Pouilly F 35 Jd45
Saint-Genix-sur-Guiers F 35 Jc47
Saint Gennys GB 18 Dc30
Saint George CH 140 Ba55
Saint-George-Motel F 23 Gb37
Saint-Georges-d'Aurac F 34 Hc49
Saint-Georges-de-Commiers F 35 Jd49
Saint-Georges-de-Didonne F 32 Fa47
Saint-Georges-de-Noisne F 32 Fc45
Saint-Georges-d'Oléron F 32 Fa46
Saint-Georges-en-Couzan F 34 Hd47
Saint-Georges-les-Baillargeux F 28 Fd44
Saint-Georges-les-Landes F 33 Gb45
Saint-Georges-s.M. B 124 Ba41
Saint-Georges-sur-la-Prée F 29 Gc42
Saint-Georges-sur-Loire F 28 Fb42
Saint-Gérand F 27 Eb39
Saint-Gérand-le-Puy F 34 Hc45
Saint-Germain F 29 Ga44
Saint-Germain-Chassenay F 30 Hc43
Saint-Germain-de-Calberte F 41 Hd52
Saint-Germain-de-Confolens F 33 Ga46
Saint-Germain-de-Coulamer F 28 Fc39
Saint-Germain-de-la-Coudre F 29 Ga39
Saint-Germain-de-la-Rivière F 32 Fc50
Saint-Germain-des-Fossés F 34 Hc45
Saint-Germain-de-Tallevende F 22 Fb37
Saint-Germain-du-Bois F 30 Jb43
Saint-Germain-du-Plain F 30 Jb43
Saint-Germain-du-Puy F 29 Ha42
Saint-Germain-en-Laye F 23 Gd37
Saint-Germain-Laval F 34 Hd46
Saint-Germain-Lavolps F 33 Gd47
Saint-Germain-Lembron F 34 Hb48
Saint-Germain-les-Arlay F 31 Jc43
Saint-Germain-les-Belles F 33 Gc47
Saint-Germain-l'Herm F 34 Hc48
Saint-Germer-de-Fly F 23 Gc35
Saint-Gervais-d'Auvergne F 33 Ha46
Saint-Gervais-de-Vic F 29 Ga40
Saint-Gervais-la-Forêt F 29 Gb41
Saint-Gervais-les-Bains F 35 Kb46
Saint-Gervais-les-Trois-Clochers F 28 Fd43
Saint-Gervais-sur-Mare F 41 Hb54
Saint-Géry F 32 Fd50
Saint-Géry F 33 Gc51
Saint-Gildas-de-Rhuys F 27 Eb41
Saint-Gildas-des-Bois F 27 Ec41
Saint-Gilles F 22 Fa36
Saint-Gilles F 28 Ed39
Saint-Gilles F 28 Fd42
Saint-Gilles F 42 Ja54
Saint-Gilles-Croix-de-Vie F 27 Ec44
Saint-Gilles-Pligeaux F 26 Ea38
Saint-Gingolph F 31 Kb44
Saint-Girons F 40 Gb56
Saint-Girons-en-Marensin F 39 Fa53
Saint-Girons-Plage F 39 Ed53
Saint-Gobain F 24 Hb34
Saint-Gondon F 29 Ha40
Saint-Gondran F 28 Ed39
Saint-Gonnery F 27 Eb39
Saint-Gravé F 27 Ec40
Saint-Guénolé F 27 Dc40
Saint-Guilhem-le-Désert F 41 Hc53
Saint-Guillaume F 35 Jc49
Saint-Haon-le-Châtel F 34 Hd46
Saint Harmon GB 15 Ea25
Saint Helens GB 15 Ec21
Saint-Helier GBJ 26 Ec36
Saint-Hilaire F 41 Ha56
Saint-Hilaire-Bonneval F 33 Gb47
Saint-Hilaire-de-Riez F 27 Ec44
Saint-Hilaire-des-Loges F 32 Fb45
Saint-Hilaire-de-Villefranche F 32 Fb47
Saint-Hilaire-du-Harcouët F 28 Fa38
Saint-Hilaire-du-Rosier F 35 Jc49
Saint-Hilaire-Foissac F 33 Gd48
Saint-Hilaire-Fontaine F 30 Hc43
Saint-Hilaire-la-Pallud F 32 Fb45
Saint-Hilaire-le-Château F 33 Gc46
Saint-Hilaire-le-Grand F 24 Hd35
Saint-Hilaire-Petitville F 22 Fa35
Saint-Hippolyte F 31 Ka41
Saint-Hippolyte F 31 Kb38
Saint-Hippolyte-du-Fort F 41 Hd53
Saint-Honoré-les-Bains F 30 Hc43
Saint-Hubert B 132 Ba43
Saint-Hubert F 28 Fd40
Saint Imier CH 141 Bc53
Saint-Inglevert F 21 Gc30
Saint-Ismier F 35 Jd48
Saint Ives GB 18 Da32
Saint Ives GB 20 Fc25
Saint-Jacques I 148 Bd58
Saint-Jacut-de-la-Mer F 26 Ec38
Saint-Jacut-du-Mené F 27 Eb39
Saint-James F 28 Fa38
Saint-Jean F 42 Ka51
Saint-Jean-Brévelay F 27 Eb40
Saint-Jean-d'Angely F 32 Fb46
Saint-Jean-d'Angle F 32 Fa47
Saint-Jean-d'Ardières F 34 Ja45
Saint-Jean-d'Avelanne F 35 Jd47
Saint-Jean-de-Barrou F 41 Hb56
Saint-Jean-de-Belleville F 35 Ka47
Saint-Jean-de-Blaignac F 32 Fc50
Saint-Jean-de Bonneval F 30 Hd39
Saint-Jean-de-Bournay F 34 Jb47
Saint-Jean-de-Côle F 33 Ga48
Saint-Jean-de-Daye F 22 Fa35
Saint-Jean-de-Durfort F 42 Jc52
Saint-Jean-de-Gonville F 35 Jd45
Saint-Jean-de-Losne F 30 Jb42
Saint-Jean-de-Luz F 39 Ed55
Saint-Jean-de-Maruéjols F 42 Ja52
Saint-Jean-de-Maurienne F 35 Ka48
Saint-Jean-de-Monts F 27 Ec43
Saint-Jean-de-Niost F 35 Jc46
Saint-Jean-de-Sauves F 28 Fd43
Saint-Jean-des-Baisants F 22 Fb36
Saint-Jean-de-Sixt F 35 Ka46
SaintJean-de-Verges F 40 Gc56
Saint-Jean-d'Illac F 32 Fb50
Saint-Jean-du-Bruel F 41 Hc53
Saint-Jean-du-Doigt F 26 Dd37
Saint-Jean-du-Gard F 41 Hd52
Saint-Jean-en-Royans F 35 Jc49
Saint-Jean-la-Rivière F 43 Kc52
Saint-Jean-le-Blanc F 29 Gc40
Saint-Jean-Pied-de-Port F 39 Fa56
Saint-Jean-Poutge F 40 Fd54
Saint-Jean-Saint-Maurice-sur-Loire F 34 Hd46
Saint-Jean-sur-Reyssouze F 30 Jb44
Saint-Jeoire F 35 Ka45
Saint-Jeure-d'Ay F 34 Jb49
Saint-Joachim F 27 Ec42
Saint John GBJ 26 Ec35
Saint John's Chapel GB 11 Ed17
Saint John's GB 10 Dc19
Saint-Jorès F 22 Fa35
Saint-Jory F 40 Gb54
Saint-Jouin F 22 Fd34
Saint-Jouin-de Marnes F 28 Fc43
Saint-Juan F 31 Ka41
Saint-Juéry F 41 Gd53
Saint-Julia F 41 Gd54
Saint-Julien F 31 Jc44
Saint-Julien F 35 Ka50
Saint-Julien Beychevelle F 32 Fb49
Saint-Julien-Chapteuil F 34 Hd49
Saint-Julien-de-Jonzy F 34 Hd45
Saint-Julien-de-Vouvantes F 28 Fa41
Saint-Julien-du Sault F 30 Hb39
Saint-Julien-en-Born F 39 Fa53
Saint-Julien-en-Genevois F 35 Jd45
Saint-Julien-en-Quint F 35 Jc50
Saint-Julien-l'Ars F 29 Ga44
Saint-Julien-le-Faucon F 22 Fd36
Saint-Julien-Molins-Molette F 34 Ja48
Saint-Julien-près-Bort F 33 Ha48
Saint-Julien-sur-Cher F 29 Gc42
Saint-Junien F 33 Ga47
Saint-Junien-la-Bregère F 33 Gc46
Saint-Junien-la-Bregère F 33 Gc47
Saint-Just F 29 Ha43
Saint Just GB 18 Cd32
Saint-Just-en-Chaussée F 23 Gd34
Saint-Just-en-Chevalet F 34 Hd46

San Pietro Vernótico – Sarleinsbach

San Pietro Vernótico I 162 Hb76
San Polo d'Enza I 149 Da62
San Presto I 156 Eb67
San Priamo I 169 Cb79
Sanquhar GB 10 Ea15
San Quirico d'Orcia I 156 Dd67
San Rafael E 46 Db63
San Remo I 43 La52
San Román E 37 Cc58
San Román de Hornija E 45 Cc61
San Román de la Cuba E 37 Cd58
San Román de los Montes E 46 Cd65
San Romolo I 43 Kd52
San Roque E 38 Da54
San Roque E 59 Cb78
San Roque (Coristanco) E 36 Ad54
San Roque (Padrenda) E 36 Ba58
San Roque Torre Guadiaro E 59 Cb77
San Rufo I 161 Fd76
Sansac-de-Marmiesse F 33 Ha50
San Sadurniño E 36 Bb53
Sansais F 32 Fb45
San Salvador E 36 Bb54
San Salvador de Cantamuda E 38 Da56
San Salvatore I 169 Bd77
San Salvatore Monferrato I 148 Ca61
San Salvatore Telesino I 161 Fb74
San Salvo I 161 Fc71
San Salvo Marina I 161 Fc71
Sansarak TR 187 Gb79
San Sebastian de Garabandal E 38 Db55
San Sebastián de los Ballesteros E 60 Cd73
San Sebastián de los Reyes E 46 Dc64
San Sebastián = Donostia E 39 Ec55
San Sebastiano Curone I 148 Cb61
San Secondo Parmense I 149 Da61
Sansepolcro I 156 Ea66
San Severino Lucano I 162 Gb77
San Severino Marche I 156 Ec67
San Severo I 161 Fd72
San Silvestre de Guzmán E 58 Ba73
Sânsimion RO 176 Ea60
Sanski Most BIH 152 Gc62
Sansol E 39 Eb57
San Sosti I 164 Gb79
San Sperate I 169 Ca79
Șanț RO 172 Dd56
Santa Agata de' Goti I 161 Fb74
Santa Agata del Bianco I 164 Gb84
Santa Agata di Esaro I 164 Gb79
Santa Agata di Militello I 167 Fb84
Santa Agata di Puglia I 161 Fd74
Santa Agata Feltria I 156 Ea65
Santa Agnès de Corona E 56 Gc69
Santa Amalia E 51 Ca68
Santa Ana E 53 Eb70
Santa Ana E 53 Ec69
Santa Ana E 60 Db74
Santa Bárbara E 54 Ed68
Santa Bárbara E 61 Ec74
Santa Bárbara P 58 Ab73
Santa Bàrbara E 48 Ga63
Santa Bárbara de Casa E 59 Bb72
Santa Bárbara de Nexe P 58 Ad74
Santa Bárbara de Padrões P 58 Ad72
Santa Brígida E 52 Da72
Santacara E 39 Ed58
Santa Catarina da Fonte do Bispo P 58 Ad74
Santa Catarina Villarmosa I 167 Fa85
Santa Caterina I 162 Hb77
Santa Caterina di Pittinuri I 169 Bd76
Santa Caterina Valfurva I 142 Db56
Santa Cecilia de Alcor E 46 Da59
Santa Cesarea Terme I 163 Hd77
Santa Clara-a-Velha P 58 Ab73
Santa Coloma de Farners E 49 Hb60
Santa Coloma de Queralt E 49 Gc61
Santa Colomba de Somoza E 37 Ca57
Santa Comba E 36 Ad55
Santa Comba da Vilariça P 45 Bc61
Santa Cristina de la Polvorosa E 45 Cb59
Santa Cristina Gela I 166 Ec84
Santa Croce Camerina I 167 Fb88
Santa Croce del Sannio I 161 Fc73
Santa Croce di Lago I 150 Eb58
Santa Croce di Magliano I 161 Fc72
Santa Croce sull' Arno I 155 Db65
Santa Croya de Tera E 45 Cb59
Santa Cruz E 36 Ba54
Santa Cruz E 37 Cb54
Santa Cruz E 60 Cd73
Santa Cruz de Campezo E 39 Eb57
Santa Cruz de Grío E 47 Ed61
Santa Cruz del Alhama o. del Comercio E 60 Da75
Santa Cruz de la Serós E 39 Fb58
Santa Cruz de la Zarza E 53 Dd66
Santa Cruz del Retamar E 46 Da65
Santa Cruz del Tozo E 38 Dc57
Santa Cruz de Moya E 54 Ed66
Santa Cruz de Mudela E 52 Dc70
Santa Cruz de Tenerife E
Santa Cruz de Yanguas E 47 Eb59
Santadi I 169 Bd80
Santa Domenica Talao I 164 Ga78
Santa Domenica Vittoria I 167 Fc84
Santadrei RO 170 Ca56
Santa Elena E 52 Dc71
Santaella E 60 Cc73
Santa Engracia E 47 Ed59
Santa Eufemia E 52 Cd70
Santa Eugènia E 57 Hb67
Santa Eugènia de Berga E 49 Ha60
Santa Eugenia (Ribeira) E 36 Ac56
Santa Eulalia E 47 Ed64
Santa Eulália P 51 Bb68
Santa Eulalia (Cabranes) E 37 Cc54
Santa Eulalia de Bóveda E 36 Bb55
Santa Eulalia de Gállego E 39 Fb58
Santa Eulalia de Oscos E 37 Bd54
Santa Eulàlia de Riuprimer E 49 Gd60
Santa Eulalia (Morcín) E 37 Cb55
Santa Eulària d'es Riu E 56 Gc69
Santa Fé E 60 Db75
Santa Fiora I 156 Dd68
Santa Flavia I 166 Ed84
Santa Gadea E 38 Dc56
Sant'Agata sul Due Golfi I 161 Fb76
Sant'Agata sul Santerno I 150 Dd63
Santa Gertrude I 142 Dc56
Santa Gertrudis de Fruitera E 56 Gc69
Santa Giusta I 169 Bd77
Sant Agustí de Lluçanès E 49 Gd59
Sant Agustí d'es Vedrà E 56 Gc69
Santahamina FIN 98 Kb40
Santa Iria P 58 Ba72
Santa Isabel E 48 Fb60
Santalha P 45 Bc59
Santa Liestra y San Quílez E 40 Fd58
Santa Luce I 155 Da66
Santa Lucia I 156 Ec70
Santa Lucia I 168 Cc75
Santa Lucia del Mela I 167 Fd84
Santa Lucía (Moraña) E 36 Ad56
Santa Luzia P 58 Ac72
Santa Maddalena Vallalta I 143 Eb55
Santa Magdalena de Pulpis E 54 Fd65
Santa Mare RO 173 Fa56
Santa Margalida E 57 Hc67
Santa Margarida da Coutada P 50 Ad66
Santa Margarida de Montbui E 49 Gc61
Santa Margarida do Sádão P 50 Ac71
Santa Margherita I 169 Ca80
Santa Margherita di Belice I 166 Eb85
Santa Margherita di Staffora I 149 Cc61
Santa Margherita Ligure I 149 Cc63
Santa Maria P 44 Ad60
Santa Maria al Bagno I 162 Hb77
Santa Maria a Mare I 157 Fa67
Santa Maria Capua Vetere I 161 Fb74
Santa Maria da Feira P 44 Ad62
Santa María de Cayón E 38 Dc55
Santa Maria de Corcó E 49 Ha59
Santa Maria degli Angeli I 156 Eb68
Santa María de Huerta E 47 Eb62
Santa Maria dei Sabbioni I 149 Cd60
Santa María del Águila E 61 Dd76
Santa María de la Peña E 39 Fb58
Santa María de las Hoyas E 46 Dd60
Santa María de la Vega E 37 Cb58
Santa María del Berrocal E 45 Cc64
Santa Maria del Camí E 57 Hb67
Santa María del Campo E 46 Db59
Santa María del Campo Rus E 53 Eb67
Santa Maria del Cedro I 164 Ga78
Santa María del Espino E 47 Eb63
Santa Maria della Versa I 149 Cc61
Santa María de los Caballeros E 45 Cc64
Santa María del Páramo E 37 Cb58
Santa María del Río E 37 Cd57
Santa María de Mare E 38 Db57
Santa María de Nieva E 61 Eb74
Santa María de Redondo E 38 Da56
Santa María de Riaza E 46 Dd61
Santa María de Trassierra E 60 Cc72
Santa Maria di Castellabate I 161 Fc77
Santa Maria di Licodia I 167 Fc85
Santa Maria im Münstertal CH 142 Db56
Santa Maria la Bruna I 161 Fb75
Santa María la Real de Nieva E 46 Da62
Santa Maria Maggiore I 148 Cb57
Santa Maria Navarrese I 169 Cc77
Sântămăria-Orlea RO 175 Cc62
Santa-Maria-Siché F 154 Cb71
Santa Marina E 37 Ca56
Santa Marina E 37 Cb55
Santa Marina del Rey E 37 Cb57
Santa Marina de Valdeón E 37 Cd55
Santa Marina Salina I 167 Fc82
Santa Marinella I 160 Dd71
Santa Marta E 51 Bc70
Santa Marta E 53 Eb69
Santa Marta P 58 Ba73
Santa Marta de Magasca E 51 Ca67
Santa Marta de Penaguião P 44 Ba61
Santana P 50 Aa69
Sântana RO 170 Bd59
Santana da Serra P 58 Ac73
Sântana de Mureș RO 171 Dc59
Sant'Anastasia I 161 Fb75
Santander E 38 Dc54
Sant' Andrea I 161 Fa74
Sant' Andrea Bagni I 149 Da62
Sant'Andrea Frius I 169 Ca79
Sant Andreu de Llavaneres E 49 Ha61
Sant'Angelo I 161 Fa75
Sant'Angelo I 161 Ga75
Sant'Angelo I 164 Gb82
Sant'Angelo a Fasanella I 161 Fd76
Sant'Angelo dei Lombardi I 161 Fd75
Sant'Angelo di Brolo I 167 Fc84
Sant'Angelo in Colle I 155 Dc68
Sant'Angelo in Formis I 161 Fb74
Sant'Angelo in Vado I 156 Eb66
Sant'Angelo Limosano I 161 Fb72
Sant'Angelo Lodigiano I 149 Cc60
Sant'Angelo Muxaro I 166 Ed86
Santa Ninfa I 166 Eb85
Sant' Anna Arresi I 169 Bd80
Sant' Anna d'Alfaedo I 149 Dc59
Sant' Anna di Valdieri I 148 Bc63
Sant' Antimo I 161 Fb75
Sant'Antioco I 169 Bd80
Sant'Antioco di Bisarcio I 168 Ca75
Sant Antoni de Calonge E 49 Hc60
Sant Antoni de Llombai E 54 Fb68
Sant Antoni de Portmany E 56 Gc69
Sant'Antonino F 154 Cb69
Sant'Antonio I 149 Db63
Sant'Antonio Abate I 161 Fb75
Sant'Antonio di Gallura I 168 Cb74
Sant'Antonio di Santadi I 169 Bd78
Santanyí E 57 Hc68
Santa Olaja E 37 Cd56
Santa Olaja de la Vega E 38 Da57
Santa Olalla E 46 Da65
Santa Olalla del Cala E 59 Bd72
Santa Panagia I 167 Fd87
Santa Pau E 49 Ha59
Santa Pola E 55 Fb72
Santa Ponça E 56 Ha67
Sant'Arcangelo I 162 Gb77
Santarcangelo di Romagna I 156 Eb64
Santarém P 50 Ac67
Sant'Arsenio I 161 Fd76
Santa Sabina I 162 Hb75
Santa Severa F 154 Cc68
Santa Severa I 160 Dd71
Santa Severina I 165 Gd80
Santaskylä FIN 89 Jb34
Santas Martas E 37 Cc57
Santa Sofia I 156 Dd65
Santa Susana P 50 Ac70
Santa Susanna E 49 Gc59
Santa Teresa di Riva I 167 Fd84
Santa Teresa Gallura I 168 Cb73
Santău RO 171 Cc55
Santăul Mare RO 170 Ca56
Santa Valburga I 142 Dc56
Santa Valha P 45 Bc59
Santa Vitória P 50 Ad71
Santa Vittoria d'Alba I 148 Bd61
Santa Vittoria in Matenano I 156 Ed68
Sant Bartomeu del Grau E 49 Gd59
Sant Boi de Llobregat E 49 Gd61
Sant Carles de la Ràpita E 48 Ga64
Sant Carles de Peralta E 56 Gc69
Sant Celoni E 49 Ha60
Sant Climenç E 49 Gc59
Sant Climent E 57 Ja66
Sant Cugat del Vallès E 49 Gd61
Santed E 47 Ed62
Sant'Egidio alla Vibrata I 156 Ed68
Sant'Elena Sannita I 161 Fb72
Sant' Elia a Pianisi I 161 Fc72
Sant'Elia Fiumerapido I 161 Fa73
Santelices E 38 Dc56
Sant' Elisabetta I 166 Ed86
Sant Elm E 56 Ha67
San Telmo E 59 Bb72
Sant'Elpidio a Mare I 156 Ed67
Santena I 148 Bd61
Santenay F 29 Gb41
Santenay F 30 Ja43
San Teodoro I 168 Cc75
Santeramo in Colle I 162 Gc75
Santervás de Campos E 37 Cd58
Santervás de la Vega E 38 Da57
Santes Creus E 49 Gc61
Santesteban E 39 Ed56
Sant'Eufemia Lamezia I 164 Gb81
Sant Feliu de Codines E 49 Gd60
Sant Feliu de Guíxols E 49 Hb60
Sant Feliu de Pallerols E 49 Ha59
Sant Feliu Sasserra E 49 Gd59
Sant Francesc de Formentera E 56 Gc70
Sant Francesc de s'Estany E 56 Gc70
Sant Gregori E 49 Hb59
Sant Guim de Freixenet E 49 Gc60
Santhià I 148 Ca59
Sant Hilari Sacalm E 49 Ha60
Sant Hipòlit de Voltregà E 49 Gd59
Santiago P 51 Bb67
Santiago de Alcántara E 51 Bb66
Santiago de Calatrava E 60 Da73
Santiago de Compostela E 36 Ad55
Santiago de Compostela = Santiago de Compostela E 36 Ad55
Santiago de la Espada E 61 Ea72
Santiago de la Puebla E 45 Cc63
Santiago de la Ribera E 55 Fa73
Santiago del Campo E 51 Bd66
Santiago de Litém P 44 Ac65
Santiago do Cacém P 50 Ab71
Santiago do Escoural P 50 Ad69
Santibáñez E 37 Cc55
Santibánez E 37 Cc57
Santibáñez de Ayllón E 46 Dd61
Santibáñez de Béjar E 45 Cb64
Santibáñez de la Peña E 38 Da56
Santibáñez de la Sierra E 45 Cb64
Santibáñez de Resova E 38 Da56
Santibáñez de Vidriales E 37 Cb58
Santibáñez el Alto E 45 Bd65
Santigoso E 37 Bd57
Sant'Ilario d'Enza I 149 Da62
Santillana de Campos E 38 Db58
Santillana del Mar E 38 Db55
Santilly F 29 Gc39
Santimbru RO 175 Da60
Santiorxo E 36 Bb57
Santiponce E 59 Bd73
Santisteban del Puerto E 53 Dd71
Santiuste de San Juan Bautista E 46 Da62
Sant Jaume d'Enveja E 48 Ga64
Sant Joan E 57 Hc67
Sant Joan d'Alacant E 55 Fb71
Sant Joan de Labritja E 56 Gc69
Sant Joan de Penyagolosa E 54 Fc65
Sant Joan les Fonts E 49 Ha59
Sant Jordi E 57 Hb67
Sant Jordi del Maestrat E 48 Fd64
Sant Josep de sa Talaia E 56 Gc69
Sant Julià de Lòria AND 40 Gc58
Sant Julià de Lòria AND 40 Gc58
Sant Julià de Ramis E 49 Hb59
Sant Llorenç de Morunys E 49 Gc59
Sant Llorenç des Cardassar E 57 Hc67
Sant Llorenç Savall E 49 Gd60
Sant Lluís E 57 Jb66
Sant Martí de Llémena E 49 Hb59
Sant Martí de Riucorb E 48 Gb61
Sant Martí de Tous E 49 Gc61
Sant Martí Sarroca E 49 Gc61
Sant Mateu E 48 Fd64
Sant Mateu d'Aubarca E 56 Gc69
Sant Miquel de Balansat E 56 Gc69
Santo Aleixo P 51 Bb68
Santo Amador P 51 Bb71
Santo André P 50 Ab71
Santo António de Alcôrrego P 50 Ad68
Santo Domingo de la Calzada E 38 Ea58
Santo Domingo de Moya E 54 Ed66
Santo Domingo de Silos E 46 Dd59
Santo Isidro de Pegões P 50 Ab69
Santok PL 120 Fd35
Santomera E 55 Fa72
Santoña E 38 Dd54
Santo-Pietro-di-Tenda F 154 Cb69
Santo Spirito I 162 Gc74
Santo Stefano Belbo I 148 Ca61
Santo Stefano d'Aveto I 149 Cc62
Santo Stefano di Cadore I 143 Eb56
Santo Stefano di Camastra I 167 Fb84
Santo Stefano di Magra I 155 Cd64
Santo Stefano di Sessanio I 156 Ed70
Santo Stefano Quisquina I 166 Ed85
Santo Stino di Livenza I 150 Eb59
Santo Tirso P 44 Ad60
Santo Tomé E 61 Dd72
Santo Tomé de Rozados E 45 Cb62
Santovenia E 45 Cb59
Santovka SK 146 Hc50
Sant Pau E 54 Fc65
Sant Pau de Segúries E 41 Ha58
Santpedor E 49 Gd60
Sant Pere de Ribes E 49 Gd62
Sant Pere de Riudebitlles E 49 Gc61
Sant Pere de Torelló E 49 Ha59
Sant Pere Pescador E 49 Hc59
Sant Pol de Mar E 49 Hb61
Santpoort NL 116 Ad35
Sant Quintí de Mediona E 49 Gc61
Sant Quirze de Besora E 49 Ha59
Sant Rafel del Maestrat E 48 Fd64
Sant Rafel de sa Creu E 56 Gc69
Sant Ramon E 49 Gc60
Santranges F 29 Ha41
Sant Sadurní d'Anoia E 49 Gd61
Sant Salvador de Guardiola E 49 Gc60
Santtio FIN 89 Ja37
Sant Tomàs E 57 Ja66
Santu Lussurgiu I 169 Bd76
Santurde E 38 Ea58
Sant Vicenç de Castellet E 49 Gd60
Sant Vicenç dels Horts E 49 Gd61
San Valentino I 149 Dc58
San Valentino alla Muta I 142 Db55
Sanvensa F 41 Gd52
San Vero Milis I 169 Bd77
San Vicente E 36 Bc57
San Vicente de Alcántara E 51 Bb67
San Vicente de Arana E 39 Eb57
San Vicente de la Barquera E 38 Db54
San Vicente de la Sonsierra E 38 Ea57
San Vicente del Grove E 36 Ac56
San Vicente de Toranzo E 38 Dc55
San Vigilio I 143 Ea55
Sanvigne F 30 Hd40
San Vincente del Raspeig E 55 Fb71
San Vincenzo I 155 Da67
San Vincenzo I 167 Fd82
San Vincenzo a Torri I 155 Dc65
San Vitero E 45 Ca59
San Vito I 161 Fd74
San Vito I 169 Cb79
San Vito al Tagliamento I 150 Ec58
San Vito Chietino I 157 Fb70
San Vito dei Normanni I 162 Hb75
San Vito di Cadore I 143 Ea56
San Vito lo Capo I 166 Eb83
San Vito Romano I 160 Ec71
San Vittore delle Chiuse I 156 Ec66
Sanxay F 32 Fc45
Sanxenxo Sangenjo E 36 Ac57
Sanza I 161 Ga77
Sânzieni RO 176 Eb61
Sanzoles E 45 Cc61
São Barnabé P 58 Ac73
São Bartolomeu P 50 Ad67
São Bartolomeu de Messines P 58 Ac73
São Bento P 36 Ad58
São Brás de Alportel P 58 Ad74
São Domingos P 50 Ab71
São Domingos de Ana Loura P 50 Ba68
São Geraldo P 50 Ad69
São Jacinto P 44 Ac62
São Joaninho P 44 Ba62
São João da Madeira P 44 Ad62
São João da Pesqueira P 44 Bb61
São João da Ribeira P 50 Ab67
São João de Negrilhos P 50 Ac71
São João dos Caldeireiros P 58 Ad72
São José da Lamarosa P 50 Ac68
São Julião de Palácios P 45 Bd59
São Leonardo P 51 Bb70
São Lourenço de Mamporcão P 50 Ba68
São Luís P 58 Ab72
São Mançôs P 50 Ba70
São Marcos da Serra P 58 Ac73
São Marcos do Campo P 50 Ba70
São Martinho das Amoreiras P 58 Ac72
São Martinho de Angueira P 45 Ca60
São Martinho do Porto P 50 Ab66
São Matias P 50 Ad71
São Miguel de Acha P 44 Bb65
São Miguel de Machede P 50 Ba69
São Miguel do Outeiro P 44 Ba63
São Pedro da Cadeira P 50 Aa67
São Pedro da Torre P 36 Ad58
São Pedro de Alva P 44 Ad64
São Pedro de Moel P 44 Ab65
São Pedro de Solis P 58 Ad73
São Pedro do Esteval P 50 Ba66
São Pedro do Sul P 44 Ba62
Saorge F 43 Kd52
São Romão P 50 Ac69
São Romão P 51 Bb69
São Romão do Sado P 50 Ac70
São Teotónio P 58 Ab73
Saou F 34 Jb50
São Vicente P 45 Bc59
São Vicente da Beira P 44 Bb65
São Vicente e Ventosa P 51 Bb68
Sapaca TR 198 Fd88
Sapakpinar TR 187 Gb78
Sapanca TR 187 Gc79
Sapanca TR 191 Ea82
Şapartoc RO 171 Da54
Şapçı TR 192 Fb81
Sapernoe RUS 202 Ea08
Sápes GR 185 Dd77
Şaphane TR 192 Fd84
Sapiãos P 44 Bb59
Säpilä FIN 89 Jb36
Sapna BIH 153 Hd63
sa Pobla E 57 Hc66
Săpoca RO 176 Ec63
Sapožok RUS 203 Fb11
Sappada I 143 Eb56
Sappee FIN 90 Kb35
Sappee FIN 90 Ka36
Sappee FIN 93 Ka36
Sappen N 63 Hb09
Sappetsele S 72 Gc24
Sappu FIN 83 Lc31
Sapri I 161 Ga77
Sapsalampi FIN 89 Jc32
Sapsoperä FIN 82 La26
Sara FIN 89 Jb33
Sarabikulovo RUS 203 Ga09
Saraby N 63 Hd07
Saracan's Head GB 17 Fd23
Saraelv N 63 Hb10
Sarafovo BG 181 Ed72
Sarai RUS 203 Fb11
Säräisniemi FIN 82 Kc25
Saraiu RO 177 Fb65
Saraja BG 179 Da73
Sarajärvi FIN 75 Kc21
Sarajärvi FIN 91 Ld34
Sarajevo BIH 159 Hc65
Sarakina GR 183 Bb79
Sarakína GR 183 Bb80
Sarakiní GR 183 Bc76
Saralog RUS 99 Ma42
Sarama CY 206 Hd97
Saramo FIN 83 Lb27
Saramon F 40 Ga54
Saranci BG 179 Cd71
Saránd H 147 Ka53
Sarandë AL 182 Ab79
Saransk RUS 203 Fc10
Saransko BG 180 Eb73
Saranskoe RUS 113 Jb58
Sarantáporo GR 183 Bc79
sa Ràpita E 57 Hb68
Sarasău RO 171 Db54
Sarašova BY 202 Dd13
Sărata Galbenă MD 173 Fc59
Sărata Nouă MD 177 Fc60
Sărata Veche MD 173 Fb56
Sărăteni MD 173 Fc59
Sărătenii Vechi MD 173 Fc56
Saratov RUS 203 Fd12
Saratovskoje RUS 113 Jd58
Saray TR 186 Fa76
Saraycık TR 187 Hb79
Saraycık TR 192 Fb85
Saraycık TR 192 Fc86
Saraycık TR 192 Ga84
Saraycık TR 199 Gb88
Sarayköy TR 193 Hb82
Sarayköy TR 198 Fc88
Saraylar TR 185 Ed79
Sarayören TR 193 Gc82
Šarbanovac SRB 179 Ca67
Sârbeni RO 176 Dd66
Sârbi RO 170 Cb56
Sarbinowo PL 120 Ga30
Sarbinowo PL 128 Fc36
Sarbka PL 121 Gb35
Sárbogárd H 146 Hc55
Sarby PL 129 Gc42
Sarcelles F 23 Gd36
Sarche I 149 Dc58
s'Archittu I 169 Bd77
Sardão P 45 Bc61
Sardara I 169 Ca78
Sardés GR 184 Db80
Sardínia GR 188 Ba83
Sardoal P 50 Ad66
Sare F 39 Ed55
s'Arenal E 57 Hb67
Šarengrad HR 153 Hd60
Sarentino I 143 Dd56
Sarentino I 143 Dd56
Särestad S 102 Ed47
Särevere EST 98 Kd44
Sarezzo I 149 Da59
Sargentes de la Lora E 38 Dc57
Sargé-sur-Braye F 29 Ga40
Sárhát H 153 Hc58
Šarhorod UA 204 Eb16
Sári H 146 Hd54
Sarıağıl TR 186 Ga79
Sariai LT 115 Lb56
Sarıbelen TR 198 Fd93
Sarıbeyler TR 191 Ed83
Sarıbeyli TR 187 Gc78
Sarıcaali TR 185 Eb77
Sarıcakaya TR 193 Gc81
Sarıcalar TR 187 Gd80
Sarıcalı TR 185 Ed76
Sarıçam TR 191 Ed85
Sarıcaova TR 193 Gc84
Sarıçayır TR 192 Fb82
Sarichioi RO 177 Fd65
Sarıdayı TR 192 Ga81
Sari-d'Orcino F 154 Ca70
Sarıgöl TR 192 Fc87
Sarıkavak TR 193 Gd82
Sarıkavak TR 193 Ha82
Sarıkaya TR 187 Hb80
Sarıkaya TR 192 Fb87
Sarıkemer TR 197 Ec89
Sarıköy TR 185 Ed80
Sarıköy TR 199 Hb88
Sarıküplü TR 193 Gd83
Sarılar TR 185 Ed77
Sarılar TR 192 Ga87
Sarılar TR 198 Fd91
Sarımahmutlu TR 192 Fc87
Sarımustafalar TR 192 Fb82
Sarinasuf RO 177 Fd64
Sariñena E 48 Fc60
Sarıöküz TR 193 Gc82
Sarıot TR 191 Eb81
Sarıot TR 192 Ga82
Sarıpınar TR 186 Fd77
Sarıpınar TR 192 Fb87
Sarıpınar TR 205 Fd20
Šarišské Dravce SK 138 Jc47
Šarišské Michal'any SK 138 Jc47
Sarısu TR 192 Fb86
Sarıyar TR 193 Ha81
Šar'ja RUS 202 Eb08
Šar'ja RUS 203 Fb08
Sarjankylä FIN 82 Ka27
Sarkad H 147 Ka55
Sarkadkeresztúr H 147 Ka55
Sarkalahti FIN 90 La36
Sarkamäki FIN 91 Lb32
Sarkaņi LV 107 Lb50
Sarkavare S 73 Hb19
Šarkavščyna BY 202 Ea11
Särkelä FIN 69 Kd16
Särkelä FIN 75 La21
Sárkeresztúr H 146 Hc54
Särkiä FIN 97 Jd40
Šarkiai LT 114 Kb53
Särkijärvi FIN 74 Ka21
Särkijärvi FIN 75 Kc23
Särkijärvi FIN 90 Kc36
Sarkikaraağaç TR 193 Ha87
Särkikylä FIN 81 Jc29
Särkilahti FIN 90 Kc35
Särkiluoma FIN 75 Lb19
Särkimo FIN 81 Ja30
Särkisalmi FIN 91 Ld34
Särkisalo FIN 82 Kc31
Särkisalo FIN 97 Jc40
Särkisjärvi FIN 68 Jb14
Särkkä FIN 83 La28
Särkkäsuo FIN 75 La20
Sarkkila FIN 83 Ld28
Särkkila FIN 89 Jc35
Šarkovo BG 185 Ec74
Şarköy TR 185 Ec79
Sarkun TR 193 Ha81
Sarlat-la-Canéda F 33 Gb50
Sarleinsbach A 136 Fa49

Sarliac-sur-l'Isle – Secuieni

Sarliac-sur-l'Isle **F** 33 Ga49
Šarlote **LV** 115 Lb53
Sărmaş **RO** 172 Ea58
Sărmăşag **RO** 171 Cc56
Sărmaşu **RO** 171 Db58
Sármellék **H** 145 Gd55
Sarmingstein **A** 144 Fc50
Sarmizegetusa **RO** 175 Cc62
Särna **S** 86 Fa36
Sarnadas de Ródão **P** 50 Ba66
Sarnaki **PL** 131 Kb36
Sarnano **I** 156 Ed68
Sārnate **LV** 105 Jb50
Sărnec **BG** 181 Ed68
Sărnegor **BG** 180 Db72
Sarnen **CH** 141 Ca54
Sărnevo **BG** 180 Dd73
Sărnevo **BG** 181 Ec73
Sarnıçköy **TR** 192 Fb82
Sarnıçköy **TR** 192 Ga81
Sarnıçköy **TR** 197 Fa88
Sarnıçköy **TR** 197 Fa90
Sarnico **I** 149 Da59
Sarn Meyllteyrn **GB** 14 Dc23
Sarno **I** 161 Fb75
Sarnowo **PL** 122 Hd34
Sarnowo **PL** 122 Ja33
Sarnowy **PL** 121 Ha31
Sarnthein **I** 143 Dd56
Sarnthein **I** 143 Dd56
Sarny **PL** 129 Hb39
Sarny **UA** 202 Ea14
Särö **S** 102 Eb49
Sarón **E** 38 Dc55
Saronída **GR** 195 Cb88
Saronída **GR** 195 Cc87
Saronno **I** 149 Cc59
Sárosd **H** 146 Hc54
Sárospatak **H** 147 Ka50
Šarovce **SK** 146 Hc51
Sarow **D** 119 Ed32
Sarpdere **TR** 185 Eb78
Sarpıncık **TR** 191 Ea85
Sarpsborg **N** 93 Ea43
Sarracín **E** 38 Dc58
Sarral **E** 48 Gb61
Sarralbe **F** 25 Ka35
Sarrance **F** 39 Fb56
Sarras **F** 34 Jb49
Sarreaus **E** 36 Bb58
Sarrebourg **F** 25 Kb36
Sarreguemines **F** 25 Ka35
Sárrétudvari **H** 147 Jd53
Sarre-Union **F** 25 Kb36
Sarrey **F** 30 Jb39
Sarria **E** 36 Bc56
Sarrià de Ter **E** 49 Hb59
Sarrians **F** 42 Jb52
Sarrikoski **FIN** 83 Lb25
Sarrión **E** 47 Fa65
Sarroca de Bellera **E** 40 Ga58
Sarroca de Lleida **E** 48 Ga61
Sarroch **I** 169 Ca80
Sarron **F** 40 Fc54
Sarry **F** 30 Hd40
Sarsina **I** 156 Ea65
Sarstedt **D** 126 Db37
Sárszentlőrinc **H** 146 Hc56
Sartaguda **E** 39 Ec58
Sarteano **I** 156 Dd68
Sartène **F** 154 Ca72
Sárti **GR** 184 Cd80
Sartilly **F** 22 Fa37
Sartininkai **LT** 113 Jc56
Sartmahmut **TR** 192 Fa86
Sarud **H** 146 Jc52
Şaru Dornei **RO** 172 Ea57
Saruhanlı **TR** 191 Ed85
Sarule **I** 169 Cb76
Sărulești **RO** 176 Ec63
Sărulești **RO** 176 Ec66
Sárvár **H** 145 Gc54
Sarvasåive **S** 72 Ha22
Sarvela **FIN** 89 Jb33
Sarves **N** 63 Hd08
Sarvi **EST** 106 Kb46
Sarvijoki **FIN** 81 Ja31
Sarvikas **FIN** 81 Jc31
Sarvikumpu **FIN** 83 Lc31
Sarvilahti **FIN** 90 Kd38
Sarviluoma **FIN** 89 Ja34
Sarvinki **FIN** 83 Ld30
Sarvisé **E** 40 Fc57
Sarvisvaara **S** 73 Hc18
Sarvivaara **FIN** 74 Kd18
Sarvlax **FIN** 90 Kd38
Särvsjön **S** 86 Fa32
Sarzana **I** 155 Cd64
Sarzeau **F** 27 Eb41
Sarzedas **P** 44 Ba65
Sarzyna **PL** 139 Ka43
Šaš **HR** 152 Gc60
Sasa **MK** 179 Ca73
Sasa del Abadiado **E** 48 Fc59
Sasamón **E** 38 Db58
sa Savina **E** 56 Gc70
Sasbach **D** 141 Bd50
Sasca Montană **RO** 174 Bd64
Saschiz **RO** 176 Dd60
Săsciori **RO** 175 Da61
Sascut **RO** 176 Ed60
Sásd **H** 152 Hb57
Sas de Penelas **E** 36 Bc57
Săseni **MD** 173 Fc57
Saševo **BG** 180 Dd70
Sasi **FIN** 89 Jc35
Sąsiadka **PL** 131 Kb41
Sasina **BIH** 152 Gc62
Sasino **PL** 121 Gd29
Sasiny **PL** 123 Kb35
Saşmalıpınar **TR** 187 Gd79
Sasnava **LV** 114 Kb58
Sason **TR** 205 Ga20
Sasovo **RUS** 203 Fb10
Sassali **FIN** 69 Jd16
Sassari **I** 168 Bd74
Sassello **I** 148 Ca62
Sassen **D** 119 Ed31
Sassenage **F** 35 Jd48
Sassenay **F** 30 Jb43
Sassenberg **D** 125 Cb37
Sassenburg **D** 126 Dc36
Sassenheim **NL** 116 Ad36
Sassetot-le Mauconduit **F** 22 Fd34
Sassetta **I** 155 Db67
Sassnitz **D** 120 Fa30
Sassocorvaro **I** 156 Eb65
Sassoferrato **I** 156 Ec66
Sasso Marconi **I** 149 Dc63
Sassonero **I** 150 Dd63
Sassuolo **I** 149 Db62
Sástago **E** 48 Fc62
Šaštín-Stráže **SK** 137 Gd49
Sas van Gent **NL** 124 Ab39
Såtåhaugen **N** 86 Eb32
Sátão **P** 44 Ba62
Šateikiai **LT** 113 Jc54
Såtenäs **S** 102 Ed46
Säter **S** 87 Fc33
Säter **S** 95 Fd40
Säter **S** 102 Fa46
Sätergården **S** 94 Fa41
Saterland **D** 117 Cb34
Sāti **LV** 105 Jd51
Satiķi **LV** 105 Jd51
Sätila **S** 102 Ec49
Satillieu **F** 34 Ja49
Sātiņi **LV** 105 Jc52
Sātiņi **LV** 105 Jd52
Satkūnai **LT** 114 Kd53
Sątoczno **PL** 122 Jb30
Såtofta **S** 110 Fa55
Satopäänkulma **FIN** 97 Jc39
Sątopy **PL** 122 Jb31
Sátoraljaújhely **H** 139 Ka49
Satosuo **FIN** 82 Kb31
Satov **CZ** 136 Ga49
Satovča **BG** 184 Cd75
Satow **D** 119 Eb31
Sätra brunn **S** 95 Ga42
Sátres **GR** 184 Db76
Satriano di Lucania **I** 161 Ga76
Satrup **D** 108 Db29
Sattajärvi **FIN** 74 Jc20
Sattajärvi **S** 68 Ja17
Sattanen **FIN** 69 Ka15
Satteins **A** 142 Cd53
Sattel **CH** 141 Cb54
Satteldorf **D** 134 Db47
Sattendorf **A** 144 Fa56
Satter **S** 73 Hd18
Sättersta **S** 96 Gc45
Sattledt **A** 144 Fa51
Satul Nou **MD** 173 Fd59
Satulung **RO** 171 Da55
Satu Mare **RO** 171 Cd54
Satu Mare **RO** 172 Eb55
Satu Nou **RO** 181 Fa67
Šatura **RUS** 203 Fa10
Saturn **RO** 181 Fc68
Saturnia **I** 155 Dc69
Saturo **I** 162 Ha76
Saubach **D** 127 Ea40
Sauca **MD** 173 Fb53
Saucats **F** 32 Fb51
Saucelle **E** 45 Bd62
Săucești **RO** 172 Ed59
Sauchen **GB** 7 Ec09
Sauclières **F** 41 Hc53
Sauda **N** 92 Cb42
Sauðárkrókur **IS** 2 Ba03
Saudasjøen **N** 92 Cb42
Saudersfoot **GB** 18 Dc27
Saudron **F** 30 Jb38
Saue **EST** 98 Kb42
Sauensiek **D** 118 Db33
Sauerlach **D** 143 Ea51
Sauga **EST** 98 Kb45
Saughtree **GB** 11 Ec15
Sauginiai **LT** 114 Ka54
Saugos **LT** 113 Jb56
Saugues **F** 34 Hc49
Sauherad **N** 93 Dc43
Saujon **F** 32 Fa47
Sauka **LV** 106 La52
Saukėnai **LT** 114 Ka54
Saukko **FIN** 83 Lb26
Saukkojärvi **FIN** 74 Kb20
Saukkokangas **FIN** 69 Kd15
Saukkola **FIN** 90 Kb33
Saukkola **FIN** 98 Ka39
Saukkomaa **FIN** 74 Kb21
Saukkoriipi **FIN** 74 Jb18
Saukonkylä **FIN** 81 Jc31
Saukonperä **FIN** 89 Jc34
Saukonsaari **FIN** 91 Lc34
Šaukotas **LV** 114 Kb55
Sauland **N** 93 Db42
Săulești **RO** 175 Cd64
Saulgau, Bad **D** 142 Cd51
Saulgrub **D** 142 Dc52
Saulheim **D** 133 Cb44
Sauļi **LV** 106 Kd48
Şăulia **RO** 171 Db58
Saulieu **F** 30 Hd42
Saulīte **LT** 114 Kb53
Saulkrasti **LV** 106 Kc49
Saulnot **F** 31 Ka40
Sault **F** 42 Jc52
Sault-de-Navailles **F** 39 Fb54
Saulx **F** 31 Jd40
Saulxerotte **F** 25 Jc37
Saulxures-sur-Moselotte **F** 31 Ka39
Saulzais-le-Potier **F** 29 Ha44
Saulzoir **F** 24 Hb32
Saumeray **F** 29 Gb39
Saumos **F** 32 Fa50
Saumur **F** 28 Fc42
Saunajärvi **FIN** 83 Lc26
Saunakylä **FIN** 82 Ka30
Saunakylä **FIN** 89 Jb34
Saunalahti **FIN** 82 La31
Saunavaara **FIN** 69 Kb16
Saurat **F** 40 Gc56
Sauris **I** 143 Ec56
Saus **N** 70 Ed24
Sausgalviai **LT** 113 Jb57
Sausnēja **LV** 106 La50
Sausset-les-Pins **F** 42 Jc55
Saussy **F** 30 Jb41
Sausvatn **N** 70 Ed23
Sauvagnat **F** 33 Ha47
Sauve **F** 41 Hd53
Sauvere **EST** 105 Jc46
Sauveterre-de-Béarn **F** 39 Fa55
Sauveterre-de-Guyenne **F** 32 Fc51
Sauveterre-de-Rouergue **F** 41 Ha52
Sauveterre-la-Lémance **F** 33 Gb51
Sauveur-Lendelin **F** 22 Fa36
Sauvo **FIN** 97 Jc39
Sauvomäki **FIN** 90 Kd32
Sauxillanges **F** 34 Hc47
Sauze d'Oulx **I** 148 Bb60
Sauzet **F** 33 Gb51
Sauzet **F** 34 Jb50
Sauzet **F** 42 Ja53
Sauzé-Vaussais **F** 32 Fd46
Sauzon **F** 27 Ea42
Sava **I** 162 Ha76
Săvădisla **RO** 171 Cd58
Savalen **N** 77 Ea33
Savália **GR** 188 Ad86
Savaloja **FIN** 82 Ka25
Sävar **S** 80 Hc28
Săvârşin **RO** 174 Cb60
Sävast **S** 73 Hd22
Savaştepe **TR** 191 Ed83
Sävastnäs **S** 73 Hd22
Savci **SLO** 145 Gb56
Sävdijári **S** 68 Hc16
Säve **S** 102 Eb48
Sävedalen **S** 102 Ec49
Saveenkylä **FIN** 89 Jb32
Savelletri **I** 162 Ha75
Savelli **I** 165 Gd80
Savenaho **FIN** 90 Kc34
Savenay **F** 27 Ec42
Săveni **RO** 172 Ed54
Săveni **RO** 177 Fa66
Saverdun **F** 40 Gc55
Saverkeit **FIN** 97 Ja40
Saverna **EST** 107 Lb46
Saverne **F** 25 Kb36
Savero **FIN** 90 La37
Sävi **FIN** 89 Jb35
Säviä **FIN** 82 Kc29
Saviaho **FIN** 82 La26
Saviena **LV** 107 Lb51
Savigliano **I** 148 Bc62
Savignac **F** 41 Gd52
Savignac-les-Eglises **F** 33 Ga49
Savignano Irpino **I** 161 Fd74
Savignano sul Rubicone **I** 156 Eb64
Savigné **F** 32 Fd46
Savigné-l'Evêque **F** 28 Fd39
Savigny **F** 31 Jc40
Savigny-en-Revermont **F** 31 Jc44
Savigny-lès-Beaune **F** 30 Ja42
Savigny-sur-Braye **F** 29 Ga40
Savijärvi **FIN** 83 Lc27
Savijoki **FIN** 90 Kc38
Savikoski **FIN** 89 Jd36
Savikummunsalo **FIN** 91 Ld33
Savikylä **FIN** 83 Lb28
Savilahti **FIN** 91 Lc35
Savimäki **FIN** 82 Kc27
Saviñao **E** 36 Bb56
Savines-le-Lac **F** 35 Ka50
Săvinești **RO** 172 Ec58
Saviniemi **FIN** 89 Jd37
Savino Selo **SRB** 153 Ja59
Saviore d'Adamello **I** 149 Db57
Savipohja **FIN** 90 Kb33
Saviranta **FIN** 82 Kd25
Şavirii Vechi **MD** 173 Fb54
Saviselkä **FIN** 82 Kb27
Savitaipale **FIN** 91 Lb35
Sävja **S** 96 Gc42
Savköy **TR** 199 Gc88
Šavnik **MNE** 159 Hd68
Savoca **I** 167 Fd84
Savognin **CH** 142 Cd55
Savolanniemi **FIN** 82 Ka28
Savolanvaara **FIN** 83 Lc27
Sávoly **H** 145 Gd56
Savona **I** 148 Ca63
Savonkylä **FIN** 81 Jc30
Savonlinna **FIN** 91 Lc33
Savonranta **FIN** 91 Lc32
Savournon **F** 42 Jd51
Sävsjö **S** 103 Fc50
Sävsjön **S** 80 Ha26
Sävsjön **S** 95 Fc41
Sävsjöström **S** 103 Fd51
Savudrija **HR** 150 Ed60
Savukoski **FIN** 69 Kc15
Savulahti **FIN** 82 La30
Sawbridgeworth **GB** 20 Fd27
Sawin **PL** 131 Kc39
Sawley **GB** 15 Ec20
Sawrey **GB** 11 Eb18
Sawston **GB** 20 Fd26
Sax **CH** 142 Cd53
Sax **E** 55 Fa71
Saxdalen **S** 95 Fc41
Saxen **A** 144 Fc51
Saxhyttan **S** 95 Fb42
Saxilby **GB** 16 Fb22
Saxlingham Nethergate **GB** 17 Gb24
Saxnäs **S** 79 Fd25
Saxon **CH** 141 Bc56
Saxton **GB** 17 Fc19
Saxtorp **S** 110 Ed55
Saxtorpsskogen **S** 110 Ed55
Saxvallen **S** 78 Ed29
Sayatón **E** 47 Ea64
Sayda **D** 127 Ed42
Sayık **TR** 192 Fb84
Säynäjä **FIN** 75 La19
Säynätsalo **FIN** 90 Kc33
Säyneinen **FIN** 83 Lb29
Säynelahti **FIN** 91 Lb32
Sazak **TR** 191 Ec81
Sazak **TR** 198 Fd91
Sazak **TR** 198 Ga89
Sázava **CZ** 136 Fc45
Sazılar **TR** 193 Hb82
Sazköy **TR** 192 Fa85
Sazköy **TR** 198 Ga88
Sazlı **TR** 191 Ea82
Sazlı **TR** 197 Ed88
Sazlıbosna **TR** 186 Fc77
Sazoba **TR** 185 Ed80
Sazoba **TR** 191 Ed85
Scaër **F** 27 Dd39
Scăești **RO** 175 Cd65
Scafa **I** 157 Fa70
Scăieni **MD** 173 Fa54
Scalasaig **GB** 6 Da12
Scalea **I** 164 Ga78
Scaletta Zanclea **I** 167 Fd84
Scalloway **GB** 5 Fa05
Scamblesby **GB** 17 Fc22
Scandiano **I** 149 Db62
Scandicci **I** 155 Dc65
Scanno **I** 161 Fa71
Scansano **I** 155 Dc69
Scânteia **RO** 173 Fa58
Scânteia **RO** 177 Fa65
Scânteiești **RO** 177 Fb62
Scanzano Jonico **I** 162 Gc77
Scarborough **GB** 17 Fc19
Scardovari **I** 150 Eb61
Scardroy **GB** 4 Dc07
Scarinish **GB** 9 Da14
Scario **I** 161 Fd77
Scărișoara **RO** 171 Cc59
Scarnagh **IRL** 13 Cd23
Scarperia **I** 155 Dc64
Scarriff **IRL** 12 Bd22
Scartaglin **IRL** 12 Bb24
Scauri **I** 160 Ed73
Scauri **I** 166 Dd88
Sceaux **F** 23 Gd37
Sceaux-sur-Huisne **F** 29 Ga39
Ščegly **RUS** 113 Jd58
Ščekino **RUS** 203 Fa11
Šćenica- Bobani **BIH** 158 Hb68
Šćepan Polje **BIH** 159 Hd66
Scerni **I** 161 Fb71
Scey-sur-Saône-et-Saint-Albin **F** 31 Jd40
Schaafheim **D** 134 Cd44
Schaan **FL** 142 Cd54
Schabs **I** 143 Dd55
Schacht-Audorf **D** 118 Db30
Schaffhausen **CH** 141 Cb52
Schafflund **D** 108 Da28
Schafstädt **D** 127 Ea40
Schafstedt **D** 118 Da31
Schäftlarn **D** 143 Dd51
Schagen **NL** 116 Ba34
Schagenbrug **NL** 116 Ba34
Schaijk **NL** 125 Bb38
Schalchen **A** 143 Ed51
Schale **D** 117 Cb36
Schalkau **D** 135 Dd43
Schalkenmehren **D** 133 Bd43
Schalkham **D** 143 Eb50
Schalksmühle **D** 125 Ca40
Schangau **CH** 141 Bd54
Schangau **CH** 141 Ca54
Schänis **CH** 142 Cc54
Schapbach, Bad Rippoldsau- **D** 133 Cb49
Schapen **D** 117 Cb36
Scharans **CH** 142 Cd55
Scharbeutz **D** 119 Dd31
Schärding **A** 143 Ed50
Scharendijke **NL** 124 Ac37
Scharfenberg **D** 127 Ed41
Scharfenstein **D** 127 Ed42
Scharfling **A** 143 Ed52
S-charl **CH** 142 Db55
Scharnebeck **D** 118 Dc33
Scharnitz **A** 143 Dd53
Scharnstein **A** 144 Fa52
Scharrel **D** 117 Cb34
Schauenburg **D** 126 Da40
Schauenstein **D** 135 Ea44
Schaufling **D** 135 Ec48
Schechen **D** 143 Eb51
Schechingen **D** 134 Da48
Scheden **D** 126 Da39
Scheemda **NL** 117 Ca33
Scheer **D** 142 Cd51
Scheeßel **D** 118 Da34
Schefflenz **D** 134 Cd46
Scheggia **I** 156 Eb66
Șcheia **RO** 172 Eb55
Șcheia **RO** 173 Fa58
Scheibbs **A** 144 Fd51
Scheidegg **D** 142 Da52
Scheifling **A** 144 Fb54
Scheinfeld **D** 134 Db45
Schela **RO** 175 Cd63
Schela **RO** 177 Fa63
Schelklingen **D** 142 Da50
Schellerten **D** 126 Db37
Schellinghout **NL** 116 Ba35
Schemmerhofen **D** 142 Da50
Schenefeld **D** 118 Db31
Schenefeld **D** 118 Db32
Schengen **L** 133 Bb45
Schenkenzell **D** 141 Cb50
Schenklengsfeld **D** 126 Db42
Schermbeck **D** 125 Bd38
Schernberg **D** 126 Dc40
Schernfeld **D** 135 Dd48
Scherpenheuvel **B** 124 Ad40
Scherpenisse **NL** 124 Ac38
Scherpenzeel **NL** 116 Bb36
Scheßlitz **D** 135 Dd44
Scheveningen **NL** 116 Ad36
Scheyern **D** 135 Dd49
Schia **I** 149 Da63
Schiavi di Abruzzo **I** 161 Fb72
Schiedam **NL** 124 Ad37
Schieder-Schwalenberg **D** 126 Cd38
Schierke **D** 126 Dc38
Schierling **D** 135 Eb48
Schiermonnikoog **NL** 117 Bd32
Schiers **CH** 142 Cd54
Schiffdorf **D** 118 Cd32
Schifferstadt **D** 133 Cb46
Schiffweiler **D** 133 Bd46
Schijndel **NL** 124 Ba38
Schildau, Gneisenaustadt **D** 127 Ec40
Schillerslage **D** 126 Db36
Schillig **D** 117 Cc32
Schillingsfürst **D** 134 Db47
Schilpario **I** 149 Da58
Schiltach **D** 141 Cb50
Schiltberg **D** 135 Dd49
Schineni **MD** 173 Fb54
Schinoúsa **GR** 196 Db90
Schio **I** 150 Dd59
Schipkau **D** 128 Fa40
Schirgiswalde **D** 128 Fb41
Schirmeck **F** 25 Kb37
Schirmitz **D** 135 Eb46
Schirnding **D** 135 Eb44
Schisò **I** 167 Fd85
Schitu **RO** 175 Db66
Schitu **RO** 180 Ea67
Schitu Duca **RO** 173 Fb58
Schitu Golești **RO** 175 Dc63
Schkeuditz **D** 127 Eb40
Schkölen **D** 127 Ea41
Schkopau **D** 127 Eb40
Schlächtenhaus **D** 141 Bd52
Schladen **D** 126 Dc38
Schladming **A** 144 Fa53
Schlägl **A** 136 Fa49
Schlalach **D** 127 Ec37
Schlanders **I** 142 Dc56
Schlangen **D** 126 Cd38
Schlanstedt **D** 127 Dd38
Schlarigna **CH** 142 Da56
Schleching **D** 143 Eb52
Schlegel **D** 128 Fc41
Schlehdorf **D** 143 Dd52
Schleiden **D** 125 Bc42
Schleitheim **D** 141 Cb51
Schleiz **D** 135 Ea43
Schlema **D** 127 Ec42
Schleswig **D** 108 Db29
Schlettau **D** 135 Ec43
Schleusingen **D** 134 Dc43
Schlieben **D** 127 Ed39
Schlierbach **A** 144 Fb51
Schliersee **D** 143 Ea52
Schlitz **D** 126 Da42
Schlögen **A** 144 Fa50
Schloßberg **A** 144 Fd56
Schloß Holte-Stukenbrock **D** 126 Cc38
Schlotheim **D** 126 Dc40
Schluchsee **D** 141 Ca51
Schlüchtern **D** 134 Da43
Schluderbach **I** 143 Ea56
Schluderns **I** 142 Db55
Schlüsselfeld **D** 134 Dc45
Schmalfeld **D** 118 Db31
Schmalkalden **D** 126 Dc42
Schmallenberg **D** 126 Cc40
Schmelz **D** 133 Bc46
Schmerzke **D** 127 Ec37
Schmidgaden **D** 135 Eb46
Schmidmühlen **D** 135 Ea47
Schmidtheim **D** 125 Bc42
Schmiedeberg **D** 128 Fa42
Schmiedefeld **D** 135 Dd43
Schmiedefeld am Rennsteig **D** 126 Dc42
Schmitten **D** 134 Cc43
Schmölln **D** 120 Fb34
Schmölln **D** 127 Eb42
Schmölln-Putzkau **D** 128 Fb41
Schmon **D** 127 Ea40
Schnackenburg **D** 119 Ea34
Schnaitsee **D** 143 Eb51
Schnaittach **D** 135 Dd46
Schnaittenbach **D** 135 Ea46
Schnarup-Thumby **D** 108 Db29
Schneeberg **D** 134 Cd45
Schneeberg **D** 135 Ec43
Schnega **D** 119 Dd35
Schneidlingen **D** 127 Ea38
Schnelldorf **D** 134 Db47
Schneverdingen **D** 118 Db34
Schobüll **D** 108 Da29
Schöder **A** 144 Fa54
Schoenberg **B** 133 Bc43
Schöftland **CH** 141 Ca53
Schöllkrippen **D** 134 Cd44
Schollene **D** 127 Eb36
Schöllnach **D** 135 Ed49
Schömberg **D** 134 Cc48
Schömberg **D** 142 Cc50
Schonach **D** 141 Cb50
Schönau **D** 128 Fb40
Schönau **D** 141 Ca51
Schönau **D** 143 Ec50
Schönau a.Königssee **D** 143 Ec53
Schönau-Berzdorf **D** 128 Fc41
Schönau (Brend) **D** 134 Db43
Schönbach **A** 144 Fc50
Schönbeck **D** 120 Fa33
Schönberg **D** 119 Dd32
Schönberg **D** 135 Ed48
Schönbergerstrand **D** 118 Dc30
Schönberg (Holstein) **D** 118 Dc30
Schönborn **D** 127 Ed39
Schönbrunn **D** 134 Cc46
Schönbrunn **D** 134 Dc43
Schönbrunn **D** 135 Dd45
Schondorf **D** 142 Dc51
Schondra **D** 134 Da43
Schönebeck **D** 118 Cd34
Schönebeck **D** 127 Ea38
Schönecken **D** 133 Bc43
Schönefeld **D** 128 Fa37
Schönermark **D** 120 Fa33
Schönewalde **D** 127 Ed39
Schönewerda **D** 127 Dd40
Schönfeld **D** 128 Fa40
Schönfelde **D** 128 Fb36
Schönfeld-Weißig **D** 128 Fa41
Schongau **D** 142 Dc52
Schöngrabern **A** 136 Ga49
Schönhausen **D** 127 Eb36
Schönheide **D** 135 Ec43
Schöningen **D** 127 Dd37
Schönkirchen **D** 118 Dc30
Schönow **D** 128 Fa36
Schönsee **D** 135 Ec46
Schonstett **D** 143 Eb51
Schönthal **D** 135 Ec47
Schonungen **D** 134 Db44
Schönwald **D** 135 Eb44
Schönwald **D** 141 Cb50
Schönwalde **D** 119 Dd30
Schönwalde **D** 128 Fa36
Schoondijke **NL** 124 Ab38
Schoonebeek **NL** 117 Ca35
Schoonhoven **NL** 124 Ba37
Schoonloo **NL** 117 Bd34
Schoonoord **NL** 117 Bd34
Schoorl **NL** 116 Ba34
Schopfheim **D** 141 Ca52
Schopfloch **D** 133 Cb49
Schopfloch **D** 134 Db47
Schöppenstedt **D** 127 Dd37
Schoppernau **A** 142 Da53
Schöppingen **D** 125 Ca37
Schöpstal **D** 128 Fc41
Schorndorf **D** 134 Cd48
Schorstedt **D** 119 Ea35
Schortens **D** 117 Cc32
Schotten **D** 126 Cd42
Schotten **D** 134 Cd43
Schramberg **D** 141 Cb50
Schraplau **D** 127 Ea40
Schrecksbach **D** 126 Cd41
Schrems **A** 136 Fc49
Schriesheim **D** 134 Cc46
Schrobenhausen **D** 135 Dd49
Schröcken **A** 142 Da53
Schrozberg **D** 134 Da46
Schruns **A** 142 Da54
Schuddebeurs **NL** 124 Ac37
Schuld **D** 125 Bd42
Schull = Skull **IRL** 12 Bb27
Schuls **CH** 142 Db55
Schulzendorf **D** 128 Fa37
Schüpfheim **CH** 141 Ca54
Schussenried, Bad **D** 142 Cd51
Schuttertal **D** 141 Ca50
Schüttorf **D** 117 Ca36
Schwaan **D** 119 Eb31
Schwabach **D** 134 Dc47
Schwabhausen **D** 143 Dd50
Schwäbisch Gmünd **D** 134 Da48
Schwäbisch Hall **D** 134 Da47
Schwabmünchen **D** 142 Dc50
Schwabstedt **D** 118 Da30
Schwadorf **A** 145 Gb51
Schwaförden **D** 118 Cd35
Schwaigern **D** 134 Cd47
Schwaikheim **D** 134 Cd48
Schwalbach **D** 133 Bc46
Schwalenberg, Schieder- **D** 126 Da38
Schwalmstadt **D** 126 Cd41
Schwalmtal **D** 125 Bc39
Schwalmtal **D** 126 Cd42
Schwanau **D** 133 Ca49
Schwanbeck **D** 120 Fa32
Schwanberg **A** 144 Fd55
Schwanden **CH** 142 Cc54
Schwandorf **D** 135 Eb47
Schwanebeck **D** 127 Dd38
Schwanebeck **D** 128 Fa36
Schwanenstadt **A** 144 Fa51
Schwanewede **D** 118 Cd33
Schwangau **D** 142 Dc52
Schwanstetten **D** 135 Dd47
Schwante **D** 119 Ed35
Schwarme **D** 118 Cd34
Schwarmstedt **D** 118 Db35
Schwarz **D** 119 Ec34
Schwarzach **D** 134 Cc46
Schwarzach **D** 135 Ec48
Schwarzach am Main **D** 134 Db45
Schwarzach im Pongau **A** 143 Ec53
Schwarzbach **D** 128 Fa40
Schwarzbach bei Rochlitz **D** 127 Ec41
Schwarzenau **A** 136 Fd49
Schwarzenau im Gebirge **A** 144 Ga52
Schwarzenbach am Wald **D** 135 Ea43
Schwarzenbach an der Saale **D** 135 Ea44
Schwarzenbek **D** 118 Dc33
Schwarzenberg **A** 136 Fa49
Schwarzenberg **D** 135 Ec43
Schwarzenborn **D** 126 Da41
Schwarzenbruck **D** 135 Dd47
Schwarzenburg **CH** 141 Bc54
Schwarzenfeld **D** 135 Eb47
Schwarzenseealm **A** 144 Fa54
Schwarze Pumpe **D** 128 Fb40
Schwarzheide **D** 128 Fa40
Schwarzhofen **D** 135 Eb47
Schwarzwaldalp **CH** 141 Ca55
Schwaz **A** 143 Ea53
Schwechat **A** 145 Gb51
Schwedt **D** 120 Fb34
Schwefelbergbad **CH** 141 Bd55
Schwei **D** 118 Cc33
Schweich **D** 133 Bc44
Schweigen-Rechtenbach **D** 133 Ca47
Schweighausen **D** 141 Ca50
Schweighof **A** 143 Ed53
Schweinfurt **D** 134 Db44
Schweinitz **D** 127 Eb37
Schweinitz **D** 127 Ed39
Schweitenkirchen **D** 135 Ea49
Schwelm **D** 125 Ca40
Schwendi **D** 142 Da50
Schwenningen, Villingen- **D** 141 Cb50
Schwepnitz **D** 128 Fa40
Schwerfen **D** 125 Bc41
Schwerin **D** 119 Ea32
Schwerte **D** 125 Ca39
Schwetzingen **D** 134 Cc46
Schwichtenberg **D** 120 Fa32
Schwieberdingen **D** 134 Cc48
Schwielochsee **D** 128 Fb38
Schwiesau **D** 127 Dd36
Schwindegg **D** 143 Eb50
Schwörstadt **D** 141 Ca52
Schwülper **D** 126 Dc36
Schwyz **CH** 141 Cb54
Sciacca **I** 166 Ec86
Sciaves **I** 143 Dd55
Scicli **I** 167 Fc88
Sciez **F** 31 Ka44
Ščigry **RUS** 203 Fa13
Scilla **I** 164 Ga83
Scillato **I** 167 Fa85
Ścinawa **PL** 129 Gb40
Ścinawa **PL** 137 Gd43
Ścinawka Średnia **PL** 137 Gb43
Scioașetea **RO** 180 Dc67
Scionzier **F** 35 Ka45
Ščir **RUS** 99 Ma44
Šćit **BIH** 158 Ha65
Scmapton **GB** 16 Fb22
Scoarța **RO** 175 Cd64
Scobinți **RO** 172 Ed56
Scoglitti **I** 167 Fb88
Sconser **GB** 4 Db08
Scopello **I** 148 Ca58
Scopello **I** 166 Eb84
Scopwick **GB** 17 Fc23
Scordia **I** 167 Fc86
Scoreni **MD** 173 Fc58
Scorniceşti **RO** 175 Db65
Ščors **UA** 202 Ec13
Scorțaru Nou **RO** 177 Fa63
Scorțeni **MD** 173 Fc56
Scorțoasa **RO** 176 Ec63
Scorzè **I** 150 Ea59
Scorzo **I** 161 Fd76
Scotch Corner **GB** 11 Fa18
Scotch Town **GB** 9 Cc16
Scoțeni **RO** 172 Ec59
Scotter **GB** 16 Fb21
Scottow **GB** 17 Gb24
Scourie **GB** 4 Dc05
Scoury **F** 29 Gb44
Scousburgh **GB** 5 Fa06
Scrabster **GB** 5 Eb04
Scramoge **IRL** 8 Ca19
Scraptoft **GB** 16 Fb24
Scredington **GB** 17 Fc23
Scribbagh **GB** 8 Ca17
Ščučja Gora **RUS** 107 Mb46
Ščučyn **BY** 202 Dd13
Sculeni **MD** 173 Fa57
Scumpia **MD** 173 Fb56
Scunthorpe **GB** 16 Fb21
Scuol **CH** 142 Db55
Scurcola Marsicana **I** 160 Ed71
Scurtu Mare **RO** 176 Dd66
Scutaru **RO** 176 Ec61
Scutelnici **RO** 176 Ec65
Sczeglino **PL** 121 Gb31
Seaca **RO** 180 Dc67
Seaca **RO** 180 Dc68
Seaca de Câmp **RO** 179 Cc67
Seaca de Pădure **RO** 175 Cc66
Seaford **GB** 20 Fd30
Seahouses **GB** 11 Fa14
Seamer **GB** 17 Fc19
Sea Palling **GB** 17 Gb24
Seascale **GB** 10 Ea18
Seaton **GB** 19 Eb30
Seaton Delaval **GB** 11 Fa16
Seave Green **GB** 11 Fb18
Sébazac-Concurès **F** 33 Ha51
Sebbersund **DK** 100 Db21
Sebečevo **SRB** 178 Ba69
Šebekino **RUS** 203 Fa14
Seben **TR** 187 Hb80
Sebenardı **TR** 187 Ha79
Sebepti **TR** 191 Ed81
Sebersdorf **A** 144 Ga54
Sebeș **RO** 175 Cd60
Šebetov **CZ** 137 Gc46
Sebež **RUS** 107 Mb51
Sebež **RUS** 202 Ea11
Sebiller **TR** 193 Hb87
Şebinkarahisar **TR** 205 Fd20
Sebiș **RO** 170 Cb59
Sebnitz **D** 128 Fb41
Seboncourt **F** 24 Hb33
Sebuzin **CZ** 136 Fb43
Seč **CZ** 136 Ga45
Sečan **SRB** 174 Bb62
Secăria **RO** 176 Ea63
Secaș **RO** 174 Ca60
Seccagrande **I** 166 Ec86
Sece **LV** 106 Kd51
Secemin **PL** 130 Ja42
Sečenovo **RUS** 203 Fc09
Séchault **F** 24 Ja35
Séchilienne **F** 35 Jd49
Seckach **D** 134 Cd46
Seckau **A** 144 Fc54
Seçköy **TR** 186 Fd80
Seclin **F** 23 Ha31
Secondigny **F** 28 Fb44
Sečovce **SK** 139 Ka48
Sečovská Polianka **SK** 139 Ka48
Secu **RO** 172 Ea57
Secu **RO** 175 Cc65
Secuieni **RO** 172 Ed58
Secuieni **RO** 172 Ed59

Siemczyno – Skødstrup

Siemczyno PL 120 Ga33
Siemianowice Śląskie PL 138 Hc43
Siemianówka PL 123 Kc34
Siemiany PL 122 Hc32
Siemiatycze PL 131 Kb36
Siemień PL 131 Kb38
Siemkowice PL 130 Hc40
Siemyśl PL 120 Fd31
Sien D 133 Ca45
Siena I 155 Dc67
Siene S 102 Ed48
Sieniawa PL 139 Kb43
Sienica PL 120 Ga33
Sienlaukis LT 114 Ka56
Siennica PL 131 Jd37
Siennica Różana PL 131 Kc40
Sienno PL 131 Jd40
Sieppijärvi FIN 68 Jb17
Sieradz PL 129 Hb39
Sieraków PL 128 Ga36
Sieraków PL 129 Hb42
Sierakowice PL 121 Gd30
Sierakowice PL 137 Hb44
Sierck-les-Bains F 25 Jd34
Siercz PL 128 Ga37
Sierentz F 31 Kc40
Sierksdorf D 119 Dd31
Sierndorf A 145 Gb50
Sierniki PL 121 Gc35
Sierning A 144 Fb51
Siero de la Reina E 37 Cd56
Sieroszewice PL 129 Ha39
Sierpc PL 122 Hd35
Sierra de Luna E 47 Fa59
Sierra de Yeguas E 60 Cc75
Sierre CH 141 Bd56
Sierre S 73 Hb19
Sierro E 61 Ea74
Siershahn D 125 Ca42
Siersleben D 127 Ea39
Siesikai LT 114 Kd56
Siestrzeń PL 130 Jb37
Siete Aguas E 54 Fa68
Siete Iglesias E 45 Cc61
Şieu RO 171 Dc57
Şieu-Măgheruş RO 171 Dc57
Şieu-Odorhei RO 171 Db57
Şieuţ RO 171 Dc57
Sieverstedt D 108 Db29
Sievi FIN 81 Jd27
Siewierz PL 138 Hc43
Sifferbo S 95 Fd39
Sig DK 108 Cd25
Sığacık TR 191 Eb86
Sigdal N 93 Dc41
Sigean F 41 Hb56
Sigerfjord N 66 Fd13
Sigetec HR 152 Gc57
Siggavuono FIN 64 Ka10
Siggelkow D 119 Eb33
Siggerud N 93 Ea42
Sighetu Marmaţiei RO 171 Db54
Sighişoara RO 175 Dc60
Sığırcık TR 193 Ha84
Sığırlık TR 199 Gd89
Sigloy F 29 Gd40
Siglufjörður IS 2 Ba03
Sigmaringen D 142 Cd50
Sigmaringendorf D 142 Cd51
Sigmarszell D 142 Da52
Sigmen BG 181 Ec72
Sigmir RO 171 Dc57
Sigmundsherberg A 136 Ga49
Signa I 155 Dc65
Signalnes N 67 Ha11
Signes F 42 Jd55
Signy-l'Abbaye F 24 Hd34
Signy-le-Petit F 24 Hd33
Sigogne F 32 Fc47
Sigonce F 42 Jd52
Sigony RUS 203 Ga10
Sigrás E 36 Ba54
Sigrí GR 191 Dd83
Sigtuna S 96 Gc42
Sigüeiro E 36 Ba55
Sigüenza E 47 Ea62
Sigüés E 39 Fa57
Sigüeya E 37 Bd57
Sigulda LV 106 Kc50
Šihany RUS 203 Fd11
Sihlea RO 176 Ed63
Sihtuuna FIN 74 Jc20
Sihva EST 106 La46
Siikainen FIN 89 Ja34
Siikajärvi FIN 98 Ka39
Siikajoki FIN 74 Jd24
Siika-Kämä FIN 74 Kb19
Siikakoski FIN 90 La34
Siikakoski FIN 91 Lb34
Siikala FIN 90 Ka38
Siikamäki FIN 82 La28
Siikamäki FIN 90 La32
Siikaselkä FIN 90 Kc33
Siikava FIN 90 Kd36
Siikavaara FIN 91 Ld32
Siiksaare EST 105 Jd46
Siilinjärvi FIN 82 La29
Siimika EST 98 Ka43
Siimusti EST 98 La44
Siipyy FIN 89 Hd34
Siironen FIN 81 Jc26
Siitama FIN 90 Ka35
Siivikko FIN 75 Kc22
Sijarinska Banja SRB 178 Bc70
Sijekovac BIH 152 Hb61
Sikakylä FIN 89 Jb32
Sikaminiá GR 183 Bd80
Sikaminia GR 191 Ea83
Sikås S 79 Fd29
Sikéa GR 195 Bd90
Sikeå S 80 Hc27
Sikeå hamn S 80 Hc27
Sikés GR 194 Bb87
Sikfőkút H 146 Jb51
Sikfors S 73 Hc22
Sikiá GR 183 Bc80
Sikiá GR 184 Cd80
Sikiés GR 189 Bc81
Sikinos GR 196 Da91
Sikióna GR 189 Bd86
Siklesciems LV 113 Ja53
Siklós H 152 Hb58
Siknäs S 73 Ja21
Sikorráhi GR 185 Dd77
Sikórz PL 130 Hd36
Sikourió GR 183 Bd80
Sikovaara FIN 83 Ld28
Sikovicy RUS 99 Ma44
Sikovuono FIN 64 Ka10
Sikrags LV 105 Jc48
Siksele S 80 Ha25
Siksjö S 79 Gb26
Siksjö S 80 Gc27
Siksjönäs S 79 Ga25
Šikšni LV 113 Jb53
Šikšniai LT 114 Ka58
Sikvaland N 92 Ca45
Sil S 79 Ga29
Sila N 70 Fa20
Šilagaliai LT 114 La54
Silagals LV 107 Lb51
Šilagalys LT 114 Kc55
Šilai LT 114 Kd55
Šilainiai LV 114 Kb56
Silajāņi LV 107 Lc52
Šilalė LT 113 Jd56
Silandro I 142 Dc56
Silanus I 169 Ca76
Šilavoas LT 114 Kc58
Silba HR 151 Fc63
Silbaš SRB 153 Ja60
Silbertal A 142 Da54
Silbodal S 94 Ec43
Silchester GB 20 Fa28
Sildhopen N 66 Fd16
Şile TR 186 Ga77
Sileby GB 16 Fa24
Silec PL 122 Jc30
Silen BG 185 Dd75
Šilėnai LT 114 Kb54
Šilėnai LT 114 La58
Silene LV 115 Lc54
Silenieki LV 106 Kb51
Siles E 53 Ea71
Silfiac F 27 Ea39
Siligo I 168 Ca75
Şilindia RO 170 Ca59
Siliqua I 169 Bd79
Siliştea RO 176 Dd66
Siliştea RO 177 Fa63
Siliştea RO 177 Fb66
Siliştea Crucii RO 179 Cd67
Siliştea Gumeşti RO 175 Dc66
Silistra BG 181 Ed67
Silius I 169 Cb79
Silivaşu de Câmpie RO 171 Db58
Silivri TR 186 Fb77
Silixen D 126 Cd37
Siljan N 93 Dc43
Siljansnäs S 95 Fc39
Siljeåsen S 79 Fd27
Silkeborg DK 108 Db24
Silla E 54 Fb68
Silla EST 98 Ka44
Silla I 155 Db64
Sillamäe EST 99 Lc41
Sillano I 149 Da63
Sillanpää FIN 81 Jc29
Sillans-la-Cascade F 42 Ka54
Silleda E 36 Ba56
Sillé-le-Guillaume F 28 Fc39
Sillenstede D 117 Cc32
Sillerud S 94 Ec43
Sillery F 24 Hd35
Sillian A 143 Eb55
Sillingebyn S 94 Ed44
s'Illot E 57 Hd67
Sillre S 87 Ga33
Sillre S 87 Gb32
Silmala LV 107 Lc51
Silnica PL 130 Hd41
Silno PL 121 Gd32
Silo HR 151 Fc61
Šilovo RUS 203 Fa12
Silovo RUS 203 Fb11
Sils CH 142 Cd56
Sils E 49 Hb60
Silsand N 67 Gc11
Silsden GB 16 Ed20
Silsjönäs S 73 Ga29
Silstrup DK 100 Da21
Siltaharju FIN 69 Ka14
Siltakylä Broby FIN 90 La38
Siltala FIN 82 Kc25
Siltala FIN 89 Jc32
Siltalanperä FIN 82 Kd26
Siltavaara FIN 83 Lc27
Silte S 104 Gd50
Siltene LV 107 Lc50
Siļukains LV 107 Lc51
Šilutė LT 113 Jb56
Šiluva LT 114 Ka55
Silva E 36 Ad54
Silván E 37 Bd57
Silvana Mansio I 164 Gc80
Silvaplana CH 142 Cd56
Silvares P 44 Ba64
Silvberg S 95 Fd40
Silveiros P 44 Ad60
Šilvėnai LT 114 Ka57
Silver Bridge GB 9 Cd19
Silverdalen S 103 Fd49
Silverdalen S 103 Ga49
Silvergruvan S 95 Fb42
Silverstone GB 20 Fb26
Silves P 58 Ab74
Silvi Marina I 157 Fa69
Silvola FIN 91 Lc33
Šima RUS 99 Ld43
Simakivka UA 202 Eb14
Simala I 169 Ca78
Simalan Metsäkulm FIN 97 Jc39
Simanala FIN 91 Lc32
Simancas E 46 Cd60
Şimand RO 170 Bd58
Simanda GR 183 Cb79
Simandre F 30 Jb44
Simanes N 63 Hd08
Šimanovci SRB 153 Jb61
Simat de la Valldigna E 54 Fc69
Simav TR 192 Fc84
Simaxis I 169 Bd77
Simbach D 135 Ec49
Simbach am Inn D 143 Ec50
Simbario I 164 Gc82
Simbirsk RUS 203 Fd09
Simeonovgrad BG 185 Dd74
Simeria RO 175 Cc61
Simested DK 100 Db22
Simferopol' UA 205 Fa17
Simi GR 197 Ed92
Şimian RO 170 Cb55
Şimian RO 174 Cb65
Simiane-la-Rotonde F 42 Jd52
Simići BIH 153 Hd63
Siminicea RO 172 Ec55
Simiö FIN 90 Ka33
Simitli BG 183 Cb74
Šimkai LT 113 Jb55
Šimkaičiai LT 114 Ka56
Simlångsdalen S 102 Ed52
Şimleu Silvaniei RO 171 Cc56
Simmelkær DK 100 Da23
Simmerath D 125 Bc42
Simmerberg D 142 Da52
Simmern D 133 Ca44
Simmersfeld D 133 Cb49
Simmershofen D 134 Db46
Simmertal D 133 Ca44
Simnas LV 114 Kb59
Simnica MK 182 Ba74
Simo FIN 74 Jd21
Simola FIN 91 Lc36
Simonburn GB 11 Ed16
Simonby FIN 97 Jb40
Şimoneşti RO 176 Dd60
Simoniemi FIN 74 Jd22
Simonkylä FIN 74 Jd22
Simonsbath GB 19 Dd29
Simonsberg D 108 Da29
Simonstad N 93 Da45
Simonstorp S 95 Ga45
Simonswald D 141 Ca50
Simontornya H 146 Hc55
Šimonys LT 114 Kd54
Simorre F 40 Ga55
Símos GR 188 Bb84
Simou CY 206 Hd97
Simpelveld NL 125 Bb41
Simpiänniemi FIN 90 Kd34
Simplon CH 148 Ca57
Simpnäs S 96 Ha41
Simremarken S 110 Ed57
Simrishamn S 111 Fb56
Simsk RUS 202 Eb09
Simskälä FIN 96 Hc40
Simskardet N 70 Fa24
Simuna EST 98 La43
Simuna FIN 90 Kc32
Sinac HR 151 Fd62
Sinaia RO 176 Ea63
Sinalunga I 156 Dd67
Sinanaj AL 182 Ab77
Sinandele TR 192 Fa83
Sinanlı TR 186 Fa76
Sinanlıballı TR 187 Gb78
Sinanoğlu TR 187 Gc78
Sinarádes GR 182 Ab80
Sinarcas E 54 Ed67
Sin'avino RUS 113 Jd59
Şinca RO 176 Dd61
Şincai RO 171 Db58
Sincan TR 205 Fd20
Sincanlı TR 193 Gb85
Şinca Nouă RO 176 Dd62
Sincansarnıç TR 192 Fc81
Sindal DK 101 Dd19
Sindel BG 181 Fa71
Sindelfingen D 134 Cc48
Sindendro GR 182 Ba79
Sindi EST 98 Kb45
Sindia I 169 Bd76
Sındırgı TR 192 Fa83
Síndos GR 183 Ca78
Sinekçi TR 185 Ed80
Sinekli TR 186 Fb77
Sinemorec BG 186 Fa74
Sinersig RO 174 Ca61
Sines P 50 Ab71
Sineşti RO 172 Ed57
Sineşti RO 175 Da64
Sineşti RO 176 Eb66
Sinettä FIN 74 Jd18
Sineu E 57 Hc67
Singen D 142 Cc51
Sîngera MD 173 Fd58
Sîngerei MD 173 Fb56
Sîngereii Noi MD 173 Fb55
Singilej RUS 203 Fd10
Singleton GB 20 Fb30
Singö S 96 Ha40
Singsby FIN 81 Hd30
Singsjön S 79 Fc31
Singureni MD 173 Fb55
Singureni RO 180 Ea67
Singusdal N 93 Db43
Sinie Lipjagi RUS 203 Fb13
Sinij Nikola RUS 107 Ma49
Sinirli TR 191 Ed85
Siniscola I 168 Cc75
Siniselkä FIN 82 Ka25
Sini Vir BG 181 Ec69
Sinj HR 158 Gc65
Sinjac MNE 159 Hd67
Sinjavka BY 202 Ea13
Sinjo Bărdo BG 179 Cd70
Sinksundet S 73 Hd22
Sin-le-Noble F 23 Ha32
Sinn D 126 Cc42
Sinnai I 169 Ca79
Sinnes N 92 Cc44
Sinntal D 134 Da43
Sinodskoe RUS 203 Fd11
Sinogóra PL 122 Hd34
Sinoie RO 177 Fc66
Sinole LV 107 Lb49
Sinop TR 205 Fb19
Sinopoli I 164 Ga83
Sins CH 141 Cb53
Sinsheim D 134 Cc47
Sinspelt D 133 Bb44
Sint Annaparochie NL 117 Bc33
Sintautai LT 114 Ka58
Sintea Mare RO 170 Ca58
Şintereag RO 171 Db57
Şinteu RO 171 Cc56
Sint Jacobiparochie NL 117 Bc33
Sint Martensbrug NL 116 Ba34
Sint Michielsgestel NL 124 Ba38
Sint Nicolaasga NL 117 Bc34
Sint-Niklaas B 124 Ac39
Sint Oedenrode NL 125 Bb38
Sint Philipsland NL 124 Ac38
Sintra P 50 Aa68
Sintsi FIN 83 Ld31
Sint-Truiden B 124 Ba41
Sinués E 39 Fb57
Sinzheim D 133 Cb48
Sinzig D 125 Bd42
Sinzing D 135 Ea48
Siófok H 145 Hb55
Sion CH 141 Bc56
Sion F 31 Jd38
Sion-les-Mines F 28 Ed40
Sion Mills GB 9 Cc16
Siorac-en-Périgord F 33 Gb50
Sipa EST 98 Kb44
Sipahi TR 185 Ec77
Sipahiler TR 199 Gd88
Šipanska Luka HR 158 Hb69
Şipca MD 173 Ga57
Sipilä FIN 82 Kb30
Sipilä FIN 90 Ka32
Sipinen FIN 82 La25
Šipka BG 180 Dc71
Šipkovica MK 183 Ca74
Šipkovo BG 180 Db71
Sipola FIN 74 Ka24
Sipola FIN 82 Kb25
Siponys LT 114 Kc58
Sipoo FIN 98 Kc39
Şipote RO 172 Ed56
Şipotele RO 181 Fb68
Şipoteni MD 173 Fc58
Šipovo BIH 158 Gd64
Sippola FIN 90 La37
Sira N 92 Cb46
Sirač HR 152 Gd59
Siracusa I 167 Fd87
Sir'ajevo RUS 107 Mb48
Siráko GR 182 Ba80
Sirakovo BG 184 Dc74
Şiran TR 205 Fd20
Şirăuţi MD 172 Ed54
Sîrcova MD 173 Fd55
Siret RO 172 Eb54
Sireţel RO 172 Ec56
Sireţi MD 173 Fd57
Sirevåg N 92 Ca45
Sirgala EST 99 Lc42
Şiria RO 170 Ca59
Sirig SRB 153 Jb59
Şirince TR 191 Ec87
Sirinçsvuş TR 185 Ed80
Sirineasa RO 175 Db64
Şirinköy TR 198 Fc88
Širitovci HR 158 Gb65
Siriu RO 176 Eb63
Sirk SK 138 Jb49
Sirkka FIN 68 Jc15
Sirkkakoski FIN 74 Jc18
Sirkkamäki FIN 82 Kc31
Sirkön S 111 Fc53
Sirma MD 173 Fb59
Sirma N 64 Ka07
Sirmione I 149 Db59
Sirna RO 176 Ea65
Sirnach CH 142 Cc53
Sirniö FIN 75 Kd20
Sirogojno SRB 178 Ad67
Sirok H 146 Jb51
Široka lăka BG 184 Da75
Široká Niva CZ 137 Gd44
Široké SK 138 Jc47
Široki Brijeg BIH 158 Ha66
Široko Polje HR 153 Hc60
Širokovo BG 180 Ea69
Sirolo I 156 Ed66
Sırpsındığı TR 185 Eb75
Siruela E 52 Cc69
Sirvaste EST 107 Lb46
Širvintos LT 114 Kd57
Sisak HR 152 Gb60
Šišan HR 151 Fa62
Sisante E 53 Eb68
Sisättö FIN 89 Jc34
Sisbacka FIN 81 Jb29
Şişcani MD 173 Fb58
Sisco F 154 Cc68
Şişeler TR 199 Ha91
Šišenci BG 179 Ca67
Sises GR 200 Da95
Şişeşti RO 171 Da55
Şişeşti RO 175 Cc64
Sislioba TR 186 Fa74
Šišljavic HR 151 Ga59
Šišmanci BG 180 Dc73
Sissach CH 141 Ca52
Sissinghurst GB 21 Ga29
Sissonne F 24 Hc34
Sista Palkino RUS 99 Ld40
Şiştărovăţ RO 174 Ca60
Sistelo P 36 Ad58
Sisteron F 42 Jd52
Sistiana I 150 Ed59
Sistín E 36 Bb57
Sisto E 36 Bb53
Sistranda N 77 Dc28
Sita Buzăului RO 176 Eb62
Sitagri GR 184 Cd76
Šit'ane RUS 107 Ma48
Sitaniec PL 131 Kc41
Sitariá GR 183 Bb77
Sitarla FIN 98 Ka39
Sitasjaurestugorna S 67 Gb15
Šitbořice CZ 137 Gc48
Sítena GR 194 Bc88
Sitges E 49 Gd62
Sitía GR 201 Dd96
Sitikala FIN 90 Kd37
Sitkowo PL 123 Kb32
Sitkunai LV 114 Kb57
Sitnica BIH 152 Gd63
Sitno PL 121 Gb32
Sitno PL 122 Hc34
Sitohóri GR 184 Cc77
Sitómena GR 188 Ba83
Sitovo BG 181 Ec68
Sitovo BG 184 Db74
Sittard NL 125 Bb40
Sittensen D 118 Da33
Sitter N 78 Eb26
Sittersdorf A 144 Fc56
Sittingbourne GB 21 Ga28
Sitzendorf an der Schmida A 136 Ga49
Siuntio FIN 98 Ka40
Siuntion kirkonkylä FIN 98 Ka40
Šiupyliai LT 114 Ka53
Siuro FIN 89 Jc36
Siurua FIN 74 Kb22
Siurunmaa FIN 69 Ka15
Siusi I 143 Dd56
Sivac SRB 153 Ja59
Sivačevo BG 180 Ea72
Sivakka FIN 83 Lb27
Sivakka FIN 83 Lc26
Sivakkajoki FIN 83 Lb27
Sivakkavaara FIN 83 Lb29
Siva reka BG 185 Ea75
Sivas TR 205 Fc20
Sivaslı TR 192 Ga86
Siverić HR 158 Gb65
Sivers LV 115 Ld53
Siverskij RUS 99 Mb41
Siverskij RUS 202 Eb09
Sivertbukt N 65 Kb07
Siviken S 102 Ec46
Sivle N 84 Cc38
Sívota GR 188 Ac81
Sivrihisar TR 193 Hb83
Sivriler TR 186 Fa75
Sívros GR 188 Ac83
Six Crosses IRL 12 Bb24
Six-Fours-les-Plages F 42 Jd55
Sixmilebrige IRL 12 Bd23
Sixmilecross GB 9 Cc17
Six Road Ends GB 10 Db17
Sixt F 35 Kb45
Sixt-sur-Aff F 27 Ec40
Siziano I 149 Cc60
Sizun F 26 Dc38
Sjabero RUS 99 Ma43
Själlarim S 73 Hb19
Sjanovo BG 180 Eb68
Sjas'stroj RUS 202 Eb08
Sjåstad N 93 Dd41
Sjava RUS 203 Fc08
Sjelle DK 108 Dc24
Sjenica SRB 178 Ad68
Sjeničak Lasinjski HR 151 Ga60
Sjerogošte MNE 159 Jb68
Sjetlina BIH 159 Hc65
Sjetnemarka N 77 Ea30
Sjeverodonec'k UA 203 Fb14
Sjisjka S 67 Ha16
Sjøåsen N 78 Eb27
Sjöberg S 71 Ga23
Sjöberg S 79 Ga25
Sjöbo S 110 Fa56
Sjöbotten S 80 Hc26
Sjöbrånet S 80 Hb26
Sjödiken S 110 Ed56
Sjogerstad S 102 Fa47
Sjögestad S 103 Fd47
Sjøholt N 76 Cd32
Sjøli N 86 Eb36
Sjöliden S 80 Gc25
Sjølund DK 108 Db26
Sjömarken S 102 Ed49
Sjona N 70 Fa20
Sjonbotn N 71 Fb20
Sjonhem S 104 Ha49
Sjørring DK 100 Da21
Sjörröd S 110 Fa54
Sjørslev DK 100 Db23
Sjørup DK 100 Da23
Sjösa S 96 Gc45
Sjötofta S 102 Ed50
Sjötorp S 95 Fb45
Sjøtun N 62 Gc10
Sjoutnäset S 79 Fc26
Sjøvegan N 67 Gc12
Sjövik S 102 Ec48
Sjugare S 95 Fc39
Sjulnäs S 73 Hc23
Sjulsmark S 73 Hd22
Sjunberget S 68 Hc17
Sjundeå FIN 98 Ka40
Sjundeå kby FIN 98 Ka40
Sjuntorp S 102 Ec47
Sjursvik N 66 Ga11
Sjusjøen N 85 Ea37
Skabland N 85 Ea40
Skaborai LT 113 Jc55
Skadovs'k UA 204 Ed17
Skælskør DK 109 Ea27
Skærbæk DK 108 Da27
Skærbæk DK 108 Db26
Skærum DK 101 Dd20
Skærup DK 108 Db25
Skævinge DK 109 Ec25
Skafidiá GR 194 Ad87
Skafså N 93 Da43
Skäfthammar S 96 Gd41
Skaftung FIN 89 Hd34
Skagaströnd IS 2 Ad03
Skage N 78 Ec26
Skagen DK 101 Dd19
Skagen N 70 Fa19
Skaiå N 92 Cd46
Skáidi N 63 Ja06
Skaill GB 5 Ec03
Skaistgiriai LT 114 Kc54
Skaistgirys LT 114 Ka53
Skaistkalne LV 106 Kc52
Skaitekojan S 73 Hb19
Skakdupiai LT 114 Ka59
Skála GR 182 Ab80
Skála GR 184 Db77
Skála GR 188 Ac85
Skála GR 189 Ca84
Skála GR 191 Ea83
Skála GR 194 Bc90
Skála GR 197 Ea89
Skała PL 138 Ja44
Skála Eressú GR 191 Dd83
Skála Foúrka GR 183 Cb80
Skałągi PL 129 Ha41
Skála Marión GR 184 Da78
Skaland N 62 Gb10
Skåland N 92 Cb46
Skála Oropoú GR 189 Cc85
Skala-Podil's'ka UA 204 Ea16
Skála Sikaminiás GR 191 Ea83
Skála Sotíros GR 184 Da78
Skálavík DK 3 Ca07
Skalbmierz PL 138 Jb43
Skålbygget S 87 Fc37
Skälderviken S 110 Ed54
Skåldö FIN 97 Jd41
Skålen S 87 Fb32
Skålevik N 84 Ca39
Skalhamn S 102 Eb47
Skalica BG 180 Ea73
Skalica SK 137 Gd48
Skalité SK 138 Hc46
Skallebølle DK 108 Dc26
Skallelv N 65 Kd06
Skällernd S 94 Ea45
Skållerud S 94 Ec45
Skallerup Klit DK 100 Dc19
Skällinge S 102 Ec51
Skallmeja S 102 Ed47
Skalltivaara FIN 64 Jd08
Skällvik S 103 Gb46
Skalmodal S 71 Fc23
Skalmsjö S 80 Gc29
Skalná CZ 135 Eb44
Skålö S 95 Fb39
Skalohóri GR 182 Ba78
Skalohóri GR 191 Dd83
Skalotí GR 184 Da76
Skalotí GR 200 Cc96
Skals DK 100 Db22
Skalsko BG 180 Dd71
Skalsvika N 71 Fc18
Skalunda S 102 Ed46
Skälvum S 102 Fa46
Skam'ja RUS 99 Lc43
Skamsdalssetra N 77 Dc33
Skandáli GR 190 Dc81
Skandawa PL 122 Jb30
Skanderborg DK 108 Dc24
Skånela S 96 Gd43
Skånes-Fagerhult S 110 Fa53
Skåne-Tranås S 111 Fb56
Skånevik N 92 Cb41
Skangali RUS 107 Ld50
Skåningbukt N 62 Ha08
Skånings-Åsaka S 102 Fa46
Skänknäsberget S 79 Ga27
Skänninge S 103 Fc47
Skanör S 110 Ed57
Skansbacken S 95 Fb40
Skansholm S 79 Ga26
Skansnäs S 71 Ga24
Skansnäs S 72 Gb22
Skansnäset S 79 Fd27
Skåpafors S 94 Ec44
Skąpe PL 128 Fd37
Skapiškis LT 114 Kd54
Skara S 102 Fa47
Skårberget N 66 Ga14
Skärblacka S 103 Ga46
Skard N 71 Fd18
Skarda S 80 Gd27
Skardet N 71 Fc20
Skardsgard N 85 Db38
Skåre N 92 Cc41
Skåre S 94 Fa43
Skares GB 10 Dd15
Skares LV 105 Jd52
Skåret N 86 Ed36
Skärgårdsstad S 96 Gd43
Skärhamn S 102 Eb48
Skärkind S 103 Ga46
Skärlöv S 111 Gb53
Skarmunken N 62 Gd09
Skarnes N 94 Eb40
Skarø By DK 109 Dd28
Skarpengland N 92 Cd46
Skärplinge S 96 Gc40
Skarpnåtö FIN 96 Hb40
Skarp Salling DK 100 Db21
Skarrild DK 108 Da24
Skärså S 87 Gb37
Skarset N 76 Cd31
Skarsfjord N 62 Gc08
Skärsjövålen S 86 Fa34
Skarstad N 66 Ga14
Skarstad S 102 Ed47
Skärstad S 103 Fb48
Skarstein N 66 Ga11
Skarsvåg N 64 Jb04
Skarszewy PL 121 Ha31
Skarszyn PL 129 Gc40
Skårup DK 109 Dd27
Skärv S 102 Fa47
Skärvången S 79 Fb29
Skarvfjordhamn N 63 Hd05
Skårvik N 67 Gc12
Skarvsjöby S 79 Gb25
Skaryszew PL 130 Jc40
Skarżyn PL 123 Jd32
Skarżysko-Kamienna PL 130 Jb40
Skasenden N 94 Ec40
Skästra S 87 Ga35
Skatelöv S 103 Fc52
Skåtøy N 93 Dc45
Skattkärr S 94 Fa43
Skattungbyn S 87 Fc37
Skatval N 78 Eb29
Skatvik N 67 Gb11
Skaudvilė LT 113 Jd56
Skaulo S 68 Hc16
Šķaune LV 107 Ma52
Skauvoll N 71 Fb18
Skavaricy RUS 99 Mb40
Skave DK 100 Da23
Skavik N 63 Ja05
Skavnakk N 63 Hb07
Skawina PL 138 Ja44
Skeagh IRL 9 Cb20
Skebobruk S 96 Ha41
Skebokvarn S 95 Gb44
Skeby S 102 Fa46
Skeda S 103 Fd47
Skėde LV 105 Jc51
Skede S 103 Fd50
Skedevi S 95 Ga45
Skedshult S 103 Gb48
Skedsmokorset N 93 Ea41
Skee S 94 Eb45
Skegness GB 17 Fd22
Skegrie S 110 Ed57
Skehanagh IRL 8 Bd20
Skehanagh IRL 12 Bd21
Skei N 70 Ec24
Skei N 77 Dc31
Skei N 78 Ec28
Skei N 84 Cc35
Skejby DK 108 Dc24
Skela SRB 153 Jb62
Skelby DK 109 Eb27
Skelby DK 109 Eb29
Skelde DK 108 Db28
Skelhøje DK 100 Db23
Skellefteå S 80 Hb25
Skelleftehamn S 80 Hc25
Skellingsted DK 109 Ea26
Skelmanthorpe GB 16 Fa21
Skelmersdale GB 15 Ec21
Skelmorlie GB 6 Dc13
Šķelteni LV 115 Lc53
Skelton GB 11 Fb18
Skėmiai LV 114 Kb55
Skender Vakuf BIH 152 Gd63
Skene S 102 Ec50
Skenfrith GB 19 Eb27
Skenshyttan S 95 Fd40
Skepasti GR 200 Cd95
Skepastó GR 184 Cc77
Skepastó GR 188 Ac81
Skępe PL 122 Hc35
Skephult S 102 Ed49
Skepperstad S 103 Fc50
Skepplanda S 102 Ec48
Skeppshult S 102 Fa51
Skeppsvik S 80 Hc28
Skepptuna S 96 Gd42
Skerike S 95 Gb42
Skerping DK 100 Db21
Skerries IRL 9 Da20
Ski N 93 Ea42
Skiadás GR 188 Ba86
Skiáthos GR 189 Cb83
Skibbereen IRL 12 Bb26
Skibbild DK 108 Da24
Skibby DK 109 Eb25
Šķibe LV 106 Kb52
Skibet DK 108 Db25
Skibice PL 128 Fd39
Skibotn N 62 Ha10
Skidal' BY 202 Dd13
Skidby GB 17 Fc20
Skidby GB 17 Fc21
Skídra GR 183 Bd77
Skieblewo PL 123 Kb31
Skiemonys LT 114 La55
Skien N 93 Dc44
Skierbieszów PL 131 Kc41
Skierniewice PL 130 Ja38
Skiftenes N 93 Da46
Skippagurra N 64 Ka06
Šķilbēni LV 107 Ld49
Skilingmark S 94 Ec42
Skille N 70 Ed23
Skillefjord N 63 Hd07
Skillerhult S 103 Ga52
Skillingaryd S 103 Fb50
Skillinge S 111 Fb56
Skimteflaten N 85 Ea40
Skinburness GB 11 Eb16
Skiniás GR 201 Db96
Skinnerup DK 100 Da21
Skinnskatteberg S 95 Fd42
Skipavig N 92 Cb43
Skipnes N 77 Dc30
Skipsea GB 17 Fc20
Skipton GB 16 Ed20
Skipton-on-Swale GB 11 Fa19
Skiptvet N 93 Ea43
Skirmantiškė LV 114 Kb56
Skirö S 103 Fd50
Skíros GR 190 Da84
Skirsnemunė LT 114 Ka57
Skirva N 93 Db41
Skíti GR 189 Ca81
Skitte N 67 Gb12
Skittenelv N 62 Gd09
Skivarp S 110 Fa57
Skive DK 100 Da22
Skivika N 70 Fa20
Skivjane KSV 178 Ad71
Skivsjön S 80 Ha27
Skjæragenta N 63 Hd08
Skjærholla N 86 Ed37
Skjærli N 84 Ca35
Skjærnes N 64 Ka06
Skjåmoen N 70 Fa22
Skjånes N 64 Jd05
Skjånes N 64 Ka04
Skjåvika N 71 Fb22
Skjeberg N 93 Ea44
Skjee N 93 Dd44
Skjeggedal N 84 Cc40
Skjeggedal N 93 Da45
Skjeggestad N 92 Cb45
Skjelbreid N 78 Fa26
Skjellelv N 67 Gb12
Skjelmoen N 71 Fc22
Skjelnes N 62 Ha10
Skjelstad N 78 Eb28
Skjelstad N 78 Ec28
Skjelten N 76 Cc32
Skjelvareid N 66 Fd15
Skjelvika N 71 Fb18
Skjern DK 108 Cd24
Skjerstad N 66 Fc17
Skjervøy N 63 Hb08
Skjevlo N 78 Ec27
Skjød DK 100 Dc23
Skjold N 92 Ca42
Skjoldastraumen N 92 Ca42
Skjoldehamn N 66 Fd12
Skjolden N 85 Da36
Skjombotn N 67 Gb14
Skjønhaug N 94 Eb42
Skjønne N 85 Db40
Sklené SK 138 Hc48
Sklithro GR 189 Ca81
Šklov BY 202 Eb12
Skoby S 96 Gd41
Skočivir MK 183 Bb76
Škocjan SLO 151 Fd58
Skocze PL 123 Jd30
Skoczów PL 138 Hc45
Skodborg DK 108 Da26
Skodje N 76 Cd32
Skødstrup DK 108 Dc24

Škofja Loka – Sømåseter

Škofja Loka SLO 151 Fb57
Škofljica SLO 151 Fb58
Skofteland N 92 Cc47
Skog N 70 Fa20
Skog S 79 Ga26
Skog S 80 Gc31
Skog S 87 Gb37
Skoga S 94 Fa41
Skoganvarre N 64 Jb08
Skógar IS 2 Ac06
Skogboda FIN 97 Hd41
Skogen S 94 Ec44
Skogen S 102 Ec47
Skoger N 93 Dd42
Skoghall S 94 Fa43
Skogly N 65 Kc09
Skogmo N 78 Ec26
Skogn N 78 Eb29
Skognes N 62 Gd10
Skognes N 62 Gc10
Skogrand N 94 Eb40
Skogså S 73 Hd21
Skogsby S 103 Gb52
Skogshamn N 67 Gb11
Skogs-Tibble S 96 Gc42
Skogstorp S 95 Gb43
Skogstorp S 102 Ec51
Skogstue N 63 Hd08
Skogum N 65 Kc09
Skogvatnet N 67 Gc13
Skoki PL 129 Gc36
Sköldinge S 95 Gb44
Sköldvik FIN 98 Kc39
Skole UA 204 Dd16
Skolebukt N 68 Ja11
Skolin PL 139 Kc44
Skollenborg N 93 Dc42
Sköllersta S 95 Fd44
Skolteplassen N 65 Kc08
Skölvene S 102 Ed48
Skołyszyn PL 139 Jd45
Skomatai LT 113 Jb56
Skomlin PL 129 Hb41
Skönberga S 103 Ga46
Skonseng N 71 Fc20
Skópelos GR 189 Cc83
Skópelos GR 191 Ea84
Skopí GR 201 Dc96
Skopiá GR 189 Bd82
Skopin RUS 203 Fa11
Skopje MK 178 Bb73
Skopós GR 183 Bb76
Skoppum N 93 Dd43
Skopun DK 3 Ca07
Skórcz PL 121 Hb32
Skordokefalos CY 206 Jb97
Skøre N 92 Cd44
Skórka PL 121 Gc34
Skorków PL 130 Ja41
Skorodnoe RUS 203 Fa13
Skorogoszcz PL 129 Gd42
Skoroszów PL 129 Gc40
Skoroszyce PL 137 Gd43
Skorovatn N 78 Fa26
Skorovot AL 182 Ad78
Skorped S 80 Gc30
Skørping DK 100 Dc22
Škorpolovci BG 181 Fa71
Skorstad N 78 Eb26
Skörstorp S 102 Fa47
Skortsinós GR 194 Bc88
Skórzec PL 131 Jd37
Skorzęcin PL 129 Ha36
Skórzyn PL 128 Fc38
Skosberg S 94 Fa41
Skotfoss N 93 Dc44
Skotina GR 183 Bd79
Skotiní GR 194 Bc87
Skotnes N 70 Ed24
Skotniki PL 129 Gd37
Skotniki PL 130 Ja40
Skotoússa GR 184 Cc76
Skotoússa GR 189 Bd82
Skoträsk S 72 Gc24
Skotsætet N 62 Gd09
Skotterud N 94 Ec41
Skottevik N 93 Da47
Skottnes N 70 Ec24
Skottorp S 110 Ed53
Skottsund S 88 Gc34
Skoulikariá GR 188 Ba82
Skoúrta GR 189 Cb86
Skoútari GR 184 Cc77
Skoutari GR 194 Bc90
Skovby DK 108 Dc28
Skovby DK 108 Dc24
Skovby DK 108 Dc26
Skövde S 102 Fa47
Skovlund DK 108 Da25
Skovorodka RUS 99 Ma44
Skovsgård DK 100 Db21
Skovs Højrup DK 108 Dc26
Skrá GR 183 Bd76
Skrad HR 151 Fc60
Skradin HR 157 Ga65
Skraičionys LT 114 Kc59
Skramstadsetra N 86 Eb37
Skrăt BG 183 Cb75
Skrautval N 85 Dc37
Skravena BG 179 Cd70
Skraverup DK 109 Eb27
Škrdlovice CZ 136 Ga46
Skrea S 102 Ec52
Skrean N 62 Gd10
Skrebatno BG 184 Cd75
Skrebinai LT 114 Kc57
Skredå N 92 Cb44
Skrede N 84 Cc34
Skredeli N 92 Cb47
Skredsvik S 102 Eb47
Skreen IRL 8 Bd18
Skreia N 85 Ea39
Skreland N 92 Cd44
Skriadžiai LV 114 Kb58
Skrivena Luka HR 158 Gd69
Skrīveri LV 106 Kd51
Skrolsvika N 66 Ga11
Skroniów PL 130 Ja42
Skrova N 66 Fc14
Skröven S 73 Hd18
Skrøyvstad N 78 Ec25
Skrudaliena LV 115 Lc53
Skrunda LV 105 Jc52
Skruv S 103 Fd52
Skrwilno PL 122 Hd34
Skrydstrup DK 108 Da27
Skryje CZ 136 Fa45
Skrzatusz PL 121 Gb34
Skrzeszew PL 131 Ka36
Skrzydlów PL 130 Hd41
Skrzynno PL 130 Jb40
Skrzypnik PL 129 Gd42
Skucani BIH 158 Gc65
Skudeneshavn N 92 Bd43
Skudutiškis LT 114 La55
Skuhrov CZ 136 Fd46
Skujene LV 106 Kd50
Skuķi LV 115 Ld53
Skulerud N 94 Eb42
Skulgam N 62 Gd08
Skull IRL 12 Bb27
Skulsfjord N 62 Gc09
Skulsk PL 129 Ha36
Skulte LV 106 Kc49
Skultorp S 102 Fa47
Skultuna S 95 Ga42
Skuodas LT 113 Jb53
Skuratovo RUS 107 Mb48
Skurträsk S 80 Ha27
Skurup S 110 Fa56
Skutari = Shkodër AL 163 Jb71
Skute N 85 Dd39
Skuteč CZ 136 Ga45
Skutskär S 96 Gc39
Skuttunge S 96 Gc41
Skutvika N 66 Fd15
Škvorec CZ 136 Fc44
Skvyra UA 204 Ec15
Skwarki PL 131 Kc42
Skwierzyna PL 128 Fd36
Skybakk N 94 Ec39
Skýcov SK 137 Hb49
Skydebjerg DK 108 Dc26
Skyllberg S 95 Fc45
Skylloura CY 206 Jb96
Skymnäs S 94 Fa42
Skyttorp S 96 Gc41
Slabadai LT 114 Ka58
Slabce CZ 136 Fa45
Slabinja HR 152 Gc60
Słaboszów PL 138 Ja43
Slade IRL 13 Cc25
Sladeburn GB 15 Ec20
Sládkovičovo SK 145 Ha51
Sladojevci HR 152 Ha59
Sladun BG 185 Eb75
Slagelse DK 109 Ea26
Slagharen NL 117 Bd35
Slagnäs S 72 Gc23
Slagstad N 66 Ga12
Slagūne LV 106 Ka52
Slaka S 103 Fd47
Slaley GB 11 Ed16
Slamannan GB 10 Ea13
Slampe LV 106 Ka51
Slančev Briag BG 181 Fa72
Slancy RUS 99 Lc42
Slancy RUS 202 Ea09
Slane IRL 9 Cd20
Slangerup DK 109 Ec25
Slănic RO 176 Ea63
Slănic-Moldova RO 176 Ec60
Slanje HR 152 Gc57
Slano HR 158 Hb68
Słanowice PL 120 Ga32
Slantrna BIH 153 Hc61
Slaný CZ 136 Fb44
Slap BIH 159 Ja64
Släp S 102 Eb49
Šlapaberžė LT 114 Kc55
Šlapanice CZ 136 Fb44
Šlapgirė LT 113 Jd55
Slap ob Idrijci SLO 151 Fa57
Släppträsk S 72 Gd24
Slåstad N 94 Eb40
Slate LV 107 Lb52
Slatina BG 180 Db70
Slatina BIH 152 Gd62
Slatina BIH 152 Hb63
Slatina BIH 158 Ha65
Slatina BIH 159 Hd66
Slatina HR 152 Ha59
Slatina KSV 178 Bb72
Slatina RO 172 Eb56
Slatina RO 175 Db66
Slatina RO 175 Dc63
Slatina SRB 153 Ja62
Slatina SRB 153 Jb63
Slatina SRB 174 Ca66
Slatina SRB 178 Ba67
Slatiňany CZ 136 Ga45
Slatina-Timiş RO 174 Cb62
Slatine HR 158 Gb66
Slatinice CZ 137 Gc46
Slatino BG 179 Cb73
Slatino MK 178 Ba72
Slatinské Lazy SK 138 Hd49
Slatinski Orenovac HR 152 Ha59
Slătioara RO 172 Eb56
Slătioara RO 175 Da63
Slătioara RO 175 Db66
Slato BIH 159 Hc67
Slättåkra S 102 Ed52
Slättberg S 73 Hc19
Slättberg S 87 Fc37
Slåttevik N 92 Ca42
Slattum N 93 Ea41
Slåttvik N 66 Fd16
Slåttvik N 79 Fb25
Slava Cercheză RO 177 Fc65
Šlavantai LT 123 Kc30
Slava Rusă RO 177 Fc65
Slaveevo BG 181 Fa69
Slavětín CZ 137 Gc46
Slavharad BY 202 Ec12
Slavičín CZ 137 Ha48
Slavikai LT 114 Ka57
Slavinja SRB 179 Cb70
Slavinsk RUS 113 Jb58
Slavjanovo BG 180 Dc69
Slavjanovo BG 180 Ea70
Slavjanovo BG 185 Dd75
Slavjansk na-Kubani RUS 205 Fc17
Slavjansko RUS 113 Jb58
Slavkoviči RUS 107 Mb47
Slavkovica SRB 153 Jc63
Slavkoviči RUS 202 Ea10
Slavkov u Brna CZ 137 Gc47
Slavonice CZ 136 Fd48
Slavonski Brod HR 152 Hb61
Slavošovce SK 138 Jb48
Slavotin BG 179 Cc68
Slavovica BG 179 Cd72
Slavovica BG 180 Db68
Slavsk RUS 113 Jc57
Slavskoe RUS 113 Ja59
Slavsko Polje HR 151 Ga60
Slavuta UA 204 Eb15
Sława PL 120 Ga32
Sława PL 128 Ga38
Sławatycze PL 131 Kc38
Sławęcin PL 121 Gd33
Sławęcin PL 122 Hd34
Sławięcice PL 137 Hb43
Sławków PL 138 Hd43
Sławkowo PL 122 Jc34
Sławniowice PL 137 Gd43
Sławno PL 121 Gb30
Sławno PL 130 Ja40
Sławoborze PL 120 Ga32
Sławsk PL 129 Ha37
Sleaford GB 17 Fc23
Słębowo PL 121 Gd35
Sledmere GB 16 Fb19
Sleen NL 117 Bd34
Sleights GB 11 Fb18
Sleme SLO 144 Fc56
Ślemie PL 138 Hd45
Slemminge DK 109 Ea29
Sleneset N 70 Ed20
Slepač most MNE 159 Jb67
Slepče MK 182 Ba75
Slepčević SRB 153 Ja62
Ślesin PL 121 Gd34
Ślesin PL 129 Ha37
Sletta N 63 Hc07
Sletta N 67 Gb12
Sletta N 77 Dd29
Slette N 85 Da34
Slettebo N 92 Ca45
Slettesetra N 85 Ea34
Slettestrand DK 100 Db20
Slettmo N 62 Gd10
Slezské Rudoltice CZ 137 Ha44
Sliač SK 138 Hd49
Sliaćkúpelele SK 138 Hd49
Slickly GB 5 Eb04
Sliedrecht NL 124 Ad37
Sliema M 166 Eb88
Šliėnava LT 114 Kc57
Sligachan GB 4 Da08
Sligeach IRL 8 Ca18
Sligglesthorne GB 17 Fc20
Sligo IRL 8 Ca18
Slimbridge GB 19 Ec27
Slimnic RO 175 Db61
Slingsby GB 16 Fb19
Sliper N 78 Eb29
Slipstensjön S 80 Ha26
Slišane SRB 178 Bc70
Šlissel'burg RUS 202 Eb08
Slite S 104 Ha49
Slītere LV 105 Jc48
Slivarava BG 186 Fa74
Slivata BG 179 Cc68
Sliven BG 180 Eb72
Slivileşti RO 175 Cc64
Slivnica BG 179 Cb70
Slivno HR 158 Gd67
Slivo Pole BG 180 Eb68
Slivovica BG 180 Ea70
Slivovica SRB 159 Jb65
Śliwa PL 122 Hd32
Śliwice PL 121 Ha32
Śliwice PL 122 Hc31
Sllatinë AL 178 Ad73
Słobity PL 122 Hd30
Sloboda LV 107 Ld52
Sloboda RUS 107 Mb47
Slobozia RO 176 Dd66
Slobozia RO 176 Ed66
Slobozia RO 180 Ea68
Slobozia Ciorăşti RO 176 Ed62
Slobozia-Cremene MD 173 Fc54
Slobozia Doamnei MD 173 Fd57
Slobozia-Duşca MD 173 Fd57
Slobozia Mândra RO 180 Db67
Slobozia Mare MD 177 Fb63
Slobozia-Raşcov MD 173 Fd55
Slobzia Conachi RO 177 Fa62
Slochteren NL 117 Ca33
Słodków PL 131 Ka41
Sloka LV 106 Ka51
Słomniki PL 138 Ja43
Slon RO 176 Eb63
Słonecznik PL 122 Hd31
Slonim BY 202 Ea13
Słonin PL 129 Gc38
Słonów PL 120 Ga35
Słońsk PL 128 Fc36
Slöta S 102 Fa47
Sloten NL 116 Bb34
Slotsbron S 94 Ed43
Slottskogen S 96 Gc42
Slough GB 20 Fb28
Slovac SRB 153 Jb63
Slovenj Gradec SLO 144 Fd56
Slovenska Bistrica SLO 151 Ga57
Slovenská L'upča SK 138 Hd48
Slovenská Ves SK 138 Jb47
Slovenské Ďarmoty SK 146 Hd51
Slovenske Konjice SLO 151 Fd57
Slovenské Nove Mesto SK 139 Ka49
Slovinci HR 152 Gc60
Slovinka RUS 203 Fb08
Slovinky SK 138 Ja48
Slov'jans'k UA 205 Fb15
Słowino PL 121 Gb30
Słubice PL 128 Fc37
Słubice PL 130 Hd36
Sluck BY 202 Ea13
Sluderno I 142 Db55
Sluis NL 124 Aa38
Sluiskil NL 124 Ab39
Šluknov CZ 128 Fb41
Slunj HR 151 Ga61
Słup PL 122 Hd33
Słupca PL 129 Ha37
Słupia PL 122 Hd35
Słupia PL 130 Ja38
Słupia PL 130 Ja42
Słupia PL 138 Jc43
Słupiec PL 137 Gb43
Słupno PL 130 Hd36
Słupsk PL 121 Gc30
Słupsk PL 122 Ja34
Slušovice CZ 137 Ha47
Slussfors S 71 Ga23
Słuszków PL 129 Ha38
Slutarp S 102 Fa48
Służewo PL 121 Hb35
Småbönders FIN 81 Jc29
Smålandsstenar S 102 Fa51
Smalåsen N 70 Fa24
Smalininkai LT 113 Jd57
Smaljavičy BY 202 Eb12
Smalley GB 16 Fa23
Smalnyčėnai LT 114 Ka59
Smalvos LT 115 Lc54
Smârdan RO 177 Fb63
Smârdan RO 177 Fb63
Smârde LV 106 Ka51
Smârdioasa RO 180 Dd68
Smardzewo PL 128 Ga37
Smarhon' BY 202 Ea12
Šmarje SLO 151 Fa60
Šmarje pri Jelšah SLO 151 Fd57
Šmarjeta SLO 151 Fd58
Smarliūnai LT 123 Kc30
Šmartno na Pohorju SLO 144 Fd56
Šmartno pri Litija SLO 151 Fc58
Šmartno pri Slovenj Gradec SLO 144 Fd56
Šmartno v Tuhinju SLO 151 Fc57
Smaszew PL 129 Ha38
Smeberg S 94 Eb45
Smečno CZ 136 Fa44
Smedås N 86 Eb33
Smedby S 103 Ga52
Smedby S 111 Gb53
Smědeč CZ 136 Fb48
Smederevo SRB 174 Bb64
Smederevska-Palanka SRB 174 Bb65
Smedjebacken S 95 Fd41
Smedjeviken S 78 Fa29
Smedmoen N 86 Ea38
Smedodden N 93 Da44
Smedsbyn S 73 Hd21
Smedstorp S 111 Fb56
Smeeni RO 176 Ec64
Smeland N 92 Cd45
Smeland N 93 Da44
Smelynė LT 115 Lb54
Smerdi RUS 99 Mb43
Smerekowiec PL 139 Jd46
Smérna GR 194 Ba87
Smértos GR 182 Ac80
Smeržaha RUS 99 Ld45
Smętowo PL 121 Hb32
Smidary CZ 136 Fd44
Śmielin PL 121 Gd33
Śmielin PL 130 Hd37
Śmierdnica PL 120 Fc33
Śmigiel PL 129 Gb38
Šmiklavž SLO 144 Fd56
Šmiklavž SLO 151 Fc57
Smila UA 204 Ed15
Smilčić HR 157 Fd64
Smilde NL 117 Bd34
Smilec BG 179 Da72
Smilec BG 181 Ed68
Smilevo MK 182 Ba75
Smilgiai LT 114 Ka54
Smilgiai LT 114 Kc54
Smilgiai LT 114 Kd57
Smiljan BG 184 Db75
Smiljan HR 151 Fd63
Smilovci SRB 179 Cb70
Śmiłowo PL 121 Gc34
Smiltene LV 106 La48
Smines N 66 Fc12
Smineset N 78 Ec25
Smiřice CZ 136 Ga44
Smirnenski BG 179 Cc68
Smirnenski BG 180 Eb68
Smithborough IRL 9 Cc18
Smithfield GB 11 Ec16
Smjadovo BG 181 Ec71
Smočevo BG 179 Cb73
Smögen S 102 Ea47
Smogorzów PL 129 Ha41
Smogulec PL 121 Gd34
Šmojlovo RUS 107 Mb47
Smojmirovo MK 183 Cb74
Smokkvica MK 183 Ca76
Smokovljani HR 158 Hb68
Smolarnia PL 137 Ha43
Smołdzino PL 121 Gc29
Smołdziński Las PL 121 Gc29
Smole PL 138 Hd43
Smolenice SK 145 Gd50
Smolensk RUS 202 Ec11
Smolino PL 122 Hd35
Smoljan BG 184 Db75
Smolmark S 94 Ec43
Smolnica PL 120 Fc35
Smolnik PL 139 Kb46
Smolník SK 138 Jc48
Smolov CZ 135 Ec46
Smolsko BG 179 Cd71
Smørda N 84 Cb34
Smørfjord N 64 Jb06
Smørholet N 94 Eb39
Smørumnedre DK 109 Ec25
Smrečje SLO 151 Fb58
Smuka SLO 151 Fc59
Smulți RO 177 Fa61
Smuniew PL 131 Ka36
Smygehamn S 110 Fa57
Smykowo PL 122 Hd32
Smyšljaevsk RUS 203 Ga10
Snäckgärdsbaden S 104 Gd49
Snagli N 67 Gc12
Snagov RO 176 Eb65
Snainton GB 16 Fb19
Snålroa N 94 Ec39
Snappertuna FIN 97 Jd40
Snaptun DK 108 Dc25
Snåre FIN 81 Jc28
Snarum N 93 Dd41
Snarup DK 108 Dc27
Šnaukštiai LT 113 Jb55
Snausen N 77 Dd30
Snave IRL 12 Bb26
Snavlunda S 95 Fc45
Snedsted DK 100 Da21
Sneek NL 117 Bc33
Sneem IRL 12 Ba25
Snefjord N 63 Ja05
Snejbjerg DK 108 Da24
Snekkersten DK 109 Ec25
Snēpele LV 105 Jc51
Snerta N 86 Ec35
Snertinge DK 109 Ea25
Snesere DK 109 Eb27
Snesudden S 73 Hb21
Snežina BG 181 Ed70
Sněžné CZ 136 Ga46
Śniadowo PL 123 Jd34
Snihurivka UA 204 Ed16
Snikere LV 106 Ka52
Snilldal N 77 Dd30
Snina SK 139 Ka47
Snitterfield GB 20 Ed25
Snjatyn UA 204 Ea16
Šnjegotina V. BIH 152 Ha62
Snøde DK 109 Dd27
Snogebæk DK 111 Fd58
Snoghøj DK 108 Db26
Snowshill GB 20 Ed26
Soalheira P 44 Bb65
Şoarş RO 175 Dc61
Soave I 149 Dc60
Soazza CH 142 Cc56
Soběšice CZ 136 Fa47
Soběslav CZ 136 Fc47
Sobibór PL 131 Kd39
Sobiechy PL 122 Jc30
Sobienie PL 130 Jc38
Sobieszewo PL 121 Hb30
Sobieszów PL 128 Ga42
Sobinka RUS 203 Fa10
Sobki PL 130 Hc40
Sobków PL 130 Jb42
Sobłówka PL 138 Hc46
Sobolevo RUS 203 Fb11
Sobolew PL 131 Jd38
Sobolice PL 128 Fc40
Søborg DK 109 Ec24
Soborzyce PL 130 Hd41
Sobota PL 130 Hd37
Soboth Ort A 144 Fc56
Sobotín CZ 137 Gc44
Sobotište SK 137 Gd49
Sobotka CZ 136 Fd43
Sobótka PL 129 Gc42
Sobótka PL 129 Ha39
Sobótka PL 131 Jd41
Sobowidz PL 121 Hb31
Sobra HR 158 Ha69
Sobradelo E 37 Bd57
Sobradillo E 45 Bd62
Sobrado E 36 Bc55
Sobrado dos Monxes E 36 Ba55
Sobral da Adiça P 51 Bb71
Sobral de Monte Agraço P 50 Aa68
Sobran TR 192 Fb86
Sobran TR 193 Gb82
Sobrance SK 139 Kb48
Sobreira P 44 Ad61
Sobreira Formosa P 50 Ba66
Sobreiro de Cima P 45 Bc59
Sobrelapeña (Lamasón) E 38 Da55
Sobrón E 38 Dd57
Søby DK 108 Dc28
Soča SLO 151 Fa57
Sočanica KSV 178 Ba69
Sočerga SLO 151 Fa60
Sochaczew PL 130 Ja37
Sochaux F 31 Ka40
Sochocin PL 122 Ja35
Soči RUS 205 Fd17
Sočkovac BIH 152 Hb62
Socodor RO 170 Bd58
Socol RO 174 Bc64
Socond RO 171 Cd55
Socovos E 53 Ec71
Socuéllamos E 53 Ea68
Soczewka PL 130 Hd36
Sodankylä FIN 69 Ka15
Sodeliai LT 114 La53
Sodeliškiai LT 114 Kc53
Söderåkra S 111 Ga53
Söderala S 87 Gb37
Söderås S 87 Fc38
Söderbärke S 95 Fd41
Söderboda S 96 Gd40
Söderby EST 97 Jd44
Söderby FIN 97 Jd40
Söderby S 96 Ha44
Söderby-Karl S 96 Ha41
Söderfors S 96 Gc40
Söderhamn S 87 Gb37
Söderhögen S 87 Fb33
Söderköping S 103 Ga46
Söderkulla FIN 98 Kc39
Söderra S 87 Gb35
Soderstorf D 118 Dc34
Södersunda FIN 96 Hc40
Södertälje S 96 Gc44
Söderudden FIN 81 Hd30
Södervik S 96 Ha42
Sødorp N 85 Dd36
Södra Åbyn S 80 Hc26
Södra Ås S 94 Fa42
Södra Åsarp S 102 Fa49
Södra Björke S 102 Ed48
Södra Borgeby S 94 Fa42
Södra Brännträsk S 73 Hb22
Södra Bredåker S 73 Hc21
Södra Fågelås S 103 Fb47
Södra Finnskoga S 94 Ed39
Södra Harads S 73 Hc21
Södra Härene S 102 Ed48
Södra Insjö S 80 Gc27
Södra Kedum S 102 Ed47
Södra Klagshamn S 110 Ed56
Södra Ljunga S 103 Fb52
Södra Löten S 86 Ed38
Södra Lundby S 102 Ed47
Södra Möckleby S 111 Gb53
Södra Ny S 94 Ed44
Södra Råda S 95 Fb45
Södra Rörum S 110 Fa55
Södra Sandby S 110 Fa56
Södra Sunderbyn S 73 Hd22
SödraTansbodarna S 95 Fc40
Södra Tresund S 79 Ga25
Södra Vallgrund FIN 81 Hd30
Södra Vi S 103 Ga49
Södra Ving S 102 Fa48
Sodražica SLO 151 Fc59
Sodupe E 38 Ea55
Soesmarke DK 109 Eb28
Soest D 125 Cb39
Soest NL 116 Bb36
Sofádes GR 189 Bc82
Sofia MD 173 Fb55
Sofia MD 173 Fc58
Sofija BG 179 Cc71
Sofijivka UA 204 Ed15
Sofikó GR 195 Ca87
Sofino RUS 107 Ma49
Şofrincani MD 173 Fa54
Şofronea RO 170 Bd59
Søfteland N 84 Ca39
Søften DK 108 Dc24
Søfting N 70 Fa22
Sofuentes E 39 Ed58
Sofuhalil TR 185 Ec76
Sofular TR 187 Hb76
Sofular TR 191 Ec81
Sofular TR 198 Fc89
Sofular TR 199 Gd88
Söğanlı TR 199 Gb89
Sögel D 117 Cb34
Sogliano al Rubicone I 156 Ea64
Soglio CH 142 Cd56
Sogndal N 84 Cd36
Sogndalstrand N 92 Cb46
Søgne N 92 Cd47
Sogn-Gions CH 141 Cb55
Sograndio E 37 Cb54
Soğucak TR 191 Ed81
Soğucak TR 192 Fb81
Soğucak TR 193 Gc86
Soğucakpınar TR 187 Gb80
Soğukpınar TR 192 Fd81
Soğuksu TR 186 Ga79
Şöğüt TR 192 Fd84
Söğüt TR 193 Gb81
Söğüt TR 193 Gb83
Söğüt TR 198 Ga88
Söğüt TR 198 Ga91
Söğüt TR 198 Ga92
Söğüt TR 199 Gb90
Söğütalan TR 192 Fb81
Söğütalanı TR 191 Ec81
Söğütköy TR 197 Fa92
Söğütlü TR 187 Gc78
Söğütlü TR 205 Ga20
Söğütlüdere TR 198 Fd91
Söğütyaylası TR 193 Gc83
Soham GB 20 Fd25
Sohatu RO 176 Eb66
Sohland D 128 Fc41
Söhlde D 126 Dc37
Sohodol RO 171 Cc59
Sohós GR 183 Cb77
Sohren D 133 Bd44
Söhrewald D 126 Da40
Soidinkumpu FIN 75 Kd19
Soidinmäki FIN 82 Ka31
Soidinvaara FIN 82 La26
Soignies B 124 Ab41
Şoimari RO 176 Eb64
Şoimi RO 170 Cb58
Soings-en-Sologne F 29 Gc41
Soini FIN 81 Jd31
Soiniemi FIN 90 Kb35
Soiniemi FIN 91 Lb34
Soininkylä FIN 89 Jd32
Soinlahti FIN 82 Kd28
Soissons F 24 Hb35
Soivio FIN 75 La20
Soizy-aux-Bois F 24 Hc37
Söjö S 87 Fd32
Söjtör H 145 Gc56
Sokal' UA 204 Ea15
Söke TR 197 Ec88
Soklot FIN 81 Ja29
Soklovo BG 181 Fb69
Sokna N 85 Dd40
Soknedal N 78 Ea31
Sökö FIN 98 Kb40
Soko Banja SRB 178 Bd68
Sokojärvi FIN 83 Ld28
Sokol BG 181 Ec68
Sokol RUS 202 Ed08
Sokolac BIH 159 Hd64
Sokolany PL 123 Kb32
Sokolare BG 179 Cd69
Sokolda PL 123 Kc33
Sokole-Kuźnica PL 121 Ha33
Sokółka PL 123 Kc32
Sokółki PL 123 Jd30
Sokolniki PL 131 Jd42
Sokolov CZ 135 Ec44
Sokolovac HR 152 Gc58
Sokolovci BG 184 Db75
Sokolovci BIH 159 Hd64
Sokolovo BG 180 Db70
Sokolovo BIH 152 Gc63
Sokołów PL 130 Hc36
Sokołów Małopolski PL 139 Ka43
Sokołowo PL 121 Gb35
Sokołowo PL 129 Hb37
Sokołów Podlaski PL 131 Ka36
Sokoły PL 123 Ka34
Sokovaara FIN 83 Ld28
Sól PL 131 Kb42
Sol' SK 139 Jd48
Sola FIN 83 Lc30
Sola N 92 Ca44
Solager DK 109 Eb25
Solalex CH 141 Bc56
Solana de los Barros E 51 Bb69
Solana del Pino E 52 Da71
Solanka PL 122 Jc30
Solares E 38 Dc55
Solarino I 167 Fd87
Solaris HR 157 Ga66
Solaro F 154 Cb71
Solarussa I 169 Bd77
Solbakken N 64 Jc05
Solbakken N 64 Jd06
Solberg N 64 Jb06
Solberg S 79 Gb28
Solberg S 79 Fd30
Solberg S 80 Gc28
Solberga S 102 Eb48
Solberga S 103 Fc49
Solberget S 73 Hc19
Solbjerg DK 100 Dc22
Solbjerg DK 108 Dc24
Solbjør N 92 Cb46
Solbozia Bradului RO 176 Ed63
Solca RO 172 Eb55
Şolcani MD 173 Fb54
Solčava SLO 151 Fc57
Sol'cy RUS 202 Eb09
Solda I 142 Db56
Şoldăneşti MD 173 Fd55
Şoldanu RO 180 Eb67
Sołdany PL 122 Jc30
Soldatovo RUS 113 Jb59
Sölden A 142 Dc55
Solduengo E 38 Dd57
Solec Kujawski PL 121 Ha34
Solec nad Wisłą PL 131 Jd40
Solec-Zdrój PL 138 Jc43
Soleggen N 85 Db35
Soleilhas F 43 Kb53
Solem N 78 Ed26
Solem N 78 Ec27
Solem N 78 Eb30
Solënoe RUS 205 Fd15
Solenzara F 154 Cb71
Solera de Gabaldón E 53 Ec67
Solesino I 150 Dd60
Solesmes F 24 Hb32
Solesmes F 28 Fc40
Soleşti RO 173 Fb59
Soleto I 163 Hc77
Solf FIN 81 Hd31
Solferino I 149 Db60
Solgne F 25 Jd36
Solhan TR 205 Ga20
Solheim N 84 Cb36
Solheim N 84 Ca37
Solheimsvik N 92 Cb42
Solignac F 33 Gb47
Soligny-lès-Étangs F 30 Hb38
Solihull GB 20 Ed25
Solin HR 158 Gc66
Solina PL 139 Kb46
Solingen D 125 Bd40
Soliny PL 123 Ka29
Solivella E 48 Gb61
Sölje S 94 Ed43
Solkan SLO 150 Ed58
Solkovo RUS 99 Ma40
Söll A 143 Eb53
Sollacaro F 154 Ca71
Sollana E 54 Fc68
Sollebrunn S 102 Ec47
Sollefteå S 79 Gb31
Sollentuna S 96 Gd43
Sóller E 57 Hb66
Søllerød DK 109 Ec25
Sollerön S 87 Fc38
Søllested DK 109 Ea28
Sollia N 85 Ea35
Söllichau D 127 Ec39
Solliès-Pont F 42 Ka55
Sollihøgda N 93 Dd41
Sollstedt D 126 Dc40
Solmaz TR 198 Fc89
Solms D 126 Cc42
Solmyra S 95 Ga42
Solncevo RUS 203 Fa13
Solnečnogorsk RUS 202 Ed10
Solnes N 65 Kc06
Solnhofen D 134 Dc48
Solnica PL 122 Hc30
Solnice CZ 137 Gb44
Solnik BG 181 Fa71
Solniki Wielkie PL 129 Gd41
Šolochovo RUS 113 Jb58
Solofra I 161 Fc75
Šolohovskij RUS 203 Fc14
Solojärvi FIN 69 Ka11
Solotarci MK 178 Bb73
Solomiac F 40 Ga53
Soloncení MD 173 Fd55
Solone UA 205 Fa15
Solonţ RO 172 Ec59
Solopaca I 161 Fb74
Solórzano E 38 Dc55
Solosancho E 46 Cd64
Solothurn CH 141 Bd53
Solovăstru RO 171 Dc58
Solov'i RUS 107 Ma47
Sölöz TR 186 Ga80
Solre-le-Château F 24 Hc32
Solrød Strand DK 109 Ec26
Sølsnes N 77 Da32
Solsona E 49 Gc59
Solstad N 67 Gc11
Solsted DK 108 Da27
Solsvik N 84 Bd39
Solt H 146 Hd55
Soltănești MD 173 Fb58
Soltau D 118 Db34
Soltendieck D 119 Dd35
Soltvadkert H 146 Hd56
Solum N 93 Dc44
Solumsmoen N 93 Dc41
Solutré-Pouilly F 34 Ja45
Solva GB 14 Db26
Solvang N 85 Dd34
Solvarbo S 95 Fd40
Sölvesborg S 111 Fc54
Solvik N 66 Fd17
Solvik S 94 Ec44
Solvorn N 84 Cd36
Solymár H 146 Hc52
Solynieve E 60 Dc75
Soma TR 191 Ed83
Somådal N 86 Ec34
Somaén E 47 Eb62
Somain F 24 Hb32
Somak TR 191 Ed87
Sømåseter N 86 Ec35

Somberek – Stănița

Somberek H 153 Hc57
Sombernon F 30 Ja42
Sombor SRB 153 Hd58
Şomcuta Mare RO 171 Da55
Someo CH 141 Cb56
Sõmera EST 105 Jc46
Somere FIN 75 Kd24
Someren NL 125 Bb39
Somerniemi FIN 89 Jd38
Somero FIN 89 Jd38
Someronkylä FIN 81 Jd26
Somerovaara FIN 74 Ka23
Sõmerpalu EST 107 Lb47
Somersham GB 20 Fd25
Somersham GB 21 Ga26
Somerton GB 19 Eb29
Someş-Oderhei RO 171 Cd56
Sominy PL 121 Gd31
Somlóvásárhely H 145 Gd54
Sommacampagna I 149 Db60
Somma Lombardo I 148 Cb58
Sommanelm N 92 Cd45
Sommariva del Bosco I 148 Bd61
Sommarøy N 62 Gc09
Sommarset N 66 Fd16
Sommatino I 167 Fa86
Sommauthe F 24 Ja34
Sommecaise F 30 Hb40
Somme-Leuze B 124 Ba42
Sommen S 103 Fc47
Sommepy-Tahure F 24 Hd35
Sömmerda D 127 Dd41
Sommerfeld D 119 Ed35
Sommerhausen D 134 Db45
Sommersete N 65 Kc05
Sommersted DK 108 Db26
Sommery F 23 Gb34
Sommesous F 24 Hd37
Somme-Tourbe F 24 Ja35
Sommevoire F 30 Ja38
Sommières F 41 Hd53
Sommières-du-Clain F 32 Fd45
Somo E 38 Dc54
Somogyapáti H 152 Ha57
Somogyaszalo H 145 Ha56
Somogycsicsó H 152 Gd57
Somogyfajsz H 145 Ha56
Somogyhárságy H 152 Ha57
Somogyjád H 145 Ha56
Somogysárd H 145 Ha56
Somogysimony H 145 Gd56
Somogytúr H 145 Ha55
Somogyudvarhely H 152 Gd57
Somogyvár H 145 Ha56
Somogyzsitfa H 145 Gd56
Somolinos E 46 Dd62
Somonino PL 121 Ha30
Somoskőújfalu H 146 Ja50
Somotor SK 139 Ka49
Somova RO 177 Fc64
Somovit BG 180 Db68
Sompa EST 99 Lb42
Sompolno PL 129 Hb36
Sompuis F 24 Hd37
Sompujärvi FIN 74 Jd21
Somsois F 24 Hd37
Somvix CH 142 Cc55
Son N 93 Ea43
Şona RO 175 Db60
Son Bou E 57 Ja66
Sonceboz CH 141 Bc53
Sonchamp F 29 Gc38
Soncillo E 38 Dc56
Soncino I 149 Cd60
Sonda EST 98 La42
Sondalo I 142 Da56
Sondby FIN 98 Kc39
Søndeled N 93 Db45
Sønder Bindslev DK 101 Dd19
Sønder Bjert DK 108 Db26
Sønderborg DK 108 Db28
Sønder Bork DK 108 Cd25
Sønderby DK 100 Da22
Sønderby DK 108 Db28
Sønder Dråby DK 100 Da21
Sønder Felding DK 108 Da24
Sønderho DK 108 Cd26
Sønderholm DK 100 Dc21
Sønder Hostrup DK 108 Db28
Sønder Hygum DK 108 Da26
Sønder Kirkeby DK 109 Eb29
Sønder Nissum DK 100 Cd23
Sønder Omme DK 108 Da25
Sønder Onsild DK 100 Dc22
Sønder Ørslev DK 109 Eb29
Sønder Rind DK 100 Db23
Sønder Rubjerg DK 100 Dc20
Sondershausen D 127 Dd40
Søndersø DK 108 Dc26
Sønder Solbjerg DK 100 Da21
Sønder Stenderup DK 108 Db26
Sønderup DK 100 Dc22
Søndervig DK 108 Cd24
Sønder Vilstrup DK 108 Db27
Sønder Vissing DK 108 Db24
Sondheim D 134 Db43
Søndre Osen N 86 Ec37
Sondrio I 149 Cd57
Söndrum S 102 Ed52
Söne S 102 Ed46
Soneja E 54 Fb66
Son en Breugel NL 125 Bb38
Songe N 93 Db45
Songeons F 23 Gc34
Songesand N 92 Cb44
Songy F 24 Hd37
Sonico I 149 Db57
Sonka FIN 74 Jd18
Sonkaja FIN 83 Ma30
Sonkajärvi FIN 82 Kd27
Sonkakoski FIN 82 Kd27
Sonkamuotka FIN 68 Ja14
Sonkari FIN 82 Kc30
Sonkovo RUS 202 Ed09
Son Macià E 57 Hc67
Son Marroig E 57 Hb67
Sonnboda FIN 97 Hd41
Sonneberg D 135 Dd43
Sonnefeld D 135 Dd44
Sonnewalde D 128 Fa39
Sonnino I 160 Ec73
Sonntag A 142 Da53
Sonogno CH 141 Cb56
Sonsbeck D 125 Bc38
Sons-de-Bretagne F 28 Ed38
Sonseca E 52 Db67
Son Servera E 57 Hc67
Sońsk PL 122 Jb35
Sonstorp S 95 Fd45
Sonta SRB 153 Hd59
Sontheim D 142 Db51
Sontheim a.d. Brenz D 134 Db49
Sonthofen D 142 Db53
Sontra D 126 Db41
Soodla EST 98 Kc42
Soomevere EST 98 Kd44
Söörmarkku FIN 89 Ja35
Sööru EST 99 Lb44
Sopeke FIN 91 Ma32
Sopelana E 38 Ea55
Sopište MK 178 Bb73
Sopje HR 152 Ha58
Sopkino RUS 122 Jb30
Soponya H 145 Hb54
Sopot AL 182 Ac75
Sopot BG 179 Da70
Sopot BG 180 Db72
Sopot PL 121 Hb30
Sopot RO 175 Cd66
Sopot SRB 153 Jc62
Sopot SRB 174 Bb64
Sopotnica MK 182 Ba75
Şopotu Nou RO 174 Bd64
Sopparjok N 64 Jc08
Soppela FIN 74 Kc18
Sopron H 145 Gc52
Sopronhorpács H 145 Gc53
Sopronkövesd H 145 Gc53
Sopsko Rudare MK 178 Bb73
Šor SRB 153 Ja62
Sora I 160 Ed72
Soragna I 149 Da61
Soråker S 88 Gc33
Sorano I 156 Dd69
Sørarnøy N 71 Fb18
Sør-Åvika N 70 Ed21
Sorbara I 149 Dc62
Sorbas E 61 Eb75
Sorbiers F 42 Jd51
Sørbø N 92 Ca43
Sorbo S 102 Eb46
Sorbolo I 149 Da61
Sörby S 94 Fa41
Sörby S 102 Fa47
Sörbygden S 87 Ga32
Sørbymagle DK 109 Ea27
Sörbyn S 73 Hd21
Sörbyn S 80 Hb26
Sord IRL 13 Cd21
Sordal N 92 Cd44
Sore F 39 Fb52
Söred H 145 Hb53
Sorede F 41 Hb57
Søreidet N 62 Gd08
Søre Moen N 78 Ed29
Sørenget N 78 Ec26
Soresina I 149 Cd60
Sørfinnset N 71 Fb18
Sörfjärden S 88 Gc34
Sørfjord N 63 Hc09
Sørfjord N 67 Gb12
Sørfjorden N 66 Fd13
Sörflärke S 80 Gc30
Sörfors S 80 Hb28
Sörforsa S 87 Gb35
Sørfossbogen N 67 Gc11
Sørgård N 71 Fb23
Sorges F 33 Ga48
Sorgono I 169 Ca77
Sør-Grunnfjord N 62 Gd08
Sorgues-l'Ouvèze F 42 Jb52
Sør-Gutvika N 70 Ec24
Sørheim N 84 Cd36
Sørhorsfjord N 70 Ec24
Sori I 148 Cb63
Soria E 47 Eb60
Soriano nel Cimino I 156 Ea70
Sorica SLO 151 Fa57
Sorico I 149 Cc57
Sorigny F 29 Ga42
Sorihuela E 45 Cb64
Sorihuela del Guadalimar E 53 Dd71
Sorila FIN 89 Jd35
Sorisdale GB 6 Da10
Sorita E 48 Fc63
Sörjön S 86 Fa36
Sørkedalen N 93 Ea41
Sorken N 86 Ec35
Sørkjos N 63 Hc08
Sørkjosen N 63 Hb09
Sørkjosen N 63 Ja05
Sorkkala FIN 89 Jd36
Sorknes N 86 Eb37
Sorkun TR 193 Gb86
Sorkuncak TR 199 Gd88
Sorkwity PL 122 Jb31
Sørland N 66 Fa16
Sør-Lenangen N 62 Ha09
Sørli N 79 Fb27
Sørlia N 78 Ec28
Sörmark S 94 Ed40
Sörmjöle S 80 Hb29
Sørmo N 67 Gc13
Sormula FIN 82 Kd26
Sorn GB 10 Dd14
Sornac F 33 Gd47
Sørnesøya N 70 Ed19
Sorno D 128 Fa39
Sörnoret S 79 Gb27
Sorø DK 109 Ea26
Soroca MD 173 Fc54
Soroc'i Gory RUS 203 Fd09
Soročkino RUS 99 Mb42
Sorokpolány H 145 Gc54
Soroní GR 197 Fa93
Sorpe E 40 Gb57
Sørreisa N 67 Gc11
Sörrenberg CH 141 Ca54
Sorrento I 161 Fb76
Sorribes E 49 Gc59
Sorring DK 108 Dc24
Sørrollnes N 66 Ga12
Sorsa FIN 82 Kc26
Sorsakoski FIN 82 La31
Sorsele S 72 Gc23
Sörskog S 87 Fd38
Sorso I 168 Bd74
Sörstafors S 95 Ga43
Sørstrand N 77 Da31
Sørstraumen N 63 Hc08
Sort E 40 Gb58
Sortino I 167 Fc87
Sortland N 66 Fd13
Sør-Tverrfjord N 63 Hb07
Sõru EST 97 Jc45
Sørum N 85 Dd39
Sørumsand N 94 Eb41
Sorunda S 96 Gd44
Sörup D 108 Db29
Sørup DK 100 Dc21
Sørvad DK 100 Da23
Sørvær N 63 Hc06
Sørvågen N 66 Fa15
Sørvágur DK 3 Ca06
Sørvik N 67 Gb12
Sørvik N 77 Dd28
Sörvik S 95 Fc41
Sørvika N 66 Ga13
Sørvika N 86 Ec33
Sörviken S 79 Ga29
Sörviken S 86 Fa33
Sørvollen N 86 Eb34
Sos F 40 Fd53
Sosa D 135 Ec43
Sösdala S 110 Fa54
Sos del Rey Católico E 39 Fa58
Sosedka RUS 203 Fc11
Sosedno RUS 99 Ma45
Soses E 48 Ga61
Sošichino RUS 107 Mb48
Sosnenskij RUS 202 Ed11
Sośnica PL 120 Ga33
Sośnica PL 139 Kc44
Sośnicowice PL 137 Hb44
Sosnicy RUS 99 Mb41
Sośnie PL 129 Gd40
Sósno PL 121 Gd33
Sosno RUS 99 Lc44
Sosnova RUS 107 Mb47
Sosnove UA 202 Ea14
Sosnovka RUS 113 Ja58
Sosnovka RUS 113 Jb58
Sosnovka RUS 203 Fb11
Sosnovka RUS 203 Fd08
Sosnovo RUS 99 Mb41
Sosnovo RUS 107 Ma46
Sosnovyj Bor RUS 99 Ld39
Sosnovyj Bor RUS 202 Ea08
Sosnowica PL 131 Kb39
Sosnowiec PL 138 Hc43
Sosnówka PL 131 Kc38
Soso FIN 74 Ka24
Sospel F 43 Kb52
Sossano I 150 Dd60
Šossejnoe RUS 113 Ja59
Sossonniemi FIN 75 La20
Sost F 40 Ga56
Šoštanj SLO 151 Fc57
Sóstis GR 184 Dc77
Šostka UA 202 Ed13
Sostógyogyfürdo H 147 Ka51
Sosynje RUS 107 Mb46
Sot SRB 153 Ja60
Şotânga RO 176 Dd64
Sotaseter N 85 Da35
Soteska SLO 151 Fa57
Soteska SLO 151 Fc59
Sotiel Coronada E 59 Bb73
Sotiello E 37 Cc54
Sotillo E 52 Db68
Sotillo de la Adrada E 46 Da65
Sotillo de la Ribera E 46 Dc60
Sotillo de las Palomas E 46 Cd65
Sotillo del Rincón E 47 Ea59
Sotillos E 37 Cd56
Sotin HR 153 Hd60
Sotira CY 206 Jd97
Sotíra GR 183 Bc77
Sotkamo FIN 82 La26
Sotkaniemi FIN 69 Jd11
Sotkanniemi FIN 82 La31
Sotkuma FIN 83 Lc30
Sotobañado y Priorato E 38 Da57
Soto de Campóo E 38 Db56
Soto de Dueñas E 37 Cd54
Soto de la Marina E 38 Dc54
Soto de la Vega E 37 Cb58
Soto del Barco E 37 Cb54
Soto de los Infantes E 37 Ca54
Soto del Real E 46 Dc63
Soto de Ribera E 37 Cb54
Soto en Cameros E 39 Eb58
Sotogrande E 59 Cb77
Sótony H 145 Gc54
Sotosalbos E 46 Db62
Sotoserrano E 45 Ca64
Sotres E 38 Da55
Sotresgudo E 38 Db57
Sotrondio E 37 Cc55
Sotta F 154 Cb72
Sotteville-lès-Rouen F 23 Gb35
Sottomarina I 150 Eb60
Sottrum D 118 Da34
Sottrupskov DK 108 Db28
Sottunga FIN 97 Hd40
Soutélamos E 53 Ea69
Soual F 41 Gd54
Souancé-au-Perche F 29 Ga39
Soubise F 32 Fa46
Soucy F 30 Hb39
Soúda GR 200 Cc95
Soudan F 28 Fa40
Soudan F 32 Fc45
Soudé F 24 Hd37
Soudes P 58 Ba73
Soues F 40 Fd55
Souesmes F 29 Gd41
Soufflenheim F 25 Kc36
Souflí GR 185 Ea77
Soúgia GR 200 Cb95
Sougy F 29 Gc39
Souillac F 33 Gc50
Souilly F 24 Jb36
Soukainen FIN 89 Ja38
Soukka FIN 98 Kb40
Soukkio FIN 90 Kb38
Soukolojärvi S 73 Jb19
Soulac-sur-Mer F 32 Fa48
Soulaines-Dhuys F 30 Ja38
Soulgé-sur-Ouette F 28 Fb39
Soúli GR 189 Bd86
Soulignonne F 32 Fb47
Soullans F 27 Ec43
Soulle F 32 Fa46
Soulópoulo GR 182 Ad80
Soultz-Haut-Rhin F 31 Kb39
Soultz-sous-Forêts F 25 Kc36
Soumoulou F 40 Fc55
Souni CY 206 Ja98
Soúnio GR 184 Db77
Souppes-sur-Loing F 29 Ha39
Souprosse F 39 Fb54
Sourdeval F 22 Fb37
Sourdon F 23 Gd34
Soure P 44 Ac64
Sourhope GB 11 Ed15
Souria F 41 Ha57
Sourpi GR 189 Ca83
Sours F 29 Gc38
Soursac F 33 Gd48
Souru FIN 82 Kd30
Souru FIN 91 Lb33
Sousceyrac F 33 Gd50
Sousel P 50 Ba68
Sous-Parsat F 33 Gd46
Soussac F 32 Fc50
Soustons F 39 Ed54
Soutelo P 45 Bd61
Southall GB 20 Fc28
Southam GB 20 Ed26
Southampton GB 20 Fa30
South Benfleet GB 21 Ga28
Southborough GB 20 Fd29
South Cave GB 16 Fb20
South Cave GB 16 Fb21
Southend GB 10 Db15
Southend-on-Sea GB 21 Ga28
Southery GB 17 Fd24
South Ferriby GB 17 Fc21
Southgate GB 20 Fc27
South Harting GB 20 Fb30
South Hayling GB 20 Fb30
South Hole GB 18 Dc29
South Kyme GB 17 Fc23
Southminster GB 21 Ga27
South Molton GB 19 Dd29
South Moreton GB 20 Fa28
South Ockendon GB 20 Fd28
South Perrott GB 19 Eb30
South Petherton GB 19 Eb30
Southport GB 15 Eb21
Southrope GB 20 Fb29
Southsea GB 20 Fa30
South Shields GB 11 Fa16
South Skirlaugh GB 17 Fc20
Southwater GB 20 Fc29
Southwell GB 16 Fb23
South Witham GB 16 Fb24
Southwold GB 21 Gc25
Soutochao E 45 Bc59
Souvála GR 195 Cb87
Souvigné F 28 Fd41
Souvigny F 30 Hb44
Sovana I 156 Dd69
Søvang DK 108 Da28
Søvang DK 109 Ec26
Søvassli N 77 Dd30
Sovata RO 172 Dd59
Söve TR 192 Fa81
Soveja RO 176 Ec61
Sover I 150 Dd57
Soverato I 164 Gc82
Sovereto I 162 Gc74
Soveria F 154 Cb69
Soveria Mannelli I 164 Gc81
Sövestad S 110 Fa56
Sovetsk RUS 113 Jc57
Sovetskaja RUS 203 Fc14
Sovetskaja RUS 205 Fd17
Sovetskij RUS 113 Ja59
Sovetskij RUS 203 Fd08
Sovetskoe RUS 205 Ga17
Sovietscoe MD 173 Fd55
Søvik N 76 Cc32
Søvika N 70 Ed22
Søvind DK 108 Dc25
Sovlje HR 157 Ga65
Sovoljano BG 179 Ca72
Sowczyce PL 129 Hb42
Sowia Góra PL 128 Ga36
Sowno PL 120 Fc33
Soye F 31 Ka41
Soyen D 143 Eb51
Soyhières CH 141 Bd52
Søyland N 92 Ca44
Søyland N 92 Ca45
Soylu TR 185 Ec77
Sozopol BG 181 Fa73
Spa B 125 Bb42
Spabrücken D 133 Ca44
Spadafora I 167 Fd83
Spahievo BG 184 Dc74
Spahnharrenstätte D 117 Cb34
Spaichingen D 142 Cc50
Spała PL 130 Ja39
Spalding GB 17 Fc24
Spálené Poříčí CZ 136 Fa46
Spálov CZ 137 Ha45
Spalt D 134 Dc47
Spalviškiai LT 106 Kd52
Spanbroek NL 116 Ba34
Spančevci BG 179 Cc69
Spandowerhagen D 120 Fa31
Spangenberg D 126 Da40
Spangereid N 92 Cc47
Spannarp S 102 Ec51
Spantekow D 120 Fa32
Spanţov RO 181 Ec67
Sparagovići HR 158 Ha68
Sparanise I 161 Fa74
Sparbu N 78 Ec28
Spāre LV 105 Jc50
Spāre LV 106 Kd49
Sparkær DK 100 Db23
Sparkford GB 19 Ec29
Sparlösa S 102 Ed47
Sparneck D 135 Ea44
Sparreholm S 95 Gb44
Sparrsätra S 95 Gb42
Sparsås N 93 Da45
Sparta I 164 Ga83
Spárti GR 194 Bc89
Spartiás GR 188 Ba84
Spárto GR 188 Ad83
Spartohóri GR 188 Ac83
Spas-Klepiki RUS 203 Fa10
Spas-Kotorsk RUS 99 Ma43
Spasovo BG 180 Dc73
Spasovo BG 181 Fb69
Spassk-Rjazanskij RUS 203 Fb11
Spáta GR 195 Cc87
Spatharéi GR 197 Eb88
Spathovúni GR 195 Bd87
Spavča HR 153 Hd61
Spean Bridge GB 6 Dc10
Specchia I 165 Hc78
Specchiarica I 162 Hb76
Specke S 94 Ed42
Speia MD 173 Ga58
Speia MD 173 Ga58
Speicher D 133 Bc44
Speichersdorf D 135 Ea45
Speikedalssetra N 86 Eb34
Spekeröd S 102 Eb48
Spelle D 117 Cb36
Spello I 156 Eb68
Spenge D 126 Cc37
Spennymoor GB 11 Fa17
Spentrup DK 100 Dc23
Sperenberg D 127 Ed37
Spergau D 127 Eb40
Sperhiáda GR 189 Bc83
Sperlinga I 167 Fb85
Sperlonga I 160 Ed73
Spermezeu RO 171 Db56
Sperone I 166 Eb84
Spessa I 150 Ed58
Spetisbury GB 19 Ec30
Spétses GR 195 Ca89
Speuld NL 116 Bb36
Spey Bay GB 5 Ec07
Speyer D 133 Cb46
Spezzano Albanese I 164 Gb79
Spezzano della Sila I 164 Gc80
Spiazzi I 149 Da58
Spicino RUS 99 Lc44
Spiddal IRL 12 Bc21
Spiegelau D 135 Ed48
Spiegelberg D 134 Cd47
Spiekeroog D 117 Cb31
Spielfeld A 144 Ga56
Spiez CH 141 Bd55
Spigno Monferrato I 148 Ca62
Spijkenisse NL 124 Ac37
Spilamberto I 149 Dc63
Spildra N 62 Gc10
Spíli GR 200 Cd96
Spiliá GR 183 Bd80
Spiliá GR 200 Cb94
Spilimbergo I 150 Ec57
Spiljani SRB 159 Jc68
Spiljani SRB 178 Ad69
Spille AL 182 Ab75
Spillum N 78 Ec26
Spilsby GB 17 Fd22
Spinazzola I 162 Gb74
Spincourt F 25 Jc35
Spind N 92 Cb47
Špindlerův Mlýn CZ 128 Fd42
Spineni RO 175 Db65
Spineta Nuova I 161 Fc76
Spinetta I 148 Cb61
Spink IRL 13 Cb22
Spiņņi LV 105 Jb49
Spino d'Adda I 149 Cd59
Spinoso I 162 Gb77
Spinuş RO 170 Cb56
Špionica BIH 153 Hc62
Spirgus LV 106 Ka51
Spiringen CH 141 Cb54
Spirovo RUS 202 Ec09
Špišić-Bukovica HR 152 Gd58
Spiss A 142 Db54
Spišská Belá SK 138 Jb47
Spišská Nová Ves SK 138 Jb48
Spišská Stará Ves SK 138 Jb46
Spišské Bystré SK 138 Jb48
Spišské Podhradie SK 138 Jc47
Spišské Vlachy SK 138 Jc48
Spišský Štvrtok SK 138 Jb47
Spital am Phyrn A 144 Fb52
Spital am Semmering A 144 Ga53
Spithami EST 97 Jd43
Spittal an der Drau A 143 Ed55
Spitz A 144 Fd50
Spjærøy N 93 Ea44
Spjald DK 108 Cd24
Spjelkavik N 76 Cc32
Spjutsbygd S 111 Fd54
Spjutsund FIN 98 Kc39
Spliding N 92 Cc47
Split HR 158 Gb66
Splügen CH 142 Cc56
Spóa GR 201 Eb95
Spodnja Kokra SLO 151 Fb57
Spodnja Pohanca SLO 151 Ga58
Spodnje Fužine SLO 151 Fb57
Spodnje Hoče SLO 144 Ga56
Spodnje Škofije SLO 151 Fa59
Spodnji Ivanjci SLO 144 Ga56
Spodnji Log SLO 151 Fc58
Spodsbjerg DK 109 Dd28
Spofforth GB 16 Fa20
Špogi LV 115 Lc53
Spohle D 118 Cc33
Špola UA 204 Ec15
Spoleto I 156 Eb69
Spondigna I 142 Db55
Spondinig I 142 Db55
Spontin B 124 Ad42
Spontour F 33 Gd49
Spora D 127 Eb41
Spore PL 121 Gb32
Spornitz D 119 Ea33
Sportgastein A 143 Ec54
Sporysz PL 121 Gc32
Spotorno I 148 Ca63
Spott GB 11 Ec13
Spraitbach D 134 Da48
Sprakensehl D 118 Dc35
Sprâncenata RO 180 Db67
Sprang-Capelle NL 124 Ba38
Sprängsviken S 88 Gc32
Spraudis LT 113 Jc55
Spreenhagen D 128 Fa37
Spremberg D 128 Fb39
Spresiano I 150 Ea59
Spridlington GB 17 Fc22
Sprimont B 132 Ba43
Şpring RO 175 Da60
Springe D 126 Da37
Springfield GB 9 Cb18
Sproatley GB 17 Fc20
Sprockhövel D 125 Ca39
Sproge S 104 Gd50
Sprogi LV 107 Lb49
Sproughton GB 21 Ga26
Spuz MNE 159 Ja69
Spychowo PL 122 Jc32
Spydeberg N 93 Ea42
Spytkowice PL 138 Hd44
Spytkowice PL 138 Ja46
Spytkowo PL 122 Jc30
Squillace I 164 Gc81
Squinzano I 162 Hb76
Sračinec HR 152 Gb57
Sraghmore IRL 13 Cd22
Srahmore IRL 8 Bc18
Sráid na Cathrach IRL 12 Bb22
Sraith Salach IRL 8 Bb20
Sramora Română RO 174 Bd61
Srbac BIH 152 Ha61
Srbica KSV 178 Ba70
Srbica MK 182 Ba74
Srbinovo MK 182 Ba74
Srbobran SRB 153 Jb59
Srbovac KSV 178 Ba69
Srđevići BIH 158 Gd65
Srdiečko SK 138 Hd48
Srebărna BG 181 Ed67
Srebrenica BIH 159 Ja64
Srebrna PL 123 Jd34
Srebrna Góra PL 137 Gb43
Sredec BG 180 Dd73
Sredec BG 181 Ed73
Središče ob Dravi SLO 152 Gb57
Središte BG 181 Ed68
Sredni Kolibi BG 180 Dd71
Srednja Besnica SLO 151 Fc58
Srednje BIH 159 Hc64
Srednjevo SRB 174 Bd64
Srednogorci BG 184 Db75
Srednogorovo BG 180 Dc72
Sredno Gradište BG 180 Dc73
Sredno Selo BG 180 Ea71
Srel'na RUS 99 Mb39
Śrem PL 129 Gc38
Sremska Kamenica SRB 153 Jb60
Sremska Mitrovica SRB 153 Ja61
Sremski Karlovci SRB 153 Jb60
Srezojevci SRB 159 Jc64
Sribne UA 202 Ed14
Srmska Rača SRB 153 Ja61
Srnetica BIH 152 Gc63
Srní CZ 135 Ed48
Srnice BIH 153 Hc62
Środa Śląska PL 129 Gb41
Środa Wielkopolska PL 129 Gd37
Srokowo PL 122 Jc30
Srpci MK 183 Bb75
Srpska Crnja SRB 174 Bb60
Srpski Hebej SRB 174 Bb61
Srpski Miletić SRB 153 Hd59
Sta S 78 Ed30
Staatz A 137 Gb49
Stabbfors S 71 Fc22
Stabbursnes N 64 Jb07
Stabulnieki LV 107 Lc51
Staburnäs S 79 Ga25
Staby DK 100 Cd23
Stachanov UA 205 Fb15
Stachy CZ 136 Fa48
Stachy PL 122 Jb33
Stačiūnai LT 114 Kb54
Staðarskáli IS 2 Ad04
Stade D 118 Da32
Stadecken-Elsheim D 133 Cb44
Stadel CH 141 Cb52
Stadelhofen D 135 Dd44
Staden B 21 Ha30
Stadensen D 118 Dc35
Stadhampton GB 20 Fa27
Stadil Kirkeby DK 100 Cd23
Stádio GR 194 Bc88
Stadland D 118 Cc33
Stadl an der Mur A 144 Fa54
Stadl Paura A 144 Fa51
Stadra S 95 Fc43
Stadskanaal NL 117 Ca34
Stadtallendorf D 126 Cd41
Stadtbergen D 142 Dc50
Stadthagen D 126 Da36
Stadtilm D 127 Dd42
Stadtkyll D 125 Bc42
Stadtlauringen D 134 Db44
Stadtlengsfeld D 126 Db42
Stadtlohn D 125 Bd37
Stadtoldendorf D 126 Da38
Stadtprozelten D 134 Cd45
Stadtroda D 127 Ea42
Stadtsteinach D 135 Ea44
Stadum D 108 Da28
Stae DK 100 Dc21
Stăeşti RO 180 Ea68
Stäfa CH 141 Cb53
Staffans S 73 Jb21
Staffanstorp S 110 Ed56
Staffarda I 148 Bc61
Staffolo I 156 Ec66
Stafford GB 16 Ed23
Staggia I 155 Dc66
Staggträsk S 72 Gc23
Stágira GR 184 Cc78
Stahnsdorf D 127 Ed37
Stahovica SLO 151 Fc57
Staicele LV 106 Kc47
Stainach A 144 Fa53
Stainforth GB 11 Ec19
Stainville F 24 Jb37
Stainz A 144 Fd55
Staithes GB 11 Fb18
Staiti I 164 Gb84
Stajčovci BG 179 Ca71
Stajićevo SRB 174 Bb62
Stajnica HR 151 Fd61
Stakčín SK 139 Kb47
Stake Pool GB 15 Eb20
Stakevci BG 179 Cb68
Stāķi LV 107 Lb49
Stakiai LT 114 Ka57
Stakkvik N 62 Gd08
Stakliškės LT 114 Kd58
Stakroge DK 108 Da25
Stalać SRB 178 Bc67
Stalbe LV 106 Kd49
Stalbridge GB 19 Ec30
Stalden CH 141 Bd56
Staldzene LV 105 Jb49
Stale PL 131 Jd42
Stalgėnai LT 113 Jc55
Stalģene LV 106 Kb52
Stalijska Mahala BG 179 Cc68
Stall A 143 Ec55
Stallarholmen S 96 Gc43
Ställberg S 95 Fc41
Ställdalen S 95 Fc41
Stalling Busk GB 11 Ed19
Stallwang D 135 Ec48
Staloluokta sameviste S 66 Ga17
Stalon S 79 Fd25
Stalowa Wola PL 131 Ka42
Stâlpeni RO 175 Dc64
Stâlpu RO 176 Ec64
Stalti LV 115 Ld53
Stalybridge GB 16 Ed21
Stambolijski BG 179 Da73
Stambulčić BIH 159 Hc65
Stamford GB 17 Fc24
Stamford Bridge GB 16 Fb20
Stamfordham GB 11 Ed16
Stammbach D 135 Ea44
Stammham D 135 Dd48
Stamnes N 66 Fd12
Stamnes N 84 Cb38
Stamora Germană RO 174 Bc62
Stams A 142 Dc54
Stamsele S 79 Fd29
Stamsried D 135 Eb47
Stamsund N 66 Fb14
Stamullin IRL 9 Cd20
Stânceni RO 172 Dd58
Stâncuţa RO 177 Fa65
Standlake GB 20 Fa27
Stăneşti RO 175 Cd63
Stăneşti RO 175 Da64
Stanevo BG 179 Cd67
Stanford-le-Hope GB 20 Fd28
Stånga S 104 Ha50
Stangaland N 92 Bd42
Stange N 94 Eb39
Stangerum DK 100 Dc22
Stanghede DK 100 Db23
Stanghella I 150 Dd61
Stanghelle N 84 Cb38
Stangnes N 67 Gb11
Stangnes N 94 Ec41
Stangvik N 77 Db31
Stanhope GB 11 Ed17
Stanica Bagaevskaja RUS 205 Fc15
Staniewice PL 121 Gb30
Stanileşti RO 173 Fb59
Stanin PL 131 Ka38
Staninci BG 179 Cb70
Stănişeşti RO 176 Ed60
Stanišić SRB 153 Hd58
Stanisławów PL 130 Jc36
Stanišovi HR 151 Fa61
Stănița RO 172 Ed58

Štanjel – Strandža

Štanjel SLO 151 Fa59
Stanjevci MK 178 Bc73
Staňkov CZ 135 Ed46
Stankovci HR 157 Ga65
Stanley GB 7 Eb11
Stanley GB 11 Fa17
Stanomino PL 120 Ga31
Stanovoe RUS 203 Fa12
Stans CH 141 Cb54
Stanton GB 21 Ga25
Stany PL 131 Ka42
Stanyčno- Luhans'ke UA 203 Fc14
Stanz A 144 Fd53
Stanzach A 142 Db53
Stapar SRB 153 Hd59
Stapari SRB 159 Jb65
Stapelburg D 126 Dc38
Staphorst NL 117 Bc35
Stapleford GB 16 Fa23
Stapleford GB 20 Ed29
Staplehurst GB 21 Ga29
Stąporków PL 130 Jb40
Stara PL 130 Ja40
Stara Baška HR 151 Fc61
Stara Błotnica PL 130 Jc39
Stará Bystrica SK 138 Hc47
Starachowice PL 130 Jc41
Stara Fužina SLO 151 Fa57
Stara Gradina HR 152 Ha58
Stará Huta SK 138 Hd49
Staraja Russa RUS 202 Eb09
Stara Jastrząbka PL 138 Jc44
Stara Kamionka PL 123 Kc32
Stara Kiszewa PL 121 Ha31
Stara Kornica PL 131 Kb36
Stara Łubianka PL 121 Gb34
Stará L'ubovňa SK 138 Jc46
Stara Moravica SRB 153 Ja58
Stara Novalja HR 151 Fc63
Stara Pazova SRB 153 Jb61
Stara Ploščica HR 152 Gc59
Stara Rečka BG 180 Ea70
Stara Reka BG 180 Ea71
Stara Rózanka PL 122 Jc30
Stará Ves nad Ondřejnicí CZ 137 Hb45
Stara Wieś PL 122 Jb33
Stara Wieś PL 131 Jd36
Stara Wiśniewka PL 121 Gc33
Stara Zagora BG 180 Dd72
Stara Žednik SRB 153 Ja58
Starchiojd RO 176 Eb63
Starcross GB 19 Ea31
Starcza PL 130 Hc42
Stare Czarnowo PL 120 Fc34
Stare Dębno PL 120 Ga32
Stare Dobrzyca PL 120 Fd32
Stare Dolistowo PL 123 Ka32
Stare Drawsko PL 120 Ga33
Stare Dyniska PL 131 Kd42
Stare Gronowo PL 121 Gd33
Staré Hamry CZ 137 Hb46
Staré Hrady CZ 136 Fd43
Stare Jabłonki PL 122 Hd32
Stare Jarosław PL 121 Gb30
Stare Jeżewo PL 123 Ka33
Stare Juchy PL 123 Jd31
Stare Kiejkuty PL 122 Jb32
Stare Kiełbonki PL 122 Jc32
Stare Komorowo PL 123 Jd34
Staré Město CZ 137 Gc44
Staré Město CZ 137 Gc45
Staré Město CZ 137 Gd48
Staré Město pod Landštejnem CZ 136 Fd48
Stare Miastko PL 129 Ha37
Stare Pole PL 122 Hc31
Staré Sedlo CZ 135 Ec46
Stare Sioło PL 139 Kc43
Stare Sobótka PL 130 Hc37
Stare Strącze PL 128 Ga38
Stare Waliszew PL 130 Hd38
Stare Wierzchowo PL 121 Gb32
Stargard Szczeciński PL 120 Fc33
Stårheim N 84 Cb34
Stari Bar MNE 159 Ja70
Starica RUS 202 Ec10
Starica RUS 202 Ed12
Starice Lisičkovo BG 179 Cb73
Staricy RUS 99 Mb42
Stari Dojran MK 183 Ca76
Stari Dulići BIH 159 Hc67
Starigrad HR 151 Fc62
Starigrad HR 158 Gc67
Stari Grad MK 183 Bc74
Stari Gradac HR 152 Gd58
Starigrad-Paklenica HR 157 Fd64
Stari Jankovci HR 153 Hd60
Stari Lec SRB 174 Bc62
Stari Log SLO 151 Fc59
Stari Majdan BIH 152 Gc62
Stari Mikanovci HR 153 Hc60
Stari Raušić KSV 178 Ad70
Stari Raušić SRB 159 Jc69
Stari trg SLO 151 Fd60
Stari Trogir HR 158 Gb66
Starkenbach A 142 Db54
Starkenbach CH 142 Cc54
Starkenberg D 127 Eb41
Starnberg D 143 Dd51
Starobil's'k UA 203 Fb14
Starobin BY 202 Ea13
Starodub RUS 202 Ec13
Staroec MK 182 Ba74
Starogard PL 120 Fd32
Starogard Gdański PL 121 Hb31
Staroglavice BIH 159 Ja64
Starojur'evo RUS 203 Fb11
Starokostjantyniv UA 204 Eb15
Starokrzepice PL 129 Hb41
Starominskaja RUS 205 Fc16
Staro Nagoričane MK 178 Bc72
Staronja RUS 107 Ma47
Staro Orjahovo BG 181 Fa71
Staropatica BG 179 Ca67
Staro Petrovo Selo HR 152 Ha60
Staropol'e RUS 99 Ld42
Starosel BG 180 Db72
Staroselci BG 179 Da69
Staroselec BG 180 Ea73
Staro Selo BG 180 Eb68
Staro Selo BIH 158 Gd64
Staro Selo Topusko HR 151 Ga60
Starosiverskaja RUS 99 Mb41
Staro Stefanje HR 152 Gc58
Starotitarovskaja RUS 205 Fb17
Starowice PL 121 Gb33
Starozagorski Bani BG 180 Dd72
Staro Železare BG 180 Db72
Starožilovo RUS 203 Fa11
Starożreby PL 130 Hd36
Starrkärr S 102 Ec48
Starše SLO 144 Ga56
Starti LV 106 Kd49
Starup DK 108 Db27
Stary Borek PL 139 Ka44
Stary Brus PL 131 Kc39
Stary Brzozów PL 130 Ja37
Stary Chwalim PL 121 Gb32
Stary Ciotusza PL 131 Kc42
Stary Dzierzgoń PL 122 Hc32
Stary Dzikowiec PL 139 Ka43
Stary Folwark PL 123 Kb30
Starý Hrozenkov CZ 137 Ha48
Staryi Oskol RUS 203 Fa13
Staryja Darohi BY 202 Eb13
Starý Jičín CZ 137 Ha46
Staryj Nizkovicy RUS 99 Mb40
Staryj Prud RUS 107 Mb52
Stary Nieskurzów PL 130 Jc41
Starý Plzenec CZ 135 Ed46
Stary Sącz PL 138 Jb46
Starý Smokovec SK 138 Jb47
Stary Szelków PL 122 Jc35
Stary Targ PL 122 Hc31
Stary Tychów PL 130 Jc40
Stary Wieś PL 131 Kb41
Starzyno PL 121 Ha29
Staševica HR 158 Hb67
Stasiówka PL 139 Jd44
Staškov SK 138 Hc46
Staßfurt D 127 Ea38
Staszów PL 130 Jc42
Stathelle N 93 Dc44
Statos Agios Fotios CY 206 Hd97
Statsås S 79 Ga26
Stăuceni MD 173 Fd58
Stăuceni RO 172 Ed55
Stauchlitz D 127 Ed40
Staufen D 141 Ca51
Staufenberg D 126 Cc42
Staughton Highway GB 20 Fc25
Staume N 84 Cb35
Staupitz D 128 Fa39
Stava S 103 Fc47
Štava SRB 178 Bb69
Stavalj SRB 178 Ad68
Stavang N 92 Ca44
Stavarygala LT 114 Kd57
Stavaträsk S 73 Hb24
Stavby S 96 Gd41
Stave N 66 Fd11
Stave N 92 Cb47
Stave SRB 153 Jb63
Stavelot B 125 Bb42
Stavely GB 16 Fa22
Stavenisse NL 124 Ac38
Stavern D 117 Cb35
Stavern N 93 Dd44
Stavnäs S 94 Ed43
Stavning DK 108 Cd24
Stavoren NL 116 Bb34
Stavós GR 184 Cc78
Stavre S 79 Fb30
Stavre S 87 Fd32
Stavreviken S 88 Gc33
Stavrodrómi GR 182 Ba78
Stavrodrómi GR 188 Ba86
Stavrodrómi GR 194 Bb87
Stavroménos GR 200 Cd95
Stavropol' RUS 205 Fd16
Stavros CY 206 Hd97
Stavrós GR 183 Bd78
Stavrós GR 184 Cc78
Stavrós GR 188 Ac84
Stavrós GR 189 Cb84
Stavrós GR 200 Cc94
Stavroskiádi GR 182 Ac79
Stavroúpoli GR 184 Db76
Stavsätra S 87 Fd36
Stavsjø N 86 Ea38
Stavsjöholm S 80 Ha29
Stavsnäs S 96 Ha43
Stavträsk S 80 Hb26
Stavtrup DK 108 Dc24
Staw PL 120 Fc35
Staw PL 129 Hb39
Stawiguda PL 122 Ja32
Stawiszyn PL 129 Ha38
Stawnica PL 121 Gc33
Staylittle GB 15 Ea24
Stazione di Mandatoriccio-Campana I 165 Gd79
Stazione di Motta Sant'Anastasia I 167 Fc86
Steane N 93 Da43
Steart GB 19 Eb29
Stębark PL 122 Hd33
Stebuliai LV 114 Kb59
Steccato I 165 Gd81
Stechelberg CH 141 Bd55
Štěchovice CZ 136 Fb45
Stechow D 127 Ec36
Steckborn CH 142 Cc52
Stede Broec NL 116 Bb34
Stedesdorf D 117 Cb32
Štědrá CZ 135 Ed44
Steeg A 142 Db54
Steenbergen NL 124 Ac38
Steenderen NL 125 Bc37
Steenvoorde F 21 Gd30
Steenwijk NL 117 Bc34
Steeple GB 21 Ga27
Steeple Aston GB 20 Fa26
Steeple Bumpstead GB 20 Fd26
Steeple Claydon GB 20 Fb26
Ştefan cel Mare RO 172 Ec58
Ştefan cel Mare RO 173 Fa59
Ştefan cel Mare RO 176 Dd66
Ştefan cel Mare RO 176 Ec60
Ştefan cel Mare RO 177 Fa66
Ştefan cel Mare RO 179 Da68
Ştefăneşti MD 173 Fc55
Ştefăneşti MD 177 Ga60
Ştefăneşti RO 172 Ed55
Ştefăneşti RO 175 Da65
Ştefăneşti RO 175 Dc64
Ştefăneşti de Jos RO 176 Eb66
Stefaniá GR 194 Bc90
Stefaniná GR 184 Cc77
Stefan Karadža BG 181 Ec68
Stefan Karadžovo BG 181 Ec73
Stefanovo BG 181 Fa69
Stefanóvouno GR 183 Bc80
Ştefan-Vodă MD 177 Ga60
Ştefan Vodă RO 176 Ed66
Steffeln D 133 Bc43
Steffenberg D 126 Cc41
Steffisburg CH 141 Bd54
Stefjordbotn N 66 Ga14
Stegaurach D 134 Dc45
Stege DK 109 Ec28
Stegelitz D 127 Eb37
Stegersbach A 145 Gb54
Stegna PL 122 Hc30
Stegny PL 122 Hd31
Stehnovo RUS 107 Mb48
Ştei RO 170 Cb58
Steikvasselva N 71 Fc22
Steimbke D 118 Da35
Stein D 134 Dc46
Stein N 78 Ea27
Stein N 93 Dd41
Steinaberg bru N 92 Cc41
Steinach A 143 Dd54
Steinach D 135 Dd43
Steinach D 135 Ec48
Steinach D 141 Ca50
Steinakirchen am Forst A 144 Fc51
Steinamanger = Szombathely H 145 Gc54
Stein am Rhein CH 142 Cc52
Stein an der Ens A 144 Fa53
Steinau D 118 Cd32
Steinau D 134 Da43
Steinbach A 143 Ed52
Steinbach am Wald D 135 Dd43
Steinbach-Hallenberg D 126 Dc42
Steinbeck D 128 Fa36
Steinberg A 143 Ea53
Steinberg D 135 Eb47
Steinberg N 92 Cb45
Steinbergkirche D 108 Db28
Steinburg D 118 Dc32
Steine N 78 Ec29
Steine N 78 Ec25
Steine N 92 Cb45
Steineien N 94 Ec41
Steinen D 141 Bd52
Steinen D 141 Ca52
Steinfeld A 143 Ed55
Steinfeld D 125 Bc42
Steinfeld D 134 Da44
Steinfeld (Oldenburg) D 117 Cc35
Steinfort L 133 Bb45
Steinfurt D 125 Ca37
Steingaden D 142 Dc52
Steinhagen D 119 Ed30
Steinhagen D 126 Cc37
Steinhaus I 143 Ea54
Steinheid D 135 Dd43
Steinheim D 126 Cd38
Steinheim D 134 Cd48
Steinheim D 134 Da49
Steinhöfel D 128 Fb37
Steinhöring D 143 Ea51
Steinibach CH 142 Cc54
Steinigtwolmsdorf D 128 Fb41
Steinkirchen D 118 Db32
Steinkirchen D 143 Eb50
Steinkirchen an der Traun A 144 Fa51
Steinkjer N 78 Ec28
Steinkjer N 78 Ed27
Steinkjernes N 65 Kc07
Steinløysa N 77 Da31
Steinnes N 62 Gd08
Steinsdal N 77 Dd29
Steinsfeld D 134 Db46
Steinshamn N 76 Cd31
Steinsholt N 93 Dc43
Steinsland N 70 Fa20
Steinsland N 93 Db44
Steinsøynes N 77 Da30
Steinsstaðabyggð IS 2 Ba04
Steinvik N 64 Ka06
Steinwiesen D 135 Dd43
Steinwiesen D 135 Ea43
Steira N 66 Fb14
Steiro N 70 Fa20
Stejari RO 175 Cd64
Stejaru RO 177 Fc65
Stejaru RO 180 Dc67
Steje MK 182 Ba76
Stekenjokk S 71 Fc24
Steķi LV 107 Lb52
Stellata I 150 Dd61
Stelle D 118 Dc33
Stellendam NL 124 Ac37
Stelmužė LT 115 Lb54
Stelnica RO 177 Fa66
Stelpe LV 106 Kc52
Stemnítsa GR 194 Bb87
Stemplės LT 113 Jc56
Stemwede D 117 Cc36
Stenaleees GB 18 Db31
Stenåsa S 111 Gb53
Stenay F 24 Jb34
Stenbacken S 67 Ha14
Stenbäcken S 80 Ha26
Stenbjerg DK 100 Cd21
Stenbrohult S 111 Fb53
Stendal D 127 Eb36
Stende LV 105 Jd50
Stenderup DK 108 Da25
Steneby S 94 Ec45
Stengårdshult S 102 Fa49
Stengelsen N 63 Hd08
Stengelsrud N 93 Dc42
Stenhamra S 96 Gc43
Stenhøj DK 101 Dd20
Stenico I 149 Dc57
Steni Dirfios GR 189 Cc85
Steniés GR 190 Da87
Stenímahos GR 183 Bc78
Steninge S 102 Ec52
Steningestrand S 102 Ec52
Stenkullen S 102 Ec49
Stenkumla S 104 Gd49
Stenkvista S 95 Gb44
Stenkyrka S 104 Ha48
Stenlille DK 109 Eb26
Stenløse DK 109 Ec25
Stennäs S 80 Gd28
Stenness GB 5 Ed04
Stenó GR 189 Bc86
Stenó GR 194 Bc88
Sténoma GR 188 Bb83
Štěnovice CZ 135 Ed46
Stensele S 72 Gb24
Stensjön S 103 Fc49
Stensryr S 102 Eb46
Stenstorp S 102 Fa47
Stensträsk S 72 Ha24
Stenstrup DK 109 Dd27
Stensund S 72 Gb23
Stensund S 72 Gc21
Stensund S 72 Gd24
Stensved DK 109 Eb28
Stenton GB 11 Ec13
Stentorp S 102 Ed48
Stenträsk S 72 Ha20
Stenudden S 72 Gc19
Stenum DK 100 Dc20
Stenungsund S 102 Eb48
Stepanci MK 183 Bc74
Štěpánov CZ 137 Gd46
Stepaside IRL 13 Cd22
Stępen BIH 159 Hc67
Stephanskirchen D 143 Eb52
Stephansposching D 135 Ec49
Stępień PL 122 Hd30
Štepivka UA 202 Ed14
Stepnica PL 120 Fc32
Stepnoe Matjunico RUS 203 Fd10
Stepnoje RUS 113 Jc58
Stepojevac SRB 153 Jc62
Stepping DK 108 Db26
Step-Soci MD 173 Fd56
Sterdyń-Osada PL 123 Ka35
Sterławki Wielkie PL 122 Jc31
Stern I 143 Ea56
Stérna GR 184 Da76
Stérna GR 185 Eb75
Sternberg D 119 Eb32
Šternberk CZ 137 Gd45
Sternenfels D 134 Cc47
Stérnes GR 200 Cc94
Sterringi N 85 Db34
Sterro I 167 Fc86
Sterup D 108 Db29
Sterup DK 100 Dc20
Sterzing I 143 Dd55
Stęszew PL 129 Gb37
Štětí CZ 136 Fb43
Stette N 76 Cd32
Stetten D 142 Cc50
Stettin = Szczecin PL 120 Fc33
Steuden D 127 Ea40
Steutz D 127 Eb38
Stevenage GB 20 Fc27
Stevenston GB 10 Dc14
Stevning DK 108 Db28
Stevnstrup DK 100 Dc23
Stevrek BG 180 Ea71
Stewarton GB 10 Db14
Stewarton GB 10 Dd14
Stewartstown GB 9 Cd17
Steyerberg D 126 Cd36
Steyning GB 20 Fc30
Steyr A 144 Fb51
Steyrbrücke A 144 Fb52
Steyregg A 144 Fb50
Stężyca PL 121 Ha31
Stężyca PL 131 Jd39
Stia I 156 Dd65
Štiavnik SK 137 Hb47
Stibanken DK 109 Ea28
Stibb Cross GB 18 Dc30
Stichill GB 11 Ec14
Stickney GB 17 Fc23
Stična SLO 151 Fc58
Stiege D 127 Dd39
Stige DK 109 Dd26
Stigen N 86 Ed36
Stigen S 102 Ec46
Stigersand N 94 Eb39
Stiglava LV 107 Ld50
Stigliano I 162 Gb76
Stigsjö S 88 Gc32
Stigsnæs DK 109 Ea27
Stigtomta S 95 Gb45
Stiklestad N 78 Ec28
Stikli LV 105 Jc49
Stilia GR 189 Bc86
Stilída GR 189 Bd83
Stilling DK 108 Dc24
Stilo I 164 Gc82
Stilton GB 20 Fc25
Stimfalia GR 189 Bc86
Štimlje KSV 178 Bb71
Stimpfach D 134 Db47
Stināpari RO 174 Bd64
Stinik MK 183 Cb75
Stinsford GB 19 Ec30
Stintino I 168 Bd74
Stio I 161 Fd77
Štip MK 183 Bd74
Stipsi GR 191 Ea83
Stira GR 190 Cd86
Stirfaka GR 189 Bc83
Stiri GR 189 Bd85
Stiring-Wendel F 25 Ka35
Stirling GB 7 Ea12
Stirniene LV 107 Lc51
Štit BG 185 Eb75
Štitar SRB 153 Ja62
Štítary CZ 136 Ga48
Štítnik SK 138 Jb49
Štíty CZ 137 Gc45
Ştiubieni RO 172 Ed54
Stiuca RO 174 Ca61
Stival F 27 Ea39
Štivan HR 151 Fb62
Stivica HR 152 Ha61
Stívos GR 183 Cb78
Stjärnfors S 95 Fc42
Stjärnhov S 95 Gb44
Stjärnorp S 103 Fd46
Stjärnsund S 95 Ga40
Stjärnvik S 95 Ga42
Stjern N 78 Ea28
Stjørdal N 78 Eb29
Støa N 78 Ec42
Stoļerova LV 107 Ld51
Stobierna PL 139 Ka43
Stobnica PL 130 Hd40
Stobno PL 121 Gb34
Stobrawa PL 129 Gd42
Stobs Castle GB 11 Ec15
Stochov CZ 136 Fa44
Stocka S 88 Gc35
Stockach D 142 Cc51
Stockamöllan S 110 Fa55
Stockaryd S 103 Fc50
Stockbridge GB 20 Fa29
Stöcke S 80 Hb28
Stockelsdorf D 119 Dd31
Stocken S 102 Eb47
Stockenboi A 143 Ed55
Stockerau A 145 Gb50
Stockheim D 134 Db43
Stockheim D 135 Dd43
Stockholm S 96 Gd43
Stockland Bristol GB 19 Eb29
Stockleigh Pomeroy GB 19 Ea30
Stocklen-Alm A 142 Dc54
Stockport GB 16 Ed22
Stocksbo S 87 Ga35
Stocksbridge GB 16 Fa21
Stöckse D 118 Da35
Stöcksjö S 80 Hb28
Stockstadt am Main D 134 Cd44
Stockton-on-Tees GB 11 Fa18
Stoczek Lukowski PL 131 Jd37
Stoczek-Osada PL 123 Jd35
Stod CZ 135 Ed46
Stöde S 87 Ga33
Stødle N 92 Cb41
Stödtlen D 134 Db48
Stöðvarfjörður IS 3 Bc06
Stoeneşti RO 176 Dd63
Stoeneşti RO 180 Db67
Stoeneşti RO 180 Ea67
Stoholm DK 100 Db23
Stoianovca MD 177 Fb60
Stoicănești RO 180 Db67
Stoiceni RO 171 Db55
Stoidraga HR 151 Ga58
Stoileşti RO 175 Db64
Stoina RO 175 Cd65
Stojakovo MK 183 Ca76
Stojan Mihajlovski BG 181 Ed70
Stojanovo BG 180 Db70
Stojanovo BG 184 Dc75
Stojkite BG 184 Db75
Stojkovo BG 185 Dd74
Stoke GB 18 Dc29
Stoke-by-Nayland GB 21 Ga26
Stoke Ferry GB 17 Fd24
Stoke Goldington GB 20 Fb26
Stoke-on-Trent GB 16 Ed23
Stokesley GB 11 Fa18
Stoke upon Tern GB 15 Ec23
Stokite BG 180 Dc71
Stokka N 70 Ed22
Stokke N 93 Dd44
Stokkeland N 92 Cd47
Stokkemarke DK 109 Ea28
Stokkseyri IS 2 Ac05
Stokksund N 78 Ea28
Stokkvågen N 70 Fa20
Stokmarknes N 66 Fc13
Stolac BIH 158 Hb67
Stolāt BG 180 Dc71
Stolberg D 125 Bc41
Stolberg D 127 Dd39
Stolbovo RUS 99 Ld43
Stolec PL 120 Fb33
Stołeczna PL 120 Fc35
Stolice SRB 153 Ja63
Stolin BY 202 Ea14
Stollberg D 127 Ec42
Stöllet S 94 Fa40
Stollhamm D 117 Cc32
Stolniceni MD 173 Fa54
Stolnici RO 175 Dc65
Stolnik BG 179 Cd71
Stolno PL 121 Hb33
Stoloiceni MD 173 Fc58
Stólos GR 194 Bc88
Stolpe D 118 Dc31
Stolpe D 119 Ed33
Stolpe D 120 Fb35
Stolpen D 128 Fb41
Stolzenau D 126 Cd36
Stolzenhain D 127 Ed38
Stómio GR 183 Ca80
Stommell S 94 Eb43
Stömne S 94 Ed43
Stomorska HR 158 Gb67
Stompetoren NL 116 Ba35
Ston HR 158 Ha68
Stone GB 16 Ed23
Stone GB 20 Fb27
Stonehaven GB 7 Ed10
Stongfjorden N 84 Ca35
Stonglandet N 67 Gb11
Stoniškiai LT 113 Jc57
Stonne F 24 Ja34
Stønnesbotn N 62 Gb10
Stonyford IRL 13 Cb24
Stopanja SRB 178 Bb68
Stopki PL 122 Jb30
Stopnica PL 138 Jc43
Stopnik SLO 151 Fa58
Storå S 95 Fc42
Stora Blåsjön S 79 Fb25
Stora Dyrön S 102 Eb48
Stora Höga S 102 Eb48
Stora Kil S 94 Fa43
Stora Levene S 102 Ed47
Stora Malm S 95 Ga45
Stora Mellby S 102 Ec47
Stora Mellösa S 95 Fd44
Stora rör S 103 Gb52
Storås N 77 Dd31
Storåsen S 79 Fc29
Stora Skedvi S 95 Fd40
Stora Stensjön S 79 Fb28
Stora Tuna S 95 Fd40
Stora Vika S 96 Gd45
Storbäck S 79 Fd26
Storbäcken S 73 Ja19
Storbacken S 73 Hb20
Storbekken N 86 Ed37
Storberg S 72 Gd23
Storberget S 73 Hd18
Storberget S 79 Gb26
Storboda S 87 Ga33
Storborgarn S 80 Gd29
Storbørja N 70 Ed23
Storbränna S 79 Fc29
Storbrännan S 80 Hb26
Storbukt N 64 Jc04
Storby FIN 96 Hb40
Stord N 92 Ca41
Stordal N 76 Cd33
Stordalen N 63 Hc07
Stordalen N 84 Cb37
Stordalen S 67 Gd14
Stordalselv N 62 Gd10
Štore SLO 151 Fd57
Store Andst DK 108 Db26
Storebro S 103 Ga49
Store Darum DK 108 Cd26
Storegarden N 86 Eb38
Storehaug N 84 Cb36
Store Heddinge DK 109 Ec27
Storekorsnes N 63 Hd07
Storelv N 63 Hd06
Storelvavoll N 86 Ec32
Stor-Elvdal N 86 Eb36
Store Lyndevad DK 108 Da28
Store Merløse DK 109 Eb26
Støren N 78 Ea31
Storeng N 63 Hb08
Storeng N 71 Fd18
Store Rise DK 108 Dc28
Store Rørbæk DK 109 Eb25
Store-Strandal N 76 Cc33
Storfall S 80 Ha29
Storfjäten S 86 Fa35
Storfjellseter N 85 Ea35
Storfjord N 62 Ha10
Storfors S 95 Fb43
Storforshei N 71 Fc20
Storfossen N 64 Jc10
Storgård FIN 97 Jc41
Storgranliden S 73 Hb23
Storhågna S 87 Fb33
Storhallaren N 77 Dc29
Storhögen S 79 Fd30
Storhöjden S 79 Fd29
Stor-Holmträsk S 80 Gd25
Štorje SLO 151 Fa59
Storjola S 79 Fc25
Storjord N 71 Fd19
Storjorda N 71 Fc18
Storjorda N 71 Fb19
Storkågeträsk S 73 Hc24
Storkow D 128 Fa37
Storkowo PL 120 Fd33
Storli N 67 Gc11
Storliden S 80 Hb26
Storlien S 78 Ec30
Stormark S 73 Hc24
Stormi FIN 89 Jc36
Stormo N 62 Gd09
Stormoen N 71 Fb23
Stormoen N 71 Fb20
Stornara I 161 Ga73
Stornarella I 161 Ga73
Stornäs S 71 Fd24
Stornäset S 79 Ga28
Stornes N 63 Hb08
Stornes N 66 Ga12
Stornoway GB 4 Da05
Störnstein D 135 Eb45
Storo I 149 Db58
Ştorobăneasa RO 180 Dd68
Storoddan N 77 Dc30
Storön S 73 Ja22
Storožinec RUS 99 Lc44
Storożynec' UA 204 Ea16
Storrington GB 20 Fc30
Storsaivis S 73 Hd19
Storsand N 93 Ea42
Storsand S 73 Hb20
Storsandsjö S 80 Hb27
Storsätern S 86 Ec34
Storsävarträsk S 80 Hb26
Storseleby S 79 Gb25
Storselet S 80 Hb25
Storsjö S 86 Fa32
Storskog N 65 Kc06
Storskog S 71 Ga23
Storslett N 63 Hb09
Storstein N 63 Hb08
Storsteinnes N 67 Gd11
Storsund S 73 Hb22
Stortinden N 63 Hd06
Storträsk S 73 Hb24
Storulvåns fjällstation S 78 Ed30
Storuman S 72 Gb24
Storvallen S 78 Ec30
Storvatnet N 66 Ga13
Storvik N 63 Hb09
Storvik S 95 Gb39
Storvika N 71 Fb18
Storvika N 78 Ea27
Storvoll N 62 Ha09
Storvollen N 62 Hc08
Storvollen N 71 Fc20
Storvollen N 71 Fb23
Storvollen N 77 Dd33
Storvorde DK 100 Dc21
Storvreta S 96 Gc41
Štós SK 138 Jc48
Stößen D 127 Ea41
Stoszowice PL 137 Gc43
Stöten S 86 Ed37
Stotfold GB 20 Fc26
Stott N 70 Fa18
Stötten D 142 Dc52
Stotternheim D 127 Dd41
Stottesdon GB 15 Ec25
Stouby DK 108 Db25
Stoulton GB 20 Ed26
Stoumont B 125 Bb42
Stoúpa GR 194 Bb90
Stourport-on-Severn GB 15 Ec25
Stovbcy BY 202 Ea13
Støvring DK 100 Dc21
Støvset N 66 Fc17
Stow GB 11 Ec14
Stowięcino PL 121 Gd29
Stowmarket GB 21 Ga26
Stow-on-the-Wold GB 20 Ed26
Stowupland GB 21 Ga26
Stožer BG 181 Fa70
Stożne PL 123 Jd30
Stra I 150 Ea60
Straach D 127 Ec38
Straasdorf an der Nordbahn A 145 Gc50
Straatsburg = Strasbourg F 25 Kc37
Strabane GB 9 Cc16
Strabla PL 123 Kb34
Strachan GB 7 Ec09
Strachomino PL 120 Ga31
Strachówka PL 130 Jc36
Strachus GB 6 Dc12
Strączno PL 121 Gb34
Strada in Chianti I 155 Dc65
Strådalen S 86 Fa34
Stradalovo BG 179 Ca73
Strada San Zeno I 156 Dd64
Stradbally IRL 13 Cb25
Stradella I 149 Cc60
Stradishall GB 20 Fd26
Stradola I 161 Fd74
Stradone IRL 9 Cc19
Stradsett GB 17 Fd24
Straduny PL 123 Jd31
Stradzde LV 105 Jd50
Straelen D 125 Bc39
Stræte N 67 Gb12
Stragan SRB 174 Bb66
Stragavallen S 86 Fa34
Strahilovo BG 180 Dd69
Strahwalde D 128 Fc41
Straimont B 132 Ba44
Straiton GB 10 Dd15
Straja RO 172 Ea54
Straja RO 181 Fc67
Stråkan S 73 Ja19
Străklevo BG 180 Ea68
Strakonice CZ 136 Fa47
Straldža BG 180 Eb72
Straloch GB 7 Eb10
Strålsnäs S 103 Fc47
Stralsund D 119 Ed30
Štramberk CZ 137 Ha46
Strambino I 148 Bd59
Strāmeriena LV 107 Lc49
Stramproy NL 125 Bb39
Strâmtura RO 171 Db55
Strand N 65 Kd08
Strand N 66 Fd13
Strand N 77 Db30
Strand N 86 Eb37
Strand N 92 Ca43
Strand S 72 Gd20
Strand S 79 Fd28
Strand S 95 Fd40
Stranda N 64 Jb05
Stranda N 76 Cd33
Strandbaden S 110 Ec54
Strandby DK 100 Db22
Strandby DK 101 Dd19
Strande D 118 Dc30
Strandebarm N 84 Cb39
Strandhill IRL 8 Bd18
Strandlykkja N 94 Eb39
Strandvalen N 78 Ec25
Strandvallen S 86 Ed36
Strandvik N 84 Ca40
Strandža BG 185 Ec74

Strangford – Svartkog

Strangford GB 10 Db18
Strängnäs S 95 Gb43
Strängsered S 102 Fa49
Strångsjö S 95 Ga45
Strání CZ 137 Ha48
Stranice SLO 151 Fd57
Stranraer GB 10 Dc16
Stransko BG 180 Dd73
Străoane RO 176 Ed61
Strasatti I 166 Ea85
Strasbourg F 25 Kc37
Strasburg D 120 Fa33
Străşeni MD 173 Fc57
Strašice CZ 136 Fa45
Strašín CZ 136 Fa47
Stråsjö S 87 Ga35
Stråskogen N 64 Jb07
Straškov Vodochody CZ 136 Fb43
Stråssa S 95 Fd42
Straßberg D 127 Dd39
Straßberg A 144 Fb55
Straßburg = Strasbourg F 25 Kc37
Straßgräbchen D 128 Fb40
Straßkirchen D 135 Ec48
Straßwalchen A 143 Ed51
Straszewo PL 121 Hb35
Straszów PL 128 Fc40
Straszyn PL 121 Hb30
Stratford-upon-Avon GB 20 Ed26
Strathan GB 6 Dc09
Strathaven GB 10 Ea14
Strathblane GB 10 Dd13
Strathcarron GB 6 Dc08
Strathconon GB 4 Dd07
Strathpeffer GB 4 Dd07
Strathyre GB 7 Dd12
Stratinista GR 182 Ac79
Stratinska BIH 152 Gc62
Stratóni GR 184 Cc78
Stratoníki GR 184 Cc78
Strátos GR 188 Ba83
Stratton GB 18 Dc30
Stratton Audley GB 20 Fa26
Straubing D 135 Eb48
Straulas I 168 Cc75
Straum N 70 Fa22
Straum N 77 Dc29
Straumen N 62 Gc10
Straumen N 66 Fd17
Straumen N 66 Ga12
Straumen N 66 Fc17
Straumen N 77 Db30
Straumen N 78 Eb28
Straumen N 78 Ec25
Straumfjord N 66 Fc13
Straumfjorden N 66 Fd15
Straumfjordnes N 63 Hb08
Straumnes N 66 Fc14
Straumnes N 67 Gb13
Straumsjøen N 66 Fc13
Straumsli N 67 Gd11
Straumsnes N 63 Hd06
Straumsnes N 65 Kd08
Straumsnes N 66 Fc13
Straumsnes N 66 Fd17
Straumsnes N 77 Db31
Straumsvika N 70 Fa19
Strijpai LT 114 Ka57
Straupe LV 106 Kc49
Straupitz D 128 Fb38
Strausberg D 128 Fa36
Straußfurt D 127 Dd41
Stravaj AL 182 Ad76
Stråvalla S 102 Ec50
Strawczyn PL 130 Jb41
Stráž CZ 135 Ec46
Straż PL 123 Kb33
Straža BG 180 Eb70
Straža SRB 174 Bc63
Strazdiņi LV 107 Lc49
Stražica BG 180 Ea70
Stražica SLO 151 Fd57
Strážnice CZ 137 Gd48
Strážný CZ 136 Fa48
Strážov CZ 135 Ed47
Stráž pod Ralskem CZ 128 Fc42
Strážske SK 139 Ka48
Štrba SK 138 Ja47
Štrbské Pleso SK 138 Ja47
Streatham GB 20 Fc28
Streatley GB 20 Fa28
Strečno SK 138 Hc47
Streda nad Bodrogom SK 139 Ka49
Street GB 19 Eb29
Streetly GB 16 Ed24
Stręgiel PL 122 Jc30
Strehaia RO 175 Cc65
Strehla D 127 Ed40
Streisângeorgiu RO 175 Cc61
Strejești RO 175 Db65
Strekov SK 145 Hb51
Strękowa Góra PL 123 Ka33
Strelča BG 179 Da72
Strelci BG 180 Db72
Strelci BG 180 Eb71
Strelec BG 180 Ea70
Střelice CZ 137 Gc45
Streliškiai LT 113 Jc53
Strelkino RUS 107 Mb48
Strelniky SK 138 Hd49
Stremț RO 175 Da60
Stremutka RUS 107 Ma47
Strenči LV 106 Kd48
Strendene N 70 Fa23
Strengberg A 144 Fc51
Strengelbach CH 141 Ca53
Strengel våg N 66 Fd12
Strengereid N 93 Db46
Stresa I 148 Cb58
Stretsbol S 94 Ed43
Stretton GB 20 Fa25
Streufdorf D 134 Dc43
Streva LT 114 Kd58
Strezimirovci SRB 179 Ca71
Strezovce KSV 178 Bc71
Strib DK 108 Db26
Striberg S 95 Fc43
Stříbrná Skalice CZ 136 Fc45
Stříbro CZ 135 Ec45
Strichen GB 5 Ed07
Striegistal D 127 Ed41
Strielčiai LT 114 Kc58
Strigno I 150 Dd58
Štrigova HR 145 Gb56
Strihovce SK 139 Kb47
Strijen NL 124 Ad37
Strikçan AL 182 Ad74
Striki LV 105 Jd52
Střílky CZ 137 Gd47
Strimasund S 71 Fc21
Strimonikó GR 183 Cb76
Strittjomvare S 72 Gd22
Strizivojna HR 153 Hc60
Strjama BG 180 Db73
Strîniceni-Prăjescu RO 172 Ec57
Strmac HR 152 Gd60
Strmica HR 158 Gb64
Strmilov CZ 136 Fd47
Strö S 102 Ed46
Strobin PL 129 Hb40
Strobl A 143 Ed52
Strøby DK 109 Ec27
Strøby Egede DK 109 Ec27
Strodi LV 107 Ld52
Stroeşti RO 175 Da63
Strofiliá GR 189 Cb84
Ströhen D 126 Cd36
Stroieşti MD 173 Fd55
Stroieşti RO 172 Eb56
Strojice BIH 158 Gd64
Strojkovce SRB 178 Bd70
Strokestown IRL 8 Ca19
Ström S 71 Fc22
Ström S 94 Ec43
Strömback S 80 Hb29
Strömbacka S 87 Gb35
Stromberg D 126 Cc38
Stromberg D 133 Ca44
Stromemore GB 4 Db08
Strömfors FIN 90 Kd38
Strömfors S 73 Hb23
Strömholm S 72 Gc22
Stromiec PL 130 Jc39
Strömma FIN 96 Hb40
Strömma FIN 97 Jc40
Strömma S 96 Ha43
Strømmen N 93 Ea41
Strömnäs S 73 Hb23
Strömnäs S 79 Ga25
Stromness GB 5 Eb03
Strömsberg S 96 Gc40
Strömsbruk S 88 Gc35
Strömsfors S 103 Ga46
Strömsholm S 95 Ga43
Strömsillret S 86 Ed35
Strömsjönäs S 80 Ha27
Strømsli N 67 Gc12
Strömsnäs S 79 Fd31
Strömsnäsbruk S 110 Fa53
Strömstad S 94 Ea45
Strömsund S 71 Ga23
Strömsund S 73 Ja21
Strömsund S 79 Fd28
Strömtorp S 95 Fd44
Stronachlachar GB 7 Dd12
Strond N 93 Da44
Strongilí GR 182 Ab80
Strongilovoúni GR 188 Ad84
Strongoli I 165 Gd80
Stronie Śląskie PL 137 Gc44
Stronsdorf A 137 Gb49
Strontian GB 6 Db10
Stroove IRL 9 Cd15
Strop LV 115 Lc53
Stropicy RUS 99 Lc44
Stropkov SK 139 Jd47
Stroppiana I 148 Ca60
Strošinci SRB 153 Hd61
Stroud GB 19 Ec27
Stroud GB 20 Fb30
Stroumpi CY 206 Hd97
Strövelstorp S 110 Ed54
Strovja MK 183 Bb74
Strovlés GR 200 Ca95
Stróża PL 138 Ja45
Stróże PL 138 Jc45
Strücklingen D 117 Cb34
Struer DK 100 Da22
Struga MK 182 Ad75
Strugari RO 172 Ec59
Strugi-Krasnye RUS 99 Mb45
Strugovo MK 182 Ba75
Struhařov CZ 136 Fc45
Štrukovec HR 145 Gb56
Strullendorf D 134 Dc45
Strumica MK 183 Ca75
Strumień PL 138 Hc45
Strumjani BG 183 Cb75
Strunga RO 172 Ed57
Strungari RO 175 Cd61
Strupina PL 129 Gc40
Struppen D 128 Fa42
Strusshamn N 84 Ca39
Struth D 126 Db40
Struy GB 7 Dd08
Stružec HR 152 Gc59
Stružna CZ 135 Ec44
Strycksele S 80 Ha26
Strycktjärn S 73 Hc22
Stryj UA 204 Dd16
Stryjno PL 131 Kb40
Stryjów PL 131 Kc41
Stryków PL 130 Hd38
Stryn N 84 Cd34
Strynø By DK 109 Dd28
Stryszawa PL 138 Hd45
Strzakły PL 131 Ka37
Strzałkowo PL 129 Ha37
Strzebin PL 130 Hc42
Strzeczona PL 121 Gc33
Strzegocin PL 122 Jb35
Strzegocin PL 130 Hc37
Strzegom PL 129 Gb41
Strzegów PL 129 Gd42
Strzegowo-Osada PL 122 Ja35
Strzelce PL 129 Gb42
Strzelce PL 129 Ha36
Strzelce PL 130 Hc37
Strzelce Krajeńskie PL 120 Fd35
Strzelce Opolskie PL 137 Hb43
Strzeleczki PL 137 Ha43
Strzelin PL 129 Gc42
Strzelniki PL 129 Gd42
Strzelno PL 112 Ha58
Strzelno PL 129 Ha36
Strzmiele PL 120 Fd32
Strzybnica PL 138 Hc43
Strzygi PL 122 Hc34
Strzyżów PL 131 Kd41
Strzyżów PL 139 Ka44
Strzyżowska PL 139 Jd45
Šttist RUS 99 Lc39
Stubal SRB 178 Bb67
Stubbæk DK 108 Db28
Stubbekøbing DK 109 Eb28
Stubben D 118 Cd33
Stubbsand S 80 Ha30
Stuben A 142 Da54
Stubenberg A 144 Ga54
Stubenberg D 143 Ec50
Stubičke toplice HR 151 Ga58
Štubik SRB 174 Ca66
Stubline SRB 153 Jb62
Stubno PL 139 Kc44
Studena BG 179 Cb72
Studená CZ 136 Fd47
Studenci HR 158 Gd66
Studenec BG 180 Eb69
Studenec CZ 136 Fd43
Studenec SLO 151 Fd58
Studénka CZ 137 Ha45
Studenzen A 144 Ga55
Studienka SK 137 Gd49
Studina RO 180 Db67
Studley GB 20 Ed25
Studley GB 20 Ed28
Studna BG 185 Eb74
Studnica PL 128 Ga41
Studsgård DK 108 Da24
Studsviken S 80 Gd29
Studzianki PL 123 Kb33
Studzianki-Pancerne PL 130 Jc38
Studzienice PL 121 Gd31
Studzieniczna PL 123 Kb31
Studzieniec PL 129 Gc36
Stūgliai LT 115 Lb55
Stugsund S 87 Gb37
Stugufläten N 77 Db33
Stugun S 79 Fd31
Stuguvollmoen N 78 Ec31
Stuhr D 118 Cd34
Stukenbrock, Schloß Holte- D 126 Cc38
Stulgiai LT 113 Jd56
Stulln D 135 Eb46
Stülpe D 127 Ed38
Stulpicani RO 172 Ea56
Stungiai LT 114 Ka53
Stunts Green GB 20 Fd30
Stuomenai LV 114 Kb58
Stuorajavrre N 68 Hd11
Stuoranjargga N 63 Ja10
Stupari BIH 153 Hc63
Stupava SK 145 Gc50
Stupino RUS 203 Fa11
Stupnik HR 151 Ga59
Stuppach D 134 Da46
Stupurai LT 114 Kb53
Stūri LV 105 Jd52
Stūri LV 106 Kc51
Sturkö S 111 Fd54
Sturla I 148 Cb63
Šturlić BIH 151 Ga61
Sturminster Newton GB 19 Ec30
Sturno I 161 Fd74
Šturovo SK 146 Hc52
Sturry GB 21 Gb29
Sturton by Stow GB 16 Fb22
Sturzelbronn F 25 Kb35
Sturzeni MD 173 Fa55
Sturzeşti MD 173 Fb55
Stutensee D 133 Cb47
Stuttgart D 134 Cd48
Stützerbach D 126 Dc42
Stuve N 86 Ea38
Stuvestøyl N 92 Cd44
Stybbersmark S 80 Ha30
Stykkishólmur IS 2 Ac03
Stylloi CY 206 Jc96
Stypułów PL 128 Fd39
Styri N 94 Eb40
Styrmannstø N 62 Ha09
Styrnäs S 80 Gc31
Styrsö S 102 Eb49
Styrvoll N 93 Dc43
Su E 49 Gc60
Suadiye TR 187 Gb79
Suances E 38 Db54
Suaningi S 73 Ja18
Suare F 154 Ca69
Suatu RO 171 Db58
Subačius LT 114 Kd54
Subaşı TR 186 Fb77
Subaşı TR 186 Fb80
Subaşı TR 187 Ha80
Subate LV 115 Lb53
Subbiano I 156 Dd66
Subcetate RO 172 Ea58
Subcetate RO 175 Cc61
Suben A 143 Ed50
Sübeylidere TR 191 Ec83
Subiaco I 160 Ec71
Subkowy PL 121 Hb31
Sublaines F 29 Gb42
Subotica HR 152 Gc57
Subotica SRB 153 Ja57
Subotiste SRB 153 Jb61
Sučany SK 138 Hd47
Sucaveni RO 177 Fb61
Suceava RO 172 Ec55
Sucé-sur-Erdre F 28 Ed42
Sučevići (Otric') HR 158 Gb64
Sucevița RO 172 Eb55
Sucha PL 129 Gd38
Sucha PL 130 Jc39
Sucha PL 137 Hb43
Sucha Beskidzka PL 138 Hd45
Suchacz PL 122 Hc30
Suchá Hora SK 138 Ja46
Sucha Koszalińska PL 121 Gb30
Suchań PL 120 Fd34
Suchdol nad Lužnicí CZ 136 Fc48
Suchedniów PL 130 Jb41
Suchodolina PL 123 Kb32
Suchorze PL 121 Gc30
Suchowola PL 123 Kb32
Suchożebry PL 131 Ka36
Suchy Dąb PL 121 Hb30
Suchy Las PL 129 Gc36
Sucina E 55 Fa73
Suciu de Sus RO 171 Db56
Sucleia MD 173 Ga59
Sucuiu RO 176 Ec62
Sücüllü TR 193 Ha86
Sucumin PL 121 Ha31
Sućuraj HR 158 Gd67
Sucy-en-Brie F 23 Ha37
Sudak UA 205 Fa17
Sudarca MD 173 Fb53
Sudargas LT 113 Jd57
Sūdava LT 114 Ka58
Súðavík IS 2 Ac02
Südbrookmerland D 117 Cb32
Sudbury GB 16 Ed23
Sudbury GB 21 Ga26
Suddesjaur S 72 Gd21
Sudeck D 126 Cd40
Sudeikiai LT 114 La55
Süderbrarup D 108 Db29
Süderburg D 118 Dc35
Süderlügum D 108 Da28
Sudervė LT 114 La57
Sudice CZ 137 Ha44
Sudik MK 178 Bd73
Sudislavl' RUS 203 Fa08
Sudiţi RO 177 Fa66
Südlohn D 125 Bd37
Sudogda RUS 203 Fa10
Sudok S 73 Hb20
Sudoměřice CZ 136 Fb47
Sudova Vyšnja UA 204 Dd15
Sudovec HR 152 Gb58
Suðureyri IS 2 Ac02
Sudwalde D 118 Cd35
Sudža RUS 202 Ed13
Sueca E 54 Fc68
Suelli I 169 Ca78
Sueros de Cepeda E 37 Cb57
Suevos E 36 Ac55
Suevos E 36 Ba54
Suèvres F 29 Gb41
Sufers CH 142 Cd55
Şugag RO 175 Da61
Sugenheim D 134 Db46
Sugères F 34 Hc47
Sugiņčiai LT 113 Jd53
Sugiņčiai LT 114 La55
Suha BIH 152 Hb63
Suha BIH 159 Hc67
Suhadoll AL 178 Ad73
Suhaia RO 180 Dd68
Suharău RO 172 Ec54
Suhindol BG 180 Dc70
Suhiniči RUS 202 Ed11
Suhl D 126 Dc42
Suhlendorf D 119 Dd35
Suhmura FIN 83 Ld31
Suhodol BG 181 Ec73
Suhodol RUS 203 Ga09
Suho Polje BIH 153 Hd62
Suhopolje HR 152 Ha58
Suhostrel BG 183 Cb74
Suhr CH 141 Ca53
Suhuluceni MD 173 Fc56
Şuhut TR 193 Gc86
Šuica BIH 158 Gd65
Şuici RO 175 Db63
Suigu EST 98 Kb45
Suijavaara S 68 Hd14
Suinula FIN 89 Jd35
Suinula FIN 90 Ka34
Suippes F 24 Hd35
Suislepa EST 106 La46
Šuja RUS 203 Fa09
Šukaičiai LT 113 Jc55
Sukë AL 182 Ac78
Sukeva FIN 82 Kd27
Šukioniai LT 114 Kb54
Sukobin MNE 163 Ja71
Sukoró H 146 Hc54
Sukošan HR 157 Fd64
Sükösd H 153 Hd57
Sukovo SRB 179 Cb70
Şükranlı TR 193 Gc83
Şükrüpaşa TR 185 Ed74
Sukth AL 182 Ab74
Sul N 78 Ec29
Šula MNE 159 Hd66
Sulåmo N 78 Ec29
Suldal N 92 Cb42
Sulden I 142 Db56
Suldrup DK 100 Dc21
Sulechów PL 128 Fd38
Sulęcin PL 128 Fc36
Sulęczyno PL 121 Gd30
Sulejów PL 130 Hd40
Sulejówek PL 130 Jc37
Suleskar N 92 Cc44
Sulesund N 76 Cc32
Şuletea RO 177 Fb60
Süleymaniye TR 185 Eb77
Süleymaniye TR 186 Ga80
Sülfeld D 118 Dc32
Sulgen D 142 Cc52
Sulhamstead GB 20 Fa28
Sulheim N 85 Db35
Suli LV 107 Lc51
Sulibórz PL 120 Fd34
Sulików PL 128 Fc41
Sulikowo PL 121 Gb32
Sulina RO 177 Ga64
Sulingen D 118 Cd35
Sulisławice PL 131 Jd42
Suliszewo PL 120 Fd34
Suliţa RO 172 Ed56
Sulitjelma N 71 Ga18
Sulkava FIN 89 Jc32
Sulkava FIN 91 Lb33
Sulkavanjärvi FIN 82 Kc28
Sulkavanjärvi FIN 82 Kc29
Sulkavankylä FIN 89 Jc32
Sulkavanperä FIN 82 Ka28
Sułkowice PL 138 Ja45
Süller TR 192 Fa83
Sullom GB 5 Fa04
Sully F 30 Ja43
Sully-la-Chapelle F 29 Gd40
Sully-sur-Loire F 29 Gd40
Sulmierzyce PL 129 Gd39
Sulmierzyce PL 130 Hc40
Sulmona I 161 Fa71
Süloğlu TR 185 Ec75
Sułoszowa PL 138 Hd43
Sułów PL 129 Gc40
Sułów PL 131 Kb41
Sulsted DK 100 Dc20
Sultançayırı TR 192 Fa81
Sultandağı TR 193 Ha86
Sultandere TR 193 Gc82
Sultanhisar TR 197 Fa88
Sultanıça TR 185 Ea78
Sultaniye TR 186 Fb80
Sultaniye TR 187 Gb79
Sultanköy TR 185 Eb77
Sultanköy TR 186 Fa77
Sultanköy TR 187 Hb79
Sultsi EST 106 Kd46
Suluca TR 185 Eb80
Sülüdere TR 199 Gb89
Sülüklü TR 186 Fc80
Sülüköy TR 192 Ga82
Sülümenli TR 192 Fd86
Sülümenli TR 193 Gd85
Sulusaray TR 205 Fc20
Sulustvere EST 98 La44
Sulva FIN 81 Hd31
Sulviken S 78 Fa29
Sülysáp H 146 Ja53
Sulz A 142 Cd53
Sulz D 134 Cc49
Sulzbach A 144 Ga55
Sulzbach D 133 Bd46
Sulzbach am Main D 134 Cd44
Sulzbach-Laufen D 134 Da48
Sulzbach (Murr) D 134 Cd47
Sulzbach-Rosenberg D 135 Ea46
Sulzberg A 142 Da52
Sulzberg D 142 Db52
Sulzburg D 141 Bd51
Sulzdorf D 119 Dd30
Sulzdorf D 134 Dc44
Sulzemoos D 143 Dd50
Sulzfeld D 134 Cc47
Sulzfeld D 134 Db43
Sulzfeld am Main D 134 Db45
Sülzhayn D 126 Dc39
Sulzheim D 134 Db44
Sumacàrcer E 54 Fb69
Sumartin HR 158 Gc67
Sumburgh GB 5 Fa06
Sümeg H 145 Gd55
Šumen BG 181 Ec70
Šumenci BG 181 Ec68
Sumer BG 179 Cc69
Šumerlja RUS 203 Fc09
Sumiainen FIN 82 Kc31
Sumiak PL 120 Fc35
Sumin PL 122 Hc33
Sumiswald CH 141 Bd54
Summa FIN 90 La38
Summalankylä FIN 91 Lb35
Summer Bridge GB 11 Ed19
Şumna MD 173 Fa55
Šumperk CZ 137 Gc45
Sumsa FIN 83 Lc25
Šumskas LT 115 Lb58
Sumstad N 78 Ea27
Sumy UA 202 Ed14
Sunākste LV 106 La52
Sunbury GB 20 Fc28
Sünching D 135 Eb48
Şuncuiuş RO 171 Cc57
Sund FIN 96 Hc40
Sund N 71 Fb18
Sund S 87 Fd34
Sund S 94 Ec44
Sund S 96 Gd40
Sund S 96 Gc45
Sund S 103 Fd48
Sundals-Ryr S 102 Ec46
Sundan N 70 Fa21
Sundborn S 95 Fd39
Sundby DK 100 Da21
Sundby DK 109 Eb29
Sundby FIN 81 Jb29
Sundbyfoss N 93 Dd43
Sunde N 65 Kd08
Sunde N 84 Cc35
Sunde N 92 Ca41
Sunde bru N 93 Db45
Sunderland GB 11 Fa17
Sundern D 125 Cb40
Sundet S 78 Ed29
Sundginge S 94 Ec44
Sundhausen D 126 Dc39
Sundhouse F 31 Kc38
Sundhultsbrunn S 103 Fc48
Sundklakk N 66 Fb14
Sundli N 77 Dd30
Sundnäs S 72 Gc20
Sundö S 103 Gb47
Sundom FIN 81 Hd31
Sundom S 73 Hd22
Sundre S 104 Gd51
Sunds DK 108 Da24
Sundsbø N 76 Cd31
Sundsbruk S 88 Gc33
Sundsby S 102 Eb48
Sundsjö S 79 Fc31
Sundsjö S 79 Fd31
Sundsli N 93 Da44
Sundsnäs S 72 Ha23
Sundsøre DK 100 Db22
Sundstrup DK 100 Db22
Sundsvall S 87 Gb33
Sundsvoll N 70 Ec22
Sundvik N 79 Fb27
Sundvollen N 93 Dd41
Sungailiškiai LT 113 Jd56
Sungurlare BG 181 Ec72
Sungurlu TR 187 Gb77
Sungurlu TR 205 Fb20
Süngüt TR 187 Gd78
Suni I 169 Bd76
Sunja HR 152 Gc60
Šunja Stijena = Šula MNE 159 Hd66
Sünlük TR 192 Fb81
Sunnan N 78 Ec28
Sunnanå S 87 Fb35
Sunnansjö S 80 Ha29
Sunnansjö S 80 Gd30
Sunnansjö S 87 Ga32
Sunnansjö S 95 Fc40
Sunnaryd S 102 Fa51
Sunndal N 84 Cb40
Sunndalsøra N 77 Db32
Sunne S 79 Fb31
Sunne S 94 Ed42
Sunnemo S 94 Fa42
Sunnersberg S 102 Ed46
Sunnet S 87 Fb36
Šunskai LV 114 Kb58
Suo-Anttila FIN 91 Lb37
Suodenniemi FIN 89 Jc35
Suojala FIN 83 Lc26
Suojanperä FIN 65 Kb09
Suojoki FIN 89 Ja34
Suojoki FIN 97 Jd39
Suokonmäki FIN 81 Jd31
Suokumaa FIN 91 Lc36
Suokylä FIN 74 Kb24
Suolahti FIN 82 Kb31
Suolgajåknjalbmi N 64 Jb10
Suolijärvi FIN 75 Kd22
Suomasema FIN 90 Ka35
Suomela FIN 98 Ka39
Suomenkylä FIN 90 La35
Suomenniemi FIN 90 La35
Suomijärvi FIN 89 Jb34
Suomu FIN 83 Ma28
Suomusjärvi FIN 97 Jd39
Suomussalmi FIN 75 La23
Suonenjoki FIN 82 Kd31
Suoniemi FIN 89 Jc36
Suonnankylä FIN 75 Kd19
Suonpää FIN 91 Ma32
Suonsalmi FIN 90 Kd34
Suontaka FIN 89 Ja38
Suontee FIN 82 Kd31
Suonttajärvi FIN 68 Ja13
Suopajärvi FIN 69 Jd17
Suopelto FIN 90 Kc35
Suora järvi FIN 75 La19
Suorsa FIN 74 Kb19
Suorva S 67 Gc16
Suotuperä FIN 82 Ka27
Suovaara FIN 82 La25
Suovanlahti FIN 82 Kc30
Super-Besse F 34 Hb48
Superdévoluy F 35 Jd50
Supersano I 163 Hc77
Super-Sauze F 43 Kb51
Supetar HR 158 Gc67
Supetarska Draga HR 151 Fc62
Supino I 160 Ec72
Suplac RO 171 Dc59
Suplacu de Barcău RO 171 Cc56
Süplingen D 127 Ea37
Supovac SRB 178 Bd68
Süpplingen D 127 Dd37
Supraśl PL 123 Kb33
Supru FIN 65 Kb09
Süpüren TR 193 Gc82
Supuru de Jos RO 171 Cc55
Supuru de Sus RO 171 Cc55
Súr H 145 Hb53
Sura S 95 Ga42
Surahammar S 95 Ga42
Suraja RO 176 Ed62
Şura Mare RO 175 Db61
Şura Mică RO 175 Da61
Šurany SK 145 Hb51
Suraż PL 123 Kb34
Suraž RUS 202 Ec12
Surberg D 143 Ec52
Surd H 152 Gc57
Surdegis LT 114 Kd54
Surdila-Găiseanca RO 176 Ed64
Surdila-Greci RO 176 Ed64
Surdoux F 33 Gc47
Surduc RO 171 Da56
Surduk SRB 153 Jc61
Surdulica SRB 178 Bd71
Surfonds F 28 Fd40
Surgères F 32 Fb46
Surheim D 143 Ec52
Surhów PL 131 Kc41
Surhuisterveen NL 117 Bc33
Şuri MD 173 Fb54
Súria E 49 Gd60
Suric MD 173 Fd59
Surier I 148 Bb58
Surin F 32 Fd46
Surju EST 106 Kc46
Surlane KSV 178 Bc72
Surlingham GB 17 Gb24
Surma RUS 203 Fd08
Sürmeli TR 187 Ha79
Surovikino RUS 203 Fd14
Surowe PL 122 Jb33
Sursee CH 141 Ca53
Surskoe RUS 203 Fd10
Surtainville F 22 Ed35
Surte S 102 Ec48
Suruceni MD 173 Fc58
Surviliškis LT 114 Kc55
Surwold D 117 Cb34
Sury-ès-Bois F 29 Ha41
Sury-le-Comtal F 34 Hd47
Surzur F 27 Eb41
Susa I 148 Bb60
Susana E 36 Ad55
Şuşani RO 175 Da65
Sušara SRB 174 Bc63
Sušary RUS 99 Mb39
Susch CH 142 Da55
Susegana I 150 Ea58
Suşehri TR 205 Fd20
Suseja LV 106 Kd52
Suseja LV 114 La53
Susek SRB 153 Ja60
Süsel D 119 Dd31
Suseni RO 171 Dc58
Suseni RO 172 Ea59
Suseni RO 175 Cc62
Suseni RO 175 Dc65
Suševo BG 181 Ec68
Sušica BG 180 Ea70
Sušice CZ 135 Ed47
Susikas FIN 89 Jd37
Šuškova LV 107 Ma52
Suskowola PL 130 Jc39
Susleni MD 173 Fd57
Suslonger RUS 203 Fd08
Sūsninkai LV 114 Kb59
Šušnjevica Valdarsa HR 151 Fb60
Suspiro del Moro E 60 Db75
Süßen D 134 Da49
Süssenborn D 127 Dd41
Süstedt D 118 Cd35
Susten CH 141 Bd56
Susteren NL 125 Bb40
Sustinente I 149 Dc61
Sustrum D 117 Ca34
Susurluk TR 192 Fb81
Susuz TR 187 Hb80
Susuz TR 192 Ga85
Susuz TR 193 Gc85
Susuzkaya TR 192 Ga83
Susuzmüsellim TR 185 Ec77
Susuzören TR 192 Fd86
Susuzşahap TR 199 Hb90
Susz PL 122 Hc32
Suszewo PL 122 Hc35
Sutanži LV 106 Kd50
Sütçüler TR 199 Gd89
Şuteşti RO 177 Fa64
Suthfeld D 126 Da36
Sutina BIH 158 Ha66
Sutivan HR 158 Gc67
Sutjeska SRB 174 Bb62
Sütlâç TR 193 Gb87
Sütlegen TR 198 Ga92
Sutlepa EST 98 Ka44
Sütlüce TR 185 Ed76
Sutomore MNE 159 Ja70
Sutri I 156 Ea70
Sutri LV 107 Lb52
Suttertjärn S 95 Fb43
Süttő H 145 Hb52
Sutton GB 20 Fc28
Sutton Coldfield GB 16 Ed24
Sutton Courtenay GB 20 Fa27
Sutton in Ashfield GB 16 Fa22
Sutton on See GB 17 Fd22
Sutton-on-the-Forest GB 16 Fb19
Sutton Saint Edmund GB 17 Fc24
Sutton Saint James GB 17 Fd24
Sutton Scotney GB 20 Fa29
Sutton-under-Whitestonecliffe GB 11 Fa19
Sutton Valence GB 21 Ga29
Sutyli RUS 99 Ma44
Suure-Jaani EST 98 Kd45
Suurejõe EST 98 Kc45
Suuremõisa EST 97 Jd44
Suurikylä FIN 91 Lc33
Suurikylä FIN 91 Ld33
Suurimäki FIN 82 La29
Suurisuo FIN 82 Kd28
Suurkylä FIN 91 Lc35
Suurlahti FIN 91 Lb35
Suurmäki FIN 83 Lc31
Suur-Miehikkälä FIN 91 Lb37
Suurtuvaara FIN 83 Ma28
Suutarinkylä FIN 82 Ka25
Suutarla FIN 89 Jc38
Suvainiškis LT 114 Kd53
Šuvalovo RUS 113 Jc59
Suvanto FIN 69 Kb16
Suva Reka KSV 178 Ba71
Suvereto I 155 Db67
Suvermez TR 193 Ha84
Suviekas LT 115 Lb54
Suvodol MK 183 Bb76
Suvorov RUS 113 Jb59
Suvorov RUS 202 Ed11
Suvorovo BG 181 Fa70
Suvorovskaja RUS 205 Ga17
Suwałki PL 123 Ka30
Süzbeyli TR 191 Eb85
Suzdal' RUS 203 Fa09
Suze-la-Rousse F 42 Jb51
Suzette F 42 Jc52
Suzzara I 149 Db61
Svabensverk S 87 Fd38
Svaipavalle sameviste S 71 Ga20
Svalbarðseyri IS 2 Ba04
Svalehult S 102 Ec47
Svalenik BG 180 Ea69
Svålestad N 92 Ca45
Svaljava UA 204 Dd16
Svallerup DK 109 Ea26
Svalöv S 110 Ed55
Svalsta S 95 Gb45
Svanabyn S 79 Gb28
Svanamyran S 80 Gc26
Svanberga S 96 Ha42
Svandal S 94 Eb45
Svaneke DK 111 Fd57
Svanelvmo N 67 Gb11
Svanesund S 102 Eb47
Svanfors S 80 Hb25
Svängsta S 111 Fc54
Švanibachovo RUS 107 Ma47
Svaningen S 79 Fc27
Svannäs S 72 Gd21
Svannäs S 79 Ga26
Svanøybukt N 84 Ca35
Svansele S 73 Hb24
Svansele S 79 Fd26
Svanshals S 103 Fc47
Svanskog S 94 Ec44
Svanstein S 74 Jb18
Svanström S 80 Hb25
Svanträsk S 72 Ha23
Svanvik N 65 Kd08
Svanvik S 102 Eb47
Svappavaara S 67 Hb16
Svarar FIN 81 Ja31
Svardal N 84 Cb35
Svardsjö S 95 Ga39
Svarinci LV 107 Ma52
Svarstad N 93 Dd43
Svartå FIN 98 Ka40
Svartå S 95 Fc44
Svärta S 95 Gb45
Svartana S 94 Ed42
Svartbäcken S 73 Hd21
Svartberget S 73 Ja20
Svartbyn S 73 Ja20
Svarte S 110 Fa57
Svarteborg S 102 Eb46
Svartehallen S 102 Eb47
Svartemyr N 84 Cb37
Svarte-nut N 92 Cc43
Svärtinge S 103 Ga46
Svartkog N 93 Ea42

287

Tigy – Torvoila

Tigy F 29 Gd40
Tiha Bârgăului RO 171 Dc57
Tihany H 145 Ha55
Tihemetsa EST 106 Kc46
Tiheró GR 185 Ea77
Tihilä FIN 82 Kc27
Tihío GR 183 Bb77
Tihkovicy RUS 99 Mb41
Tihoreck RUS 205 Fc16
Tihusniemi FIN 90 La32
Tihvin RUS 202 Eb08
Tihvinka RUS 99 Ld42
Tiilää FIN 90 Kc38
Tiimola FIN 91 Lb34
Tiirimetsa EST 105 Jc47
Tiironkylä FIN 82 Ka30
Tiistenjoki FIN 81 Jc31
Tijesno HR 157 Ga65
Tíjola E 61 Ea74
Tijovac SRB 179 Ca68
Tikinmaa FIN 89 Jd36
Tikkakoski FIN 90 Kb32
Tikkala FIN 83 Ld31
Tikkala FIN 90 Kb33
Tikkurila FIN 98 Kb39
Tikøb DK 109 Ec24
Tilaj H 145 Gd55
Tilburg NL 124 Ba38
Tilbury GB 20 Fd28
Til-Châtel F 30 Jb41
Tileagd RO 170 Cb56
Tilisca RO 175 Da61
Tílisos GR 200 Da95
Tillac F 40 Fd55
Tillay-le-Péneux F 29 Gc39
Tillberga S 95 Gb42
Tilleda D 127 Dd40
Tillicoultry GB 7 Ea12
Tillières-sur-Avre F 23 Gb37
Tillinge S 95 Gb42
Tilly F 33 Gb45
Tilly-sur-Seulles F 22 Fb36
Tilsaperä FIN 90 Kb33
Tilshead GB 20 Ed29
Tilst DK 108 Dc24
Tilstock GB 15 Ec23
Tiltai LT 114 Kd59
Tiltiņi LV 106 Kb51
Tiltrem N 78 Ea28
Tilža LV 107 Ld50
Tilže LT 115 Lc54
Tim DK 100 Cd23
Tim RUS 203 Fa13
Timahoe IRL 13 Cb22
Timár H 147 Jd50
Timaševsk RUS 205 Fc16
Timau I 143 Ec56
Timbáki GR 200 Cd96
Timberscombe GB 19 Ea29
Time N 92 Ca44
Timfristós GR 188 Bb83
Timi CY 206 Hd98
Timirjazevo RUS 113 Jc57
Ţimişeşti RO 172 Ec57
Timişoara RO 174 Bd60
Timişu de Sus RO 176 Ea62
Timmele S 102 Fa48
Timmendorfer Strand D 119 Dd31
Timmenrode D 127 Dd38
Timmernabben S 103 Gb51
Timmersdala S 102 Fa46
Timmervik S 102 Ec46
Timofeevo RUS 113 Jd57
Timohino RUS 202 Ec08
Timola FIN 90 La32
Timoleague IRL 12 Bc26
Timoniemi FIN 83 Lb25
Timošino RUS 203 Fb08
Timovaara FIN 83 Lc29
Timpinvaara FIN 75 Lb21
Timrå S 88 Gc33
Timring DK 108 Da24
Timsbury GB 20 Fa29
Timsfors S 110 Fa53
Tinahely IRL 13 Cd23
Tinajas E 47 Ea65
Tinalhas P 44 Bb65
Tınaztepe TR 193 Gc85
Tinca RO 170 Ca57
Tinchebray F 22 Fb37
Tinchi I 162 Gc76
Tinden N 77 Dd29
Tineo E 37 Ca54
Tingere LV 105 Jd49
Tinglev DK 108 Da28
Tingsbekk N 93 Da46
Tingsryd S 111 Fc53
Tingstad S 103 Ga46
Tingstäde S 104 Ha49
Tingsted DK 109 Eb28
Tingvoll N 77 Db31
Tinieblas E 46 Dd59
Tinja BIH 153 Hc62
Tinjan HR 151 Fa60
Tinlot B 124 Ba42
Tinnura I 169 Bd76
Tínos GR 196 Db88
Tiñosillos E 46 Cd62
Tinosu RO 176 Ea65
Tinqueux F 24 Hc35
Tintagel GB 18 Db30
Tinţareni MD 173 Fc56
Ţînţăreni MD 173 Fd58
Tinténiac F 28 Ed38
Tintern Parva GB 19 Eb27
Ţinteşti RO 176 Ec64
Tintigny B 132 Ba44
Tinūži LV 106 Kc51
Tiobraid Árann IRL 13 Ca24
Tione di Trento I 149 Db58
Ţipala MD 173 Fd58
Tipasoja FIN 83 Lb26
Tipčenica BG 179 Cd70
Tipperary IRL 13 Ca24
Tiptree GB 21 Ga27
Tipu EST 98 Kc45
Tiranë AL 182 Ab74
Tiranges F 34 Hd48
Tirano I 149 Da57
Tiraspol MD 173 Ga58
Tirazli TR 191 Ec86
Tire TR 191 Ed87
Tiream RO 171 Cc55
Tirebolu TR 205 Fd19
Tireļi LV 106 Ka51
Tîrgul Vertiujeni MD 173 Fc54
Tiriez E 53 Eb69
Tirig E 48 Fd64
Tiriolo I 164 Gc81
Tirivolo I 164 Gc80
Tirkiliškiai LT 114 Kc57
Tirkšliai LT 113 Jd53
Tirley GB 15 Ec26
Tirmo FIN 98 Kd39
Tirmonperä FIN 75 Kc22
Tirnaneill IRL 9 Cc18
Tîrnauca MD 173 Ga59
Tirnava TR 192 Fb81
Tírnavos GR 183 Bd80
Tîrnova MD 173 Fa54
Tîrnova MD 173 Fb54
Tirol I 142 Dc55
Tirolo I 142 Dc55
Tirós GR 195 Bd89
Tirrenia I 155 Da65
Tirro FIN 69 Jd11
Tirschenreuth D 135 Eb45
Tîrşiţei MD 173 Fc56
Tirstrup DK 101 Dd23
Tīrumbaltgalvji LV 106 La51
Tirza LV 107 Lb49
Tisău RO 176 Ec64
Tiscar Don Pedro E 61 Dd73
Tiset DK 108 Da27
Tiševica BG 179 Cd69
Tišino RUS 107 Ma48
Tišino RUS 113 Ja59
Tiskādi LV 107 Lc51
Tiskolovo RUS 99 Lc40
Tismana RO 175 Cc63
Tišnov CZ 137 Gb47
Tisovac BIH 158 Hb64
Tisovec SK 138 Ja49
Tisselskog S 94 Ec45
Tistedal N 94 Eb44
Tistrup DK 108 Da25
Tisvilde DK 109 Eb24
Tisvildeleje DK 109 Eb24
Tiszaadony H 147 Kb50
Tiszaalpár H 146 Jb55
Tiszabecs H 147 Kc50
Tiszabura H 146 Jc53
Tiszacsege H 147 Jd52
Tiszacsermely H 147 Ka50
Tiszadada H 147 Jd51
Tiszadob H 147 Jd51
Tiszadorogma H 146 Jc52
Tiszaeszlár H 147 Jd51
Tiszaföldvár H 146 Jb54
Tiszafüred H 146 Jc52
Tiszajenő H 146 Jb54
Tiszakécske H 146 Jb54
Tiszakeszi H 147 Jd51
Tiszakürt H 146 Jb55
Tiszalök H 147 Jd51
Tiszalúc H 147 Jd51
Tiszanána H 146 Jc52
Tiszaörs H 146 Jc52
Tiszaroff H 146 Jb53
Tiszaszőlős H 146 Jc52
Tiszatelek H 147 Ka50
Tiszaújváros H 147 Jd51
Tiszavasvári H 147 Jd51
Titaguas E 54 Fa66
Titáni GR 189 Bd86
Titeikiai LT 114 Kd55
Titel SRB 153 Jc60
Ţiţeşti RO 175 Dc64
Tithoréa GR 189 Bd84
Tithróni GR 189 Bd84
Titioniai LT 114 Kb53
Titisee-Neustadt D 141 Ca51
Titkoniai LT 114 Kc53
Tito I 161 Ga76
Titran N 77 Db29
Titreyengöl TR 199 Ha91
Titting D 135 Dd48
Tittling D 135 Ed49
Tittmoning D 143 Ec51
Titu RO 176 Dd65
Titulcia E 46 Dc65
Titz D 125 Bc40
Tiuccia F 154 Ca70
Tiukka FIN 89 Hd33
Tiukurova FIN 69 Kc17
Tiurajärvi FIN 68 Jb15
Tivat MNE 159 Hd69
Tived S 95 Fc45
Tivenys E 48 Ga63
Tiverton GB 19 Ea30
Tivissa E 48 Ga62
Tivoli I 160 Eb71
Tizzano F 154 Ca72
Tizzano Val Parma I 149 Da62
Tjačiv UA 204 Dd16
Tjæreborg DK 108 Cd26
Tjällmo S 103 Fd46
Tjåmotis S 72 Gd18
Tjamšča RUS 107 Ld47
Tjappsåive S 72 Ha22
Tjärn S 80 Gc28
Tjärnberg S 72 Gd23
Tjärnmyrberget S 79 Fd26
Tjärnö S 94 Ea45
Tjärstad S 103 Fd47
Tjäruträsk S 73 Ja20
Tjåure S 78 Fa28
Tjåurek S 67 Ha16
Tjautjas S 67 Hb17
Tjeldnes N 66 Ga13
Tjeldstø N 84 Bd38
Tjeldsundbrua N 66 Ga13
Tjelle N 77 Da32
Tjenndalen N 93 Db44
Tjentište BIH 159 Hc66
Tjernagel N 92 Ca41
Tjöck FIN 89 Hd33
Tjøme N 93 Dd44
Tjong N 70 Fa19
Tjønnefoss N 93 Da44
Tjønnvik N 78 Fa25
Tjørhom N 92 Cc44
Tjörnarp S 110 Fa55
Tjörnekalv S 102 Eb48
Tjøtta N 70 Ed22
Tjuda FIN 97 Jc40
Tjulenovo BG 181 Fc69
Tjulträsk S 71 Ga21
Tjuonajåkk S 67 Gd16
Tjurkö S 111 Fd54
Tjusk PL 122 Hc30
Tjuvkil S 102 Eb48
Tjuvö FIN 98 Kd39
Tjuvskjær N 67 Gb12
Tkon HR 157 Fd65
Tlačene BG 179 Cd69
Tleń PL 121 Ha32
Tlmače SK 145 Hb50
Tłuchowo PL 122 Hc35
Tlučná CZ 135 Ed45
Tlumačov CZ 137 Gd47
Tłuściec PL 131 Kb37
Tłuszcz PL 130 Jc36
Toano I 149 Db63
Toba SRB 174 Bb60
Toba de Valdivieso E 38 Dc56
Tobar E 38 Dc58
Tobar an Choire IRL 8 Bd18
Tobarra E 53 Ec70
Tobercurry IRL 8 Bd18
Toberdoney GB 9 Cd15
Tobermore GB 9 Cd16
Tobermory GB 6 Da10
Toberonochy GB 6 Db12
Toberscanavan IRL 8 Ca18
Toblach I 143 Eb55
Tobo S 96 Gc40
Tobolac SRB 178 Bb68
Tobru N 86 Ea38
Tobson GB 4 Da05
Toby FIN 81 Ja31
Tobyn S 94 Ed42
Tocane-Saint-Apre F 33 Ga49
Toceni MD 177 Fb60
Tocha P 44 Ac63
Tocina E 59 Ca73
Töcksfors S 94 Eb43
Töcksmark S 94 Eb43
Tocón E 60 Db74
Tocuz MD 173 Ga59
Todal N 77 Dc30
Todalsøra N 77 Dc32
Toddington GB 20 Fb26
Todendorf D 118 Dc30
Todendorf D 119 Dd30
Todenham GB 20 Ed26
Todi I 156 Ea68
Todireni RO 172 Ed56
Todireşti MD 173 Fb57
Todireşti RO 172 Eb55
Todireşti RO 172 Ed57
Todireşti RO 173 Fa58
Todmorden GB 16 Ed20
Todolella E 48 Fc64
Todoričene BG 179 Da70
Todor Ikonomovo BG 181 Ed69
Todorovo BG 181 Ec68
Tødsø DK 100 Da21
Todtmoos D 141 Ca51
Todtnau D 141 Ca51
Tõdva EST 98 Kb43
Todzia PL 122 Jc33
Toft GB 5 Fa04
Tofta S 102 Ec51
Tofta S 104 Gd49
Toftbyn S 95 Fd39
Tofte N 70 Ed23
Tofte N 85 Dc34
Tofte N 93 Ea43
Töftedal S 94 Eb45
Tofterup DK 108 Da25
Tofteryd S 103 Fb50
Tofteseter N 85 Dd36
Toftesetra N 85 Dc34
Toftevåg N 84 Bd39
Toftir DK 3 Ca06
Toftlund DK 108 Da27
Töfű H 152 Hb57
Togher IRL 9 Cd20
Togher IRL 12 Bb26
Töging D 143 Eb50
Tohanu Nou RO 176 Dd62
Tohatin MD 173 Fd58
Tohmajärvi FIN 83 Ma31
Tohmo FIN 69 Kb17
Tohni FIN 81 Jc31
Toholampi FIN 81 Jd28
Tohvri EST 98 Kd45
Toiano I 155 Db66
Toija FIN 97 Jd40
Toijala FIN 89 Jd36
Toikkala FIN 90 La36
Toikkala FIN 91 Lb36
Toila EST 99 Lb41
Toirano I 148 Bd63
Toivakka FIN 90 Kc33
Toivala FIN 82 La30
Toiviaiskylä FIN 82 Kc28
Toivola FIN 83 Lb26
Toivola FIN 90 Kd35
Töjby FIN 89 Hd32
Tokačka BG 185 Dd76
Tokaj H 147 Jd50
Tokarevka RUS 203 Fb12
Tokarnia PL 130 Jb42
Tokarnia PL 138 Ja45
Tokary PL 131 Kb36
Tokat TR 192 Fd83
Tokat TR 205 Fc20
Tokatbaşı TR 191 Ed87
Toklucak TR 193 Ha84
Tokmacık TR 193 Gd87
Tokmak UA 205 Fa16
Tokmaklı TR 192 Fb85
Tokod H 146 Hc52
Tököl H 146 Hc53
Tokrajärvi FIN 83 Ma29
Tokuşlar TR 193 Gb85
Tolbaños E 46 Da63
Tölby FIN 81 Ja31
Tolca TR 199 Ha88
Tolcsva H 147 Jd50
Toldaos E 36 Bc56
Toledo E 52 Db66
Tolentino I 156 Ec67
Tolfa I 156 Dd70
Tolfta S 96 Gc40
Tolg S 103 Fc51
Tolga N 86 Eb33
Tolinas E 37 Cb55
Toliočiai LT 114 Ka54
Tolivia E 37 Cc55
Tolja FIN 74 Kb20
Tol'jatti RUS 203 Ga10
Tolk D 108 Db29
Tolkee FIN 83 Lc27
Tołkiny PL 122 Jb30
Tolkis FIN 98 Kc39
Tolkkinen FIN 98 Kc39
Tolkmicko PL 122 Hc30
Tolko PL 122 Ja30
Tolköyü TR 199 Hb89
Tollarp S 111 Fb55
Tolle I 150 Eb61
Tollesbury GB 21 Ga27
Tollikko FIN 81 Jb29
Töllinperä FIN 82 Ka27
Tollo I 157 Fb70
Tølløse DK 109 Eb26
Töllsjö S 102 Ed49
Tolmačevo RUS 99 Mb42
Tolmezzo I 143 Ec56
Tolmin SLO 151 Fa57
Tolna H 146 Hc56
Tolnanémedi H 146 Hc55
Tolne DK 101 Dd19
Toló GR 195 Bd88
Tolonen FIN 69 Ka12
Tolonen FIN 69 Jd17
Tolosa E 39 Ec55
Tolosa P 50 Ba67
Tolosenjoki FIN 75 Kd24
Tolosenmäki FIN 91 Ld32
Tolox E 60 Cc76
Tolsa FIN 98 Kb40
Tolsta GB 4 Db05
Tolva E 48 Ga59
Tolva FIN 75 Kd19
Tölvä FIN 82 Kd29
Tolvādia RO 174 Bc62
Tolve I 162 Gb75
Tomai MD 173 Fc59
Tomai MD 177 Fd61
Tomaiul Nou MD 173 Fc59
Tomakivka UA 205 Fa16
Tömäperä FIN 81 Jd26
Tomar P 50 Ac66
Tomarovka RUS 203 Fa14
Tomaševac SRB 153 Jc60
Tomaševac SRB 174 Bb62
Tomaševo MNE 159 Jb67
Tomašica BIH 152 Gc62
Tomašica HR 152 Gd59
Tomašići HR 151 Fd60
Tomášikovo SK 145 Ha51
Tomášovce SK 146 Ja50
Tomašpil' UA 204 Eb16
Tomaszowice PL 131 Ka40
Tomaszów Lubelski PL 131 Kc42
Tomaszów Mazowiecki PL 130 Ja39
Tomatin GB 7 Ea08
Tombebœuf F 32 Fd51
Tomcrasky GB 7 Dd09
Tome LV 106 Kc51
Tomelilla S 111 Fb56
Tomellosa E 47 Ea64
Tomelloso E 53 Dd68
Tomeşti RO 171 Cc59
Tomeşti RO 173 Fa57
Tomeşti RO 174 Cb61
Tometino SRB 159 Jb64
Tomice PL 129 Gd38
Tomich GB 7 Dd08
Tomintoul GB 7 Eb08
Tomislavgrad BIH 158 Gd65
Tomiszowice PL 130 Hd42
Tomma N 70 Fa20
Tommarp S 111 Fb56
Tømmerbakk N 84 Cb36
Tømmerneset N 66 Fd15
Tommerup DK 108 Dc27
Tommerup Stationsby DK 108 Dc27
Tømmervåg N 77 Db30
Tommola FIN 90 La35
Tompa H 153 Ja57
Tomperi FIN 82 Kc26
Tompter N 93 Ea42
Tømra N 78 Eb30
Tomrefjord N 76 Cd32
Tomşani RO 175 Da63
Tomşani RO 176 Eb64
Tomsino RUS 107 Mb51
Tôň SK 145 Ha52
Tona E 49 Ha60
Tonara I 169 Cb77
Tonbridge GB 20 Fd29
Tondela P 44 Ad63
Tønder DK 108 Da28
Tondorf D 125 Bc42
Tondu GB 19 Ea28
Toneby S 94 Ed42
Tonezza I 150 Dd58
Tongeren B 124 Ba41
Tongue GB 5 Ea04
Toninek PL 121 Gd33
Tönisvorst D 125 Bc39
Tønjum N 84 Cd37
Tonkino RUS 203 Fc08
Tonna GB 19 Dd27
Tonnay-Boutonne F 32 Fb46
Tonnay-Charente F 32 Fb46
Tonneins F 40 Fd52
Tonnerre F 30 Hd40
Tönnersjö S 102 Ed52
Tonnes N 70 Fa20
Tønnesland N 92 Cd46
Tönning D 118 Da30
Tönnö FIN 90 Kc37
Tono I 167 Fd83
Tonšaevo RUS 203 Fc08
Tønsberg N 93 Dd44
Tønsnes N 62 Gd09
Tonstad N 92 Cb45
Tõnumaa EST 98 Kb44
Tonya TR 205 Fd19
Toome GB 9 Cd16
Toomyvara IRL 13 Ca22
Tootsi EST 98 Kc45
Topağaç TR 185 Ed79
Topala MD 177 Fc60
Topalak TR 192 Fb83
Topalar TR 198 Fb91
Topallı TR 199 Gd91
Topalu RO 177 Fb66
Topana RO 175 Db64
Topârcea RO 175 Da61
Topas E 45 Cb61
Topçam TR 197 Fa89
Topčić-Polje BIH 152 Hb63
Topčii BG 180 Eb69
Topcliffe GB 11 Fa19
Topçukoy TR 186 Fa76
Topçular TR 186 Ga79
Topczewo PL 123 Kb34
Töpen D 135 Ea43
Topeno FIN 90 Ka38
Tophisar TR 186 Fb80
Topla RO 174 Ca60
Topla SLO 144 Fc56
Toplet RO 174 Cb64
Topli Do SRB 179 Cb69
Topliţa RO 172 Ea58
Topliţa RO 175 Cc61
Topola SRB 174 Bb65
Topolany PL 123 Kc34
Topolcafő H 145 Ha54
Topolčane BG 180 Eb72
Topolčani MK 183 Bb75
Topoľčany SK 137 Hb49
Topoľčianky SK 145 Hb50
Topólia GR 200 Ca95
Topólka PL 129 Hb36
Topolnica SRB 174 Ca65
Topólno PL 130 Hd36
Topolog RO 177 Fc65
Topolovăţu Mare RO 174 Bd61
Topoloveni RO 175 Dc65
Topolovgrad BG 185 Eb74
Topolovnik SRB 174 Bc64
Topolovo BG 184 Dc74
Topolšica SLO 151 Fc57
Toponár H 145 Ha56
Toponica SRB 174 Bb66
Toponica SRB 178 Bd69
Toporów PL 128 Fd37
Toporu RO 180 Dd67
Toppenstedt D 118 Dc33
Topraisar RO 181 Fc68
Topuk TR 192 Fc81
Topusko HR 151 Ga60
Topyaka TR 193 Gd82
Torà E 49 Gc60
Torajärvi FIN 89 Jd37
Toral E 37 Cb58
Toral de los Guzmanes E 37 Cc58
Tõramaa EST 98 Kc45
Toranj HR 151 Fa61
Torás E 54 Fb66
Torasjärvi S 73 Hd18
Toasperä FIN 81 Jd31
Toras-Sieppi FIN 68 Jb14
Töravere EST 98 La45
Torba TR 197 Ec90
Torbalı TR 191 Ec87
Torbay GB 19 Ea31
Torbel CH 141 Bd56
Tørberget N 86 Ec37
Torbjörntorp S 102 Fa47
Torcé-en Vallée F 28 Fd39
Torcello I 150 Eb59
Torcross GB 19 Dd32
Torcy F 23 Ha37
Torcy F 30 Ja43
Torcy-le-Grand F 23 Gb34
Torda SRB 153 Jc59
Torda SRB 174 Bb61
Tørdal N 93 Db44
Tordehumos E 46 Cd59
Tordera E 49 Hb60
Tordesillas E 46 Cd61
Tordesilos E 47 Ed64
Tordillos E 45 Cc63
Tordómar E 46 Dc59
Tore GB 5 Ea07
Töre S 73 Ja21
Töreboda S 103 Fb46
Toreby DK 109 Ea29
Toreby DK 109 Eb29
Torekov S 110 Ec53
Torella dei Lombardi I 161 Fd75
Torella del Sannio I 161 Fb72
Torelló E 49 Ha59
Toreno E 37 Ca56
Torestorp S 102 Ed50
Toresund S 96 Gc43
Torete E 47 Ec63
Torfou F 28 Fa43
Torgåsmon S 86 Fa38
Torgau D 127 Ed39
Torgelow D 120 Fb33
Torgu EST 105 Jc47
Torhamn S 111 Ga54
Torheim N 84 Cb34
Torhout B 21 Ha29
Torhult S 102 Fa49
Tori EST 98 Kc45
Torigni-sur-Vire F 22 Fb36
Torija E 46 Dd63
Torikka FIN 97 Jc40
Toril E 47 Ed65
Torino I 148 Bc60
Torino di Sangro Marina I 157 Fb70
Tõrise EST 105 Jc46
Toritto I 162 Gc74
Torjulvågen N 77 Db31
Tõrma EST 98 La42
Tõrma EST 99 Lb44
Törmä FIN 83 Lb26
Tormac RO 174 Bd61
Törmäkylä FIN 82 Kc25
Tormaleo E 37 Bd55
Törmänen FIN 69 Ka11
Törmänki FIN 74 Jc18
Törmänmäki FIN 75 Kd24
Tormantos E 38 Dd58
Tormás H 152 Hb57
Tormäsenvaara FIN 75 La20
Tormäsjärvi FIN 74 Jc19
Tormestorp S 110 Fa54
Törmörkény H 146 Jb55
Tornal'a SK 138 Jb49
Tornanádska H 138 Jc49
Törnävä FIN 81 Jb31
Tornavacas E 45 Cb64
Tornby DK 100 Dc19
Torndrup Strand DK 101 Dd21
Tornefors S 68 Hd16
Tornehamn S 67 Gc13
Tornes N 76 Cd31
Tørnes N 93 Db44
Tornesch D 118 Db32
Torneträsk S 67 Ha14
Tornimäe EST 97 Jd45
Tornin E 37 Cd55
Tornio FIN 74 Jc21
Tornio FIN 90 Kc36
Tornioniemi FIN 91 Lb32
Tornjoš SRB 153 Jb58
Torno I 149 Cc58
Tornos E 47 Ed63
Törnsfall S 103 Gb49
Tornyosnémeti H 139 Jd49
Toro E 45 Cc60
Torö S 96 Gd45
Törökbálint H 146 Hc53
Törökkoppány H 145 Hb56
Törökszentmiklós H 146 Jc54
Toróni GR 184 Cc80
Torony H 145 Gb54
Toropec RUS 202 Eb10
Torošino RUS 107 Ma46
Torp FIN 96 Hb40
Torp S 102 Eb46
Torp S 102 Eb47
Torpa S 95 Ga43
Torpa S 102 Fa52
Torpa S 103 Fd48
Torpao N 85 Dd38
Torpè I 168 Cc75
Torphins GB 7 Ec09
Torpo N 85 Db39
Torpoint GB 18 Dc31
Torpsbruk S 103 Fc51
Torpshammar S 87 Ga33
Torquay GB 19 Ea31
Torquemada E 46 Db59
Torraca I 161 Ga77
Torralba E 47 Eb65
Torralba de Aragón E 48 Fb60
Torralba de Calatrava E 52 Db69
Torralba del Moral E 47 Eb62
Torralba de los Frailes E 47 Ed62
Torralba del Río E 39 Eb57
Torralba de Oropesa E 52 Cc66
Torrão P 50 Ac70
Torrão do Lameiro P 44 Ac62
Torrböle S 80 Hb29
Torre E 59 Cb77
Torre F 154 Cb72
Torre P 44 Ac59
Torre P 50 Ab70
Torre-Alháquime E 59 Cb75
Torre a Mare I 162 Gd74
Torre Annunziata I 161 Fb75
Torrebaja E 54 Ed66
Torrebarrio E 37 Cb55
Torrebeleña E 46 Dd63
Torre Beretti I 148 Cb60
Torreblacos E 47 Ea60
Torreblanca E 54 Fd65
Torreblanca de los Caños E 59 Ca74
Torreblascopedro E 60 Db72
Torrebruna I 161 Fb71
Torrebueit E 53 Ea66
Torrecaballeros E 46 Db62
Torrecampo E 52 Cd70
Torre Canne I 162 Ha75
Torre Cardela E 60 Dc74
Torrechiara I 149 Da62
Torrecilla E 47 Eb65
Torrecilla E 52 Da72
Torrecilla de Alcañiz E 48 Fc63
Torrecilla de la Jara E 52 Cd66
Torrecilla del Pinar E 46 Db61
Torrecilla de Valmadrid E 47 Fa61
Torrecilla en Cameros E 38 Ea58
Torrecillas de la Tiesa E 51 Cb67
Torre das Vargens P 50 Ad67
Torre de Dom Chama P 45 Bc60
Torre de Juan Abad E 53 Dd70
Torre de la Higuera E 59 Bc75
Torre del Bierzo E 37 Ca57
Torre del Campo E 60 Db73
Torre del Greco I 161 Fb75
Torre del Lago Puccini I 155 Da65
Torre dell'Impiso I 166 Eb84
Torre dell'Orso I 163 Hc77
Torre del Mar E 60 Da76
Torre del Peñón E 61 Ec75
Torredembarra E 49 Gc62
Torre de Miguel Sesmero E 51 Bc69
Torre de Moncorvo P 45 Bc61
Torre d'en Doménec E 54 Fd65
Torre de'Passeri I 157 Fa70
Torre di Porticello I 162 Gb71
Torre d'Isola I 149 Cc60
Torredonjimeno E 60 Db73
Torre Faro I 164 Ga83
Torrefarrera E 48 Ga60
Torregrossa E 48 Ga61
Torreira P 44 Ac62
Torrejoncillo E 45 Bd65
Torrejoncillo del Rey E 53 Ea66
Torrejón de Ardoz E 46 Dc64
Torrejón del Rey E 46 Dd64
Torrejón el Rubio E 51 Ca66
Torrelabatón E 46 Cd60
Torrelacárcel E 47 Ed64
Torrelaguna E 46 Dc63
Torrelapaja E 47 Ec61
Torre Lapillo I 162 Hb77
Torrelavega E 38 Db55
Torrellano Alto E 55 Fb71
Torrelodones E 46 Db64
Torremaggiore I 161 Fd72
Torremayor E 51 Bd69
Torremazanas E 55 Fb70
Torremegía E 51 Bd69
Torre Melissa I 165 Gd80
Torremendo E 55 Fa72
Torre Mileto I 161 Ga71
Torremocha E 51 Ca67
Torremolinos E 60 Cd76
Torremormojón E 46 Da59
Torremuelle E 60 Cd77
Torrenieri I 156 Dd67
Torrenostra E 54 Fd65
Torrent E 54 Fb68
Torrente de Cinca E 48 Fd61
Torrenueva E 60 Dc76
Torreorgaz E 51 Bd67
Torre Orsaia I 161 Fd77
Torre-Pacheco E 55 Fa73
Torre Pedrera I 156 Eb64
Torre Pellice I 148 Bc61
Torreperogil E 52 Dc72
Torrequebradilla E 60 Db72
Torrequemada E 51 Ca67
Torre Rinalda I 163 Hc76
Torre Ruffa I 164 Ga82
Torres E 60 Dc73
Torresandino E 46 Db60
Torre San Gennaro I 163 Hc76
Torre San Giovanni I 165 Hc78
Torre Santa Susanna I 162 Hb76
Torres de Albánchez E 53 Ea71
Torres de Berrellén E 47 Fa60
Torres de la Alameda E 46 Dd64
Torres del Carrizal E 45 Cb60
Torres del Obispo E 48 Fd59
Torres de Montes E 48 Fc59
Torres de Segre E 48 Ga61
Torres Novas P 50 Ac66
Torrestio E 37 Cb55
Torres-Torres E 54 Fc67
Torres Vedras P 50 Aa67
Torretta I 149 Dc61
Torretta I 155 Da66
Torrette I 156 Ed66
Torrette di Fano I 156 Ec65
Torre Vado I 165 Hc78
Torrevelilla E 48 Fc63
Torrevicente E 47 Ea61
Torrevieja E 55 Fb72
Torricela I 162 Ha76
Torricella Peligna I 161 Fb71
Torrico E 52 Cc66
Torri del Benaco I 149 Db59
Torridon GB 4 Dc07
Torriglia I 149 Cc62
Torrijas E 54 Fa66
Torrijo del Campo E 47 Ed63
Torrijos E 52 Da66
Torrild DK 108 Dc24
Torrin GB 4 Db08
Tørring DK 108 Db25
Torring N 78 Eb27
Torrita di Siena I 156 Dd67
Torrivaara S 73 Hd19
Torro FIN 89 Jd38
Torroal P 50 Ab70
Torroella de Fluvià E 49 Hb59
Torroella de Montgrí E 49 Hc59
Torrox E 60 Da76
Torrox Costa E 60 Da76
Torrskog S 94 Ec44
Torrubia del Campo E 53 Dd66
Torsåker S 80 Gc31
Torsåker S 95 Ga40
Torsåker S 96 Gc45
Torsång S 95 Fd40
Torsansalo FIN 91 Ld34
Torsås S 111 Ga53
Torsbo S 102 Fa49
Torsborg S 86 Fa32
Torsby S 94 Ed41
Torsby S 94 Fa42
Torsdalsdammen N 92 Cd43
Torsebro S 111 Fb54
Torsetnes N 77 Dc30
Torsfjärden S 79 Fc27
Torshälla S 95 Gb43
Tórshavn DK 3 Ca07
Torsholma FIN 97 Hd40
Torsjöåsen S 86 Fa38
Torskefjord N 64 Jd05
Torsken N 62 Gb10
Torskinge S 102 Fa51
Torskors S 111 Fd54
Torslanda S 102 Eb49
Torslunde DK 109 Ea28
Torsnes N 93 Ea44
Torsö S 94 Fa45
Torstuna S 95 Gb42
Torsvi S 96 Gc43
Törtel H 146 Jb54
Torthorwald GB 10 Ea16
Tortinmäki FIN 89 Jb38
Tortola E 53 Eb66
Tórtola de Heneras E 46 Dd63
Tórtoles de Esgueva E 46 Db60
Tortoli I 169 Cc77
Tortoman RO 181 Fb67
Tortona I 148 Cb61
Tortora I 164 Ga78
Tortora Marina I 164 Ga78
Tortorella I 161 Ga77
Tortoreto Lido I 157 Fa68
Tortorici I 167 Fc84
Tortosa E 48 Ga63
Tortosendo P 44 Bb64
Tortuera E 47 Ec63
Tortuna S 95 Gb42
Torul TR 205 Fd19
Toruń PL 121 Hb34
Torup S 102 Ed51
Tõrva EST 106 La46
Tor Vaianica I 160 Ea72
Torvastad N 92 Bd42
Torvela FIN 82 Kd25
Torvenkylä FIN 81 Jc27
Torver GB 11 Eb18
Tørvik N 77 Dd28
Torvik N 77 Db31
Torvikbukt N 77 Da31
Tørvikbygd N 84 Cb39
Torvinen FIN 69 Ka16
Torvizcón E 60 Dc76
Torvoila FIN 90 Ka36

Torvsjö – Turany

Torvsjö S 79 Gb27
Torysa SK 138 Jc47
Torysky SK 138 Jc47
Toržok RUS 202 Ec10
Torzym PL 128 Fc37
Tosåsen S 87 Fb32
Tosaunet N 70 Ed24
Tosbotn N 70 Fa23
Toscaig GB 4 Db08
Toscolano-Maderno I 149 Db59
Tösens A 142 Db54
Tosno RUS 202 Eb08
Tossa S 73 Jb20
Tossa de Mar E 49 Hb60
Tossåsen S 87 Fb32
Tossavanlahti FIN 82 Kc29
Tosse F 39 Ed54
Tösse S 94 Ed45
Tosseberg S 94 Ed41
Tossene S 102 Eb46
Tõstamaa EST 106 Ka46
Tostared S 102 Ec50
Tostedt D 118 Db33
Tosunlar TR 192 Fc87
Tosya TR 205 Fb20
Tószeg H 146 Jb54
Toszek PL 137 Hb43
Totana E 55 Ed73
Totebo S 103 Ga49
Totenviken N 85 Ea39
Tôtes F 23 Gb34
Totești RO 175 Cc62
Tótkomlós H 146 Jc56
Totland GB 20 Fa31
Tøtlandsvik N 92 Cb43
Totleben BG 180 Dc69
Totnes GB 19 Dd31
Totsås N 78 Fa26
Tótszerdahely H 152 Gc57
Tøttdal N 78 Eb26
Tottenham GB 20 Fc28
Tottijärvi FIN 89 Jc36
Totton GB 20 Fa30
Tótvázsony H 145 Ha54
Touça P 45 Bc62
Toucy F 30 Hb40
Toudon F 43 Kc52
Touët-sur-Var F 43 Kc52
Touillon F 30 Ja40
Toul F 25 Jc37
Toulat FIN 82 Kc30
Toulon F 42 Ka55
Toulon-sur-Arroux F 30 Hd44
Toulouse F 40 Gc54
Toulx Sainte-Croix F 33 Gd45
Toúmba GR 183 Ca77
Tourcoing F 21 Ha30
Tourigo P 44 Ad63
Touriñán E 36 Ac54
Tourlaville F 22 Ed34
Tourlída GR 188 Ba85
Tourmakeady IRL 8 Bc19
Tournai B 124 Aa41
Tournan-en-Brie F 23 Ha37
Tournay F 40 Fd56
Tournecoupe F 40 Ga53
Tournefeuille F 40 Gb54
Tournefort F 43 Kc52
Tournehem-sur-la-Hem F 21 Gc30
Tournon-d'Agenais F 33 Gb51
Tournon-Saint-Martin F 29 Ga44
Tournon-sur-Rhône F 34 Jb49
Tournus F 30 Jb44
Tourny F 23 Gc36
Tourouvre F 29 Ga38
Tours F 29 Ga42
Tours-en-Vimeu F 23 Gc33
Tourteron F 24 Ja34
Tourtoirac F 33 Gb49
Tourtour F 42 Ka53
Tourula FIN 89 Jb37
Tourves F 42 Ka54
Tourville-sur-Sienne F 22 Ed36
Toury F 29 Gc39
Toutencourt F 23 Gd33
Touvois F 28 Ed43
Touzac F 33 Gb51
Toužim CZ 135 Ec44
Tovačov CZ 137 Gd46
Tovariševo SRB 153 Ja60
Tovarkovskij RUS 203 Fa11
Tovarnik HR 153 Hd60
Tovdal N 93 Da45
Tøvelde DK 109 Ec28
Toven N 70 Fa21
Tovrljane SRB 178 Bc69
Tovsli N 92 Cd44
Towcester GB 20 Fb26
Tow Law GB 11 Ed17
Town Yetholm GB 11 Ed14
Toxotes GR 184 Db77
Toya E 61 Dd73
Toybelen TR 192 Fa81
Tøymskardlia N 70 Fa23
Töysä FIN 89 Jd32
Töysänperä FIN 90 Ka32
Tozaklı TR 185 Ed76
Tozalmoro E 47 Eb60
Trabada E 36 Bc54
Trabadelo E 37 Bd56
Trabanca E 45 Ca61
Trabazos E 45 Ca59
Traben-Trarbach D 133 Bd44
Trabia I 166 Ed84
Trabitz D 135 Ea45
Traboch A 144 Fc53
Trabotivište MK 183 Ca74
Trabzon TR 205 Fd19
Trachslau CH 141 Cb54
Tracino I 166 Dd88
Tradate I 148 Cb58
Træna N 70 Ed20
Trættlia N 78 Eb29
Trafask IRL 12 Ba26
Trafoi I 142 Db56
Tragacete E 47 Ec65
Traganó GR 188 Ad86
Traghetto I 150 Dd62
Tragöss-Oberort A 144 Fc53
Tragwein A 144 Fc50
Trahiá GR 195 Ca88
Trahíla GR 194 Bb90
Trahíli GR 189 Cc85
Trahütten A 144 Fd55
Traian RO 172 Ed59
Traian RO 177 Fa64
Traian RO 177 Fb64
Traian RO 177 Fc66
Traian RO 180 Db67
Traian Vuia RO 174 Ca61
Traiguera E 48 Fd64
Trainel F 30 Hb38
Trainou F 29 Gd40
Traisen A 144 Ga51
Traiskirchen A 145 Gb51
Traismauer A 144 Ga50
Trăisteni RO 176 Ea63
Traitsching D 135 Ec47
Trakai LT 114 Kd58
Trakai LT 114 La58
Trakija BG 180 Dd73
Trakiszki PL 123 Kb30
Trakošćan HR 151 Ga57
Trakšėdžiai LT 113 Jb56
Träkumla S 104 Gd49
Tralee IRL 12 Bb24
Trá Lí IRL 12 Bb24
Tramacastilla E 47 Ed64
Tramariglio I 168 Bc75
Tramatza I 169 Bd77
Tramayes F 34 Ja45
Tramelan CH 141 Bc53
Trá Mhór IRL 13 Cb25
Tramm D 119 Ea33
Tramonti di Sopra I 150 Ec57
Tramore IRL 13 Cb25
Trampot F 30 Jb38
Tramutola I 161 Ga77
Trăn BG 179 Ca70
Trana I 148 Bc60
Tranås S 103 Fc48
Tranbjerg DK 108 Dc24
Tranby N 93 Dd42
Trancault F 30 Hc38
Tranco E 61 Ea72
Trancoso P 44 Bb62
Trandal N 76 Cc33
Tranebjerg DK 109 Dd25
Tranekær DK 109 Dd28
Tranemo S 102 Fa50
Tranent GB 11 Ec13
Tranestederne DK 101 Dd19
Trångmon S 79 Fc26
Trångslet S 86 Fa37
Trångsviken S 79 Fb30
Trani I 162 Gc73
Trănica BG 181 Ed69
Traniș RO 171 Cd56
Trankil S 94 Ec44
Trănkovo BG 180 Dd73
Trannes F 30 Ja38
Tranóvalto GR 183 Bc79
Tranøya N 66 Fd14
Trans F 28 Ed38
Transinne B 132 Ad43
Transtrand S 86 Fa38
Tranum DK 100 Db20
Tranum Enge DK 100 Db20
Tranvik S 96 Ha43
Tranvikan N 77 Dc29
Trapani I 166 Ea84
Trapene LV 107 Lb48
Trapoklovo BG 180 Eb72
Trapp GB 19 Dd27
Trappenkamp D 118 Dc31
Trappes F 23 Gc37
Trappeto I 166 Eb84
Trappstadt D 134 Dc43
Traryd S 110 Fa53
Trasacco I 160 Ed71
Trasadingen CH 141 Cb52
Trasanquelos E 36 Ba54
Trascastro E 36 Ba56
Trasdorf A 144 Ga50
Trashan AL 163 Jb71
Trasierra E 51 Ca71
Träskholm S 73 Hb24
Träskvik FIN 89 Ja33
Träslövsläge S 102 Ec51
Trasmonte E 36 Bb55
Traspinedo E 46 Da60
Trässberg S 102 Ed46
Trassem D 133 Bc45
Trästena S 103 Fb46
Trăstenik BG 180 Db69
Trăstenik BG 180 Ea69
Trăstikovo BG 181 Ed73
Tratnach A 144 Fa51
Traun A 144 Fb51
Traunkirchen A 144 Fa52
Traunreut D 143 Eb51
Traunstein D 143 Ec52
Traupis LT 114 Kd55
Trausnitz D 135 Eb46
Trauten N 94 Eb40
Trautskirchen D 134 Dc46
Trävad S 102 Ed47
Travassós P 44 Ba60
Trävattna S 102 Fa47
Travemünde D 119 Dd31
Travers CH 141 Bb54
Traversella I 148 Bd59
Traversetolo I 149 Da62
Traves F 31 Jd40
Traviesas E 36 Ba54
Travnik BIH 158 Ha64
Travnik SLO 151 Fb59
Travo F 154 Cb71
Trawniki PL 131 Kb40
Trawsfynydd GB 15 Dd23
Trazo E 36 Ad55
Trbovlje SLO 151 Fc57
Trbuk BIH 152 Hb62
Trbušani SRB 159 Jc64
Trbušnica SRB 153 Jc63
Trdevac KSV 178 Ba71
Trean IRL 8 Bc20
Trearddur Bay GB 14 Dc22
Trébago E 47 Ec60
Tréban F 34 Hb45
Třebařov CZ 137 Gc45
Trebbin D 127 Ed37
Trebbus D 128 Fa39
Třebechovice pod Orebem CZ 136 Ga44
Trebel D 119 Ea34
Třeben CZ 135 Eb44
Treben D 127 Eb41
Trebenište MK 182 Ba75
Trebenow D 120 Fa33
Trèbes F 41 Ha55
Trébeurden F 26 Dd37
Trebgast D 135 Ea44
Třebíč CZ 136 Ga47
Trebinjë AL 182 Ad76
Trebinje BIH 159 Hc69
Trebisacce I 164 Gc78
Trebisăuți MD 173 Fa53
Trebisht AL 182 Ad74
Trebisov SK 139 Ka48
Trebitz D 127 Ec39
Treblinka PL 123 Jd35
Trebnje SLO 151 Fc58
Třebohostice CZ 136 Fa47
Třeboň CZ 136 Fc48
Tréboul F 27 Dc39
Třebovice CZ 137 Gb45
Trebsen D 127 Ec40
Trebujena E 59 Bd75
Trebujeni MD 173 Fd57
Trebur D 134 Cc44
Treburley GB 18 Dc31
Trecastagni I 167 Fd85
Trecastle GB 15 Ea26
Trecate I 148 Cb59
Trecchina I 161 Ga77
Trecenta I 150 Dd61
Trechtlingshausen D 133 Ca44
Trecwn GB 14 Db26
Tredegar GB 19 Ea27
Trédion F 27 Eb40
Tredòs E 40 Ga57
Tredozio I 156 Dd64
Treehoo IRL 9 Cc19
Treen GB 18 Da32
Trefeglwys GB 15 Ea24
Tréfeuntec F 27 Dc39
Treffelstein D 135 Ec46
Treffen A 144 Fa56
Treffieux F 28 Ed41
Treffort-Cuisat F 35 Jc45
Treffurt D 126 Db41
Trefnant GB 15 Ea22
Tre Fontane I 166 Eb85
Trefor GB 15 Dd22
Trefriw GB 15 Ea22
Tregaron GB 15 Dd25
Trégastel-Plage F 26 Dd37
Treglio I 157 Fb70
Tregnago I 149 Dc59
Trégomeur F 26 Eb38
Tregony GB 18 Db32
Trégourez F 27 Dd39
Tréguier F 26 Ea37
Trégunc F 27 Dd40
Trehörna S 103 Fc47
Trehörningsjö S 80 Ha29
Treia D 108 Da29
Treia I 156 Ed67
Treignac F 33 Gc48
Treignat F 33 Gd45
Treignes B 132 Ac43
Treigny F 30 Hb41
Treillières F 28 Ed42
Treimani EST 106 Kb47
Treis-Karden D 133 Bd43
Trekanten S 103 Ga52
Trekilen S 79 Gb30
Trekljano BG 179 Ca71
Trelawnyd GB 15 Ea22
Trélazé F 28 Fc41
Trélaze F 28 Fc41
Trelde DK 108 Db26
Trelech GB 14 Dc26
Treleth GB 11 Eb19
Trélissac F 33 Ga49
Trelkowo PL 122 Jb32
Trelleborg S 110 Ed57
Trelleck GB 19 Eb27
Trélon F 24 Hc32
Treluminjt AL 182 Ad77
Tremblay F 28 Ed38
Tremblois-lès-Rocroi F 24 Hd33
Tremedal E 45 Cb64
Tremedal de Tormes E 45 Ca62
Tremelo B 124 Ad40
Trémentines F 28 Fb42
Tremês P 50 Ab67
Třemešná CZ 137 Gd44
Tremezzo I 149 Cc57
Tréminis F 35 Jd50
Tremoli I 164 Ga78
Tremor de Arriba E 37 Ca56
Tremosine I 149 Db58
Třemošná CZ 135 Ed45
Třemošnice CZ 136 Fd45
Tremp E 48 Ga59
Trenance GB 18 Db31
Trénči LV 106 Kb51
Trenčianska Turná SK 137 Ha48
Trenčianske Stankovce SK 137 Ha48
Trenčianske Teplice SK 137 Hb48
Trenčín SK 137 Ha48
Trend DK 100 Db21
Trendelburg D 126 Da39
Trengereiddal N 84 Ca39
Trensacq F 39 Fb52
Trent D 119 Ed30
Trenta SLO 151 Fa57
Trento I 149 Dc58
Trentola I 161 Fa74
Tréogan F 27 Dd39
Tréon F 23 Gb37
Treorchy GB 19 Ea27
Trepča HR 151 Ga60
Trepča KSV 178 Bb70
Trepča Atomska SRB 159 Jc64
Treppeln D 128 Fb38
Trept F 35 Jc47
Trepuzzi I 163 Hc76
Trerulefoot GB 18 Dc31
Třešť CZ 136 Fd47
Trescares E 38 Da55
Trescore Balneario I 149 Cd59
Trescore Cremasco I 149 Cd59
Tresfjord N 76 Cd32
Tresigallo I 150 Ea62
Tresjuncos E 53 Ea67
Treskë AL 182 Ad77
Treski EST 107 Lc46
Treskog S 94 Ed42
Tresnja SRB 153 Jc62
Tresnja SRB 174 Bb64
Trešnjevica SRB 178 Ad67
Trešnjevo MNE 159 Hd69
Tresnuraghes I 169 Bd76
Tresonče MK 182 Ba74
Trespaderne E 38 Dd56
Tressait GB 7 Ea10
Tresson F 29 Ga40
Treteau F 34 Hc45
Tretjakovo RUS 114 Ka58
Trets F 42 Jd54
Tretten N 63 Hb09
Tretten N 85 Dd37
Treuchtlingen D 134 Dc48
Treuen D 135 Eb43
Treuenbrietzen D 127 Ec38
Treungen N 93 Da44
Trevalampi FIN 98 Ka39
Trevélez E 60 Dc75
Tréveray F 24 Jb37
Trevi I 156 Eb68
Treviana E 38 Ea57
Trévières F 22 Fb35
Treviglio I 149 Cd59
Trevignano Romano I 156 Ea70
Trévignon F 27 Dd40
Treviño E 38 Ea57
Treviso I 150 Ea59
Trevor GB 14 Dc23
Trewithian GB 18 Db32
Trézelles F 34 Hc45
Trezzano sul Naviglio I 149 Cc59
Trezzo sull' Adda I 149 Cd59
Trgovište SRB 178 Bd72
Trhanov CZ 135 Ec47
Trhová Kamenice CZ 136 Ga45
Trhovište SK 139 Ka48
Triacastela E 36 Bc56
Triaize F 32 Fa45
Triana I 156 Dd68
Triánda GR 197 Fa92
Triangelen N 65 Kc09
Triantafillià GR 183 Bb77
Triaucourt-en-Argonne F 24 Ja36
Triberg D 141 Cb50
Tribsees D 119 Ec31
Tribunj HR 157 Ga65
Tricarico I 162 Gb76
Tricase I 165 Hc78
Tricase Porto I 165 Hc78
Tricesimo I 150 Ed57
Tricot F 23 Ha34
Triebel D 135 Eb43
Trieben A 144 Fb53
Triebes D 127 Eb42
Trie-Château F 23 Gc35
Triefenstein D 134 Da45
Triei I 169 Cc77
Triengen CH 141 Ca53
Trier D 133 Bc44
Trierweiler D 133 Bc44
Trieste I 151 Fa59
Triest = Trieste I 151 Fa59
Trie-sur-Baïse F 40 Fd55
Trifănești MD 173 Fb55
Trifești MD 173 Fd56
Trifești RO 172 Ed58
Trifești RO 173 Fa56
Triftern D 143 Ec50
Trigance F 43 Kb53
Triglitz D 119 Eb34
Trignac F 27 Ec42
Trigóna GR 182 Ba80
Trígono GR 182 Ba77
Trigrad BG 184 Da75
Triguères F 30 Hb40
Trigueros E 59 Bb73
Trigueros del Valle E 46 Da60
Trijebine SRB 159 Jb67
Trijebine SRB 178 Ad68
Trijueque E 46 Dd63
Trikala GR 183 Bd78
Trikala GR 188 Bb81
Trikāta LV 106 La48
Trikéri GR 189 Ca83
Tri Kladenci BG 179 Cd69
Trikokiá GR 183 Bb80
Trikomo CY 206 Jd96
Trikorfo GR 182 Ba79
Trilj HR 158 Gc66
Trillevallen S 78 Fa30
Trillo E 47 Ea63
Trilofos GR 183 Bd78
Trim IRL 9 Cc20
Trimbach CH 141 Ca53
Trimiklini CY 206 Ja97
Trimsaran GB 19 Dd27
Trin CH 142 Cd55
Trinay F 29 Gc39
Trinca MD 172 Ed54
Trindade P 45 Bc60
Trindade P 58 Ad72
Třinec CZ 137 Hb45
Tring GB 20 Fb27
Trinità I 148 Bc63
Trinità I 148 Bd62
Trinità d'Agultu I 168 Ca74
Trinitapoli I 162 Gb73
Trinity GBJ 26 Ec35
Trino I 148 Ca60
Trinta P 44 Bb63
Triodos GR 194 Bb89
Triogo E 37 Cd54
Triollo E 38 Da56
Triora I 43 Kc52
Trípes GR 194 Bb87
Trípiti GR 184 Cd79
Trípiti GR 194 Ba87
Trípoli GR 194 Bc88
Triponzo I 156 Ec68
Tripótama GR 188 Bb86
Tripótama GR 188 Ba83
Tripótamos GR 183 Bd78
Triptis D 127 Ea42
Trispen GB 18 Db31
Tři Studně CZ 136 Ga46
Tritenii de Jos RO 171 Db58
Trittau D 118 Dc32
Trittenheim D 133 Bd44
Trivalea-Moșteni RO 176 Dd66
Trivento I 161 Fb72
Trivero I 148 Ca58
Trivignano Udinese I 150 Ed58
Trivigno I 162 Gb76
Trizac F 33 Ha48
Trizelnieki LV 107 Lb51
Trizina GR 195 Ca88
Trjavna BG 180 Dd71
Trnakovac HR 152 Gd60
Trnava SK 145 Ha50
Trnava SRB 159 Jb64
Trnavce KSV 178 Ba70
Trnjane SRB 178 Bc68
Trnjani BIH 152 Gc61
Trnjani HR 152 Hb60
Trnovac SRB 179 Ca68
Trnovec HR 152 Gb57
Trnovec nad Váhom SK 145 Ha51
Trnovica BIH 159 Hc66
Trnovica HR 158 Hb68
Trnovo BIH 159 Hc65
Trnovska vas SLO 144 Ga56
Troarn F 22 Fc36
Tröbitz D 127 Ed39
Trobo E 36 Bb54
Tročany SK 139 Jd47
Trochry GB 7 Ea11
Trochtelfingen D 142 Cd50
Trödje S 88 Gc38
Troedyrhiw GB 19 Ea27
Troekurovo RUS 203 Fb11
Troense DK 109 Dd28
Trofa P 44 Ad60
Trofa P 44 Ad60
Trofaiach A 144 Fc53
Trofors N 70 Fa23
Trogen CH 142 Cd53
Trogir HR 158 Gb66
Troglan Bara SRB 178 Bd67
Tröglitz D 127 Eb41
Troia I 161 Fd73
Tróia P 50 Ab70
Troianul RO 180 Dc67
Troickaja RUS 205 Fc17
Troina I 167 Fb85
Troisdorf D 125 Bd41
Trois Ponts B 125 Bb42
Troistorrents CH 141 Bb56
Troisvierges L 133 Bb43
Troița Nouă MD 173 Ga59
Troițcoe MD 173 Fd59
Trojaci MK 183 Bc75
Trojan BG 180 Db71
Trojane SLO 151 Fc57
Trojanovo BG 181 Ec72
Trojanów PL 131 Jd38
Trójca PL 128 Fc41
Trökörna S 102 Ed47
Troldhede DK 108 Da24
Trolla N 78 Ea29
Trollfjord N 63 Ja04
Trollhättan S 102 Ec47
Trollknuten N 93 Db43
Trollshovda FIN 97 Jc40
Trollvik N 63 Hb10
Trømborg N 94 Eb43
Tromello I 148 Cb60
Tromøy N 93 Db46
Tromsdal N 78 Ec29
Tromsdalen N 62 Gd09
Tromsø N 62 Gd09
Tromvik N 62 Gc09
Trönbyn S 87 Gb37
Troncedo E 40 Fd58
Tronco P 45 Bc59
Trondheim N 77 Ea30
Trondstad N 92 Cd47
Trones N 71 Fc18
Trones N 78 Fa25
Trönninge S 102 Ec51
Trönninge S 102 Ed52
Trönö S 87 Gb36
Trontveit N 93 Da44
Tronvik N 78 Eb29
Tronvik N 84 Cb36
Trôo F 29 Ga40
Troodos CY 206 Ja97
Troon GB 10 Dd14
Troøyen N 78 Ea31
Trooz B 124 Ba41
Trópea GR 194 Bb87
Tropea I 164 Ga82
Tropojë AL 159 Jc69
Tropojë AL 178 Ad71
Tröpolach A 143 Ed56
Tropy Sztumskie PL 122 Hc31
Trory GB 9 Cb17
Trosa S 96 Gc45
Trosby N 93 Dc44
Troškas LV 107 Lb51
Troškūnai LT 114 Kd55
Trošmarija HR 151 Fd60
Trosna RUS 202 Ed12
Trossin D 127 Ec39
Trossingen D 141 Cb50
Trostan' RUS 202 Ec13
Tröstau D 135 Ea44
Trostberg D 143 Eb51
Trostjanec' UA 202 Ed14
Trostjanskij RUS 203 Fc13
Troszczyno PL 120 Fd32
Troszyn PL 122 Jc34
Trotby FIN 97 Jc40
Trouans F 24 Hd37
Troubelice CZ 137 Gc45
Troubky CZ 137 Gd46
Troulloi CY 206 Jc97
Troutbeck GB 11 Eb18
Trouville-sur-Mer F 22 Fd35
Troviscal P 44 Ad65
Trowbridge GB 19 Ec28
Troyes F 30 Hd38
Trpanj HR 158 Gd68
Trpezi MNE 159 Jc68
Trpezi MNE 178 Ad69
Trpezica MK 182 Ad76
Trpinja HR 153 Hd60
Trsa MNE 159 Hd67
Tršće HR 151 Fc59
Tršic SRB 153 Ja63
Trstená SK 138 Hd46
Trstenik HR 158 Ha68
Trstenik SRB 178 Bb67
Trsteno HR 158 Hb69
Trstice SK 145 Ha51
Trübbach CH 142 Cd54
Trubčevsk RUS 202 Ed13
Trubetčino RUS 203 Fb12
Trubia E 37 Cb54
Trubjela MNE 159 Hd68
Trubschachen CH 141 Bd54
Trucco I 43 Kd52
Truchas E 37 Ca58
Trud BG 180 Db73
Trudovec BG 179 Cd70
Trujillanos E 51 Bd69
Trujillo E 51 Ca67
Trulben D 133 Ca47
Trumieje PL 122 Hc32
Trumiejki PL 122 Hc32
Trumpji LV 105 Jc49
Trun CH 142 Cc55
Trun F 22 Fd37
Trundön S 73 Hd23
Trupel PL 122 Hc32
Truro GB 18 Db32
Trușeni MD 173 Fc58
Trușești RO 172 Ed55
Trusetal D 126 Dc42
Truskava LT 114 Kc55
Truskolasy PL 130 Hc42
Truskolasy-Lachy PL 123 Ka34
Trustrup DK 101 Dd23
Trutnov CZ 136 Ga43
Trutnowy PL 121 Hb30
Try N 92 Cd47
Tryczówka PL 123 Kb34
Trydal N 92 Cd43
Tryde S 111 Fb56
Tryggelev DK 109 Dd28
Tryggestad N 84 Cd34
Trygort PL 122 Jc30
Tryland N 92 Cc46
Tryńcza PL 139 Kb43
Trypimeni CY 206 Jc96
Tryserum S 103 Gb47
Trysil N 86 Ec37
Tryškiai LT 113 Jd54
Trysnes N 92 Cd47
Tryszczyn PL 121 Ha34
Tržac BIH 151 Ga61
Trzciana PL 139 Ka44
Trzcianka PL 121 Gb34
Trzcianka PL 122 Jc35
Trzcianka PL 123 Kb32
Trzcianne PL 123 Ka33
Trzciel PL 128 Ga37
Trzcinica PL 129 Ha41
Trzcinna PL 120 Fc35
Trzcinno PL 121 Gc31
Trzcińsk PL 121 Hb31
Trzcińsko-Zdrój PL 120 Fc35
Trzebce PL 130 Hd41
Trzebiatów PL 120 Fd31
Trzebicz PL 120 Ga35
Trzebiel PL 128 Fc39
Trzebielino PL 121 Gc31
Trzebień PL 128 Fd40
Trzebieszów PL 131 Ka37
Trzebieszowice PL 137 Gc43
Trzebież PL 120 Fb32
Trzebin PL 120 Ga34
Trzebinia PL 138 Hd44
Trzebnica PL 129 Gc40
Trzebnice PL 128 Ga40
Trzebów PL 128 Fc36
Trzeciewiec PL 121 Ha34
Trzemeszno PL 129 Gd36
Trzemżal PL 129 Ha36
Trzepnica PL 130 Hd40
Trześcianka PL 123 Kc34
Trześń PL 131 Jd42
Trześniów PL 139 Ka45
Trzęsów PL 129 Gb39
Trzeszczany PL 131 Kd41
Tržič SLO 151 Fb57
Trzin SLO 151 Fb57
Tržišće SLO 151 Fd58
Trzydnik Duży PL 131 Ka41
Tsada CY 206 Hd97
Tsangaráda GR 189 Cb82
Tsaritsáni GR 183 Bc80
Tschenstochau = Częstochowa PL 130 Hc42
Tschernitz D 128 Fc39
Tschiertschen CH 142 Cd55
Tschierv CH 142 Db56
Tschlin I 142 Db55
Tsepélovo GR 182 Ad79
Tseri CY 206 Jb97
Tséria GR 194 Bb89
Tševetjävri FIN 65 Kb08
Tsikalariá GR 200 Cb95
Tsilivi GR 188 Ac86
Tsirguliina EST 106 La47
Tsirgumäe EST 107 Lb48
Tsitália GR 195 Bd89
Tsjernobyl UA 202 Ec14
Tsooru EST 107 Lb47
Tsotili GR 182 Ba78
Tsoúka GR 189 Bc83
Tsoukaládes GR 188 Ac83
Tsoútsouros GR 200 Da96
Tsz-lakótelep H 146 Hd55
Tua N 78 Eb28
Tua P 44 Bb61
Tuaim IRL 8 Bd20
Tuam IRL 8 Bd20
Tuapse RUS 205 Fc17
Tuar Mhic Éadaigh IRL 8 Bc19
Tūbausiai LT 113 Jb54
Tubbergen NL 117 Bd36
Tubilla de Agua E 38 Dc57
Tubilleja E 38 Dc56
Tübinės LT 113 Jb56
Tübingen D 134 Cc49
Tučapy CZ 136 Fc47
Tučepi HR 158 Gd67
Tuchan F 41 Ha56
Tüchen D 119 Eb34
Tuchheim D 127 Eb37
Tuchlino PL 121 Gd30
Tuchola PL 121 Gd33
Tuchomie PL 121 Gc31
Tuchów PL 138 Jc44
Tuckur FIN 81 Ja30
Tučovo RUS 202 Ed10
Tuczki PL 122 Hd33
Tuczna PL 131 Kc37
Tuczno PL 120 Fd35
Tuczno PL 121 Gb34
Tuczno PL 120 Ga34
Tudanca E 38 Db55
Tuddal N 93 Db41
Tuddenham GB 20 Fd25
Tudeils F 33 Gc49
Tudela E 47 Ed59
Tudela de Duero E 46 Da60
Tudela Veguín E 37 Cc54
Tudora RO 172 Ec56
Tudor Vladimirescu RO 177 Fa64
Tudor Vladimirescu RO 177 Fa62
Tudu EST 98 La42
Tudulinna EST 99 Lb43
Tudweiliog GB 14 Dc23
Tuéjar E 54 Fa67
Tuen DK 101 Dd19
Tuenno I 149 Dc57
Tufeni RO 175 Dc66
Tufești RO 177 Fa64
Tuffé F 29 Ga39
Tufjord N 63 Ja05
Tufjord N 64 Jb04
Tugford GB 15 Ec25
Tuggensele S 80 Gd26
Țuglui RO 175 Cd66
Tugotino RUS 107 Mb46
Tuhala EST 98 Kc43
Tuhalaane EST 106 Kd46
Tuhaň CZ 136 Fb43
Tuhkakylä FIN 82 La26
Tui E 36 Ad58
Tuin MK 182 Ba74
Tuiskula FIN 89 Jb32
Tuixén E 49 Gc59
Tuiza E 37 Cb55
Tūja LV 106 Kb49
Tuk Mrkopaljski HR 151 Fc60
Ţukovicy RUS 99 Ma45
Ţukovo RUS 107 Ld48
Tukums LV 106 Ka51
Tula I 168 Ca75
Tula RUS 203 Fa11
Tulach Mhór IRL 13 Cb21
Tulare SRB 178 Bc70
Tülau D 127 Dd36
Tulawki PL 122 Ja31
Tulca RO 170 Ca57
Tulcea RO 177 Fc64
Tul'cevo RUS 107 Ld48
Tulčik SK 139 Jd47
Tul'čyn UA 204 Eb16
Tulette F 42 Jb51
Tulgheș RO 172 Ea58
Tuliharju FIN 82 Kd25
Tuliszków PL 129 Ha38
Tulje BIH 158 Hb68
Tulla IRL 12 Bc22
Tullaghanstown IRL 9 Cc20
Tullamore IRL 13 Cb21
Tulle F 33 Gc49
Tullebølle DK 109 Dd28
Tulleråsen S 79 Fb30
Tullins F 35 Jc48
Tulln A 144 Ga50
Tullow IRL 13 Cc23
Tully GB 9 Cb17
Tullyamalra IRL 9 Cc19
Tulnici RO 176 Ec61
Tulovo BG 180 Dd72
Tułowice PL 130 Ja36
Tułowice PL 137 Gd43
Tulppio FIN 69 Kd14
Tulsk IRL 8 Ca19
Tulstrup DK 108 Db24
Tulstrup DK 109 Ec25
Tulucești RO 177 Fb63
Tum PL 130 Hc38
Tuma RUS 203 Fb10
Tumba S 96 Gd44
Tumbo E 36 Bc54
Tumbo S 95 Ga43
Tume LV 106 Ka51
Tumleberg S 102 Ed47
Tummel Bridge GB 7 Ea10
Tun S 102 Ed46
Tuna S 87 Gb33
Tuna S 96 Gd41
Tuna S 103 Ga49
Tunaberg S 103 Gb46
Tunadal S 88 Gc33
Tuna-Hästberg S 95 Fd40
Tunari RO 176 Eb66
Tunby S 87 Gb33
Tunçbilek TR 192 Ga82
Tunceli TR 205 Fd20
Tune DK 109 Eb26
Tune N 93 Ea43
Tungaseter N 77 Da33
Tunge S 102 Ec48
Tungelsta S 96 Gd44
Tunhovd N 85 Db39
Tuningen D 141 Cb51
Tunjë AL 182 Ac76
Tunkkari FIN 81 Jc29
Tunneberga S 110 Ec54
Tunnerstad S 103 Fb48
Tunnsjørørvika N 78 Fa25
Tunnstad N 66 Fc12
Tunø By DK 109 Dd25
Tunstall GB 11 Ec19
Tunstall GB 17 Fc21
Tunstall GB 21 Gb26
Tuntenhausen D 143 Ea51
Tunturikeskus Kiilopää FIN 69 Kb12
Tunvågen S 87 Fc32
Tuohikotti FIN 90 La36
Tuohikylä FIN 69 Kd16
Tuohisaari FIN 91 Lc33
Tuohittu FIN 97 Jd40
Tuolluvaara S 67 Hb15
Tuolpukka S 68 Hc15
Tuomela FIN 74 Ka18
Tuomikylä FIN 81 Jb31
Tuomioja FIN 81 Jd25
Tuomiperä FIN 81 Jd27
Tuomiperä FIN 82 Ka28
Tuopanjoki FIN 83 Lc29
Tuorila FIN 89 Ja35
Tuoro sul Trasimeno I 156 Ea67
Tuovila FIN 81 Ja31
Tuovilanlahti FIN 82 Kd29
Tupicino RUS 99 Ld44
Tupilați RO 172 Ec57
Tupilați RO 177 Fb60
Tuplice PL 128 Fc39
Tupos FIN 74 Ka24
Tuppu FIN 74 Kb24
Tuppurinmäki FIN 82 La31
Tur PL 121 Gd34
Tur PL 130 Hc38
Tura H 146 Ja52
Turaida LV 106 Kc49
Turajärvi FIN 89 Ja37
Turanj HR 157 Fd65
Turanköy TR 186 Fd80
Turanlar TR 197 Ed88
Turany SK 138 Hc47

Usson-les-Bains F 41 Gd57
Ussy F 22 Fc36
Ustaritz F 39 Ed55
Ust'Džeguta RUS 205 Fd17
Ust'e RUS 99 Ma41
Ŭštěk CZ 136 Fb43
Uster CH 141 Cd53
Ustia MD 173 Fa56
Ustia MD 173 Fd57
Ustibar BIH 159 Ja66
Ustikolina BIH 159 Hd66
Ústí nad Labem CZ 128 Fa42
Ústí nad Orlicí CZ 137 Gb45
Ustiprača BIH 159 Hd65
Ustjužna RUS 202 Ec08
Ustka PL 121 Gc29
Ust'-Labinsk RUS 205 Fc17
Ust'-Luga RUS 99 Lc40
Ust'Luga RUS 202 Ea08
Ustovo BG 184 Db75
Ustrem BG 185 Eb74
Ustronie Morskie PL 120 Ga31
Ust'-Rudicy RUS 99 Ma39
Ustrzyki Dolne PL 139 Kb46
Ustrzyki Górne PL 106 Kb47
Üstünler TR 199 Hb89
Ustyluh UA 202 Dd14
Usvjaty RUS 202 Eb11
Uszyce PL 129 Hb41
Utajärvi FIN 74 Kb24
Utåker N 92 Cd41
Utakleiv N 66 Fb14
Utanen FIN 74 Kb24
Utäng S 94 Gb45
Utansjö S 88 Gc32
Utbjoa N 92 Ca41
Utby S 102 Ec47
Utby S 103 Fb46
Utebo E 47 Fa60
Utekáč SK 138 Ja49
Utena LT 114 La55
Úterý CZ 135 Ec45
Uthaug N 77 Dd29
Uthmöden D 127 Ea37
Utiel E 54 Fa67
Utne N 84 Cc39
Utnes N 65 Kd08
Utö S 96 Gd45
Utoslahti FIN 74 Kb24
Utrasniemi FIN 91 Ld33
Utrecht NL 116 Ba36
Utrera E 59 Ca74
Utriala FIN 90 La32
Utrillas E 47 Fa63
Utrine SRB 153 Jb58
Utset N 77 Dc29
Utsiktstårn N 65 Kd08
Utsjö S 94 Fa39
Utsjoki FIN 64 Jd07
Utskarpen N 71 Fb20
Uttendorf A 143 Eb54
Uttenweiler D 142 Cd50
Utterbyn S 94 Ed41
Utterliden S 72 Ha23
Uttermossa FIN 89 Ja34
Uttersberg S 95 Fd42
Uttersjöbäcken S 81 Hd26
Utterslev DK 109 Ea28
Utti FIN 90 La37
Utting D 142 Dc51
Uttoxeter GB 16 Ed23
Utula FIN 91 Lc35
Utvängstorp S 102 Fa48
Utvik N 84 Cc34
Utvin RO 174 Bc61
Útvina CZ 135 Ec44
Utvorda N 78 Eb26
Uue-Kariste EST 106 Kd46
Uukuniemen kirkonkylä FIN 91 Ma33
Uukuniemi FIN 91 Ld33
Uulu EST 106 Kb46
Uura FIN 82 Kd25
Uurainen FIN 90 Kb32
Uuro FIN 83 Lc27
Uuro FIN 89 Ja33
Uusijoki FIN 69 Ka14
Uusikaarlepyy FIN 81 Ja29
Uusikartano FIN 89 Jb38
Uusikaupunki FIN 89 Ja38
Uusikylä FIN 81 Jc27
Uusikylä FIN 81 Jd30
Uusikylä FIN 90 Kc37
Uusi-Värtsilä FIN 83 Ma31
Uusküla EST 99 Lb43
Uutela FIN 69 Ka14
Uva FIN 82 Kd27
Uvac SRB 159 Ja65
Úvaly CZ 136 Fc44
Uvanå S 94 Fa40
Uvarovo RUS 203 Fc12
Uvdal N 85 Db40
Üvecik TR 191 Ea81
Uxbridge GB 20 Fc22
Uyanık TR 193 Hb85
Üyük TR 187 Gb80
Úžava LV 105 Jb50
Užbičiai LT 113 Jc57
Uzdin SRB 174 Bb62
Uzdowo PL 122 Hd33
Uzel F 27 Eb39
Uzemain F 31 Jd39
Uzerche F 33 Gc48
Uzès F 42 Ja52
Uzeste F 32 Fc51
Užhorod UA 204 Dd16
Úžice SRB 159 Jb65
Užliekné LT 113 Jd53
Užlieknis LT 113 Jc54
Uzlovaja RUS 203 Fa11
Uzlovoe RUS 113 Ja58
Uzlovoe RUS 113 Jd58
Užovka RUS 203 Fc10
Užpaliai LT 114 La54
Uzsa H 145 Gd53
Uztarroz E 39 Fa56
Užtiltė LT 115 Lb54
Užuguostis LT 114 Kd58
Üzümdere TR 199 Hb90
Üzümler TR 191 Ed87
Üzümlü TR 192 Fa86
Üzümlü TR 198 Fd91
Üzümlü TR 199 Hb89
Üzümlü TR 205 Fd20
Üzümlüpınar TR 199 Gc89
Uzundere TR 191 Ec86
Uzundžovo BG 185 Dd74
Uzunköprü TR 185 Eb76
Uzunkoyu TR 191 Ea86
Uzunpınar TR 192 Fd87
Uzunpınar TR 193 Gc86
Uzuntarla TR 187 Gb79
Uzunyurt TR 198 Fc92
Uzupis LT 115 Lc54
Užusaliai LT 114 Kc57
Užusienis LT 114 La58
Užventis LT 113 Jd54
Uzyn UA 204 Ec15

Vå N 92 Cd41
Vä S 111 Fb55
Vaabina EST 107 Lb47
Vaadinselkä FIN 69 Kd17
Vaahersalo FIN 91 Ld33
Vaajakoski FIN 90 Kc32
Vaajasalmi FIN 82 Kd31
Vääkiö FIN 75 La22
Vaala FIN 82 Kc25
Vaalajärvi FIN 69 Ka16
Vaale D 118 Da31
Vaalimaa FIN 91 Lb37
Vaaljoki FIN 89 Jb38
Vaals NL 125 Bb41
Väänänen FIN 90 Kc36
Vääräkoski FIN 89 Jd32
Vaarakylä FIN 83 Lb27
Väärämäki FIN 81 Jd30
Vaaraniva FIN 75 Kd22
Vaarankylä FIN 82 Kd25
Vaaranperä FIN 74 Jb18
Vaaraperä FIN 75 La21
Vaaraslahti FIN 82 Kc29
Väärinmaja FIN 89 Jd34
Vaartsi EST 107 Lc46
Vaas F 28 Fd41
Vaasa FIN 81 Hd30
Vaassen NL 117 Bc36
Väästa EST 98 Kd44
Väätäiskylä FIN 90 Kd37
Vaattojärvi FIN 68 Jb17
Vabaliai LT 113 Jc53
Vabalninkas LT 114 Kd53
Vaida EST 98 Kc42
Vaideeni RO 175 Da63
Vaiges F 28 Fb39
Vaiguva LT 113 Jd55
Vaihingen (Enz) D 134 Cc48
Vaikantonys LT 114 Kd57
Väike-Maarja EST 98 La43
Väike Rakke EST 98 La45
Vaikko FIN 83 Lb28
Vaillant F 30 Jb40
Vailly F 35 Ka65
Vailly-sur-Aisne F 24 Hb35
Vailly-sur-Sauldre F 29 Ha41
Vaimaro FIN 89 Ja38
Vaimastvere EST 98 La44
Väimela EST 107 Lb47
Vaimõisa EST 98 Kd44
Vaimosuo FIN 75 La19
Vainikkala FIN 91 Lc36
Vainiūai LT 123 Kc49
Vainiži LV 106 Kc49
Vaiņode LV 113 Jc53
Vainova LV 107 Lc52
Vainutas LT 113 Jc56
Väisälä FIN 75 La24
Väisälä FIN 90 La33
Väisälänmäki FIN 82 Kd29
Vaisi EST 98 Ka43
Vaisodžiai LT 114 Kc59
Vaison-la-Romaine F 42 Jc52
Vaiste EST 106 Ka46
Vaišvydava LT 114 Kc57
Vaite F 31 Jc40
Vaiteliai LT 113 Jb55
Vaitkūnai LT 114 La54
Vaivadiškiai LT 114 Kc56
Vaivara EST 99 Lc41
Vaivio FIN 83 Lc30
Vajangu EST 98 Kd43
Vaje N 93 Da46
Väjern S 102 Ea46
Vajkijaur S 72 Ha19
Vajmat S 72 Ha19
Vajska SRB 153 Hd60
Vajszló H 152 Hb58
Vajta H 146 Hc55
Vajze AL 182 Ab77
Vakern S 95 Fb40
Vakfıkebir TR 205 Fd19
Vadu Moţilor RO 171 Cc59
Vakıf TR 185 Ea79
Vakıf TR 187 Gd79
Vakıflaro TR 186 Fa77
Vakıftaş TR 187 Ha80
Vakkola FIN 90 Kc38
Vakkotavare S 67 Gc16
Vaklino BG 181 Fc69
Vaksala S 96 Gc42
Vaksdal N 84 Cb39
Vākšēni LV 106 Kd48
Vaksevo BG 179 Cb73
Vaksvik N 76 Cd32
Val E 36 Ba53
Vál H 146 Hc53
Valada P 50 Ab68
Vålådalen S 78 Ed31
Valadares E 36 Ad57
Valady F 33 Ha51
Valainiai LT 114 Kb54
Valajärvi FIN 89 Jc37
Valajaskoski FIN 74 Jd19
Valakbždis LT 114 Ka57
Valalta HR 150 Ed61
Valand N 92 Cd47
Valandovo MK 183 Ca75
Valanhamn N 63 Hb08
Valanida GR 183 Bc80
Vălani de Pomezeu RO 170 Cb57
Valareña E 47 Ed59
Valaská SK 138 Hd48
Valaská Belá SK 137 Hb48
Vålåskaret N 77 Dd31
Valašská Polanka CZ 137 Ha47
Valašské Klobouky CZ 137 Ha47
Valašské Meziříčí CZ 137 Ha46
Valasti EST 98 Kd43
Vålax FIN 98 Kc39
Valay F 31 Jc41
Valbella CH 142 Cc56
Valberg F 43 Kc52
Valberg N 66 Fb14
Valberg S 94 Fa43
Valbiska HR 151 Fb61
Valbo S 95 Gb39
Valboa E 36 Ba56
Valbonnè AL 159 Jb69
Valbondione I 149 Da57
Valbonilla E 38 Db58
Valbonne F 43 Kc53
Valbo-Ryr S 102 Ea46
Valbruna I 143 Ed56
Valbuena de Duero E 46 Db60
Valbukta N 65 Kc07
Valby DK 109 Ec26
Valcabadillo E 38 Da57
Vălcănești RO 176 Eb64
Vălcani RO 170 Bb59
Valcau de Jos RO 171 Cc56
Valcavado E 37 Cb58
Vălcele RO 175 Db66
Vălcele RO 176 Ea61
Vălcelele RO 176 Ed63
Vălcelele RO 176 Ed66
Valčevo BG 180 Db71
Vălčidol BG 181 Fa70
Vălcineţ MD 173 Fb57
Valcivières F 34 Hd47
Valdagno I 149 Dc59
Valdahon F 31 Ka42
Valdaj RUS 202 Ec09
Valdanzo E 46 Dd61
Valdaora I 143 Ea55
Valdearcos E 37 Cc57
Valdearcos de la Vega E 46 Db60
Val de Asón E 38 Dc55
Valdeazores E 52 Cc67
Valdebeix F 34 Hb48
Valdebótoa E 51 Bc68
Valdecaballeros E 52 Cc68
Valdecabras E 47 Ec65
Valdecañas de Cerrato E 46 Db59
Valdecarros E 45 Cc63
Valdecastillo E 37 Cd56
Valdecuenca E 47 Ed65
Valdeflores S 58 Dc72
Valdefuentes E 51 Ca67
Valdefuentes del Páramo E 37 Cb58
Valdeganga E 53 Ec69
Valdeganga de Cuenca E 53 Eb66
Valdehierro E 52 Db68
Valdeki LV 105 Jd51
Valdelacasa de Tajo E 52 Cc66
Valdelagrana E 59 Bd76
Valdelamusa E 59 Bb72
Valdelinares E 54 Fb65
Valdelosa E 45 Cc61
Valdeltormo E 48 Fd63
Valdemaluque E 46 Dd60
Valdemārpils LV 105 Jd49
Valdemarsvik S 103 Gb47
Valdemeca E 47 Ec65
Valdemorales E 51 Ca68
Valdemorillo E 46 Db63
Valdemoro E 46 Dc65
Valdemoro-Sierra E 47 Ec65
Valdenebro de los Valles E 46 Cd59
Valdenoceda E 38 Dc56
Valdenoguera E 45 Bd62
Valdeobispo E 45 Ca65
Valdepeñas E 52 Dc70
Valdepeñas de Jaén E 60 Db73
Valdepeñas de la Sierra E 46 Dc63
Valdepolo E 37 Cd57
Valderas E 45 Cc59
Val-de-Reuil F 23 Gb35
Valderice I 166 Ea84
Valderiès F 41 Gd53
Valderrama E 38 Dd57
Valderrobres E 48 Fd63
Valderrodilla E 47 Ea61
Val-de-Saâne F 23 Ga34
Valdesalor E 51 Bd67
Valdesamario E 37 Cb56
Valdesimonte E 46 Dc62
Val de San Román E 37 Ca57
Valdestillas E 46 Cd61
Valdetorres E 51 Ca69
Valdetorres de Jarama E 46 Dc63
Valdeverdeja E 52 Cc66
Valdevimbre E 37 Cc57
Valdgale LV 105 Jd50
Valdieri I 148 Bc63
Valdilecha E 46 Dd65
Valdín E 37 Bd58
Valdivia E 51 Ca68
Valdivienne F 29 Ga44
Val-d'Izé F 28 Fa39
Valdobbiadene I 150 Ea58
Valdongo dos Azeites P 44 Bb61
Valdrôme F 42 Jd51
Valdshult S 102 Fa50
Valdunquillo E 45 Cc59
Valdurna I 143 Dd55
Vale Adînca MD 173 Fd55
Vale Argovei RO 176 Ec66
Valea Călugărească RO 176 Eb64
Valea Chioarului RO 171 Da56
Valea Ciorii RO 177 Fa65
Valea Crisului RO 176 Ea61
Valea Dacilor RO 181 Fb67
Valea Danului RO 175 Dc63
Valea de Brazi RO 175 Cc62
Valea Doftanei RO 176 Ea63
Valea Iaşului RO 175 Dc63
Valea Ierii RO 171 Cd58
Valea Largă RO 171 Db58
Valea lui Mihai RO 170 Cb55
Valea Lungă RO 175 Db60
Valea Lungă RO 176 Ea64
Valea Măcrişului RO 176 Ec65
Valea Mare MD 173 Fb57
Valea Mare RO 175 Da65
Valea Mare RO 176 Dd63
Valea Mare-Pravăț RO 176 Dd63
Valea Mărului RO 177 Fa62
Valea Mică RO 175 Cd60
Valea Moldovei RO 172 Eb56
Valea Neagră RO 171 Da55
Valea Nucarilor RO 177 Fd64
Valea Perjei MD 173 Fc59
Valea Perjei MD 177 Fd61
Valea Râmnicului RO 176 Ed63
Valea Sării RO 176 Ec61
Valea Seacă RO 172 Ec57
Valea Seacă RO 176 Ed60
Valea Stanciului RO 179 Da67
Valea-Trestieni MD 173 Fb58
Valea Ursului RO 172 Ed58
Valea Viilor RO 175 Db60
Valea Vinului RO 171 Db56
Valea Vinului RO 172 Dd56
Valebjørg N 93 Da43
Valebø N 93 Dc43
Valen N 63 Ja05
Vale da Telha P 58 Aa73
Vale da Vinha P 50 Ad70
Vale de Açor P 58 Ad72
Vale de Cambra P 44 Ad62
Vale de Moura P 50 Ad70
Vale de Nogueira P 45 Bd60
Vale de Salgueiro P 45 Bc60
Vale de Vargo P 50 Ba71
ValGorde N 59 Ha40
Valeia CY 206 Jd96
Valiena S 58 Bd76
Valfabbrica I 156 Eb67
Vale do Lobo P 58 Ac74
Valeggio sul Mincio I 149 Db60
Valeia CY 206 Jd96
Valen N 63 Ja05
Valença do Minho P 36 Ad58
Valençay F 29 Gc42
Valence F 32 Fd47
Valence F 34 Jb49
Valence F 40 Ga52
Valence-d'Albigeois F 41 Ha53
Valence-en-Brie F 29 Ha38
Valence-sur-Baïse F 40 Fd53
València E 54 Fc68
Valencia de Alcántara E 51 Bb67
Valencia de Don Juan E 37 Cc58
Valencia de las Torres E 51 Ca70
Valencia del Mombuey E 51 Bb71
Valencia del Ventoso E 51 Bd71
Valenciennes F 24 Hb32
Văleni MD 177 Fb62
Văleni RO 173 Fa59
Văleni RO 175 Dc66
Văleni-Dâmbovita RO 176 Dd63
Văleni de Munte RO 176 Eb63
Văleni-Stânişoara RO 172 Eb57
Valensole F 42 Ka53
Valentano I 156 Dd69
Valentigney F 31 Ka41
Valentin E 61 Ec72
Valentinovo HR 151 Ga57
Valenza E 60 Da73
Valenzuela de Calatrava E 52 Db69
Våler N 93 Ea43
Våler N 94 Ec34
Valera de Abajo E 53 Eb67
Valera Fratta I 149 Cc60
Valeria E 53 Eb66
Valero E 45 Ca63
Vales Mortos P 58 Ba72
Valestrand N 92 Ca41
Valestrandsfossen N 84 Ca39
Valevåg N 92 Ca41
Valfabbrica I 156 Eb67
Valfarta E 48 Fc61
Valflaunès F 41 Hd53
Valfréjus F 35 Kb48
Valga EST 106 La47
Valgale LV 105 Jd50
Valgejõgi EST 98 Kd42
Vālgi EST 99 Lb44
Valgorge F 34 Hd51
Valgu EST 98 Kd43
Valgunde LV 106 Kb51
Valguta EST 106 La46
Valhelhas P 44 Bb64
Valhuon F 23 Gd31
Valie S 111 Fc54
Välijoki FIN 74 Ka19
Välijoki FIN 91 Lb36
Välikangas FIN 74 Ka19
Väli-Kannus FIN 81 Jc27
Välikylä FIN 81 Jc28
Valin F 32 Fc49
Valinge S 102 Ec51
Väli-Olhava FIN 74 Ka22
Valira GR 194 Bb89
Väljala EST 105 Jd46
Väljataló RO 169 Fd77
Valjevo SRB 153 Jb63
Valjok N 64 Jc08
Valjunquera E 48 Fd63
Valka LV 106 La47
Valkeakoski FIN 89 Jd36
Valkeala FIN 90 La37
Valkealuomi FIN 90 Kb33
Valkeavaara FIN 91 Ma32
Valkeiskylä FIN 82 Kc28
Valkeiskylä FIN 82 La29
Valkenburg aan de Geul NL 125 Bb41
Valkenswaard NL 124 Ba39
Valkininkai LT 114 La59
Valkla EST 98 Kc42
Valko FIN 90 Kd38
Valkola FIN 90 Kb32
Valkom FIN 90 Kd38
Valkosel BG 184 Cd75
Valky UA 203 Fa14
Vall S 104 Gd49
Vall S 79 Fb29
Valla S 79 Ga31
Vallada E 54 Fb69
Valladolid E 46 Da60
Vållåkra S 110 Ed55
Vallada S 45 Cb61
Vallata I 161 Fd74
Vallauris-Golfe-Juan F 43 Kc53
Vallberga S 110 Ed53
Vallbona de les Monges E 48 Gb61
Vallby S 95 Gb43
Valida S 102 Eb50
Valldal N 76 Cd33
Valldemossa E 57 Hb67
Valldossera E 49 Gc61
Valle LV 106 Kc52
Valle N 76 Cc32
Valle N 92 Cd43
Valleberga S 111 Fb57
Valle Castellana I 156 Ed69
Vallecillo E 37 Cd58
Vallecorsa I 160 Ed73
Valle Dame I 156 Ea67
Valle de Abdalajís E 60 Cd75
Valle de Cabuérniga E 38 Db55
Valle de Cerrato E 46 Da59
Valle de Finolledo E 37 Bd56
Valle de la Serena E 51 Ca69
Valle de Santa Ana E 51 Bc70
Valledolmo I 166 Ed85
Valleiry F 35 Jd45
Vallelado E 46 Da61
Valle Lomellina I 148 Cb60
Vallelunga Pratameno I 166 Ed85
Valle Mosso I 148 Ca58
Vallen S 79 Ga29
Vallen S 79 Gb29
Vallen S 80 Hc26
Vallentuna S 96 Gd43
Vallepietra I 160 Ec71
Vallerås S 94 Fa39
Valleraugue F 41 Hc52
Vallerheim N 92 Cd43
Vallermosa I 169 Bd79
Vallerstad S 103 Fd46
Vallersund N 77 Dd28
Vallery F 30 Hb39
Vallespinoso de Aguilar E 38 Db56
Vallestad N 84 Ca35
Vallet F 28 Fa42
Valletta M 166 Eb88
Valleviken S 104 Ha48
Valley D 143 Ea51
Valley GB 14 Dc22
Vallfogona de Ripollès E 49 Ha59
Vallibona E 48 Fd64
Valligrund S 81 Ja30
Vallmoll E 48 Gb62
Vallo N 93 Dd43
Vallobal E 37 Cd54
Vålløby DK 109 Ec27
Vallo della Lucania I 161 Fd77
Valloire F 35 Ka48
Vallombrosa I 156 Dd65
Vallon-Pont-d'Arc F 34 Ja51
Vallon-sur-Gée F 28 Fc40
Vallorbe CH 140 Ba54
Vallouise F 35 Ka49
Vallrun S 79 Fb29
Valls E 48 Gb62
Vallsbo S 87 Gb38
Vallset N 94 Eb39
Vallsjärv S 73 Ja19
Vallsta S 87 Ga36
Vallstena S 104 Ha49
Vallvik S 87 Gb37
Valmadrera I 149 Cc58
Valmiera LV 106 Kd48
Valmigère F 41 Ha56
Valmo EST 98 La45
Valmojado E 46 Db65
Valmont F 22 Fd34
Valmontone I 160 Ec72
Valmorel F 35 Ka47
Vālnari BG 181 Ed69
Valnontey I 148 Bc58
Valö S 96 Gd40
Valognes F 22 Fa35
Valongo P 44 Ad61
Valoria la Buena E 46 Da60
Valøya N 78 Eb25
Valøya N 78 Ec27
Valožyn BY 202 Ea12
Valpaços P 45 Bc60
Valpalmas E 48 Fb59
Valpelline I 148 Bc58
Valperga I 148 Bd59
Valpiana I 155 Db67
Valpovo HR 153 Hc59
Valras-Plage F 41 Hc55
Valréas F 42 Jc51
Vals CH 142 Cc55
Valsaín E 46 Db63
Valsavarenche I 148 Bc58
Valsebo S 94 Ec44
Valseca E 46 Db62
Valseco E 37 Ca56
Valsemé F 22 Fd36
Valsenestre F 35 Ka49
Valsequillo E 51 Cb70
Valserres F 42 Ka51
Valset N 77 Dd29
Valgård DK 100 Dc22
Valsinni I 162 Gc77
Valsjöbyn S 79 Fb28
Valsjön S 87 Ga34
Valskog S 95 Ga43
Vals-les-Bains F 34 Ja50
Valsøllile DK 109 Ec26
Valsonne F 34 Ja46
Valsøybotn N 77 Dc31
Valsøyfjord N 77 Db30
Vålsta S 87 Gb35
Valstad S 102 Fa47
Valstagna I 150 Dd58
Valsted DK 100 Db21
Valtaiki LV 105 Jc52
Valtessiniko GR 194 Bb87
Valtétsi GR 194 Bc88
Val-Thorens F 35 Kb48
Valtice CZ 137 Gc49
Valtierra E 47 Ed59
Valtimo FIN 83 Lb27
Valtola FIN 90 La36
Valtola FIN 91 Lc34
Valtopina I 156 Eb68
Valtorp S 102 Fa47
Valtorta I 149 Cd58
Váltos GR 185 Eb76
Valtournenche I 148 Bd57
Valtura HR 151 Fa62
Valujki RUS 203 Fb14
Valu lui Traian RO 181 Fc67
Valun HR 151 Fb62
Valvåg N 77 Db29
Valverde E 47 Ec59
Valverde de Burgillos E 51 Bc71
Valverde de Júcar E 53 Eb67
Valverde de la Vera E 45 Cb65
Valverde de la Virgen E 37 Cc57
Valverde del Camino E 59 Bc73
Valverde de Leganés E 51 Bb69
Valverde del Fresno E 45 Bc64
Valverde de Lierena E 51 Ca71
Valverde del Majano E 46 Db62
Valverde de Mérida E 51 Bd69
Valverdón E 45 Cb62
Vallières S 33 Gd46
Vallières S 35 Jd46
Vama RO 171 Da54
Vama RO 172 Ea56
Vama Buzăului RO 176 Eb62
Vama Veche BG 181 Fc69
Vamberk CZ 137 Gb44
Vamdrup DK 108 Db26
Vámhus S 87 Fb37
Vamlingbo S 104 Gd51
Vamma N 93 Ea43
Vammala FIN 89 Jc36
Vammen DK 100 Db22
Vámos GR 200 Cc95
Vámosgyörk I 146 Ja52
Vámospércs H 147 Ka52
Vampula FIN 89 Jc37
Vanagi LV 107 Lb52
Vanaja FIN 90 Kd32
Vanaja FIN 90 Ka37
Vana-Kojola EST 107 Lb46
Vana-Kuuste EST 99 Lb45
Vana-Roosa EST 107 Lb47
Vänatori RO 170 Ca58
Vânători RO 172 Ed56
Vânători RO 175 Cc66
Vânători RO 175 Dc60
Vânători RO 176 Dd60
Vânători RO 176 Ed62
Vânători RO 177 Fb63
Vânătorii Mici RO 176 Dd66
Vânători-Neamţ RO 172 Ec57
Vanattara FIN 89 Jd36
Vančé F 29 Ga40
Vanda FIN 98 Kb39
Vandāni LV 107 Lb52
Vandans A 142 Da54
Vandel DK 108 Db25
Vandenesse F 30 Hc43
Vandesse A 30 Hc43
Vandoies I 143 Ea55
Vändra EST 98 Kc45
Vändträsk S 73 Hc22
Vandzene LV 105 Jd49
Vandžiogala LT 114 Kc57
Väne LV 105 Jd51
Väne-Åsaka S 102 Ec47
Vänersborg S 102 Ec47
Vänersnäs S 102 Ec47
Väne-Ryr S 102 Ec47
Vaneze I 149 Dc58
Vang DK 100 Da21
Vang N 85 Db37
Vang S 94 Eb43
Vänga S 103 Fd46
Vånga S 111 Fb54
Vangaži LV 106 Kc50
Vänge S 96 Gc42
Vänge S 104 Ha50
Vängel S 79 Ga29
Vangsåsen DK 100 Da21
Vangshamn N 62 Gc10
Vangshylla N 78 Eb30
Vangsnes N 84 Cc37
Vangsvik N 67 Gb11

Vendœuvres – Villafranca di Verona

Vendœuvres F 29 Gb44
Vendôme F 29 Gb40
Vendranges F 34 Hd46
Vendrennes F 28 Fa43
Vendzavae LV 105 Jb50
Venec BG 181 Ec69
Venec BG 181 Ec72
Veneheitto FIN 82 Kb25
Venejärvi FIN 68 Jb16
Venejoki FIN 83 Ld29
Venelin BG 181 Fa71
Venesjärvi FIN 89 Jb35
Veneskoski FIN 81 Jb31
Veneskoski FIN 89 Jb35
Venetmäki FIN 82 Kd29
Venetmäki FIN 90 Kd32
Venetpalo FIN 82 Kb27
Venetti FIN 68 Jb17
Venev RUS 203 Fa11
Venevere EST 98 La43
Venezia I 150 Eb60
Vengasaho FIN 74 Kb22
Vengja N 84 Ca40
Venhuizen NL 116 Bb34
Venialbo E 45 Cc61
Vénissieux F 34 Jb47
Venjan S 87 Fb38
Venlo NL 125 Bc39
Venn N 77 Ea30
Vénna GR 184 Dc77
Vennermoor D 117 Cc36
Vennesla N 92 Cd46
Vennesund N 70 Ed24
Venosa I 161 Ga74
Venray NL 125 Bb38
Vensac F 32 Fa48
Venset N 66 Fd17
Venstøp N 93 Dc43
Vent A 142 Dc55
Venta LT 113 Jd53
Ventabren F 42 Jc54
Venta de Ballerías E 48 Fc60
Venta de Baños E 46 Da59
Ventade Gaeta E 54 Fa68
Venta de la Chata E 52 Dc72
Venta de las Ranas E 37 Cc54
Venta de la Vigen E 55 Fa73
Venta del Charco E 52 Da71
Venta del Moro E 54 Ed68
Venta de los Santos E 53 Dd71
Ventanilla E 38 Da56
Venta Nueva E 37 Ca55
Ventas de Barreira E 36 Bc58
Ventas de Huelma E 60 Db75
Ventas de Muniesa E 48 Fb62
Ventė LT 113 Jb56
Vent del Tollo E 55 Ed71
Ventelä FIN 98 Ka39
Ventelay F 24 Hc35
Venticano I 161 Fc74
Ventimiglia I 43 Kd53
Ventimiglia di Sicilia I 166 Ed84
Ventiseri F 154 Cb71
Ventlinge S 111 Gb54
Ventnor GB 20 Fa31
Ventorros de Balerma E 60 Da74
Ventosa del Río Almar E 45 Cc62
Ventosa de Pisuerga E 38 Db57
Ventotene I 160 Ed75
Ventry IRL 12 Ad24
Ventschow D 119 Ea32
Ventspils LV 105 Jb49
Venturina I 155 Da67
Venus RO 181 Fc68
Venzone I 150 Ec57
Vepriai LT 114 Kd56
Veprinac HR 151 Fb60
Vepsä FIN 74 Kb24
Vepsä FIN 83 Lb26
Ver F 22 Fa37
Vera E 61 Ec75
Vera HR 153 Hd59
Vera N 78 Ed28
Vera-de Bidaosa E 39 Ed55
Vera de Moncayo E 47 Ed60
Vera de Rey E 53 Eb68
Verbania I 148 Cb57
Verberie F 23 Ha35
Verbicaro I 164 Gb78
Verbier CH 148 Bc57
Verbița RO 175 Cc66
Verbūnai LT 114 Ka54
Vercelli I 148 Ca59
Vercel-Villedieu-le Camp F 31 Ka42
Verchen D 119 Ed32
Vercheny F 35 Jc50
Verchnjadzvinsk BY 202 Ea11
Verchnje Syn'ovydne UA 204 Dd16
Verchn'odniprovs'k UA 204 Ed15
Vercorin CH 141 Bd56
Verçun AL 182 Ad76
Verdaches F 42 Ka51
Verdalsøra N 78 Ec28
Verdeggia I 43 Kd52
Verdello I 149 Cd59
Verden D 118 Da34
Verdes F 29 Gb40
Verdikoússa GR 183 Bc80
Verdille F 32 Fc47
Verdonnet F 30 Hd40
Verdun F 24 Jb35
Verdun-sur-Garonne F 40 Gb53
Verdun-sur-le-Doubs F 30 Jb43
Véreaux F 29 Ha43
Verebiejai LV 114 Kb59
Verebkovo RUS 107 Lc47
Vereide N 84 Cc34
Verejeni MD 173 Fc56
Veren BG 180 Dc73
Verenci BG 180 Eb71
Vereniki GR 182 Ac80
Veresegyház H 146 Hd52
Verest RUS 99 Mb42
Vereşti RO 172 Ec56
Veret'e RUS 107 Ma48
Vereteni RUS 107 Mb46
Verfeil F 40 Gc54
Verfeil F 41 Gd52
Vērgale LV 105 Jb52
Vergato I 149 Dc63
Vergel E 55 Fc70
Vergeletto CH 141 Cb56
Verges E 49 Hb59
Verghereto I 156 Ea65
Vergi EST 98 Kd41
Vérgi GR 184 Cc77
Vergiate I 148 Cb58
Vergína GR 183 Bd78
Vergt F 33 Ga49
Verguleasa RO 175 Db65
Verhnij Most RUS 107 Mb47
Verholino RUS 107 Ld46
Véria GR 183 Bd78
Verići BIH 152 Gd61
Vérignon F 42 Ka53
Vérigny F 29 Gb38
Verin E 44 Bb59
Veriña Tremañes E 37 Cc54
Veringenstadt D 142 Cd50
Verinsko BG 179 Cd72
Veriora EST 107 Lc46
Verkenseter N 85 Dd34
Verkkojoki FIN 83 Lb27
Verl D 126 Cc38
Verla FIN 90 Kd36
Verlar D 126 Cc38
Vermand F 24 Hb33
Vermenton F 30 Hc40
Vermeș RO 174 Bd61
Vermiglio I 149 Db57
Vermoim P 44 Ad60
Vermosh AL 159 Jb69
Vermuntila FIN 89 Ja37
Vernantes F 28 Fd42
Vernár SK 138 Jb48
Vernazza I 155 Cd64
Vern-d'Anjou F 28 Fb41
Vernes N 77 Dd29
Vernești RO 176 Ec64
Vernet F 40 Gc55
Vernet-les-Bains F 41 Ha57
Verneuil F 24 Hc36
Verneuil-en-Bourbonnais F 34 Hb45
Verneuil-sur-Avre F 23 Ga37
Verneuil-sur-Indre F 29 Gb43
Verninge DK 108 Dc27
Verningen N 93 Dd44
Vernio I 155 Dc64
Vernoil F 28 Fd42
Vernole I 163 Hc76
Vernon F 23 Gb36
Vernon F 32 Fd45
Vernou-en-Sologne F 29 Gc41
Vernouillet F 23 Gb37
Vernou-sur-Brenne F 29 Ga41
Vernoux-en-Vivarais F 34 Ja50
Vern-sur-Seiche F 28 Ed39
Vero F 154 Ca70
Verőce H 146 Hd52
Verolanuova I 149 Da60
Veroli I 160 Ed72
Véron F 30 Hb39
Verona I 149 Dc59
Verpelét H 146 Jb51
Verrabotn N 78 Ea28
Verrès I 148 Bd58
Verrières F 33 Ga45
Verrone I 148 Ca59
Versailles F 23 Gd37
Versam CH 142 Cd55
Verseg H 146 Ja52
Veršiai LT 114 Ka58
Versmold D 126 Cc37
Versols-et-Lapeyre F 41 Hb53
Verstaminai LV 114 Kb59
Vertavillo E 46 Db60
Verteillac F 32 Fd48
Vertelim RUS 203 Fc10
Vértesacsa H 146 Hc53
Verteuil-sur-Charente F 32 Fd46
Vertijivka UA 202 Ec14
Vertimai LT 113 Jd57
Vertiskos GR 183 Cb77
Vertiujeni MD 173 Fc55
Vertjačij RUS 203 Fd14
Vērtmuiža LV 106 Kd47
Vertolaye F 34 Hc47
Vërtop AL 182 Ac77
Vertou F 28 Ed42
Vert-Saint-Denis F 29 Ha38
Vertus F 24 Hc36
Vertuu FIN 89 Jb35
Verucchio I 156 Eb64
Verum S 110 Fa53
Verviers B 125 Bb41
Vervins F 24 Hc33
Vervnäs S 86 Fa37
Verwood GB 20 Ed30
Veržej SLO 145 Gb56
Verzino I 165 Gd80
Verzuolo I 148 Bc62
Vesala FIN 74 Kb23
Vesala FIN 75 La20
Vesamäki FIN 82 Kc30
Vesanka FIN 90 Kb32
Vesanto FIN 82 Kc30
Vescona I 156 Dd67
Vescovato F 154 Cc69
Vesdun F 29 Ha44
Vése H 152 Gd57
Ves'egonsk RUS 202 Ed08
Vesela BIH 158 Ha64
Veselava LV 106 Kd49
Vesele UA 205 Fa16
Veselec BG 181 Ec68
Veselie BG 181 Fa73
Veselí nad Lužnicí CZ 136 Fc47
Veselí nad Moravou CZ 137 Gd48
Veselinovo BG 180 Eb72
Veselinovo BG 181 Ec71
Veselovka RUS 113 Jd59
Veselynove UA 204 Ed16
Vešenskaja RUS 203 Fc13
Vesijako FIN 90 Kb36
Vesijärvi FIN 89 Ja34
Vesilahti FIN 89 Jd36
Vesivehmaa FIN 90 Kc36
Vesjärvi FIN 89 Jc35
Veskoniemi FIN 69 Kb11
Veskonjarga FIN 69 Kb11
Vesløs DK 100 Da21
Vesmajärvi FIN 69 Jd15
Vesnovo RUS 113 Jd58
Vesoul F 31 Jd40
Vespolate I 148 Cb59
Véssa GR 191 Dd86
Vessigebro S 102 Ec51
Veståskapellet N 85 Dc38
Vestbjerg DK 100 Dc21
Vestby N 86 Ec37
Vestby N 93 Ea42
Vestbygd N 92 Cb47
Vestbygda N 66 Fd14
Vestenanova I 149 Dc59
Vestenbergsgreuth D 134 Dc45
Vester Åby DK 108 Dc27
Vesterby DK 109 Ea28
Vester Egense DK 108 Dc26
Vester Egesborg DK 109 Eb27
Vesterelv N 65 Kb07
Vesterelva N 65 Kc05
Vester Hæsinge DK 108 Dc27
Vester Hassing DK 100 Dc21
Vester Hjermitslev DK 100 Dc20
Vester Hornum DK 100 Db21
Vesterli N 71 Fc18
Vesterli N 71 Fb23
Vestermarie DK 111 Fc58
Vester Nebel DK 108 Db26
Vesterø Havn DK 101 Ea20
Vestertana N 64 Ka06
Vester Torup DK 100 Db20
Vester Vedsted DK 108 Cd26
Vestervig DK 100 Cd22
Vester Vistorp DK 100 Da23
Vestfossen N 93 Dc42
Vestfossen N 93 Dd42
Vestiena LV 106 La50
Vestlax FIN 97 Jc40
Vestmanna DK 3 Ca06
Vestmannaeyjar IS 2 Ac06
Vestnes N 76 Cd32
Vestola FIN 90 Kb36
Vestone I 149 Db59
Vestpollen N 66 Fc14
Vestre Jakobselv N 65 Kc06
Vestre Kile N 92 Cd44
Vestre Moland N 93 Da47
Vestre Slidre N 85 Dc37
Vestre Spone N 93 Dd41
Vestre Vallesverd N 93 Da47
Vestro N 92 Ca42
Vestvågan N 70 Ed21
Vestvik N 78 Eb28
Vesunti FIN 89 Jc36
Veszprém H 145 Ha54
Veszprémvarsány H 145 Ha53
Vésztő H 147 Jd54
Vetaherrado E 59 Ca75
Vețca RO 171 Dc59
Vețel RO 175 Cc60
Veteli FIN 81 Jc29
Vetheuil F 23 Gc36
Vetiș RO 171 Cd54
Vetla EST 98 Kc43
Vetlanda S 103 Fc50
Vetluga RUS 203 Fb08
Vetovo BG 180 Eb68
Vetralla I 156 Ea70
Vetren BG 179 Cd73
Vetren BG 180 Dd72
Vetren BG 181 Ed67
Vetren BG 181 Ed72
Vetren MK 179 Cb73
Vetrești-Herăstrău RO 176 Ec62
Vetrino BG 181 Ed70
Vetriolo Terme I 150 Dd58
Vetrișoaia RO 177 Fb60
Větrný Jeníkov CZ 136 Fd46
Vetrovo RUS 113 Jc57
Vetschau D 128 Fb39
Vetsikko FIN 64 Ka07
Vettasjärvi S 68 Hc16
Vettelschoß D 125 Ca42
Vetterslev DK 109 Eb27
Vetterud N 94 Eb40
Vetting N 93 Da46
Vetto I 149 Da63
Vettweiß D 125 Bc41
Vetulonia I 155 Db68
Vetunica MK 178 Bd72
Vetvenik RUS 99 Lc44
Veules-les-Roses F 23 Ga33
Veulettes-sur-Mer F 23 Ga33
Veum N 93 Da43
Veurne B 21 Ha29
Vevang N 77 Da31
Vevčani MK 182 Ad75
Vevey CH 141 Bb55
Vévi GR 183 Bb77
Vevring N 84 Cb35
Vex CH 141 Bc56
Vexala FIN 81 Ja29
Veynes F 35 Jd50
Veyrier F 35 Ka46
Veysel TR 193 Ha84
Vežaičiai LT 113 Jb55
Vezdemarbán E 45 Cc60
Vézelay F 30 Hc41
Vézelise F 25 Jd37
Vézelois F 31 Kb40
Vezels-Roussy F 33 Ha50
Vezenkovo BG 181 Ec71
Vézénobres F 42 Ja52
Vezins F 28 Fb42
Vézins-de-Lévézou F 41 Hb52
Vezionys LT 114 Kc58
Vežionys LT 114 La59
Vezirhan TR 187 Gb80
Vezirköprü TR 205 Fb20
Vezza d'Oglio I 149 Db57
Vezzani F 154 Cb70
Vezzano I 149 Dc57
Vezzano sul Crostolo I 149 Db62
Vi S 88 Gc33
Viabon F 29 Gc39
Viadana I 149 Db61
Viana E 39 Eb58
Viana de Bolo E 36 Bc58
Viana do Alentejo P 50 Ad70
Viana do Castelo P 44 Ac59
Vianden L 133 Bb44
Viane F 41 Ha54
Vianen NL 124 Ba37
Viano I 149 Db62
Viaño Pequeño E 36 Ad55
Vianos E 53 Ea70
Vianta FIN 82 Kd29
Viarano Scalo I 161 Fa73
Viareggio I 155 Da65
Viarmes F 23 Gd36
Vias F 41 Hc55
Viasvesi FIN 89 Ja36
Viatodos P 44 Ad60
Vibble S 104 Gd49
Vibbyn S 73 Hd21
Viblemo N 92 Cc46
Viborg DK 100 Db23
Vibo Valentia I 164 Gb82
Vibo Valentia Marina I 164 Gb82
Vibraye F 29 Ga39
Viby DK 109 Eb26
Viby S 95 Fc44
Viby S 103 Fd47
Vic E 49 Ha59
Vič SLO 144 Fc56
Viča SRB 178 Ba67
Vicarello I 155 Da65
Vicari I 166 Ed85
Vicarstown IRL 13 Cc22
Vicchio I 156 Dd64
Vicdessos F 40 Gc57
Vicedo E 36 Bc53
Vic-en-Bigorre F 40 Fd55
Vicenza I 150 Dd59
Vic-Fezensac F 40 Fd54
Vicherey F 31 Jc38
Vichy F 34 Hc46
Vicién E 48 Fb59
Vickan S 102 Eb50
Vickleby S 111 Gb53
Vic-le-Comte F 34 Hb47
Vic-le-Fesq F 41 Hd53
Vico F 154 Ca70
Vico I 149 Da62
Vico del Gargano I 162 Gb71
Vico Equense I 161 Fb75
Vicoforte I 148 Bd62
Vicopisano I 155 Db65
Vicosoprano CH 142 Cd56
Vicovaro I 160 Eb71
Vicovu de Jos RO 172 Eb55
Vicovu de Sus RO 172 Ea54
Vicq-Exemplet F 29 Gd44
Vic-sur-Aisne F 24 Hb35
Vic-sur-Cère F 33 Ha49
Vic-sur-Seille F 25 Jd36
Victoria M 166 Ea87
Victoria RO 173 Fa57
Victoria RO 175 Dc62
Victoria RO 177 Fa65
Victor Vlad Delamarina RO 174 Ca61
Vičuga RUS 203 Fb09
Vidaga LV 107 Lb48
Vidago P 44 Bb59
Vidale LV 105 Jc49
Vidanes E 37 Cd56
Vidángoz E 39 Fa57
Viðareiði DK 3 Ca06
Vidauban F 43 Kb54
Vidbo S 96 Gd42
Viddal N 76 Cc33
Videbæk DK 108 Da24
Videle RO 176 Dd66
Videm pri Ptuju SLO 151 Ga57
Videniškiai LT 114 La56
Videsæter N 84 Cd34
Videstøyl N 92 Cd44
Vidiago E 38 Da54
Vidice CZ 135 Ec46
Vidigal P 50 Ac69
Vidigueira P 50 Ad71
Vidin BG 179 Cb67
Vidiškiai LT 114 Kd56
Vidlin GB 5 Fa04
Vidnava CZ 137 Gc43
Vidön S 94 Fa43
Vidouze F 40 Fc55
Vidra RO 171 Cc59
Vidra RO 176 Ec61
Vidra RO 180 Eb67
Vidrare BG 179 Da70
Vidrenjak HR 152 Gc59
Vidreres E 49 Hb60
Vidriži LV 106 Kc49
Vidsel S 73 Hb22
Vidsmuiža LV 107 Lc51
Vidsodis LT 113 Jd54
Vidstrup DK 100 Dc19
Viduklė LT 114 Ka56
Vidzy BY 202 Ea11
Viechtach D 135 Ec48
Vieille-Brioude F 34 Hc48
Vieille-Soubiran F 40 Fc53
Vieillespesse F 34 Hb49
Vieillevigne F 28 Ed43
Vieira do Minho P 44 Ba59
Vieki FIN 83 Lc27
Viekšnaliai LT 113 Jd54
Viekšniai LT 113 Jd53
Vielank D 119 Dd34
Vielha E 40 Ga57
Viella E 37 Cc54
Vielle F 39 Fa53
Vielleségure F 39 Fb55
Vielmur-sur-Agout F 41 Gd54
Vielsam B 125 Bb42
Viels-Maisons F 24 Hb36
Viemose DK 109 Eb28
Vienenburg D 126 Dc38
Vienne F 34 Jb47
Vienne-en-Val F 29 Gd40
Vienne-le-Château F 24 Ja35
Viens F 42 Jd53
Viensuu FIN 83 Lc28
Viereck D 120 Fb33
Vieremä FIN 82 Kc27
Viereth-Trunstadt D 134 Dc45
Vierhouten NL 117 Bc36
Vierlingsbeek NL 125 Bc38
Viernau D 126 Dc42
Viernheim D 134 Cc46
Vierraden D 120 Fb34
Viersen D 125 Bc39
Vieru RO 180 Ea68
Vierumäki FIN 90 Kc36
Vierville-sur-Mer F 22 Fb35
Vierzon F 29 Gd42
Viesati LV 105 Jd51
Viešintos LT 114 Kd54
Viesīte LV 106 La52
Viesītes LV 106 Kd52
Vieste I 162 Gb71
Vieštovėnai LT 113 Jc55
Viešvėnai LT 113 Jd54
Viešvilė LT 113 Jd57
Vietalva LV 106 La51
Vietas S 67 Gc16
Vietlübbe D 119 Ea32
Vietri di Potenza I 161 Ga76
Vietri sul Mare I 161 Fc75
Vieux-Boucau-les-Bains F 39 Ed53
Vieux-Fume F 22 Fc36
Vievis LT 114 Kd57
Vieyes I 148 Bc58
Vif F 35 Jd49
Vig DK 109 Eb25
Viganj HR 158 Gd68
Vigante LV 106 La51
Vigarano Mainarda I 150 Dd62
Vigeland N 92 Cc47
Vigevano I 148 Cb60
Vigge S 87 Fb32
Viggianello I 164 Gb78
Viggiano I 161 Ga76
Viggiù I 148 Cb58
Viglaš SK 138 Hd49
Vigmostad N 92 Cc47
Vignacourt F 23 Gd33
Vignale Monferrato I 148 Ca60
Vignanello I 156 Ea70
Vignes-la-Côte F 30 Jb38
Vigneulles-lès-Hattonchâtel F 25 Jc36
Vignola I 149 Dc63
Vignola Mare I 168 Cb73
Vignole I 150 Ea57
Vignory F 30 Jb38
Vigny F 23 Gc36
Vigo E 36 Ad57
Vigo di Cadore I 143 Eb56
Vigo di Fassa I 143 Dd56
Vigoleno I 149 Cd61
Vigone I 148 Bc61
Vigo Rendena I 149 Db57
Vigre N 92 Ca45
Vigrestad N 92 Ca45
Vigrieži LV 107 Lb48
Vigsnæs DK 109 Eb28
Viguzzolo I 148 Cb61
Vihajärvi FIN 75 Kd24
Vihakse EST 106 Kb46
Vihantasalmi FIN 90 Kd35
Vihanti FIN 81 Jd25
Vihasjärvi FIN 90 Ka35
Vihasoo EST 98 Kd41
Viherlahti FIN 97 Ja39
Vihiers F 28 Fb42
Vihren BG 184 Cc74
Vihtakangas FIN 83 Ld29
Vihtari FIN 83 Lc31
Vihtasuo FIN 83 Lc28
Vihtavaara FIN 91 Ld32
Vihtavuori FIN 90 Kb32
Vihteljärvi FIN 89 Jb35
Vihterpalu EST 98 Ka43
Vihti FIN 98 Ka39
Vihtiälä FIN 89 Jc36
Vihtijärvi FIN 90 Ka38
Vihtola FIN 91 Lb36
Vihtra EST 98 Kc45
Vihu FIN 89 Jb35
Vihula EST 98 Kd41
Viiala FIN 89 Jd36
Viidu EST 105 Jc46
Viiksimo FIN 83 Ld25
Viikusjärvi S 68 Hd14
Viile Satu Mare RO 171 Cd55
Viinijärvi FIN 83 Lc30
Viinikka FIN 81 Jc30
Viinikoski FIN 74 Kb23
Viinistu EST 98 Kd41
Viira EST 97 Jd45
Viiratsi EST 98 Kd45
Viirilä FIN 90 Kd38
Viisarimäki FIN 90 Kc33
Viișoara MD 173 Fa56
Viișoara RO 171 Cc55
Viișoara RO 171 Da59
Viișoara RO 172 Eb58
Viișoara RO 172 Ed54
Viișoara RO 175 Dc60
Viișoara RO 177 Fb60
Viitaila FIN 90 Kb36
Viitakangas FIN 82 Kb29
Viitala FIN 81 Jb31
Viitalahti FIN 83 Lb31
Viitalankylä FIN 81 Jb31
Viitamäki FIN 82 Kc27
Viitaniemi FIN 83 Lb29
Viitaperä FIN 75 Kc23
Viitapohja FIN 89 Jd35
Viitaranta FIN 69 Kc16
Viitaranta FIN 75 Kd19
Viitasaari FIN 82 Kb30
Viitavaara FIN 75 Lb24
Viitka EST 107 Lc47
Viitna EST 98 Kd42
Viivikonna EST 99 Lc42
Vijciems LV 106 La48
Vijtala FIN 89 Jb32
Vik N 66 Fc13
Vik N 70 Ed24
Vik N 70 Fa21
Vik N 76 Cb33
Vik N 76 Cd32
Vik N 78 Eb26
Vik N 84 Cc37
Vik N 92 Ca42
Vik N 93 Da44
Vik N 93 Da46
Vik S 111 Fb56
Vika FIN 74 Ka18
Vika N 63 Hd07
Vika N 78 Eb29
Vika S 87 Fb38
Vika S 95 Fd40
Vikajärvi FIN 74 Ka18
Vikan N 76 Cd31
Vikan N 77 Db30
Vikane N 92 Cb46
Vikane N 93 Ea44
Vikanes N 84 Cb38
Vikarbyn S 87 Fc38
Vikebuk N 76 Cd32
Vikedal N 92 Ca42
Vikeid N 66 Fd12
Vikeland N 92 Cd46
Viken S 110 Ec54
Vikene S 94 Ec42
Viker N 85 Dd39
Viker S 94 Ec43
Viker S 95 Fc43
Vikersund N 93 Dd41
Vikeså N 92 Ca45
Vikevåg N 92 Ca43
Vikhamar N 77 Ea30
Viķi LV 106 Kc48
Vikingstad S 103 Fd47
Vikja N 84 Cc36
Vikna N 78 Eb25
Vikøy N 84 Cb39
Vikran N 62 Gc10
Vikran N 63 Ja04
Vikran N 66 Ga12
Viksfjord N 93 Dd44
Viksjö S 88 Gc32
Viksna LV 107 Lc49
Vikšņi LV 107 Lc50
Viksøyri N 84 Cc37
Viksta S 96 Gc41
Vikstøl N 92 Cd45
Vikten N 66 Fa14
Viktring A 144 Fb56
Vikvallen S 72 Ha22
Vilaboa E 36 Bb53
Vila Chã P 44 Ac60
Vila Chã P 44 Bb63
Vilachá E 36 Bc57
Vila Cova de Alva P 44 Ba64
Vila da Ponte P 44 Ba59
Vila de Cruces E 36 Ba56
Vila de Rei P 50 Ad66
Vila do Bispo P 58 Aa74
Vila do Conde P 44 Ac60
Vilafamés E 54 Fc65
Vilafant E 41 Hb58
Vila Fernando P 51 Bb68
Vila Flor P 45 Bc61
Vila Franca das Naves P 44 Bb63
Vilafranca de Bonany E 57 Hc67
Vilafranca del Maestrat E 48 Fc64
Vilafranca del Penedès E 49 Gc61
Vila Franca de Xira P 50 Ab68
Vilafrío E 36 Bb56
Vilagarcía de Arousa E 36 Ad56
Vilajuïga E 41 Hb58
Viļaka LV 107 Ld49
Vilalba E 36 Bb54
Vilalba dels Arcs E 48 Fd62
Vilalbite E 36 Bb55
Vilaller E 40 Ga58
Vilamadat E 49 Hb59
Vilamaior E 36 Bc56
Vilamarxant E 54 Fb67
Vilamitjana E 48 Gb59
Vilamoura P 58 Ac74
Viļāni LV 107 Lc51
Vila Nogueira de Azeitão P 50 Ab69
Vilanova E 36 Ac57
Vilanova E 36 Ad56
Vilanova E 37 Bd58
Vila Nova de Anços P 44 Ac64
Vilanova de Bellpuig E 48 Gb61
Vila Nova de Cerveira P 36 Ac58
Vila Nova de Famalição P 44 Ad60
Vila Nova de Foz Côa P 45 Bc61
Vila Nova de Gaia P 44 Ac61
Vilanova del Camí E 49 Gc61
Vilanova de Meià E 48 Gb59
Vila Nova de Milfontes P 58 Ab72
Vila Nova de Paiva P 44 Ba62
Vila Nova de Santo André P 50 Ab71
Vila Nova de São Bento P 58 Ba72
Vilanova de Sau E 49 Ha59
Vila Nova do Ceira P 44 Ad64
Vilanova i la Geltrú E 49 Gc62
Vilanova (Lourenzá) E 36 Bc54
Vilapedre E 36 Bc56
Vilapedre E 36 Bb54
Vila Pouca de Aguiar P 44 Bb60
Vila Praia de Âncora P 44 Ac59
Vilar P 44 Ba62
Vilarandelo P 45 Bc59
Vilarbacu E 36 Bc57
Vilarchán E 36 Ad57
Vilar de Amargo P 45 Bc62
Vilar de Barrio E 36 Bb58
Vilar de Murteda P 44 Ac59
Vilar de Olalla E 53 Eb66
Vilar de Ossos P 45 Bc59
Vilar de Perdizes P 44 Bb59
Vilar de Pinheiro P 44 Ac60
Vilar de Rei E 36 Bb58
Vilardevós E 45 Bc59
Vila Real P 44 Ba61
Vila-real E 54 Fc66
Vila Real de Santo Antonio P 58 Ba74
Vilares P 45 Bc60
Vilares del Saz E 53 Ea66
Vilar Formoso P 45 Bc63
Vilarinho do Bairro P 44 Ac63
Vilariño das Poldras E 36 Bb58
Vilariño de Conso E 36 Bc58
Vilariño Frío E 36 Bb57
Vilarmeao E 36 Bc58
Vila-rodona E 49 Gc62
Vilarouco P 44 Bb61
Vilarrube E 36 Bb53
Vila Ruva P 50 Ad70
Vilasantar E 36 Ba55
Vilas de Turbón E 40 Ga58
Vila Seca P 44 Ac60
Vila Seca P 44 Ad64
Vila-seca E 48 Gb62
Vilasobroso E 36 Ad57
Vilassar de Dalt E 49 Ha61
Vilassar de Mar E 49 Ha61
Vilasund S 71 Fc21
Vilatuxe E 36 Ba56
Vila Velha de Ródão P 50 Ba66
Vilavella E 36 Bc58
Vila Verde P 44 Ad59
Vila Verde de Ficalho P 58 Ba72
Vila Verde dos Francos P 50 Ab67
Vila Viçosa P 50 Ba69
Vilce LV 106 Kb52
Vilcele MD 177 Fc60
Vilches E 52 Dc71
Vildbjerg DK 100 Da23
Vildecans E 49 Gd61
Vilejka BY 202 Ea12
Vilela E 36 Bb56
Vilémov CZ 136 Fd45
Vilers E 49 Hb59
Vilgale LV 105 Jb51
Vilhelmina S 79 Ga26
Vilhula FIN 90 Kd32
Vilia GR 189 Ca86
Vilikkala FIN 97 Jd39
Viliošiai LT 113 Jd53
Viljakkala FIN 89 Jc35
Viljandi EST 98 Kd45
Viljaniemi FIN 90 Kc37
Viljaspohja FIN 90 Kb33
Viljevo HR 152 Hb59
Viljolahti FIN 91 Lb32
Vilkaviškis LT 114 Ka58
Vilkėnai LV 114 Kb56
Viļķene LV 106 Kc48
Vilkija LV 114 Kb57
Vilkjärvi FIN 91 Lb36
Vilkkilä FIN 91 Lb38
Vilkla EST 98 Ka44
Vilkovo BG 181 Ec69
Vilkumiešts LV 115 Lb54
Vilkyčiai LT 113 Jb56
Vilkyškiai LT 113 Jd57
Villa CH 142 Cc55
Villabáñez E 46 Da60
Villabassa I 143 Ea55
Villablanca E 58 Ba74
Villablino E 37 Ca56
Villaboa E 36 Bc54
Villabon F 29 Ha42
Villabona E 37 Cb54
Villabona E 39 Ec55
Villabrágima E 46 Cd59
Villabuena del Puente E 45 Cc61
Villacañas E 52 Dc67
Villacarillo E 61 Dd72
Villacarriedo E 38 Dc55
Villa Castelli I 162 Ha76
Villacastín E 46 Da63
Villach A 144 Fa56
Villacián E 38 Dd56
Villacibrán E 37 Ca55
Villacidro I 169 Bd79
Villaciervos E 47 Ea60
Villacintor E 37 Cd57
Villaconejos E 46 Dc65
Villaconejos de Trabaque E 47 Eb64
Villada E 37 Cd58
Villa d'Agri I 161 Ga76
Villa d'Almè I 149 Cd58
Villadangos del Páramo E 37 Cb57
Villa del Prado E 46 Da65
Villa del Rey E 51 Bc66
Villa del Río E 52 Da72
Villadiego E 38 Db57
Villadoro I 167 Fa85
Villadose I 150 Ea61
Villadossola I 148 Ca57
Villaeles de Valdavia E 38 Da57
Villaescusa de Haro E 53 Ea67
Villaescusa la Sombría E 38 Dd58
Villaespesa E 47 Fa65
Villafáfila E 45 Cc59
Villafalletto I 148 Bc62
Villafernando E 37 Bd54
Villaferrueña E 37 Cb58
Villaflores E 45 Cc62
Villafontana I 149 Dc60
Villafranca E 39 Ec58
Villafranca de Córdoba E 60 Cd72
Villafranca de Ebro E 48 Fb61
Villafranca del Bierzo E 37 Bd56
Villafranca del Campo E 47 Ed64
Villafranca de los Barros E 51 Bd70
Villafranca de los Caballeros E 52 Dc67
Villafranca di Verona I 149 Db60

Vizzini – Wąsosz

Vizzini I 167 Fc87
Vjatskie Poljany RUS 203 Ga08
Vjatskoe RUS 203 Fa08
Vjaz'ma RUS 202 Ec11
Vjazniki RUS 203 Fb09
V. Kolaro (Pamporovo) BG 184 Db75
Vlaardingen NL 124 Ac37
Vlachovo SK 138 Jb48
Vlachovo Březí CZ 136 Fa48
Vlad AL 159 Jc70
Vlad AL 178 Ad71
Vlădaia RO 175 Cc66
Vladaja BG 179 Cc71
Vlădeni RO 172 Ec55
Vlădeni RO 173 Fa56
Vlădeni RO 177 Fa66
Vlădești RO 175 Db63
Vlădești RO 175 Dc63
Vlădești RO 177 Fb62
Vladičin-Han SRB 178 Bd71
Vlădila RO 180 Db67
Vladilovce MK 183 Bc74
Vladimir MNE 163 Ja71
Vladimir RO 175 Cd64
Vladimir RUS 203 Fa10
Vladimirci SRB 153 Jb62
Vladimirescu RO 170 Bd59
Vladimirovac SRB 174 Bb63
Vladimirovci BG 181 Ec69
Vladimirovo BG 179 Cc68
Vladimirovo BG 181 Fa69
Vladimirovo MK 183 Ca74
Vladimirovo RUS 113 Ja59
Vladinja BG 180 Db70
Vladinos MNE 163 Ja71
Vladislav CZ 136 Ga47
Vlad Țepeș RO 176 Ed66
Vladyčkino RUS 99 Mb42
Vlagtwedde NL 117 Ca34
Vlaháta GR 188 Ac85
Vlaháva GR 183 Bb80
Vlahi BG 183 Cb74
Vlahiá GR 189 Cb84
Vlahióti GR 194 Bc90
Vlăhița RO 176 Ea60
Vlahokerassiá GR 194 Bc88
Vlahović HR 152 Gb60
Vlahović BIH 158 Hb68
Vlăiculești RO 176 Ec66
Vlaina Okruglica SRB 179 Ca71
Vlajkovac SRB 174 Bc63
Vlajkovci SRB 178 Bb68
Vlas BG 181 Fa72
Vlasenica BIH 159 Hd64
Vlashuk AL 182 Ab76
Vlasi SRB 179 Ca70
Vlašici HR 157 Fd64
Vlašim CZ 136 Fc46
Vlașin RO 180 Ea67
Vlasina Rid SRB 179 Ca71
Vlăsinești RO 172 Ed55
Vlaški Drenovac KSV 178 Ba71
Vlasotince SRB 178 Bd70
Vlastiboř CZ 136 Fc47
Vlatten D 125 Bc41
Vledder NL 117 Bc34
Vlesno RUS 107 Ma49
Vleuten NL 116 Ba36
Vlijmen NL 124 Ba38
Vlissingen NL 124 Ab38
Vlorë AL 182 Aa77
Vlotho D 126 Cd37
V. Nedelja SLO 152 Gb57
Vnorovy CZ 137 Gd48
Vobbia I 148 Cb62
Vocance F 34 Ja49
Voćin HR 152 Ha59
Vockerode D 127 Eb38
Vöcklabruck A 144 Fa51
Vöcklamarkt A 143 Ed51
Vodable F 34 Hb48
Vodanj SRB 174 Bb64
Voden BG 185 Dd74
Voden BG 185 Ec74
Vodenica BIH 152 Gb62
Vodeničane BG 180 Eb72
Vodica BG 180 Ea70
Vodica BIH 158 Gd64
Vodicë AL 182 Ad78
Vodice HR 151 Fa60
Vodice HR 157 Ga65
Vodice SLO 151 Fb57
Vodňany CZ 136 Fb47
Vodnjan HR 151 Fa61
Vodnjanci BG 179 Cb68
Vodno BG 180 Ea70
Vodovrat MK 183 Bc74
Vodskov DK 100 Dc21
Vodstrup DK 100 Da21
Voe GB 5 Fa04
Voel DK 108 Db24
Voerde D 125 Bd38
Voerladegård DK 108 Db24
Voerså DK 101 Dd20
Vœu F 29 Gc43
Voganj SRB 153 Jb61
Vogatsikó GR 183 Bb78
Vogelsdorf, Petershagen- D 128 Fa36
Vögelsen D 118 Dc33
Voggenau A 144 Fc52
Voghera I 148 Cb61
Voghiera I 150 Dd62
Vognill N 77 Dd32
Vognsild DK 100 Db22
Vogogna I 148 Ca57
Vogorno CH 148 Cb57
Vogt D 142 Da52
Vogtareuth D 143 Eb51
Vogtsburg D 141 Bd50
Vogüe F 34 Ja51
Vohburg D 135 Dd49
Vohburg D 135 Ea49
Vohenstrauß D 135 Eb46
Vöhl D 126 Cd40
Võhma EST 97 Jc45
Võhma EST 98 Ka45
Võhma EST 98 Kd41
Võhma EST 98 Kd44
Vohonjoki FIN 74 Kb20
Vohonovo RUS 99 Mb40
Vöhrden, Neuenkirchen- D 117 Cc36
Vöhrenbach D 141 Cb50
Vöhringen D 142 Cc50
Vöhringen D 142 Da50
Voicești RO 175 Db65
Void-Vacon F 25 Jc37
Voievoda RO 180 Dc68
Voigtsdorf D 120 Fa33
Voigtstedt D 127 Dd40
Voikoski FIN 90 Kd35
Voila RO 175 Dc61
Voiluoto FIN 89 Ja37
Voineasa RO 175 Da62
Voineasa RO 175 Da66
Voinescu MD 173 Fc59
Voinești RO 173 Fa57
Voinești RO 173 Fa59
Voinești RO 176 Dd64
Voiron F 35 Jc48
Voise F 29 Gc38
Võisiku EST 98 Kd44
Voisines F 30 Jb40
Võiste EST 106 Kb46
Voiteg RO 174 Bc61
Voiteur F 31 Jc43
Voitoinen FIN 89 Jb37
Voitsberg A 144 Fd54
Voivodeni RO 171 Dc58
Vojakkala FIN 74 Jc21
Vojakkala FIN 90 Ka38
Vojčice SK 139 Ka48
Vojens DK 108 Db27
Vojinka UA 205 Fa17
Vojka SRB 153 Jb61
Vojkovice CZ 135 Ec44
Vojkovići BIH 159 Hc65
Vojmån S 79 Gb25
Vojnić HR 151 Ga60
Vojnik SLO 151 Fd57
Vojnika BG 181 Ec73
Vojnjagovo BG 180 Db72
Vojno-Selo MNE 159 Jb69
Vojnovo BG 181 Ed68
Vojšanci MK 183 Bd75
Vojsil BG 180 Db73
Vojska SRB 174 Bc66
Vojtjajaure S 71 Fd23
Vojvoda BG 181 Ed69
Vojvoda Stepa SRB 174 Bb61
Vojvodino BG 181 Fa70
Vojvodinovo BG 180 Db73
Voka EST 99 Lc41
Voladilla Alta E 60 Cc77
Vólakas GR 184 Cd76
Volargne I 149 Db59
Volary CZ 136 Fa48
Vólax GR 196 Db89
Volbu N 85 Dc37
Volče SLO 151 Fa57
Volciano I 149 Db59
Volčki RUS 203 Fb12
Volda N 76 Cc33
Voldby DK 101 Dd23
Volden N 78 Ea31
Volders A 143 Dd54
Voldi EST 98 La44
Voldum DK 100 Dc23
Volendam NL 116 Ba35
Volga RUS 202 Ed09
Volgelsheim F 31 Kc39
Volgodonsk RUS 205 Fd15
Volgograd RUS 203 Fd14
Volgorečensk RUS 203 Fa09
Volgovo RUS 99 Ma40
Volgsele S 79 Gb25
Volhov RUS 202 Eb08
Volimes GR 188 Ac86
Volintiri MD 177 Ga60
Volissós GR 191 Dd85
Voljice BIH 158 Ha65
Volkach D 134 Db45
Volkenschwand D 135 Ea49
Völkermarkt A 144 Fc56
Völklingen D 133 Bc46
Volkmarsen D 126 Cd39
Volkovija MK 178 Ba73
Volkovo RUS 107 Ld48
Volkstedt D 127 Ea39
Voll N 86 Ea38
Vollen N 62 Gc10
Vollen N 78 Ec28
Vollenhove NL 117 Bc35
Vollersode D 118 Cd33
Vollerup DK 108 Db28
Vollheim N 79 Fb26
Vollore-Montagne F 34 Hc47
Vollore-Ville F 34 Hc47
Vollsjö S 110 Fa56
Volmsjö S 80 Gc27
Volna RUS 99 Ma42
Volnay F 28 Fd40
Volnovacha UA 205 Fb15
Voloave MD 173 Fc54
Voločaevskij RUS 205 Fd15
Voločajevskoje RUS 113 Hd59
Vološ'k UA 204 Ea15
Volodarka UA 204 Ec15
Volodarovka RUS 113 Jc59
Volodarsk RUS 203 Fb09
Volodarskij Toriki RUS 99 Mb39
Volodymyrec' UA 202 Ea14
Volodymyr-Volyns'kyj UA 202 Dd14
Vologda RUS 202 Ed08
Voloiac RO 175 Cc65
Volokolamsk RUS 202 Ed10
Volokonovka RUS 203 Fb13
Volonne F 42 Ka52
Vólos GR 189 Ca82
Volosovo RUS 99 Ld43
Volosovo RUS 99 Ma41
Vološovo RUS 99 Mb43
Volosovo RUS 202 Ea08
Volotovo RUS 203 Fb13
Volovăț RO 172 Eb55
Volovec' UA 204 Dd16
Volovița MD 173 Fc54
Volovo BG 180 Ea69
Volpiano I 148 Bd60
Völpke D 127 Dd37
Völschow D 119 Ed32
Vol'sk RUS 203 Ga11
Voltaggio I 148 Cb62
Volta Mantovana I 149 Db60
Volterra I 155 Db66
Voltlage D 117 Cb36
Voltri I 148 Cb62
Voltti FIN 81 Jb30
Volturara Appula I 161 Fc73
Volturara Irpina I 161 Fc75
Volvic F 34 Hb46
Volyně CZ 136 Fa47
Volžsk RUS 203 Fd09
Volžskij RUS 203 Fd13
Vömmorski EST 107 Lc47
Vomp A 143 Dd53
Vonêche B 132 Ad43
Vonešta Voda BG 180 Dd71
Vóni GR 200 Da96
Vónitsa GR 188 Ad82
Vonnas F 34 Jb45
Võnnu EST 99 Lb45
Vonsild DK 108 Db26
Vööpste EST 99 Lb45
Vööpsu EST 107 Lc46
Voorburg NL 116 Ad36
Voore EST 99 Lb44
Voorschoten NL 116 Ad36
Voorthuizen NL 116 Bb36
Vopnafjörður IS 3 Bc04
Vörå FIN 81 Ja30
Vorau A 144 Ga53
Voray-sur-l'Ognon F 31 Jd41
Vorbasse DK 108 Da25
Vorchdorf A 144 Fa51
Vorden NL 125 Bc37
Vordernberg A 144 Fc53
Vorderriß D 143 Dd53
Vorderstoder A 144 Fb52
Vorderweissenburg A 136 Fb49
Vordingborg DK 109 Eb28
Vordónia GR 194 Bc89
Vordorf D 126 Dc37
Vorë AL 182 Ab74
Voreppe F 35 Jd48
Vorey F 34 Hd49
Vóri GR 200 Cd96
Vorinó GR 183 Bc76
Vorly F 29 Ha43
Vormsele S 80 Gd25
Vormsund N 94 Eb41
Vormträsk S 80 Gd25
Vorna FIN 82 Kb26
Vorniceni RO 172 Ec54
Vorning DK 100 Dc22
Vorona RO 172 Ec56
Voroncovo RUS 107 Mb48
Voroneț RO 172 Eb56
Voronež RUS 203 Fb13
Voronkina RUS 107 Lc47
Voronovo RUS 99 Ld42
Vorožba UA 202 Ed13
Vorpbukta N 78 Ea28
Vorra D 135 Dd46
Vorsma RUS 203 Fb09
Vorța RO 175 Cc60
Vorterøyskagen N 62 Ha08
Võru EST 107 Lb47
Vorzova LV 115 Ma53
Vosbutai LV 114 Kb56
Voshod RUS 203 Ga14
Vosiliškis LV 114 Kb55
Voskop AL 182 Ad77
Voskopojë AL 182 Ad77
Voskresensk RUS 203 Fa10
Voskresenskoe RUS 202 Ed09
Voskresenskoe RUS 203 Fc08
Vosläbeni RO 172 Ea59
Voss N 84 Cc38
Võsu EST 98 Kd41
Vothylakas CY 206 Jd95
Votice CZ 136 Fc46
Võtikvere EST 99 Lb43
Voudenay-l'Église F 30 Ja42
Voúdia GR 195 Cd91
Voue F 30 Hd38
Vougécourt F 31 Jd39
Vougeot F 30 Jb42
Vouguinha P 44 Ba62
Vouhé F 32 Fb46
Vouillé F 28 Fd44
Vouillé F 32 Fc45
Voukoliés GR 200 Cb95
Voúla GR 195 Cb87
Vouliagméni GR 195 Cb87
Vouliásta GR 188 Ad81
Voúlpi GR 188 Ba82
Voulx F 29 Ha38
Voumajärvi S 73 Jb20
Voúnargo GR 188 Ba86
Vounihóra GR 189 Bc85
Vourgareli GR 188 Ba81
Vourijärvi FIN 89 Jc34
Vourkári GR 195 Cd88
Vourvouroú GR 184 Cc79
Vousnainen FIN 97 Ja39
Voussac F 34 Hb45
Voutás GR 200 Ca95
Voutenay-sur-Cure F 30 Hc41
Voutiáni GR 194 Bc89
Voutsarás GR 182 Ac80
Voútsis GR 194 Bb87
Vouvant F 28 Fb44
Vouvray F 29 Ga41
Vouzailles F 28 Fd44
Vouzela P 44 Ba62
Vouzeron F 29 Gd42
Voúzi GR 189 Bd82
Vouziers F 24 Ja35
Vouzon F 29 Gd41
Vovčans'k UA 203 Fa14
Voves F 29 Gc39
Voxna S 87 Fd37
Voxtorp S 103 Fb51
Voxtorp S 111 Ga53
Vöyri FIN 81 Ja30
Vozneseni MD 173 Fc59
Voznesens'k UA 204 Ed16
Voznesenskoe RUS 203 Fb10
Voznice CZ 136 Fb45
Vrå DK 100 Dc20
Vrå S 102 Fa52
Vrabča BG 179 Cb70
Vrabevo BG 180 Db70
Vráble SK 145 Hb50
Vraca BG 179 Cd69
Vračeš BG 179 Cd71
Vračev Gaj SRB 174 Bc63
Vračević SRB 153 Jc63
Vracov CZ 137 Gd48
Vrådal N 93 Da43
Vradijivka UA 204 Ec16
Vrads DK 108 Db24
Vragočanica SRB 153 Jb63
Vrahneika GR 188 Ba85
Vráhos GR 188 Ac82
Vråliosen N 93 Da43
Vrana HR 151 Fb62
Vrana HR 157 Ga65
Vrančе MK 183 Bb75
Vrâncioaia RO 176 Ec61
Vranduk BIH 152 Hb63
Vranes MD 173 Fa56
Vrangiana GR 188 Ba82
Vrångö S 102 Eb49
Vrani RO 174 Bd63
Vranić SRB 153 Jc62
Vrani Kon BG 180 Eb71
Vranilovci BG 180 Dc71
Vranino BG 181 Fb69
Vranja HR 151 Fa60
Vranjak BG 179 Cd69
Vranje SRB 178 Bd71
Vranjska Banja SRB 178 Bd71
Vranov nad Dyjí CZ 136 Ga48
Vranov nad Topl'ou SK 139 Ka48
Vranovo SRB 174 Bc64
Vranovská ves CZ 136 Ga48
Vransko SLO 151 Fc57
Vrap AL 182 Ab75
Vrapce Polje MNE 159 Jb67
Vrapčište MK 178 Ba73
Vrassná GR 184 Cc78
Vrástama GR 184 Cc79
Vrata SLO 144 Fd56
Vratarnica SRB 179 Ca67
Vratěnín CZ 136 Ga48
Vratimov CZ 137 Hb45
Vratlo MNE 159 Ja68
Vrátna SK 138 Hc47
Vratnica MK 178 Bb72
Vravróna GR 195 Cc87
Vrba MNE 159 Ja66
Vrbanj HR 158 Gc67
Vrbanja BIH 152 Gd62
Vrbanja HR 153 Hd61
Vrbanjci BIH 152 Ha62
Vrbanje MNE 159 Hc69
Vrbas SRB 153 Ja59
Vrbaška BIH 152 Gd61
Vrbeštica KSV 178 Ba72
Vrbnica KSV 178 Ad72
Vrbnik HR 151 Fc61
Vrbno pod Pradědem CZ 137 Gd44
Vrboska HR 158 Gc67
Vrbov SK 138 Jb47
Vrbovce SK 137 Gd48
Vrbové SK 137 Ha49
Vrbovec HR 152 Gb58
Vrbovski SRB 153 Jc61
Vrbovsko HR 151 Fd60
Vrchlabí CZ 136 Fd43
Vrčice SLO 151 Fd59
Vrcin SRB 174 Bb64
Vrdy CZ 136 Fd45
Vrebac HR 151 Fd63
Vrécourt F 31 Jc38
Vreden D 125 Bd37
Vrees D 117 Cb34
Vrela KSV 178 Ad70
Vrela SRB 159 Jc68
Vrelo SRB 178 Bd68
Vremski Britof SLO 151 Fa59
Vrena S 95 Gb45
Vrensted DK 100 Dc20
Vreoci SRB 153 Jc62
Vresovo BG 181 Ed71
Vresse-s.-Semois B 132 Ad44
Vréstena GR 194 Bc88
Vreta FIN 97 Jc40
Vreta kloster S 103 Fd46
Vreten S 95 Gb39
Vretstorp S 95 Fc44
Vrgada HR 157 Fd65
Vrgorac HR 158 Ha67
Vrhnika SLO 151 Fb58
Vrhopolje BIH 152 Gc62
Vrhovine HR 151 Fd62
Vrhovo SLO 151 Fd58
Vries NL 117 Bd33
Vriezenveen NL 117 Bd36
Vrigne-au-Bois F 24 Ja33
Vrigstad S 103 Fb50
Vrin CH 142 Cc55
Vrinners DK 109 Dd24
Vrisári GR 188 Bb86
Vríses GR 200 Cc95
Vríssa GR 191 Ea84
Vrissiá GR 189 Bc82
Vrissohóri GR 182 Ad79
Vrissoúla GR 188 Ad81
Vrizy F 24 Ja34
Vrlika HR 158 Gb65
Vrnjačka Banja SRB 178 Bb67
Vrnograč BIH 151 Ga61
Vrodoú GR 183 Bd79
Vron F 23 Gc32
Vrondádos GR 191 Dd86
Vronderó GR 182 Ba77
Vrontamás GR 194 Bc89
Vroomshoop NL 117 Bd35
Vrossina GR 182 Ac80
Vroutek CZ 135 Ed44
Vrpolje HR 153 Hc60
Vrpolje HR 158 Gb66
Vršac SRB 174 Bc63
Vršani BIH 153 Hd62
Vrsar HR 150 Ed61
Vrsi HR 157 Fd64
Vrtoče BIH 152 Gb62
Vruda RUS 99 Ma41
Vrujci SRB 153 Jc63
Vrulja MNE 159 Ja67
Vrulje HR 157 Fd65
Vrútky SK 138 Hc47
Vrutok MK 178 Ba73
Všeruby CZ 135 Ec47
Všestary CZ 136 Ga44
Všetaty CZ 136 Fc44
Vsetín CZ 137 Ha47
Vsevoložsk RUS 202 Eb08
Vtroja RUS 99 Lc43
Vuarrens CH 141 Bb55
Vučedo HR 153 Hd60
Vučić SRB 174 Bb65
Vučijak BIH 152 Ha62
Vučince SRB 178 Ba69
Vučinići HR 151 Fc60
Vučitrn KSV 178 Bb70
Vučja Lokva KSV 178 Ba69
Vučja Luka BIH 159 Hc65
Vučje SRB 178 Bd70
Vučkovica SRB 178 Ad67
Vught NL 124 Ba38
Vuillafons F 31 Jd42
Vukan BG 179 Ca71
Vukosanka FIN 83 Lb25
Vukovar HR 153 Hd60
Vukovina HR 152 Gb59
Vuku N 78 Ec29
Vulaines-sur-Seine F 29 Ha38
Vulcan RO 175 Cd62
Vulcan RO 176 Dd62
Vulcana-Băi RO 176 Dd64
Vulcănești MD 177 Fc62
Vulcănești UA 204 Ec18
Vulcano Piano I 167 Fc83
Vulcano Porto I 167 Fc83
Vulpeni RO 175 Da65
Vultureni RO 171 Da57
Vultureni RO 176 Ed60
Vulturești RO 172 Ec56
Vulturești RO 173 Fa58
Vulturești RO 175 Db65
Vulturu RO 177 Fa62
Vulturu RO 177 Fb66
Vuobmaved FIN 64 Jc10
Vuoggatjålme S 71 Ga19
Vuohèèu FIN 69 Ka13
Vuohijärvi FIN 90 Kd36
Vuohiniemi FIN 90 Ka37
Vuohtomäki FIN 82 Kb28
Vuojalahti FIN 90 Kd33
Vuojärvi FIN 69 Ka17
Vuokatti FIN 82 La26
Vuoksenniska FIN 91 Lc35
Vuolenkoski FIN 90 Kd36
Vuolijoki FIN 82 Kc26
Vuolinko FIN 90 La34
Vuolle FIN 81 Jc28
Vuolledalen N 63 Ja09
Vuollerim S 73 Hb20
Vuonamo FIN 82 Kc29
Vuonisjärvi FIN 83 Ld28
Vuonislahti FIN 83 Ld28
Vuono S 74 Jc21
Vuonos FIN 83 Lc30
Vuontee FIN 90 Kc32
Vuontisjärvi FIN 68 Jb13
Vuorenkylä FIN 90 Kc34
Vuorenmaa FIN 89 Jb37
Vuorenmaa FIN 90 La33
Vuoreslahti FIN 82 Kd26
Vuorilahti FIN 82 Kb30
Vuorimäki FIN 89 Jd32
Vuoriniemi FIN 91 Ld34
Vuosaari FIN 98 Kb39
Vuoskojaure sameviste S 67 Ha13
Vuostimo FIN 69 Kb17
Vuostimojärvi FIN 69 Kb17
Vuotinainen FIN 90 Ka38
Vuotjärvi FIN 82 La29
Vuotner S 72 Ha22
Vuotsa FIN 83 Ma29
Vuotso FIN 69 Ka13
Vuottas S 73 Hd20
Vuottolahti FIN 82 Kc26
Vuotunki FIN 75 La19
Vuovdakuoihka FIN 64 Jc09
Vurnary RUS 203 Fc09
Vurpăr RO 175 Db61
Vust DK 100 Db20
Vutcani RO 177 Fb60
Vybor RUS 107 Mb48
Vybor RUS 202 Ea10
Vyborg RUS 202 Ea08
Výčapy CZ 136 Ga47
Výčapy Opatovce SK 145 Hb50
Východná SK 138 Ja47
Vydeniai LT 114 Kd59
Vydmantai LT 113 Jb54
Vygoniči RUS 202 Ed12
Vygréliai LT 114 Ka59
Vyksa RUS 203 Fb10
Vy-lès-Lure F 31 Ka40
Vylkove UA 204 Ec18
Vynnyky UA 204 Dd15
Vypolzovo RUS 202 Ec09
Vyra RUS 99 Mb41
Vyrica RUS 202 Eb08
Vyšgorodok RUS 107 Ld49
Vyšhorod UA 202 Ec14
Vyskatka RUS 99 Ld42
Vyškov CZ 137 Gd47
Vyskytná CZ 136 Fd46
Vyšné Nemecké SK 139 Kb48
Vyšné Ružbachy SK 138 Jb46
Vyšnij Voloček RUS 202 Ec09
Vysockoe RUS 107 Mb49
Vysoká SK 137 Hb46
Vysoké Mýto CZ 137 Gb45
Vysokij Most RUS 107 Ld47
Vysokoe RUS 113 Jc58
Vysokoje RUS 113 Jd58
Vysokovsk RUS 202 Ed10
Vysoký Chlumec CZ 136 Fb46
Vyšší Brod CZ 136 Fb49
Vystavka RUS 107 Mb46
Vyžiai LT 113 Jc56
Vyžnycja UA 204 Ea16
Vyžuonos LT 114 La55
Vzmor'e RUS 113 Hd59

W

Waabs D 108 Dc29
Waake D 126 Db39
Waakirchen D 143 Ea52
Waal D 142 Dc51
Waalre NL 124 Ba39
Waalwijk NL 124 Ba38
Waase D 119 Ed30
Wabcz PL 121 Hb33
Waben F 23 Gc32
Wabern D 126 Da40
Wabienice PL 129 Gd41
Wąbrzeźno PL 121 Hb33
Wach PL 122 Jc33
Wachenheim D 133 Cb46
Wachenroth D 134 Dc45
Wąchock PL 130 Jc41
Wachow D 127 Ec36
Wachów PL 129 Hb42
Wachtberg D 125 Bd42
Wachtendonk D 125 Bc39
Wächtersbach D 134 Cd43
Wacken D 118 Da31
Wackersdorf D 135 Eb47
Wackersleben D 127 Dd37
Waddesdon GB 20 Fb27
Waddewarden D 117 Cc32
Waddington GB 17 Fc22
Waddingtown IRL 13 Cc25
Waddinxveen NL 116 Ad36
Wadebridge GB 18 Db31
Wädenswil CH 141 Cb53
Wadern D 133 Bc45
Wadersloh D 126 Cc38
Wadhurst GB 20 Fd29
Wadlew PL 130 Hd39
Wadowice PL 138 Hd45
Waffenbrunn D 135 Ec47
Wagenfeld D 126 Cd36
Wageningen NL 125 Bb37
Waghäusel D 134 Cc47
Waging am See D 143 Ec51
Wagna A 144 Fd55
Wagrain A 143 Ed53
Wągrowiec PL 121 Gc35
Wahlstedt D 118 Dc31
Wahrenberg D 119 Ea35
Wahrenholz D 126 Dc36
Waiblingen D 134 Cd48
Waibstadt D 134 Cc46
Waidhaus D 135 Eb46
Waidhofen an der Thaya A 136 Fd49
Waidhofen an der Ybbs A 144 Fc51
Waidring A 143 Eb53
Waimes B 125 Bb42
Wainfleet All Saints GB 17 Fd23
Wainhouse Corner GB 18 Dc30
Waischenfeld D 135 Dd45
Waizenkirchen A 144 Fa50
Wakefield GB 16 Fa21
Walbeck D 125 Bc39
Walbeck D 127 Dd37
Walberswick GB 21 Gc25
Wałbrzych PL 129 Gb42
Walchen A 143 Dd54
Walchum D 117 Ca34
Walchwil CH 141 Cb54
Wałcz PL 121 Gb34
Wald A 143 Ed54
Wald A 144 Fc53
Wald CH 142 Cc53
Wald D 142 Cd51
Waldaschaff D 134 Cd44
Waldbach A 144 Ga53
Waldböckelheim D 133 Ca44
Waldbreitbach D 125 Ca42
Waldbröl D 125 Ca41
Waldbronn D 133 Cb48
Waldbrunn D 134 Cd46
Waldbrunn (Westerwald) D 125 Cb42
Waldburg D 142 Da52
Walddrehna D 128 Fa39
Wälde, Betzweiler- D 133 Cb49
Waldeck D 126 Cd40
Waldems D 133 Cb43
Waldenbuch D 134 Cd49
Waldenburg D 127 Ec42
Waldenburg D 134 Da47
Waldenstein-Twimberg A 144 Fc55
Walderbach D 135 Eb47
Walderton GB 20 Fb30
Waldfeucht D 125 Bb40
Waldfischbach-Burgalben D 133 Ca46
Waldhausen im Strudengau A 144 Fc50
Waldheim D 127 Ed41
Waldkappel D 126 Db40
Waldkirch CH 142 Cd53
Waldkirch D 141 Ca50
Waldkirchen D 127 Ed42
Waldkirchen D 136 Fa49
Waldkraiburg D 143 Eb50
Wald-Michelbach D 134 Cc46
Waldmohr D 133 Bd46
Waldmünchen D 135 Ec47
Waldneukirchen A 144 Fb51
Wałdowo PL 121 Gd33
Waldringfield GB 21 Gb26
Waldsassen D 135 Eb45
Waldsee D 133 Cb46
Waldsee, Bad D 142 Da51
Waldshut-Tiengen D 141 Ca52
Waldsieversdorf D 128 Fb36
Waldsolms D 134 Cc43
Waldstetten D 134 Cd46
Wałdyki PL 122 Hd32
Waldzell A 143 Ed51
Walenstadt CH 142 Cd54
Wales GB 16 Fa22
Walewice PL 130 Hd37
Walferdange L 133 Bb45
Walgherton GB 15 Ec23
Walichnowy PL 129 Hb40
Walim PL 129 Gb42
Walincourt-Selvigny F 24 Hb33
Walkenried D 126 Dc39
Walkerburn GB 11 Eb14
Walkern GB 20 Fc27
Walkowice PL 121 Gb34
Wallasey GB 15 Eb21
Walldorf D 126 Dc42
Walldorf D 134 Cc46
Walldürn D 134 Cd46
Wallendorf D 133 Bb44
Wallenfels D 135 Dd44
Wallenhorst D 117 Cb36
Wallerfing D 135 Ec49
Wallern A 144 Fa50
Wallern im Burgenland A 145 Gc52
Wallers F 24 Hb32
Wallersdorf D 135 Ec49
Wallerstein D 134 Db48
Wallgau D 143 Dd53
Wallhalben D 133 Ca46
Wallhausen D 127 Dd40
Wallhausen D 134 Db47
Wallingford GB 20 Fa28
Wallisellen CH 141 Cb53
Wallmoden D 126 Dc38
Walls GB 5 Ed05
Wallsee A 144 Fc51
Wallstawe D 119 Dd35
Walluf D 133 Cb44
Wallwitz D 127 Eb39
Walmerod D 125 Cb42
Wałowice PL 128 Fc38
Walpertskirchen D 143 Ea50
Walpole Saint Andrew GB 17 Fd24
Walsall GB 16 Ed24
Walschleben D 127 Dd41
Walsdorf D 134 Dc45
Walsrode D 118 Db35
Waltenhofen D 142 Db52
Waltersdorf D 128 Fc42
Waltershausen D 126 Dc41
Waltham GB 17 Fc21
Waltham-on-the-Wolds GB 16 Fb24
Walton East GB 14 Db26
Walton-on-the-Naze GB 21 Gb27
Waltrop D 125 Ca38
Waly F 24 Jb36
Wamba E 46 Cd60
Wambierzyce PL 137 Gb43
Wanborough GB 20 Ed28
Wanderup D 108 Da29
Wandlitz D 119 Ed35
Wanfried D 126 Db40
Wangen CH 141 Bd53
Wangenbourg F 25 Kb37
Wangen im Allgäu D 142 Da52
Wangerland D 117 Cc32
Wangerooge D 117 Cc31
Wängi CH 142 Cc52
Wanlockhead GB 10 Ea15
Wanna D 118 Cd32
Wansleben D 127 Ea40
Wanssum NL 125 Bc38
Wantage GB 20 Fa28
Wanzleben D 127 Ea38
Wapenveld NL 117 Bc35
Wąpielsk PL 122 Hc34
Wapienne PL 139 Jd45
Waplewo PL 122 Ja33
Wapnica PL 120 Fd34
Wapno PL 121 Gd35
Warberg D 127 Dd37
Warbomont B 124 Ba42
Warboys GB 20 Fc25
Warburg D 126 Cd39
Warchlino PL 120 Fc33
Warcino PL 121 Gb31
Warcq F 25 Jc35
Ward IRL 13 Cd21
Wardenburg D 117 Cc34
Wardin B 133 Bb43
Wardington GB 20 Fa26
Ware GB 20 Fc27
Waregem B 124 Aa40
Wareham GB 19 Ec31
Waremme B 124 Ba41
Waren D 119 Ec33
Warendorf D 125 Cb37
Warffum NL 117 Bd32
Warga NL 117 Bc33
Warin D 119 Ea32
Warka PL 130 Jc38
Warkworth GB 11 Fa15
Warley GB 20 Ed25
Warlingham GB 20 Fc29
Warlubie PL 121 Hb32
Warluis F 23 Gd35
Warmenhuizen NL 116 Ba34
Warmensteinach D 135 Ea44
Warminster GB 19 Ec29
Warmsen D 126 Cd36
Warmwell GB 19 Ec31
Warnemünde D 119 Eb31
Warnford GB 20 Fa30
Warngau D 143 Ea52
Warnice PL 120 Fc35
Warnikajmy PL 122 Jb30
Warnino PL 120 Ga31
Warnołęka PL 120 Fb32
Warnowo PL 120 Fb32
Warrenpoint IRL 9 Cd19
Warrington GB 15 Ec21
Warschau = Warszawa PL 130 Jb37
Warslow GB 16 Ed22
Warsop GB 16 Fa22
Warsow D 119 Ea33
Warstein D 126 Cc39
Warszawa PL 130 Jb37
Warszkowo PL 121 Gb30
Wart, Altensteig- D 134 Cc49
Warta PL 129 Hb39
Warta Bolesławiecka PL 128 Ga41
Wartenberg D 126 Da42
Wartenberg D 143 Ea50
Wartenburg D 127 Ec39
Warth A 142 Da53
Warthausen D 142 Da50
Warthe D 120 Fa31
Wartin D 120 Fb34
Wartkowice PL 130 Hc38
Wartmannsroth D 134 Da44
Warton GB 11 Ed15
Warwick GB 20 Fa25
Wasbek D 118 Db31
Wasbister GB 5 Ec02
Waschleithe D 127 Ec42
Washaway GB 18 Db31
Washington GB 11 Fa17
Wasigny F 24 Hd34
Wasilków PL 123 Kb33
Waskemeer NL 117 Bd33
Waśniów PL 130 Jc41
Wąsosz PL 121 Gd35

Wólka Pełkińska – Zalegošč

Wólka Pełkińska PL 139 Kb43
Wolkenstein D 127 Ed42
Wolkenstein I 143 Dd56
Wolkersdorf A 145 Gb50
Wolkowe PL 122 Jc33
Wołkowyja PL 139 Kb46
Wolkramshausen D 126 Dc40
Wollbach D 134 Db43
Wollersheim D 125 Bc41
Wöllstadt D 134 Cc43
Wöllstein D 133 Cb45
Wolmirstedt D 127 Ea37
Wolnica PL 122 Ja31
Wolnzach D 135 Ea49
Wołomin PL 130 Jc36
Wołosate PL 139 Kc47
Wołow PL 129 Gb40
Wołowe Lasy PL 121 Gb34
Wolpertshausen D 134 Da47
Wolpertswende D 142 Cd51
Wolphaartsdijk NL 124 Ab38
Wolsingham GB 11 Ed17
Wolsztyn PL 128 Ga38
Woltersdorf D 119 Dd35
Wolvega NL 117 Bc34
Wolverhampton GB 16 Ed24
Wolverley GB 15 Ec25
Wombourn GB 15 Ec24
Wommels NL 116 Bb33
Wonersh GB 20 Fb29
Wonfurt D 134 Dc44
Woodborough GB 16 Fb23
Woodbridge GB 21 Gb26
Woodchurch GB 21 Ga29
Woodcuts GB 20 Ed30
Wood Dalling GB 17 Ga24
Woodenbridge IRL 13 Cd23
Woodford GB 20 Fd28
Woodford IRL 12 Bd22
Woodhall Spa GB 17 Fc22
Woodhouse GB 16 Fa22
Woodhouse Eaves GB 16 Fa24
Wooding-Dean GB 20 Fc30
Woodseaves GB 15 Ec23
Woodstock GB 20 Fa27
Woodton GB 21 Gb25
Wool GB 19 Ec31
Woolacombe GB 18 Dc29
Wooler GB 11 Ed14
Woolpit GB 21 Ga26
Woolverstone GB 21 Gb26
Woolwich GB 20 Fd28
Wooperton GB 11 Ed15
Wootton GB 20 Fb26
Wootton Bassett GB 20 Ed28
Wootton-Wawen GB 20 Ed25
Worb CH 141 Bd54
Worbis, Leinefelde- D 126 Dc40
Worcester GB 15 Ec26
Wördern A 145 Gb50
Wörgl A 143 Ea53
Woringen D 142 Db51
Wörishofen, Bad D 142 Db51
Workington GB 10 Ea17
Worksop GB 16 Fa22
Workum NL 116 Bb33
Wörlitz D 127 Ec38
Wormeldange L 25 Jd34
Wormeldange L 133 Bc45
Wormerveer NL 116 Ba35
Wormhout F 21 Gd30
Worms D 133 Cb45
Wörnharts A 136 Fc49
Wörnitz D 134 Db47
Worpswede D 118 Cd33
Wörrstadt D 133 Cb44
Wört D 134 Db47
Wörth A 143 Ec54
Wörth D 133 Cb47
Wörth D 135 Eb49
Wörth D 143 Ea50
Wörth am Main D 134 Cd45
Wörth an der Donau D 135 Eb48
Worthen GB 15 Eb24
Worthing GB 20 Fc30
Worton GB 20 Ed28
Woskowice Górne PL 129 Ha41
Woszczyce PL 138 Hc44
Woudenberg NL 116 Bb36
Woudsend NL 116 Bb34
Woumen B 21 Ha29
Woziwoda PL 121 Gd32
Wozławki PL 122 Jb30
Woźnawieś PL 123 Ka32
Woźnice PL 122 Jc31
Woźniki PL 130 Hc42
Wożuczyn PL 131 Kd42
Wragby GB 17 Fc22
Wrangle GB 17 Fd23
Wręczyca Wielka PL 130 Hc42
Wredenhagen D 119 Ec34
Wrelton GB 16 Fb19
Wremen D 118 Cd32
Wrentham GB 21 Gc25
Wrestedt D 118 Dc35
Wrexham GB 15 Eb23
Wriedel D 118 Dc34
Wriezen D 128 Fb36
Wrist D 118 Db31
Wróblew PL 129 Hb39
Wróblewo PL 129 Gb36
Wróblewo PL 130 Ja36
Wróbliniec PL 129 Gd39
Wroceń PL 123 Ka32
Wrocki PL 122 Hc34
Wrocław PL 129 Gc41
Wroczyny PL 130 Hc37
Wroniawy PL 128 Ga38
Wronki PL 129 Gb36
Wronki Wielkie PL 123 Jd30
Wronowy PL 129 Ha36
Wrotnów PL 131 Jd36
Wroughton GB 20 Ed28
Wroxham GB 17 Gb24
Wrząca PL 121 Gb34
Wrzesina PL 122 Ja32
Września PL 122 Hd34
Września PL 129 Gd37
Wrzoski PL 121 Ha35
Wrzosowo PL 120 Ga31
Wschowa PL 129 Gb39
Wulfen D 127 Eb38
Wülfershausen D 134 Db43
Wülfrath D 125 Bd39
Wulfsen D 118 Dc33
Wulften D 126 Db39
Wulkau D 119 Eb35
Wülknitz D 127 Ed40
Wulsbüttel D 118 Cd33
Wunderstetten A 144 Fc56
Wünnenberg D 126 Cd39
Wünschendorf D 127 Eb42
Wünsdorf D 127 Ed37
Wunsiedel D 135 Eb44
Wunstorf D 126 Da36
Wuppertal D 125 Ca40
Würenlos CH 141 Cb53
Wurmannsquick D 143 Ec50
Wurmsham D 143 Eb50
Würnsdorf A 144 Fd50
Würselen D 125 Bb41
Wurzach, Bad D 142 Da51
Würzburg D 134 Da45
Wurzen D 127 Ec40
Wüstenrot D 134 Cd47
Wusterhausen D 119 Ec35
Wusterhusen D 120 Fa31
Wustermark D 127 Ed36
Wusterwitz D 127 Eb37
Wüsting D 117 Cc34
Wustrow D 119 Dd35
Wustrow D 119 Ec30
Wustrow D 119 Ed34
Wuustwezel B 124 Ad38
Wybcz PL 121 Hb34
Wyborów PL 130 Jc38
Wyczechy PL 121 Gc32
Wycześniak PL 130 Ja38
Wydmusy PL 122 Jc33
Wydrza PL 131 Jd42
Wye GB 21 Ga29
Wygoda PL 123 Jd34
Wygoda PL 129 Hb38
Wygoda PL 130 Hc42
Wygoda PL 131 Jd39
Wyk auf Föhr D 108 Cd29
Wykrot PL 122 Jc33
Wylatowo PL 129 Ha36
Wymondham GB 17 Ga24
Wyningen CH 141 Bd53
Wyryki-Połód PL 131 Kc38
Wyrzysk PL 121 Gc34
Wysall GB 16 Fa23
Wyśmierzyce PL 130 Jb39
Wysocice PL 138 Ja43
Wysoka PL 120 Fc35
Wysoka PL 121 Gc34
Wysoka PL 128 Ga40
Wysoka PL 138 Hd43
Wysoka PL 139 Jd44
Wysoka Cerkiew PL 129 Gb39
Wysoka Lelowska PL 130 Hd42
Wysokie PL 123 Ka31
Wysokie PL 131 Kb41
Wysokie Mazowieckie PL 123 Ka34
Wysoki Most PL 123 Kb30
Wysowa PL 138 Jc46
Występ PL 122 Jc32
Wystok PL 128 Fc37
Wyszanów PL 129 Ha40
Wyszki PL 123 Kb34
Wyszków PL 122 Jc35
Wyszków PL 131 Jd36
Wyszogród PL 130 Ja36
Wyszomierz Wielki PL 123 Jd34
Wyszonki-Kościelny PL 123 Ka35
Wyszyna PL 129 Hb37
Wyszyny PL 121 Gc35
Wyszyny PL 122 Ja34
Wythall GB 20 Ed25
Wyvis Lodge GB 4 Dd07
Wziąchowo PL 129 Gd39

X

Xàbia E 55 Fd70
Xanten D 125 Bc38
Xánthi GR 184 Db77
Xàtiva E 54 Fb69
Xendive E 36 Ba58
Xeraco E 54 Fc69
Xermaménil F 25 Jd37
Xert E 48 Fd64
Xerta E 48 Ga63
Xertigny F 31 Jd39
Xesta E 36 Ba56
Xestoso E 36 Bb54
Xhyrë AL 182 Ad75
Xibrrakë AL 182 Ac75
Xifianí GR 183 Bc76
Xilagani GR 184 Dc77
Xilókastro GR 189 Bd86
Xilokeratiá GR 195 Cc91
Xiloúpoli GR 183 Cb77
Xilxes E 54 Fc67
Xinó Neró GR 183 Bb77
Xinorlet E 55 Fa71
Xinóvrisi GR 189 Cb82
Xinzo de Limia E 36 Bb58
Xirokámbi GR 194 Bc89
Xirókambo GR 197 Eb90
Xirolímni GR 183 Bb78
Xirólofos GR 188 Ac81
Xironda E 44 Bb59
Xiropígado GR 188 Bb85
Xiropótamos GR 184 Cd76
Xitta I 166 Ea84
Xixona E 55 Fb71
Xove E 36 Bc53
Xuño E 36 Ac56
Xunqueira de Ambia E 36 Bb58
Xylofagou CY 206 Jd97
Xylóskalo GR 200 Cb95
Xylotymvou CY 206 Jc97

Y

Yabacı TR 192 Fb85
Yağca TR 199 Gc90
Yağcı TR 191 Ed83
Yağcıdereköy TR 197 Ed88
Yağcılar TR 186 Ga78
Yağcılar TR 191 Eb86
Yağcılar TR 192 Fa81
Yağcılar TR 192 Fb83
Yağdiran TR 191 Ed82
Yağhane TR 197 Ec89
Yağlılar TR 198 Fc88
Yağmurlar TR 192 Ga84
Yağmurlu TR 191 Ed83
Yahşieli TR 191 Ea81
Yaka TR 199 Ha88
Yakaafşar TR 199 Ha88
Yakacık TR 198 Fd92
Yakaköy TR 191 Ec85
Yakaköy TR 197 Ec91
Yakaköy TR 197 Ed90
Yakaören TR 199 Gc88
Yakasinek TR 193 Ha86
Yakuplar TR 192 Fd84
Yalakdere TR 186 Ga79
Yalding GB 20 Fd29
Yalıçiftlik TR 197 Ed90
Yalıkavak TR 197 Ec90
Yalıköy TR 186 Fb76
Yalımkaya TR 193 Ha81
Yalnız TR 199 Gb92
Yalnızdam TR 191 Ed83
Yalova TR 185 Ea80
Yalova TR 186 Fd79
Yalvaç TR 193 Ha86
Yamaç TR 197 Ec88
Yamadı TR 198 Ga90
Yamanlar TR 191 Ec85
Yancıklar TR 185 Ed76
Yanguas E 47 Eb59
Yanıkağıl TR 186 Fa77
Yanıköy TR 193 Gd83
Yanişehir TR 192 Fc85
Yanuslar TR 191 Ec83
Yapıldak TR 185 Eb80
Yapıldak TR 193 Gc84
Yarbasan TR 192 Fc84
Yarbasan TR 193 Gc83
Yarbaşı TR 199 Gc91
Yarcombe GB 19 Eb30
Yarıkkaya TR 193 Gd86
Yarıkkaya TR 193 Ha84
Yarımca TR 193 Gc81
Yariş TR 192 Fd83
Yarışlı TR 193 Gc86
Yarpuz TR 199 Hb90
Yassıbel TR 193 Ha87
Yassıgeçit TR 187 Gc78
Yassıören TR 186 Fc77
Yassıören TR 192 Fc83
Yassıören TR 193 Gc87
Yaşyer TR 191 Ec82
Yatağan TR 197 Fa89
Yátova E 54 Fa68
Yattendon GB 20 Fa28
Yavaşça TR 185 Ed77
Yavaşlar TR 193 Gb86
Yavaşlı TR 193 Hb85
Yaverören TR 193 Ha83
Yaxham GB 17 Ga24
Yayaağaç TR 185 Ec78
Yayakent TR 191 Ec84
Yayakent TR 191 Ed84
Yayakırıldık TR 192 Fa84
Yayalar TR 192 Ga86
Yayıklı TR 193 Gd82
Yaykın TR 192 Fa84
Yayla TR 191 Ed82
Yaylaalan TR 199 Ha91
Yaylabaşı TR 192 Fb82
Yaylabayır TR 192 Fa81
Yaylaçayırı TR 192 Fb81
Yaylacık TR 191 Ea82
Yaylaköy TR 185 Ea78
Yaylaköy TR 191 Ea85
Yaylaköy TR 192 Ga84
Yaylaköy TR 198 Ga88
Yaylaköy TR 199 Gb90
Yaylalı TR 186 Ga77
Yaylapınar TR 198 Fd90
Yaylasöğüt TR 198 Fb90
Yaylatepe TR 187 Hb78
Yazıbaşı TR 192 Fd82
Yazıca TR 187 Hb80
Yazıcık TR 187 Hb78
Yazıdere TR 193 Gd83
Yazıkent TR 198 Fb88
Yazıköy TR 197 Ec91
Yazıköy TR 199 Gb89
Yazılıkaya TR 193 Gc84
Yazıpınar TR 199 Gc89
Yazır TR 198 Ga89
Yazır TR 199 Gb91
Yazır TR 199 Gb92
Yazırköy TR 198 Fb88
Yazıtepe TR 193 Gb85
Yazla TR 193 Hb86
Yazlık TR 186 Fc77
Ybbs an der Donau A 144 Fc51
Ybbsitz A 144 Fc51
Ychoux F 39 Fa52
Ydby DK 100 Cd22
Yderby DK 109 Dd28
Yeadon GB 16 Ed20
Yealmpton GB 19 Dd31
Yebra E 46 Dd65
Yebra de Basa E 40 Fc58
Yéchar E 55 Ed72
Yecla E 55 Fa70
Yediburun TR 198 Fd93
Yedisu TR 205 Ga20
Yekli TR 192 Fd84
Yeleğen TR 192 Fc86
Yeles E 46 Db65
Yelken TR 198 Fd92
Yelland GB 19 Dd29
Yelten TR 199 Gb90
Yelvertoft GB 20 Fa25
Yelverton GB 19 Dd31
Yemişendere TR 198 Fb90
Yenibağarası TR 191 Eb85
Yenibosna TR 186 Fc78
Yeniçam TR 192 Fc87
Yenice TR 185 Ea78
Yenice TR 185 Ec78
Yenice TR 186 Fa75
Yenice TR 186 Fa80
Yenice TR 191 Ec81
Yenice TR 192 Fa82
Yenice TR 192 Fa84
Yenice TR 192 Fb81
Yenice TR 192 Fd83
Yenice TR 192 Ga85
Yenice TR 193 Gc84
Yenice TR 193 Gd81
Yenice TR 198 Fb88
Yenicekent TR 192 Fc87
Yeniceköy TR 186 Fa77
Yeniceşehler TR 187 Gd79
Yeniçiftlik TR 185 Ec80
Yeniçiftlik TR 186 Fa77
Yeni Çiftlik TR 191 Ed87
Yenidibek TR 185 Eb78
Yenidoğan TR 197 Ec88
Yenidoğan TR 199 Hb88
Yenierenköy = Aigialousa CY 206 Jd95
Yenifoça TR 191 Eb85
Yenigürle TR 186 Fd80
Yenikarabağ TR 193 Ha85
Yeni Karpuzlu TR 185 Ea78
Yenikavak TR 192 Fa81
Yenikent TR 193 Gd82
Yenikızılelma TR 192 Fc81
Yeniköy TR 185 Eb76
Yeniköy TR 185 Ec79
Yeniköy TR 185 Ed78
Yeniköy TR 186 Fb80
Yeniköy TR 186 Fc77
Yeniköy TR 186 Fd79
Yeniköy TR 187 Gb79
Yeniköy TR 187 Gc78
Yeniköy TR 191 Ea81
Yeniköy TR 191 Ec84
Yeniköy TR 191 Ec86
Yeniköy TR 191 Ec86
Yeniköy TR 191 Ec87
Yeniköy TR 191 Ec87
Yeniköy TR 191 Ed85
Yeniköy TR 191 Ed85
Yeniköy TR 192 Fa81
Yeniköy TR 192 Fa82
Yeniköy TR 192 Fa85
Yeniköy TR 192 Fc85
Yeniköy TR 192 Fd82
Yeniköy TR 192 Fd85
Yeniköy TR 193 Gb81
Yeniköy TR 193 Ha84
Yeniköy TR 193 Ha87
Yeniköy TR 198 Ga93
Yenimahalle TR 185 Ec75
Yenimahalle TR 187 Gc77
Yenimuhacir TR 185 Eb78
Yenioba TR 191 Ed87
Yenipazar TR 187 Gc80
Yenipazar TR 197 Fa88
Yenişakran TR 191 Ec84
Yenişarbademli TR 199 Ha88
Yenişehir TR 186 Ga80
Yenişehir TR 192 Fa87
Yeniyurt TR 193 Ha82
Yeniziraatlı TR 186 Fa80
Yenne F 35 Jd47
Yeovil GB 19 Eb30
Yepes E 52 Dc66
Yera E 38 Dc55
Yerkesik TR 197 Fa90
Yerlisu TR 185 Eb78
Yeroluk TR 192 Fa81
Yerseke NL 124 Ac38
Yerville F 23 Ga34
Yesa E 39 Fa57
Yeşilbağ TR 199 Ha89
Yeşilbağcılar TR 197 Fa89
Yesilçay = Ağva TR 187 Gb77
Yeşilce TR 186 Fa75
Yeşilçukurca TR 192 Ga82
Yeşildağ TR 199 Gb89
Yeşildağ TR 199 Ha89
Yeşildon TR 193 Gd82
Yeşilhisar TR 191 Ed83
Yeşilhüyük TR 193 Gb87
Yeşilkaraman TR 199 Gd90
Yeşilkavak TR 192 Fc86
Yeşilköy TR 191 Ed85
Yeşilköy TR 192 Fc84
Yeşilköy TR 192 Ga82
Yeşilköy TR 193 Gd87
Yeşilköy TR 197 Ec89
Yeşilköy TR 198 Fc88
Yeşilköy TR 198 Fd93
Yeşilköy TR 198 Ga90
Yeşiller TR 192 Fc81
Yeşilova TR 185 Ec76
Yeşilova TR 192 Fa81
Yeşilova TR 192 Fd87
Yeşilova TR 198 Ga89
Yeşiltepe TR 193 Gc83
Yeşilvadi TR 186 Fd77
Yeşilyayla TR 199 Gb90
Yeşilyurt TR 185 Ed77
Yeşilyurt TR 191 Eb82
Yeşilyurt TR 192 Fc86
Yeşilyurt TR 192 Ga85
Yeşilyurt TR 197 Fa90
Yeşilyuva TR 198 Fd89
Yesnaby GB 5 Eb03
Yeste E 53 Eb71
Yetre Brenna N 64 Jc06
Yetre Kjæs N 64 Jc05
Yetterlännäs S 80 Gc31
Yetts o'Muckhart GB 7 Ea12
Yg S 87 Ga35
Ygos-Saint-Saturnin F 39 Fb53
Ygrande F 30 Hb44
Yığılca TR 187 Ha78
Yiğitler TR 185 Ed79
Yiğitler TR 191 Eb81
Ylipää FIN 81 Jd26
Yıldızeli TR 205 Fc20
Yıldızköy TR 192 Fb81
Yıldızören TR 193 Ha83
Yılmazlı TR 198 Ga91
Yırcaköy TR 191 Ed83
Yitäkylä FIN 97 Jd39
Ykspihlaja FIN 81 Jb28
Ylakiai LT 113 Jc53
Ylä-Kintaus FIN 90 Kb32
Ylä-Kolkki FIN 89 Jd33
Ylä-Kuona FIN 91 Lc32
Ylä-Luosta FIN 83 Lb28
Ylämaa FIN 91 Lb37
Ylämylly FIN 83 Lc30
Yläne FIN 89 Jb38
Ylä-Valtimo FIN 83 Lb27
Ylemmäinen FIN 90 Kc35
Ylhäisi FIN 97 Jc39
Ylihärmä FIN 81 Jb30
Yli-Ii FIN 74 Ka22
Ylijärvi FIN 81 Lb37
Ylijoki FIN 89 Jc32
Yli-Kannus FIN 81 Jc28
Yli-Kärppä FIN 74 Ka21
Ylikiiminki FIN 74 Kb23
Yli-Körkkö FIN 74 Ka19
Ylikulma FIN 97 Jd40
Yli-Kurki FIN 75 Kd22
Ylikylä FIN 69 Kb17
Ylikylä FIN 81 Jd29
Ylikylä FIN 81 Jc31
Ylikylä FIN 81 Jb30
Ylikylä FIN 83 Lb27
Ylikylä FIN 89 Jb32
Ylikylä FIN 89 Ja33
Yli-Kyrö FIN 68 Jb14
Yli-Lesti FIN 82 Ka29
Yli-Livo FIN 75 Kc21
Ylimarkku FIN 89 Hd32
Yli-Muonio FIN 68 Ja14
Yli-Nampa FIN 74 Ka18
Yli-Olhava FIN 74 Ka22
Ylipää FIN 74 Jd24
Ylipää FIN 74 Jd24
Ylipää FIN 74 Ka24
Ylipää FIN 81 Jd25
Ylipää FIN 81 Jc30
Ylipää FIN 81 Jd25
Ylipää FIN 82 Kb25
Ylipää FIN 82 Ka28
Yli-Paakkola FIN 74 Jc20
Yli-Siurua FIN 74 Kb21
Yliskulma FIN 97 Jc39
Yliskylä FIN 89 Jc34
Yliskylä FIN 90 Ka35
Ylistaro FIN 81 Jb31
Yli-Tannila FIN 74 Ka22
Ylitornio FIN 73 Jb20
Yli-Tynkä FIN 81 Jc27
Yli-Utos FIN 75 Kc24
Yli-Valli FIN 89 Jb33
Ylivesi FIN 90 La34
Ylivieska FIN 81 Jd27
Yli-Vuotto FIN 74 Kb23
Ylläsjärvi FIN 68 Jb16
Ylläsjokisuu FIN 68 Jb16
Ylläsmaja FIN 68 Jb15
Yllestad S 102 Fa48
Ylöjärvi FIN 89 Jd35
Ylönkylä FIN 97 Jc40
Ylvingen N 70 Ed22
Ymonville F 29 Gc39
Yngsjö S 111 Fb55
Ynyslas GB 15 Dd24
Yoğunpelit TR 187 Hb78
Yoğuntaş TR 185 Ec75
Yolağazı TR 185 Ea79
Yolağzı TR 186 Fb80
Yolçatı TR 186 Fc80
Yolören TR 186 Ga80
Yolüstü TR 192 Fa87
Yolüstü TR 198 Fb89
Yorazlar TR 193 Hb86
Yörgüç TR 185 Ec78
York GB 16 Fb20
Yortanlı TR 191 Ec83
Youghal IRL 13 Ca26
Youlgreave GB 16 Ed22
Yoxford GB 21 Gb25
Ypäjä FIN 89 Jc38
Ypäjankyla FIN 89 Jc38
Yppäri FIN 81 Jc26
Ypsonas CY 206 Ja98
Ypyä FIN 81 Jd27
Ypykänvaara FIN 75 La22
Yrittäperä FIN 75 Kd23
Yrkje N 92 Ca42
Yrouerre F 30 Hc40
Yrttivaara S 73 Hc18
Ysane S 111 Fc54
Yset N 86 Ea32
Ysjö S 79 Gb29
Ysselsteyn NL 125 Bb39
Yssingeaux F 34 Hd49
Ystad S 110 Fa57
Ystebrød N 92 Ca45
Ystrad-Aeron GB 15 Dd25
Ystradfellte GB 19 Ea27
Ystradowen GB 19 Ea28
Yterturingen S 87 Fc33
Ytre Andersdal N 62 Gd10
Ytre Arna N 84 Ca39
Ytre Dåsvatn N 92 Cd45
Ytre Enebakk N 93 Ea42
Ytre Kårvik N 62 Gc09
Ytre Leirpollen N 64 Jc06
Ytre Ølydna N 92 Cc46
Ytre Oppedal N 84 Ca37
Ytre Ramse N 93 Da45
Ytre Sandvik N 64 Jb06
Ytre Snillfjord N 77 Dd30
Ytre Søndeled N 93 Db45
Ytre Veines N 64 Jb06
Ytterån S 79 Fb30
Ytteräng S 78 Fa29
Ytterås N 78 Eb30
Ytteråträsk S 80 Hb27
Ytterberg S 87 Fc34
Ytterboda S 80 Hc28
Ytterboda S 95 Fc39
Ytterbråtö FIN 81 Jb28
Ytter-Busjö S 80 Ha26
Ytterby S 102 Eb48
Yttergran S 96 Gc42
Ytterhogdal S 87 Fc34
Ytterjärna S 96 Gc44
Ytterjeppo FIN 81 Jb29
Yttermalung S 95 Fb39
Ytterrissjö S 80 Gc28
Yttersby S 96 Ha40
Ytterselö S 96 Gc43
Yttersjön S 80 Ha26
Yttersta S 73 Hc23
Ytterstad N 66 Fd14
Yttertällmo S 80 Gc29
Yttertavle S 80 Hc28
Ytter-Torga N 70 Ed23
Yttervik S 71 Fd23
Yttervik S 80 Hc25
Yttilä FIN 89 Jb37
Yttre Lansjärv S 73 Hd19
Yücebağ TR 205 Ga20
Yukarıdudullu TR 186 Fd78
Yukarıaliçomak TR 193 Hb84
Yukarıballı TR 192 Fc81
Yukarıbey TR 191 Ec83
Yukarıçamozü TR 205 Fd20
Yukarıdereköy TR 198 Fd91
Yukarıdinek TR 193 Ha87
Yukarıdolaylar TR 192 Fc83
Yukarı Dumanlı TR 185 Ec80
Yukarıfındıklı TR 187 Gc78
Yukarıgökdere TR 199 Gd88
Yukarıgüllüce TR 192 Fc85
Yukarıgüney TR 187 Ha79
Yukarıiğdeağacı TR 193 Ha82
Yukarıkadıköy TR 185 Ed75
Yukarıkalabak TR 193 Gc82
Yukarıkaraçay TR 198 Fd88
Yukarıkaraman TR 199 Gc91
Yukarıkılıçlı TR 185 Ed78
Yukarıkızılca TR 191 Ed86
Yukarı Kocayatak TR 199 Gd91
Yukarımusalar TR 192 Fb82
Yukarıotluk TR 193 Gb86
Yukarıpiribeyli TR 193 Hb84
Yukarısapçı TR 191 Eb81
Yukarısoku TR 187 Hb78
Yumaklar TR 199 Gd90
Yumaklı TR 193 Gc83
Yumaklı TR 198 Fb89
Yumrutaı TR 198 Fd89
Yunak TR 193 Hb85
Yuncos E 46 Db65
Yunquera E 60 Cc76
Yunquera de Henares E 46 Dd63
Yunuseli TR 186 Fd80
Yunusemre TR 193 Ha82
Yunuslar TR 192 Ga84
Yunuslar TR 199 Hb88
Yüreğil TR 192 Fb84
Yüreğil TR 198 Fd89
Yüreğil TR 198 Ga88
Yürekli TR 191 Ec82
Yürücekler TR 192 Fc81
Yürük TR 185 Ec78
Yürükkaracaören TR 193 Gd85
Yürükler TR 185 Ed77
Yürükler TR 186 Ga79
Yürükmezarı TR 193 Gb85
Yürükoğlu TR 198 Fc90
Yusufca TR 197 Ed89
Yusufça TR 198 Ga90
Yusufeli TR 205 Ga19
Yuva TR 185 Ec78
Yuva TR 187 Hb78
Yuva TR 198 Ga91
Yuvacık TR 187 Gb79
Yuvacık TR 197 Fa91
Yuvalı TR 186 Fa76
Yuvalı TR 199 Gd88
Yuvalıdere TR 187 Gc78
Yüylük TR 193 Gb84
Yverdon CH 141 Bb54
Yvetot F 23 Ga34
Yvignac F 26 Ec38
Yvoire F 31 Ka44
Yvré-le-Pôlin F 28 Fd40
Yxnerum S 103 Ga47
Yxpila FIN 81 Jb28
Yxsjö S 80 Gc27
Yxskaftkälen S 79 Fd29
Yzeron F 34 Ja47

Z

Zaamslag NL 124 Ab39
Zaanstad NL 116 Ba35
Zăbala RO 176 Eb61
Žabalj SRB 153 Jb60
Zabalocce BY 202 Ec13
Zabar H 146 Jb50
Zabărdo BG 184 Db74
Žabari SRB 174 Bc65
Zabartowo PL 121 Gd34
Zabeltitz D 127 Ed40
Zaberfeld D 134 Cc47
Żabia Wola PL 130 Jb37
Zabica BIH 159 Hc68
Zabierzów PL 138 Ja44
Żabin PL 122 Jc34
Żabin PL 129 Gb39
Žabinka BY 202 Dd14
Żabiny PL 122 Hd33
Ząbki PL 130 Jc36
Ząbkowice Śląskie PL 137 Gc43
Zablaće BIH 152 Gc63
Záblatí CZ 136 Fa48
Zăblava LV 107 Lc48
Žabljak MNE 159 Ja67
Zabłocie PL 128 Fc39
Zabłocie PL 139 Kb46
Zabłudów PL 123 Kb34
Żabno PL 129 Gc37
Żabno PL 131 Kb41
Żabno PL 138 Jc44
Zabok HR 151 Ga58
Zabolotje LV 107 Lc51
Zabór PL 128 Ga38
Zaboreni MD 173 Fd56
Zaborov'e RUS 99 Lc44
Zaborovka RUS 99 Ld45
Zaborów PL 129 Gb40
Zaborowice PL 129 Gb39
Zaborowo PL 122 Ja33
Żabów PL 120 Fc34
Zăbrani RO 174 Bd60
Zabrđe SRB 159 Ja66
Zábřeh CZ 137 Gc45
Zabrežje SRB 153 Jc62
Zăbriceni MD 173 Fa54
Zabrodzie PL 122 Jb31
Zabrodzie PL 130 Jc36
Zabrodzie PL 139 Kb46
Zabrost Wielki PL 122 Jc30
Ząbrowo PL 120 Fd32
Zabrze PL 138 Hc43
Zabrzeż PL 138 Jb46
Zaburalan TR 198 Fd91
Zabzuni AL 182 Ad75
Zacharzyn PL 121 Gc34
Zachenberg D 135 Ec48
Zaclău RO 177 Fb63
Žaclér CZ 128 Ga42
Zadar HR 157 Fd64
Zădăreni RO 170 Bd59
Zaddžje RUS 107 Mb49
Žadeikiai LT 113 Jc55
Žadeikiai LT 113 Jc55
Žadeikiai LT 114 Kd53
Zadonsk RUS 203 Fb12
Zadruga BG 180 Eb68
Zadworzany PL 123 Kc32
Zadzim PL 130 Hc39
Zafarraya E 60 Da75
Zafferana Etnea I 167 Fd85
Zafirovo BG 181 Ec68
Zafra E 51 Bd70
Zafra de Záncara E 53 Ea66
Zafrilla E 47 Ed65
Žaga SLO 150 Ed57
Żagań PL 128 Fd39
Zagăr RO 171 Dc59
Zagarancea MD 173 Fb57
Žagarė LT 114 Ka53
Žagariai LT 114 Kc59
Zagarise I 164 Gc81
Zaglavak SRB 159 Jb64
Zaglav HR 157 Fd65
Zagnańsk PL 130 Jb41
Zagon RO 176 Eb62
Zagorá GR 189 Ca82
Zagorci BG 180 Ea72
Zagorci BG 181 Ec73
Zagor'e RUS 99 Ld42
Zagorje RUS 107 Mb46
Zagorje ob Savi SLO 151 Fc57
Zagórów PL 129 Ha37
Zagorskoe RUS 113 Jc58
Zagórz PL 139 Kb45
Zagórze Śląskie PL 129 Gb42
Zagość PL 138 Jb43
Zagra E 60 Da74
Zagra RO 171 Db56
Zagražden BG 180 Db68
Zagreb HR 151 Ga58
Zagrilla E 60 Da74
Zagrodno PL 128 Ga41
Žagubica SRB 174 Bd66
Zagvozd HR 158 Gd66
Zahara de la Sierra E 59 Cb76
Zahara de los Atunes E 59 Ca78
Zaháro GR 194 Ba87
Zahinos E 51 Bb70
Zahman TR 192 Fd85
Zahna D 127 Ec38
Zahody RUS 99 Ld45
Zahody RUS 107 Ld49
Záhony H 139 Kb49
Zahora E 59 Bd77
Záhoří CZ 136 Fb47
Záhorská Bystrica SK 145 Gc50
Záhorská Ves SK 145 Gc50
Zahrádky CZ 136 Fb43
Zăicana MD 173 Fd57
Zăicani MD 173 Fa55
Zaiceva LV 107 Lc48
Zaidín E 48 Fd61
Žaiginys LT 114 Kb55
Zaim MD 173 Ga59
Zaimčevo BG 181 Ed71
Zaimovo KSV 178 Ba71
Zainsk RUS 203 Ga08
Zaisenhausen D 134 Cc47
Zaistovec HR 152 Gb58
Zajača SRB 153 Ja63
Zajač'e RUS 203 Fa13
Zajączek PL 128 Fc39
Zajan'e RUS 99 Ld43
Zajas MK 182 Ba74
Zajcevo RUS 107 Ma47
Zaječar SRB 179 Ca67
Zaječov CZ 136 Fa45
Zajęczniki PL 131 Ka36
Zajezierze PL 120 Ga33
Zajezierze PL 131 Jd39
Zajk H 145 Gc56
Zakaki CY 206 Ja98
Zákamenné SK 138 Hd46
Zákány H 152 Gc57
Zákányszék H 153 Jb57
Žakarovce SK 138 Jc48
Zákas GR 182 Ba79
Zaķi LV 106 La48
Zákinthos GR 188 Ac86
Zakl SLO 151 Ga57
Zakliczyn PL 138 Jc45
Zaklików PL 131 Ka41
Zaklopača BIH 159 Hd64
Zakobjakino RUS 203 Fa08
Zakomo BIH 159 Hd65
Zakopane PL 138 Ja47
Zakroczym PL 130 Jb36
Zákros GR 201 Dd96
Zakrzew PL 130 Jc39
Zakrzew PL 131 Kb41
Zakrzewo PL 121 Gc33
Zakrzewo PL 121 Hb35
Zakrzewo PL 129 Gc37
Zakrzówek Osada PL 131 Ka41
Zákupy CZ 128 Fc42
Zalaapáti H 145 Gd55
Zalabaska H 145 Gc56
Zalaegerszeg H 145 Gc55
Zalęnieki LV 106 Ka52
Zalahaláp H 145 Gd55
Zalahtov'e RUS 99 Lc44
Zalaistvánd H 145 Gc55
Zalakaros H 145 Gd56
Zalakomár H 145 Gd56
Zalakoppány H 145 Gd55
Zalalövő H 145 Gc55
Zalamea de la Serena E 51 Cb70
Zalamea la Real E 59 Bc73
Zalamillas E 37 Cc58
Zalas PL 122 Jc33
Zalasowa PL 138 Jc44
Zalaszabar H 145 Gd56
Zalaszántó H 145 Gd55
Zalaszentbalázs H 145 Gc56
Zalaszentgrót H 145 Gd55
Zalaszentgyörgy H 145 Gc55
Zalatárnok H 145 Gc56
Zalău RO 171 Cd56
Zalavár H 145 Gd56
Zalavas LT 115 Lb56
Załazy PL 131 Jd39
Zalec PL 122 Jc31
Žalec SLO 151 Fd57
Załęcze PL 129 Gc39
Zalegošč' RUS 203 Fa12

Żalesa – Żywocice

Žalesa LT 114 La57
Zales'e RUS 107 Lc47
Zales'e RUS 113 Jc58
Zalesie PL 121 Gc33
Zalesie PL 121 Gd35
Zalesie PL 130 Jb37
Zalesie PL 131 Kc37
Zalesie PL 139 Kc43
Zalesina HR 151 Fc60
Zalesje LV 107 Ma51
Zaleskie PL 121 Gb30
Zaleszany PL 131 Ka42
Zalewo PL 122 Hc31
Załęże PL 122 Ja33
Žalgiriai LT 113 Jb56
Zalha RO 171 Da56
Žalioji LT 114 Ka58
Zališčyky UA 204 Ea16
Zaliszewo PL 120 Fd34
Zalivino RUS 113 Jb57
Zalivino RUS 113 Jb58
Zalivnoe RUS 113 Ja58
Zalizci UA 204 Ea15
Zall-Dardhë AL 178 Ad73
Zaļmežnieki LV 107 Lb50
Žalno PL 121 Gd32
Zalogovac SRB 178 Bc67
Załom PL 128 Ga36
Žalpiai LT 114 Ka56
Zaltbommel NL 124 Ba37
Záltsa GR 189 Bd85
Zaluč'e RUS 202 Eb09
Załuski PL 130 Ja36
Zalustež'e RUS 99 Ma42
Zalužje BIH 159 Ja64
Zalužnica HR 151 Fd62
Zalve LV 106 Kd52
Zam RO 174 Cb60
Zamárdi H 145 Ha55
Zamarte PL 121 Gd33
Žamberk CZ 137 Gb44
Zambra E 60 Da74
Zambrana E 38 Ea57
Zâmbreasca RO 175 Dc66
Zambrów PL 123 Jd34
Zambski-Kościelne PL 122 Jc35
Zambujeira do Mar P 58 Ab72
Zamch PL 139 Kc43
Zamęcin PL 120 Fd34
Zamfirovo BG 179 Cc69
Zamłynie PL 130 Hc42
Zamogil'e RUS 99 Lc44
Zámoly H 145 Hb53
Zamora E 45 Cb60
Zamość PL 121 Gd34
Zamość PL 122 Jc34
Zamość PL 131 Kc41
Zamoš'e RUS 99 Lc43
Zamostea RO 172 Eb55
Zámutov SK 139 Jd48
Zana LV 105 Jc52
Zanat H 145 Gc54
Žandov CZ 128 Fb42
Zandvoort NL 116 Ad35
Zănești RO 172 Ec58
Zangliveri GR 183 Cb78
Zangora E 39 Fa57
Zaniemyśl PL 129 Gc37
Zánka H 145 Ha55
Zante LV 105 Jd51
Zaokskij RUS 203 Fa11
Zaorejas E 47 Eb63
Zaozen'e RUS 99 Ma45
Zaozer'e RUS 99 Mb42
Zaoz'ernoje RUS 113 Jc59
Zapadnaja Dvina RUS 202 Ec10
Zapałow PL 139 Kc43
Zapesen'e RUS 99 Mb44
Zapfendorf D 134 Dc44
Zapljus'e RUS 99 Mb44
Zápodeni RO 173 Fa59
Zapole PL 129 Hb39
Zapol'e RUS 99 Ld41
Zapol'e RUS 99 Ma41
Zapol'e RUS 99 Mb44
Zaporižžja UA 205 Fa15
Zaporožskoe RUS 202 Ea08
Zapovednoe RUS 113 Jb57
Zappendorf D 127 Ea39
Zapponeta I 162 Gb73
Zaprešić HR 151 Ga58
Zaprudnja RUS 202 Ed10
Zapyškis LV 114 Kb57
Žár CZ 136 Fc49
Zara TR 205 Fd20
Zaraevo BG 180 Eb69
Zaragoza E 47 Fa61
Zarajsk RUS 203 Fa11
Zărand RO 170 Ca58
Zarańsko PL 120 Ga33
Zarasai LT 115 Lb54
Zaratán E 46 Cd60
Zarautz E 39 Ec55
Zarbince KSV 178 Bc71
Zar'binka RUS 99 Ma44
Zarcilla de Ramos E 61 Ec73
Żarczyn PL 120 Fb34
Zaręby PL 122 Jb33
Zaręby Kościelne PL 123 Jd35
Zaręby-Warchoły PL 123 Ka34
Zareč'e RUS 113 Jb58
Zareč'e RUS 113 Jb59
Zarečnoe RUS 113 Jd57
Žarėnai LT 113 Jc54
Žarėnai LT 114 Ka53
Zarga de Alange E 51 Bd69
Žarki PL 128 Fc39
Žarki PL 130 Hd42
Zárko GR 189 Bc81
Žarkovo RUS 107 Mb51
Zărnești RO 176 Dd62
Zărnești RO 176 Ec63
Zărnevo BG 181 Ed69
Žarnovica SK 138 Hc49
Żarnów PL 130 Ja40
Żarnowiec PL 112 Ha58
Żarnowiec PL 138 Ja43
Żarnowo PL 120 Fc32
Zarojeni MD 173 Fb55
Zarós GR 200 Da96
Žarošice CZ 137 Gc48
Zaroúhla GR 189 Bc86
Žarovnica HR 152 Gb57
Żarów PL 129 Gb41
Zarrentin D 119 Dd33
Zarskoe Selo RUS 202 Eb08
Zarszyn PL 139 Ka45
Zaruč'e RUS 99 Ld43
Zaručejnoe RUS 113 Jb58
Žary PL 128 Fd39
Zarza Capilla (Nueva) E 52 Cc69
Zarza de Granadilla E 45 Ca64
Zarza de Tajo E 53 Dd66
Zarzadilla de Totana E 61 Ec73
Zarza la Mayor E 45 Bc65
Zarzecze PL 131 Jd40
Zarzecze PL 131 Ka42
Zarzecze PL 139 Kb44
Zarzosa E 47 Eb59
Zarzuela E 47 Eb65
Zarzuela del Monte E 46 Da63
Żarzyn PL 128 Fd37
Zás E 36 Ad54
Zasa LV 107 Lb52
Zasavica SRB 153 Ja61
Zaseki RUS 107 Ma46
Zasieki PL 128 Fc39
Zasip SLO 151 Fa57
Zasitino RUS 107 Ma51
Zaškiv UA 204 Ec15
Žasliai LT 114 Kd57
Zásmuky CZ 136 Fc45
Zasos'e RUS 99 Ld42
Zasów PL 139 Jd44
Zaspy Małe PL 120 Ga31
Zastávka CZ 137 Gb47
Zastinca MD 173 Fc54
Zastražišće HR 158 Gc67
Zaszków PL 123 Ka35
Žatec CZ 136 Fa44
Zatom PL 120 Ga34
Zaton HR 157 Ga65
Zaton MNE 159 Jb67
Zatonie PL 128 Fd38
Zator PL 138 Hd44
Zatory PL 122 Jc35
Zătreni RO 175 Da64
Zatwarnica PL 139 Kb46
Zaube LV 106 Kd50
Zauchwitz D 127 Ed37
Zau de Câmpie RO 171 Db58
Zavala BIH 158 Hb68
Zavala HR 158 Gc67
Zavalatica HR 158 Gd68
Zavalinë AL 182 Ac76
Zavalje BIH 151 Ga62
Zavattarello I 149 Cc61
Zavelstein, Bad Teinach- D 134 Cc48
Zavet BG 181 Ec68
Zavetvoe RUS 205 Ga15
Zavidov CZ 136 Fa44
Zavidovići BIH 152 Hb63
Zavitne UA 205 Fb17
Zavlaka SRB 153 Ja63
Zăvoaia RO 177 Fa64
Zăvoi RO 174 Cb62
Zavoj MK 182 Ba75
Zavoj SRB 179 Cb69
Zavolž'e RUS 203 Fb09
Zawada PL 121 Gb34
Zawada PL 128 Fd38
Zawada PL 129 Gd40
Zawada PL 130 Hd41
Zawada PL 130 Ja40
Zawada PL 131 Kc41
Zawady PL 123 Ka33
Zawady PL 123 Kb33
Zawady PL 130 Ja38
Zawady PL 131 Kd42
Zawadzkie PL 129 Hb42
Zawda PL 122 Hc32
Zawichost PL 131 Jd41
Zawidów PL 128 Fc41
Zawidz Kościelny PL 122 Hd35
Zawiercie PL 138 Hd43
Zawierki PL 123 Kb33
Zawoja PL 138 Hd45
Zawonia PL 129 Gc40
Zazid SLO 151 Fa59
Zázrivá SK 138 Hd47
Zazuela del Pinar E 46 Db61
Zbaraž UA 204 Ea15
Zbarzewo PL 129 Gb38
Zbąszyń PL 128 Ga37
Zbąszynek PL 128 Ga37
Zbečno CZ 136 Fa44
Zbelovo SLO 151 Fd57
Zberki PL 129 Gd37
Zbiczno PL 122 Hc33
Zbiersk PL 129 Ha38
Zbiroh CZ 136 Fa45
Zbiewo PL 121 Ha31
Zboj SK 139 Kb47
Zbójno PL 122 Hc34
Zbojštica SRB 159 Jb65
Zboriv UA 204 Ea15
Zborov SK 139 Jd46
Zborowice PL 138 Jc45
Zborowskie PL 129 Hb42
Zbože PL 121 Gd33
Zbraslavice CZ 136 Fd45
Zbrosławice PL 138 Hc43
Zbrudzewo PL 129 Gc37
Zbůch CZ 135 Ed46
Zbucznka PL 131 Ka37
Zbýšov CZ 136 Fd45
Zbýšov CZ 137 Gb47
Žďár CZ 136 Fc43
Ždala HR 152 Gd57
Ždaňa SK 139 Jd49
Ždánice CZ 137 Gc48
Žďár CZ 135 Ed44
Ždár CZ 135 Ed47
Žďárec CZ 137 Gb47
Žďár nad Sázavou CZ 136 Ga46
Zdbice PL 121 Gb33
Zdenci HR 152 Hb59
Zdenska vas SLO 151 Fc58
Ždiar SK 138 Jb47
Zdice CZ 136 Fa45
Zdíkov CZ 136 Fa48
Ždírec nad Doubravou CZ 136 Ga46
Zdobnice CZ 137 Gb44
Zdolbuniv UA 204 Ea15
Zdounky CZ 137 Gd47
Zdrajsh AL 182 Ac75
Ždralovac BIH 158 Gc65
Zdravec BG 180 Eb70
Zdravec BG 181 Fa71
Ždrelo SRB 174 Bc65
Zdroisko PL 120 Fd35
Zdunje MK 178 Bb73
Zduńska Wola PL 130 Hc39
Zduny PL 129 Gd39
Zduny PL 130 Hd37
Zdżary PL 129 Ha37
Zdżary PL 130 Jb39
Zdziebórz PL 122 Jc35
Zdzieszowice PL 137 Ha43
Zdziłowice PL 131 Kb41
Zębowice PL 129 Hb42
Żebrak PL 131 Jd37
Zebreira P 45 Bc65
Zebrene LV 105 Jd52
Žebrokai LT 113 Jb53
Żebry-Wierzchlas PL 122 Jc34
Zebrzydowa PL 128 Fd40
Zebrzydowice PL 137 Hb45
Zechlin D 119 Ec34
Zechlinerhütte D 119 Ed34
Zeddam NL 125 Bc37
Zedelgem B 21 Ha29
Zedenac HR 151 Fd60
Zederhaus A 143 Ed54
Zedricy RUS 107 Mb49
Zeebrugge B 21 Ga28
Zeeland NL 125 Bb38
Zeesen D 128 Fa37
Zeewolde NL 116 Bb36
Zegama E 39 Eb56
Żegar SLO 151 Fd57
Zegiestów PL 123 Kb30
Zegerscappel F 21 Gd30
Żegiestów PL 138 Jc46
Żeglarci BG 181 Ed69
Żegocina PL 138 Jb45
Żegoty PL 122 Ja31
Żegra KSV 178 Bc72
Zegrze PL 130 Jb36
Zegrze Pomorskie PL 120 Ga31
Zegrzynek PL 130 Jb36
Zehdenick D 119 Ed35
Zehlendorf D 119 Ed35
Zehren, Diera- D 127 Ed41
Zeil D 134 Dc44
Zeilarn D 143 Ec50
Žeimelis LT 114 Kb53
Žeimiai LT 114 Ka54
Žeimiai LT 114 Kc56
Zeist NL 116 Ba36
Zeithain D 127 Ed40
Zeitlarn D 135 Eb48
Zeitlofs D 134 Da43
Zeitz D 127 Eb41
Žejane HR 151 Fb60
Zekeriyaköy TR 186 Fd77
Zekeriyaköy TR 187 Gd78
Żelazków PL 129 Ha38
Żelazna PL 121 Gd29
Żelazna Góra PL 122 Hd30
Żelazno PL 137 Gc43
Żelazowa Wola PL 130 Ja37
Żelechlinek PL 130 Ja39
Żelechów PL 131 Jd38
Zelencovo RUS 113 Jc59
Zelenčukskaja RUS 205 Fd17
Zeleni Jadar BIH 159 Ja64
Zelenik SRB 174 Bd65
Zelenika MNE 159 Hc69
Zelenikovo BG 180 Dc72
Zelenivka UA 205 Fb16
Zelenodol'sk RUS 203 Fd09
Zelenodol's'k UA 204 Ed16
Zelenograd RUS 202 Ed10
Zelenogradsk RUS 113 Ja58
Zelenokumsk RUS 205 Ga16
Želenov CZ 136 Fa47
Zelenovo RUS 113 Jb58
Želetava CZ 136 Ga47
Železan BG 185 Ea76
Železino BG 185 Ea76
Železná Ruda CZ 135 Ed47
Železné SK 138 Hd48
Železnica BG 179 Cc72
Železnik BG 181 Ec72
Železnik SRB 153 Jc62
Železniki SLO 151 Fb57
Železnodorožnyj RUS 122 Jb30
Železnogorsk RUS 202 Ed13
Železný Brod CZ 128 Fd42
Zelgauska LV 107 Lb50
Zelhem NL 125 Bc37
Żelichów PL 138 Jc43
Želiezovce SK 146 Hc51
Želinja BIH 152 Hb62
Zélio GR 189 Ca84
Želisławice PL 130 Ja42
Żeliszew PL 131 Jd37
Želizna PL 131 Kb38
Žeļjazkovo BG 185 Ec74
Želiuša BIH 158 Hb66
Želju Vojoda BG 180 Eb72
Zelki PL 123 Jd31
Żelkowo PL 121 Gc29
Zell A 144 Fa50
Zell D 133 Ca49
Zell D 134 Da45
Zell D 135 Eb47
Zell D 141 Ca51
Zella-Mehlis D 126 Dc42
Zell am Moos A 143 Ed52
Zell am See A 143 Ec53
Zell am Ziller A 143 Ea54
Zellerfeld, Clausthal- D 126 Dc38
Zellingen D 134 Da45
Zell (Mosel) D 133 Bd44
Zell-Pfarre A 144 Fb56
Želnava CZ 136 Fa49
Želovce SK 146 Hd51
Zelovo HR 158 Gc65
Żelów PL 130 Hc39
Želsva LV 114 Kb59
Želtiņi LV 107 Lb48
Zeltweg A 144 Fc54
Želva LT 114 La56
Žemaičių Kalvarija LT 113 Jc54
Žemaičių Naumiestis LT 113 Jc56
Žemaitkiemis LT 114 Kd56
Žemaitkiemis LV 123 Kb30
Žemalė LT 113 Jc53
Žemberovce SK 146 Hc50
Zemblak AL 182 Ba77
Zembry PL 131 Ka37
Zembrze PL 122 Hd33
Zembrzyce PL 138 Hd45
Zemen BG 179 Cb72
Zemeș RO 172 Ec59
Zemgale LV 115 Lc54
Zemianska Oľča SK 145 Ha52
Zemite LV 105 Jd51
Zemitz D 120 Fa31
Zemmer D 133 Bc44
Zemné SK 145 Ha51
Zemplénagárd H 139 Kb49
Zemplínska Teplica SK 139 Jd48
Zemsko PL 128 Fd36
Zemun SRB 153 Jc61
Zenica BIH 158 Hb64
Zennor GB 18 Da32
Zentene LV 105 Jd50
Zenting D 135 Ed49
Zepa BIH 159 Hd64
Žepče BIH 152 Hb63
Zepernick D 128 Fa36
Žeravna BG 180 Eb71
Zerbisia GR 194 Bb88
Zerbst D 127 Eb38
Żerczyce PL 123 Kb35
Zerdevka RUS 203 Fc12
Zerenikovo MK 178 Bc73
Zerf D 133 Bc45
Zeri I 149 Cd63
Zerind RO 170 Bd58
Żerków PL 129 Gd38
Żerkowice PL 128 Fd41
Zermatt CH 148 Bd57
Zernez CH 142 Da55
Zernien D 119 Dd34
Žerniki PL 129 Gd38
Zernograd RUS 205 Fc15
Zernsdorf D 128 Fa37
Žeronys LT 114 Kd58
Zerpenschleuse D 120 Fa35
Zerqan AL 182 Ad74
Zervynos LT 123 Kd30
Zestoa E 39 Eb55
Žetale SLO 151 Ga57
Zetea RO 172 Dd59
Zetel D 118 Cc33
Zetjovo BG 180 Dc73
Zeulenroda D 127 Eb42
Zeuthen D 128 Fa37
Zeven D 118 Da33
Zevenaar NL 125 Bc37
Zevenbergen NL 124 Ad38
Zevgolatió GR 188 Bd86
Zevio I 149 Dc60
Zevloki RUS 107 Mb50
Zeybekçayırı TR 191 Ec81
Zeyköyü TR 193 Ha82
Zeytin TR 197 Fa89
Zeytinbağı TR 186 Fc80
Zeytindağ TR 191 Ec84
Zeytineli TR 191 Ea86
Zeytinköy TR 191 Ec87
Zeytinli TR 185 Dd80
Zeytinli TR 191 Ea81
Zeytinli TR 191 Ec82
Zeževo HR 157 Ga66
Zgalevo BG 180 Db69
Zgărdești MD 173 Fb56
Zgierz PL 130 Hc38
Zgłobień PL 139 Ka44
Zgniłoche PL 122 Ja32
Zgon PL 122 Jc32
Zgornja Kungota SLO 144 Ga56
Zgornje Jezersko SLO 151 Fb57
Zgórsko PL 138 Jc43
Zgorzelec PL 128 Fc41
Zgozhd AL 182 Ad75
Zgurița MD 173 Fb54
Zhukë AL 182 Aa77
Žiar nad Hronom SK 138 Hc49
Zibello I 149 Da61
Žibikai LT 113 Jd53
Žiča SRB 178 Ba67
Zicavo F 154 Cb71
Zichow D 120 Fb34
Zicisht AL 182 Ba77
Zidani Most SLO 151 Fd58
Zidarovo BG 181 Ed73
Ziddorf D 119 Ec32
Židikai LT 113 Jc53
Židina LV 115 Lc53
Židlochovice CZ 137 Gc48
Ziduri RO 176 Ed63
Ziębice PL 137 Gc43
Zięby PL 122 Ja30
Ziegenhagen D 126 Da40
Ziegenrück D 127 Ea42
Ziegra-Knobelsdorf D 127 Ed41
Ziēkas LV 105 Jb50
Zielenice PL 129 Gc42
Zieleniec PL 137 Gb43
Zieleniewo PL 120 Fd34
Zieleniewo PL 120 Fd31
Zielin PL 121 Gc30
Zielitz D 127 Ea37
Zielona PL 122 Hd34
Zielona Góra PL 128 Fd38
Zielonka PL 130 Jc36
Zieluń PL 122 Hd34
Ziemeris LV 107 Lc48
Ziemetshausen D 142 Db50
Ziemiełowice PL 129 Ha41
Ziemupe LV 105 Ja52
Ziērbena E 38 Ea55
Zierenberg D 126 Da40
Zierikzee NL 124 Ac37
Ziersdorf A 136 Ga49
Zierzow D 119 Ea34
Ziesar D 127 Eb37
Ziethen D 120 Fa32
Zieuwent NL 125 Bd37
Žiežmariai LT 114 Kd57
Zigós GR 184 Da77
Žiguri LV 107 Ld48
Žihle CZ 135 Ed44
Žilaiskalns LV 106 Kd48
Zilāni LV 106 La51
Zile LV 106 La47
Zile TR 205 Fc20
Žiliai LT 113 Jd54
Žilina SK 138 Hc47
Žilinai LT 114 Kd59
Žilino RUS 113 Jc58
Zillis CH 142 Cd55
Zilly D 127 Dd38
Zilshausen D 133 Ca43
Ziltendorf D 128 Fc37
Zilupe LV 107 Ma51
Zimandu-Nou RO 170 Bd59
Zimány H 145 Ha56
Zimari RUS 107 Mb49
Zimbor RO 171 Cd57
Zimbreni MD 173 Fd58
Zimlje = Rujišta BIH 158 Hb66
Zimmern D 141 Cb50
Zimna Brzeźnica PL 128 Ga39
Zimna Woda PL 122 Ja33
Zimnica BG 180 Eb72
Zimnicea RO 180 Dd68
Zimnice Wielkie PL 137 Ha43
Zimovniki RUS 205 Fd15
Zinal CH 148 Bd57
Zinasco Vecchio I 148 Cb60
Žindaičiai LT 114 Ka57
Zingst D 119 Ec30
Zinkgruvan S 95 Fc45
Zin'kiv UA 202 Ed14
Žinkovy CZ 135 Ed46
Zinnowitz D 120 Fa31
Žiopeliai LT 113 Jd53
Zipári GR 197 Ec91
Ziras LV 105 Jb50
Zirc H 145 Ha54
Zirchow D 120 Fb32
Žiri SLO 151 Fa58
Žirje HR 157 Ga66
Zirl A 143 Dd53
Zirndorf D 134 Dc46
Zirņi LV 105 Jc52
Zirnovsk RUS 203 Fd12
Ziros GR 201 Dd96
Žirovica MK 182 Ad74
Žirovnica SLO 151 Fb57
Žirovnice CZ 136 Fd47
Zistersdorf A 137 Gc49
Žitište SRB 153 Jc59
Žitište SRB 174 Bb61
Žitkovac SRB 178 Bd68
Žitnica BG 180 Db72
Žitnica BG 181 Ed71
Žitni Potok SRB 178 Bc69
Žitomislići BIH 158 Hb67
Žitoradja SRB 178 Bd69
Žitosvjat BG 181 Ec73
Zitsa GR 182 Ad80
Zittau D 128 Fc42
Žiūronys LT 114 Kc59
Živaja HR 152 Gc60
Živinice BIH 153 Hc63
Živkovo BG 179 Cd72
Živojno MK 183 Bb76
Ziyamet TR 187 Gc77
Złaków Kościelny PL 130 Hd37
Zlarin HR 157 Ga66
Zlata SRB 178 Bc69
Zlatá Baňa SK 139 Jd47
Zlatá Idka SK 138 Jc48
Zlatar BG 181 Ec70
Zlatar HR 152 Gb58
Zlatar Bistrica HR 152 Gb58
Zlatarevo BG 183 Cb75
Zlatari SRB 178 Bb68
Zlatarica BG 180 Ea71
Zlaté Hory CZ 137 Gd44
Zlaté Klasy SK 145 Gd51
Zlaté Moravce SK 145 Hb50
Zlatica BG 179 Da71
Zlatini BG 185 Eb74
Zlati Vojvoda BG 180 Ea72
Zlatna RO 175 Cd60
Zlatna Greda HR 153 Hd59
Zlatna Ostrove SK 145 Ha52
Zlatna Panega BG 179 Da70
Zlatni Pjasăci BG 181 Fb70
Zlatograd BG 184 Dc76
Zlatoklas BG 181 Ed68
Zlatokop SRB 178 Bd71
Zlatoličje SLO 144 Ga56
Zlatopole BG 185 Dd74
Zlatovo SRB 174 Bc66
Žlebič SLO 151 Fc59
Žlibinai LT 113 Jc54
Zliechov SK 137 Hb48
Zlín CZ 137 Ha47
Zliv CZ 136 Fb48
Žljebovi BIH 159 Hd64
Złobek PL 139 Kb46
Žlobin BY 202 Eb13
Zlobin HR 151 Fc60
Złochowice PL 130 Hc41
Złocieniec PL 120 Ga33
Złoczew PL 129 Hb40
Zlogonje HR 152 Gb57
Zlogoš BG 179 Ca72
Zlosela BIH 158 Gd64
Zlostup MNE 159 Hd68
Zlot SRB 174 Bd66
Złotniki Kujawskie PL 121 Ha35
Złotoria PL 121 Hb34
Złotoryja PL 128 Ga41
Złotów PL 121 Gc33
Złotowo PL 122 Hd33
Złotowo PL 129 Hb36
Złoty Stok PL 137 Gc43
Žlunice CZ 136 Fd44
Žlutice CZ 135 Ed44
Zmajevac BIH 152 Gb61
Zmajevac HR 153 Hc58
Zmajevo SRB 153 Ja59
Žman HR 157 Fd65
Žmerynka UA 204 Eb15
Zmievka RUS 203 Fa12
Żmigród PL 129 Gc40
Żmigródek PL 129 Gc40
Žmijiv UA 203 Fa14
Zminica MNE 159 Ja67
Žminj HR 151 Fa61
Znamenka RUS 99 Ld45
Znamenosec BG 180 Ea73
Znamensk RUS 113 Jb59
Znamenskoe RUS 202 Ed12
Znam'janka UA 204 Ed15
Żnin PL 121 Gd35
Znojmo CZ 136 Ga48
Zoagli I 149 Cc63
Zocca I 149 Dc63
Žocene LV 105 Jd49
Zodzina BY 202 Eb12
Zoetermeer NL 116 Ad36
Zofingen CH 141 Ca53
Zogaj AL 163 Ja71
Žogi LV 107 Lc50
Zogno I 149 Cd58
Żogotas LV 107 Lc51
Žogotas LV 107 Ld50
Zohor SK 145 Gc50
Zoio P 45 Bd59
Zoldo Alto I 143 Ea56
Zoljan HR 152 Hb60
Żółkiewka PL 131 Kb41
Zollhaus CH 141 Bc55
Zolling D 143 Ea50
Zollino I 163 Hc77
Zoločiv UA 204 Ea15
Zolote UA 203 Fb14
Zolotievca MD 173 Fd59
Zolotonoša UA 204 Ed15
Żółwino PL 120 Ga34
Żołynia PL 139 Ka43
Zomba H 146 Hc56
Zonguldak TR 187 Hb76
Zonhoven B 124 Ba40
Zoni GR 185 Ea76
Zóni GR 194 Bb88
Zonianá GR 200 Cd95
Zonza F 154 Cb71
Zórawina PL 129 Gc41
Zörbig D 127 Eb39
Zorge D 126 Dc39
Zorile MD 173 Fd56
Zorita E 51 Cb68
Zorita de la Loma E 37 Cd58
Zorita de los Canes E 47 Ea65
Zorlar TR 198 Fd92
Zorleni RO 177 Fa60
Zorlenţu Mare RO 174 Ca62
Zorneding D 143 Ea51
Zornica BG 181 Ec73
Zory PL 137 Hb44
Zosna LV 107 Ld52
Zossen D 127 Ed37
Zoutkamp NL 117 Bd33
Zoutleeuw B 124 Ba41
Zoúzouli GR 182 Ba78
Zovka RUS 99 Ma44
Žovkva UA 204 Dd15
Žovti Vody UA 204 Ed15
Žovtneve UA 202 Ed14
Zreče SLO 151 Fd57
Zrenjanin SRB 153 Jc60
Zrenjanin SRB 174 Bb61
Zrin HR 152 Gb61
Zrinski Topolovac HR 152 Gc58
Zrmanja-Vrelo HR 158 Gb64
Zrnovci MK 183 Ca74
Žrnovnica HR 158 Gc66
Zruč nad Sázavou CZ 136 Fd45
Zruč-Senec CZ 135 Ed45
Zrze KSV 178 Ba71
Zrze MK 183 Bb74
Zsadány H 147 Ka54
Zsámbék H 146 Hc53
Zsámbok H 146 Ja52
Zsana H 146 Ja56
Zschadraß D 127 Ec41
Zscherben D 127 Ea40
Zschocken D 127 Ec42
Zschopau D 127 Ed42
Zschoppach D 127 Ec41
Zschornewitz D 127 Eb39
Zschortau D 127 Eb40
Zsedeny H 145 Gc53
Zsurk H 139 Kb49
Zuazo de Cuartango E 38 Ea56
Zubcov RUS 202 Ec10
Zuberec SK 138 Hd47
Zubia E 60 Db75
Zubialde E 38 Ea55
Zubići BIH 158 Ha64
Zubieta E 39 Ec56
Zubiškes LT 114 Kd57
Zubova Poljana RUS 203 Fb11
Zubowo PL 123 Kb34
Zubrești MD 173 Fc57
Żubrówka PL 123 Kb30
Zubrzyca Górna PL 138 Hd46
Žuč SRB 178 Bb69
Zucaina E 54 Fb65
Zudaire E 39 Ec57
Zudar D 119 Ed30
Zudibiarte E 38 Ea55
Zuera E 48 Fb60
Zufia E 39 Ec57
Zufre E 59 Bd72
Zug CH 141 Cb53
Zuheros E 60 Da73
Zuid-Beijerland NL 124 Ac37
Zuidhorn NL 117 Bd33
Zuidlaren NL 117 Bd33
Zuidwolde NL 117 Bd35
Zújar E 51 Cb70
Zújar E 61 Ed74
Zuji LV 107 Lc51
Zujkovo RUS 107 Mb50
Žukai LT 113 Jd57
Žukovka RUS 202 Ed12
Żuków PL 131 Kc38
Żukowice PL 128 Ga39
Żukowo PL 121 Ha30
Žuljana HR 158 Ha68
Žulová CZ 137 Gc44
Zülpich D 125 Bc41
Zumaia E 39 Eb55
Zumarraga E 39 Eb56
Zundert NL 124 Ad38
Zundi LV 107 Ld52
Zuoz CH 142 Da56
Zupa HR 158 Gd67
Županja HR 153 Hc61
Župelevec SLO 151 Ga58
Žur KSV 178 Ba72
Zūras LV 105 Jb50
Żurawica PL 139 Kb44
Zurbarán E 51 Cb68
Zurgena E 61 Eb74
Zürich CH 141 Cb53
Zurich NL 116 Bb33
Zuriza E 39 Fb57
Zurndorf A 145 Gc51
Żurobice PL 123 Kb35
Żuromin PL 122 Hd34
Żurominek PL 122 Ja34
Zurrieq M 166 Eb88
Zürs A 142 Da54
Zurzach CH 141 Cb52
Zusmarshausen D 142 Db50
Züssow D 120 Fa31
Žuta Lokva HR 151 Fd61
Zutphen NL 117 Bc36
Zuydcoote F 21 Gd29
Zuzela PL 123 Jd35
Žužemberk SLO 151 Fc58
Zvăničevo BG 179 Da73
Zvārtava LV 107 Lb48
Zvečan KSV 178 Ba70
Zvegor MK 179 Cb73
Zvenejnieciems LV 106 Kc49
Zvenigorod RUS 202 Ed10
Zvenigovo RUS 203 Fd09
Zvenimir BG 181 Ec68
Zvenyhorodka UA 204 Ec15
Zverino BG 179 Cd70
Zvezd SRB 153 Jb62
Zvezdec BG 185 Ed74
Zvezdel BG 185 Dd75
Zvidziena LV 107 Lc50
Žvingiai LT 113 Jc56
Žvirče SLO 151 Fc59
Žvirgždaičiai LT 114 Ka58
Zvirgzde LV 106 Kc51
Žvirgždėnai LT 114 Kd59
Zvirinë AL 182 Ad76
Zvole CZ 137 Gb46
Zvole CZ 137 Gc45
Zvolen SK 138 Hd49
Zvollenská Slatina SK 138 Hd49
Zvonce SRB 179 Ca70
Zvony RUS 107 Mb50
Zvoriștea RO 172 Ec55
Zvornik BIH 153 Hd63
Zwaagwesteinde NL 117 Bc33
Zwanenburg NL 116 Ba35
Zwardoń PL 138 Hc46
Zwaring A 144 Fd55
Zwartemeer NL 117 Ca35
Zwartsluis NL 117 Bc35
Zweeloo NL 117 Bd34
Zweibrücken D 133 Bd46
Zweiflingen D 134 Cd47
Zweisimmen CH 141 Bc55
Zwenkau D 127 Eb40
Zwethau D 127 Ed39
Zwettl A 136 Fd49
Zwettl an der Rodl A 144 Fb50
Zwiastowice PL 137 Ha43
Zwickau D 127 Ec42
Zwiefalten D 142 Cd50
Zwiernik PL 138 Jc44
Zwierzno PL 122 Hc31
Zwierzyn PL 120 Fd35
Zwierzyniec PL 131 Kc42
Zwiesel D 135 Ed48
Zwieselstein A 142 Dc55
Zwillbrock D 125 Bd37
Zwingenberg D 134 Cc45
Zwischenwasser I 143 Ea55
Zwochau D 127 Eb40
Zwoleń PL 131 Jd39
Zwolle NL 117 Bc35
Zwönitz D 127 Ec42
Żychlin PL 130 Hd37
Żydačiv UA 204 Ea15
Żydów PL 129 Ha39
Żydowo PL 121 Gb31
Żydowo PL 129 Gd36
Žygaičiai LT 113 Jc56
Zygi CY 206 Jb98
Zygmantiškė LV 114 Kb57
Zypliai LT 114 Ka57
Żyraków PL 139 Jd44
Żyrardów PL 130 Ja37
Żyrowa PL 137 Ha43
Żyrzyn PL 131 Ka39
Žytkavičy BY 202 Eb13
Żytkiejmy PL 123 Ka29
Żytniów PL 129 Hb41
Żytno PL 130 Hd41
Žytomyr UA 204 Eb15
Żywiec PL 138 Hd45
Żywocice PL 137 Ha43

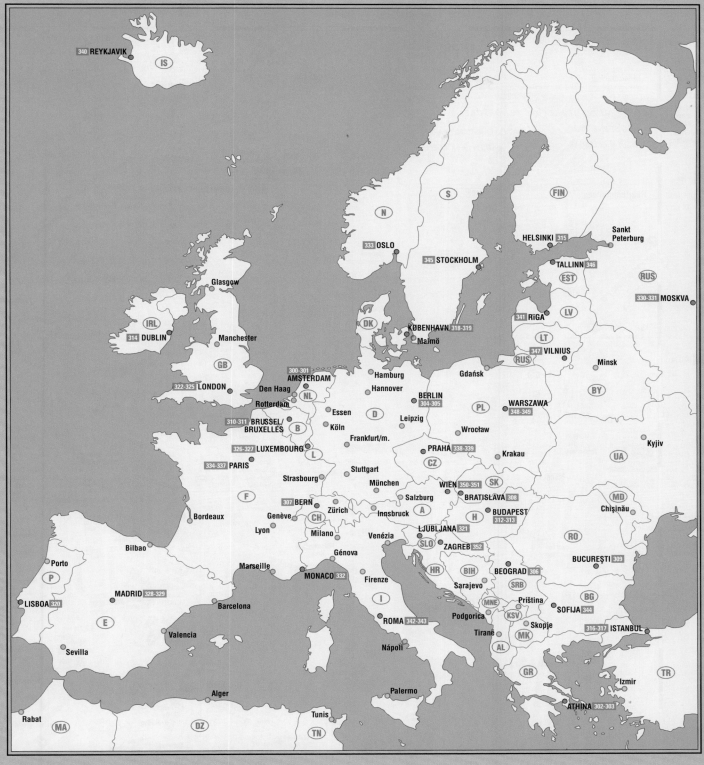

340 REYKJAVIK
IS

N
S
FIN

333 OSLO
345 STOCKHOLM

HELSINKI 315
Sankt Peterburg

TALLINN 346
EST
RUS
330-331 MOSKVA

341 RĪGA
LV

KØBENHAVN 318-319
DK
Malmö

LT
347 VILNIUS
RUS
Minsk
BY

Glasgow

IRL
314 DUBLIN
Manchester

GB

322-325 LONDON

300-301
AMSTERDAM
Den Haag
Rotterdam
NL
Hamburg
Hannover
Gdańsk

BERLIN
304-305
PL
WARSZAWA
348-349

310-311 BRUSSEL/
BRUXELLES
B
Essen
Köln
D
Leipzig
Wrocław

Frankfurt/m.
Kyjiv

326-327 LUXEMBOURG
L
PRAHA 338-339
CZ
Krakau
UA

334-337 PARIS
Stuttgart

Strasbourg
München
WIEN 350-351
SK
MD

F
307 BERN
Zürich
Salzburg
BRATISLAVA 308
Chişinău

Genève
Innsbruck
A
H
BUDAPEST
312-313
RO

CH
Milano
LJUBLJANA 321

Bordeaux
Lyon
Venézia
SLO
ZAGREB 352

Bilbao
Génova
HR
BIH
BEOGRAD 306

Porto
Marseille
Sarajevo
SRB

P
MONACO 332
Firenze
MNE
Prištína
BG

LISBOA 320
MADRID 328-329
KSV
SOFIJA 344

E
Barcelona
Podgorica
316-317 ISTANBUL
RO

Sevilla
Valencia
I
ROMA 342-343
Tiranë
Skopje
MK

AL

Alger
Palermo
GR
Izmir
TR

Rabat
Tunis
ATHINA 302-303
MA
DZ
TN

	GB	D	F	NL		GB	D	F	NL
	City map	**Stadtplan**	**Plan de ville**	**Plattegrond**	**1:15.000**	**City map**	**Stadtplan**	**Plan de ville**	**Plattegrond**
	Motorway	Autobahn	Autoroute	Autosnelweg		Central station, bus station	Hauptbahnhof, Busbahnhof	Gare centrale, gare routière	Centraal station, busstation
	Major road	Wichtige Hauptstraße	Route principale importante	Hoofdroute		Hospital	Krankenhaus	Hôpital	Ziekenhuis
	Main road	Hauptstraße	Route régionale	Belangrijke verbindingsweg		Information, post office	Information, Post	Information, bureau de poste	Informatie, postkantoor
	Pedestrian zone	Fußgängerzone	Zone piétonne	Voetgangerzone		Church, mosque	Kirche, Moschee	Église, mosquèe	Kerk, moskee
	Railway	Bahnlinie	Ligne de tramway	Spoorweg		Synagogue	Synagoge	Synagogue	Synagoge
	Stadium	Stadion	Stade	Stadion		Theatre	Theater	Théâtre	Theater
	Parking, garage parking	Parkplatz, Parkhaus	Parking	Parkeerplaats		Museum	Museum	Musée	Museum
	Exhibition Hall	Messe	Palais des expositions	Beurs		Library	Bibliothek	Bibliothèque	Bibliotheek

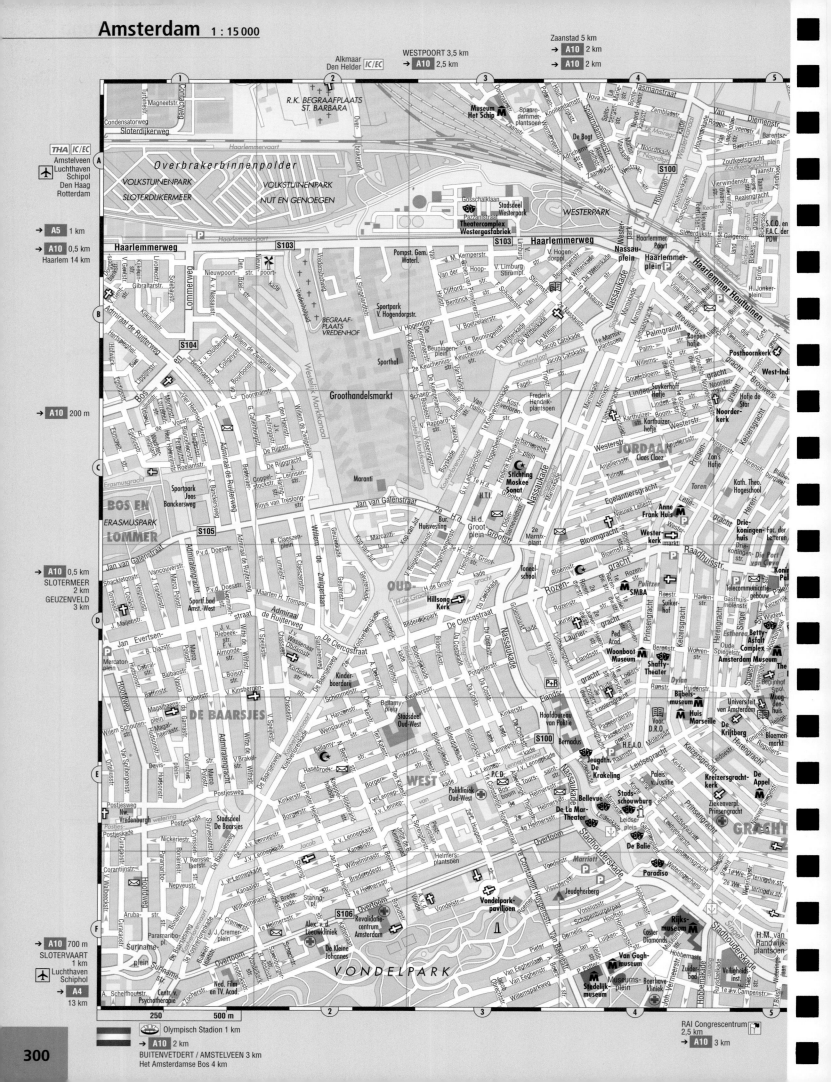

Volendam 15 km
→ N 247 1,5 km
BUIKSLOOT 1 km
→ A10 1,5 km
⇤ Noord
NIEUWENDAM 0,5 km

NOORD 8

Het IJ

Westerdok
Westerdoks
Westerdoksdijk

NOORD 5

Rijkspolitie te Water

EYE, Film Institut Nederland

NOORD
NOORDERPARK

Nieuwe

Johan van Hasseltweg

Leeuwarderweg

Johan van Hasseltweg

VOLKSTUINEN
BUITENZORG

Viegenbos

Sporthal

S 116

Plein Spanje 36-39

NOORD 6

Hamerkanaal

Pomhaven

K.v.K.
Haven-gebouw

Nieuwe Westerdok

S100

Ibis Amsterdam centre

De Ruijterkade

THA
i ICE IC/EC
Centraal Station
CENTRAAL STATION

Voorhaven v.h. Noord Hollandschkanaal

Adelaarswegveer

IJ-Tunnel

Oosterdokseiland

Muziekgebouw aan 't IJ
Mövenpick Hotel

Bimhuis

Passenger Terminal Amsterdam

De Ruijterkade

De Chocoladefabrik

Piet Heinkade

Sumatrakade

Sumatrakade

IJhaven

HAVENS OOST 1 km

Oostelijk Havengebied

Piet Heinkade

S100

Piet Heinkade

Veemkade

HAVENS OOST 0,5 km

Nieuwe of Ronde Lutherse Kerk
Renaissance

Dominicus-kerk

Crowne Plaza City Centre
Victoria
Barbizon Palace

St. Nicolaaskerk

Museum Ons' Lieve Heer op Solder
Schreierstoren

OBA – Openbare Bibliotheek Amsterdam
Conservatorium

Oosterdokskade

Oosterdok

Dijksgracht

NEMO Science & Technology Museum

Marine Etablissement

Mariniers-kade

Ravenwerf

Beurs van Berlage (Koopmansbeurs)

Oude Kerk
Koffie en Theemuseum
't Kolkje ('t Sluisje)

CHINATOWN

Scheepvaarthuis Grand Hotel Amrâth

Het Scheepvaart-museum

Kattenburgerstr.

Leeuwen-werf
Olifants-werf

Windroos-plein

Nieuwe Kerk
Swissôtel
Krasnapolsky

Effecten-beurs

De Waag

NIEUWMARKT

Oosterkerk

Witten-burgervaart

Windroosvaart

Dam
National Mon.
Mme. Tussaud Scenerama

Montelbaans-toren

Prins Hendrikkade

ARCAM Architectuur Centrum Amsterdam

Kattenburger-plein

Oosterkerk

De Brakke Grond
Vm. Stadhuis Oost-Indisch Huis
Zuiderkerk

Hash Marih. & Hemp Mus.

T.M.F.

Oostenburgervaart

Frascati
Sofitel The Grand Amsterdam
Radisson SAS

Nieuwe Vlienburgerstr.

Rapenburger-str.

Brandweer

Amsterdam Dungeon

Doelen-zaal
Theater-school

Museum Het Rembrandthuis

Amsterdamse Hoogeschool voor de Kunsten

Entrepotdok

Oostenburgergracht

Museumswerf 't Kromhout

De Molen De Gooyer
Zeeburgerpad

Allard Pierson Museum

Universiteits-theater

Stadhuis Stopera
Muziek-theater

WATERLOOPLEIN

Mr. Visser-plein
Portugese Synagoge

Verzetsmus.

Planetarium

De Kleine Komedie

Joods Historisch Mus.

Hortus Botanicus
Universiteit

Hollandsche Schouwburg

Herv. Ped. Acad.

NATURA

Artisbibliotheek
ARTIS

EnergeticA

→ A10 5 km

Zeeburgerdijk

Singelgracht

FOAM

Museum Willet-Holthuysen

Amstelhof
Hermitage

Wittenberg

St. Jacob

Zoo Artis
MAGISTRA
Aquarium

S113

Muidergracht

EASTERN DOCKLANDS

ENGORDEL UID

Museum Van Loon

Amstelkerk
Prinsengracht

De Duif

Theater Carré

WEESPER-PLEIN

Fac. Org. Chem.

Fac. Nat. en Sterrenk.

Natuurk. Lab.

Fac. Wisk./Inf.

Alexander-plein

Muiderkade

Tropenmuseum

Soeterijn-theater

Muider-kerk

→ A10 5 km

Prinsenhof

Amstel Intercontinental

S100

OOSTERPARK

S113

ICE IC/EC

Utrecht Arnhem

P.D.I.S.

Den Texstr.

Nederlandse Bank

Wibaut-huis

Rijksbel-kantoor

Sporthal

O.L.V. Gasthuis

Stadsdeel Oost

Arbeids bureau

Heineken Experience
Stadhouderskade

De IJsbreker Muziekcentrum en TV-Studio

Rhijn-spoorpl.

→ A2 / A10 3,5 km
Utrecht 24 km

→ A10 3 km
DUIVENDRECHT 3,5 km
ArenA 5 km
⇤ Gaasperplas Gein

WATERGRAAFSMEER 200 m
→ A10 2,5 km

301

Athina 1 : 15 000

A8 5,5 km
DAFNI 5,5 km
PERISTERI 3,5 km

ELEFSINA 17 km
Skaramagkas 9,5 km

PERISTERI 3 km
VERDI 7 km

Stathmos
Peloponissou 0,2 km

Stathmos
Larissis 0,5 km

Ag. Antonios

Egaleo
A8 9 km
EGALEO 1 km
DAFNI 9,5 km

NIKEA 11 km
PERAMA 12,5 km
(N. Salamina)

Stadio Karaiskaki
(Pireas) 3,5 km
Stadio
Irinis & Filias
4,5 km
Pireas 5 km
NIKEA 6,5 km
(N. Salamina,
Kriti, Kiklades,
Dodekanissa,
Izmir (TR), Rodos)
PERAMA 14 km
(N. Salamina)

Pireas

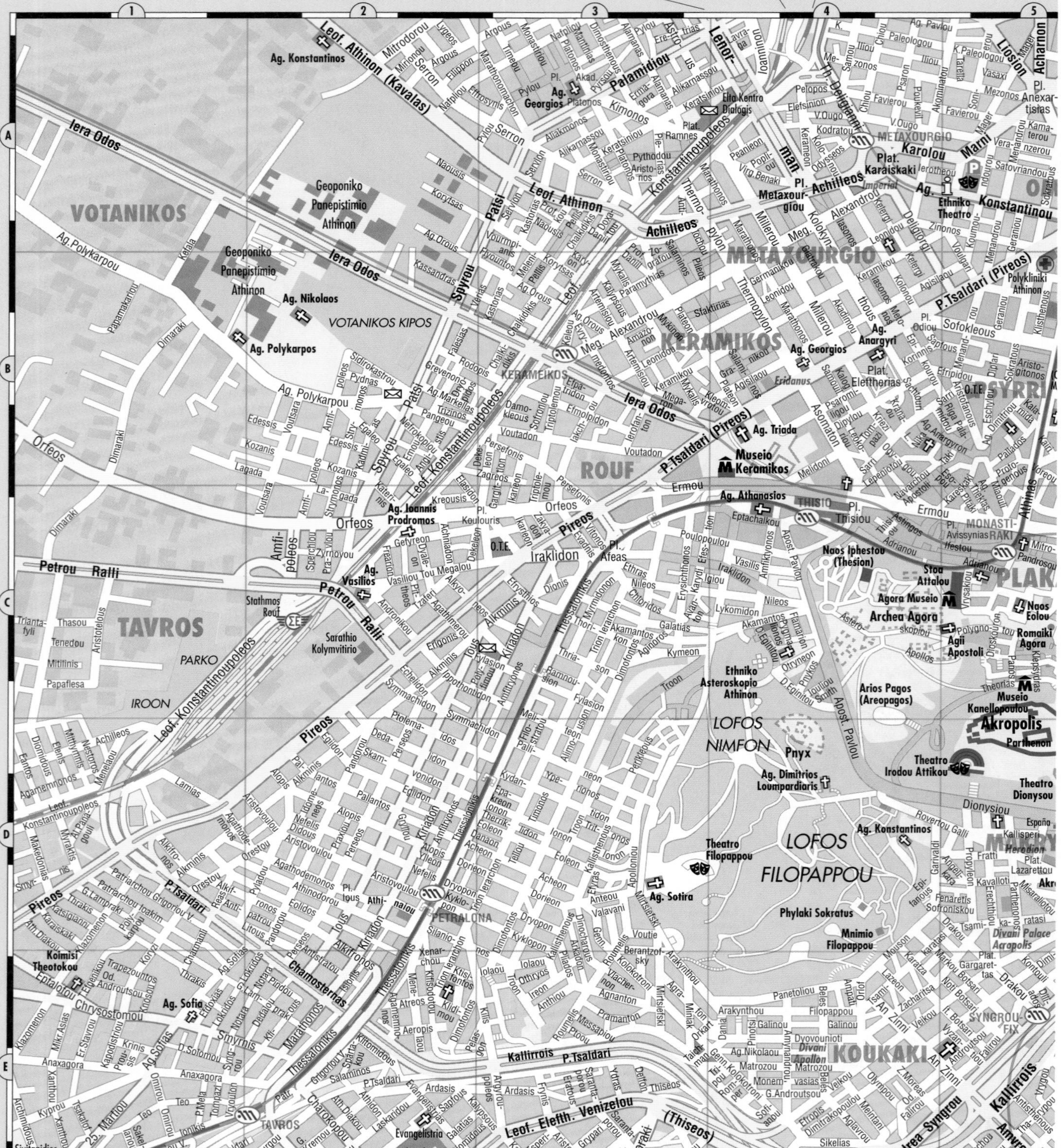

VOTANIKOS
Geoponiko Panepistimio Athinon
Geoponiko Panepistimio Athinon
VOTANIKOS KIPOS
Ag. Nikolaos
Ag. Polykarpos
METAXOURGIO
KERAMIKOS
ROUF
Museio Keramikos
THISIO
PLAK
Naos Iphestou (Thesion)
Stoa Attalou
Agora Museio
Archea Agora
Agii Apostoli
Romeiki Agora
Naos Eolou
Arios Pagos (Areopagos)
Museio Kanellopoulou
Akropolis
Parthenon
TAVROS
PARKO
IROON
Sarathio Kolymvitirio
Petrou Ralli
Stathmos Rouf
LOFOS NIMFON
Pnyx
Theatro Irodou Attikou
Theatro Dionysou
Ethniko Asteroskopio Athinon
Ag. Dimitrios Loumpardiaris
LOFOS FILOPAPPOU
Theatro Filopappou
Ag. Sotira
Phylaki Sokratus
Mnimio Filopappou
Divani Palace Akropolis
KOUKAKI
SYNGROU-FIX
PETRALONA
Kallirrois
Leof. Eleftn. Venizelou (Thiseos)
TAVROS
KALLITHEA
Stadio Kallitheas
DOURGOUTI
Platia Machis Analatou

Pireas 5 km
KALAMAKI 9 km

Kareskaki Stadio 5 km
Pireas 6 km

91 3 km
KALAMAKI 7 km
ELLINIKO 9 km
Vouliagmeni 21 km

DAFNI 0,5 km

250   500 m

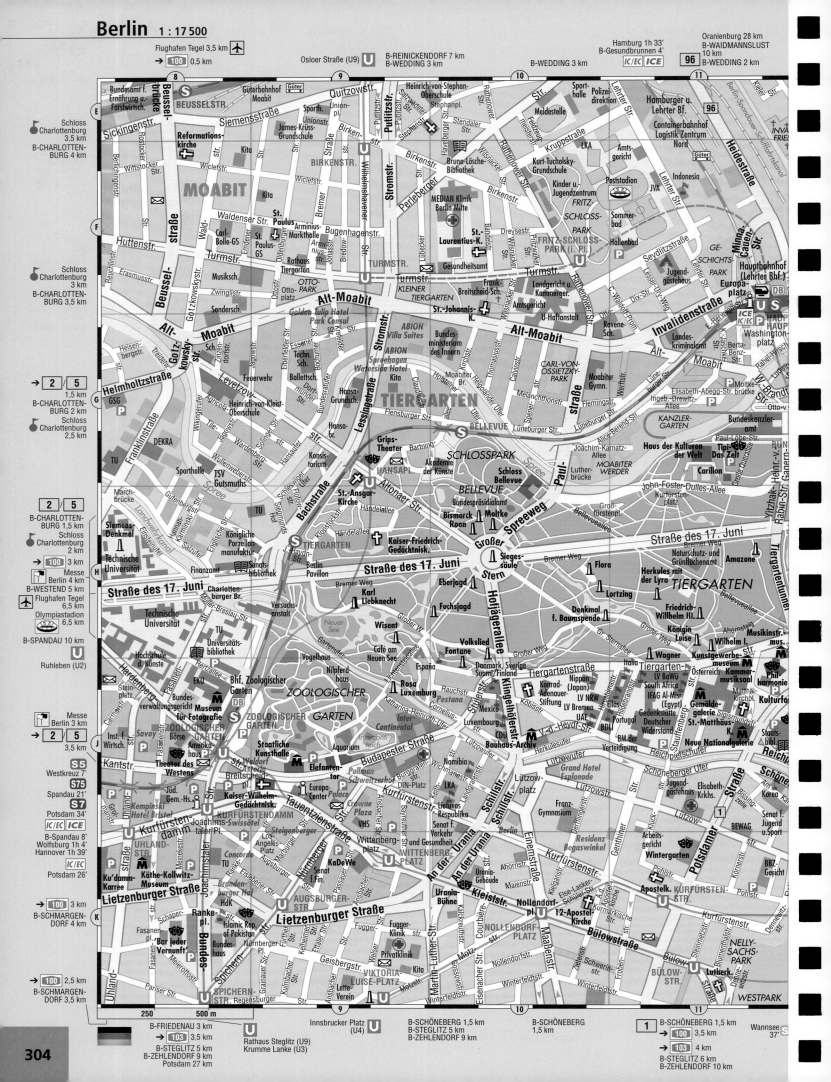

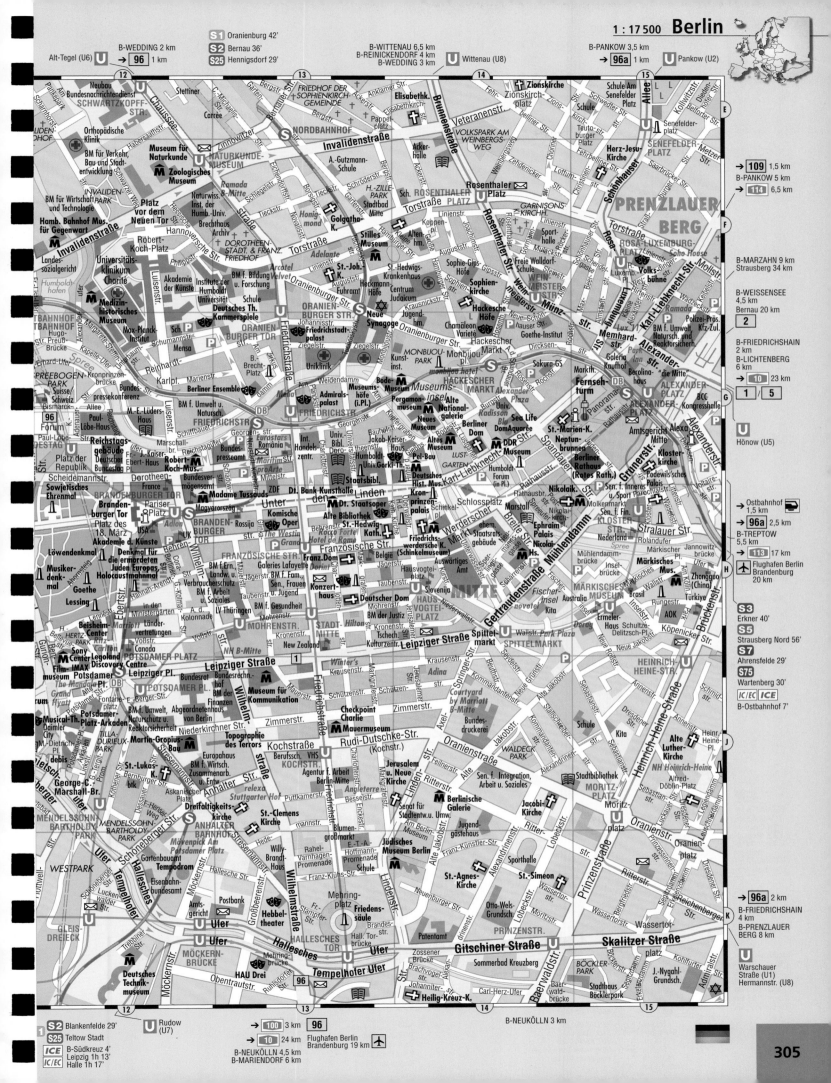

Dunav

DORĆOL

Sportski centar

Oslobodiocima Beograda

Nebojša kula

Bulevar vojvode Bojovića

Defektološki fakultet

ZOO

Crkva Svete Petke
Crkva Ružica

Kalemegdan

Šeih-Mustafino turbe
Pobednik
Zavod za zaštitu spomenika kulture

Muzej šumarstva i lova

Vojni muzej

Galerija fresaka

Izložbeni Pavilion

Bajrakli džamija

Muzej nauke i tehnike

Jevrejski istorijski muzej
Muzej pozorišne umetnosti, Vukov i Dositejev muzej

Pedagoški muzej

Etnografski muzej

Cara Dušana

Crkva Svetog Aleksandra Nevskog
Bajlonova pijaca

STARI GRAD

Makedonija
Prirodno-matematički fakultet

Hellas

Slovenija
Narodni Univerzitet
UNIVERZITETSKI PARK Studentski trg

Saborna crkva

Muzej Srpske pravoslavne crkve

Filološki fakultet
Akademski trg
Filozofski fakultet

Nederland

Bitef teatar

France

Australia

Bulevar despota Stefana

Narodno pozorište

Muzej primenjene umetnosti
Muzej grada Beograda
Narodni muzej
Trg Republike

Gradski zavod

Crkva Svetog Petra

KRNJAČA 3 km
BORČA 8 km
ZRENJANIN 70 km

24-1

KARABURMA 2,5 km
ZVEZDARA 3 km
VIŠNJIČKA BANJA 4 km
Višnjica 6,5 km

1-9

Pančevo 17 km
Kovin 53 km
Vršac 80 km
Timişoara (RO) 156 km

Brankov Most
Brankova

22-1

Pijaca
Zeleni venac

Prizrenska
Terazije

Moskva

Crkva Svetog Marka na Tašmajdanu

Hilandarska

Peru
Majestic
Union

22-1

Institut za mentalno zdravlje

Botanička bašta

Rudarsko-geološki fakultet

Takovska

Pozorište na Terazijama
Muzej istorije kulture Jugoslavije

Atelje 212

ZEMUN 3,5 km
GORNJI GRAD 4 km
NOVA GALENIKA 5,5 km
Batajnica 15,5 km
Stara Pazova 31 km
Novi Sad 74 km

Omen teatar

Ekonomski fakultet

Trg Nikole Pašića
Skupština SRJ

PTT muzej

Ruska pravoslavna crkva
Duško Radović

Splendid

Prag

Skupština Beograd
Ministarstvo

100

Stadion Tašmajdan

PALILULA

Autobuska stanica Lasta

Ginekološko-akušerska klinika
Kosovska bolnica

PIONIRSKI PARK

Predsednik Republike Srbije

Češka Republika
Türkiye

Kneza Miloša

Bulevar Kralja Aleksandra

TAŠMAJDAN

Crkva Krista Kralja
Dadov

Autobuska stanica Beograd

Astoria

Skupština Srbije

Učiteljski fakultet

Bosna i Hercegovina
Brasil
Belgije i Belgique

Ministarstvo ekonomije i regionalnog razvoja

Metropol

Mašinski fakultet

Železnička stanica Beograd
Savski Trg

Vaznesenjska crkva
Milošev Amam

1-9

Vlada Republike Srbije
Ministarstvo finansija

rudarstva i energetike

Pravni fakultet

Arhiv Srbije
Univ. biblioteka

100

Arhitektonski, elektrotehnički i građevinski fakultet

Bolnica Sv. Sava
Železnički muzej

Min. za državnu upravu i lokalnu samoupravu

Ministarstvo spoljnih poslova

España

Jug. dramsko pozorište

Spomenik Nikoli Tesli

Palata pravde

Ministarstvo odbrane

Istorijski muzej Srbije

PARK MANJEŽ

Muzej N. Tesle

Ministarstvo za ljudska i manjinska prava, dr-žavnu upravu i lokalnu samoupravu

Polska

Ministarstvo pravde

Park

100

ZVEZDARA 3,5 km
MALI MOKRI LUG 5,5 km
Grocka 30 km
Smederevo 49 km

Kneza
United Kingdom
USA

Rex
Hrvatska

România

Narodna banka Srbije
Trg Slavija

Prirodnjački muzej

Igralište FK "Železničar"

Myanmar
Canada

Italia
Balgaria

Suisse/Svizzera
Best Western M
Suomi/Finland
Slavija Lux

ĆUBURA

1

BEŽANIJA 4 km
ZEMUN 5,5 km
Aerodrom Beograd-Surčin 15 km
Sremska Mitrovica 73 km
Slavonski Brod 207 km

Deutschland
Zavod za zdravstvenu zaštitu radnika
Ministarstvo unutrašnjih poslova

Urgentni centar

Rossija

Dečja klinika

Pozorište Slavija

Belarus

Guinée
Vatikan

ŠAVSKI VENAC

Klinički centar Srbije
Kapela Svetih vračeva Kozme i Damjana

Medicinski stomatološki i farmaceutski fakultet

Crkva Sv. Save

Narodna biblioteka

VRAČAR

Cara Nikolaja II

Poliklinika

Stanica za hitnu pomoć

Plućne bolesti

19

Beogradski sajam 0,5 km
ČUKARICA 3,5 km
RAKOVICA 7 km
Železnik 10,5 km
Obrenovac 23 km

Kneza Miloša
Bulevar Franše d'Eperea

Beogradska industrija piva

Zavod za protetiku

Infektivni i tropske bolesti

KARA-DEV PARK

1

E 75

Sava

Sremska

250   500 m

Stadion FK Partizan 1 km
Stadion FK Crvena Zvezda 1,5 km

SENJAK 200 m
BANJICA 3 km
VOŽDOVAC 5 km
Mladenovac Varoš 58 km
Kragujevac 124 km

1

Stadion FK Crvena Zvezda 1,5 km
ZVEZDARA 5 km
Vrčin 18 km
Velika Plana 85 km
Kragujevac 138 km

1   300 m

Stadion FK Crvena Zvezda 1,5 km
VOŽDOVAC 2 km
BANJICA 2,5 km
JAJINCI 5 km

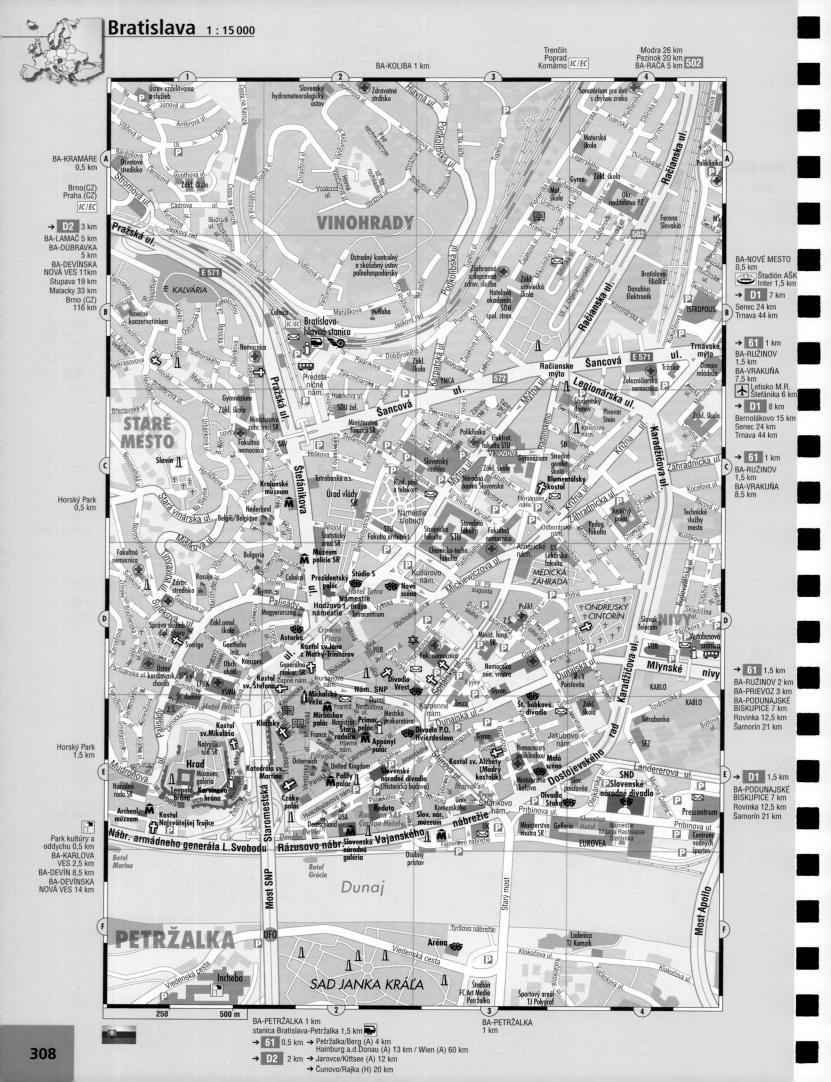

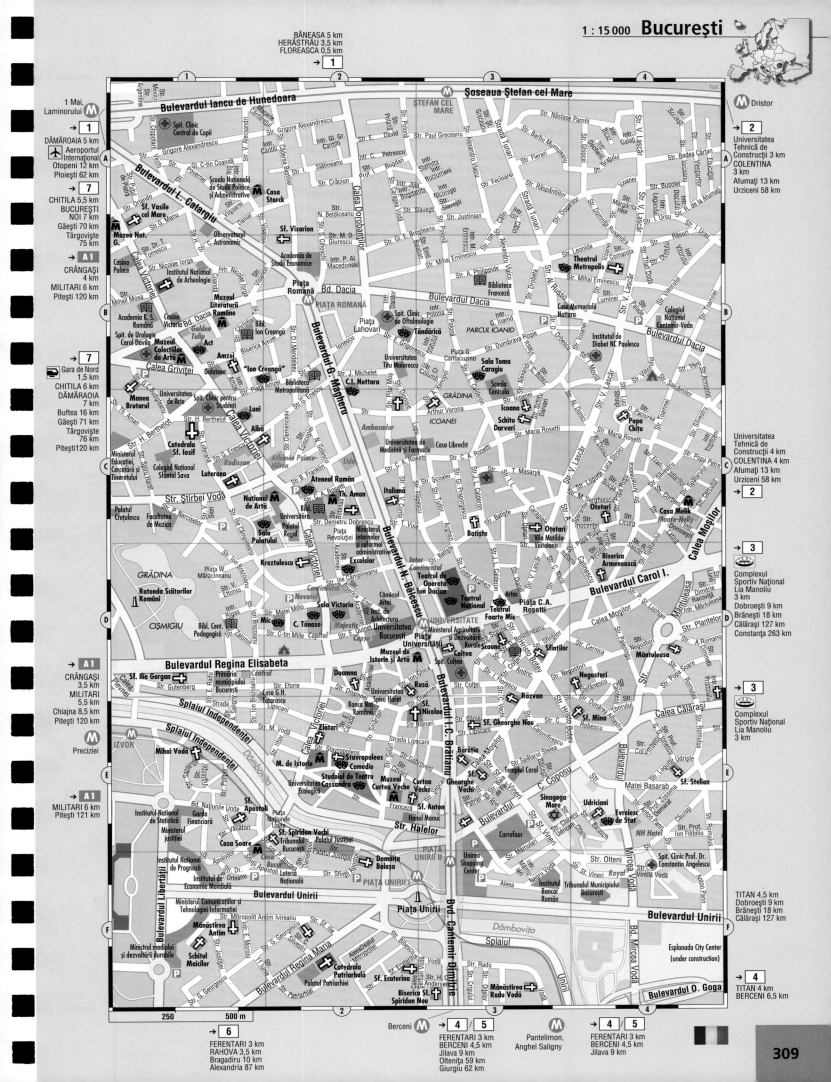

BĂNEASA 5 km
HERĂSTRĂU 3,5 km
FLOREASCA 0,5 km
→ 1

Şoseaua Ştefan cel Mare

Ⓜ Dristor
→ 2

1 Mai,
Laminorului Ⓜ
→ 1

Universitatea
Tehnică de
Construcţii 3 km
COLENTINA
3 km
Afumaţi 13 km
Urziceni 58 km

DĂMĂROAIA 5 km
✈ Aeroportul
International
Otopeni 12 km
Ploieşti 62 km

7
CHITILA 5,5 km
BUCUREŞTI
NOI 7 km
Găeşti 70 km
Târgovişte
75 km

→ A1
CRÂNGAŞI
4 km
MILITARI 6 km
Piteşti 120 km

7
Gara de Nord
1,5 km
CHITILA 6 km
DĂMĂROAIA
7 km
Buftea 16 km
Găeşti 71 km
Târgovişte
76 km
Piteşti120 km

Universitatea
Tehnică de
Construcţii 4 km
COLENTINA 4 km
Afumaţi 13 km
Urziceni 58 km
→ 2

→ 3
Complexul
Sportiv Naţional
Lia Manoliu
3 km
Dobroeşti 9 km
Brăneşti 18 km
Călăraşi 127 km
Constanţa 263 km

→ A1
CRÂNGAŞI
3,5 km
MILITARI
5,5 km
Chiajna 8,5 km
Piteşti 120 km

Ⓜ
Preciziei

→ 3
Complexul
Sportiv Naţional
Lia Manoliu
3 km

→ A1
MILITARI 6 km
Piteşti 121 km

TITAN 4,5 km
Dobroeşti 9 km
Brăneşti 18 km
Călăraşi 127 km

Esplanada City Center
(under construction)

→ 4
TITAN 4 km
BERCENI 6,5 km

250   500 m

→ 6
FERENTARI 3 km
RAHOVA 3,5 km
Bragadiru 10 km
Alexandria 87 km

Berceni Ⓜ → 4 / 5
FERENTARI 3 km
BERCENI 4,5 km
Jilava 9 km
Olteniţa 59 km
Giurgiu 62 km

Ⓜ Pantelimon,
Anghel Saligny

→ 4 / 5
FERENTARI 3 km
BERCENI 4,5 km
Jilava 9 km

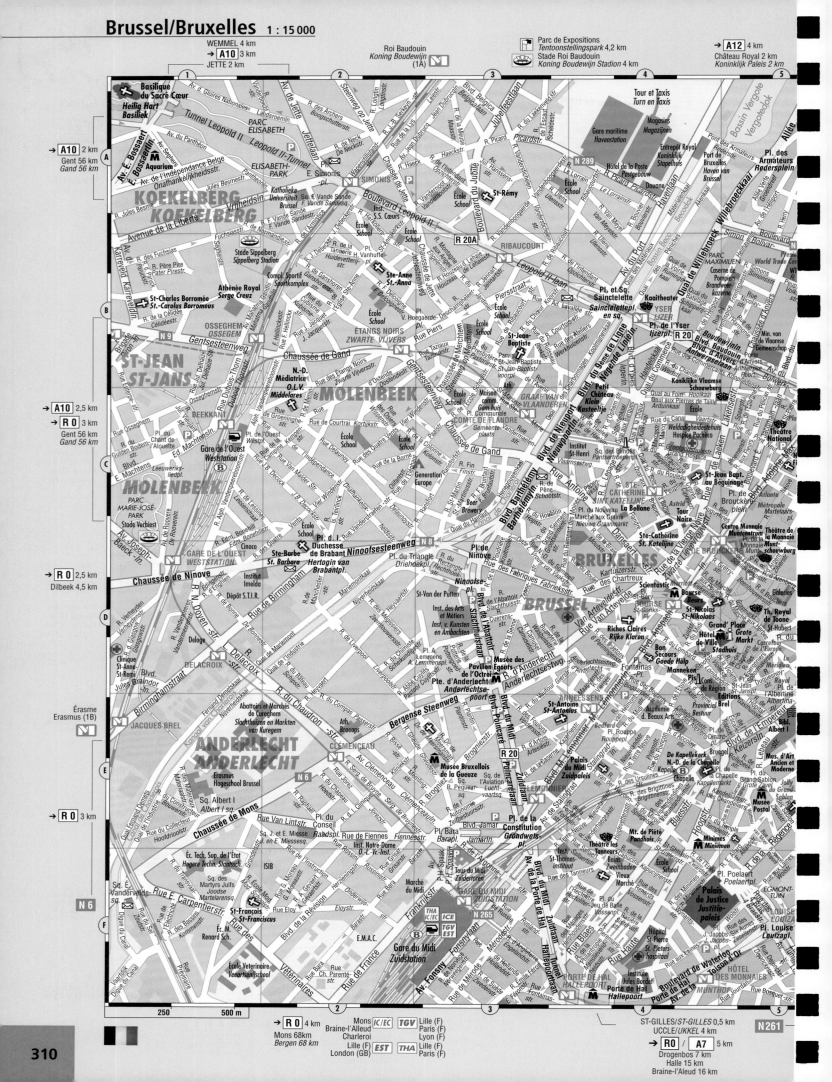

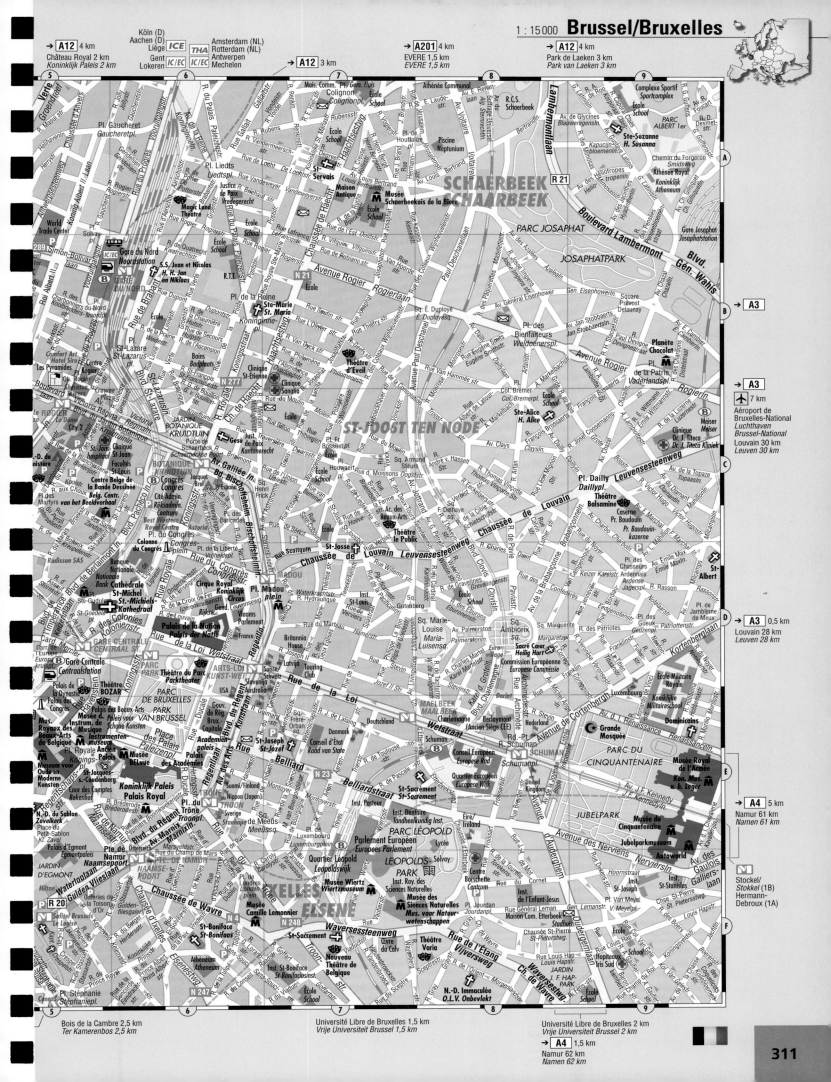

Budapest 1 : 15 000

Esztergom 44 km
Szentendre 15 km
Pilisvörösvár 14 km
BÉKÁSMEGYER 9 km · ÓBUDA · Szentendre
ÓBUDA 2 km

ÚJLIPÓTVÁROS 0,5 km

HÜVÖSVÖLGY 5 km
NAGYKOVÁCSI 9 km

ISTENHEGY 1,5 km

NÉMETVÖLGY 1 km

NÉMETVÖLGY 0,5 km

250 · 500 m

KELENFÖLD 2 km · KELENFÖLD 2 km
M1 / M7 2,5 km
Érd 14 km
Tatabánya 54 km
Székesfehérvár 60 km

312

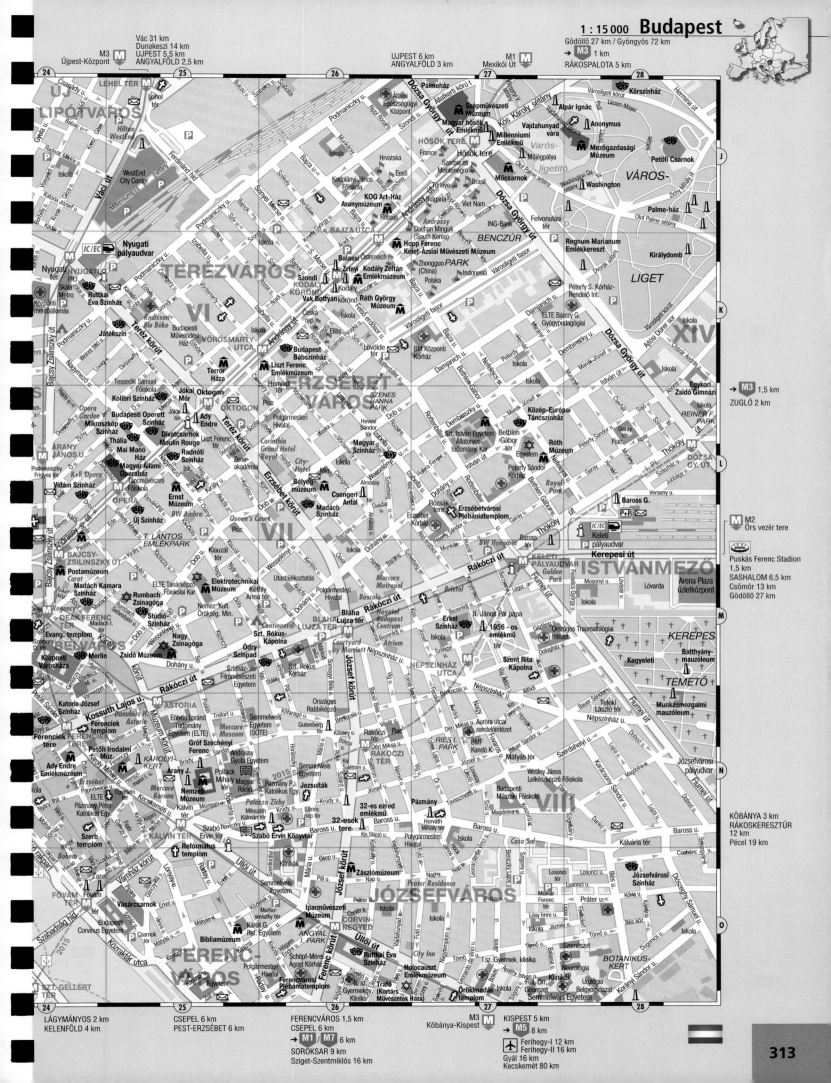

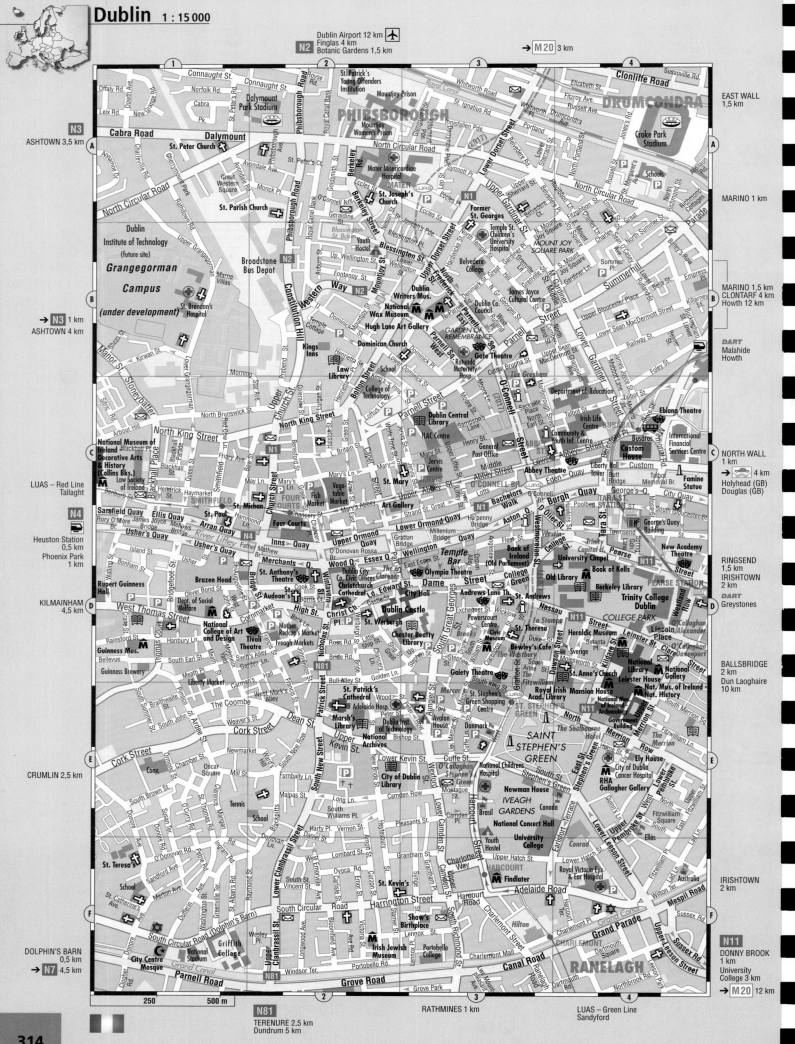

Dublin 1 : 15 000

EAST WALL 1,5 km

DRUMCONDRA

PHIBSBOROUGH

MARINO 1 km

N3
ASHTOWN 3,5 km

Cabra Road

MARINO 1,5 km
CLONTARF 4 km
Howth 12 km

→ N3 1 km
ASHTOWN 4 km

Dublin Institute of Technology (future site)
Grangegorman Campus (under development)

DART Malahide Howth

NORTH WALL 1 km

LUAS – Red Line Tallaght

→ 🚢 4 km
Holyhead (GB)
Douglas (GB)

N4
Heuston Station 0,5 km
Phoenix Park 1 km

RINGSEND 1,5 km
IRISHTOWN 2 km

KILMAINHAM 4,5 km

DART Greystones

BALLSBRIDGE 2 km
Dun Laoghaire 10 km

CRUMLIN 2,5 km

SAINT STEPHEN'S GREEN

IRISHTOWN 2 km

DOLPHIN'S BARN 0,5 km
→ N7 4,5 km

RANELAGH

N11
DONNY BROOK 1 km
University College 3 km

→ M20 12 km

250   500 m

N81
TERENURE 2,5 km
Dundrum 5 km

RATHMINES 1 km

LUAS – Green Line
Sandyford

314

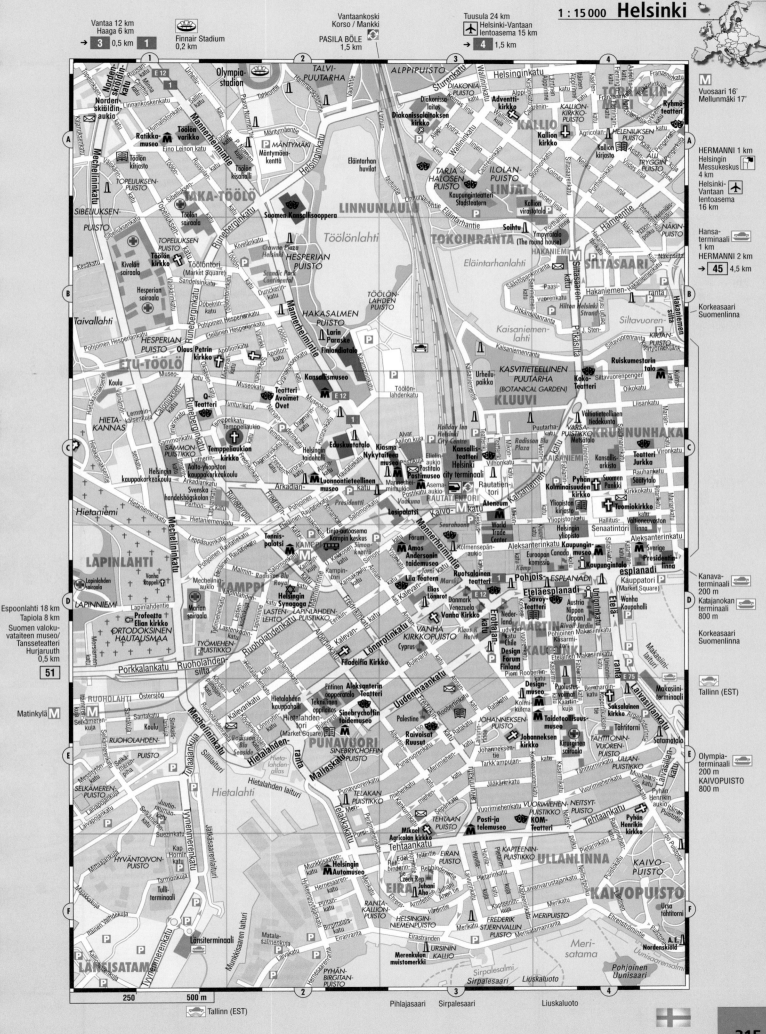

Istanbul 1 : 15 000

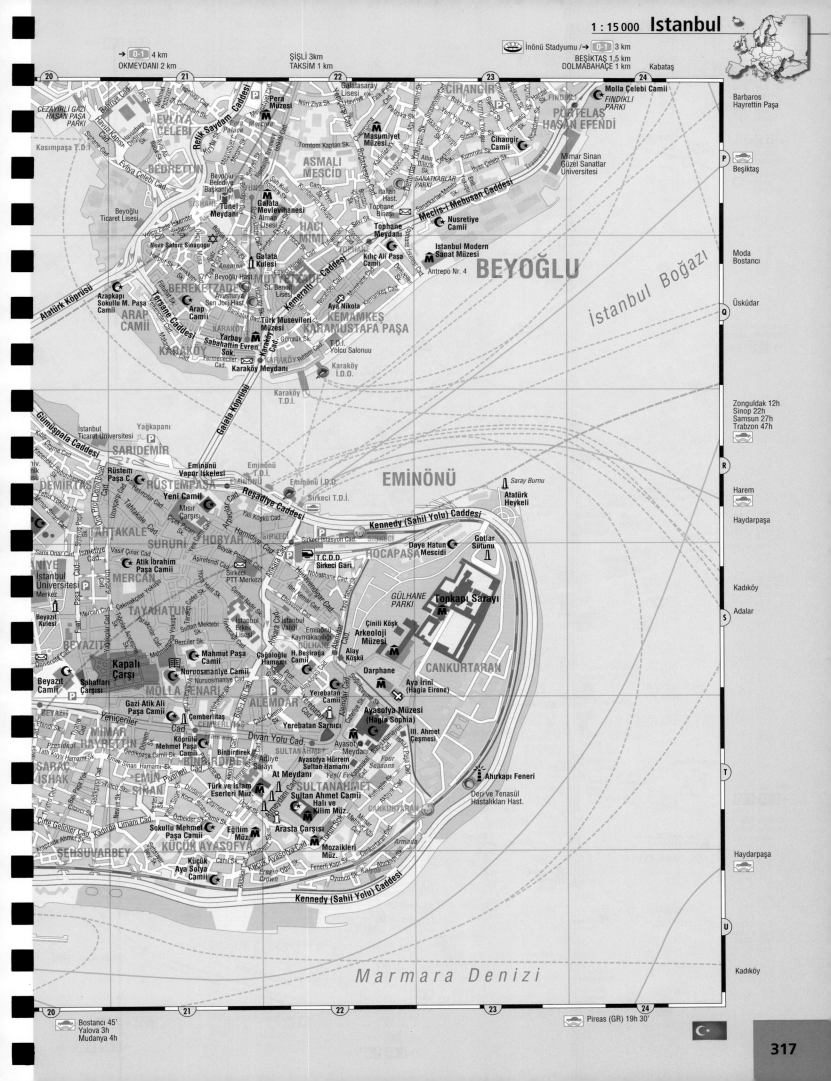

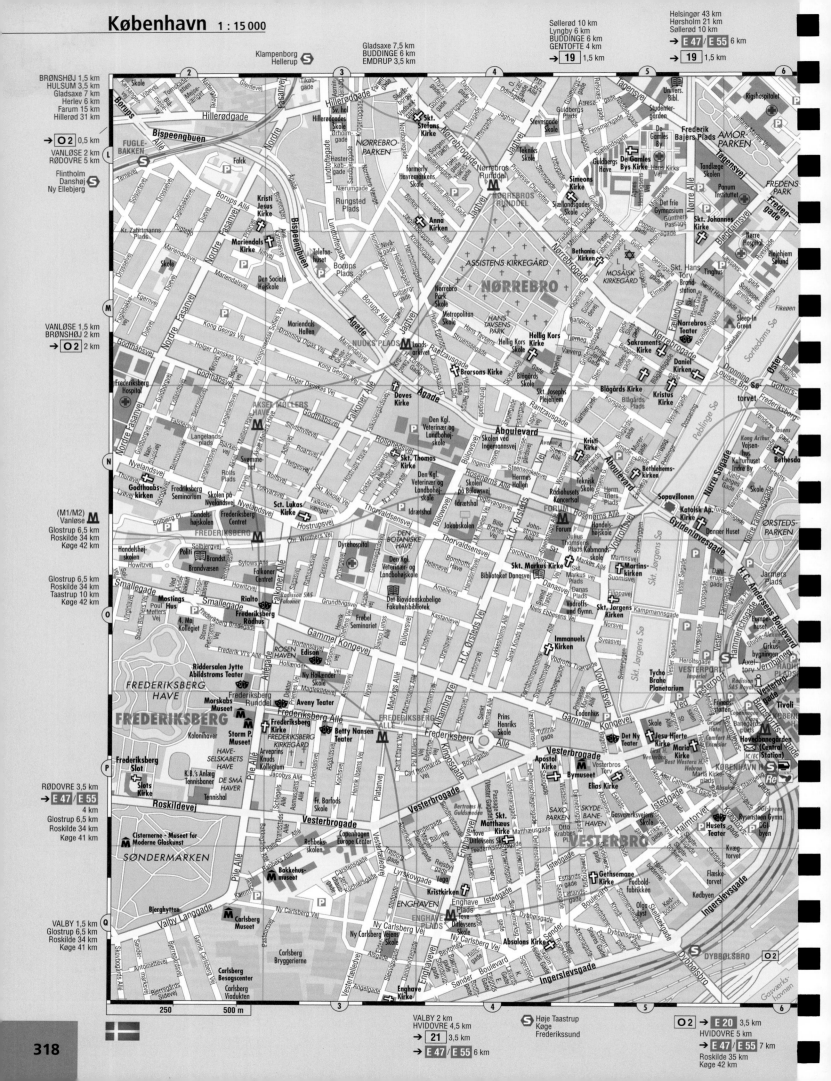

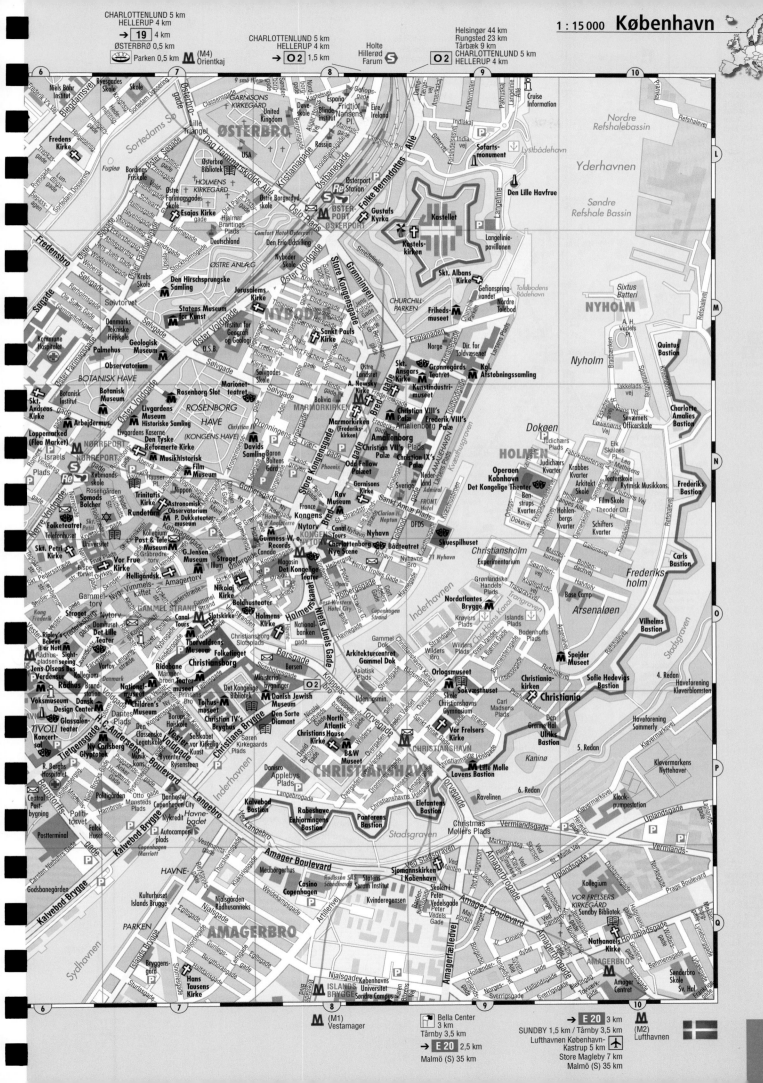

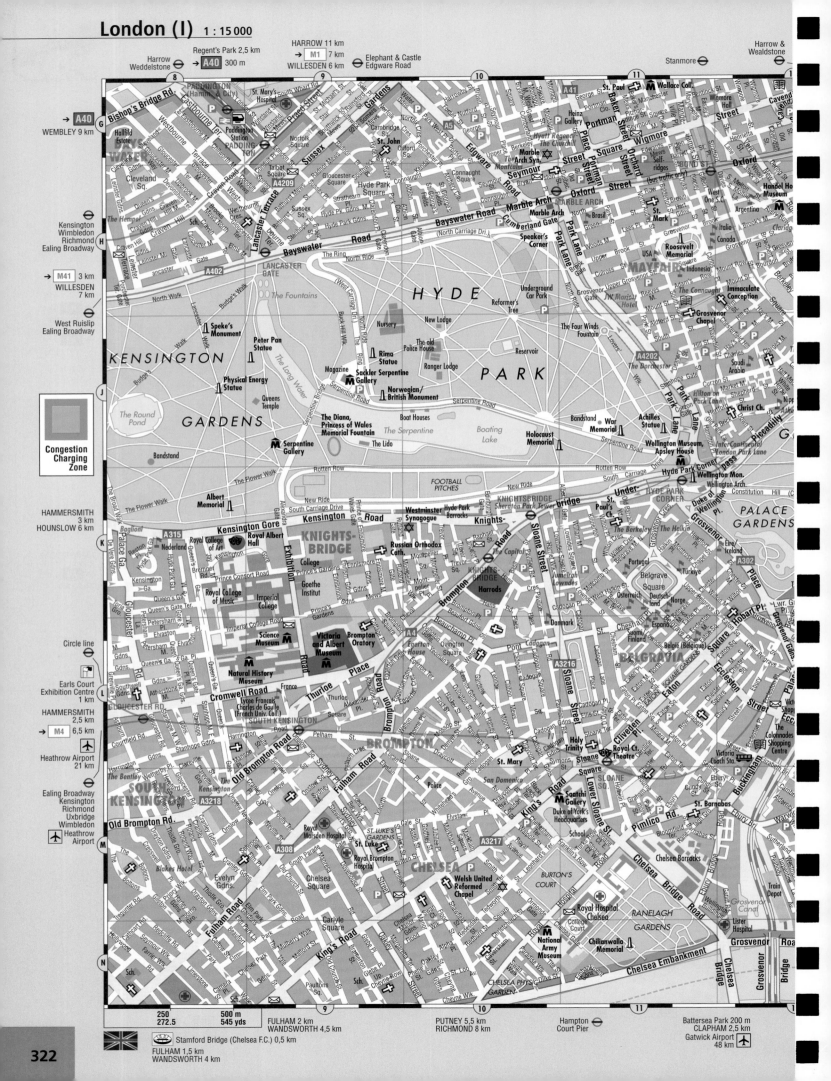

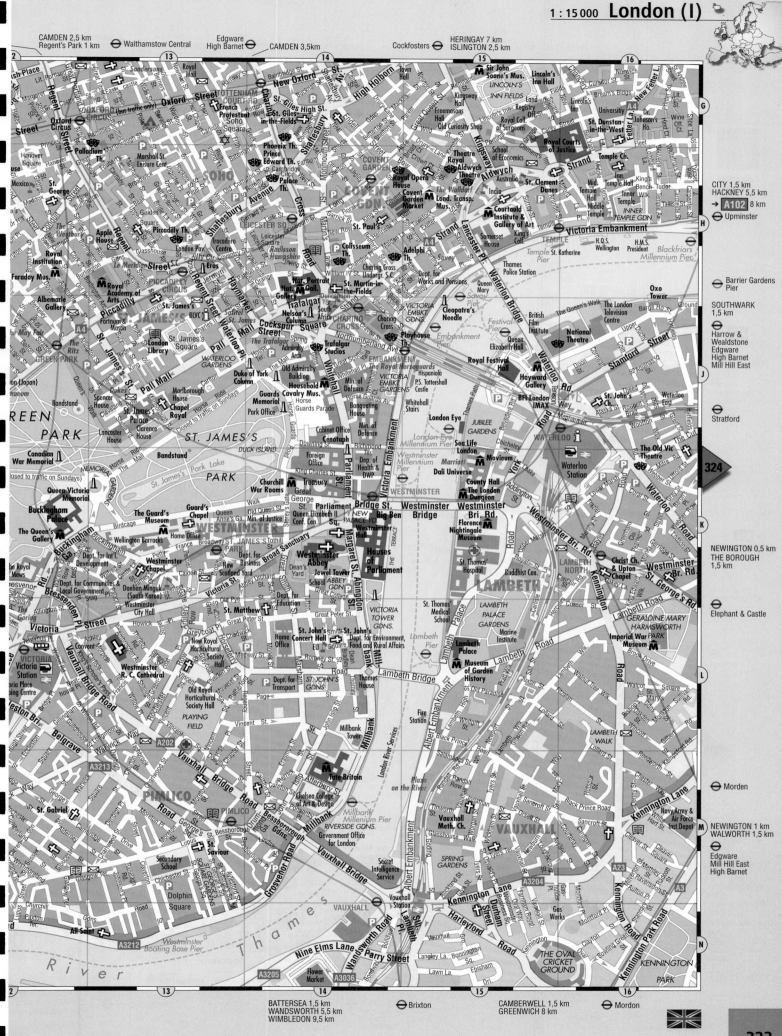

Congestion Charging Zone

REGENT'S PARK · SOMERS TOWN · ST. PANCRAS · PENTONVILLE · BLOOMSBURY · HOLBORN · SOHO · COVENT GDN · ST. JAMES'S · GREEN PARK · WESTMINSTER · WATERLOO · PALACE GARDENS

Buckingham Palace · Houses of Parliament · Big Ben · Westminster Bridge · London Eye · Trafalgar Square · Nelson's Column · British Museum · Euston Station · King's Cross Station · St Pancras International

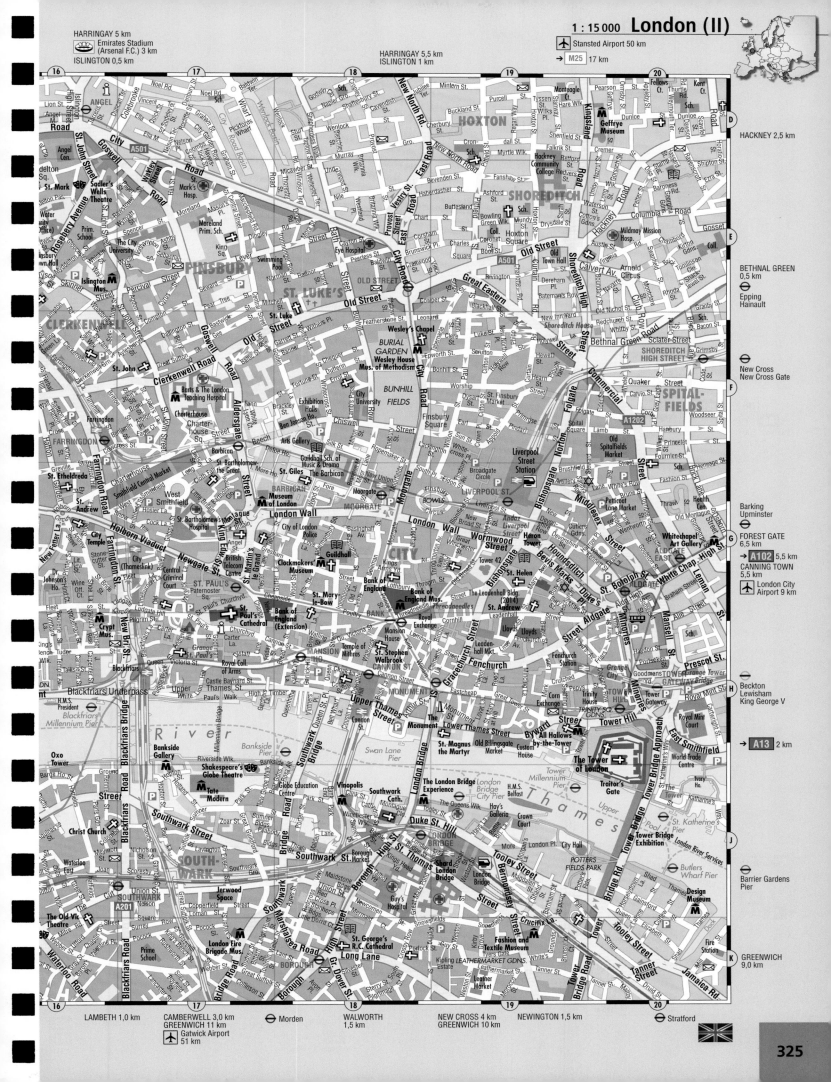

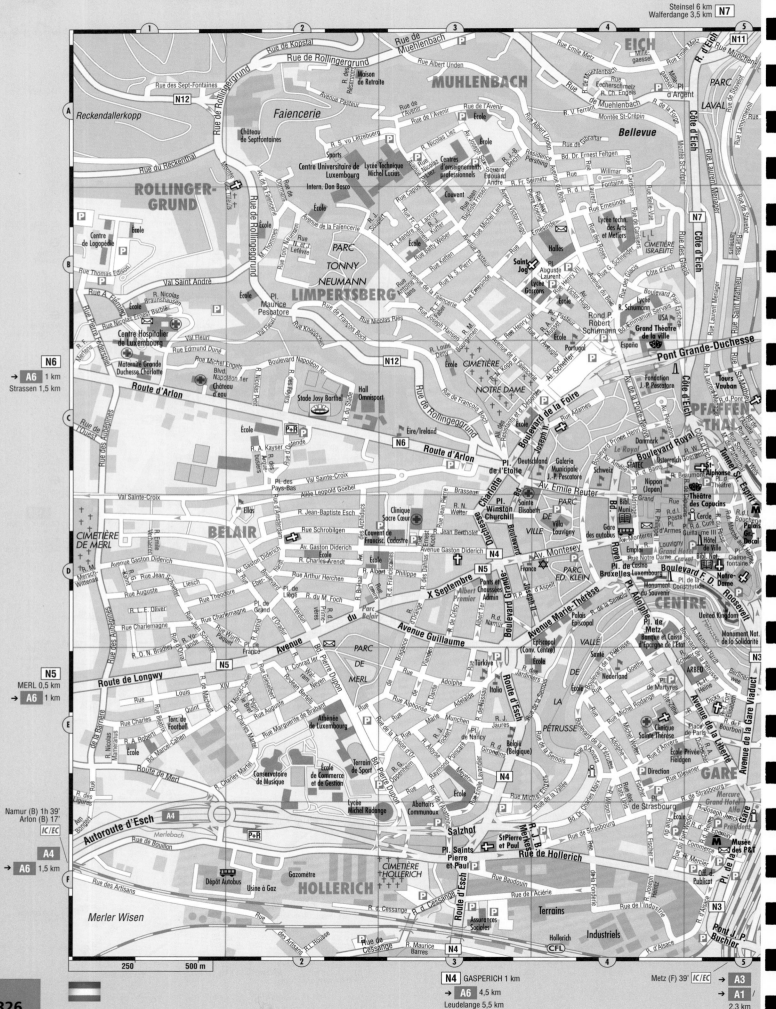

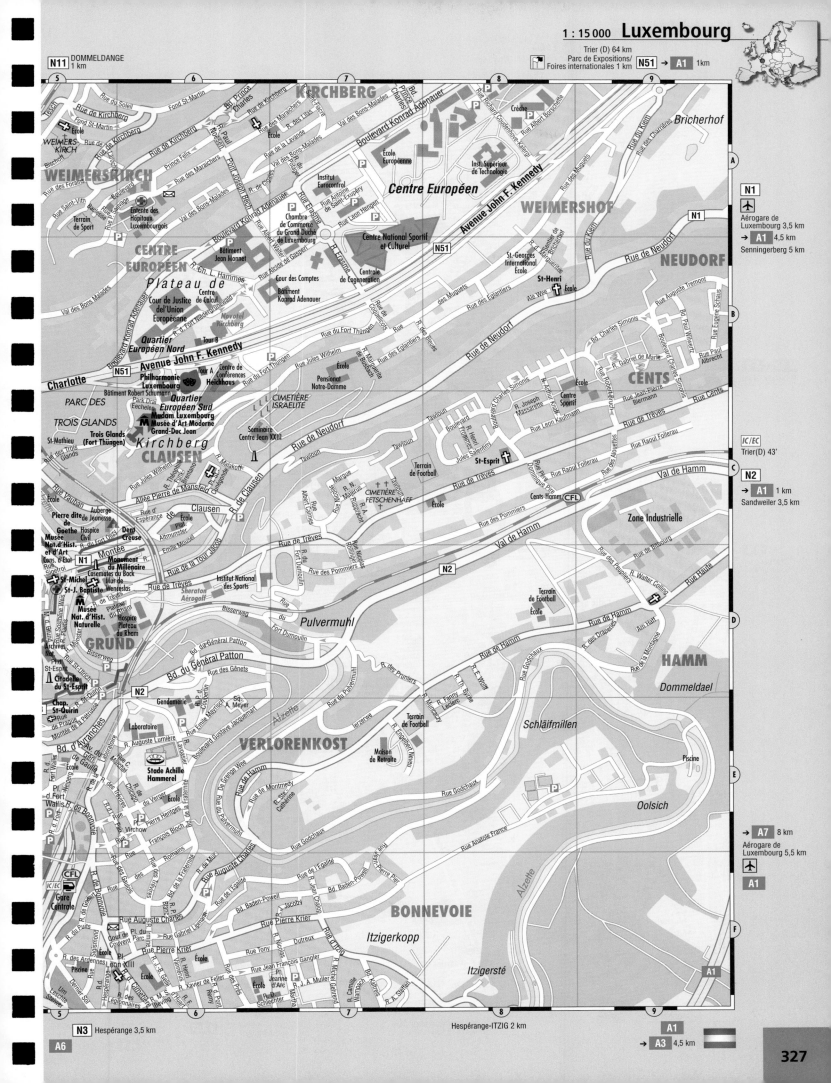

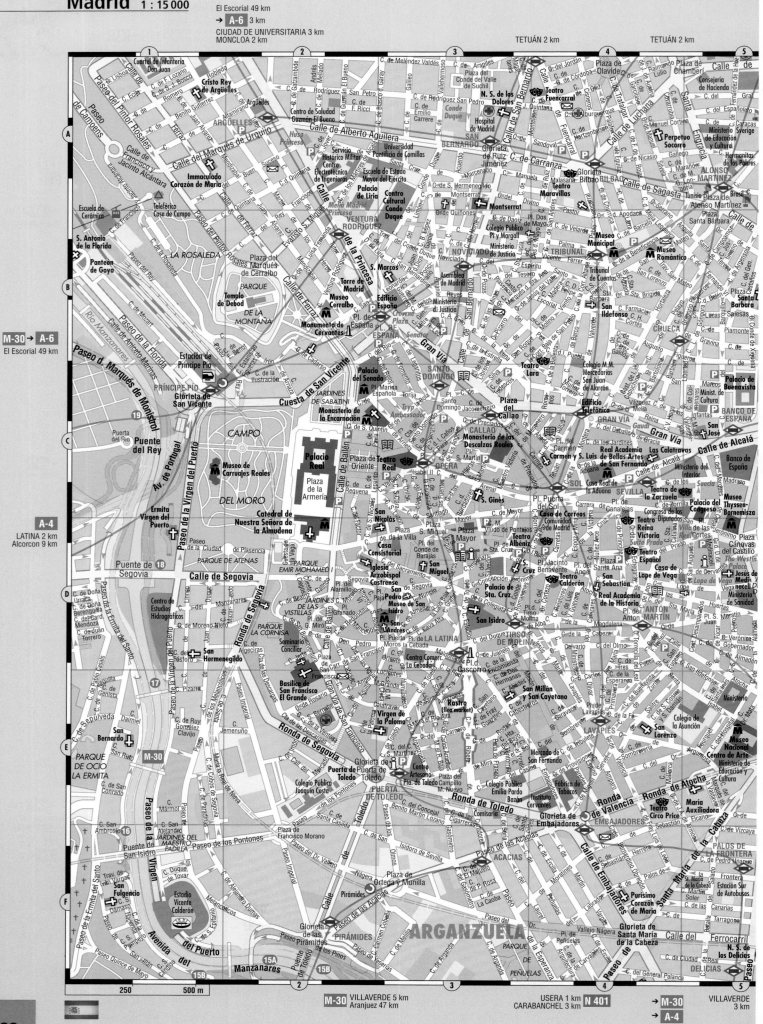

El Escorial 49 km
→ A-6 3 km
CIUDAD DE UNIVERSITARIA 3 km
MONCLOA 2 km

TETUÁN 2 km

TETUÁN 2 km

M-30 → A-6
El Escorial 49 km

A-4
LATINA 2 km
Alcorcon 9 km

250   500 m

M-30 VILLAVERDE 5 km
Aranjuez 47 km

USERA 1 km
CARABANCHEL 3 km   N 401

→ M-30
VILLAVERDE
3 km

→ A-4

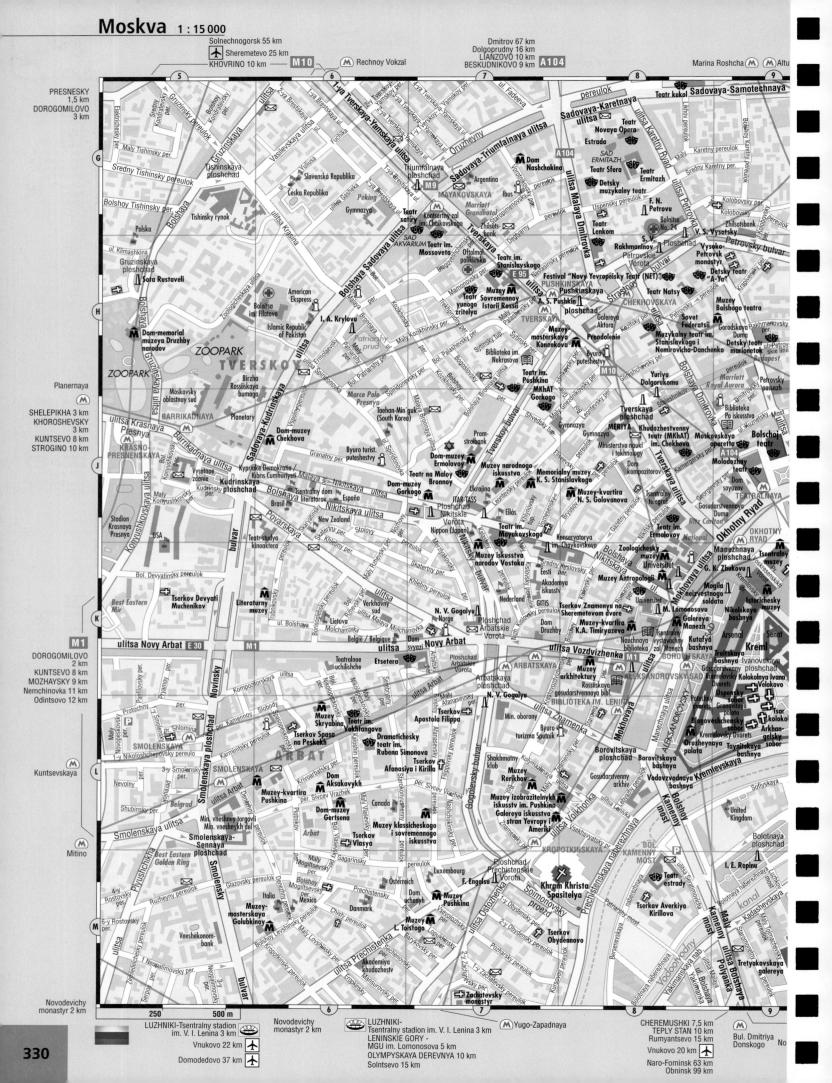

Monaco 1 : 15 000

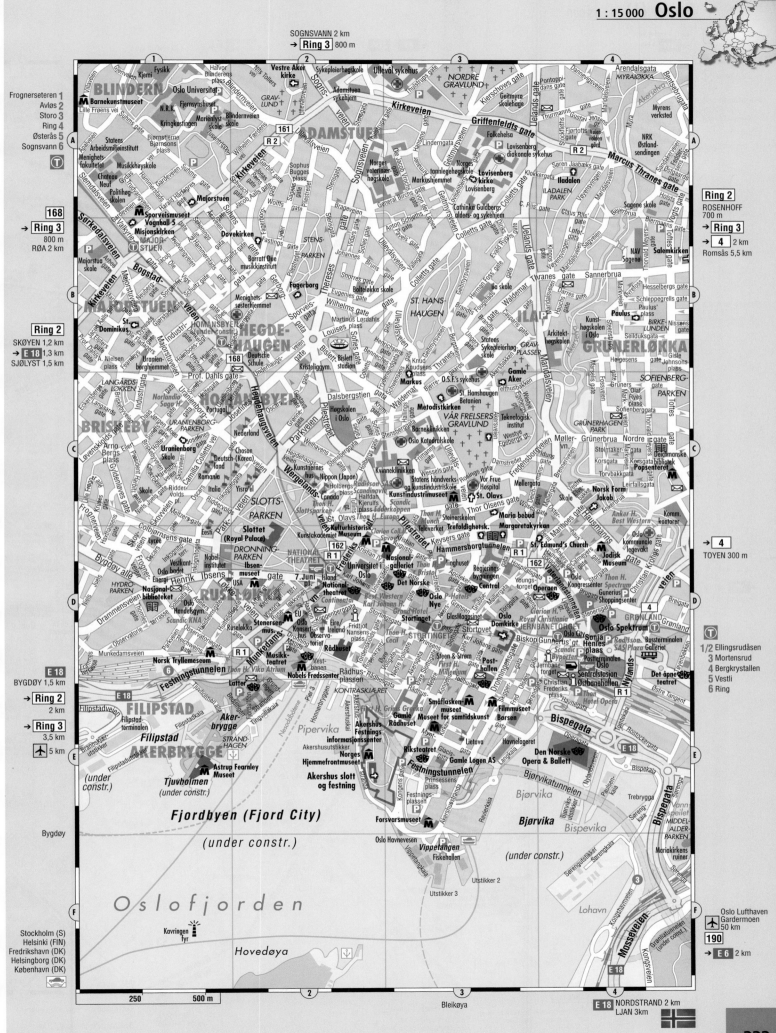

SOGNSVANN 2 km
→ Ring 3 800 m

Frognerseteren 1
Avløs 2
Storo 3
Ring 4
Østerås 5
Sognsvann 6

168
→ Ring 3
800 m
RØA 2 km

Ring 2
SKØYEN 1,2 km
→ E 18 1,3 km
SJØLYST 1,5 km

168

Ring 2

E 18
BYGDØY 1,5 km
→ Ring 2
2 km
→ Ring 3
3,5 km
✈ 5 km

Stockholm (S)
Helsinki (FIN)
Fredrikshavn (DK)
Helsingborg (DK)
København (DK)

Ring 2
ROSENHOFF
700 m
→ Ring 3
→ 4 2 km
Romsås 5,5 km

→ 4
TOYEN 300 m

1/2 Ellingsrudåsen
3 Mortensrud
4 Bergkrystallen
5 Vestli
6 Ring

✈ Oslo Lufthaven
Gardermoen
50 km
190
→ E 6 2 km

BLINDERN
ADAMSTUEN
MAJORSTUEN
Kirkeveien
HEGDE-HAUGEN
BRISKEBY
HOMANSBYEN
ILA
GRÜNERLØKKA
SOFIENBERG-PARKEN
SLOTTS-PARKEN
RUSELØKKA
FILIPSTAD
AKERBRYGGE

Fjordbyen (Fjord City)
(under constr.)

Bygdøy

O s l o f j o r d e n

Hovedøya

GRØNLAND
Bispegata
Bjørvika
Bispevika
MIDDEL-ALDER-PARKEN
Mariakirkens ruiner

Kavringen fyr

250   500 m

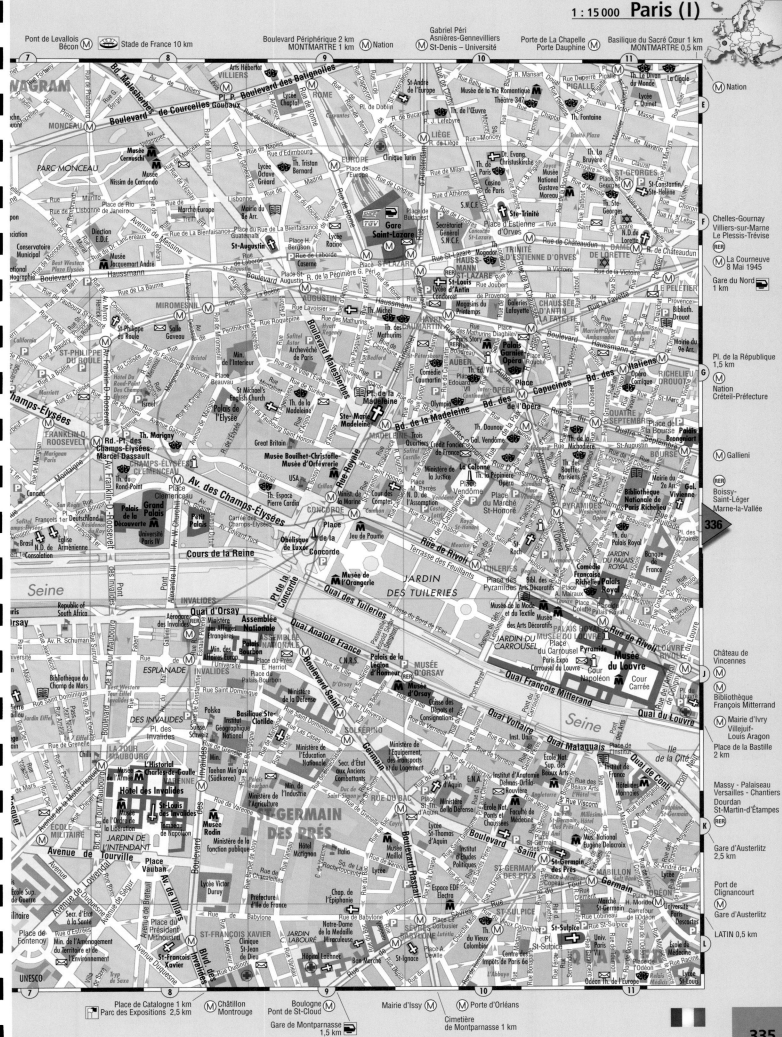

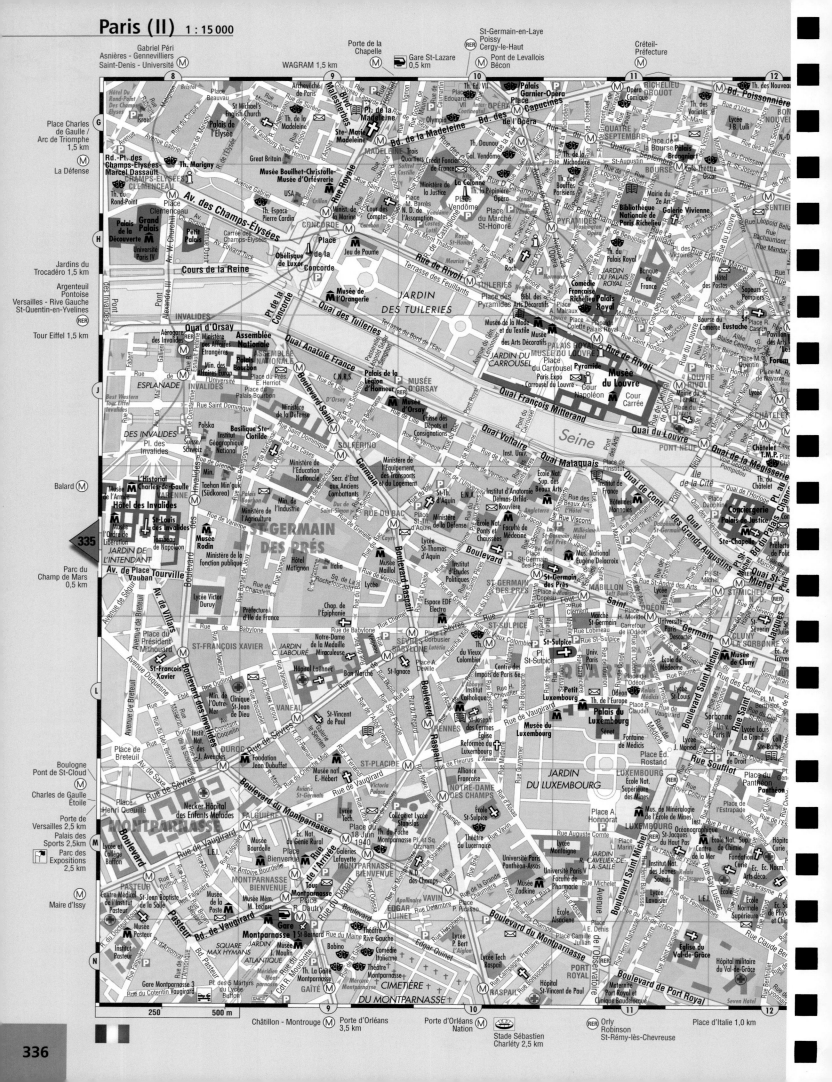

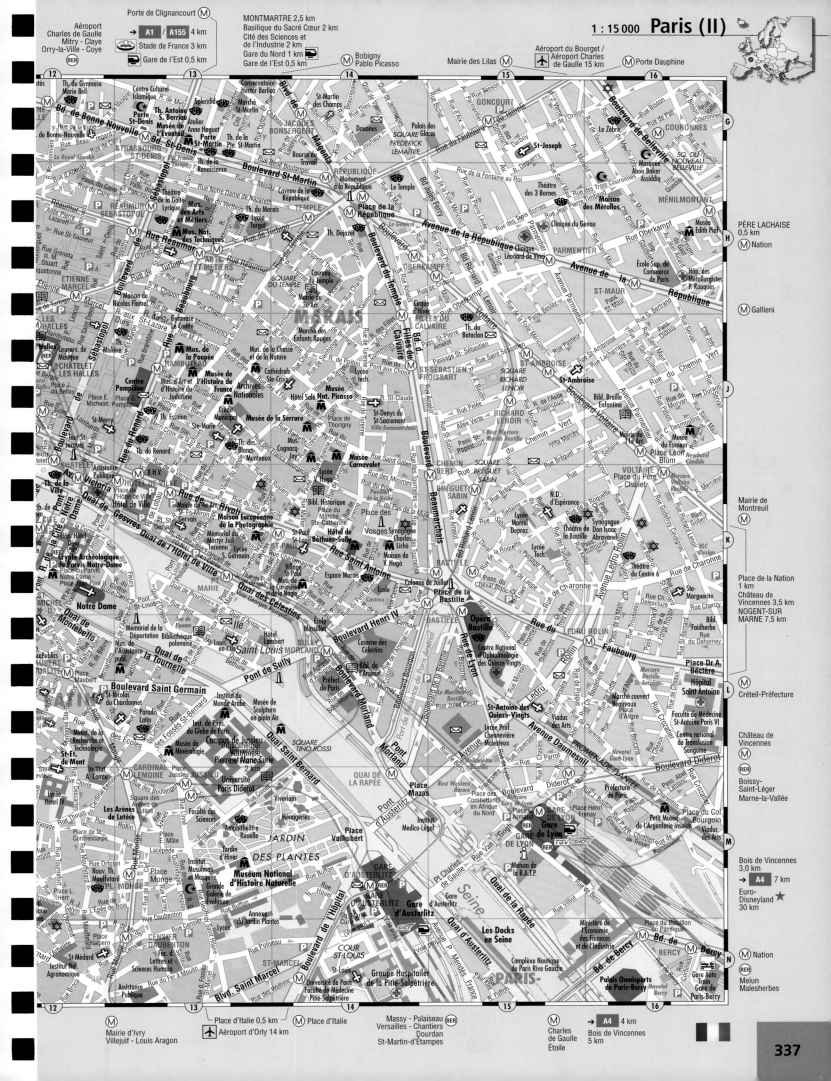

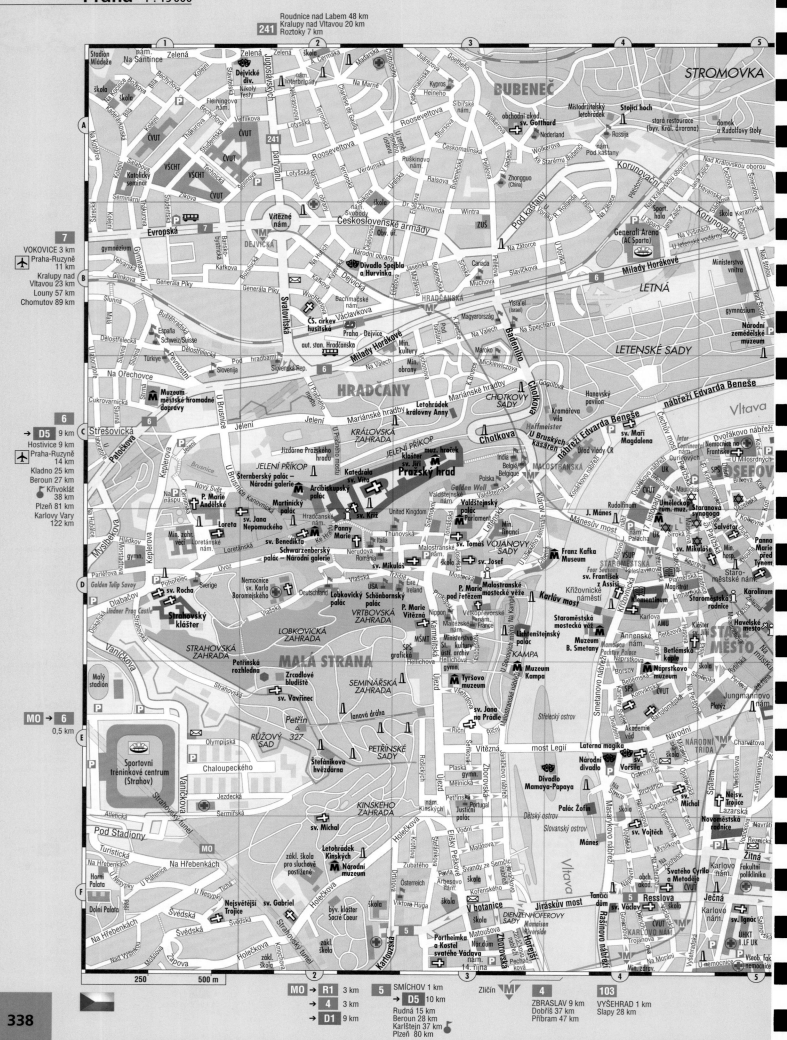

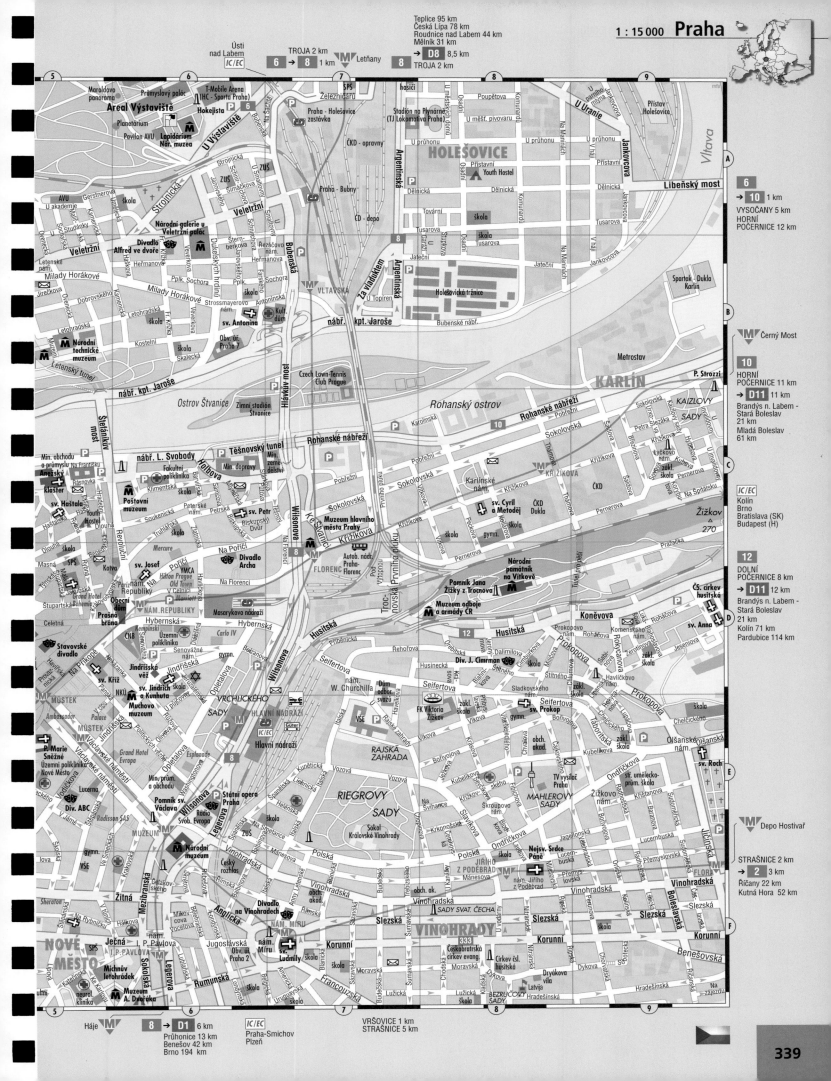

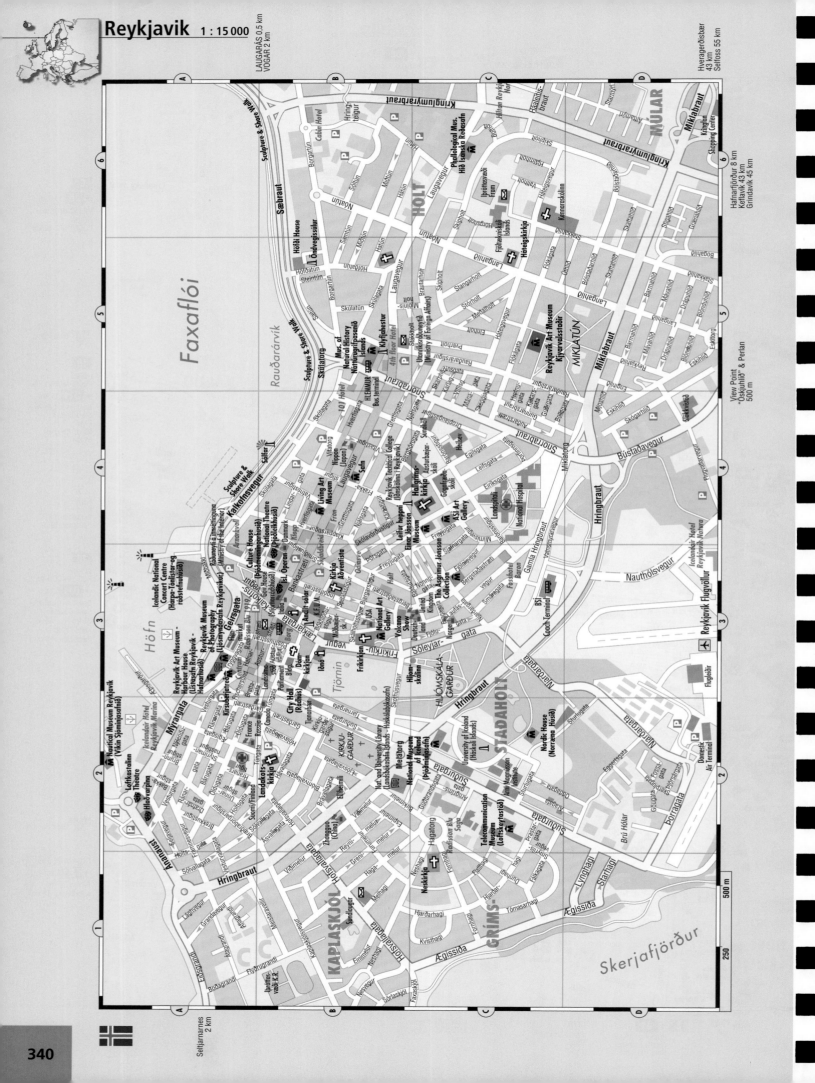

Faxaflói

Skerjafjörður

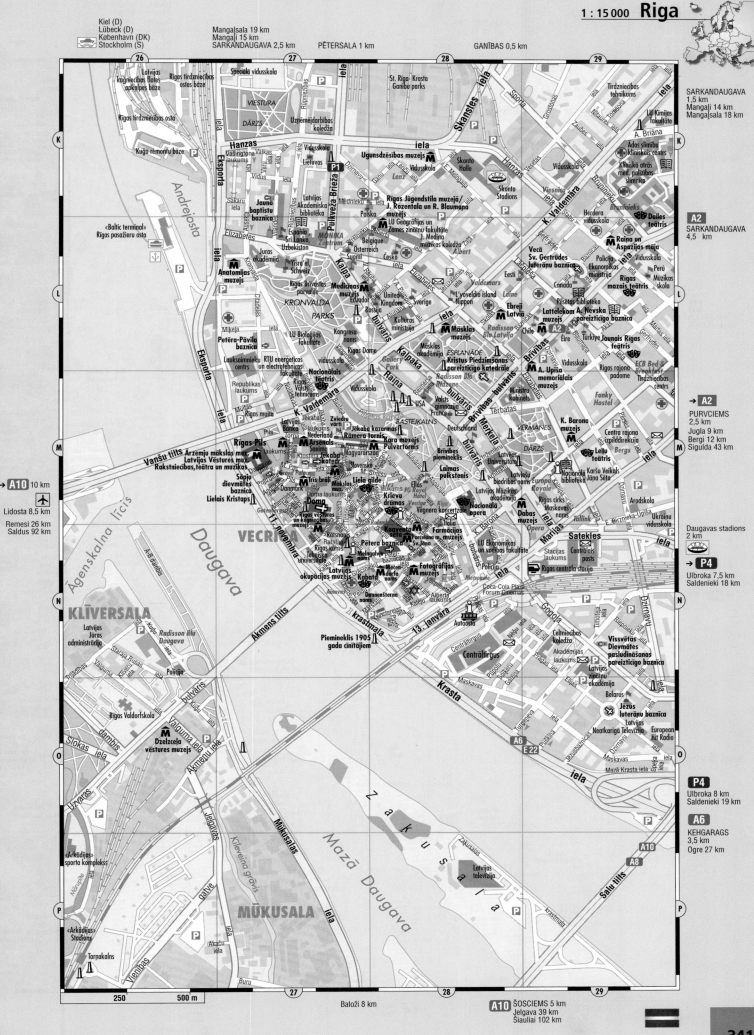

Kiel (D)
Lübeck (D)
København (DK)
Stockholm (S)

Mangaļsala 19 km
Mangaļi 15 km
SARKANDAUGAVA 2,5 km

PĒTERSALA 1 km

GANĪBAS 0,5 km

SARKANDAUGAVA
1,5 km
Mangaļi 14 km
Mangaļsala 18 km

A2
SARKANDAUGAVA
4,5 km

A2
PURVCIEMS
2,5 km
Jugla 9 km
Bergi 12 km
Sigulda 43 km

A10 10 km

Lidosta 8,5 km

Remesi 26 km
Saldus 92 km

Daugavas stadions
2 km

P4
Ulbroka 7,5 km
Saldenieki 18 km

P4
Ulbroka 8 km
Saldenieki 19 km

A6
KEHGARAGS
3,5 km
Ogre 27 km

A10
A8

250   500 m

Baloži 8 km

A10 ŠOSCIEMS 5 km
Jelgava 39 km
Šiauliai 102 km

341

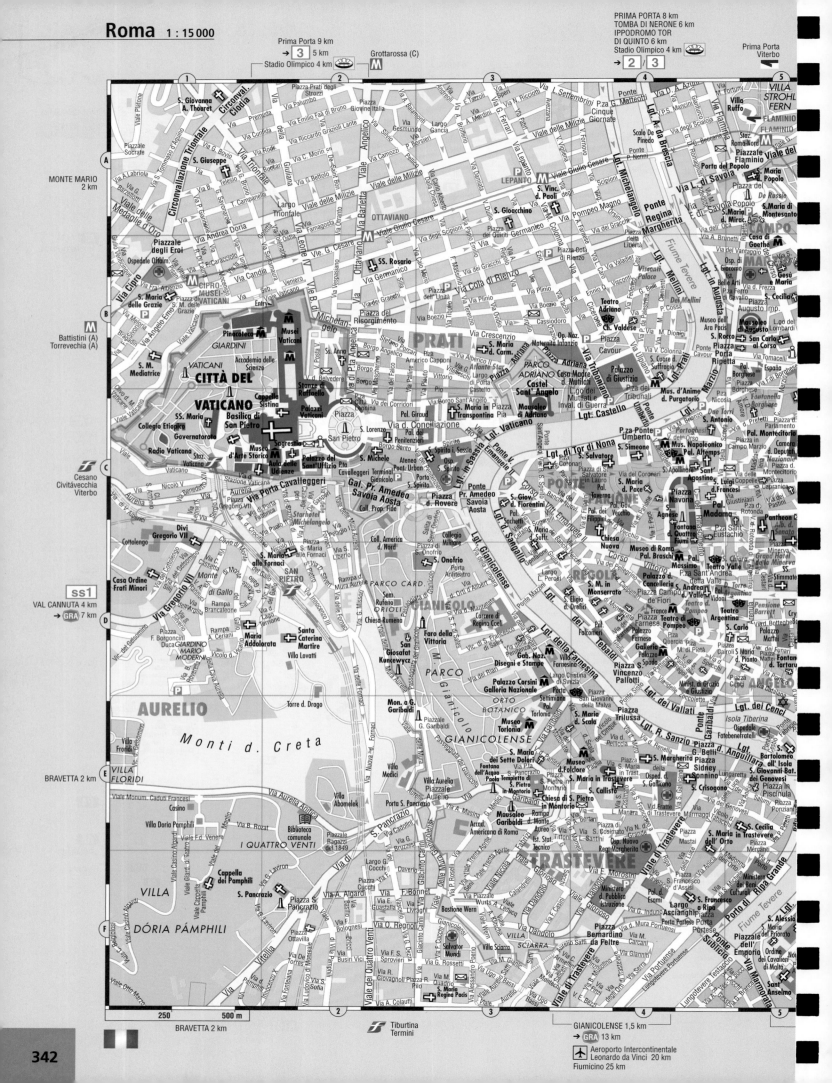

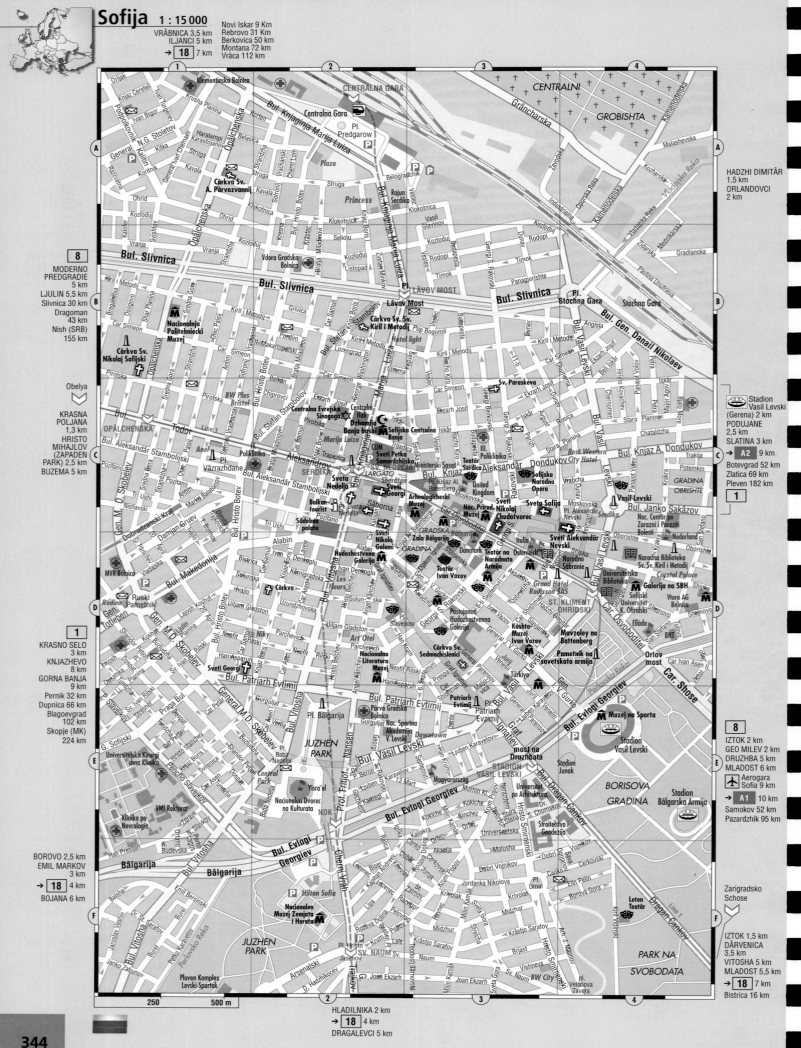

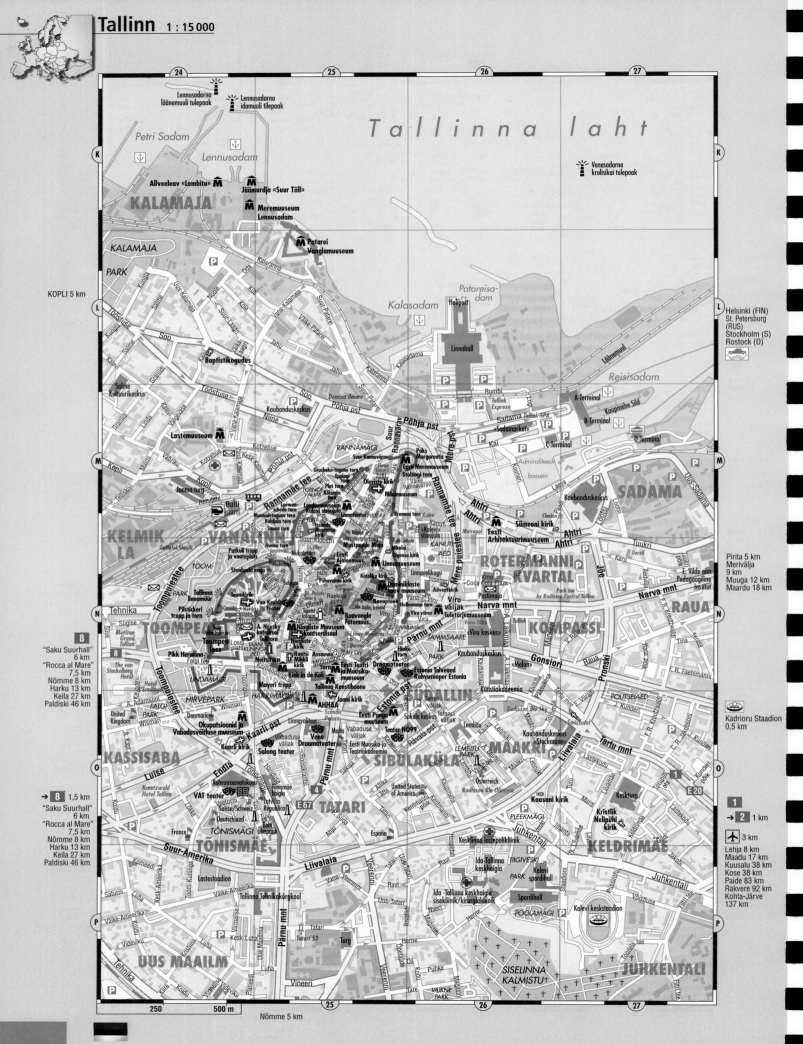

Tallinna laht

Lennusadarna läänemuuli tulepaak
Lennusadarna idamuuli tilepaak

Vanasadarna krulisikai tulepaak

Petri Sadam
Lennusadam

KALAMAJA

Allveeleav «Lembitu»
Jäämurdja «Suur Töll»
Meremuuseum Lennusadam

KALAMAJA PARK

Patarei Vanglamuuseum

KOPLI 5 km

Kalasadam
Heliport
Linnahall
Patareisa-dam

Reisisadam

Helsinki (FIN)
St. Petersburg (RUS)
Stockholm (S)
Rostock (D)

Baptistikogudus

Salme Kultuurikeskus

Jaama turg

Lastemuuseum

Kaubanduskeskus

Põhja pst

Sadama Tallink SPA
Sadamarkets

A-Terminal
Tallink Express
B-Terminal

C-Terminal

D-Terminal

RANNAMÄGI
Suur Rannavärav
Paks Margareeta
Eesti Meremuuseum

SADAMA

Balti jaam

Rannamäe tee
Gruseke-togune torn
Eppingi torn
Oleviste kirik
Nunnadetagune torn
Kuldjala torn
Sauna torn

Stoltingi torn
Väike Rannavärav
Miinimuuseum

Kaubanduskeskus

KELMIK-LA

VANALINN

Loewen-schede torn
Plat torn
Kalevi siseujul
Linnateater

Bremeni torn
Kalev
«Kalevi» siseujula
Metropol

Ahtri
Siimeoni kirik
Eesti Arhitektuurimuuseum

Patkuli trepp ja vaateplats
Nunna torn
Nukuteater
Stenbocki maja

Mustpeade Maja
Suurgilde hoone
Pühavaimu kirik

Rootsi-Mihkli
Nikolai
Oigeusu kirik

Linnamuuseum
Linnavolikogu

ROTERMANNI KVARTAL

Pirita 5 km
Merivälja 9 km
Muuga 12 km
Maardu 18 km

Tallinna linnamüür
Toomkirik
Pilstickeri trepp ja torn

Katoliku kirik
Dominiklaste klov muuseum

KANUTI AED

Kino «Coca Cola Plaza»
Postimaja

Adventkirik

E. Vilde nim. Pedagoogiline Instit

TOOMPEA

Von Krahliti Teater
Niguliste Muuseum
konsertsiaal
Niguliste kirik

Raeapteek
Raekoja plats
Raevangla Fotomuus.

Tuletõrjemuuseum

RAUA

Toompea loss
Pikk Hermann

A. Nevsky katedraal

Hellemanni torn
Viru värav
Viru väljak
Narva mnt

KOMPASS

«Saku Suurhall» 6 km
«Rocca al Mare» 7,5 km
Nõmme 8 km
Harku 13 km
Keila 27 km
Paldiski 46 km

Neitsitorn
Kiek in de Kök

Eesti Teatri ja Muusika-muuseum
Tallinna Kunstihoone

Dramaateater
Estonia Talveaed
Rahvusooper Estonia

Kunstiakadeemia

POLITSEIAED

Kadrioru Staadion 0,5 km

Mayeri trepp

AHHAA

Jaani kirik

Okupatsiooni ja Vabadusvõitluse muuseum

Eesti Panga muuseum

Teater NO99

SÜDALINN

Sokala keskus
Sakala väljak

Kaubanduskeskus Stockmann

MAAKRI

KASSISABA

Kaarli kirik

Vene Draamateater

Vabaduse väljak
Salong teater
Eesti Muusika-ja Teatriakadeemia

SIBULAKÜLA

United States of America

Kaasani kirik

Kristlik Nelipühi kirik

KELDRIMAE

→ 8 1,5 km
«Saku Suurhall» 6 km
«Rocca al Mare» 7,5 km
Nõmme 8 km
Harku 13 km
Keila 27 km
Paldiski 46 km

Rahvusraamatukogu
VAT teater

Tõnismäe haigla

E67
TATARI

Kesklinna lastepolikliinik

Keskturg

PLEEKMÄGI

→ 2 1 km

→ 3 km
Lehja 8 km
Maadu 17 km
Kuusalu 38 km
Kose 38 km
Paide 83 km
Rakvere 92 km
Kohta-Järve 137 km

TÕNISMÄE

Liivalaia

UUS MAAILM

Tallinna Tehnikakõrgkool

Ida-Tallinna keskhaigla

Ida-Tallinna keskhaigla siseklinik/kirurgiaklinik

Kalevi spordihall

Spordihall

Kalevi keskstadion

SISELINNA KALMISTU

JUHKENTALI

250   500 m

Nõmme 5 km

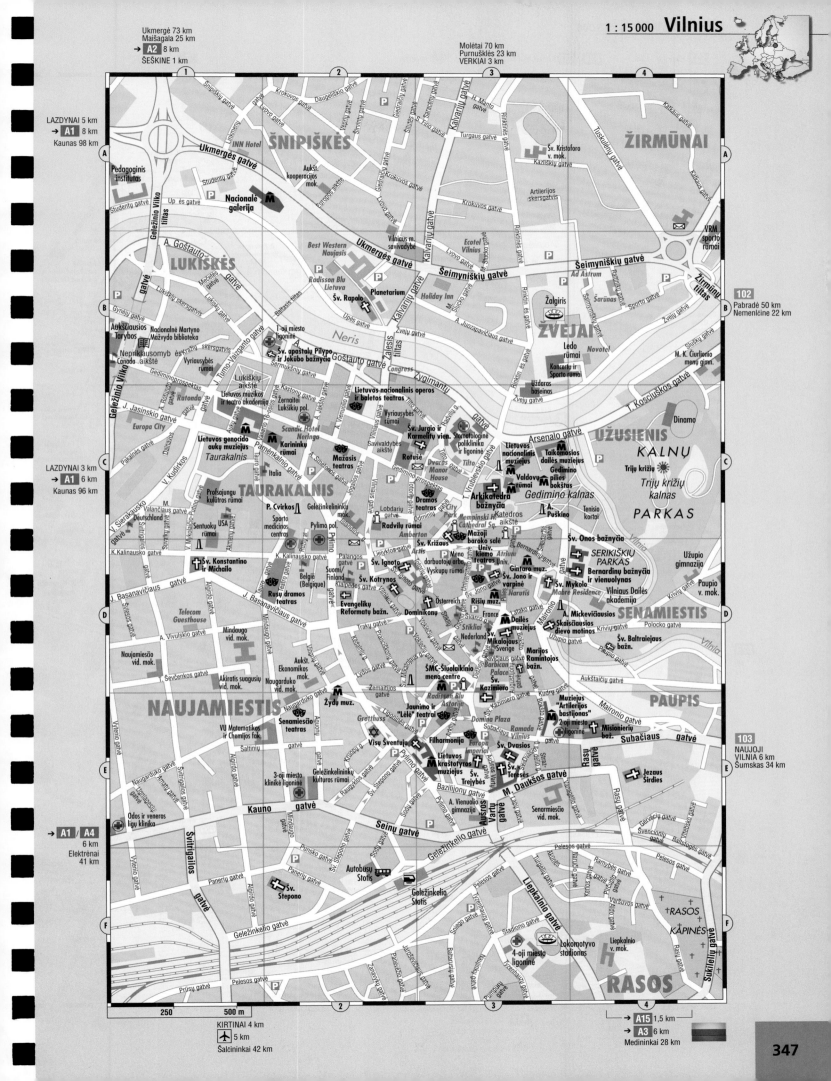

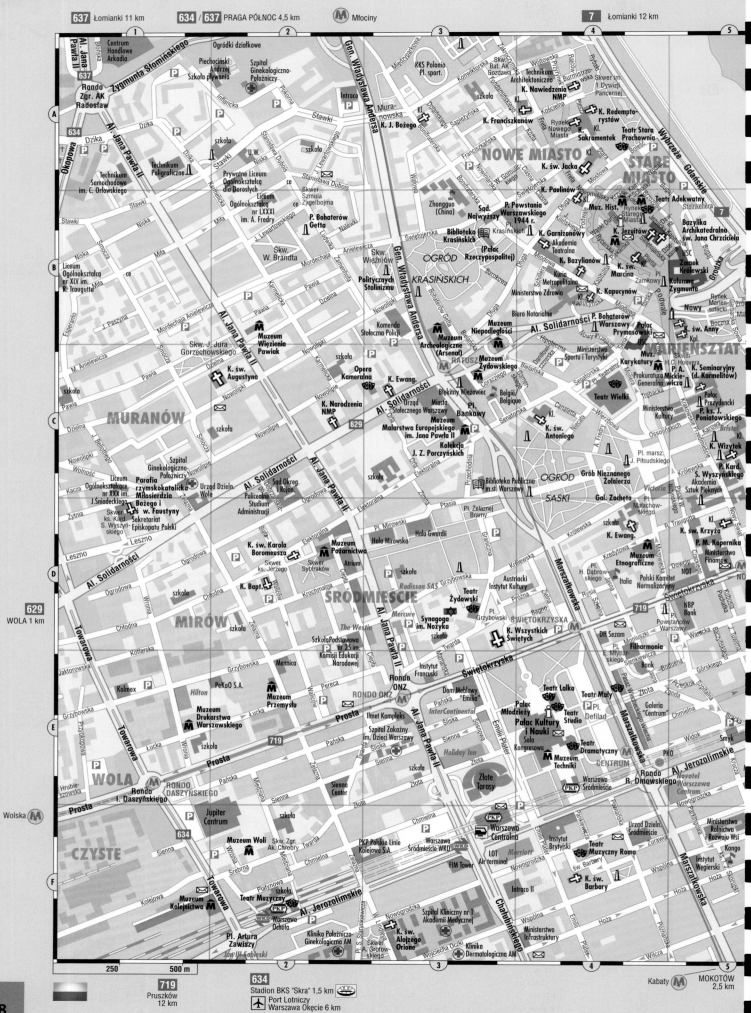

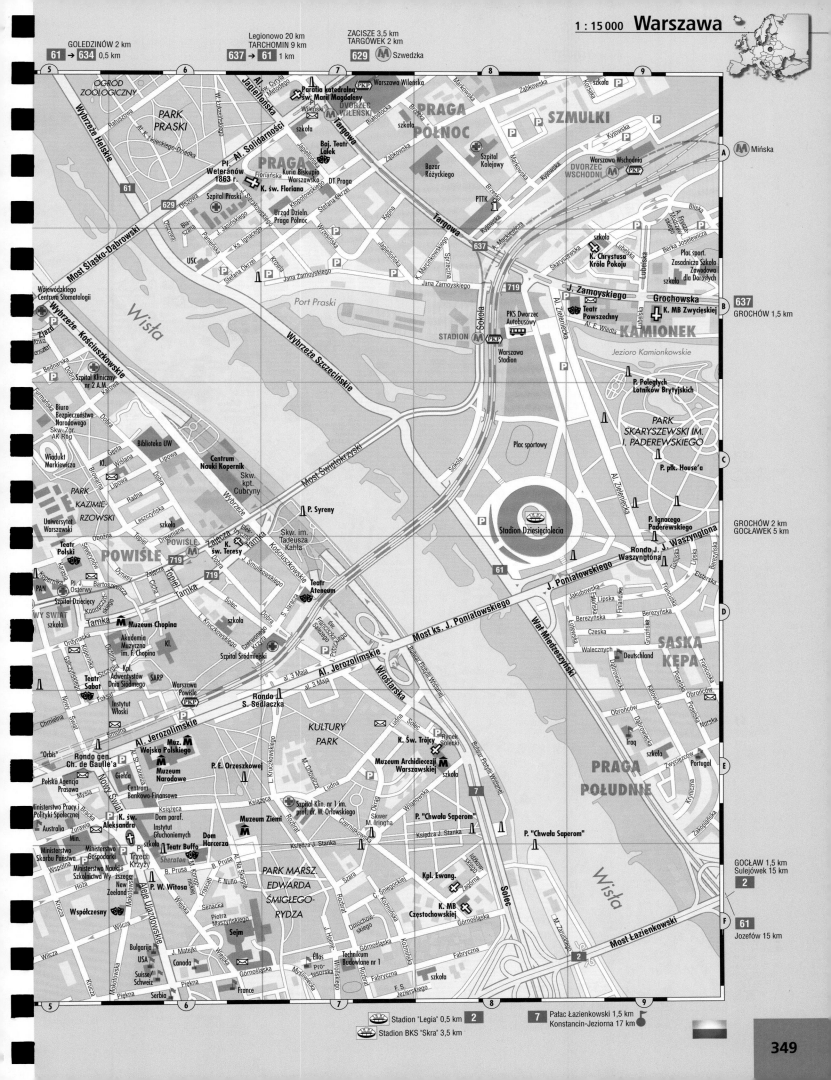

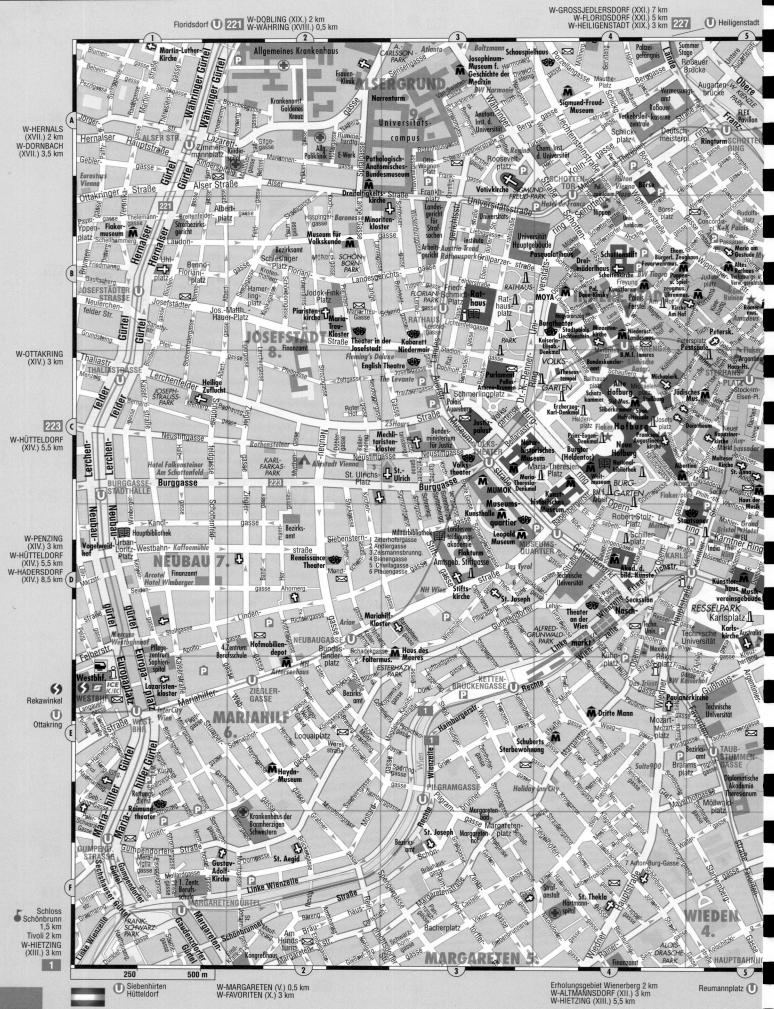

Wien 1 : 15 000

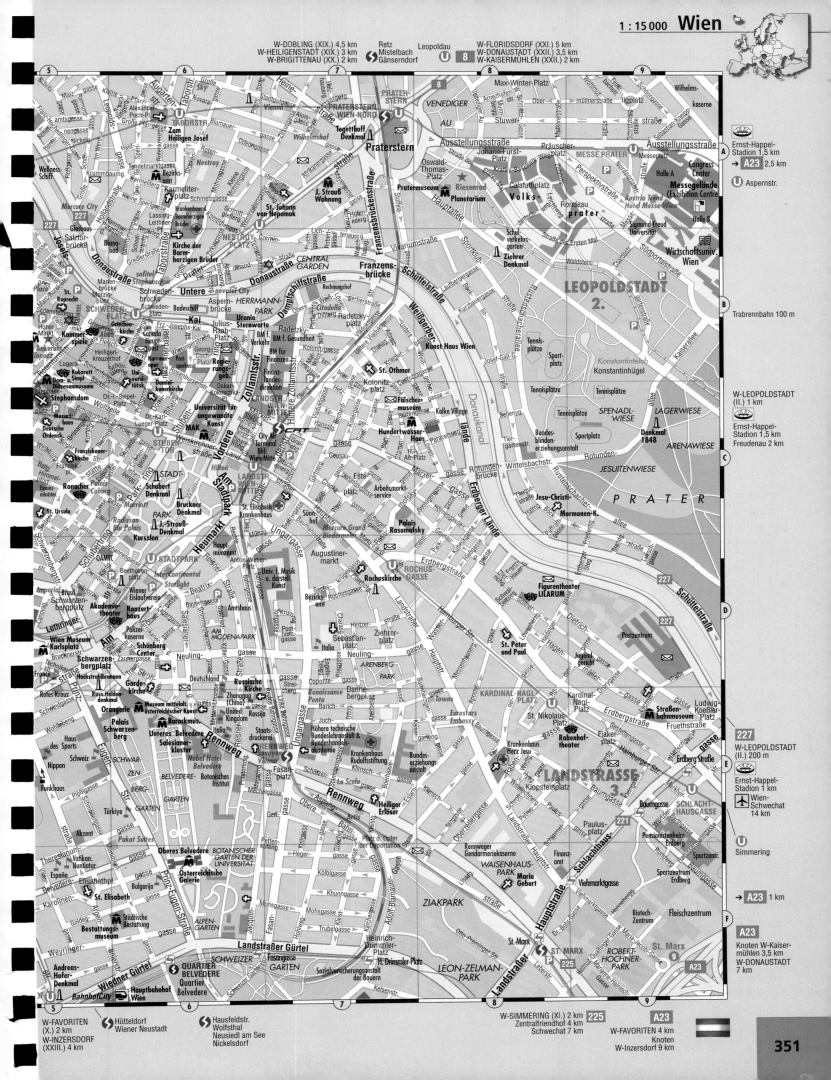

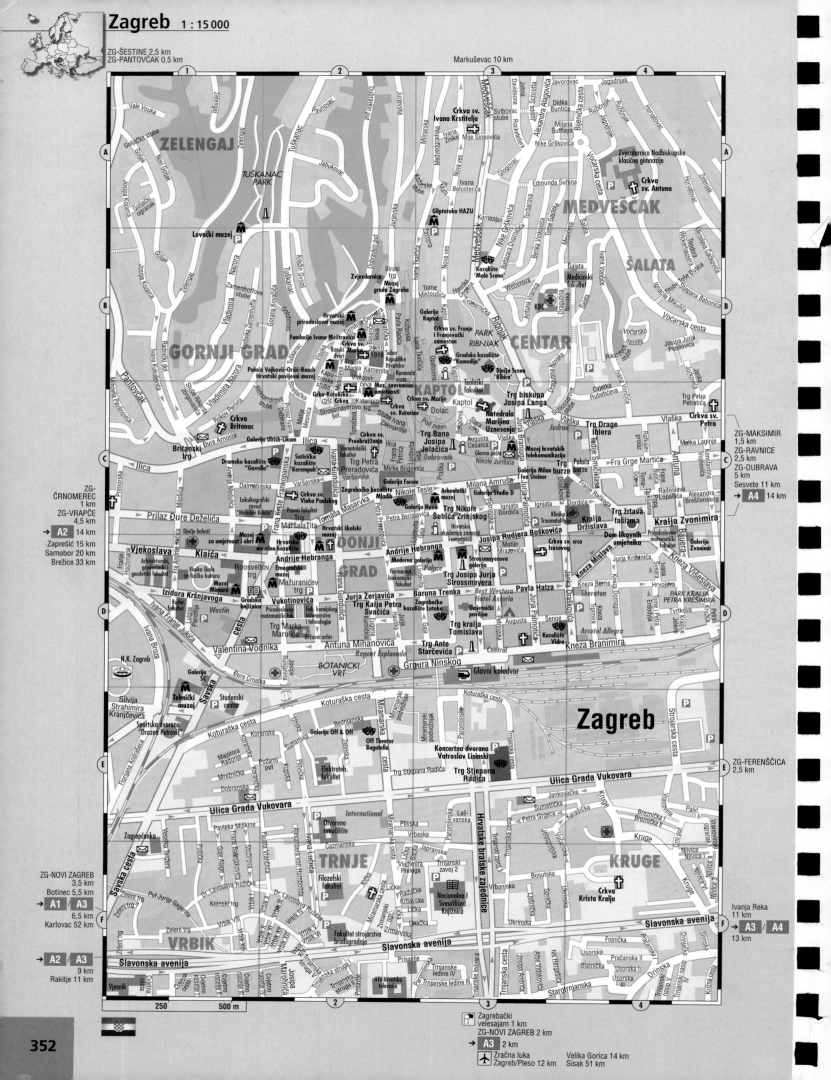